INTRODUCING THE NEXT MILLENNIUM

From The Undisputed Leader
In Accounting Instruction

SOUTH-WESTERN

Introducing
The Most Complete
High School Accounting
Instructional Package.

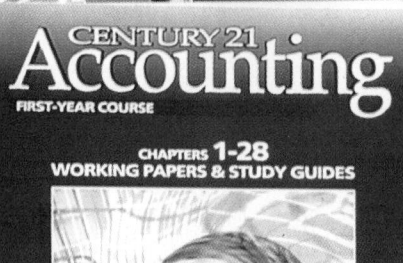

Century 21 Accounting
First-Year Course

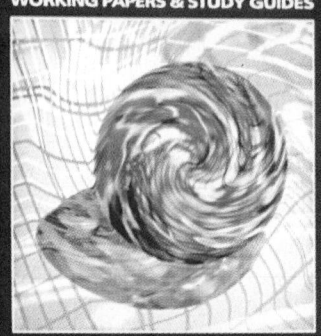

- *Right For The Way You Teach Now*
- *Ready To Adapt For Your Needs In The Future*
- *Not Just Pieces, But A Fully-Integrated Teaching/Learning System*

Century 21 Accounting
First-Year Course
General Journal Approach

Automated
Accounting 6.0

Century 21 Accounting
Advanced Course

Now, The Future Of Accounting Is In Your Hands.

Open The Door To The Future.

Think about how the world has changed since you started teaching. Now you have less time than ever before. There's a bewildering array of new technology available. Students raised on MTV don't relate well to the old instructional methods.

Imagine...

Now imagine a future where you spend more time teaching and less time with preparation and paperwork. Imagine a new approach to technology which allows you to harness its power easily. Imagine your students interacting easily with the material as participants rather than spectators.

CENTURY 21
Accounting
FIRST-YEAR COURSE

ROSS, HANSON, GILBERTSON, LEHMAN & SWA
SIXTH EDITION

Suddenly, The Future Is Here.

The new editions of *Century 21 Accounting* will help give you all you imagined and more. Starting right now, the tools you need for the next century are in your hands.

Use The Only First-Year Text With 3 Complete Accounting Cycles.

Our unique approach allows the accounting cycle to be applied 3 times during the course so your students learn the material in a real-world way.

Students begin to get the concepts they need early in the course, rather than saving them for the end where they may never be covered.

Choose The First-Year Version That Fits The Way You Teach.

We are the only publisher who offers you two choices:
- *Century 21 Accounting* (traditional multi-column journal approach)

OR
- *Century 21 Accounting— General Journal* (general journal/special journals approach)

Either way, we have everything you need to cover more material better with these two new *Century 21 Accounting* instructional packages.

Computer Applications Flow Directly From Manual Concepts.

We will help you guide your students smoothly from understanding concepts to manual applications to computer applications. The new edition of *Century 21 Accounting* continues to be the only instructional package that integrates automated accounting right into the text.

The Way Accounting Will Be Taught From Now On.

An Easier Way To A More Successful Tomorrow

The new edition of *Century 21 Accounting* is easy for you to use. It's based on the proven principles and concepts which you are used to teaching. But, while it is as comfortable as your favorite slippers, it will change the way high school accounting is taught from this day forward.

Because the learning is interactive and intuitive, your students will be able to jump right in and begin to build skills and confidence. But don't take our word for it, check out these features for yourself.

More Transactions Than Any Other Text.

Other texts provide many problems but relatively few actual transactions. *Century 21 Accounting* has a better method. We give your students a carefully selected group of problems with an appropriate number of transactions. The language and construction of problems are always the same. This focus on complete problems and consistent presentation reflects the real world of accounting.

The Computer Advantage.

The new edition of *Century 21 Accounting* is the only instructional package which continues to integrate automated accounting right into the text. This feature is valuable to your students because it allows them to work specially iconed regular chapter problems with automated accounting software.
The mini-chapters integrate manual and automated accounting and provide students the opportunity to complete 31 problems, 3 reinforcement activities, and 3 simulations with our *Automated Accounting 6.0* software.

Additionally, the Application Program disk provides 23 problems; the Spreadsheet Template enables the student to work 17 problems; and the Tutorial is used with 20 different chapters.

ILLUSTRATION 9-12

FYI

Capital is not co the work sheet ance sheet. Ca lated using be tal, minus dra income or m

Now Your Students Can Check Their Own Progress.

With our new Audit Your Understanding feature at the end of each part of the chapter, it's easy for students to see how well they understand the work that they have covered. Students can uncover the gaps in knowledge and take the necessary corrective action by themselves. It's a confidence-builder for them; it's a time-saver for you.

AUDIT YOUR UNDERSTANDING

Challenge Your Students To Think For Themselves.

Every chapter ends with a

CASES FOR CRITICAL THINKING

critical-thinking feature that you may use to stretch your students and help them assimilate the material covered.

The cases also encourage the use of language and writing skills, which provides an important cross-discipline opportunity.

Put Your Students On The Job.

Give your students "on the job" training and hands-on experience with our three "real-life" simulations. Available in both manual and automated versions, *Video Transfer*, *Viking Marine*, and *Western Rider* are fictitious but realistic companies which let your students do real accounting and learn by putting theory into practice.

We Place Math In The Spotlight.

All math formulas are featured in boxes and noted with icons to emphasize their importance.

MATHEMATICS

Prepare Your Students For A Changing World.

Give Your Class An Ethical Overview Of Business.

Our Professional Business Ethics feature raises important, relevant questions for discussion. Topics include truthfulness on resumes, software pirating, and what is and isn't a legitimate business expense. Students are given a 3-step checklist to help evaluate each situation.

PROFESSIONAL BUSINESS ETHICS

Show How Accounting Can Lead To An Exciting Career.

Many different accounting and accounting-related careers are show-cased throughout the text. This helps students set career goals and demonstrates the ultimate value of the skills and information which they will learn in your class.

Take Your Classroom Into The Boardroom.

Interviews with top business people give your students the "facts of life" about the importance of accounting in a future career. These vivid profiles also highlight various multicultural groups.

PERSONAL VISIONS IN BUSINESS

PROFESSIONAL BUSINESS ETHICS

Is This Really a Business Expense?

Randall Stovall, an architect, owns and operates a business known as Stovall Designs. Each year the federal government requires Mr. Stovall to report the amount of revenue and expenses of the business. Reported expenses are limited to those expenses required to operate the business. Mr. Stovall must pay federal income tax on the amount by which revenues exceed expenses.

As the bookkeeper for Stovall Designs, you know that Mr. Stovall is not fond of paying income taxes. In fact, you believe his actions are often motivated by his desire to minimize his income tax liability.

INSTRUCTIONS Use the three-step checklist to analyze whether each of the following actions by Mr. Stovall demonstrates ethical behavior.

After this transaction is recorded, the sum of the balances on the left side of the equation equals the sum of the balances on the right side, $11,590.00. The equation is still in balance.

Other expense transactions might be for advertising, equipment rental or repairs, charitable contributions, and other miscellaneous items. All expense transactions affect the accounting equation in the same way as Transactions 7 and 8.

Paid Cash to Owner for Personal Use

Assets taken out of a business for the owner's personal use are called **withdrawals**. A withdrawal decreases owner's equity. Although an owner may withdraw any kind of asset, usually an owner withdraws cash. The withdrawal decreases the account balance of the withdrawn asset, such as Cash.

Transaction 9   August 12, 19--. Paid cash to owner for personal use, $100.00.

The effect of this transaction on the accounting equation is shown in Illustration 3-5 on the next page. The asset account, Cash, is decreased by $100.00, the amount of cash paid out. This decrease is on the left side of the accounting equation. The owner's equity account, Ben Furman, Capital, is also decreased by $100.00. This decrease is on the right side of the equation.

After this transaction is recorded, the sum of the balances on the left side of the equation equals the sum of the balances on the right side, $11,490.00. The equation is still in balance. ...rease in owner's equity because of a withdrawal is not a ...rations of a business. Therefore, a with-

The BCCI Scandal and the Savings & Loan Crisis are merely two examples of how important it will be for your students to have a sense of their ethical responsibilities as they leave the classroom for the real world of business.

Increasing international competition makes understanding of various cultures a top priority. Your students need to acquire an appreciation for the many opportunities accounting will provide them in the future. *Century 21 Accounting* helps you cover all these important topics and more in the exciting, new student editions.

Give Your Class A Global Perspective.

In selected chapters, we provide practical information relating to accounting and business practices in the global community. In today's ever-smaller world, this is a must for your students.

Broaden Your Students' Awareness Of Multicultural Issues.

This feature exposes your class to the many different cultures in our country and world. It shows the contributions of each as well as the advantages of having different cultures within one harmonious society.

We Highlight The Important Information.

These short, impactful FYI features are sprinkled throughout each chapter to emphasize important points and provide interesting information about accounting and business.

Spreadsheet Options Illustrate Flexibility.

This feature shows your class a variety of ways to use spreadsheets. They may use their spreadsheet software to duplicate the examples given and may create new sets of data so they can do "What If" scenarios.

1. Mr. Stovall often makes personal long-distance phone calls office. He charges these calls to the business account.

2. A lover of fine furniture, Mr. Stovall equipped his office with .00 leather chair rather than a $400.00 vinyl model.

3. Mr. Stovall prepared a design for a lumber company in ange for $1,500.00 of wood and paint used to build a porch at Mr. ll's summer cottage. Mr. Stovall instructed you not to record the action in Stovall Designs' accounting records.

tion 4. Mr. Stovall hired a floral company to install and maintain ts in his office.

ILLUSTRATION 3-5

Paying cash to owner for personal use decreases assets and owner's equity

	Assets			=	Liabilities	+	Owner's Equity
	Cash +	Supplies +	Prepaid Insurance	=	Butler Cleaning Supplies +		Ben Furman Capit
		$4,297	$1,200		$1,360		$10,230 −100 (withdrawal)
Balances Transaction 9	$6,093 −100	$4,297	$1,200		$1,360		$10,130
New Balances	$5,993						Total of right side: $1,360 + $10,130 = $11,490

Total of left side: $5,993 + $4,297 + $1,200 = $11,490

have affected owner's equity. In Chapter 2, Ben Furman made a $10,000.00 investment. In this chapter, four transactions that changed owner's equity were recorded in the accounting equation.

SPREADSHEET OPTIONS

Transaction Number	Kind of Transaction	Chang Owner's E
6	Revenue	+525
7	Expense (rent)	−250.0
8	Expense (telephone)	−45.00
9	Withdrawal	−100.00
		+130.00
	Net change in owner's equity	

A revenue transaction increased owner's equity. Expense and withdrawal transactions decreased owner's equity. These transactions together increased total owner's equity by $130.00, from $10,000.00 to $10,130.00.

Audit Your Understanding

1. How is owner's equity affected when cash is received from sales?

2. How is owner's equity affected when cash is paid for expenses?

3. How is owner's equity affected when cash is paid to the owner for personal use?

That Affect Owner's Equity

Gain The Freedom and Flexibility To Teach Your Best.

Our New Wraparound Format Puts Everything You Need For Daily Teaching Right At Your Fingertips.

New "Wraparound" Teacher's Editions

Our new Teacher's Editions give you the same basic concepts in the same proven way that you've probably relied on since you started teaching high school accounting. But now, we've given you more help than ever before. And we've wrapped it right around every page so it's in front of you, every minute of every teaching day. This makes it easier to keep your class on schedule and makes your preparation time more productive.

8

MULTICULTURAL AWARENESS

The MULTICULTURAL AWARENESS feature is intended to expose students to the concept that our society is composed of people from many different cultural backgrounds. These features show both past contributions of many cultures and benefits of a culturally diverse society. Teachers should (1) have students read the brief feature; (2) discuss the concepts explored in the feature; (3) clarify any terms or questions that students may have; and (4) do the additional multicultural activity.

provides. Write the accounting equation on the board and explain the analyzing procedure. Present the accounting equation as a review of a basic algebraic concept, the equation. Remind students that an equation must always have equal amounts on each side.

APPLY

- Review the importance of keeping a business' financial information separate from the owner's personal financial information.

- Draw the accounting equation on the board and show how changes on one side can affect the other side.

Guided Practice

Invite a student to the board. Have the class list assets they own while the student lists them. Continue this for equities and liabilities. It is important to encourage students to participate in class. Participation gives students a sense of importance and enhances the learning process.

Independent Practice

Assign Terms 1–7 and Questions 1–3.

ASSESS

- Assess student understanding by checking solutions to the Independent Practice activities.

- Ask students why personal and business items should be kept separate.

- Write the accounting equation on the board. Then write a mathematical equation and omit one number. Ask students to furnish the missing number and explain how they arrived at that answer.

A = L + OE
10 = 5 + ___

20

MULTICULTURAL AWARENESS

Professional Organizations

Professional organizations provide important social and economic benefits to their members. For example, the National Association of Black Accountants is a professional organization. Members of this association are CPAs, accountants, and accounting students. The organizational purpose is to unite accountants and accounting students who have similar interests and ideals, who are committed to professional and academic excellence, who possess a sense of professional and civic responsibility, and who are concerned with enhancing opportunities for minorities in the accounting profession. Activities include free income tax preparation, student scholarships, high school and university career seminars, regional student conferences, technical seminars and lecturers, a speakers' bureau, a placement service, and publication of a journal and newsletter.

A complete list of accounting concepts is in Appendix A.

A person who chooses to start a business must m_ sions. To make these decisions, a businessperson _ information about the business. To provide the info_ records and reports relating to the business must be to create useful records and reports, financial inform_ kept in an organized way. Planning, recording, analyzi_ preting financial information is known as accounting_ process for providing financial information that will _ management is known as an accounting system.

THE BUSINESS

A business that performs an activity for a fee is called a **se_ness.** Ben Furman worked for a service business that clear_ for a fee. Mr. Furman wants to be in control of his hours_ earnings. Therefore, he decided to start his own carpet-_ business. A business owned by one person is called a **pr_ship.** A proprietorship is also referred to as a sole proprie_ Mr. Furman has named his new proprietorship *Rugcare.* R_ will rent office space and the equipment used to opera_ business.

Since a new business is being started, Mr. Furman must c_ the accounting system that will be used to keep Rugcare's acc_ ing records. In the accounting system, Mr. Furman's acc_ ful to keep Rugcare's accounting records separate from his_ personal financial records. For example, Mr. Furman owns a ho_ and a personal car. Rugcare's financial records must *not* inc_ information about Mr. Furman's house, car, or other perso_ belongings. For example, Mr. Furman must use one check_ account for his personal expenses and another checking account f_ Rugcare. The financial records for Rugcare and Mr. Furman's pe_ sonal belongings must be kept separate. The accounting concep_ *Business Entity,* is applied when a business' financial informatio_ is recorded and reported separately from the owner's persona_ financial information. *(CONCEPT: Business Entity)*

Accounting concepts are described throughout this textbook when an application of a concept first occurs. When additional applications occur, a concept reference, such as *(CONCEPT: Business Entity)*, indicates an application of a specific accounting concept. A brief description of each accounting concept used in this text is also provided in Appendix A.

THE ACCOUNTING EQUATION

A business has many items that have value. Rugcare will own items such as cash and supplies that will be used to conduct daily operations. Anything of value that is owned is called an **asset**. Assets have value because they can be used to acquire other assets or be used to operate a business. For example, Rugcare will use cash to

PART 2   Accounting for a Service Business Organized as a Proprietorship

---

MULTICULTURAL AWARENESS ACTIVITY

For additional exposure to diversity in professional organizations, explain to students that most professions have their own professional organizations. Furthermore, in many professions, such as accounting, people of similar minority or ethnic backgrounds often form additional professional organizations. Ask students to research professional organizations for different professions and to identify professional organizations organized for particular minority or ethnic groups. Students may wish to do this research as a group activity.

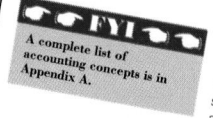

TEACHING TIPS

APPLIED SKILLS

You told us how helpful our Teaching Tips are. So we gave you more of them than ever before—in the margins, just where you need them the most.

Lesson Plans Keep You On Course Every Day.

Now, your lesson plans are in the margins, so you'll never need to hunt for them or spend time preparing for class the old-fashioned way.

Special Interleaf Pages Organize Each Unit and Chapter.

Now, planning your presentation of material is simpler and more rewarding because the material is laid out for you. Each unit and chapter has a Teacher Overview so you know where you want to go right from the start.

The points you want to emphasize, and appropriate teaching techniques for them, come immediately to mind.

You'll also like the chapter grids that correlate Enabling Performance tasks with lesson plans, chapter activities, and tests. The grids ensure appropriate teaching, application, and assessment of tasks to be mastered.

FOCUS

TEACH

APPLY

ASSESS

CLOSURE

UNIT & CHAPTER OVERVIEWS

GRIDS

---

deci-
ncial
any
rder
be
er-
ed
to

...siness. Rugcare will then use the asset, sup-
...of the rug-cleaning business.
...e assets of a business are called **equities.**
...es of equities. (1) Equity of those to whom
...ple, Rugcare may buy some supplies and
...plies at a later date. The business from
...t will have a right to some of Rugcare's
...called a **liability.** (2) Equity of the owner. Mr. Furman
will own Rugcare and invest in the assets of the business. Therefore, he will have a right to decide how the assets will be used. The
amount remaining after the value of all liabilities is subtracted from the value of all assets is called **owner's equity.**

The relationship among assets, liabilities, and owner's
equity can be written as an equation. An equation showing
the relationship among assets, liabilities, and owner's equity
is called the **accounting equation.** The accounting equation
is most often stated as:

$$Assets = Liabilities + Owner's\ Equity$$

The accounting equation must be in balance to be correct. Thus, the total of the amounts on the left side of the
equation must always equal the total of the amounts on
the right side. Before Mr. Furman actually starts the business, Rugcare's accounting equation would show the following amounts.

Assets		Liabilities + Owner's Equity
Left side amount	=	Right side amounts
$0	=	$0 + $0

Audit Your Understanding
1. What is a proprietorship?
2. State the accounting equation.
3. What kinds of accounts go on the left side of the accounting equation?
4. What kinds of accounts go on the right side of the accounting equation?

FYI

The left side of the accounting equation must always equal the right side.

HOW BUSINESS ACTIVITIES CHANGE THE ACCOUNTING EQUATION

Business activities change the amounts in the accounting equation.
A business activity that changes assets, liabilities, or owner's equity
is called a **transaction.** For example, a business that pays cash for
supplies is engaging in a transaction. After each transaction, the
accounting equation must remain in balance.

The accounting concept, *Unit of Measurement*, is applied when
business transactions are stated in numbers that have common values—that is, using a common unit of measurement. (CONCEPT:
Unit of Measurement) For example, in the United States, business
transactions are recorded in dollars. In Switzerland, business transactions are recorded in Swiss francs. The unit of measurement concept is followed so that the financial reports of businesses can be
clearly stated and understood in numbers that have comparable values. For example, reports would not be clear if some information
was reported in United States dollars and some in Swiss francs.

CHAPTER 2 Starting a Proprietorship

21

MULTICULTURAL AWARENESS ACTIVITY (continued)
Each group or individual could choose a profession that is of personal interest. Students should be
encouraged to explore beyond the traditional medical and legal fields. For example, police officers and
firefighters also have professional organizations. Once an organization is researched, the activity can be
expanded to include writing to an organization to obtain their literature and information about the organization and its purpose.

AUDIT YOUR UNDERSTANDING

The AUDIT YOUR UNDERSTANDING
feature appears at the end of each
section of the chapter. Explain to your
students that the word *audit* means to
check or verify. AUDIT YOUR UNDER-
STANDING may be used to check student comprehension of the section
just studied. The answers are provided in Appendix D in the back of the
textbook.

1. A business owned by one person.
2. Assets = Liabilities + Owner's Equity.
3. Assets.
4. Liabilities and Owner's Equity.

Reteach

If students are having difficulty understanding the difference between personal and business assets and equities,
start two lists on the board—one for
personal items, one for business items.
Ask for student input.

Extend

Assign Cases for Critical Thinking 1.

Enrich

Assign the GLOBAL PERSPECTIVE feature on page 28. Discuss the feature and
distribute the GLOBAL PERSPECTIVE
Activity sheet in the Masters and Solutions Section in the Enrichment/Application Activities Section in the Teacher's Resource
Guide.

CLOSURE

Use Audit Your Understanding
questions.

LESSON PLAN 2-2

Materials
- Student pages 21–26
- Transparency 2-1, Blank Accounting Equation and Balance Sheet
- Demonstration Problem 2A, Accounting Equation
- Software: Accounting Tutorial

Objectives (Enabling Performance Task
a. Define accounting terms...
starting a service business...
as a proprietorship.

Check Figures Simplify Use Of Chapter Problems.

End-Of-Chapter Problems have Check Figures to save you time. This will mean you have more time to concentrate on helping your students master the concepts.

CHECK FIGURES

21

9

A Complete Package Of Teacher Support To Save You Time.

Teacher's Resource Guide
Now you can make more effective presentations with less preparation time. Includes Enrichment materials, Test Masters, blank ruling masters and solutions to tests.

TEACHER'S RESOURCE GUIDE

Bring complex concepts to life with skillfully designed **Transparency Masters**. Includes 90 all-new masters, with at least one per chapter.

TRANSPARENCIES

Test-giving is easier with the right **Printed Tests**. Both Problem Tests and Objective Tests are available.

TESTS

Working Papers with Demonstration and Recycling Problems provide additional problems you can use to demonstrate concepts within each chapter, and we've included rulings for the Recycling Problems.

WORKING PAPERS

New Teaching Support Options Help You Use Your Time More Effectively.

Now, *Century 21 Accounting* makes more help available. You can select the individual products you need to help you implement your instructional plan and give you more planning choices.

MicroExam. Now tests are easier to prepare and give with this test bank. It supplies 50 questions for each chapter and makes it simple to modify the tests or add your own.

> MICROEXAM

Electronic Auditor means you won't have to check your students' automated problems the time-consuming manual way ever again. This software does it for you, effortlessly and accurately.

> ELECTRONIC AUDITOR

Enhance your classroom instruction with the power of sight, sound, and motion. **Video Cassettes** involve your class in a way that no oral or written presentation can and make the material easier to understand. We make it easy for you to match this exciting new product with your own teaching style. The technology of tomorrow is available to you now from *Century 21 Accounting's* unsurpassed package of teacher support options.

> VIDEO

The Most Advanced Package For Advanced Accounting Instruction.

- Builds Upon The First-Year Course With The Same Approach And Features

- Continuity Helps Your Second-Year Students Learn Faster

- All New Package Helps You Teach More Efficiently

A Complete Package To Help You Achieve Your Teaching Goals

CENTURY 21 Accounting
ADVANCED COURSE
TEACHER'S RESOURCE GUIDE

CENTURY 21 Accounting
ADVANCED COURSE
CHAPTERS 1-24
WORKING PAPERS & STUDY GUIDES
ROSS, HANS...

CENTURY 21 Accounting
ADVANCED COURSE
TEACHER'S EDITION

CENTURY 21 Accounting
ADVANCED COURSE
ROSS, HANSON, GILBERT
SIXTH EDIT...

ROSS, HANSON, GILBERTSON & LEHMA...
SIXTH EDITION

Realistic Software For The Real World Beyond The Classroom.

- Provides Hands-On Experience With Computer Business Applications
- State-Of-The-Art Appearance And Function
- Works Like Popular Commercial Packages
- Uses Mouse Or Keyboard

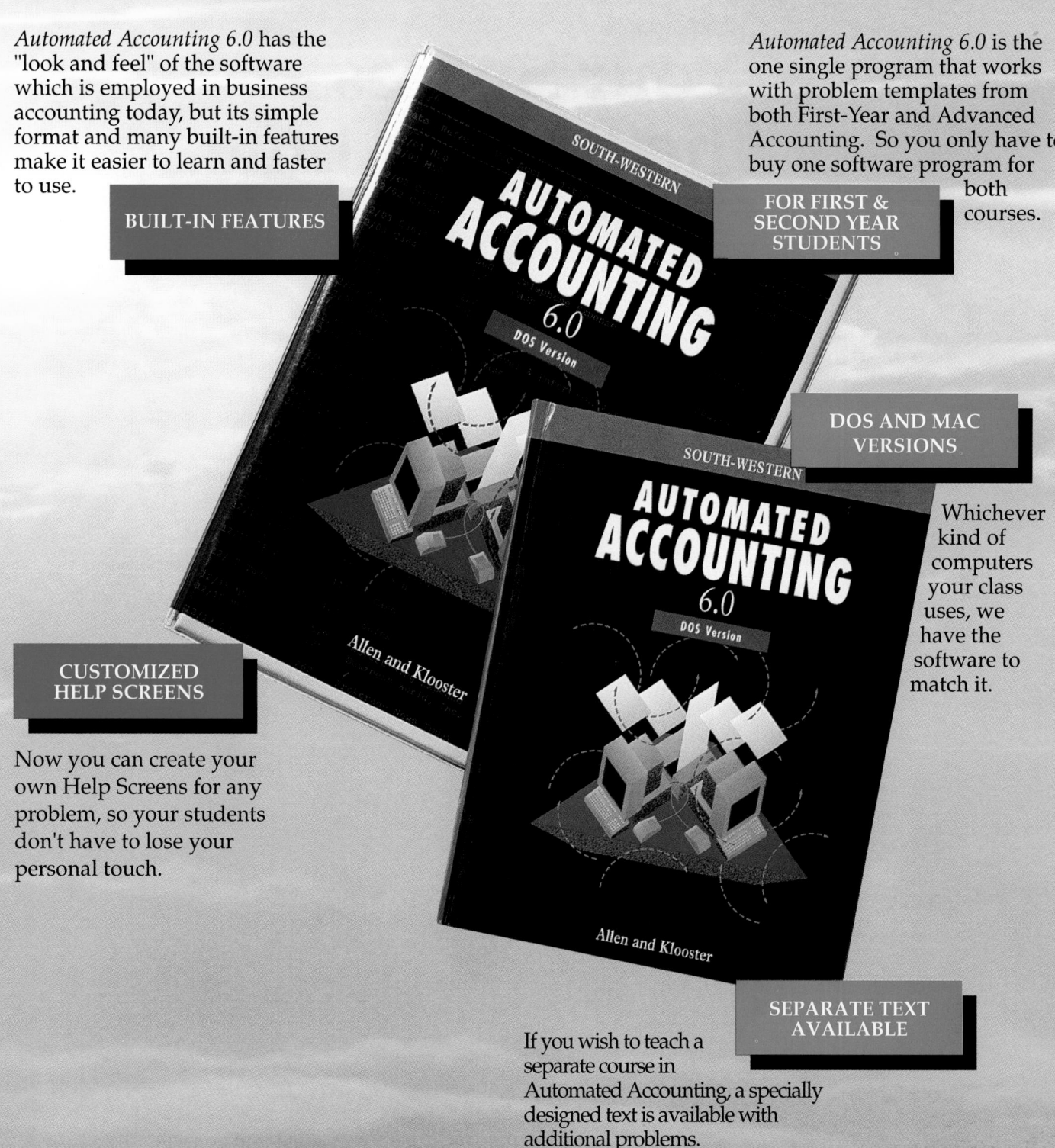

Automated Accounting 6.0 has the "look and feel" of the software which is employed in business accounting today, but its simple format and many built-in features make it easier to learn and faster to use.

BUILT-IN FEATURES

Automated Accounting 6.0 is the one single program that works with problem templates from both First-Year and Advanced Accounting. So you only have to buy one software program for both courses.

FOR FIRST & SECOND YEAR STUDENTS

DOS AND MAC VERSIONS

Whichever kind of computers your class uses, we have the software to match it.

CUSTOMIZED HELP SCREENS

Now you can create your own Help Screens for any problem, so your students don't have to lose your personal touch.

SEPARATE TEXT AVAILABLE

If you wish to teach a separate course in Automated Accounting, a specially designed text is available with additional problems.

13

Your Success Is The Bottom Line.

We know that no matter how good your teaching materials and support may be, you are the one who makes it happen for your students in the classroom.

For that reason, these new editions of *Century 21 Accounting* are dedicated to you.

We invite you to examine this text, and we welcome your comments or questions.

For help, or just to tell us how you feel about the enhancements we've made, please give us a call at 1-800-543-7972.

We are looking forward to hearing from you.

SOUTH WESTERN
PUBLISHING CO.

ISBN 0-538-62998-3

Stock No. BA20EAEG95

CENTURY 21
Accounting

CENTURY 21 Accounting

FIRST-YEAR COURSE

WRAPAROUND TEACHER'S EDITION

SIXTH EDITION

Kenton E. Ross, CPA
Professor of Accounting
East Texas State University
Commerce, Texas

Robert D. Hanson
Associate Dean
College of Business Administration
Central Michigan University
Mount Pleasant, Michigan

Claudia Bienias Gilbertson, CPA
Teaching Professor
Anoka-Ramsey Community College
Coon Rapids, Minnesota

Mark W. Lehman, CPA
Instructor
School of Accountancy
Mississippi State University
Starkville, Mississippi

Robert M. Swanson
Professor Emeritus of Business Education
and Office Administration
Ball State University
Muncie, Indiana

South-Western Publishing Co.
BA20FW

Teacher's Edition Photo Credits:

Photography by Alan Brown/Photonics: pages T5, T6 (top, middle), T7, 15A, 241A, 467A, 747A

Picture provided by Ameritech Mobile Communications, Inc.: page T6 (bottom)

Cover Design: The Optimum Group

Internal Design: Lesiak/Crampton Design

ISBN: 0-538-62953-3

1 2 3 4 5 6 7 8 9 0 KI 99 98 97 96 95 94

Printed in the United States of America

I(T)P
International Thomson Publishing

South-Western Publishing Co. is an ITP Company. The ITP trademark is used under license.

TEACHER'S EDITION CONTENTS

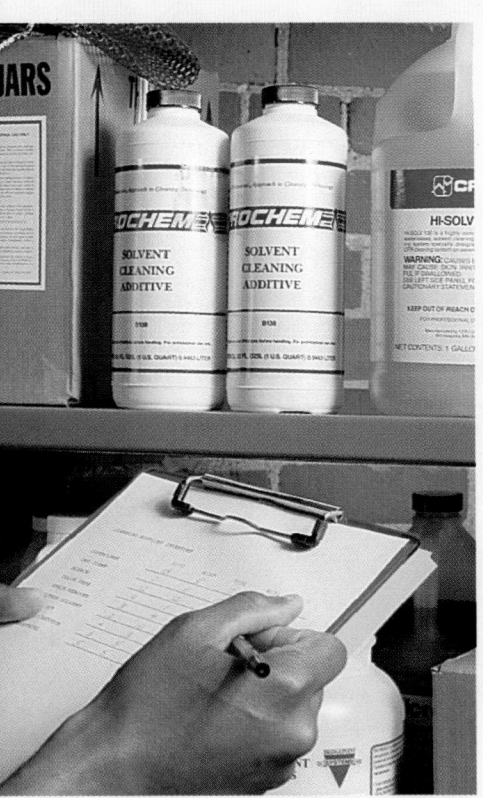

PART 3

Accounting for a Merchandising Business Organized as a Partnership (Overview)

PART 4

Accounting for a Merchandising Business Organized as a Corporation (Overview)

PART 5

The Legal Environment of Business (Overview)   747A

BREAKTHROUGH EDITION

This new 6th Edition of *CENTURY 21 ACCOUNTING, First-Year Course* has been completely redesigned to provide you and your students with a textbook and supplemental items that make accounting easy to teach and easy to learn. This new text, with many new features, supports various approaches to teaching accounting.

1. Traditional: *CENTURY 21 ACCOUNTING, First-Year Course* continues to support the traditional course in which accounting procedures are done manually within the framework of the accounting cycle.
2. Automated: Frequent integrated accounting topics show how manual concepts are practiced in an automated environment. *Automated Accounting 6.0* and higher software is used for illustrations and for solving textbook problems.
3. Contemporary curriculum: All of the features of the traditional course can be taught and automated accounting concepts can be integrated. However, with the new *CENTURY 21 ACCOUNTING, First-Year Course* you can also devote time to issues that concern educators today and concepts that are increasingly being integrated in college accounting courses. The textbook provides opportunities to focus on multicultural issues, ethical dilemmas, global (international) topics, communication activities, careers, math applications, and spreadsheet topics, without neglecting any of the traditional and automated accounting topics.

The textbook has new, relevant topics and features. This wraparound teacher's edition provides lesson plans, answers, and teaching tips and suggestions. All these enhancements make accounting easy to teach so that you can put your energies into the classroom where they benefit your students most. As you examine the new edition of *CENTURY 21 ACCOUNTING, First-Year Course* you will find the familiar basic skills and procedures of accounting still there, but greatly enhanced with new features.

INNOVATIVE ENHANCEMENTS FOR STUDENTS

Many new enhancements have been made to the student text and student support materials.

New Graphic Design

A new, larger trim size provides spacious margins and more readable pages.

Emphasis on Critical Thinking

Critical thinking activities are emphasized in the content of the text and through Multicultural Awareness activities, Professional Business Ethics, and Global Perspective activities which require thoughtful analysis of the situations described. Also critical thinking analysis has been added to end-of-chapter activities.

End-of-Chapter Activities

Two new activities have been added—Cases for Critical Thinking and Applied Communications. Cases for Critical Thinking require application and synthesis of accounting knowledge acquired in the chapter to new situations encountered by accounting professionals. Applied Communication activities require students to accurately communicate solutions to accounting activities.

Also, each end-of-chapter activity is correlated with the enabling performance tasks so students can see that they have met the learning objectives.

Special Features

New special interest features have been added to this edition. These features may be used as part of the accounting instruction to add interest to the course. However, if the instructor prefers, these features can be omitted without affecting the integrity of the course.

Multicultural Awareness

Student awareness of many cultural groups and their contributions to accounting is heightened in these articles. Teacher annotations suggest additional activities for further appreciation of multicultural contributions.

Professional Business Ethics

Business courses are often criticized for teaching business concepts but ignoring the ethical application of these concepts. Professional Business Ethics exposes students to ethical issues in the workplace. A 3-step checklist, first presented in Chapter 1, is used for solving the ethical dilemmas presented in each case.

Global Perspective

Students learn practical aspects of doing business in the international environment. Additional student worksheets are presented in the Teacher's Resource Guide (TRG) as blackline masters for additional exploration of these topics.

Personal Visions in Business

Interviews with successful businesspeople take students out of the classroom and into the community and beyond. Personal Visions in Business emphasize the importance of business/accounting study for success and highlight contributions of individuals with diverse cultural backgrounds.

Careers in Accounting

Information about accounting positions and the job world in general appear frequently. Job titles and descriptions of duties are correlated with the *Dictionary of Occupational Titles.*

Spreadsheet Options

Students discover various uses of spreadsheets that are relevant in current accounting practice.

FYI (For Your Information)

FYI notes in the margins of the student edition emphasize points to remember and provide enrichment information about accounting and business. Students will eagerly turn the pages to discover each new FYI.

Audit Your Understanding

Questions at the end of each section of each chapter provide an informal review of comprehension. Answers are printed in the wraparound teacher's edition. Answers are also printed in Appendix D of the student edition for self-checking.

Applied Mathematics

All formulas are highlighted and icons in the end-of-chapter activities indicate the first occurrence of each math skill. A full grid of math competencies and their first occurrence in the end-of-chapter activities is presented in the Applied Math Grid section in this teacher edition.

Applied Communications

Selected chapters have new Applied Communications activities that require responding to a situation in a written or verbal mode.

Glossary

The glossary presents every term defined in the text and its definition, including a reference to the page on which the term is defined.

Technology Enhancements

Technology has been integrated into this text through the use of software. As with other special features, instructors may choose to omit these activities without sacrificing the integrity of the accounting course.

Integrating Automated Accounting Topics is a new technology feature. These topics are mini-chapters that explain the application of *Automated Accounting 6.0* program software. Described in each are the procedures for completing input forms and instructions for automating selected problems from the chapters in the text.

Along with the new mini-chapters on automated accounting, students are given the opportunity to use the following software in conjunction with end-of-chapter activities.
* *Automated Accounting 6.0*
* *Accounting Tutorial*
* *Application Program*
* *Spreadsheet Templates*
* *Electronic Study Guide Software*

A comprehensive grid for using all software is within this Instructional Strategies material on page T38.

STUDENT SUPPORT MATERIALS

Three major supplements exist outside the textbook to aid student understanding and reinforcement of skills.

Working Papers and Study Guides

Using the working papers is the most efficient method of assuring that students complete problems accurately and in the least time possible. Beginning balances for ledger accounts and work sheet trial balances are provided where required. This eliminates tedious copying work before a problem can be started. Each workbook provides the following:
* An objective, short-answer study guide for each chapter.
* Sufficient ruled paper for completing the Drills for Understanding, Application Problems, Enrichment Problems, and Reinforcement Activities 1, 2, and 3.
* Input forms for completing the Integrating Automated Accounting Problems.

Demonstration and Recycling Problems Working Papers

Demonstration problems are a new problem set that demonstrate procedures from each chapter. The workbook furnishes all the accounting forms needed to complete all the demonstration and recycling problems. The narrative of the recycling problems is in Appendix C of the student textbook.

Simulations

A variety of business simulations may be used with *CENTURY 21 ACCOUNTING, First Year Course.* Business simulations should be used at intervals to integrate all the principles studied up to a certain point. Use of at least one simulation a semester is recommended. Simulations provide a capstone experience for each accounting cycle as well as provide realistic exposure to the business world.

All simulations are available in both manual and automated versions, except the payroll pegboard simulation, which is a manual version only. Separate teacher's keys are needed for the manual and automated versions.

Automated simulations require *Automated Accounting 6.0* plus the appropriate template disk. The template disk is recommended since the beginning balances and the charts of accounts for general ledger and subsidiary ledgers are already entered for the students.

The simulations available are:

Video Transfer, a service business organized as a proprietorship, is recommended for use after Chapter 10. One month's transactions are recorded in the books of account. The narrative of transactions is provided in the simulation envelope.

Viking Marine, a merchandising business organized as a partnership, is recommended for use after Chapter 18. One month's transactions are recorded in the books of account. Manual and automated versions are available in narrative or source document format.

Western Rider, Inc., a merchandising business organized as a corporation, is recommended for use after Chapter 27. One month's transactions are recorded in the books of account. This set is available in source document format.

Stellar Attractions Pegboard Payroll System, for use after Chapter 15, is self-contained and includes a pegboard device, payroll registers, employee's earning records, and paychecks, similar to those provided commercially to thousands of small and large businesses throughout the nation. Payroll transactions and instructions for using the pegboard system are provided in a narrative booklet. Use of this simulation provides the students with experiences very much like those in a real office.

The complete replacement package includes 4 earnings records, 30 checks, 2 payroll registers, and 1 narrative booklet. Each prepackaged set will accommodate 25 students and will be sold only in prepackaged sets. The pegboard and plastic bag will not be provided with this replacement set.

INNOVATIVE ENHANCEMENTS FOR TEACHERS

With this edition, we have also enhanced the teacher support materials with many new features. The major enhancement is the Wraparound Teacher's Edition.

Wraparound Annotated Teacher's Edition

The wraparound annotated teacher's edition contains the complete student text and an examination guide, teacher information, lesson plans and margin notes on reduced student pages, and chapter and part interleaf pages.

Using the Wraparound Teacher's Edition

The wraparound teacher's edition has margin notes on reduced student pages that contain lesson plans for each section of each chapter, teaching suggestion boxes that address relevant topics, answers to end-of-chapter activities, and check figures.

Lesson Plans

Lesson plans are printed in the margins of the wraparound teacher's edition. Most chapters have two or more lesson plans and they are positioned to show how each chapter can be broken down into several smaller parts. Abbreviated lesson plans are also printed in the TRG as blackline masters.

The lesson plans have been designed to satisfy the needs of teachers following various formats. The following parts are included in each lesson plan:

- **Materials.** Each lesson plan begins with a list of the items needed to complete the lesson, such as student pages covered, applicable software, and transparencies.
- **Goals.** Specific enabling performance tasks covered by each lesson plan are listed.
- **Focus.** Focus provides motivation for student learning and a setting or background for the work to be done as well as a transition from past lessons to the current one.
- **Teach.** Suggestions describes how the teacher presents material to the students and emphasizes important concepts.
- **Apply.** The use of specific transparencies and illustrations suggest how to prepare students for Guided and Independent Practice.
  Guided Practice. The instructor and students do the suggested guided practice activities together. The teacher's role is to demonstrate, monitor, observe, and answer questions. Students follow the demonstration step-by-step until readiness for independent practice activities is achieved.
  Independent Practice. Students perform suggested independent practice activities by themselves. The teacher does not normally intervene with instructional assistance.
- **Assess.** Each lesson plan ends with suggestions for informally assessing student comprehension as the lesson progresses.
  Reteach. Reteaching suggestions are used if students are having difficulty understanding the material to present the material in a different way.
  Extend/Enrich. Suggestions for extension and enrichment activities take students beyond the traditional assignments to stretch their ability and knowledge.
- **Closure.** Closure suggestions describe ways to review and reinforce the material.

- **Assess.** The last lesson plan for each chapter lists tests that can be used for formal assessment.

Teaching Suggestions

In addition to the lesson plans, marginal boxes describe various teaching strategies or tips. These can be categorized in three general areas:

1. *Suggestions Related to Building Student Skills.* Blue boxes describe actions the teacher can take to build applied skills in the following areas:
   - Communications
   - Mathematics
   - Building Study Skills
   - Language Arts
   - Word Processing
   - Writing Across the Curriculum
2. *Suggestions Related to Other Teaching Methodology.* Black boxes describe actions the teacher can take to reinforce concepts developed in the chapter. They can be categorized in the following areas:
   - Accounting Pedagogy
   - Assessment by Portfolio
   - Different Learning Abilities (covering Gifted Students, Limited English Proficiency (LEP) Students, Specific Learning Disability (SLD) Students, At-Risk Students, and Visually-Impaired Students)
   - Different Learning Styles (covering print learners, visual learners, auditory learners, tactile learners, and kinesthetic learners)
   - Cooperative Learning
   - Expanding Beyond the Classroom
   - Applying Visuals
   - Teaching Tip
   - Safety and Health
3. *Suggestions Related to Student Features.* Color coordinated boxes highlight special student features and their benefits. Additional optional activities, such as the Multicultural Awareness Activity, are suggested.
   - Multicultural Awareness
   - Professional Business Ethics
   - Global Perspective
   - Careers in Accounting
   - Personal Visions in Business
   - Spreadsheet Options
   - Audit Your Understanding
   - Software Focus

Check Figures

Check figures are given for end-of-chapter activities and reinforcement activities. When student solutions match these check figures, it can be assumed that the student's solutions are significantly correct. A blackline master of check figures is provided in the TRG to use as a student handout if desired.

OTHER TEACHER SUPPORT MATERIALS

We have also greatly enhanced our other teacher support material with new ideas to make organizing your lessons easier.

Teacher's Resource Guide

Some of the teacher aids available in this resource guide are as follows:

1. Lesson plans
2. Schedules for planning the year's work
3. Blackline masters for
   - Supplemental Global Perspective activities
   - Applied Math worksheets
   - Accounting forms
   - 3-step checklist for ethical decisions
   - Handbook for finding and correcting errors
   - Check figures handout
   - Assessment by portfolio
   - Resume checklist
4. Competency-based education outline and competency statements
5. Supplemental topics
   - Safety and health considerations
   - Personal income tax
   - Statement of changes in financial position
   - Voucher system
   - Completing a sales invoice
   - Calculating compound interest using an interest table
   - Personal attributes for success in business
6. Test section
   - Blackline masters for Unit Problem Tests
   - Answers for Unit Problem Tests
   - Blackline masters for Chapter Problem Tests
   - Answers for Chapter Problem Tests
   - Blackline masters for Unit Objective Tests
   - Answers for Unit Objective Tests
7. Integrating Automated Accounting section with solutions to all automated problems

Teacher's Editions of the Working Papers and Study Guides

The teacher's editions provide full solutions for all problems in the end-of-chapter sections of each student chapter, including reinforcement activities and integrating automated accounting problems.

Teacher's Edition of Demonstration and Recycling Problems

The teacher's edition for this student book provides full solutions for all problems. Teachers may wish to make transparencies of either the student or the teacher versions of the problems to demonstrate chapter applications.

Unit and Chapter Problem Tests

Solutions and blackline masters of the problem tests are provided in the TRG. Multiple copies of both sets of problem tests may be purchased from the publisher.

Unit Objective Tests

Answer keys and blackline masters of the objective tests are provided in the TRG. Multiple copies of the objective tests may be purchased from the publisher.

Overhead Transparencies

The overhead transparency package consists of 90 transparencies to illustrate the course. They are referenced in the lesson plans.

Wall Charts

The wall charts can be prominently displayed in the classroom and show the major summary illustrations from the chapters.

Simulation Keys

Each simulation has a separate key. Manual and automated versions of the simulation have separate keys. The automated keys show solutions to the input forms and required output.

MicroExam

This test preparation software can be used to produce objective tests or daily quizzes for one or more chapters. Problems may be selected by question or randomly generated. Answer key strips are also generated by the software.

Electronic Auditor

This piece of software will check student solutions to automated problems.

ORGANIZATION OF THE TEXT

The student text is organized in a logical manner. Learning progresses from the simple to the complex using a spiral approach as shown in the five parts of the textbook.

Scope and Sequence

Part 1: The accounting environment, ethics, and communications

Part 2: Service business organized as a proprietorship

Part 3: Merchandising business organized as a partnership

Part 4: Merchandising business organized as a corporation

Part 5: Forming and dissolving different forms of business organizations

Part Opener Page

Each part in the student edition begins with a page that lists the goals for the part so students understand the purpose of that part.

In the wraparound teacher's edition, the part opener also gives an overview of all the chapters in that part. An additional interleave page lists all special features for both student edition and teacher edition to assist the instructor in planning the lessons.

Chart of Accounts

Each part begins with a chart of accounts to provide a point of reference to account titles and account numbers.

Chapter Opener Page

Each chapter in the student edition begins with a page that shows a photograph related to the chapter, a list of the enabling performance tasks (goals/learning objectives) for the chapter, and a preview of the accounting terms to be defined within the chapter.

In the wraparound teacher's edition, an additional interleave page features planning grids to assist the instructor in teaching the content of that chapter.

Smaller Parts

Each chapter can be divided into smaller parts based on the lesson plans in the margins of the wraparound teacher's edition.

Enabling Performance Tasks (EPTs)

The Enabling Performance Tasks describe what the student will be able to achieve and demonstrate proficiency in after completing the chapter. End-of-chapter activities are labeled to show which EPTs are demonstrated by each activity.

Emphasis on Vocabulary

Accounting terms are carefully defined in complete sentences ending with the term printed in bold type.

Illustrations

The chapters are copiously illustrated to demonstrate the concepts presented in the chapter. In addition, each chapter has at least one chapter summary illustration and frequent interim summary illustrations.

End-of-Chapter Activities

These activities include Accounting Terms, Questions for Individual Study, Cases for Critical Thinking, Drills for Understanding, and Application, Mastery, and Challenge Problems. Applied Communications activities are interspersed throughout the text. Recycling Problems for students who need additional reinforcement are included in Appendix C.

Reinforcement Activities

Reinforcement Activities in the middle and end of each accounting cycle provide an opportunity to synthesize all learnings from the part and complete an entire accounting cycle project.

Simulations

Four accounting simulations, Video Transfer, Viking Marine, Stellar Attractions, and Western Rider, Inc. provide realistic simulations of daily business activities for students to apply the principles learned in an accounting cycle.

Special Features

This edition includes many new features that are specifically described in the section titled "Innovative Enhancements for Students." These include Multicultural Awareness, Professional Business Ethics, Global Perspective, Personal Visions in Business, Careers in Accounting, Spreadsheet Options, FYI (For Your Information), Audit Your Understanding, Applied Math, Applied Communications, and Integrating Automated Accounting Topics.

USING SOFTWARE AND TECHNOLOGY

After manual accounting procedures are mastered, computer software may be used as an enrichment activity to facilitate the processing of accounting data and experience the use of computers in accounting.

Five software packages are available to use with *CENTURY 21 ACCOUNTING, First-Year Course* to augment teacher instruction: *Study Guide Software, Accounting Tutorial: A Transaction Analysis Approach; Application Program Diskette for CENTURY 21 ACCOUNTING; Spreadsheet Template for CENTURY 21 ACCOUNTING;* and *Automated Accounting 6.0* or higher, and the accompanying templates.

All activities for which software may be used are designated by an icon next to the activity in the text. This makes identification easy for both the teacher and student. Also, software applicable to individual chapters is noted in lesson plans and interleave pages.

Each software package and its documentation is available from South-Western Publishing Company.

A complete correlation grid for using software is in the Teacher's Resource Guide.

Study Guide Software

Study Guide Software for CENTURY 21 ACCOUNTING enables students to complete the study guide from the working papers at the computer. This software is available for every chapter in the text. Therefore, there is not an icon in the text to indicate its use.

This software is self-contained and does not involve the use of templates.

Accounting Tutorial

Accounting Tutorial: A Transaction Analysis Approach provides for the use of a software to analyze daily transactions, adjusting entries, closing entries, and reversing entries. This software is self-contained and does not involve the use of templates.

Application Program

Application Program Diskette for CENTURY 21 ACCOUNTING may be used with selected end-of-chapter problems from *CENTURY 21 ACCOUNTING, First-Year Course* text. This software is self-contained and does not involve the use of templates.

Twenty-three problems from *CENTURY 21 ACCOUNTING* may be used with this program.

Spreadsheet Template

Spreadsheet Template for CENTURY 21 ACCOUNTING, First-Year and *Advanced Courses* may be used with selected Application Problems and Enrichment Problems. In order to use the templates, Lotus® 1-2-3® or Microsoft® Works™ are needed for DOS computers. For Macintosh computers, Microsoft Works for the Macintosh™ or Microsoft Excel® are needed.

Seventeen problems from *CENTURY 21 ACCOUNTING, First-Year Course* may be used with spreadsheet software.

Automated Accounting

Automated Accounting 6.0 or higher may be used to complete selected Application Problems, Enrichment Problems, Integrating Automated Accounting Problems, Reinforcement Activities, and Simulations. The *CENTURY 21 ACCOUNTING, First-Year Course* Template Disk is also needed to complete the Automated Accounting problems and reinforcement activities in the text. Separate templates are needed for each simulation that is completed.

A total of 31 problems, 3 reinforcement activities, and 3 simulations from *CENTURY 21 ACCOUNTING, First Year Course* may be automated using *Automated Accounting 6.0.*

It is suggested that the text that accompanies *Automated Accounting 6.0.* be used as reference. The correlation for that text is listed in the last column of the grid.

Startup

To boot the *Automated Accounting 6.0* software, key A1 at the prompt. Students will be prompted to enter the path to which a template file can be retrieved. After the file is retrieve, a help screen will appear. This student help screen contains step-by-step instructions for completing the problem. Direct your students to print a copy to use throughout the completion of the problem. You may want to file a copy of the help screen for reference.

The student text for *Automated Accounting 6.0* gives complete operational instructions for the software.

Documentation

Teachers who plan to use the *Automated Accounting 6.0* software in conjunction with *CENTURY 21 AC-COUNTING*, should also obtain at least one copy of the Automated Accounting student text and teacher's manual as complete documentation for the software. The student text gives instructions for using the software, including all software operations. The teacher's manual gives additional instructions including how to use the *Electronic Auditor 6.0*.

Saving Work in Progress on Template Disk

The keying of accounting data often must be halted before all data have been entered. For example, students may only be partially finished keying data for a computer application when a class period ends. *Automated Accounting 6.0* allows students to save a problem at any stage of completion. The software also allows the student to save a problem under more than one name. See the student text for complete instructions.

Building and Solving Additional Problems

Additional problems can be added to the template disk. Complete documentation of the procedures for doing so are in the teacher's manual.

Electronic Auditor 6.0. The Electronic Auditor helps you check your students' work. The software will compare student data files (stored on data disks or a hard disk) with solution data files stored on the *Electronic Auditor 6.0*. In addition, a summary report of the results will be provided.

You may also add solutions to the *Electronic Auditor 6.0* for problems you create. Once added, these solutions will appear in the solutions directory and can be used to check your student's solutions.

A full explanation of how to use the *Electronic Auditor 6.0* is provided in the teacher's manual.

STRATEGIES FOR OPTIMIZING INDIVIDUAL LEARNING

The student population not only reflects the cultural diversity in American society as a whole, but it also consists of students with different abilities and different styles of learning. Many of these individual student differences require an adjustment in teaching style or presentation. This section describes teaching strategies for students with different learning abilities, students with different learning styles, and cooperative learning.

Teaching Strategies for Students with Different Learning Abilities

Classrooms typically contain students with a wide variation of ability, intelligence, and motivation. Although the instructor must direct a majority of the instruction to the "average" student, optimal learning will occur only when the curriculum is modified to meet the needs of each individual student.

The first and greatest challenge facing the instructor is identifying the special abilities of each student. Whereas physical disabilities are usually relatively easy to identify, learning disabilities can be very difficult to detect and classify. Classifying students solely on examination scores and prior classroom performance may be misleading and should be avoided. For example, poor subject examination scores and short attention spans may be the symptoms of either a student with a specific learning disability or a gifted student who is bored.

The correct assessment of students should be a combined effort of the instructor, the school counselor or special education instructor, and the student. Together, this team can design an individualized program that will challenge the student while providing adequate opportunity to achieve attainable goals.

Gifted Students

One objective of programs for gifted students should be the development of leadership skills. Current literature suggests that four skill areas are involved in the development of effective leadership.

1. Cognition—The ability to identify, research, and learn factual knowledge.
2. Problem Solving—The ability to identify problems and develop creative solutions.
3. Interpersonal Communication—The ability to work with other people.
4. Decision Making—The ability to develop and implement realistic goals, and evaluate performance of the goals.

Different hemispheres of the brain control these functions. Cognition and Problem Solving are typically associated with left-brain functions; Interpersonal Communication and Decision Making are associated with right-brain functions. Therefore, effective leadership training must target development of both hemispheres. Most students will enter the classroom with stronger development in some skill areas more than others. Thus, a student lacking interpersonal communication skills should undertake projects to develop those skills.

The Professional Business Ethics and Applied Communications activities in the student textbook provide opportunities for gifted students to develop these leadership skills. Encourage gifted students to extend these activities by developing related activities.

Gifted students may need to move through the accounting program at an accelerated pace. It may not be appropriate for gifted students to work every problem provided. For example, after a chapter has been reviewed, gifted students may demonstrate mastery by working only the mastery or recycling problem. Others may need to work one or more of the application problems. In some cases the *Accounting Tutorial* software may substitute for working the application problems so students may go directly to the mastery problem. The challenge problem should always be assigned to gifted students to provide the "stretch" for exploring alternatives to the chapter content.

Additional activities might include:

1. Gifted students should master transaction analysis quickly; therefore, challenge them to identify a special research project that interests them. The students should be encouraged to identify a project that requires interaction with a businessperson. For example, a student could contact a bank loan officer to learn how a proprietor would apply for a loan, research formats for a business plan, and develop a business plan for a hypothetical business. Finally, the student could invite the bank loan officer to class and use role-playing to demonstrate how communication skills can enhance an individual's chance of getting the loan.

2. Partnerships require effective communication and cooperation among partners. Gifted students can best learn about the opportunities, problems, and challenges of a partnership by forming a real partnership. Encourage gifted students to form a partnership to sell a service or product of their selection. The students should prepare the partnership agreement, operate the business, and report the results of operations. Suggest that the students consult businesspersons, such as lawyers and accountants, for assistance.

3. Using gifted students as tutors for other students can be an effective way of teaching the topics students find most difficult. Allow the gifted student to complete one of these chapters while the class completes the first two chapters of a cycle. The gifted students can then assist you in presenting the concepts and procedures on their chapter to the class. Encourage the students to use visual aids and develop methods to assess student learning.

Limited-English-Proficiency Students

Limited-English-Proficiency (LEP) students are individuals whose native or dominant language is a language other than English. Although these students may be involved in special English-as-a-Second-Language (ESL) classes, the instructor can significantly improve learning by adopting several strategies.

1. Provide students with translations of key terms prior to presenting each chapter. Encourage students to use dictionaries.

2. Create visual instructional methods, such as posters and bulletin boards, that reinforce accounting concepts in both English and the other dominant language(s).

3. Use simple words in oral presentations and testing materi-als. Avoid polysyllabic words. Simplify the non-technical vocabulary.

4. At early levels, LEP students have limited comprehension of English and can respond with one or two word answers. Assess understanding by having students match, choose, move, draw, or point. Students at this level can respond to directions that require them to name, list, categorize, label, or reply with one or two words.

5. LEP students, like visual learners, require a variety of visual clues to support the lesson and help them understand abstract ideas. Use transparencies, textbook illustrations, and software demonstrations to provide these clues.

6. Allow for longer pauses when you ask questions. Non-native speakers need more time to formulate their answers.

7. Stress accounting terms so that LEP students learn the language of accounting.

8. Speak directly. Avoid negative constructions and passive verbs, such as "Don't forget that Cash is not debited in this transaction." Instead, say "Remember to credit Cash in this transaction."

9. Rather than asking students whether they understand what you have said, ask them to restate what you have said in their own words.

10. Adjust the length of time allotted to complete assignments and tests. Remember that the primary objective is to assess knowledge of accounting rather than the ability to translate and comprehend the question or problem.

11. Coordinate classroom activities with the school's ESL support staff.

12. Don't misinterpret a nod as understanding. The nod may instead mean that the listener did not understand.

13. Be cautious if there are no interruptions or questions. It may mean that very little has been understood.

14. In some cultures, "Yes" is the response to every question. It may mean "I heard your question" rather than "I understand."

15. In some cultures, giggling or inappropriate laughter may indicate embarrassment at poor comprehension rather than disrespect for the teacher.

Additional activities might include:

1. Recruit businesspersons willing to act as mentors for LEP students. These mentors should be invited to speak to the class and periodically meet with LEP students to assist with assignments. The instructor should be actively involved in any meetings with LEP students to show support for both the mentor and the students.

2. In many cases, LEP students come from cultures different from the predominant culture in the United States. LEP students should research the cultural differences that may impact how an individual conducts business. Cultural differences can be identified by reading books and current magazines as well as interviewing businesspersons. Encourage students to orally present their findings to the class; role-playing is an entertaining way to demonstrate how an individual's ignorance of cultural differences can have disastrous results.

3. Although LEP students may feel handicapped in the classroom, their knowledge of two languages provides them with excellent career opportunities in today's international business environment. LEP students should identify what unique career opportunities exist for them in various types of organizations, such as international businesses and government. Students could create a bulletin board to inform other students of these opportunities. Successful bulletin boards could also be used in the classrooms of younger students, or in elementary schools.

Specific Learning Disability (SLD) Students

Instructors need not be reminded that adolescence is a period of turmoil and adjustment. What many instructors often view as adolescent behavior may, however, be caused by a student's specific learning disability (SLD). The correct assessment of SLD students is difficult because adolescent behavior is similar to the typical characteristics of SLD students.

Passive Learners

When faced with making a decision, SLD students avoid making a decision in favor of waiting for a teacher to provide specific direction.

Poor Self-Concept

Years of failure cause SLD students to have low self-esteem, thus reducing their confidence that they can achieve academic success.

Inept Social Skills

SLD students often have difficulty making and keeping friends.

Attention Deficits

SLD students often lack the ability to concentrate on one topic for an extended period.

Lack of Motivation

Years of failure have conditioned SLD students to doubt their abilities and, therefore, view their efforts as being futile.

Once an SLD student is correctly assessed, the instructor should work with the student to develop an individualized program. The basic objective of the program should be the development of functional (life) skills. The student should be counseled to established challenging yet attainable goals and provide frequent feedback as to the attainment of these goals. The student's academic success should be measured on the demonstrated ability to learn as much as the mastery of a defined body of knowledge.

Several general instructional strategies are effective in teaching SLD students:

1. When asking questions during class, ask SLD students questions that they can likely answer successfully. Save more difficult or unstructured questions for better students.

2. Rotate instructional materials rather than trying to complete a single text. Supplemental instructional materials may include additional texts, business magazines, government publications, etc.

3. Incorporate current literature (magazines and newspapers) to identify current topics of interest to students.

4. Encourage students to maintain a daily log or journal that describes their academic progress. Students can share this log, if they desire, with the teacher when updating their individual program.

5. When feasible, SLD students should become involved in work-study programs that are consistent with course content. When work-study opportunities are unavailable, simulations can be used to provide a simulated work environment. Field trips are an excellent method to expose students to the business world.

Additional activities might include:

1. The popular board game *Monopoly* is well known as an enjoyable way to practice mathematical skills. The game also provides students the opportunity to analyze and record their transactions. Playing *Monopoly* enables students to see how transaction analysis and the accounting equation provide information for business decisions. Students should use T accounts until they have

completed the cycle. The instructor may need to assist students with identifying accounts, such as plant assets, that are not presented in the cycle.

2. Specific Learning Disability (SLD) Students. Exposing students to actual business situations can be an excellent motivational device. Arrange a field trip to a local business familiar to the students, such as a grocery store. Before the field trip, require the students to identify questions to ask the managers of the business during the field trip. After the field trip, lead a class discussion which allows students the opportunity to share what they learned.

3. Specific Learning Disability (SLD) Students. Many students will ultimately work in inventory-related jobs. Simulating the inventory of a business will enable students to actively participate in the accounting for inventory. For example, students could establish a classroom store carrying school supplies, snacks, or other low cost items. The students would record the purchase and sales transactions and update the perpetual inventory. Students would periodically take inventory and reconcile the periodic and perpetual inventory quantities.

At-Risk Students

Many environmental factors may negatively impact a student's ability and motivation to succeed academically. Any student who is a potential dropout may be classified as an at-risk student. At-risk students typically are deficient in mathematics, reading, and language skills. These students provide a unique challenge to the accounting instructor since the instructor has little, if any, power to correct problems in the home environment.

Effective instructional strategies for at-risk students should be based on the premise that all individuals have a need for achievement and social acceptance. Within the accounting classroom, these needs can be fulfilled by developing a curriculum that promotes academic success and acceptance by the instructor. Techniques for working with at-risk students include:

1. Develop a personal profile of the student. Avoid placing too much significance on past academic performance as this may represent a symptom rather than the underlying problem.

2. Together with the student, develop an individualized program that allows the student to attain both short-term and long-term goals. When identifying goals, consider the student's anticipated career goals.

3. Utilize the lesson plans provided in the teacher's edition to divide each chapter into smaller parts to

create short units that provide frequent opportunities for assessment and goal attainment.

4. Modify presentation strategies to include more visual displays and supplement explanations with current, realistic examples.

5. Organize field trips and mentor programs to expose students to the business environment.

Additional activities might include:

1. Assist students to understand how accounting is a useful skill in careers which interest them. This could be accomplished many ways. For example, a student who shows interest in auto mechanics could be introduced to the owner of a local auto repair business. The student could then report his/her observations to the instructor in oral or written form. If no mentor is available, trade magazines often present articles to assist their readers in managing their businesses.

2. Many at-risk students can become motivated to begin self-improvement only when they recognize that they have a need to improve. One method of promoting self-evaluation is to have students identify the qualities they would require of another individual. Have students imagine that they are partners in a business that is considering hiring employees for both service and office positions. Require the student to prepare a job description that includes both skill and personal characteristics that applicants should possess. This activity should enable students to compare their qualifications with the job descriptions they have developed.

3. Allow the students to identify and complete a project that interests them. For example, a student who shows special interest in both art and computers could prepare a presentation using graphic or presentation software. Shareware companies, as advertised in many computer magazines, provide an inexpensive source of software. The instructor should assist the student in learning the software and developing a business-related class presentation.

Visually Impaired Students

Students with mild visual impairments are typically mainstreamed and may elect to enroll in accounting. The nature and degree of students' visual impairments will vary. A student's visual impairment may include a difficulty in reading print, an inability to distinguish colors, a sensitivity to light, and a limited field of vision. The instructor must identify each student's exact impairment and adapt teaching strategies appropriately.

Many sources exist for providing alternative teaching materials. Most states have schools for the blind and rehabilitation service agencies that can enlarge the textbook and working papers. Consult these organizations to identify the latest technologies available for assisting the students.

The instructor and student should develop an individualized program that establishes a time frame for achieving specific learning objectives. The learning objectives should be consistent with the student's anticipated career goals. The time frame should consider the student's impairment and the availability of technical assistance, such as enlarged materials and closed circuit television. The use of software should not be overlooked for visually impaired students, particularly if oversized monitors with larger displays are available.

Additional activities might include:

1. It is important for visually impaired students to have confidence in their ability to participate fully within the business world. Require students to prepare an oral or written report which profiles a successful visually impaired business professional.
2. New technologies are continually being developed that assist visually impaired students to participate fully in both school and business. Students must be aware of these technologies and know how to continually learn of new technologies. Using government agencies as a resource, assist the students in preparing a report concerning anticipated technologies.
3. The additional time required for visually impaired students to complete the first cycles will minimize the time available to complete additional cycles. The instructor should consider skipping chapters 19 and 20 in favor of beginning chapters that present the new topics of uncollectible accounts receivable, plant assets, and inventory.

Teaching Strategies for Students with Different Learning Styles

There are many different learning styles. Some people learn best from reading material. Others need to see a demonstration or learn by feeling. Still others may learn best from auditory cues. It is important to remember, however, that no matter what learning style works best for any individual, learning style is not an indicator of intelligence. Two people of similar levels of intelligence may learn best in two different styles of learning. Learning style is also not necessarily a rigid behavior. Many individuals may have a dominant learning style; however, most also have the flexibility to adapt learning style to the demands of the material to be learned. Different learning styles include print, visual, auditory, tactile, and kinesthetic learning.

Print Learners

The print learner prefers to see the data in print— preferably printed in words.

1. When introducing the T account, a print learner would prefer to study the illustration in the textbook which shows a T account, labelled with the words "DEBIT" and "CREDIT."
2. When covering journal entries, the instructor should discuss the entries, using the textbook examples and referring to the textbook. The print learner can later go back and study the entries.
3. When learning how to post, the print learner would prefer to see the process in print. This can be done by distributing a handout which explains the steps in the posting process. Allow the student to study the handout.
4. When learning formulas, the print learner would prefer to be able to study the formula as given in the textbook or as printed on a separate handout. The print material should show the formula as well as an example of performing the calculations.

Visual Learners

The visual learner needs to "see" the concept. One way for the learner to "see" the concept is mental visualization. Illustrations and visual aids are important to the visual learner.

1. Ask the student (with eyes closed) picture a T account. The student should be able to see both sides of the account. Next, the student should visualize the word "DEBIT" on the left side of the account. Finally, the student should visualize the word "CREDIT" on the right side of the account. Once this concept takes on a visual form, the student will be able to access it when needed.
2. When covering journal entries, the instructor should discuss the entries, using a transparency or the chalkboard to record the entry. In addition, the student should be asked to mentally picture each part of the entry before the instructor actually writes it on the transparency or chalkboard.
3. To teach posting, the instructor could use a transparency to assist in the lecture. The transparency could be (1) a blank transparency that the instructor completes or (2) a prepared transparency that uses arrows to trace the steps involved in posting.
4. Formulas, such as those used to calculate component percentages, should be illustrated on the chalkboard to assist visual learners. For depreciation, the instructor should complete the calculations for a few depreciable assets to show the process to visual learners.

Auditory Learners

The auditory learner will best learn by hearing. Auditory learners who read a textbook chapter benefit from hearing reinforcement of key concepts spoken out loud.

1. When introducing the T account, have the student say out loud that the "left side is the debit side of the account." Repeating this statement a few times will increase the chances of its being reinforced. Repeat the process with the statement the "right side is the credit side of the account."
2. To reinforce the learning of journal entries, the auditory learner should verbally repeat the analysis of the transaction. The student should also verbally list the steps involved in making the entry.
3. When learning how to post, the auditory learner would prefer to hear the steps involved in posting. This can be done via a live lecture or a taped tutorial. To reinforce learning, the student could recite the posting steps to another student or group of students.
4. The auditory learner can reinforce the learning of formulas by verbally explaining the formula and/or calculations to other students in a small group. In a group of three, for example, each student should get the opportunity to "teach" the formula to the other two students. Through this process, each student in the group will "teach" the formula once and "learn" the formula two times.

Tactile Learners

The tactile learner learns best by touching or handling objects.
1. Using play money, have the student touch the right side of the desk and place an amount of money on it to reinforce an amount in the right side or credit side of an account. Repeat the process for the left/debit side.
2. Tactile learners may benefit from using the computer to key journal entries and then print reports. A ruler can be positioned on the input forms as a guide when keying the entries. The student should also be encouraged to place a finger on each account title in the journal entries report and trace it over to the amount in the amount column of the report to check it for accuracy. Tactile learners should also be given the opportunity to journalize transactions from at least one simulation that contains source documents which must be handled to analyze, journalize, and file.
3. The tactile learner can use a group of index cards to represent the general ledger. Each card should represent an account and should have 3 vertical lines to distinguish between the debit and credit columns, and balance columns. Have the tactile learner post each example of a journal entry to the appropriate cards (accounts).
4. Suggest using a calculator with a printed tape to perform mathematical calculations. Better calculators also print the operational signs of calculations (+, −, etc.) for students to trace the steps in a calculation.

Kinesthetic Learners

The kinesthetic learner learns best by taking an active part in the instruction. Motion is an important part of kinesthetic learning.
1. Have the student draw a T account in the air or use a finger to draw a T account on the back of the hand or arm. Next, have the student label the left side with the word "DEBIT" and the right side with the word "CREDIT."
2. To teach journal entries, the instructor should give the student journal paper and have the student complete the entries as the instructor demonstrates on a transparency or chalkboard.
3. The kinesthetic learner would prefer to participate in the posting process. Use a transparency of the ledger account and have each student complete one or more steps of the posting process at the overhead projector. Other students can be completing the posting process individually on printed ledger accounts.
4. Provide the opportunity to perform the calculations to solve formulas. One way to accomplish this is to develop a work sheet with several examples listed or use appropriate drills from the working papers.

COOPERATIVE LEARNING

Cooperative learning activities should be an integral part of accounting pedagogical strategies. Cooperative learning involves small heterogeneous groups of students who work together to share the responsibility for learning. Cooperative learning activities should be designed with the following goals in mind.
1. All students should be able to participate.
2. Groups should be heterogeneous.
3. Each student needs to be held accountable for his or her contribution to the group.

Cooperative learning is more successful with heterogeneous rather than homogeneous groups. Research further supports cooperative learning as a teaching strategy to increase students' motivation, achievement, and behavior. The teacher should select team members for a cooperative learning activity. Group composition should include a mixture of gender, ability level, cultural or ethnic background, and learning style. For example, placing a visual learner with an auditory learner enhances and strengthens the group's performance. Group members should be rotated frequently.

The time needed to complete an activity will vary among groups. Therefore, the teacher needs to provide additional activities to be completed by groups as they finish. These activities might include, for example, specific questions about the activity. These additional activities are often referred to as debriefing.

Cooperative learning promotes the development of higher-order thinking skills where brighter students explain concepts or principles to slower students. Using higher-order thinking skills to articulate ideas in accounting will normally result in material's being learned more effectively with improved retention rates.

To be successful, each student must be held accountable for his/her contribution to the cooperative learning activity. A variety of evaluation methods may be employed. These methods may include (1) a short quiz taken individually, (2) teacher observation of individual contributions to a group activity, or (3) bonus points assigned to individuals only if all group members do well individually. Performance on cooperative learning activities in accounting should range from no more than 5 to 10 percent of the final grade.

One of the goals of cooperative learning is to have students work out the roles of the group members themselves. Some groups will assign a role to an individual, such as when a representative of the group will need to record results and present them to the class, and sometimes individuals within a group will assume roles within the group without being asked to do so.

Some cooperative learning activities are as follows:

1. *Research project:* Assign students to groups of two. Each group researches the financial statements (through the annual report) of a company in which they are interested, perhaps because they are familiar with the product. Students look for a list of specific items such as what kinds of stock is the corporation authorized to issue, what categories of assets are listed on the balance sheet, what is the total of current liabilities, did net income increase/decrease from the previous period, etc. The group must then plan and deliver a presentation of the data to the entire class. Additional time outside of class is needed to complete research and prepare presentation. Timeframe: 45 minutes.

2. *Designing a better journal:* Before introducing special journals, assign students to groups of three. Ask students to design a more efficient journal or journal system. Limit the amount of direction given to students to encourage creativity. Each group should develop the new journal on poster-size paper and present/explain the journal to the rest of the class. Timeframe: 45 minutes.

3. *Develop a better way to classify assets:* Assign students to groups of three. Give students a deck of cards with one asset listed on each card. Ask each group to physically group these asset cards to develop a better system of classifying assets. Each group should explain their system to one other group. Timeframe: 30 minutes.

4. *Explain what component percentages measure:* Assign students to groups of three. Each group is to plan, prepare, and deliver a presentation to NON ACCOUNTANTS. The presentation should explain what component percentages are and how they are used to analyze financial statements. Timeframe: 30 minutes over several class periods.

5. *Divide the class into groups of two or three students each.* Have each group discuss and prepare a list of service businesses found in the local community. Each group should appoint a leader who will present the list of businesses and services to the class. Timeframe: 20 minutes.

6. *Divide the class into groups of two students each.* Using a drill that involves analyzing transactions, have students orally analyze transactions to each other, alternating transactions. Timeframe: 20 minutes.

7. *Divide the class into two groups.* Each group stands and faces each other. The teacher or a student moderator states an accounting term. The first student to raise a hand has the opportunity to give the correct definition. The group with the most correctly defined terms is declared the winner. As an alternative to this game, the teacher or moderator may read the definition of a term, such as "Anything of value that is owned," while the groups must identify the term. The answer should be given in a question format, such as "What is an asset?" if you wish to imitate a popular television game show.

8. *Reinforcement Activities.* Assign reinforcement activities as homework. Divide the class into groups of two students each. Each pair of students exchange and evaluate each other's work in class. Students are permitted to correct their work based on their partner's evaluation. Timeframe: 15 minutes.

9. *Divide the class into groups of four or five students each.* Using Cases for Critical Thinking, each group analyzes the cases and arrives at agreed-upon solutions. One member of each group is appointed the recorder and presents the group's analysis to the class. Timeframe: 20 minutes.

10. *Divide the class into groups of two or three students each.* Each group will discuss and prepare a list of merchandising businesses found in the local community. The group-appointed leader presents to the class the list and merchandise being sold. Timeframe: 25 minutes.

11. *Divide the class into groups of two students.* Each group decides on a merchandising business to form as a partnership. The teacher provides a list of sample transactions as well as all forms necessary to complete a partnership accounting cycle. This activity is completed utilizing both in-class and out-of-class time throughout the study of Part 3. The teacher meets periodically with each group to offer assistance and determine progress.

12. *Divide the class into auditing groups of three or four students per group.* Each auditing group is responsible for assisting other class members as well as correcting homework assignments. A lead auditor is appointed by the group and is responsible for turning in completed homework assignments for each group member to the teacher.

SUGGESTIONS FOR TEACHING PROFESSIONAL BUSINESS ETHICS

Businesses have recently become aware of the severe implications of the unethical behavior of employees. In response, many businesses have begun training their employees to make ethical decisions and establishing company codes of conduct. The message from businesses today is clear—employees must be capable of making ethical decisions to protect the business from legal liability and to maximize long-term profits.

Most students' principles of right and wrong are well established prior to their enrolling in high school accounting. Thus, the presentation of business ethics does not involve the teaching of right and wrong. Instead, students need to learn how to apply their principles of right and wrong to business situations.

Professional Business Ethics

There are nine Professional Business Ethics features in this text to give instructors an opportunity to teach ethics in the accounting class.

Causes of Unethical Behavior

Chapter 1 provides an introduction to business ethics. The major causes of unethical behavior are presented to assist students in recognizing the forces that can cause unethical behavior. Recognizing the causes of unethical behavior is the first step in making business decisions that prevent employees from being placed in compromising situations.

Steps for Analyzing Ethical Situations

A three-step checklist is presented to help students analyze the ethics of an action. This approach encourages students to collect pertinent information that will provide a basis for their decision. Ultimately, students'

decisions are based on their personal ethics applied to the facts of the situation.

Assessment

Correct solutions are generally obvious if the action is either illegal or violates a business or professional standard. For example, most students will agree that it is unethical to dispose of hazardous waste into the water supply. However, students may challenge compliance with other laws and standards. A class discussion of whether the truck drivers of a business should be required to drive the speed limit and wear safety belts may demonstrate many students' willingness to disregard selected laws.

Many of the situations in the Professional Business Ethics activities provide situations where the line between right and wrong is unclear. As a result, students will likely differ on their decision as to whether the action is ethical. Assessment of Professional Business Ethics activities should be based on the students' analysis of the facts and the objective support for their decisions. The students' decisions about whether a case demonstrates ethical behavior should not be assessed. Therefore, no conclusions are provided with the solutions.

Teachers can adopt several strategies to cover a Professional Business Ethics activity. The activity can be presented initially as a classroom discussion. Alternately, the activity can be assigned as an individual or group project. Whichever method is used, students should be given the opportunity to discuss the case in class. This exchange of ideas enables students to observe how other individuals make and support their decisions. When asking questions and making observations, the instructor should be careful not to reveal his or her personal bias.

Communication Skills

The Professional Business Ethics activities provide an opportunity for students to practice communication skills. For example, the Professional Business Ethics activity in Chapter 1 requires students to determine what action, if any, a manager should take when an employee obtained a position by falsifying a resume. Students could assume the position of manager and prepare the appropriate message to the employee. In this case, the students would also be required to identify the correct method of communication.

Solutions for Professional Business Ethics

Chapter 1: Can I Say This in My Resume?

Students are required to evaluate the ethical behavior of a person who overstated a resume. Students are instructed to use the three-step checklist to determine whether Kenneth demonstrated ethical behavior in preparing his resume.

This first Professional Business Ethics activity has been completed in the chapter for the students to walk them through the three-step checklist of analyzing ethical behavior. The Professional Business Ethics activities in future chapters will not provide answers in the textbook.

Since personal ethics are unique, students' solutions will vary. Although there is no one correct solution, the solution given illustrates the use of the three-step checklist.

Guide students through this checklist and encourage different solutions from them.

Chapter 3: Is This Really a Business Expense?

Students will evaluate the ethical behavior of a business owner. Students must determine whether a series of situations illegally avoids federal income taxes. Situations 1 and 3 describe illegal activities since they contradict federal income tax regulations. Although situations 2 and 4 are not illegal, some students may view the situations as unethical.

Since personal ethics are unique, students' solutions will vary. Although there is no one correct solution, the following solution illustrates the use of the three-step checklist.

Situation 1:

Step 1. Is the action illegal? Yes. The government only allows expenses to include those items necessary to conduct business. Unless Mr. Stovall could prove a business purpose for the phone calls, reporting the cost of the personal calls on the tax return would be illegal.

Steps 2 and 3. Because the action is illegal, no evaluation of these questions is necessary.

Situation 2:

Step 1. Is the action illegal? No. The government does not have limits on the quality or cost of assets purchased by businesses.

Step 2. Does the action violate company or professional standards? No. Company or professional standards do not apply.

Step 3. Who is affected, and how, by the action? *(See Table 1.)*

TABLE 1

PEOPLE AFFECTED	NEGATIVE	POSITIVE
Proprietor		Enjoys luxury of leather chair. Reduces tax liability.
Society	Lost tax revenues may be offset with higher taxes on other taxpayers.	Economy benefits from his spending $1,200.00 rather than $400.00 for the chair.

Situation 3:

Step 1. Is the action illegal? Yes. Although the transaction is not illegal, failure to report the transaction for income tax purposes is illegal. The transaction should have been recorded as a sale in Stovall Designs' accounting records. The fact that Mr. Stovall personally received wood and paint does not mean he can avoid recording the transaction in Stovall Design's accounting records. Not recording the transaction will result in an incorrect amount being recorded for revenue on the income tax return.

Steps 2 and 3. Because the action is illegal, no evaluation of these questions is necessary.

Situation 4:

Step 1. Is the action illegal? No. The government allows a business to record as an expense all services necessary to conduct business.

Step 2. Does the action violate company or professional standards? No. Company or professional standards do not apply.

Step 3. Who is affected, and how, by the action? *(See Table 2.)*

TABLE 2

PEOPLE AFFECTED	NEGATIVE	POSITIVE
Proprietor		Enjoys beauty of plants without having to personally maintain them. Reduces tax liability.
Employees		Enjoy beauty of plants.
Society	Lost tax revenues may be offset with higher taxes on other taxpayers.	Economy benefits from hiring the floral company to maintain plants.

Chapter 8: Am I a Software Pirate?

Students will evaluate the ethical behavior in three situations involving computer software. The activity also introduces the concept of shareware. The instructor may have students research information about shareware before assigning this activity.

The action of each situation may violate copyright laws. Students will typically recognize that situations 1 and 3 are illegal and agree that such behavior is unethical.

The discussion of this activity can be extended by asking students to evaluate whether making a copy of a cassette tape is ethical. This situation closely parallels the software issue, yet is common behavior among students. Many students will admit to copying musical recordings but may rationalize that their behavior is not unethical. This discussion could be used to illustrate how difficult it is to evaluate ethical situations objectively, especially when an objective evaluation indicates that our actions are unethical.

Since personal ethics are unique, students' solutions will vary. Although there is no one correct solution, the following solution illustrates the use of the three-step checklist.

Situation 1:

Step 1. Is the action illegal? Yes. The company's copying of software violates the license agreement.

Steps 2 and 3. Because the action is illegal, no evaluation of these questions is necessary.

Situation 2:

Step 1. Is the action illegal? No. however, it is usually requested that a fee be sent to the creator of the software.

Step 2. Does the action violate company or professional standards? Yes. Professional standards dictate that such a request be honored.

Step 3. Who is affected, and how, by the action? The shareware author will lose revenue. *(See Table 3.)*

TABLE 3

PEOPLE AFFECTED	NEGATIVE	POSITIVE
Shareware Authors	Lose revenue.	
Individual		Enjoys free use of software.
Society	Shareware authors have no incentive to continue to develop new software.	

Situation 3:

Step 1. Is the action illegal? Yes. The university's copying of the software violates the license agreement. The fact that the university is a public organization is irrelevant.

Steps 2 and 3. Because the action is illegal, no evaluation of these questions is necessary.

Chapter 11: Am I Cheating the Company?

Students will evaluate a partner's taking of inventory for personal use. Since personal ethics are unique, students' solutions will vary. Although there is no one correct solution, the following solution illustrates the use of the three-step checklist.

Instruction 1:

Step 1. Is the action illegal? No. Ms. Rushing's taking items home is not illegal. However, if the cost of the food is recorded as a business expense, the action would be illegal since it avoided federal income taxes. The transaction should be recorded as a drawing from Ms. Rushing's capital account rather than as a business expense.

Step 2. Does the action violate company or professional standards? No. However, Ms. Rushing's taking items home without recording the transaction in the accounting records may violate the partnership agreement. All assets of the partnership are owned equally by the partners. By using an asset for personal use, Ms. Rushing receives all the benefits of the asset while paying for only half of its cost.

Step 3. Who is affected, and how, by the action? *(See Table 4.)*

TABLE 4

PEOPLE AFFECTED	NEGATIVE	POSITIVE
Stella Rushing		Consumes quality food without paying for its full cost.
Frances Phillips	Must share the cost of the food consumed by her partner.	
Partnership	Future of partnership may be endangered if negative feelings develop between partners.	
Society	Food available for orphanage decreased.	

Instruction 2:

Ms. Phillips should not permit Ms. Rushing to take any items home without establishing policies that are included in the partnership agreement. Even the taking of expired items should be governed by the partnership agreement. Ms. Phillips must communicate her disapproval of Ms. Rushing's actions and make positive suggestions to correct the situation. Ms. Phillips must consider that Ms. Rushing's action may not be intentional; she may simply not understand the full effect of her actions.

Chapter 15: Who Owns My Time?

Students will evaluate three employment practices. These employment practices are legal and none violate individual company policies or professional standards. Thus, each practice must be evaluated by analyzing the affect on each group. Since personal ethics are unique, students' solutions will vary. Although there is no one correct solution, the following solution illustrates the use of the three-step checklist.

Encourage students to identify other employment-related behavior that they have witnessed or experienced. Discuss the factors that may have caused the unethical behavior and ask students what actions should be taken to correct these practices.

Situation 1:

Step 1. Is the action illegal? No. The receptionist has no legal obligation to perform tasks not specifically assigned by management.

Step 2. Does the action violate company or professional standards? No. Unless the company has a policy that prohibits employees from using idle time for personal activities, such as reading books or completing crossword puzzles, no company standard has been violated.

Step 3. Who is affected, and how, by the action? *(See Table 5.)*

TABLE 5

PEOPLE AFFECTED	NEGATIVE	POSITIVE
Receptionist	Failure to spend time improving skills may lead to her termination. May be resented by other employees.	Provides recreation.
Employees	Employees without idle time may resent receptionist's light work schedule.	
Company	Fails to fully utilize employee. Customers and vendors who observe receptionist question quality of company's management.	

Situation 2:

Step 1. Is the action illegal? No. Laws generally do not require businesses to provide an employee with a minimum number of hours or health care benefits.

Step 2. Does the action violate company or professional standards? No. No company or professional standards apply.

Step 3. Who is affected, and how, by the action? *(See Table 6.)*

Situation 3:

Step 1. Is the action illegal? No. Laws do not require employers to pay overtime wages to salaried employees.

Step 2. Does the action violate company or professional standards? No. No company or professional standards apply.

Step 3. Who is affected, and how, by the action? *(See Table 7.)*

Chapter 22: What Does the Policy Manual Say?

Students will evaluate the ethical behavior of four actions in which employees are using company assets for personal use. Most students will conclude that the actions violate the company's policies. Since personal

TABLE 6

PEOPLE AFFECTED	NEGATIVE	POSITIVE
Customers		May reduce the cost of hamburgers.
Part-time employees	Part-time employees must buy their own health insurance policy.	Reducing total employee expenses provides more employment opportunities for typical part-time employees such as students.
Full-time employees		Benefits may be better than would be available if all employees were insured. Company can spend its benefit dollars to buy better coverage for fewer employees.
Sandi's Hamburgers		Reduces total employee expenses.
Local Community		Provides good source of employment for traditional part-time employees.

TABLE 7

PEOPLE AFFECTED	NEGATIVE	POSITIVE
Accountants	Receive no immediate reward for overtime.	Extra vacation time provides additional leisure.
Adams and Associates	Accountants work many hours and are often tired. The accountants may not be efficient and may make more errors.	Not required to hire additional accountants to handle busy season.

ethics are unique, students' solutions will vary. Although there is no one correct solution, the following solution illustrates the use of the three-step checklist.

Since the actions violate company policy, students would not normally use step three of the checklist. However, students are instructed to use step three to help decide whether the company's board of directors should make an exception to its standard policy and allow the action. Although suggested actions of the board of directors are presented here, students' answers may vary based on their analysis.

Situation 1:

Step 1. Is the action illegal? No. There are no laws that prohibit employees from using company assets for legal activities.

Step 2. Does the action violate company or professional standards? Yes. Ms. Huckaby's personal phone calls provide no economic benefit to the company and violate company policy. Thus, the action is unethical.

Step 3. Who is affected, and how, by the action? Based on the following analysis, the board of directors should probably not permit employees to use the WATTS lines for personal calls. The small positive benefit received by each employee does not appear to offset the negative impact on other employees and the company's operations. *(See Table 8.)*

TABLE 8

PEOPLE AFFECTED	NEGATIVE	POSITIVE
Ella Huckaby	Reduces personal productivity; violates company policy; impacts job security and promotion opportunities.	Personal long-distance phone costs paid by Pathanos Technologies.
Employees	Other employees may not have access to the WATTS line to conduct company business.	
Managers	Inability to control use of company assets reflects negatively on management's abilities.	
Company	Increases telephone expenses and reduces net income.	
Owners	Reduces return on investment.	

Situation 2:

Step 1. Is the action illegal? No. There are no laws that prohibit employees from using company assets for legal activities.

Step 2. Does the action violate company or professional standards? Yes. Ms. Iverson's personal use of the computer provides no economic benefit to the company and violates company policy. Thus, the action is unethical.

Step 3. Who is affected, and how, by the action? Based on the following analysis, the board of directors should not permit employees to use the computer to conduct personal business. The positive benefit received by Ms. Iverson does not appear to offset the negative impact on other employees and the company's operations. *(See Table 9.)*

Situation 3:

Step 1. Is the action illegal? No. There are no laws that prohibit employees from using company assets for legal activities.

Step 2. Does the action violate company or professional standards? Yes. Mr. Crowley's use of the company car for personal travel provides no economic benefit to the company and violates company policy.

TABLE 9

PEOPLE AFFECTED	NEGATIVE	POSITIVE
Janice Iverson	May prevent her from improving her professional skills or finding opportunities for improving company profitability. Violation of company policies may impact her job security or promotion opportunities.	Earns money in addition to company salary.
Employees	Other employees may not have access to computer for company business. Action may encourage employees to violate other company policies.	
Managers	Inability to control use of company assets reflects negatively on management's abilities.	
Company	Additional use of computer reduces its useful life and increases maintenance expenses.	
Owners	Higher maintenance expenses reduce net income. Idle time not used to increase net income.	

Although Mr. Crowley is paying for the gas used, he is not reimbursing the company for the additional mileage incurred. Thus, the action is unethical.

Step 3. Who is affected, and how, by the action? Based on the following analysis, the board of directors may elect to permit sales representatives to use company cars for personal use. This action would provide a substantial positive affect to the sales representatives since they could avoid owning a personal car. Management should consider the value of this benefit when evaluating the salaries of sales representatives. *(See Table 10 on page T27.)*

Situation 4:

Step 1. Is the action illegal? No. There are no laws that prohibit employees from using company assets for legal activities.

Step 2. Does the action violate company or professional standards? Yes. The baseball field provides a direct benefit to Ms. Powell without providing a clear economic benefit to the company. However, the field may improve the company' public image, providing the company with an indirect benefit. Without the appropriate approval of the board of directors, this action violates company policy.

TABLE 10

PEOPLE AFFECTED	NEGATIVE	POSITIVE
Lorenzo Crowley	Violation of company policies impacts his job security or promotion opportunities.	Not required to own or maintain a personal car.
Employees	Action may encourage employees to violate other company policies.	
Managers	Inability to control use of company assets reflects negatively on management's abilities.	
Company	Additional use of car reduces its useful life and increases maintenance expenses.	
Owners	Higher maintenance expenses reduce net income.	

Step 3. Who is affected, and how, by the action? Based on the following analysis, the board of directors may approve the building of the baseball field. Most businesses contribute to the improvement of their community. If the board of directors views this action as an appropriate contribution, the use of company assets may be appropriate. The board of directors should, however, clearly study and define the company's involvement in the community. *(See Table 11.)*

TABLE 11

PEOPLE AFFECTED	NEGATIVE	POSITIVE
Faye Powell		Coach of little league team is provided with a practice field.
Employees	Employees involved in other civic organizations may not have use for the field and therefore may not receive equal benefit.	Other employees who coach little league provided with practice field.
Company	Land not available for productive use or resale.	Improves public relations.
Owners	Reduces net income. Owners contributing to community without their approval.	Owners contribute to local community.
Local Community		Provides children with additional recreation opportunities.

Chapter 27: Should Tax Fraud be Reported?

This activity requires students to evaluate the decision of a public accountant who learns that her client has filed a fraudulent tax return. The teacher could ask a CPA to attend class the day this activity is presented. The CPA should be able to defend why the accounting profession does not permit its members to report illegal acts to the government. Since personal ethics are unique, students' solutions will vary. Although there is no one correct solution, the following solution illustrates the use of the three-step checklist.

Step 1. Is the action illegal? No. Laws do not require accountants to report fraudulent tax returns to the government.

Step 2. Does the action violate company or professional standards? No. Professional standards require that information obtained while performing professional services must be kept confidential.

Step 3. Who is affected, and how, by the action? *(See Table 12.)*

TABLE 12

PEOPLE AFFECTED	NEGATIVE	POSITIVE
Profession		Professional standards require a confidential relationship between CPAs and their clients. Therefore, Rhonda Bender is precluded from reporting the fraudulent tax return to anyone outside of her firm.
Rhonda Bender		Complying with professional standards protects her professional certification.
Sutton and Associates	Lose revenue.	Protected from working with a company whose management is willing to approve fraudulent activities.
Walker Company	If fraudulent tax return is discovered by the government, company is subject to severe penalties and managers could be criminally prosecuted.	Company "gets away" with filing a fraudulent tax return and underpaying income taxes.
Society	Tax underpayment is not reported.	

Chapter 28: Can You Make Too Much Money?

This activity allows students to consider the topic of excessive management salaries. This issue was being debated by Congress as this textbook was being written. One alternative being proposed is to place an extra tax on "exorbitant salaries." Consult a CPA to determine whether any limitations have been placed on management salaries. Since personal ethics are unique, students' solutions will vary. Although there is no one correct solution, the following solution illustrates the use of the three-step checklist.

Step 1. Is the action illegal? No. There are no laws that limit the salary that any individual can earn in private business.

Step 2. Does the action violate company or professional standards? No. Professional standards do not limit the salary an individual can earn.

Step 3. Who is affected, and how, by the action? *(See Table 13.)*

TABLE 13

PEOPLE AFFECTED	NEGATIVE	POSITIVE
Chief Executive Officer	Increases pressure to generate higher company profits to justify salary.	Earns high salary and financial security.
Other Managers	Significant differences in salary cause resentment. Managers may be motivated to take unethical actions to earn promotions to highly paid positions.	Provides motivation to increase performance and earn promotions.
Employees	Large differences in salary between chief financial officer and employees may cause resentment and reduced productivity.	
Owners	Resentment of employees may result in lower productivity and net income.	Motivation for managers to earn promotions may increase productivity and net income.
Society	May reduce competitiveness with companies from other nations that prohibit high management salaries.	

SUGGESTIONS FOR TEACHING APPLIED COMMUNICATIONS

Chapter 1 contains a brief introduction to the importance of communication and language arts skills for career success. Several accounting organizations have emphasized that successful accounting professionals must possess good oral and written communication skills. Since effective communication is a skill developed with practice, this textbook has incorporated several opportunities for students to develop their skills. There are eight Applied Communications activities that are interspersed throughout the chapters in the end-of-chapter section after the Cases for Critical Thinking. Suggested solutions are printed in the margin of this Annotated Teacher's Edition.

Students' knowledge of communication and language arts skills will vary. You may consider asking an English or communications instructor to assist you in reviewing communication skills that students have learned previously in other classes.

Whether preparing an outline for an oral presentation or a letter for a written assignment, students should be encouraged to use word processing software to prepare their messages. Word processing software is now used extensively by both public and private accountants and proficiency in its use is essential. By using word processing to complete Applied Communications activities you will be able to emphasize the importance of computer skills from the first week of the semester.

Assessment

Since the activities allow students to prepare unique messages, there are no "correct" answers. Your students may create excellent solutions that differ significantly from the sample solution. Thus, evaluate each student's solution on its ability to transmit the message in an efficient, effective, and professional manner. The activities should be evaluated for both content and format. Each instructor must determine the importance of errors.

Revising Written Documents

A significant amount of learning occurs when students are provided the opportunity to correct mistakes in their original written documents. Require students to revise documents and incorporate your suggestions. The revised document should be assessed and, if necessary, revised again. Teachers should consider giving students credit for successful revisions.

Cases for Critical Thinking

Most of the Cases for Critical Thinking in this textbook require students to prepare a written answer. You can adapt these cases to further reinforce students' communication skills. Rather than simply answering the questions, require students to prepare an oral or written message to an individual or business mentioned in the case. For example, Case 2 of Chapter 1 requires a decision as to whether Duane, the student in the case, should take his counselor's advice regarding the educational requirements necessary for an accounting career. Vary the requirements of each activity by requiring different types of oral and written messages.

ASSESSMENT BY PORTFOLIO

Assessment by portfolio is a growing education trend in assessing student performance. A portfolio enables the teacher to assess student goals and accomplishments while providing the student with the opportunity to collect information that will help set and accomplish current and future goals.

A portfolio should be organized across the curriculum with each discipline making a contribution. A complete portfolio should include the following:

1. A resume.
2. Copies of personal information such as social security card and driver's license.
3. A completed job application to use as a guide.
4. Copies of awards and achievements.
5. Samples of letters of applications, cover memos to attach with a resume, and thank you letters for interviews.
6. Reference letters.
7. Copies of performance in skills, communications, and any other evaluation that would contribute to success in a job.

The accounting class can contribute as many of these items to the portfolio as the instructor desires. Most instructors will want to have accounting students complete a resume (number 1) and documentation of performance (number 7).

Writing a resume is an Applied Communications activity in Chapter 1 which provides the opportunity for Writing Across the Curriculum. This can be a positive writing experience for students and is a good way to start off the school year.

Documenting performance in accounting should include a variety of accounting material that is produced by the student. A portfolio might include items such as problems the student has completed, a personal journal describing references and procedures the student used to complete the problem, and a summary report on what was learned from the project. The portfolio should be based on the accounting cycle to produce the most desirable results. Each documentation of performance should have an evaluation sheet that the student completes to explain what activity has been accomplished. The instructor should review and sign this evaluation. A sample PORTFOLIO ASSESSMENT sheet is in the Teacher's Resource Guide.

The portfolio should be an example of the student's best work that will reflect the skills and knowledge the student has learned. Each student should have a binder or folder so that the work may be organized and presented in an attractive manner. Suggested organization of the portfolio is as follows:

1. Table of contents.
2. Personal information (resume, job applications, etc.).

3. Documentation of performance (work samples, personal journals).

The following is a guideline for content coverage in the portfolio.

Objective

The student will demonstrate the skills necessary to record business transactions and analyze the financial condition of a service business organized as a proprietorship. (The business organization will change depending on the accounting cycle that is being evaluated.)

Documentation of Performance

1. The major component of the portfolio is a complete accounting problem that encompasses the entire accounting cycle. The problem should include journals, ledgers, a work sheet, and financial statements. There should be examples for each form of ownership—proprietorship, partnership, and corporation.
   a. *Manual cycle.* Accounting cycle for a service business organized as a proprietorship. This could be Reinforcement Activity 1 or the Video Transfer simulation.
   b. *Automated cycle.* Comprehensive problem of your choice. This could be a Reinforcement Activity, simulation, or selected reports from the automated accounting problems.
2. A daily personal journal should be kept in which the student records activities such as the number of problem instructions completed each day, references necessary to perform various tasks, how difficult tasks were solved, what equipment was used, and any other activity that contributed to the successful completion of the assignment.
3. A written report is another important part of the portfolio. The report should include experiences encountered by the student while completing the activity, such as instructions that took more or less time to complete than anticipated, accessibility to equipment, student time management and organizational skills that enabled the project to flow smoothly, and how things could have been done differently. A second part of the report should include an analysis of the business in the problem, such as, are the component percentages acceptable for that type of business, is the chart of accounts appropriate for the business, and suggestions on how to make the business operate more efficiently from an accounting point of view.

Assessment

1. The accounting problem should be complete and in correct format, all words should be spelled correctly, the information should be neat and accurate, and the problem should be submitted in an orderly fashion.
2. The personal journal should be set up on a daily basis and entries should be recorded for each day. Personal experiences should be documented neatly and accurately. Language arts skills should be evaluated (grammar, spelling, punctuation, and sentence structure).
3. The written report should be in complete sentences and word processed or typewritten. It should be an accurate assessment of the student's experience. Language arts skills should be evaluated (grammar, spelling, punctuation, and sentence structure).
4. The student will complete a PORTFOLIO ASSESSMENT and describe the project. The teacher should then complete the evaluation portion of the assessment sheet.

CENTURY 21 ACCOUNTING—A COMPLETE COMPETENCY-BASED ACCOUNTING PROGRAM

CENTURY 21 ACCOUNTING is organized into a complete competency-based instructional program. A competency-based instructional program is an organization of subject matter consisting of one or more courses designed to lead students to predetermined goals and objectives. A competency-based instructional program identifies what the student must "do" to successfully complete the program. A minimum acceptable level of performance is clearly specified before instruction and learning begin. In a competency-based instructional program, attention is focused on learner outcomes rather than on teaching activities. The teaching activities or delivery of instruction is directed toward the predetermined goals and objectives. A competency-based instructional program may be used effectively in a traditional classroom setting. The competency-based *CENTURY 21 ACCOUNTING* program model is given in Figure 1.

Program Goals

Program goals are general, student-oriented competency statements which take two or more general behavioral goals to demonstrate. The complete *CENTURY 21 ACCOUNTING* program has the following program goals:

1. Know accounting as it relates to careers.
2. Know accounting terminology.

3. Understand accounting concepts, principles, and practices.
4. Apply accounting procedures.

FIGURE 1

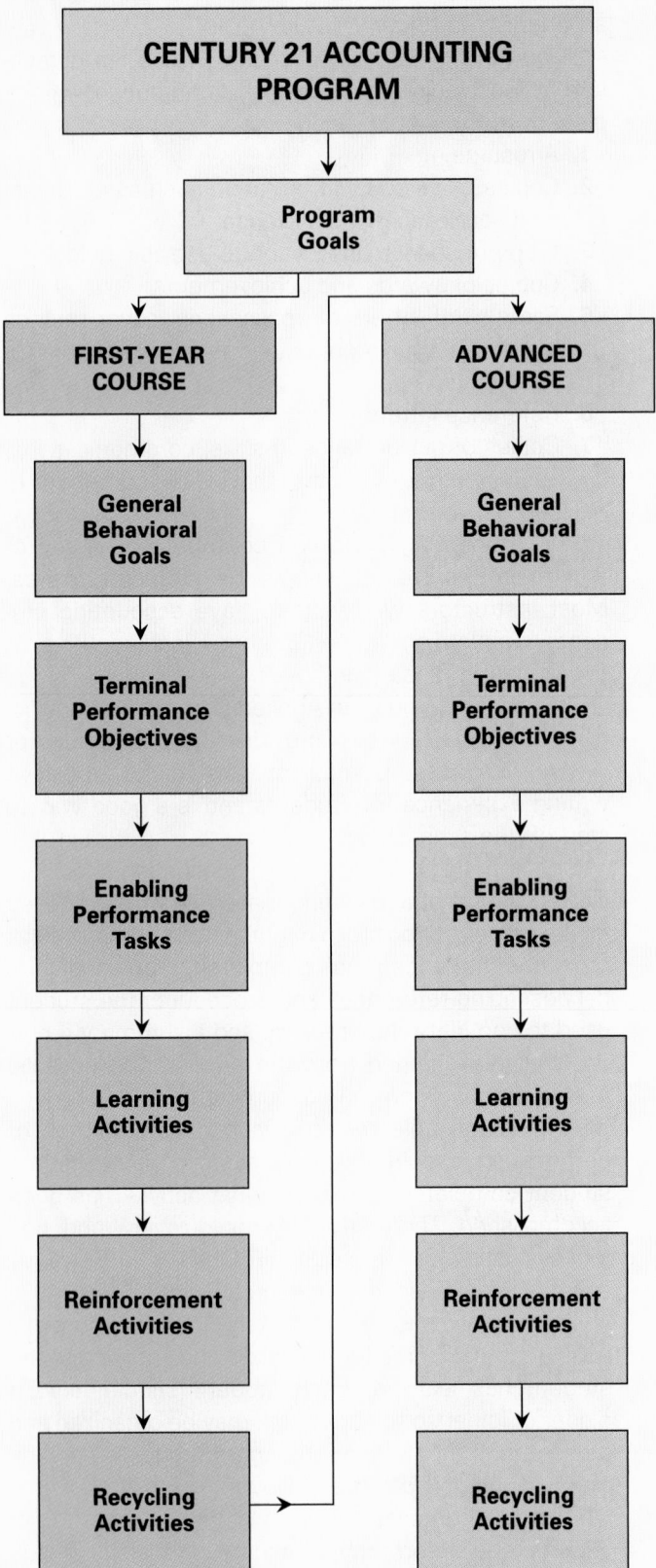

Learning outcomes that demonstrate knowledge involve recall of previously learned subject matter. Being able to identify the correct definition of an accounting term would be an example of a learning outcome that demonstrates knowledge. Knowledge represents the lowest level of learning outcomes.

Learning outcomes that demonstrate understanding involve the ability to interpret subject matter. Being able to distinguish between correct and incorrect accounting principles and practices would be an example of a learning outcome that demonstrates understanding. Understanding goes one step beyond the simple remembering of material. Understanding assumes the knowledge level of learning.

Learning outcomes that demonstrate application involve the ability to use learned material in realistic situations. Being able to record transactions in a journal would be an example of a learning outcome that demonstrates application. Application represents a higher level of learning than either knowledge or understanding levels of learning.

General Behavioral Goals

General behavioral goals are student-oriented behavioral statements which take one or more terminal performance objectives to demonstrate. General behavioral goals specify the content required to satisfy the learning outcomes described in the program goals.

Terminal Performance Objectives

Terminal performance objectives are statements that indicate the behavior a student will demonstrate upon successful completion of a learning experience. Terminal performance objectives consists of three basic elements.

1. The condition under which the performance is to take place.
2. The behavior (things to be done) expected of a student.
3. The criteria (standards) used to determine how well the behavior is to be done.

Determining Criteria (Standards) of Performance

A terminal performance objective specifies the minimum level of performance needed to demonstrate successful completion of a block of subject matter. The minimum level of performance may be related to assessment standards or to employment standards. For example, a minimum of 75 percent of the behavior specified in the terminal performance objective may meet school requirements for a passing score. However, a higher minimum (perhaps 95 percent) may be required to meet the minimum acceptable employment standards.

Many schools now require that the criteria specified in a terminal performance objective be based on minimum employment standards. Using employment standards allows schools to better communicate with prospective employers concerning the specific behaviors students have obtained and those that may require on-the-job training to meet the minimum requirements of the position.

To establish the minimum level of performance required for employment, teachers must follow local employment standards. The establishment of an advisory committee made up of prospective employers of accounting graduates is an approach often used to determine the minimum levels of performance required for employment. An advisory committee may also be used to review the behaviors specified in the terminal performance objectives. Local condition may require that additional behaviors be specified or may allow the deletion of some of the behaviors.

The evaluation of performance for assessment purposes under a competency-based instructional program is the same as for noncompetency-based programs. Local school assessment standards are followed. A student may perform at a level satisfactory to pass the course but may not perform at a level necessary for employment. Typically, a student achieving minimum employment standards will pass the course and meet minimum employment standards.

Availability of Terminal Performance Objectives

Teachers should distribute copies of terminal performance objectives to all students before they begin their study of each part of the accounting program. Each terminal performance objective should be reviewed with students so that they understand the specific behaviors required.

Level of Specificity of Terminal Performance Objectives

The writing of terminal performance objectives related to specific evaluation instruments is fully explained in the TRG.

Enabling Performance Tasks

Enabling performance tasks are the steps a student must go through to prepare for the successful demonstration of the behavior specified in terminal performance objectives. Enabling performance tasks are performance statements designed to guide the student through the learning experiences required.

Learning Activities

Learning activities are teacher-directed activities planned for one or more students so that they may be able to demonstrate predetermined terminal performance objectives. The learning activities should be directed to the knowledge, understanding, and application specified in the terminal performance objectives.

Reinforcement Activities

Reinforcement activities should be provided in a competency-based instructional program to strengthen student learnings. In a competency-based accounting program, each reinforcement activity should cover a complete accounting cycle.

Recycling Activities

Some students do not reach the minimum level of performance specified in a terminal performance objective as easily as others. For these students, additional learning activities are needed. Recycling activities are the student-oriented learning activities used by students who need more practice than most students. Not all students need to complete recycling activities. After students have completed the teacher-directed

recycling activities, they should be given a second opportunity to demonstrate performance on the terminal performance objective for which they did not reach the minimum level of performance on the first try.

CENTURY 21 ACCOUNTING, First-Year Course

The specific elements within each component in the competency-based program model are provided in outline form in the TRG. This material is provided as a guide for teachers conducting competency-based education.

The general behavioral goals are also given on each part opener within the textbook to guide students through the learning experiences. The specific criteria (standards) of performance have been purposely omitted from the terminal performance objectives to allow each teacher to provide for local differences in student abilities, job requirements, and school conditions.

APPLIED MATHEMATICS GRID

Basic applied mathematics skills are not specifically identified in *CENTURY 21 ACCOUNTING* since all problems apply the basic skills that are listed in the table below. Adding columns of numbers is demonstrated in all chapters that contain journalizing, posting, work sheets, and financial statements. Subtracting numbers is demonstrated in chapters that involve posting, calculating net income/net loss on work sheets, and preparing financial statements. Multiplying numbers is demonstrated in chapters that cover payroll, depreciation, sales tax, discounts, and interest.

Dividing numbers is demonstrated in chapters that include component percentages, depreciation, and interest. Finding unknown numbers is covered in chapters in which transactions are analyzed using the accounting equation.

The Mathematics icon appears in the end-of-chapter activities the first time a specific math skill that demonstrates a specific accounting skill is introduced. The following table depicts the math skill and the first application in the end-of-chapter activities of that skill. Repeated applications are not noted.

APPLIED MATHEMATICS GRID	
Applied Mathematics/Accounting Skill	**Application**
Chapter 5	
A: Proving a journal page and proving debits and credits	5-1
B: Proving cash	5-1
Chapter 6	
A: Calculating new account balances	6-2
Chapter 7	
A: Calculating new balances on a check stub	7-2
B: Reconciling bank statements	7-D1
C: Calculating amount of petty cash replenishment	7-D3
Chapter 8	
A: Analyzing adjustments	8-1
B: Calculating net income/net loss	8-D2
C: Checking for typical arithmetic errors	8-3
Chapter 9	
A: Calculating net income	9-D2
B: Calculating component percentages	9-1
C: Calculating owner's equity	9-D2
Chapter 12	
A: Calculating sales tax	12-D2
B: Proving an expanded journal	12-1
C: Proving cash	12-M
Chapter 14	
A: Calculating hours worked	14-1
B: Calculating employee total earnings	14-D1
C: Calculating FICA taxes	14-D2
D: Calculating deductions in a payroll register	14-2
E: Calculating net pay in a payroll register	14-2
F: Calculating accumulated earnings	14-3
Chapter 15	
A: Calculating unemployment taxes	15-D2
B: Calculating employer tax liabilities	15-3
Chapter 16	
A: Calculating net income	16-D2
Chapter 17	
A: Calculating cost of merchandise sold	17-D1
B: Calculating component percentages for an income statement	17-D3

(continued on page T-34)

(continued from page T-33)

APPLIED MATHEMATICS GRID

Applied Mathematics/Accounting Skill	Application
Chapter 19 A: Calculating purchases discounts B: Calculating petty cash short and over	19-D1 19-D2
Chapter 20 A: Calculating sales discounts B: Calculating sales tax reductions for sales discounts C: Calculating sales tax on sales returns and allowances	20-D3 20-D3 20-D3
Chapter 21 A: Calculating estimated uncollectible accounts expense B: Calculating book value of accounts receivable	21-D1 21-D1
Chapter 22 A: Calculating depreciation expense for a year (straight-line method) B: Calculating depreciation expense for a partial year (straight-line method) C: Calculating book value of plant assets D: Calculating gain or loss on a plant asset E: Calculating depreciation expense (declining-balance method) F: Calculating property tax	22-D1 22-D2 22-D2 22-5 22-6 22-7
Chapter 23 A: Calculating inventory using the first-in, first-out inventory costing method B: Calculating inventory using the last-in, first-out inventory costing method C: Calculating inventory using the weighted-average inventory costing method D: Estimating inventory using the gross profit method	23-D2 23-D2 23-D2 23-2
Chapter 24 A: Calculating interest for a year B: Calculating interest for a fraction of a year C: Calculating maturity date D: Calculating maturity value of a note E: Calculating bank discount and proceeds for a discounted note	24-D1 24-D1 24-D2 24-C 24-C
Chapter 25 A: Calculating accrued interest income B: Calculating maturity value of a note C: Calculating accrued interest expense	25-1 25-C 25-2
Chapter 26 A: Calculating net income before federal income tax expense B: Calculating the adjustment for federal income tax expense	26-C 26-2
Chapter 27 A: Calculating component percentages B: Calculating retained earnings C: Calculating working capital and the current ratio	27-1 27-1 27-1
Chapter 28 A: Calculating the loss on sale of assets B: Calculating the gain on sale of assets	28-D1 28-D2

SPECIAL FEATURES GRID

CENTURY 21 ACCOUNTING has been expanded to cover many contemporary special features. The following grid illustrates the features and their location.

SPECIAL FEATURES GRID							
Chapter	Professional Business Ethics	Spreadsheet Options	Multicultural Awareness	Global Perspective	Personal Visions in Business	Careers in Accounting	Applied Communications
1	Can I Say This in My Resume?						Writing a Resume
2			Professional Organizations	Foreign Currency			
3	Is This Really a Business Expense?						
4			Fra Luca Pacioli		Joe Arriola, Avanti Press		
5			Debit/Credit	Professional Accounting Associations			
6					Belinda Hughes, Boo Boo Baby	General Ledger Bookkeeper	Writing a Fax Communication
7		Using an Electronic Spreadsheet to Prepare a Bank Reconciliation				Cashier I/Cash Accounting Clerk	
8	Am I a Software Pirate?		Abacus				
9		Electronic Spreadsheets Help Answer "What If?" Questions				Accountant	
10			Accountants in Ancient Civilizations		Tom Richardson, Holder, McCall & Richardson		Creating Questions to Interview a Business Manager
A3						Data Entry Clerk	
11	Am I Cheating the Company?		Diversity in the Workplace				
12				International Work Week			Creating a Comparison of Rising Prices
13			Ancient Greece and Egypt		Jan Robbins, NAS, Inc.		
14		Using Functions to Prepare a Payroll Register	Arabic Numerals			Timekeeper	Writing a Memo Concerning Time System

(continued on page T-36)

(continued from page T-35)

SPECIAL FEATURES GRID

Chapter	Professional Business Ethics	Spreadsheet Optons	Multicultural Awareness	Global Perspective	Personal Visions in Business	Careers in Accounting	Applied Communications
15	Who Owns My Time?					Payroll Clerk	
16			Peru		Bryan Choi, Architects Associated		
17				International Telephone Communication			Creating an Outline
18			Asia Minor		Judy Sims, Software Spectrum		
A6						Computer Programmer	
19					Philip Showalter, D.D.S.		Writing a Letter of Request for an Annual Stock Report
20			Early Egypt			Letter-of-Credit Document Examiner	
21				International Weights and Measures			
22	What Does the Policy Manual Say?					Credit Reporting Clerk	Creating a Comparison of Prices
23			Ancient China		Bert N. Mitchell Mitchell, Titus & Co.		
24							Preparing a Graph for a Presentation
25			Historical Records		Jean Myong VanHorn Amikor Cleaners		
26				International Travel		Accountant, Tax	
27	Should Tax Fraud Be Reported?	Graphics Enhance Financial Statement Analysis					
28	Can You Make Too Much Money?		Ancient Accounting				Writing a Report Summarizing Speaking Techniques

PLANNING THE YEAR'S WORK
**Manual Approach and/or
Limited Use of Computers**

A time schedule for a complete year should be planned before the year begins. Five steps for planning the year's work are given below.

1. Review what has been previous experience with the pace of work that students have maintained in past accounting classes.
2. Determine how many business simulations and reinforcement activities are to be used during the current year.
3. Decide how much allowance should be made for interruptions in the school day that occur on short notice.
4. Determine if computers will be used in the class. Optional automated accounting activities are indicated with parentheses. If you choose not to use computers, disregard the information in the parentheses.
5. If you choose to use computers on a limited basis, use the information in the parentheses. Learning how to use software may require additional class time. However, if computers are used to complete some problems, reinforcement activities, and simulations, rather than working them manually, time may be saved in the schedule.
6. If you prefer to completely automate your course, use the grid that follows this time schedule.
7. Prepare a proposed schedule of work to be completed. Inspect the schedule to determine if typical breaks in the school year (vacations, special events, and scheduled reporting periods) come at a logical time.

A sample time schedule is given for planning the year's work.

SAMPLE TIME SCHEDULE (FOR THREE QUARTERS—180 DAYS TOTAL)

Week	First Quarter—12 Weeks (Chapters 1–10) Lesson Plans for	Second Quarter—12 Weeks (Chapters 11–18) Lesson Plans for	Third Quarter—12 Weeks (Chapters 19–28) Lesson Plans for
1	Chapter 1 Chapter 2	Chapter 11	Chapter 19 Integrating Automated Accounting Topic 7
2	Chapter 3	Chapter 12	Chapter 20 Integrating Automated Accounting Topic 8
3	Chapter 4	Chapter 13 Integrating Automated Accounting Topic 4	Reinforcement Activity 3, Part A (optional automate)
4	Chapter 5	Chapter 14	Chapter 21
5	Chapter 6 Integrating Automated Accounting Topic 1	Chapter 15 Integrating Automated Accounting Topic 5	Chapter 22 Integrating Automated Accounting Topic 9
6	Chapter 7 Integrating Automated Accounting Topic 2	Reinforcement Activity 2, Part A (optional automate)	Chapter 23
7	Reinforcement Activity 1, Part A (optional automate)	Stellar Attractions Pegboard Payroll Simulation	Chapter 24
8	Chapter 8	Chapter 16	Chapter 25
9	Chapter 9	Chapter 17	Chapter 26
10	Chapter 10	Chapter 18 Integrating Automated Accounting Topic 6	Chapter 27 Integrating Automated Accounting Topic 10
11	Integrating Automated Accounting Topic 3 Reinforcement Activity 1, Part B (optional automate)	Reinforcement Activity 1, Part B (optional automate)	Reinforcement Activity 3, Part B Western Rider, Inc. Simulation (optional automate)
12	Video Transfer Simulation (optional automate)	Viking Marine Business Simulation (optional automate)	Chapter 28

SOFTWARE CORRELATION

After manual accounting procedures are mastered, computer software may be used as an enrichment activity to facilitate the processing of accounting data and experience the use of computers in accounting.

Five software packages are available to use with *CENTURY 21 ACCOUNTING, First-Year Course* to augment teacher instruction: *STUDY GUIDE SOFTWARE; ACCOUNTING TUTORIAL: A TRANSACTION ANALYSIS APPROACH; APPLICATION PROGRAM DISKETTE FOR CENTURY 21 ACCOUNTING; SPREADSHEET TEMPLATE FOR CENTURY 21 ACCOUNTING; and AUTOMATED ACCOUNTING 6.0* or higher, and the accompanying templates.

All activities for which software may be used are designated by an icon next to the activity in the text. This makes identification easy for both the teacher and student.

Each software package and its documentation is available from South-Western Publishing Company.

Study Guide Software: *STUDY GUIDE SOFTWARE FOR CENTURY 21 ACCOUNTING* enables students to complete the study guide from the working papers at the computer. This software is available for every chapter in the text. Therefore, there is not an icon in the text to indicate its use.

This software is self-contained and does not involve the use of templates.

Accounting Tutorial: *ACCOUNTING TUTORIAL: A TRANSACTION ANALYSIS APPROACH* provides for the use of software to analyze daily transactions, adjusting entries, closing entries, and reversing entries.

This software is self-contained and does not involve the use of templates.

Application Program: *APPLICATION PROGRAM DISKETTE FOR CENTURY 21 ACCOUNTING* may be used with selected end-of-chapter problems from *CENTURY 21 ACCOUNTING, First-Year Course* text. This software is self-contained and does not involve the use of templates.

Twenty-three problems from *CENTURY 21 ACCOUNTING* may be used with this program.

Spreadsheet Template: *SPREADSHEET TEMPLATE FOR CENTURY 21 ACCOUNTING*, First-Year and Advanced Courses may be used with selected Application Problems and Enrichment Problems. In order to use the templates, *Lotus® 1-2-3®* or *Microsoft® Works™* are needed for DOS computers. For Macintosh computers, *Microsoft Works* for the *Macintosh™* or *Microsoft Excel®* are needed.

Seventeen problems from *CENTURY 21 ACCOUNTING* may be used with spreadsheet software.

Automated Accounting: *AUTOMATED ACCOUNTING 6.0* or higher may be used to complete selected Application Problems, Enrichment Problems, Integrating Automated Accounting Problems, Reinforcement Activities, and Simulations. The *CENTURY 21 ACCOUNTING, First-Year Course Template Disk* is also needed to complete the *AUTOMATED ACCOUNTING* problems and reinforcement activities in the text. Separate templates are needed for each simulation that is completed.

A total of 31 problems, 3 reinforcement activities, and 3 simulations from *CENTURY 21 ACCOUNTING* may be automated using *AUTOMATED ACCOUNTING 6.0*.

It is suggested that the text that accompanies *AUTOMATED ACCOUNTING 6.0* be used for reference. The correlation for that text is listed in the last column of the grid below.

CENTURY 21 ACCOUNTING SOFTWARE CORRELATION						*Automated Accounting 6.0 Text Chapter*
Text Chapter	**Template Problems**	**Tutorial**	**Application Program Disk**	**Spreadsheet Template**	**Study Guide Disk**	
1					x	
2		Unit 1			x	
3		Unit 1			x	
4		Unit 1			x	
5			5-M, 5-C		x	
6	6-M, 6-C		6-M, 6-C		x	
*IA-1	Optional Problem DB-1A					1, 2
7	7-M, 7-C	Unit 1	7-4, 7-5, 7-M	7-D1, 7-M	x	

(continued on page T-39)

(continued from page T-38)

CENTURY 21 ACCOUNTING SOFTWARE CORRELATION

Text Chapter	Template Problems	Tutorial	Application Program Disk	Spreadsheet Template	Study Guide Disk	Automated Accounting 6.0 Text Chapter
*IA-2	Optional Problems DB-2A, DB-2B					
8		Unit 2	8-M, 8-C		x	
9				9-M, 9-C	x	
10	10-M, 10-C	Units 2 and 3	10-M		x	
Reinforcement Activity 1 Video Transfer Simulation (A separate template disk is needed)						
*IA-3	Optional Problem DB-3A					3
11		Unit 4	11-M		x	
12		Unit 4	12-M		x	
13	13-C				x	
*IA-4	Optional Problem DB-4A					4, 5
14				14-2, 14-3, 14-C	x	
15	15-M, 15-C	Unit 4	15-M, 15-C	15-2	x	
*IA-5	Optional Problem DB-5A					10
16		Unit 5	16-M		x	
17				17-M, 17-C	x	
18	18-1, 18-M, 18-C	Units 5, 6	18-M		x	
Reinforcement Activity 2 Viking Marine Simulation (A separate template disk is needed)						
*IA-6	Optional Problem DB-6A					6
19	19-3, 19-M	Unit 7	19-M		x	
*IA-7	Optional Problem DB-7A					7, 9
20	20-M, 20-C	Unit 7	20-M		x	
*IA-8	Optional Problem DB-8A					7, 9
21		Unit 8	21-M		x	
22	22-6, 22-M, 22-C	Unit 8	22-5, 22-7	22-6, 22-M	x	
*IA-9	Optional Problem DB-9A					8
23				23-1, 23-2	x	11
24		Unit 7	24-M	24-D1, 24-D3	x	
25		Units 8, 9, 10			x	
26		Unit 8	26-M		x	
27	27-C	Units 8, 9, 10		27-M	x	
*IA-10	Optional Problem DB-10A					
Reinforcement Activity 3 Western Rider Simulation (A separate template disk is needed)						
28					x	12

*Integrating Automated Accounting Topics

LOCATION OF ANSWERS AND SOLUTIONS

Due to the abundance of teacher support material available with this course, the table below is provided to guide you in locating solutions to student activities.

Item	Found In
KEY TO LOCATION OF ANSWERS AND SOLUTIONS	
Audit Your Understanding Questions	Margins of Wraparound Teacher's Edition Appendix D of Student Text
Accounting Terms	Margins of Wraparound Teacher's Edition
Questions for Individual Study	Margins of Wraparound Teacher's Edition
Cases for Critical Thinking	Margins of Wraparound Teacher's Edition
Applied Communications	Margins of Wraparound Teacher's Edition
Professional Business Ethics	Instructional Strategies of Wraparound Teacher's Edition
Drills	Check figures in Margins of Wraparound Teacher's Edition Balance of Solution in Teacher's Edition of Working Papers
Application Problems	Check figures in Margins of Wraparound Teacher's Edition Balance of Solution in Teacher's Edition of Working Papers
Mastery Problems	Check figures in Margins of Wraparound Teacher's Edition Balance of Solution in Teacher's Edition of Working Papers
Challenge Problems	Check figures in Margins of Wraparound Teacher's Edition Balance of Solution in Teacher's Edition of Working Papers
Recycling Problems	Check figures in Margins of Wraparound Teacher's Edition Balance of Solution in Teacher's Edition of Demonstration and Recycling Problems
Reinforcement Activities	Check figures in Margins of Wraparound Teacher's Edition Balance of Solution in Teacher's Edition of Working Papers
Integrating Automated Accounting Problems	Check figures in Margins of Wraparound Teacher's Edition Input Form Solutions in Teacher's Edition of Working Papers and repeated in TRG Reports in TRG
Demonstration Problems	Teacher's Edition of Demonstration and Recycling Problems
Study Guides	Teacher's Edition of Working Papers
Tests	TRG
Manual Simulations	Key for manual simulations
Automated Simulations	Key for automated simulations
Supplemental Global Business Worksheets	TRG
Supplemental Math Worksheets	TRG

PROFESSIONAL REFERENCES AND RESOURCES

Periodicals

Accounting Horizons, American Accounting Association, Sarasota, FL.

Accounting News, Warren, Gorham & Lamont, New York, NY.

Accounting, Organizations and Society, Pergamon Press, Inc., Tarrytown, NY.

Accounting Review, American Accounting Association, Sarasota, FL.

Accounting Technology (formerly *Computers in Accounting*), Faulkner & Gray, Eleven Penn Plaza, 17th Floor, New York, NY 10001.

Accounting Today, Lebhar-Friedman, Inc., New York, NY.

American Accounting Association Newsletter, Sarasota, FL.

Black Enterprise, New York, NY. (Multicultural awareness)

CPA Digest, CPA Services, Inc., Brookfield, WI.

CPA Journal, New York State Society of CPAs, New York, NY.

Forbes, New York, NY (Business news).

Fortune, New York, NY (Business news).

Hispanic, Washington, D.C. (Multicultural awareness)

Inc. (Business)

Journal of Accountancy, AICPA, Jersey City, NJ.

Journal of Accounting Education, Pergamon Press, Inc., Tarrytown, NY.

Journal of Business Ethics, Kluwer Academic Publishers, Norwell, CA.

Nattive, A. "Cooperative Learning: An Overview." *Journal of Humanistic Education.* 1988.

Management Accounting, National Association of Accountants, 10 Paragon Drive, Montvale, NJ.

Multicultural Review, Greenwood Press Inc., Westport, CT. (Multicultural awareness)

Multinational Business, Economist Newspaper, New York NY. (Global business)

Native Peoples, Phoenix, AZ. (Multicultural awareness)

Practical Accountant, Faulkner & Gray, Inc., New York, NY.

Transpacific, Malibu, CA. (Multicultural awareness)

Wall Street Journal, New York, NY. (Business newspaper)

Working Woman, New York, NY. (Multicultural awareness)

Books

AICPA. *A Survey of Perceptions, Knowledge and Attitudes Towards CPAs and the Accounting Profession,* 1986.

AICPA. *Accounting Trends and Techniques,* 1991.

AICPA. *FASB Accounting Standards.*

AICPA. *Upward Mobility of Women Special Committee: Report to the AICPA Board of Directors.*

African America: Portrait of a People. Detroit: Visible Ink Press, 1994.

Albrecht, W. Steve. *Ethical Issues in the Practice of Accounting.* Cincinnati: South-Western Publishing Co., 1992.

AT&T, *International Telephone Guide.*

Bieg, Bernard J., and B. Lewis Keeling. *Payroll Accounting.* (Revised Annually). Cincinnati: South-Western Publishing Co.

Bloom, Benjamin S., ed., et. al. *Taxonomy of Educational Objectives: Handbook I, Cognitive Domain.* White Plains: Longman, Inc., 1977.

Cantlon, T. *Structuring the Classroom Successfully for Cooperative Team Learning.* Portland, OR: Prestige Publishers, 1991.

Champagne, Duane. *Native America: Portrait of a People.* Detroit: Visible Ink Press, 1994.

Chatfield, Michael. *A History of Accounting Thought.* Second Edition. Huntington, NY: Robert E. Krieger Publishing, 1977.

Cohen, E. *Designing Group Work.* New York: Teachers College Press, 1986.

Diamond, Michael A. *Financial Accounting.* Third Edition. Cincinnati: South-Western Publishing Co., 1993.

Duranti, Luciana. "The Odyssey of Records Managers." *ARMA Quarterly,* July, 1989.

Ehrlich, Virginia Z. *Gifted Children: A Guide for Parents and Teachers.* Unionville, NY: Trillium Press, 1985.

Elashmawi, Farid, and Philip R. Harris. *Multicultural Management: New Skills for Global Success.* Houston: Gulf Publishing Company, 1993.

Estes, Ralph. *Dictionary of Accounting.* Second Edition. Cambridge: The MIT Press, 1986.

Evans, Thomas G., Martin E. Taylor, and Oscar Holzmann. *International Accounting and Reporting.* Cincinnati: South-Western Publishing Co., 1985.

Fess, Philip E., and Carl S. Warren. *Accounting Principles.* Seventeenth Edition. Cincinnati: South-Western Publishing Co., 1993.

Gelinas, Ulric J., Jr., Allan E. Oram, and William P. Wiggins. *Accounting Information Systems.* Second Edition. Cincinnati: South-Western Publishing Co., 1993.

Gibson, Charles H. *Financial Statement Analysis: Using Financial Accounting Information.* Fifth Edition. Cincinnati: South-Western Publishing Co., 1992.

Gilbertson, Claudia. *Accounting: Learning and Instruction.* Second Edition. Cincinnati: South-Western Publishing Co., 1992.

Gordon, Gus. *Understanding Financial Statements.* Cincinnati: South-Western Publishing Co., 1992.

Gronlund, Norman E. *Stating Objectives for Classroom Instruction.* 3d. ed. New York: Macmillan Publishing Co., Inc., 1985.

Hamilton, D. *Cooperative Learning in the Classroom.* Bloomington, IN: Phi Delta Kappa Educational Foundation, 1990.

Harrell, Earl, and Cassandra Harrell. *Surviving in the Workplace: A Resource for Individuals, Educational Institutions, and Businesses for Promoting Safety and Awareness in the Workplace.* Milwaukee: E.T. Publishing Company, 1994.

Harris, Philip R., and Robert T. Moran. *Managing Cultural Differences.* Houston: Gulf Publishing Company, 1992.

Heintz, James, and Robert Parry. *College Accounting.* Fourteenth Edition. Cincinnati: South-Western Publishing Co., 1993.

Hendrickson, Aletha. *Writing for Accountants.* Cincinnati: South-Western Publishing Co., 1993.

Henke, Emerson O. *Introduction to Nonprofit Organization Accounting.* Fourth Edition. Cincinnati: South-Western Publishing Co., 1992.

Johnson, D., and R. Johnson. *Cooperation and Competition.* Hillsdale, NJ: Lawrence Eribaum, 1987.

Johnson, D., and R. Johnson. *Social Skills for Successful Group Work. Educational Leadership,* 1990.

Kagan, S. *Cooperative Learning Resources for Teachers.* San Juan Capistrano: Resources for Teachers, 1989.

Langenderfer, Harold Q., Willis C. Stevenson, Herbert C. Sieg, and James B. Bower. *Federal Income Taxation.* (Revised Annually). Cincinnati: South-Western Publishing Co.

Langenderfer, Harold Q., Willis C. Stevenson, Herbert C. Sieg, and James B. Bower. *Personal Income Taxation.* (Revised Annually). Cincinnati: South-Western Publishing Co.

Lerner, Janet. *Learning Disabilities: Theories, Diagnosis, and Teaching Strategies,* Fifth Edition. Boston: Houghton Mifflin, 1988.

Mager, Robert F. *Preparing Instructional Objectives.* 2d. ed., rev. Belmont: Pitman Learning, Inc., 1984.

Magill, Harry T., and Gary J. Previts. *CPA Professional Responsibilities: A Guide.* Cincinnati: South-Western Publishing Co., 1991.

Marzano, Robert J. *A Different Kind of Classroom: Teaching with Dimensions of Learning.* Association for Supervision and Curriculum Development, Alexandria, VA, 1992.

McCabe and McCabe. *Writing Effective Resumes, A Complete Guide.* Cincinnati: South-Western Publishing Co., 1993.

Miller, Sidney R., and Patrick J. Schloss. *Career-Vocational Education for Handicapped Youth.* Rockville, MD: Aspen Systems Corporation, 1982.

Moran, Robert T., and William G. Stripp. *Dynamics of Successful International Business Negotiations.* Houston: Gulf Publishing Company, 1991.

Moran, Robert T., Philip R. Harris, and William G. Stripp. *Developing the Global Organization.* Houston: Gulf Publishing Company, 1993.

Nash, John F., and Cynthia D. Heagy. *Accounting Information Systems.* Third Edition. Cincinnati: South-Western Publishing Co., 1993.

National Society of Public Accountants. *Portfolio of Accounting Systems for Small and Medium-Sized Businesses.* Revised. Englewood Cliffs, NJ: Prentice Hall, 1977.

Parker, Jeanette P. *Instructional Strategies for Teaching the Gifted.* Boston: Allyn and Bacon, 1989.

Sarkees, Michelle Donnelly, and John L. Scott. *Vocation Special Needs,* Second Edition. American Technical Publishers, 1986.

Secretary's Commission on Achieving Necessary Skills. *What Work Requires of Schools: A SCANS Report for America 2000.* Washington, DC: U.S. Department of Labor, 1991.

Sheth, Jagdish N., and Abdolreza Eshghi, eds. *Global Accounting Perspectives.* Cincinnati: South-Western Publishing Co., 1989.

Shim, Jay K., and Joel G. Siefel. *Encyclopedic Dictionary of Accounting & Finance.* Englewood Cliffs, NJ: Prentice Hall, 1989.

Simons, George F., Carmen Vazquez, and Philip R. Harris. *Transcultural Leadership: Empowering the Diverse WorkForce.* Houston: Gulf Publishing Company, 1993.

Skousen, K. Fred, Harold Q. Langenderfer, and W. Steve Albrecht. *Accounting Principles and Applications.* Cincinnati: South-Western Publishing Co., 1993.

Slavin, R. *Using Student Team Learning.* Baltimore: John Hopkins University Press, 1986.

Swartz, R. *The Effects of Attitudes and Aptitudes in Predicting Final Course Grades: Implications for Multi-Group Organization in Business Communication Classes.* Unpublished paper presented in Teacher Education 883, Michigan State University, East Lansing, 1987.

U.S. Department of Commerce. *Basic Guide to Exporting.* 1986.

U.S. Department of Labor. *Dictionary of Occupational Titles.*

U.S. Department of Labor. *Occupational Outlook Handbook.*

Weirich, Thomas R., and Alan Reinstein. *Accounting and Auditing Research: A Practical Guide.* Third Edition. Cincinnati: South-Western Publishing Co., 1992.

Zedlitz. *Getting a Job, Process Kit.* Third Edition. Cincinnati: South-Western Publishing Co., 1993.

Technology

AICPA. *The Bottom Line: Inside Accounting Today,* 1987. (Video)

AICPA. *It All Adds Up,* 1989. (Video)

AICPA. *A License to Succeed,* 1990. (Video)

AICPA. *Luca Pacioli: Unsung Hero of the Renaissance.* (Video)

AICPA. *Serving America: A Tradition of Excellence,* 1986. (Video)

AICPA. *TOTAL (Total On-line Tax and Accounting Library)* (Tax and accounting on-line database)

Dun & Bradstreet Information Services. *Dun's Direct Access* (On-line database of U.S. companies)

Excel (spreadsheet software)

Lotus (spreadsheet software)

Mead Data Central, Inc. *LEXIS/NEXIS* (On-line database)

Pagemaker (desktop publishing software)

Research Institute of America. *OnPoint CD-ROM Tax Library* (Tax research CD-ROM database)

Ventura Publisher (desktop publishing software)

Windows (operating system software)

WordPerfect (word processing software)

Works (integrated software)

CENTURY 21
Accounting

CENTURY 21 Accounting

FIRST-YEAR COURSE

SIXTH EDITION

Kenton E. Ross, CPA
Professor of Accounting
East Texas State University
Commerce, Texas

Robert D. Hanson
Associate Dean
College of Business Administration
Central Michigan University
Mount Pleasant, Michigan

Claudia Bienias Gilbertson, CPA
Teaching Professor
Anoka-Ramsey Community College
Coon Rapids, Minnesota

Mark W. Lehman, CPA
Instructor
School of Accountancy
Mississippi State University
Starkville, Mississippi

Robert M. Swanson
Professor Emeritus of Business Education
and Office Administration
Ball State University
Muncie, Indiana

South-Western Publishing Co.
BA20FA

Vice-President/Editor-in-Chief: Dennis M. Kokoruda
Senior Developmental Editor: Carol Volz
Art Director: John Robb
Design Coordinator: Darren Wright
Marketing Manager: Larry Qualls
Coordinating Editor: Mark Beck
Production Manager: Carol Sturzenberger
Senior Production Editor: Mark Cheatham
Production Editor: Kimberlee Kusnerak
Production Editor I: Denise Wheeler
Associate Director/Photo Editing: Devore Nixon
Photo Editor: Kimberly A. Larson

Cover Design: The Optimum Group

Internal Design: Lesiak/Crampton Design

ISBN: 0-538-62952-5

Library of Congress Catalog Card Number: 93-085316

1 2 3 4 5 6 7 8 9 0 D 99 98 97 96 95 94

Printed in the United States of America

I(T)P
International Thomson Publishing

South-Western Publishing Co. is an ITP Company. The ITP trademark is used under license.

Preface

This preface is addressed primarily to the student. A complete examination guide for the CENTURY 21 ACCOUNTING, First-Year Course, learning package is included in the wraparound teacher's edition of this text.

This first-year accounting text will give you a thorough background in the basic accounting procedures used to operate a business. The accounting procedures presented will also serve as a sound background for employment in office jobs and preparation for studying business courses in college. Because the complete accounting cycle is covered, it is easy to see how each employee's job fits into the cycle for a business, an important qualification to employers. After this textbook is mastered, an advanced, or second-year, text is also available for learning more complex accounting concepts.

How to Use This Text

This textbook is carefully designed to function as a learning tool. The overall organization is in five parts, with one or more chapters in each part. Parts 1 and 5 are special parts that have only one chapter each. Parts 2, 3, and 4 each consist of several chapters that present a complete accounting cycle. For each part, a business is identified and described and that business is used to illustrate all the concepts for the rest of that part. In addition, each of these parts begins with a chart of accounts that is used throughout the part; it is an excellent preview for the part and serves as a convenient reference as you study each chapter.

Each chapter begins with a set of enabling performance tasks, or learning objectives, that describe what you will be able to do after studying the chapter. The task statements preview the chapter. A list of new terms that are defined and used within the chapter is also printed at the start of the chapter. Begin your study of each chapter with reading the enabling performance tasks and new accounting terms.

Each chapter has a number of headings that should be previewed to help understand the chapter. These headings can also function as a topical outline for a chapter if your studying method includes taking notes in outline format. Abundant illustrations highlight concepts in the chapter narrative. Note that each illustration has both an illustration number that is referenced within the narrative of the chapter and a descriptive caption that describes what is being illustrated. A summary illustration at the end of each chapter ties the main points of the chapter together in graphic terms. All new accounting vocabulary terms are printed in bold type within the sentence that defines the term so these definitions can be easily found.

Special Features

The following special features appear throughout the textbook:

Multicultural Awareness: This feature describes the contributions of a variety of cultures to accounting and business. Some of these features focus on historical contributions while others describe a situation in the United States today. This feature will help strengthen your awareness of the value of diversity in the work force and society.

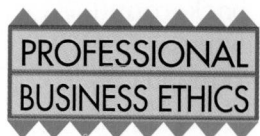

Professional Business Ethics: The news media are full of stories about unethical behavior in business and the effect of this unethical behavior on businesses and individuals. Boxed features throughout the text present ethical dilemmas that employees and business owners encounter in real life. Chapter 1 discusses ethical behavior in general and presents a 3-step checklist as a model for analyzing ethical decisions.

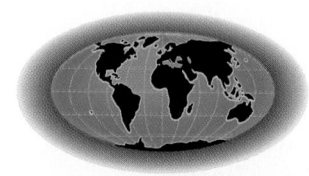

Global Perspective: Global business topics provide information and activities to enhance preparation for working in the global economy. These topics provide practical real-life information about trading across national boundaries and furnish activities to demonstrate how this information is applied.

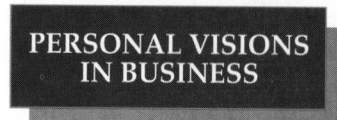

Personal Visions in Business: These personality profiles describe individuals in the business world today from a variety of occupations and cultural backgrounds. The individuals portrayed describe how an accounting background can be useful when starting and maintaining your own business and what they have learned about business from their own experiences.

Careers in Accounting: This feature presents a list of job duties for different job titles. This feature can help you select the kinds of jobs you might want to pursue based on the responsibilities of each job.

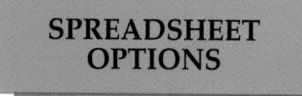

Spreadsheet Options: Features of spreadsheet software can help streamline business practices. The Spreadsheet Options feature describes some of the techniques used by businesses to make their financial reporting and analysis more efficient.

Applied Mathematics: If accounting is the language of business, then numbers are probably the words of the language. Many different mathematical calculations are involved in accounting for a business. Within a chapter, each time a new mathematical calculation is presented, the formula is highlighted by a color box and the Applied Math icon appears beside it. The Applied Math Icon is repeated next to end-of-chapter activities that first apply each calculation.

AUDIT
YOUR
UNDERSTANDING

Audit Your Understanding Questions: At the end of each short section of a chapter, a list of questions are given for assessing your grasp of the concepts covered. Self-check answers are provided in Appendix D.

FYI ("For Your Information"):   Boxes in the margins emphasize important points from the chapter and sometimes present additional interesting information about accounting and business.

End-of-Chapter Activities

The end of each chapter provides questions, cases, drills, and problems for practicing the new skills learned in the chapter and demonstrating your grasp of the concepts. Each section identifies the enabling performance tasks to be performed. The identifying letters of the tasks are placed in parentheses next to the heading of each activity.

The first section at the end of each chapter presents a list of all the new accounting terms defined in the chapter. You should be sure you know the meaning of each of these terms. This activity is followed by questions that help you review the concepts in the chapter. The next section, called Cases for Critical Thinking, describes case scenarios based on chapter concepts for which you are required to stretch your knowledge to provide the best answer or select the best alternative from those presented. Frequent Applied Communications sections furnish opportunities for honing your communication skills in the context of topics that are related to accounting.

The remaining end-of-chapter activities are drills and problems. The drills require you to analyze procedures from the chapter in a short-answer format. Application Problems apply your new accounting skills as you complete a problem for each section of the chapter. The Mastery Problem is a further application of all the new skills from the chapter in one single problem. The Challenge Problem concludes the chapter by stretching your knowledge to cover new applications. A Recycling Problem is available at the end of the textbook, in Appendix C, to use for additional practice or review. Reinforcement Activities and simulations for each of the three accounting cycles are milestone activities that synthesize all the activities from the chapters in the part.

Software

There are four pieces of software that may be used to complete end-of-chapter activities. Each piece of software is represented by an icon. These icons are placed on the appropriate drills and problems that may be completed using the computer.

Automated Accounting: This icon identifies a problem that is appropriate for solving using the *Automated Accounting 6.0* or higher software. A template for this problem is available that contains the chart of accounts and opening balances for selected problems.

Application Program: This icon identifies a problem that is available on the Application Program Disk software.

Accounting Tutorial: This icon identifies a section for which learning can be enhanced using the Accounting Tutorial software.

Spreadsheet Template: This icon identifies a problem for which a template file is available that can be used with commercial spreadsheet software for solving the problem.

All problems that are identified as being appropriate for solving with the use of software can also be completed manually with pencil and paper.

Reference Material

Reference material at the end of the book includes four appendices, a glossary of terms, and an index. Appendix A briefly describes each of the major accounting concepts described in more detail within the text narrative. Appendix B includes information about using a 10-key calculator and computer keypad. Appendix C presents a recycling problem for each chapter in the textbook for additional practice, or review. Appendix D provides the answers to the Audit Your Understanding questions in each chapter so that the questions can be used for self-review. The glossary of terms lists all the terms defined in the text and their definitions for easy reference. The index shows the page location for each topic in the text. This can be useful if you need to look up a topic but do not know where to find it.

ACKNOWLEDGMENTS

We thank the following individuals who contributed to the review process for this edition:

Mrs. Pam Caldwell
Godwin High School
Richmond, Virginia

Ms. Carolyn Francis
Robert E. Lee High School
Baytown, Texas

Mr. Neil Yeager
Cordova High School
Rancho Cordova, California

Dr. Arvella Jones
Commerce High School
Commerce, Texas

Mr. Robert Greer
John Jay High School
San Antonio, Texas

Dr. De Lois Gibson
Cass Technical High School
Detroit, Michigan

Mr. Peter Eisen
Murry Bergtraum High School
New York, New York

Mrs. Linda Songer
Orange Park High School
Orange Park, Florida

Mr. Joe McFarland
Shasta High School
Redding, California

We also appreciate the ongoing feedback provided by the classroom professionals who use CENTURY 21 ACCOUNTING every day.

Contents

PART 3

Accounting for a Merchandising Business Organized as a Partnership

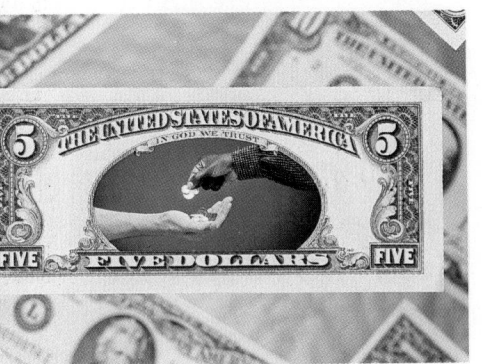

PART 4

Accounting for a Merchandising Business Organized as a Corporation

PART 5

The Legal Environment of Business

PHOTO CREDITS

STUDENT EDITION

STUDENT FEATURES

Professional Business Ethics

Can I Say This In My Resume? pages 8-9

Audit Your Understanding

This student activity can be found on pages 11 and 13

APPLIED SKILLS

Applied Communications

Page 15

SOFTWARE APPLICATIONS

Study Guide Software for Chapter 1

APPLIED SKILLS

Communications, page 10
Language Arts, page 9
Writing Across the Curriculum, page 13
Word Processing, page 13

TEACHING STRATEGIES

Accounting Pedagogy, page 4
Assessment by Portfolio, page 11
Different Learning Abilities, page 7
Cooperative Learning, page 8
Expanding Beyond the Classroom, page 5
Applying Visuals, page 10
Teaching Tip, pages 6, 7, 9
Software Focus, page 12

ASSESSMENT

Assessment by Portfolio
MicroExam software

SOFTWARE

Study Guide Software
MicroExam
WordPerfect (word processing)
Windows (operating system)

BIBLIOGRAPHY

AICPA. *A Survey of Perceptions, Knowledge and Attitudes Towards CPAs and the Accounting Profession,* 1986.

Albrecht, W. Steve. *Ethical Issues in the Practice of Accounting.* Cincinnati: South-Western Publishing Co., 1992.

Bloom, Benjamin S., ed., et al. *Taxonomy of Educational Objectives: Handbook I, Cognitive Domain.* White Plains: Longman, Inc., 1977.

Estes, Ralph. *Dictionary of Accounting.* Second Edition. Cambridge: The MIT Press, 1986.

Gilbertson, Claudia. *Accounting: Learning and Instruction.* Second Edition. Cincinnati: South-Western Publishing Co., 1992.

Hendrickson, Aletha. *Writing for Accountants.* Cincinnati: South-Western Publishing Co., 1993.

McCabe and McCabe. *Writing Effective Resumes, A Complete Guide.* Cincinnati: South-Western Publishing Co., 1993.

Periodicals

Accounting Review, American Accounting Association, Sarasota, FL
Fortune, New York, NY (Business news)
Hispanic, Washington, D.C. (Multicultural awareness)
Practical Accountant, Faulkner & Gray, Inc., New York, NY
Wall Street Journal, New York, NY (Business newspaper)

Technology

AICPA. *A License to Succeed,* 1990. (Video)

Accounting as a Career

Part 1 lays the foundation for the accounting program. In Chapter 1, an overview is presented that introduces students to accounting and career opportunities in the accounting profession. Two additional important and timely topics are also presented—communication skills and ethics.

Good communication skills play an important role for today's worker. Employers seek individuals with good written and oral communication skills. Chapter 1 introduces students to the importance of effective communication. As the chapters progress, students are given the opportunity to apply their skills in the end-of-chapter Applied Communications activities. Students are also given opportunities to apply their writing skills in portfolio assessment, writing across the curriculum, and practicing language arts skills as suggested in the margin of the teacher's edition. All communication activities are accounting related to be more meaningful and applicable to the subject area.

Ethical decision making skills also play an important role for today's worker. Chapter 1 discusses business ethics and some of the causes of unethical behavior. A three-step checklist is outlined for making ethical decisions which gives students a framework to stretch their critical thinking skills. Throughout the text, the student feature Professional Business Ethics gives students the opportunity to apply this three-step checklist and analyze situations that they may encounter in the real world.

GENERAL GOALS

1. Know accounting terminology related to accounting careers.

2. Understand entry-level positions, educational requirements, and career opportunities in accounting.

3. Understand that success in the accounting profession depends on the ability to communicate and make ethical decisions.

CHAPTER 1 OVERVIEW

Chapter 1 is an introduction to the accounting profession, communication skills, and ethical business be-havior. The accounting profession is encouraging educators to develop all the skills needed for profes-sional success. Therefore, it is important for students to be aware of accounting career opportunities and professional organizations. It is also important that communication skills and business ethics awareness are taught.

Chapter 1 is an informational chapter. Therefore, end-of-chapter drills and problems are not in-cluded. However, Cases for Critical Thinking and an Applied Communications activity are provided.

GUIDE TO ACHIEVING LEARNING OBJECTIVES

Enabling Performance Tasks	TEACH	APPLY		EXTEND/ENRICH					
	Lesson Plans	Drills for Understanding	Application Problems	Mastery Problems	Challenge Problems	Cases for Critical Thinking	Recycling Problems	Reinforcement Activity	
a. Define accounting terms related to accounting careers.	1-1								
b. Identify how accounting serves as a basis for careers.	1-1					Cases 1, 2			
c. Identify the tasks of various accounting occupations.	1-1								
d. Describe how communi-cation skills are im-portant in reporting accounting information.	1-2								
e. Describe how individ-uals make ethical business decisions.	1-2								

ENRICHMENT

SPECIAL FEATURES	TECHNOLOGY CONNECTION
Professional Business Ethics, page 8	Electronic Study Guide
Applied Communications, page 15	

	INFORMAL ASSESSMENT		FORMAL ASSESSMENT				
	Study Guide	Audit Your Understanding	Chapter MicroExam	Chapter Problem Test	Unit Problem Test	Unit Objective Test	Portfolio
	Unit A	✓	✓			✓	
	Unit B	✓	✓			✓	✓
	Unit B	✓	✓			✓	✓
	Unit C	✓	✓			✓	✓
	Unit C	✓	✓			✓	

NEW, REVIEW, AND EXTENSION

ACTIVITIES/CONCEPTS/TRANSACTIONS	NEW	REVIEW/ EXTENSION
Accounting careers	✓	
Accounting career ladder	✓	
Communication in accounting	✓	
Ethical decision-making	✓	
3-step checklist for making ethical decisions	✓	

TEACHING MATERIALS

Teacher's Wraparound Edition of Text

Teacher's Resource Guide

Teacher's Edition of Working Papers

Teaching Transparencies

MicroExam

1

Accounting Careers: Communication and Ethics in the Workplace

ENABLING PERFORMANCE TASKS

After studying Chapter 1, you will be able to:

a Define accounting terms related to accounting careers.

b Identify how accounting serves as a basis for careers.

c Identify the tasks of various accounting occupations.

d Describe how communication skills are important in reporting accounting information.

e Describe how individuals make ethical business decisions.

TERMS PREVIEW

accounting • accounting system • accounting records • accountant • public accounting firm • private accountant • bookkeeper • accounting clerk • general office clerk • ethics • business ethics

4

A successful business is involved in numerous financial activities. Summary reports of these financial activities are needed by several people. Owners and managers must understand financial reports to make good business decisions. *How much should be charged for the product or service? Are profits sufficient? Should new products be sold? Should new services be provided? Can costs be decreased?*

Individuals outside the business also use summary reports to make decisions that affect the business. The business' banker uses these summary reports to make loan decisions. *How much should the bank allow the business to borrow? Is the business likely to be able to repay the loan?*

A business must also submit summary reports to certain government agencies. The government requires that the business report financial information when it pays taxes. Other government agencies examine the financial activities of the business to assure that it follows various federal and state laws.

Persons responsible for nonprofit organizations also need accounting information as the basis for making financial decisions. The mayor of a community uses summary reports to determine how taxpayers' money should be spent. *How efficient is the community's water department? Can the community afford to purchase a new fire truck? Must taxes be raised to pay for a new high school building?* Nonprofit organizations, such as churches, public service organizations, and city governments, must keep spending within available financial resources.

Career opportunities exist for individuals to provide businesses, government, and nonprofit organizations with necessary financial information. Many young people choose to prepare for a career in the field of accounting.

☞ ☞ FYI ☜ ☜

The six largest accounting firms in the United States are referred to as the Big Six. They are:
- Arthur Andersen & Co.
- Coopers & Lybrand
- Deloitte & Touche
- Ernst & Young
- KMPG Peat Marwick
- Price Waterhouse

WHAT IS ACCOUNTING?

To create useful reports, financial information must be maintained in an organized way. Planning, recording, analyzing, and interpreting financial information is called **accounting**. A planned process for providing financial information that will be useful to management is called an **accounting system**. Organized summaries of a business' financial activities are called **accounting records**.

Inaccurate accounting records often contribute to business failure and bankruptcy. Failure to understand accounting information can result in poor business decisions for both businesses and nonprofit organizations. Accounting education helps managers and owners make better business decisions.

Accounting is the language of business. Many individuals in a business complete accounting forms and prepare accounting reports. Owners, managers, and accounting personnel use their knowledge of accounting to understand the information provided in the accounting reports. Regardless of their responsibilities within an organization, individuals can perform their jobs more efficiently if they know the language of business—accounting.

Materials

Student pages 4–11

Objectives (Enabling Performance Tasks)

a. Define accounting terms related to accounting careers.

b. Identify how accounting serves as a basis for careers.

c. Identify the tasks of various accounting occupations.

FOCUS

- Explain that the career opportunities for people with accounting training and experience will be presented in this lesson.

- Introduce new vocabulary: accounting, accounting system, accounting records, accountant, public accounting firm, private accountant, bookkeeper, accounting clerk, general office clerk.

TEACHING STRATEGIES: EXPANDING BEYOND THE CLASSROOM

Stress the importance of accounting in everyday jobs. Students need to realize that accounting is important for everyone, not just people who are going to be accountants. Set up a day where several people from the community are invited to be members of a professional panel. Try to get a person such as a hair stylist who can tell students how important it is to understand accounting to keep track of the books. A builder might explain to students how costs are tracked for building a house and the role accounting plays. This could be a good recruiting tool to emphasize the importance of accounting in everyday living.

Cover student pages 4–11, "What is Accounting?", "Job Opportunities in Accounting", and "A Career in Accounting." Accounting is the language of business. Most employees and professionals need to have some knowledge of accounting to complete their day-to-day tasks, if for no other reason than all individuals use accounting when completing their federal tax returns. Review the various career opportunities and educational requirements for those in accounting. The *Directory of Occupational Titles* is a good source of accounting occupation titles.

APPLY

Define each new vocabulary term and discuss each term.

Guided Practice

Guide students through the classified advertisements illustrated in the chapter. Ask students where on the career ladder each position can be found and what education and experience is required for each job.

Independent Practice

Assign Terms 1–9 and Questions 1–10.

TEACHING STRATEGIES:
TEACHING TIP

The first few days in class will set the tone for the entire term. Therefore, involve students in identifying the importance of accounting information in various organizations. Have students identify how accounting is used in familiar organizations, such as the business where they work, a family member's employer, and the local school system. Stress the importance of good accounting records and the decisions that are made based on these records. This will help students understand the importance of accounting and the value they will gain with a knowledge of accounting procedures.

Accounting is used by most individuals in everyday life. Nearly everyone in the United States earns money and must submit income tax reports to the federal and state governments. Everyone, personally or for a business, must plan ways to keep spending within available income. Individuals having accounting skills are better prepared to keep personal financial records.

JOB OPPORTUNITIES IN ACCOUNTING

Accounting positions fit into several classifications that include accountants, bookkeepers, accounting clerks, and other general office workers. An increasing amount of accounting work is done using computers. However, the increase in the use of computers does not appear to be decreasing the need for all kinds of accounting personnel.

FYI

According to a survey by the Gallup organization, approximately 1 in 20 high school and college students expects to be an accountant by age 30.

Accountants

A person who plans, summarizes, analyzes, and interprets accounting information is called an **accountant**. Accountants prepare various accounting reports and assist owners and managers in making financial decisions. Accountants also supervise the work of other accounting personnel and check the accuracy of financial statements.

CONTROLLER

Accountant needed to maintain accounting system and supervise accounting personnel. Five or more years experience, professional certification, and computer skills required.

ACCOUNTANT

Local business needs an accountant to supervise all accounting functions. Good interpersonal and communications skills are required.

Some accountants work as members of accounting firms that sell accounting services to other businesses. A business selling accounting services to the general public is called a **public accounting firm**. Public accounting firms provide a variety of accounting services to businesses and individuals. These accounting services may include planning an accounting system, preparing accounting reports, and submitting income tax reports to the government. For example, a medical clinic may not need a full-time accountant. The doctor, a nurse, or another office employee may do the day-to-day accounting tasks. The doctor may hire a public accounting firm to help plan the accounting system and analyze, report, and interpret the accounting information.

PART 1   Accounting as a Career

TEACHING STRATEGIES: TEACHING TIP

Instruct students to clip accounting employment advertisements from local and national newspapers. Use these advertisements for class discussion. The advertisements will demonstrate the variety and quantity of accounting positions available within your community as well as across the nation.

An accountant who is employed by a single business is called a **private accountant**. The work of private accountants is similar to that done by public accounting firms. However, a private accountant works for only one business.

Bookkeepers

A person who does general accounting work plus some summarizing and analyzing of accounting information is called a **bookkeeper**. In some businesses bookkeepers may supervise the work of other accounting personnel. In small to medium-size businesses, bookkeepers may also help owners and managers interpret accounting information.

BOOKKEEPER

Work without supervision. Experience in general ledger and payroll required. Experience in supervising accounting clerks desirable. Electronic spreadsheet and word processing skills required.

BOOKKEEPER-CLERICAL

Bookkeeper required to supervise accounts receivable and general ledger. Computer and keyboarding skills a must.

Bookkeepers in small businesses may do additional general office work. Many businesses require that bookkeepers have filing and keyboarding skills. Filing skills are needed for storing accounting records. Keyboarding skills are necessary to efficiently use computers to prepare accounting records and reports.

Accounting Clerks

A person who records, sorts, and files accounting information is often called an **accounting clerk**. Some businesses have large amounts of routine accounting tasks that are assigned to accounting clerks.

PAYROLL CLERK

Opening for responsible payroll clerk. Coordination of all payroll activities. Salary depends on training and experience.

ACCOUNTS PAYABLE CLERK

Retail store. Automated system. Will train person with general accounting background.

- Assess student understanding by checking solutions to the Independent Practice activities.
- Review the job opportunities in accounting and the educational requirements and promotional possibilities in accounting careers.

Reteach

Use actual newspaper advertisements for accounting positions to illustrate the number of different types of jobs available and the educational requirements of each position.

Extend

Assign Cases for Critical Thinking 1 and 2.

CLOSURE

Use Audit Your Understanding questions.

TEACHING STRATEGIES: TEACHING TIP

Field trips to local businesses should be made to help students see accounting personnel in actual work situations. Students will benefit from contact with local business persons. These contacts should include obtaining information about job opportunities in the local employment area. Students should use these experiences to find answers to the following questions:

a. What kinds of entry-level accounting jobs are available in the local community?

b. What business courses should students take to prepare for available jobs?

c. What nonbusiness courses should students take to prepare for available jobs?

d. What must employees do to earn a promotion?

e. What post-high school education should students complete?

TEACHING STRATEGIES: DIFFERENT LEARNING ABILITIES

Limited English Proficiency (LEP) Students. Ask students to make a list of words or concepts they do not understand in the chapter. Assign a student mentor to work individually with the LEP student to review the list and provide the meanings of the words or concepts.

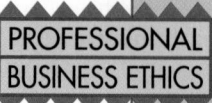

FYI

Analyzing ethical behavior is discussed in more detail on pages 12–14.

PROFESSIONAL BUSINESS ETHICS

Can I Say This In My Resume?

Kenneth Reed just graduated from high school with one year of high school accounting. Not sure of his long-term career goal, Kenneth decided to apply for a position as bookkeeper with Jackson Industries. In an effort to improve his chances to get the job, Kenneth overstated the leadership experience he had acquired in several part-time jobs. For example, Kenneth's experience as a janitor was exaggerated on his resume as ''Asset Maintenance Engineer—accountable for the acquisition and maintenance of productive assets.'' In the same way, Kenneth's job as a lifeguard was exaggerated as ''Recreational Director—responsible for coordinating customers' recreational activities.''

Based on the impressive nature of his resume, Kenneth was hired for the bookkeeping position. After one year of employment, Kenneth received above average ratings on his annual employment evaluation. Shortly thereafter, the accountant met Kenneth's former employers and learned the truth of Kenneth's work experience.

The three-step checklist presented in this chapter is useful in determining whether Kenneth demonstrated ethical behavior in preparing his resume.

INSTRUCTIONS Use the following three-step checklist for making ethical decisions. The first activity has been completed for you as follows.

1. Is the action illegal? No. Overstating qualifications is not illegal, but it does provide the employer the opportunity to terminate employment.

2. Does the action violate company or professional standards? No. Since Kenneth was neither an employee of the company nor a member of any profession, this question does not apply.

Accounting clerks are often given a title, such as payroll clerk or accounts payable clerk, to describe the specific accounting activities they perform. These clerks usually work with only a small part of the total accounting system. However, accounting clerks who understand the total accounting system will understand the importance of the work being done. With accounting knowledge and some experience, accounting clerks may earn promotions to more responsible accounting positions.

General Office Clerks

A person who does general kinds of office tasks, including some accounting tasks, is called a **general office clerk**. Many office personnel and computer operators perform some accounting tasks. For example, a secretary may be in charge of a small cash fund. A telephone operator may key-enter sales order information directly into a computer. A computer operator may key-enter data from special accounting documents. Regardless of who completes the accounting activities, the work must be done according to established

---

TEACHING STRATEGIES: COOPERATIVE LEARNING

Newspapers and magazines regularly report on illegal or unethical actions by individuals and businesses. Select a group of five students to collect examples from the local media of illegal or unethical actions. Each member of the group should find an example and write a summary of these actions and analyze the ethics involved. Allow five days for the collection of material. Appoint a group leader to present the findings to the class.

3. Who is affected, and how, by the action?

People Affected	Negative	Positive
Kenneth Reed	Could be terminated since management can no longer rely on his honesty. If retained, he could lose any chance of promotion.	Obtains employment.
Other Job Applicants	More highly qualified applicants lost an opportunity for employment.	
Company	Managers may lose trust and may delegate important tasks to other employees.	

As a bookkeeper, Kenneth has been placed in a position of trust. Management must be able to have faith in the accounting records and reports prepared by a bookkeeper. Knowing that Kenneth has the capacity to misrepresent the facts, management may lose faith in Kenneth's honesty.

Kenneth's success in performing the functions of bookkeeper may affect management's decisions. Management may forgive Kenneth for his previous actions since he has proved to be a loyal employee. Although Kenneth may not be terminated, his relationship with management has been damaged.

TEACHING STRATEGIES:
TEACHING TIP

Share information with the guidance counselors on the importance of accounting for all students. Educate them to the fact that students who are going on to college will benefit by taking an accounting course even though they are not planning to be accountants. Anyone majoring in Business Administration will take an accounting course in college. Those entering into Law will also take an accounting course. Students going directly into the work force will have a better chance of employment with an accounting background.

accounting concepts and procedures. General office clerks with some knowledge of accounting will be able to understand the importance of the accounting tasks they complete.

SECRETARY

Requires 3 years secretarial experience, word processing, communication skills, and bookkeeping experience or accounting education.

SALES REPRESENTATIVE

Direct merchandising company. Key phone orders into automated sales/inventory system. Keyboarding and communications skills required. Knowledge of accounting a plus.

APPLIED SKILLS: LANGUAGE ARTS

Paraphrasing, writing complete sentences. For additional practice in language arts skills, direct students to answer the Accounting Terms and Questions for Individual Study at the end of the chapter. Students should write the definitions in their own words and in complete sentences.

A CAREER IN ACCOUNTING

The career ladder shown in Illustration 1-1 represents the educational requirements and promotional possibilities in accounting careers.

ILLUSTRATION 1-1   Career Ladder

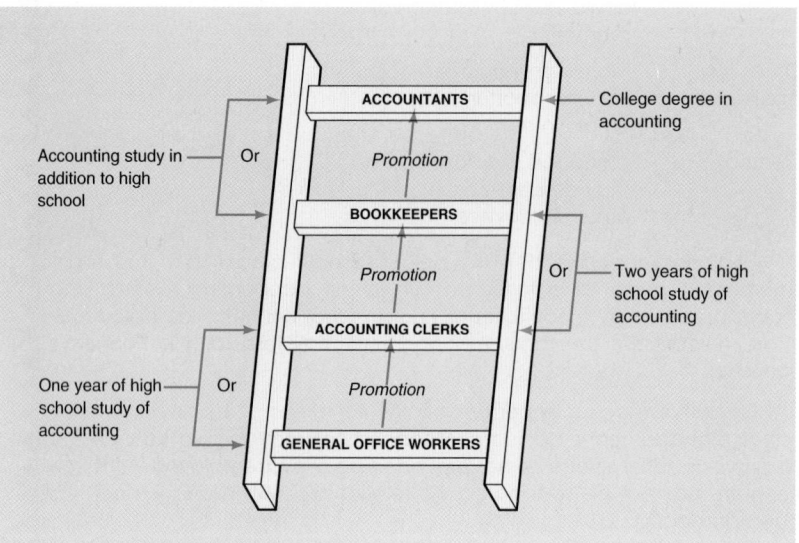

Immediately after high school graduation, individuals may start an accounting career as accounting clerks or general office clerks. A few of the better students may start as bookkeepers. High school study in accounting is useful as preparation for these accounting positions. The study of high school accounting is also good preparation for the study of accounting in college. With experience and additional accounting study, accounting personnel can earn a promotion to a higher position on the career ladder.

Professional Certification

Almost all persons seeking positions as accountants must complete some study of accounting beyond high school and must gain accounting experience. Most public accountants also earn the Certified Public Accountant (CPA) designation. Each state sets the standards for earning a CPA certificate. Usually, the requirements include the study of college accounting, some accounting experience, and a passing score on a professional test covering all aspects of the accounting field.

Many private accountants often earn certification from a variety of professional accounting organizations. Private accountants can demonstrate their expertise in specific fields of accounting by earning certification such as the Certified Management Accountant (CMA) or the Certified Internal Auditor (CIA).

Professional Organizations

During the past one hundred years accountants have joined to form many professional organizations. The oldest and largest of these organizations is the American Institute of Certified Public Accountants (AICPA). The AICPA has a diverse membership of both public and private accountants. Other organizations, such as the American Woman's Society of Certified Public Accountants, the National Association of Black Accountants, and the International Federation of Accountants provide unique services to meet the needs of their members. Together, these organizations strive to promote job opportunities in accounting, to support and develop the professional skills of their members, and to improve the usefulness of accounting information.

Audit Your Understanding

1. What is accounting?
2. List several classifications of accounting positions.
3. What is the full name of the AICPA?

THE IMPORTANCE OF COMMUNICATION AND ETHICS IN ACCOUNTING

Your knowledge of accounting will provide you with an important skill necessary for success in any profession or business. Yet, accounting knowledge alone will not assure success. Your ability to communicate and make ethical decisions will increase your chances of achieving professional success.

Communication

Effective accounting records can provide individuals with accurate and timely information regarding the financial activities of a business. Yet this information is of little value unless it can be communicated effectively to individuals responsible for making business decisions. Effective communication is essential because managers and accountants must often communicate accounting information to individuals with little or no accounting knowledge. Business leaders emphasize that communication skills are as important as technical skills in achieving career success.

Communication is the transfer of information between two or more individuals. Communication can be either oral or written. Oral communication includes phone conversations, one-on-one meetings, and group meetings. Written communication includes memorandums, letters, and reports.

Effective communication requires both a knowledge of good communication skills and regular practice using those skills. You have learned communication skills in a variety of language and communication classes. This textbook provides you the opportunity

FYI

Examples of other professional associations are: Institute of Management Accountants, American Accounting Association, Work in America Institute, and Families and Work Institute.

AUDIT YOUR UNDERSTANDING

The AUDIT YOUR UNDERSTANDING feature appears at the end of each section of the chapter. Explain to your students that the word *audit* means to check or verify. AUDIT YOUR UNDERSTANDING may be used to check student comprehension of the section just studied. The answers are provided in Appendix D in the back of the textbook.

1. The language of business.
2. Accountants, bookkeepers, accounting clerks, and other general office workers.
3. The American Institute of Certified Public Accountants (AICPA).

LESSON PLAN 1-2

Materials

- Student pages 11–14
- Software: Electronic Study Guide
- Assess: MicroExam Chapter 1

Objectives (Enabling Performance Tasks)

d. Describe how communication skills are important in reporting accounting information.

e. Describe how individuals make ethical business decisions.

FOCUS

- Career opportunities in accounting were presented earlier in this chapter. Explain that now we will discuss how the ability to communicate and make ethical business decisions will increase a person's chances of achieving success in an accounting career.

- Introduce new vocabulary: ethics, business ethics.

TEACH

Cover student pages, 11–14, "The Importance of Communication and Ethics in Accounting." Communication skills can be improved by learning good communication techniques and practicing those techniques.

APPLY

Have students read the Professional Business Ethics case and give their opinions on the answers given in the three-step checklist.

Guided Practice

Have students write a solution to the Applied Communications activity. This activity provides the opportunity to prepare a resume and apply the ethics learned in this chapter. Guide students through the steps of completing a resume.

Independent Practice

Assign Terms 10–11, Questions 11–15, and Study Guide 1.

ASSESS

- Assess student understanding by checking solutions to the Independent Practice activities.
- Review the three-step checklist for making ethical decisions.
  a. Is the action legal?
  b. Does the action violate company or professional standards?
  c. Who is affected, and how, by the action?

Reteach

If students do not understand the reasons that cause unethical behavior, write each of the six factors on the chalkboard.

Enrich

Assign the Electronic Study Guide Chapter 1 to complete the study guide from the working papers at the computer. Ask students to identify a current event that requires an ethical decision and apply the three-step checklist and recommend a decision.

to practice your communication and language arts skills. Throughout the textbook you will be presented with a variety of business situations that require you to prepare an oral or written message.

Business Ethics

In your personal life you are faced daily with making decisions between right and wrong. The principles of right and wrong that guide an individual in making decisions are called **ethics**. Your personal ethics enable you to make decisions that consider the impact of your actions on others as well as yourself. Personal ethics are developed throughout your life from your relationships with family, friends, teachers, and other individuals that influence your life.

The use of personal ethics in making business decisions is called **business ethics**. Regardless of your position in an organization, you will be challenged to apply business ethics in making business decisions. The increasing complexity of today's business environment is also increasing the number of difficult business decisions that must be made.

Causes of Unethical Behavior. Unethical behavior occurs when an individual disregards his or her principles of right and wrong by choosing the wrong action. An understanding of the causes of unethical behavior is critical to preventing unethical behavior. Effective managers can identify and correct situations that would allow their employees to make decisions that may be unethical.

Six different factors may cause an individual to make an unethical decision.

1. Excessive emphasis on profits. Business managers are often judged on their ability to increase business profits. The salaries of business managers are often based on the amount of profits earned.
2. Misplaced business loyalty. Business managers often develop a misplaced dedication to their company. Disregarding their business ethics, managers may make decisions that appear to benefit the business without considering the negative impact on others.
3. Personal advancement. Some individuals have a "whatever it takes" attitude toward their personal careers. Their decisions are based solely on the degree that an action will advance their personal careers.
4. Expectation of not getting caught. An individual can recognize that an action is ethically wrong yet select that action because the chance of getting caught is small.
5. Unethical business environment. Individuals working in a business are less likely to apply business ethics if their managers are also making unethical decisions. The ethical environment set by business managers influences the ethical behavior of everyone in the business.

SOFTWARE FOCUS

Software may be used for independent practice or enrichment/extension as the instructor deems appropriate. For this chapter, the Electronic Study Guide Chapter 1 may be assigned to complete the study guide from the working papers at the computer.

6. Unwillingness to take a stand. How often have you seen something wrong but not taken any action to correct it? Individuals can be unwilling to take a stand against unethical behavior because they fear losing their jobs, missing a deserved promotion, or alienating other employees.

Competition and the pursuit of success are the foundation of the free enterprise system. However, these factors are also common elements of unethical behavior. The desire to gain a competitive edge can motivate some individuals and businesses to make unethical decisions. The pursuit of success can motivate some individuals to overlook their principles of right and wrong. Fortunately, most business leaders now recognize that ethical behavior is the only way to attain long-term success.

Making Ethical Decisions. The increasing complexity of today's business environment requires that you be able to apply ethics in making business decisions. Determining whether an action is ethical can be difficult. In many business situations the line between right and wrong is not clear.

Analyzing a situation is the first step in deciding whether an action is ethical. The following three-step checklist will serve as a guide in collecting all relevant information regarding an action.

FYI

Three-step checklist for making ethical decisions:
1. Is the action illegal?
2. Does the action violate company or professional standards?
3. Who is affected, and how, by the action?

Audit Your Understanding

1. What is communication?
2. When does unethical behavior occur?
3. What are the three questions for analyzing ethical situations?

1 *Is the action illegal?* Does the action violate international, federal, state, or local laws? You should not consider an action if it is illegal. Obeying the law is in your best interest and the best interest of your business. Individuals will often encourage you to violate laws when the chance of being caught is small or the fine is minimal. Such an approach is shortsighted and does not consider all people who may be effected by the action.

2 *Does the action violate company or professional standards?* Public laws often set only minimum standards of behavior. Many businesses and professions set even higher standards of behavior. Thus, an action may be legal, yet still violate standards of the business or profession. Violating these standards may affect your job security and professional certification. The action may also have a negative effect on your business.

Several professional accounting organizations have adopted codes of professional conduct to assist their members in making ethical decisions. These codes have been written by the organizations' members to encourage their members to act and uphold the professional image of the accounting profession.

3 *Who is affected, and how, by the action?* If an action is legal and complies with business and professional standards, you must rely on your principles of right and wrong to determine if the action is ethical. Determine

CHAPTER 1 Accounting Careers: Communication and Ethics in the Workplace **13**

CLOSURE

Use Audit Your Understanding questions.

ASSESS

Administer a MicroExam test for Chapter 1.

APPLIED SKILLS: WRITING ACROSS THE CURRICULUM

Writing paragraphs and short essays. Surveys of business managers show that communication skills are one of the most desired traits in new employees. The Cases for Critical Thinking are short, practical applications of the accounting principles developed in the chapter. Some cases are planned to present problems related to the chapter but not specifically discussed and answered in the chapter. These cases present an opportunity for critical thinking and decision making. These cases also require more than a short objective-type response. Therefore, they provide ideal practice in writing paragraphs and short essays.

APPLIED SKILLS: WORD PROCESSING

If you wish to integrate word processing into your accounting course, you may direct students to answer the end-of-chapter Accounting Terms, Questions for Individual Study, and Cases for Critical Thinking using their word processing software.

AUDIT YOUR UNDERSTANDING

1. Communication is the transfer of information between two or more individuals.
2. When an individual disregards his or her principles of right and wrong by choosing the wrong action.
3. (1) Is the action illegal? (2) Does the action violate company or professional standards? (3) Who is affected, and how, by the action?

13

1. **accounting:** Planning, recording, analyzing, and interpreting financial information. (p. 5)

2. **accounting system:** A planned process for providing financial information that will be useful to management. (p. 5)

3. **accounting records:** Organized summaries of a business' financial activities. (p. 5)

4. **accountant:** A person who plans, summarizes, analyzes, and interprets accounting information. (p. 6)

5. **public accounting firm:** A business selling accounting services to the general public. (p. 6)

6. **private accountant:** An accountant who is employed by a single business. (p. 7)

7. **bookkeeper:** A person who does general accounting work plus some summarizing and analyzing of accounting information. (p. 7)

8. **accounting clerk:** A person who records, sorts, and files accounting information. (p. 7)

9. **general office clerk:** A person who does general kinds of office tasks, including some accounting tasks. (p. 8)

10. **ethics:** The principles of right and wrong that guide an individual in making decisions. (p. 12)

11. **business ethics:** The use of personal ethics in making business decisions. (p. 12)

1. Owners, managers, the business' banker, and government. (p. 5)

2. As the basis for making financial decisions. (p. 5)

3. To prepare income tax reports and to keep expenditures within available income. (p. 6)

4. Accountants prepare various accounting reports and assist owners and managers in making financial decisions. Accountants also supervise the work of other accounting personnel and check the accuracy of financial statements. (p. 6)

5. Planning an accounting system, preparing accounting reports, and submitting income tax reports to the government. (p. 6)

6. Both do essentially the same accounting work. A private accountant is employed by a single business; a public accountant works for a public accounting firm that sells its services to other businesses. (pp. 6, 7)

7. In some businesses, bookkeepers may supervise the work of other accounting personnel. In small to medium-size businesses, bookkeepers may also help owners and managers interpret accounting information. (p. 7)

8. General office clerks with some knowledge of accounting will be able to understand the importance of the accounting tasks they complete. (p. 9)

9. Individuals may start an accounting career as accounting clerks or general office clerks. A few of the better students may start as bookkeepers. (p. 10)

how the action affects a variety of people or groups, including the business employees and owners, customers, the local community, and society. In evaluating ethical situations, individuals often fail to consider how their actions affect a wide range of people.

Throughout this textbook you will have the opportunity to analyze common business situations. Use this three-step checklist to help determine whether each action demonstrates ethical behavior.

ACCOUNTING TERMS

What is the meaning of each of the following?

1. accounting
2. accounting system
3. accounting records
4. accountant
5. public accounting firm
6. private accountant
7. bookkeeper
8. accounting clerk
9. general office clerk
10. ethics
11. business ethics

QUESTIONS FOR INDIVIDUAL STUDY

1. Who uses summary reports of the financial activities of a business?
2. Why do persons responsible for nonprofit organizations need accounting information?
3. What personal reasons do individuals have for learning accounting facts and procedures?
4. What are the responsibilities of accountants?
5. What accounting services do public accounting firms offer?
6. What is the difference between a private accountant and a public accountant?
7. What does a bookkeeper do?
8. Why do general office clerks need to study accounting?
9. What entry-level accounting jobs might be obtained by persons who have studied high school accounting?
10. How can a person earn a designation as a CPA?
11. Why must managers and accountants have effective communication skills?
12. How are personal ethics developed?
13. What are the causes of unethical behavior?
14. What do most business leaders now recognize about ethical behavior?
15. What is the three-step checklist for collecting information for making an ethical decision?

CASES FOR CRITICAL THINKING

CASE 1   Cynthia's career goal is to be the accountant responsible for her community's accounting system. After completing one year of high school accounting, she hopes to obtain an accounting clerk job in city government. She believes that several years of hard work in city government will provide her with the experience necessary to assume the accountant's job. Do you think Cynthia can reach her goal? Explain.

CASE 2   When planning his high school course selections, Duane selects accounting as a career field. He plans to complete two years of high school accounting study. Duane is not planning to complete any other high school business courses. Duane's school counselor suggests that he also complete at least one year of keyboarding. Should Duane take the counselor's advice? Explain.

APPLIED COMMUNICATIONS

A resume provides a statement of your education, experience, and qualifications for a prospective employer. Your resume should be accurate, honest, and perfect in every respect.

Your resume should include all work experience along with the companies and dates of employment. Education, activities, and interests are all important items that should be included. It is preferable to keep the resume to one typed page.

INSTRUCTIONS:

1. Go to the library and research how to prepare an appropriate resume.
2. Prepare a personal resume that you could send to a prospective employer.

---

13. (a) Excessive emphasis on profits. (b) Misplaced business loyalty. (c) Personal advancement. (d) Expectation of not getting caught. (e) Unethical business environment. (f) Unwillingness to take a stand. (p. 12)

14. Ethical behavior is the only way to attain long-term success. (p. 13)

15. (1) Is the action illegal? (2) Does the action violate company or professional standards? (3) Who is affected, and how, by the action? (p. 13)

CASES FOR CRITICAL THINKING

Case 1   Cynthia is not prepared for the accountant's job. Only persons with college accounting education are qualified for jobs as accountants. A city government may also require that its top accounting job be held by someone with professional certification. Cynthia should consider continuing her education to obtain the necessary qualifications.

Case 2   Duane should take the school counselor's advice to enroll in a keyboarding class. Many businesses require that bookkeepers have keyboarding skills. Keyboarding skills are necessary to efficiently use computers to prepare and communicate accounting records and reports.

APPLIED COMMUNICATIONS

The resume should be keyed, one page in length, and in the most current style. Individual student resumes will vary; however, they should include the following elements: (1) Name, address, telephone number, social security number. (2) Education, including grade average, courses, any special skills. (3) Work experience and any special training. (4) Relevant school activities. (5) Honors or awards.

---

10. Each state sets the standards for earning a CPA certificate. Usually, the requirements include the study of college accounting, some accounting experience, and a passing score on a professional test covering all aspects of the accounting field. (p. 10)

11. Effective communication skills are essential because managers and accountants must often communicate accounting information to individuals with little or no accounting knowledge. (p. 11)

12. Personal ethics are developed throughout your life from your relationships with family, friends, instructors, and other individuals that influence your life. (p. 12)

STUDENT EDITION

STUDENT FEATURES

Multicultural Awareness

Professional Organizations, page 20
Fra Luca Pacioli, page 57
Debit/Credit, page 81
Abacus, page 171
Accountants In Ancient Civilizations, page 215

Professional Business Ethics

Is This Really A Business Expense? pages 40–41
Am I A Software Pirate? pages 184–185

Global Perspective

Foreign Currency, page 28
Professional Accounting Associations, page 88

Careers In Accounting

General Ledger Bookkeeper, page 101
Cashier I/Cash-Accounting Clerk, page 146
Accountant, page 196
Data Entry Clerk, page 234

Personal Visions In Business

Joe Arriola, page 60
Belinda Hughes, page 109
Tom Richardson, page 212

Spreadsheet Options

Using An Electronic Spreadsheet To Prepare A Bank
Reconciliation, page 145
Electronic Spreadsheets Help Answer "What If?" Questions,
page 203

Audit Your Understanding

This student activity can be found on pages 21, 26, 29, 41, 43,
55, 64, 76, 83, 87, 103, 112, 140, 147, 153, 183, 187, 199, 204,
213, 223, 227

APPLIED SKILLS

Applied Communications

Pages 118, 229

Applied Math

Pages 87, 93, 94, 104, 105, 106, 109, 110, 111, 119, 151, 153,
156, 157, 175, 176D, 180, 182, 183, 189, 190, 196, 197, 201,
202, 207

SOFTWARE APPLICATIONS

Automated Accounting 6.0 Problems 6-M, 6-C, (Optional
Problem DB-1A); 7-M, 7-C, (Optional Problems DB-2A, DB-2B);
10-M, 10-C, (Optional Problem DB-3A), Reinforcement Activity 1
Spreadsheet Template Drill 7-D1, Problems 7-M, 9-M, 9-C
Accounting Tutorial Units 1-3
Application Program Disk Problems 5-M, 5-C, 6-M, 6-C, 7-4, 7-5,
7-M, 8-M, 8-C, 10-M

TEACHER'S EDITION

APPLIED SKILLS

Communications, pages 107, 217, 230

Language Arts, pages 32, 45, 63, 76, 111, 144, 178, 204, 212

Writing Across the Curriculum, pages 33, 48, 62, 89, 99, 149, 185, 227

Building Study Skills, pages 61, 62, 77, 104, 137, 174

Mathematics, pages 84, 105, 139, 177, 193

Word Processing, pages 34, 42, 65, 90, 113, 146, 182, 205, 222

TEACHING STRATEGIES

Accounting Pedagogy, pages 18, 19, 36, 52, 72, 98, 123, 134, 160, 170, 192, 210, 232

Assessment by Portfolio, pages 159, 167, 228, 241

Different Learning Abilities, pages 19, 41, 56, 74, 108, 131, 143, 152, 160, 176D, 179, 195, 210, 219, 236

Different Learning Styles, pages 55, 57, 58, 59, 60, 81, 82, 85, 86, 87, 103, 106, 108, 109, 110, 193, 196, 198, 203

Cooperative Learning, pages 24, 46, 64, 75, 105, 129, 154, 161, 168, 197, 220, 236, 240

Expanding Beyond the Classroom, pages 25, 125, 138, 140, 148, 176, 216

Applying Visuals, pages 30, 44, 65, 80, 90, 116, 141, 149, 172, 205, 228

Teaching Tip, pages 18, 22, 23, 24, 25, 26, 27, 28, 29, 31, 37, 38, 39, 40, 53, 54, 63, 64, 65, 73, 78, 79, 132, 136, 150, 165, 175, 184, 186, 194, 199, 200, 201, 202, 203, 218, 220, 226, 237

Software Focus, pages 24, 40, 63, 88, 116, 126, 127, 130, 134, 164, 169, 180, 204, 221, 234

Safety and Health, pages 50, 128, 162, 181, 237

Simulation, page 231

Milestone, page 231

Reinforcement Activity, pages 159, 167, 230, 240

Work Sheet Overlay, page 173

ASSESSMENT

Assessment by Portfolio
MicroExam software for each chapter
Problem Test for each chapter
Unit Problem Test No. 1 (2-5)
Unit Problem Test No. 2 (6-10)
Unit Objective Test No. 1 (1-5)
Unit Objective Test No. 2 (6-10)

SOFTWARE

Automated Accounting 6.0   MicroExam
Accounting Tutorial   *Lotus* (spreadsheet)
Electronic Auditor   *WordPerfect* (word processing)
Application Program Disk   *Windows* (operating system)
Study Guide Software

BIBLIOGRAPHY

AICPA. *FASB Accounting Standards.*
Cantlon, T. *Structuring the Classroom Successfully for Cooperative Team Learning.* Portland, OR: Prestige Publishers, 1991.
Chatfield, Michael. *A History of Accounting Thought.* Huntington, N.Y.: Robert E. Krieger Publishing, 1977.
U.S. Department of Labor. *Dictionary of Occupational Titles.*

Periodicals

Accounting Technology, New York, NY
Black Enterprise, New York, NY (Multicultural awareness)
Forbes, New York, NY (Business news)
Working Woman, New York, NY (Multicultural awareness)

Technology

AICPA. *Luca Pacioli: Unsung Hero of the Renaissance.* (Video)

PART 2 OPENER

Accounting for a Service Business Organized as a Proprietorship

GENERAL GOALS

1. Know accounting terminology related to an accounting system for a service business organized as a proprietorship.

2. Understand accounting concepts and practices related to an accounting system for a service business organized as a proprietorship.

3. Demonstrate accounting procedures used in an accounting system for a service business organized as a proprietorship.

The business described in Part 2 begins a proprietorship with only a cash investment by the owner. Chapter 2 describes how a proprietorship is started and the transactions that occur when the business is organized. The accounting equation is used to analyze the transactions. A balance sheet is then prepared and the relationship of the accounting equation to the balance sheet is emphasized. Chapter 3 continues with additional transactions for starting a business. Likewise, a balance sheet is completed.

Chapter 4 analyzes the transactions from Chapter 2 and Chapter 3 using T accounts. The theory of debit and credit is built around the relationship between the left and right sides of the accounting equation and the left and right sides of a T account.

Chapter 5 begins the journalizing process. Once again, the same transactions from Chapters 2 and 3 are used for consistency and follow through. Chapter 6 analyzes the procedures for posting. After Chapter 6, Integrating Automated Accounting Topic 1 is presented to integrate computer applications with the manual procedures that have been introduced in Chapters 2–6. For those teachers who wish to fully integrate the accounting program, *Automated Accounting 6.0* may be used to actually automate selected problems in the text.

Chapter 7 includes information on bank accounts and petty cash as they apply to a proprietorship. Cash control systems are important to each form of business. After Chapter 7, Integrating Automated Accounting Topic 2 is presented to automate cash control systems.

Chapter 8 guides students through the preparation of a work sheet through the use of the Work Sheet Overlay feature that appears in the text. All businesses must complete adjusting entries. Therefore, adjusting entries are introduced as they apply to a proprietorship.

Chapter 9 presents financial statements and basic financial statement analysis for critical thinking.

Chapter 10 wraps up the accounting cycle for a proprietorship and explains how to record adjusting entries and closing entries in the journal. After Chapter 10, Integrating Automated Accounting Topic 3 presents the opportunity to automate the end-of-fiscal-period activities.

Chapters 2–10 present the entire cycle for a proprietorship. It is important that the students see the entire accounting cycle as it applies to a proprietorship. It is also important that the students apply these concepts through the completion of a simulation, Video Transfer, and/or the reinforcement activity.

Reinforcement Activity 1 is divided into Parts A and B. Part A may be completed after Chapter 7. Part B may be completed after Chapter 10. However, some teachers may wish to delay work on Part A until after Chapter 10 is completed. Then both Parts A and B can be completed as a single unit. The audit test is also divided into two parts.

Chapter 2 describes how a proprietorship is started. The owner begins the business with a cash investment. Five transactions are introduced in this chapter: owner invests money, buys supplies for cash, buys insurance for cash, buys supplies on account, and pays cash on account. A balance sheet is then completed to show the relationship of the accounting equation to the balance sheet. This approach eliminates the need for an opening entry.

GUIDE TO ACHIEVING LEARNING OBJECTIVES

Enabling Performance Tasks	TEACH Lesson Plans	APPLY Drills for Understanding	APPLY Application Problems	EXTEND/ENRICH Mastery Problems	EXTEND/ENRICH Challenge Problems	EXTEND/ENRICH Cases for Critical Thinking	EXTEND/ENRICH Recycling Problems	EXTEND/ENRICH Reinforcement Activity	
a. Define accounting terms related to starting a service business organized as a proprietorship.	2-1, 2-2								
b. Identify accounting concepts and practices related to starting a service business organized as a proprietorship.	2-1, 2-2					Cases 1, 2			
c. Classify accounts as assets, liabilities, or owner's equity.	2-2	2-D1				Case 1			
d. Analyze how transactions related to starting a service business organized as a proprietorship affect accounts in an accounting equation.	2-2	2-D2	2-1, 2-3	2-M	2-C		2-R		
e. Prepare a balance sheet for a service business organized as a proprietorship from information in an accounting equation.	2-3	2-D3	2-2, 2-3	2-M			2-R		

ENRICHMENT

SPECIAL FEATURES	TECHNOLOGY CONNECTION
Multicultural Awareness, page 20	Accounting Tutorial Unit 1
Global Perspective, page 28	Electronic Study Guide

Chapter 2 introduces the following concepts: business entity, unit of measurement, and going concern. Appendix A contains a listing of all the accounting concepts presented in the text. When a concept is first mentioned in the text, a detailed explanation of that concept is given. The concept is explained in relationship to the topic being presented at that point. After the concept has been defined and when it is applicable to the content, it is noted in parentheses with the word CONCEPT in uppercase letters.

	INFORMAL ASSESSMENT		FORMAL ASSESSMENT				
	Study Guide	Audit Your Understanding	Chapter MicroExam	Chapter Problem Test	Unit Problem Test	Unit Objective Test	Portfolio
	Unit A	✓	✓			✓	
	Units B, D	✓	✓			✓	
		✓	✓			✓	
	Unit C	✓	✓	✓	✓	✓	
				✓	✓		

NEW, REVIEW, AND EXTENSION

ACTIVITIES/CONCEPTS/TRANSACTIONS	NEW	REVIEW/ EXTENSION
Analyze transactions on an accounting equation	✓	
Received cash from owner as an investment	✓	
Paid cash for supplies	✓	
Paid cash for insurance	✓	
Bought supplies on account	✓	
Paid cash on account	✓	

TEACHING MATERIALS

Teacher's Wraparound Edition of Text

Teacher's Resource Guide

Teacher's Edition of Working Papers

Teacher's Edition of Demonstration/Recycling Problems

Teaching Transparencies

Accounting Tutorial Manual

Global Perspective Work Sheets

MicroExam

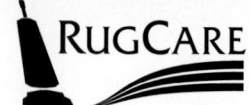

CHART OF ACCOUNTS

Balance Sheet Accounts	Income Statement Accounts
(100) ASSETS	**(400) REVENUE**
110 Cash	410 Sales
120 Petty Cash	
130 Supplies	**(500) EXPENSES**
140 Prepaid Insurance	510 Advertising Expense
	520 Insurance Expense
(200) LIABILITIES	530 Miscellaneous Expense
210 Butler Cleaning Supplies	540 Rent Expense
220 Dale Office Supplies	550 Repair Expense
	560 Supplies Expense
(300) OWNER'S EQUITY	570 Utilities Expense
310 Ben Furman, Capital	
320 Ben Furman, Drawing	
330 Income Summary	

The chart of accounts for Rugcare is illustrated above for ready reference as you study Part 2 of this textbook.

Starting a Proprietorship

ENABLING PERFORMANCE TASKS

After studying Chapter 2, you will be able to:

a Define accounting terms related to starting a service business organized as a proprietorship.

b Identify accounting concepts and practices related to starting a service business organized as a proprietorship.

c Classify accounts as assets, liabilities, or owner's equity.

d Analyze how transactions related to starting a service business organized as a proprietorship affect accounts in an accounting equation.

e Prepare a balance sheet for a service business organized as a proprietorship from information in an accounting equation.

TERMS PREVIEW

service business • proprietorship • asset • equities • liability • owner's equity • accounting equation • transaction • account • account title • account balance • capital • balance sheet

provides. Write the accounting equation on the board and explain the analyzing procedure. Present the accounting equation as a review of a basic algebraic concept, the equation. Remind students that an equation must always have equal amounts on each side.

APPLY

- Review the importance of keeping a business' financial information separate from the owner's personal financial information.

- Draw the accounting equation on the board and show how changes on one side can affect the other side.

Guided Practice

Invite a student to the board. Have the class list assets they own while the student lists them. Continue this for equities and liabilities. It is important to encourage students to participate in class. Participation gives students a sense of importance and enhances the learning process.

Independent Practice

Assign Terms 1–7 and Questions 1–3.

ASSESS

- Assess student understanding by checking solutions to the Independent Practice activities.

- Ask students why personal and business items should be kept separate.

- Write the accounting equation on the board. Then write a mathematical equation and omit one number. Ask students to furnish the missing number and explain how they arrived at that answer.

$A = L + OE$

$10 = 5 + \_\_\_$

20

FYI

A complete list of accounting concepts is in Appendix A.

A person who chooses to start a business must make many decisions. To make these decisions, a businessperson needs financial information about the business. To provide the information, many records and reports relating to the business must be kept. In order to create useful records and reports, financial information must be kept in an organized way. Planning, recording, analyzing, and interpreting financial information is known as accounting. A planned process for providing financial information that will be useful to management is known as an accounting system.

THE BUSINESS

A business that performs an activity for a fee is called a **service business.** Ben Furman worked for a service business that cleans carpets for a fee. Mr. Furman wants to be in control of his hours and his earnings. Therefore, he decided to start his own carpet-cleaning business. A business owned by one person is called a **proprietorship.** A proprietorship is also referred to as a sole proprietorship. Mr. Furman has named his new proprietorship *Rugcare*. Rugcare will rent office space and the equipment used to operate the business.

Since a new business is being started, Mr. Furman must design the accounting system that will be used to keep Rugcare's accounting records. In the accounting system, Mr. Furman must be careful to keep Rugcare's accounting records separate from his own personal financial records. For example, Mr. Furman owns a house and a personal car. Rugcare's financial records must *not* include information about Mr. Furman's house, car, or other personal belongings. For example, Mr. Furman must use one checking account for his personal expenses and another checking account for Rugcare. The financial records for Rugcare and Mr. Furman's personal belongings must be kept separate. The accounting concept, *Business Entity*, is applied when a business' financial information is recorded and reported separately from the owner's personal financial information. *(CONCEPT: Business Entity)*

> Accounting concepts are described throughout this textbook when an application of a concept first occurs. When additional applications occur, a concept reference, such as *(CONCEPT: Business Entity)*, indicates an application of a specific accounting concept. A brief description of each accounting concept used in this text is also provided in Appendix A.

THE ACCOUNTING EQUATION

A business has many items that have value. Rugcare will own items such as cash and supplies that will be used to conduct daily operations. Anything of value that is owned is called an **asset.** Assets have value because they can be used to acquire other assets or be used to operate a business. For example, Rugcare will use cash to

---

buy supplies for the business. Rugcare will then use the asset, supplies, in the operation of the rug-cleaning business.

Financial rights to the assets of a business are called **equities**. A business has two types of equities. (1) Equity of those to whom money is owed. For example, Rugcare may buy some supplies and agree to pay for the supplies at a later date. The business from whom supplies are bought will have a right to some of Rugcare's assets until Rugcare pays for the supplies. An amount owed by a business is called a **liability**. (2) Equity of the owner. Mr. Furman will own Rugcare and invest in the assets of the business. Therefore, he will have a right to decide how the assets will be used. The amount remaining after the value of all liabilities is subtracted from the value of all assets is called **owner's equity**.

The relationship among assets, liabilities, and owner's equity can be written as an equation. An equation showing the relationship among assets, liabilities, and owner's equity is called the **accounting equation**. The accounting equation is most often stated as:

$$\text{Assets} = \text{Liabilities} + \text{Owner's Equity}$$

The accounting equation must be in balance to be correct. Thus, the total of the amounts on the left side of the equation must always equal the total of the amounts on the right side. Before Mr. Furman actually starts the business, Rugcare's accounting equation would show the following amounts.

Assets	=	Liabilities + Owner's Equity
Left side amount		Right side amounts
$0	=	$0 + $0

Audit Your Understanding

1. What is a proprietorship?
2. State the accounting equation.
3. What kinds of accounts go on the left side of the accounting equation?
4. What kinds of accounts go on the right side of the accounting equation?

HOW BUSINESS ACTIVITIES CHANGE THE ACCOUNTING EQUATION

FYI

The left side of the accounting equation must always equal the right side.

Business activities change the amounts in the accounting equation. A business activity that changes assets, liabilities, or owner's equity is called a **transaction**. For example, a business that pays cash for supplies is engaging in a transaction. After each transaction, the accounting equation must remain in balance.

The accounting concept, *Unit of Measurement*, is applied when business transactions are stated in numbers that have common values—that is, using a common unit of measurement. *(CONCEPT: Unit of Measurement)* For example, in the United States, business transactions are recorded in dollars. In Switzerland, business transactions are recorded in Swiss francs. The unit of measurement concept is followed so that the financial reports of businesses can be clearly stated and understood in numbers that have comparable values. For example, reports would not be clear if some information was reported in United States dollars and some in Swiss francs.

CHAPTER 2   Starting a Proprietorship   **21**

AUDIT YOUR UNDERSTANDING

The AUDIT YOUR UNDERSTANDING feature appears at the end of each section of the chapter. Explain to your students that the word *audit* means to check or verify. AUDIT YOUR UNDERSTANDING may be used to check student comprehension of the section just studied. The answers are provided in Appendix D in the back of the textbook.

1. A business owned by one person.
2. Assets = Liabilities + Owner's Equity.
3. Assets.
4. Liabilities and Owner's Equity.

Reteach

If students are having difficulty understanding the difference between personal and business assets and equities, start two lists on the board—one for personal items, one for business items. Ask for student input.

Extend

Assign Cases for Critical Thinking 1.

Enrich

Assign the GLOBAL PERSPECTIVE feature on page 28. Discuss the feature and distribute the GLOBAL PERSPECTIVE Activity sheet in the Masters and Solutions to Enrichment/Application Activities Section in the Teacher's Resource Guide.

CLOSURE

Use Audit Your Understanding questions.

LESSON PLAN 2-2

Materials

- Student pages 21–26
- Transparency 2-1, Blank Accounting Equation and Balance Sheet
- Demonstration Problem 2A, Accounting Equation
- Software: Accounting Tutorial

Objectives (Enabling Performance Tasks)

a. Define accounting terms related to starting a service business organized as a proprietorship.

MULTICULTURAL AWARENESS ACTIVITY (*continued*)

Each group or individual could choose a profession that is of personal interest. Students should be encouraged to explore beyond the traditional medical and legal fields. For example, police officers and firefighters also have professional organizations. Once an organization is researched, the activity can be expanded to include writing to an organization to obtain their literature and information about the organization and its purpose.

Received Cash from Owner as an Investment

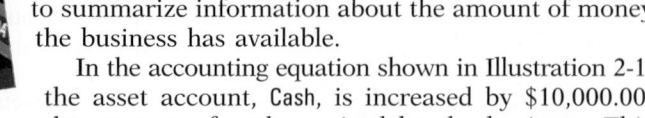

Mr. Furman uses $10,000.00 of his own money to invest in Rugcare. Rugcare should only be concerned with the effect of this transaction on Rugcare's records. The business should *not* be concerned about Mr. Furman's personal records. (CONCEPT: Business Entity)

> Transaction 1   August 1, 19--. Received cash from owner as an investment, $10,000.00.

A record summarizing all the information pertaining to a single item in the accounting equation is called an **account**. The name given to an account is called an **account title**. Each part of the accounting equation consists of one or more accounts. For example, one of the asset accounts is titled Cash. The cash account is used to summarize information about the amount of money the business has available.

In the accounting equation shown in Illustration 2-1, the asset account, Cash, is increased by $10,000.00, the amount of cash received by the business. This increase is on the left side of the accounting equation. The amount in an account is called the **account balance**. Before the owner's investment, the account balance of Cash was zero. After the owner's investment, the account balance of Cash is $10,000.00.

| | | | ILLUSTRATION 2-1 | Receiving cash from owner as an investment changes one asset and owner's equity |

	Assets	=	Liabilities	+	Owner's Equity
	Cash	=			Ben Furman, Capital
Beg. Balances	$0		$0		$0
Transaction 1	+10,000				+10,000 (investment)
New Balances	$10,000		$0		$10,000

The account used to summarize the owner's equity in business is called **capital**. The capital account is an owner's equity account. Rugcare's capital account is titled Ben Furman, Capital. In the accounting equation shown in Illustration 2-1, the owner's equity account, Ben Furman, Capital, is increased by $10,000.00. This increase is on the right side of the accounting equation. Before the owner's investment, the account balance of Ben Furman, Capital was zero. After the owner's investment, the account balance of Ben Furman, Capital is $10,000.00.

The accounting equation has changed as a result of the receipt of cash as the owner's investment. However, both sides of the equation are changed by the same amount, $10,000.00. The $10,000.00 increase on the left side of the equation equals the $10,000.00

increase on the right side of the equation. Therefore, the accounting equation is still in balance.

Paid Cash for Supplies

Rugcare needs supplies to operate the business. Ben Furman uses some of Rugcare's cash to buy supplies.

> Transaction 2   *August 3, 19--. Paid cash for supplies, $1,577.00.*

The effect of this transaction on the accounting equation is shown in Illustration 2-2. In this transaction, two asset accounts are changed. One asset, cash, has been exchanged for another asset, supplies. The asset account, Cash, is decreased by $1,577.00, the amount of cash paid out. This decrease is on the left side of the accounting equation. The asset account, Supplies, is increased by $1,577.00, the amount of supplies bought. This increase is also on the left side of the accounting equation.

ILLUSTRATION 2-2   Paying cash for supplies changes two assets

	Assets		=	Liabilities	+	Owner's Equity
	Cash	+ Supplies	=			Ben Furman, Capital
Balances	$10,000	$0		$0		$10,000
Transaction 2	−1,577	+1,577				
New Balances	$8,423	$1,577		$0		$10,000
	Total of left side: $8,423 + $1,577 = $10,000			Total of right side: $10,000		

For this transaction, two assets are changed. Therefore, the two changes are both on the left side of the accounting equation. When changes are made on only one side of the accounting equation, the equation must still be in balance. Therefore, if one account is increased, another account on the same side of the equation must be decreased. After this transaction, the new account balance of Cash is $8,423.00. The new account balance of Supplies is $1,577.00. The sum of the amounts on the left side is $10,000.00 (Cash, $8,423.00 + Supplies, $1,577.00). The amount on the right side is also $10,000.00. Therefore, the accounting equation is still in balance.

Paid Cash for Insurance

Insurance premiums must be paid in advance. For example, Rugcare pays a $1,200.00 insurance premium for future insurance coverage.

> Transaction 3   *August 4, 19--. Paid cash for insurance, $1,200.00.*

Guide students through Drill 2-D2. Direct students to complete the drill using the form in the working papers as the students decide the change caused by each transaction as a group. All students should agree with the analysis of a transaction before proceeding to the next transaction.

Independent Practice

Assign Terms 8–12, Questions 4–9, and Problem 2-1.

ASSESS

- Assess student understanding by checking solutions to the Independent Practice activities.

- Review how transactions change the accounting equation. Ask students to describe what happens in the accounting equation when cash is paid and when cash is received. Ask if it is possible to have a transaction that does not involve cash; if so, ask for a description of such a transaction.

Reteach

Use Demonstration Problem 2A. This problem can be done on the overhead as the students complete the problem at their desks.

Extend

Assign Cases for Critical Thinking 2.

Enrich

Assign the Accounting Tutorial software, Unit 1, to be completed at the computer.

CLOSURE

Use Audit Your Understanding questions.

TEACHING STRATEGIES: TEACHING TIP

Recording the transactions on the overhead will prepare students to analyze transactions on their own. Using Transparency 2-1, Blank Accounting Equation and Balance Sheet, to record the transactions presented in the chapter will enable students to watch and participate in the analysis process.

In return for this payment, Rugcare is entitled to insurance coverage for the length of the policy. The insurance coverage is something of value owned by Rugcare. Therefore, the insurance coverage is an asset. Because insurance premiums are paid in advance, or *prepaid*, the premiums are recorded in an asset account titled Prepaid Insurance.

The effect of this transaction on the accounting equation is shown in Illustration 2-3. In this transaction, two assets are changed. One asset, cash, has been exchanged for another asset, prepaid insurance. The asset account, Cash, is decreased by $1,200.00, the amount of cash paid out. This decrease is on the left side of the accounting equation. The asset account, Prepaid Insurance, is increased by $1,200.00, the amount of insurance bought. This increase is also on the left side of the accounting equation.

ILLUSTRATION 2-3 Paying cash for insurance changes two assets

	Assets			= Liabilities + Owner's Equity	
	Cash	+ Supplies	+ Prepaid Insurance =		Ben Furman, Capital
Balances	$8,423	$1,577	$0	$0	$10,000
Transaction 3	−1,200		+1,200		
New Balances	$7,223	$1,577	$1,200	$0	$10,000

Total of left side:
$7,223 + $1,577 + $1,200 = $10,000

Total of right side:
$10,000

Since two assets are changed by this transaction, both changes are on the left side of the accounting equation. Since one account is increased, the other account on the same side of the equation must be decreased. After this transaction, the new account balance of Cash is $7,223.00. The new account balance of Prepaid Insurance is $1,200.00. The sum of the amounts on the left side is $10,000.00 (Cash, $7,223.00 + Supplies, $1,577.00 + Prepaid Insurance, $1,200.00). The amount on the right side is also $10,000.00. Therefore, the accounting equation is still in balance.

Bought Supplies on Account

Rugcare needs to buy additional supplies. The supplies are obtained from Butler Cleaning Supplies, which is located in a different city. It is a common business practice to buy items and pay for them at a future date. Another way to state this activity is to say that these items are bought *on account*.

> Transaction 4 August 7, 19--. Bought supplies on account from Butler Cleaning Supplies, $2,720.00.

The effect of this transaction on the accounting equation is shown in Illustration 2-4. In this transaction, one asset and one liability are changed. The asset account, Supplies, is increased by $2,720.00, the amount of supplies bought. This increase is on the left side of the accounting equation. Butler Cleaning Supplies will have a claim against some of Rugcare's assets until Rugcare pays for the supplies bought. Therefore, Butler Cleaning Supplies is a liability account. The liability account, Butler Cleaning Supplies, is increased by $2,720.00, the amount owed for the supplies. This increase is on the right side of the accounting equation.

ILLUSTRATION 2-4   Buying supplies on account changes one asset and one liability

	Assets			= Liabilities	+ Owner's Equity
				Butler	
			Prepaid	Cleaning	Ben Furman,
	Cash	+ Supplies	+ Insurance =	Supplies	+ Capital
Balances	$7,223	$1,577	$1,200	$0	$10,000
Transaction 4		+2,720		+2,720	
New Balances	$7,223	$4,297	$1,200	$2,720	$10,000

Total of left side: Total of right side:
$7,223 + $4,297 + $1,200 = $12,720 $2,720 + $10,000 = $12,720

This transaction changes both sides of the accounting equation. When changes are made on both sides of the equation, the change on the left side must equal the change on the right side. After this transaction, the new account balance of Supplies is $4,297.00. The new account balance of Butler Cleaning Supplies is $2,720.00. The sum of the amounts on the left side is $12,720.00 (Cash, $7,223.00 + Supplies, $4,297.00 + Prepaid Insurance, $1,200.00). The sum of the amounts on the right side is also $12,720.00 (Butler Cleaning Supplies, $2,720.00 + Ben Furman, Capital, $10,000.00). Therefore, the accounting equation is still in balance.

Paid Cash on Account

Since Rugcare is a new business, Butler Cleaning Supplies has not done business with Rugcare before. Butler Cleaning Supplies allows Rugcare to buy supplies on account but requires Rugcare to send a check for one-half of the amount immediately. Rugcare will pay the remaining liability at a later date.

> Transaction 5   August 11, 19--. Paid cash on account to Butler Cleaning Supplies, $1,360.00.

The effect of this transaction on the accounting equation is shown in Illustration 2-5. In this transaction, one asset and one lia-

ILLUSTRATION 2-5   Paying cash on account changes one asset and one liability

		Assets		= Liabilities +	Owner's Equity
	Cash +	Supplies +	Prepaid Insurance =	Butler Cleaning Supplies +	Ben Furman, Capital
Balances	$7,223	$4,297	$1,200	$2,720	$10,000
Transaction 5	−1,360			−1,360	
New Balances	$5,863	$4,297	$1,200	$1,360	$10,000

Total of left side:
$5,863 + $4,297 + $1,200 = $11,360

Total of right side:
$1,360 + $10,000 = $11,360

Audit Your Understanding

1. What does it mean if the accounting equation is "in balance?"

2. What must be done if a transaction increases the left side of the accounting equation?

3. How can a transaction affect only one side of the accounting equation?

bility are changed. The asset account, Cash, is decreased by $1,360.00, the amount of cash paid out. This decrease is on the left side of the accounting equation. After this payment, Rugcare owes less money to Butler Cleaning Supplies. Therefore, the liability account, Butler Cleaning Supplies, is decreased by $1,360.00, the amount paid on account. This decrease is on the right side of the accounting equation.

This transaction changes both sides of the accounting equation. When changes are made on both sides of the equation, the change on the left side must equal the change on the right side. After this transaction, the new account balance of Cash is $5,863.00. The new account balance of Butler Cleaning Supplies is $1,360.00. The sum of the amounts on the left side is $11,360.00 (Cash, $5,863.00 + Supplies, $4,297.00 + Prepaid Insurance, $1,200.00). The sum of the amounts on the right side is also $11,360.00 (Butler Cleaning Supplies, $1,360.00 + Ben Furman, Capital, $10,000.00). Therefore, the accounting equation is still in balance.

REPORTING FINANCIAL INFORMATION ON A BALANCE SHEET

FYI

Every financial statement has a three-line heading that consists of the name of the company, the name of the statement, and the date.

Periodically a business reports details about its assets, liabilities, and owner's equity. The financial details about assets, liabilities, and owner's equity could be found on the last line of the accounting equation. However, most businesses prepare more formal financial statements that may be copied and sent to interested persons. A financial statement that reports assets, liabilities, and owner's equity on a specific date is called a **balance sheet.**

When a business is started, it is expected that the business will continue to operate indefinitely. For example, Ben Furman assumes that he will own and operate Rugcare for many years. When he retires, he expects to sell Rugcare to someone else who will con-

PART 2   Accounting for a Service Business Organized as a Proprietorship

tinue its operation. The accounting concept, *Going Concern*, is applied when financial statements are prepared with the expectation that a business will remain in operation indefinitely. *(CONCEPT: Going Concern)*

Body of a Balance Sheet

A balance sheet has three major sections. (1) *Assets* are on the left side of the accounting equation. Therefore, Rugcare lists its assets on the left side of the balance sheet. (2) *Liabilities* are on the right side of the accounting equation. Therefore, Rugcare lists its liabilities on the right side of the balance sheet. (3) *Owner's equity* is also on the right side of the accounting equation. Therefore, Rugcare lists its owner's equity on the right side of the balance sheet.

Rugcare's balance sheet, prepared after the transaction on August 11, is shown in Illustration 2-6.

ILLUSTRATION 2-6

Balance sheet for a service business organized as a proprietorship

	Assets		= Liabilities + Owner's Equity	
	Cash +	Supplies +	Prepaid Insurance =	Butler Cleaning Supplies +	Ben Furman, Capital
Balances	$5,863	$4,297	$1,200	$1,360	$10,000

Rugcare				
Balance Sheet				
August 11, 19--				
Assets		**Liabilities**		
Cash	5 86 3 00	Butler Cleaning Supplies	1 36 0 00	
Supplies	4 29 7 00	Owner's Equity		
Prepaid Insurance	1 20 0 00	Ben Furman, Capital	10 00 0 00	
Total Assets	11 36 0 00	Total Liab. and Owner's Eq.	11 36 0 00	

Preparing a Balance Sheet

Rugcare's balance sheet is prepared in six steps.

1 Write the *heading* on three lines at the top of the balance sheet. Center each line. The heading for Rugcare's balance sheet is:

Name of the business:	Rugcare
Name of the report:	Balance Sheet
Date of the report:	August 11, 19--

2 Prepare the *assets section* on the LEFT side. Center the word *Assets* on the first line of the wide column on the left side. Under this heading, write each asset account title and

CHAPTER 2   Starting a Proprietorship   **27**

Global Perspective

The GLOBAL PERSPECTIVE feature is intended to expose students to some of the ways in which accounting and business in general differ in other countries. Use the GLOBAL PERSPECTIVE ACTIVITY in the Masters and Solutions to Enrichment/Application Activities Section in the Teacher's Resource Guide to allow students to apply the concept of foreign currency conversion.

Global Perspective

FOREIGN CURRENCY

As our world becomes smaller and global trade increases, more and more United States businesses will get involved in business transactions with companies in foreign countries. Transactions with foreign businesses may be stated in terms of U.S. dollars or the currency of the other country. If the transaction involves foreign currency, the U.S. business must convert the foreign currency into U.S. dollars before the transaction can be recorded. *(CONCEPT: Unit of Measurement)*

The value of foreign currency can change daily. The **exchange rate** is the value of foreign currency in relation to the U.S. dollar. Current exchange rates can be found in many daily newspa-

COUNTRY	CURRENCY	U.S. $ EQUIVALENT
Australia	Dollar	.7303
Canada	Dollar	.7908
Germany	Mark	.6757
Hong Kong	Dollar	.12935
Mexico	New Peso	.323154
Peru	New Sol	.7931
South Africa	Rand	.2519

pers or by contacting a bank. The above list of exchange rates is taken from a newspaper. Because the

rates change daily, the current exchange rates could be quite different than these rates which were current when this book was published.

The exchange rate is stated in terms of one unit of foreign currency. Using Germany as an example, the rate means that one German mark is worth .6757 U.S. dollars (or 68

U.S. cents). This rate would be used when exchanging German marks for U.S. dollars.

A **conversion formula** can be used to find out how many foreign currency units can be purchased with one U.S. dollar. The formula is:

---
1 ÷ exchange rate = foreign currency per U.S. dollar

1 dollar ÷ .6757 = 1.4799 marks per dollar

Applying the conversion formula to Germany, one U.S. dollar would buy 1.48 German marks. The formula could be applied to each rate stated above to determine how many foreign currency units can be purchased with one U.S. dollar.

Extend

Assign Challenge Problem 2-C (the challenge is that Transaction 5 is personal and does not appear in the equation. Transaction 6 is recorded at $100.00).

Enrich

- Assign students to read the MULTICULTURAL AWARENESS feature on page 20. Discuss the various professional accounting organizations and how they span various cultures.

- Assign the Electronic Study Guide Chapter 2 to complete the study guide from the working papers at the computer.

CLOSURE

- Use Audit Your Understanding questions.

ASSESS

- Administer Problem Test Chapter 2.

- Administer a MicroExam test for Chapter 2.

amount. The asset accounts are: Cash, $5,863.00; Supplies, $4,297.00; and Prepaid Insurance, $1,200.00.

3 Prepare the *liabilities section* on the RIGHT side. Center the word *Liabilities* on the first line of the wide column on the right side. Under this heading, write each liability account title and amount. Rugcare has only one liability account to be listed, Butler Cleaning Supplies, $1,360.00.

4 Prepare the *owner's equity section* on the RIGHT side. Center the words *Owner's Equity* on the next blank line of the wide column on the right side. Under this heading, write the owner's equity account title and amount. Rugcare's owner's equity account is Ben Furman, Capital, $10,000.00.

5 Determine if the balance sheet is *in balance*. Use a calculator, if available, or a sheet of scratch paper. Add all the asset amounts on the LEFT side. The total on the left side of Rugcare's balance sheet is $11,360.00 ($5,863.00 + $4,297.00 + $1,200.00). Add the liabilities and owner's equity amounts on the RIGHT side. The total on the right side of Rugcare's balance sheet is $11,360.00 ($1,360.00 + $10,000.00). The total of the LEFT side is the same as the total of the RIGHT side, $11,360.00. Therefore, Rugcare's balance sheet is in balance.

TEACHING STRATEGIES: TEACHING TIP

Demonstrating the completion of a balance sheet on the overhead will make it easy for students to follow the six steps. Use Transparency 2-2, Blank Accounting Equation and Balance Sheet, and demonstrate the example in the chapter. You may want students to have a blank balance sheet at their desk to work along with you. A blackline master for a balance sheet is available in the Accounting Forms Masters section of the Teacher's Resource Guide.

If the balance sheet is NOT in balance, find the errors before completing any more work.

6 Complete the balance sheet. Rule a single line across both amount columns. A single line means that amounts are to be added or subtracted. On the next line, write *Total Assets* in the wide column on the left side. On the same line, write the total asset amount, $11,360.00, in the left amount column. On the same line, write *Total Liabilities and Owner's Equity* in the wide column on the right side. On the same line, write the total liabilities and owner's equity amount, $11,360.00, in the right amount column. Rule double lines below the amount column totals. Double lines mean that the totals have been verified as correct.

When possible, words are spelled in full so there can be no doubt about what word was intended. However, in a few situations, where there is insufficient room to spell the words in full, words may be abbreviated. On Rugcare's balance sheet, it is necessary to abbreviate the words *Total Liab. and Owner's Eq.*

SUMMARY OF HOW TRANSACTIONS CHANGE THE ACCOUNTING EQUATION

Changes in the accounting equation caused by Transactions 1 to 5 are summarized in Illustration 2-7 on the following page.

Four basic rules relate to how transactions affect the accounting equation

1 Each transaction changes at least two accounts in the accounting equation.

2 When all the changes occur on one side of the accounting equation, increases on that side must be matched by decreases on the same side. Transactions 2 and 3 are examples of this rule.

3 When a transaction increases one side of the accounting equation, the other side of the equation must also be increased by the same amount. Transactions 1 and 4 are examples of this rule.

4 When a transaction decreases one side of the accounting equation, the other side of the equation must also be decreased by the same amount. Transaction 5 is an example of this rule.

SUMMARY ILLUSTRATION 2-7

Summary of how transactions change the accounting equation

Four basic rules relate to how transactions affect the accounting equation.

1 Each transaction changes at least two accounts in the accounting equation.

2 When all the changes occur on one side of the accounting equation, increases on that side must be matched by decreases on the same side. Transactions 2 and 3 are examples of this rule.

3 When a transaction increases one side of the accounting equation, the other side of the equation must also be increased by the same amount. Transactions 1 and 4 are examples of this rule.

4 When a transaction decreases one side of the accounting equation, the other side of the equation must also be decreased by the same amount. Transaction 5 is an example of this rule.

Transaction	Cash	+ Supplies +	Prepaid Insurance	=	Butler Cleaning Supplies	+	Ben Furman, Capital
				Assets =	Liabilities +		Owner's Equity
Beginning Balance	$0	$0	$0		$0		$0
1. Received cash from owner as an investment	+10,000						+10,000 (investment)
New Balances	$10,000	$0	$0		$0		$10,000
2. Paid cash for supplies	−1,577	+1,577					
New Balances	$8,423	$1,577	$0		$0		$10,000
3. Paid cash for insurance	−1,200		+1,200				
New Balances	$7,223	$1,577	$1,200		$0		$10,000
4. Bought supplies on account		+2,720			+2,720		
5. New Balances	$7,223	$4,297	$1,200		$2,720		$10,000
Paid cash on account	−1,360				−1,360		
New Balances	$5,863	$4,297	$1,200		$1,360		$10,000

Total of left side:
$5,863 + $4,297 + $1,200 = $11,360

Total of right side:
$1,360 + $10,000 = $11,360

ACCOUNTING TERMS   EPT(a)

What is the meaning of each of the following?

1. **service business**
2. **proprietorship**
3. **asset**
4. **equities**
5. **liability**
6. **owner's equity**
7. **accounting equation**
8. **transaction**
9. **account**
10. **account title**
11. **account balance**
12. **capital**
13. **balance sheet**

1. Which accounting concept is being applied when a business records and reports financial information separate from the owner's personal financial information?
2. What are the two types of equities of a business?
3. What must be true about the accounting equation after each transaction?
4. Which accounting concept is being applied when a business in the United States reports financial information in dollars?
5. What accounts are affected, and how, when the owner invests cash in a business?
6. What accounts are affected, and how, when a business pays cash for supplies?
7. Why is Prepaid Insurance an asset?
8. How are liabilities affected when a business buys supplies on account?
9. How are liabilities affected when a business pays cash for a liability?
10. Which accounting concept is being applied when financial statements are prepared with the expectation that a business will remain in operation indefinitely?
11. What three items are included in the heading of a balance sheet?
12. What six steps are followed in preparing a balance sheet?
13. What do double lines below a column total mean?
14. What are the four basic rules relating to how transactions affect the accounting equation?

CASES FOR CRITICAL THINKING   EPT(a,b)

CASE 1 James Patton starts a new business. Mr. Patton uses his personal car in the business with the expectation that later the business can buy a car. All expenses for operating the car, including license plates, gasoline, oil, tune-ups, and new tires, are paid for out of business funds. Is this an acceptable procedure? Explain.

CASE 2 At the end of the first day of business, Quick Clean Laundry has the following assets and liabilities:

Assets	
Cash	$3,500.00
Supplies	950.00
Prepaid Insurance	1,200.00
Liabilities	
Smith Office Supplies	$ 750.00
Super Supplies Company	1,500.00

The owner, Susan Whiteford, wants to know the amount of her equity in Quick Clean Laundry. Determine this amount and explain what this amount represents.

DRILLS FOR UNDERSTANDING   EPT(c,d,e)

DRILL 2-D1   Classifying assets, liabilities, and owner's equity

Use a form similar to the following.

Item	Asset	Liability	Owner's Equity
1. Cash	√		

INSTRUCTIONS:

Classify each item listed below as an asset, liability, or owner's equity. Place a check mark in the appropriate column. Item 1 is given as an example.

1. Cash
2. Alice Jones, Capital
3. Prepaid Insurance
4. Steward Supply Company
5. Supplies
6. Any amount owed
7. Owner's capital account
8. Anything owned

CHAPTER 2   Starting a Proprietorship   **31**

TEACHING STRATEGIES: TEACHING TIP

Students are just beginning to learn the process involved in analyzing and recording business transactions. Therefore, begin the drill exercises together with the students, doing the first few items in each drill as a group. Students can finish each drill during class and the correct answers can be discussed.

1. Business Entity concept. (p. 20)
2. Equity of those to whom money is owed and equity of the owner. (p. 21)
3. After each transaction, the accounting equation must remain in balance. (p. 21)
4. Unit of Measurement concept. (p. 21)
5. The asset account, Cash, is increased by the amount of cash received by the business. The owner's equity account, Capital, is increased by the same amount. (p. 22)
6. The asset account, Cash, is decreased by the amount of cash paid out. The asset account, Supplies, is increased by the same amount. (p. 23)
7. The business is entitled to insurance coverage for the length of the policy. The insurance coverage is something of value owned by the business. Therefore, the insurance coverage is an asset. (p. 24)
8. Liabilities increase because the business now owes more money. (p. 25)
9. Liabilities decrease because the business now owes less money. (p. 26)
10. Going Concern concept. (p. 27)
11. (1) The name of the business, (2) the name of the report, and (3) the date of the report. (p. 27)
12. (1) Write the heading on three lines. (2) Prepare the assets section on the LEFT side. (3) Prepare the liabilities section on the RIGHT side. (4) Prepare the owner's equity section on the RIGHT side. (5) Determine if the balance sheet is in balance. (6) Complete the balance sheet. (pp. 27–29)
13. Double lines mean that totals have been verified as correct. (p. 29)
14. (1) Each transaction changes at least two accounts in the accounting equation. (2) When all the changes occur on one side of the accounting equation, increases on that side must be matched by decreases on the same side. (3) When a transaction increases one side of the accounting equation, the other side of the equation must also be increased by the same amount. (4) When a transaction decreases one side of the accounting equation, the other side of the equation must also be decreased by the same amount. (p. 30)

Case 1 No, this is not an acceptable accounting procedure. One of the basic accounting concepts—Business Entity—requires that personal and business expenses be kept separate. Only those car expenses directly connected with business activities should be paid for out of business funds.

Case 2 The amount of Susan Whiteford's equity in Quick Clean Laundry is the amount remaining after the value of all liabilities is subtracted from the value of all assets. In this case, assets equal $5,650.00 and liabilities equal $2,250.00. Therefore, Ms. Whiteford's equity is $3,400.00. This amount represents the value of Ms. Whiteford's financial rights to the assets of Quick Clean Laundry.

CHECK FIGURES

See Teacher's Edition of Working Papers for complete solutions to drills and problems.

Drill 2-D1 Asset; Owner's Equity; Asset; Liability; Asset; Liability; Owner's Equity; Asset

Drill 2-D2 Trans. 1: Assets and Liab. −. Trans. 2 and 4: Assets + and −. Trans. 3.: Assets and Owner's Equity +. Trans. 5: Assets and Liab. −.

Drill 2-D3 Nos. 1, 3, 4, and 6 are Asset left side. Nos. 2 and 8 are Owner's Equity right side. Nos. 5 and 7 are Liability right side.

Problem 2-1 Last Line New Bal.: 1,000; 1,100; 600; 0; 200; 2,500

DRILL 2-D2 Determining how transactions change an accounting equation

Use a form similar to the following.

Trans. No.	Assets	=	Liabilities	+	Owner's Equity
1.	+		+		

Transactions
1. Bought supplies on account.
2. Paid cash for insurance.
3. Received cash from owner as an investment.
4. Paid cash for supplies.
5. Paid cash on account to Konroy Company.

INSTRUCTIONS:

Decide which classification(s) are changed by each transaction. Place a plus (+) in the appropriate column if the classification is increased. Place a minus (−) in the appropriate column if the classification is decreased. Transaction 1 is given as an example.

DRILL 2-D3 Determining where items are listed on a balance sheet

Use a form similar to the following.

1	2	3
Items	Balance Sheet	
	Left Side	Right Side
1. Cash	*Asset*	

INSTRUCTIONS:

Classify each item as an asset, liability, or owner's equity. Write the classification in Column 2 or 3 to show where each item is listed on a balance sheet. Item 1 is given as an example.

1. Cash
2. Gretchen Murphy, Capital
3. Supplies
4. Prepaid Insurance
5. Action Laundry
6. Anything owned
7. Any amount owed
8. Owner's capital account

APPLICATION PROBLEMS   EPT(d,e)

PROBLEM 2-1 Determining how transactions change an accounting equation

Frank Mori is starting Mori Repair Shop, a small service business. Mori Repair Shop uses the accounts shown in the following accounting equation. Use a form similar to the following to complete this problem.

Trans. No.	Assets			=	Liabilities			+	Owner's Equity
	Cash +	Supplies +	Prepaid Insurance	=	Swan's Supply Company +	York Company	+		Frank Mori, Capital
Beg. Bal. 1.	0 +2,000	0	0		0	0			0 +2,000 (investment)
New Bal. 2.	2,000	0	0		0	0			2,000

APPLIED SKILLS: LANGUAGE ARTS

Paraphrasing, writing complete sentences, identifying nouns. For additional practice in language arts skills, direct students to answer the Accounting Terms and Questions for Individual Study at the end of the chapter. Students should write the definitions in their own words and in complete sentences. To further practice language arts skills, ask students to underline all nouns in their answers.

Transactions
1. Received cash from owner as an investment, $2,000.00.
2. Paid cash for insurance, $600.00.
3. Bought supplies on account from Swan's Supply Company, $100.00.
4. Bought supplies on account from York Company, $500.00.
5. Paid cash on account to Swan's Supply Company, $100.00.
6. Paid cash on account to York Company, $300.00.
7. Paid cash for supplies, $500.00.
8. Received cash from owner as an investment, $500.00.

INSTRUCTIONS:

For each transaction, complete the following. Transaction 1 is given as an example.

a. Analyze the transaction to determine which accounts in the accounting equation are affected.

b. Write the amount in the appropriate columns using a plus (+) if the account increases or a minus (−) if the account decreases.

c. For transactions that change owner's equity, write in parentheses a description of the transaction to the right of the amount.

d. Calculate the new balance for each account in the accounting equation.

e. Before going on to the next transaction, determine that the accounting equation is still in balance.

PROBLEM 2-2 Preparing a balance sheet from information in an accounting equation

On September 30 the Steffens Company's accounting equation indicated the following account balances.

Trans. No.	Assets						= Liabilities	+ Owner's Equity
	Cash	+	Supplies	+	Prepaid Insurance	=	Morton Company	+	Steve Steffens, Capital
New Bal.	1,200		150		300		250		1,400

INSTRUCTIONS:

Using the September 30 balance in the accounting equation, prepare a balance sheet for the Steffens Company.

PROBLEM 2-3 Determining how transactions change an accounting equation and preparing a balance sheet

Nancy Dirks is starting Dirks Company, a small service business. Dirks Company uses the accounts shown in the following accounting equation. Use a form similar to the following to complete this problem.

Trans. No.	Assets						= Liabilities	+ Owner's Equity
	Cash	+	Supplies	+	Prepaid Insurance	=	Helfrey Company	+	Nancy Dirks, Capital
Beg. Bal.	0		0		0		0		0
1.	+350								+350 *(investment)*
New Bal.	350		0		0		0		350
2.									

APPLIED SKILLS: WRITING ACROSS THE CURRICULUM

Writing paragraphs and short essays. The Cases for Critical Thinking are short, practical applications of the accounting principles developed in the chapter. Some cases are planned to present problems related to the chapter but not specifically discussed and answered in the chapter. These cases present an opportunity for critical thinking and decision making. These cases also require more than a short objective-type response. Therefore, they provide ideal practice in writing paragraphs and short essays.

Transactions

1. Received cash from owner as an investment, $350.00.
2. Bought supplies on account from Helfrey Company, $100.00.
3. Paid cash for insurance, $150.00.
4. Paid cash for supplies, $50.00.
5. Received cash from owner as an investment, $300.00.
6. Paid cash on account to Helfrey Company, $75.00.

INSTRUCTIONS:

1. For each transaction, complete the following. Transaction 1 is given as an example.
   a. Analyze the transaction to determine which accounts in the accounting equation are affected.
   b. Write the amount in the appropriate columns, using a plus (+) if the account increases or a minus (−) if the account decreases.
   c. For transactions that change owner's equity, write in parentheses a description of the transaction to the right of the amount.
   d. Calculate the new balance for each account in the accounting equation.
   e. Before going on to the next transaction, determine that the accounting equation is still in balance.
2. Using the final balances in the accounting equation, prepare a balance sheet for Dirks Company. Use July 31 of the current year as the date of the balance sheet.

ENRICHMENT PROBLEMS   EPT(d,e)

MASTERY PROBLEM 2-M   Determining how transactions change an accounting equation and preparing a balance sheet

Gregory Morgan is starting a limousine service called Luxury Limo. Luxury Limo uses the accounts shown in the following accounting equation. Use a form similar to the following to complete this problem.

Trans. No.	Assets			=	Liabilities	+	Owner's Equity
	Cash	+ Supplies	+ Prepaid Insurance	=	Limo Supply Company	+	Gregory Morgan, Capital
Beg. Bal.	0	0	0		0		0
1.	+2,000						+2,000 (investment)
New Bal.	2,000	0	0		0		2,000
2.							

Transactions

1. Received cash from owner as an investment, $2,000.00.
2. Paid cash for supplies, $250.00.
3. Bought supplies on account from Limo Supply Company, $300.00.
4. Paid cash for insurance, $600.00.
5. Paid cash on account to Limo Supply Company, $150.00.

INSTRUCTIONS:

1. For each transaction, complete the following. Transaction 1 is given as an example.
   a. Analyze the transaction to determine which accounts in the accounting equation are affected.
   b. Write the amount in the appropriate columns, using a plus (+) if the account increases or a minus (−) if the account decreases.

c. For transactions that change owner's equity, write in parentheses a description of the transaction to the right of the amount.

d. Calculate the new balance for each account in the accounting equation.

e. Before going on to the next transaction, determine that the accounting equation is still in balance.

2. Using the final balances in the accounting equation, prepare a balance sheet for Luxury Limo. Use February 5 of the current year as the date of the balance sheet.

CHALLENGE PROBLEM 2-C **Applying accounting concepts to determine how transactions change the accounting equation**

Olson Delivery Service, a new business owned by Jerome Olson, uses the accounts shown in the following accounting equation. Use a form similar to the following to complete this problem.

Trans. No.	Assets			=	Liabilities		+	Owner's Equity
	Cash +	Supplies +	Prepaid Insurance	=	Mutual Savings Bank	+ Nelson Supply Co.	+	Jerome Olson, Capital
Beg. Bal.	0	0	0		0	0		0
1.	+1,500							+1,500 (investment)
New Bal.	1,500	0	0		0	0		1,500
2.								

Transactions

1. Owner invested cash, $1,500.00.
2. Bought supplies for cash, $400.00.
3. Paid cash for insurance, $240.00.
4. Supplies were bought on account from Nelson Supply Company, $80.00.
5. The owner, Jerome Olson, paid $1,000.00 of his personal cash to Mutual Savings Bank for the car payment on his personal car.
6. Wrote a check for supplies. The supplies were bought from a Canadian company. The supplies cost $120.00 in Canadian dollars, which is equivalent to $100.00 in United States dollars.

INSTRUCTIONS:

For each transaction, complete the following. Transaction 1 is given as an example.

a. Analyze the transaction to determine which business accounts in the accounting equation, if any, are affected. You will need to apply the Business Entity and Unit of Measurement concepts in this problem.

b. If business accounts are affected, determine the appropriate amount of the change. Write the amount in the appropriate columns, using a plus (+) if the account increases or a minus (−) if the account decreases.

c. For transactions that change owner's equity, write in parentheses a description of the transaction to the right of the amount.

d. Calculate the new balance for each account in the accounting equation.

e. Before going on to the next transaction, determine that the accounting equation is still in balance.

Chapter 3 is a continuation of the accounting practices presented in Chapter 2. Both chapters require students to analyze transactions using the accounting equation.

The owner's investment of cash in the business is introduced in Chapter 2. Three transactions related to changes in owner's equity are included in Chapter 3: owner collects revenue, owner pays expenses, owner withdraws cash. A balance sheet is completed once again to show the relationship of the accounting equation to the balance sheet.

GUIDE TO ACHIEVING LEARNING OBJECTIVES

Enabling Performance Tasks	TEACH Lesson Plans	APPLY Drills for Understanding	APPLY Application Problems	EXTEND/ENRICH Mastery Problems	EXTEND/ENRICH Challenge Problems	EXTEND/ENRICH Cases for Critical Thinking	EXTEND/ENRICH Recycling Problems	EXTEND/ENRICH Reinforcement Activity	
a. Define accounting terms related to changes that affect owner's equity for a service business organized as a proprietorship.	3-1								
b. Identify accounting practices related to changes that affect owner's equity for a service business organized as a proprietorship.	3-1					Cases 1, 2			
c. Analyze changes that affect owner's equity for a service business organized as a proprietorship in an accounting equation.	3-1	3-D1, 3-D2	3-1, 3-2	3-M	3-C		3-R		
d. Prepare a balance sheet for a service business organized as a proprietorship from information in the accounting equation.	3-2		3-2	3-M			3-R		

ENRICHMENT

SPECIAL FEATURES
Professional Business Ethics, pages 40–41

TECHNOLOGY CONNECTION
Accounting Tutorial Unit 1
Electronic Study Guide

	INFORMAL ASSESSMENT		FORMAL ASSESSMENT				
	Study Guide	Audit Your Understanding	Chapter MicroExam	Chapter Problem Test	Unit Problem Test	Unit Objective Test	Portfolio
Unit C			✓			✓	
Units B, D		✓	✓			✓	
Unit A		✓	✓	✓	✓	✓	
				✓	✓		

NEW, REVIEW, AND EXTENSION

ACTIVITIES/CONCEPTS/TRANSACTIONS	NEW	REVIEW/ EXTENSION
Analyze transactions in an accounting equation		✓
Received cash from owner as an investment		✓
Paid cash for supplies		✓
Paid cash for insurance		✓
Bought supplies on account		✓
Paid cash on account		✓
Received cash from sales	✓	
Paid cash for expenses	✓	
Paid cash to owner for personal use	✓	

TEACHING MATERIALS

Teacher's Wraparound Edition of Text
Teacher's Resource Guide
Teacher's Edition of Working Papers
Teacher's Edition of Demonstration/Recycling Problems
Teaching Transparencies
Accounting Tutorial Manual
MicroExam

Starting a Proprietorship: Changes That Affect Owner's Equity

ENABLING PERFORMANCE TASKS

After studying Chapter 3, you will be able to:

a Define accounting terms related to changes that affect owner's equity for a service business organized as a proprietorship.

b Identify accounting practices related to changes that affect owner's equity for a service business organized as a proprietorship.

c Analyze changes that affect owner's equity for a service business organized as a proprietorship in an accounting equation.

d Prepare a balance sheet for a service business organized as a proprietorship from information in the accounting equation.

TERMS PREVIEW

revenue • expense • withdrawals

A business activity that changes assets, liabilities, or owner's equity is known as a transaction. Chapter 2 describes five transactions involved in starting Rugcare, a proprietorship. Rugcare is now ready to open for business. This chapter presents the transactions that commonly occur during the daily operations of a business. Each of these transactions changes Ben Furman's equity in Rugcare.

HOW TRANSACTIONS CHANGE OWNER'S EQUITY IN AN ACCOUNTING EQUATION

The accounting equation for Rugcare as of August 11, showing the effect of transactions for starting a business, is shown in Illustration 3-1.

The sum of the balances on the left side of the accounting equation, $11,360.00, equals the sum of the balances on the right side of the equation, $11,360.00. The equation is in balance.

Many transactions involved in the daily operations of a business increase or decrease owner's equity. Detailed information about these changes in owner's equity is needed by owners and managers to make sound business decisions.

FYI

Each transaction changes at least two accounts in the accounting equation.

ILLUSTRATION 3-1   Accounting equation after transactions for starting a proprietorship

	Assets			= Liabilities +	Owner's Equity
	Cash	+ Supplies +	Prepaid Insurance =	Butler Cleaning Supplies +	Ben Furman, Capital
Balances	$5,863	$4,297	$1,200	$1,360	$10,000
	Total of left side: $5,863 + $4,297 + $1,200 = $11,360			Total of right side: $1,360 + $10,000 = $11,360	

Received Cash from Sales

A transaction for the sale of goods or services results in an increase in owner's equity. An increase in owner's equity resulting from the operation of a business is called **revenue.** When cash is received from a sale, the total amount of assets and owner's equity is increased.

When Rugcare receives cash for services performed, two accounts in the accounting equation are affected. The asset account, Cash, is increased by the amount of cash received. The owner's equity account, Ben Furman, Capital, is increased by the same amount.

> *Transaction 6   August 12, 19--. Received cash from sales, $525.00.*

CHAPTER 3   Starting a Proprietorship: Changes That Affect Owner's Equity   **37**

LESSON PLAN 3-1

Materials

- Student pages 37–42
- Transparency 2-1, Blank Accounting Equation and Balance Sheet
- Software: Accounting Tutorial
- Demonstration Problem 3A, Accounting Equation

Objectives (Enabling Performance Tasks):

a. Define accounting terms related to changes that affect owner's equity for a service business organized as a proprietorship.

b. Identify accounting practices related to changes that affect owner's equity for a service business organized as a proprietorship.

c. Analyze changes that affect owner's equity for a service business organized as a proprietorship in an accounting equation.

FOCUS

- In Chapter 2, transactions related to starting a business were analyzed to determine the effect on the accounting equation. Explain that changes that affect owner's equity will be analyzed on the accounting equation. Previously students saw that the initial investment of the owner increased owner's equity. In this lesson they will see that the normal business operations of a company also affect owner's equity.
- Introduce new vocabulary: revenue, expense, withdrawals.

TEACHING STRATEGIES: TEACHING TIP

Review the definition of transaction. A business activity that changes assets, liabilities, or owner's equity is called a transaction.

Cover student pages 37–42 "How Transactions Change Owner's Equity in an
Accounting Equation." This lesson continues to use the accounting equation to
analyze transactions. However, new
kinds of transactions are analyzed —
those that affect owner's equity.
Emphasize that revenue (sales) transactions increase owner's equity. Expenses
decrease owner's equity. Withdrawals
by the owner also decrease owner's
equity. Revenue, expense, and withdrawal transactions will be encountered
in every part of the accounting text
because they are important transactions
in the accounting cycle. Review the definition of transaction. Emphasize that the
words "Received cash" in a transaction
statement always means cash
increases; "Paid cash" always means
cash decreases.

Use Transparency 2-1 to record the
transactions as they are presented.

Guided Practice

Guide students through Drills 3-D1 and
3-D2. Direct students to complete the
drills using the forms in the working
papers as the students decide the
change caused by each transaction as a
group. All students should agree with
the analysis of a transaction before proceeding to the next transaction.

Independent Practice

Assign Terms 1–3, Questions 1–10,
Problem 3-1, and Problem 3-2,
Instruction 1.

The effect of this transaction on the accounting equation is
shown in Illustration 3-2. The asset account, Cash, is increased by
$525.00, the amount of cash received. This increase is on the left
side of the equation. The owner's equity account, Ben Furman, Capital,
is also increased by $525.00. This increase is on the right side of
the equation.

ILLUSTRATION 3-2   Receiving cash from sales increases assets and owner's equity

	Assets			= Liabilities + Owner's Equity	
	Cash	+ Supplies	+ Prepaid Insurance =	Butler Cleaning Supplies +	Ben Furman, Capital
Balances	$5,863	$4,297	$1,200	$1,360	$10,000
Transaction 6	+525				+525 (revenue)
New Balances	$6,388	$4,297	$1,200	$1,360	$10,525
	Total of left side: $6,388 + $4,297 + $1,200 = $11,885			Total of right side: $1,360 + $10,525 = $11,885	

After this transaction is recorded, the sum of the balances on
the left side of the equation equals the sum of the balances on the
right side, $11,885.00. The equation is still in balance.

In this chapter, three different kinds of transactions that affect
owner's equity are described. Therefore, a description of the transaction is shown in parentheses to the right of the amount in the
accounting equation. Transaction 6 is a revenue transaction. Therefore, *(revenue)* is shown beside the $525.00 change in owner's equity
in Illustration 3-2.

> **FYI**
>
> When all the changes
> occur on one side of the
> accounting equation,
> increases on that side must
> be matched by decreases on
> the same side.

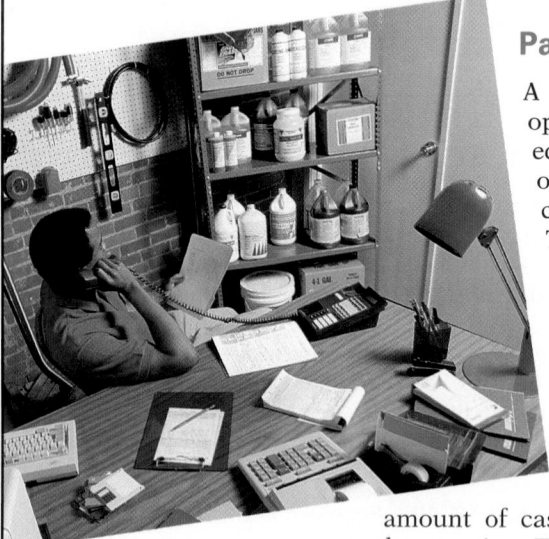

Paid Cash for Expenses

A transaction to pay for goods or services needed to
operate a business results in a decrease in owner's
equity. A decrease in owner's equity resulting from the
operation of a business is called an **expense**. When
cash is paid for expenses, the business has less cash.
Therefore, the asset account, Cash, is decreased. The
owner's equity account, Ben Furman, Capital, is also
decreased by the same amount.

> *Transaction 7   August 12, 19--. Paid cash for
> rent, $250.00.*

The effect of this transaction on the accounting equation is shown in Illustration 3-3. The
asset account, Cash, is decreased by $250.00, the
amount of cash paid out. This decrease is on the left side of
the equation. The owner's equity account, Ben Furman, Capital, is also

---

TEACHING STRATEGIES: TEACHING TIP

Make liberal use of the chalkboard or an overhead projector as the class is discussing the analysis of
transactions. The demonstration problems are provided for this purpose.

ILLUSTRATION 3-3 Paying cash for an expense decreases assets and owner's equity

	Assets			= Liabilities +	Owner's Equity
	Cash	+ Supplies +	Prepaid Insurance =	Butler Cleaning Supplies +	Ben Furman, Capital
Balances	$6,388	$4,297	$1,200	$1,360	$10,525
Transaction 7	−250				−250 (expense)
New Balances	$6,138	$4,297	$1,200	$1,360	$10,275

Total of left side: $6,138 + $4,297 + $1,200 = $11,635   Total of right side: $1,360 + $10,275 = $11,635

decreased by $250.00. This decrease is on the right side of the equation.

After this transaction is recorded, the sum of the balances on the left side of the equation equals the sum of the balances on the right side, $11,635.00. The equation is still in balance.

Transaction 8   August 12, 19--. Paid cash for telephone bill, $45.00.

Most businesses must make payments for goods and services provided by public utilities, such as telephone companies. These goods and services are often referred to as utilities. In addition to telephone services, electricity, gas, water, and sanitation are also considered to be utilities.

The effect of this transaction on the accounting equation is shown in Illustration 3-4. The asset account, Cash, is decreased by $45.00, the amount of cash paid out. This decrease is on the left side of the equation. The owner's equity account, Ben Furman, Capital, is also decreased by $45.00. This decrease is on the right side of the equation.

ILLUSTRATION 3-4 Paying cash for an expense decreases assets and owner's equity

	Assets			= Liabilities +	Owner's Equity
	Cash	+ Supplies +	Prepaid Insurance =	Butler Cleaning Supplies +	Ben Furman, Capital
Balances	$6,138	$4,297	$1,200	$1,360	$10,275
Transaction 8	−45				−45 (expense)
New Balances	$6,093	$4,297	$1,200	$1,360	$10,230

Total of left side: $6,093 + $4,297 + $1,200 = $11,590   Total of right side: $1,360 + $10,230 = $11,590

PROFESSIONAL BUSINESS ETHICS

Is This Really a Business Expense?

Randall Stovall, an architect, owns and operates a business known as Stovall Designs. Each year the federal government requires Mr. Stovall to report the amount of revenue and expenses of the business. Reported expenses are limited to those expenses required to operate the business. Mr. Stovall must pay federal income tax on the amount by which revenues exceed expenses.

As the bookkeeper for Stovall Designs, you know that Mr. Stovall is not fond of paying income taxes. In fact, you believe his actions are often motivated by his desire to minimize his income tax liability.

INSTRUCTIONS Use the three-step checklist to analyze whether each of the following actions by Mr. Stovall demonstrates ethical behavior.

After this transaction is recorded, the sum of the balances on the left side of the equation equals the sum of the balances on the right side, $11,590.00. The equation is still in balance.

Other expense transactions might be for advertising, equipment rental or repairs, charitable contributions, and other miscellaneous items. All expense transactions affect the accounting equation in the same way as Transactions 7 and 8.

Paid Cash to Owner for Personal Use

Assets taken out of a business for the owner's personal use are called **withdrawals**. A withdrawal decreases owner's equity. Although an owner may withdraw any kind of asset, usually an owner withdraws cash. The withdrawal decreases the account balance of the withdrawn asset, such as Cash.

Transaction 9   August 12, 19--. Paid cash to owner for personal use, $100.00.

The effect of this transaction on the accounting equation is shown in Illustration 3-5 on the next page. The asset account, Cash, is decreased by $100.00, the amount of cash paid out. This decrease is on the left side of the accounting equation. The owner's equity account, Ben Furman, Capital, is also decreased by $100.00. This decrease is on the right side of the equation.

After this transaction is recorded, the sum of the balances on the left side of the equation equals the sum of the balances on the right side, $11,490.00. The equation is still in balance.

A decrease in owner's equity because of a withdrawal is not a result of the normal operations of a business. Therefore, a withdrawal is not an expense.

Summary of Changes in Owner's Equity

After recording the transactions for starting Rugcare as a proprietorship, the total owner's equity was $10,000.00. Five transactions

40

Situation 1. Mr. Stovall often makes personal long-distance phone calls from his office. He charges these calls to the business account.

Situation 2. A lover of fine furniture, Mr. Stovall equipped his office with a $1,200.00 leather chair rather than a $400.00 vinyl model.

Situation 3. Mr. Stovall prepared a design for a lumber company in exchange for $1,500.00 of wood and paint used to build a porch at Mr. Stovall's summer cottage. Mr. Stovall instructed you not to record the transaction in Stovall Designs' accounting records.

Situation 4. Mr. Stovall hired a floral company to install and maintain plants in his office.

| ILLUSTRATION 3-5 | Paying cash to owner for personal use decreases assets and owner's equity |

	Assets				=	Liabilities	+	Owner's Equity
	Cash	+	Supplies	+	Prepaid Insurance	=	Butler Cleaning Supplies	+	Ben Furman, Capital
Balances	$6,093		$4,297		$1,200		$1,360		$10,230
Transaction 9	−100								−100 (withdrawal)
New Balances	$5,993		$4,297		$1,200		$1,360		$10,130

Total of left side:
$5,993 + $4,297 + $1,200 = $11,490

Total of right side:
$1,360 + $10,130 = $11,490

have affected owner's equity. In Chapter 2, Ben Furman made a $10,000.00 investment. In this chapter, four transactions that changed owner's equity were recorded in the accounting equation.

Transaction Number	Kind of Transaction	Change in Owner's Equity
6	Revenue	+525.00
7	Expense (rent)	−250.00
8	Expense (telephone)	−45.00
9	Withdrawal	−100.00
	Net change in owner's equity	+130.00

A revenue transaction increased owner's equity. Expense and withdrawal transactions decreased owner's equity. These transactions together increased total owner's equity by $130.00, from $10,000.00 to $10,130.00.

Audit Your Understanding

1. How is owner's equity affected when cash is received from sales?

2. How is owner's equity affected when cash is paid for expenses?

3. How is owner's equity affected when cash is paid to the owner for personal use?

CHAPTER 3 Starting a Proprietorship: Changes That Affect Owner's Equity **41**

For a business to succeed, revenues must be greater than expenses during most periods of time. An established business should rarely experience a decrease in its owner's equity.

FYI

The Small Business Administration (SBA) was created by Congress in 1953. Its purpose is to advise and assist small businesses in the United States.

REPORTING A CHANGED ACCOUNTING EQUATION ON A BALANCE SHEET

A balance sheet may be prepared on any date to report information about the assets, liabilities, and owner's equity of a business. The balance sheet prepared in Chapter 2, Illustration 2-6, reports Rugcare's financial condition at the end of business on August 11. The transactions recorded in Chapter 3 have changed the account balances of Cash and Ben Furman, Capital in the accounting equation. A revised balance sheet is prepared to report Rugcare's financial condition after recording these transactions.

The last transaction on August 12 is recorded in the accounting equation as shown in Illustration 3-5. The new account balances in the accounting equation after Transaction 9 are used to prepare the balance sheet. Rugcare's balance sheet as of August 12 is shown in Illustration 3-6.

The August 12 balance sheet is prepared using the same steps as described in Chapter 2.

ILLUSTRATION 3-6   Balance sheet

	Assets			= Liabilities + Owner's Equity	
	Cash	+ Supplies	+ Prepaid Insurance =	Butler Cleaning Supplies +	Ben Furman, Capital
New Balances	$5,993	$4,297	$1,200	$1,360	$10,130

Rugcare
Balance Sheet
August 12, 19--

Assets			Liabilities		
Cash	5 9 9 3 00		Butler Cleaning Supplies	1 3 6 0 00	
Supplies	4 2 9 7 00		Owner's Equity		
Prepaid Insurance	1 2 0 0 00		Ben Furman, Capital	10 1 3 0 00	
Total Assets	11 4 9 0 00		Total Liab. and Owner's Eq.	11 4 9 0 00	

The accounts on the left side of the accounting equation are reported on the left side of Rugcare's balance sheet. The accounts on the right side of the accounting equation are shown on the right side of the balance sheet. The total of the left side of the balance

PART 2   Accounting for a Service Business Organized as a Proprietorship

APPLIED SKILLS: WORD PROCESSING

If you wish to integrate word processing into your accounting course, you may direct students to answer the end-of-chapter Accounting Terms, Questions for Individual Study, and Cases for Critical Thinking using their word processing software.

sheet, $11,490.00, is equal to the total of the right side of the balance sheet. The balance sheet is in balance.

A comparison of the August 11 and August 12 balance sheet totals is shown in Illustration 3-7.

The balance sheet has an increase of $130.00 on the left side (Assets) and an increase of $130.00 on the right side (Liabilities + Owner's Equity).

ILLUSTRATION 3-7·   Comparison of balance sheet totals

	Assets			= Liabilities + Owner's Equity	
	Cash	+ Supplies	+ Prepaid Insurance =	Butler Cleaning Supplies +	Ben Furman, Capital
August 11	$5,863	$4,297	$1,200	$1,360	$10,000
August 12	$5,993	$4,297	$1,200	$1,360	$10,130
	+$130	$0	$0	$0	+$130

Few businesses need to prepare a balance sheet every day. Many businesses prepare a balance sheet only on the last day of each month. Monthly balance sheets provide business owners and managers with frequent and regular information for making business decisions.

SUMMARY OF TRANSACTIONS THAT AFFECT OWNER'S EQUITY

Revenue, expense, and withdrawal transactions affect owner's equity. A revenue transaction increases owner's equity. Expense and withdrawal transactions decrease owner's equity.

The accounting equation has two sides. The left side of the equation shows assets. The right side of the equation shows liabilities and owner's equity. A transaction changes the account balances of two or more accounts. After each transaction, the total of accounts on the left side must equal the total of accounts on the right side. The effects of the transactions analyzed in Chapters 2 and 3 on the accounting equation are shown in Illustration 3-8 on the following page. After these transactions are recorded, the total of the balances on the left side equals the total of the balances on the right side, $11,490.00. Therefore, the accounting equation is in balance.

The new balances of the accounting equation are used to prepare a balance sheet. The left side of the balance sheet contains asset accounts. The right side contains liability and owner's equity accounts.

Audit Your Understanding

1. What is the heading on the left side of the balance sheet?

2. What are the headings on the right side of the balance sheet?

3. What is the total on the left side of the balance sheet?

4. What is the total on the right side of the balance sheet?

TEACHING STRATEGIES:
APPLYING VISUALS

Direct the students to the Summary Illustration 3-8. Review the summary illustration and each type of transaction presented in the chapter.

SUMMARY ILLUSTRATION 3-8

Summary of how transactions affect the accounting equation

Transaction	Assets			= Liabilities + Owner's Equity	
	Cash +	Supplies +	Prepaid Insurance	Butler Cleaning Supplies +	Ben Furman, Capital
Beginning Balance	$0	$0	$0	$0	$0
1. Received cash from owner as an investment	+10,000				+10,000 (investment)
New Balances	$10,000	$0	$0	$0	$10,000
2. Paid cash for supplies	−1,577	+1,577			
New Balances	$ 8,423	$1,577	$0	$0	$10,000
3. Paid cash for insurance	−1,200		+1,200		
New Balances	$ 7,223	$1,577	$1,200	$0	$10,000
4. Bought supplies on account		+2,720		+2,720	
New Balances	$ 7,223	$4,297	$1,200	$2,720	$10,000
5. Paid cash on account	−1,360			−1,360	
New Balances	$ 5,863	$4,297	$1,200	$1,360	$10,000
6. Received cash from sales	+525				+525 (revenue)
New Balances	$ 6,388	$4,297	$1,200	$1,360	$10,525
7. Paid cash for rent	−250				−250 (expense)
New Balances	$ 6,138	$4,297	$1,200	$1,360	$10,275
8. Paid cash for telephone bill	−45				−45 (expense)
New Balances	$ 6,093	$4,297	$1,200	$1,360	$10,230
9. Paid cash to owner for personal use	−100				−100 (withdrawal)
New Balances	$ 5,993	$4,297	$1,200	$1,360	$10,130

Total of left side:
$5,993 + $4,297 + $1,200 = $11,490

Total of right side:
$1,360 + $10,130 = $11,490

Enrich

- Assign the Electronic Study Guide Chapter 3 to complete the study guide from the working papers at the computer.
- Discuss the PROFESSIONAL BUSINESS ETHICS feature on pages 40–41. You may wish to distribute copies of the 3-step Checklist for Making Ethical Decisions. A blackline master is furnished in the Masters and Solutions to the Enrichment/Application Activities Section in the Teacher's Resource Guide.

CLOSURE

Use Audit Your Understanding questions.

ASSESS

- Administer Problem Test Chapter 3.
- Administer a MicroExam test for Chapter 3.

ACCOUNTING TERMS

1. **revenue:** An increase in owner's equity resulting from the operation of a business. (p. 37)

2. **expense:** A decrease in owner's equity resulting from the operation of a business. (p. 38)

3. **withdrawals:** Assets taken out of a business for the owner's personal use. (p. 40)

ACCOUNTING TERMS   EPT(a)

What is the meaning of each of the following?

1. **revenue**
2. **expense**
3. **withdrawals**

QUESTIONS FOR INDIVIDUAL STUDY   EPT(b)

1. Why do owners and managers need information about changes in owner's equity?

2. What accounts are affected, and how, when cash is received from sales?

3. How does a cash payment for goods or services needed to operate a business affect owner's equity?

4. What accounts are affected, and how, by a cash payment for an expense?

5. What must be true of the accounting equation after each transaction is recorded?

6. What are four expense transactions other than rent and utilities?

7. Which asset is normally withdrawn by an owner for personal use?

8. What accounts are affected, and how, when an owner withdraws $200.00 for personal use?

9. What transactions decrease owner's equity?

10. What must be true of changes in owner's equity if a business is to be successful?

11. What are three accounts that might be found on the left side of a balance sheet?

12. How often might a business be expected to prepare a balance sheet?

QUESTIONS FOR INDIVIDUAL STUDY

1. To make sound business decisions. (p. 37)

2. Cash is increased; the capital account is increased. (p. 37)

3. Owner's equity is decreased. (p. 38)

4. Cash is decreased; the capital account is decreased. (p. 38)

5. The equation must still be in balance. (p. 39)

6. Advertising, equipment rental or repairs, charitable contributions, and miscellaneous expenses. (p. 40)

7. Cash. (p. 40)

8. Cash is decreased by $200.00; the capital account is decreased by $200.00. (p. 40)

9. Expenses and withdrawals. (p. 41)

10. The business must have more increases than decreases in owner's equity. (p. 42)

11. Cash, Supplies, and Prepaid Insurance. (p. 42)

12. Many businesses prepare a balance sheet monthly. (p. 43)

CASES FOR CRITICAL THINKING   EPT(b)

CASE 1 Garcia Books received an investment from its owner, Mrs. Juanita Garcia. This transaction is recorded in the following accounting equation. Is the analysis correct? Explain.

	Assets		=	Liabilities	+	Owner's Equity
Cash +	Supplies +	Prepaid Insurance =		Panther Supply Company	+	Juanita Garcia, Capital
$1,000	$3,000	$2,000		$2,500		$3,500
+750						
$1,750	$3,000	$2,000		$2,500		$3,500

CASE 2 The manager of Phillip's Department Store prepares a balance sheet at the end of each business day. Is this a satisfactory procedure? Explain.

CASES FOR CRITICAL THINKING

Case 1   When one account is changed on the left side of the equation, either another account on the left side or an account on the right side must also be changed. This is necessary so that the changes to equation accounts are in balance. Also, the new balances on the last line of the analysis must be in balance. As the analysis stands, the total of the balances on the left side of the accounting equation is $6,750.00. The total of the balances on the right side of the accounting equation is only $6,000.00. This transaction should also increase owner's equity by $750.00.

APPLIED SKILLS: LANGUAGE ARTS

Paraphrasing, writing complete sentences, identifying singular and plural nouns. For additional practice in language arts skills, direct students to answer the Accounting Terms and Questions for Individual Study at the end of the chapter. Students should write in their own words and in complete sentences. To further practice language arts skills, ask students to underline the singular nouns and circle the plural nouns in their definitions.

Case 2 This is probably not a satis-factory procedure. Few businesses need to have a balance sheet prepared as often as every day. Many businesses prepare a balance sheet once a month. Therefore, business owners and man-agers receive frequent and regular infor-mation that can be used to make business decisions.

CHECK FIGURES

See Teacher's Edition of Working Papers for complete solutions to drills and problems.

Drill 3-D1 Trans. No. 1, 2, and 7 are "+" for Cash and Susan Sanders, Capi-tal; rest are "−" for both accounts

Drill 3-D2 Trans. No. 3 and 5 are "+" for Cash, Trans. 1 does not affect Cash, rest are "−" for Cash

DRILLS FOR UNDERSTANDING

EPT(c)

DRILL 3-D1 Determining how revenue, expense, and withdrawal transactions change an accounting equation

TUTORIAL

Use a form similar to the following.

| Trans. No. | Assets | | | | = Liabilities | + Owner's Equity |
	Cash	+ Supplies	+ Prepaid Insurance	= Maxwell Company	+ Susan Sanders, Capital
1.	+				+

Transactions

1. Received cash from owner as an investment.
2. Received cash from sales.
3. Paid cash for telephone bill.
4. Paid cash for advertising.
5. Paid cash to owner for personal use.
6. Paid cash for rent.
7. Received cash from sales.
8. Paid cash for equipment repairs.

INSTRUCTIONS:

Decide which accounts in the accounting equation are changed by each transaction. Place a plus (+) in the appropriate column if the account is increased. Place a minus (−) in the appro-priate column if the account is decreased. Transaction 1 is given as an example.

DRILL 3-D2 Determining how transactions change an accounting equation

Use a form similar to the following.

| Trans. No. | Assets | | | | = Liabilities | + Owner's Equity |
	Cash	+ Supplies	+ Prepaid Insurance	= Barrett Company	+ Sue Marist, Capital
1.		+		+	

Transactions

1. Bought supplies on account from Barrett Company.
2. Paid cash for electric bill.
3. Received cash from owner as an investment.
4. Paid cash for insurance.

TEACHING STRATEGIES: COOPERATIVE LEARNING

Divide the class into groups of four or five students each. Using Cases for Critical Thinking, each group analyzes the cases and arrives at agreed-upon solutions. One member of each group is appointed the recorder and presents the group's analysis to the class. This cooperative learning activity should not take more than 20 to 25 minutes of class time.

5. Received cash from sales.
6. Paid cash for rent.
7. Paid cash for supplies.
8. Paid cash for advertising.
9. Paid cash on account to Barrett Company.
10. Paid cash to owner for personal use.

INSTRUCTIONS:

Decide which accounts in the accounting equation are changed by each transaction. Place a plus (+) in the appropriate column if the account is increased. Place a minus (−) in the appropriate column if the account is decreased. Transaction 1 is given as an example.

APPLICATION PROBLEMS

EPT(c,d)

PROBLEM 3-1 Determining how revenue, expense, and withdrawal transactions change an accounting equation

Peter Smith operates a service business called Peter's Service Company. Peter's Service Company uses the accounts shown in the following accounting equation. Use a form similar to the following to complete this problem.

| Trans. No. | Assets | | | | | = Liabilities | + Owner's Equity |
	Cash	+	Supplies	+	Prepaid Insurance	= Kline Company	+ Peter Smith, Capital
Beg. Bal.	625		375		300	200	1,100
1.	−300						−300 (expense)
New Bal.	325		375		300	200	800
2.							

Transactions

1. Paid cash for rent, $300.00.
2. Paid cash to owner for personal use, $150.00.
3. Received cash from sales, $800.00.
4. Paid cash for equipment repairs, $100.00
5. Paid cash for telephone bill, $60.00.
6. Received cash from sales, $650.00.
7. Paid cash for charitable contributions, $35.00.
8. Paid cash for miscellaneous expenses, $25.00.

INSTRUCTIONS:

For each transaction, complete the following. Transaction 1 is given as an example.

a. Analyze the transaction to determine which accounts in the accounting equation are affected.

b. Write the amount in the appropriate columns, using a plus (+) if the account increases or a minus (−) if the account decreases.

c. For transactions that change owner's equity, write in parentheses a description of the transaction to the right of the amount.

d. Calculate the new balance for each account in the accounting equation.

e. Before going on to the next transaction, determine that the accounting equation is still in balance.

PROBLEM 3-2 Determining how transactions change an accounting equation and preparing a balance sheet

Doris Becker operates a typing business called QuickType. QuickType uses the accounts shown in the following accounting equation. Use a form similar to the following to complete this problem.

| Trans. No. | Assets | | | | | = Liabilities | + | Owner's Equity |
	Cash	+	Supplies	+	Prepaid Insurance	= Teale Company	+	Doris Becker, Capital
Beg. Bal. 1.	500 −50		260		300	100		960 −50 (expense)
New Bal. 2.	450		260		300	100		910

Transactions
1. Paid cash for equipment repair, $50.00.
2. Received cash from sales, $325.00.
3. Paid cash for supplies, $200.00.
4. Bought supplies on account from Teale Company, $1,200.00.
5. Paid cash for advertising, $200.00.
6. Received cash from sales, $280.00.
7. Paid cash for water bill, $60.00.
8. Paid cash for insurance, $400.00.
9. Paid cash to owner for personal use, $125.00.
10. Received cash from sales, $260.00.
11. Paid cash for equipment rental, $45.00.
12. Paid cash for charitable contributions, $25.00.
13. Received cash from sales, $300.00.
14. Paid cash on account to Teale Company, $100.00.
15. Received cash from owner as an investment, $1,000.00.
16. Paid cash for rent, $600.00.
17. Received cash from sales, $430.00.
18. Paid cash on account to Teale Company, $750.00.

INSTRUCTIONS:

1. For each transaction, complete the following. Transaction 1 is given as an example.
   a. Analyze the transaction to determine which accounts in the accounting equation are affected.
   b. Write the amount in the appropriate columns, using a plus (+) if the account increases or a minus (−) if the account decreases.
   c. For transactions that change owner's equity, write in parentheses a description of the transaction to the right of the amount.

APPLIED SKILLS: WRITING ACROSS THE CURRICULUM

Writing paragraphs and short essays. The Cases for Critical Thinking are short, practical applications of the accounting principles developed in the chapter. Some cases are planned to present problems related to the chapter but not specifically discussed and answered in the chapter. These cases present an opportunity for critical thinking and decision making. These cases also require more than a short objective-type response. Therefore, they provide ideal practice in writing paragraphs and short essays.

PART 2   Accounting for a Service Business Organized as a Proprietorship

d. Calculate the new balance for each account in the accounting equation.

e. Before going on to the next transaction, determine that the accounting equation is still in balance.

2. Using the final balances in the accounting equation, prepare a balance sheet for Quick-Type. Use the date July 17 of the current year.

ENRICHMENT PROBLEMS

EPT(c,d)

MASTERY PROBLEM 3-M Determining how transactions change an accounting equation and preparing a balance sheet

Fred Nance operates a service business called Nance Company. Nance Company uses the accounts shown in the following accounting equation. Use a form similar to the following to complete this problem.

Trans. No.	Assets				= Liabilities	+ Owner's Equity	
	Cash	+	Supplies	+	Prepaid Insurance	= Sickle Company	+ Fred Nance, Capital
Beg. Bal. 1.	1,400 −100		300		400	1,500	600 −100 (expense)
New Bal. 2.	1,300		300		400	1,500	500

Transactions
1. Paid cash for telephone bill, $100.00.
2. Received cash from owner as an investment, $200.00.
3. Paid cash for rent, $500.00.
4. Paid cash for equipment rental, $100.00.
5. Received cash from sales, $895.00.
6. Bought supplies on account from Sickle Company, $600.00.
7. Paid cash for equipment repair, $15.00.
8. Paid cash for miscellaneous expense, $30.00.
9. Received cash from sales, $920.00.
10. Paid cash for advertising, $50.00.
11. Paid cash for charitable contribution, $10.00.
12. Paid cash for supplies, $400.00.
13. Paid cash for advertising, $250.00.
14. Received cash from sales, $795.00.
15. Paid cash on account to Sickle Company, $1,500.00.
16. Paid cash for insurance, $250.00.
17. Received cash from sales, $960.00.
18. Paid cash to owner for personal use, $1,000.00.

INSTRUCTIONS:

1. For each transaction, complete the following. Transaction 1 is given as an example.

   a. Analyze the transaction to determine which accounts in the accounting equation are affected.

b. Write the amount in the appropriate columns, using a plus (+) if the account increases or a minus (−) if the account decreases.

c. For transactions that change owner's equity, write in parentheses a description of the transaction to the right of the amount.

d. Calculate the new balance for each account in the accounting equation.

e. Before going on to the next transaction, determine that the accounting equation is still in balance.

2. Using the final balances in the accounting equation, prepare a balance sheet for Nance Company. Use the date April 30 of the current year.

CHALLENGE PROBLEM 3-C Calculating the missing amounts in an accounting equation

Each of the following statements includes four of the five amounts needed to complete an accounting equation.

Statements

1. Cash, $400.00; Supplies, $300.00; Prepaid Insurance, $800.00; Dexter Company, $500.00.
2. Cash, $200.00; Prepaid Insurance, $400.00; Dexter Company, $250.00; Pat Bouwman, Capital, $900.00.
3. Cash, $300.00; Supplies, $1,000.00; Prepaid Insurance, $750.00; Pat Bouwman, Capital, $1,200.00.
4. Supplies, $2,000.00; Prepaid Insurance, $1,200.00; Dexter Company, $2,400.00; Pat Bouwman, Capital, $3,500.00.
5. Cash, $100.00; Supplies, $2,700.00; Dexter Company, $1,100.00; Pat Bouwman, Capital, $2,500.00.
6. Cash, $250.00; Supplies, $400.00; Prepaid Insurance, $300.00; Pat Bouwman, Capital, $500.00.
7. Cash, $600.00; Supplies, $2,200.00; Prepaid Insurance, $900.00; Dexter Company, $500.00.
8. Supplies, $100.00; Prepaid Insurance, $400.00; Dexter Company, $150.00; Pat Bouwman, Capital, $500.00.

INSTRUCTIONS:

1. Use a form similar to the following. Record the information from each of the statements. Statement 1 is given as an example.

State-ment	Assets			= Liabilities + Owner's Equity	
	Cash +	Supplies +	Prepaid Insurance	= Dexter Company +	Pat Bouwman, Capital
1.	400	300	800	500	_____
	Total: _____			Total: _____	

2. Use a form similar to the one shown on page 51. Calculate the sum of the balances on the side of the accounting equation that is complete. The totals of the balances on the left and right sides must be equal for the accounting equation to be in balance.

3. For each line of the form, calculate the amount of the missing item in the accounting equation. Statement 1 is given as an example.

State-ment	Assets					= Liabilities + Owner's Equity	
	Cash	+	Supplies	+	Prepaid Insurance	= Dexter Company	+ Pat Bouwman, Capital
1.	400		300		800	500	1,000
	Total: 1,500					Total: 1,500	

Chapter 4 analyzes transactions into debit and credit parts using T accounts. All transactions that were introduced in Chapters 2 and 3 are used for demonstration purposes throughout the chapter. The repetition of using these same transactions enables students to see the continuity of the analyzation process. At this juncture, transaction statements begin to take on importance. All transaction statements are worded consistently so that students may model the analyzation process to the examples in the text.

GUIDE TO ACHIEVING LEARNING OBJECTIVES

Enabling Performance Tasks	TEACH	APPLY		EXTEND/ENRICH				
	Lesson Plans	Drills for Understanding	Application Problems	Mastery Problems	Challenge Problems	Cases for Critical Thinking	Recycling Problems	Reinforcement Activity
a. Define accounting terms related to analyzing transactions into debit and credit parts.	4-1, 4-2							
b. Identify accounting practices related to analyzing transactions into debit and credit parts.	4-1, 4-2	4-D1				Cases 1, 2		
c. Use T accounts to analyze transactions showing which accounts are debited or credited for each transaction.	4-2	4-D1, 4-D2	4-1, 4-2	4-M	4-C		4-R	
d. Verify the equality of debits and credits for each transaction.	4-2	4-D2	4-1, 4-2	4-M	4-C		4-R	

ENRICHMENT

SPECIAL FEATURES	TECHNOLOGY CONNECTION
Multicultural Awareness, page 57	Accounting Tutorial Unit 1
Personal Visions in Business, page 60	Electronic Study Guide

	INFORMAL ASSESSMENT		FORMAL ASSESSMENT				
Study Guide		Audit Your Understanding	Chapter MicroExam	Chapter Problem Test	Unit Problem Test	Unit Objective Test	Portfolio
Unit A			✓			✓	
Units B, C		✓	✓			✓	
				✓	✓		
				✓	✓		

NEW, REVIEW, AND EXTENSION

ACTIVITIES/CONCEPTS/TRANSACTIONS	NEW	REVIEW/ EXTENSION
The effect of transactions on the accounting equation		✓
Normal balance of an account	✓	
Analyzing transactions into debit and credit parts	✓	
Received cash from owner as an investment		✓
Paid cash for supplies		✓
Paid cash for insurance		✓
Bought supplies on account		✓
Paid cash on account		✓
Received cash from sales		✓
Paid cash for an expense		✓
Paid cash to owner for personal use		✓

TEACHING MATERIALS

Teacher's Wraparound Edition of Text

Teacher's Resource Guide

Teacher's Edition of Working Papers

Teacher's Edition of Demonstration/Recycling Problems

Teaching Transparencies

Accounting Tutorial Manual

MicroExam

Analyzing Transactions into Debit and Credit Parts

ENABLING PERFORMANCE TASKS

After studying Chapter 4, you will be able to:

a Define accounting terms related to analyzing transactions into debit and credit parts.

b Identify accounting practices related to analyzing transactions into debit and credit parts.

c Use T accounts to analyze transactions showing which accounts are debited or credited for each transaction.

d Verify the equality of debits and credits for each transaction.

TERMS PREVIEW

T account • debit • credit • chart of accounts • contra account

52

How business transactions affect accounts in an accounting equation is described in Chapters 2 and 3. Even though the effects of transactions *can* be recorded in an accounting equation, the procedure is not practical in an actual accounting system. Accountants need more detail about the changes affecting each account than will appear in an accounting equation. Also, the number of accounts used by most businesses would make the accounting equation cumbersome to use as a major financial record. Therefore, a separate record is commonly used for each account.

ACCOUNTS

The accounting equation can be represented as a *T*, as shown in Illustration 4-1.

ILLUSTRATION 4-1

Sides of an accounting equation

Assets =	Liabilities + Owner's Equity
Left side	Right side

FYI

Always draw T accounts when analyzing transactions so that you can see the debit and credit sides.

The values of all things owned (assets) are on the left side of the accounting equation. The values of all equities or claims against the assets (liabilities and owner's equity) are on the right side of the accounting equation.

The total of amounts on the left side of the accounting equation must always equal the total of amounts on the right side. Therefore, the total of all assets on the left side of the accounting equation must always equal the total of all liabilities and owner's equity on the right side.

A record summarizing all the information pertaining to a single item in the accounting equation is known as an account. Transactions change the balances of accounts in the accounting equation. Accounting transactions must be analyzed to determine how account balances are changed. An accounting device used to analyze transactions is called a **T account**. The relationship of a T account to the accounts in the accounting equation is shown in Illustration 4-2.

ILLUSTRATION 4-2

Relationship of a T account to the accounting equation

Assets =	Liabilities + Owner's Equity
Left side	Right side

T Account	
Left side DEBIT SIDE	Right side CREDIT SIDE

CHAPTER 4   Analyzing Transactions into Debit and Credit Parts   **53**

54

ASSESS

- Assess student understanding by checking solutions to the Independent Practice activities.

- Review the two basic accounting rules that regulate increases and decreases of account balances.

  1. Account balances increase on the normal side of an account.

  2. Account balances decrease on the opposite side of the normal balance of an account.

Reteach

If students have difficulty understanding the debit and credit sides of accounts, all of the questions can be repeated, using the two sides of the classroom to represent an account rather than a T. Once these concepts are mastered, however, the connection to T accounts needs to be made by relating the T to the sides of the classroom.

Extend

Assign students to read the MULTICULTURAL AWARENESS feature on page 57.

Enrich

Assign the Accounting Tutorial software, Unit 1, to be completed at the computer.

CLOSURE

Use Audit Your Understanding questions.

FYI

When drawing T accounts, stack the accounts instead of writing them horizontally. This will make it easier to recognize debits and credits.

Accountants have special names for amounts recorded on the left and right sides of a T account. An amount recorded on the left side of a T account is called a **debit**. An amount recorded on the right side of a T account is called a **credit**. The T account is the basic device used to analyze the effect of transactions on accounts.

The normal balance side of an asset, liability, or capital account is based on the location of the account in the accounting equation, as shown in Illustration 4-3.

ILLUSTRATION 4-3

Relationship of asset, liability, and capital accounts to the accounting equation

Assets	=	Liabilities	+	Owner's Equity

Left side	Right side
ASSETS	LIABILITIES

Left side	Right side		Left side	Right side
Debit side	Credit side		Debit side	Credit side
NORMAL BALANCE				NORMAL BALANCE

OWNER'S CAPITAL ACCOUNT

Left side	Right side
Debit side	Credit side
	NORMAL BALANCE

Asset accounts have normal debit balances (left side) because assets are on the left side of the accounting equation. Liability accounts have normal credit balances (right side) because liabilities appear on the right side of the accounting equation. The owner's capital account has a normal credit balance (right side) because the capital account appears on the right side of the accounting equation.

The sides of a T account are also used to show increases and decreases in account balances, as shown in Illustration 4-4.

ILLUSTRATION 4-4

Increase and decrease sides of asset, liability, and capital accounts

Assets	=	Liabilities	+	Owner's Equity

Left side	Right side
ASSETS	LIABILITIES

Left side	Right side		Left side	Right side
Debit side	Credit side		Debit side	Credit side
Normal balance				Normal balance
INCREASE	DECREASE		DECREASE	INCREASE

OWNER'S CAPITAL

Left side	Right side
Debit side	Credit side
	Normal balance
DECREASE	INCREASE

TEACHING STRATEGIES: TEACHING TIP

Review the definition of account. A record summarizing all the information pertaining to a single item in the accounting equation is called an account.

Audit Your Understanding

1. Draw the accounting equation on a T account.

2. What are the two accounting rules that regulate increases and decreases of account balances?

Two basic accounting rules regulate increases and decreases of account balances. (1) Account balances increase on the normal balance side of an account. (2) Account balances decrease on the side opposite the normal balance side of an account.

Asset accounts have normal debit balances; therefore, asset accounts increase on the debit side and decrease on the credit side. Liability accounts have normal credit balances; therefore, liability accounts increase on the credit side and decrease on the debit side. The owner's capital account has a normal credit balance; therefore, the capital account increases on the credit side and decreases on the debit side.

ANALYZING HOW TRANSACTIONS AFFECT ACCOUNTS

Before a transaction is recorded in the records of a business, the information is analyzed to determine which accounts are changed and how. Each transaction changes the balances of at least two accounts. In addition, debits equal credits for each transaction, as shown in Illustration 4-5.

ILLUSTRATION 4-5

Debits equal credits for each transaction

Supplies		Cash	
Left side Debit side Normal balance Increase 1,577.00	Right side Credit side Decrease	Left side Debit side Normal balance Increase	Right side Credit side 1,577.00 Decrease

DEBITS --------------------------------- equal -------------------------------- CREDITS

The total debits, $1,577.00, equal the total credits, $1,577.00, for this transaction.

Four questions are used in analyzing a transaction into its debit and credit parts.

1 *What accounts are affected?* A list of accounts used by a business is called a **chart of accounts**. The account titles used by Rugcare are found on the chart of accounts on page 18.

2 *How is each account classified?* Rugcare's accounts are classified as assets, liabilities, owner's equity, revenue, and expenses.

3 *How is each account balance changed?* Is each account increased or decreased?

4 *How is each amount entered in the accounts?* The amount is either debited or credited to the account.

CHAPTER 4 Analyzing Transactions into Debit and Credit Parts   **55**

AUDIT YOUR UNDERSTANDING

The AUDIT YOUR UNDERSTANDING feature appears at the end of each section of the chapter. Explain to your students that the word *audit* means to check or verify. AUDIT YOUR UNDERSTANDING may be used to check student comprehension of the section just studied. The answers are provided in Appendix D in the back of the textbook.

1. Assets = Liabilities + Owner's Equity

2. (1) Account balances increase on the normal balance side of an account. (2) Account balances decrease on the side opposite the normal balance side of an account.

LESSON PLAN 4-2

Materials

- Student pages 55–65
- Demonstration Problem 4A, Analyzing Transactions into Debit and Credit Parts
- Transparencies: 4-1, Blank T Accounts; 4-2, Chapter Summary
- Software: Electronic Study Guide
- Demonstration Problem: Problem 4-A, Analyzing Transactions
- Assess: Problem Test 4, MicroExam 4

Objectives (Enabling Performance Tasks)

a. Define accounting terms related to analyzing transactions into debit and credit parts.

b. Identify accounting practices related to analyzing transactions into debit and credit parts.

c. Use T accounts to analyze transactions showing which accounts are debited or credited for each transaction.

d. Verify the equality of debits and credits for each transaction.

TEACHING STRATEGIES: Different Learning Styles

Auditory Learner. The auditory learner will best learn by hearing. When introducing the T account to an auditory learner, have the student say out loud that the "left side is the debit side of the account." Repeating this statement a few times will increase the chances of its being reinforced. Repeat the process with the statement the "right side is the credit side of the account."

- The T account was introduced earlier in this chapter. Explain that T accounts will be used to analyze the transactions that were presented earlier in Chapters 2 and 3 to determine which accounts are changed and how.

- Introduce new vocabulary: chart of accounts, contra account.

TEACH

Cover student pages 55–65 "Analyzing How Transactions Affect Accounts." Transactions must be analyzed into debit and credit parts before they can be recorded in the records of a business. All transactions are analyzed using the same four questions: (1) What accounts are affected? (2) How is each account classified? (3) How is each account balance changed? (4) How is each amount entered in the accounts? Establish the habit of using the four questions to analyze each transaction. Students need to remember that the words "Paid cash" always mean cash decreases and "Received cash" always means cash increases.

FYI

For a transaction in which cash is received, the cash account is always increased.

ILLUSTRATION 4-6

Received Cash from Owner as an Investment

August 1, 19--. Received cash from owner as an investment, $10,000.00.

The effect of this transaction in the accounting equation is shown in Illustration 4-6.

How debits and credits affect accounts when receiving cash from owner as an investment

Assets		=	Liabilities	+	Owner's Equity	
Left side Cash +10,000.00					Right side Ben Furman, Capital +10,000.00 (investment)	

Any Asset			Owner's Capital	
Left side Debit side Normal balance Increase	Right side Credit side Decrease		Left side Debit side Decrease	Right side Credit side Normal balance Increase

Cash			Ben Furman, Capital	
Left side Debit side Normal balance Increase 10,000.00	Right side Credit side Decrease		Left side Debit side Decrease	Right side Credit side Normal balance Increase 10,000.00

DEBITS ------------------------------- equal ----------------------------- CREDITS

Four questions are used to analyze this transaction.

1 *What accounts are affected?* Cash and Ben Furman, Capital.

2 *How is each account classified?* Cash is an asset account with a normal debit balance. Ben Furman, Capital is an owner's equity account with a normal credit balance.

3 *How is each account balance changed?* Cash is increased. Ben Furman, Capital is increased.

4 *How is each amount entered in the accounts?* The asset account, Cash, has a normal debit balance and is increased by a debit, $10,000.00. The owner's equity account, Ben Furman, Capital, has a normal credit balance and is increased by a credit, $10,000.00.

For this transaction, the total debits, $10,000.00, equal the total credits, $10,000.00.

Paid Cash for Supplies

August 3, 19--. Paid cash for supplies, $1,577.00.

The effect of this transaction is shown in Illustration 4-7.

TEACHING STRATEGIES: DIFFERENT LEARNING ABILITIES

Gifted Students. Gifted students need to be presented with additional challenges in order to maintain a high level of motivation. Assign gifted students to tutor other students on material in this chapter.

Assets		=	Liabilities	+	Owner's Equity
Cash −1,577.00	Supplies +1,577.00				

Any Asset

Left side	Right side
Debit side	Credit side
Normal balance	
Increase	Decrease

Supplies

Left side	Right side
Debit side	Credit side
Normal balance	
Increase 1,577.00	Decrease

Cash

Left side	Right side
Debit side	Credit side
Normal balance	
Increase	Decrease 1,577.00

DEBITS ------------- equal ------------ CREDITS

Four questions are used to analyze this transaction.

1 What accounts are affected?   Cash and Supplies.

2 How is each account classified?   Cash is an asset account with a normal debit balance. Supplies is an asset account with a normal debit balance.

3 How is each account balance changed?   Cash is decreased. Supplies is increased.

4 How is each amount entered in the accounts?   The asset account, Supplies, has a normal debit balance and is increased by a debit, $1,577.00. The asset account, Cash, has a normal debit balance and is decreased by a credit, $1,577.00.

For this transaction, the total debits, $1,577.00, equal the total credits, $1,577.00.

Paid Cash for Insurance

August 4, 19--. Paid cash for insurance, $1,200.00.

The effect of this transaction is shown in Illustration 4-8.
    Four questions are used to analyze this transaction.

1 What accounts are affected?   Cash and Prepaid Insurance.

2 How is each account classified?   Cash is an asset account with a normal debit balance. Prepaid Insurance is an asset account with a normal debit balance.

58

APPLY

While explaining the transactions, use Transparency 4-1, Blank T Account, to demonstrate each.

Guided Practice

Guide students through Drills 4-D1 and 4-D2. Students should have the forms from the working papers to complete as you guide them through the drills. For Drill 4-D1, for each account title, ask students which labels should be used for each side of each account's T account. All students should agree with the labels for an account before proceeding to the next account title. For Drill 4-D2, for each transaction, ask students to answer each of the analysis questions. All students should agree with the analysis for a transaction before proceeding to the next transaction.

Independent Practice

Assign Terms 4–5, Questions 6–17, Problems 4-1 and 4-2, Study Guide 4, and Mastery Problem 4-M.

ILLUSTRATION 4-8   How debits and credits affect accounts when paying cash for insurance

Assets		=	Liabilities	+	Owner's Equity

Cash	Prepaid Insurance
−1,200.00	+1,200.00

Any Asset

Left side	Right side
Debit side	Credit side
Normal balance	
Increase	Decrease

Prepaid Insurance

Left side	Right side
Debit side	Credit side
Normal balance	
Increase 1,200.00	Decrease

Cash

Left side	Right side
Debit side	Credit side
Normal balance	
Increase	Decrease 1,200.00

DEBITS ------------ equal ------------ CREDITS

3 *How is each account balance changed?* Cash is decreased. Prepaid Insurance is increased.

4 *How is each amount entered in the accounts?* The asset account, Prepaid Insurance, has a normal debit balance and is increased by a debit, $1,200.00. The asset account, Cash, has a normal debit balance and is decreased by a credit, $1,200.00.

For this transaction, the total debits, $1,200.00, equal the total credits, $1,200.00.

Bought Supplies on Account

August 7, 19--. Bought supplies on account from Butler Cleaning Supplies, $2,720.00.

The effect of this transaction is shown in Illustration 4-9.
    Four questions are used to analyze this transaction.

1 *What accounts are affected?* Supplies and Butler Cleaning Supplies.

2 *How is each account classified?* Supplies is an asset account with a normal debit balance. Butler Cleaning Supplies is a liability account with a normal credit balance.

3 *How is each account balance changed?* Supplies is increased. Butler Cleaning Supplies is increased.

4 *How is each amount entered in the accounts?* The asset account, Supplies, has a normal debit balance and is increased

---

👈👈 **FYI** 👈👈

Always use the four steps of analyzing transactions. This will make the analyzing process easier.

PART 2   Accounting for a Service Business Organized as a Proprietorship

---

TEACHING STRATEGIES: DIFFERENT LEARNING STYLES

Print Learner. The print learner prefers to see the data in print—preferably words. When introducing the T account, a print learner would prefer to study the illustration in the textbook which shows a T account, labelled with the words "DEBIT" and "CREDIT."

ILLUSTRATION 4-9

How debits and credits affect accounts when buying supplies on account

Assets		=	Liabilities	+	Owner's Equity

Supplies +2,720.00			Butler Cleaning Supplies +2,720.00	

Any Asset			Any Liability	
Left side Debit side Normal balance Increase	Right side Credit side Decrease		Left side Debit side Decrease	Right side Credit side Normal balance Increase

Supplies			Butler Cleaning Supplies	
Left side Debit side Normal balance Increase 2,720.00	Right side Credit side Decrease		Left side Debit side Decrease	Right side Credit side Normal balance Increase 2,720.00

DEBITS -------------------------------- equal -------------------------------- CREDITS

by a debit, $2,720.00. The liability account, Butler Cleaning Supplies, has a normal credit balance and is increased by a credit, $2,720.00.

For this transaction, the total debits, $2,720.00, equal the total credits, $2,720.00.

Paid Cash on Account

August 11, 19--. Paid cash on account to Butler Cleaning Supplies, $1,360.00.

The effect of this transaction is shown in Illustration 4-10.

ILLUSTRATION 4-10

How debits and credits affect accounts when paying cash on account

Assets		=	Liabilities	+	Owner's Equity

Cash -1,360.00			Butler Cleaning Supplies -1,360.00	

Any Asset			Any Liability	
Left side Debit side Normal balance Increase	Right side Credit side Decrease		Left side Debit side Decrease	Right side Credit side Normal balance Increase

Cash			Butler Cleaning Supplies	
Left side Debit side Normal balance Increase	Right side Credit side Decrease 1,360.00	Left side Debit side Decrease 1,360.00	Right side Credit side Normal balance Increase

CREDITS ----- equal ------ DEBITS

- Assess student understanding by checking solutions to the Independent Practice activities.
- Review the four questions to analyze transactions.
  1. What accounts are affected?
  2. How is each account classified?
  3. How is each account balance changed?
  4. How is each amount entered in the accounts?
- Review "Summary of Analyzing Transactions Into Debit and Credit Parts." Use Transparency 4-2, Chapter Summary.

Reteach

- Use Demonstration Problem 4A. This problem can be done on the overhead with the students completing the problem at their desks.
- Assign Recycling Problem 4R-1.

Extend

Assign Cases for Critical Thinking 1 and 2 and Challenge Problem 4-C (the challenge is that the students must reconstruct transactions from completed T accounts).

Enrich

- Assign the Electronic Study Guide Chapter 4 to complete the study guide from the working papers at the computer.
- Assign the PERSONAL VISIONS IN BUSINESS feature on page 60. Discuss the feature.

TEACHING STRATEGIES: DIFFERENT LEARNING STYLES

Tactile Learner. Tactile learners need to handle or touch materials to learn concepts. Using play money, have the student touch the right side of the desk and place an amount of money on it to reinforce an amount in the right side or credit side of an account. Repeat the process for the left/debit side.

ASSESS

- Administer Problem Test Chapter 4.
- Administer a MicroExam Test for Chapter 4.

Four questions are used to analyze this transaction.

1 *What accounts are affected?* Cash and Butler Cleaning Supplies.

2 *How is each account classified?* Cash is an asset account with a normal debit balance. Butler Cleaning Supplies is a liability account with a normal credit balance.

3 *How is each account balance changed?* Cash is decreased. Butler Cleaning Supplies is decreased.

4 *How is each amount entered in the accounts?* The liability account, Butler Cleaning Supplies, has a normal credit balance and is decreased by a debit, $1,360.00. The asset account, Cash, has a normal debit balance and is decreased by a credit, $1,360.00.

For this transaction, the total debits, $1,360.00, equal the total credits, $1,360.00.

Received Cash from Sales

Revenue increases the owner's capital. The increases from revenue could be recorded directly in the owner's capital account. However, to avoid a capital account with a large number of entries and to

FYI

The Small Business Administration (SBA) offers two major types of loans to small businesses. One type of loan is made by private lending institutions. Another type of loan is made directly by the SBA.

■ Joe Arriola ■

AVANTI PRESS, MIAMI, FLORIDA

Cuban-born Joe Arriola is the chairperson and chief executive officer of Avanti Press in Miami, Florida. Avanti Press prints high-quality catalogs and brochures. Clients include Walt Disney Company, Avon, Royal Caribbean Cruise Line, J.C. Penney, and many others. Avanti has sales of over $65 million a year. Winning the Minority Supplier of the Year Award has also attracted national attention and resulted in new business for the firm.

When he was 25 years old Arriola joined his father's printing business, which he began to expand when his father retired. A high school friend, Gene Martinez, helped in the expansion and is now president of the firm. Together, the two friends expanded the firm from 12 employees to over 425. In the process, the small offset printing company expanded into a full-service business offering different kinds of printing, design, photography, copy writing, and graphics. New areas for the

business are telemarketing and fulfillment services for their customers.

Arriola admits that when he and Martinez began the expansion they thought they knew a lot more than they really did about how to run a business. However, with hard work and some luck they prospered. Arriola says, "Back then we worked a lot of twenty-hour days. Now that we've been very successful, we've cut back to 16-hour workdays."

Arriola also maintains that the two best courses he has ever taken were the two years of accounting courses he took in high school in Miami. The accounting courses gave him the background to be able to read and understand financial statements and to communicate with bankers and financial institutions in the language of business, accounting.

Looking back on the early days of his business, Arriola said that the biggest surprise was that he thought "you open your doors, work hard, sell a lot, and make a lot of money. But it's not as easy as that. You have to plan for cash flows so that you can pay your accounts payable, and so many other things that you never thought of."

Personal Visions in Business

TEACHING STRATEGIES: DIFFERENT LEARNING STYLES

Visual Learner. The visual learner needs to "see" the concept. One way for the learner to "see" the concept is mental visualization. When introducing the T account, have the student (with eyes closed) picture a T account. The student should be able to see both sides of the account. Next, the student should visualize the word "DEBIT" on the left side of the account. Finally, the student should visualize the word "CREDIT" on the right side of the account. Once this concept takes on a visual form, the student will be able to access it when needed.

summarize revenue information separately from the other records, Rugcare uses a separate revenue account.

August 12, 19--. Received cash from sales, $525.00.

The effect of this transaction is shown in Illustration 4-11.

ILLUSTRATION 4-11 How debits and credits affect accounts when receiving cash from sales

Assets	=	Liabilities	+	Owner's Equity
Cash +525.00				Owner's Capital +525.00 (revenue)

Owner's Capital

Left side Debit side	Right side Credit side
	Normal balance
Decrease	Increase

Any Revenue Account

Left side Debit side	Right side Credit side
	Normal balance
Decrease	Increase

Cash

Left side Debit side	Right side Credit side
Normal balance	
Increase 525.00	Decrease

Sales

Left side Debit side	Right side Credit side
	Normal balance
Decrease	Increase 525.00

DEBITS ----------------------------- equal ----------------------------- CREDITS

The owner's capital account has a normal credit balance. A revenue account shows increases in capital. Therefore, a revenue account also has a normal credit balance. Revenue accounts increase on the credit side and decrease on the debit side. Rugcare's revenue account is titled Sales.

Four questions are used to analyze this revenue transaction.

1 *What accounts are affected?* Cash and Sales.

2 *How is each account classified?* Cash is an asset account with a normal debit balance. Sales is a revenue account with a normal credit balance.

3 *How is each account balance changed?* Cash is increased. Sales is increased.

4 *How is each amount entered in the accounts?* The asset account, Cash, has a normal debit balance and is increased by a debit, $525.00. The revenue account, Sales, has a normal credit balance and is increased by a credit, $525.00.

For this transaction, the total debits, $525.00, equal the total credits, $525.00.

FYI

Do not confuse the word debit with increase or decrease. Debit only means the left side of an account.

Paid Cash for an Expense

Expenses decrease the owner's capital. Expenses could be recorded directly in the owner's capital account. However, to avoid a capital account with a large number of entries and to summarize expense information separately from the other records, Rugcare uses separate expense accounts.

The titles of Rugcare's expense accounts are shown on the chart of accounts, page 18. The expense account, Utilities Expense, is used to record all payments of utility bills. These include payments made for electricity, telephone, gas, water, and sanitation.

August 12, 19--. Paid cash for rent, $250.00.

The effect of this transaction is shown in Illustration 4-12.

ILLUSTRATION 4-12   How debits and credits affect accounts when paying cash for an expense

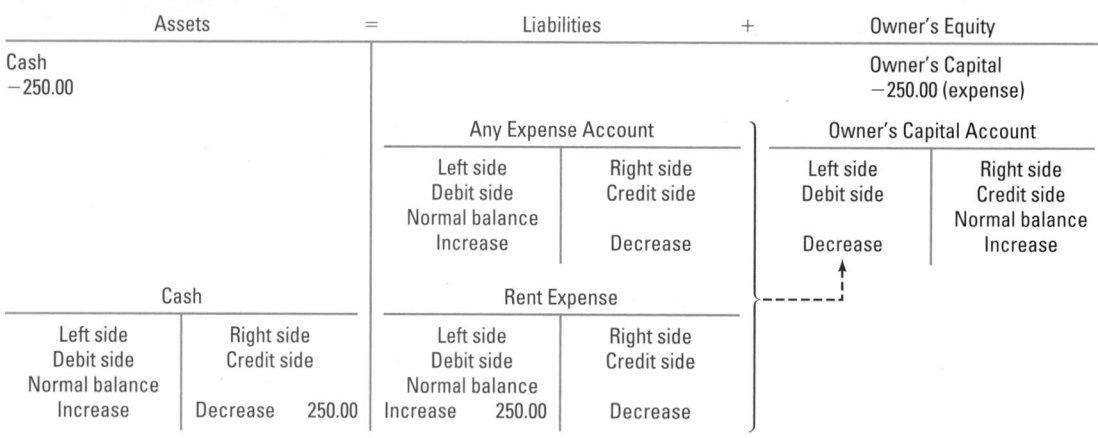

The owner's capital account has a normal credit balance. Decreases in the owner's capital account are shown as debits. An expense account shows decreases in owner's equity. Therefore, an expense account has a normal debit balance. An expense account increases on the debit side and decreases on the credit side.

Four questions are used to analyze this expense transaction.

1 *What accounts are affected?*   Cash and Rent Expense.

2 *How is each account classified?*   Cash is an asset account with a normal debit balance. Rent Expense is an expense account with a normal debit balance.

3 *How is each account balance changed?*   Cash is decreased. Rent Expense is increased.

4 *How is each amount entered in the accounts?* The expense account, Rent Expense, has a normal debit balance and is increased by a debit, $250.00. The asset account, Cash, has a normal debit balance and is decreased by a credit, $250.00.

For this transaction, the total debits, $250.00, equal the total credits, $250.00.

Paid Cash to Owner for Personal Use

Assets taken out of a business for the personal use of the owner are known as withdrawals. Withdrawals are considered to be part of the owner's equity taken out of a business. Therefore, withdrawals decrease the owner's equity. Withdrawals could be recorded as decreases directly in the owner's capital account. However, common accounting practice is to record withdrawals in a separate account to provide a separate record of the withdrawals for each fiscal period. In this way, the owner knows how much has been withdrawn from the business each fiscal period.

An account that reduces a related account on a financial statement is called a **contra account.** The drawing account is a contra capital account because the account shows decreases in capital.

August 12, 19--. Paid cash to owner for personal use, $100.00.

The effect of this transaction is shown in Illustration 4-13.

ILLUSTRATION 4-13	How debits and credits affect accounts when paying cash to owner for personal use

Assets	=	Liabilities	+	Owner's Equity

Cash
−100.00

Owner's Capital
−100.00 (withdrawal)

A Contra Capital Account

Left side Debit side Normal balance Increase	Right side Credit side Decrease

Owner's Capital Account

Left side Debit side Decrease	Right side Credit side Normal balance Increase

Cash

Left side Debit side Normal balance Increase	Right side Credit side Decrease 100.00

Ben Furman, Drawing

Left side Debit side Normal balance Increase 100.00	Right side Credit side Decrease

The owner's capital account has a normal credit balance. Decreases in the owner's capital account are shown as debits. Because a drawing account shows decreases in capital, a drawing account has a normal debit balance. A drawing account increases on the debit side and decreases on the credit side.

CHAPTER 4 Analyzing Transactions into Debit and Credit Parts   **63**

..
AUDIT YOUR
UNDERSTANDING

1. (1) What accounts are affected?
(2) How is each account classified? (3) How is each account balance changed? (4) How is each
amount entered in the accounts?
2. Debit.
3. Credit.
4. Debit.
5. Credit.
6. Debit.

Audit Your Understanding

1. State the four questions to analyze a transaction.
2. Are asset accounts increased on the debit side or credit side?
3. Are liability accounts increased on the debit side or credit side?
4. Is the owner's drawing account increased on the debit side or credit side?
5. Are revenue accounts increased on the debit side or credit side?
6. Are expense accounts increased on the debit side or credit side?

Four questions are used to analyze this transaction.

1 *What accounts are affected?*   Cash and Ben Furman, Drawing.

2 *How is each account classified?*   Cash is an asset account with a normal debit balance. Ben Furman, Drawing is a contra capital account with a normal debit balance.

3 *How is each account balance changed?*   Cash is decreased. Ben Furman, Drawing is increased.

4 *How is each amount entered in the accounts?*   The contra capital account, Ben Furman, Drawing, has a normal debit balance and is increased by a debit, $100.00. The asset account, Cash, has a normal debit balance and is decreased by a credit, $100.00.

For this transaction, the total debits, $100.00, equal the total credits, $100.00.

SUMMARY OF ANALYZING TRANSACTIONS INTO DEBIT AND CREDIT PARTS

The total debits and total credits for a transaction must be equal, as shown in the following T accounts.

Supplies			Cash	
Debits	Credits		Debits	Credits
1,577.00				1,577.00

DEBITS -------------------- equal ------------------- CREDITS

Debits and credits affect account balances as shown in the following.

Assets	=	Liabilities	+	Owner's Equity
Equation's left side				Equation's right side

Asset Accounts		Liability Accounts		Owner's Capital Account	
Left side	Right side	Left side	Right side	Left side	Right side
Debit side	Credit side	Debit side	Credit side	Debit side	Credit side
Normal balance			Normal balance		Normal balance
Increases	Decreases	Decreases	Increases	Decreases	Increases

Owner's Drawing Account	
Left side	Right side
Debit side	Credit side
Normal balance	
Increases	Decreases

Expense Accounts		Sales	
Left side	Right side	Left side	Right side
Debit side	Credit side	Debit side	Credit side
Normal balance			Normal balance
Increases	Decreases	Decreases	Increases

TEACHING STRATEGIES:
TEACHING TIP

It is important that transactions are always analyzed using T accounts. Students who establish the habit of analyzing transactions will have fewer problems understanding journalizing in future chapters. If working with the entire class, put the T accounts on the board and fill them in as students analyze a transaction. If working with an individual student, have that student put T accounts on a piece of paper. Avoid placing T accounts side by side on the board. Place T accounts one below another. With this stacked arrangement students can more easily check the analysis to determine if debits equal credits for the transaction.

TEACHING STRATEGIES: COOPERATIVE LEARNING

Divide students into teams according to rows in the classroom. Each team should appoint a spokesperson. Give each team a list of transactions. The team must work together to analyze the transactions and draw T accounts. The team that finishes with the best time and the most accurate solutions is the winner.

A summary analysis of transactions is shown in Illustration 4-14.

SUMMARY ILLUSTRATION 4-14
Summary analysis of transactions into debit and credit parts

Transaction	Accounts Affected	Account Classification	How is Account Affected?		Entered in Account as a	
			Increase	Decrease	Debit	Credit
Received cash from owner as an investment	Cash	Asset	X		X	
	Ben Furman, Capital	Owner's Equity	X			X
Paid cash for supplies	Supplies	Asset	X		X	
	Cash	Asset		X		X
Paid cash for insurance	Prepaid Insurance	Asset	X		X	
	Cash	Asset		X		X
Bought supplies on account	Supplies	Asset	X		X	
	Butler Cleaning Supplies	Liability	X			X
Paid cash on account	Butler Cleaning Supplies	Liability		X	X	
	Cash	Asset		X		X
Received cash from sales	Cash	Asset	X		X	
	Sales	Revenue	X			X
Paid cash for rent	Rent Expense	Expense	X		X	
	Cash	Asset		X		X
Paid cash to owner for personal use	Ben Furman, Drawing	Contra Capital	X		X	
	Cash	Asset		X		X

TEACHING STRATEGIES: APPLYING VISUALS

Direct students to Summary Illustration 4-14 and review how debits and credits affect account balances.

TEACHING STRATEGIES: TEACHING TIP

At this stage in their learning, students need much practice in classifying accounts, recognizing the balance side of each account, and recognizing the increase and decrease side of each account. Drills that require quick responses from students should supplement end-of-chapter drills.

a. Prepare flash cards with one account title to a card. On the back of each card, for your reference, place information related to that account: the account classification, the normal balance side, increase side, and decrease side.

b. Use about five minutes at the beginning of a class period to drill students on quickly responding to any of the accounts' characteristics. For example, go through all the cards and ask the students to respond by saying the account classification for each card. Then go through the cards again asking for the normal balance side, and so on.

APPLIED SKILLS: WORD PROCESSING

If you wish to integrate word processing into your accounting course, you may direct students to answer the end-of-chapter Accounting Terms, Questions for Individual Study, and Cases for Critical Thinking using their word processing software.

ACCOUNTING TERMS

1. **T account:** An accounting device used to analyze transactions. (p. 53)

2. **debit:** An amount recorded on the left side of a T account. (p. 54)

3. **credit:** An amount recorded on the right side of a T account. (p. 54)

4. **chart of accounts:** A list of accounts used by a business. (p. 55)

5. **contra account:** An account that reduces a related account on a financial statement. (p. 63)

QUESTIONS FOR INDIVIDUAL STUDY

1. The T account. (p. 53)

2. The location of an account in the accounting equation. The normal balance side of an account is the same as the side of the equation on which the account appears. (p. 54)

3. Asset, debit; liability, credit; capital, credit. (p. 54)

4. (a) Accounts increase on the normal balance side. (b) Accounts decrease on the side opposite the normal balance side. (p. 55)

5. Asset accounts: Increase, debit; decrease, credit. Liability accounts, increase, credit; decrease, debit. Capital account, increase, credit; decrease, debit. (p. 55)

6. Total debits equal total credits. (p. 55)

7. Cash is increased with a debit; the owner's capital account is increased with a credit. (p. 56)

8. Supplies is increased with a debit; Cash is decreased with a credit. (pp. 56–57)

9. Prepaid Insurance is increased with a debit; Cash is decreased with a credit. (pp. 57–58)

10. Supplies is increased with a debit; the liability account is increased with a credit. (pp. 58–59)

11. The liability account is decreased with a debit; Cash is decreased with a credit. (pp. 59–60)

12. The right or credit side. (p. 61)

13. Cash is increased with a debit; Sales is increased with a credit. (pp. 60–61)

14. The left or debit side. (p. 62)

ACCOUNTING TERMS EPT(a)

What is the meaning of each of the following?

1. **T account**
2. **debit**
3. **credit**
4. **chart of accounts**
5. **contra account**

QUESTIONS FOR INDIVIDUAL STUDY EPT(b)

1. What basic accounting device is used to help analyze transactions?

2. What determines which side of a T account will be the normal balance side?

3. What is the normal balance side of an asset account? Of a liability account? Of a capital account?

4. What two basic accounting rules regulate the increases and decreases of an account?

5. On which sides of a T account are increases and decreases recorded for asset accounts? For liability accounts? For the capital account?

6. What is the relationship between total debits and total credits in accounting records?

7. What accounts are affected, and how, when cash is received from an owner as an investment?

8. What accounts are affected, and how, when cash is paid for supplies?

9. What accounts are affected, and how, when cash is paid for insurance?

10. What accounts are affected, and how, when supplies are bought on account?

11. What accounts are affected, and how, when cash is paid on account?

12. What is the normal balance side of a revenue account?

13. What accounts are affected, and how, when cash is received from sales?

14. What is the normal balance side of an expense account?

15. What accounts are affected, and how, when cash is paid for rent?

16. What is the normal balance side of a drawing account?

17. What accounts are affected, and how, when cash is paid to an owner for personal use?

CASES FOR CRITICAL THINKING EPT(b)

CASE 1 Sharon Morris records *all* cash receipts as revenue and *all* cash payments as expenses. Is Miss Morris recording her cash receipts and cash payments correctly? Explain your answer.

CASE 2 Thomas Bueler records all investments, revenue, expenses, and withdrawals in his capital account. At the end of each month, Mr. Bueler sorts the information to prepare a summary of what has caused the changes in his capital account balance. To help Mr. Bueler prepare this summary in the future, what changes would you suggest he make in his records?

DRILL 4-D1 Determining the normal balance, increase, and decrease sides for accounts

TUTORIAL

Jeff Dixon owns a service business called HouseClean. HouseClean uses the following accounts.

Cash
Supplies
Prepaid Insurance
Miller Supplies
Wayne Office Supplies
Jeff Dixon, Capital
Jeff Dixon, Drawing

Sales
Advertising Expense
Miscellaneous Expense
Rent Expense
Repair Expense
Utilities Expense

INSTRUCTIONS:

1. Prepare a T account for each account. Label the debit and credit sides of each account. The T account for Cash is given as an example.
2. For each account, label the side of the T account that is used for each of the following. The T account for Cash is given as an example.
   a. Normal balance
   b. Increase side
   c. Decrease side

Cash	
Debit Side	Credit Side

Cash	
Debit Side Normal balance Increase	Credit Side Decrease

DRILL 4-D2 Analyzing how transactions affect accounts

Use a form similar to the following. Transaction 1 is given as an example.

1	2	3	4	5	6	7	8	9
Trans. No.	Accounts Affected	Account Classification	Account's Normal Balance		How is Account Affected?		Entered in Account as a	
			Debit	Credit	(+)	(−)	Debit	Credit
1.	Cash	Asset	√		√		√	
	Jeff Dixon, Capital	Owner's Equity		√	√			√

Transactions
1. Received cash from owner as an investment.
2. Paid cash for supplies.
3. Paid cash for insurance.
4. Bought supplies on account from Miller Supplies.
5. Received cash from sales.
6. Paid cash on account to Miller Supplies.
7. Paid cash for rent.
8. Paid cash for repairs.
9. Paid cash for miscellaneous expense.
10. Paid cash for telephone bill (utilities expense).
11. Paid cash to owner for personal use.

15. Rent Expense is increased with a debit; Cash is decreased with a credit. (p. 62)
16. The left or debit side. (p. 63)
17. The owner's drawing account is increased with a debit; Cash is decreased by a credit. (p. 63)

CASES FOR CRITICAL THINKING

Case 1 No, she is not recording the receipts and payments correctly. Some cash received could be from owner's investments, which is not revenue. Cash payments can be for transactions that do not affect expenses: (a) paying cash to owner for personal use, (b) paying cash for supplies, (c) paying cash for insurance, and (d) paying cash on account.

Case 2 Mr. Bueler should use separate accounts for capital, revenue, expenses, and withdrawals. At the end of a month, the information will already be separated and summarized for him. In addition, his capital account will contain only summary information about changes in the account.

CHECK FIGURES

See Teacher's Edition of Working Papers for complete solutions to drills and problems.

Drill 4-D1 9 accounts have normal debit balances; the liability, owner's capital, and sales accounts have normal credit balances.

Drill 4-D2 Column 6 has 13 check marks; column 7 has 9 check marks. Cash is debited in Trans. No. 1 and 5; Cash is not affected in Trans. No. 4; Cash is credited in the rest.

CHECK FIGURES (cont'd)

Problem 4-1 Cash is affected in 11 transactions. Cash is debited only in Apr. 1, 7, and 14 transactions.

Problem 4-2 Cash has 6 debits (1, 7, 14, 21, 28, and 31) and 10 credits.

INSTRUCTIONS:

1. Use the account titles given in Drill 4-D1. In Column 2, write the accounts affected by each transaction.
2. For each account title, write the account classification in Column 3.
3. For each account title, place a check mark in either Column 4 or 5 to indicate the normal balance.
4. For each account title, place a check mark in either Column 6 or 7 to indicate if the account is increased (+) or decreased (−) by this transaction.
5. For each account title, place a check mark in either Column 8 or 9 to indicate if the account is changed by a debit or a credit.

APPLICATION PROBLEMS   EPT(c,d)

PROBLEM 4-1 Analyzing transactions into debit and credit parts

Dixie Conastar owns a business called Conastar Company. Conastar Company uses the following accounts.

Cash	Sales
Supplies	Advertising Expense
Prepaid Insurance	Miscellaneous Expense
Bales Office Supplies	Rent Expense
Dixie Conastar, Capital	Utilities Expense
Dixie Conastar, Drawing	

Transactions

Apr. 1. Received cash from owner as an investment, $5,000.00.
  2. Paid cash for supplies, $50.00.
  3. Paid cash for insurance, $75.00.
  6. Bought supplies on account from Bales Office Supplies, $100.00.
  7. Received cash from sales, $400.00.
  8. Paid cash for water bill (utilities expense), $25.00.
  9. Paid cash for advertising, $40.00.
  13. Paid cash on account to Bales Office Supplies, $50.00.
  14. Received cash from sales, $400.00.
  15. Paid cash for miscellaneous expense, $5.00.
  16. Paid cash to owner for personal use, $50.00.
  18. Paid cash for rent, $250.00.

INSTRUCTIONS:

April 1.

Cash	
5,000.00	

Dixie Conastar, Capital	
	5,000.00

1. Prepare two T accounts for each transaction. On each T account, write the account title of one of the accounts affected by the transaction.
2. Write the debit or credit amount in each T account to show how the transaction affected that account. T accounts for the first transaction are given as an example.

PROBLEM 4-2 Analyzing transactions into debit and credit parts

Buelah VanBorne owns a business called VanBorne Services. VanBorne Services uses the following accounts.

Cash	Sales
Supplies	Advertising Expense
Prepaid Insurance	Miscellaneous Expense
Fortune Supplies	Rent Expense
Herdle Office Supplies	Repair Expense
Buelah VanBorne, Capital	Utilities Expense
Buelah VanBorne, Drawing	

Transactions

May 1. Received cash from owner as an investment, $2,000.00.
4. Bought supplies on account from Herdle Office Supplies, $500.00.
6. Paid cash for rent, $500.00.
7. Received cash from sales, $400.00.
11. Paid cash on account to Herdle Office Supplies, $250.00.
13. Paid cash for repairs, $80.00.
14. Received cash from sales, $500.00.
15. Paid cash for supplies, $600.00.
19. Paid cash for insurance, $240.00.
20. Bought supplies on account from Fortune Supplies, $50.00.
21. Paid cash for supplies, $500.00.
21. Received cash from sales, $750.00.
25. Paid cash for telephone bill (utilities expense), $90.00.
26. Paid cash for advertising, $130.00.
28. Paid cash for miscellaneous expense, $15.00.
28. Received cash from sales, $520.00.
29. Paid cash to owner for personal use, $600.00.
31. Received cash from sales, $400.00.

INSTRUCTIONS:

1. Prepare a T account for each account.
2. Analyze each transaction into its debit and credit parts. Write the debit and credit amounts in the proper T accounts to show how each transaction changes account balances. Write the date of the transaction in parentheses before each amount. The amounts for Transaction 1 are given in T accounts as an example.

Cash	
(1) 2,000.00	

Buelah VanBorne, Capital	
	(1) 2,000.00

CHECK FIGURES *(cont'd)*

Mastery Problem 4-M Cash has 7 debits (1, 4, 11, 11, 18, 25, and 30) and 9 credits.

Challenge Problem 4-C Transactions affect 13 asset accounts. Cash is debited in Trans. No. 1, 6, 8, and 9.

ENRICHMENT PROBLEMS   EPT(c,d)

MASTERY PROBLEM 4-M Analyzing transactions into debit and credit parts

James Lands owns a business called LandScape. LandScape uses the following accounts.

Cash	Sales
Supplies	Advertising Expense
Prepaid Insurance	Miscellaneous Expense
Derner Office Supplies	Rent Expense
Janitor Supplies	Repair Expense
James Lands, Capital	Utilities Expense
James Lands, Drawing	

Transactions

June 1. Received cash from owner as an investment, $3,000.00.
2. Paid cash for supplies, $60.00.
4. Paid cash for rent, $200.00.
4. Received cash from sales, $350.00.
5. Paid cash for repairs, $10.00.
9. Bought supplies on account from Janitor Supplies, $500.00.
10. Paid cash for insurance, $100.00.
11. Received cash from owner as an investment, $900.00.
11. Received cash from sales, $300.00.
12. Bought supplies on account from Derner Office Supplies, $50.00.
15. Paid cash for miscellaneous expense, $5.00.
16. Paid cash on account to Janitor Supplies, $50.00.

18. Received cash from sales, $400.00.
22. Paid cash for electric bill (utilities expense), $35.00.
23. Paid cash for advertising, $30.00.
25. Received cash from sales, $220.00.
26. Paid cash to owner for personal use, $600.00.
30. Received cash from sales, $100.00.

INSTRUCTIONS:

1. Prepare a T account for each account.
2. Analyze each transaction into its debit and credit parts. Write the debit and credit amounts in the proper T accounts to show how each transaction changes account balances. Write the date of the transaction in parentheses before each amount.

CHALLENGE PROBLEM 4-C Analyzing transactions recorded in T accounts

Edward Burns owns a business for which the following T accounts show the current financial situation.

	Cash					Sales	
(1)	5,000.00	(2)	80.00			(6)	475.00
(6)	475.00	(4)	15.00			(8)	350.00
(8)	350.00	(5)	16.00			(9)	400.00
(9)	400.00	(7)	900.00				
		(10)	150.00				
		(11)	95.00				
		(12)	50.00				

	Supplies			Advertising Expense	
(3)	300.00		(5)	16.00	
(11)	95.00				

	Midwest Supplies				Miscellaneous Expense	
(10)	150.00	(3)	300.00	(4)	15.00	

	Edward Burns, Capital				Rent Expense	
		(1)	5,000.00	(7)	900.00	

	Edward Burns, Drawing			Utilities Expense	
(2)	80.00		(12)	50.00	

INSTRUCTIONS:

1. Use a form similar to the following.

1	2	3	4	5	6
Trans. No.	Accounts Affected	Account Classification	Entered in Account as a		Description of Transaction
			Debit	Credit	
1.	Cash Edward Burns, Capital	Asset Owner's Equity	√	√	Received cash from owner as an investment

2. Analyze each numbered transaction in the T accounts. Write the titles of accounts affected in Column 2. For each account, write the classification of the account in Column 3.

3. For each account, place a check mark in either Column 4 or 5 to indicate if the account is affected by a debit or a credit.

4. For each transaction, write a brief statement in Column 6 describing the transaction. Information for Transaction 1 is given as an example.

Chapter 5 introduces source documents for the first time. This chapter also describes the multicolumn journal and the journalizing process. All transactions that were introduced in Chapters 2 and 3 are used

GUIDE TO ACHIEVING LEARNING OBJECTIVES

Enabling Performance Tasks	TEACH Lesson Plans	APPLY Drills for Understanding	APPLY Application Problems	EXTEND/ENRICH Mastery Problems	EXTEND/ENRICH Challenge Problems	EXTEND/ENRICH Cases for Critical Thinking	EXTEND/ENRICH Recycling Problems	EXTEND/ENRICH Reinforcement Activity	
a. Define accounting terms related to journalizing transactions.	5-1, 5-3								
b. Identify accounting concepts and practices related to journalizing transactions.	5-1, 5-2, 5-3	5-D1, 5-D2				Cases 1, 2			
c. Record selected transactions in a five-column journal.	5-2		5-1, 5-2	5-M	5-C		5-R	1A	
d. Prove equality of debits and credits in a five-column journal.	5-3		5-1, 5-2	5-M	5-C		5-R	1A	
e. Prove cash.	5-3		5-1, 5-2	5-M	5-C		5-R	1A	
f. Forward totals from one journal page to another.	5-3		5-2	5-M	5-C		5-R	1A	
g. Rule a five-column journal.	5-3		5-1, 5-2	5-M	5-C		5-R	1A	

ENRICHMENT

SPECIAL FEATURES

Multicultural Awareness, page 81

Global Perspective, page 88

TECHNOLOGY CONNECTION

Application Program Disk Problems 5-M, 5-C

Electronic Study Guide

NEW, REVIEW, AND EXTENSION

ACTIVITIES/CONCEPTS/TRANSACTIONS	NEW	REVIEW/ EXTENSION
Analyzing transactions into debit and credit parts		✓
Using a 5-column multicolumn journal	✓	
Using a journal with special amount columns	✓	
Received cash from owner as an investment		✓
Paid cash for supplies		✓
Paid cash for insurance		✓
Bought supplies on account		✓
Paid cash on account		✓
Received cash from sales		✓
Paid cash for an expense		✓
Paid cash to owner for personal use		✓
Starting a new journal page/forwarding journal totals	✓	
Proving and ruling a journal	✓	
Proving cash	✓	
Generally accepted accounting practices	✓	

for demonstration purposes throughout the chapter. The repetition of using these same transactions enables students to see the continuity of the analyzation process. The accounting concept, *Objective Evidence*, is presented and described in full for the first time in Chapter 5.

| | INFORMAL ASSESSMENT | | FORMAL ASSESSMENT | | | | |
	Study Guide	Audit Your Understanding	Chapter MicroExam	Chapter Problem Test	Unit Problem Test	Unit Objective Test	Portfolio
Unit A			✓			✓	
Units B, D		✓	✓			✓	
Unit C				✓	✓		✓
				✓	✓		✓
				✓	✓		✓
				✓	✓		✓
				✓	✓		✓

TEACHING MATERIALS

Teacher's Wraparound Edition of the Text

Teacher's Resource Guide

Teacher's Edition of Working Papers

Teacher's Edition of Demonstration/Recycling Problems

Teaching Transparencies

Global Perspective Work Sheets

Applied Math Work Sheets

MicroExam

APPLIED MATHEMATICS

APPLIED MATH/ACCOUNTING SKILL	APPLICATION
Proving a journal page and proving debits and credits	Prob. 5-1
Proving cash	Prob. 5-1

5

Journalizing Transactions

ENABLING PERFORMANCE TASKS

After studying Chapter 5, you will be able to:

a Define accounting terms related to journalizing transactions.

b Identify accounting concepts and practices related to journalizing transactions.

c Record selected transactions in a five-column journal.

d Prove equality of debits and credits in a five-column journal.

e Prove cash.

f Forward totals from one journal page to another.

g Rule a five-column journal.

TERMS PREVIEW

journal • journalizing • special amount column • general amount column • entry • double-entry accounting • source document • check • receipt • memorandum • proving cash

As described in Chapter 4, transactions are analyzed into debit and credit parts before information is recorded. A form for recording transactions in chronological order is called a **journal**. Recording transactions in a journal is called **journalizing.**

Transactions could be recorded in the accounting equation. However, generally accepted accounting practice is to make a more permanent record by recording transactions in a journal.

A JOURNAL

Each business uses the kind of journal that best fits the needs of that business. The nature of a business and the number of transactions to be recorded determine the kind of journal to be used.

Journal Form

Rugcare uses a journal that has five amount columns, as shown in Illustration 5-1.

ILLUSTRATION 5-1   Five-column journal

The five amount columns in Rugcare's journal are General Debit, General Credit, Sales Credit, Cash Debit, and Cash Credit. A journal amount column headed with an account title is called a **special amount column.** Special amount columns are used for frequently occurring transactions. For example, most of Rugcare's transactions involve receipt or payment of cash. A large number of the transactions involve receipt of cash from sales. Therefore, Rugcare uses three special amount columns in its journal: Sales Credit, Cash Debit, and Cash Credit.

Using special amount columns eliminates writing an account title in the Account Title column. Therefore, recording transactions in a journal with special amount columns saves time.

A journal amount column that is not headed with an account title is called a **general amount column.** In Rugcare's journal, the General Debit and General Credit columns are general amount columns.

Accuracy

Information recorded in a journal includes the debit and credit parts of each transaction recorded in one place. The information

---

LESSON PLAN 5-1

Materials

- Student pages 73–76
- Transparency A, Blank Journal

Objectives (Enabling Performance Tasks)

a. Define accounting terms related to journalizing transactions.
b. Identify accounting concepts and practices related to journalizing transactions.

FOCUS

- In Chapter 4, transactions were analyzed into debit and credit parts. Explain that after transactions are analyzed, they are recorded in a journal. Explain that the information needed to record entries in the journal is obtained from source documents.
- Introduce new vocabulary: journal, journalizing, special amount column, general amount column, entry, double-entry accounting, source document, check, receipt, memorandum.

TEACHING STRATEGIES: TEACHING TIP

Journals are considered permanent accounting records of a business. Usually a business requires that permanent records be kept in ink. However, at this stage of the learning process, doing the work in ink inhibits students. Students should not be required to do the work in ink for at least Parts 2, 3, and 4 of this textbook. The use of pencil removes some of the tension related to making mistakes in ink that cannot be easily corrected.

Cover student pages 73–76 "A Journal" and "Source Documents." This lesson introduces the five-column journal which will be used to record all transactions in the first accounting cycle. Important concepts related to the use of a journal are accuracy, chronological order, and double-entry accounting. Emphasize that all transactions are recorded by date. Students will also be introduced to common source documents such as checks, calculator tapes, receipts, and memorandums. Explain that the information needed to record entries in the journal is obtained from these source documents.

APPLY

Use Transparency A, blank journal, to point out and explain the amount columns of the journal. Point out the document number column will be used when transactions are recorded.

Guided Practice

Direct students' attention to Illustration 5-1, the five-column journal. Ask for student input on what might be recorded in each column. Give special emphasis to the difference between a general and a special amount column. Also direct student attention to the source documents, Illustrations 5-2 through 5-5. Solicit student comments on what kinds of information would be important to include on these documents.

Independent Practice

Assign Terms 1–10 and Questions 1–6.

FYI

Of all service businesses in the United States, only 4 percent employ 50 or more people and 80 percent have fewer than 10 employees.

FYI

The Small Business Administration (SBA) has programs that offer free management and accounting advice to small business owners. The SBA sponsors various workshops and publishes a variety of booklets for small business owners.

can be verified by comparing the data in the journal with the source document data to assure that all information is correct.

Chronological Record

Transactions are recorded in a journal by date in the order in which the transactions occur. All the information about each transaction is recorded in one place making the information for a specific transaction easy to locate.

Double-Entry Accounting

Information for each transaction recorded in a journal is called an **entry.** The recording of debit and credit parts of a transaction is called **double-entry accounting.** In double-entry accounting, each transaction affects at least two accounts. Both the debit part and the credit part are recorded for each transaction. This procedure reflects the dual effect of each transaction on the business' records. For example, cash paid for advertising causes (1) a decrease in cash and (2) an increase in expenses. Double-entry accounting assures that debits equal credits.

SOURCE DOCUMENTS

A business paper from which information is obtained for a journal entry is called a **source document.** Each transaction is described by a source document that proves that the transaction did occur. For example, Rugcare prepares a check stub for each cash payment made. The check stub describes information about the cash payment transaction for which the check is prepared. The accounting concept, *Objective Evidence,* is applied when a source document is prepared for each transaction. *(CONCEPT: Objective Evidence)*

A transaction should be journalized only if it actually occurs. The amounts recorded must be accurate and true. Nearly all transactions result in the preparation of a source document. One way to verify the accuracy of a specific journal entry is to compare the entry with the source document. Rugcare uses four source documents: checks, calculator tapes, receipts, and memorandums.

Checks

A business form ordering a bank to pay cash from a bank account is called a **check.** The source document for cash payments is a check. Rugcare makes all cash payments by check. The checks are prenumbered to help Rugcare account for all checks. Rugcare's record of information on a check is the check stub prepared at the same time as the check. A check and check stub prepared by Rugcare are shown in Illustration 5-2.

TEACHING STRATEGIES: DIFFERENT LEARNING ABILITIES

At-Risk Students. Some students need concrete examples before they understand a concept like journalizing a source document. Pass sample source documents around the room and let students see what a typical document looks like.

ILLUSTRATION 5-2   Check and check stub

NO. 1	$ 1,577.00		
Date _August 3_	19 __		
To _Janitorial Supplies Co._			
For _Supplies_			
BAL. BRO'T. FOR'D.		0	00
AMT. DEPOSITED ... 8 / 1 / -- Date	10,000	00	
SUBTOTAL		10,000	00
OTHER:			
SUBTOTAL		10,000	00
AMT. THIS CHECK		1,577	00
BAL. CAR'D. FOR'D.		8,423	00

RugCare 623 Walnut Street
Billings, MT 59101-1946

NO. 1   93-109
           929

August 3,   19 __

PAY TO THE
ORDER OF _Janitorial Supplies Co._ $ 1,577.00

One thousand five hundred seventy-seven and ⁿᵒ⁄₁₀₀   DOLLARS
For Classroom Use Only

Peoples national bank
Billings, MT 59101-2320

FOR _Supplies_   _Ben Furman_

⑆092901094⑆ 43⑈452119⑈

Procedures for preparing checks and check stubs are described in Chapter 7.

Calculator Tapes

Rugcare collects cash at the time services are rendered to customers. At the end of each day, Rugcare uses a printing electronic calculator to total the amount of cash received from sales for that day. By totaling all the individual sales, a single source document is produced for the total sales of the day. Thus, time and space are saved by recording only one entry for all of a day's sales. The calculator tape is the source document for daily sales. *(CONCEPT: Objective Evidence)* A calculator tape used as a source document is shown in Illustration 5-3.

ILLUSTRATION 5-3   Calculator tape used as a source document

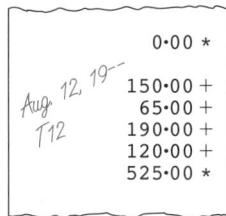

Aug. 12, 19--
T12

0·00	*
150·00	+
65·00	+
190·00	+
120·00	+
525·00	*

Rugcare dates and numbers each calculator tape. For example, in Illustration 5-3, the number, *T12*, indicates that the tape is for the twelfth day of the month.

Receipts

A business form giving written acknowledgement for cash received is called a **receipt**. When cash is received from sources other than sales, Rugcare prepares a receipt. The receipts are prenumbered to help account for all the receipts. A receipt is the source document

FYI

If you misspell words in your written communications, people may mistrust the quality of your accounting skills. Note that in the word receipt the "e" comes before the "i" and there is a silent "p" before the "t" at the end of the word.

for cash received from transactions other than sales. *(CONCEPT: Objective Evidence)* Rugcare's receipt is shown in Illustration 5-4.

ILLUSTRATION 5-4 Receipt used as a source document

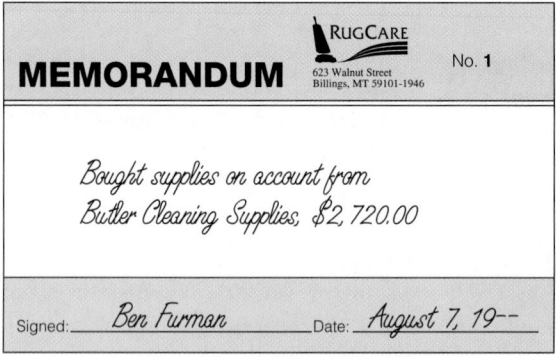

Audit Your Understanding

1. What are the five amount columns in Rugcare's journal?
2. In what order are transactions recorded in a journal?
3. List four types of source documents.
4. Why are source documents important?

Memorandums

A form on which a brief message is written describing a transaction is called a **memorandum.** When no other source document is prepared for a transaction, or when additional explanation is needed about a transaction, Rugcare prepares a memorandum. *(CONCEPT: Objective Evidence)* Rugcare's memorandums are prenumbered to help account for all the memorandums. A brief note is written on the memorandum to describe the transaction. The memorandum used by Rugcare is shown in Illustration 5-5.

ILLUSTRATION 5-5 Memorandum used as a source document

MEMORANDUM   **RugCare** 623 Walnut Street Billings, MT 59101-1946   No. 1

Bought supplies on account from Butler Cleaning Supplies, $2,720.00

Signed: *Ben Furman*   Date: *August 7, 19--*

APPLIED SKILLS: LANGUAGE ARTS

Paraphrasing, writing complete sentences, and identifying subjects. For additional practice in language arts skills, direct students to answer the Questions for Individual Study at the end of the chapter. Students should write the answers in their own words and in complete sentences. To further practice language arts skills, ask students to underline the subject(s) in each sentence of their answers.

RECORDING TRANSACTIONS IN A FIVE-COLUMN JOURNAL

Information for each transaction recorded in a journal is known as an entry. An entry consists of four parts: (1) date, (2) debit, (3) credit, and (4) source document. Before a transaction is recorded in a journal, the transaction is analyzed into its debit and credit parts.

Received Cash from Owner as an Investment

August 1, 19--. Received cash from owner as an investment, $10,000.00. Receipt No. 1.

The source document for this transaction is Receipt No. 1. *(CONCEPT: Objective Evidence)* The analysis of this transaction is shown in the T accounts.

    All T account analysis in Chapter 5 is described in detail in Chapter 4.

The asset account, Cash, is increased by a debit, $10,000.00. The owner's capital account, Ben Furman, Capital, is increased by a credit, $10,000.00. The journal entry for this transaction is shown in Illustration 5-6.

Cash	
10,000.00	

Ben Furman, Capital	
	10,000.00

ILLUSTRATION 5-6   Journal entry to record receiving cash from owner as an investment

	DATE		ACCOUNT TITLE	DOC. NO.	POST. REF.	GENERAL DEBIT	GENERAL CREDIT	SALES CREDIT	CASH DEBIT	CASH CREDIT	
1	19-- Aug.	1	Ben Furman, Capital	R1			10 000 00		10 000 00		1

1 Date. Write the date, *19--, Aug. 1,* in the Date column. This entry is the first one on this journal page. Therefore, the year and month are both written for this entry. Neither the year nor the month are written again on the same page.

2 Debit. The journal has a special amount column for debits to Cash. The title of the account is in the column heading. Therefore, the account title does not need to be written in the Account Title column. Write the debit amount, *$10,000.00,* in the Cash Debit column.

3 Credit. Write the title of the account credited, *Ben Furman, Capital,* in the Account Title column. There is no special amount column with the title of the account credited, Ben Furman, Capital, in its heading. Therefore, the credit amount is recorded in the General Credit column. Write the credit amount, *$10,000.00,* in the General Credit column.

FYI

If you draw T accounts for transactions, it will make journalizing easier.

CHAPTER 5   Journalizing Transactions   **77**

Cover student pages 77–83, "Recording Transactions in a Five-Column Journal." Review the definition of an entry and stress the four parts. Explain to the students that it is important to always draw T accounts for each transaction. Stacking the T accounts allows for easy identification of debits and credits.

Point out that if neither account affected by a transaction has a special column in the journal, both accounts must be written in the Account Title column. Another important point to convey is that a check mark in the Account Title Column means that each amount in the entry is recorded in a special column.

APPLY

As transactions are presented in the chapter, journalize each using Transparency A.

Guided Practice

Guide students through Drills 5-D1 and 5-D2. Students should have the forms from the working papers to complete as you guide them through the drills. For each transaction in Drill 5-D1, ask students which accounts are affected and how. All students should agree with the analysis before proceeding to the next transaction. For each transaction in Drill 5-D2, ask students which accounts are affected, the classification of each account, and how the accounts are affected. Students should record their answers in the working papers before proceeding to the next transaction. All students should agree with the analysis before proceeding to the next transaction.

Independent Practice

Assign Questions 7–15 and Problem 5-1, instruction 1, and Problem 5-2, instruction 1.

All amounts recorded in the General Debit or General Credit amount columns must have an account title written in the Account Title column.

4 *Source document.* Write the source document number, *R1*, in the Doc. No. column. The source document number, *R1*, indicates that this is Receipt No. 1.

The source document number is a cross reference from the journal to the source document. If more details are needed about this transaction, a person can refer to Receipt No. 1.

Paid Cash for Supplies

August 3, 19--. Paid cash for supplies, $1,577.00. Check No. 1.

The source document for this transaction is Check No. 1. *(CONCEPT: Objective Evidence)* The analysis of this transaction is shown in the T accounts.

The asset account, Supplies, is increased by a debit, $1,577.00. The asset account, Cash, is decreased by a credit, $1,577.00. The journal entry for this transaction is shown in Illustration 5-7.

ILLUSTRATION 5-7 Journal entry to record paying cash for supplies

	DATE	ACCOUNT TITLE	DOC. NO.	POST. REF.	GENERAL DEBIT	GENERAL CREDIT	SALES CREDIT	CASH DEBIT	CASH CREDIT	
2	3	Supplies	C1		1 5 7 7 00				1 5 7 7 00	2

JOURNAL   PAGE **1**

1 *Date.* Write the date, *3*, in the Date column. This is not the first entry on the journal page. Therefore, the year and month are not written for this entry.

2 *Debit.* Write the title of the account debited, *Supplies*, in the Account Title column. There is no special amount column with the title of the account debited, Supplies, in its heading. Therefore, the debit amount is recorded in the General Debit column. Write the debit amount, *$1,577.00*, in the General Debit column.

3 *Credit.* The journal has a special amount column for credits to Cash. The title of the account is in the column heading. Therefore, the account title does not need to be written in the Account Title column. Write the credit amount, *$1,577.00*, in the Cash Credit column.

4 *Source document.* Write the source document number, *C1*, in the Doc. No. column. The source document number, *C1*, indicates that this is Check No. 1.

78   PART 2   Accounting for a Service Business Organized as a Proprietorship

TEACHING STRATEGIES: TEACHING TIP

Read each transaction as presented in the chapter. Ask students to list the 4 parts of each entry. This routine will make it easier for the students to journalize transactions.

Paid Cash for Insurance

August 4, 19--. Paid cash for insurance, $1,200.00. Check No. 2.

Prepaid Insurance

| 1,200.00 | |

Cash

| | 1,200.00 |

The source document for this transaction is Check No. 2. *(CONCEPT: Objective Evidence)* The analysis of this transaction is shown in the T accounts.

The asset account, Prepaid Insurance, is increased by a debit, $1,200.00. The asset account, Cash, is decreased by a credit, $1,200.00. The journal entry for this transaction is shown in Illustration 5-8.

ILLUSTRATION 5-8 Journal entry to record paying cash for insurance

JOURNAL   PAGE 1

| | | | | | 1 | 2 | 3 | 4 | 5 | |
DATE	ACCOUNT TITLE	DOC. NO.	POST. REF.	GENERAL DEBIT	GENERAL CREDIT	SALES CREDIT	CASH DEBIT	CASH CREDIT	
4	Prepaid Insurance	C2		1 2 0 0 00				1 2 0 0 00	3

1 Date. Write the date, *4*, in the Date column.

2 Debit. Write the title of the account debited, *Prepaid Insurance*, in the Account Title column. There is no special amount column with the title of the account debited, Prepaid Insurance, in its heading. Therefore, the debit amount is recorded in the General Debit column. Write the debit amount, *$1,200.00*, in the General Debit column.

3 Credit. The journal has a special amount column for credits to Cash. The title of the account is in the column heading. Therefore, the account title does not need to be written in the Account Title column. Write the credit amount, *$1,200.00*, in the Cash Credit column.

4 Source document. Write the source document number, *C2*, in the Doc. No. column.

Bought Supplies on Account

August 7, 19--. Bought supplies on account from Butler Cleaning Supplies, $2,720.00. Memorandum No. 1.

Supplies

| 2,720.00 | |

Butler Cleaning Supplies

| | 2,720.00 |

Rugcare ordered these supplies by telephone. Rugcare wishes to record this transaction immediately. Therefore, a memorandum is prepared that shows supplies were received on account.

The source document for this transaction is Memorandum No. 1. *(CONCEPT: Objective Evidence)* The analysis of this transaction is shown in the T accounts.

The asset account, Supplies, is increased by a debit, $2,720.00. The liability account, Butler Cleaning Supplies, is increased by a credit, $2,720.00. The journal entry for this transaction is shown in Illustration 5-9.

CHAPTER 5 Journalizing Transactions **79**

ILLUSTRATION 5-9   Journal entry to record buying supplies on account

	DATE	ACCOUNT TITLE	DOC. NO.	POST. REF.	GENERAL		SALES CREDIT	CASH	
					DEBIT	CREDIT		DEBIT	CREDIT
4	7	Supplies	M1		2 7 2 0 00					4
5		Butler Cleaning Supplies				2 7 2 0 00				5

JOURNAL   PAGE *1*

1 Date. Write the date, 7, in the Date column.

2 Debit. The journal does not have a special amount column for either the debit to Supplies or credits to Butler Cleaning Supplies. Therefore, both account titles need to be written in the Account Title column. The debit and credit amounts are recorded in the General Debit and General Credit columns. Write the title of the account debited, *Supplies*, in the Account Title column. Write the debit amount, $2,720.00, in the General Debit column.

3 Credit. On the next line, write the title of the account credited, *Butler Cleaning Supplies*, in the Account Title column. Write the credit amount, $2,720.00, in the General Credit column on the same line as the account title.

This entry requires two lines in the journal because account titles for both the debit and credit amounts must be written in the Account Title column.

4 Source document. Write the source document number, *M1*, in the Doc. No. column on the first line of the entry.

Paid Cash on Account

August 11, 19--. Paid cash on account to Butler Cleaning Supplies, $1,360.00. Check No. 3.

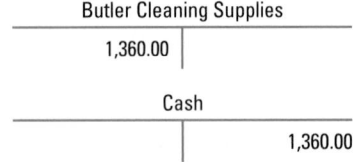

The source document for this transaction is Check No. 3. *(CONCEPT: Objective Evidence)* The analysis of this transaction is shown in the T accounts.

The liability account, Butler Cleaning Supplies, is decreased by a debit, $1,360.00. The asset account, Cash, is decreased by a credit, $1,360.00. The journal entry for this transaction is shown in Illustration 5-10.

ILLUSTRATION 5-10   Journal entry to record paying cash on account

JOURNAL   PAGE *1*

	DATE	ACCOUNT TITLE	DOC. NO.	POST. REF.	GENERAL		SALES CREDIT	CASH	
					DEBIT	CREDIT		DEBIT	CREDIT
6	11	Butler Cleaning Supplies	C3		1 3 6 0 00				1 3 6 0 00	6

TEACHING STRATEGIES: APPLYING VISUALS

Journalizing from source documents will prepare students for working simulations. Prepare a real source document for each transaction that is presented in the chapter. Show the source document, analyze the transaction on the board, then record the transaction on Transparency A.

MULTICULTURAL
AWARENESS

The MULTICULTURAL AWARENESS feature is intended to expose students to the concept that our society is composed of people from many different cultural backgrounds. These features show both past contributions of many cultures and benefits of a culturally diverse society. (1) Read the feature. (2) Discuss the specific information in the feature. (3) Clarify any terms or questions. (4) Do the following multicultural activity.

MULTICULTURAL AWARENESS

Debit/Credit

The terms "debit" and "credit" are often abbreviated as "dr." and "cr." These terms are derived from the Latin and Italian words "debere" and "credere." Ledger accounts with debit and credit sides became popular in the early seventeenth century throughout Europe. Sometimes the abbreviations for debit (dr.) and credit (cr.) were used as column headings for the ledger accounts.

1 Date. Write the date, *11*, in the Date column.

2 Debit. Write the title of the account debited, *Butler Cleaning Supplies*, in the Account Title column. There is no special amount column with the title of the account debited, *Butler Cleaning Supplies*, in its heading. Therefore, the debit amount is recorded in the General Debit column. Write the debit amount, *$1,360.00*, in the General Debit column.

3 Credit. The journal has a special amount column for credits to *Cash*. The title of the account is in the column heading. Therefore, the account title does not need to be written in the Account Title column. Write the credit amount, *$1,360.00*, in the Cash Credit column.

4 Source document. Write the source document number, *C3*, in the Doc. No. column.

Received Cash from Sales

August 12, 19--. Received cash from sales, $525.00. Tape No. 12.

The source document for this transaction is Calculator Tape No. 12. *(CONCEPT: Objective Evidence)* The analysis of this transaction is shown in the T accounts.

The asset account, *Cash*, is increased by a debit, $525.00. The revenue account, *Sales*, is increased by a credit, $525.00. The journal entry for this transaction is shown in Illustration 5-11.

Cash	
525.00	

Sales	
	525.00

ILLUSTRATION 5-11   Journal entry to record receiving cash from sales

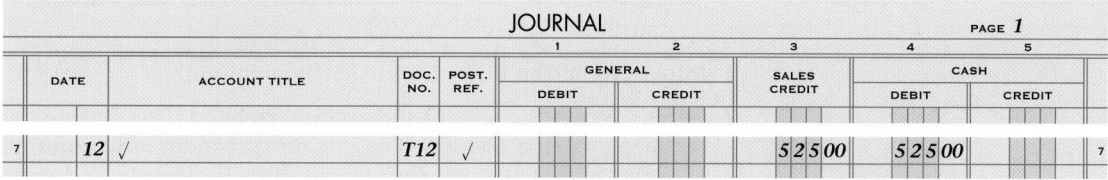

1 Date. Write the date, *12*, in the Date column.

2 Debit. The journal has a special amount column for debits to *Cash*. The title of the account is in the column heading. Therefore, the account title does not need to be written in the Account Title column. Write the debit amount, *$525.00*, in the Cash Debit column.

3 Credit. The journal also has a special amount column for credits to *Sales*. The title of the account is in the column heading. Therefore, the account title does not need to be written in the Account Title column. Write the credit amount, *$525.00*, in the Sales Credit column.

Because both amounts for this entry are recorded in special amount columns, no account titles are written in the

☞ FYI ☞

Remember that a check mark in the Account Title Column means that each amount in the entry is recorded in a special column. Therefore, no account titles need to be written.

MULTICULTURAL AWARENESS ACTIVITY

Write the Latin words "debere" and "credere" on the board. Underline the D and R and emphasize that DR. is sometimes used as an abbreviation for debit. Underline the C and R and emphasize that CR. is sometimes used as an abbreviation for credit. For further exploration of these terms in other cultures, have students look up the terms "debit" and "credit" in dictionaries for other languages and bring the new foreign words to class. More sophisticated students may also bring the suggested derivations of the words as stated for that language. In using dictionaries, you should caution students that the terms "debit" and "credit" are part of the technical language of accounting and that the dictionary definitions may differ slightly because they will emphasize the common meaning of the terms rather than the technical meaning.

CHAPTER 5   Journalizing Transactions   **81**

TEACHING STRATEGIES: DIFFERENT LEARNING STYLES

Auditory Learner. To reinforce the learning of journal entries, the auditory learner should verbally repeat the analysis of the transaction. The student should also verbally list the steps involved in making the entry.

Account Title column. Therefore, a check mark is placed in the Account Title column to show that no account titles need to be written for this transaction. A check mark is also placed in the Post. Ref. column to show that no separate amounts on this line are to be posted individually.

Posting procedures are described in Chapter 6.

4 Source document. Write the source document number, *T12*, in the Doc. No. column.

Paid Cash for an Expense

August 12, 19--. Paid cash for rent, $250.00. Check No. 4.

The source document for this transaction is Check No. 4. *(CONCEPT: Objective Evidence)* The analysis of this transaction is shown in the T accounts.

The expense account, Rent Expense, is increased by a debit, $250.00. The asset account, Cash, is decreased by a credit, $250.00. The journal entry for this transaction is shown on line 8 in Illustration 5-12.

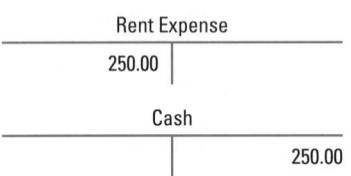

ILLUSTRATION 5-12   Journal entries to record paying cash for expenses

	DATE	ACCOUNT TITLE	DOC. NO.	POST. REF.	GENERAL DEBIT	GENERAL CREDIT	SALES CREDIT	CASH DEBIT	CASH CREDIT	
8	12	Rent Expense	C4		250 00				250 00	8
9	12	Utilities Expense	C5		45 00				45 00	9

JOURNAL   PAGE 1

1 Date. Write the date, *12*, in the Date column.

2 Debit. Write the title of the account debited, *Rent Expense*, in the Account Title column. There is no special amount column with the title of the account debited, Rent Expense, in its heading. Therefore, the debit amount is recorded in the General Debit column. Write the debit amount, *$250.00*, in the General Debit column.

3 Credit. The journal has a special amount column for credits to Cash. The title of the account is in the column heading. Therefore, the account title does not need to be written in the Account Title column. Write the credit amount, *$250.00*, in the Cash Credit column.

4 Source document. Write the source document number, *C4*, in the Doc. No. column.

The journal entry shown in Illustration 5-12 includes a cash payment for another expense, Utilities Expense. This transaction is journalized in the same way as the cash payment for rent.

Paid Cash to Owner for Personal Use

August 12, 19--. Paid cash to owner for personal use, $100.00. Check No. 6.

Ben Furman, Drawing

| 100.00 | |

Cash

| | 100.00 |

The source document for this transaction is Check No. 6. (*CONCEPT: Objective Evidence*) The analysis of this transaction is shown in the T accounts.

The contra capital account, Ben Furman, Drawing, is increased by a debit, $100.00. The asset account, Cash, is decreased by a credit, $100.00. The journal entry for this transaction is shown in Illustration 5-13.

ILLUSTRATION 5-13 Journal entry to record paying cash to owner for personal use

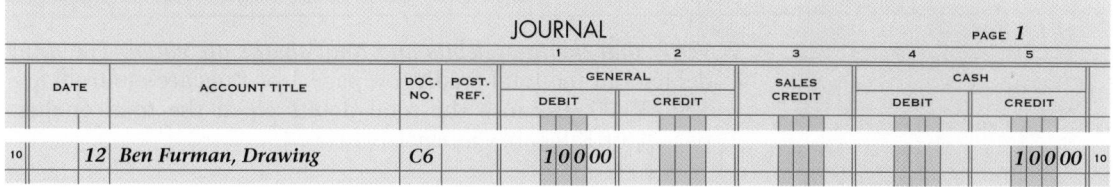

					1	2	3	4	5	
					GENERAL		SALES	CASH		
	DATE	ACCOUNT TITLE	DOC. NO.	POST. REF.	DEBIT	CREDIT	CREDIT	DEBIT	CREDIT	
10	12	Ben Furman, Drawing	C6		100 00				100 00	10

JOURNAL — PAGE 1

1 *Date.* Write the date, *12*, in the Date column.

2 *Debit.* Write the title of the account debited, *Ben Furman, Drawing*, in the Account Title column. There is no special amount column with the title of the account debited, Ben Furman, Drawing, in its heading. Therefore, the debit amount is recorded in the General Debit column. Write the debit amount, *$100.00*, in the General Debit column.

3 *Credit.* The journal has a special amount column for credits to Cash. The title of the account is in the column heading. Therefore, the account title does not need to be written in the Account Title column. Write the credit amount, *$100.00*, in the Cash Credit column.

4 *Source document.* Write the source document number, *C6*, in the Doc. No. column.

PROVING AND RULING A JOURNAL

After Rugcare uses all but the last line on a journal page, columns are proved and ruled before totals are carried forward to the next page. At the end of each month, Rugcare also proves and rules the journal.

After all entries on August 20 are recorded, page 1 of Rugcare's journal is filled, as shown in Illustration 5-14 on the next page.

Page 1 is proved and ruled before totals are carried forward to page 2.

Proving a Journal Page

To prove a journal page, Rugcare verifies that the total debits on the page equal the total credits. Three steps are followed in proving a journal page.

FYI

Instructions are given in Appendix B for using a calculator.

Audit Your Understanding

1. List the four parts of a journal entry.

AUDIT YOUR UNDERSTANDING

1. Date, debit, credit, source document.

LESSON PLAN 5-3

Materials

- Student pages 83–90
- Transparencies: A, Blank Journal; 5-1, Chapter Summary
- Software: Application Program Disk, Electronic Study Guide
- Tests: Problem Test Chapter 5, MicroExam Chapter 5, Objective Test No. 1, Unit Problem Test No. 1
- Demonstration Problem: Problem 5A, Journalizing Transactions

Objectives (Enabling Performance Tasks)

a. Define accounting terms related to journalizing transactions.

b. Identify accounting concepts and practices related to journalizing transactions.

d. Prove equality of debits and credits in a five-column journal.

e. Prove cash.

f. Forward totals from one journal page to another.

g. Rule a five-column journal.

FOCUS

- Journalizing was introduced earlier in this chapter. Explain that now the journal will be proved and ruled.
- Introduce new vocabulary: proving cash.

TEACH

Cover student pages 83–90 "Proving and Ruling a Journal" and "Generally Accepted Accounting Practices." This section of Chapter 5 covers the procedures for completing a journal at the end of a page and at the end of the month and proving cash. These activities ensure accuracy of the journal entries and are critically important to the accuracy of posting which will be covered in the next chapter. Keep reinforcing that debits must equal credits. It is important that students use a straight edge to draw total lines. Reinforce that double lines mean the totals are verified as correct. Use Illustrations 5-14 and 5-15 to emphasize procedures for starting a new journal page. Use Illustration 5-16 to emphasize procedures for proving and ruling a journal.

1 *Add each of the amount columns.* Use a calculator if one is available. If a calculator is not available, total the columns on a sheet of paper.

2 *Add the debit column totals, and then add the credit column totals.* The figures from page 1 of Rugcare's journal are below.

Column	Debit Column Totals	Credit Column Totals
General	$ 7,920.00	$12,920.00
Sales		2,319.00
Cash	12,319.00	5,000.00
Totals	$20,239.00	$20,239.00

3 *Verify that the total debits and total credits are equal.* The total debits and the total credits on page 1 of Rugcare's journal are $20,239.00. Because the total debits equal the total credits, page 1 of Rugcare's journal is proved.

ILLUSTRATION 5-14   Completed page 1 of a journal

JOURNAL   PAGE 1

	DATE		ACCOUNT TITLE	DOC. NO.	POST. REF.	GENERAL DEBIT	GENERAL CREDIT	SALES CREDIT	CASH DEBIT	CASH CREDIT	
1	Aug.	1	Ben Furman, Capital	R1			1000000		1000000		1
2		3	Supplies	C1		157700				157700	2
3		4	Prepaid Insurance	C2		120000				120000	3
4		7	Supplies	M1		272000					4
5			Butler Cleaning Supplies				272000				5
6		11	Butler Cleaning Supplies	C3		136000				136000	6
7		12	✓	T12	✓			52500	52500		7
8		12	Rent Expense	C4		25000				25000	8
9		12	Utilities Expense	C5		4500				4500	9
10		12	Ben Furman, Drawing	C6		10000				10000	10
11		13	Repair Expense	C7		2000				2000	11
12		13	Miscellaneous Expense	C8		2500				2500	12
13		13	✓	T13	✓			22900	22900		13
14		14	Advertising Expense	C9		6800				6800	14
15		14	✓	T14	✓			36000	36000		15
16		17	Petty Cash	C10		20000				20000	16
17		17	✓	T17	✓			35000	35000		17
18		18	Miscellaneous Expense	C11		7000				7000	18
19		18	✓	T18	✓			32000	32000		19
20		19	✓	T19	✓			29000	29000		20
21		20	Repair Expense	C12		8500				8500	21
22		20		T20	✓			24500	24500		22
23		20	Supplies	M2		20000					23
24			Dale Office Supplies				20000				24
25		20	Carried Forward		✓	792000	1292000	231900	1231900	500000	25

84   PART 2   Accounting for a Service Business Organized as a Proprietorship

---

APPLIED SKILLS: MATHEMATICS

Use the MATH WORK SHEET in the Masters and Solutions to Enrichment/Application section of the Teacher's Resource Guide to integrate applied mathematics. In this work sheet students will total and prove a journal page, prove debits and credits, and prove cash.

If the total debits do not equal the total credits, the errors must be found and corrected before any more work is completed.

Ruling a Journal Page

After a journal page is proved, the page is ruled as shown in Illustration 5-14.

1 Rule a single line across all amount columns directly below the last entry to indicate that the columns are to be added.

2 On the next line, write the date, *20*, in the Date column.

3 Write the words, *Carried Forward*, in the Account Title column. A check mark is also placed in the Post. Ref. column to show that nothing on this line needs to be posted.

4 Write each column total below the single line.

5 Rule double lines below the column totals across all amount columns. The double lines mean that the totals have been verified as correct.

Starting a New Journal Page

The column totals from the previous page are carried forward to a new page. The totals are recorded on the first line of the new page as shown in Illustration 5-15.

ILLUSTRATION 5-15   Starting a new journal page

| | | | | | | GENERAL | | SALES CREDIT | CASH | |
	DATE	ACCOUNT TITLE	DOC. NO.	POST. REF.		DEBIT	CREDIT		DEBIT	CREDIT
1	Aug. 20	Brought Forward		✓		7 9 2 0 00	12 9 2 0 00	2 3 1 9 00	12 3 1 9 00	5 0 0 0 00
2										

JOURNAL   PAGE *2*

1 Write the page number, *2*, at the top of the journal.

2 Write the date, *19--, Aug. 20*, in the Date column. Because this is the first time that a date is written on page 2, the year, month, and day are all written in the Date column.

3 Write the words, *Brought Forward*, in the Account Title column. A check mark is also placed in the Post. Ref. column to show that nothing on this line needs to be posted.

4 Record the column totals brought forward from the previous page.

Completing a Journal at the End of a Month

Rugcare always proves and rules a journal at the end of each month even if the last page for the month is not full. Page 2 of Rugcare's journal on August 31 is shown in Illustration 5-16.

ILLUSTRATION 5-16   Ruling a journal at the end of a month

JOURNAL   PAGE 2

	DATE		ACCOUNT TITLE	DOC. NO.	POST. REF.	GENERAL DEBIT	GENERAL CREDIT	SALES CREDIT	CASH DEBIT	CASH CREDIT	
1	Aug.	20	Brought Forward		✓	7920 00	12920 00	2319 00	12319 00	5000 00	1
2		21	✓	T21	✓			270 00	270 00		2
3		24	✓	T24	✓			300 00	300 00		3
4		25	✓	T25	✓			310 00	310 00		4
5		26	✓	T26	✓			245 00	245 00		5
6		27	Utilities Expense	C13		70 00				70 00	6
7		27	✓	T27	✓			290 00	290 00		7
8		28	Supplies	C14		434 00				434 00	8
9		28	✓	T28	✓			267 00	267 00		9
10		28	Miscellaneous Expense	M3		3 00				3 00	10
11		31	Miscellaneous Expense	C15		7 00				12 00	11
12			Repair Expense			5 00					12
13		31	Ben Furman, Drawing	C16		500 00				500 00	13
14		31	✓	T31	✓			290 00	290 00		14
15		31	Totals			8939 00	12920 00	4291 00	14291 00	6019 00	15

The entries on lines 10, 11, and 12, Illustration 5-16, are described in Chapter 7.

FYI

Double lines ruled below totals mean the totals have been verified as correct.

Proving Page 2 of a Journal. The last page of a journal for a month is proved using the same steps previously described. Then, cash is proved and the journal is ruled. The proof of page 2 of Rugcare's journal is shown below.

Column	Debit Column Totals	Credit Column Totals
General	$ 8,939.00	$12,920.00
Sales		4,291.00
Cash	14,291.00	6,019.00
Totals	$23,230.00	$23,230.00

Page 2 of Rugcare's journal is proved because the total debits are equal to the total credits, $23,230.00.

Proving Cash. Determining that the amount of cash agrees with the accounting records is called **proving cash**. Cash can be proved at any time Rugcare wishes to verify the accuracy of the cash records. However, Rugcare *always* proves cash at the end of a month when the journal is proved. Rugcare uses two steps to prove cash.

1 *Calculate the cash balance.*

Cash on hand at the beginning of the month. . . $0.00

Rugcare began the month with no cash balance. Mr. Furman invested the initial cash on August 1.

Plus total cash received during the month . . . . .   +14,291.00

This amount is the total of the journal's Cash Debit column.

Equals total $14,291.00
Less total cash paid during the month . . . .   − 6,019.00

This amount is the total of the journal's Cash Credit column.

Equals cash balance at the end of the month. . . $ 8,272.00

Checkbook balance on the next unused
check stub . . . . $ 8,272.00

2 *Verify that the cash balance equals the checkbook balance on the next unused check stub in the checkbook.* Because the cash balance calculated using the journal and the checkbook balance are the same, *$8,272.00,* cash is proved.

Always use a straight edge to draw lines.

Ruling a Journal at the End of a Month. A journal is ruled at the end of each month even if the last journal page is not full. Rugcare's journal is ruled as shown in Illustration 5-16.

The procedures for ruling a journal at the end of a month are similar to those for ruling a journal page to carry the totals forward.

Rugcare uses five steps in ruling a journal at the end of each month.

1 Rule a single line across all amount columns directly below the last entry to indicate that the columns are to be added.

2 On the next line, write the date, *31*, in the Date column.

3 Write the word, *Totals*, in the Account Title column.

Some of the column totals will be posted as described in Chapter 6. Therefore, a check mark is not placed in the Post. Ref. column for this line.

4 Write each column total below the single line.

5 Rule double lines below the column totals across all amount columns. The double lines mean that the totals have been verified as correct.

Audit Your Understanding

1. List the formula for proving cash.

2. List the 5 steps to rule a journal at the end of a month.

Global Perspective

PROFESSIONAL ACCOUNTING ASSOCIATIONS

tle. Some countries also have special requirements and title designations for individuals who perform tax accounting work.

The following is a selected list of countries and their professional accounting title designation and the organization that grants that title.

Accounting for financial activities of businesses around the world has many similarities as well as differences. In many countries, accounting associations grant a title to designate accountants as professionals in their field.

Qualification requirements for a title designation are generally established by a professional accounting organization. The requirements normally consist of a stated amount of education and experience in accounting. Upon meeting these requirements, individuals are designated with a special ti-

COUNTRY	TITLE	ORGANIZATION
Australia	Chartered Accountant	Institute of Chartered Accountants in Australia
Bangladesh	Chartered Accountant	Institute of Chartered Accountants of Bangladesh
Canada	Chartered Accountant	Canadian Institute of Chartered Accountants
India	Chartered Accountant	Institute of Chartered Accountants of India
Japan	Certified Public Accountant	Japanese Institute of Certified Public Accountants
Mexico	Contador Público (Public Accountant)	Mexican Institute of Public Accountants Federation of Societies of Public Accountants
Nigeria	Chartered Accountant	Institute of Chartered Accountants of Nigeria
Pakistan	Chartered Accountant	Institute of Chartered Accountants of Pakistan
Republic of China (Taiwan)	Certified Public Accountant	National Federation of Certified Public Accountants Associations of the Republic of China Chartered Accountants
South Africa	Chartered Accountant	South African Institute of Chartered Accountants

The Summary Illustration on page 90 analyzes the procedure for journalizing transactions.

GENERALLY ACCEPTED ACCOUNTING PRACTICES

In completing accounting work, Rugcare is guided by generally accepted accounting practices, including those shown in Illustration 5-17.

1. Errors are corrected in a way that does not cause doubts about what the correct information is. If an error is recorded, cancel the error by neatly drawing a line through the incorrect item. Write the correct item immediately above the canceled item, as

shown in the Cash Debit column on line 17 of Illustration 5-17.

2. Sometimes an entire entry is incorrect and is discovered before the next entry is journalized. Draw neat lines through all parts of the incorrect entry. Journalize the entry correctly on the next blank line, as shown on lines 18 and 19, Illustration 5-17.

ILLUSTRATION 5-17   Some generally accepted accounting practices

JOURNAL — PAGE 2

	DATE	ACCOUNT TITLE	DOC. NO.	POST. REF.	GENERAL DEBIT	GENERAL CREDIT	SALES CREDIT	CASH DEBIT	CASH CREDIT	
17	28	✓ **4**	T28		**5**		3 5 0 00	3̶5̶0̶0̶0̶ ← **1**		17
18	**2** → 29	~~Rent Expense~~	~~C22~~		~~5 00~~				~~5 00~~	18
19	29	Repair Expense	C22		5 0 00			**7**	5 0 00	19
20	**3** → 29	~~Miscellaneous Expense~~ *Supplies*	C21		1 0 0 00				1 0 0 00	20
21	30	Don Better, Drawing	C24		5 0 0 00 ← **6**				5 0 0 00	21
22	30	Totals			8 7 5 0 00	9 2 0 0 00	4 0 0 0 00	12 3 0 0 00	7 8 5 0 00	22
23				**8** ↗	**9** →					23

3. Sometimes several correct entries are recorded after an incorrect entry is made. The next blank lines are several entries later. Draw neat lines through all incorrect parts of the entry. Record the correct items on the same lines as the incorrect items, directly above the canceled parts. This procedure is shown on line 20 of Illustration 5-17.

4. Words in accounting records are written in full when space permits. Words may be abbreviated only when space is limited. All items are written legibly.

5. Dollars and cents signs and decimal points are not used when writing amounts on ruled accounting paper. Sometimes a color tint or a heavy vertical rule is used on printed accounting paper to separate the dollars and cents columns.

6. Two zeros are written in the cents column when an amount is in even dollars, such as $500.00. If the cents column is left blank, doubts may arise later about the correct amount.

7. A single line is ruled across amount columns to indicate addition or subtraction as shown on line 21, Illustration 5-17.

8. A double line is ruled across amount columns to indicate that the totals have been verified as correct.

9. Neatness is very important in accounting records so that there is never any doubt about what information has been recorded. A ruler is used to make single and double lines.

CHAPTER 5   Journalizing Transactions   **89**

APPLIED SKILLS: WRITING ACROSS THE CURRICULUM

Writing paragraphs and short essays.   The Cases for Critical Thinking are short, practical applications of the accounting principles developed in the chapter. Some cases are planned to present problems related to the chapter but not specifically discussed and answered in the chapter. These cases present an opportunity for critical thinking and decision making. These cases also require more than a short objective-type response. Therefore, they provide ideal practice in writing paragraphs and short essays.

TEACHING STRATEGIES:
APPLYING VISUALS

Direct the students to Summary
Illustration 5-18. Review the summary
of journalizing transactions.

SUMMARY ILLUSTRATION 5-18

Summary of journalizing transactions

1 Analyze transactions

a. From source document information

Receipts	Calculator Tapes	Checks	Memorandums

Rent Expense	Cash
50.00	50.00

b. Using T accounts

Debits ⟶ equal ⟶ Credits

c. Verify for each entry that:

2 Record entries in a journal

Transactions	Written in Account Title Column	Journal Amount Columns Used				
		General		Sales	Cash	
		Debit	Credit	Credit	Debit	Credit
Received cash from owner as an investment	Capital Account Title		✓		✓	
Paid cash for supplies	Supplies	✓				✓
Paid cash for insurance	Prepaid Insurance	✓				✓
Bought supplies on account	Supplies Liability Account Title	✓	✓			
Paid cash on account	Liability Account Title	✓				✓
Received cash from sales	✓			✓	✓	
Paid cash for an expense	Expense Account Title	✓				✓
Paid cash to owner for personal use	Drawing Account Title	✓				✓

3 Prove the journal

a. Rule a single line across amount columns.

b. Add amount columns.

c. Add all debit totals and add all credit totals.

d. Verify that total debits equal total credits.

4 Prove cash

a. Cash at beginning + Total cash received = Total
Total − Total cash paid = Ending cash balance

b. Verify that the cash balance is the same as the amount shown on the next unused check stub.

5 Complete the journal by ruling double lines across all amount columns.

APPLIED SKILLS: WORD PROCESSING

If you wish to integrate word processing into your accounting course, you may direct students to answer
the end-of-chapter Accounting Terms, Questions for Individual Study, and Cases for Critical Thinking using
their word processing software.

ACCOUNTING TERMS   EPT(a)

What is the meaning of each of the following?

1. **journal**
2. **journalizing**
3. **special amount column**
4. **general amount column**
5. **entry**
6. **double-entry accounting**
7. **source document**
8. **check**
9. **receipt**
10. **memorandum**
11. **proving cash**

QUESTIONS FOR INDIVIDUAL STUDY   EPT(b)

1. What are the five amount columns in the journal used by Rugcare?
2. Which of the columns in Rugcare's journal are special amount columns?
3. What is the source document for a cash payment transaction?
4. What is the source document for a sales transaction?
5. What is the source document for cash received from transactions other than sales?
6. What is the source document for a transaction when no other source document is prepared or when additional explanation is needed?
7. What are the four parts of a journal entry?
8. What two journal amount columns are used to record cash received from the owner as an investment?
9. What two journal amount columns are used to record cash paid for supplies?
10. What two journal amount columns are used to record cash paid for insurance?
11. What two journal amount columns are used to record supplies bought on account?
12. What two journal amount columns are used to record cash paid on account?
13. What two journal amount columns are used to record cash received from sales?
14. What two journal amount columns are used to record cash paid for an expense?
15. What two journal amount columns are used to record cash paid to the owner for personal use?
16. What is the procedure for proving a journal page?
17. What are the two steps that Rugcare uses in proving cash?

CASES FOR CRITICAL THINKING   EPT(b)

CASE 1 During the summer, Willard Kelly does odd jobs to earn money. Mr. Kelly keeps all his money in a single checking account. He writes checks to pay for personal items and for business expenses. These payments include personal clothing, school supplies, gasoline for his car, and recreation. Mr. Kelly uses his check stubs as his accounting records. Are Mr. Kelly's accounting procedures and records correct? Explain your answer.

CASE 2 In his business, Michael Rock uses a journal with the following columns: Date, Account Title, Check No., Cash Debit, and Cash Credit. Mr. Rock's wife, Jennifer, suggests that he needs three additional amount columns: General Debit, General Credit, and Sales Credit. Mr. Rock states that all his business transactions are for cash, and he never buys on account. Therefore, he does not see the need for more than the Cash Debit and Cash Credit special amount columns. Who is correct, Mr. or Mrs. Rock? Explain your answer.

ACCOUNTING TERMS

1. **journal:** A form for recording transactions in chronological order. (p. 73)
2. **journalizing:** Recording transactions in a journal. (p. 73)
3. **special amount column:** A journal amount column headed with an account title. (p. 73)
4. **general amount column:** A journal amount column that is not headed with an account title. (p. 73)
5. **entry:** Information for each transaction recorded in a journal. (p. 74)
6. **double-entry accounting:** The recording of debit and credit parts of a transaction. (p. 74)
7. **source document:** A business paper from which information is obtained for a journal entry. (p. 74)
8. **check:** A business form ordering a bank to pay cash from a bank account. (p. 74)
9. **receipt:** A business form giving written acknowledgement for cash received. (p. 75)
10. **memorandum:** A form on which a brief message is written describing a transaction. (p. 76)
11. **proving cash:** Determining that the amount of cash agrees with the accounting records. (p. 86)

QUESTIONS FOR INDIVIDUAL STUDY

1. (a) General Debit, (b) General Credit, (c) Sales Credit, (d) Cash Debit, and (e) Cash Credit. (p. 73)
2. (a) Sales Credit, (b) Cash Debit, and (c) Cash Credit. (p. 73)
3. A check. (p. 74)
4. A calculator tape. (p. 75)
5. A receipt. (p. 75)
6. A memorandum. (p. 76)
7. (a) Date, (b) debit, (c) credit, and (d) source document. (p. 77)
8. Cash Debit and General Credit. (p. 77)
9. General Debit and Cash Credit. (p. 78)
10. General Debit and Cash Credit. (p. 79)
11. General Debit and General Credit. (pp. 79–80)
12. General Debit and Cash Credit. (pp. 80–81)
13. Cash Debit and Sales Credit. (p. 81)
14. General Debit and Cash Credit. (p. 82)

15. General Debit and Cash Credit. (p. 83)

15. General Debit and Cash Credit. (p. 83)

16. (a) Add each of the amount columns. (b) Add the debit column totals, and then add the credit column totals. (c) Verify that the total debits and total credits are equal. (pp. 83–84)

17. (a) Calculate the cash balance. (b) Verify that the cash balance equals the checkbook balance on the next unused check stub in the checkbook. (pp. 86–87)

CASES FOR CRITICAL THINKING

Case 1 Neither Mr. Kelly's procedures nor his records are correct. First, he mixes his personal records with his business records. Second, he has all his records in chronological order only in the check stubs. If he needs to know how much he spent for gasoline for personal use and gasoline for business use, he must go through the check stubs and sort the information. Mr. Kelly should at least keep his personal and business records separate.

Case 2 Mrs. Rock is correct. Mr. Rock's journal provides only for a record of how much cash is received and paid. The record does not show the sources of revenue or the reasons for the payments. Mr. Rock should expand his journal to include the three additional amount columns Mrs. Rock suggests.

DRILL 5-D1   **Analyzing transactions**

This drill provides continuing practice in analyzing transactions into debit and credit parts. Use Rugcare's chart of accounts, page 18.

Transactions
1. Paid cash for supplies, $100.00.
2. Bought supplies on account from Butler Cleaning Supplies, $500.00.
3. Paid cash to owner for personal use, $50.00.
4. Received cash from sales, $300.00.
5. Paid cash for rent, $200.00.
6. Paid cash for insurance, $250.00.
7. Received cash from owner as an investment, $1,000.00.
8. Paid cash for repairs, $25.00.
9. Paid cash for telephone bill, $30.00.
10. Paid cash for advertising, $40.00.
11. Paid cash on account to Butler Cleaning Supplies, $300.00.
12. Paid cash for miscellaneous expense, $3.00.

```
        Supplies
  100.00  |
          |
          Cash
          |
          |  100.00
```

INSTRUCTIONS:

1. For each transaction, prepare two T accounts. On the T accounts, write the account titles affected by the transaction.
2. Write the debit or credit amount in each T account to show how the transaction affected that account. T accounts for Transaction 1 are given as an example.

DRILL 5-D2   **Analyzing transactions**

This drill continues the practice in analyzing transactions. Mark Jacobs owns a service business called Jacobs Secretarial Services. Jacobs Secretarial Services uses the following accounts.

Cash	Sales
Supplies	Advertising Expense
Prepaid Insurance	Miscellaneous Expense
Gable Supplies	Rent Expense
Mark Jacobs, Capital	Repair Expense
Mark Jacobs, Drawing	Utilities Expense

Use a form similar to the following. Transaction 1 is given as an example.

1	2	3	4	5	6	7
			How is Account Affected?		**Entered in Account as a**	
Trans. No.	**Accounts Affected**	**Account Classification**	(+)	(−)	**Debit**	**Credit**
1.	Advertising Expense	Expense	✓		✓	
	Cash	Asset		✓		✓

Transactions
1. Paid cash for advertising.
2. Paid cash for repairs.
3. Received cash from owner as an investment.
4. Paid cash for miscellaneous expense.
5. Bought supplies on account from Gable Supplies.

6. Paid cash on account to Gable Supplies.
7. Paid cash for water bill.
8. Paid cash for supplies.
9. Paid cash for rent.
10. Paid cash to owner for personal use.
11. Received cash from sales.
12. Paid cash for insurance.

INSTRUCTIONS:

1. In Column 2, write the titles of the accounts affected by each transaction.
2. For each account title, write the account classification in Column 3.
3. For each account title, place a check mark in either Column 4 or 5 to indicate if each account is increased (+) or decreased (−) by this transaction.
4. For each account title, place a check mark in either Column 6 or 7 to indicate if the amount is entered in the account as a debit or a credit.

APPLICATION PROBLEMS   EPT(c,d,e,f,g)

PROBLEM 5-1   Journalizing transactions

Dorothy Gilbert owns a service business called Lane Company. Lane Company uses the following accounts.

Cash	Sales
Supplies	Advertising Expense
Prepaid Insurance	Miscellaneous Expense
Mertz Supplies	Rent Expense
Dorothy Gilbert, Capital	Repair Expense
Dorothy Gilbert, Drawing	Utilities Expense

INSTRUCTIONS:

1. Journalize the following transactions completed during February of the current year. Use page 1 of a journal similar to the one described in this chapter for Rugcare. Source documents are abbreviated as follows: check, C; memorandum, M; receipt, R; calculator tape, T.

Transactions

Feb. 1. Received cash from owner as an investment, $12,000.00. R1.
       3. Paid cash for rent, $600.00. C1.
       4. Paid cash for insurance, $1,200.00. C2.
       5. Bought supplies on account from Mertz Supplies, $1,500.00. M1.
       6. Paid cash for supplies, $1,000.00. C3.
       7. Paid cash on account to Mertz Supplies, $750.00. C4.
      10. Paid cash for miscellaneous expense, $5.00. C5.
      12. Received cash from sales, $500.00. T12.
      14. Received cash from sales, $450.00. T14.
      17. Paid cash for repairs, $75.00. C6.
      17. Received cash from sales, $300.00. T17.
      20. Received cash from sales, $370.00. T20.
      21. Received cash from sales, $470.00. T21.
      24. Received cash from sales, $400.00. T24.
      25. Paid cash for electric bill, $50.00. C7.
      25. Received cash from sales, $450.00. T25.
      26. Paid cash for advertising, $90.00. C8.
      26. Received cash from sales, $300.00. T26.
      27. Received cash from sales, $350.00. T27.
      28. Paid cash to owner for personal use, $250.00. C9.
      28. Received cash from sales, $500.00. T28.

2. Prove the journal. Rule a single line across all amount columns. Write the amount column totals below the single line.

3. Prove cash. The beginning cash balance on February 1 is zero. The ending cash balance on the next unused check stub is $12,070.00.

4. Rule the journal.

PROBLEM 5-2 Journalizing transactions

Rona Dowling owns a service business called LawnCare. LawnCare uses the following accounts.

Cash	Sales
Supplies	Advertising Expense
Prepaid Insurance	Miscellaneous Expense
Main Office Supplies	Rent Expense
Westley Supplies	Repair Expense
Rona Dowling, Capital	Utilities Expense
Rona Dowling, Drawing	

INSTRUCTIONS:

1. Journalize the following transactions completed during April of the current year. Use page 1 of a journal similar to the one described in this chapter for Rugcare. Source documents are abbreviated as follows: check, C; memorandum, M; receipt, R; calculator tape, T.

Transactions

Apr. 1. Received cash from owner as an investment, $10,000.00. R1.
    2. Paid cash for rent, $800.00. C1.
    3. Paid cash for insurance, $3,000.00. C2.
    6. Bought supplies on account from Westley Supplies, $2,000.00. M1.
    7. Paid cash for supplies, $700.00. C3.
    8. Paid cash on account to Westley Supplies, $1,000.00. C4.
    8. Received cash from sales, $500.00. T8.
    9. Paid cash for telephone bill, $60.00. C5.
    9. Received cash from sales, $650.00. T9.
   10. Paid cash for repairs, $85.00. C6.
   10. Received cash from sales, $600.00. T10.
   13. Paid cash for miscellaneous expense, $15.00. C7.
   13. Received cash from sales, $700.00. T13.
   14. Received cash from sales, $650.00. T14.
   15. Paid cash to owner for personal use, $350.00. C8.
   15. Received cash from sales, $500.00. T15.
   16. Paid cash for supplies, $1,000.00. C9.
   16. Received cash from sales, $600.00. T16.
   17. Received cash from sales, $650.00. T17.
   20. Bought supplies on account from Main Office Supplies, $500.00. M2.
   20. Received cash from sales, $570.00. T20.
   21. Received cash from sales, $670.00. T21.

2. Prove and rule page 1 of the journal. Carry the column totals forward to page 2 of the journal.

3. Use page 2 of the journal. Journalize the following transactions completed during April of the current year.

Apr. 22. Paid cash for electric bill, $55.00. C10.
   22. Received cash from sales, $600.00. T22.
   23. Bought supplies on account from Main Office Supplies, $50.00. M3.
   23. Received cash from sales, $650.00. T23.
   24. Paid cash for advertising, $100.00. C11.

24. Received cash from sales, $500.00. T24.
27. Received cash from sales, $550.00. T27.
28. Received cash from sales, $500.00. T28.
29. Paid cash for supplies, $150.00. C12.
29. Received cash from sales, $650.00. T29.
30. Paid cash to owner for personal use, $350.00. C13.
30. Received cash from sales, $500.00. T30.

4. Prove page 2 of the journal.
5. Prove cash. The beginning cash balance on April 1 is zero. The balance on the next unused check stub is $12,375.00.
6. Rule page 2 of the journal.

ENRICHMENT PROBLEMS

MASTERY PROBLEM 5-M Journalizing transactions

APPLICATION

Rachel Frank owns a service business called Frank's Car Wash. Frank's Car Wash uses the following accounts.

Cash	Sales
Supplies	Advertising Expense
Prepaid Insurance	Miscellaneous Expense
Delancy Supplies	Rent Expense
Long Supplies	Repair Expense
Rachel Frank, Capital	Utilities Expense
Rachel Frank, Drawing	

INSTRUCTIONS:

1. Journalize the following transactions completed during June of the current year. Use page 1 of a journal similar to the one described in this chapter for Rugcare. Source documents are abbreviated as follows: check, C; memorandum, M; receipt, R; calculator tape, T.

Transactions

June 1. Received cash from owner as an investment, $18,000.00. R1.
2. Paid cash for rent, $900.00. C1.
3. Paid cash for supplies, $1,500.00. C2.
4. Bought supplies on account from Delancy Supplies, $3,000.00. M1.
5. Paid cash for insurance, $4,500.00. C3.
8. Paid cash on account to Delancy Supplies, $1,500.00. C4.
8. Received cash from sales, $750.00. T8.
9. Paid cash for electric bill, $75.00. C5.
9. Received cash from sales, $700.00. T9.
10. Paid cash for miscellaneous expense, $7.00. C6.
10. Received cash from sales, $750.00. T10.
11. Paid cash for repairs, $100.00. C7.
11. Received cash from sales, $850.00. T11.
12. Received cash from sales, $700.00. T12.
15. Paid cash to owner for personal use, $350.00. C8.
15. Received cash from sales, $750.00. T15.
16. Paid cash for supplies, $1,500.00. C9.
16. Received cash from sales, $650.00. T16.
17. Bought supplies on account from Long Supplies, $750.00. M2.
17. Received cash from sales, $600.00. T17.
18. Received cash from sales, $800.00. T18.
19. Received cash from sales, $750.00. T19.

2. Prove and rule page 1 of the journal. Carry the column totals forward to page 2 of the journal.

3. Use page 2 of the journal. Journalize the following transactions completed during June of the current year.

Transactions

June 22. Bought supplies on account from Long Supplies, $80.00. M3.
22. Received cash from sales, $700.00. T22.
23. Paid cash for advertising, $130.00. C10.
23. Received cash from sales, $650.00. T23.
24. Paid cash for telephone bill, $60.00. C11.
24. Received cash from sales, $600.00. T24.
25. Received cash from sales, $550.00. T25.
26. Paid cash for supplies, $70.00. C12.
26. Received cash from sales, $600.00. T26.
29. Received cash from sales, $750.00. T29.
30. Paid cash to owner for personal use, $375.00. C13.
30. Received cash from sales, $800.00. T30.

4. Prove page 2 of the journal.

5. Prove cash. The beginning cash balance on June 1 is zero. The balance on the next unused check stub is $18,883.00.

6. Rule page 2 of the journal.

CHALLENGE PROBLEM 5-C   Journalizing transactions

APPLICATION

Wilbur Moore owns a service business called Moore's Tailors. Moore's Tailors uses the following accounts.

Cash	Sales
Supplies	Advertising Expense
Prepaid Insurance	Miscellaneous Expense
Marker Supplies	Rent Expense
O'Brien Supplies	Repair Expense
Wilbur Moore, Capital	Utilities Expense
Wilbur Moore, Drawing	

INSTRUCTIONS:

1. Use page 1 of a journal similar to the following.

Journal								Page 1
Cash		Date	Account Title	Doc. No.	Post Ref.	General		Sales Credit
Debit	Credit					Debit	Credit	

Journalize the following transactions completed during June of the current year. Source documents are abbreviated as follows: check, C; memorandum, M; receipt, R; calculator tape, T.

Transactions

June 1. Owner invested money, $17,000.00. R1.
2. Wrote a check for supplies, $1,400.00. C1.
3. Paid June rent, $800.00. C2.
4. Wrote a check for insurance, $3,000.00. C3.
5. Bought supplies on account from Marker Supplies, $2,500.00. M1.
7. Received cash from sales, $550.00. T7.

June 9. Paid monthly telephone bill, $70.00. C4.
9. Wrote a check to Marker Supplies on account, $1,300.00. C5.
10. Received cash from sales, $550.00. T10.
11. Paid for miscellaneous expense, $6.00. C6.
11. Received cash from sales, $550.00. T11.
12. Wrote a check for repairs, $90.00. C7.
12. Cash was received from sales, $600.00. T12.
15. Paid for supplies, $1,300.00. C8.
15. Total cash sales, $540.00. T15.
16. Owner withdrew money for personal use, $300.00. C9.
16. Cash was received from sales, $400.00. T16.
17. Total cash sales, $780.00. T17.
18. Bought supplies on account from O'Brien Supplies, $900.00. M2.
18. Received cash from sales, $600.00. T18.
19. Wrote a check for supplies, $85.00. C10.
19. Cash was received from sales, $850.00. T19.

2. Prove and rule page 1 of the journal. Carry the column totals forward to page 2 of the journal.

3. Use page 2 of the journal. Journalize the following transactions completed during June of the current year.

Transactions

June 22. Received cash from sales, $700.00. T22.
23. Bought supplies on account from Marker Supplies, $95.00. M3.
23. Received cash from sales, $720.00. T23.
24. Paid for July advertising, $100.00. C11.
24. Received cash from sales, $550.00. T24.
25. Paid water bill, $75.00. C12.
25. Received cash from sales, $600.00. T25.
26. Received cash from sales, $450.00. T26.
29. Wrote a check to O'Brien Supplies on account, $900.00. C13.
29. Received cash from sales, $630.00. T29.
30. Owner withdrew cash for personal use, $450.00. C14.
30. Received cash from sales, $360.00. T30.

4. Prove page 2 of the journal.

5. Prove cash. The cash balance on June 1 is zero. The balance on the next unused check stub is $16,554.00.

6. Rule page 2 of the journal.

CHAPTER 6 OVERVIEW

Chapter 6 analyzes the procedures for posting from the journal to the general ledger. Arranging accounts in a general ledger, preparing a chart of accounts, and opening accounts are important activities that are completed before students begin the posting process. The five steps in posting are emphasized to make the posting procedures easy to follow and perform.

For Mastery Problem 6-M and Recycling Problem 6-R, students are required to record transactions in a journal as well as post from a journal to a general ledger. This requirement provides additional practice for students on analyzing transactions into debit and credit parts.

GUIDE TO ACHIEVING LEARNING OBJECTIVES

Enabling Performance Tasks	TEACH	APPLY		EXTEND/ENRICH					
	Lesson Plans	Drills for Understanding	Application Problems	Mastery Problems	Challenge Problems	Cases for Critical Thinking	Recycling Problems	Reinforcement Activity	
a. Define accounting terms related to posting from a journal to a general ledger.	6-1, 6-2								
b. Identify accounting concepts and practices related to posting from a journal to a general ledger.	6-1, 6-2	6-D2				Cases 1, 2			
c. Prepare a chart of accounts for a service business organized as a proprietorship.	6-1	6-D1	6-1						
d. Post amounts from a journal to a general ledger.	6-2	6-D2	6-2	6-M	6-C		6-R	1A	

ENRICHMENT

SPECIAL FEATURES

Personal Visions in Business, page 109

Careers in Accounting, page 101

Applied Communications, page 118

TECHNOLOGY CONNECTION

Automated Accounting 6.0 Problems 6-M, 6-C

Integrating Automated Accounting Topic 1 Optional Problem DB-1A

Application Program Disk Problems 6-M, 6-C

Electronic Study Guide

NEW, REVIEW, AND EXTENSION

ACTIVITIES/CONCEPTS/TRANSACTIONS	NEW	REVIEW/ EXTENSION
File maintenance	✓	
Assigning account numbers	✓	
Opening accounts	✓	
Posting	✓	
Posting to a general ledger	✓	
Posting separate amounts individually	✓	
Posting totals of special amount columns	✓	

INFORMAL ASSESSMENT		FORMAL ASSESSMENT					
Study Guide	Audit Your Understanding	Chapter MicroExam	Chapter Problem Test	Unit Problem Test	Unit Objective Test	Portfolio
Unit A		✓			✓	
Units B, C	✓	✓			✓	
			✓			
Unit D			✓	✓		✓

TEACHING MATERIALS

Teacher's Wraparound Edition of Text

Teacher's Resource Guide

Teacher's Edition of Working Papers

Teacher's Edition of Demonstration/Recycling Problems

Teaching Transparencies

Applied Math Work Sheets

MicroExam

APPLIED MATHEMATICS

APPLIED MATH/ACCOUNTING SKILL	APPLICATION
Calculating new account balances	Prob. 6-2

Posting to a General Ledger

ENABLING PERFORMANCE TASKS

After studying Chapter 6, you will be able to:

a Define accounting terms related to posting from a journal to a general ledger.

b Identify accounting concepts and practices related to posting from a journal to a general ledger.

c Prepare a chart of accounts for a service business organized as a proprietorship.

d Post amounts from a journal to a general ledger.

TERMS PREVIEW

ledger • general ledger • account number • file maintenance • opening an account • posting

98

Rugcare records transactions in a journal as described in Chapter 5. A journal is a permanent record of the debit and credit parts of each transaction with transactions recorded in chronological order. A journal does not show in one place all the changes in a single account. If only a journal is used, a business must search through all journal pages to find items affecting a single account balance. For this reason, a form is used to summarize in one place all the changes to a single account. A separate form is used for each account.

An account form is based on and includes the debit and credit sides of a T account as shown in Illustration 6-1.

ILLUSTRATION 6-1

Relationship of a T account to an account form

In addition to debit and credit columns, space is provided in the account form for recording the transaction date and journal page number. This information can be used to trace a specific entry back to where a transaction is recorded in a journal.

The major disadvantage of the account form shown in Illustration 6-1 is that no current, up-to-date account balance is shown. If the form in Illustration 6-1 is used, an up-to-date balance must be calculated each time the account is examined. Also, the balance is difficult and time consuming to calculate when an account has a large number of entries. Therefore, a more commonly used account form has Debit and Credit Balance columns as shown in Illustration 6-2. Because the form has columns for the debit and credit balance, it is often referred to as the balance-ruled account form.

ILLUSTRATION 6-2

Account form

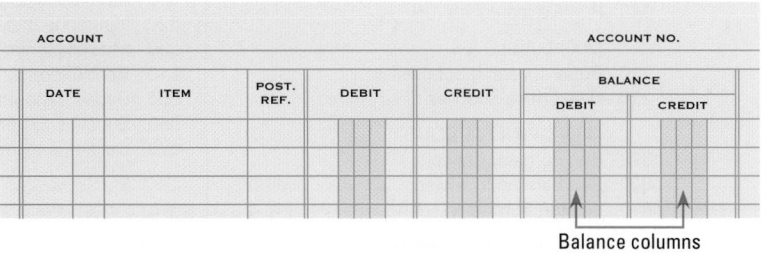

The account balance is calculated and recorded as each entry is recorded in the account. Recording information in an account is described later in this chapter. The T account is a useful device for analyzing transactions into debit and credit parts. However, the balance-ruled account form is more useful as a permanent record of changes to account balances than is the T account. Rugcare uses the balance-ruled account form.

LESSON PLAN 6-1

Materials

- Student pages 99–103
- Transparency B, Blank General Ledger
- Demonstration Problems: Problem 6A, Preparing a Chart of Accounts; Problem 6B, Posting to a General Ledger

Objectives (Enabling Performance Tasks)

a. Define accounting terms related to posting from a journal to a general ledger.

b. Identify accounting concepts and practices related to posting from a journal to a general ledger.

c. Prepare a chart of accounts for a service business organized as a proprietorship.

FOCUS

- Recording transactions in a journal was covered in Chapter 5. In this lesson, we will introduce the ledger account form to which the journalized transactions are posted.
- Introduce new vocabulary: ledger, general ledger, account number, file maintenance, opening an account.

FYI

The account numbers in the chart of accounts play an important role in both manual and automated accounting. In manual accounting, the account number in the journal's Post. Ref. column shows where information has been posted. In automated accounting, the account number is also used to identify the account when journalizing.

ARRANGING ACCOUNTS IN A GENERAL LEDGER

A group of accounts is called a **ledger**. A ledger that contains all accounts needed to prepare financial statements is called a **general ledger**. The name given to an account is known as an account title. The number assigned to an account is called an **account number**.

Preparing a Chart of Accounts

A list of account titles and numbers showing the location of each account in a ledger is known as a chart of accounts. Rugcare's chart of accounts is shown in Illustration 6-3.

ILLUSTRATION 6-3   Chart of accounts

RUGCARE

CHART OF ACCOUNTS

Balance Sheet Accounts	Income Statement Accounts
(100) ASSETS	**(400) REVENUE**
110 Cash	410 Sales
120 Petty Cash	
130 Supplies	**(500) EXPENSES**
140 Prepaid Insurance	510 Advertising Expense
	520 Insurance Expense
(200) LIABILITIES	530 Miscellaneous Expense
210 Butler Cleaning Supplies	540 Rent Expense
220 Dale Office Supplies	550 Repair Expense
	560 Supplies Expense
(300) OWNER'S EQUITY	570 Utilities Expense
310 Ben Furman, Capital	
320 Ben Furman, Drawing	
330 Income Summary	

ILLUSTRATION 6-4

For ease of use while studying Part 2, Rugcare's chart of accounts is also shown on page 100.

Accounts in a general ledger are arranged in the same order as they appear on financial statements. Rugcare's chart of accounts, Illustration 6-3, shows five general ledger divisions. (1) Assets, (2) Liabilities, (3) Owner's Equity, (4) Revenue, and (5) Expenses.

Numbering General Ledger Accounts

Rugcare assigns a three-digit account number to each account. For example, Supplies is assigned the number *130* as shown in Illustration 6-4.

Account numbers

<u>1</u> <u>3</u> <u>0</u>   **Supplies**

General ledger division   Location within general ledger division

The first digit of each account number shows the general ledger division in which the account is located. For example, the asset division accounts are numbered in the 100s. Therefore, the number for the asset account, Supplies, begins with a *1*.

The second two digits indicate the location of each account within a general ledger division. The *1* in the account number 130, Supplies, indicates that the account is located in the asset division. The *30* in the account number for Supplies indicates that the account is located between account number 120 and account number 140.

Rugcare initially assigns account numbers by 10s so that new accounts can be added easily. Nine numbers are unused between each account on Rugcare's chart of accounts, Illustration 6-3. For example, numbers 111 to 119 are unused between accounts numbered 110 and 120. New numbers can be assigned between existing account numbers without renumbering all existing accounts. The procedure for arranging accounts in a general ledger, assigning account numbers, and keeping records current is called **file maintenance.**

Unused account numbers are assigned to new accounts. Rugcare records payments for gasoline in Miscellaneous Expense. If Mr. Furman found that the amount paid each month for gasoline had become a major expense, he might decide to use a separate account. The account might be titled Gasoline Expense. Rugcare arranges expense accounts in alphabetic order in its general ledger. Therefore, the new account would be inserted between Advertising Expense and Insurance Expense.

510	Advertising Expense	(Existing account)
	GASOLINE EXPENSE	(NEW ACCOUNT)
520	Insurance Expense	(Existing account)

- Assess student understanding by checking solutions to the Independent Practice activities.

- Ask students to name the five divisions (assets, liabilities, owner's equity, revenue, expenses) of the chart of accounts. Also ask them to name the two steps to open a general ledger account (account title and account number.)

Reteach

- Use Demonstration Problem 6A and Demonstration Problem 6B, instruction 1. These problems can be done on the overhead with the students completing the problems at their desks.

- Direct student attention to the chart of accounts at the beginning of Part 2. Discuss each classification, the accounts within each classification, and the account number assigned to each account. Ask students what numbers would be assigned to various new accounts assigned to the existing chart of accounts, such as Automobile Expense (515) Smith Supplies (230), and Equipment (answers may vary).

Enrich

- Assign the PERSONAL VISIONS IN BUSINESS feature on page 109.

- Assign the CAREERS IN ACCOUNTING feature on page 101.

CLOSURE

Use Audit Your Understanding questions.

The number selected for the new account should leave some unused numbers on either side of it for other accounts that might need to be added. The middle, unused account number between existing numbers 510 and 520 is 515. Therefore, 515 is assigned as the account number for the new account.

510	Advertising Expense	(Existing account)
515	GASOLINE EXPENSE	(NEW ACCOUNT)
520	Insurance Expense	(Existing account)

When an account is no longer needed, it is removed from the general ledger and the chart of accounts. For example, if Rugcare were to buy its own equipment and building, there would be no need for the rent expense account. The account numbered 540 would be removed, and that number would become unused and available to assign to another account if the need should arise.

When a new account is added at the end of a ledger division, the next number in a sequence of 10s is used. For example, suppose Rugcare needs to add another expense account, Water Expense, to show more detail about one of the utility expenses. The expense accounts are arranged in alphabetic order. Therefore, the new account would be added at the end of the expense section of the chart of accounts. The last used expense account number is 570, as shown on the chart of accounts, Illustration 6-3. The next number in the sequence of 10s is 580, which is assigned as the number of the new account.

560	Supplies Expense	(Existing account)
570	Utilities Expense	(Existing account)
580	WATER EXPENSE	(NEW ACCOUNT)

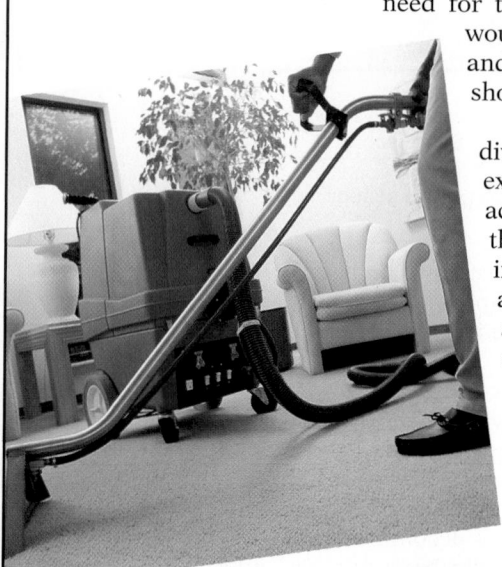

Rugcare has relatively few accounts in its general ledger and does not anticipate adding many new accounts in the future. Therefore, a three-digit account number adequately provides for the few account numbers that might be added. However, as the number of general ledger accounts increases, a business may change to four or more digits.

Charts of accounts with more than three digits are described in later chapters.

Opening General Ledger Accounts

Writing an account title and number on the heading of an account is called **opening an account**. A general ledger account is opened for each account listed on a chart of accounts. Accounts are opened and arranged in a general ledger in the same order as on the chart of accounts.

Cash, account number 110, is the first account on Rugcare's chart of accounts. The cash account is opened as shown in Illustration 6-5.

FYI

There are two steps to opening an account: Write the account title and account number on the heading of the account.

PART 2   Accounting for a Service Business Organized as a Proprietorship

ILLUSTRATION 6-5   Opening an account in a general ledger

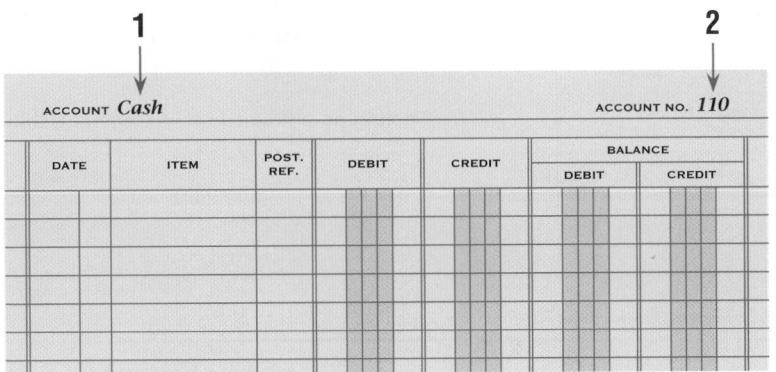

1 Write the account title, *Cash*, after the word *Account* in the heading.

2 Write the account number, *110*, after the words *Account No.* in the heading.

The same procedure is used to open all accounts listed on Rugcare's chart of accounts.

Audit Your Understanding

1. Describe the two parts of an account number.

2. List the two steps for opening an account.

POSTING FROM A JOURNAL TO A GENERAL LEDGER

Transferring information from a journal entry to a ledger account is called **posting.** Posting sorts journal entries so that all debits and credits affecting each account are brought together in one place. For example, all changes to Cash are brought together in the cash account.

Amounts in journal entries are recorded in either general amount columns or special amount columns. There are two rules for posting amounts from a journal. (1) Separate amounts in a journal's general amount columns are posted individually to the account written in the Account Title column. (2) Separate amounts in a journal's special amount columns are not posted individually. Instead, the special amount column totals are posted to the account named in the heading of the special amount column.

Posting Separate Amounts

For most, but not all journal entries, at least one separate amount is posted individually to a general ledger account. When an entry in a journal includes an amount in a general amount column and an account title in the Account Title column, the amount is posted individually.

FYI

Each separate amount in the general debit and credit columns is posted individually. The totals of these columns are not posted.

CHAPTER 6   Posting to a General Ledger   **103**

TEACH

Cover student pages 103–116 "Posting from a Journal to a General Ledger." The type of journal amount column an amount is recorded in determines how that amount is posted to the general ledger. Amounts in general amount columns are posted individually. Amounts in special amount columns are posted as part of the total of the amount column. Posting totals saves time and reduces errors because only the total of many of the same kinds of transactions must be posted as opposed to posting each amount each time a frequently occurring transaction is journalized. Review the purposes of the Post. Ref. columns. Emphasize the importance of the last step in posting as a record of what entries have been posted. Stress that a check mark in the Post. Ref. column means that nothing on that line is posted.

Posting a Separate Amount from a General Debit Column. Each separate amount in the General Debit and General Credit columns of a journal is posted to the account written in the Account Title column. Posting an amount from the General Debit column is shown in Illustration 6-6.

ILLUSTRATION 6-6 Posting an amount from a General Debit column

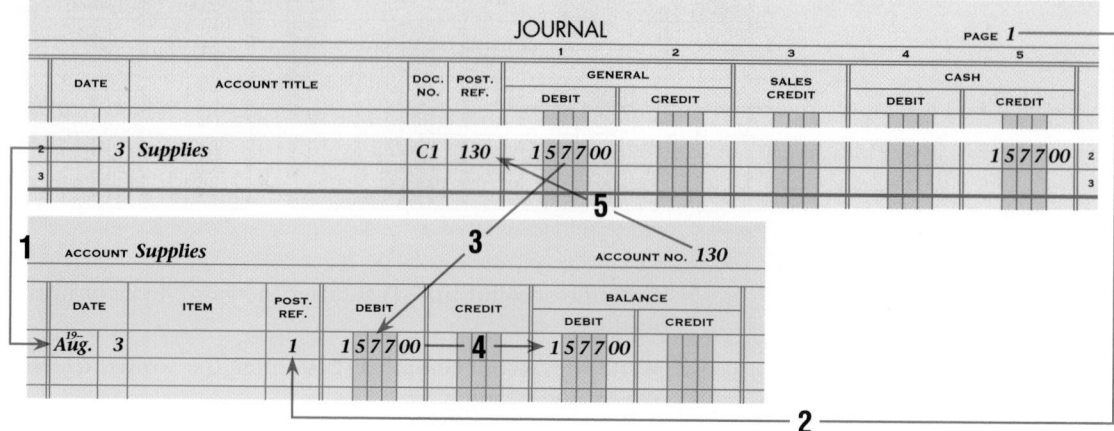

1 Write the date, *19--, Aug. 3*, in the Date column of the account, Supplies.

2 Write the journal page number, *1*, in the Post. Ref. column of the account. Post. Ref. is an abbreviation for Posting Reference.

3 Write the debit amount, *$1,577.00*, in the Debit amount column.

4 Write the new account balance, *$1,577.00*, in the Balance Debit column. Because this entry is the first in the supplies account, the previous balance is zero. The new account balance is calculated as shown below.

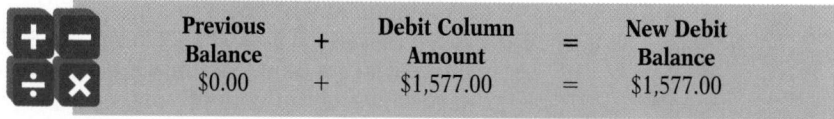

	Previous Balance	+	Debit Column Amount	=	New Debit Balance
	$0.00	+	$1,577.00	=	$1,577.00

5 Return to the journal and write the account number, *130*, in the Post. Ref. column of the journal.

The numbers in the Post. Ref. columns of the general ledger account and the journal serve three purposes. (1) An entry in an account can be traced to its source in a journal. (2) An entry in a journal can be traced to where it was posted in an account. (3) If posting is interrupted, the accounting personnel can easily see

APPLIED SKILLS: BUILDING STUDY SKILLS

Direct students to create a Quick Reference Guide (QRG) on a small card or sheet of paper to use as an aid in posting. Students should write the five steps for posting on an index card to use as a QRG. Have them use this QRG whenever they post transactions.

which entries in the journal still need to be posted. A blank in the Post. Ref. column of the journal indicates that posting for that line still needs to be completed. *Therefore, the posting reference is always recorded in the journal as the last step in the posting procedure.*

A second amount is posted to the supplies account from Rug-care's journal, line 4, as shown in Illustration 6-7.

APPLY

Use Transparency 6-1 to demonstrate posting.

Guided Practice

Guide students through Drill 6-D2. Direct students to complete the drill using the form in the working papers as the students decide which amounts are posted individually for each of the lines given as a group. All students should agree with the answer before proceeding to the next line. The questions in Instruction 2 should be answered and discussed with the class as a group.

Independent Practice

Assign Term 6 and Questions 8–15, Problem 6-2, Study Guide 6, and Mastery Problem 6-M.

ILLUSTRATION 6-7   Posting a second amount to an account

FYI

Remember to always post amounts in the ledger from left to right.

1 Write the date, 7, in the Date column of the account. The month and year are written only once on a page of a ledger account unless the month or year changes.

2 Write the journal page number, *1*, in the Post. Ref. column of the account.

3 Write the debit amount, *$2,720.00*, in the Debit amount column.

4 Write the new account balance, *$4,297.00*, in the Balance Debit column. The new account balance is calculated as shown below.

	Previous Debit Balance	+	Debit Column Amount	=	New Debit Balance
	$1,577.00	+	$2,720.00	=	$4,297.00

5 Return to the journal and write the account number, *130*, in the Post. Ref. column of the journal.

APPLIED SKILLS:
MATHEMATICS

Use the MATH WORK SHEET in the Teacher's Resource Guide to integrate applied mathematics. In this work sheet, students will apply math concepts to calculate new account balances.

CHAPTER 6   Posting to a General Ledger   **105**

TEACHING STRATEGIES: COOPERATIVE LEARNING

Select a group of three students to prepare a bulletin board that includes the five steps for posting. Allow five days for this project. Appoint a spokesperson to make a presentation to the class of these five steps and how they are necessary to post correctly.

- Assess student understanding by checking solutions for the Independent Practice activities.

- Review "Summary of Posting to a General Ledger." Use Transparency 6-2, Chapter Summary.

Reteach

- Use Demonstration Problem 6B, instructions 2 and 3. This problem can be done on the overhead with the students completing the problem at their desks.

- Duplicate and assign Math Work Sheet Chapter 6, Calculating New Account Balances from the Masters and Solutions to Enrichment/Application Activities Section in the Teacher's Resource Guide to provide additional practice on the mathematics of calculating new account balances in the general ledger.

- Assign Recycling Problem 6R.

Extend

Assign Cases for Critical Thinking 1 and 2 and Challenge Problem 6-C (the challenge is that the columns of the journal have been rearranged).

Enrich

- Assign the Application Program Disk software to be used with Problems 6-M and 6-C.

- Use *Automated Accounting 6.0* or higher with Mastery Problem 6-M and Challenge Problem 6-C to enable students to reinforce the concept of posting.

- Assign the Electronic Study Guide Chapter 6 to complete the study guide from the working papers at the computer.

- Assign students the Applied Communications activity on page 118.

Posting a Separate Amount from a General Credit Column. An amount in the General Credit column of a journal is posted as shown in Illustration 6-8.

ILLUSTRATION 6-8   Posting an amount from a General Credit column

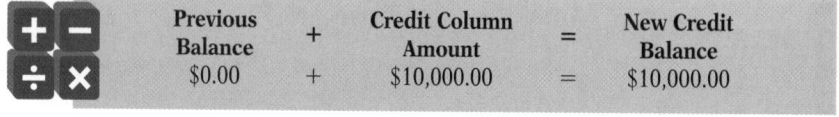

1 Write the date, *19--, Aug. 1*, in the Date column of the account.

2 Write the journal page number, *1*, in the Post. Ref. column of the account.

3 Write the credit amount, *$10,000.00*, in the Credit amount column.

4 Write the new account balance, *$10,000.00*, in the Balance Credit column. The new account balance is calculated as shown below.

	Previous Balance		Credit Column Amount		New Credit Balance
	$0.00	+	$10,000.00	=	$10,000.00

5 Return to the journal and write the account number, *310*, in the Post. Ref. column of the journal.

Journal Entries that are not Posted Individually. Several lines in Rugcare's journal contain separate amounts that are not to be posted individually. These include forwarding totals and amounts recorded in special amount columns.

The totals brought forward from page 1 are shown on line 1 of the journal in Illustration 6-9. None of these separate total amounts on line 1 are posted individually to general ledger accounts. To assure that no postings are overlooked, no blank posting reference

106   PART 2   Accounting for a Service Business Organized as a Proprietorship

---

TEACHING STRATEGIES: DIFFERENT LEARNING STYLES

Kinesthetic Learner. When learning how to post, the kinesthetic learner would prefer to participate in the posting process. This can be done by using a transparency of the ledger account and having each student complete one or more steps of the posting process at the overhead projector. Other students can be completing the posting process individually on printed ledger accounts.

spaces should be left in the Post. Ref. column of the journal. Therefore, when the totals were forwarded to page 2 of the journal, a check mark was placed in the Post. Ref. column of line 1 to show that no separate amounts are posted individually.

CLOSURE

Use Audit Your Understanding questions.

ASSESS

- Administer Problem Test Chapter 6.
- Administer a MicroExam test for Chapter 6.

ILLUSTRATION 6-9   Check marks show that amounts are not posted

JOURNAL   PAGE 2

					1 GENERAL DEBIT	2 GENERAL CREDIT	3 SALES CREDIT	4 CASH DEBIT	5 CASH CREDIT	
DATE		ACCOUNT TITLE	DOC. NO.	POST. REF.						
1	Aug. 20	Brought Forward		✓	7 9 2 0 00	12 9 2 0 00	2 3 1 9 00	12 3 1 9 00	5 0 0 0 00	1
11	31	Miscellaneous Expense	C15	530	7 00				1 2 00	11
12		Repair Expense		550	5 00					12
13	31	Ben Furman, Drawing	C16	320	5 0 00				5 0 0 00	13
14	31 ✓		T31	✓			2 9 0 00	2 9 0 00		14
15	31	Totals			8 9 3 00	12 9 2 0 00	4 2 9 1 00	14 2 9 1 00	6 0 1 9 00	15
16					(✓)	(✓)				16
17										17

Check mark indicates that amounts ARE NOT posted individually

Check marks indicate that general amount column totals ARE NOT posted

Remember that a check mark in the Post. Ref. column means nothing on that line is posted.

Separate amounts in the special amount columns, Sales Credit, Cash Debit, and Cash Credit, are not posted individually. For example, on line 14 of the journal, Illustration 6-9, two separate $290.00 amounts are recorded in two special amount columns, Sales Credit and Cash Debit.

A check mark was placed in the Post. Ref. column on line 14 when the entry was journalized. The check mark indicates that no separate amounts are posted individually from this line. Instead, the totals of the special amount columns are posted.

Posting the Totals of Amount Columns

Separate amounts in special amount columns *are not* posted individually. The separate amounts are part of the special amount column totals. Only the totals of special amount columns *are* posted.

Remember that only the totals of special amount columns are posted.

Totals of General Debit and General Credit Amount Columns. The General Debit and General Credit columns are not special amount columns because the column headings do not contain the name of an account. All of the separate amounts in the General Debit and General Credit amount columns are posted individually.

APPLIED SKILLS: COMMUNICATIONS

Surveys of business managers show that communication skills are one of the most desired traits in new employees. The student activity APPLIED COMMUNICATIONS provides an opportunity for students to practice their communication and language arts skills on topics that directly relate to accounting. This Applied Communication activity gives students some background information on the use of office fax machines. This activity also requires students to compose a memorandum and prepare a cover sheet for transmitting the memorandum using a fax machine. If a fax machine is available, you may wish to include instruction on how to operate it to send the student memo.

Therefore, the column totals *are not* posted. A check mark in parentheses is placed below each general amount column total as shown in Illustration 6-9. The check mark indicates that the totals of the General Debit and General Credit columns are not posted.

A check mark in the Post. Ref. column indicates that amounts are not to be posted individually. On the totals line, the amounts in the special amount columns are posted. Therefore, a check mark is not placed in the Post. Ref. column for the totals line.

Posting the Totals of Special Amount Columns. Rugcare's journal has three special amount columns for which only totals are posted: Sales Credit, Cash Debit, and Cash Credit.

Posting the Total of the Sales Credit Column. The Sales Credit column of a journal is a special amount column with the account title Sales in the heading. Each separate amount in a special amount column could be posted individually. However, all of the separate amounts are debits or credits to the same account. Therefore, an advantage of a special amount column is that only the column total needs to be posted. For example, 14 separate sales transactions are recorded in the Sales Credit column of Rugcare's August journal. Instead of making 14 separate credit postings to Sales, only the column total is posted. As a result, only one posting is needed, which saves 13 postings. The smaller number of postings means 13 fewer opportunities to make a posting error. Posting special amount column totals saves time and results in greater accuracy.

The total of Rugcare's Sales Credit column is posted as shown in Illustration 6-10.

ILLUSTRATION 6-10   Posting the total of the Sales Credit column

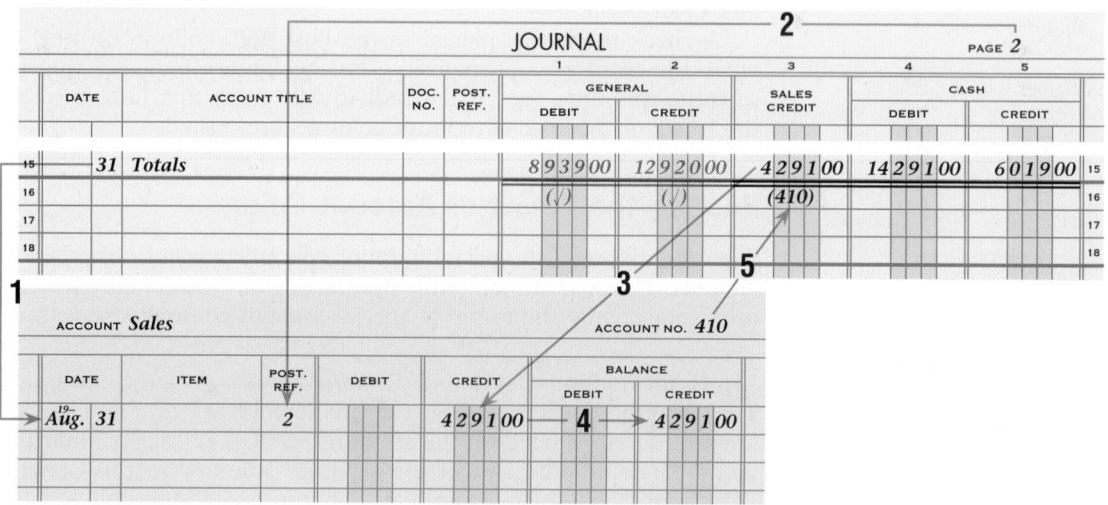

1 Write the date, *19--, Aug. 31*, in the Date column of the account, Sales.

2 Write the journal page number, *2*, in the Post. Ref. column of the account.

3 Write the column total, *$4,291.00*, in the Credit amount column.

4 Write the new account balance, *$4,291.00*, in the Balance Credit column. The new account balance is calculated as shown below.

Previous Balance	+	Credit Column Amount	=	New Credit Balance
$0.00	+	$4,291.00	=	$4,291.00

5 Return to the journal and write the account number in parentheses, *(410)*, below the Sales Credit column total.

■ Belinda Hughes ■
BOO-BOO-BABY, INC., NEW YORK, NEW YORK

Belinda Hughes is looking for investors with $250,000 to help turn her company into a large corporation. Her business, Boo-Boo-Baby, Inc., based in New York, makes a designer line of children's coats and accessories. It all started for Hughes, formerly head designer of women's coats in a New York company, when she became an aunt and made her first children's coat in 1986. Then she turned an interest into an opportunity by starting her own company designing children's outerwear.

Hughes started her business with an investment of $15,000 from her personal savings. By 1991 she had sold $240,000 of children's wear and expects solid future growth. Five years after the start of her Boo-Boo-Baby line, her children's coats were carried in over 100 stores across the country, including major department stores such as Macy's, Bloomingdale's, Sak's, and Nordstrom's.

Hughes uses bold colors, unusual fabrics, and her own creative designs to distinguish her products in the large children's apparel market. She describes her coats as "funky" and says, "I design coats so that when people see them, they absolutely must have them."

She has a plan for the future of her business which includes the continued distribution of her coats to major department stores. Her ambitions also include a moderately priced line for chain stores.

Hughes is a graduate of the Parsons School of Design and has strong opinions about the value of education. When asked what she would recommend to students who would like to be successful business owners, she said "a good education is very important." She also believes that a course in accounting is crucial for business success because "you have to know the numbers to succeed." Although her degree is in design, her degree program included business courses. Drawing from personal experience, she emphasized that students should pay attention in school because you can't know today what will be important in real life later.

Personal Visions in Business

TEACHING STRATEGIES: DIFFERENT LEARNING STYLES

Print Learner. When learning how to post, the print learner would prefer to see the process in print. This can be done by distributing a handout which explains the steps in the posting process. Allow the student to study the handout.

Posting the Total of the Cash Debit Column. The Cash Debit column of a journal is posted as shown in Illustration 6-11.

ILLUSTRATION 6-11   Posting the total of the Cash Debit column

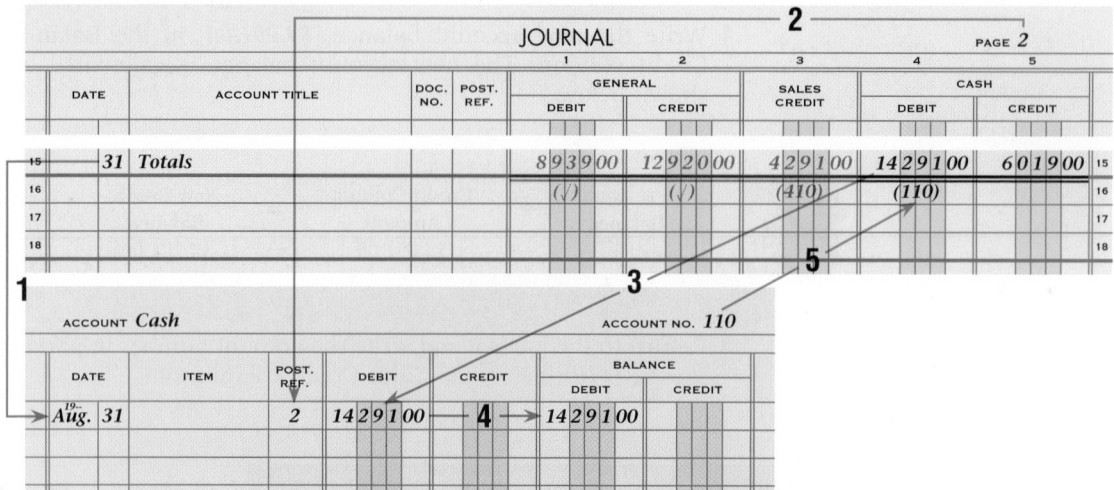

FYI

Two zeros are written in the cents column when an amount is in even dollars, such as $500.00. If the cents column is left blank, doubts may arise later about the correct amount.

1 Write the date, *19--, Aug. 31,* in the Date column of the account, Cash.

2 Write the journal page number, *2,* in the Post. Ref. column of the account.

3 Write the column total, *$14,291.00,* in the Debit amount column.

4 Write the new account balance, *$14,291.00,* in the Balance Debit column. The new account balance is calculated as shown below.

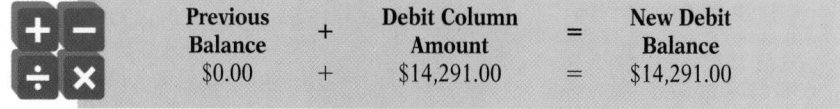

	Previous Balance	+	Debit Column Amount	=	New Debit Balance
	$0.00	+	$14,291.00	=	$14,291.00

5 Return to the journal and write the account number in parentheses, *(110),* below the Cash Debit column total.

Posting the Total of the Cash Credit Column. Posting the total of a journal's Cash Credit column is shown in Illustration 6-12.

110   PART 2   Accounting for a Service Business Organized as a Proprietorship

ILLUSTRATION 6-12   Posting the total of the Cash Credit column

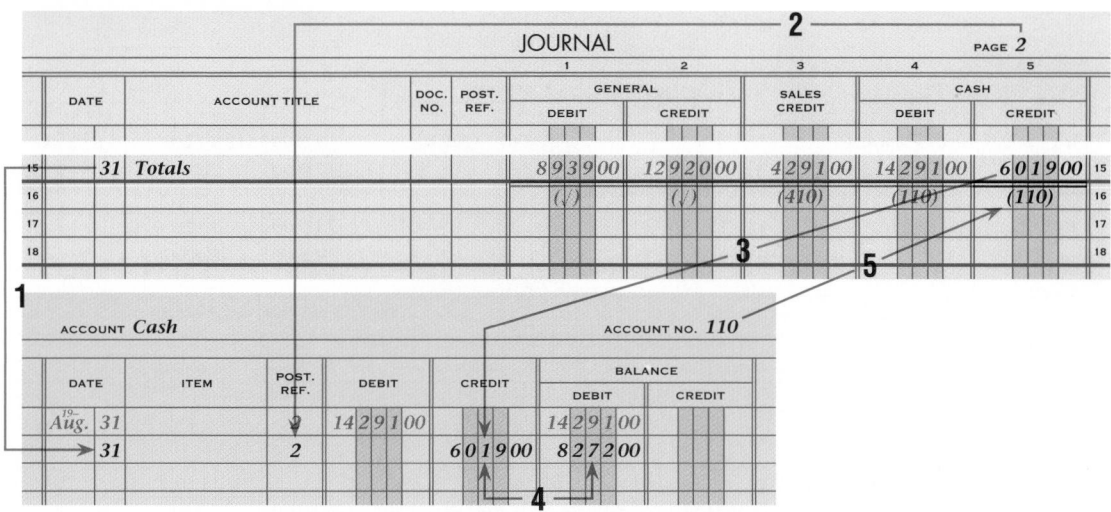

1 Write the date, *31*, in the Date column of the account, Cash.

2 Write the journal page number, *2*, in the Post. Ref. column of the account.

3 Write the column total, *$6,019.00*, in the Credit amount column.

4 Write the new account balance, *$8,272.00*, in the Balance Debit column. The new account balance is calculated as shown below.

	Previous Debit Balance	–	Credit Column Amount	=	New Debit Balance
	$14,291.00	–	$6,019.00	=	$8,272.00

Whenever the debits in an account exceed the credits, the account balance is a debit. Whenever the credits in an account exceed the debits, the account balance is a credit.

5 Return to the journal and write the account number in parentheses, *(110)*, below the Cash Credit column total.

Journal Page with Posting Completed

Page 2 of Rugcare's August journal, after all posting has been completed, is shown in Illustration 6-13.

Errors are corrected in a way that does not cause doubts about what the correct information is. If an error is recorded, cancel the error by neatly drawing a line through the incorrect item. Write the correct item immediately above the canceled item.

ILLUSTRATION 6-13   A journal page after posting has been completed

JOURNAL

PAGE 2

	DATE	ACCOUNT TITLE	DOC. NO.	POST. REF.	GENERAL DEBIT	GENERAL CREDIT	SALES CREDIT	CASH DEBIT	CASH CREDIT	
					1	2	3	4	5	
1	Aug. 20	Brought Forward		√	7 9 2 0 00	12 9 2 0 00	2 3 1 9 00	12 3 1 9 00	5 0 0 0 00	1
2	21	√	T21	√			2 7 0 00	2 7 0 00		2
3	24	√	T24	√			3 0 0 00	3 0 0 00		3
4	25	√	T25	√			3 1 0 00	3 1 0 00		4
5	26	√	T26	√			2 4 5 00	2 4 5 00		5
6	27	Utilities Expense	C13	570	7 0 00				7 0 00	6
7	27	√	T27	√			2 9 0 00	2 9 0 00		7
8	28	Supplies	C14	130	4 3 4 00				4 3 4 00	8
9	28	√	T28	√			2 6 7 00	2 6 7 00		9
10	28	Miscellaneous Expense	M3	530	3 00				3 00	10
11	31	Miscellaneous Expense	C15	530	7 00				1 2 00	11
12		Repair Expense		550	5 00					12
13	31	Ben Furman, Drawing	C16	320	5 0 0 00				5 0 0 00	13
14	31	√	T31	√			2 9 0 00	2 9 0 00		14
15	31	Totals			8 9 3 9 00	12 9 2 0 00	4 2 9 1 00	14 2 9 1 00	6 0 1 9 00	15
16					(√)	(√)	(410)	(110)	(110)	16
17										17

Audit Your Understanding

1. List the five steps of posting from the journal to the general ledger.

General Ledger with Posting Completed

Rugcare's general ledger, after all posting from the August journal is completed, is shown in Illustration 6-14.

The use of the accounts, Income Summary, Insurance Expense, and Supplies Expense, is described in Chapter 8.

ILLUSTRATION 6-14   A general ledger after posting has been completed

ACCOUNT **Cash**   ACCOUNT NO. **110**

DATE	ITEM	POST. REF.	DEBIT	CREDIT	BALANCE DEBIT	BALANCE CREDIT
Aug. 31		2	14 2 9 1 00		14 2 9 1 00	
31		2		6 0 1 9 00	8 2 7 2 00	

ACCOUNT **Petty Cash**   ACCOUNT NO. **120**

DATE	ITEM	POST. REF.	DEBIT	CREDIT	BALANCE DEBIT	BALANCE CREDIT
Aug. 17		1	2 0 0 00		2 0 0 00	

ILLUSTRATION 6-14 A general ledger after posting has been completed (continued)

ACCOUNT **Supplies**   ACCOUNT NO. *130*

DATE	ITEM	POST. REF.	DEBIT	CREDIT	BALANCE DEBIT	BALANCE CREDIT
Aug. 3		1	1 5 7 7 00		1 5 7 7 00	
7		1	2 7 2 0 00		4 2 9 7 00	
20		1	2 0 0 00		4 4 9 7 00	
28		2	4 3 4 00		4 9 3 1 00	

ACCOUNT **Prepaid Insurance**   ACCOUNT NO. *140*

DATE	ITEM	POST. REF.	DEBIT	CREDIT	BALANCE DEBIT	BALANCE CREDIT
Aug. 4		1	1 2 0 0 00		1 2 0 0 00	

ACCOUNT **Butler Cleaning Supplies**   ACCOUNT NO. *210*

DATE	ITEM	POST. REF.	DEBIT	CREDIT	BALANCE DEBIT	BALANCE CREDIT
Aug. 7		1		2 7 2 0 00		2 7 2 0 00
11		1	1 3 6 0 00			1 3 6 0 00

ACCOUNT **Dale Office Supplies**   ACCOUNT NO. *220*

DATE	ITEM	POST. REF.	DEBIT	CREDIT	BALANCE DEBIT	BALANCE CREDIT
Aug. 20		1		2 0 0 00		2 0 0 00

ACCOUNT **Ben Furman, Capital**   ACCOUNT NO. *310*

DATE	ITEM	POST. REF.	DEBIT	CREDIT	BALANCE DEBIT	BALANCE CREDIT
Aug. 1		1		10 0 0 0 00		10 0 0 0 00

APPLIED SKILLS: WORD PROCESSING

If you wish to integrate word processing into your accounting course, you may direct students to answer the end-of-chapter Accounting Terms, Questions for Individual Study, and Cases for Critical Thinking using their word processing software.

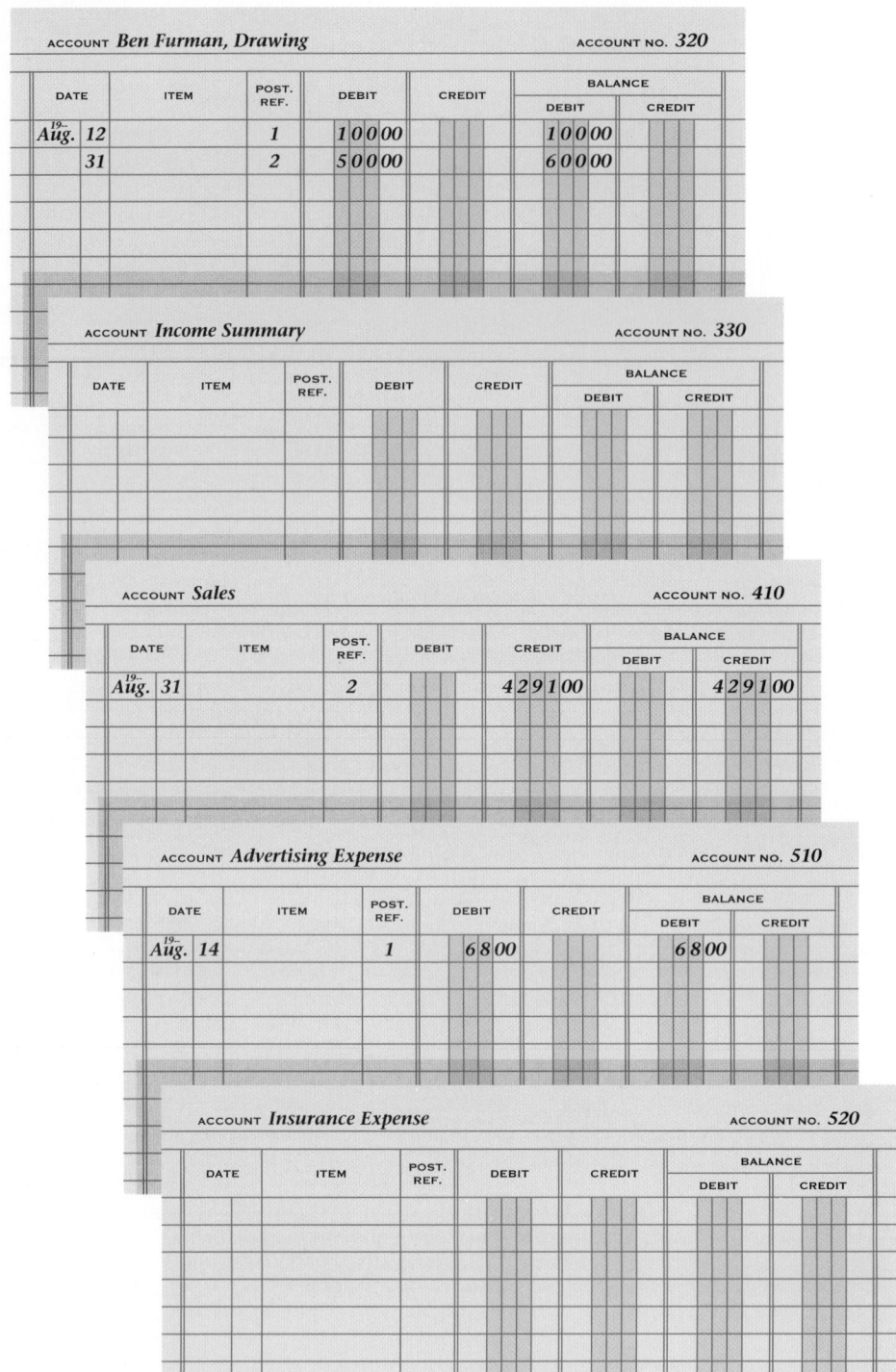

ACCOUNT **Ben Furman, Drawing**   ACCOUNT NO. *320*

DATE	ITEM	POST. REF.	DEBIT	CREDIT	BALANCE DEBIT	BALANCE CREDIT
Aug. 12		1	1000 00		1000 00	
31		2	500 00		600 00	

ACCOUNT **Income Summary**   ACCOUNT NO. *330*

DATE	ITEM	POST. REF.	DEBIT	CREDIT	BALANCE DEBIT	BALANCE CREDIT

ACCOUNT **Sales**   ACCOUNT NO. *410*

DATE	ITEM	POST. REF.	DEBIT	CREDIT	BALANCE DEBIT	BALANCE CREDIT
Aug. 31		2		4291 00		4291 00

ACCOUNT **Advertising Expense**   ACCOUNT NO. *510*

DATE	ITEM	POST. REF.	DEBIT	CREDIT	BALANCE DEBIT	BALANCE CREDIT
Aug. 14		1	68 00		68 00	

ACCOUNT **Insurance Expense**   ACCOUNT NO. *520*

DATE	ITEM	POST. REF.	DEBIT	CREDIT	BALANCE DEBIT	BALANCE CREDIT

ILLUSTRATION 6-14

A general ledger after posting has been completed (concluded)

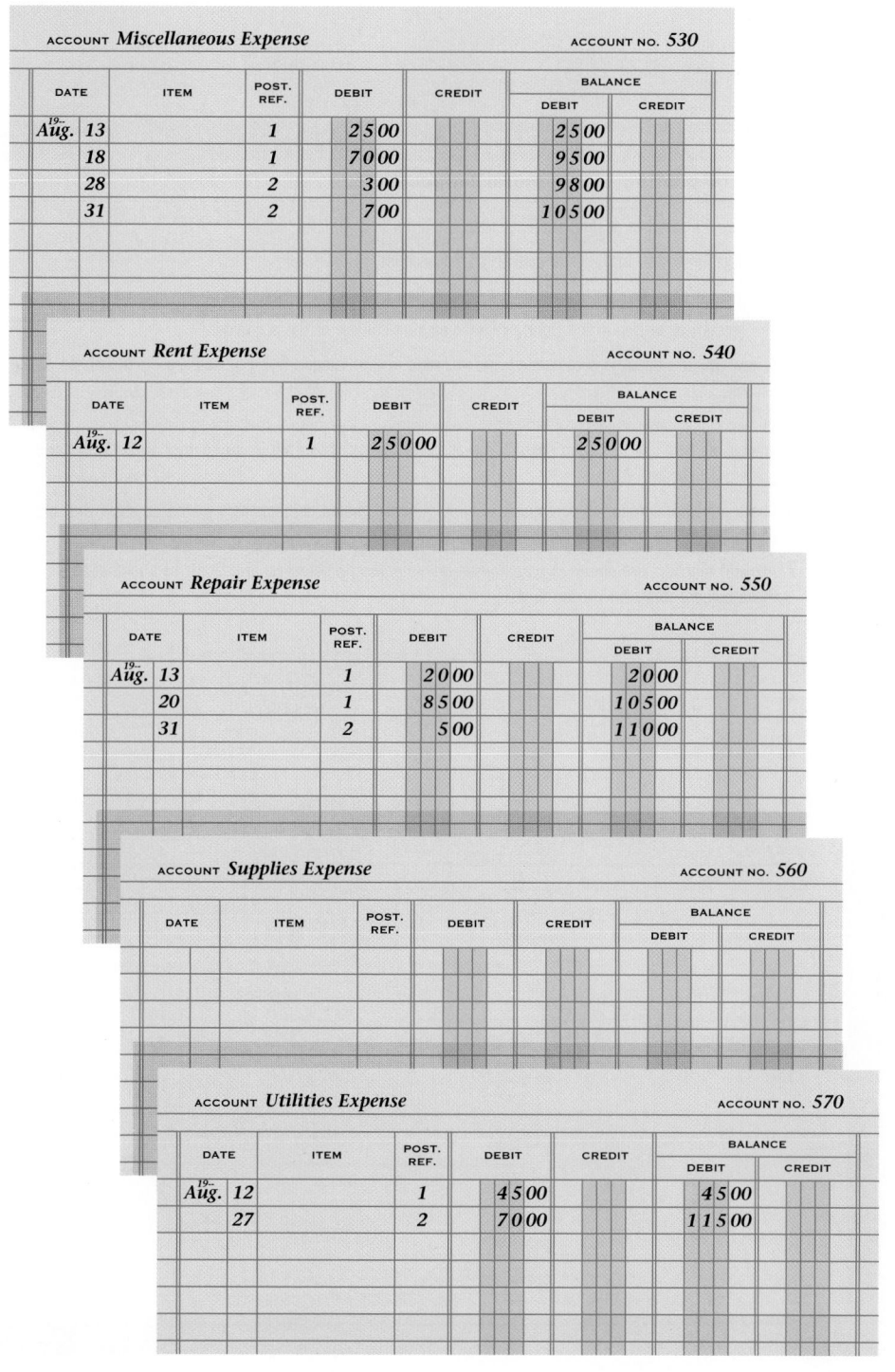

ACCOUNT *Miscellaneous Expense*   ACCOUNT NO. *530*

DATE	ITEM	POST. REF.	DEBIT	CREDIT	BALANCE DEBIT	BALANCE CREDIT
Aug. 13		1	25 00		25 00	
18		1	70 00		95 00	
28		2	3 00		98 00	
31		2	7 00		105 00	

ACCOUNT *Rent Expense*   ACCOUNT NO. *540*

DATE	ITEM	POST. REF.	DEBIT	CREDIT	BALANCE DEBIT	BALANCE CREDIT
Aug. 12		1	250 00		250 00	

ACCOUNT *Repair Expense*   ACCOUNT NO. *550*

DATE	ITEM	POST. REF.	DEBIT	CREDIT	BALANCE DEBIT	BALANCE CREDIT
Aug. 13		1	20 00		20 00	
20		1	85 00		105 00	
31		2	5 00		110 00	

ACCOUNT *Supplies Expense*   ACCOUNT NO. *560*

DATE	ITEM	POST. REF.	DEBIT	CREDIT	BALANCE DEBIT	BALANCE CREDIT

ACCOUNT *Utilities Expense*   ACCOUNT NO. *570*

DATE	ITEM	POST. REF.	DEBIT	CREDIT	BALANCE DEBIT	BALANCE CREDIT
Aug. 12		1	45 00		45 00	
27		2	70 00		115 00	

The procedures for posting from Rugcare's journal are summarized in Illustration 6-15.

TEACHING STRATEGIES:
APPLYING VISUALS

Direct students to Summary Illustration 6-15 and review posting to a general ledger.

SUMMARY ILLUSTRATION 6-15

Summary of posting to a general ledger

Seven steps are followed in posting amounts from a journal to a general ledger.

1 The date is written in the Date column of the account.

2 The journal page number is written in the Post. Ref. column of the account.

3 The amount is written in the Debit or Credit amount column of the account.

4 A new account balance is calculated and recorded in the Balance Debit or Balance Credit column of the account.

5 An account number is placed in the Post. Ref. column of the journal to show to which account a separate amount on that line has been posted. The account number is written in the journal *as the last step* in the posting procedure.

6 Check marks are placed in parentheses below general amount columns of a journal to show that the totals of these columns *are not* posted.

7 Account numbers are placed in parentheses below special amount column totals of a journal to show that these column totals have been posted.

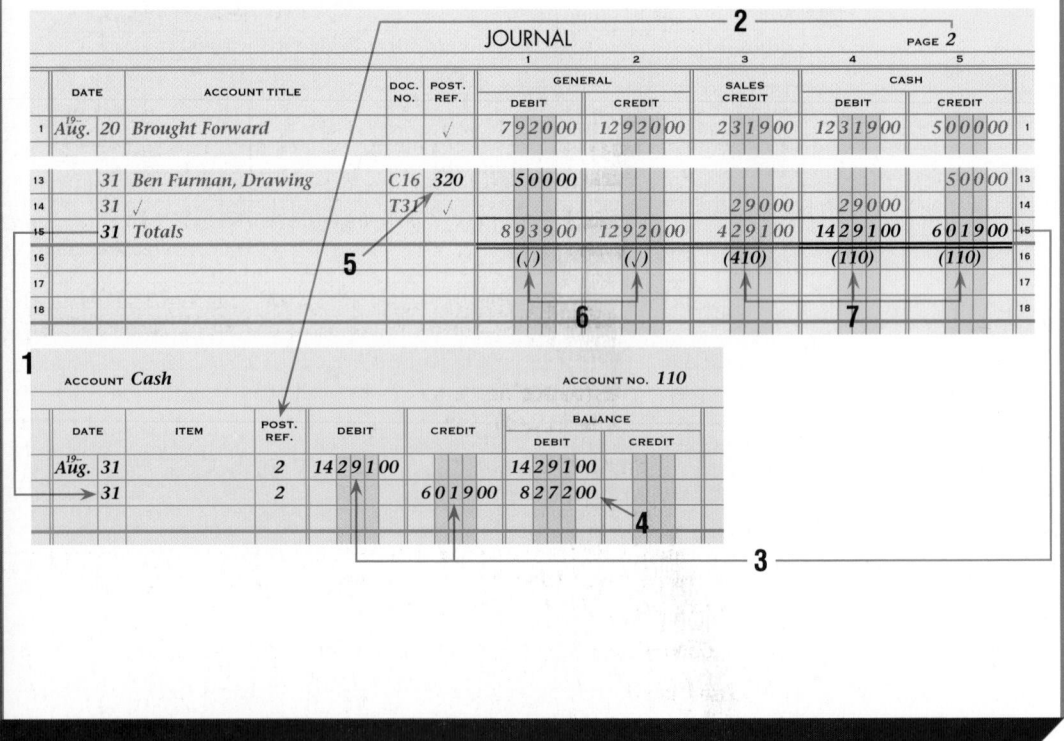

SOFTWARE FOCUS

Software may be used for independent practice or enrichment/extension as the instructor deems appropriate. For this chapter, the following software may be used: *Automated Accounting 6.0* or higher with Mastery Problem 6-M and Challenge Problem 6-C; Application Program Disk with Mastery Problem 6-M and Challenge Problem 6-C; the Electronic Study Guide Chapter 6.

ACCOUNTING TERMS   EPT(a)

What is the meaning of each of the following?

1. **ledger**
2. **general ledger**
3. **account number**
4. **file maintenance**
5. **opening an account**
6. **posting**

QUESTIONS FOR INDIVIDUAL STUDY   EPT(b)

1. Why are general ledger accounts used in an accounting system?
2. In what order are accounts arranged in a general ledger?
3. On Rugcare's chart of accounts, what is indicated by each digit in an account number?
4. Why are unused numbers usually left between account numbers on a chart of accounts?
5. What number is assigned to a new account inserted in a chart of accounts between accounts numbered 530 and 540?
6. What number is assigned to a new account added at the end of a division in which the last account is numbered 550?
7. What are the two steps in opening a new account?
8. Why are amounts posted from a journal to general ledger accounts?
9. What three purposes are served by recording posting reference numbers in journals and accounts?
10. How is a new account balance calculated when the previous balance is a debit and a debit entry is posted?
11. Why are separate amounts in special amount columns of a journal not posted individually?
12. Why are totals of a journal's general amount columns not posted?
13. What is done to indicate that the general amount column totals are not posted?
14. What is done to indicate that a special amount column total in a journal has been posted?
15. How is a new account balance calculated when the previous balance is a debit, a credit entry is posted, and the previous debit balance is larger than the credit entry?

CASES FOR CRITICAL THINKING   EPT(b)

CASE 1 Angela Silva does not use a journal in her business records. She records the debits and credits for each transaction directly in the general ledger accounts. Is Ms. Silva using the correct procedure? Explain your answer.

CASE 2 Philip Westing does the accounting work for his business. When posting, he first transfers all of the information to the general ledger accounts. Then he returns to the journal and, all at one time, writes the account numbers in the Post. Ref. column of the journal. Diana Young also does the accounting work for her business. When posting, she writes all the account numbers in the Post. Ref. column of the journal before she transfers any information to the accounts. Is Mr. Westing or Miss Young following the correct procedure? Explain your answer.

ACCOUNTING TERMS

1. **ledger:** A group of accounts. (p. 100)
2. **general ledger:** A ledger that contains all accounts needed to prepare financial statements. (p. 100)
3. **account number:** The number assigned to an account. (p. 100)
4. **file maintenance:** The procedure for arranging accounts in a general ledger, assigning account numbers, and keeping records current. (p. 101)
5. **opening an account:** Writing an account title and number on the heading of an account. (p. 102)
6. **posting:** Transferring information from a journal entry to a ledger account. (p. 103)

QUESTIONS FOR INDIVIDUAL STUDY

1. To summarize in one place all changes to a single account. (p. 99)
2. In the same order as the accounts appear on financial statements. (p. 101)
3. The first digit indicates in which general ledger division the account is located. The second and third digits indicate the location of the account within that division. (p. 101)
4. So there will be unused numbers available if new accounts are to be inserted. (p. 101)
5. The new number is 535, halfway between the existing accounts. (p. 102)
6. The new number is 560. (p. 102)
7. (a) Write the account title after the word *Account.* (b) Write the account number after the words *Account No.* (p. 103)
8. So that all debits and credits affecting each account balance are brought together in one place. (p. 103)
9. (a) An entry in a general ledger account can be traced to its source in a journal. (b) An entry in a journal can be traced to where it was posted in an account. (c) If posting is interrupted, the accounting personnel can easily see which entries in the journal still need to be posted. (p. 104)
10. Previous debit balance + debit column amount = new debit balance. (p. 105)
11. Because only totals of the special amount columns are posted to save time in posting. (p. 107)

12. Because all separate amounts in the general amount columns are posted individually. (p. 107)

13. A check mark in parentheses is placed below the general amount column totals. (p. 108)

14. The account number in parentheses is placed below the column total showing to which account the column total has been posted. (p. 109)

15. Previous debit balance − credit column amount = new debit balance. (p. 111)

CASES FOR CRITICAL THINKING

Case 1 No, Ms. Silva is not using the correct procedure. If she needed to find the information about a specific transaction on a specific date, she would have to search through all her accounts because the information would not be recorded in one place in chronological order. Ms. Silva needs to use both a journal and general ledger accounts.

Case 2 Neither Mr. Westing nor Miss Young is following the correct procedure. If Mr. Westing is interrupted, or forgets to post an amount on a journal line, he has no way of knowing that an amount has not been posted. Miss Young has the same problem. A basic accounting rule is that the last step in the posting procedure is to return to the journal and record the account number in the Post. Ref. column of the journal as each amount is posted.

APPLIED COMMUNICATIONS

Student solutions will vary, since this activity requires original composition. However, the memorandum should include the elements required in Instruction 1 (an introductory sentence or paragraph and a concluding statement). The cover sheet should include the four items specified in the Applied Communications case.

APPLIED COMMUNICATIONS

A fax machine allows a business to send documents anywhere in a matter of minutes using a telephone line. Business managers no longer have to wait days to obtain the information needed to make timely business decisions. Some businesses use fax machines to increase sales, allowing customers to order items without leaving their offices or homes.

Most fax machines in offices are located in one or more central locations and used by a number of different workers for both sending and receiving documents. To facilitate directing the document to the intended receiver, it is usual practice to include a cover sheet in the fax transmission. The cover sheet should include the information below.

1. Name of the person sending the message.
2. Name of the person to receive the message.
3. Phone number of both sending and receiving fax machines.
4. Total number of pages being transmitted, including the cover sheet.

INSTRUCTIONS:

1. Write a memorandum responding to the following scenario: Ben Furman is at the bank applying for a business loan. The bank's loan officer has asked for a list of Rugcare's asset, liability, owner's equity, sales, and expense accounts, and their current balances. Mr. Furman has just called you and asked that you fax him at the bank with this information. In your memorandum include an introductory sentence or paragraph and end with a concluding statement.

2. Prepare a cover sheet for transmitting a fax message. The bank's fax machine telephone number is 800-555-3333. Use your own name and personal telephone number or school telephone number.

DRILLS FOR UNDERSTANDING EPT(b,c,d)

DRILL 6-D1 Preparing a chart of accounts

The following account descriptions refer to the location of accounts in a chart of accounts similar to the one for Rugcare, page 100.

1. The first asset account
2. The first liability account
3. The first owner's equity account
4. The first revenue account
5. The first expense account
6. The third asset account
7. The fourth expense account
8. The owner's drawing account
9. The cash account
10. The sales account
11. The owner's capital account

Use a form similar to the following. Account description 1 is given as an example.

1	2
Account Description	**Account Number**
1. The first asset account	*110*

INSTRUCTIONS:

1. In Column 1, write the account description.
2. In Column 2, write the account number. Account numbers are assigned by 10s.
3. Check your answers with Rugcare's chart of accounts, page 100. Determine if your answers are the same for each account as shown on the chart of accounts.
4. Cover your answers in Column 2. Practice rapidly recalling the account numbers for each account.

DRILL 6-D2 Analyzing posting from a journal

INSTRUCTIONS:

1. Use completed page 2 of the journal shown in Illustration 6-13. For each of the following lines in that illustration, write the separate amount, if any, that is posted individually. Also, write the account title to which the amount is posted.

   a. Line 6   **c.** Line 10   **e.** Line 12
   b. Line 9   **d.** Line 11   **f.** Line 13

2. Use the general ledger accounts shown in Illustration 6-14. Answer the following questions.

   a. What item or transaction is represented by the amount in the cash account's Credit column?
   b. What item or transaction is represented by the amount in the prepaid insurance account's Debit Balance column?
   c. What item or transaction is represented by the amount in the sales account's Credit column?
   d. Where in the journal is the information found about the item or transaction recorded in the advertising expense account's Debit column?

CHECK FIGURES

See Teacher's Edition of Working Papers for complete solutions to drills and problems.

Drill 6-D1   Account numbers: 110, 210, 310, 410, 510, 130, 540, 320, 110, 410, 310

Drill 6-D2   (1) All are posted individually except item b. (2a) 6,019 total cash paid.

Problem 6-1   Two new accounts are 515 and 550.

Problem 6-2   Cash account balance, 4,790; Supplies, 1,500; Donard Supplies, 310.00.

APPLICATION PROBLEMS   EPT(c,d)

PROBLEM 6-1 Preparing a chart of accounts

Marie Wilson owns a service business called Wilson's Services. Wilson's Services uses the following accounts.

Automobile Expense	Miscellaneous Expense
Bartel Supplies	Novack Office Supplies
Cash	Prepaid Insurance
Insurance Expense	Sales
Marie Wilson, Capital	Supplies
Marie Wilson, Drawing	Supplies Expense

INSTRUCTIONS:

1. Prepare a chart of accounts similar to the one described in this chapter. Arrange expense accounts in alphabetic order. Use 3-digit account numbers and number the accounts within a division by 10s.
2. Two new accounts, Gasoline Expense and Utilities Expense, are to be added to the chart of accounts prepared in Instruction 1. Assign account numbers to the two new accounts.

PROBLEM 6-2 Posting to a general ledger

Don Ley owns a service business called AquaCare. AquaCare's journal, which is needed to complete this problem, is in the working papers that accompany this textbook.

INSTRUCTIONS:

1. Open a general ledger account for each of the following accounts.

Assets	**Revenue**
110 Cash	410 Sales
120 Supplies	**Expenses**
130 Prepaid Insurance	510 Advertising Expense
Liabilities	520 Miscellaneous Expense
210 Donard Supplies	530 Rent Expense
220 Fell Office Supplies	540 Utilities Expense
Owner's Equity	
310 Don Ley, Capital	
320 Don Ley, Drawing	

2. Post the separate amounts on each line of the journal that need to be posted individually.
3. Post the journal's special amount column totals.

ENRICHMENT PROBLEMS   EPT(d)

MASTERY PROBLEM 6-M Journalizing and posting to a general ledger

AUTOMATED

APPLICATION

Al Hiatt owns a service business called Hiatt Cleaning. Hiatt Cleaning's general ledger accounts are given in the working papers that accompany this textbook.

INSTRUCTIONS:

1. Open an account for Utilities Expense. Use the 3-digit numbering system described in the chapter.
2. Journalize the following transactions completed during November of the current year. Use page 1 of a journal. Source documents are abbreviated as follows: check, C; memorandum, M; receipt, R; calculator tape, T.

Nov. 1. Received cash from owner as an investment, $7,000.00. R1.
3. Paid cash for rent, $300.00. C1.
5. Paid cash for insurance, $200.00. C2.
6. Received cash from sales, $750.00. T6.
9. Paid cash for miscellaneous expense, $5.00. C3.
11. Paid cash for supplies, $500.00. C4.
13. Bought supplies on account from Major Supplies, $600.00. M1.
13. Received cash from sales, $700.00. T13.
16. Paid cash for electric bill, $40.00. C5.
18. Paid cash on account to Major Supplies, $300.00. C6.
20. Paid cash for advertising, $30.00. C7.
20. Received cash from sales, $770.00. T20.
25. Paid cash for supplies, $150.00. C8.
27. Paid cash for supplies, $100.00. C9.
27. Received cash from sales, $1,150.00. T27.
30. Paid cash to owner for personal use, $300.00. C10.
30. Received cash from sales, $410.00. T30.

3. Prove the journal.
4. Prove cash. The beginning cash balance on November 1 is zero. The balance on the next unused check stub is $8,855.00.
5. Rule the journal.
6. Post from the journal to the general ledger.

CHALLENGE PROBLEM 6-C Journalizing and posting to a general ledger

AUTOMATED

Dee Worthy owns a service business called HouseCare. HouseCare's general ledger accounts are given in the working papers that accompany this textbook.
HouseCare uses the following journal.

JOURNAL							Page	
Debit		Date	Account Title	Doc. No.	Post Ref.	Credit		
Cash	General					General	Sales	Cash
1								

INSTRUCTIONS:

1. Journalize the following transactions completed during March of the current year. Use page 5 of a journal. Source documents are abbreviated as follows: check, C; memorandum, M; receipt, R; calculator tape, T.

Mar. 1. Owner invested money, $8,000.00. R1.
    3. Paid March rent, $350.00. C1.
    5. Wrote a check for miscellaneous expense, $5.00. C2.
    9. Paid for quarterly insurance, $250.00. C3.
   11. Paid for supplies, $400.00. C4.
   13. Cash sales, $450.00. T13.
   16. Supplies were bought on account from Hartwood Supplies, $700.00. M1.
   18. Hartwood Supplies was paid on account, $350.00. C5.
   19. Paid telephone bill, $60.00. C6.
   20. Cash was received from sales, $1,100.00. T20.
   23. Wrote a check for June advertising, $50.00. C7.
   23. Paid for supplies, $150.00. C8.
   27. Paid for supplies, $150.00. C9.
   27. Received cash from sales, $1,830.00. T27.
   30. Owner withdrew cash for personal use, $400.00. C10.
   31. Received cash from sales, $410.00. T31.

2. Prove the journal.
3. Prove cash. The beginning cash balance on March 1 is zero. The balance on the next unused check stub is $9,625.00.
4. Rule the journal.
5. Post from the journal to the general ledger.

Safety and Health Considerations

ELECTRICAL EQUIPMENT

The following rules protect the operator of the equipment, other persons in the environment, and the equipment itself.

1. Do not unplug equipment by pulling on the electrical cord. Instead, grasp the plug at the outlet and remove it.
2. Do not stretch electrical cords across an aisle where someone might trip over them.
3. Avoid food and beverages near equipment where a spill might result in an electrical short.
4. Do not attempt to remove the cover of equipment for any reason while the power is turned on.
5. Do not attempt to repair equipment while it is plugged in. To avoid damage most repairs should be done by an authorized service technician.
6. Always turn the power off when finished using equipment.
7. Do not overload extension cords.
8. Follow manufacturer recommendations for safe use.
9. Replace frayed electrical cords immediately.

MICROCOMPUTERS

1. To avoid damage to the drives, do not insert pencils or other implements in floppy disk drives.
2. To prevent overheating, avoid blocking air vents.
3. Position keyboards to prevent bumping or dropping them off the work surface.

MONITORS

1. Most manufacturers advise repair by authorized service technicians only.
2. Adjust brightness and focus for comfortable viewing.
3. Avoid glare on the monitor screen.
4. Do not leave fingerprints on the screen. Keep the screen clear of dust. Only use a soft cloth for cleaning the screen.

PRINTERS

1. Do not let jewelry, ties, scarves, loose sleeves, or other clothing get caught in the machinery. This could result in damage to the machinery and could cause personal injury.
2. Exercise caution when using toxic chemicals such as toner in order to avoid spills.

DISKETTES

1. Write/protect all program software to avoid accidental erasure.
2. Do not bend or fold diskettes.
3. Do not write on a diskette with a hard or sharp-pointed pen or pencil; use a felt-tip marker.
4. Do not touch exposed surfaces of diskettes.
5. Be sure the disk drive is not running when you insert or remove a diskette.
6. Keep diskettes away from extreme hot or cold temperatures. Do not leave diskettes in a car during very hot or cold weather.
7. Keep diskettes away from magnetic fields such as transformers and magnets.
8. Store diskettes in the storage envelopes.
9. Keep diskettes away from smoke, ashes, and dust, including chalk dust.
10. Do not leave diskettes in the disk drive for prolonged periods, such as overnight.

Recording Transactions for a Proprietorship

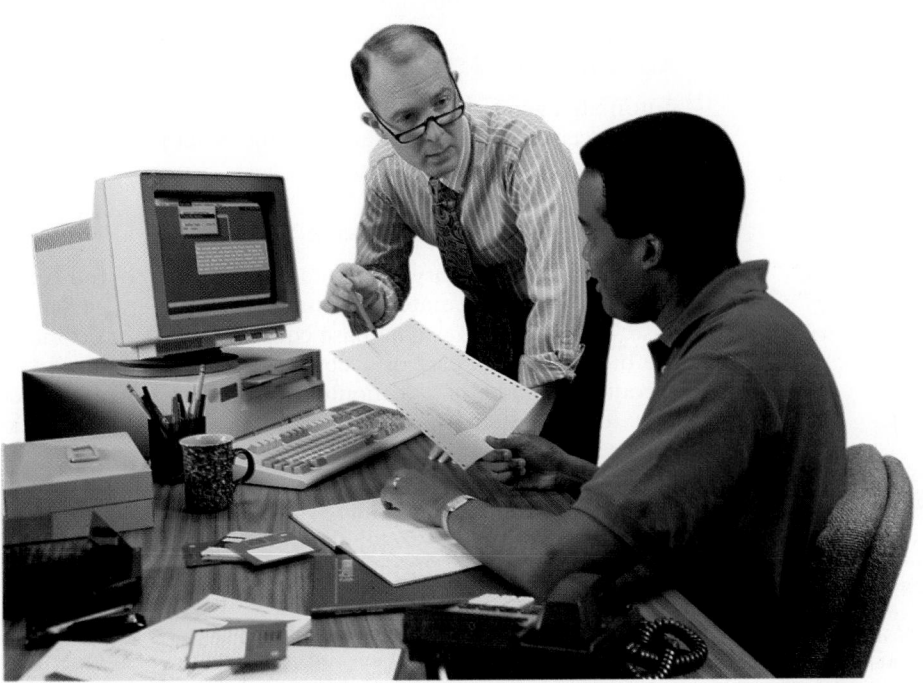

Financial data may be recorded and reported by hand or by machine. An accounting system in which data are recorded and reported mostly by hand is referred to as **manual accounting**. Some businesses use automated machines to speed the recording and reporting process. An accounting system in which data are recorded and reported mostly by using automated machines is **automated accounting**. However, even in automated accounting, some procedures are done by hand.

Rugcare, the service business described in Part 2, uses a manual accounting system. Rugcare's manual journalizing and posting procedures are described in Chapters 5 and 6. Integrating Automated Accounting Topic 1 describes procedures for using automated accounting software to journalize and post Rugcare's transactions. The Automated Accounting Problems contain instructions for using automated accounting software to solve Mastery Problem 6-M and Challenge Problem 6-C, Chapter 6.

123

COMPUTER PROGRAMMING

A **computer program** is a set of instructions followed by a computer to process data. The programs used to direct the operations of a computer are **software**. An **automated accounting system** is a collection of computer programs designed to automate accounting procedures.

A person needs special training to be a **computer programmer**. Understanding accounting concepts and procedures is helpful to a computer programmer. Just as important, an accountant needs to know basic computer concepts and procedures in order to assist a computer programmer and to use a computer.

AUTOMATED GENERAL LEDGER ACCOUNTING

Automated general ledger accounting is based on the same accounting concepts as a manual accounting system. The only differences are equipment and procedures.

General Ledger Data Base

A pre-arranged file in which data can be entered and retrieved is a **data base**. In automated accounting the general ledger is a data base. A general ledger data base contains general information about the business, the chart of accounts, and financial activity for each account. A model of a computer application stored on a computer disk for repeated use is a **template**. Rugcare stores its general ledger data base as a template.

To perform accounting procedures, the general ledger data base is retrieved from the template. The file is saved as a new file using another file name, which allows the template to remain in its original format. Changes to the original template should be made only when necessary to update the file for future repeated use.

The new file is then used to complete accounting activities. Transaction data may then be recorded in the general ledger accounts. At the end of a fiscal period, financial data are retrieved and financial reports are prepared.

Chart of Accounts Numbering Systems

Chart of accounts numbering systems are similar for both automated and manual accounting. Rugcare's three-digit numbering system is described in Chapter 6. The procedures for arranging accounts in a general ledger, assigning account numbers, and keeping records current are **file maintenance**.

File Maintenance

File maintenance procedures are similar for both automated and manual accounting. In automated accounting the chart of accounts is part of the general ledger data base. The chart of accounts requires maintenance periodically to add and change accounts. File maintenance requires five steps. (1) A chart of accounts input form is prepared. (2) The general ledger data base is retrieved. (3) Data

FYI

To save a file under another name, pull down the File menu and choose the Save As menu command. Key the path to the drive and directory that contains the data files. Save your data base with a file name of XXX1A (where XXX are your initials).

from the chart of accounts input form are keyed into the computer to change the chart of accounts. (4) A revised chart of accounts report is prepared to verify the accuracy of the data that was keyed. (5) The revised chart of accounts is stored as part of the general ledger data base.

Adding an Account Within a Ledger Division. Rugcare decided to add a new account titled Gasoline Expense within the expenses division of the chart of accounts. The entry on the chart of accounts input form to add Gasoline Expense is shown on line 1 of Illustration T1-1.

Entry for file maintenance

A new account number added within a ledger division is determined using procedures described in Chapter 6. Using the unused middle number, the new account number for Gasoline Expense is 515.

510	Advertising Expense	(Existing Account)
515	Gasoline Expense	(NEW ACCOUNT)
520	Insurance Expense	(Existing Account)

Three steps are followed to complete a chart of accounts input form.

1 The run date, *08/12/--*, is written in the space provided at the top of the form. The **run date** is the date to be printed on reports prepared by a computer.

2 Each account number is written in the Account Number column.

3 Each account title is written in the Account Title column just as it will appear on the output. The automated accounting software specifies the maximum number of spaces that can be used for account numbers and account titles. Any account title that contains more than 25 characters must be abbreviated when recorded on the chart of accounts input form. All of Rugcare's account titles fit the 25-character space allowed, so none have to be abbreviated.

Adding an Account at the End of a Ledger Division. A new account number added at the end of a ledger division is determined following procedures described in Chapter 6. The next number in a

☞ FYI ☜

Automated Accounting 6.0 software limits account titles to 25 characters. Therefore, abbreviations may be necessary.

TEACH

Cover student pages 123–127, "Computer Programming" and "Automated General Ledger Accounting." This lesson introduces some terms and concepts that students will need to understand whenever they use an automated accounting system. An automated general ledger accounting system is based on the same accounting concepts as a manual accounting system. Therefore, Rugcare's three-digit numbering system does not change.

Review the definition of file maintenance. (File maintenance is the procedure for arranging accounts in a general ledger, assigning account numbers, and keeping records current.) Summarize the five steps needed for file maintenance so that students have an understanding of the procedure.

It is important to emphasize that *Automated Accounting 6.0* software limits account titles to 25 characters. When students are completing input forms, account titles may need to be abbreviated.

APPLY

Use Transparency AA-1, Blank Chart of Accounts Maintenance Input Form, to point out and explain the three steps that are followed when completing a chart of accounts maintenance input form.

Guided Practice

Students should be at the computers. Guide students through booting the software and loading Optional Problem DB-1A from the template. Instruct students to complete the file maintenance activities only as you go step-by-step through the procedures.

Independent Practice

Assign Automating Problem 6-M Instruction 1a. Students should complete input forms for file maintenance only.

TEACHING STRATEGIES: EXPANDING BEYOND THE CLASSROOM

Small business owners who recently automated their company's accounting system may be invited to the classroom to share their experiences. The speaker could describe the benefits such as time savings and also the problems and frustrations involved in automating an accounting system.

- Assess student understanding by checking solutions to Independent Practice activity.
- Ask students to explain the numbering system for adding an account to the chart of accounts.

Reteach

Use Transparency AA-1 to add "Gasoline Expense" to the chart of accounts while pointing out the file maintenance procedures.

Extend

Assign students to add "Water Expense" to the chart of accounts on Optional Problem DB-1A.

Enrich

Assign students to find an article from a magazine that discusses computers in business. Have them share the article with the class.

CLOSURE

Ask students to list the steps for file maintenance.

sequence of 10 is used for a new account added at the end of a chart of accounts division.

Processing File Maintenance Data

In automated accounting the activities are arranged so that each activity may be selected using a keyboard or some other input device such as a mouse. A list of options from which an activity may be selected is a **menu**. Rugcare's software has a menu bar and a series of pull-down menus. When a menu is selected from the menu bar, a pull-down list of commands will appear. The menu bar shown in Illustration T1-2 contains six different menus. (1) File. (2) Options. (3) Journals. (4) Ledgers. (5) Reports. (6) Help.

ILLUSTRATION T1-2   Menu bar and pull-down file menu

The general ledger data base is retrieved from the template disk by first selecting File from the menu bar. The Open Accounting File command is then chosen from the File menu, as shown in Illustration T1-2, to retrieve a specific general ledger data base from the template disk.

To process file maintenance data, select the Ledgers menu from the menu bar. The Maintain Accounts command is then chosen from the Ledgers menu to display the data entry window for entering file maintenance data. File maintenance data are keyed from the chart of accounts input form. The entry for Gasoline Expense is shown in Illustration T1-3.

SOFTWARE FOCUS

Automated Accounting 6.0 is available in both DOS and Mac versions. For illustration purposes, the DOS version has been used in this text. Refer to the documentation that accompanies the software for specific instructions for operating *Automated Accounting 6.0.*

After all file maintenance data have been keyed, the Reports menu is selected from the menu bar. The Accounts command is chosen from the Reports menu to display the Report Selection window. When the Report Selection window appears, select the Chart of Accounts option to display the revised chart of accounts report. The revised chart of accounts report is checked for accuracy by comparing the report with the chart of accounts input form. The revised chart of accounts report, as shown in Illustration T1-4 on the next page, is printed and filed for future reference.

RECORDING TRANSACTIONS

In manual accounting, transactions are analyzed into debit and credit parts as described in Chapter 4 and recorded in a journal as described in Chapter 5. Transaction data are then periodically posted from a journal to a general ledger as described in Chapter 6.

In automated accounting, transactions are also analyzed into debit and credit parts. A general journal input form is used to journalize transactions. After each transaction has been keyed, the software is directed to post to the general ledger accounts.

INTEGRATING AUTOMATED ACCOUNTING—TOPIC 1   **127**

TEACH

Cover student pages 127–132, "Recording Transactions." This lesson shows the procedures for recording transactions on general journal input forms and for processing journal entries. Emphasize that automated accounting also requires that transactions be analyzed into debit and credit parts. For that reason, it is necessary to record transactions on input forms prior to entering data into the computer.

ILLUSTRATION T1-4   Revised chart of accounts report

```
                Rugcare
          Chart of Accounts
               08/12/--
-------------------------------------
Account    Account
Number     Title
-------------------------------------
110        Cash
120        Petty Cash
130        Supplies
140        Prepaid Insurance
210        Butler Cleaning Supplies
220        Dale Office Supplies
310        Ben Furman, Capital
320        Ben Furman, Drawing
410        Sales
510        Advertising Expense
515        Gasoline Expense
520        Insurance Expense
530        Miscellaneous Expense
540        Rent Expense
550        Repair Expense
560        Supplies Expense
570        Utilities Expense
```

The following transactions completed by Rugcare are analyzed into debit and credit parts in Chapter 4.

Received Cash from Owner as an Investment

August 1, 19--. Received cash from owner as an investment, $10,000.00. Receipt No. 1.

Dollar and cent signs are not entered on input forms.

The journal entry to record this transaction is on lines 1 and 2 of the general journal input form shown in Illustration T1-5.

The run date, *08/12/--*, is written in the space provided at the top of the input form. The run date indicates the date to be printed on the report.

On line 1, the date, *08/01*, is written in the Date column. The source document number, *R1*, is entered in the Reference column. The cash account number, *110*, is recorded in the Account No. column. The Customer/Vendor No. column is left blank. Entries requiring the use of this column are described in Part 3, Integrating Automated Accounting Topic 4. The amount debited to Cash, *$10,000.00*, is written in the Debit column.

On line 2, the account number for Ben Furman, Capital, *310*, is written in the Account No. column. The Date and Reference numbers are entered only once for each complete transaction. Therefore, the Date and Reference columns are left blank starting with the second line of an entry. The amount credited to Ben Furman, Capital, *$10,000.00*, is recorded in the Credit column.

128   INTEGRATING AUTOMATED ACCOUNTING—TOPIC 1

ILLUSTRATION T1-5 General journal input form with transactions recorded

RUN DATE 08/12/--
MM DD YY

GENERAL JOURNAL
Input Form

	DATE MM/DD	REFERENCE	ACCOUNT NO.	CUSTOMER/ VENDOR NO.	DEBIT	CREDIT	
1	08/01	R1	110		10000 00		1
2	/		310			10000 00	2
3	/03	C1	130		1577 00		3
4	/		110			1577 00	4
5	/04	C2	140		1200 00		5
6	/		110			1200 00	6
7	/07	M1	130		2720 00		7
8	/		210			2720 00	8
9	/11	C3	210		1360 00		9
10	/		110			1360 00	10
11	/12	T12	110		525 00		11
12	/		410			525 00	12
13	/12	C4	540		250 00		13
14	/		110			250 00	14
15	/12	C5	570		45 00		15
16	/		110			45 00	16
17	/12	C6	320		100 00		17
18	/		110			100 00	18
19	/						19
25	/						25
				PAGE TOTALS	17777 00	17777 00	
				FINAL TOTALS	17777 00	17777 00	

Use Transparency AA-2, Blank General Journal Input Form, to explain how to record journal entries. Emphasize that the totals of a general journal input form should be compared to ensure that debits equal credits. This should always be done before entering data into the computer.

Guided Practice

Students should be at the computers. Guide students through booting the software and loading Optional Problem DB-1A from the template. Instruct students to journalize each transaction as you go step-by-step through the procedures.

Independent Practice

Assign students to complete the remaining activities for Automating Problem 6-M.

Paid Cash for Supplies

August 3, 19--. Paid cash for supplies, $1,577.00. Check No. 1.

The journal entry to record this transaction is on lines 3 and 4 of Illustration T1-5. Supplies is debited and Cash is credited for $1,577.00.

Paid Cash for Insurance

August 4, 19--. Paid cash for insurance, $1,200.00. Check No. 2.

The journal entry to record this transaction is on lines 5 and 6 of Illustration T1-5. Prepaid Insurance is debited and Cash is credited for $1,200.00.

Bought Supplies on Account

August 7, 19--. Bought supplies on account from Butler Cleaning Supplies, $2,720.00. Memorandum No. 1.

The journal entry to record this transaction is on lines 7 and 8 of Illustration T1-5. Supplies is debited and Butler Cleaning Supplies is credited for $2,720.00.

FYI

Dollar signs and cent signs are not keyed when using Automated Accounting 6.0 software. When the cents are zero (.00), key only the dollar amount. For example, if the amount is 15.00, key 15. The software automatically assigns the .00.

TEACHING STRATEGIES: COOPERATIVE LEARNING

Using automated accounting software to complete accounting problems is an ideal cooperative learning experience. Students working in groups can collaborate on completing input forms and keying data.

- Assess student understanding by checking solutions to Automating Problem 6-M.
- Ask students to explain the procedures for keying transactions into the software.

Reteach

Review Illustrations T1-5 through T1-7. These illustrations can be used to reinforce the procedures for recording and processing journal entries using an automated accounting system. Use Transparency AA-2 to review the steps in keying the transactions into the software.

Extend

Assign Automating Problem 6-C.

CLOSURE

Review the steps for recording transactions using automated accounting software.

Paid Cash on Account

August 11, 19--. Paid cash on account to Butler Cleaning Supplies, $1,360.00. Check No. 3.

The journal entry to record this transaction is on lines 9 and 10 of Illustration T1-5. Butler Cleaning Supplies is debited and Cash is credited for $1,360.00.

Received Cash from Sales

August 12, 19--. Received cash from sales, $525.00. Tape No. 12.

The journal entry to record this transaction is on lines 11 and 12 of Illustration T1-5. Cash is debited and Sales is credited for $525.00.

Paid Cash for an Expense

August 12, 19--. Paid cash for rent, $250.00. Check No. 4.

The journal entry to record this transaction is on lines 13 and 14 of Illustration T1-5. Rent Expense is debited and Cash is credited for $250.00.

Illustration T1-5 includes a journal entry, lines 15 and 16, for Utilities Expense. This transaction is journalized in the same way as the cash payment for rent.

Paid Cash to Owner for Personal Use

August 12, 19--. Paid cash to owner for personal use, $100.00. Check No. 6.

The journal entry to record this transaction is on lines 17 and 18 of Illustration T1-5. Ben Furman, Drawing is debited and Cash is credited for $100.00.

Completing a General Journal Input Form

After all transactions have been journalized, Rugcare totals the Debit and Credit amount columns. The totals are recorded on the Page Totals line provided at the bottom of the input form.

A journal entry should not be split on two different general journal input forms. Therefore, if a complete journal entry cannot be entered on an input form, a new input form is started. The totals for all pages are then entered *only* on the last page on the Final Totals line. The two totals are compared to assure that debits equal credits. If only one general journal input form is required then the totals are recorded on the Page Totals line and the Final Totals line.

FYI

A journal entry should not be split on two different general journal input forms.

Processing Journal Entries

To process journal entries, the Journals menu is selected from the menu bar. The General Journal command is chosen from the Journals menu to display the data entry window for entering transaction data from the general journal input form. Rugcare keys the

INTEGRATING AUTOMATED ACCOUNTING—TOPIC 1

transaction data from the general journal input form one line at a time. Lines 1 and 2 are shown entered in Illustration T1-6.

ILLUSTRATION T1-6   Data entry window with a general journal entry recorded

**TEACHING STRATEGIES:
DIFFERENT LEARNING ABILITIES**

Limited English Proficiency (LEP) Students. Teachers report that LEP students are particularly successful using software to complete accounting problems. When working at the computer, LEP students are independent, work at their own pace, and do not feel the need to compete with other students in the classroom. LEP students can successfully complete automated problems because the problems do not require strong verbal skills.

FYI

To avoid damage to disk drives on the computer, do not insert any implements such as pencils in the disk drive.

After all lines on the input form have been keyed and posted, the Reports menu is selected from the menu bar. The Journals command is chosen from the Reports menu. The General Journal report is chosen from the Report Selection window. This selection displays the Selection Options screen shown in Illustration T1-7.

The data to be printed on reports can be restricted by specifying the date range or reference numbers as shown on Illustration T1-7. As Rugcare wants to print all transactions recorded on the general journal input form, pushing the *Ok* box directs the software to display a general journal report. The displayed general journal report is checked for accuracy by comparing the report totals, $17,777.00, with the totals on the general journal input form. Because the totals are the same, the general journal report is assumed to be correct. The general journal report is printed, as shown in Illustration T1-8, and is filed for future reference.

```
╔═══════ Selection Options ═══════╗
║           (Journals)            ║
║                                 ║
║  Date range: 08/01/-- to 08/12/-- ║
║                                 ║
║  Reference restriction:         ║
║                                 ║
╠═════════════════════════════════╣
║    [ OK ]      [ Cancel ]       ║
╚═════════════════════════════════╝
```

```
                        Rugcare
                    General Journal
                       08/12/--
-----------------------------------------------------------------
Date   Refer.  V/C Acct.  Title                   Debit     Credit
-----------------------------------------------------------------
08/01  R1          110    Cash                  10000.00
08/01  R1          310    Ben Furman, Capital              10000.00

08/03  C1          130    Supplies               1577.00
08/03  C1          110    Cash                              1577.00

08/04  C2          140    Prepaid Insurance      1200.00
08/04  C2          110    Cash                              1200.00

08/07  M1          130    Supplies               2720.00
08/07  M1          210    Butler Cleaning Supplies          2720.00

08/11  C3          210    Butler Cleaning Supplies 1360.00
08/11  C3          110    Cash                              1360.00

08/12  T12         110    Cash                    525.00
08/12  T12         410    Sales                              525.00

08/12  C4          540    Rent Expense            250.00
08/12  C4          110    Cash                               250.00

08/12  C5          570    Utilities Expense        45.00
08/12  C5          110    Cash                                45.00

08/12  C6          320    Ben Furman, Drawing     100.00
08/12  C6          110    Cash                               100.00
                                                ---------- ----------
                         Totals                 17777.00   17777.00
                                                ========== ==========
```

OPTIONAL PROBLEM DB-1A

Rugcare's general ledger data base is on the accounting textbook template. If you wish to complete these file maintenance activities and record transactions using automated accounting software, load the *Automated Accounting 6.0* or higher software. Select Data Base 1A (DB-1A) from the template disk. Read the Problem Instructions screen. Use the completed input forms in Illustrations T1-1 and T1-5, and follow the procedures described to process Rugcare's file maintenance activities and to record transactions.

AUTOMATED ACCOUNTING PROBLEMS

AUTOMATING MASTERY PROBLEM 6-M Journalizing and posting to a general ledger

INSTRUCTIONS:

1. Prepare input forms for Mastery Problem 6-M, Chapter 6.
   a. Prepare a chart of accounts input form to add Utilities Expense to the general ledger chart of accounts using the 3-digit numbering system described in Chapter 6. Use November 30 of the current year as the run date. Hiatt Cleaning uses the following chart of accounts.

Assets	**Revenue**
110 Cash	410 Sales
120 Supplies	**Expenses**
130 Prepaid Insurance	510 Advertising Expense
Liabilities	520 Miscellaneous Expense
210 Major Supplies	530 Rent Expense
Owner's Equity	
310 Al Hiatt, Capital	
320 Al Hiatt, Drawing	

   b. Record Hiatt Cleaning's transactions on a general journal input form. Use November 30 of the current year as the run date.
2. Load the *Automated Accounting 6.0* or higher software. Select data base *F6-M (First-Year Course Problem 6-M)* from the accounting textbook template. Read the Problem Instructions screen.
3. Select File from the menu bar and choose the Save As menu command. Key the path to the drive and directory that contains your data files. Save the data base with a file name of XXX6M (where XXX are your initials).
4. Key the data from the completed chart of accounts input form.
5. Display/print the revised chart of accounts report. Check the report for accuracy.
6. Key the transactions from the completed general journal input form.
7. Display/print the general journal report. Check the report for accuracy by comparing the report totals with the totals on the input form.

AUTOMATING CHALLENGE PROBLEM 6-C Journalizing and posting to a general ledger

INSTRUCTIONS:

1. Prepare input forms for Challenge Problem 6-C, Chapter 6.
2. Load the *Automated Accounting 6.0* or higher software. Select data base *F6-C (First-Year Course Problem 6-C)* from the accounting textbook template. Read the Problem Instructions screen.
3. Select File from the menu bar and choose the Save As menu command. Key the path to the drive and directory that contains your data files. Save the data base with a file name of XXX6C (where XXX are your initials).
4. Key the transactions from the completed general journal input form.
5. Display/print the general journal report. Check the report for accuracy by comparing the report totals with the totals on the input form.

OPTIONAL PROBLEM

OPTIONAL PROBLEM DB-1A provides students a hands-on learning activity. By keying the input forms illustrated in this topic, students have an opportunity for guided practice before actually working a problem independently. Refer to OPTIONAL PROBLEM DB-1A for information about automating this topic.

CHECK FIGURES

See the Teacher's Resource Guide for complete solutions to automating problems.
- Automating Problem 6-M: General Journal totals $13,305.00
- Automating Problem 6-C: General Journal totals $14,655.00

CHAPTER 7 OVERVIEW

Chapter 7 describes cash control systems for a sole proprietorship. Checking accounts, including writing checks and reconciling bank statements, are covered. Basic procedures are also introduced for petty cash usage for a proprietorship. It is important that cash control systems be described and applied for all forms of ownership. By doing so, the complete accounting cycle may be covered in its entirety for proprietorships, partnerships, and corporations.

GUIDE TO ACHIEVING LEARNING OBJECTIVES

Enabling Performance Tasks	TEACH Lesson Plans	APPLY Drills for Understanding	APPLY Application Problems	Mastery Problems	Challenge Problems	Cases for Critical Thinking	Recycling Problems	Reinforcement Activity
a. Define accounting terms related to using a checking account and a petty cash fund.	7-1, 7-2, 7-3							
b. Identify accounting concepts and practices related to using a checking account.	7-1, 7-2							
c. Prepare business papers related to using a checking account.	7-1		7-1, 7-2		7-C			
d. Reconcile a bank statement.	7-2	7-D1, 7-D2	7-3	7-M	7-C	Case 1	7-R	1A
e. Establish and replenish a petty cash fund.	7-3	7-D3	7-5	7-M		Case 2	7-R	1A
f. Record selected transactions related to using a checking account and a petty cash fund.	7-2, 7-3		7-3, 7-4, 7-5	7-M			7-R	1A

ENRICHMENT

SPECIAL FEATURES

Spreadsheet Options, page 145

Careers in Accounting, page 146

TECHNOLOGY CONNECTION

Automated Accounting 6.0 Problems 7-M, 7-C
Integrating Automated Accounting Topic 2 Optional Problems DB-2A, DB-2B

Accounting Tutorial Unit 1

Application Disk Program Problems 7-4, 7-5, 7-M

Spreadsheet Template Drill 7-D1, Problem 7-M

Electronic Study Guide

NEW, REVIEW, AND EXTENSION

ACTIVITIES/CONCEPTS/TRANSACTIONS	NEW	REVIEW/ EXTENSION
Checking accounts	✓	
Writing checks	✓	
Reconciling a bank statement	✓	
Electronic Funds Transfer (EFT)	✓	
Journalizing transactions		✓
Recording a bank service charge	✓	
Recording a dishonored check	✓	
Petty cash	✓	
Establishing a petty cash fund	✓	
Making payments from a petty cash fund	✓	
Replenishing a petty cash fund	✓	

For Mastery Problem 7-M and Recycling Problem 7-R, students are required to record transactions in a journal as well as post from a journal to a general ledger. This requirement provides additional practice for students on analyzing transactions into debit and credit parts.

	INFORMAL ASSESSMENT		FORMAL ASSESSMENT				
	Study Guide	Audit Your Understanding	Chapter MicroExam	Chapter Problem Test	Unit Problem Test	Unit Objective Test	Portfolio
Unit A			✓			✓	
Units B, C		✓	✓			✓	
				✓			
				✓	✓		✓
				✓			✓
				✓			✓

TEACHING MATERIALS

Teacher's Wraparound Edition of the Text

Teacher's Resource Guide

Teacher's Edition of Working Papers

Teacher's Edition of Demonstration/Recycling Problems

Teaching Transparencies

Accounting Tutorial Manual

Applied Math Work Sheets

MicroExam

APPLIED MATHEMATICS

APPLIED MATH/ACCOUNTING SKILL	APPLICATION
Reconciling bank statements	Prob. 7-D1
Calculating new balances on a check stub	Prob. 7-2
Calculating amount of petty cash replenishment	Prob. 7-D3

7

Cash Control Systems

ENABLING PERFORMANCE TASKS

After studying Chapter 7, you will be able to:

a Define accounting terms related to using a checking account and a petty cash fund.

b Identify accounting concepts and practices related to using a checking account.

c Prepare business papers related to using a checking account.

d Reconcile a bank statement.

e Establish and replenish a petty cash fund.

f Record selected transactions related to using a checking account and a petty cash fund.

TERMS PREVIEW

checking account • endorsement • blank endorsement • special endorsement • restrictive endorsement • postdated check • bank statement • dishonored check • electronic funds transfer • petty cash • petty cash slip

134

In accounting, money is usually referred to as cash. Most businesses make major cash payments by check. However, small cash payments for items such as postage and some supplies may be made from a cash fund kept at the place of business.

Because cash transactions occur more frequently than other types of transactions, more chances occur to make recording errors affecting cash. Cash can be transferred from one person to another without any question about ownership. Also, cash may be lost as it is moved from one place to another.

As a safety measure, Rugcare keeps most of its cash in a bank. Because all cash receipts are placed in a bank, Rugcare has written evidence to support its accounting records. Rugcare can compare its record of checks written with the bank's record of checks paid. Greater control of Rugcare's cash and greater accuracy of its cash records result from these procedures.

CHECKING ACCOUNTS

A business form ordering a bank to pay cash from a bank account is known as a check. A bank account from which payments can be ordered by a depositor is called a **checking account.**

Authorizing Signatures

When a checking account is opened, the bank customer must provide a signature on a signature card for the bank records. If several persons are authorized to sign checks, each person's signature must be on the signature card. Checks should always be signed with the same signature as on the signature card. Only Ben Furman is authorized to sign checks for Rugcare.

Depositing Cash

A bank customer prepares a deposit slip each time cash or checks are placed in a bank account. Deposit slips may differ slightly from one bank to another. Each bank designs its own deposit slips to fit the bank's recording machines. However, all deposit slips contain the same basic information as the slip shown in Illustration 7-1.

Checks are listed on a deposit slip according to the bank number on each check. For example, in Illustration 7-1, the number *93-108* identifies the bank on which the $10,000.00 check is written.

When a deposit is made, a bank gives the depositor a receipt. Many banks use a copy of the deposit slip with a printed or stamped verification as the receipt. The printed verification, *AUG 1 19-- D10000.00 RDS*, is shown along the top left edge of the deposit slip in Illustration 7-1. This printed verification means that a total of $10,000.00 was deposited on August 1. The initials *RDS* next to the amount are those of the bank employee who accepted the deposit.

CHAPTER 7   Cash Control Systems   **135**

LESSON PLAN 7-1

Materials

- Student pages 135–140
- Transparency 7-1 Blank Deposit Slip, Check and Stub
- Math Work Sheet Chapter 7, Part A: Calculating New Balances on a Check Stub (TRG)

Objectives (Enabling Performance Tasks)

a. Define accounting terms related to using a checking account and a petty cash fund.

b. Identify accounting concepts and practices related to using a checking account.

c. Prepare business papers related to using a checking account.

FOCUS

- In Chapter 5, cash receipts and cash payments transactions were journalized. Because of the large number of cash transactions a business has, more chances occur to make recording errors. Also, cash may be easily lost or stolen. Explain that a bank checking account provides safety and a record of cash payments.
- Introduce new vocabulary: checking account, endorsement, blank endorsement, special endorsement, restrictive endorsement, postdated check.

Cover student pages 135–140 "Check-ing Accounts." This lesson introduces some of the procedures followed when writing and depositing checks. Empha-size that endorsements should be writ-ten in ink and that there are space limitations on the back of a check for an endorsement (see Illustration 7-3). Write examples of the three types of endorse-ments on the board, explain each, and convey that the blank endorsement is most common. Stress that a restrictive endorsement should always be used if mailing a deposit to the bank or if endorsing a check before going to the bank.

Encourage good check writing habits. Before writing a check, the stub should always be completed. Writing the purpose of the check on the check stub is a good recordkeeping practice. Numbers should be written very close on a check so no one can change the amount. The check should be signed as the signature appears on the signature card. It is important to write the signa-ture the same each time. A check on which an error has been made should not be destroyed. Write void on the stub and check and file the check.

APPLY

Use Transparency 7-1 Blank Deposit Slip, Check, and Stub to demonstrate how to complete a deposit slip, record a deposit on a check stub, complete a check stub, and complete a check.

Guided Practice

Have students write the various types of endorsements on a sheet of paper while you explain each and write them on a blank transparency.

Independent Practice

Assign Terms 1–6, Questions 1–4, and Problems 7-1 and 7-2.

ILLUSTRATION 7-1   Deposit slip

Rugcare records the August 1 deposit on the next unused check stub, as shown in Illustration 7-2.

ILLUSTRATION 7-2   Deposit recorded on a check stub

After the deposit is recorded on the check stub, a checkbook subtotal is calculated. The balance brought forward on Check Stub No. 1 is zero. The previous balance, $0.00, *plus* the deposit, $10,000.00, *equals* the subtotal, $10,000.00.

Cash receipts are journalized at the time cash is received. Later, the cash receipts are deposited in the checking account. Therefore, no journal entry is needed for deposits because the cash receipts have already been journalized.

Endorsing Checks

Ownership of a check can be transferred. The name of the first owner is stated on a check following the words *Pay to the order of*. Therefore, the person to whom payment is to be made must indi-

TEACHING STRATEGIES: TEACHING TIP

Students will gain a better understanding of how to complete a deposit slip and check stub if the proce-dures are demonstrated on the overhead. This can be accomplished by using Transparency 7-1 to demon-strate completing a deposit slip and recording a deposit on a check stub.

cate that ownership of the check is being transferred. One person transfers ownership to another person by signing on the back of a check. A signature or stamp on the back of a check transferring ownership is called an **endorsement.**

An endorsement should be signed exactly as the person's name appears on the front of the check. For example, a check made payable to B.E. Furman is endorsed on the back as *B.E. Furman.* Immediately below that endorsement, Mr. Furman writes his official signature, *Ben Furman.*

Ownership of a check might be transferred several times, resulting in several endorsements. Each endorser guarantees payment of the check. If a bank does not receive payment from the person who signed the check, each endorser is individually liable for payment.

Three types of endorsements are commonly used, each having a specific use in transferring ownership.

Blank Endorsement. An endorsement consisting only of the endorser's signature is called a **blank endorsement.** A blank endorsement indicates that the subsequent owner is whoever has the check. A blank endorsement is shown in Illustration 7-3.

ILLUSTRATION 7-3   Blank endorsement

Federal regulations require that an endorsement be confined to a limited amount of space that is indicated on the back of a check.

If a check with a blank endorsement is lost or stolen, the check can be cashed by anyone who has it. Ownership may be transferred without further endorsement. A blank endorsement should be used *only* when a person is at the bank ready to cash or deposit a check.

Special Endorsement.   An endorsement indicating a new owner of a check is called a **special endorsement.** Special endorsements are sometimes known as endorsements in full. A special endorsement is shown in Illustration 7-4.

ILLUSTRATION 7-4   Special endorsement

CHAPTER 7   Cash Control Systems   **137**

138

TEACHING STRATEGIES: EXPANDING BEYOND THE CLASSROOM

Arrange a field trip to a bank. Inform the bank contact that the major purpose of the trip is to learn about checking accounts for businesses. However, other information about personal use of banking services should be included in the topics described. Ask the bank personnel to describe the following items that will be of personal interest to students:

a. *NOW checking accounts.* Most banks restrict the NOW, interest-bearing checking accounts to individuals. Businesses usually cannot use the NOW accounts.

b. *Joint accounts.* This is a common arrangement for a husband and wife.

c. *Canceled checks.* Are canceled checks returned with a bank statement by local banks?

d. *Endorsements on checks.* Ask for a demonstration of the written and stamped endorsements the bank recommends. Ask for an explanation of the federal regulations about endorsing checks.

e. *Check forms.* Ask for information about the checkbook arrangements that individuals and businesses may use. Ask for an explanation of the register form of checks used for most personal accounts and the printed forms used by most businesses.

f. *Electronic funds transfer.* Ask for an explanation of when businesses and individuals might use electronic funds transfer. Ask also how the transfer is accomplished.

Special endorsements include the words *Pay to the order of* and the name of the new check owner. Only the person or business named in a special endorsement can cash, deposit, or further transfer ownership of the check.

Restrictive Endorsement. An endorsement restricting further transfer of a check's ownership is called a **restrictive endorsement.** A restrictive endorsement limits use of the check to whatever purpose is stated in the endorsement. A restrictive endorsement is shown in Illustration 7-5.

ILLUSTRATION 7-5   Restrictive endorsement

On all checks received, Rugcare stamps a restrictive endorsement which states that the check is for deposit only. This restrictive endorsement prevents unauthorized persons from cashing a check if it is lost or stolen.

Writing Checks

Rugcare uses printed checks with check stubs attached. Consecutive numbers are preprinted on Rugcare's checks. Consecutive numbers on checks provide an easy way of identifying each check. Also, the numbers help keep track of all checks to assure that none are lost or misplaced.

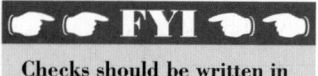

FYI

Checks should be written in ink so that no one can alter them.

Preparing Check Stubs.   A check stub is a business' record of each check written for a cash payment transaction. *(CONCEPT: Objective Evidence)* To avoid forgetting to prepare a check stub, the check stub is prepared before the check is written. Rugcare's check stub and check are shown in Illustration 7-6.

ILLUSTRATION 7-6   Completed check stub and check

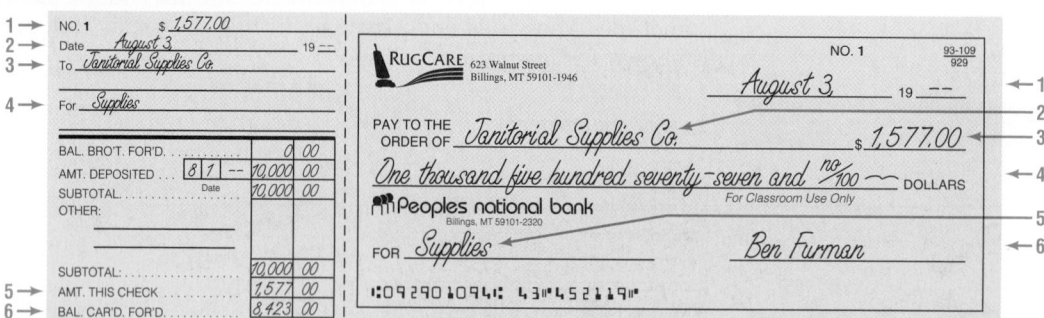

Six steps are used to complete Rugcare's Check Stub No. 1.

1 Write the amount of the check, *$1,577.00*, in the space after the dollar sign at the top of the stub.

2 Write the date of the check, *August 3, 19--*, on the Date line at the top of the stub.

3 Write to whom the check is to be paid, *Janitorial Supplies Co.*, on the To line at the top of the stub.

4 Record the purpose of the check, *Supplies*, on the For line.

5 Write the amount of the check, *$1,577.00*, in the amount column at the bottom of the stub on the line with the words "Amt. this Check."

6 Calculate the new checking account balance, *$8,423.00*, and record the new balance in the amount column on the last line of the stub. The new balance is calculated as shown below.

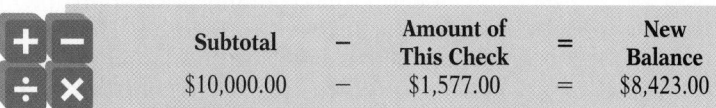

	Subtotal	–	Amount of This Check	=	New Balance
	$10,000.00	–	$1,577.00	=	$8,423.00

During the Great Depression of the 1930s, over 10,000 commercial banks failed.

Preparing Checks. After the check stub is completed, the check is written. The check shown in Illustration 7-6 is prepared as follows.

1 Write the date, *August 3, 19--*, in the space provided.

> The date should be the month, day, and year on which the check is issued. A check with a future date on it is called a **postdated check.** Most banks will not accept postdated checks because money cannot be withdrawn from a depositor's account until the date on the check.

2 Write to whom the check is to be paid, *Janitorial Supplies Co.*, following the words "Pay to the order of."

> If the person to whom a check is to be paid is a business, use the business' name rather than the owner's name. *(CONCEPT: Business Entity)* If the person to whom the check is to be paid is an individual, use that person's name.

3 Write the amount in figures, *$1,577.00*, following the dollar sign.

> Write the figures close to the printed dollar sign. This practice prevents anyone from writing another digit in front of the amount to change the amount of the check.

4 Write the amount in words, *One thousand five hundred seventy-seven and no/100*, on the line with the word "Dollars."

> This written amount verifies the amount written in figures after the dollar sign. Begin the words at the extreme left. Draw a line through the unused space up to the word "Dollars." This line prevents anyone from writing in additional words to change the amount.

FYI

Always complete the check stub before writing the check. Otherwise you may forget to record the amount of the check on the stub.

Audit Your Understanding

1. List the three types of endorsements.

2. List the six steps for preparing a check stub.

FYI

Not all banks return canceled checks with the bank statement. Occasionally a canceled check is needed as proof of payment. When a canceled check is needed, a copy of the check can be obtained from the bank for a small fee.

If the amounts in words and in figures are not the same, a bank may pay only the amount in words. Often, when the amounts do not agree, a bank will refuse to pay the check.

5 Write the purpose of the check, *Supplies*, on the line labeled "For."

On some checks this space is labeled "Memo." Some checks do not have a line for writing the purpose of the check.

6 Sign the check.

A check should not be signed until each item on the check and its stub has been verified for accuracy.

Voiding Checks. Banks usually refuse to accept altered checks. If any kind of error is made in preparing a check, a new check should be prepared. Because checks are prenumbered, all checks not used should be retained for the records. This practice helps account for all checks and assures that no checks have been lost or stolen.

A check that contains errors must be marked so that others will know that it is not to be used. The word *VOID* is written in large letters across both the check and its stub.

When Rugcare records a check in its journal, the check number is placed in the journal's Doc. No. column. If a check number is missing from the Doc. No. column, there is a question whether all checks have been journalized. To assure that all check numbers are listed in the journal, Rugcare records voided checks in the journal. The date is recorded in the journal's Date column. The word *VOID* is written in the Account Title column. The check number is recorded in the Doc. No. column. A check mark is entered in the Post. Ref. column. A dash is placed in the Cash Credit column.

BANK STATEMENT

Banks keep separate records for each depositor. Information from deposit slips and checks is recorded daily in depositors' accounts. A report of deposits, withdrawals, and bank balance sent to a depositor by a bank is called a **bank statement.** Rugcare's bank statement for August 27 is shown in Illustration 7-7.

The balance for Rugcare's checking account on August 27, according to the bank's records, is $8,731.00.

When a bank receives checks, the amount of each check is deducted from the depositor's account. Then, the bank stamps the checks to indicate that the check is canceled and is not to be transferred further. Canceled checks are returned to a depositor with a bank statement. Outstanding checks are those checks issued by a depositor but not yet reported on a bank statement. Outstanding deposits are those deposits made at a bank but not yet shown on a bank statement. A bank may assess a charge for maintaining a checking account. Account service charges are also listed on a bank statement.

TEACHING STRATEGIES: EXPANDING BEYOND THE CLASSROOM

Speakers. Bank personnel may also be invited to speak to the class about banking services. Or invite someone from a local business to describe to the class how a petty cash fund is used and controlled.

Banks may have different kinds of checking accounts to fit special needs of depositors. Each bank has its own regulations for its services, and fees are not charged for some checking accounts.

ILLUSTRATION 7-7   Bank statement

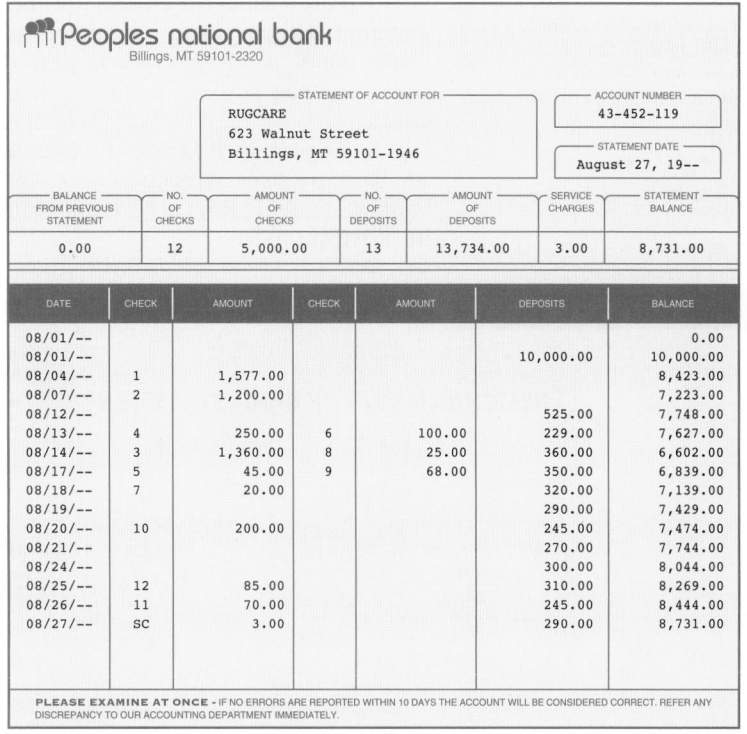

Objectives (Enabling Performance Tasks)

a. Define accounting terms related to using a checking account and a petty cash fund.

b. Identify accounting concepts and practices related to using a checking account.

d. Reconcile a bank statement.

f. Record selected transactions related to using a checking account and a petty cash fund.

FOCUS

- Using a checking account was introduced earlier in this chapter. Explain that the bank periodically sends a report of deposits, withdrawals, and the bank balance to the depositor.

- Introduce new vocabulary: bank statement, dishonored check.

TEACH

Cover student pages 140–148 "Bank Statement" and "Dishonored Checks." Review the bank statement in Illustration 7-7 and the bank statement reconciliation in Illustration 7-8. Point out canceled checks, outstanding checks, and outstanding deposits as they appear on the statements. When a bank statement is received, canceled checks usually accompany it. The canceled checks should be compared with check stubs and a check mark placed on each stub for canceled checks. The same should be done with deposits. When the reconciliation is completed, the two adjusted balances should be the same. Remind students that the service charge should be written on a check stub so that the checking account is not overstated.

Discuss dishonored checks and the seriousness of insufficient funds and forging a check. Some stores post signs to inform customers of the charge that will be imposed for a dishonored check. Ask students to find out charges for the stores where they most commonly purchase tapes, compact disks, clothes, and so on.

Verifying a Bank Statement

Although banks seldom make mistakes, occasionally a check or deposit might be recorded in a wrong account. When a bank statement is received, a depositor should verify its accuracy. If errors are discovered, the bank should be notified at once. However, a bank's records and a depositor's records may differ and still be correct. The difference may exist for several reasons.

1. A service charge may not have been recorded in the depositor's business records.
2. Outstanding deposits may be recorded in the depositor's records but not yet reported on a bank statement.
3. Outstanding checks may be recorded in the depositor's records but not yet reported on a bank statement.
4. A depositor may have made errors in doing arithmetic or in recording information in the business records. The most common mistakes made by depositors are arithmetic errors.
5. The bank may have made an error.

CHAPTER 7   Cash Control Systems   **141**

Use Transparency 7-2 to complete a reconciliation. Use Transparency 7-1 to demonstrate recording a service charge on a check stub and to record a dishonored check on a check stub. Draw T accounts to explain the transaction to journalize a bank service charge. Use Transparency A to journalize the transaction.

Guided Practice

Guide students through Drill 7-D1. Students should have the forms from the working papers to complete as you guide them through the drill using the three steps discussed in the lesson. All students should agree with the action taken for each step before proceeding to the next step.

Independent Practice

Assign Terms 7–8, Questions 5–8, Drill 7-D2, and Problem 7-3.

Reconciling a Bank Statement

A bank statement is reconciled by verifying that information on a bank statement and a checkbook are in agreement. Rugcare reconciles a bank statement on the same day that the statement is received. Reconciling immediately is an important aspect of cash control.

Rugcare's canceled checks are received with the bank statement. The returned checks are arranged in numeric order. For each canceled check, a check mark is placed on the corresponding check stub. A check stub with no check mark indicates an outstanding check.

On August 28 Rugcare receives a bank statement dated August 27. Rugcare uses a reconciliation form printed on the back of the bank statement. Rugcare's bank statement reconciliation is shown in Illustration 7-8.

FYI

Banks are not the only institutions that offer checking account services. Many credit unions also offer accounts on which an individual can also write checks.

ILLUSTRATION 7-8   Bank statement reconciliation

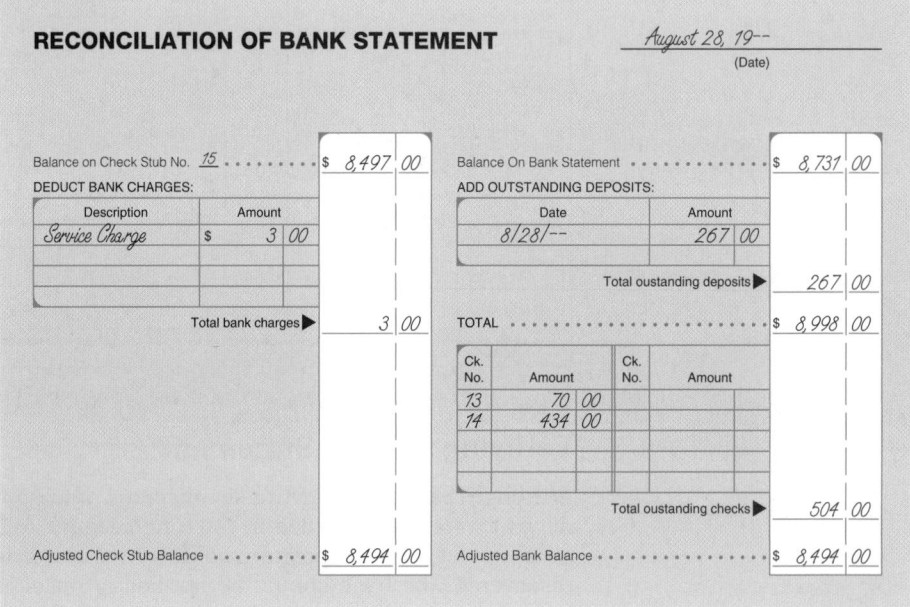

Rugcare uses three steps to reconcile a bank statement.

1 Calculate the adjusted check stub balance.

* Write the date on which the reconciliation is prepared, *August 28, 19--.*

* In the left amount column, list the balance brought forward on Check Stub No. 15, the next unused check stub, *$8,497.00.*

* In the space for bank charges, list any charges. The only such charge for Rugcare is the bank service charge, *$3.00.*

The bank service charge is labeled *SC* on the bank statement.

- Write the adjusted checkbook balance, *$8,494.00*, in the space provided at the bottom of the left amount column. The balance on the check stub, $8,497.00, *minus* the bank's service charge, $3.00, *equals* the adjusted check stub balance, $8,494.00.

2 Calculate the adjusted bank balance.

- Write the ending balance shown on the bank statement, *$8,731.00*, in the right amount column.

- Write the date, *8/28/--* and the amount, *$267.00*, of any outstanding deposits in the space provided. Add the outstanding deposits. Write the total outstanding deposits, *$267.00*, in the right amount column.

- Add the ending bank statement balance to the total outstanding deposits. Write the total, *$8,998.00*, in the space for the Total.

- List the outstanding checks, *Nos. 13 and 14*, and their amounts, *$70.00 and $434.00*, in the space provided. Add the amounts of the outstanding checks, and write the total, *$504.00*, in the right amount column.

- Calculate the adjusted bank balance, and write the amount, *$8,494.00*, in the space provided at the bottom of the right amount column. The total, $8,998.00, *minus* the total outstanding checks, $504.00, *equals* the adjusted bank balance, $8,494.00.

3 Compare adjusted balances.

- The adjusted balances must be the same. The adjusted check stub balance is the same as the adjusted bank balance, *$8,494.00*. Because the two amounts are the same, the bank statement is reconciled. The completed reconciliation form is filed for future reference.

- If the two adjusted balances are not the same, the errors must be found and corrected before any more work is done.

Recording a Bank Service Charge on a Check Stub

The bank deducts the service charge from Rugcare's checking account each month. Although Rugcare did not write a check for the bank service charge, this cash payment must be recorded in Rugcare's accounting records as a cash payment. Rugcare makes a record of a bank service charge on a check stub as shown in Illustration 7-9.

Three steps are used to record a bank service charge on a check stub.

1 Write the words, *Service charge, $3.00*, on the check stub under the heading "Other."

2 Write the amount, *$3.00*, in the check stub's amount column.

3 Calculate and record the new balance, *$8,494.00*, on the Subtotal line.

ILLUSTRATION 7-9   Bank service charge recorded on a check stub

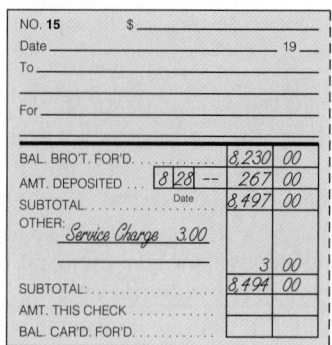

Journalizing a Bank Service Charge

Because the bank service charge is a cash payment for which no check is written, Rugcare prepares a memorandum as the source document. Rugcare's bank service charges are relatively small and occur only once a month. Therefore, a separate ledger account for the expense is not used. Instead, Rugcare records the bank service charge as a miscellaneous expense.

August 28, 19--. Received bank statement showing August bank service charge, $3.00. Memorandum No. 3.

A memorandum is the source document for a bank service charge transaction. *(CONCEPT: Objective Evidence)* The analysis of this transaction is shown in the T accounts.

Miscellaneous Expense is debited for $3.00 to show the increase in this expense account balance. Cash is credited for $3.00 to show the decrease in this asset account balance. The journal entry to record Rugcare's bank service charge is shown in Illustration 7-10.

ILLUSTRATION 7-10   Journal entry to record a bank service charge

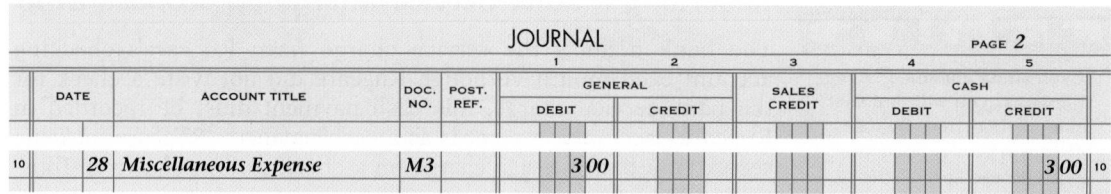

This entry is journalized using four steps.

1 Date. Write the date, *28*, in the Date column.

2 Debit. Write the title of the account to be debited, Miscellaneous Expense, in the Account Title column. Record the amount

144   PART 2   Accounting for a Service Business Organized as a Proprietorship

SPREADSHEET OPTIONS

USING AN ELECTRONIC SPREADSHEET TO PREPARE A BANK RECONCILIATION

Businesses often use forms to prepare accounting reports. The bank reconciliation form in Illustration 7-8 increases the efficiency of verifying a bank statement. Electronic spreadsheet software is another useful tool for preparing accounting reports. Unlike paper forms, however, electronic spreadsheets contain formulas that automatically perform calculations.

An **electronic spreadsheet** displayed on a computer monitor is a group of rows and columns. The space where a column intersects with a row is a **cell**. Cell A17 is located at the intersection of column A and row 17. This is known as the **cell address**.

A spreadsheet prepared for reconciling a bank statement would look like the one in the following illustration. Electronic spreadsheets can be extremely large, having hundreds of columns and thousands of rows.

The power of the electronic spreadsheet comes from the ability to let the software make calculations. This is accomplished by attaching formulas to different cells. This spread-sheet was created with all the formulas necessary to complete a bank reconciliation. For example, the formula at cell I15, +H12+H13, calculates the total outstanding deposits. The spreadsheet adds the values in cells H12 and H13, and displays the value, $1,131.00, in cell I15.

After the bank reconciliation is printed, the same spreadsheet can be used to reconcile other bank statements. Preparing a bank reconciliation using an electronic spreadsheet assures the preparer that the calculations are accurate.

```
       A         B         C    D    E    F       G        H          I
 1  General Ledger: 110                        Date: March 31, 19--
 2  Account Number: 34-2353-26
 3
 4  RECONCILIATION OF BANK STATEMENT
 5
 6  Balance on Check Stub.. 6,234.00      Balance on Bank Statement.. 6,247.00
 7
 8  DEDUCT BANK CHARGES:                   ADD OUTSTANDING DEPOSITS:
 9
10    Description    Amount                Date              Amount
11   ----------------------                ---------------------------
12  Service Charge    8.00                 3/30/--              436.00
13                                         3/31/--              695.00
14                                         ---------------------------
15                                         Total outstanding deposits. 1,131.00
16   ----------------------                                    ----------
17  Total bank charges.....    8.00        TOTAL..................... 7,378.00
18                          ----------
19                                         DEDUCT OUTSTANDING CHECKS:
20
21                                         Ck.          Ck.
22                                         No.  Amount  No.  Amount
23                                         ---------------------------
24                                         423   85.00  458    54.00
25                                         455  343.00  459   147.00
26                                         457  523.00
27                                         ---------------------------
28                                         Total outstanding checks... 1,152.00
29                          ----------                              ----------
30  Adjusted Check Stub
31    Balance..............  6,226.00      Adjusted Bank Balance......  6,226.00
32                          ==========                              ==========
33
34
35
```

debited to Miscellaneous Expense, *$3.00*, in the General Debit column.

3 *Credit.* Record the amount credited to Cash, *$3.00*, in the Cash Credit column.

4 *Source document.* Write the source document number, *M3*, in the Doc. No. column.

Rugcare reconciled its bank statement on August 28. The entry for the bank service charge is journalized on the same date. Rugcare continues to record entries in the journal until the end of the month as shown in Illustration 6-10, Chapter 6.

CHAPTER 7   Cash Control Systems   **145**

CAREERS IN ACCOUNTING

CASHIER I/CASH-ACCOUNTING CLERK

- *Receives cash from customers/employees*
- *Issues change and cashes checks*
- *Reconciles cash receipts with cash register balances*
- *Prepares checks for authorized disbursements*
- *Prepares bank deposit slips*

DISHONORED CHECKS

A check that a bank refuses to pay is called a **dishonored check.** Banks may dishonor a check for a number of reasons. (1) The check appears to be altered. (2) The signature of the person who signed the check does not match the one on the signature card at the bank. (3) The amounts written in figures and in words do not agree. (4) The check is postdated. (5) The person who wrote the check has stopped payment on the check. (6) The account of the person who wrote the check has insufficient funds to pay the check.

Issuing a check on an account with insufficient funds is illegal in most states. Altering or forging a check is illegal in all states. A dishonored check may affect the credit rating of the person or business who issued the check. Checking accounts and records should be maintained in such a way that all checks will be honored when presented to the bank.

Sometimes money for a dishonored check can be collected directly from the person or business who wrote the check. Often, however, the value of a dishonored check cannot be recovered and becomes an expense to the business.

Most banks charge a fee for handling dishonored checks that have been previously accepted for deposit. This fee is an expense of the business receiving a dishonored check. Rugcare's bank charges a $5.00 fee for handling dishonored checks. Rugcare attempts to collect the $5.00 fee in addition to the amount of the dishonored check.

Rugcare records a check as a cash debit and deposits the check. When a check is dishonored, the bank deducts the amount of the check plus the fee, $5.00, from Rugcare's checking account. Therefore, Rugcare records a dishonored check in its journal as a cash payment transaction.

Recording a Dishonored Check on a Check Stub

A dishonored check recorded on a check stub is shown in Illustration 7-11.

ILLUSTRATION 7-11   Dishonored check recorded on a check stub

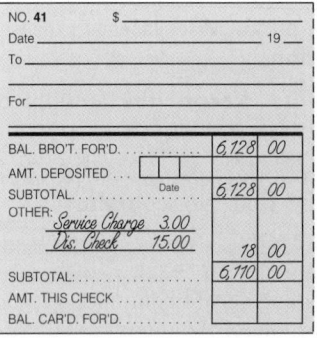

APPLIED SKILLS: WORD PROCESSING

If you wish to integrate word processing into your accounting course, you may direct students to answer the end-of-chapter Accounting Terms, Questions for Individual Study, and Cases for Critical Thinking using their word processing software.

The words, *Dishonored check*, are written on the line below the words "Other." The total amount of the dishonored check plus the fee, *$15.00*, is written in the amount column on the same line. A new subtotal is calculated by subtracting the total, $18.00 ($3.00 service charge *plus* $15.00 dishonored check), from the balance brought forward, $6,128.00. The new subtotal, *$6,110.00*, is written on the Subtotal line. A new Balance Carried Forward is not calculated until after Check No. 41 is written.

Journalizing a Dishonored Check

During August, Rugcare received no checks that were subsequently dishonored. However, in November Rugcare did receive a check that was dishonored.

> *November 29, 19--. Received notice from the bank of a dishonored check, $10.00, plus $5.00 fee; total, $15.00. Memorandum No. 6.*

Because Rugcare did not write a check for this cash payment, a memorandum is prepared as the source document. *(CONCEPT: Objective Evidence)*

All checks received are deposited in Rugcare's checking account. The entry for each cash receipts transaction includes a debit to Cash. If a check is subsequently returned as dishonored, the previous cash debit for the amount of the check must be offset by a cash credit. The analysis of this transaction is shown in the T accounts.

Miscellaneous Expense

Miscellaneous Expense	
15.00	

Cash	
	15.00

Miscellaneous Expense is debited for $15.00 to show the increase in this expense account balance. Cash is credited for $15.00 to show the decrease in this asset account balance. The journal entry to record this transaction is shown in Illustration 7-12.

This entry is journalized using four steps.

1 *Date.* Write the date, *29*, in the Date column.

2 *Debit.* Write the title of the account to be debited, Miscellaneous Expense, in the Account Title column. Record the amount debited to Miscellaneous Expense, *$15.00*, in the General Debit column.

3 *Credit.* Record the amount credited to Cash, *$15.00*, in the Cash Credit column.

4 *Source document.* Write the source document number, *M6*, in the Doc. No. column.

ILLUSTRATION 7-12   Journal entry to record a dishonored check

	JOURNAL								PAGE 10	
				1	2	3		4	5	
DATE	ACCOUNT TITLE	DOC. NO.	POST. REF.	GENERAL DEBIT	GENERAL CREDIT	SALES CREDIT		CASH DEBIT	CASH CREDIT	
29	Miscellaneous Expense	M6		15 00					15 00	19

FYI

Individuals can also use a form of electronic funds transfer. Personal accounts can be accessed through Automated Teller Machines (ATMs) to make inquiries, withdraw money, deposit money, and transfer funds from one account to another.

Kelson Enterprises

350.00	

Cash

	350.00

FYI

Financial Management Service of the Department of the Treasury issues over 250 million Electronic Funds Transfer (EFT) payments annually.

ELECTRONIC FUNDS TRANSFER

A computerized cash payments system that uses electronic impulses to transfer funds is called **electronic funds transfer.** Many businesses use electronic funds transfer to pay vendors. To use electronic funds transfer (EFT), a business makes arrangements with its bank to process EFT transactions. Arrangements are also made with vendors to accept EFT on account. After arranging for EFT payments on account, a telephone call is all that is needed to transfer funds from the business' account to the vendor's account.

To control cash payments through EFT, the person responsible for requesting transfers should be given a password. The bank should be instructed to not accept EFT requests from any person unable to provide an established password.

Superior Cleaning Service uses electronic funds transfer to make payments on account to vendors. The journal entry for making payments on account through electronic funds transfer is the same as when a check is written. The only change is the source document used to prove that the transaction did occur. Superior Cleaning Service uses a memorandum as the source document for an electronic funds transfer. A note is written on the memorandum to describe the transaction.

September 2. Paid cash on account to Kelson Enterprises, $350.00, using EFT. Memorandum No. 10.

The source document for this transaction is Memorandum No. 10. (CONCEPT: *Objective Evidence*) The analysis of this transaction is shown in the T accounts.

The liability account, Kelson Enterprises, is decreased by a debit, $350.00. The asset account, Cash, is decreased by a credit, $350.00.

A cash payment made by EFT is recorded on the check stub as "Other." This procedure keeps the checkbook in balance during the time lag from when the EFT is made until receipt of the bank statement. The EFT payments are verified as part of the regular bank statement reconciliation process. EFT payments are identified in the Check column of the bank statement by the notation *EFT* rather than by a check number.

A summary of procedures for using checking accounts is shown in Illustration 7-13.

Summary of checking account procedures

1 A deposit slip is prepared to deposit cash and checks in a checking account.

2 Checks are written to make payments from the checking account.

3 Cash payments transactions are journalized from check stubs.

4 A bank statement showing details of deposits, checks, and service charges.

5 The bank statement is reconciled to assure that the bank statement and checkbook information agree.

6 Bank service changes are journalized and recorded in the checkbook.

7 Dishonored checks are recorded in the checkbook and in the journal.

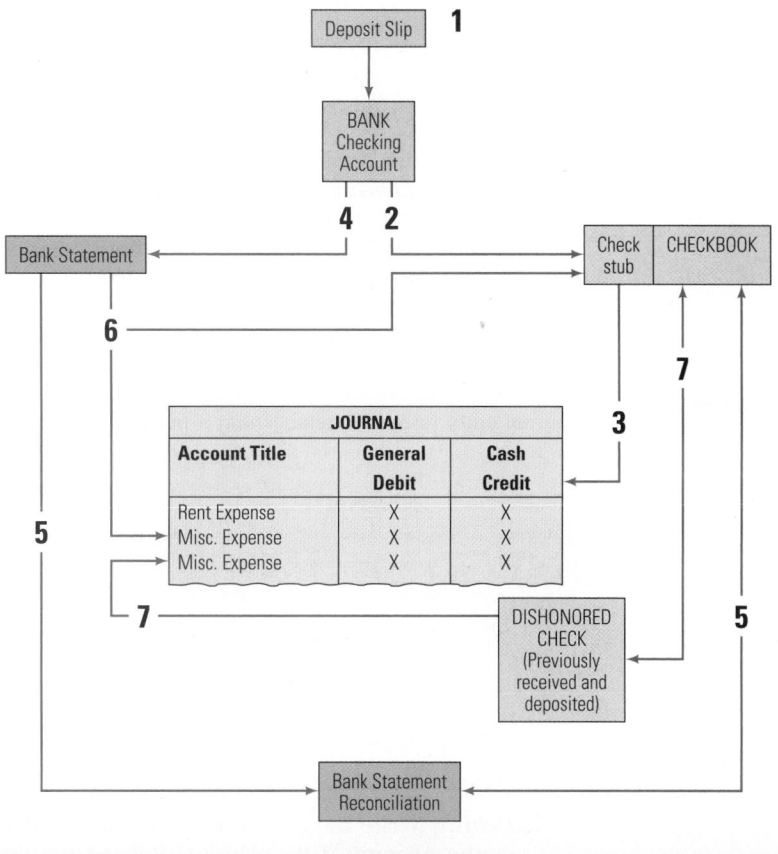

PETTY CASH

An amount of cash kept on hand and used for making small payments is called **petty cash.** Cash control is effective if all cash payments are made by check and cash receipts are deposited in the bank. However, a business usually has some small payments for

CHAPTER 7 Cash Control Systems

149

TEACHING STRATEGIES:
APPLYING VISUALS

Direct the students to Summary Illustrations 7-13 and 7-18. Review checking account and petty cash procedures.

TEACH

Cover student pages 148–154 "Electronic Funds Transfer" and "Petty Cash." Explain how electronic funds transfer (EFT) works and what type of controls should be in place to safeguard the funds. Use Transparency A to journalize an EFT transaction.

Give examples of how petty cash is used in businesses. Perhaps the school office has a petty cash fund. Point out that very large businesses may have several petty cash funds throughout their offices and plants. It is very important to keep accurate records of the petty cash fund. Only one person should be authorized to use it.

Guided Practice

Guide students through Drill 7-D3. Students should have the forms from the working papers to complete as you guide them through the drill using Transparency 4-1 Blank T Accounts. All students should agree with the analysis before proceeding to the next transaction.

Independent Practice

- Assign Terms 9–11, Questions 9–15, Problems 7-4 and 7-5, Study Guide 7, and Problem 7-M.

- Duplicate and assign Math Work Sheet Chapter 7 Part C, Calculating Amount of Petty Cash Replenishment from the Masters and Solutions to Enrichment/Application Activities Section in the Teacher's Resource Guide to provide additional practice on the mathematics of replenishing petty cash.

which writing a check is not time or cost effective. Therefore, a business may maintain a separate cash fund for making small cash payments. The actual dollar amount considered to be a small payment differs from one business to another. Mr. Furman has set $5.00 as the maximum amount to be paid at any one time from the petty cash fund.

The petty cash account is an asset with a normal debit balance. The balance of the petty cash account increases on the debit side and decreases on the credit side.

Petty Cash	
Debit side **NORMAL BALANCE** Increases	Credit side Decreases

Establishing a Petty Cash Fund

On August 17 Mr. Furman decided that Rugcare needed a petty cash fund of $200.00. This amount should provide for the small cash payments anticipated during a month.

August 17, 19--. Paid cash to establish a petty cash fund, $200.00. Check No. 10.

The source document for this transaction is Check No. 10. (CONCEPT: Objective Evidence) The analysis of this transaction is shown in the T accounts.

Petty Cash	
200.00	

Cash	
	200.00

Petty Cash is debited for $200.00 to show the increase in this asset account balance. Cash is credited for $200.00 to show the decrease in this asset account balance. The journal entry to record this transaction is shown in Illustration 7-14.

ILLUSTRATION 7-14   Journal entry to record establishing a petty cash fund

					GENERAL		SALES CREDIT	CASH	
	DATE	ACCOUNT TITLE	DOC. NO.	POST. REF.	DEBIT	CREDIT		DEBIT	CREDIT
16	17	*Petty Cash*	C10		2 0 0 00				2 0 0 00

JOURNAL — PAGE 1

This entry is journalized using four steps.

1 *Date.*   Write the date, *17*, in the Date column.

2 *Debit.*   Write the title of the account to be debited, *Petty Cash*, in the Account Title column. Record the amount debited to Petty Cash, *$200.00*, in the General Debit column.

3 *Credit.*   Record the amount credited to Cash, *$200.00*, in the Cash Credit column.

4 *Source document.*   Write the source document number, *C10*, in the Doc. No. column.

Mr. Furman cashed the check and placed the $200.00 in a locked petty cash box kept at Rugcare's place of business. Only Mr. Furman is authorized to make payments from the petty cash fund.

TEACHING STRATEGIES: TEACHING TIP

Make the subject of petty cash relevant. Use a small box and label it PETTY CASH. Put 25 play dollars in the box and 5 petty cash slips. Pass the box around the class and have several students take a few dollars out and record the amount on the petty cash slip. After most of the money has been removed, appoint someone to be the accountant and complete the petty cash report. Have a student go to the board and draw T accounts for replenishing the petty cash.

Making Payments from a Petty Cash Fund

Each time a small payment is made from the petty cash fund, Mr. Furman prepares a form showing the purpose and amount of the payment. A form showing proof of a petty cash payment is called a **petty cash slip**.

A petty cash slip used by Rugcare is shown in Illustration 7-15.

ILLUSTRATION 7-15   Petty cash slip

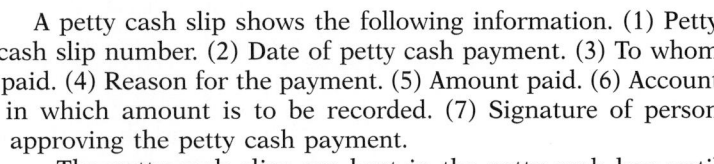

PETTY CASH SLIP	No. 1
Date: *August 18, 19--*	
Paid to: *Bernie's Repair Shop*	
For: *Hose Repair*	$ *5.00*
Account: *Repair Expense*	
Approved: *Ben Furman*	

A petty cash slip shows the following information. (1) Petty cash slip number. (2) Date of petty cash payment. (3) To whom paid. (4) Reason for the payment. (5) Amount paid. (6) Account in which amount is to be recorded. (7) Signature of person approving the petty cash payment.

The petty cash slips are kept in the petty cash box until the fund must be replenished. No entries are made in the journal for the individual petty cash payments.

Replenishing a Petty Cash Fund

As petty cash is paid out, the amount in the petty cash box decreases. Eventually, the petty cash fund must be replenished and the petty cash payments recorded. Rugcare replenishes its petty cash fund whenever the amount on hand is reduced to $75.00. Also, the petty cash fund is always replenished at the end of each month so that all of the expenses are recorded in the month they are incurred. Rugcare completes four steps in replenishing the petty cash fund.

    1 *Prove the petty cash fund.* On August 31 Mr. Furman proves petty cash as shown below.

Petty cash on hand.................................... $188.00
Count the cash remaining in the petty cash fund
Plus total of petty cash slips.......................... + 12.00
Add the amounts on the petty cash slips
Equals petty cash fund.............................. $200.00

ASSESS

- Assess student understanding by checking solutions to Independent Practice activities.
- Review Summary Illustration 7-13, Summary of Checking Account Procedures.
- Review Summary Illustration 7-18, Summary of Petty Cash Fund Procedures.
- Use Transparency 7-3, Summary of Checking Account Procedures, and Transparency 7-4, Summary of Petty Cash Fund Procedures.

Reteach

- Use Demonstration Problem 7C. This problem can be done on the overhead with the students completing the problem at their desks.
- Assign Recycling Problem 7R-1.

Extend

- Assign Cases for Critical Thinking 2 and Challenge Problem 7-C (the challenge is to use canceled checks and a bank statement to do a reconciliation and find errors).
- Assign students to read the CAREERS IN ACCOUNTING feature on page 146. Have the students discuss what a career as a CASHIER I/ CASH-ACCOUNTING CLERK might be like.

Enrich

- Assign the Application Program Disk software to be used with Problem 7-4, 7-5, and Mastery Problem 7-M.
- Use *Automated Accounting 6.0* or higher and Accounting Textbook Template with Mastery Problem 7-M and Challenge Problem 7-C.
- Assign the Electronic Study Guide Chapter 7 to complete the study guide from the working papers at the computer.

CLOSURE

Use Audit Your Understanding questions.

ASSESS

- Administer Problem Test Chapter 7.
- Administer a MicroExam test for Chapter 7.

The last line of the proof must show the same total as the original balance of the petty cash fund, $200.00. If petty cash does not prove, the errors must be found and corrected before any more work is done.

2 *Prepare a petty cash report.* At the end of August, Mr. Furman totals the petty cash slips and prepares a report. Rugcare's August petty cash report is shown in Illustration 7-16.

Petty cash report

PETTY CASH REPORT	Date: August 31, 19--		
Explanation	Amounts		
Fund total			200 00
Payments:			
Miscellaneous Expense	7 00		
Repair Expense	5 00		
Less total payments			12 00
Equals recorded amount on hand			188 00
Actual amount on hand			188 00

The report shows that a total of $12.00 has been paid out of petty cash for repairs and miscellaneous expenses. Thus, $12.00 needs to be added to the remaining $188.00 to bring the petty cash fund back to its normal size, $200.00.

3 *Write a check to replenish the petty cash fund.*

4 *Journalize the entry to replenish petty cash.*

Miscellaneous Expense
7.00	

Repair Expense
7.00	

Cash
	12.00

August 31, 19--. Paid cash to replenish the petty cash fund, $12.00: miscellaneous expense, $7.00; repairs, $5.00. Check No. 15.

The source document for this transaction is Check No. 15. (CONCEPT: *Objective Evidence*) The analysis of this transaction is shown in the T accounts.

Miscellaneous Expense is debited for $7.00 and Repair Expense is debited for $5.00 to show the increases in these expense account balances. Cash is credited for $12.00 to show a decrease in this asset account balance.

Unless the petty cash fund is permanently increased or decreased, the balance of the account is always the original amount of the fund. The check issued to replenish petty cash is a credit to Cash and does not affect Petty Cash. When the check is cashed, the money is placed in the petty cash box. The amount in the petty cash box changes as shown below.

Amount in petty cash box before fund is replenished			$188.00
Amount from check issued to replenish petty cash			+ 12.00
Amount in petty cash box after fund is replenished			$200.00

The total amount in the petty cash box, $200.00, is again the same as the balance of the petty cash account. The journal entry to record the transaction to replenish petty cash is shown in Illustration 7-17.

ILLUSTRATION 7-17   Journal entry to record replenishing of petty cash

JOURNAL   PAGE *2*

	DATE	ACCOUNT TITLE	DOC. NO.	POST. REF.	GENERAL DEBIT	GENERAL CREDIT	SALES CREDIT	CASH DEBIT	CASH CREDIT	
11	31	*Miscellaneous Expense*	*C15*		7 00				12 00	11
12		*Repair Expense*			5 00					12

This entry is journalized using four steps.

1 Date.   Write the date, *31*, in the Date column.

2 Debit.   Write the title of the first account to be debited, Miscellaneous Expense, in the Account Title column. Write the amount to be debited to Miscellaneous Expense, *$7.00*, in the General Debit column on the same line as the account title. Write the title of the second account to be debited, Repair Expense, on the next line in the Account Title column. Record the amount to be debited to Repair Expense, *$5.00*, in the General Debit column on the same line as the account title.

3 Credit.   Record the amount to be credited to Cash, *$12.00*, in the Cash Credit column on the first line of this entry.

4 Source document.   Write the source document number, *C15*, in the Doc. No. column.

The check is cashed, and the money is placed in the petty cash box. The amount in the petty cash box is now the original amount of the petty cash fund, $200.00. Petty cash on hand, $188.00, *plus* the cash to replenish, $12.00, *equals* the original amount of the petty cash fund, $200.00. The amount in the petty cash fund is now the same as the balance of the petty cash account, $200.00.

A summary of procedures for using a petty cash fund is shown in Illustration 7-18.

Audit Your Understanding

Draw T accounts to analyze the following transactions:

1. An EFT transaction to pay cash on account to Kelson Enterprises.

2. Establishment of a petty cash fund.

3. Replenishment of a petty cash fund with payments for miscellaneous and repair expenses.

AUDIT YOUR UNDERSTANDING

1.   Kelson Enterprises

X	

Cash

	X

2.   Petty Cash

X	

Cash

	X

3.   Miscellaneous Expense

X	

Repair Expense

X	

Cash

	X

Summary of petty cash fund procedures

1 A check is issued to establish a petty cash fund.

2 The cash payment to establish a petty cash fund is journalized.

3 A petty cash slip is prepared for each payment from the petty cash fund.

4 When the petty cash fund needs to be replenished, a petty cash report is prepared summarizing the petty cash slips.

5 A check is issued to replenish the petty cash fund.

6 The cash payment to replenish petty cash is journalized.

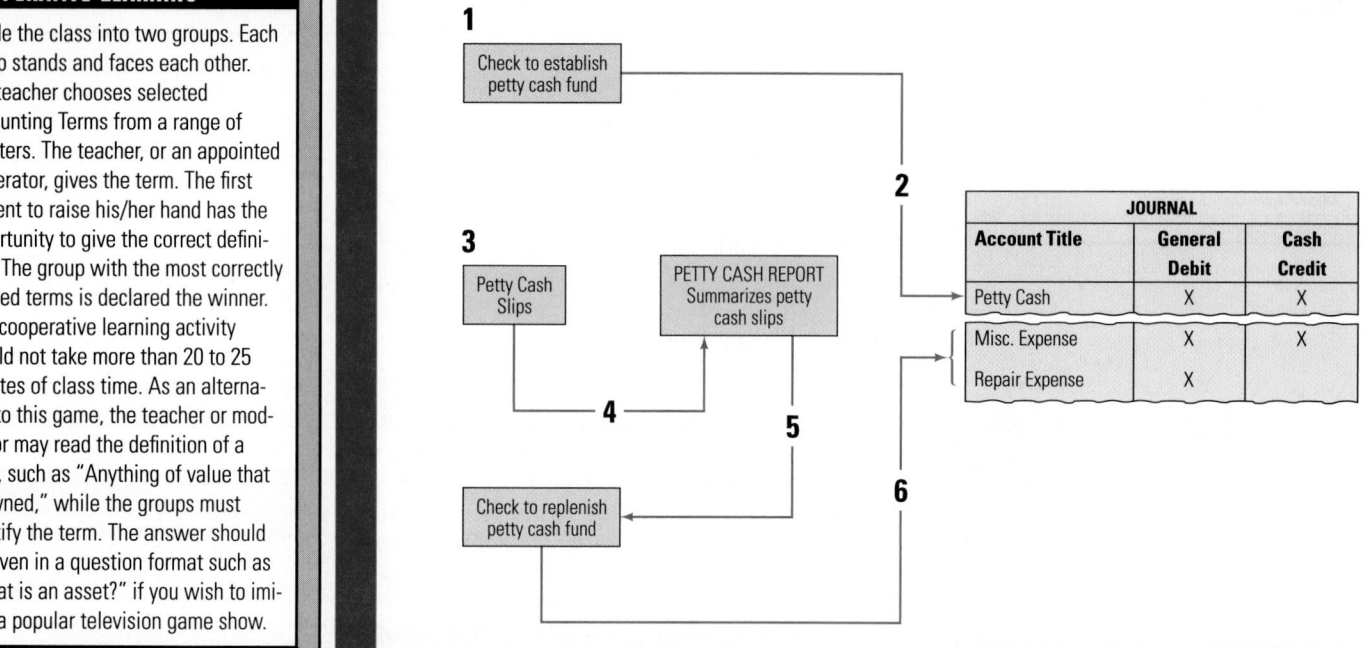

What is the meaning of each of the following?

1. **checking account**
2. **endorsement**
3. **blank endorsement**
4. **special endorsement**
5. **restrictive endorsement**
6. **postdated check**
7. **bank statement**
8. **dishonored check**
9. **electronic funds transfer**
10. **petty cash**
11. **petty cash slip**

QUESTIONS FOR INDIVIDUAL STUDY   EPT(b)

1. What evidence does a depositor have that money has been deposited in a checking account?
2. Why is no journal entry made by a business for a deposit in a checking account?
3. Why is the amount written in both numbers and words on a check?
4. What is the most common way of voiding a check?
5. Under what circumstances can a depositor assume that a bank statement reconciliation is correct?
6. Which accounting concept is being applied when a memorandum is prepared for the service charges deducted from a checking account?
7. What accounts are affected, and how, by an entry to record a bank service charge for a checking account?
8. What accounts are affected, and how, when Rugcare is notified that a deposited check has been dishonored?
9. What is the source document for an electronic funds transfer (EFT) transaction?
10. What is the purpose of a petty cash fund?
11. What accounts are affected, and how, when a petty cash fund is established?
12. What is Rugcare's initial record of amounts that have been paid from the petty cash fund?
13. How is the petty cash fund proved?
14. What accounts are affected, and how, by an entry to replenish petty cash when the petty cash slips show payments for miscellaneous expense and repair expense?
15. When is a journal entry made to record payments from the petty cash fund?

CASES FOR CRITICAL THINKING   EPT(d,e)

CASE 1 Iris Velez has a personal checking account in which she maintains a small balance. She receives a bank statement every three months. She files the statement and does not prepare a reconciliation. Sueanne Merker also has a personal checking account in which she maintains a balance of several hundred dollars. She receives bank statements once a month. She prepares a bank statement reconciliation for each bank statement received. Is Mrs. Velez or Ms. Merker following the better procedure? Explain your answer.

CASE 2 Dorset Company decides to establish a petty cash fund. The owner, Edna Dorset, wants to establish a $100.00 petty cash fund and limit payments to $5.00 or less. The manager, Roy Evans, suggests a petty cash fund of $3,000.00 limited to payments of $50.00 or less. Mr. Evans claims this limit will help him avoid writing so many checks. Do you agree with Ms. Dorset or Mr. Evans? Explain your answer.

ACCOUNTING TERMS

1. **checking account:** A bank account from which payments can be ordered by a depositor. (p. 135)
2. **endorsement:** A signature or stamp on the back of a check transferring ownership. (p. 137)
3. **blank endorsement:** An endorsement consisting only of the endorser's signature. (p. 137)
4. **special endorsement:** An endorsement indicating a new owner of a check. (p. 137)
5. **restrictive endorsement:** An endorsement restricting further transfer of a check's ownership. (p. 138)
6. **postdated check:** A check with a future date on it. (p. 139)
7. **bank statement:** A report of deposits, withdrawals, and bank balance sent to a depositor by a bank. (p. 140)
8. **dishonored check:** A check that a bank refuses to pay. (p. 146)
9. **electronic funds transfer:** A computerized cash payments system that uses electronic impulses to transfer funds. (p. 148)
10. **petty cash:** An amount of cash kept on hand and used for making small payments. (p. 149)
11. **petty cash slip:** A form showing proof of a petty cash payment. (p. 151)

QUESTIONS FOR INDIVIDUAL STUDY

1. The depositor is given a receipt by the bank at the time of the deposit. (p. 135)
2. Because the cash deposited was recorded previously in the journal at the time the cash was received (p. 136)
3. The amount in words verifies the amount in numbers. If the two do not agree, the bank may not accept the check. (pp. 139–140)
4. Writing the word "VOID" across both the check and its stub. (p. 140)
5. When the adjusted check stub balance equals the adjusted bank statement balance. (p. 143)
6. Objective Evidence. (p. 144)
7. Miscellaneous Expense is debited; Cash is credited. (p. 144)
8. Miscellaneous Expense is debited; Cash is credited. (p. 147)
9. A memorandum. (p. 148)
10. A petty cash fund is used for small cash payments. (pp. 149–150)
11. Petty Cash is debited; Cash is credited. (p. 150)

12. A petty cash slip is prepared for each petty cash payment. (p. 151)

13. Petty cash on hand *plus* total of petty cash slips *equals* original balance of petty cash fund. (p. 151)

14. Miscellaneous Expense is debited; Repair Expense is debited; Cash is credited. (p. 152)

15. When the petty cash fund is replenished. (p. 153)

CASES FOR CRITICAL THINKING

Case 1 Ms. Merker is following the better procedure. Even though Mrs. Velez has a relatively small checking account balance, she still needs to know the correct account balance against which she can write checks. A bank statement should be reconciled when it is received, regardless of the size of the account.

Case 2 Agree with Ms. Dorset. One of the purposes of a petty cash fund is to provide for *small* cash payments. Limiting petty cash payments to $50.00 or less is providing for large payments as well as small. Ms. Dorset's $5.00 limit is more reasonable for petty cash. The size of the fund, whether $100.00 or $3,000.00, depends upon the size of the company and the number and amount of payments to be made from the fund. For a small company, a $100.00 petty cash fund may be reasonable. For a large company, $3,000.00 may be reasonable.

CHECK FIGURES

See Teacher's Edition of Working Papers for complete solutions to drills and problems.

Drill 7-D1 Adjusted balance 1,573

Drill 7-D2 Adjusted balance 3,573

Drill 7-D3 Cash credits 57, 46, 75, 30

DRILL 7-D1 **Reconciling a bank statement**

TUTORIAL

SPREADSHEET

On July 29 of the current year, DeepClean received a bank statement dated July 28. The following information is obtained from the bank statement and from the records of the business.

Bank statement balance	$1,528.00
Bank service charge	2.00
Outstanding deposit, July 28	150.00
Outstanding checks:	
No. 103	70.00
No. 105	35.00
Checkbook balance on Check Stub No. 106	1,575.00

INSTRUCTIONS:

Prepare a bank statement reconciliation. Use July 29 of the current year as the date.

DRILL 7-D2 **Reconciling a bank statement**

On September 30 of the current year, Ajax Service Co. received a bank statement dated September 29. The following information is obtained from the bank statement and from the records of the business.

Bank statement balance	$3,208.00
Bank service charge	5.00
Outstanding deposits:	
September 29	310.00
September 30	330.00
Outstanding checks:	
No. 214	90.00
No. 215	135.00
No. 217	50.00
Checkbook balance on Check Stub No. 218	3,578.00

INSTRUCTIONS:

Prepare a bank statement reconciliation. Use September 30 of the current year as the date.

DRILL 7-D3 **Replenishing a petty cash fund**

MATHEMATICS

KeepClean replenished petty cash on the dates shown in Column 2 of the following table. The information in Columns 3 to 5 is obtained from the petty cash reports.

1	2	3	4	5
Trans.	Replenished on	**Summary of Petty Cash Slips**		
		Supplies	Advertising	Miscellaneous
A	July 31	32.00	25.00	
B	August 31	21.00	20.00	5.00
C	September 30	40.00	20.00	15.00
D	October 31	10.00		20.00

INSTRUCTIONS:

Prepare T accounts for Cash, Supplies, Advertising Expense, and Miscellaneous Expense. Use the T accounts to analyze each transaction given in the table. Label each amount in the T accounts with the corresponding transaction letter.

APPLICATION PROBLEMS   EPT(c,d,e,f)

PROBLEM 7-1   Endorsing checks

For each of the following situations, prepare the appropriate endorsement.

INSTRUCTIONS:

1. Write a blank endorsement. Use your own signature.
2. Write a special endorsement to transfer a check to Delbert Richardson. Use your own signature.
3. Write a restrictive endorsement to deposit a check in the account of OddJobs. Use your own signature.

PROBLEM 7-2   Writing checks

MATHEMATICS

You are authorized to sign checks for OddJobs.

INSTRUCTIONS:

1. Record the balance brought forward on Check Stub No. 50, $1,396.35.
2. Record a deposit of $390.00 made on October 30 of the current year on Check Stub No. 50.
3. Prepare check stubs and write the following checks. Use October 30 of the current year as the date.

Check No. 50. To Corner Garage for repairs, $138.00.
Check No. 51. To OfficeWorld for supplies, $50.00.
Check No. 52. To Dixon Papers for supplies, $15.00.

PROBLEM 7-3   Reconciling a bank statement and recording a bank service charge

Use the bank statement, canceled checks, and check stubs given in the working papers accompanying this textbook.

INSTRUCTIONS:

1. Compare the canceled checks with the check stubs. For each canceled check, place a check mark next to the appropriate check stub number.
2. For each deposit shown on the bank statement, place a check mark next to the deposit amount on the appropriate check stub.
3. Prepare a bank statement reconciliation. Use August 29 of the current year as the date.
4. Record the following transactions on page 8 of a journal. The abbreviation for memorandum is M.

Sept. 1. Received bank statement showing August bank service charge, $5.00. M25.
    1. Received notice from the bank of a dishonored check, $170.00, plus $5.00 fee; total, $175.00. M26.

5. Record the bank service charge and dishonored check on Check Stub No. 165.

CHECK FIGURES (cont'd)

Problem 7-4 Each account payable dr.; cash cr.

Problem 7-5 All entries each account dr.; cash cr.

Mastery Problem 7-M New account numbers 115; 535. Adjusted balance 1,596.

Challenge Problem 7-C Corrected statement adjusted balance 11,647

PROBLEM 7-4 Paying cash on account using electronic funds transfer

Century Service uses electronic funds transfer to make payments on account.

INSTRUCTIONS:

Journalize the following transactions completed during July of the current year. Use page 8 of a journal. The abbreviation for memo is M.

July 8. Paid cash on account to Central Supply, $268.00, using EFT. M32.
     12. Paid cash on account to Lapham Enterprises, $420.00, using EFT. M33.
     16. Paid cash on account to Miller Sales, $355.00, using EFT. M34.

PROBLEM 7-5 Establishing and replenishing a petty cash fund

SweepUp established a petty cash fund on August 3 of the current year. At the end of August, the business replenished the petty cash fund.

INSTRUCTIONS:

Journalize the following transactions completed during August of the current year. Use page 10 of a journal. The abbreviation for check is C.

Aug. 3. Paid cash to establish a petty cash fund, $100.00. C57.
     31. Paid cash to replenish the petty cash fund, $78.00: supplies, $25.00; miscellaneous expense, $8.00; repairs, $45.00. C97.

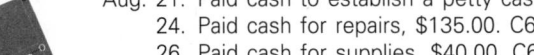

ENRICHMENT PROBLEMS   EPT(c,d,e,f)

MASTERY PROBLEM 7-M File maintenance; reconciling a bank statement; journalizing a bank service charge, a dishonored check, and petty cash transactions

Joseph Cruz owns a business called LawnMow. Selected general ledger accounts are given below.

110	Cash	520	Miscellaneous Expense
115	Petty Cash	530	Rent Expense
120	Supplies	535	Repair Expense
130	Prepaid Insurance	540	Supplies Expense
320	Joseph Cruz, Drawing	550	Utilities Expense

INSTRUCTIONS:

1. Journalize the following transactions completed during August of the current year. Use page 20 of a journal. Source documents are abbreviated as follows: check, C; memorandum, M.

Aug. 21. Paid cash to establish a petty cash fund, $100.00. C61.
     24. Paid cash for repairs, $135.00. C62.
     26. Paid cash for supplies, $40.00. C63.
     27. Received notice from the bank of a dishonored check, $35.00, plus $5.00 fee; total, $40.00. M22.
     28. Paid cash for miscellaneous expense, $12.00. C64.
     31. Paid cash to owner for personal use, $300.00. C65.
     31. Paid cash to replenish the petty cash fund, $55.00: supplies, $35.00; miscellaneous expense, $20.00. C66.

2. On August 31 of the current year, LawnMow received a bank statement dated August 30. Prepare a bank statement reconciliation. Use August 31 of the current year as the

date. The following information is obtained from the August 30 bank statement and from the records of the business.

Bank statement balance	$1,521.00
Bank service charge..................................	5.00
Outstanding deposit, August 31......................	430.00
Outstanding checks, Nos. 65 and 66.	
Checkbook balance on Check Stub No. 67..............	1,601.00

3. Continue using the journal and journalize the following transaction.

Aug. 31. Received bank statement showing August bank service charge, $5.00. M23.

CHALLENGE PROBLEM 7-C Reconciling a bank statement

AUTOMATED

On November 30 of the current year, Johnson Company received a bank statement dated November 29. Miss Johnson placed a check mark beside the amount on each check stub for which a canceled check was received. She also placed a check mark on the check stub beside the amount of each deposit shown on the bank statement. She then prepared a bank statement reconciliation.

The last eight check stubs for the month of November and the bank statement reconciliation are given in the working papers accompanying this textbook. Both the check stubs and reconciliation contain errors.

INSTRUCTIONS:

1. Verify the amounts on the check stubs. Assume that the check amounts in the upper right corner of each stub are correct. Also assume that all deposits have been entered correctly on the check stubs.

2. Draw a line through all incorrect amounts on the check stubs. Write the correct amounts either above or below the incorrect amounts, depending on where space is available.

3. Prepare a correct bank statement reconciliation. Assume that the check marks written beside check and deposit amounts on the check stubs are correct. Therefore, the outstanding deposits and checks are those that are not checked.

Automated Cash Control Systems

Rugcare's manual cash control systems are described in Chapter 7. Integrating Automated Accounting Topic 2 describes procedures for using automated accounting software to reconcile a bank statement. Topic 2 also describes procedures to record selected transactions for using a checking account and petty cash fund. The Automated Accounting Problems contain instructions for using automated accounting software to solve Mastery Problem 7-M and Challenge Problem 7-C, Chapter 7.

RECONCILING A BANK STATEMENT

To reconcile a bank statement using automated accounting software, File is selected from the menu bar. The Payroll/Assets/Bank

Rec. command is selected from the File menu. File is again selected from the menu bar. The Open Data File command is then chosen to retrieve the bank reconciliation data base from the template disk.

System is selected from the menu bar and the Bank Reconciliation option is chosen. Reconciliation is selected from the menu bar. The Reconciliation Data command is then chosen to display the data entry window for keying bank reconciliation data. The following information is obtained from the August 28 bank statement and from the records of Rugcare.

Bank statement balance	$7,586.00
Checkbook balance	8,497.00
Bank service charge	3.00
Outstanding deposit	1,412.00
Outstanding checks:	
No. 13	70.00
No. 14	434.00

The bank statement reconciliation data are keyed as shown in Illustration T2-1.

ILLUSTRATION T2-1   Completed bank reconciliation data entry window

FYI

Automated Accounting 6.0 software is broken into three modules. Module 1—general ledger, accounts payable, accounts receivable, financial statement analysis, and budgeting. Module 2—payroll, plant asset accounting, and bank reconciliation. Module 3—inventory accounting.

After the bank reconciliation data are keyed, Reports is selected from the menu bar. The Bank Reconciliation command is chosen from the Reports menu to display the bank reconciliation report. The report is checked for accuracy by comparing the Adjusted Checkbook Balance with the Adjusted Bank Balance. As these two totals are the same, the bank statement reconciliation is assumed to be correct. The bank statement reconciliation report is printed, as shown in Illustration T2-2, and filed for future reference.

ILLUSTRATION T2-2   Bank statement reconciliation report

```
                              Rugcare
                        Bank Reconciliation
                            08/28/--

Checkbook Balance                                          8497.00
                                              3.00
                                          -----------
Less Bank Charges                                             3.00
                                                          -----------
Adjusted Checkbook Balance                                 8494.00
                                                          ===========


Bank Balance                                               7586.00
                                           1412.00
                                          -----------
Plus Outstanding Deposits                                  1412.00
                                 13           70.00
                                 14          434.00
                                          -----------
Less Outstanding Checks                                      504.00
                                                          -----------
Adjusted Bank Balance                                      8494.00
                                                          ===========
```

RECORDING CASH CONTROL TRANSACTIONS

A general journal input form is used to journalize cash control transactions. Transaction data are journalized on an input form and keyed. The software is directed to post to the general ledger accounts.

Rugcare's cash control transactions are analyzed into debit and credit parts in Chapter 7.

Establishing a Petty Cash Fund

FYI

The run date is usually the date of the last transaction or the last day of a fiscal period.

August 17, 19--. Paid cash to establish a petty cash fund, $200.00. Check No. 10.

The journal entry to record this transaction is on lines 1 and 2 of the general journal input form shown in Illustration T2-3. Petty Cash is debited and Cash is credited for $200.00.

General journal input form with transactions recorded

RUN DATE 08,31,--						
MM DD YY			**GENERAL JOURNAL** Input Form			

GENERAL JOURNAL — Input Form

	DATE MM/DD	REFERENCE	ACCOUNT NO.	CUSTOMER/ VENDOR NO.	DEBIT	CREDIT	
1	08, 17	C10	120		200 00		1
2	/		110			200 00	2
3	,28	M3	530		3 00		3
4	/		110			3 00	4
5	,29	M6	530		15 00		5
6	/		110			15 00	6
7	,31	C15	530		7 00		7
8			550		5 00		8
9	/		110			12 00	9
10	/						10
11	/						11
12	/						12
25							25
				PAGE TOTALS	230 00	230 00	
				FINAL TOTALS	230 00	230 00	

Recording a Bank Service Charge

August 28, 19--. Received bank statement showing August bank service charge, $3.00. Memorandum No. 3.

The journal entry to record this transaction is on lines 3 and 4 of Illustration T2-3. Miscellaneous Expense is debited and Cash is credited for $3.00.

Recording a Dishonored Check

August 29, 19--. Received notice from the bank of a dishonored check, $10.00, plus $5.00 fee; total, $15.00. Memorandum No. 6.

The journal entry to record this transaction is on lines 5 and 6 of Illustration T2-3. Miscellaneous Expense is debited and Cash is credited for $15.00.

Replenishing a Petty Cash Fund

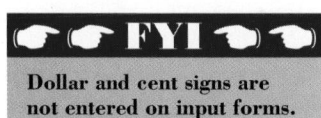

Dollar and cent signs are not entered on input forms.

August 31, 19--. Paid cash to replenish the petty cash fund, $12.00: miscellaneous expense, $7.00; repairs, $5.00. Check No. 15.

The journal entry to record this transaction is on lines 7 through 9 of Illustration T2-3. Miscellaneous Expense is debited for $7.00. Repair Expense is debited for $5.00. Cash is credited for $12.00.

INTEGRATING AUTOMATED ACCOUNTING — TOPIC 2   **163**

FOCUS

In Chapter 7, manual journalizing and posting procedures for cash control transactions were described. Emphasize that automated accounting software may be used to speed the journalizing and posting procedures. Explain that using automated accounting software, however, does not change accounting concepts. Only the methods change.

TEACH

Cover student pages 162–166 "Recording Cash Control Transactions." This lesson covers the procedures for journalizing cash control transactions on input forms and then processing them using automated accounting software. These transactions are the same as those in the text for Chapter 7. Review the definition of dishonored check and petty cash. (A dishonored check is a check the bank refuses to pay. Petty cash is an amount of cash kept on hand and used for making small payments.)

Module 1, Accounting System, must be loaded in order to process cash control transactions. Key A1 at the DOS prompt to load this module. Or, if the File menu contains the Payroll, Assets, Bank Rec. command, Module 1 is already loaded.

OPTIONAL PROBLEMS

OPTIONAL PROBLEMS DB-2A and DB-2B provide students with hands-on learning activities. By keying the input forms illustrated in this topic, students have an opportunity for guided practice before actually working a problem independently. Refer to the OPTIONAL PROBLEMS for information about automating this topic.

Use Transparency AA-2, Blank General Journal Input Form, to explain how to record cash control transactions. Emphasize that the totals of a general journal input form should be compared to ensure that debits equal credits. This should always be done before entering data into the computer.

Guided Practice

Students should be at the computers. Guide students through booting the software and loading Optional Problem DB-2B from the template. Instruct students to journalize the transactions as you go step-by-step through the procedures.

Independent Practice

Assign Automating Problem 7-M Instructions 1–5.

- Assess student understanding by checking solutions to Independent Practice Activities.

- Review the steps for keying transactions into the automated accounting software.

Reteach

Review Illustrations T2-3 and T2-4. These illustrations can be used to reinforce the procedures for recording and processing cash control transactions using an automated accounting system. Use Transparency AA-2 to journalize cash control transactions on the overhead.

Enrich

Invite a local software merchant to speak to the class on the methods for recording transactions using commercial automated software.

Review the process of using automated accounting software to journalize transactions.

Dollar signs and cent signs are not keyed when using Automated Accounting 6.0 software. When the cents are zero (.00), key only the dollar amount. The software automatically assigns the .00.

After all transactions have been journalized, Rugcare totals the Debit and Credit amount columns. The totals are recorded on the Page Totals and Final Totals lines provided at the bottom of the input form. The totals are compared to assure that debits equal credits.

Processing Cash Control Journal Entries

To process cash control journal entries, File is selected from the menu bar. The Open Accounting File command is chosen from the File menu to retrieve the general ledger data base from the template disk. The Journals menu is selected from the menu bar. The General Journal command is chosen from the Journals menu to key the cash control transaction data.

After all lines on the input form have been keyed and posted, the Reports menu is selected from the menu bar. The Journals command is chosen from the Reports menu. The General Journal report is selected from the Reports Selection menu. This selection displays the Selection Options screen. As Rugcare wants to print all transactions journalized on Illustration T2-3, pushing the *Ok* button directs the software to display a general journal report. The displayed general journal report is checked for accuracy by comparing the report totals, $230.00, with the totals on the general journal input form. Because the totals are the same, the general journal report is assumed to be correct. The general journal report is printed, as shown in Illustration T2-4, and filed for future reference.

ILLUSTRATION T2-4   General journal report

```
                              Rugcare
                          General Journal
                            08/31/--
---------------------------------------------------------------------
Date    Refer.   V/C Acct.  Title                   Debit      Credit
---------------------------------------------------------------------
08/17   C10          120    Petty Cash             200.00
08/17   C10          110    Cash                               200.00

08/28   M3           530    Miscellaneous Expense    3.00
08/28   M3           110    Cash                                 3.00

08/29   M6           530    Miscellaneous Expense   15.00
08/29   M6           110    Cash                                15.00

08/31   C15          530    Miscellaneous Expense    7.00
08/31   C15          550    Repair Expense           5.00
08/31   C15          110    Cash                                12.00

                                                   ----------  ----------
                            Totals                 230.00      230.00
                                                   ==========  ==========
```

The Automated Accounting Problems in this Integrating Automated Accounting Topic use Mastery Problem 7-M and Challenge Problem 7-C, Chapter 7, which students have already completed manually. Refer students back to these problems to complete the input forms. The problem instructions in *Automated Accounting 6.0* will lead students through automating the problems.

OPTIONAL PROBLEM DB-2A

Rugcare's general ledger data base is on the accounting textbook template. If you wish to reconcile Rugcare's bank statement using automated accounting software, load the *Automated Accounting 6.0* or higher software. Pull down the File menu from the menu bar and choose the Payroll/Assets/Bank Rec. command. Pull down the File menu and choose the Open Data File command to retrieve Data Base 2A (DB-2A) from the template disk. Read the Problem Instructions screen. Use Illustration T2-1 and follow the procedures described to reconcile Rugcare's bank statement.

OPTIONAL PROBLEM DB-2B

Rugcare's general ledger data base is on the accounting textbook template. If you wish to process Rugcare's cash control transactions using automated accounting software, load the *Automated Accounting 6.0* or higher software. If you just completed Optional Problem DB-2A, you must first load the Accounting System module before you begin. Pull down the File menu and choose the Accounting System command. Pull down the File menu and choose the Open File menu command to retrieve Data Base 2B (DB-2B) from the template disk. Read the Problem Instructions screen. Use Illustration T2-3 and follow the procedures described to process Rugcare's cash control journal entries.

AUTOMATED ACCOUNTING PROBLEMS

AUTOMATING MASTERY PROBLEM 7-M Reconciling a bank statement; journalizing a bank service charge, a dishonored check, and petty cash transactions

INSTRUCTIONS:

1. Journalize transactions from Mastery Problem 7-M, Chapter 7 on a general journal input form. Use August 31 of the current year as the run date.
2. Load the *Automated Accounting 6.0* or higher software. Select data base F7-M (First-Year Course Problem 7-M) from the accounting textbook template. Read the Problem Instructions screen.
3. Select File from the menu bar and choose the Save As menu command. Key the path to the drive and directory that contains your data files. Save the data base with a file name of XXX7M (where XXX are your initials).
4. Key the transactions from the completed general journal input form.
5. Display/print the general journal report. Check the report for accuracy by comparing the report totals with the totals on the input form.
6. Save your file.
7. To complete the bank reconciliation, select File from the menu bar and select the Payroll/Assets/Bank Rec. command. Select File and then the Open Data File command to retrieve data base F7-M from the template disk. The following information is obtained from the bank statement and from the records of the business.

Bank statement balance	$1,521.00
Checkbook balance	1,601.00
Bank service charge	5.00
Outstanding deposit	430.00
Outstanding checks:	
No. 65	300.00
No. 66	55.00

8. Key the bank statement reconciliation data.
9. Display/print the bank statement reconciliation.

TEACHING STRATEGIES: TEACHING TIP

It is important for students to save a template file under another name before they begin work. This will keep the template file intact for future use.

AUTOMATING CHALLENGE PROBLEM 7-C Reconciling a bank statement

INSTRUCTIONS:

1. Load the *Automated Accounting 6.0* or higher software. Select File from the menu bar and select the Payroll/Assets/Bank Rec. command. Select File and then the Open Data File command to retrieve data base F7-C from the template disk.
2. Use the manual solution prepared for Challenge Problem 7-C. Key the bank statement reconciliation data.
3. Display/print the bank statement reconciliation.

An Accounting Cycle for a Proprietorship: Journalizing and Posting Transactions

Reinforcement activities strengthen the learning of accounting concepts and procedures. Reinforcement Activity 1 is a single problem divided into two parts. Part A includes learnings from Chapters 2 through 7. Part B includes learnings from Chapters 8 through 10. An accounting cycle is completed in Parts A and B for a single business—The Fitness Center.

TEACHING STRATEGIES: REINFORCEMENT ACTIVITY

Reinforcement Activity 1 begins with Part A and continues with Part B after Chapter 10. Reinforcement Activity 1 presents the whole accounting cycle for a service business organized as a proprietorship. You may prefer to have your students begin Part A and continue with Part B later. Or you may reserve Part A to be completed with Part B after Chapter 10. Blackline masters for audit tests for Reinforcement Activity 1 are available in the Teacher's Resource Guide in three options: Part A only, Part B only, and Parts A and B combined. In addition, *Automated Accounting 6.0* or higher can be used to automate Reinforcement Activity 1.

THE FITNESS CENTER

In May of the current year, Gail Davis starts a service business called The Fitness Center. The business provides exercise facilities for its clients. In addition, Miss Davis, a professional dietician, offers diet and exercise counseling for clients who request her assistance. The business rents the facilities with which it operates, pays the utilities, and is responsible for maintenance. The Fitness Center charges clients for each visit.

CHART OF ACCOUNTS

The Fitness Center uses the following chart of accounts.

CHART OF ACCOUNTS

Balance Sheet Accounts	Income Statement Accounts
(100) ASSETS	(400) REVENUE
110 Cash	410 Sales
120 Petty Cash	(500) EXPENSES
130 Supplies	510 Advertising Expense
140 Prepaid Insurance	520 Insurance Expense
(200) LIABILITIES	530 Miscellaneous Expense
210 Dunnel Supplies	540 Rent Expense
220 Morgan Office Supplies	550 Repair Expense
(300) OWNER'S EQUITY	560 Supplies Expense
310 Gail Davis, Capital	570 Utilities Expense
320 Gail Davis, Drawing	
330 Income Summary	

TEACHING STRATEGIES: ASSESSMENT BY PORTFOLIO

If you assign Reinforcement Activity 1, Part A and intend to use it as part of an assessment by portfolio evaluation, advise students that their work on this activity will be included in their portfolio.

RECORDING TRANSACTIONS

INSTRUCTIONS:

1. Journalize the following transactions completed during May of the current year. Use page 1 of the journal. Source documents are abbreviated as follows: check stub, C; memorandum, M; receipt, R; calculator tape, T.

May 1. Received cash from owner as an investment, $15,000.00. R1.
    1. Paid cash for rent, $1,000.00. C1.
    2. Paid cash for electric bill, $45.00. C2.
    4. Paid cash for supplies, $500.00. C3.
    4. Paid cash for insurance, $960.00. C4.
    7. Bought supplies on account from Dunnel Supplies, $800.00. M1.
  11. Paid cash to establish a petty cash fund, $200.00. C5.
  12. Received cash from sales, $550.00. T12.
  13. Paid cash for repairs, $25.00. C6.
  13. Paid cash for miscellaneous expense, $35.00. C7.
  13. Received cash from sales, $185.00. T13.
  14. Paid cash for advertising, $100.00. C8.
  14. Received cash from sales, $335.00. T14.
  15. Paid cash to owner for personal use, $250.00. C9.
  15. Paid cash on account to Dunnel Supplies, $300.00. C10.
  15. Received cash from sales, $325.00. T15.
  18. Paid cash for miscellaneous expense, $100.00. C11.
  18. Received cash from sales, $295.00. T18.
  19. Received cash from sales, $155.00. T19.
  20. Paid cash for repairs, $125.00. C12.
  20. Bought supplies on account from Morgan Office Supplies, $150.00. M2.
  20. Received cash from sales, $195.00. T20.

2. Prove and rule page 1 of the journal. Carry the column totals forward to page 2 of the journal.

3. Post the separate amounts on each line of page 1 of the journal that need to be posted individually.

4. Use page 2 of the journal. Journalize the following transactions.

May 21. Paid cash for water bill, $110.00. C13.
  21. Received cash from sales, $235.00. T21.
  25. Paid cash for supplies, $50.00. C14.
  25. Received cash from sales, $295.00. T25.
  26. Paid cash for miscellaneous expense, $25.00. C15.
  26. Received cash from sales, $300.00. T26.
  27. Received cash from sales, $195.00. T27.
  28. Paid cash for telephone bill, $210.00. C16.
  28. Received cash from sales, $275.00. T28.

5. The Fitness Center received a bank statement dated May 27. The following information is obtained from the bank statement and from the records of the business. Prepare a bank statement reconciliation. Use May 29 as the date.

Bank statement balance	$14,312.00
Bank service charge	3.00
Outstanding deposit, May 28	275.00
Outstanding checks:	
No. 14	50.00
No. 15	25.00
No. 16	210.00
Checkbook balance on Check Stub No. 17	14,305.00

6. Continue using page 2 of the journal, and journalize the following transactions.

May 29. Received bank statement showing May bank service charge, $3.00. M3.
    29. Paid cash for supplies, $60.00. C17.
    29. Received cash from sales, $240.00. T29.
    31. Paid cash to replenish the petty cash fund, $17.00: miscellaneous expense, $10.00; repairs, $7.00. C18.
    31. Paid cash to owner for personal use, $250.00. C19.
    31. Received cash from sales, $280.00. T31.

7. Prove page 2 of the journal.
8. Prove cash. The beginning cash balance on May 1 is zero. The balance on the next unused check stub is $14,495.00.
9. Rule page 2 of the journal.
10. Post the separate amounts on each line of page 2 of the journal that need to be posted individually.
11. Post the column totals on page 2 of the journal.

The general ledger prepared in Reinforcement Activity 1, Part A, is needed to complete Reinforcement Activity 1, Part B.

Chapter 8 introduces the 8-column work sheet. The Work Sheet Overlay in the chapter is an excellent visual summary of the steps in preparing a work sheet.

In order to complete a work sheet, adjustments must be made. Chapter 8 describes two simple adjustments for a proprietorship—supplies and prepaid insurance. A proprietorship, like other forms of business organizations, must adjust certain accounts. By introducing two basic adjustments in this chapter, this allows the text to present a complete, realistic accounting cycle for a proprietorship.

The accounting concepts, *Consistent Reporting, Accounting Period Cycle,* and *Matching Expenses with Revenue,* are introduced for the first time in this chapter.

GUIDE TO ACHIEVING LEARNING OBJECTIVES

Enabling Performance Tasks	TEACH — Lesson Plans	APPLY — Drills for Understanding	APPLY — Application Problems	EXTEND/ENRICH — Mastery Problems	EXTEND/ENRICH — Challenge Problems	EXTEND/ENRICH — Cases for Critical Thinking	EXTEND/ENRICH — Recycling Problems	EXTEND/ENRICH — Reinforcement Activity	
a. Define accounting terms related to a work sheet for a service business organized as a proprietorship.	8-1								
b. Identify accounting concepts and practices related to a work sheet for a service business organized as a proprietorship.	8-1								
c. Plan adjustments for supplies and prepaid insurance.	8-1		8-1, 8-2	8-M	8-C	Case 1	8-R	1B	
d. Complete a work sheet for a service business organized as a proprietorship.	8-1	8-D1, 8-D2	8-1, 8-2	8-M	8-C		8-R	1B	
e. Identify selected procedures for finding and correcting errors in accounting records.	8-2		8-3			Case 2			

ENRICHMENT

SPECIAL FEATURES

Professional Business Ethics, page 184

Multicultural Awareness, page 171

TECHNOLOGY CONNECTION

Accounting Tutorial Unit 2

Application Program Disk Problems 8-M, 8-C

Electronic Study Guide

NEW, REVIEW, AND EXTENSION

ACTIVITIES/CONCEPTS/TRANSACTIONS	NEW	REVIEW/ EXTENSION
Preparing an 8-column work sheet	✓	
Preparing a trial balance	✓	
Planning adjustments on a work sheet	✓	
Adjustment for supplies	✓	
Adjustment for prepaid insurance	✓	
Completing a work sheet	✓	
Finding and correcting errors	✓	

	INFORMAL ASSESSMENT		FORMAL ASSESSMENT				
	Study Guide	Audit Your Understanding	Chapter MicroExam	Chapter Problem Test	Unit Problem Test	Unit Objective Test	Portfolio
	Unit A		✓			✓	
	Units B, C, D	✓	✓			✓	
				✓	✓		✓
	Unit B			✓	✓		✓
		✓	✓			✓	

TEACHING MATERIALS

Teacher's Wraparound Edition of Text

Teacher's Resource Guide

Teacher's Edition of Working Papers

Teacher's Edition of Demonstration/Recycling Problems

Teaching Transparencies

Accounting Tutorial Manual

Applied Math Work Sheets

MicroExam

APPLIED MATHEMATICS

APPLIED MATH/ACCOUNTING SKILL	APPLICATION
Analyzing adjustments	Prob. 8-1
Calculating net income/net loss	Prob. 8-D2
Checking for typical arithmetic errors	Prob. 8-3

8

Work Sheet for a Service Business

ENABLING PERFORMANCE TASKS

After studying Chapter 8, you will be able to:

a Define accounting terms related to a work sheet for a service business organized as a proprietorship.

b Identify accounting concepts and practices related to a work sheet for a service business organized as a proprietorship.

c Plan adjustments for supplies and prepaid insurance.

d Complete a work sheet for a service business organized as a proprietorship.

e Identify selected procedures for finding and correcting errors in accounting records.

TERMS PREVIEW

fiscal period • work sheet • trial balance • adjustments • income statement • net income • net loss

170

General ledger accounts contain information needed by managers and owners. Before the information can be used, however, it must be analyzed, summarized, and reported in a meaningful way. The accounting concept, *Consistent Reporting*, is applied when the same accounting procedures are followed in the same way in each accounting period. *(CONCEPT: Consistent Reporting)* For example, in one year a delivery business might report the number of deliveries made. The next year the same business reports the amount of revenue received for the deliveries made. The information for the two years cannot be compared because the business has not been consistent in reporting information about deliveries.

FISCAL PERIODS

The length of time for which a business summarizes and reports financial information is called a **fiscal period**. A fiscal period is also known as an accounting period. Businesses usually select a period of time, such as a month, six months, or a year, for which to summarize and report financial information. The accounting concept, *Accounting Period Cycle*, is applied when changes in financial information are reported for a specific period of time in the form of financial statements. *(CONCEPT: Accounting Period Cycle)* Each business chooses a fiscal period length that meets its needs. Because federal and state tax reports are based on one year, most businesses use a one-year fiscal period. However, because Rugcare is a new business, Mr. Furman wishes to have financial information reported frequently to help him make decisions. For this reason, Rugcare uses a one-month fiscal period.

A fiscal period can begin on any date. However, most businesses begin their fiscal periods on the first day of a month. Rugcare started business on August 1. Therefore, Rugcare's monthly fiscal period is for the period from August 1 through August 31, inclusive. Another business might use a one-year fiscal period from August 1 of one year through July 31 of the next year. Many businesses use a calendar year starting on January 1 and ending on December 31. Businesses often choose a one-year fiscal period that ends during a period of low business activity. In this way, the end-of-year accounting work comes at a time when other business activities are the lightest. For example, a store with a large volume of Christmas holiday sales might prefer to begin its fiscal period on February 1 or March 1.

> Most individuals use a one-year fiscal period that begins on January 1 and ends on December 31. This fiscal period corresponds to the period for which they must file income tax returns for the federal and state governments. However, individuals may use a different fiscal period if approved by the Internal Revenue Service.

Financial information may be analyzed, summarized, and reported on any date a business needs the information. However,

- In Chapter 6, financial information was posted from the journal to the general ledger. Explain that before this information can be used, it must be analyzed, summarized, and reported in a meaningful way. This lesson will look at how a business determines the period of time it will use for summarizing and reporting financial information. This lesson will also introduce the accounting form used to summarize the general ledger information needed to prepare financial statements.

- Introduce new vocabulary: fiscal period, work sheet, trial balance, adjustments, income statement, net income, net loss.

A summary of preparing a work sheet is shown on the Work Sheet Overlay on pages 176A through 176C.

financial information is always summarized and reported at the end of a fiscal period.

WORK SHEET

A columnar accounting form used to summarize the general ledger information needed to prepare financial statements is called a **work sheet.**

Accountants use a work sheet for four reasons. (1) To summarize general ledger account balances to prove that debits equal credits. (2) To plan needed changes to general ledger accounts to bring account balances up to date. (3) To separate general ledger account balances according to the financial statements to be prepared. (4) To calculate the amount of net income or net loss for a fiscal period.

Journals and ledgers are permanent records of a business and are usually prepared in ink. However, a work sheet is a planning tool and is not considered a permanent accounting record. Therefore, a work sheet is prepared in pencil.

Preparing the Heading of a Work Sheet

The heading on a work sheet consists of three lines. (1) Name of the business. (2) Name of the report. (3) Date of the report. The heading for Rugcare's work sheet is shown in Illustration 8-1.

FYI

The work sheet has a three-line heading which includes the name of the company, the name of the form, and the time period the work sheet covers.

ILLUSTRATION 8-1

Heading on a work sheet

Rugcare
Work Sheet
For Month Ended August 31, 19--

The date on Rugcare's work sheet indicates that the work sheet covers the 31 days from August 1 through and including August 31. If the work sheet were for a calendar year fiscal period, it might have a date stated as *For Year Ended December 31, 19--. (CONCEPT: Accounting Period Cycle)*

Preparing a Trial Balance on a Work Sheet

The equality of debits and credits in the general ledger must be proved. The total of all debit account balances must equal the total of all credit account balances. A proof of the equality of debits and credits in a general ledger is called a **trial balance.** Rugcare prepares a trial balance on a work sheet. Rugcare's August 31 trial balance on a work sheet is shown in Illustration 8-2.

172   PART 2   Accounting for a Service Business Organized as a Proprietorship

TEACHING STRATEGIES: APPLYING VISUALS

Direct students to the summary Work Sheet Overlay for a visual reinforcement of the procedures for completing a work sheet.

Information for the trial balance is taken from the general ledger. General ledger account titles are listed on a trial balance in the same order as listed on the chart of accounts. All the account titles are listed, even if some accounts do not have balances. The accounts that do not have balances in the Trial Balance columns will be needed in other parts of the work sheet.

ILLUSTRATION 8-2

Trial balance on a work sheet

	ACCOUNT TITLE	TRIAL BALANCE	
		DEBIT	CREDIT
1	Cash	8 2 7 2 00	
2	Petty Cash	2 0 0 00	
3	Supplies	4 9 3 1 00	
4	Prepaid Insurance	1 2 0 0 00	
5	Butler Cleaning Supplies		1 3 6 0 00
6	Dale Office Supplies		2 0 0 00
7	Ben Furman, Capital		1 0 0 0 0 00
8	Ben Furman, Drawing	6 0 0 00	
9	Income Summary		
10	Sales		4 2 9 1 00
11	Advertising Expense	6 8 00	
12	Insurance Expense		
13	Miscellaneous Expense	1 0 5 00	
14	Rent Expense	2 5 0 00	
15	Repair Expense	1 1 0 00	
16	Supplies Expense		
17	Utilities Expense	1 1 5 00	
18		1 5 8 5 1 00	1 5 8 5 1 00

Rugcare
Work Sheet
For Month Ended August 31, 19--

Seven steps are used in preparing a trial balance on a work sheet.

1 Write the general ledger account titles in the work sheet's Account Title column.

2 Write the general ledger account debit balances in the Trial Balance Debit column. Write the general ledger account credit

Cover student pages 171–183. "Fiscal Periods" and "Work Sheet." Emphasize that it is easier to keep track of an accounting period cycle that begins the first day of the month and ends the last day of the month. Emphasize that the work sheet has a typical three-line heading as any financial statement. All accounts are listed on a work sheet from the general ledger whether they have a balance or not. Account titles are not abbreviated unless there is not enough room to write the title in full.

Students should establish the habit of asking the four questions to analyze each adjustment. Draw T accounts on the board to analyze adjustments for supplies and insurance. Emphasize that when recording the adjustments on a work sheet, follow the three steps of (1) writing the debit amount in work sheet's Adjustments Debit column; (2) writing the credit amount in the work sheet's Adjustments Credit column; and (3) label the two parts of the adjustment with the next available small letter. The first adjustment on each work sheet begins with a. When extending balances, assets, liabilities, and owner's equity always go in the Balance Sheet columns. Revenue and expenses always go in the Income Statement columns.

The work sheet overlay feature on student pages 176A–176C can be an invaluable teaching tool for helping students to understand the procedures for preparing a work sheet.

WORK SHEET OVERLAY

Frequently refer to the work sheet overlay that appears in this chapter. This is an excellent step-by-step instructional method to help explain making adjustments and completing the work sheet.

- Relate auto insurance premiums that students pay to calculating adjustments. Ask students how much they pay for coverage. Break it down to a price per day that they are paying for coverage. Then relate how impractical it would be to record this expense every day.

- Use Transparency C to illustrate completing a work sheet using the data from Illustrations 8-1 through 8-7 in the textbook.

Guided Practice

Guide students through Drills 8-D1 and 8-D2. Students should have the forms from the working papers to complete as you guide them through the drills. All students should agree with the action taken for each step before proceeding to the next step.

Independent Practice

Assign Terms 1–7, Questions 1–13, and Problems 8-1 and 8-2.

FYI

Complete the Trial Balance columns of the work sheet before going on to the other columns. If the Trial Balance columns are not correct, the remaining columns will also be incorrect.

balances in the Trial Balance Credit column. If an account does not have a balance, the space in the Trial Balance columns is left blank.

3 Rule a single line across the two Trial Balance columns below the last line on which an account title is written. This single line shows that the two columns are to be added.

4 Add both the Trial Balance Debit and Credit columns. Use a calculator if one is available. For Rugcare's work sheet, the totals are Debit, $15,851.00 and Credit, $15,851.00.

5 Check the equality of the two amount column totals. If the two column totals are the same, then debits equal credits in the general ledger accounts. Because the totals, $15,851.00, are the same, the Trial Balance columns on Rugcare's work sheet are in balance.

If the two column totals are not the same and the trial balance is not in balance, recheck the Trial Balance columns to find the error. Other parts of a work sheet are not completed until the Trial Balance columns are proved. Suggestions for locating errors are described later in this chapter.

6 Write each column's total, *$15,851.00*, below the single line.

7 Rule double lines across both Trial Balance columns. The double lines mean that the Trial Balance column totals have been verified as correct.

Planning Adjustments on a Work Sheet

Sometimes a business will pay cash for an expense in one fiscal period, but the expense is not used until a later period. The expense should be reported in the same fiscal period that it is used to produce revenue. The accounting concept, *Matching Expenses with Revenue*, is applied when revenue from business activities and expenses associated with earning that revenue are recorded in the same accounting period. For example, Rugcare buys supplies in quantity in August, but some of the supplies are not used until September. Only the value of the supplies used in August should be reported as expenses in August. In this way, August revenue and the supplies expense associated with earning the August revenue are recorded in the same accounting period. *(CONCEPT: Matching Expenses with Revenue)*

In order to give accurate information on financial statements, some general ledger accounts must be brought up to date at the end of a fiscal period. For example, Rugcare debits an asset account, Supplies, each time supplies are bought. Supplies on hand are items of value owned by a business until the supplies are used. The value of supplies that are used becomes an expense to the business. However, recording an expense each time an individual supply, such as a pencil, is used would be impractical. Therefore, on August 31 the balance of the asset account, Supplies, is the value of all supplies bought rather than the value of only the supplies that

APPLIED SKILLS: BUILDING STUDY SKILLS

Direct students to create a Quick Reference Guide (QRG) on a small card or sheet of paper to use as an aid in analyzing adjustments. Students should write the four questions to analyze an adjustment on an index card to use as a QRG. Have them use this QRG whenever they analyze adjustments.

have not been used. The amount of supplies that have been used must be deducted from the asset account, Supplies, and recorded in the expense account, Supplies Expense.

Likewise, the amount of insurance that has been used during the fiscal period is also an expense of the business. When the insurance premium for a year of insurance coverage is paid, the entire amount is debited to an asset account, Prepaid Insurance. Each day during August a portion of the insurance coverage is used. The value of the insurance used is an expense of the business. However, recording each day's amount of insurance used is impractical. Therefore, at the end of a fiscal period, the balance of Prepaid Insurance is the value of all insurance coverage bought, rather than the value of only the insurance coverage that still remains. The amount of the insurance coverage used must be deducted from the asset account, Prepaid Insurance, and recorded in the expense account, Insurance Expense.

Changes recorded on a work sheet to update general ledger accounts at the end of a fiscal period are called **adjustments**. The assets of a business, such as supplies and prepaid insurance, are used to earn revenue. The portion of the assets consumed in order to earn revenue become expenses of the business. The portions consumed are no longer assets but are now expenses. Therefore, adjustments must be made to both the asset and expense accounts for supplies and insurance. After the adjustments are made, the expenses incurred to earn revenue are reported in the same fiscal period as the revenue is earned and reported. (CONCEPT: *Matching Expenses with Revenue*)

A work sheet is used to plan adjustments. Changes are not made in general ledger accounts until adjustments are journalized and posted. The accuracy of the planning for adjustments is checked on a work sheet before adjustments are actually journalized.

Procedures for journalizing Rugcare's adjustments are described in Chapter 10.

Supplies Adjustment. On August 31, before adjustments, the balance of Supplies is $4,931.00, and the balance of Supplies Expense is zero, as shown in the T accounts.

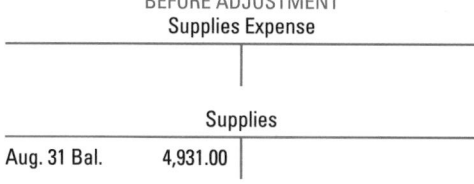

BEFORE ADJUSTMENT
Supplies Expense

Supplies

| Aug. 31 Bal. | 4,931.00 |

On August 31 Mr. Furman counted the supplies on hand and found that the value of supplies still unused on that date was $2,284.00. The value of the supplies used is calculated as shown below.

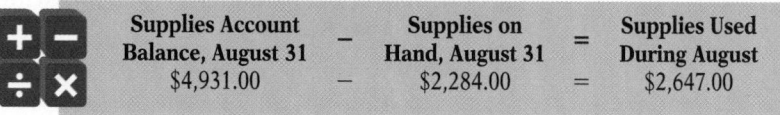

Supplies Account Balance, August 31	–	Supplies on Hand, August 31	=	Supplies Used During August
$4,931.00	–	$2,284.00	=	$2,647.00

Four questions are asked in analyzing the adjustment for the asset account, Supplies.

1.	What is the balance of Supplies?.	$4,931.00
2.	What should the balance be for this account?. . . .	$2,284.00
3.	What must be done to correct the account balance?	
	Decrease	$2,647.00
4.	What adjustment is made?	
	Debit Supplies Expense	$2,647.00
	Credit Supplies.	$2,647.00

AFTER ADJUSTMENT

Supplies Expense

Adj. (a)	2,647.00

Supplies

Aug. 31 Bal.	4,931.00	Adj. (a)	2,647.00
(New Bal.	2,284.00)		

The expense account, Supplies Expense, is increased by a debit, $2,647.00, the value of supplies used. The balance of Supplies Expense, $2,647.00, is the value of supplies used during the fiscal period from August 1 to August 31. *(CONCEPT: Matching Expenses with Revenue)*

The asset account, Supplies, is decreased by a credit, $2,647.00, the value of supplies used. The debit balance, $4,931.00, *less* the credit adjustment, $2,647.00, *equals* the new balance, $2,284.00. The new balance of Supplies is the same as the value of supplies on hand on August 31.

Rugcare's supplies adjustment is shown on lines 3 and 16 of the work sheet in Illustration 8-3.

ILLUSTRATION 8-3   Supplies adjustment on a work sheet

		1	2	3	4	
	ACCOUNT TITLE	TRIAL BALANCE		ADJUSTMENTS		
		DEBIT	CREDIT	DEBIT	CREDIT	
3	*Supplies*	4 9 3 1 00			(a) 2 6 4 7 00	3
16	*Supplies Expense*			(a) 2 6 4 7 00		16
17						17
18						18
19						19
20						20

Three steps are used to record the supplies adjustment on the work sheet.

1 Write the debit amount, *$2,647.00*, in the work sheet's Adjustments Debit column on the line with the account title Supplies Expense (line 16).

2 Write the credit amount, *$2,647.00*, in the Adjustments Credit column on the line with the account title Supplies (line 3).

3 Label the two parts of this adjustment with a small letter *a* in parentheses *(a)*. The letter *a* identifies the debit and credit amounts as part of the same adjustment.

TEACHING STRATEGIES: EXPANDING BEYOND THE CLASSROOM

Invite an auditor to talk about the importance of the accuracy of the data on the work sheet.

SUMMARY OF PREPARATION OF A WORK SHEET FOR A SERVICE BUSINESS

The following overlay summarizes the preparation of a work sheet. Follow the directions below in using the overlay.

1. Before using the overlay, be sure the pages and transparent overlays are arranged correctly. The correct arrangement is shown below.

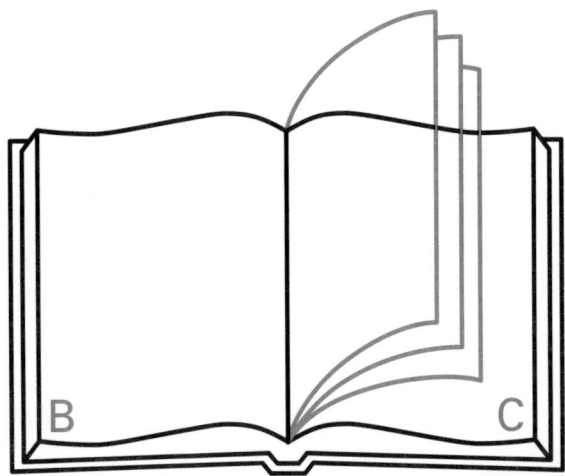

2. Place your book in a horizontal position. Study the steps on page C in preparing the work sheet. You will be able to read the text through the transparent overlays. When directed, carefully lift the transparent overlays and lay them over the work sheet as shown below.

PREPARING A WORK SHEET

To correctly use the insert, read the steps below. Apply the transparent overlays when directed to do so in the steps.

Rugcare
Work Sheet
For Month Ended August 31, 19--

	ACCOUNT TITLE	TRIAL BALANCE DEBIT	TRIAL BALANCE CREDIT	ADJUSTMENTS DEBIT	ADJUSTMENTS CREDIT	INCOME STATEMENT DEBIT	INCOME STATEMENT CREDIT	BALANCE SHEET DEBIT	BALANCE SHEET CREDIT
1	Cash	827200							
2	Petty Cash	20000							
3	Supplies	493100							
4	Prepaid Insurance	120000							
5	Butler Cleaning Supplies		136000						
6	Dale Office Supplies		20000						
7	Ben Furman, Capital		1000000						
8	Ben Furman, Drawing	60000							
9	Income Summary								
10	Sales		429100						
11	Advertising Expense	6800							
12	Insurance Expense								
13	Miscellaneous Expense	10500							
14	Rent Expense	25000							
15	Repair Expense	11000							
16	Supplies Expense								
17	Utilities Expense	11500							
18		1585100	1585100						
19									
20									
21									
22									
23									
24									
25									

PREPARING A WORK SHEET

1 Write the heading.

2 Record the trial balance.
- Write the general ledger account titles in the Account Title column.
- Write the account balances in either the Trial Balance Debit or Credit column.
- Rule a single line across the Trial Balance columns.
- Add the Trial Balance columns, and compare the totals.
- Rule double lines across both Trial Balance columns. *Carefully apply the first overlay.*

3 Record the supplies adjustment.
- Write the debit amount in the Adjustments Debit column on the line with the account title Supplies Expense.
- Write the credit amount in the Adjustments Credit column on the line with the account title Supplies.
- Label this adjustment *(a)*.

4 Record the prepaid insurance adjustment.
- Write the debit amount in the Adjustments Debit column on the line with the account title Insurance Expense.
- Write the credit amount in the Adjustments Credit column on the line with the account title Prepaid Insurance.
- Label this adjustment *(b)*.

5 Prove the Adjustments columns.
- Rule a single line across the Adjustments columns.
- Add the Adjustments columns, and compare the totals to assure that they are equal.
- Write the proving totals below the single line.
- Rule double lines across both Adjustments columns. *Carefully apply the second overlay.*

6 Extend all balance sheet account balances.
- Extend the up-to-date asset account balances to the Balance Sheet Debit column.
- Extend the up-to-date liability account balances to the Balance

Sheet Credit column.
- Extend the owner's capital and drawing account balances to the Balance Sheet columns.

7 Extend all income statement account balances.
- Extend the up-to-date revenue account balance to the Income Statement Credit column.
- Extend the up-to-date expense account balances to the Income Statement Debit column. *Carefully apply the third overlay.*

8 Calculate and record the net income (or net loss).
- Rule a single line across the Income Statement and Balance Sheet columns.
- Add the columns, and write the totals below the single line.
- Calculate the net income or net loss amount.
- Write the amount of net income (or net loss) below the smaller of the two Income Statement column totals. Write the words *Net Income* or *Net Loss* in the Account Title column.
- Extend the amount of net income (or net loss) to the Balance Sheet columns. Write the amount under the smaller of the two column totals. Write the amount on the same line as the words *Net Income (or Net Loss)*.

9 Total and rule the Income Statement and Balance Sheet columns.
- Rule a single line across the Income Statement and Balance Sheet columns immediately below the net income (or net loss) amounts.
- Add the net income (or net loss) to the previous column totals. Compare the column totals to assure that totals for each pair of columns are in balance.
- Write the proving totals for each column below the single line.
- Rule double lines across the Income Statement and Balance Sheet columns immediately below the proving totals.

Prepaid Insurance Adjustment. When Rugcare pays for insurance, the amount is debited to the asset account, Prepaid Insurance. However, to debit Insurance Expense daily for the amount of that day's insurance premium used is impractical. Therefore, at the end of a fiscal period, Rugcare's prepaid insurance account does not show the actual value of the remaining prepaid insurance.

BEFORE ADJUSTMENT

Insurance Expense

Prepaid Insurance

Aug. 31 Bal.	1,200.00

On August 31, before adjustments, the balance of Prepaid Insurance is $1,200.00, and the balance of Insurance Expense is zero, as shown in the T accounts.

On August 31 Mr. Furman checked the insurance records and found that the value of insurance coverage remaining was $1,100.00. The value of insurance coverage used during the fiscal period is calculated as shown below.

	Prepaid Insurance Balance, August 31	–	Insurance Coverage Remaining Unused, August 31	=	Insurance Coverage Used During August
	$1,200.00	–	$1,100.00	=	$100.00

FYI

If you use the four questions for analyzing adjustments, it will be easier to calculate the correct amounts for the adjustment.

Four questions are asked in analyzing the adjustment for the asset account, Prepaid Insurance.

1. What is the balance of Prepaid Insurance? $1,200.00
2. What should the balance be for this account? $1,100.00
3. What must be done to correct the account balance?
   Decrease . . . . $ 100.00
4. What adjustment is made?
   Debit Insurance Expense . . . . $ 100.00
   Credit Prepaid Insurance . . . . $ 100.00

AFTER ADJUSTMENT

Insurance Expense

Adj. (b)	100.00	

Prepaid Insurance

Aug. 31 Bal.	1,200.00	Adj. (b)	100.00
(New Bal.	1,100.00)		

FYI

Dun and Bradstreet estimates that since 1985, an average of 250,000 new businesses will start each year.

The expense account, Insurance Expense, is increased by a debit, $100.00, the value of insurance used. The balance of Insurance Expense, $100.00, is the value of insurance coverage used from August 1 to August 31. (CONCEPT: *Matching Expenses with Revenue*)

The asset account, Prepaid Insurance, is decreased by a credit, $100.00, the value of insurance used. The debit balance, $1,200.00, *less* the credit adjustment, $100.00, *equals* the new balance, $1,100.00. The new balance of Prepaid Insurance is the same as the amount of insurance coverage unused on August 31.

Rugcare's prepaid insurance adjustment is shown on lines 4 and 12 of the work sheet in Illustration 8-4.

ILLUSTRATION 8-4   Prepaid insurance adjustment on a work sheet

APPLIED SKILLS:
MATHEMATICS

Use the MATH WORK SHEETS in the Masters and Solutions to Enrichment/Application Activities section of the Teacher's Resource Guide to integrate applied mathematics. In these work sheets, students will apply math concepts to analyze adjustments, calculate net income/net loss, and correct arithmetic errors in the general ledger.

		1	2	3	4	
	ACCOUNT TITLE	**TRIAL BALANCE**		**ADJUSTMENTS**		
		DEBIT	**CREDIT**	**DEBIT**	**CREDIT**	
1	Cash	8 2 7 2 00				1
2	Petty Cash	2 0 0 00				2
3	Supplies	4 9 3 1 00			(a) 2 6 4 7 00	3
4	Prepaid Insurance	1 2 0 0 00			(b) 1 0 0 00	4
12	Insurance Expense			(b) 1 0 0 00		12
13	Miscellaneous Expense	1 0 5 00				13
14	Rent Expense	2 5 0 00				14
15	Repair Expense	1 1 0 00				15
16	Supplies Expense			(a) 2 6 4 7 00		16
17	Utilities Expense	1 1 5 00				17
18		1 5 8 5 1 00	1 5 8 5 1 00	2 7 4 7 00	2 7 4 7 00	18
19						19

Three steps are used to record the prepaid insurance adjustment on a work sheet.

1 Write the debit amount, *$100.00*, in the work sheet's Adjustments Debit column on the line with the account title Insurance Expense (line 12).

2 Write the credit amount, *$100.00*, in the Adjustments Credit column on the line with the account title Prepaid Insurance (line 4).

3 Label the two parts of this adjustment with a small letter *b* in parentheses *(b)*. The letter *b* identifies the debit and credit amounts as part of the same adjustment.

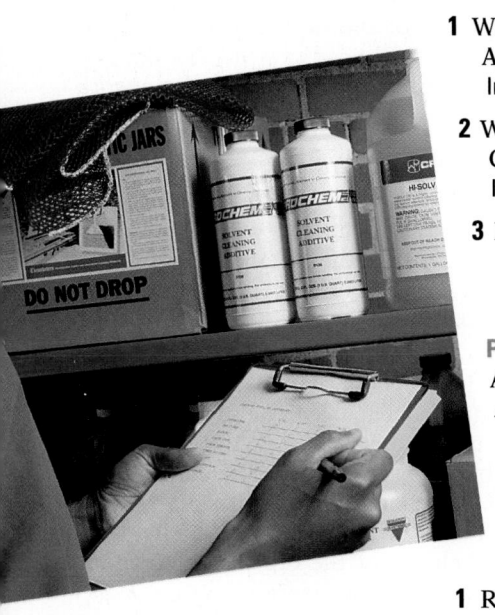

Proving the Adjustments Columns of a Work Sheet. After all adjustments are recorded in a work sheet's Adjustments columns, the equality of debits and credits for the two columns is proved. Rugcare's completed Adjustments columns are shown in Illustration 8-4.

Three steps are used in proving a work sheet's Adjustments columns.

1 Rule a single line across the two Adjustments columns on the same line as the single line for the Trial Balance columns.

2 Add both the Adjustments Debit and Credit columns. If the two column totals are the same, then debits equal credits for these two columns, and the work sheet's Adjustments columns are in balance. On Rugcare's work sheet, the Adjustments Debit and Credit column totals are $2,747.00. Therefore, the

FYI

A work sheet is prepared in manual accounting to adjust the accounts and sort amounts needed to prepare financial statements. However, in automated accounting adjustments are prepared from the trial balance and the software automatically generates the financial statements with no need for a work sheet.

Adjustments columns on Rugcare's work sheet are in balance. Write each column's total below the single line.

If the two Adjustments column totals are not the same, the Adjustments columns are rechecked and errors corrected before completing the work sheet.

3 Rule double lines across both Adjustments columns. The double lines mean that the totals have been verified as correct.

Extending Financial Statement Information on a Work Sheet

At the end of each fiscal period, Rugcare prepares two financial statements from information on a work sheet. *(CONCEPT: Accounting Period Cycle)* A financial statement that reports assets, liabilities, and owner's equity on a specific date is known as a balance sheet. A financial statement showing the revenue and expenses for a fiscal period is called an **income statement.** The up-to-date account balances on a work sheet are extended to columns for the two financial statements.

Extending Balance Sheet Account Balances on a Work Sheet. The balance sheet accounts are the asset, liability, and owner's equity accounts. Up-to-date balance sheet account balances are extended to the Balance Sheet Debit and Credit columns of the work sheet. The extension of Rugcare's balance sheet account balances is shown on lines 1 through 9 of the work sheet in Illustration 8-5.

Three steps are used in extending balance sheet items on a work sheet.

1 Extend the up-to-date balance of each asset account.

- The balance of Cash in the Trial Balance Debit column is up to date because no adjustment affects this account. Extend the balance of Cash, *$8,272.00*, to the Balance Sheet Debit column. Balances of all asset accounts not affected by adjustments are extended in the same way.

- The balance of Supplies in the Trial Balance Debit column is not up to date because it is affected by an adjustment. Calculate the up-to-date adjusted balance. The debit balance, $4,931.00, *minus* the credit adjustment, $2,647.00, *equals* the up-to-date adjusted balance, $2,284.00. Extend the up-to-date balance, *$2,284.00*, to the Balance Sheet Debit column. The same procedure is used to calculate and extend the up-to-date adjusted balance of the other asset account affected by an adjustment, Prepaid Insurance.

2 Extend the up-to-date balance of each liability account.

- The balance of Butler Cleaning Supplies is the up-to-date balance because no adjustment affects this account. Extend the up-to-date balance, *$1,360.00*, to the Balance Sheet Credit column. The balance of the other liability account is extended in the same way.

ILLUSTRATION 8-5   Balance sheet account balances extended on a work sheet

TEACHING STRATEGIES:
DIFFERENT LEARNING ABILITIES

Gifted students. Students who are gifted often enjoy the challenge of getting to the heart of a problem. Assign Challenge Problem 8-C which is reconstructing a trial balance. Have the students complete the problem and then present it to the class explaining the steps taken to reconstruct the trial balance.

Rugcare

Work Sheet

For Month Ended August 31, 19--

	ACCOUNT TITLE	TRIAL BALANCE DEBIT	TRIAL BALANCE CREDIT	ADJUSTMENTS DEBIT	ADJUSTMENTS CREDIT	INCOME STATEMENT DEBIT	INCOME STATEMENT CREDIT	BALANCE SHEET DEBIT	BALANCE SHEET CREDIT	
1	Cash	8 2 7 2 00						8 2 7 2 00		1
2	Petty Cash	2 0 0 00						2 0 0 00		2
3	Supplies	4 9 3 1 00			(a) 2 6 4 7 00			2 2 8 4 00		3
4	Prepaid Insurance	1 2 0 0 00			(b) 1 0 0 00			1 1 0 0 00		4
5	Butler Cleaning Supplies		1 3 6 0 00						1 3 6 0 00	5
6	Dale Office Supplies		2 0 0 00						2 0 0 00	6
7	Ben Furman, Capital		10 0 0 0 00						10 0 0 0 00	7
8	Ben Furman, Drawing	6 0 0 00						6 0 0 00		8
9	Income Summary									9
10										10

3 Extend the up-to-date balances of the owner's equity accounts.

- The balance of Ben Furman, Capital in the Trial Balance Credit column is the up-to-date balance because no adjustment affects this account. Extend the balance, *$10,000.00*, to the Balance Sheet Credit column.

- The balance of Ben Furman, Drawing in the Trial Balance Debit column is the up-to-date balance because no adjustment affects this account. Extend the balance, *$600.00*, to the Balance Sheet Debit column.

- Income Summary has no balance in the Trial Balance columns. Therefore, no amount needs to be extended for this account.

Extending Income Statement Account Balances on a Work Sheet. Rugcare's income statement accounts are the revenue and expense accounts. The extension of income statement account balances is shown on lines 10 through 17 of the work sheet in Illustration 8-6.

Two steps are used in extending income statement accounts on a work sheet.

1 Extend the up-to-date balance of the revenue account.

- The balance of Sales in the Trial Balance Credit column is the up-to-date balance because no adjustment affects this account. Extend the balance, *$4,291.00*, to the Income Statement Credit column.

2 Extend the up-to-date balance of each expense account.

- The balance of Advertising Expense in the Trial Balance Debit column is the up-to-date balance because no adjustment affects this account. Extend the balance, *$68.00*, to the Income Statement Debit column. Balances of all expense

FYI

Use a ruler when extending amounts on a work sheet to keep track of the line you are on.

ILLUSTRATION 8-6   Income statement account balances extended on a work sheet

Rugcare
Work Sheet
For Month Ended August 31, 19--

		1	2	3	4	5	6	7	8	
	ACCOUNT TITLE	TRIAL BALANCE		ADJUSTMENTS		INCOME STATEMENT		BALANCE SHEET		
		DEBIT	CREDIT	DEBIT	CREDIT	DEBIT	CREDIT	DEBIT	CREDIT	
10	Sales		4 29 1 00				4 29 1 00			10
11	Advertising Expense	6 8 00				6 8 00				11
12	Insurance Expense			(b) 1 0 0 00		1 0 0 00				12
13	Miscellaneous Expense	1 0 5 00				1 0 5 00				13
14	Rent Expense	2 5 0 00				2 5 0 00				14
15	Repair Expense	1 1 0 00				1 1 0 00				15
16	Supplies Expense			(a) 2 6 4 7 00		2 6 4 7 00				16
17	Utilities Expense	1 1 5 00				1 1 5 00				17
18		15 8 5 1 00	15 8 5 1 00	2 7 4 7 00	2 7 4 7 00					18
19										19

accounts not affected by adjustments are extended in the same way.

- The balance of Insurance Expense in the Trial Balance columns is zero. This zero balance is not the up-to-date balance because this account is affected by an adjustment. Calculate the up-to-date adjusted balance. The debit balance, $0.00, *plus* the debit adjustment, $100.00, *equals* the adjusted balance, $100.00. Extend the up-to-date adjusted debit balance, *$100.00*, to the Income Statement Debit column. The same procedure is used to calculate and extend the up-to-date adjusted balance of each expense account affected by an adjustment.

Calculating and Recording Net Income on a Work Sheet. The difference between total revenue and total expenses when total revenue is greater is called **net income**. Rugcare's August net income is shown on line 19 of the work sheet in Illustration 8-7.

Five steps are used in calculating net income on a work sheet.

1 Rule a single line across the four Income Statement and Balance Sheet columns.

2 Add both the Income Statement and Balance Sheet columns. Write the totals below the single line.

3 Calculate the net income. Rugcare's net income is calculated as shown below.

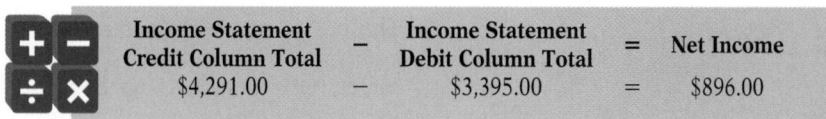

	Income Statement Credit Column Total	−	Income Statement Debit Column Total	=	Net Income
	$4,291.00	−	$3,395.00	=	$896.00

ILLUSTRATION 8-7   Completed work sheet

Rugcare

Work Sheet

For Month Ended August 31, 19--

	ACCOUNT TITLE	TRIAL BALANCE DEBIT	TRIAL BALANCE CREDIT	ADJUSTMENTS DEBIT	ADJUSTMENTS CREDIT	INCOME STATEMENT DEBIT	INCOME STATEMENT CREDIT	BALANCE SHEET DEBIT	BALANCE SHEET CREDIT	
1	Cash	8272.00						8272.00		1
2	Petty Cash	200.00						200.00		2
3	Supplies	4931.00			(a) 2647.00			2284.00		3
4	Prepaid Insurance	1200.00			(b) 100.00			1100.00		4
5	Butler Cleaning Supplies		1360.00						1360.00	5
6	Dale Office Supplies		200.00						200.00	6
7	Ben Furman, Capital		10000.00						10000.00	7
8	Ben Furman, Drawing	600.00						600.00		8
9	Income Summary									9
10	Sales		4291.00				4291.00			10
11	Advertising Expense	68.00				68.00				11
12	Insurance Expense			(b) 100.00		100.00				12
13	Miscellaneous Expense	105.00				105.00				13
14	Rent Expense	250.00				250.00				14
15	Repair Expense	110.00				110.00				15
16	Supplies Expense			(a) 2647.00		2647.00				16
17	Utilities Expense	115.00				115.00				17
18		15851.00	15851.00	2747.00	2747.00	3395.00	4291.00	12456.00	11560.00	18
19	Net Income					896.00			896.00	19
20						4291.00	4291.00	12456.00	12456.00	20
21										21

Rugcare's August work sheet shows a net income because the Income Statement Credit column (revenue) exceeds the Income Statement Debit column (expenses).

4 Write the amount of net income, *$896.00*, below the Income Statement Debit column total. Write the words, *Net Income*, on the same line in the Account Title column.

5 Extend the amount of net income, *$896.00*, to the Balance Sheet Credit column on the same line as the words *Net Income*. The owner's equity account, Ben Furman, Capital, is increased by a credit. Therefore, the net income amount is extended to the Balance Sheet Credit column.

Totaling and Ruling a Work Sheet. Four steps are used in totaling and ruling a work sheet.

1 Rule a single line across the four Income Statement and Balance Sheet columns just below the net income amounts.

2 Add the subtotal and net income amount for each column to get proving totals for the Income Statement and Balance Sheet columns. Write the proving totals below the single line.

FYI

A single line is ruled across amount columns to indicate addition or subtraction. A double line is ruled across amount columns to indicate that the totals have been verified as correct.

CHAPTER 8 Work Sheet for a Service Business   **181**

Proving totals are used to determine that the debits equal credits for each pair of column totals.

3 Check the equality of the proving totals for each pair of columns. A summary of preparing a work sheet is shown on the Work Sheet Overlay on pages 176A through 176C.

- As shown on line 20 of the work sheet in Illustration 8-7, the proving totals for the Income Statement columns, $4,291.00, are the same.

- As shown on line 20 of the work sheet in Illustration 8-7, the proving totals for the Balance Sheet columns, $12,456.00, are the same.

4 Rule double lines across the Income Statement and Balance Sheet columns. The double lines mean that the totals have been verified as correct.

Calculating and Recording a Net Loss on a Work Sheet. Rugcare's completed work sheet shows a net income. However, a business might have a net loss to report. The difference between total revenue and total expenses when total expenses is greater is called a **net loss.** A net loss on a work sheet is shown in Illustration 8-8.

ILLUSTRATION 8-8   Net loss shown on a work sheet

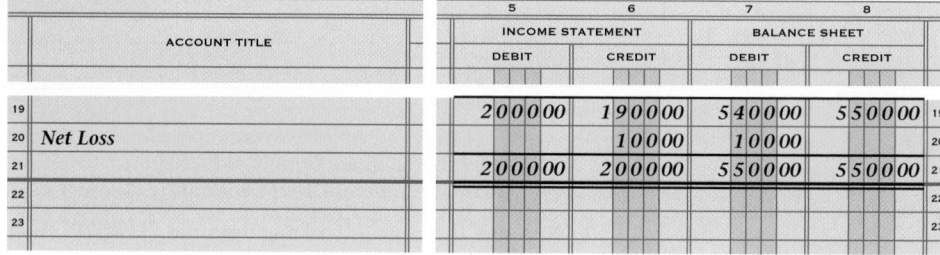

	ACCOUNT TITLE		5 INCOME STATEMENT DEBIT	6 INCOME STATEMENT CREDIT	7 BALANCE SHEET DEBIT	8 BALANCE SHEET CREDIT	
19			2 0 0 0 00	1 9 0 0 00	5 4 0 0 00	5 5 0 0 00	19
20	*Net Loss*			1 0 0 00	1 0 0 00		20
21			2 0 0 0 00	2 0 0 0 00	5 5 0 0 00	5 5 0 0 00	21
22							22
23							23

Six steps are used in completing a work sheet with a net loss.

1 Rule a single line across the four Income Statement and Balance Sheet columns.

2 Add both the Income Statement and Balance Sheet columns. Write the totals below the single line.

3 The net loss is calculated as shown below.

	Income Statement Debit Column Total	–	Income Statement Credit Column Total	=	Net Loss
	$2,000.00	–	$1,900.00	=	$100.00

APPLIED SKILLS: WORD PROCESSING

If you wish to integrate word processing into your accounting course, you may direct students to answer the end-of-chapter Accounting Terms, Questions for Individual Study, and Cases for Critical Thinking using their word processing software.

Audit Your Understanding

1. What is the length of the fiscal period for most businesses?

2. What is written on the three-line heading on a work sheet?

3. List the four questions to analyze an adjustment on a work sheet.

4. Which accounts are extended into the Balance Sheet columns of the work sheet?

5. Which accounts are extended into the Income Statement columns of the work sheet?

The Income Statement Debit column total (expenses) is greater than the Income Statement Credit column total (revenue). Therefore, because expenses exceed revenue, there is a net loss.

4 Write the amount of net loss, *$100.00*, below the Income Statement Credit column total. Write the words, *Net Loss*, on the same line in the Account Title column.

5 Extend the amount of net loss, *$100.00*, to the Balance Sheet Debit column on the same line as the words *Net Loss*. The owner's capital account is decreased by a debit. Therefore, a net loss is extended to the Balance Sheet Debit column.

6 Total and rule the work sheet using the same steps as when there is net income.

FINDING AND CORRECTING ERRORS

Some errors in accounting records are not discovered until a work sheet is prepared. For example, a debit to the supplies account may not have been posted from a journal to the general ledger supplies account. The omission may not be discovered until the work sheet's trial balance does not balance. Also, information may be transferred incorrectly from general ledger accounts to the work sheet's trial balance. Additional errors may be made on a work sheet, such as recording adjustment information incorrectly or adding columns incorrectly. In addition, errors may be made in extending amounts to the Income Statement and Balance Sheet columns.

Any errors found on a work sheet must be corrected before any further work is completed. If an incorrect amount is found on a work sheet, erase the error and replace it with the correct amount. If an amount is written in an incorrect column, erase the amount and record it in the correct column. If column totals do not balance, add the columns again.

> ☞☞ **FYI** ☜☜
>
> **Use the Work Sheet Overlay to review the steps for preparing a work sheet.**

Checking for Typical Arithmetic Errors

When two column totals are not in balance, subtract the smaller total from the larger total to find the difference. Check the difference between the two amounts against the following guides.

1 *The difference is 1, such as $.01, $.10, $1.00, or $10.00.* For example, if the totals of the two columns are Debit, $12,542.00 and Credit, $12,543.00, the difference between the two columns is $1.00. The error is most likely in addition. Add the columns again.

2 *The difference can be divided evenly by 2.* For example, the difference between two column totals is $48.00. The differ-

CHAPTER 8   Work Sheet for a Service Business   **183**

AUDIT YOUR UNDERSTANDING

The AUDIT YOUR UNDERSTANDING feature appears at the end of each section of the chapter. Explain to your students that the word *audit* means to check or verify. AUDIT YOUR UNDERSTANDING may be used to check student comprehension of the section just studied. The answers are provided in Appendix D in the back of the textbook.

1. One year.

2. Name of business, name of report, date of report.

3. (a) What is the balance of the account? (b) What should the balance be for this account? (c) What must be done to correct the account balance? (d) What adjustment is made?

4. Assets, liabilities, and owner's equity accounts.

5. Revenue and expense accounts.

LESSON PLAN 8-2

Materials

- Student pages 183–187
- Transparency: 8-1, Chapter Summary
- Math Work Sheet Chapter 8, Part C: Checking for Typical Arithmetic Errors (TRG)
- 3-Step Checklist for Making Ethical Decisions (TRG)
- Software: Application Program Disk, Electronic Study Guide
- Assess: Problem Test Chapter 8, MicroExam Chapter 8

Objectives (Enabling Performance Tasks)

e. Identify selected procedures for finding and correcting errors in accounting records.

FOCUS

Preparing a work sheet was presented earlier in this chapter. Explain that if errors are found while preparing the work sheet, the errors must be found and corrected as shown in this lesson. Emphasize how important it is to work accurately and prevent errors whenever possible.

PROFESSIONAL BUSINESS ETHICS

Am I a Software Pirate?

Computer software is created by a variety of companies and individuals. Some software is created by large companies that employ many computer programmers. However, a large selection of software is also created by individual computer programmers.

Software created by large companies is typically sold in stores. Included with the software is a user's manual and a license agreement. The license agreement usually states that the company retains legal ownership of the software. The company gives the buyer the right to use the software according to stipulations provided in the license agreement. For example, most companies require that software be used only on a single computer and that no copies be made. Thus, a business with 15 computers is required to purchase 15 copies of the software.

Many individuals also create software. Lacking the financial resources of the large companies, these software authors have developed a concept referred to as "shareware" to distribute their software. Individuals are encouraged to copy shareware and distribute copies to others. In return,

---

ence, $48.00, *divided* by 2 *equals* $24.00 with no remainder. Look for a $24.00 amount in the Trial Balance columns of the work sheet. If the amount is found, check to make sure it has been recorded in the correct Trial Balance Debit or Credit column. A $24.00 debit amount recorded in a credit column results in a difference between column totals of $48.00. If the error is not found on the work sheet, check the general ledger accounts and journal entries. An entry for $24.00 may have been recorded in an incorrect column in the journal or in an account.

3   ***The difference can be divided evenly by 9.***   For example, the difference between two columns is $45.00. The difference, $45.00, *divided* by 9 *equals* $5.00 with no remainder. When the difference can be divided equally by 9, look for transposed numbers such as 54 written as 45 or 19 written as 91. Also, check for a "slide." A "slide" occurs when numbers are moved to the right or left in an amount column. For example, $12.00 is recorded as $120.00 or $350.00 is recorded as $35.00.

4   ***The difference is an omitted amount.***   Look for an amount equal to the difference. If the difference is $50.00, look for an account balance of $50.00 that has not been extended. Look for any $50.00 amount on the work sheet and determine if it has been handled correctly. Look in the accounts and journals for a $50.00 amount, and check if that amount has been handled correctly. Failure to record a $50.00 account balance will make a work sheet's Trial Balance column totals differ by $50.00.

the individual is instructed to send the author a registration fee if the individual uses the software. Some shareware authors request a specific dollar amount while other authors ask users to pay whatever they consider to be a fair amount.

INSTRUCTIONS Use the three-step checklist to analyze whether each of the following situations demonstrates ethical behavior.

Situation 1. A large company purchased one copy of a copyrighted software program and made numerous copies for use on other computers.

Situation 2. An individual used a shareware program extensively but did not send the shareware author the requested registration fee.

Situation 3. A public university, lacking adequate funds to purchase the required number of copies of a copyrighted electronic spreadsheet program, purchased a single copy and made numerous copies. A label stating "For educational purposes only" was attached to each copy of the software. Students regularly copy the software for personal use.

Checking for Errors in the Trial Balance Columns

1 Have all general ledger account balances been copied in the Trial Balance columns correctly?

2 Have all general ledger account balances been recorded in the correct Trial Balance column?

Correct any errors found and add the columns again.

Checking for Errors in the Adjustments Columns

1 Do the debits equal the credits for each adjustment? Use the small letters that label each part of an adjustment to help check accuracy and equality of debits and credits.

2 Is the amount for each adjustment correct?

Correct any errors found and add the columns again.

Checking for Errors in the Income Statement and Balance Sheet Columns

1 Has each amount been copied correctly when extended to the Income Statement or Balance Sheet column?

2 Has each account balance been extended to the correct Income Statement or Balance Sheet column?

3 Has the net income or net loss been calculated correctly?

4 Has the net income or net loss been recorded in the correct Income Statement or Balance Sheet column?

Correct any errors found and add the columns again.

CHAPTER 8 Work Sheet for a Service Business   **185**

APPLY

Use Illustration 8-9 to show students how to correct an error in posting to the wrong account. Use Illustration 8-10 to show students how to correct an amount written incorrectly and to correct an error in posting to the wrong column of an account.

Guided Practice

Duplicate and assign Math Work Sheet Chapter 8 Part C, Checking for Typical Arithmetic Errors from the Masters and Solutions to Enrichment/Application Activities Section in the Teacher's Resource Guide to provide additional practice on the mathematics of checking for typical arithmetic errors. Guide students through this work sheet by showing the work sheet on the overhead projector and completing it as a group.

Independent Practice

Assign Questions 14–15, Problem 8-3, Study Guide 8, and Mastery Problem 8-M. Students should follow appropriate procedures for finding and correcting errors when they occur.

APPLIED SKILLS: WRITING ACROSS THE CURRICULUM

Writing paragraphs and short essays. The CASES FOR CRITICAL THINKING are short, practical applications of the accounting principles developed in the chapter. Some cases are planned to present problems related to the chapter but not specifically discussed and answered in the chapter. These cases present an opportunity for critical thinking and decision making. These cases also require more than a short objective-type response. Therefore, they provide ideal practice in writing paragraphs and short essays.

- Assess student understanding by checking solutions to Independent Practice activities.

- Review "Summary of Preparation of a Work Sheet for a Service Business." Use Transparency 8-1, Chapter Summary.

Reteach

- Show a work sheet that contains errors. Ask students to explain how they would find and correct the errors.
- Assign Recycling Problem 8R.

Extend

- Assign Cases for Critical Thinking 2.
- Assign Challenge Problem 8-C (the challenge is students have to reconstruct events to establish trial balance accounts and their balances). Students should follow appropriate procedures for finding and correcting errors when they occur.
- For students who need to complete an additional activity to master the enabling performance tasks, assign the Application Program Disk software to be used with Mastery Problem 8-M and Challenge Problem 8-C.

Enrich

- Discuss the PROFESSIONAL BUSINESS ETHICS feature on page 184. You may wish to distribute copies of the 3-step Checklist for Making Ethical Decisions. A blackline master is furnished in the Masters and Solutions to Enrichment/Application Activities Section in the Teacher's Resource Guide.

- Assign the Electronic Study Guide Chapter 8 to complete the study guide from the working papers at the computer.

CLOSURE

Use Audit Your Understanding questions.

ASSESS

- Administer Problem Test Chapter 8.
- Administer a MicroExam test for Chapter 8.

Checking for Errors in Posting to General Ledger Accounts

Sometimes a pair of work sheet columns do not balance, and an error cannot be found on the work sheet. If this is the situation, check the posting from the journal to the general ledger accounts. As each item in an account or a journal entry is verified, a check mark should be placed next to it. The check mark indicates that the item has been checked for accuracy.

1 Have all amounts that need to be posted actually been posted from the journal?

- For an amount that has not been posted, complete the posting to the correct account.

- In all cases where posting is corrected, recalculate the account balance and correct it on the work sheet.

    When an omitted posting is recorded as described above, the dates in the general ledger accounts may be out of order.

2 Have all amounts been posted to the correct accounts?

- For an amount posted to the wrong account, draw a line through the entire incorrect entry. Recalculate the account balance.

- Record the posting in the correct account. Recalculate the account balance, and correct the work sheet. Make the correction in the general ledger accounts, as shown in Illustration 8-9.

FYI

When correcting errors in the ledger, draw a line through the error using a straight edge. Write the correct number above the correction.

ILLUSTRATION 8-9

Correcting an error in posting to the wrong account

ACCOUNT	Supplies						ACCOUNT NO. 130	
						BALANCE		
DATE	ITEM	POST. REF.	DEBIT	CREDIT	DEBIT	CREDIT		
Feb. 1		1	40000		40000			
25		2	9000		49000			
12		1	5000		54000			

ACCOUNT	Prepaid Insurance						ACCOUNT NO. 140	
						BALANCE		
DATE	ITEM	POST. REF.	DEBIT	CREDIT	DEBIT	CREDIT		
Feb. 9		1	60000		60000			
12		1	5000		65000			

Errors in permanent records should *never* be erased. Erasures in permanent records raise questions about whether important financial information has been altered.

3 Have all amounts been written correctly? Have all amounts been posted to the correct Debit or Credit columns of an account?

TEACHING STRATEGIES: TEACHING TIP

If students need instruction on using a calculator, refer them to Appendix B in this textbook.

- If an amount has been written incorrectly, draw a line through the incorrect amount. Write the correct amount just above the correction in the same space. Recalculate the account balance, and correct the account balance on the work sheet. Correcting an error in writing an amount incorrectly is shown on the first line of the utilities expense account in Illustration 8-10.

ILLUSTRATION 8-10 Correcting an amount written incorrectly and an error in posting to the wrong column of an account

ACCOUNT	Utilities Expense				ACCOUNT NO.	570	
					BALANCE		
DATE	ITEM	POST. REF.	DEBIT	CREDIT	DEBIT	CREDIT	
Sept. 19-- 8		1	70 00		7̶0̶ 0̶0̶ 00 (70 00)		
17		1	27 00	2̶7̶ 0̶0̶	9̶ 7̶ 00 6̶7̶3̶ 00		

- For an amount posted to the wrong amount column, draw a line through the incorrect item in the account. Record the posting in the correct amount column. Recalculate the account balance, and correct the work sheet. Correcting an error in posting to a wrong amount column is shown on the second line of the utilities expense account in Illustration 8-10.

Checking for Errors in Journal Entries

1 Do debits equal credits in each journal entry?

2 Is each journal entry amount recorded in the correct journal column?

3 Is information in the Account Title column correct for each journal entry?

4 Are all of the journal amount column totals correct?

5 Does the sum of debit column totals equal the sum of credit column totals in the journal?

6 Have all transactions been recorded?

Some suggestions for correcting errors in journal entries are described in Chapter 5.

Preventing Errors

The best way to prevent errors is to work carefully at all times. Check the work at each step in an accounting procedure. Most errors occur in doing the required arithmetic, especially in adding columns. When possible, use a calculator to add columns. When an error is discovered, do no more work until the cause of the error is found and corrections are made.

🖝🖝 FYI 🖝🖝

Never erase ink or it will look as if the numbers were altered. Altered numbers arouse suspicion of wrongdoing.

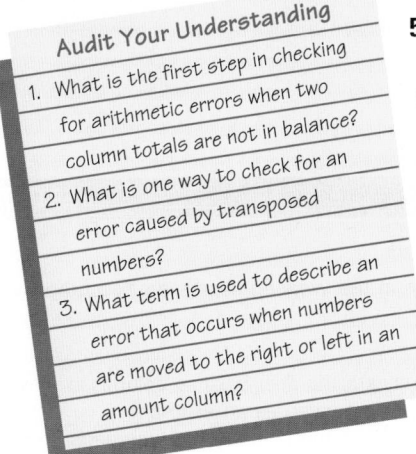

Audit Your Understanding

1. What is the first step in checking for arithmetic errors when two column totals are not in balance?

2. What is one way to check for an error caused by transposed numbers?

3. What term is used to describe an error that occurs when numbers are moved to the right or left in an amount column?

AUDIT YOUR UNDERSTANDING

1. Subtract the smaller total from the larger total to find the difference.
2. The difference between two column totals can be divided evenly by 9.
3. A slide.

TEACHING STRATEGIES: COOPERATIVE LEARNING

Rap song. Assign students to groups of five. Each group composes a short rap song about an accounting concept/issue. Allow each group to perform the rap for the rest of the class. Time frame: approximately 45 minutes of class time.

ACCOUNTING TERMS

ACCOUNTING TERMS   EPT(a)

1. **fiscal period:** The length of time for which a business summarizes and reports financial information. (p. 171)

2. **work sheet:** A columnar accounting form used to summarize the general ledger information needed to prepare financial statements. (p. 172)

3. **trial balance:** A proof of the equality of debits and credits in a general ledger. (p. 172)

4. **adjustments:** Changes recorded on a work sheet to update general ledger accounts at the end of a fiscal period. (p. 175)

5. **income statement:** A financial statement showing the revenue and expenses for a fiscal period. (p. 178)

6. **net income:** The difference between total revenue and total expenses when total revenue is greater. (p. 180)

7. **net loss:** The difference between total revenue and total expenses when total expenses is greater. (p. 182)

ACCOUNTING TERMS   EPT(a)

What is the meaning of each of the following?

1. **fiscal period**
2. **work sheet**
3. **trial balance**
4. **adjustments**
5. **income statement**
6. **net income**
7. **net loss**

QUESTIONS FOR INDIVIDUAL STUDY   EPT(b)

1. What are typical lengths of fiscal periods?
2. Which accounting concept is being applied when a business summarizes and reports financial information for a fiscal period?
3. What are four reasons for preparing a work sheet?
4. Why is a work sheet prepared in pencil?
5. How is the equality of debits and credits proved in a general ledger?
6. Why is an adjustment for supplies planned at the end of a fiscal period?
7. What accounts are affected, and how, by the adjustment for supplies?
8. After a supplies adjustment, what does the supplies account balance represent?
9. What accounts are affected, and how, by the adjustment for prepaid insurance?
10. Why are the Adjustments columns on a work sheet totaled?
11. What two financial statements are prepared from information on a work sheet?
12. If a work sheet shows a net income, in which two columns will the net income be recorded?
13. How are the amounts in the Income Statement and Balance Sheet columns of a work sheet proved?
14. If two work sheet column totals are not equal and the difference between the totals is one, what is the most likely error?
15. If two work sheet column totals are not equal and the difference between the totals is evenly divisible by nine, what is the most likely error?

CASES FOR CRITICAL THINKING   EPT(c,e)

CASE 1 Peter Dowther owns a small business. At the end of a fiscal period, he does not make an adjustment for supplies. Are Mr. Dowther's accounting procedures correct? What effect will Mr. Dowther's procedures have on the business' financial reporting? Explain your answer.

CASE 2 When posting amounts from a journal to general ledger accounts, a $10.00 debit to Supplies is mistakenly posted as a credit to Utilities Expense. Will this error be discovered when the work sheet is prepared? Explain.

DRILLS FOR UNDERSTANDING   EPT(d)

DRILL 8-D1   **Extending account balances on a work sheet**

A partial work sheet form with account titles is given in the working papers that accompany this textbook.

INSTRUCTIONS:

1. Place a check mark in either Column 1 or 2 to indicate the Trial Balance column in which each account's balance will appear. The first account is given as an example.
2. Place a check mark in Columns 5, 6, 7, or 8 to indicate the column to which each up-to-date account balance will be extended.

QUESTIONS FOR INDIVIDUAL STUDY

1. A month, six months, or a year. (p. 171)

2. Accounting Period Cycle. (p. 171)

3. (a) To summarize general ledger account balances to prove that debits equal credits. (b) To plan needed changes to general ledger accounts to bring the account balances up to date. (c) To separate general ledger account balances according to the financial statements to be prepared. (d) To calculate the amount of net income or net loss for a fiscal period. (p. 172)

4. A work sheet, unlike journals and ledgers, is not considered a permanent accounting record. (p. 172)

5. By preparing a trial balance on a work sheet. (p. 172)

6. The supplies account balance is not up to date. The value of supplies bought has been recorded. However, the expense for the supplies used has not been recorded. (pp. 174–175)

7. Supplies Expense is debited; Supplies is credited. (p. 176)

8. The value of supplies unused. (p. 176)

9. Insurance Expense is debited; Prepaid Insurance is credited. (p. 176D)

10. To assure that debits equal credits in the adjustments. (p. 177)

---

188   PART 2   Accounting for a Service Business Organized as a Proprietorship

DRILL 8-D2   Calculating net income or net loss on a work sheet

The column totals from the work sheets of five different businesses are given in the working papers that accompany this textbook.

INSTRUCTIONS:

Complete the following for each company. The amounts for Company A are given as an example.

1. Calculate the amount of net income or net loss. Write the amount on line 2 in the correct columns. Label the amount as *Net Income* or *Net Loss*.
2. Add the amounts in each column. Write the totals on line 3.
3. Verify the accuracy of your proving totals.

APPLICATION PROBLEMS   EPT(c,d,e)

PROBLEM 8-1   Completing a work sheet

On September 30 of the current year, CleanLawn has the following general ledger accounts and balances. The business uses a monthly fiscal period.

	Account Balances	
Account Titles	**Debit**	**Credit**
Cash.	$3,000.00	
Petty Cash	100.00	
Supplies.	2,000.00	
Prepaid Insurance	900.00	
Bix Supplies		$ 600.00
OfficeWorld.		100.00
Dorothy Daily, Capital		4,100.00
Dorothy Daily, Drawing	200.00	
Income Summary.	—	—
Sales		2,505.00
Advertising Expense	75.00	
Insurance Expense.	—	
Miscellaneous Expense.	110.00	
Rent Expense.	600.00	
Repair Expense	180.00	
Supplies Expense.	—	
Utilities Expense	140.00	

INSTRUCTIONS:

1. Prepare the heading and trial balance on a work sheet. Total and rule the Trial Balance columns.
2. Analyze the following adjustment information into debit and credit parts. Record the adjustments on the work sheet.

Adjustment Information, September 30

Supplies on hand	$1,100.00
Value of prepaid insurance	600.00

3. Total and rule the Adjustments columns.
4. Extend the up-to-date balances to the Balance Sheet or Income Statement columns.
5. Rule a single line across the Income Statement and Balance Sheet columns. Total each column. Calculate and record the net income or net loss. Label the amount in the Account Title column.
6. Total and rule the Income Statement and Balance Sheet columns.

PROBLEM 8-2   Completing a work sheet

On October 31 of the current year, Village Service Co. has the following general ledger accounts and balances. The business uses a monthly fiscal period.

11. A balance sheet and an income statement. (p. 178)
12. Income Statement Debit and Balance Sheet Credit. (p. 181)
13. The columns are totaled, and the net income or net loss is calculated and recorded on the work sheet. The columns are totaled again, and each pair of columns should be in balance. (pp. 181–182)
14. An error in addition. (p. 183)
15. A transposition error, such as writing 16 as 61, or a slide, such as writing $12.00 as $120.00. (p. 184)

CASES FOR CRITICAL THINKING

Case 1   Mr. Dowther's procedures are not correct. Adjustments for supplies must be made to bring the accounts up to date. *(CONCEPT: Matching Expenses with Revenue)* If the adjustments are not made, the asset (Supplies) will be overstated and the expense (Supplies Expense) will be understated. This will result in reporting a larger net income or smaller net loss than is actually true.

Case 2   Yes, the error will be discovered when the work sheet is prepared. The Trial Balance columns will not be in balance because a debit was posted as a credit.

CHECK FIGURES

See Teacher's Edition of Working Papers for complete solutions to drills and problems.

Drill 8-D1   5 check marks in Income Statement Debit column. 4 check marks in Balance Sheet Debit column.

Drill 8-D2   Company B and D have a net income. Company C and E have a net loss.

Problem 8-1   Net Income 200
Problem 8-2   Net Loss 600

Account Titles	Account Balances Debit	Credit
Cash.	$4,900.00	
Petty Cash	300.00	
Supplies.	2,500.00	
Prepaid Insurance	2,100.00	
National Supplies		$ 1,400.00
Office Distributors		1,200.00
Wensk Movies		800.00
Susan Haile, Capital.		6,000.00
Susan Haile, Drawing	1,200.00	
Income Summary.	—	—
Sales		20,100.00
Advertising Expense	4,200.00	
Insurance Expense.	—	
Miscellaneous Expense.	600.00	
Rent Expense.	8,000.00	
Repair Expense	2,400.00	
Supplies Expense.	—	
Utilities Expense	3,300.00	

INSTRUCTIONS:

1. Prepare the heading and trial balance on a work sheet. Total and rule the Trial Balance columns.
2. Analyze the following adjustment information into debit and credit parts. Record the adjustments on the work sheet.

Adjustment Information, October 31

Supplies on hand.	$1,500.00
Value of prepaid insurance	900.00

3. Total and rule the Adjustments columns.
4. Extend the up-to-date balances to the Balance Sheet or Income Statement columns.
5. Rule a single line across the Income Statement and Balance Sheet columns. Total each column. Calculate and record the net income or net loss. Label the amount in the Account Title column.
6. Total and rule the Income Statement and Balance Sheet columns.

PROBLEM 8-3 Finding and correcting errors in accounting records

Paul Coty has completed the September monthly work sheet for his business, LeafyLift. The work sheet and general ledger accounts are given in the working papers accompanying this textbook.

Mr. Coty believes that he has made one or more errors in preparing the work sheet. He asks you to help him verify the work sheet.

INSTRUCTIONS:

1. Examine the work sheet and the general ledger accounts. Make a list of the errors you find.
2. Correct any errors you find in the general ledger accounts.
3. Prepare a corrected work sheet.

ENRICHMENT PROBLEMS
EPT(c,d)

MASTERY PROBLEM 8-M Completing a work sheet

On April 30 of the current year, FastGrow has the following general ledger accounts and balances. The business uses a monthly fiscal period.

Account Titles	Account Balances Debit	Credit
Cash.	$5,800.00	
Petty Cash	200.00	

PART 2 Accounting for a Service Business Organized as a Proprietorship

Supplies..	4,000.00	
Prepaid Insurance	1,000.00	
Wheaton Supplies		$ 200.00
Norton Company		115.00
Roger Bently, Capital.........................		7,200.00
Roger Bently, Drawing	400.00	
Income Summary.............................	—	—
Sales		5,300.00
Advertising Expense	325.00	
Insurance Expense...........................	—	
Miscellaneous Expense........................	140.00	
Rent Expense................................	500.00	
Supplies Expense.............................	—	
Utilities Expense	450.00	

INSTRUCTIONS:

1. Prepare the heading and trial balance on a work sheet. Total and rule the Trial Balance columns.
2. Analyze the following adjustment information into debit and credit parts. Record the adjustments on the work sheet.

Adjustment Information, April 30

Supplies inventory...............................	$2,050.00
Value of prepaid insurance........................	450.00

3. Extend the up-to-date account balances to the Balance Sheet or Income Statement columns.
4. Complete the work sheet.

CHALLENGE PROBLEM 8-C Completing a work sheet

APPLICATION

Clean and Mow had a small fire in its office. The fire destroyed some of the accounting records. On November 30 of the current year, the end of a monthly fiscal period, the following information was constructed from the remaining records and other sources.

Remains of the general ledger:

Account Titles	Account Balances
Supplies...	$1,800.00
Donna Edwards, Drawing...........................	150.00
Sales	4,000.00
Advertising Expense	420.00
Rent Expense.....................................	700.00
Utilities Expense	490.00

Information from the business' checkbook:
Cash balance on last unused check stub, $3,400.00
Total payments for miscellaneous expense, $60.00
Total payments for insurance, $325.00

Information obtained through inquiries to other businesses:
Owed to Outdoor Supplies, $2,000.00
Value of prepaid insurance, November 30, $250.00

Information obtained by counting supplies on hand after the fire:
Supplies on hand, $1,100.00

INSTRUCTIONS:

1. From the information given, prepare a heading and reconstruct a trial balance on a work sheet. The owner's capital account balance is the difference between the total of all debit account balances minus the total of all credit account balances.
2. Complete the work sheet.

Chapter 9 introduces the preparation of an income statement and balance sheet for a proprietorship. The procedures for completing these two statements are covered thoroughly to prepare students for the culminating activities of completing the accounting cycle. Not only is statement preparation covered but the financial statement analysis of these statements are introduced in the simplest form. Component percentages for total expenses and net income are calculated and discussed for the income statement.

Financial statement analysis is emphasized to cultivate critical thinking. It is important to begin the critical thinking skills of financial statement analysis in the first cycle so that these skills can be built upon in the cycles to follow.

The accounting concept, *Adequate Disclosure,* is presented and described in full for the first time in this chapter.

GUIDE TO ACHIEVING LEARNING OBJECTIVES

Enabling Performance Tasks	TEACH Lesson Plans	APPLY Drills for Understanding	Application Problems	Mastery Problems	Challenge Problems	Cases for Critical Thinking	Recycling Problems	Reinforcement Activity	
a. Define the accounting terms related to financial statements for a service business organized as a proprietorship.	9-1								
b. Identify accounting concepts and practices related to preparation of financial statements for a service business organized as a proprietorship.	9-1, 9-2	9-D1, 9-D2				Cases 1, 2			
c. Prepare an income statement for a service business organized as a proprietorship.	9-1		9-1	9-M	9-C		9-R	1B	
d. Analyze an income statement using component percentages.	9-1		9-1	9-M	9-C		9-R	1B	
e. Prepare a balance sheet for a service business organized as a proprietorship.	9-2		9-2	9-M	9-C		9-R	1B	

ENRICHMENT

SPECIAL FEATURES

Spreadsheet Options, page 203

Careers in Accounting, page 196

TECHNOLOGY CONNECTION

Spreadsheet Template Problems 9-M, 9-C

Electronic Study Guide

NEW, REVIEW, AND EXTENSION

ACTIVITIES/CONCEPTS/TRANSACTIONS	NEW	REVIEW/ EXTENSION
Financial statements for a proprietorship	✓	
Preparing an income statement	✓	
Calculating component percentages	✓	
Component percentage for total expenses	✓	
Component percentage for net income	✓	
Preparing a balance sheet		✓

	INFORMAL ASSESSMENT		FORMAL ASSESSMENT				
	Study Guide	Audit Your Understanding	Chapter MicroExam	Chapter Problem Test	Unit Problem Test	Unit Objective Test	Portfolio
			✓			✓	
Unit C		✓	✓			✓	
Unit A				✓	✓		✓
				✓	✓		✓
Unit B				✓	✓		✓

TEACHING MATERIALS

Teacher's Wraparound Edition of Text

Teacher's Resource Guide

Teacher's Edition of Working Papers

Teacher's Edition of Demonstration/Recycling Problems

Teaching Transparencies

Applied Math Work Sheets

MicroExam

APPLIED MATHEMATICS

APPLIED MATH/ACCOUNTING SKILL	APPLICATION
Calculating net income	Prob. 9-D2
Calculating component percentages	Prob. 9-1
Calculating owner's equity	Prob. 9-D2

9

Financial Statements for a Proprietorship

ENABLING PERFORMANCE TASKS

After studying Chapter 9, you will be able to:

a Define the accounting term related to financial statements for a service business organized as a proprietorship.

b Identify accounting concepts and practices related to preparation of financial statements for a service business organized as a proprietorship.

c Prepare an income statement for a service business organized as a proprietorship.

d Analyze an income statement using component percentages.

e Prepare a balance sheet for a service business organized as a proprietorship.

TERMS PREVIEW

component percentage

The financial information needed by managers and owners to make good business decisions can be found in the general ledger accounts. However, the information in the general ledger is very detailed. Therefore, to make this general ledger information more usable, the information is summarized, organized, and reported to the owners and managers.

Also, *all* financial information *must* be reported if good business decisions are to be made. A financial statement with incomplete information is similar to a book with missing pages. The complete story is not told. If a business has both rent and utilities expenses but reports only the rent expense, managers will have incomplete information on which to base decisions. The accounting concept, *Adequate Disclosure*, is applied when financial statements contain all information necessary to understand a business' financial condition. *(CONCEPT: Adequate Disclosure)*

Rugcare prepares two financial statements: an income statement and a balance sheet. Rugcare always prepares financial statements at the end of each monthly fiscal period. *(CONCEPT: Accounting Period Cycle)* The time periods covered by Rugcare's financial statements are shown in Illustration 9-1.

ILLUSTRATION 9-1   Time periods for financial statements

An income statement reports financial *progress* from August 1 through August 31.

A balance sheet reports financial *condition* on August 31.

An income statement reports financial information over a *specific period of time*, indicating the financial *progress* of a business in earning a net income or net loss.

A balance sheet reports financial information on a *specific date*, indicating the financial *condition* of a business. The financial condition of a business refers to its financial strength. If a business has adequate available assets and few liabilities, that business is financially strong. If the business' financial condition is not strong, adverse changes in the economy might cause the business to fail.

CHAPTER 9 Financial Statements for a Proprietorship   **193**

Materials

- Student pages 193–199

- Transparencies: D, Blank Income Statement; 9-1, Completed Income Statement and Balance Sheet

- Math Work Sheet Chapter 9: Part A: Calculating Net Income (TRG); Part B: Calculating Component Percentages (TRG)

- Demonstration Problem: 9A, Preparing an Income Statement

Objectives (Enabling Performance Tasks)

a. Define the accounting term related to financial statements for a service business organized as a proprietorship.

b. Identify accounting concepts and practices related to preparation of financial statements for a service business organized as a proprietorship.

c. Prepare an income statement for a service business organized as a proprietorship.

d. Analyze an income statement using component percentages.

FOCUS

- In Chapter 8, the work sheet was presented as an accounting form used to summarize general ledger information needed to prepare financial statements. Explain that in this lesson the information from the Income Statement columns of the work sheet will be used to prepare the first financial statement.

- Introduce new vocabulary: component percentage.

INCOME STATEMENT

Revenue is the earnings of a business from business activities. Expenses are the amounts a business pays to operate the business and earn the revenue. The revenue earned and the expenses incurred to earn that revenue are reported in the same fiscal period. (CONCEPT: *Matching Expenses with Revenue*)

Information needed to prepare financial statements could be obtained from the general ledger accounts. However, a work sheet is prepared to assist in planning the financial statements. Rugcare's income statement information on a work sheet is shown in Illustration 9-2.

Information needed to prepare Rugcare's income statement is obtained from two places on the work sheet. Account titles are obtained from the work sheet's Account Title column. Account balances are obtained from the work sheet's Income Statement columns.

The income statement for a service business has four sections: (1) heading, (2) revenue, (3) expenses, and (4) net income or net loss.

FYI

Information needed to prepare the income statement is obtained from two places on the work sheet. Account titles are obtained from the work sheet's Account Title column. Account balances are obtained from the work sheet's Income Statement columns.

ILLUSTRATION 9-2

Income statement information on a work sheet

		5	6	7	8	
	ACCOUNT TITLE	INCOME STATEMENT		BALANCE SHEET		
		DEBIT	CREDIT	DEBIT	CREDIT	
10	Sales		4 2 9 1 00			10
11	Advertising Expense	6 8 00				11
12	Insurance Expense	1 0 0 00				12
13	Miscellaneous Expense	1 0 5 00				13
14	Rent Expense	2 5 0 00				14
15	Repair Expense	1 1 0 00				15
16	Supplies Expense	2 6 4 7 00				16
17	Utilities Expense	1 1 5 00				17
18		3 3 9 5 00	4 2 9 1 00			18
19	Net Income	8 9 6 00				19
20		4 2 9 1 00	4 2 9 1 00			20

Heading of an Income Statement

All financial statements have similar information in their three-line headings. (1) The name of the business. (2) The name of the statement. (3) The date of the statement. The three-line heading for Rugcare's income statement is shown in Illustration 9-3.

ILLUSTRATION 9-3

Heading of an income statement

Rugcare
Income Statement
For Month Ended August 31, 19--

TEACHING STRATEGIES: TEACHING TIP

Review the definitions of revenue and expenses. An increase in owner's equity resulting from the operation of a business is called revenue. A decrease in owner's equity resulting from the operation of a business is called an expense.

The income statement's date shows that this income statement reports information for the one-month fiscal period from August 1 through August 31.

Revenue Section of an Income Statement

Information from the work sheet's Account Title column and Income Statement Credit column is used to prepare the revenue section. The revenue section of an income statement is shown in Illustration 9-4.

ILLUSTRATION 9-4

Revenue section of an income statement

Revenue:		
Sales		4 2 9 1 00

Write the name of this section, *Revenue:*, at the extreme left of the wide column on the first line. Write the title of the revenue account, *Sales*, on the next line indented about one centimeter. Record the balance of the account, *$4,291.00*, on the same line in the second amount column.

Expenses Section of an Income Statement

Information from the work sheet's Account Title column and Income Statement Debit column is used to prepare the expenses section. The expenses section of Rugcare's income statement is shown in Illustration 9-5.

ILLUSTRATION 9-5

Expenses section of an income statement

Expenses:		
Advertising Expense	6 8 00	
Insurance Expense	1 0 0 00	
Miscellaneous Expense	1 0 5 00	
Rent Expense	2 5 0 00	
Repair Expense	1 1 0 00	
Supplies Expense	2 6 4 7 00	
Utilities Expense	1 1 5 00	
Total Expenses		3 3 9 5 00

Write the name of this section, *Expenses:*, at the extreme left of the wide column on the next blank line. Write the title of each expense account in the wide column indented about one centimeter. Record the balance of each expense account in the first amount column on the same line as the account title.

FYI

Not all businesses call their revenue account Sales. Some businesses use account titles such as Fees, Services, or Income.

FYI

If there is more than one revenue account on the income statement, indent each account under the heading "Revenue:".

TEACH

Cover student pages 193–199 "Income Statement." From the onset of this lesson it is important that students understand that an income statement reports information over a period of time while a balance sheet reports information for a specific date. Review the definition of revenue and expenses.

This lesson introduces students to some important concepts regarding the preparation of an income statement, such as (1) account balances for the income statement are taken from the Income Statement columns of the work sheet; (2) all financial statements have a three-line heading; (3) account titles are indented; (4) the two columns on the income statement are not debit and credit columns; (5) account balances are listed in the first column, totals in the second column; and (6) it should always be verified that the amount of net income or net loss is the same as that on the work sheet.

Point out to students that component percentages allow a business to compare its percentages to comparable businesses. If the expenses percentage is higher than industry standards, it might be wise to review spending practices. Businesses should also compare their own component percentages from one fiscal period with the percentages of previous fiscal periods.

TEACHING STRATEGIES: DIFFERENT LEARNING ABILITIES

At-Risk Students. One of the techniques for encouraging at-risk students is to keep lessons relevant. While financial statements in this chapter are presented for businesses, you can also make links between personal assets and liabilities. Have students create a personal balance sheet and explain that such a balance sheet will contain information necessary to apply for a loan for an automobile. To further extend this relevance, ask students to describe the expenses in owning a car and relate them to the expenses section of the income statement.

Guided Practice

Write a company's name and some revenue and expense account titles and amounts on the board. Guide students through preparing an income statement. Students should have a blank income statement form to complete as you guide them through the exercise. Direct students' attention to Illustration 9-6, an income statement, for correct formatting.

Independent Practice

- Assign Term 1, Questions 1–11, and Problem 9-1.

- Duplicate and assign Math Work Sheets Chapter 9 Parts A and B, Calculating Net Income, and Calculating Component Percentages from the Masters and Solutions to Enrichment/Application Activities Section in the Teacher's Resource Guide to provide additional practice on the mathematics of calculating net income and component percentages.

CAREERS IN ACCOUNTING

The CAREERS feature box, ACCOUNTANT, comes from the Dictionary of Occupational Titles (DOT). The entry number for this job title is D.O.T. 160.162-018. Bring this dictionary to class and explain its purpose and how to use it. The career feature is designed to expose students to the exploration of different careers in accounting. The feature gives a realistic description of actual job duties. This feature can be used to demonstrate that the skills learned in this course are relevant.

FYI

The two columns on the income statement are not debit and credit columns. The first column is for listing numbers, the second column is for totals.

CAREERS IN ACCOUNTING

ACCOUNTANT

- *Analyzes financial information to prepare entries*
- *Verifies invoices and other accounting documents*
- *Analyzes financial information detailing assets, liabilities, and capital*
- *Applies principles of accounting to analyze financial information and prepare financial reports*
- *Prepares balance sheet, income statement, and other reports*
- *Establishes, modifies, documents, and coordinates implementation of accounting and accounting control procedures*

To indicate addition, rule a single line across the first amount column under the last expense account balance. Write the words, *Total Expenses*, on the next blank line in the wide column. Record the amount of total expenses, *$3,395.00*, on the same line in the second amount column.

Net Income Section of an Income Statement

The amount of net income is calculated and verified using two steps.

1 The net income is calculated from information on the income statement as shown below.

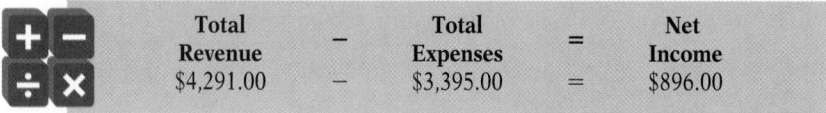

	Total Revenue	–	Total Expenses	=	Net Income
	$4,291.00	–	$3,395.00	=	$896.00

2 The amount of net income, *$896.00*, is compared with the net income shown on the work sheet, Illustration 9-2. The net income calculated for the income statement and the net income shown on the work sheet must be the same. The net income calculated for Rugcare's income statement, $896.00, is the same as that on the work sheet.

If the net income calculated for the income statement is not the same as that shown on the work sheet, an error has been made. No more work on the income statement should be completed until the error is found and corrected.

A single line is drawn across the second amount column just below the amount of total expenses, as shown in Illustration 9-6.

Write the words, *Net Income*, on the next line at the extreme left of the wide column. On the same line, record the amount of net income, *$896.00*, in the second amount column. Rule double lines across both amount columns below the amount of net income to show that the amount has been verified as correct. Rugcare's completed income statement is shown in Illustration 9-6.

If total expenses exceed total revenue, a net loss is reported on an income statement. When a net loss is reported, write the words, *Net Loss*, in the wide column. Subtract the total expenses from the revenue to calculate the net loss. Record the amount of net loss in the second amount column in parentheses. An amount written in parentheses on a financial statement indicates a negative amount.

Component Percentage Analysis of an Income Statement

For a service business, the revenue reported on an income statement includes two components: (1) total expenses and (2) net income. To make decisions about future operations, Mr. Furman

---

TEACHING STRATEGIES: DIFFERENT LEARNING STYLES

Visual Learner. Formulas, such as those used to calculate component percentages, should be illustrated on the chalkboard to assist visual learners. The instructor should also complete the calculations for a few income statement items to show the process to visual learners.

ILLUSTRATION 9-6   An income statement

Rugcare					
Income Statement					
For Month Ended August 31, 19--					
					% OF SALES
Revenue:					
Sales				4 2 9 1 00	100.0
Expenses:					
Advertising Expense		6 8 00			
Insurance Expense		1 0 0 00			
Miscellaneous Expense		1 0 5 00			
Rent Expense		2 5 0 00			
Repair Expense		1 1 0 00			
Supplies Expense		2 6 4 7 00			
Utilities Expense		1 1 5 00			
Total Expenses				3 3 9 5 00	79.1
Net Income				8 9 6 00	20.9

analyzes relationships between these two income statement components and the total sales. The percentage relationship between one financial statement item and the total that includes that item is called a **component percentage**. On an income statement, component percentages are calculated by dividing the amount of each component by the total amount of sales. Rugcare calculates a component percentage for total expenses and net income. The relationship between each component and total sales is shown in a separate column on the income statement at the right of the amount columns.

Acceptable Component Percentages. For a component percentage to be useful, Mr. Furman needs to know what component percentages are acceptable for businesses similar to Rugcare. Various industry organizations publish average percentages for similar businesses. In the future Mr. Furman could also compare Rugcare's component percentages from one fiscal period with the percentages of previous fiscal periods.

Total Expenses Component Percentage. The total expenses component percentage, based on information from the August income statement shown in Illustration 9-6, is calculated as shown below.

Total Expenses	÷	Total Sales	=	Total Expenses Component Percentage
$3,395.00	÷	$4,291.00	=	79.1%

CHAPTER 9 Financial Statements for a Proprietorship **197**

ASSESS

- Assess student understanding by checking solutions to Independent Practice activities.
- Review the procedures for preparing the income statement. Use Transparency 9-1, the completed income statement.

Reteach

Use Demonstration Problem 9A. This problem can be done on the overhead with the students completing the problem at their desks.

Extend

Assign Cases for Critical Thinking 1 and 2.

Enrich

- Assign the SPREADSHEET OPTIONS feature on page 203.
- Assign the students to read the CAREERS IN ACCOUNTING feature on page 196.

CLOSURE

Use Audit Your Understanding questions.

TEACHING STRATEGIES: COOPERATIVE LEARNING

When explaining what component percentages measure, assign students to groups of three. Each group is to plan, prepare, and deliver a presentation to NON ACCOUNTANTS. The presentation should explain what component percentages are and how they are used to analyze financial statements. Time frame: Class time should equal 30 minutes over a few class periods; additional time outside of class will be required to prepare the presentation.

TEACHING STRATEGIES:
DIFFERENT LEARNING STYLES

Auditory Learner. The auditory learner can reinforce the learning of formulas by verbally explaining the formula and/or calculations to other students in a small group. In a group of three, for example, each student should get the opportunity to "teach" the formula to the other two students. Through this process, each student in the group will "teach" the formula once and "learn" the formula two times.

For businesses similar to Rugcare, an acceptable total expenses component percentage is not more than 80.0%. Therefore, Rugcare's percentage, 79.1%, is less than 80.0% and is acceptable.

Net Income Component Percentage. The net income component percentage, based on information from the August income statement, is calculated as shown below.

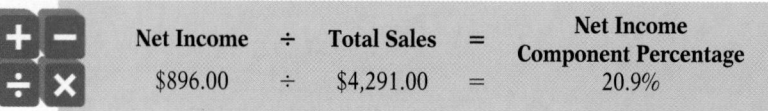

	Net Income	÷	Total Sales	=	Net Income Component Percentage
	$896.00	÷	$4,291.00	=	20.9%

For businesses similar to Rugcare, an acceptable net income component percentage is not less than 20.0%. Therefore, Rugcare's percentage, 20.9%, is greater than 20.0% and is acceptable. The net income component percentage will improve if Rugcare can reduce total expenses in future months. Also, the net income component percentage will improve if Rugcare can increase the amount of revenue in future months.

> When there is a net loss, the component percentage for net loss is written in parentheses. A net loss is considered unacceptable.

Income Statement with Two Sources of Revenue

Rugcare receives revenue from only one source, the sale of services for rug and carpet cleaning. Milton Lawn Service receives revenue from two sources, the sale of services to fertilize lawns and the sale of services to trim and care for trees. The business' owner wants to know how much revenue is earned from each source. Therefore, the business uses two revenue accounts: Sales—Lawns and Sales—Tree Care.

When an income statement is prepared for Milton Lawn Service, both revenue accounts are listed, as shown in Illustration 9-7.

ILLUSTRATION 9-7

Revenue section of an income statement showing two sources of revenue

				% OF SALES
Milton Lawn Service				
Income Statement				
For Month Ended August 31, 19--				
Revenue:				
Sales—Lawns	3 3 6 0 00			
Sales—Tree Care	2 2 5 0 00			
Total Sales		5 6 1 0 00	100.0	
Expenses:				

TEACHING STRATEGIES: DIFFERENT LEARNING STYLES

Print Learner. When learning formulas, the print learner would prefer to be able to study the formula as given in the textbook or as printed on a separate handout. The print material should show the formula as well as an example of performing the calculations.

Audit Your Understanding

1. List the four sections of an income statement.

2. What is the formula for calculating the total expenses component percentage?

3. What is the formula for calculating the net income component percentage?

Only the revenue section of Milton Lawn Service's income statement differs from the income statement prepared by Rugcare. Write the section heading, *Revenue:*, at the left of the wide column. Write the titles of both revenue accounts in the wide column indented about one centimeter. Record the balance of each account in the first amount column on the same line as the account title. Total the two revenue account balances. Write the total amount on the next line in the second amount column. Write the words, *Total Sales*, in the wide column indented about one centimeter on the same line as the total revenue amount.

BALANCE SHEET

Information about assets, liabilities, and owner's equity might be obtained from the general ledger accounts or from a work sheet. However, the information is easier to use if reported in an organized manner such as on a balance sheet. Rugcare's balance sheet information on a work sheet is shown in Illustration 9-8.

ILLUSTRATION 9-8

Balance sheet information on a work sheet

	ACCOUNT TITLE	BALANCE SHEET		
		7 DEBIT	**8** CREDIT	
1	Cash	8 2 7 2 00		1
2	Petty Cash	2 0 0 00		2
3	Supplies	2 2 8 4 00		3
4	Prepaid Insurance	1 1 0 0 00		4
5	Butler Cleaning Supplies		1 3 6 0 00	5
6	Dale Office Supplies		2 0 0 00	6
7	Ben Furman, Capital		1 0 0 0 0 00	7
8	Ben Furman, Drawing	6 0 0 00		8
17				17
18		1 2 4 5 6 00	1 1 5 6 0 00	18
19	Net Income		8 9 6 00	19
20		1 2 4 5 6 00	1 2 4 5 6 00	20

FYI

Information needed to prepare the balance sheet is obtained from two places on the work sheet. Account titles are obtained from the work sheet's Account Title column. Account balances are obtained from the work sheet's Balance Sheet columns.

Information needed to prepare Rugcare's balance sheet is obtained from two places on the work sheet. Account titles are obtained from the work sheet's Account Title column. Account balances are obtained from the work sheet's Balance Sheet columns.

A balance sheet has four sections: (1) heading, (2) assets, (3) liabilities, and (4) owner's equity.

Heading of a Balance Sheet

The heading of a balance sheet consists of three lines. (1) The name of the business. (2) The name of the statement. (3) The date of the

CHAPTER 9   Financial Statements for a Proprietorship   **199**

The AUDIT YOUR UNDERSTANDING feature appears at the end of each section of the chapter. Explain to your students that the word *audit* means to check or verify. AUDIT YOUR UNDERSTANDING may be used to check student comprehension of the section just studied. The answers are provided in Appendix D in the back of the textbook.

1. Heading, revenue, expenses, and net income or net loss.
2. Total Expenses ÷ Total Sales = Total Expenses Component Percentage.
3. Net Income ÷ Total Sales = Net Income Component Percentage.

LESSON PLAN 9-2

Materials

- Student pages 199–205
- Transparencies: 2-1, Blank Accounting Equation and Balance Sheet; 2-2, Preparing a Balance Sheet; 9-1, Completed Income Statement and Balance Sheet; 9-2, Chapter Summary
- Math Work Sheet Chapter 9, Part C: Calculating Owner's Equity (TRG)
- Software: Spreadsheet Template, Electronic Study Guide
- Demonstration Problem: 9B, Preparing a Balance Sheet
- Assess: Problem Test Chapter 9, MicroExam Chapter 9

Objectives (Enabling Performance Tasks)

b. Identify accounting concepts and practices related to preparation of financial statements for a service business organized as a proprietorship.

e. Prepare a balance sheet for a service business organized as a proprietorship.

TEACHING STRATEGIES: TEACHING TIP

Review the accounting equation. Assets = Liabilities + Owner's Equity.

ILLUSTRATION 9-9

Heading of a balance sheet

Rugcare
Balance Sheet
August 31, 19--

Assets, liabilities, and owner's equity are reported on Rugcare's balance sheet as of a specific date, August 31.

Assets Section of a Balance Sheet

A balance sheet reports information about the elements of the accounting equation.

Assets = Liabilities + Owner's Equity

The assets are on the LEFT side of the accounting equation and on the LEFT side of Rugcare's balance sheet.

   The information needed to prepare the assets section is obtained from the work sheet's Account Title column and the Balance Sheet Debit column. The assets section of Rugcare's balance sheet is shown in Illustration 9-10.

ILLUSTRATION 9-10

Assets section of a balance sheet

Assets		
Cash	8 2 7 2 00	
Petty Cash	2 0 0 00	
Supplies	2 2 8 4 00	
Prepaid Insurance	1 1 0 0 00	

Write the title of the section, *Assets*, in the middle of the left wide column. Under the heading write the titles of all asset accounts. Record the balance of each asset account in the left amount column on the same line as the account title.

Equities Section of a Balance Sheet

Two kinds of equities are reported on a balance sheet: (1) liabilities and (2) owner's equity. Liabilities and owner's equity are on the RIGHT side of the accounting equation and on the RIGHT side of Rugcare's balance sheet.

Liabilities Section of a Balance Sheet. The information needed to prepare the liabilities section is obtained from the work sheet's Account Title column and the Balance Sheet Credit column. The liabilities are reported on a balance sheet as shown in Illustration 9-11.

ILLUSTRATION 9-11

Liabilities section of a balance sheet

				Liabilities		
				Butler Cleaning Supplies	1 3 6 0 00	
				Dale Office Supplies	2 0 0 00	
				Total Liabilities	1 5 6 0 00	

Write the title of the section, *Liabilities*, in the middle of the right wide column. Under this heading write the titles of all liability accounts. Record the balance of each liability account in the right amount column on the same line as the account title. To indicate addition, rule a single line across the right amount column under the last amount. Write the words, *Total Liabilities*, in the right wide column on the next blank line. Record the total of all liabilities, *$1,560.00*, in the right amount column.

Remember that there are two kinds of equity: Liabilities and Owner's Equity.

Owner's Equity Section of a Balance Sheet. Only the amount of current capital is reported on Rugcare's balance sheet. The amounts needed to calculate the current capital are found in the work sheet's Balance Sheet Debit and Credit columns. The amount of current capital is calculated as shown below.

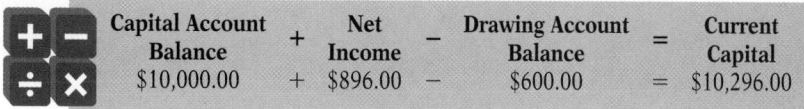

Capital Account Balance	+	Net Income	−	Drawing Account Balance	=	Current Capital
$10,000.00	+	$896.00	−	$600.00	=	$10,296.00

The title of the owner's capital account is obtained from the work sheet's Account Title column. Owner's equity is reported on a balance sheet as shown in Illustration 9-12.

Write the title of the section, *Owner's Equity*, in the middle of the right wide column on the next line. On the next line, write the title of the owner's capital account, *Ben Furman, Capital.* Record the current amount of owner's equity, *$10,296.00*, in the right amount column.

Rugcare's balance sheet prepared on August 31 is shown in Illustration 9-12. Rule a single line across both amount columns under the last amount in the amount column that is the longest. For Rugcare's balance sheet, the longest column is the right amount

The word Equity can be abbreviated as "Eq."

Use Transparency 2-1 to demonstrate completing a balance sheet.

Guided Practice

Guide students through Drills 9-D1 and 9-D2. Students should have the forms from the working papers to complete as you guide them through the drills. For Drill 9-D1, for the first 3 accounts, ask students to name the account classification and determine on which financial statement will it appear. For Drill 9-D2, calculate the net income or net loss and current capital on the chalkboard for Companies A and B. Check the accuracy of your work by using the accounting equation. The balance of Drills 9-D1 and 9-D2 can be completed as Independent Practice.

Independent Practice

- Assign Questions 12–13, Drills 9-D1 and 9-D2, Problem 9-2, Study Guide 9, and Mastery Problem 9-M.

- Duplicate and assign Math Work Sheets Chapter 9 Part B, Calculating Owner's Equity from the Masters and Solutions to Enrichment/Application Activities Section in the Teacher's Resource Guide to provide additional practice on the mathematics of calculating owner's equity.

TEACHING STRATEGIES: TEACHING TIP

Review the two types of equities. (1) Equity of those to whom money is owed. (2) Equity of the owner.

ASSESS

- Assess student understanding by checking solutions to Independent Practice activities.

- Review the procedures for preparing the balance sheet. Use Transparency 9-1, the completed balance sheet.

Reteach

- Use Demonstration Problem 9B. This problem can be done on the overhead with the students completing the problem at their desks.

- Assign Recycling Problem 9R.

Extend

Assign Challenge Problem 9-C (the challenge is to complete a work sheet that has a net loss instead of net income).

Enrich

- Assign the Spreadsheet Template for Problems 9-M and 9-C.

- Assign the Electronic Study Guide Chapter 9 to complete the study guide from the working papers at the computer.

CLOSURE

- Use Audit Your Understanding questions.

- Review "Summary of Financial Statements for a Proprietorship." Use Transparency 9-2, Chapter Summary.

ASSESS

- Administer Problem Test Chapter 9.

- Administer a MicroExam test for Chapter 9.

ILLUSTRATION 9-12   A balance sheet

Rugcare				
Balance Sheet				
August 31, 19--				
Assets		**Liabilities**		
Cash	8 2 7 2 00	Butler Cleaning Supplies	1 3 6 0 00	
Petty Cash	2 0 0 00	Dale Office Supplies	2 0 0 00	
Supplies	2 2 8 4 00	Total Liabilities	1 5 6 0 00	
Prepaid Insurance	1 1 0 0 00	Owner's Equity		
		Ben Furman, Capital	10 2 9 6 00	
Total Assets	11 8 5 6 00	Total Liab. and Owner's Eq.	11 8 5 6 00	

👈👈 FYI 👉👉

Capital is not copied from the work sheet to the balance sheet. Capital is calculated using beginning capital, minus drawing, plus net income or minus net loss.

column. The line is ruled under the amount of Ben Furman's capital, $10,296.00. On the next line, in the right wide column, write the words, *Total Liab. and Owner's Eq.* Record the amount of total liabilities and owner's equity, *$11,856.00*, in the right amount column.

The total assets amount is not recorded at the time the rest of the assets section is prepared. The placement of the total assets line is determined after the equities section is prepared so that the two final totals are on the same line.

Write the words, *Total Assets*, in the left wide column on the same line as the words *Total Liab. and Owner's Eq.* Record the amount of total assets, *$11,856.00*, in the left amount column.

Compare the totals of the two amount columns. Because the totals are the same on both sides of Rugcare's balance sheet, $11,856.00, the balance sheet is in balance. The accounting equation being reported is also in balance.

	Assets	=	Liabilities	+	Owner's Equity
	$11,856.00	=	$1,560.00	+	$10,296.00

If the total assets do not equal the total liabilities and owner's equity, the error or errors must be found and corrected before the balance sheet is completed.

Rule double lines across both the left and right amount columns just below the column totals to show that the totals have been verified as correct.

When a business has a net loss, current capital is calculated as shown below.

Capital Account Balance	–	Net Loss	–	Drawing Account Balance	=	Current Capital
$15,000.00	–	$200.00	–	$500.00	=	$14,300.00

TEACHING STRATEGIES: TEACHING TIP

Review ruling a balance sheet.

ELECTRONIC SPREADSHEETS HELP ANSWER "WHAT IF?" QUESTIONS

Ben Furman analyzes the income statement in Illustration 9-6 to make decisions about Rugcare's future operations. Mr. Furman may analyze several "what if?" questions to determine what action might improve net income and the net income component percentage. What if the amount spent on advertising was increased to $300.00? Mr. Furman estimated that this would increase sales to $5,000.00. However, if sales increase, Rugcare will also need additional supplies to clean more rugs. Therefore, Mr. Furman estimates that supplies expense will increase to $2,900.00.

Electronic spreadsheets eliminate the need to manually erase data and recalculate totals each time a change is made. When data is keyed on the spreadsheet, formulas use the new data to recalculate other values. Formulas may consist of a combination of values, mathematical operations, and cell addresses. The electronic spreadsheet uses the standard mathematical operations of addition (+), subtraction (−), multiplication (*), and division (/). For example,

the formula to calculate the net income component percentage, +E19/E7, divides the value currently displayed at E19 by the value currently displayed at E7.

The analysis indicates that spending $300.00 on advertising would improve net income and the net income component percentage. Mr. Furman will save the spreadsheet on a computer disk for use in answering other "what if?" questions. In the future, Mr. Furman can retrieve the spreadsheet, key new data, and instantly analyze the revised net income and net income component percentage.

```
F7    (P1) +E7/E7
      A         B              C         D          E         F         G
 1                             Rugcare
 2                         Income Statement
 3                       Projection of Net Income
 4                                                          % of
 5                                                          Sales
 6    Revenue:                                            -------
 7       Sales                                 5,000.00   100.0%
 8    Expenses:
 9       Advertising Expense         300.00
10       Insurance Expense           100.00
11       Miscellaneous Expense       105.00
12       Rent Expense                250.00
13       Repair Expense              110.00
14       Supplies Expense          2,900.00
15       Utilities Expense           115.00
16                                ----------
17       Total Expenses                        3,880.00   77.6%
18                                            ----------
19    Net Income                               1,120.00   22.4%
20                                            ==========
```

The current capital, $14,300.00, is reported on the balance sheet in the same way as shown in Illustration 9-12.

Owner's Equity Reported in Detail on a Balance Sheet

Rugcare's balance sheet reports the current capital on August 31 but does not show how this amount was calculated. Rugcare is a small business with relatively few changes in owner's equity to report. Therefore, Ben Furman decided that the business does not need to report all the details in the owner's equity section. However, some businesses prefer to report the details about how owner's equity is calculated.

If Rugcare were to report details about owner's equity, the balance sheet would be prepared as shown in Illustration 9-13.

SPREADSHEET OPTIONS

The SPREADSHEET OPTIONS feature is intended to expose students to a variety of ways to use spreadsheets. As an optional activity, students may use their spreadsheet software to duplicate the example shown in the spreadsheet options feature. They may also create new sets of data to do what-if analyses.

TEACHING STRATEGIES: TEACHING TIP

Review that a double rule means totals are verified as correct.

TEACHING STRATEGIES: DIFFERENT LEARNING STYLES

Kinesthetic Learner. The kinesthetic learner should have the opportunity to perform the calculations to solve the formula. One way to accomplish this is to use the math work sheet.

ILLUSTRATION 9-13 Owner's equity reported in detail on a balance sheet

Total Liabilities			1 5 6 0 00
Owner's Equity			
Ben Furman, Capital, August 1		10,000.00	
Net Income	896.00		
Less Ben Furman, Drawing	600.00	296.00	
Ben Furman, Capital, August 31			10 2 9 6 00
Total Liabilities and Owner's Equity			11 8 5 6 00

Audit Your Understanding

1. List the four sections of a balance sheet.
2. What is the formula for calculating current capital?

First, the owner's capital account balance, $10,000.00, is reported. Second, the balance of the drawing account, $600.00, is subtracted from the net income for the fiscal period, $896.00. The difference, $296.00, is added to the previous capital account balance. The current capital, $10,296.00, is recorded as the amount of Ben Furman, Capital on August 31.

A summary of financial statements for a service business organized as a proprietorship is shown in Illustration 9-14.

SUMMARY OF FINANCIAL STATEMENTS FOR A PROPRIETORSHIP

1 An income statement is prepared using information from the Account Title column and Income Statement columns of a work sheet.

2 Component percentages for total expenses and net income are calculated as shown below.

Total Expenses ÷ Total Sales = Total Expenses Component Percentage

Net Income ÷ Total Sales = Net Income Component Percentage

3 A balance sheet is prepared using information obtained from the work sheet's Account Title column and Balance Sheet columns. Current capital to be reported on the balance sheet is calculated as shown below:

Capital Account Balance + Net Income − Drawing Account Balance = Current Capital

SUMMARY ILLUSTRATION 9-14

Summary of financial statements for a proprietorship

1 An income statement is prepared using information from the Account Title column and Income Statement columns of a work sheet.

2 Component percentages for total expenses and net income are calculated as shown below.

Total Expenses ÷ Total Sales = Total Expenses Component Percentage
Net Income   ÷ Total Sales = Net Income Component Percentage

3 A balance sheet is prepared using information obtained from the work sheet's Account Title column and Balance Sheet columns. Current capital to be reported on the balance sheet is calculated as shown below.

$$\text{Capital Account Balance} + \text{Net Income} - \text{Drawing Account Balance} = \text{Current Capital}$$

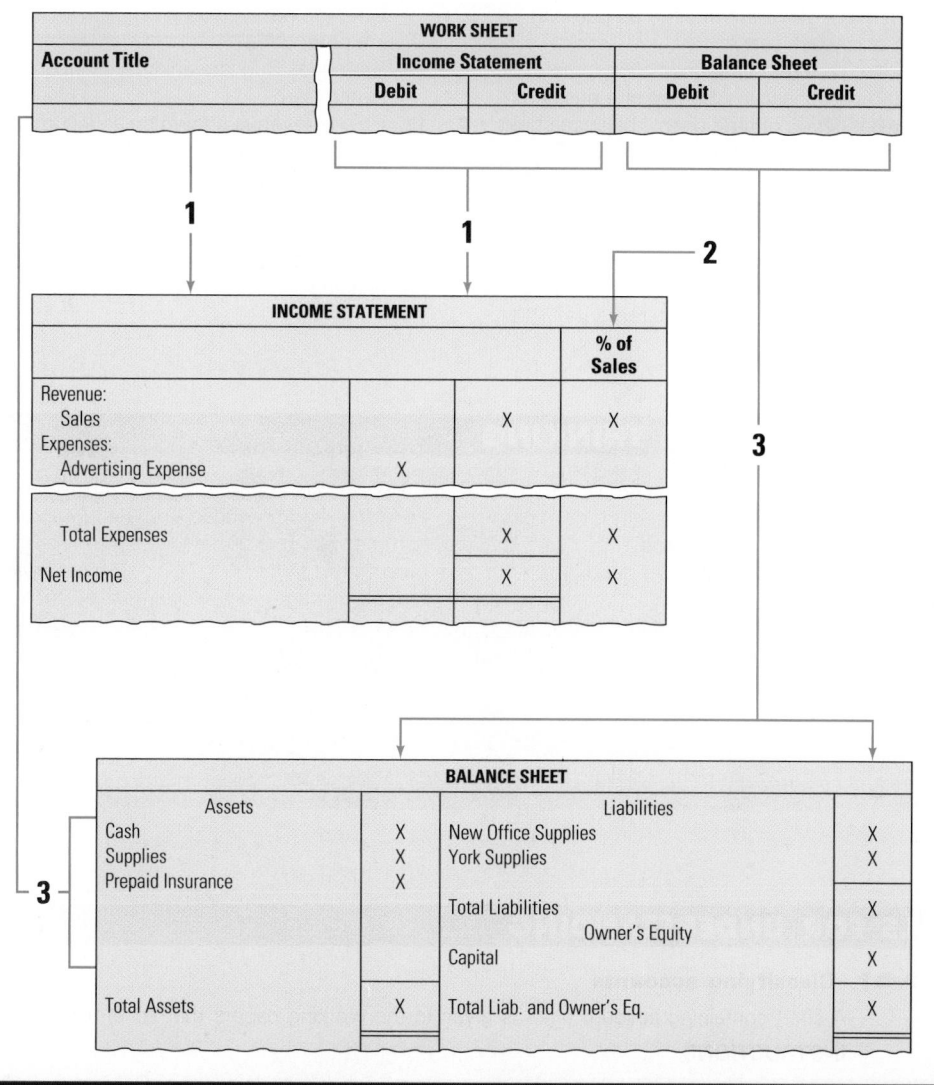

TEACHING STRATEGIES:
APPLYING VISUALS

Direct students to Summary Illustration 9-14 to review financial statements for a proprietorship.

APPLIED SKILLS:
WORD PROCESSING

If you wish to integrate word processing into your accounting course, you may direct students to answer the end-of-chapter Accounting Terms, Questions for Individual Study, and Cases for Critical Thinking using their word processing software.

APPLIED SKILLS: WRITING ACROSS THE CURRICULUM

Writing paragraphs and short essays. The Cases for Critical Thinking are short, practical applications of the accounting principles developed in the chapter. Some cases are planned to present problems related to the chapter but not specifically discussed and answered in the chapter. These cases present an opportunity for critical thinking and decision making. These cases also require more than a short objective-type response. Therefore, they provide ideal practice in writing paragraphs and short essays.

ACCOUNTING TERM

1. **component percentage:** The percentage relationship between one financial statement item and the total that includes that item. (p. 197)

QUESTIONS FOR INDIVIDUAL STUDY

1. Adequate Disclosure. (p. 193)

2. Accounting Period Cycle. (p. 193)

3. An income statement reports financial information over a specific period of time. (p. 193)

4. A balance sheet reports financial information on a specific date. (p. 193)

5. Matching Expenses with Revenue. (p. 194)

6. Prepares a work sheet. (p. 194)

7. From the Account Title column and the Income Statement columns of a work sheet. (p. 194)

8. (a) The name of the business; (b) the name of the statement; and (c) the date of the statement. (p. 194)

9. (a) The net income is calculated from information on the income statement (Total Revenue – Total Expenses = Net Income). (b) The amount of net income calculated is compared to the amount of net income shown on the work sheet. The two amounts must be the same. (p. 196)

10. By calculating the total expenses component percentage and the net income component percentage. (pp. 196–197)

11. Both revenue account titles and account balances are listed in the revenue section of the income statement. The two revenue account balances are totaled, and the total sales is recorded. (p. 199)

12. From the Account Title column and the Balance Sheet columns of a work sheet. (p. 199)

13. (a) The name of the business; (b) the name of the statement; and (c) the date of the statement. (p. 199)

ACCOUNTING TERM EPT(a)

What is the meaning of the following?

1. **component percentage**

QUESTIONS FOR INDIVIDUAL STUDY EPT(b)

1. Which accounting concept is being applied when all the information about a business' financial condition is reported on financial statements?

2. Which accounting concept is being applied when financial statements are prepared at least once each year?

3. For what period of time does an income statement report financial progress of a business?

4. For what period of time does a balance sheet report financial condition of a business?

5. Which accounting concept is being applied when revenue earned and the expenses incurred to earn that revenue are recorded in the same fiscal period?

6. What does Rugcare do to assist in planning the preparation of financial statements?

7. Where does Rugcare obtain the information for preparing an income statement?

8. What information is found in an income statement heading?

9. What are the two steps in calculating and verifying the net income on Rugcare's income statement?

10. How does Rugcare analyze its income statement?

11. How is revenue shown on an income statement when a business has two sources of revenue?

12. Where does Rugcare obtain the information for preparing a balance sheet?

13. What information is found in a balance sheet heading?

CASES FOR CRITICAL THINKING EPT(b)

CASE 1 James Worth and Mary Derner each own small businesses. Mr. Worth prepares an income statement and balance sheet at the end of each day for his business. He claims that he needs the information to make business decisions. Mrs. Derner prepares an income statement and balance sheet for her business only at the end of each one-year fiscal period. She claims that she needs the information only at the end of the year when preparing tax reports. Which owner is using the better procedure? Explain your answer.

CASE 2 Ralph Macy owns and manages a business that has produced an average annual net income of $21,600.00 for five years. George Wayne has offered to buy Mr. Macy's business and retain him as manager at a monthly salary of $2,000.00. What should Mr. Macy consider before selling his business and accepting the position as manager?

DRILLS FOR UNDERSTANDING EPT(b)

DRILL 9-D1 Classifying accounts

A chart containing account titles is given in the working papers that accompany this textbook.

INSTRUCTIONS:

1. For each account title on the chart, place a check mark in either Column 2, 3, 4, 5, or 6 to indicate the classification of each account.

CHECK FIGURES

See Teacher's Edition of Working Papers for complete solutions to drills and problems.

Drill 9-D1   There are 3 assets, 2 liab., 2 owner's eq., 1 rev., 5 exp., 6 inc. stmt., and 7 bal. sheet.

Drill 9-D2   Net Inc. A 1,400; B 1,900; D 1,890; E 3,015; G 4,050. Net Loss C 840; F 1,420; H 7,000.

2. Place a check mark in either Column 7 or 8 to indicate on which financial statement each account will be reported.

DRILL 9-D2 Calculating net income or net loss and owner's current capital

MATHEMATICS

A chart containing information for 8 companies is given in the working papers that accompany this textbook.

INSTRUCTIONS:

Complete the following for each company given in the chart.

1. Use the information in Columns 5 and 6. Calculate the amount of net income or net loss for each company. For example, Company A: Revenue, $2,300, − expenses, $900, = net income, $1,400.
2. Calculate the amount of current capital for each company using the net income or net loss from Instruction 1 and the information in Columns 3 and 4. For example, Company A: Capital account balance, $2,320, + net income, $1,400, − drawing, $120, = current capital, $3,600.
3. Use the accounting equation to check the accuracy of your answers in Instructions 1 and 2. For example, Company A: Assets, $5,600, = liabilities, $2,000, + owner's equity, $3,600. If the equation is not in balance, recalculate and correct your answers to Instructions 1 and 2.

APPLICATION PROBLEMS   EPT(c,d,e)

PROBLEM 9-1 Preparing an income statement

MATHEMATICS

The following information is obtained from the work sheet of LawnMow for the month ended June 30 of the current year.

				5	6	7	8	
	ACCOUNT TITLE			INCOME STATEMENT		BALANCE SHEET		
				DEBIT	CREDIT	DEBIT	CREDIT	
10	Sales				3 1 0 0 00			10
11	Advertising Expense			3 0 00				11
12	Insurance Expense			1 4 0 00				12
13	Miscellaneous Expense			6 5 00				13
14	Rent Expense			8 0 0 00				14
15	Supplies Expense			4 0 0 00				15
16	Utilities Expense			7 5 00				16
17				1 5 1 0 00	3 1 0 0 00			17
18	Net Income			1 5 9 0 00				18
19				3 1 0 0 00	3 1 0 0 00			19
20								20

INSTRUCTIONS:

Prepare an income statement for the month ended June 30 of the current year. Calculate and record the component percentages for total expenses and net income. Round percentage calculations to the nearest 0.1%.

PROBLEM 9-2 Preparing a balance sheet

The information on page 208 is obtained from the work sheet of LawnMow for the month ended June 30 of the current year.

INSTRUCTIONS:

Prepare a balance sheet for June 30 of the current year.

ACCOUNT TITLE	BALANCE SHEET DEBIT	CREDIT	
1 Cash	7 5 3 0 00		1
2 Petty Cash	2 0 0 00		2
3 Supplies	6 8 6 0 00		3
4 Prepaid Insurance	2 5 0 0 00		4
5 Barker Supplies		4 4 0 0 00	5
6 Richmond Office Supplies		1 3 0 0 00	6
7 Clem Sutter, Capital		11 0 0 0 00	7
8 Clem Sutter, Drawing	1 2 0 0 00		8
9 Income Summary			9
16			16
17	18 2 9 0 00	16 7 0 0 00	17
18 Net Income		1 5 9 0 00	18
19	18 2 9 0 00	18 2 9 0 00	19

MASTERY PROBLEM 9-M   Preparing financial statements

SPREADSHEET

The following information is obtained from the work sheet of Ace Delivery Service for the month ended July 31 of the current year.

ACCOUNT TITLE	INCOME STATEMENT DEBIT	CREDIT	BALANCE SHEET DEBIT	CREDIT	
1 Cash			7 5 0 0 00		1
2 Petty Cash			2 0 0 00		2
3 Supplies			7 8 0 0 00		3
4 Prepaid Insurance			2 6 0 0 00		4
5 Down Supplies				4 7 0 0 00	5
6 Melton Office Supplies				1 2 0 0 00	6
7 Clark Smith, Capital				12 0 0 0 00	7
8 Clark Smith, Drawing			1 4 0 0 00		8
9 Income Summary					9
10 Sales		5 6 7 0 00			10
11 Advertising Expense	3 9 0 00				11
12 Insurance Expense	1 9 0 00				12
13 Miscellaneous Expense	1 5 0 00				13
14 Rent Expense	3 0 0 00				14
15 Supplies Expense	2 0 0 00				15
16 Utilities Expense	1 4 0 00				16
17	4 0 7 0 00	5 6 7 0 00	19 5 0 0 00	17 9 0 0 00	17
18 Net Income	1 6 0 0 00			1 6 0 0 00	18
19	5 6 7 0 00	5 6 7 0 00	19 5 0 0 00	19 5 0 0 00	19

INSTRUCTIONS:

1. Prepare an income statement for the month ended July 31 of the current year. Calculate and record the component percentages for total expenses and net income. Round percentage calculations to the nearest 0.1%.

2. Prepare a balance sheet for July 31 of the current year.

CHALLENGE PROBLEM 9-C Preparing financial statements with two sources of revenue and a net loss

The following information is obtained from the work sheet of Mercer Lawn Service for the month ended August 31 of the current year.

	ACCOUNT TITLE	INCOME STATEMENT DEBIT	INCOME STATEMENT CREDIT	BALANCE SHEET DEBIT	BALANCE SHEET CREDIT	
1	Cash			6 0 2 0 00		1
2	Petty Cash			2 0 0 00		2
3	Supplies			6 0 0 0 00		3
4	Prepaid Insurance			2 5 0 0 00		4
5	Choice Supplies				3 0 0 0 00	5
6	Poll Office Supplies				2 0 0 00	6
7	Lydia Roland, Capital				13 0 0 0 00	7
8	Lydia Roland, Drawing			1 3 0 0 00		8
9	Income Summary					9
10	Sales—Lawn Care		4 7 0 0 00			10
11	Sales—Shrub Care		2 6 0 0 00			11
12	Advertising Expense	3 9 0 00				12
13	Insurance Expense	3 0 0 00				13
14	Miscellaneous Expense	4 5 0 00				14
15	Rent Expense	3 0 0 0 00				15
16	Supplies Expense	3 1 0 0 00				16
17	Utilities Expense	2 4 0 00				17
18		7 4 8 0 00	7 3 0 0 00	16 0 2 0 00	16 2 0 0 00	18
19	Net Loss		1 8 0 00	1 8 0 00		19
20		7 4 8 0 00	7 4 8 0 00	16 2 0 0 00	16 2 0 0 00	20

INSTRUCTIONS:

1. Prepare an income statement for the month ended August 31 of the current year. Calculate and record the component percentages for total expenses and net loss. Place the percentage for net loss in parentheses to show that it is for a net loss. Round percentage calculations to the nearest 0.1%.

2. Prepare a balance sheet for August 31 of the current year.

CHAPTER 10 OVERVIEW

Chapter 10 presents journalizing adjusting entries for a proprietorship. Adjusting entries play an important role in the accounting cycle for all forms of business. It is important for students to understand how these entries are journalized.

Journalizing closing entries is also covered in this chapter. Recording closing entries has been made easier in this edition. Students are instructed to take the information directly from a work sheet when journalizing the closing entries. A direct tie-in between the work sheet and the closing entries is shown in the illustrations.

After the adjusting and closing entries are journalized and posted, the post-closing trial balance is completed.

GUIDE TO ACHIEVING LEARNING OBJECTIVES

Enabling Performance Tasks	TEACH — Lesson Plans	APPLY — Drills for Understanding	APPLY — Application Problems	EXTEND/ENRICH — Mastery Problems	EXTEND/ENRICH — Challenge Problems	EXTEND/ENRICH — Cases for Critical Thinking	EXTEND/ENRICH — Recycling Problems	EXTEND/ENRICH — Reinforcement Activity	
a. Define accounting terms related to adjusting and closing entries for a service business organized as a proprietorship.	10-1, 10-2, 10-3								
b. Identifying accounting concepts and practices related to adjusting and closing entries for a service business organized as a proprietorship.	10-1, 10-2, 10-3	10-D1				Cases 1, 2			
c. Record adjusting entries for a service business organized as a proprietorship.	10-1		10-1	10-M	10-C		10-R	1B	
d. Record closing entries for a service business organized as a proprietorship.	10-2		10-1	10-M	10-C		10-R	1B	
e. Prepare a post-closing trial balance for a service business organized as a proprietorship.	10-3		10-1	10-M				1B	

ENRICHMENT

SPECIAL FEATURES	TECHNOLOGY CONNECTION
Multicultural Awareness, page 215	*Automated Accounting 6.0* Problems 10-M, 10-C
Personal Visions in Business, page 212	Integrating Automated Accounting Topic 3 Optional Problem DB-3A
Careers in Accounting, page 234	Accounting Tutorial Units 2, 3
Applied Communications, page 229	Application Program Disk Problem 10-M
	Electronic Study Guide

	INFORMAL ASSESSMENT		FORMAL ASSESSMENT				
	Study Guide	Audit Your Understanding	Chapter MicroExam	Chapter Problem Test	Unit Problem Test	Unit Objective Test	Portfolio
	Unit A		✓			✓	
	Units B, C, D	✓	✓			✓	
				✓	✓		✓
				✓	✓		✓
				✓			✓

NEW, REVIEW, AND EXTENSION

ACTIVITIES/CONCEPTS/TRANSACTIONS	NEW	REVIEW/ EXTENSION
Journalizing and posting		✓
Recording adjusting entries	✓	
Adjusting entry for supplies		✓
Adjusting entry for prepaid insurance		✓
Recording closing entries	✓	
Preparing a post-closing trial balance	✓	

TEACHING MATERIALS

Teacher's Wraparound Edition of Text

Teacher's Resource Guide

Teacher's Edition of Working Papers

Teacher's Edition of Demonstration/Recycling Problems

Teaching Transparencies

Accounting Tutorial Manual

MicroExam

Key for Video Transfer

10

Recording Adjusting and Closing Entries for a Service Business

ENABLING PERFORMANCE TASKS

After studying Chapter 10, you will be able to:

a Define accounting terms related to adjusting and closing entries for a service business organized as a proprietorship.

b Identify accounting concepts and practices related to adjusting and closing entries for a service business organized as a proprietorship.

c Record adjusting entries for a service business organized as a proprietorship.

d Record closing entries for a service business organized as a proprietorship.

e Prepare a post-closing trial balance for a service business organized as a proprietorship.

TERMS PREVIEW

adjusting entries • permanent accounts • temporary accounts • closing entries • post-closing trial balance • accounting cycle

Rugcare prepares a work sheet at the end of each fiscal period to summarize the general ledger information needed to prepare financial statements. (CONCEPT: Accounting Period Cycle) Financial statements are prepared from information on the work sheet. (CONCEPT: Adequate Disclosure)

RECORDING ADJUSTING ENTRIES

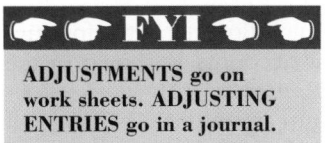

ADJUSTMENTS go on work sheets. ADJUSTING ENTRIES go in a journal.

Rugcare's adjustments are analyzed and planned on a work sheet. However, these adjustments must be journalized so that they can be posted to the general ledger accounts. Journal entries recorded to update general ledger accounts at the end of a fiscal period are called **adjusting entries.**

Adjusting entries are recorded on the next journal page following the page on which the last daily transactions for the month are recorded. The adjusting entries are entered in the General Debit and General Credit columns of a journal.

Rugcare records two adjusting entries. (1) An adjusting entry to bring the supplies account up to date. (2) An adjusting entry to bring the prepaid insurance account up to date.

Adjusting Entry for Supplies

The information needed to journalize the adjusting entry for supplies is obtained from lines 3 and 16 of Rugcare's work sheet. A partial work sheet and the adjusting entry for supplies are shown in Illustration 10-1.

ILLUSTRATION 10-1

Adjusting entry for supplies recorded in a journal

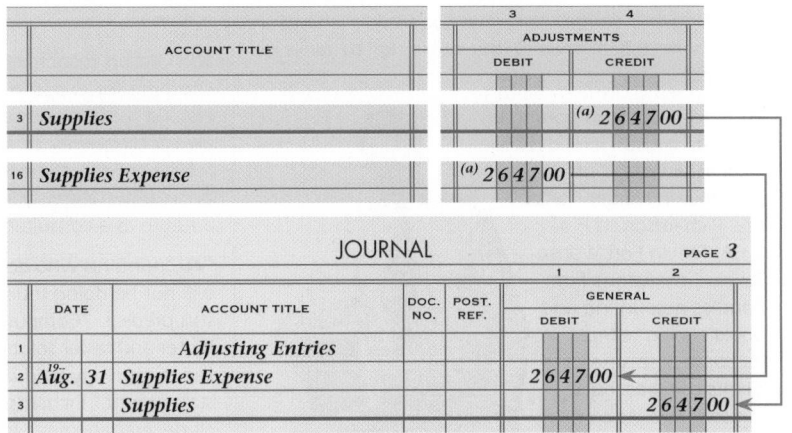

The heading, *Adjusting Entries*, is written in the middle of the Account Title column of the journal. Because no source document is prepared for adjusting entries, the entries are identified with a

CHAPTER 10 Recording Adjusting and Closing Entries for a Service Business **211**

Materials

- Student pages 211–214
- Transparencies: A, Blank Journal; 10-1, Summary of Adjusting Entries
- Software: Accounting Tutorial
- Demonstration Problem: 10A, Journalizing and Posting Adjusting Entries

Objectives (Enabling Performance Tasks)

a. Define accounting terms related to adjusting and closing entries for a service business organized as a proprietorship.

b. Identify accounting concepts and practices related to adjusting and closing entries for a service business organized as a proprietorship.

c. Record adjusting entries for a service business organized as a proprietorship.

FOCUS

- In Chapter 8, adjustments were analyzed and planned on the work sheet. Explain that in this lesson we will look at how these adjustments are journalized so that they can be posted to the general ledger accounts.
- Introduce new vocabulary: adjusting entries.

TEACH

Cover student pages 211–214 "Recording Adjusting Entries." To begin this lesson, review the definition of adjustments and why they are necessary. Changes recorded on a work sheet to update general ledger accounts at the end of a fiscal period are called adjustments. Use Transparency 10-1 to describe journalizing adjusting entries. Explain that adjusting entries are recorded on a new journal page with the heading Adjusting Entries centered on the first line of the journal. Point out that no source document is necessary when journalizing adjusting entries.

heading in the journal. This heading explains all of the adjusting entries that follow. Therefore, the heading is written only once for all adjusting entries.

The date, *19--, Aug. 31*, is written in the Date column. The title of the account debited, *Supplies Expense*, is written in the Account Title column. The debit amount, *$2,647.00*, is recorded in the General Debit column on the same line as the account title. The title of the account credited, *Supplies*, is written on the next line. The credit amount, *$2,647.00*, is recorded in the General Credit column on the same line as the account title.

The effect of posting the adjusting entry for supplies to the general ledger accounts is shown in the T accounts.

Supplies Expense has an up-to-date balance of $2,647.00, which is the value of the supplies used during the fiscal period. Supplies has a new balance of $2,284.00, which is the value of the supplies on hand at the end of the fiscal period.

Supplies Expense		
Adj. (a)	2,647.00	

Supplies			
Bal.	4,931.00	Adj. (a)	2,647.00
(New Bal.	2,284.00)		

■ Tom Richardson ■

HOLDER, MCCALL, AND RICHARDSON, LLP, FORT WORTH, TEXAS

Tom Richardson started his career as a C.P.A., but then he began importing fish. Richardson was in business with a partner in Scotland who bought and shipped fish to the United States by airplane. This seafood importing business led to Richardson's first major exposure to the use of personal computers and software to manage a business and keep its records. During the course of pulling the computer system together, Richardson also connected a Telex to the computer to facilitate transmitting his overseas orders.

After leaving the importing business, Richardson joined a large local accounting firm. He is now a partner in Holder, McCall, and Richardson, LLP, a C.P.A. firm in Fort Worth, Texas. Richardson's firm handles accounting and bookkeeping services for some of its smaller clients using accounting software. As companies become larger, many of them want to bring the accounting system in-house and do their own accounting. Richardson helps these companies bridge the gap by providing consulting services on accounting software and technology. Richardson says that his firm's goal is "to provide a solution." Richardson analyzes a company's needs and recommends the software that will best fill those needs. Richardson can also provide software installation and training.

Richardson recommends the study of high school accounting for exposure to accounting as a career field. He also recommends a college degree in accounting as an excellent way to learn how a business works. He feels a college degree in accounting can open a lot of doors down the way and is an excellent background for a future as a consultant.

"Accountants who do not get involved with computers will not be doing much business in ten years," Richardson predicts. "Computer software is constantly offering better and faster solutions to business problems. In fact, the technology field is so dynamic that it is difficult to stay current." Richardson recommends that students include management information system (MIS) courses with their accounting courses so that they are not left behind in the business world.

Personal Visions in Business

Adjusting Entry for Prepaid Insurance

The information needed to journalize the adjusting entry for prepaid insurance is obtained from lines 4 and 12 of Rugcare's work sheet. A partial work sheet and the adjusting entry for prepaid insurance are shown in Illustration 10-2.

ILLUSTRATION 10-2

Adjusting entry for prepaid insurance recorded in a journal

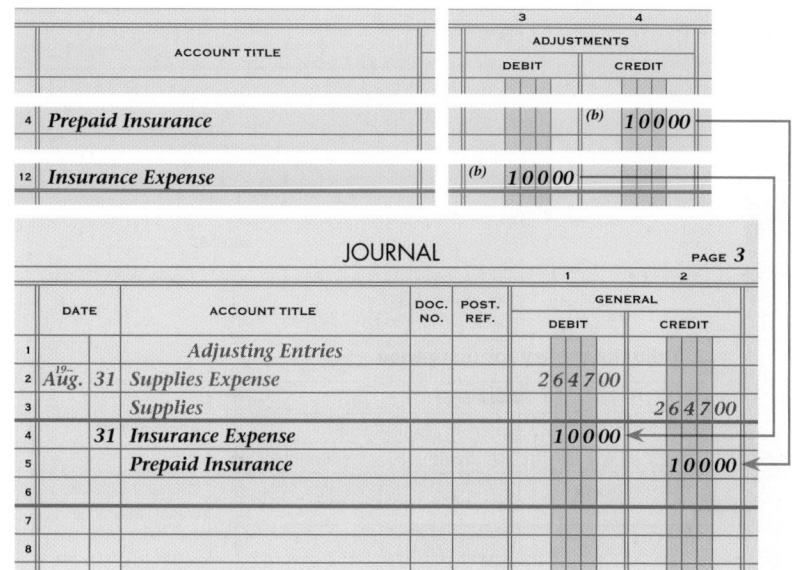

The date, *31*, is written in the Date column. The title of the account debited, *Insurance Expense*, is written in the Account Title column. The debit amount, *$100.00*, is recorded in the General Debit column on the same line as the account title. The title of the account credited, *Prepaid Insurance*, is written on the next line in the Account Title column. The credit amount, *$100.00*, is recorded in the General Credit column on the same line as the account title.

The effect of posting the adjusting entry for insurance to the general ledger accounts is shown in the T accounts. Insurance Expense has an up-to-date balance of $100.00, which is the value of insurance premiums used during the fiscal period. Prepaid Insurance has a new balance of $1,100.00, which is the value of insurance premiums that remain unused at the end of the fiscal period. (*CONCEPT: Matching Expenses with Revenue*)

The two adjusting entries for a service business organized as a proprietorship are summarized in Illustration 10-3.

Audit Your Understanding

1. Why are adjustments journalized?
2. Where is the information obtained to journalize adjusting entries?
3. What accounts are increased from zero balances after adjusting entries for supplies and prepaid insurance are journalized and posted?

Insurance Expense	
Adj. (b) 100.00	

Prepaid Insurance	
Bal. 1,200.00	Adj. (b) 100.00
(New Bal. 1,100.00)	

ASSESS

Assess student understanding by checking solutions to Independent Practice activities. Review "Summary of Adjusting Entries for a Service Business Organized as a Proprietorship." Use Transparency 10-1, Summary of Adjusting Entries.

Reteach

Use Demonstration Problem 10A. This problem can be done on the overhead with the students completing the problem at their desks.

Extend

- Assign Cases for Critical Thinking 1.
- Assign the Accounting Tutorial, Unit 2, to be completed at the computer.

Enrich

Assign students to read the MULTICULTURAL AWARENESS feature on page 215. Discuss with them how an understanding and appreciation of history and other cultures contributes to understanding civilization today.

CLOSURE

Use Audit Your Understanding questions.

AUDIT YOUR UNDERSTANDING

The AUDIT YOUR UNDERSTANDING feature appears at the end of each section of the chapter. Explain to your students that the word *audit* means to check or verify. AUDIT YOUR UNDERSTANDING may be used to check student comprehension of the section just studied. The answers are provided in Appendix D in the back of the textbook.

1. To update general ledger accounts.
2. Adjustments column of the work sheet.
3. Insurance Expense and Supplies Expense.

Summary of adjusting entries for a service business organized as a proprietorship

1. Adjusting entry for supplies

WORK SHEET				JOURNAL			
Account Title	Adjustments			Account Title	General		
	Debit	Credit			Debit	Credit	
Supplies		(a) X		Supplies Expense	X		
				Supplies		X	
Supplies Expense	(a) X						

```
            Supplies Expense
    Adjusting   |

               Supplies
    Balance     |   Adjusting
```

2. Adjusting entry for insurance

WORK SHEET				JOURNAL			
Account Title	Adjustments			Account Title	General		
	Debit	Credit			Debit	Credit	
Prepaid Insurance		(b) X		Insurance Expense	X		
				Prepaid Insurance		X	
Insurance Expense	(b) X						

```
            Insurance Expense
    Adjusting   |

            Prepaid Insurance
    Balance     |   Adjusting
```

RECORDING CLOSING ENTRIES

FYI

Permanent accounts are sometimes referred to as real accounts.

Accounts used to accumulate information from one fiscal period to the next are called **permanent accounts**. Permanent accounts are also referred to as real accounts. Permanent accounts include the asset and liability accounts and the owner's capital account. The ending account balances of permanent accounts for one fiscal period are the beginning account balances for the next fiscal period.

FYI

Only temporary accounts are closed.

Accounts used to accumulate information until it is transferred to the owner's capital account are called **temporary accounts.** Temporary accounts are also referred to as nominal accounts. Temporary accounts include the revenue, expense, and owner's drawing accounts plus the income summary account. Temporary accounts show changes in the owner's capital for a single fiscal period. Therefore, at the end of a fiscal period, the balances of temporary accounts are summarized and transferred to the owner's capital account. The temporary accounts begin a new fiscal period with zero balances.

Need for Closing Temporary Accounts

Journal entries used to prepare temporary accounts for a new fiscal period are called **closing entries.** The temporary account balances must be reduced to zero at the end of each fiscal period. This procedure prepares the temporary accounts for recording information about the next fiscal period. Otherwise, the amounts for the next fiscal period would be added to amounts for previous fiscal periods. *(CONCEPT: Matching Expenses with Revenue)* The net income for the next fiscal period would be difficult to calculate because amounts from several fiscal periods remain in the accounts. Therefore, the temporary accounts must start each new fiscal period with zero balances.

To close a temporary account, an amount equal to its balance is recorded in the account on the side opposite to its balance. For example, if an account has a credit balance of $4,291.00, a debit of $4,291.00 is recorded to close the account.

Need for the Income Summary Account

Whenever a temporary account is closed, the closing entry must have equal debits and credits. If an account is debited for $3,000.00 to close the account, some other account must be credited for the same amount. A temporary account titled *Income Summary* is used to summarize the closing entries for the revenue and expense accounts.

The income summary account is unique because it does not have a normal balance side. The balance of this account is determined by the amounts posted to the account at the end of a fiscal period. When revenue is greater than total expenses, resulting in a net income, the income summary account has a credit balance, as shown in the T account.

Income Summary	
Debit side Total expenses	Credit side Revenue (greater than expenses) (Credit balance is the net income.)

When total expenses are greater than revenue, resulting in a net loss, the income summary account has a debit balance, as shown in the T account on the following page.

FOCUS

- In Chapter 8, the work sheet was prepared at the end of the fiscal period. Explain that in this lesson we will look at how amounts taken from the income statement and balance sheet columns of the work sheet are used to prepare some of the accounts for recording information about the next fiscal period.

- Introduce new vocabulary: permanent accounts, temporary accounts, closing entries.

TEACH

Cover student pages 214–222 "Recording Closing Entries." Explain to students that permanent accounts (real accounts) remain open but temporary accounts (nominal accounts) are closed. The temporary account balances must be reduced to zero at the end of the fiscal period to prepare the temporary accounts for recording information about the next fiscal period. Income Summary is a temporary account and does not have a normal balance. Emphasize that the four closing entries are taken from the Income Statement and Balance Sheet columns of the work sheet. Point out that the heading Closing Entries is centered on the journal line.

Income Summary	
Debit side	Credit side
Total expenses (greater than revenue)	Revenue
(Debit balance is the net loss.)	

Thus, whether the balance of the income summary account is a debit or a credit depends upon whether the business earns a net income or incurs a net loss. Because Income Summary is a temporary account, the account is also closed at the end of a fiscal period when the net income or net loss is recorded.

Rugcare records four closing entries. (1) An entry to close income statement accounts with credit balances. (2) An entry to close income statement accounts with debit balances. (3) An entry to record net income or net loss and close Income Summary. (4) An entry to close the owner's drawing account.

Information needed to record the four closing entries is found in the Income Statement and Balance Sheet columns of the work sheet.

FYI

Amounts for closing entries are taken from the Income Statement and Balance Sheet columns of the work sheet.

Closing Entry for an Income Statement Account with a Credit Balance

Rugcare has one income statement account with a credit balance, Sales, as shown on the partial work sheet in Illustration 10-4. This credit balance must be reduced to zero to prepare the account for the next fiscal period. To reduce the balance to zero, Sales is debited for the amount of the balance. Because debits must equal credits for each journal entry, some other account must be credited. The account used for the credit part of this closing entry is Income Summary. The closing entry for Sales is journalized as shown in Illustration 10-4.

ILLUSTRATION 10-4

Closing entry for an income statement account with a credit balance

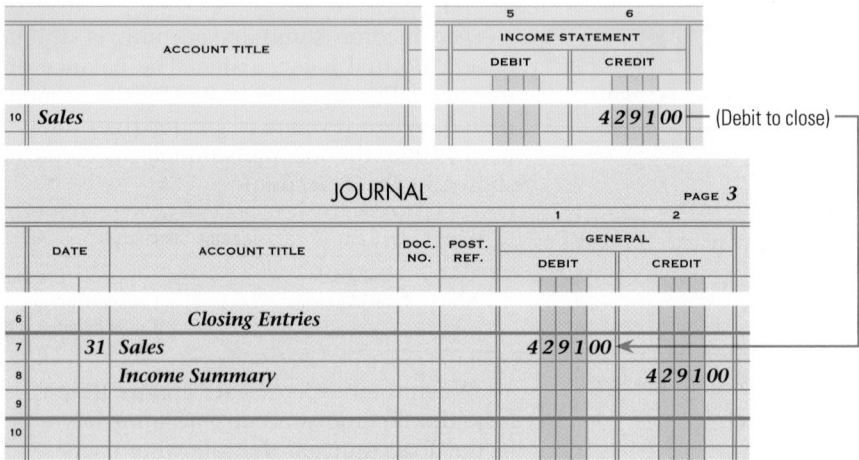

No source document is used for closing entries. Therefore, the heading, *Closing Entries*, is written in the Account Title column of the journal. For Rugcare, this heading is placed in the journal on the first blank line after the last adjusting entry.

The date, *31*, is written on the next line in the Date column. The title of the account debited, *Sales*, is written in the Account Title column. The debit amount, *$4,291.00*, is recorded in the General Debit column on the same line as the account title. The title of the account credited, *Income Summary*, is written in the Account Title column on the next journal line. The credit amount, *$4,291.00*, is recorded in the General Credit amount column on the same line as the account title.

The effect of this closing entry on the general ledger accounts is shown in the T accounts.

The balance of Sales is now zero, and the account is ready for the next fiscal period. The credit balance of Sales is transferred to Income Summary.

Sales			
Closing	4,291.00	Bal.	4,291.00
		(New Bal. zero)	

Income Summary	
	Closing (revenue) 4,291.00

Closing Entry for Income Statement Accounts with Debit Balances

Rugcare has several income statement accounts with debit balances. The seven expense accounts have normal debit balances at the end of a fiscal period, as shown on the partial work sheet in Illustration 10-5, on page 218. The balances of the expense accounts must be reduced to zero to prepare the accounts for the next fiscal period. Each expense account is credited for an amount equal to its balance, and Income Summary is debited for the total of all the expense account balances. The closing entry for the expense accounts is journalized as shown in Illustration 10-5.

The heading for closing entries is written only once. Therefore, the closing entry for expenses starts on the next blank line in the journal.

The date, *31*, is written in the Date column. The title of the account debited, *Income Summary*, is written in the Account Title column. The amount debited to Income Summary is not entered in the amount column until all expenses have been journalized and the total amount calculated. The account title and balance of each expense account is recorded in the Account Title and General Credit columns. After all expense accounts and their balances have been written in the journal, the credit amounts for this entry are added. The total of all expenses, *$3,395.00*, is recorded in the General Debit column on the same line as the account title, Income Summary.

CHAPTER 10   Recording Adjusting and Closing Entries for a Service Business   **217**

⚞ FYI ⚟

The reasons for recording closing entries can be compared to a trip odometer. Closing entries are recorded to prepare the temporary accounts for the next fiscal period by reducing their balances to zero. Likewise a trip odometer must be reset to zero to begin recording the miles for the next trip.

APPLY

Use Transparencies 10-2 and 10-3 to describe journalizing closing entries. Use Transparency A to journalize the entries as the lesson progresses.

Guided Practice

Guide students through Drill 10-D1, Instructions 2-3. Students should have the form from the working papers to complete as you guide them through the drill. For each general ledger account, ask the students if the account is affected by a closing entry and whether the account has a balance after the closing entries are posted. All students should agree with the analysis before proceeding to the next general ledger account.

Independent Practice

Assign Terms 2–4, Questions 5–11, and Problem 10-1, Instruction 2.

APPLIED SKILLS: COMMUNICATIONS

Surveys of business managers show that communication skills are one of the most desired traits in new employees. The applied communications activity provides an opportunity for students to practice their communication and language arts skills on topics that directly relate to accounting.

Assess student understanding by checking solutions to Independent Practice
activities. Review "Summary of Closing
Entries for a Service Business Organized
as a Proprietorship." Use Transparency
10-2, Closing Entries for Income Statement Accounts with a Credit Balance
and Debit Balances, and Transparency
10-3, Closing Entry to Record Net
Income and Close the Income Summary
Account and the Drawing Account.

Reteach

Use Demonstration Problem 10B. This
problem can be done on the overhead
with the students completing the problem at their desks.

Extend

- Assign Cases for Critical Thinking 2.
- Assign the Accounting Tutorial, Unit
  3, to be completed at the computer.

Enrich

- Assign the PERSONAL VISIONS IN
  BUSINESS feature on page 212.
- Assign the Applied Communications
  special feature on page 229.

CLOSURE

Use Audit Your Understanding
questions.

ILLUSTRATION 10-5   Closing entry for income statement accounts with debit balances

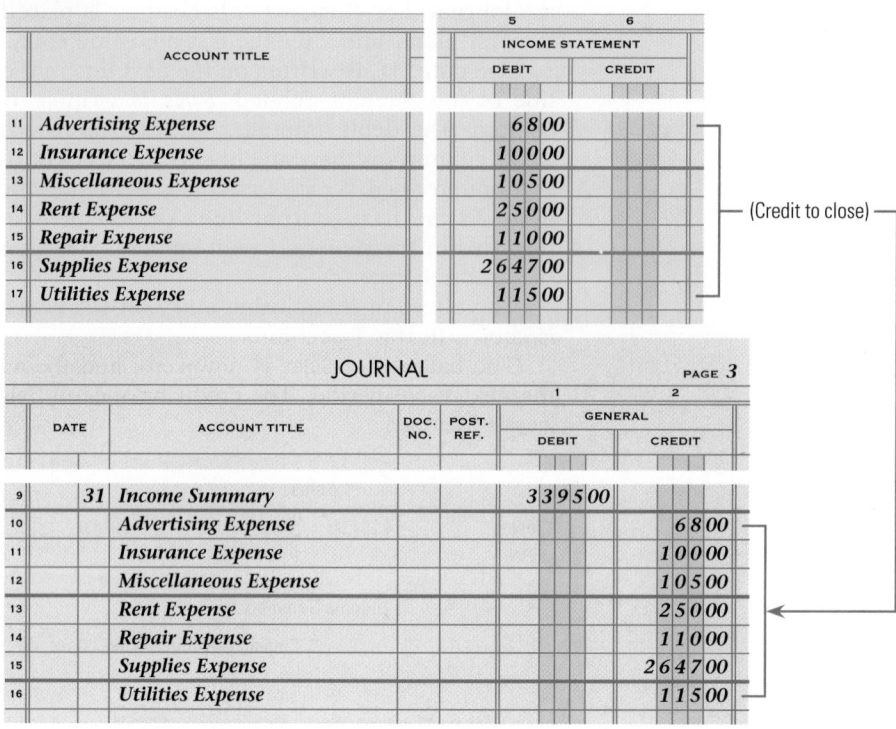

The effect of the closing entry for Rugcare's expense accounts is shown in the T accounts.

Income Summary			
Closing (expenses)	3,395.00	Closing (revenue)	4,291.00
		(New Bal.	896.00)

Advertising Expense			
Bal.	68.00	Closing	68.00
(New Bal. zero)			

Repair Expense			
Bal.	110.00	Closing	110.00
(New Bal. zero)			

Insurance Expense			
Bal.	100.00	Closing	100.00
(New Bal. zero)			

Supplies Expense			
Bal.	2,647.00	Closing	2,647.00
(New Bal. zero)			

Miscellaneous Expense			
Bal.	105.00	Closing	105.00
(New Bal. zero)			

Utilities Expense			
Bal.	115.00	Closing	115.00
(New Bal. zero)			

Rent Expense			
Bal.	250.00	Closing	250.00
(New Bal. zero)			

TEACHING STRATEGIES: TEACHING TIP

First year accounting students often find closing entries the most difficult accounting concept to master. It
is important for students to understand the "why" of closing entries which is to bring temporary accounts
to a zero balance. However, the mechanics of recording closing entries should not be difficult if students
follow the model of taking amounts directly from the work sheet.

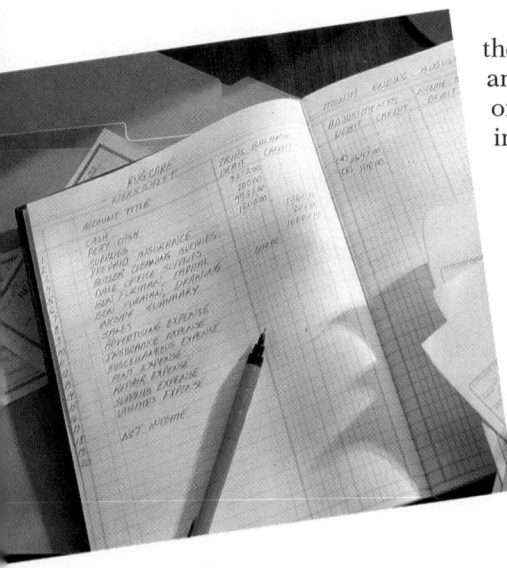

The balance of each expense account is returned to zero, and the accounts are ready for the next fiscal period. The debit balances of the expense accounts are recorded in Income Summary as one debit amount. The balance of Income Summary is the net income for the fiscal period, $896.00.

Closing Entry to Record Net Income or Loss and Close the Income Summary Account

Rugcare's net income is on the partial work sheet shown in Illustration 10-6. The amount of net income increases the owner's capital and, therefore, must be credited to the owner's capital account. The balance of the temporary account, Income Summary, must be reduced to zero to prepare the account for the next fiscal period. The closing entry to record net income and close the income summary account is journalized as shown in Illustration 10-6.

ILLUSTRATION 10-6   Closing entry to record net income and close the income summary account

ACCOUNT TITLE	INCOME STATEMENT	
	5 DEBIT	**6** CREDIT
17		
18	3 3 9 5 00	4 2 9 1 00
19 *Net Income*	8 9 6 00	
20	4 2 9 1 00	4 2 9 1 00
21		
22		
23		

(Capital: credit to record net income)

JOURNAL   PAGE *3*

	DATE	ACCOUNT TITLE	DOC. NO.	POST. REF.	GENERAL	
					1 DEBIT	**2** CREDIT
17	31	*Income Summary*			8 9 6 00	
18		*Ben Furman, Capital*				8 9 6 00
19						
20						
21						
22						
23						

(Income Summary: debit to close)

The date, *31*, is written in the Date column. The title of the account debited, *Income Summary*, is written in the Account Title column. The debit amount, *$896.00*, is recorded in the General Debit column on the same line as the account title. The title of the account credited, *Ben Furman, Capital*, is written in the Account Title column on the next line. The credit amount, *$896.00*, is recorded in the General Credit column on the same line as the account title.

The effect of this closing entry on the general ledger accounts is shown in the T accounts.

The debit to the income summary account, $896.00, reduces the account balance to zero and prepares the account for the next fiscal period. The credit, $896.00, increases the balance of the owner's capital account, Ben Furman, Capital.

If the business incurs a net loss, the closing entry is a debit to the owner's capital account and a credit to the income summary account.

Income Summary

Closing (expenses)		Closing (revenue)	
	3,395.00		4,291.00
Closing	896.00	*(New Bal. zero)*	

Ben Furman, Capital

		Bal.	10,000.00
		Closing (net income)	
			896.00
		(New Bal.	*10,896.00)*

☜☜ **FYI** ☞☞

Most small businesses use the calendar year as their fiscal year because it matches the way the owners have to file their personal income tax returns.

Closing Entry for the Owner's Drawing Account

Withdrawals are assets that the owner takes out of a business and which decrease the amount of the owner's equity. The drawing account is a temporary account that accumulates information separately for each fiscal period. Therefore, the drawing account balance is reduced to zero at the end of one fiscal period to prepare the account for the next fiscal period.

The drawing account is neither a revenue nor an expense account. Therefore, the drawing account is not closed through Income Summary. The drawing account balance is closed directly to the owner's capital account.

The closing entry for the owner's drawing account is journalized as shown in Illustration 10-7. The closing entry is on lines 19 and 20 of the journal.

The date, *31*, is written in the Date column. The title of the account debited, *Ben Furman, Capital*, is written in the Account Title column. The debit amount, *$600.00*, is recorded in the General Debit column on the same line with the account title. The title of the account credited, *Ben Furman, Drawing*, is written in the Account Title column on the next line. The credit amount, *$600.00*, is written in the General Credit column on the same line as the account title.

The effect of the entry to close the drawing account is shown in the T accounts.

The drawing account has a zero balance and is ready for the next fiscal period. The capital account's new balance, $10,296.00, is verified by checking the balance with the amount of capital shown on the balance sheet prepared at the end of the fiscal period. The capital account balance shown on Rugcare's balance sheet in Chapter 9, Illustration 9-12, is $10,296.00. The two amounts are the same, and the capital account balance is verified.

Ben Furman, Capital

Closing	600.00	Bal.	10,000.00
		Net Income	896.00
		(New Bal.	*10,296.00)*

Ben Furman, Drawing

Bal.	600.00	Closing	600.00
(New Bal. zero)			

	ACCOUNT TITLE	BALANCE SHEET	
		7 DEBIT	**8** CREDIT
7	Ben Furman, Capital		1000000
8	Ben Furman, Drawing	60000	— (Credit to close)
9			
10			
11			

JOURNAL   PAGE 3

	DATE	ACCOUNT TITLE	DOC. NO.	POST. REF.	DEBIT	CREDIT	
6		**Closing Entries**					6
7	31	Sales			429100		7
8		Income Summary				429100	8
9	31	Income Summary			339500		9
10		Advertising Expense				6800	10
11		Insurance Expense				10000	11
12		Miscellaneous Expense				10500	12
13		Rent Expense				25000	13
14		Repair Expense				11000	14
15		Supplies Expense				264700	15
16		Utilities Expense				11500	16
17	31	Income Summary			89600		17
18		Ben Furman, Capital				89600	18
19	31	Ben Furman, Capital			60000		19
20		Ben Furman, Drawing				60000	20
21							21
22							22
23							23

FYI

The Department of Labor estimates that by the year 2005, 25 million jobs will be added to the U.S. economy. Most of these new jobs will be in service businesses.

Closing entries are journalized and posted to prepare temporary accounts for the next fiscal period. The income summary account is used to summarize all revenue and expense accounts before recording net income or net loss in the owner's capital account. A summary of closing entries is shown in Illustration 10-8.

To complete a fiscal period, Rugcare records four journal entries to close temporary accounts.

1 Close income statement accounts with credit balances.

2 Close income statement accounts with debit balances.

3 Record the net income or net loss in the owner's capital account and close Income Summary.

4 Close the owner's drawing account.

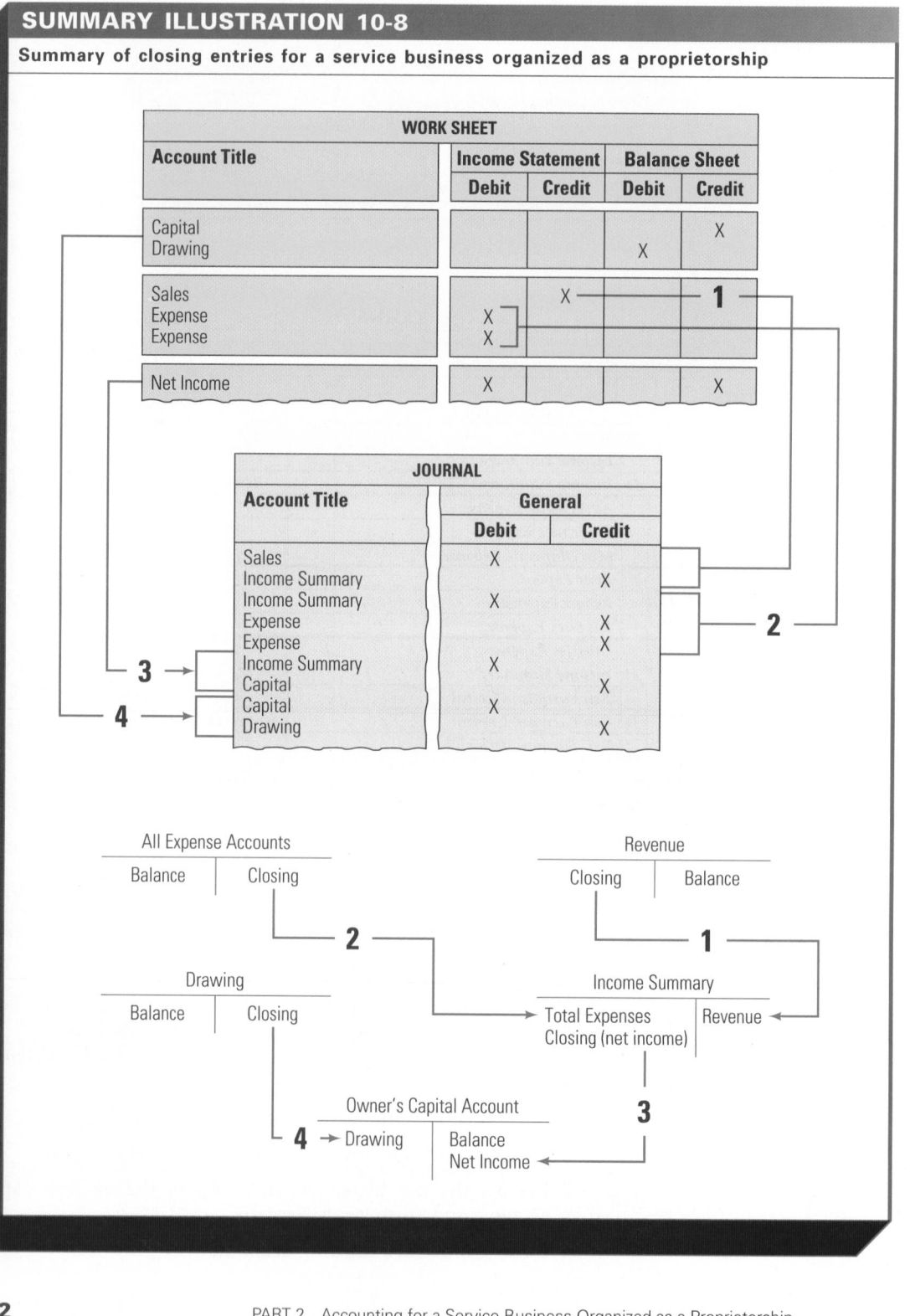

SUMMARY ILLUSTRATION 10-8

Summary of closing entries for a service business organized as a proprietorship

APPLIED SKILLS:
WORD PROCESSING

If you wish to integrate word processing in your accounting course, you may direct students to answer the end-of-chapter Accounting Terms and Questions for Individual Study using their word processing software.

GENERAL LEDGER AFTER ADJUSTING AND CLOSING ENTRIES ARE POSTED

Rugcare's general ledger after the adjusting and closing entries are posted is shown in Illustration 10-9. When an account has a zero balance, lines are drawn in both the Balance Debit and Balance Credit columns. The lines assure a reader that a balance has not been omitted.

ILLUSTRATION 10-9   General ledger accounts after adjusting and closing entries are posted

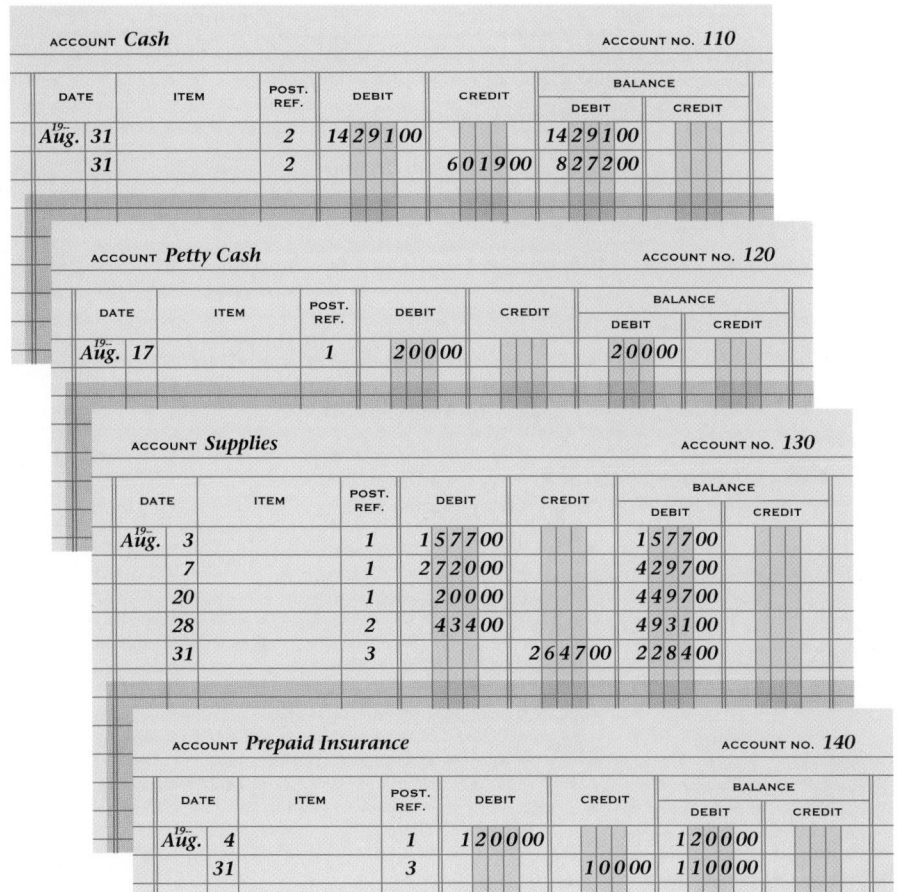

ACCOUNT **Cash**   ACCOUNT NO. **110**

DATE	ITEM	POST. REF.	DEBIT	CREDIT	BALANCE DEBIT	BALANCE CREDIT
Aug. 31		2	14 29 1 00		14 29 1 00	
31		2		6 0 1 9 00	8 27 2 00	

ACCOUNT **Petty Cash**   ACCOUNT NO. **120**

DATE	ITEM	POST. REF.	DEBIT	CREDIT	BALANCE DEBIT	BALANCE CREDIT
Aug. 17		1	2 0 0 00		2 0 0 00	

ACCOUNT **Supplies**   ACCOUNT NO. **130**

DATE	ITEM	POST. REF.	DEBIT	CREDIT	BALANCE DEBIT	BALANCE CREDIT
Aug. 3		1	1 5 7 7 00		1 5 7 7 00	
7		1	2 7 2 0 00		4 2 9 7 00	
20		1	2 0 0 00		4 4 9 7 00	
28		2	4 3 4 00		4 9 3 1 00	
31		3		2 6 4 7 00	2 2 8 4 00	

ACCOUNT **Prepaid Insurance**   ACCOUNT NO. **140**

DATE	ITEM	POST. REF.	DEBIT	CREDIT	BALANCE DEBIT	BALANCE CREDIT
Aug. 4		1	1 2 0 0 00		1 2 0 0 00	
31		3		1 0 0 00	1 1 0 0 00	

- Journalizing and posting adjusting and closing entries was presented earlier in this chapter. Explain that in this lesson we will look at how the debits and credits in the general ledger accounts are verified after the adjusting and closing entries are posted.

- Introduce new vocabulary: post-closing trial balance, accounting cycle.

TEACH

Cover student pages 223–228 "General Ledger After Adjusting and Closing Entries Are Posted," "Post-Closing Trial Balance," and "The Accounting Cycle for a Service Business." Emphasize to students that when posting, if an account has a zero balance lines are drawn in both the Balance Debit and Balance Credit columns to assure the reader that a balance has not been omitted. Direct students' attention to the eight steps for preparing a post-closing trial balance. Point out that these steps can be followed for Rugcare and businesses in general.

ILLUSTRATION 10-9   General ledger accounts after adjusting and closing entries are posted (continued)

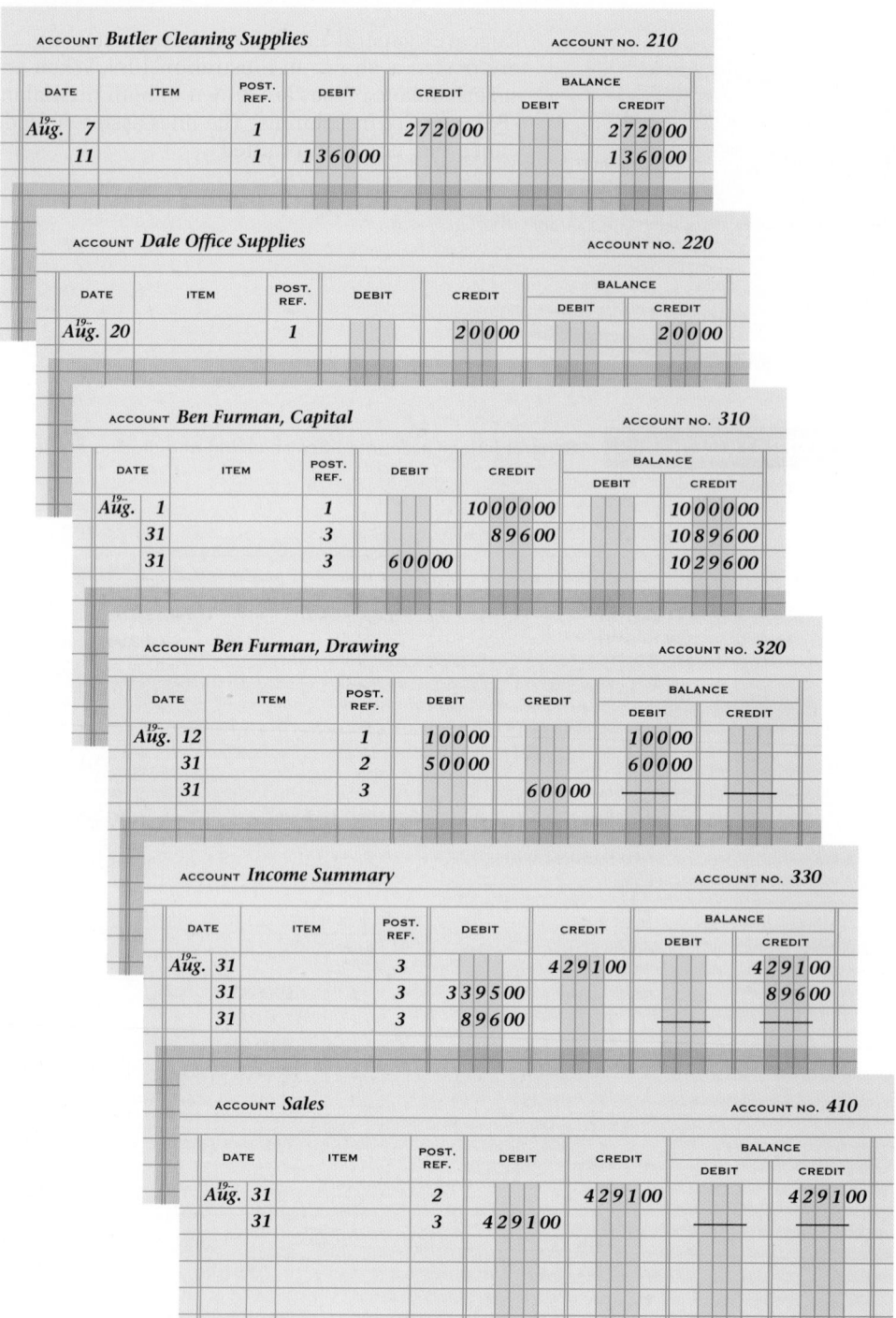

PART 2   Accounting for a Service Business Organized as a Proprietorship

ILLUSTRATION 10-9

General ledger accounts after adjusting and closing entries are posted (continued)

ACCOUNT *Advertising Expense*   ACCOUNT NO. *510*

DATE	ITEM	POST. REF.	DEBIT	CREDIT	BALANCE DEBIT	BALANCE CREDIT
Aug. 14		1	6 8 00		6 8 00	
31		3		6 8 00		

ACCOUNT *Insurance Expense*   ACCOUNT NO. *520*

DATE	ITEM	POST. REF.	DEBIT	CREDIT	BALANCE DEBIT	BALANCE CREDIT
Aug. 31		3	1 0 0 00		1 0 0 00	
31		3		1 0 0 00		

ACCOUNT *Miscellaneous Expense*   ACCOUNT NO. *530*

DATE	ITEM	POST. REF.	DEBIT	CREDIT	BALANCE DEBIT	BALANCE CREDIT
Aug. 13		1	2 5 00		2 5 00	
18		1	7 0 00		9 5 00	
28		2	3 00		9 8 00	
31		2	7 00		1 0 5 00	
31		3		1 0 5 00		

ACCOUNT *Rent Expense*   ACCOUNT NO. *540*

DATE	ITEM	POST. REF.	DEBIT	CREDIT	BALANCE DEBIT	BALANCE CREDIT
Aug. 12		1	2 5 0 00		2 5 0 00	
31		3		2 5 0 00		

ACCOUNT *Repair Expense*   ACCOUNT NO. *550*

DATE	ITEM	POST. REF.	DEBIT	CREDIT	BALANCE DEBIT	BALANCE CREDIT
Aug. 13		1	2 0 00		2 0 00	
20		1	8 5 00		1 0 5 00	
31		2	5 00		1 1 0 00	
31		3		1 1 0 00		

ACCOUNT *Supplies Expense*   ACCOUNT NO. *560*

DATE	ITEM	POST. REF.	DEBIT	CREDIT	BALANCE DEBIT	BALANCE CREDIT
Aug. 31		3	2 6 4 7 00		2 6 4 7 00	
31		3		2 6 4 7 00		

Use Transparency E to demonstrate preparing a post-closing trial balance.

Guided Practice

Write a company's name and some asset, liability, and owner's equity account titles and amounts on the board. Guide students through preparing a post-closing trial balance. Students should have a blank post-closing trial balance form to complete as you guide them through the exercise. Direct students' attention to Illustration 10-10, a post-closing trial balance, for correct formatting.

Independent Practice

Assign Terms 5–6 and Questions 12–13. Assign Problem 10-1, Instruction 3, Study Guide 10, and Mastery Problem 10-M.

ASSESS

Assess student understanding by checking solutions to Independent Practice activities. Review "Summary of an Accounting Cycle for a Service Business." Use Transparency 10-4, Chapter Summary.

Reteach

- Use Demonstration Problem 10C. This problem can be done on the overhead with the students completing the problem at their desks.
- Assign Recycling Problem 10-R.
- Assign the Application Program Disk software to be used with Problem 10-M.

Extend

- Assign Challenge Problem 10-C (the challenge is to complete the work sheet before journalizing adjusting and closing entries).
- Assign Reinforcement Activity 1 Part B.

Enrich

- Use *Automated Accounting 6.0* or higher with Mastery Problem 10-M and Challenge Problem 10-C.
- Assign the Electronic Study Guide Chapter 10.
- Assign *Video Transfer: A Business Simulation.*

ASSESS

• Administer Problem Test Chapter 10.
• Administer a MicroExam test for
  Chapter 10.
• Administer Objective Test No. 2.
• Administer Unit Problem Test No. 2.

| ILLUSTRATION 10-9 | General ledger accounts after adjusting and closing entries are posted (concluded) |

ACCOUNT Utilities Expense   ACCOUNT NO. 570

DATE	ITEM	POST. REF.	DEBIT	CREDIT	BALANCE DEBIT	BALANCE CREDIT
Aug. 12		1	4 5 00		4 5 00	
27		2	7 0 00		1 1 5 00	
31		3		1 1 5 00	—	—

POST-CLOSING TRIAL BALANCE

The word "Post" means "after." The *Post*-Closing Trial Balance is prepared *after* closing entries.

After the closing entries are posted, Rugcare verifies that debits equal credits in the general ledger accounts by preparing a trial balance. A trial balance prepared after the closing entries are posted is called a **post-closing trial balance**.

Only general ledger accounts with balances are included on a post-closing trial balance. The permanent accounts (assets, liabilities, and owner's capital) have balances and do appear on a post-closing trial balance. Because the temporary accounts (income summary, revenue, expense, and drawing) are closed and have zero balances, they do not appear on a post-closing trial balance. Rugcare's post-closing trial balance is shown in Illustration 10-10.

| ILLUSTRATION 10-10 | Post-closing trial balance |

Rugcare
Post-Closing Trial Balance
August 31, 19--

ACCOUNT TITLE	DEBIT	CREDIT
Cash	8 2 7 2 00	
Petty Cash	2 0 0 00	
Supplies	2 2 8 4 00	
Prepaid Insurance	1 1 0 0 00	
Butler Cleaning Supplies		1 3 6 0 00
Dale Office Supplies		2 0 0 00
Ben Furman, Capital		10 2 9 6 00
Totals	11 8 5 6 00	11 8 5 6 00

TEACHING STRATEGIES: TEACHING TIP

As this chapter concludes the accounting cycle for a service business organized as a proprietorship, ask students to describe in their own words the steps for completing the accounting cycle. This will prepare students for the next accounting cycle which is a merchandising business organized as a partnership.

Rugcare uses eight steps to prepare a post-closing trial balance.

1 Write the heading on three lines.

2 Write the titles of all general ledger accounts with balances in the Account Title column.

3 On the same line with each account title, write each account's balance in either the Debit or Credit column.

4 Rule a single line across both amount columns below the last amount, and add each amount column.

5 Compare the two column totals. The two column totals must be the same. The total of all debits must equal the total of all credits in a general ledger. The totals of both columns on Rugcare's post-closing trial balance are the same, $11,856.00. Rugcare's post-closing trial balance shows that the general ledger account balances are in balance and ready for the new fiscal period. If the two column totals are not the same, the errors must be found and corrected before any more work is completed.

6 Write the word, *Totals*, on the line below the last account title.

7 Write the column totals, *$11,856.00*, below the single line.

8 Rule double lines across both amount columns to show that the totals have been verified as correct.

Audit Your Understanding

1. Why are lines drawn in both the Balance Debit and Balance Credit columns when an account has a zero balance?

2. Which accounts go on the post-closing trial balance?

3. Why are temporary accounts omitted from a post-closing trial balance?

AUDIT YOUR UNDERSTANDING

1. To assure a reader that a balance has not been omitted.

2. Only those with balances (permanent accounts).

3. Because they are closed and have zero balances.

THE ACCOUNTING CYCLE FOR A SERVICE BUSINESS

Chapters 2 through 10 describe Rugcare's accounting activities for a one-month fiscal period. The series of accounting activities included in recording financial information for a fiscal period is called an **accounting cycle**. *(CONCEPT: Accounting Period Cycle)* Rugcare's accounting cycle is summarized in Illustration 10-11.

For the next fiscal period, the cycle begins again at Step 1.

APPLIED SKILLS: WRITING ACROSS THE CURRICULUM

Writing paragraphs and short essays. The Cases for Critical Thinking are short, practical applications of the accounting principles developed in the chapter. Some cases are planned to present problems related to the chapter but not specifically discussed and answered in the chapter. These cases present an opportunity for critical thinking and decision making. These cases also require more than a short objective-type response. Therefore, they provide ideal practice in writing paragraphs and short essays.

TEACHING STRATEGIES:
APPLYING VISUALS

Direct students to Summary Illustration 10-11 to review the summary of the accounting cycle for a service business.

SUMMARY ILLUSTRATION 10-11

Summary of an accounting cycle for a service business

1 Source documents are checked for accuracy, and transactions are analyzed into debit and credit parts.

2 Transactions, from information on source documents, are recorded in a journal.

3 Journal entries are posted to the general ledger.

4 A work sheet, including a trial balance, is prepared from the general ledger.

5 Financial statements are prepared from the work sheet.

6 Adjusting and closing entries are journalized from the work sheet.

7 Adjusting and closing entries are posted to the general ledger.

8 Post-closing trial balance of the general ledger is prepared.

PART 2   Accounting for a Service Business Organized as a Proprietorship

TEACHING STRATEGIES: ASSESSMENT BY PORTFOLIO

An ideal specimen for inclusion in a portfolio to demonstrate mastery of the procedures and concepts involved in the complete accounting cycle is an extended activity that simulates the accounting cycle. For this part, the accounting cycle for a service business organized as a proprietorship, you may wish to have students complete and include in their portfolios either Reinforcement Activity 1 Parts A and B or *Video Transfer: A Business Simulation.* You may also wish to include both a manual version and an automated version for either or both of these activities.

ACCOUNTING TERMS

EPT(a)

What is the meaning of each of the following?

1. **adjusting entries**
2. **permanent accounts**
3. **temporary accounts**
4. **closing entries**
5. **post-closing trial balance**
6. **accounting cycle**

QUESTIONS FOR INDIVIDUAL STUDY

EPT(b)

1. Which accounting concept is being applied when information in a general ledger is summarized on a work sheet at the end of each fiscal period?
2. How are adjusting entries identified in a journal?
3. What accounts are affected, and how, by the adjusting entry for supplies?
4. What accounts are affected, and how, by the adjusting entry for prepaid insurance?
5. Why are closing entries journalized and posted at the end of a fiscal period?
6. How is the income summary account used?
7. Why is the income summary account considered unique?
8. What kind of balance will the income summary account have if a business has a net income?
9. What four closing entries are recorded by Rugcare?
10. What effect do withdrawals have on the owner's equity?
11. After the closing entries are posted, how is the balance of the capital account verified?
12. Why is a post-closing trial balance prepared after the closing entries have been posted?
13. What are the eight steps of an accounting cycle?

CASES FOR CRITICAL THINKING

EPT(b)

CASE 1 Thomas Westcott forgot to journalize and post the adjusting entry for prepaid insurance at the end of the June fiscal period. What effect will this omission have on the records of Mr. Westcott's business as of June 30? Explain your answer.

CASE 2 Jason Fields states that his business is so small that he just records supplies and insurance as expenses when he pays for them. Thus, at the end of a fiscal period, Mr. Fields does not record adjusting and closing entries for his business. Do you agree with his accounting procedures? Explain your answer.

APPLIED COMMUNICATIONS

You have learned that accounting information is used by managers to make business decisions. But exactly what kind of decisions does the owner of a local business make? How does accounting information enable the manager to make better decisions?

INSTRUCTIONS:

Identify a local business of personal interest to you. Write five questions you would ask the manager to learn how accounting information is used to make decisions.

ACCOUNTING TERMS

1. **adjusting entries:** Journal entries recorded to update general ledger accounts at the end of a fiscal period. (p. 211)
2. **permanent accounts:** Accounts used to accumulate information from one fiscal period to the next. (p. 214)
3. **temporary accounts:** Accounts used to accumulate information until it is transferred to the owner's capital account. (p. 215)
4. **closing entries:** Journal entries used to prepare temporary accounts for a new fiscal period. (p. 215)
5. **post-closing trial balance:** A trial balance prepared after the closing entries are posted. (p. 226)
6. **accounting cycle:** The series of accounting activities included in recording financial information for a fiscal period. (p. 227)

QUESTIONS FOR INDIVIDUAL STUDY

1. Accounting Period Cycle. (p. 211)
2. By writing the heading "Adjusting Entries" on the line before the first adjusting entry. (p. 211)
3. Supplies Expense is debited; Supplies is credited. (p. 212)
4. Insurance Expense is debited; Prepaid Insurance is credited. (p. 213)
5. To prepare the temporary accounts for recording information for the next fiscal period. (p. 215)
6. To summarize the closing entries for revenue and expense accounts. (p. 215)
7. Because the account does not have a normal balance side. (p. 215)
8. A credit balance. (p. 215)
9. (1) Close income statement accounts with credit balances. (2) Close income statement accounts with debit balances. (3) Record the net income or net loss in the owner's capital account and close Income Summary. (4) Close the owner's drawing account. (p. 220)
10. Withdrawals decrease the amount of the owner's equity. (p. 220)
11. By checking the balance of the capital account with the amount of capital shown on the balance sheet. The two amounts must be the same. (p. 220)
12. To verify that debits equal credits in the general ledger accounts. (p. 226)

13. (a) Check the source documents for accuracy and analyze transactions. (b) Journalize transactions. (c) Post journal entries to the general ledger. (d) Prepare a work sheet. (e) Prepare financial statements. (f) Journalize adjusting and closing entries. (g) Post adjusting and closing entries. (h) Prepare a post-closing trial balance. (p. 228)

CASES FOR CRITICAL THINKING

Case 1 The amount of reported net income will be overstated because Mr. Westcott did not record the amount of insurance expense. In addition, the value of total assets will be overstated. The prepaid insurance account balance will be larger than it should be because the insurance used has not been deducted from the account.

Case 2 No, disagree with his procedures. Even if the business is small, a better picture of assets and expenses will be reported if the asset amounts of supplies and insurance are reported separately from the expense amounts (Adequate Disclosure Concept).

APPLIED COMMUNICATIONS

Student solutions will vary. Possible questions that may be asked are: How often are financial statements prepared? Are any account balances, such as sales, reported during a fiscal period? Why are they reported more often than other account balances? Are employee wages based on sales (e.g., commissions); if so, how are sales determined for payroll purposes?

DRILL FOR UNDERSTANDING   EPT(b)

DRILL 10-D1 Determining accounts affected by adjusting and closing entries

TUTORIAL

Rapid Service Company uses the general ledger accounts that appear on the chart in the working papers that accompany this textbook.

INSTRUCTIONS:

1. For each account title, place a check mark in either Column 2 or 3 to indicate whether the account is affected by an adjusting entry.
2. For each account title, place a check mark in either Column 4 or 5 to indicate whether the account is affected by a closing entry.
3. For each account title, place a check mark in either Column 6 or 7 to indicate whether the account has a balance after the closing entries are posted.

APPLICATION PROBLEM   EPT(c,d,e)

PROBLEM 10-1 Journalizing and posting adjusting and closing entries; preparing a post-closing trial balance

Eiler Company's partial work sheet for the month ended October 31 of the current year is given below. The general ledger accounts are given in the working papers that accompany this textbook. (The general ledger accounts do not show all details for the fiscal period. The "Balance" shown in each account is the account's balance before adjusting and closing entries are posted.)

		3	4	5	6	7	8	
	ACCOUNT TITLE	ADJUSTMENTS		INCOME STATEMENT		BALANCE SHEET		
		DEBIT	CREDIT	DEBIT	CREDIT	DEBIT	CREDIT	
1	Cash					2 6 0 0 00		1
2	Supplies		(a) 1 4 5 00			5 6 0 00		2
3	Prepaid Insurance		(b) 1 9 0 00			2 1 0 00		3
4	Kurtz Supplies						3 0 0 00	4
5	Wiley Supplies						9 0 00	5
6	Norma Delk, Capital						2 8 5 0 00	6
7	Norma Delk, Drawing					2 5 0 00		7
8	Income Summary							8
9	Sales				1 1 0 0 00			9
10	Insurance Expense	(b) 1 9 0 00		1 9 0 00				10
11	Miscellaneous Expense			6 5 00				11
12	Rent Expense			3 2 0 00				12
13	Supplies Expense	(a) 1 4 5 00		1 4 5 00				13
14		3 3 5 00	3 3 5 00	7 2 0 00	1 1 0 0 00	3 6 2 0 00	3 2 4 0 00	14
15	Net Income			3 8 0 00			3 8 0 00	15
16				1 1 0 0 00	1 1 0 0 00	3 6 2 0 00	3 6 2 0 00	16
17								17
18								18
19								19

INSTRUCTIONS:

1. Use page 3 of a journal. Journalize and post the adjusting entries.
2. Continue to use page 3 of the journal. Journalize and post the closing entries.
3. Prepare a post-closing trial balance.

TEACHING STRATEGIES: REINFORCEMENT ACTIVITY

Reinforcement Activity 1, Part B continues Reinforcement Activity 1 beginning with completing a trial balance on a work sheet through adjusting entries, financial statements, closing entries, and a post-closing trial balance. Reinforcement Activity 1, Part A was presented after Chapter 7 and included journalizing and posting daily transactions. Blackline masters for audit tests for Reinforcement Activity 1 are available in the Teacher's Resource Guide in three options: Part A only, Part B only, and Parts A and B combined. In addition, *Automated Accounting 6.0* or higher can be used to automate Reinforcement Activity 1.

MASTERY PROBLEM 10-M **Journalizing and posting adjusting and closing entries; preparing a post-closing trial balance**

AUTOMATED

APPLICATION

Kellerman Services' partial work sheet for the month ended November 30 of the current year is given below. The general ledger accounts are given in the working papers that accompany this textbook. (The general ledger accounts do not show all details for the fiscal period. The "Balance" shown in each account is the account's balance before adjusting and closing entries are posted.)

INSTRUCTIONS:

1. Use page 3 of a journal. Journalize and post the adjusting entries.
2. Continue to use page 3 of the journal. Journalize and post the closing entries.
3. Prepare a post-closing trial balance.

	ACCOUNT TITLE	ADJUSTMENTS 3 DEBIT	ADJUSTMENTS 4 CREDIT	INCOME STATEMENT 5 DEBIT	INCOME STATEMENT 6 CREDIT	BALANCE SHEET 7 DEBIT	BALANCE SHEET 8 CREDIT	
1	Cash					3 5 0 00		1
2	Supplies		(a) 1 9 5 00			7 5 0 00		2
3	Prepaid Insurance		(b) 2 6 0 00			2 8 0 00		3
4	Kern Supplies						5 0 0 00	4
5	Waite Supplies						1 2 0 00	5
6	A. Kellerman, Capital						3 7 2 5 00	6
7	A. Kellerman, Drawing					3 5 0 00		7
8	Income Summary							8
9	Sales				1 5 0 0 00			9
10	Insurance Expense	(b) 2 6 0 00		2 6 0 00				10
11	Miscellaneous Expense			8 5 00				11
12	Rent Expense			4 2 5 00				12
13	Supplies Expense	(a) 1 9 5 00		1 9 5 00				13
14		4 5 5 00	4 5 5 00	9 6 5 00	1 5 0 0 00	4 8 8 0 00	4 3 4 5 00	14
15	Net Income			5 3 5 00			5 3 5 00	15
16				1 5 0 0 00	1 5 0 0 00	4 8 8 0 00	4 8 8 0 00	16

CHALLENGE PROBLEM 10-C **Completing end-of-fiscal-period work**

AUTOMATED

A trial balance on a work sheet for Reed Company is given in the working papers that accompany this textbook.

INSTRUCTIONS:

1. Complete the work sheet.

Adjustment Information, December 31

Supplies on hand	$980.00
Value of prepaid insurance	700.00

2. Use page 3 of a journal. Journalize the adjusting entries.
3. Continue to use page 3 of the journal. Journalize the closing entries.

SIMULATION

To give students an opportunity to apply accounting concepts from the first accounting cycle, assign students to complete *Video Transfer: A Business Simulation. Video Transfer* may also be automated using *Automated Accounting 6.0* or higher.

End-of-Fiscal-Period Work
for a Proprietorship

LESSON PLAN A3

Materials

- Student pages 232–239
- Transparency AA-2 Blank General Journal Input Form
- Input forms for Automating Problems 10-M and 10-C are provided in the working papers that accompany this textbook. If additional input forms are needed, blackline masters are provided in the Accounting Ruling Masters section of the Teacher's Resource Guide.
- Complete solutions for automated problems are provided in the Teacher's Resource Guide.
- *Video Transfer An Automated Business Simulation*
- Software: *Automated Accounting 6.0* or higher; Accounting Textbook Template

Objective

Complete end-of-fiscal period work for a proprietorship using an automated accounting system.

Chapters 8 through 10 describe Rugcare's manual accounting procedures for completing end-of-fiscal-period work. Integrating Automated Accounting Topic 3 describes procedures for using automated accounting software to complete Rugcare's end-of-fiscal-period work. The Automated Accounting Problems contain instructions for using automated accounting software to solve Mastery Problem 10-M and Challenge Problem 10-C, Chapter 10.

COMPLETING END-OF-FISCAL-PERIOD WORK

In automated accounting end-of-fiscal-period reports are generated by the software. The run date used for all end-of-fiscal-period reports is the ending date of the accounting period. Before printing financial statements, the software is directed to prepare a trial balance. The trial balance is prepared to prove equality of general ledger debits and credits. The trial balance is also used to plan adjustments to general ledger accounts.

Preparing a Trial Balance

To prepare a trial balance, the File menu is selected from the menu bar. The Open Accounting File command is then chosen to retrieve the general ledger data base from the template disk.

The Reports menu is selected from the menu bar. The Ledgers command is then chosen from the Reports menu. The Trial Balance is then selected from the Report Selection menu to display the trial balance as shown in Illustration T3-1.

```
                            Rugcare
                         Trial Balance
                           08/31/--
-----------------------------------------------------------------
Acct.    Account
Number   Title                              Debit          Credit
-----------------------------------------------------------------
110      Cash                              8272.00
120      Petty Cash                         200.00
130      Supplies                          4931.00
140      Prepaid Insurance                 1200.00
210      Butler Cleaning Supplies                         1360.00
220      Dale Office Supplies                              200.00
310      Ben Furman, Capital                             10000.00
320      Ben Furman, Drawing                600.00
410      Sales                                            4291.00
510      Advertising Expense                 68.00
530      Miscellaneous Expense              105.00
540      Rent Expense                       250.00
550      Repair Expense                     110.00
570      Utilities Expense                  115.00
                                        ----------      ----------
         Totals                          15851.00        15851.00
                                        ==========      ==========
```

Recording Adjusting Entries

Adjusting entries are recorded on a general journal input form. Rugcare records two adjusting entries. (1) An adjusting entry to bring the supplies account up to date. (2) An adjusting entry to bring the prepaid insurance account up to date.

Rugcare has the following adjustment data on August 31.

Adjustment Information, August 31

Supplies on hand...............................	$2,284.00
Value of prepaid insurance	1,100.00

The information needed to journalize the adjusting entries is obtained from the trial balance. The expense account, Supplies

FYI

Dollar signs and cent signs are not keyed when using Automated Accounting 6.0 software. When the cents are zero (.00), key only the dollar amount. The software automatically assigns the .00.

Guided Practice

Students should be at the computers. Guide students through booting the software and loading Optional Problem DB-3A from the template. Instruct students to complete the end-of-fiscal-period work as you go step-by-step through the procedures.

Independent Practice

Assign Automating Problem 10-M.

Expense, is increased by a debit, $2,647.00, the value of supplies used. The asset account, Supplies, is decreased by a credit, $2,647.00, the value of the supplies used. The journal entry to record this adjustment is on lines 1 and 2 of the general journal input form shown in Illustration T3-2. The abbreviation for adjusting entries, *Adj. Ent.*, is written in the Reference column for each entry.

The expense account, Insurance Expense, is increased by a debit, $100.00, the value of insurance used. The asset account, Prepaid Insurance, is decreased by a credit, $100.00, the value of insurance used. The journal entry to record this adjustment is shown on lines 3 and 4 of Illustration T3-2.

ILLUSTRATION T3-2	General journal report for adjusting entries

GENERAL JOURNAL
Input Form

RUN DATE *08,31,--* MM DD YY

	DATE MM/DD	REFERENCE	ACCOUNT NO.	CUSTOMER/ VENDOR NO.	DEBIT	CREDIT	
1	08,31	Adj. Ent.	560		2647 00		1
2	/		130			2647 00	2
3	,31	Adj. Ent.	520		100 00		3
4	/		140			100 00	4
21	/						21
22	/						22
23	/						23
24	/						24
25	/						25
	PAGE TOTALS				2747 00	2747 00	
	FINAL TOTALS				2747 00	2747 00	

Processing Adjusting Entries

To process adjusting entries, the Journals menu is selected from the menu bar. The General Journal command is chosen to display the data entry window for keying adjustment data.

After all lines on the input form have been keyed and posted, the Reports menu is selected from the menu bar. The Journals command is selected from the Reports menu. The General Journal report is chosen from the Report Selection menu. This selection displays the Selection Options screen. The *Ok* button is pushed to display the general journal report. The general journal report is checked for accuracy by comparing the report totals, $2,747.00, with the totals on the general journal input form. Because the totals are the same, the general journal report is assumed to be correct. The general journal report is printed, as shown in Illustration T3-3, and filed for future reference.

CAREERS IN ACCOUNTING

DATA ENTRY CLERK

- *Compiles, sorts, and verifies accuracy of source documents*
- *Prepares computer input forms*
- *Enters data from input forms into computer*
- *Verifies accuracy of data entered with computer printouts*

SOFTWARE FOCUS

The Automated Accounting Problems in this Integrating Automated Accounting Topic use Mastery Problem 10-M and Challenge Problem 10-C, Chapter 10, which students have already completed manually. Refer students back to these problems to complete the input forms. The problem instructions in *Automated Accounting 6.0* will lead students through automating the problems.

```
                            Rugcare
                         General Journal
                           08/31/--
------------------------------------------------------------------------
Date   Refer.   V/C Acct.  Title                    Debit      Credit
------------------------------------------------------------------------
08/31  Adj.Ent.     560    Supplies Expense        2647.00
08/31  Adj.Ent.     130    Supplies                            2647.00

08/31  Adj.Ent.     520    Insurance Expense        100.00
08/31  Adj.Ent.     140    Prepaid Insurance                    100.00

                                                   ---------  ---------
                           Totals                   2747.00    2747.00
                                                   =========  =========
```

PROCESSING FINANCIAL STATEMENTS

To process the income statement, the Reports menu is selected from the menu bar. The Financial Statements command is then selected from the menu. The Income Statement option is chosen from the Report Selection window to display the income statement. The income statement is printed, as shown in Illustration T3-4, and filed for future reference.

ILLUSTRATION T3-4   Income statement

```
                               Rugcare
                          Income Statement
                       For Period Ended 08/31/--
------------------------------------------------------------------------
                          *****Monthly*****      *****Yearly*****
                          Amount    Percent      Amount    Percent
------------------------------------------------------------------------
Operating   Revenue
--------------------------
Sales                     4291.00    100.00      4291.00    100.00
                         --------- ---------    --------- ---------
Total Operating Revenue   4291.00    100.00      4291.00    100.00

Operating   Expenses
--------------------------
Advertising Expense         68.00      1.58        68.00      1.58
Insurance Expense          100.00      2.33       100.00      2.33
Miscellaneous Expense      105.00      2.45       105.00      2.45
Rent Expense               250.00      5.83       250.00      5.83
Repair Expense             110.00      2.56       110.00      2.56
Supplies Expense          2647.00     61.69      2647.00     61.69
Utilities Expense          115.00      2.68       115.00      2.68
                         --------- ---------    --------- ---------
Total Operating Expenses  3395.00     79.12      3395.00     79.12
                         --------- ---------    --------- ---------
Net Income                 896.00     20.88       896.00     20.88
                         ========= =========    ========= =========
```

The income statement prepared by Rugcare's automated accounting software provides both current month and yearly amounts and percentages. This additional data allows Mr. Furman to analyze both monthly and yearly performance. As the month of August was Rugcare's first month of operation, monthly and yearly amounts are the same.

To process the balance sheet, the Reports menu is selected from the menu bar. The Financial Statements command is then selected from the Reports menu. The Balance Sheet option is selected from the Report Selection window to display the balance sheet. The balance sheet is printed, as shown in Illustration T3-5, and filed for future reference.

A balance sheet may be prepared in one of two forms: (1) account form or (2) report form. An account form of balance sheet lists assets on the left and equities on the right. Rugcare's manual accounting system uses the account form of balance sheet. A report form of balance sheet lists the assets, liabilities, and owner's equity vertically. Illustration T3-5 is a report form of balance sheet.

FYI

To prevent the computer from overheating, avoid blocking air vents.

ILLUSTRATION T3-5   Balance sheet

```
                              Rugcare
                          Balance Sheet
                            08/31/--

Assets
----------
Cash                          8272.00
Petty Cash                     200.00
Supplies                      2284.00
Prepaid Insurance             1100.00
                            ----------
Total Assets                              11856.00
                                          ==========
Liabilities
----------------------
Butler Cleaning Supplies      1360.00
Dale Office Supplies           200.00
                            ----------
Total Liabilities                          1560.00
Owner's  Equity
----------------------------
Ben Furman, Capital          10000.00
Ben Furman, Drawing           -600.00
Net Income                     896.00
                            ----------
Total Owner's Equity                      10296.00
                                          ----------
Total Liabilities & Equity                11856.00
                                          ==========
```

Closing Temporary Accounts

In automated accounting the software contains instructions for closing temporary accounts. The Options menu is selected from the menu bar. The Period-End Closing command is selected from the Options menu to close all temporary accounts.

Processing a Post-Closing Trial Balance

After the financial statements have been prepared and closing entries have been posted, a post-closing trial balance is prepared. A **post-closing trial balance** is a trial balance that is prepared after closing entries have been posted.

To process a post-closing trial balance, the Reports menu is selected from the menu bar. The Ledgers menu command is selected and the Trial Balance is then chosen from the Report Selection menu. The post-closing trial balance is printed, as shown in Illustration T3-6, and is filed for future reference.

ILLUSTRATION T3-6   Post-closing trial balance

```
                        Rugcare
                     Trial Balance
                       08/31/--
------------------------------------------------------------
Acct.   Account
Number  Title                          Debit          Credit
------------------------------------------------------------
110     Cash                         8272.00
120     Petty Cash                    200.00
130     Supplies                     2284.00
140     Prepaid Insurance            1100.00
210     Butler Cleaning Supplies                     1360.00
220     Dale Office Supplies                          200.00
310     Ben Furman, Capital                         10296.00
                                    ----------      ----------
        Totals                      11856.00        11856.00
                                    ==========      ==========
```

COMPARISON OF MANUAL AND AUTOMATED ACCOUNTING CYCLE

The accounting cycle is the same for both manual and automated accounting, only the procedures change. A comparison is shown in Illustration T3-7.

Comparison of manual and automated accounting cycle

Manual Accounting Cycle	Automated Accounting Cycle
Analyze source documents	Analyze source documents
Record transactions in a journal	Record transactions on an input form and key
Post journal entries	Select posting command
Prepare a work sheet	Print a trial balance
(Adjustments are planned on the work sheet)	Analyze adjusting entries using the trial balance; record adjusting entries on input form, key, and post
Prepare financial statements	Print financial statements
Journalize and post adjusting entries	(Adjusting entries already recorded)
Record closing entries	Select closing command
Prepare a post-closing trial balance	Print a post-closing trial balance

OPTIONAL PROBLEM DB-3A

Rugcare's general ledger data base is on the accounting textbook template. If you wish to process Rugcare's end-of-fiscal-period work using automated accounting software, load the *Automated Accounting 6.0* or higher software. Select Data Base 3A (DB-3A) from the template disk. Read the Problem Instructions screen. Use Illustration T3-2 and follow the procedures described to process Rugcare's end-of-fiscal-period work.

AUTOMATED ACCOUNTING PROBLEMS

AUTOMATING MASTERY PROBLEM 10-M Journalizing and posting adjusting entries; end-of-fiscal-period work for a proprietorship

INSTRUCTIONS:

1. Use the end-of-fiscal period work for Mastery Problem 10-M, Chapter 10. Use November 30 of the current year as the run date.

2. Load the *Automated Accounting 6.0* or higher software. Select data base F10-M (First-Year Course Problem 10-M) from the accounting textbook template. Read the Problem Instructions screen.

3. Select File from the menu bar and choose the Save As menu command. Key the path to the drive and directory that contains your data files. Save the data base with a file name of XXX10M (where XXX are your initials).

4. Display/print a trial balance.

5. Record the adjusting entries on a general journal input form using the following information. Use the account numbers from the trial balance that was printed in Instruction 4.

Adjustment Information, November 30

Supplies on hand.	$750.00
Value of prepaid insurance.	280.00

6. Key the adjusting entries from the general journal input form.

INTEGRATING AUTOMATED ACCOUNTING—TOPIC 3

OPTIONAL PROBLEM

OPTIONAL PROBLEM DB-3A provides students with a hands-on learning activity. By keying the input forms illustrated in this topic, students have an opportunity for guided practice before actually working a problem independently. Refer to the OPTIONAL PROBLEM DB-3A for information about automating this topic.

7. Display/print the general journal report.
8. Display/print the income statement.
9. Display/print the balance sheet.
10. Perform period-end closing.
11. Display/print the post-closing trial balance.

AUTOMATED

AUTOMATING CHALLENGE PROBLEM 10-C Completing end-of-fiscal period work

INSTRUCTIONS:

1. Load the *Automated Accounting 6.0* or higher software. Select data base F10-C from the accounting textbook template. Read the Problem Instructions screen.
2. Select File from the menu bar and choose the Save As menu command. Key the path to the drive and directory that contains your data files. Save the data base with a file name of XXX10C (where XXX are your initials).
3. Display/print a trial balance.
4. Record the adjusting entries on a general journal input form using the following information. Use the account numbers from the trial balance that was printed in Instruction 3.

Adjustment Information, December 31

Supplies on hand.	$980.00
Value of prepaid insurance.	700.00

5. Key the adjusting entries from the general journal input form.
6. Display/print the general journal report.
7. Display/print the income statement.
8. Display/print the balance sheet.
9. Perform period-end closing.
10. Display/print the post-closing trial balance.

An Accounting Cycle for a Proprietorship: End-of-Fiscal-Period Work

AUTOMATED

The general ledger prepared in Reinforcement Activity 1, Part A, is needed to complete Reinforcement Activity 1, Part B.

Reinforcement Activity 1, Part B, includes end-of-fiscal-period activities studied in Chapters 8 through 10.

WORK SHEET

INSTRUCTIONS:

12. Prepare a trial balance on a work sheet. Use a one-month fiscal period ended May 31 of the current year.

13. Analyze the following adjustment information into debit and credit parts. Record the adjustments on the work sheet.

Adjustment Information, May 31

Supplies on hand $515.00
Value of prepaid insurance 800.00

14. Total and rule the Adjustments columns.

15. Extend the up-to-date account balances to the Balance Sheet and Income Statement columns.

16. Complete the work sheet.

FINANCIAL STATEMENTS

17. Prepare an income statement. Figure and record the component percentages for sales, total expenses, and net income. Round percentage calculations to the nearest 0.1%.

18. Prepare a balance sheet.

ADJUSTING ENTRIES

19. Use page 3 of the journal. Journalize and post the adjusting entries.

CLOSING ENTRIES

20. Continue using page 3 of the journal. Journalize and post the closing entries.

POST-CLOSING TRIAL BALANCE

21. Prepare a post-closing trial balance.

240

Top border: "A BUSINESS SIMULATION A BUSINESS SIMULATION A BUSINESS SIMULATION A BUSINESS SIMULATION A BUSINESS SIMULATION"

This simulation covers the transactions completed by Video Transfer, a service business organized as a proprietorship. Video Transfer begins business on September 1 of the current year. The business produces personal videos for such events as weddings and family reunions. In addition, the business also transfers home movies and slides to video tape.

The activities included in the accounting cycle for Video Transfer are listed below. The company uses a journal and a general ledger similar to those described for Rugcare in Part 2.

This simulation is available from the publisher in either manual or automated versions.

VIDEO TRANSFER

A BUSINESS SIMULATION

The following activities are included in this simulation.

1. Journalizing transactions in a journal.
2. Forwarding column totals to a new journal page.
3. Preparing a bank statement reconciliation and recording a bank service charge.
4. Proving cash.
5. Proving and ruling a journal.
6. Posting from a journal to a general ledger.
7. Preparing a trial balance on a work sheet.
8. Recording adjustments on a work sheet.
9. Completing a work sheet.
10. Preparing financial statements (income statement and balance sheet).
11. Journalizing and posting adjusting entries.
12. Journalizing and posting closing entries.
13. Preparing a post-closing trial balance.

241

Now the teaching strategies box.

TEACHING STRATEGIES: ASSESSMENT BY PORTFOLIO

An ideal specimen for inclusion in a portfolio to demonstrate mastery of the procedures and concepts involved in the complete accounting cycle is an extended activity that simulates the accounting cycle. For this part, the accounting cycle for a service business organized as a proprietorship, you may wish to have students complete and include in their portfolios either Reinforcement Activity 1, Parts A and B or *Video Transfer: A Business Simulation*. You may also wish to include both a manual version and an automated version for either or both of these activities.

PART 3 OVERVIEW

STUDENT EDITION

STUDENT FEATURES

Multicultural Awareness

Diversity Today, page 246
Ancient Greece and Egypt, page 286
Arabic Numerals, page 332
Peru, page 393
Asia Minor, page 438

Professional Business Ethics

Am I Cheating The Company? page 254
Who Owns My Time? pages 358, 359

Global Perspective

International Work Week, page 271
International Telephone Communication, page 415

Careers In Accounting

Timekeeper, page 328
Payroll Clerk, page 351
Computer Programmer, page 460

Personal Visions In Business

Jan Robbins, page 287
Brian Choi, page 403
Judy Sims, page 443

Spreadsheet Options

Using Functions To Prepare A Payroll Register, page 333

Audit Your Understanding

This student activity can be found on pages 253, 259, 273, 277, 290, 298, 302, 330, 334, 341, 344, 360, 364, 368, 398, 399, 404, 420, 428, 437, 452

APPLIED SKILLS

Applied Communications

Pages 279, 346, 431

Applied Math

Pages 267, 275, 276, 279, 280, 281, 328, 329, 330, 336, 338, 339, 342, 343, 346, 347, 357, 360, 362, 370, 371, 407, 413, 417

SOFTWARE APPLICATIONS

Automated Accounting 6.0 Problems 13-C, (Optional Problem DB-4A); 15-M, 15-C, (Optional Problem DB-5A); 18-1, 18-C, 18-M, (Optional Problem DB-6A); Reinforcement Activity 2
Spreadsheet Template, Problems 14-2, 14-3, 14-C, 15-2, 17-M, 17-C
Accounting Tutorial, Units 4–6
Application Program Disk, Problems 11-M, 12-M, 15-M, 15-C, 16-M, 18-M
Study Guide Software for each chapter

APPLIED SKILLS

Communications, pages 279, 329, 431

Language Arts, pages 260, 270, 299, 340, 359, 402, 426, 440

Writing Across the Curriculum, pages 252, 277, 297, 338, 368, 397, 422, 445

Building Study Skills, pages 249, 268, 287, 352, 355, 439

Mathematics, pages 267, 356, 403, 413

Word Processing, pages 255, 272, 303, 335, 366, 395, 425, 448

TEACHING STRATEGIES

Accounting Pedagogy, pages 244, 245, 266, 284, 309, 326, 350, 374, 386, 410, 434, 458

Assessment by Portfolio, pages 373, 382, 450, 466

Different Learning Abilities, pages 249, 256, 257, 275, 296, 299, 301, 314, 337, 360, 362, 364, 366, 376, 397, 398, 423, 424, 447, 463

Different Learning Styles, pages 248, 250, 253, 255, 259, 269, 270, 272, 276, 286, 288, 291, 292, 294, 417, 418, 419

Cooperative Learning, pages 252, 254, 258, 269, 317, 338, 367, 378, 383, 391, 416, 461, 466

Expanding Beyond the Classroom, pages 339, 390

Applying Visuals, pages 260, 277, 302, 315, 336, 344, 357, 368, 375, 402, 429, 453, 460

Teaching Tip, pages 244, 247, 251, 256, 268, 271, 274, 275, 285, 289, 290, 291, 293, 295, 300, 324, 327, 331, 334, 353, 358, 365, 367, 379, 387, 388, 392, 394, 395, 396, 399, 412, 414, 415, 419, 427, 444, 446, 464

Software Focus, pages 245, 266, 284, 323, 326, 350, 374, 381, 400, 410, 434, 451, 458, 466

Optional Problem, pages 310, 375, 462

Safety and Health, pages 316, 377, 463

Simulation, pages 372, 450

Milestone, page 451

Reinforcement Activity, pages 373, 381, 449, 466

ASSESSMENT

Assessment by Portfolio
MicroExam software for each chapter
Problem Test for each chapter
Unit Problem Test No. 3 (11–13)
Unit Problem Test No. 4 (14–15)
Unit Problem Test No. 5 (16–18)
Unit Objective Test No. 3 (11–13)
Unit Objective Test No. 4 (14–15)
Unit Objective Test No. 5 (16–18)

SOFTWARE

Automated Accounting 6.0
Accounting Tutorial
Electronic Auditor
Application Program Disk
Study Guide Software

MicroExam
Excel (spreadsheet software)
Pagemaker (desktop publishing software)
Works (integrated software)

BIBLIOGRAPHY

AICPA. *Upward Mobility of Women Special Committee: Report to the AICPA Board of Directors.*

Bieg, Bernard J., and B. Lewis Keeling. *Payroll Accounting.* (Revised Annually) Cincinnati: South-Western Publishing Co.

Gordon, Gus. *Understanding Financial Statements.* Cincinnati: South-Western Publishing Co., 1992.

Kagan, S. *Cooperative Learning Resources for Teachers.* San Juan Capistrano: Resources for Teachers, 1989.

Marzano, Robert J. *A Different Kind of Classroom: Teaching with Dimensions of Learning.* Association for Supervision and Curriculum Development, Alexandria, VA, 1992.

U.S. Department of Labor. *Occupational Outlook Handbook.*

Periodicals

Accounting, Organizations and Society, Pergamon Press, Inc., Tarrytown, NY.

American Accounting Association Newsletter, Sarasota, FL.

Journal of Accounting Education, Pergamon Press, Inc., Tarrytown, NY.

Transpacific, Malibu, CA. (Multicultural awareness)

Technology

AICPA. *It All Adds Up,* 1989. (Video)

AICPA. *TOTAL (Total On-line Tax and Accounting Library).* (Tax and accounting on-line database)

PART 3 OPENER

Accounting for a Merchandising Business Organized as a Partnership

Access to Capital

Management Talent

Ease of Formation

Tax Benefits

GENERAL GOALS

1. Know accounting terminology related to an accounting system for a merchandising business organized as a partnership.

2. Understand accounting concepts and practices related to an accounting system for a merchandising business organized as a partnership.

3. Demonstrate accounting procedures used in an accounting system for a merchandising business organized as a partnership.

presented to automate recording of the transactions presented in Chapters 11 and 12 and posting procedures from Chapter 13.

Chapters 14 and 15 guide students through payroll concepts. Chapter 14 covers the calculations for employee earnings and deductions and the completion of a payroll register and employee earnings records. Chapter 15 completes the presentation with the calculations for employer payroll taxes, the journal entries for payroll transactions, and payroll reports. After Chapter 15, Integrating Automated Accounting Topic 5 provides the opportunity to automate payroll procedures.

Chapter 16 begins the end-of-fiscal-period work by describing the work sheet and adjustments for a merchandising business.

Chapter 17 continues the end-of-fiscal-period work with the preparation of financial statements.

Chapter 18 completes the accounting cycle with the recording of adjusting and closing entries and the preparation of a post-closing trial balance. After Chapter 18, Integrating Automated Accounting Topic 6 furnishes instruction and practice in automating end-of-fiscal-period work to complete the automated accounting cycle.

Chapters 11–18 model the accounting cycle for the second time. This time, the business is a merchandising business and a partnership and has more kinds of transactions than the service business in Part 2. All accounting concepts and procedures in this part are described within the context of the accounting cycle so students can see how each procedure contributes to the overall financial picture of the business. Students will benefit from applying these concepts to completing a simulation, Viking Marine, and/or a reinforcement activity. The Stellar Attractions Pegboard Payroll Simulation can also be used to reinforce payroll procedures and provide realistic experience in using a pegboard.

Reinforcement Activity 1 is divided into Parts A and B. Part A may be completed after Chapter 15. Part B may be completed after Chapter 18. However, Part A may be delayed until after Chapter 18 to complete Parts A and B as a single unit. The audit test is divided into two parts that may be completed either separately or as a single test.

Part 3 presents a complete accounting cycle for a merchandising business organized as a partnership. The primary differences between a merchandising business and a service business are that a merchandising business purchases merchandise for resale, charges sales tax on sales of merchandise, and includes a cost of merchandise sold section on the income statement.

The partnership form of business organization requires additional capital accounts for the partners. The business in this part uses subsidiary ledgers and has a payroll system for compensating the employees.

Chapters 11 and 12 present the daily transactions of a merchandising business. Merchandise is purchased for

cash and on account, and merchandise is sold for cash and on account; in addition, credit card sales are described.

Chapter 13 ties the previous two chapters together by describing posting to the general ledger and the accounts payable and accounts receivable subsidiary ledgers. After Chapter 13, Integrating Automated Accounting Topic 4 is

CHAPTER 11 OVERVIEW

Chapter 11 begins by describing the 11-column expanded multi-column journal that is used to record transactions in this part. The journal's evolution from the 5-column journal is described and illustrated to show how the needs of the business determine what form of journal is used. The purchase of merchandise, a transaction unique to merchandising businesses, is introduced. Purchasing merchandise on account incurs a liability that must be paid; therefore, cash payments comprise the second part of this

GUIDE TO ACHIEVING LEARNING OBJECTIVES

Enabling Performance Tasks	TEACH	APPLY		EXTEND/ENRICH					
	Lesson Plans	Drills for Understanding	Application Problems	Mastery Problems	Challenge Problems	Cases for Critical Thinking	Recycling Problems	Reinforcement Activity	
a. Define accounting terms related to purchases and cash payments for a merchandising business.	11-1, 11-2								
b. Identify accounting concepts and practices related to purchases and cash payments for a merchandising business.	11-1, 11-2					Case 1			
c. Analyze purchases and cash payments transactions for a merchandising business.	11-1, 11-2	11-D1	11-1	11-M	11-C	Case 2	11-R	2A	
d. Journalize purchases and cash payments transactions for a merchandising business.	11-1, 11-2	11-D2	11-1	11-M	11-C		11-R	2A	

ENRICHMENT

SPECIAL FEATURES	TECHNOLOGY CONNECTION
Professional Business Ethics, page 254	Accounting Tutorial Unit 4
Multicultural Awareness, page 246	Application Program Disk Problem 11-M
	Electronic Study Guide

chapter. The chapter concludes with the analysis of transactions for partners' withdrawals of cash and merchandise and correcting entries. T accounts illustrate the normal balance sides of the new accounts Purchases and Accounts Payable.

The accounting concept, *Historical Cost,* is described for the first time in this chapter.

	INFORMAL ASSESSMENT		FORMAL ASSESSMENT				
	Study Guide	Audit Your Understanding	Chapter MicroExam	Chapter Problem Test	Unit Problem Test	Unit Objective Test	Portfolio
Unit A		✓	✓			✓	
		✓	✓			✓	
Unit B		✓		✓	✓		✓
Unit B				✓	✓		✓

NEW, REVIEW, AND EXTENSION

ACTIVITIES/CONCEPTS/TRANSACTIONS	NEW	REVIEW/ EXTENSION
Partnerships	✓	
Analyzing transactions into debit and credit parts		✓
Using an expanded 11-column multi-column journal	✓	
Using a journal with special amount columns		✓
Purchase merchandise for cash	✓	
Purchase merchandise on account	✓	
Buying supplies for cash		✓
Buying supplies on account		✓
Cash payment on account		✓
Cash payment of an expense		✓
Cash payment to replenish petty cash		✓
Cash withdrawals by owners	✓	
Merchandise withdrawals by owners		✓
Correcting entries	✓	

TEACHING MATERIALS

Teacher's Wraparound Edition of Text
Teacher's Resource Guide
Teacher's Edition of Working Papers
Teacher's Edition of the Demonstration/Recycling Problems
Teaching Transparencies
Accounting Tutorial Manual
MicroExam

A chart of accounts for the business that is used to illustrate each part of this textbook is provided at the beginning of each part. Charts of accounts are extremely important to companies because they drive the accounting system. Employees usually cannot even receive reimbursement for expenses without knowing which account the expense should be charged to. Pedagogically, the chart of accounts provides the following information: (1) Classification for each account—needed to determine how a transaction is analyzed. (2) Permanent accounts (balance sheet accounts) and temporary accounts (income statement accounts)—assist in analyzing transactions and recording closing entries. (3) Account number for every general ledger and subsidiary ledger account—critical information in automated accounting, since transactions are entered by account number rather than account title.

CHART OF ACCOUNTS

This second chart of accounts is for a merchandising business organized as a partnership. The cost of merchandise section is new to this part which introduces merchandising businesses. In the assets section, the asset account Merchandise Inventory also appears for the first time.

The subsidiary ledgers are shown at the bottom of the page and the controlling accounts are shown in the assets and liabilities sections. Other new liability accounts are the payroll tax liability accounts and Sales Tax Payable.

The owners' equity section is similar to that of a proprietorship, except that there are capital and drawing accounts for each of the partners.

CHART OF ACCOUNTS
GENERAL LEDGER

Balance Sheet Accounts

(1000) ASSETS

1110	Cash
1120	Petty Cash
1130	Accounts Receivable
1140	Merchandise Inventory
1145	Supplies—Office
1150	Supplies—Store
1160	Prepaid Insurance

(2000) LIABILITIES

2110	Accounts Payable
2120	Employee Income Tax Payable
2130	FICA Tax Payable
2140	Sales Tax Payable
2150	Unemployment Tax Payable—Federal
2160	Unemployment Tax Payable—State
2170	Health Insurance Premiums Payable
2180	U.S. Savings Bonds Payable
2190	United Way Donations Payable

(3000) OWNERS' EQUITY

3110	Amy Kramer, Capital
3120	Amy Kramer, Drawing
3130	Dario Mesa, Capital
3140	Dario Mesa, Drawing
3150	Income Summary

Income Statement Accounts

(4000) OPERATING REVENUE

4110	Sales

(5000) COST OF MERCHANDISE

5110	Purchases

(6000) OPERATING EXPENSES

6110	Advertising Expense
6120	Credit Card Fee Expense
6130	Insurance Expense
6140	Miscellaneous Expense
6150	Payroll Taxes Expense
6160	Rent Expense
6170	Salary Expense
6175	Supplies Expense—Office
6180	Supplies Expense—Store
6190	Utilities Expense

SUBSIDIARY LEDGERS

Accounts Receivable Ledger

110	Ashley Delivery
120	Autohaus Service
130	Friendly Auto Service
140	Keystone Delivery
150	Powell Rent-A-Car
160	Wood Sales & Service

Accounts Payable Ledger

210	Antelo Supply
220	Bell Office Products
230	Filtrex Tires
240	Nilon Motor Parts
250	Q-Ban Distributors
260	Veloz Automotive

The charts of accounts for CarLand are illustrated above for ready reference as you study Part 3 of this textbook.

TEACHING STRATEGIES: TEACHING TIP

Emphasize that students should refer to this chart of accounts throughout their study of Part 3. It will help them determine classification of accounts, which accounts are temporary and permanent accounts, and what account numbers to use for automated accounting. It will also be a useful reference for performing file maintenance activities.

11

Journalizing Purchases and Cash Payments

ENABLING PERFORMANCE TASKS

After studying Chapter 11, you will be able to:

a Define accounting terms related to purchases and cash payments for a merchandising business.

b Identify accounting concepts and practices related to purchases and cash payments for a merchandising business.

c Analyze purchases and cash payments transactions for a merchandising business.

d Journalize purchases and cash payments transactions for a merchandising business.

TERMS PREVIEW

partnership • partner • merchandising business • merchandise • cost of merchandise • markup • vendor • purchase on account • invoice • purchase invoice • terms of sale • correcting entry

245

MULTICULTURAL AWARENESS

The MULTICULTURAL AWARENESS feature is intended to expose students to the concept that our society is composed of people from many different cultural backgrounds. These features show both past contributions of many cultures and benefits of a culturally diverse society. (1) Read the feature. (2) Discuss the specific information in the feature. (3) Clarify any terms or questions. (4) Do the Multicultural Awareness Activity.

LESSON PLAN 11-1

Materials

- Student pages 246–253
- Transparencies: F, Blank Expanded Journal, Left Side; G, Blank Expanded Journal, Right Side; 11-1, Blank Expanded Journal, Partial
- 3-Step Checklist for Making Ethical Decisions (TRG)
- Software: Accounting Tutorial

Objectives (Enabling Performance Tasks)

a. Define accounting terms related to purchases and cash payments for a merchandising business.

b. Identify accounting concepts and practices related to purchases and cash payments for a merchandising business.

c. Analyze purchases and cash payments transactions for a merchandising business.

d. Journalize purchases and cash payments transactions for a merchandising business.

MULTICULTURAL AWARENESS

Diversity in the Workplace

Today's workplace reflects society in the cultural diversity of employees. For example, a workplace might have a mixture of employees from different heritages, such as Asian, African, or Hispanic. A company might also have a mix of employees who may be younger or older than average, who may be physically handicapped, or who may speak English as a second language. Furthermore, there may be differences between employees raised in an urban environment and a rural environment, differences based on what part of the country employees were raised, or lifestyle differences.

Enlightened companies encourage sensitivity to individual differences so that each employee is treated fairly and is able to contribute appropriately to the company's productivity.

FYI

The number and arrangement of columns in a journal is determined by the type and frequency of transactions.

Rugcare, the business described in Part 2, is owned by one person. A business owned by one person is known as a proprietorship.

Businesses often require the skills of more than one person. Many businesses also need more capital than one owner can provide. Therefore, some businesses are owned by two or more persons. A business in which two or more persons combine their assets and skills is called a **partnership.** Each member of a partnership is called a **partner.** Partners must agree on how each partner will share the business' profit or loss. As in proprietorships, reports and financial records of the business are kept separate from the personal records of the partners. *(CONCEPT: Business Entity)*

Rugcare, the business described in Part 2, sells services for a fee. A business that sells a service for a fee is known as a service business. However, many other businesses purchase goods to sell. A business that purchases and sells goods is called a **merchandising business.** Goods that a merchandising business purchases to sell are called **merchandise.** The selling of merchandise rather than a service is what makes the activities of a merchandising business different from those of a service business.

CarLand, the business described in this part, is a merchandising business organized as a partnership. The business is owned by Amy Kramer and Dario Mesa. The business purchases and sells automotive supplies. CarLand rents the building in which the business is located as well as the equipment used for operation. CarLand expects to make money and continue in business indefinitely. *(CONCEPT: Going Concern)*

USING AN EXPANDED JOURNAL

A service business generally has a large number of cash transactions and a limited number of noncash transactions. Noncash transactions are those that do not involve either the receipt or payment of cash. Rugcare uses a 5-column journal to record all cash and noncash transactions.

Need for Expanded Journal

CarLand, a merchandising business, has many noncash and other frequently occurring transactions that affect single accounts. CarLand could use the same journal as the one used by Rugcare. However, without adding more special amount columns to the journal, the large number of transactions would require many entries in the General Debit and Credit columns.

Form of Expanded Journal

To save time and space in journalizing transactions, CarLand uses an 11-column journal. The journal includes additional special amount columns for recording frequently occurring transactions that affect single accounts. A journal expanded to provide for the

---

MULTICULTURAL AWARENESS ACTIVITY

Research what local businesses are doing in terms of cultural diversity within their workforces. (Note that this activity will be more successful with larger companies that have Human Resources departments.) Students may call or write to companies to do such research. Students should inquire about the ethnic makeup of the employees, official company policies on including ethnic diversity in the workforce, and the nature and availability of special recruiting and training programs. Students should advise the company recording of frequently occurring transactions that affect single accounts is shown in Illustration 11-1.

ILLUSTRATION 11-1   Amount columns of an expanded journal

An expanded journal is commonly used by small merchandising businesses in which only one person records transactions. Amy Kramer records all transactions for CarLand.

CarLand's journal, Illustration 11-1, has special amount columns for the recording of frequently occurring transactions related to the purchasing and selling of merchandise. The columns are arranged to make accurate journalizing and posting easier. Debit and credit columns for **Cash, Accounts Receivable,** and **Accounts Payable** are arranged in pairs. This arrangement helps avoid errors in recording amounts in the wrong columns. All columns are placed to the right of the Account Title column. The General Debit and Credit amount columns are placed first so that amounts in these columns will be close to the titles in the Account Title column.

The number and arrangement of columns in a journal is determined by the type and frequency of transactions. CarLand determined that the journal described above would best meet the needs of the business.

JOURNALIZING PURCHASES OF MERCHANDISE

FYI

The cost account, Purchases, is only used to record the value of merchandise purchased. All other items bought, such as supplies, are recorded in the appropriate asset account.

The price a business pays for goods it purchases to sell is called **cost of merchandise.** The selling price of merchandise must be greater than the cost of merchandise for a business to make a profit. The amount added to the cost of merchandise to establish the selling price is called **markup.** Revenue earned from the sale of merchandise includes both the cost of merchandise and markup. Only the markup increases capital. Accounts for the cost of merchandise are kept in a separate division of the general ledger. The cost of merchandise division is shown in CarLand's chart of accounts, page 244.

CHAPTER 11   Journalizing Purchases and Cash Payments   **247**

FOCUS

- Review the complete accounting cycle that was presented for a service business organized as a proprietorship in the first cycle of the text. Explain that now we are going to work through the complete accounting cycle for a merchandising business organized as a partnership.

- Introduce new vocabulary: partnership, partner, merchandising business, merchandise, cost of merchandise, markup, vendor, purchase on account, invoice, purchase invoice, terms of sale.

TEACHING STRATEGIES:
TEACHING TIP

Review the reasons why Rugcare's journal, Part 2, has special columns. Discuss reasons why CarLand uses an 11-column expanded journal. Use an overhead projector or chalkboard to demonstrate how the 5-column journal used in Part 2 can easily be expanded by the addition of more special columns. This teaching method enables students to see that an expanded journal is merely a simple enlargement of the journal used by Rugcare. Through discussion and demonstration, develop the expanded journal used by CarLand in Part 3. Help students to see the relationship between the 5-column and the 11-column expanded journal.

Cover student pages 246–253 "Using an Expanded Journal," "Journalizing Purchases of Merchandise," and "Journalizing Buying Supplies." Give examples of noncash transactions such as buying on credit. Ask a student to identify the similarities and differences between the 5-column journal and the expanded journal. Explain that special amount columns are needed for recording frequently occurring transactions that affect single accounts.

Draw a T account for Purchases. Label the sides. Explain the purpose of the account, its classification, and normal balance. Emphasize that a purchase of merchandise is merchandise purchased to sell to customers. Supplies are to be used by the company and will not be resold. "Purchased merchandise" always means that Purchases is debited. Continue drawing T accounts for each transaction as it is presented. Emphasize that a check mark in the Account Title column means that all accounts affected have their own column; a check mark in the Post. Ref. column means don't post.

Draw a T account and label it Accounts Payable. Draw 4 vendor T accounts with balances. Put the total of the balances in the Accounts Payable account. Explain that this one account summarizes the individual vendor accounts. Explain that invoices should always be verified when the items are received. If there is an error, the vendor should be contacted immediately. Emphasize that when a purchase on account has been made, the vendor name must always be written in the Account Title column.

Explain that even though an invoice is received for buying supplies on account, it is not the source document. Purchase invoices are source documents only for purchases. Therefore, a memorandum is written and attached to the invoice explaining that it is for supplies.

Purchases	
Debit side	Credit side
Normal balance	
Increase	Decrease

In addition to purchasing merchandise to sell, a merchandising business also buys supplies and other assets for use in the business. A business from which merchandise is purchased or supplies or other assets are bought is called a **vendor.**

The account used for recording the cost of merchandise purchased to sell is titled Purchases. Purchases is classified as a cost account because it is in the cost of merchandise division in the chart of accounts. The cost account, Purchases, is a temporary account. Because the cost of merchandise purchased for resale reduces capital when the merchandise is purchased, the cost account, Purchases, has a normal debit balance. Therefore, the purchases account is increased by a debit and decreased by a credit, as shown in the T account.

The cost account, Purchases, is used only to record the value of merchandise purchased. Therefore, only purchases of merchandise are recorded in the Purchases Debit column of the journal. All other items bought, such as supplies, are recorded in the General Debit column of the journal. Merchandise and other items bought are recorded and reported at the price agreed upon at the time the transactions occur. The price agreed upon at the time the transaction occurs may be lower than the given price. The accounting concept, *Historical Cost,* is applied when the actual amount paid for merchandise or other items bought is recorded. *(CONCEPT: Historical Cost)*

Purchase of Merchandise for Cash

CarLand pays cash for some purchases. All cash payments are made by check.

November 2, 19--. Purchased merchandise for cash, $483.00. Check No. 259.

A cash purchase transaction increases the purchases account balance and decreases the cash account balance.

Because the purchases account has a normal debit balance, Purchases is debited for $483.00 to show the increase in this cost account. The cash account also has a normal debit balance. Therefore, Cash is credited for $483.00 to show the decrease in this asset account.

The journal entry to record this transaction is shown in Illustration 11-2.

ILLUSTRATION 11-2 Journal entry to record a purchase of merchandise for cash

						9	10	11	
PAGE 21		JOURNAL						PAGE 21	
						PURCHASES DEBIT	CASH		
DATE		ACCOUNT TITLE		DOC. NO.	POST. REF.		DEBIT	CREDIT	
1	Nov. 19-- 2	√		C259	√	483 00		483 00	1
2									2

TEACHING STRATEGIES: DIFFERENT LEARNING STYLES

Auditory Learner. To reinforce the learning of journal entries, the auditory learner should verbally repeat the analysis of the transaction. The student should also verbally list the steps involved in making the entry.

A check mark in the Account Title column means that all account titles have their own column. A check mark in the Post. Ref. column means don't post.

The date, *19--, Nov. 2*, is recorded in the Date column. Both the debit and credit amounts will be recorded in special amount columns. Therefore, a check mark is placed in the Account Title column to show that no account title needs to be written. The check number, *C259*, is recorded in the Doc. No. column. Both the debit and credit amounts will be posted as part of special amount column totals. Therefore, a check mark is placed in the Post. Ref. column to show that amounts on this line are not to be posted individually. The debit to Purchases, *$483.00*, is entered in the Purchases Debit column. The credit to Cash, *$483.00*, is entered in the Cash Credit column.

Purchase of Merchandise on Account

A transaction in which the merchandise purchased is to be paid for later is called a **purchase on account.** Some businesses that purchase on account from only a few vendors keep a separate general ledger account for each vendor to whom money is owed. Businesses that purchase on account from many vendors will have many accounts for vendors. To avoid a bulky general ledger, the total amount owed to all vendors can be summarized in a single general ledger account. A liability account that summarizes the amounts owed to all vendors is titled Accounts Payable. CarLand uses an accounts payable account.

The liability account, Accounts Payable, has a normal credit balance. Therefore, the accounts payable account is increased by a credit and decreased by a debit, as shown in the T account.

When a vendor sells merchandise to a buyer, the vendor prepares a form showing what has been sold. A form describing the goods sold, the quantity, and the price is called an **invoice.** An invoice used as a source document for recording a purchase on account transaction is called a **purchase invoice.** *(CONCEPT: Objective Evidence)* A purchase invoice received by CarLand is shown in Illustration 11-3.

Accounts Payable	
Debit side	Credit side
	Normal balance
Decrease	Increase

ILLUSTRATION 11-3   Purchase invoice

veloz automotive
2611 Industrial
Fremont, NH 03044-2672

REC'D 11/02/-- P74

TO: CarLand
1374 Parklane
Rockville, RI 02873-4121

DATE: 10/26/--
INV. NO.: 2768
TERMS: 30 days
ACCT. NO.: 260

QUANTITY	CAT. NO.	DESCRIPTION	UNIT PRICE	TOTAL
8	4422	All-season tires	73.00	584.00
6	4424	All-season tires	73.00	438.00
12	6620	Floor mats	16.00	192.00
12	7715	Seat covers	45.00	540.00
		Total		1,754.00

Pst

CHAPTER 11   Journalizing Purchases and Cash Payments   **249**

ASSESS

Assess student understanding by checking solutions to Independent Practice activities.

Reteach

Use Unit 4 of the Accounting Tutorial to reteach analyzing transactions. Students may work at the computer at their own pace.

Extend

Assign Cases for Critical Thinking 1 and 2.

Enrich

Discuss the PROFESSIONAL BUSINESS ETHICS feature on page 254. You may wish to distribute copies of the 3-Step Checklist for Making Ethical Decisions. A blackline master is furnished in the Masters and Solutions to Enrichment/ Application Activities Section in the Teacher's Resource Guide.

A purchase invoice lists the quantity, the description, the price of each item, and the total amount of the invoice. A purchase invoice provides the information needed for recording a purchase on account.

When CarLand receives a purchase invoice, a date and a number are stamped in the upper right-hand corner. The date stamped is the date the invoice is received. CarLand received the invoice in Illustration 11-3 on 11/02/--. This date should not be confused with the vendor's date on the invoice, 10/26/--. CarLand assigns numbers in sequence to easily identify all purchase invoices. The number stamped on the invoice, *P74*, is the number assigned by CarLand to this purchase invoice. This number should not be confused with the invoice number, *2768*, assigned by the vendor. Each vendor uses a different numbering system. Therefore, vendor invoice numbers could not be recorded in sequence, which would make it impossible to detect a missing invoice.

A buyer needs to know that all items ordered have been received and that the prices are correct. The check marks on the invoice show that the items have been received and that amounts have been checked and are correct. The initials near the total are those of the person at CarLand who checked the invoice.

An agreement between a buyer and a seller about payment for merchandise is called the **terms of sale.** The terms of sale on the invoice, Illustration 11-3, are 30 days. These terms mean that payment is due within 30 days from the date of the invoice. The invoice is dated October 26. Therefore, payment must be made by November 25.

> *November 2, 19--. Purchased merchandise on account from Veloz Automotive, $1,754.00. Purchase Invoice No. 74.*

A purchase on account transaction increases the amount owed to a vendor. This transaction increases the purchases account balance and increases the accounts payable account balance.

Because the purchases account has a normal debit balance, Purchases is debited for $1,754.00 to show the increase in this cost account. The accounts payable account has a normal credit balance. Therefore, Accounts Payable is credited for $1,754.00 to show the increase in this liability account.

The journal entry to record this purchase on account transaction is shown in Illustration 11-4.

FYI

The check marks on an invoice show that the items have been received and that amounts have been checked and are correct. The initials near the total are those of the person who checked the invoice.

Purchases
1,754.00

Accounts Payable
1,754.00

ILLUSTRATION 11-4   Journal entry to record a purchase of merchandise on account

						7	8	9
PAGE 21			JOURNAL					
	DATE	ACCOUNT TITLE	DOC. NO.	POST. REF.		ACCOUNTS PAYABLE		PURCHASES DEBIT
						DEBIT	CREDIT	
2	2	Veloz Automotive	P74				1 7 5 4 00	1 7 5 4 00

TEACHING STRATEGIES: DIFFERENT LEARNING STYLES

Kinesthetic Learner.   When covering journal entries with a kinesthetic learner, the instructor should give the student journal paper and have the student complete the entries as the instructor demonstrates on a transparency or chalkboard.

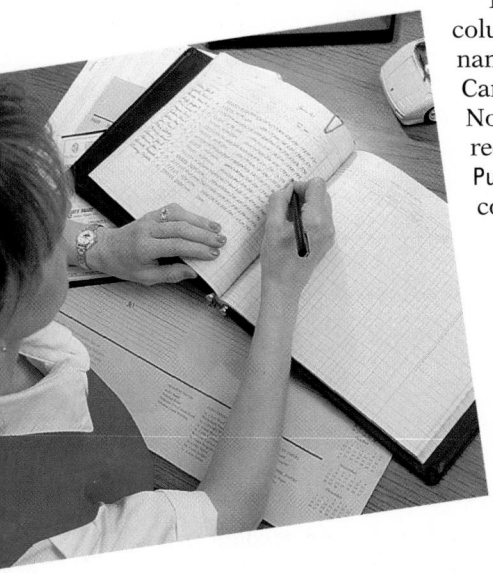

The date, *2*, is written in the Date column. No special amount column is provided for Veloz Automotive Therefore, the vendor name, *Veloz Automotive*, is recorded in the Account Title column. CarLand's purchase invoice number, *P74*, is entered in the Doc. No. column. The credit to Accounts Payable, *$1,754.00*, is recorded in the Accounts Payable Credit column. The debit to Purchases, *$1,754.00*, is recorded in the Purchases Debit column.

The debit to Purchases and the credit to Accounts Payable are recorded in special amount columns. Therefore, writing the titles of either general ledger account in the Account Title column is not necessary. However, the name of the vendor is written in the Account Title column to show to whom the amount is owed. The way CarLand keeps records of the amount owed to each vendor is described in Chapter 13.

JOURNALIZING BUYING SUPPLIES

CarLand buys supplies for use in the business. Supplies are not recorded in the purchases account because supplies are not intended for sale. Cash register tapes and price tags are examples of supplies used in a merchandising business.

Buying Supplies for Cash

CarLand buys most of its supplies for cash.

November 5, 19--. Paid cash for office supplies, $87.00. Check No. 261.

Supplies—Office
| 87.00 | |

Cash
| | 87.00 |

This transaction increases the office supplies account balance and decreases the cash account balance.

Because the office supplies account has a normal debit balance, Supplies—Office is debited for $87.00 to show the increase in this asset account. The cash account also has a normal debit balance. Therefore, Cash is credited for $87.00 to show the decrease in this asset account.

The journal entry to record this buying supplies for cash transaction is shown in Illustration 11-5, page 252.

The date, *5*, is recorded in the Date column. No special amount column is provided for Supplies—Office. Therefore, the account title, *Supplies—Office*, is written in the Account Title column. The check number, *C261*, is entered in the Doc. No. column. The debit to Supplies—Office, *$87.00*, is recorded in the General Debit column. The credit to Cash, *$87.00*, is recorded in the Cash Credit column.

FYI

Supplies are not recorded in the Purchases account because supplies are not intended for sale.

CHAPTER 11   Journalizing Purchases and Cash Payments   **251**

ILLUSTRATION 11-5

Journal entry to record buying supplies for cash

	DATE	ACCOUNT TITLE	DOC. NO.	POST. REF.	GENERAL DEBIT	GENERAL CREDIT		CASH DEBIT	CASH CREDIT	
6	5	Supplies—Office	C261		8700				8700	6
7										7
8										8

PAGE 21   JOURNAL   PAGE 21

FYI

When supplies are bought on account, an invoice is received from the vendor. To avoid confusion with purchase invoices received when merchandise is purchased, a memorandum is attached noting that the invoice is for supplies and not for purchases.

Buying Supplies on Account

CarLand usually buys supplies for cash. Occasionally, however, CarLand buys some supplies on account.

November 6, 19--. Bought store supplies on account from Antelo Supply, $160.00. Memorandum No. 43.

When CarLand buys supplies on account, an invoice is received from the vendor. This invoice is similar to the purchase invoice received when merchandise is purchased. To assure that no mistake is made, a memorandum is attached to the invoice noting that the invoice is for supplies and not for purchases. Memorandum 43 is shown in Illustration 11-6.

ILLUSTRATION 11-6

Memorandum for buying supplies on account

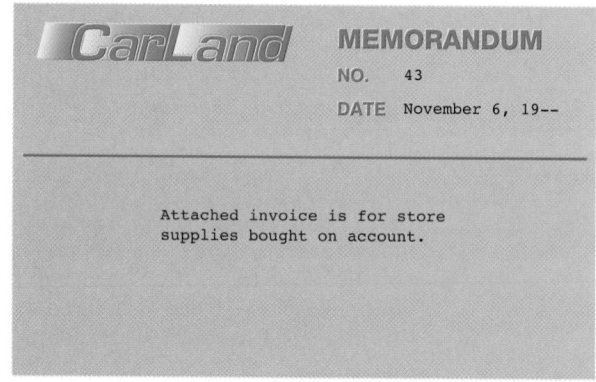

CarLand

MEMORANDUM

NO. 43

DATE November 6, 19--

Attached invoice is for store
supplies bought on account.

Supplies—Store	
160.00	

Accounts Payable	
	160.00

This transaction increases the store supplies account balance and increases the accounts payable account balance.

Because the store supplies account has a normal debit balance, Supplies—Store is debited for $160.00 to show the increase in this asset account. The accounts payable account has a normal credit balance. Therefore, Accounts Payable is credited for $160.00 to show the increase in this liability account.

The journal entry to record this buying supplies on account transaction is shown in Illustration 11-7.

ILLUSTRATION 11-7   Journal entry to record buying supplies on account

					GENERAL		ACCOUNTS PAYABLE	
	DATE	ACCOUNT TITLE	DOC. NO.	POST. REF.	DEBIT	CREDIT	DEBIT	CREDIT
9	6	Supplies—Store	M43		16000			
10		Antelo Supply						16000

PAGE *21*   JOURNAL

The date, *6*, is written in the Date column. No special amount column is provided for Supplies—Store Therefore, the account title, *Supplies—Store*, is recorded in the Account Title column. The memorandum number, *M43*, is entered in the Doc. No. column. The debit to Supplies—Store, *$160.00*, is written in the General Debit column on the same line. An account title is also required for the credit part of the entry. Therefore, the vendor name, *Antelo Supply*, is recorded in the Account Title column on the next line. The credit to Accounts Payable, *$160.00*, is entered in the Accounts Payable Credit column on the same line.

JOURNALIZING CASH PAYMENTS

Most of CarLand's cash payments are to vendors or for expenses. Payment to vendors is made according to the terms of sale on the purchase invoices. Payment for an expense is usually made at the time the expense occurs.

Cash Payment on Account

CarLand pays by check for all cash purchases and for payments on account.

> *November 7, 19--. Paid cash on account to Filtrex Tires, $970.00, covering Purchase Invoice No. 72. Check No. 263.*

This cash payment on account transaction decreases the amount owed to vendors. This transaction decreases the accounts payable account balance and decreases the cash account balance.

Because the accounts payable account has a normal credit balance, Accounts Payable is debited for $970.00 to show the decrease in this liability account. The cash account has a normal debit balance. Therefore, Cash is credited for $970.00 to show the decrease in this asset account.

Accounts Payable	
970.00	

Cash	
	970.00

CHAPTER 11 Journalizing Purchases and Cash Payments   **253**

Objectives (Enabling Performance Tasks)

a. Define accounting terms related to purchases and cash payments for a merchandising business.

b. Identify accounting concepts and practices related to purchases and cash payments for a merchandising business.

c. Analyze purchases and cash payments transactions for a merchandising business.

d. Journalize purchases and cash payments transactions for a merchandising business.

PROFESSIONAL BUSINESS ETHICS

Am I Cheating the Company?

Frances Phillips and Stella Rushing are partners in a frozen food market named The Fishing Net. The partners continually monitor the expiration dates of their inventory to assure that only fresh products are stored in the freezers.

Rather than discarding the inventory, the partners agreed to donate the inventory to an orphanage just prior to its expiration date. After several months, Ms. Rushing began to take some expiring items home for personal use. Lately, Ms. Rushing has even taken home new items.

INSTRUCTIONS:

1. Use the three-step checklist to analyze whether Stella Rushing's latest actions demonstrate ethical behavior.

2. What actions should Ms. Phillips take?

The journal entry to record this cash payment on account transaction is shown in Illustration 11-8.

ILLUSTRATION 11-8   Journal entry to record a cash payment on account

The date, 7, is written in the Date column. No special amount column is provided for Filtrex Tires. Therefore, the vendor name, *Filtrex Tires*, is recorded in the Account Title column. The check number, *C263*, is entered in the Doc. No. column. The debit to Accounts Payable, *$970.00*, is written in the Accounts Payable Debit column. The credit to Cash, *$970.00*, is written in the Cash Credit column.

Cash Payment of an Expense

CarLand usually pays for an expense at the time the transaction occurs.

November 9, 19--. Paid cash for advertising, $125.00. Check No. 265.

This cash payment increases the advertising expense account balance and decreases the cash account balance.

Advertising Expense

| 125.00 | |

Cash

| | 125.00 |

Because the advertising expense account has a normal debit balance, **Advertising Expense** is debited for $125.00 to show the increase in this expense account. The cash account also has a normal debit balance. Therefore, **Cash** is credited for $125.00 to show the decrease in this asset account.

The journal entry to record this cash payment of an expense transaction is shown in Illustration 11-9.

ILLUSTRATION 11-9   Journal entry to record a cash payment of an expense

PAGE *21*					JOURNAL					PAGE *21*	
						1	2		10	11	
					GENERAL				CASH		
	DATE	ACCOUNT TITLE	DOC. NO.	POST. REF.	DEBIT	CREDIT		DEBIT	CREDIT	
17	9	*Advertising Expense*	C265		125 00				125 00	17

The date, *9*, is written in the Date column. No special amount column is provided for **Advertising Expense**. Therefore, the account title, *Advertising Expense*, is recorded in the Account Title column. The check number, *C265*, is entered in the Doc. No. column. The debit to **Advertising Expense**, *$125.00*, is written in the General Debit column. The credit to **Cash**, *$125.00*, is written in the Cash Credit column.

Cash Payment to Replenish Petty Cash

FYI

The account title Petty Cash is used only when establishing the petty cash account.

CarLand deposits all cash in a bank. Some cash, however, is kept in a petty cash fund for making change at the cash register and for making small cash payments. CarLand has a petty cash fund of $500.00, which is replenished whenever the petty cash on hand drops below $200.00.

> *November 9, 19--. Paid cash to replenish the petty cash fund, $301.00: office supplies, $58.00; store supplies, $65.00; advertising, $92.00; miscellaneous, $86.00. Check No. 266.*

This cash payment increases the balances of the supplies accounts and several expense accounts and decreases the cash account balance.

Supplies—Office

| 58.00 | |

Supplies—Store

| 65.00 | |

Advertising Expense

| 92.00 | |

Miscellaneous Expense

| 86.00 | |

Cash

| | 301.00 |

The supplies accounts have normal debit balances. Therefore, **Supplies—Office** is debited for $58.00 and **Supplies—Store** is debited for $65.00 to show the increases in these two asset accounts. The expense accounts also have normal debit balances. Therefore, **Advertising Expense** is debited for $92.00 and **Miscellaneous Expense** is debited for $86.00 to show the increases in these expense accounts. The cash account has a normal debit balance. Therefore, **Cash** is credited for $301.00, the total amount needed to replenish the petty cash fund, to show the decrease in this asset account.

The journal entry to record this cash payment to replenish petty cash transaction is shown in Illustration 11-10.

CHAPTER 11   Journalizing Purchases and Cash Payments   **255**

Cover student pages 253–260 "Journalizing Cash Payments" and "Journalizing
Other Transactions." Draw T accounts
for each transaction as it is presented.
Use Transparencies F and G or Transparency 11-1 to journalize the transaction. Emphasize that when cash is paid
on account, the vendor name must
always be written in the Account Title
column. Any account title on a T account
that does not have a special column in
the journal is written in the Account
Title column. Reinforce that the account
title Petty Cash is used only when
establishing the petty cash account.
Review the definition for withdrawal.

ILLUSTRATION 11-10 Journal entry to record a cash payment to replenish petty cash

| | | | | | GENERAL | | | CASH | |
DATE	ACCOUNT TITLE	DOC. NO.	POST. REF.	DEBIT	CREDIT			DEBIT	CREDIT
18	9 Supplies—Office	C266		5 8 00					3 0 1 00	18
19	Supplies—Store			6 5 00						19
20	Advertising Expense			9 2 00						20
21	Miscellaneous Expense			8 6 00						21

PAGE 21 — JOURNAL — PAGE 21

The date, 9, is written once in the Date column, line 18. No special amount columns are provided for any of the accounts for which
the petty cash fund was used. Therefore, the account titles are
recorded in the Account Title column. The check number, C266, is
entered once in the Doc. No. column, line 18. The debit amounts
are written in the General Debit column. The credit amount is
recorded in the Cash Credit column.

JOURNALIZING OTHER TRANSACTIONS

Most transactions of merchandising businesses are related to purchasing and selling merchandise. A merchandising business, however, has other transactions that must be recorded. CarLand records
these other transactions in its journal.

Withdrawals by Partners

Amy Kramer, Drawing	
Debit side	Credit side
Normal balance	
Increase	Decrease

Dario Mesa, Drawing	
Debit side	Credit side
Normal balance	
Increase	Decrease

Assets taken out of a business for the personal use of an owner
are known as withdrawals. The two assets generally taken out of
a merchandising business are cash and merchandise. Withdrawals reduce the amount of a business' capital. The account
titles of the partners' drawing accounts are Amy Kramer, Drawing and
Dario Mesa, Drawing. The drawing accounts are classified as contra
capital accounts. Since capital accounts have credit balances,
partners' drawing accounts have normal debit balances. Therefore, the drawing accounts are increased by a debit and decreased
by a credit, as shown in the T accounts.

Withdrawals could be recorded as debits directly to the partners'
capital accounts. However, withdrawals are normally recorded in
separate accounts so that the total amounts are easily determined
for each accounting period.

Cash Withdrawal. When either Amy Kramer or Dario Mesa withdraws cash from CarLand, a check is written for the payment.

*November 10, 19--. Dario Mesa, partner, withdrew cash for
personal use, $1,500.00. Check No. 267.*

Dario Mesa, Drawing

| 1,500.00 | |

Cash

| | 1,500.00 |

This cash withdrawal increases Dario Mesa's drawing account balance and decreases the cash account balance.

Because the drawing account has a normal debit balance, Dario Mesa, Drawing is debited for $1,500.00 to show the increase in this contra capital account. The cash account also has a normal debit balance. Therefore, Cash is credited for $1,500.00 to show the decrease in this asset account.

The journal entry to record this cash withdrawal is shown in Illustration 11-11.

Guided Practice

Guide students through Drill 11-D1, Transactions 8–16, and Drill 11-D2, Transactions 8–16. Students should have the forms from the working papers to complete as you guide them through the drills. For Drill 11-D1, for each transaction, ask students which accounts are affected, and how. All students should agree with the analysis before proceeding to the next transaction. For Drill 11-D2, for each transaction, ask the students the column, the amount, and whether it is a debit or a credit. All students should agree with the analysis before proceeding to the next transaction.

Independent Practice

- Assign Term 12, Questions 17–20, Problem 11-1, transactions for Sept. 8–30, Study Guide 11, and Mastery Problem 11-M.

- Assign Study Guide 11. If you prefer to have your students complete the study guide at the computer, use the Electronic Study Guide.

ILLUSTRATION 11-11   Journal entry to record a cash withdrawal by a partner

PAGE 21 — JOURNAL — PAGE 21

	DATE	ACCOUNT TITLE	DOC. NO.	POST. REF.	GENERAL DEBIT	GENERAL CREDIT	CASH DEBIT	CASH CREDIT	
22	10	Dario Mesa, Drawing	C267		1 5 0 0 00			1 5 0 0 00	22

The date, *10*, is written in the Date column. No special amount column is provided for Dario Mesa, Drawing. Therefore, the contra capital account title, *Dario Mesa, Drawing*, is recorded in the Account Title column. The check number, *C267*, is entered in the Doc. No. column. The debit to Dario Mesa, Drawing, *$1,500.00*, is written in the General Debit column. The credit to Cash, *$1,500.00*, is written in the Cash Credit column.

Merchandise Withdrawal.   A partner may also withdraw merchandise for personal use.

November 12, 19--. Dario Mesa, partner, withdrew merchandise for personal use, $200.00. Memorandum No. 44.

This merchandise withdrawal increases Dario Mesa's drawing account balance and decreases the purchases account balance.

Dario Mesa, Drawing

| 200.00 | |

Purchases

| | 200.00 |

Because the drawing account has a normal debit balance, Dario Mesa, Drawing is debited for $200.00 to show the increase in this contra capital account. The purchases account also has a normal debit balance. Therefore, Purchases is credited for $200.00 to show the decrease in this cost account.

The journal entry to record this merchandise withdrawal is shown in Illustration 11-12.

ILLUSTRATION 11-12   Journal entry to record a merchandise withdrawal by a partner

PAGE 21 — JOURNAL

	DATE	ACCOUNT TITLE	DOC. NO.	POST. REF.	GENERAL DEBIT	GENERAL CREDIT
26	12	Dario Mesa, Drawing	M44		2 0 0 00	
27		Purchases				2 0 0 00

CHAPTER 11   Journalizing Purchases and Cash Payments   **257**

TEACHING STRATEGIES: DIFFERENT LEARNING ABILITIES

Visually-Impaired Students.   New technologies are continually being developed that assist visually impaired students to participate fully in both school and business. Students must be aware of these technologies and know how to continually learn of new technologies. Using government agencies as a resource, assist the students in preparing a report concerning anticipated technologies.

Assess student understanding by checking solutions to Independent Practice activities. Review Summary Illustration 11-15, "Summary of Entries for Purchases, Cash Payments, and Other Transactions in an Expanded Journal." Use Transparency 11-2, Chapter Summary.

Reteach

- Use Demonstration Problem 11A. This problem can be done on the overhead with the students completing the problem at their desks.
- Assign Recycling Problem 11-R.

Extend

- Assign Challenge Problem 11-C (the challenge is that students must journalize a variety of correcting entries).
- Assign the Accounting Tutorial, Unit 4.

Enrich

- Assign the Application Program disk to be completed at the computer using Mastery Problem 11-M.
- Assign students to read the MULTI-CULTURAL AWARENESS feature on page 246. Discuss with them how an understanding and appreciation of history and other cultures contribute to understanding civilization today.

FYI

Gross National Product (GNP) is the total market value of all goods and services produced by a nation each year.

FYI

CFO represents Chief Financial Officer.

The date, *12*, is written in the Date column. Neither a Drawing Debit nor a Purchases Credit column is provided in the journal because merchandise withdrawals do not occur frequently. Therefore, the account title, *Dario Mesa, Drawing*, is recorded in the Account Title column. The memorandum number, *M44*, is entered in the Doc. No. column. The debit to Dario Mesa, Drawing, *$200.00*, is written in the General Debit column. The account title, *Purchases*, is recorded in the Account Title column on the next line. The credit to Purchases, *$200.00*, is entered in the General Credit column.

Correcting Entry

Errors may be made even though care is taken in recording transactions. Simple errors may be corrected by ruling through the incorrect item, as described in Chapter 5. However, a transaction may have been improperly journalized and posted to the ledger. When an error in a journal entry has already been posted, the incorrect journal entry should be corrected with an additional journal entry. A journal entry made to correct an error in the ledger is called a **correcting entry.**

> *November 13, 19--. Discovered that a payment of cash for advertising in October was journalized and posted in error as a debit to* Miscellaneous Expense *instead of* Advertising Expense, *$120.00. Memorandum No. 45.*

If an accounting error is discovered, a memorandum is prepared describing the correction to be made. The source document for a correcting entry is the memorandum. *(CONCEPT: Objective Evidence)* A memorandum for this correcting entry is shown in Illustration 11-13.

ILLUSTRATION 11-13   Memorandum for a correcting entry

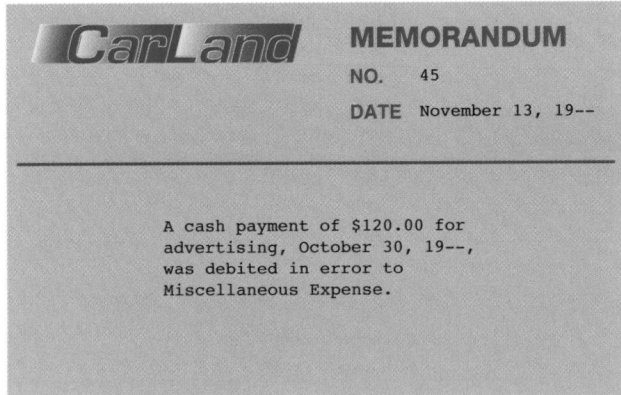

TEACHING STRATEGIES: COOPERATIVE LEARNING

Divide the class into groups of two or three students each. Have each group discuss and prepare a list of merchandising businesses found in the local community. Each group appoints a leader who will present the list and merchandise being sold to the class. This cooperative learning activity should not take more than 20 to 30 minutes of class time.

To correct the error, an entry is made to add $120.00 to the advertising expense account. The entry must also deduct $120.00 from the miscellaneous expense account. The correcting entry increases the advertising expense account balance and decreases the miscellaneous expense account balance.

Because the advertising expense account has a normal debit balance, Advertising Expense is debited for $120.00 to show the increase in this expense account. The miscellaneous expense account also has a normal debit balance. Therefore, Miscellaneous Expense is credited for $120.00 to show the decrease in this expense account.

The journal entry to record this correcting entry is shown in Illustration 11-14.

```
       Advertising Expense
        120.00      |
                    |
     Miscellaneous Expense
                    |   120.00
                    |
```

ILLUSTRATION 11-14   Journal entry to record a correcting entry

				1	2
PAGE 21	JOURNAL				
				GENERAL	
DATE	ACCOUNT TITLE	DOC. NO.	POST. REF.	DEBIT	CREDIT
28	13	Advertising Expense	M45	1 2 0 00	
29		Miscellaneous Expense			1 2 0 00
30					
31					
32					
33					
34					

Audit Your Understanding

1. When cash is paid on account, what is the effect on the cash account?

2. What are two assets normally withdrawn by the partners of a business?

3. What is a correcting entry?

The date, *13*, is written in the Date column. The account title, *Advertising Expense*, is recorded in the Account Title column. The memorandum number, *M45*, is entered in the Doc. No. column. The debit to Advertising Expense, *$120.00*, is entered in the General Debit column. The account title, *Miscellaneous Expense*, is written in the Account Title column on the next line. The credit to Miscellaneous Expense, *$120.00*, is recorded in the General Credit column.

The chart shown in Illustration 11-15 summarizes the entries for purchases, cash payments, and other transactions in an expanded journal.

CLOSURE

Use Audit Your Understanding questions.

ASSESS

- Administer Problem Test Chapter 11.
- Administer a MicroExam test for Chapter 11.

AUDIT YOUR UNDERSTANDING

1. Cash is decreased by a credit.
2. Cash and merchandise.
3. A journal entry made to correct an error in the ledger.

TEACHING STRATEGIES: DIFFERENT LEARNING STYLES

Visual Learner. When covering journal entries with a visual learner, the instructor should discuss the entries, using a transparency or the chalkboard to record the entry. In addition, the student should be asked to mentally picture each part of the entry before the instructor actually writes it on the transparency or chalkboard.

TEACHING STRATEGIES:
APPLYING VISUALS

Direct students to Summary Illustration 11-15 and review entries for purchases, cash payments, and other transactions in an expanded journal.

SUMMARY ILLUSTRATION 11-15

Summary of entries for purchases, cash payments, and other transactions in an expanded journal

TRANSACTION	JOURNAL										
	1 GENERAL DEBIT	2 GENERAL CREDIT	3 ACCOUNTS RECEIVABLE DEBIT	4 ACCOUNTS RECEIVABLE CREDIT	5 SALES CREDIT	6 SALES TAX PAYABLE CREDIT	7 ACCOUNTS PAYABLE DEBIT	8 ACCOUNTS PAYABLE CREDIT	9 PURCHASES DEBIT	10 CASH DEBIT	11 CASH CREDIT
Purchase merchandise for cash									X		X
Purchase merchandise on account								X	X		
Buying supplies for cash	X										X
Buying supplies on account	X							X			
Cash payment on account							X				X
Cash payment of an expense	X										X
Cash payment to replenish petty cash	X										X
Cash withdrawal	X										X
Merchandise withdrawal	X	X									

What is the meaning of each of the following?

1. **partnership**
2. **partner**
3. **merchandising business**
4. **merchandise**
5. **cost of merchandise**
6. **markup**
7. **vendor**
8. **purchase on account**
9. **invoice**
10. **purchase invoice**
11. **terms of sale**
12. **correcting entry**

QUESTIONS FOR INDIVIDUAL STUDY   EPT(b)

1. Why would two or more persons want to own a single business?

2. What makes the activities of a merchandising business different from those of a service business?

3. What are noncash transactions?

4. Why does CarLand use an 11-column journal rather than a 5-column journal like the one used by Rugcare?

5. What is the title of the account that shows the cost of merchandise purchased for sale?

6. What is the account classification of Purchases?

7. Which accounting concept is being applied when merchandise and other items bought are recorded and reported at the price agreed upon at the time the transactions occur?

8. What accounts are affected, and how, when merchandise is purchased for cash?

9. Why is a check mark placed in the Account Title column of an expanded journal for a cash purchase transaction?

10. Why would a business use a single general ledger account to summarize the amount owed to all vendors?

11. What is the name of the liability account that summarizes the amounts owed to all vendors?

12. Why does CarLand use its own set of sequential purchase invoice numbers rather than using the numbers assigned by vendors?

13. What accounts are affected, and how, when merchandise is purchased on account?

14. Why are the account titles (Purchases and Accounts Payable) for a purchase on account entry not written in the Account Title column in the expanded journal?

15. Why are supplies bought recorded in a separate supplies account rather than in the purchases account?

16. What accounts are affected, and how, when store supplies are bought on account?

17. What accounts are affected, and how, when a cash payment on account is made?

18. How does CarLand use a petty cash fund?

19. What accounts are affected, and how, when a withdrawal of merchandise is made?

20. When should a journal entry be made to correct errors in recording transactions?

1. **partnership:** A business in which two or more persons combine their assets and skills. (p. 246)

2. **partner:** Each member of a partnership. (p. 246)

3. **merchandising business:** A business that purchases and sells goods. (p. 246)

4. **merchandise:** Goods that a merchandising business purchases to sell. (p. 246)

5. **cost of merchandise:** The price a business pays for goods it purchases to sell. (p. 247)

6. **markup:** The amount added to the cost of merchandise to establish the selling price. (p. 247)

7. **vendor:** A business from which merchandise is purchased or supplies or other assets are bought. (p. 248)

8. **purchase on account:** A transaction in which the merchandise purchased is to be paid for later. (p. 249)

9. **invoice:** A form describing the goods sold, the quantity, and the price. (p. 249)

10. **purchase invoice:** An invoice used as a source document for recording a purchase on account transaction. (p. 249)

11. **terms of sale:** An agreement between a buyer and a seller about payment for merchandise. (p. 250)

12. **correcting entry:** A journal entry made to correct an error in the ledger. (p. 258)

QUESTIONS FOR INDIVIDUAL STUDY

1. The type of business might require the skills of more than one person or more capital than one owner can provide. (p. 246)

2. A merchandising business purchases and sells goods; a service business sells services. (p. 246)

3. Noncash transactions are those that do not involve either the receipt or payment of cash. (p. 246)

4. To save time and space in journalizing transactions. (p. 246)

5. Purchases. (p. 248)

6. Purchases is classified as a cost account. (p. 248)

7. Historical Cost concept. (p. 248)

8. Purchases is debited; Cash is credited. (p. 248)

9. The check mark shows that no ledger account title needs to be entered. (p. 249)

10. To avoid a bulky general ledger. (p. 249)

11. Accounts Payable. (p. 249)

12. Because each vendor uses a different numbering system, detecting missing invoices would be impossible. (p. 250)

13. Purchases is debited; Accounts Payable is credited. (p. 250)

14. Special amount columns have been provided for both of these debit and credit amounts. (p. 251)

15. Supplies are not intended for sale. (p. 251)

16. Supplies—Store is debited; Accounts Payable is credited. (p. 252)

17. Accounts Payable is debited; Cash is credited. (p. 253)

18. To make change at the cash register and to make small cash payments. (p. 255)

19. The drawing account is debited; Purchases is credited. (p. 257)

20. When it is discovered that an incorrect entry has been posted to the ledger. (p. 258)

CASES FOR CRITICAL THINKING

Case 1 The decision should be based on the following: (1) Would forming a partnership result in increased profits for Ms. Butler? (2) Would forming a partnership make the operation of the business easier for Ms. Butler? If the answers to these questions are positive, forming a partnership would be the best method of obtaining additional capital. Facts to consider:

Borrow money

1. Money borrowed, plus a fee for the use of the money, must be paid back.

2. The salary of the additional employee would be paid from revenue received.

3. Ms. Butler would receive all net income.

4. Ms. Butler would make all decisions about business operations.

CASES FOR CRITICAL THINKING

CASE 1 Deborah Butler owns and operates a gift shop in a downtown shopping area. Because of a shopping mall that has opened in one of the suburbs, the gift shop's business has been declining. Ms. Butler has an opportunity to move the business to the shopping mall. Additional capital, however, is required to move and operate the business in a new location. The local bank has agreed to lend the money needed. The business hours would be extended at the new location. The business would also be open seven days a week. The extended hours plus the expected increase in business would require the hiring of one additional employee. Ms. Butler has been contacted by Fred Chaney, a person with similar merchandising experience, who would like to become a partner. As an alternative to borrowing cash, Mr. Chaney would provide the capital necessary to move the business to the new location. For the capital provided, Mr. Chaney would share equally in the net income or loss of the business. Mr. Chaney would also share equally in the operation of the business. Should Ms. Butler (1) borrow the money from the bank or (2) bring in a partner? Explain your answer.

CASE 2 Daryl Hodges is a high school student who works part-time in a local clothing store. As part of his duties, he records daily transactions in a journal. One day he asks the owner: "You use the purchase invoice as your source document for recording purchases of merchandise on account. You use a memorandum as your source document for recording the entry when supplies are bought on account. Why don't you use the invoice for both entries?" How would you respond to this question?

DRILLS FOR UNDERSTANDING

DRILL 11-D1 Analyzing transactions into debit and credit parts

TUTORIAL

INSTRUCTIONS:

Prepare two T accounts for each of the following transactions. Use the T accounts to analyze each transaction. Use account titles similar to CarLand's, as shown in the chart of accounts, page 244. The partners' names are Irma Gilbert and Alex Jensen. The first transaction is given as an example.

Purchases	
200.00	

Cash	
	200.00

1. Purchased merchandise for cash, $200.00.
2. Purchased merchandise on account from Klein Co., $900.00.
3. Paid cash for office supplies, $75.00.
4. Bought store supplies on account from Central Supply, $240.00.
5. Bought office supplies on account from Cratin Supply, $125.00.
6. Purchased merchandise for cash, $175.00.
7. Paid cash for office supplies, $70.00.
8. Paid cash on account to Matson Company, $750.00.
9. Purchased merchandise on account from Garber Company, $1,200.00.
10. Paid cash for advertising, $85.00.
11. Irma Gilbert, partner, withdrew cash for personal use, $1,000.00.
12. Alex Jensen, partner, withdrew cash for personal use, $1,000.00.
13. Irma Gilbert, partner, withdrew merchandise for personal use, $130.00.
14. Paid cash on account to Butler Enterprises, $360.00.

15. Discovered that a transaction for office supplies bought last month was journalized and posted in error as a debit to Prepaid Insurance instead of Supplies—Office, $60.00.
16. Alex Jensen, partner, withdrew merchandise for personal use, $95.00.

The solution to Drill 11-D1 is needed to complete Drill 11-D2.

DRILL 11-D2 Analyzing journal entries

The solution to Drill 11-D1 is needed to complete Drill 11-D2.

INSTRUCTIONS:

A form for analyzing transactions is given in the working papers that accompany this textbook. Based on the answers in Drill 11-D1, write the amounts in the amount columns to be used to journalize each transaction. Transaction 1 is given as an example in the working papers.

APPLICATION PROBLEM   EPT(c,d)

PROBLEM 11-1 Journalizing purchases, cash payments, and other transactions

Mary Demski and Eileen Ivan, partners, own a gift shop.

INSTRUCTIONS:

Journalize the following transactions completed during September of the current year. Use page 21 of a journal similar to the one described in this chapter for CarLand. Source documents are abbreviated as follows: check, C; memorandum, M; purchase invoice, P.

Sept. 1. Purchased merchandise for cash, $150.00. C220.
1. Purchased merchandise on account from Kemp Fashions, $1,350.00. P60.
2. Paid cash for office supplies, $75.00. C221.
2. Purchased merchandise on account from Bonner & Co., $740.00. P61.
3. Purchased merchandise on account from Burton Fabrics, $585.00. P62.
4. Paid cash for office supplies, $55.00. C222.
7. Bought store supplies on account from Pulver Supply, $135.00. M42.
7. Purchased merchandise for cash, $120.00. C223.
8. Paid cash for telephone bill, $120.00. C224.
9. Bought office supplies on account from Lorand Supply, $85.00. M43.
11. Purchased merchandise for cash, $110.00. C225.
12. Paid cash for store supplies, $60.00. C226.
14. Mary Demski, partner, withdrew cash for personal use, $1,200.00. C227.
14. Eileen Ivan, partner, withdrew cash for personal use, $1,200.00. C228.
18. Paid cash on account to Kemp Fashions, $1,350.00, covering P60. C229.
21. Paid cash for advertising, $87.00. C230.
22. Paid cash on account to Bonner & Co., $740.00, covering P61. C231.
24. Mary Demski, partner, withdrew merchandise for personal use, $160.00. M44.
25. Discovered that a transaction for office supplies bought in August was journalized and posted in error as a debit to Purchases instead of Supplies—Office, $88.00. M45.
26. Paid cash on account to Burton Fabrics, $585.00, covering P62. C232.
29. Eileen Ivan, partner, withdrew merchandise for personal use, $120.00. M46.
30. Paid cash to replenish the petty cash fund, $305.00: office supplies, $63.00; store supplies, $51.00; advertising, $88.00; miscellaneous, $103.00. C233.
30. Paid cash on account to Pulver Supply, $135.00, covering M42. C234.

CHECK FIGURES (cont'd)

Mastery Problem 11-M   There are 16 General Debit entries; Accounts Payable is credited 6 times.

Challenge Problem 11-C   There are 7 General Debit and 9 General Credit entries; Purchases is debited 2 times.

ENRICHMENT PROBLEMS

MASTERY PROBLEM 11-M   Journalizing purchases, cash payments, and other transactions

APPLICATION

Sylvia Prior and Julia Steger, partners, own a bookstore.

INSTRUCTIONS:

Journalize the following transactions completed during November of the current year. Use page 23 of a journal similar to the one described in this chapter for CarLand. Source documents are abbreviated as follows: check, C; memorandum, M; purchase invoice, P.

Nov. 2. Paid cash for rent, $1,250.00. C261.
2. Sylvia Prior, partner, withdrew cash for personal use, $1,500.00. C262.
2. Julia Steger, partner, withdrew cash for personal use, $1,500.00. C263.
3. Purchased merchandise for cash, $130.00. C264.
4. Paid cash on account to BFL Publishing, $920.00, covering P71. C265.
4. Purchased merchandise on account from Quality Books, $1,450.00. P74.
5. Paid cash for office supplies, $48.00. C266.
7. Julia Steger, partner, withdrew merchandise for personal use, $42.00. M32.
9. Paid cash for electric bill, $154.00. C267.
9. Paid cash on account to Quality Books, $1,235.00, covering P72. C268.
10. Bought store supplies on account from Carson Supply Co., $106.00. M33.
11. Paid cash on account to Matson Book Service, $975.00, covering P73. C269.
14. Purchased merchandise on account from Falk Book Co., $1,525.00. P75.
16. Paid cash for store supplies, $62.00. C270.
16. Sylvia Prior, partner, withdrew merchandise for personal use, $64.00. M34.
17. Bought store supplies on account from Gray Supplies, $214.00. M35.
18. Purchased merchandise for cash, $145.00. C271.
18. Paid cash to replenish the petty cash fund, $302.00: office supplies, $73.00; store supplies, $47.00; advertising, $92.00; miscellaneous, $90.00. C272.
19. Paid cash on account to Quality Books, $1,450.00, covering P74. C273.
21. Purchased merchandise on account from Voss Publishing, $925.00. P76.
24. Paid cash on account to Falk Book Co., $1,525.00, covering P75. C274.
26. Discovered that a transaction for office supplies bought in October was journalized and posted in error as a debit to Purchases instead of Supplies—Office, $94.00. M36.
28. Bought store supplies on account from Carson Supply, $118.00. M37.
30. Purchased merchandise for cash, $68.00. C275.

CHALLENGE PROBLEM 11-C   Journalizing correcting entries

A review of Meir Decorating's accounting records for last month revealed the following errors.

INSTRUCTIONS:

Journalize the needed correcting entries on page 8 of a journal similar to the one described in this chapter for CarLand. Use December 2 of the current year.

Dec. 2. Merchandise withdrawn by Alice Reyes, partner, was journalized and posted in error as a credit to Cash instead of Purchases, $116.00. M35.
2. Office supplies bought for cash were journalized and posted in error as a debit to Purchases instead of Supplies—Office, $95.00. M36.
2. A check written for advertising was journalized and posted in error as a debit to Miscellaneous Expense instead of Advertising Expense, $125.00. M37.
2. Store supplies bought on account were journalized and posted in error as a debit to Utilities Expense instead of Supplies—Store, $52.00. M38.
2. Merchandise purchased on account was journalized and posted in error as a debit to Supplies—Office instead of Purchases, $850.00. M39.

Dec. 2. A check written for rent was journalized and posted in error as a debit to Salary Expense instead of Rent Expense, $1,200.00. M40.

2. A cash withdrawal by Harold Atkins, partner, was journalized and posted in error as a credit to Purchases instead of Cash, $200.00. M41.

2. A check written for miscellaneous expense was journalized and posted in error as a debit to Supplies Expense—Store instead of Miscellaneous Expense, $89.00. M42.

2. Office supplies bought for cash were journalized and posted in error as a debit to Prepaid Insurance instead of Supplies—Office, $160.00. M43.

2. A check written for store supplies was journalized and posted in error as a debit to Supplies—Office instead of Supplies—Store, $151.00. M44.

Chapter 12 continues the daily transactions of a merchandising business. Revenue is generated by the sale of merchandise. Calculating and recording the liability for sales tax on the sale of merchandise is presented. Cash, credit card, and on account sales are described. T accounts illustrate the normal balance sides of the new accounts Sales Tax Payable and Accounts Receivable.

GUIDE TO ACHIEVING LEARNING OBJECTIVES

	TEACH	APPLY		EXTEND/ENRICH					
Enabling Performance Tasks	Lesson Plans	Drills for Understanding	Application Problems	Mastery Problems	Challenge Problems	Cases for Critical Thinking	Recycling Problems	Reinforcement Activity	
a. Define accounting terms related to sales and cash receipts for a merchandising business.	12-1								
b. Identify accounting concepts and practices related to sales and cash receipts for a merchandising business.	12-1					Cases 1, 2			
c. Analyze sales and cash receipts transactions for a merchandising business.	12-1	12-D1, 12D-2	12-1	12-M	12-C		12-R	2A	
d. Journalize sales and cash receipts transactions for a merchandising business.	12-1	12-D3	12-1	12-M	12-C		12-R	2A	
e. Prove and rule a journal.	12-2		12-1	12-M	12-C		12-R	2A	

ENRICHMENT

SPECIAL FEATURES

Global Perspective, page 271

Applied Communications, page 279

TECHNOLOGY CONNECTION

Accounting Tutorial Unit 4

Application Program Disk Problem 12-M

Electronic Study Guide

NEW, REVIEW, AND EXTENSION

ACTIVITIES/CONCEPTS/TRANSACTIONS	NEW	REVIEW/ EXTENSION
Analyzing transactions into debit and credit parts		✓
Using an expanded 11-column multi-column journal		✓
Using a journal with special amount columns		✓
Sales on account	✓	
Sales tax on sales	✓	
Cash sales		✓
Credit card sales	✓	
Cash receipts on account	✓	
General ledger account Accounts Receivable	✓	
Proving a journal		✓
Forwarding totals of a journal		✓
Proving cash		✓
Ruling a journal		✓

The accounting concept, *Realization of Revenue,* is described for the first time in this chapter.

Mastery Problem 12-M includes transactions from both Chapters 11 and 12 for additional reinforcement and realism.

	INFORMAL ASSESSMENT		FORMAL ASSESSMENT				
Study Guide	Audit Your Understanding	Chapter MicroExam	Chapter Problem Test	Unit Problem Test	Unit Objective Test	Portfolio
Unit A	✓	✓			✓	
Unit B	✓	✓			✓	
Units B, C	✓		✓	✓		✓
Unit C			✓	✓		✓
			✓	✓		✓

TEACHING MATERIALS

Teacher's Wraparound Edition of Text

Teacher's Resource Guide

Teacher's Edition of Working Papers

Teacher's Edition of Demonstration/Recycling Problems

Teaching Transparencies

Accounting Tutorial Manual

MicroExam

Applied Math Work Sheet

APPLIED MATHEMATICS

APPLIED MATH/ACCOUNTING SKILL	APPLICATION
Calculating sales tax	Drill 12-D2
Proving an expanded journal	Prob. 12-1
Proving cash	Prob. 12-M

Journalizing Sales and Cash Receipts

ENABLING PERFORMANCE TASKS

After studying Chapter 12, you will be able to:

a Define accounting terms related to sales and cash receipts for a merchandising business.

b Identify accounting concepts and practices related to sales and cash receipts for a merchandising business.

c Analyze sales and cash receipts transactions for a merchandising business.

d Journalize sales and cash receipts transactions for a merchandising business.

e Prove and rule a journal.

TERMS PREVIEW

customer • sales tax • cash sale • credit card sale • sale on account • sales invoice

Purchases and sales of merchandise are the two major activities of a merchandising business. A person or business to whom merchandise or services are sold is called a **customer**. Rugcare, described in Part 2, sells services. CarLand, described in this part, sells merchandise. Other businesses may sell both services and merchandise.

SALES TAX

Laws of most states and some cities require that a tax be collected from customers for each sale made. A tax on a sale of merchandise or services is called a **sales tax.** Sales tax rates are usually stated as a percentage of sales. Regardless of the tax rates used, accounting procedures are the same.

Every business collecting a sales tax needs accurate records of the amount of tax collected. Businesses must file reports with the proper government unit and pay the amount of sales tax collected. Records need to show (1) total sales and (2) total sales tax. The amount of sales tax collected by CarLand is a business liability until paid to the state government. Therefore, the sales tax amount is recorded in a separate liability account titled *Sales Tax Payable.* The liability account, Sales Tax Payable, has a normal credit balance. This account is increased by a credit and decreased by a debit, as shown in the T account.

Sales Tax Payable	
Debit side	Credit side
	Normal balance
Decrease	Increase

CarLand operates in a state with a 6% sales tax rate. A customer must pay for the price of the goods plus the sales tax. The total amount of a sale of merchandise priced at $200.00 is calculated as shown below.

Price of Goods	×	Sales Tax Rate	=	Sales Tax
$200.00	×	6%	=	$12.00
Price of Goods	+	Sales Tax	=	Total Amount Received
$200.00	+	$12.00	=	$212.00

A customer must pay $212.00 for the merchandise ($200.00 for the goods plus $12.00 for the sales tax). CarLand records the price of goods sold, the sales tax, and the total amount received.

JOURNALIZING SALES AND CASH RECEIPTS FOR SALES

A sale of merchandise may be (1) for cash or (2) on account. A sale of merchandise increases the revenue of a business. Regardless of when payment is made, the revenue should be recorded at the time of a sale, not on the date cash is received. For example, on June 15 CarLand sells merchandise on account to a customer. The customer pays CarLand for the merchandise on July 12. CarLand records the

CHAPTER 12   Journalizing Sales and Cash Receipts   **267**

LESSON PLAN 12-1

Materials

- Student pages 267–273
- Transparencies: F, Blank Expanded Journal, Left Side; G, Blank Expanded Journal, Right Side; 12-1, Blank Expanded Journal, Partial
- Math Work Sheet Chapter 12 Part A, Calculating Sales Tax
- Software: Accounting Tutorial, Unit 4
- Global Perspective Activity Work Sheet (TRG)

Objectives (Enabling Performance Tasks)

a. Define accounting terms related to sales and cash receipts for a merchandising business.

b. Identify accounting concepts and practices related to sales and cash receipts for a merchandising business.

c. Analyze sales and cash receipts transactions for a merchandising business.

d. Journalize sales and cash receipts transactions for a merchandising business.

APPLIED SKILLS: MATHEMATICS

Use the MATH WORK SHEET in the Masters and Solutions to Enrichment/Application Activities section of the Teacher's Resource Guide to integrate applied mathematics. In this worksheet, students will apply math concepts to calculate sales tax, prove the equality of debits and credits in an expanded journal, and prove cash.

- In Chapter 11, the expanded journal was introduced, and journalizing purchases and cash payments transactions was presented. In this lesson, we will record sales and cash receipts transactions in an expanded journal. Introduce the topic of sales of merchandise by having students list local companies that sell services, merchandise, or both services and merchandise.

- Introduce new vocabulary: customer, sales tax, cash sale, credit card sale, sale on account, sales invoice.

APPLIED SKILLS:
BUILDING STUDY SKILLS

Instruct students to continue using the Quick Reference Guide (QRG) for transactions that they prepared in Chapter 11.

1. Use a new heading for SALES AND CASH RECEIPTS.

2. Draw a T account for the two new accounts introduced in this chapter, Sales Tax Payable and Accounts Receivable, and label the debit, credit, increase, and decrease sides.

3. Copy the transactions out of the chapter narrative that illustrate the new accounts. Draw the T accounts that analyze the transactions.

4. Use another new heading PROVING CASH and write the formula for proving cash.

This QRG can then be used when students are completing end-of-chapter activities.

revenue on June 15, the date of the sale. The accounting concept, *Realization of Revenue*, is applied when revenue is recorded at the time goods or services are sold. *(CONCEPT: Realization of Revenue)*

Cash and Credit Card Sales

CarLand sells most of its merchandise for cash. A sale in which cash is received for the total amount of the sale at the time of the transaction is called a **cash sale**. CarLand also sells merchandise to customers who have a bank approved credit card. A sale in which a credit card is used for the total amount of the sale at the time of the transaction is called a **credit card sale**. Major bank approved credit cards include VISA, MasterCard, Discover Card, and Carte Blanche. CarLand accepts all major bank approved credit cards from customers. A customer who uses a credit card promises to pay the amount due for the credit card transaction to the bank issuing the credit card.

CarLand prepares a credit card slip for each credit card sale. At the end of each week, these credit card slips are included with CarLand's bank deposit. CarLand's bank accepts the credit card slips the same way it accepts checks and cash for deposit. The bank increases CarLand's bank account by the total amount of the credit card sales deposited. If a credit card was issued by another bank, CarLand's bank sends the credit card slips to the issuing bank. The bank that issues the credit card then bills the customer and collects the amount owed. The bank that accepts and processes the credit card slips for a business charges a fee for this service. This fee is included on CarLand's monthly bank statement.

Cash and credit card sales are both revenue items that increase the revenue account, Sales. Because the bank accepts credit card slips the same way it accepts cash, CarLand's bank account increases after each deposit as though cash had been deposited. Therefore, CarLand combines all cash and credit card sales and records the two revenue items as a single cash sales transaction.

November 7, 19--. Recorded cash and credit card sales, $6,450.00, plus sales tax, $387.00; total, $6,837.00. Cash Register Tape No. 7.

CarLand uses a cash register to list all cash and credit card sales. When a transaction is entered on the cash register, a paper tape is printed as a receipt for the customer. The cash register also internally accumulates data about total cash and credit card sales.

At the end of each week, a cash register tape is printed showing total cash and credit card sales. The tape is removed from the cash register and marked with a *T* and the date (T7). The cash register tape is used by CarLand as the source document for weekly cash and credit card sales transactions. *(CONCEPT: Objective Evidence)*

A cash and credit card sales transaction increases the balances of the cash account, the sales account, and the sales tax payable account.

	Cash	
6,837.00		

	Sales	
		6,450.00

	Sales Tax Payable	
		387.00

TEACHING STRATEGIES: TEACHING TIP

Review the debit and credit parts of a cash sale without sales tax to reinforce prior learning. Following this review, introduce the topic of sales tax and how the debit and credit parts of the cash sales entry change. Emphasize that the only new learning is the treatment of sales tax and that Cash increases by the amount of the sales tax liability.

The fee assessed on credit card sales usually varies between 1% and 5% of the total sale amount.

Because the asset account, Cash, has a normal debit balance, Cash is debited for the total sales and sales tax, $6,837.00, to show the increase in this asset account. The sales account has a normal credit balance. Therefore, Sales is credited for the total price of all goods sold, $6,450.00, to show the increase in this revenue account. The sales tax payable account also has a normal credit balance. Therefore, Sales Tax Payable is credited for the total sales tax, $387.00, to show the increase in this liability account.

The journal entry to record this cash and credit card sales transaction is shown in Illustration 12-1.

ILLUSTRATION 12-1   Journal entry to record cash and credit card sales

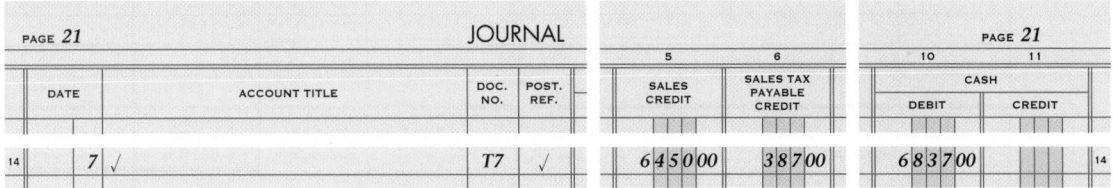

The date, 7, is written in the Date column. Special amount columns are provided for all accounts in this transaction. Therefore, a check mark is placed in the Account Title column to show that no account title needs to be written. The cash register tape number, *T7*, is recorded in the Doc. No. column. A check mark is also placed in the Post. Ref. column to show that amounts on this line do not need to be posted individually. The credit to Sales, *$6,450.00*, is written in the Sales Credit column. The credit to Sales Tax Payable, *$387.00*, is recorded in the Sales Tax Payable Credit column. The debit to Cash, *$6,837.00*, is entered in the Cash Debit column.

Sales on Account

A sale for which cash will be received at a later date is called a **sale on account**. A sale on account is also referred to as a charge sale. CarLand sells on account only to businesses. Other customers must either pay cash or use a credit card.

Accounts Receivable	
Debit side	Credit side
Normal balance	
Increase	Decrease

CarLand summarizes the total due from all charge customers in a general ledger account titled *Accounts Receivable*. Accounts Receivable is an asset account with a normal debit balance. Therefore, the accounts receivable account is increased by a debit and decreased by a credit, as shown in the T account.

When merchandise is sold on account, the seller prepares a form showing what has been sold. A form describing the goods sold, the quantity, and the price is known as an invoice. An invoice used as a source document for recording a sale on account is called a **sales invoice**. *(CONCEPT: Objective Evidence)* A sales invoice is also referred to as a sales ticket or a sales slip. The sales invoice used by CarLand is shown in Illustration 12-2.

CHAPTER 12   Journalizing Sales and Cash Receipts   **269**

Use Illustrations 12-1, 12-3, and 12-4 to point out the arrangement of the columns. Draw T accounts for the cash sales, sales on account, and the cash receipts on account transactions. Use Transparencies F and G or Transparency 12-1 to journalize the transactions.

Guided Practice

Guide students through Drill 12-D1. Direct students to complete the drill using the T accounts in the working papers as the students analyze each transaction. All students should agree with the analysis of a transaction before proceeding to the next transaction.

Independent Practice

Assign Terms 1–6, Questions 1–18, Drills 12-D2 and 12-D3, and Problem 12-1, Instruction 1.

TEACHING STRATEGIES:
DIFFERENT LEARNING STYLES

Kinesthetic Learner. When covering journal entries with a kinesthetic learner, the instructor should give the student journal paper and have the student complete the entries as the instructor demonstrates on a transparency or chalkboard.

ILLUSTRATION 12-2   Sales invoice

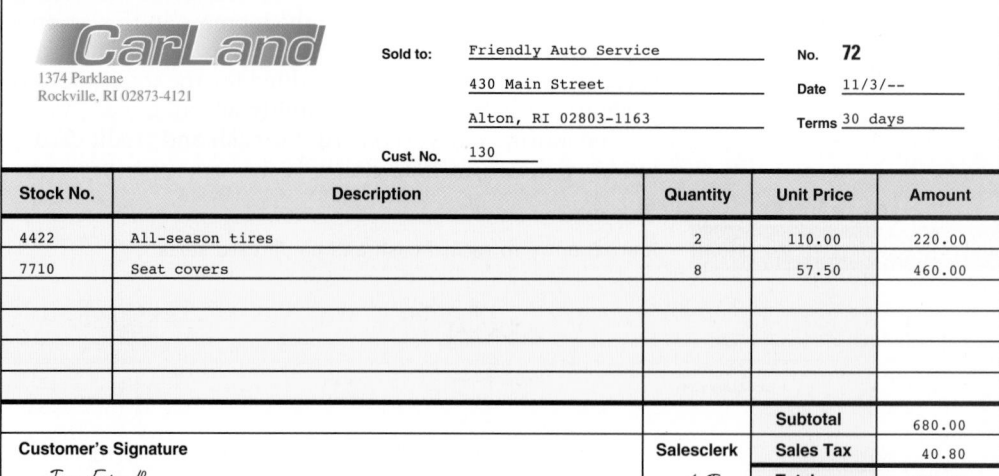

FYI

About 115 million people in the United States use credit cards to buy goods and services.

```
      Accounts Receivable
      720.80 |

            Sales
                  | 680.00

      Sales Tax Payable
                  | 40.80
```

The seller considers an invoice for a sale on account to be a sales invoice. The same invoice is considered by the customer to be a purchase invoice.

A sales invoice is prepared in duplicate. The original copy is given to the customer. The carbon copy is used as the source document for the sale on account transaction. *(CONCEPT: Objective Evidence)* Sales invoices are numbered in sequence. The number 72 is the number of the sales invoice issued to Friendly Auto Service.

November 3, 19--. Sold merchandise on account to Friendly Auto Service, $680.00, plus sales tax, $40.80; total, $720.80. Sales Invoice No. 72.

A sale on account transaction increases the amount to be collected later from a customer. Payment for this sale will be received at a later date. However, the sale is recorded at the time the sale is made because the sale has taken place and payment is due to CarLand. *(CONCEPT: Realization of Revenue)*

Because the accounts receivable account has a normal debit balance, Accounts Receivable is debited for the total sales and sales tax, $720.80, to show the increase in this asset account. The sales account has a normal credit balance. Therefore, Sales is credited for the price of the goods, $680.00, to show the increase in this revenue account. The sales tax payable account also has a normal credit balance. Therefore, Sales Tax Payable is credited for the amount of sales tax, $40.80, to show the increase in this liability account.

The journal entry to record this sale on account transaction is shown in Illustration 12-3.

APPLIED SKILLS: LANGUAGE ARTS

Paraphrasing, writing complete sentences, and identifying adverbs and the words they modify.
For additional practice in language arts skills, direct students to answer the Cases for Critical Thinking at the end of the chapter. Students should write the answers in their own words and in complete sentences. These cases also require more than a short objective-type response. Therefore they provide ideal practice in writing paragraphs and short essays. To further practice language arts skills, ask students to underline all adverbs and circle the words they modify in their answers.

INTERNATIONAL WORK WEEK

American business offices normally operate Monday through Friday, eight hours a day, with a 30 to 45 minute lunch break. However, that is not necessarily true in other countries. When doing business internationally, the business day must be taken into consideration when telephone communication is made.

For example, in Spain, many businesses close at 2:00 p.m. so that employees may eat lunch with their families. The office reopens at 5:00 p.m. and stays open until about 8:00 p.m.

In the People's Republic of China, employees usually work Monday through Saturday, eight hours a day, with lunch from 1:00 p.m. to 2:00 p.m.

Before attempting to telephone or fax communication to foreign countries, the time differences and working hours must be taken into consideration. The following chart shows the time zones around the world.

World Time Zone Map

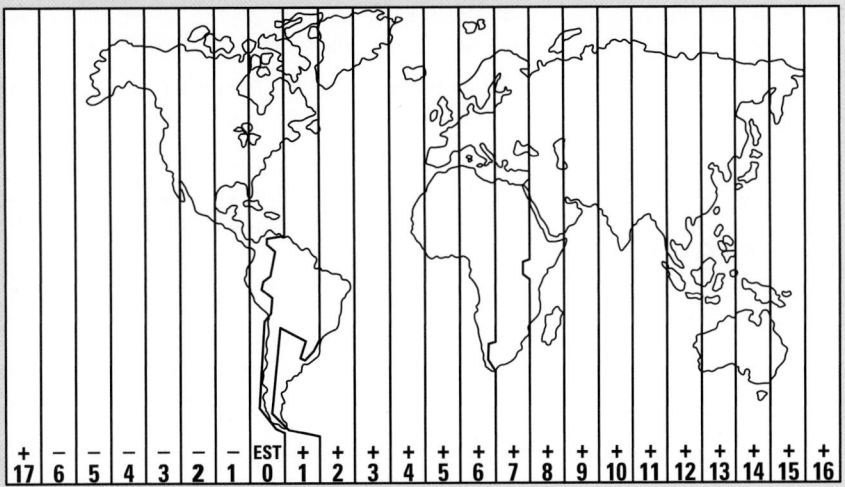

| + 17 | – 6 | – 5 | – 4 | – 3 | – 2 | – 1 | EST 0 | + 1 | + 2 | + 3 | + 4 | + 5 | + 6 | + 7 | + 8 | + 9 | + 10 | + 11 | + 12 | + 13 | + 14 | + 15 | + 16 |

ILLUSTRATION 12-3   Journal entry to record a sale on account

PAGE 21   JOURNAL

	DATE	ACCOUNT TITLE	DOC. NO.	POST. REF.	3 ACCOUNTS RECEIVABLE DEBIT	4 ACCOUNTS RECEIVABLE CREDIT	5 SALES CREDIT	6 SALES TAX PAYABLE CREDIT
4	3	Friendly Auto Service	S72		7 2 0 80		6 8 0 00	4 0 80
5								

The date, *3*, is written in the Date column. The customer name, *Friendly Auto Service*, is recorded in the Account Title column. The sales invoice number, *S72*, is entered in the Doc. No. column. The

---

TEACHING STRATEGIES: TEACHING TIP

Analyzing transactions on the blackboard and then journalizing on the overhead is a very valuable teaching method. It is more meaningful for students to see the actual process when journalizing is being taught.

CLOSURE

- Use Audit Your Understanding questions.
- Review the procedures for journalizing sales and cash receipts transactions.

debit to Accounts Receivable $720.80, is written in the Accounts Receivable Debit column. The credit to Sales, $680.00, is recorded in the Sales Credit column. The credit to Sales Tax Payable, $40.80, is entered in the Sales Tax Payable Credit column.

The debit and credit amounts are recorded in special amount columns. Therefore, writing the titles of the ledger accounts in the Account Title column is not necessary. However, the name of the customer is written in the Account Title column to show from whom the amount is due. CarLand's procedures for keeping records of the amounts to be collected from each customer are described in Chapter 13.

Cash Receipts on Account

When cash is received on account from a customer, CarLand prepares a receipt. The receipts are prenumbered so that all receipts can be accounted for. Receipts are prepared in duplicate. The original copy of the receipt is given to the customer. The carbon copy of the receipt is used as the source document for the cash receipt on account transaction. (CONCEPT: Objective Evidence)

November 6, 19--. Received cash on account from Autohaus Service, $1,802.00, covering S65. Receipt No. 86.

A cash receipt on account transaction decreases the amount to be collected from a customer. This transaction increases the cash account balance and decreases the accounts receivable account balance.

Because the cash account has a normal debit balance, Cash is debited for the amount of cash received, $1,802.00, to show the increase in this asset account. The accounts receivable account also has a normal debit balance. Therefore, Accounts Receivable is credited for $1,802.00 to show the decrease in this asset account.

The journal entry to record this cash receipt on account transaction is shown in Illustration 12-4.

APPLIED SKILLS:
WORD PROCESSING

If you wish to integrate word processing in your accounting course, you may direct students to answer the end-of-chapter Accounting Terms, Questions for Individual Study, and Cases for Critical Thinking using their word processing software.

```
              Cash
          1,802.00 |
       Accounts Receivable
                  | 1,802.00
```

TEACHING STRATEGIES:
DIFFERENT LEARNING STYLES

Print Learner. When covering journal entries with a print learner, the instructor should discuss the entries, using the textbook examples and referring to the textbook. The print learner can later go back and study the entries.

ILLUSTRATION 12-4   Journal entry to record a cash receipt on account

	DATE	ACCOUNT TITLE	DOC. NO.	POST. REF.	ACCOUNTS RECEIVABLE DEBIT	ACCOUNTS RECEIVABLE CREDIT	CASH DEBIT	CASH CREDIT	
11	6	*Autohaus Service*	R86			1 8 0 2 00	1 8 0 2 00		11
12									12

The date, 6, is written in the Date column. The customer name, *Autohaus Service*, is recorded in the Account Title column. The

TEACHING STRATEGIES: DIFFERENT LEARNING STYLES

Tactile Learner. Tactile learners may benefit from using the computer to key journal entries and then print reports. A ruler can be positioned on the input forms as a guide when keying the entries. The student should also be encouraged to place a finger on each account title in the journal entries report and trace it over to the amount in the amount column of the report to check it for accuracy.

Tactile learners should also be given the opportunity to journalize transactions from at least one simulation that contains source documents which must be handled to analyze, journalize, and file.

receipt number, *R86*, is entered in the Doc. No. column. The credit to Accounts Receivable, *$1,802.00*, is written in the Accounts Receivable Credit column. The debit to Cash, *$1,802.00*, is recorded in the Cash Debit column.

The Summary Illustration on page 277 summarizes the entries for sales and cash receipts transactions in an expanded journal.

PROVING AND RULING AN EXPANDED JOURNAL

A journal is proved and ruled whenever a journal page is filled and always at the end of a month.

Totaling and Proving an Expanded Journal Page

After all November 14 entries are recorded, page 21 of CarLand's journal is filled. Page 21 is totaled and proved before column totals are forwarded to page 22. To prove a journal page, CarLand uses a calculator to verify that the total debit amounts equal the total credit amounts. CarLand's debit totals equal the credit totals on page 21 of the journal. Therefore, the equality of debits and credits has been proved.

Ruling an Expanded Journal Page to Carry Totals Forward

After a journal page has been proved, the journal must be prepared for forwarding. CarLand's journal column totals prepared for forwarding are shown on line 34, Illustration 12-5 on pages 274 and 275.

Five steps are followed to rule CarLand's journal.

1 Rule a single line across all amount columns directly below the last entry to indicate that the columns are to be added.

2 On the next line write the date, *14*, in the Date column.

3 Write the words, *Carried Forward*, in the Account Title column. A check mark is also placed in the Post. Ref. column to show that nothing on this line needs to be posted.

4 Write each column total below the single line.

5 Rule double lines below the column totals across all amount columns to show that the totals have been verified as correct.

FYI

To prove a journal page, use a calculator to verify that total debit amounts equal total credit amounts.

Starting a New Expanded Journal Page

The totals from the previous journal page are carried forward to the next journal page. The totals are recorded on the first line of the new page. Column totals brought forward to a new page are shown on line 1, Illustration 12-6 on pages 274 and 275.

CHAPTER 12   Journalizing Sales and Cash Receipts   **273**

ILLUSTRATION 12-5   Journal prepared for forwarding (left page)

PAGE 21

JOURNAL

	DATE		ACCOUNT TITLE	DOC. NO.	POST. REF.	GENERAL DEBIT (1)	GENERAL CREDIT (2)	ACCOUNTS RECEIVABLE DEBIT (3)	ACCOUNTS RECEIVABLE CREDIT (4)	
1	Nov. 19--	2	✓	C259	✓					1
2		2	Veloz Automotive	P74						2
32		14	Powell Rent-A-Car	R89					3 1 8 00	32
33		14	✓	T14	✓					33
34		14	Carried Forward		✓	4 2 9 3 00	3 2 0 00	3 3 9 2 00	3 9 7 5 00	34

ILLUSTRATION 12-6   Journal totals brought forward to a new page (left page)

PAGE 22

JOURNAL

	DATE		ACCOUNT TITLE	DOC. NO.	POST. REF.	GENERAL DEBIT (1)	GENERAL CREDIT (2)	ACCOUNTS RECEIVABLE DEBIT (3)	ACCOUNTS RECEIVABLE CREDIT (4)	
1	Nov. 19--	14	Brought Forward		✓	4 2 9 3 00	3 2 0 00	3 3 9 2 00	3 9 7 5 00	1
2										2
3										3
4										4

Four steps are followed for forwarding totals.

1 Write the page number, *22*, at the top of the journal.

2 Write the date, *19--, Nov. 14*, in the Date column.

3 Write the words, *Brought Forward*, in the Account Title column. A check mark is also placed in the Post. Ref. column to show that nothing on this line needs to be posted.

4 Record the column totals brought forward from page 21 of the journal.

Proving an Expanded Journal at the End of a Month

Equality of debits and credits in a journal is proved at the end of each month. The proof for CarLand's journal, Illustration 12-7 on pages 276 and 277, is calculated as follows.

ILLUSTRATION 12-5   Journal prepared for forwarding (right page)

PAGE 21

	5 SALES CREDIT	6 SALES TAX PAYABLE CREDIT	7 ACCOUNTS PAYABLE DEBIT	8 ACCOUNTS PAYABLE CREDIT	9 PURCHASES DEBIT	10 CASH DEBIT	11 CASH CREDIT	
1					483 00		483 00	1
2				1754 00	1754 00			2
32						318 00		32
33	5100 00	306 00				5406 00		33
34	14750 00	885 00	5360 00	11690 00	12013 00	16218 00	9656 00	34

ILLUSTRATION 12-6   Journal totals brought forward to a new page (right page)

PAGE 22

	5 SALES CREDIT	6 SALES TAX PAYABLE CREDIT	7 ACCOUNTS PAYABLE DEBIT	8 ACCOUNTS PAYABLE CREDIT	9 PURCHASES DEBIT	10 CASH DEBIT	11 CASH CREDIT	
1	14750 00	885 00	5360 00	11690 00	12013 00	16218 00	9656 00	1
2								2
3								3
4								4

Col. No.	Column Title	Debit Totals	Credit Totals
1	General Debit	$15,686.22	
2	General Credit		$ 2,029.02
3	Accounts Receivable Debit	9,222.00	
4	Accounts Receivable Credit		7,950.00
5	Sales Credit		31,600.00
6	Sales Tax Payable Credit		1,896.00
7	Accounts Payable Debit	10,820.00	
8	Accounts Payable Credit		15,870.00
9	Purchases Debit	14,773.00	
10	Cash Debit	32,224.00	
11	Cash Credit		23,380.20
	Totals	$82,725.22	$82,725.22

FYI

Double lines below totals show that the totals have been verified as correct.

The two totals, *$82,725.22*, are equal. Equality of debits and credits in CarLand's journal for November is proved.

Use Transparencies F and G to rule an expanded journal, carry forward, and start a new page.

Guided Practice

Guide students through Demonstration Problem 12A. Demonstrate this problem on the overhead with the students completing the problem at their desks. For each transaction read the transaction, ask how it is analyzed, and ask how it is recorded in the journal. All students should agree with the analysis of the transaction before proceeding to the next transaction.

Independent Practice

- Assign Questions 19–20, Problem 12-1, Instructions 2–3, Study Guide 12, and Mastery Problem 12-M.
- Assign Study Guide 12. If you prefer to have your students complete the study guide at the computer, use the Electronic Study Guide.

TEACHING STRATEGIES: TEACHING TIP

Double lines mean that the totals have been verified as correct. It is important to reinforce this step.

TEACHING STRATEGIES: DIFFERENT LEARNING ABILITIES

Gifted Students. Partnerships are an effective form of business organization only when there is effective communication and cooperation among partners. Gifted students can best learn about the opportunities, problems, and challenges of a partnership by forming a real partnership. Encourage gifted students to form a partnership to sell a service or product of their selection. The students should prepare the partnership agreement, operate the business, and report the results of operations. Suggest that the students consult businesspersons, such as lawyers and accountants, for assistance.

- Assess student understanding by checking solutions to Independent Practice activities.
- Review Summary Illustration 12-8, "Summary of Entries for Sales and Cash Receipts Transactions in an Expanded Journal."

Reteach

- Assign Recycling Problem 12-R.
- Duplicate and assign Math Work Sheet Chapter 12 Part B, Proving an Expanded Journal and Part C, Proving Cash from the Masters and Solutions to Enrichment/Application Activities Section in the Teacher's Resource Guide to provide additional practice on the mathematics of proving an expanded journal and proving cash.

Extend

- Assign Challenge Problem 12-C (the challenge is the columns have been rearranged in the expanded journal).
- Assign the Application Program Disk software with Problem 12-M.
- Assign Electronic Study Guide

Enrich

Assign the Applied Communications special feature on page 279.

ILLUSTRATION 12-7   Journal page totaled and ruled at the end of a month (left page)

	DATE	ACCOUNT TITLE	DOC. NO.	POST. REF.	GENERAL DEBIT	GENERAL CREDIT	ACCOUNTS RECEIVABLE DEBIT	ACCOUNTS RECEIVABLE CREDIT	
15	30 ✓		T30	✓					15
16	30	Totals			15 686 22	2 029 02	9 222 00	7 950 00	16
17									17
18									18
19									19
20									20

PAGE 23 — JOURNAL

Proving Cash at the End of a Month

CarLand's cash proof at the end of November is calculated as shown below.

Cash on hand at the beginning of the month . . . . (November 1 balance of cash account in general ledger)	$14,706.20
Plus total cash received during the month . . . . (Cash Debit column total, line 16, Illustration 12-7)	32,224.00
Equals total	$46,930.20
Less total cash paid during the month . . . . (Cash Credit column total, line 16, Illustration 12-7)	23,380.20
Equals cash balance on hand at end of the month . . .	$23,550.00
Checkbook balance on the next unused check stub . .	$23,550.00

Since the balance on the next unused check stub is the same as the cash proof, cash is proved.

FYI

When cash is proved, it must always equal the amount on the next unused check stub.

Ruling an Expanded Journal at the End of a Month

CarLand's journal is ruled at the end of each month. CarLand's expanded journal totaled and ruled at the end of November is shown on line 16, Illustration 12-7. Five steps are followed to rule a journal.

1 Rule a single line across all amount columns directly below the last entry to indicate that the columns are to be added.

TEACHING STRATEGIES: DIFFERENT LEARNING STYLES

Visual Learner. When covering journal entries with a visual learner, the instructor should discuss the entries, using a transparency or the chalkboard to record the entry. In addition, the student should be asked to mentally picture each part of the entry before the instructor actually writes it on the transparency or chalkboard.

PAGE 23

	SALES CREDIT	SALES TAX PAYABLE CREDIT	ACCOUNTS PAYABLE DEBIT	ACCOUNTS PAYABLE CREDIT	PURCHASES DEBIT	CASH DEBIT	CASH CREDIT	
	5	6	7	8	9	10	11	
15	1150 00	69 00				1219 00		15
16	31600 00	1896 00	10820 00	15870 00	14773 00	32224 00	23380 20	16
17								17
18								18
19								19
20								20

2 On the next line write the date, *30*, in the Date column.

3 Write the word, *Totals*, in the Account Title column.

4 Write each column total below the single line.

5 Rule double lines across all amount columns to show that the totals have been verified as correct.

Some of the column totals will be posted as described in Chapter 13. Therefore, a check mark is not placed in the Post. Ref. column for this line.

The chart shown in Illustration 12-8 summarizes the entries for sales and cash receipts transactions in an expanded journal.

SUMMARY ILLUSTRATION 12-8

Summary of entries for sales and cash receipts transactions in an expanded journal

TRANSACTION	GENERAL DEBIT	GENERAL CREDIT	ACCOUNTS RECEIVABLE DEBIT	ACCOUNTS RECEIVABLE CREDIT	SALES CREDIT	SALES TAX PAYABLE CREDIT	ACCOUNTS PAYABLE DEBIT	ACCOUNTS PAYABLE CREDIT	PURCHASES DEBIT	CASH DEBIT	CASH CREDIT
	1	2	3	4	5	6	7	8	9	10	11
Cash and credit card sale					X	X				X	
Sale on account			X		X	X					
Cash receipt on account				X						X	

CLOSURE

- Use Audit Your Understanding questions.
- Review Summary Illustration 12-8 and Transparency 12-2, Chapter Summary.

ASSESS

- Administer Problem Test Chapter 12.
- Administer a MicroExam test for Chapter 12.

AUDIT YOUR UNDERSTANDING

1. The columns are totaled and the equality of debits and credits is verified.
2. (1) Write the page number at the top of the journal. (2) Write the date in the Date column. (3) Write the words, Brought Forward, in the Account Title column. A check mark is also placed in the Post. Ref. column to show that nothing on this line needs to be posted. (4) Record the column totals brought forward from the previous page of the journal.
3. Cash on hand at the beginning of the month, plus total cash received during the month, less total cash paid during the month, equals cash balance on hand at end of the month. Cash is proved if the balance on the next unused check stub is the same as the cash proof.

TEACHING STRATEGIES: APPLYING VISUALS

Direct students to Summary Illustration 12-8 to review the summary of entries for sales and cash receipts transactions in an expanded journal.

APPLIED SKILLS: WRITING ACROSS THE CURRICULUM

Writing paragraphs and short essays. The Cases for Critical Thinking are short, practical applications of the accounting principles developed in the chapter. Some cases are planned to present problems related to the chapter but not specifically discussed and answered in the chapter. These cases present an opportunity for critical thinking and decision making. These cases also require more than a short objective-type response. Therefore they provide ideal practice in writing paragraphs and short essays.

1. **customer:** A person or business to whom merchandise or services are sold. (p. 267)

2. **sales tax:** A tax on a sale of merchandise or services. (p. 267)

3. **cash sale:** A sale in which cash is received for the total amount of the sale at the time of the transaction. (p. 268)

4. **credit card sale:** A sale in which a credit card is used for the total amount of the sale at the time of the transaction. (p. 268)

5. **sale on account:** A sale for which cash will be received at a later date. (p. 269)

6. **sales invoice:** An invoice used as a source document for recording a sale on account. (p. 269)

QUESTIONS FOR INDIVIDUAL STUDY

1. The purchase and sale of merchandise. (p. 267)

2. As a percentage of sales. (p. 267)

3. Because businesses must file reports with the proper government unit and pay the amount of sales tax collected. (p. 267)

4. Total sales and total sales tax. (p. 267)

5. Because the sales tax collected is owed to the state government. (p. 267)

6. The sales tax payable account has a normal credit balance; the account is increased by a credit and decreased by a debit. (p. 267)

7. Realization of Revenue concept. (p. 268)

8. Objective Evidence concept. (p. 268)

9. Weekly. (p. 268)

10. Cash is debited; Sales and Sales Tax Payable are credited. (p. 269)

11. Special amount columns are provided for all accounts in this transaction. (p. 269)

12. Charge sale. (p. 269)

13. Accounts Receivable. (p. 269)

14. Sales invoice. (p. 269)

15. Sales ticket and sales slip. (p. 269)

16. Accounts Receivable is debited; Sales and Sales Tax Payable are credited. (p. 270)

ACCOUNTING TERMS   EPT(a)

What is the meaning of each of the following?

1. customer	4. credit card sale
2. sales tax	5. sale on account
3. cash sale	6. sales invoice

QUESTIONS FOR INDIVIDUAL STUDY   EPT(b)

1. What are the two major activities of a merchandising business?

2. How are sales tax rates usually stated?

3. Why must every business that collects a sales tax keep accurate records of the amount of tax collected?

4. What two amounts must sales tax records show?

5. Why is sales tax collected considered a liability?

6. What is the normal balance of the sales tax payable account, and how is the account increased and decreased?

7. Which accounting concept is being applied when revenue is recorded at the time a sale is made, regardless of when payment is made?

8. Which accounting concept is being applied when a cash register tape is used as the source document for cash and credit card sales?

9. How often does CarLand journalize cash sales?

10. What accounts are affected, and how, for a cash and credit card sales transaction?

11. Why is a check mark placed in the Account Title column of an expanded journal when journalizing cash and credit card sales?

12. What is another name used for a sale on account?

13. What is the title of the general ledger account used to summarize the total amount due from all charge customers?

14. What is the source document for a sale on account transaction?

15. What are other names used for a sales invoice?

16. What accounts are affected, and how, for a sale on account transaction?

17. Which amount columns in a journal are used to record a sale on account transaction?

18. What accounts are affected, and how, for a cash receipt on account transaction?

19. How often is the equality of debits and credits in a journal proved?

20. How often is a journal page ruled?

CASES FOR CRITICAL THINKING   EPT(b)

CASE 1 Carrie and Karl Lott, partners, operate a shoe store. A 5-column journal similar to the one described in Chapter 5 is used to record all transactions. The business sells merchandise for cash and on account. The business also purchases most of its merchandise on account. Mrs. Lott asked an accountant to check the accounting system and recommend changes. The accountant suggests that an expanded journal similar to the one described in Chapters 11 and 12 be used. Which journal would be better? Why?

CASE 2 Amy Pryor, an accountant for a sporting goods store, has noted a major increase in overdue amounts from charge customers. All invoice amounts from sales on account are due within 30 days. The amounts due have reduced the amount of cash available for the day-to-day operation of the business. Miss Pryor recommends that the business (1) stop all sales on account and (2) begin accepting bank credit cards. The owner is reluctant to accept the recommendations because the business might lose some reliable customers who do not have credit cards. Also, the business will have increased expenses because of the credit card fee. How would you respond to Miss Pryor's recommendations? What alternatives might the owner consider?

17. Accounts Receivable Debit; Sales and Sales Tax Payable Credit. (pp. 271–272)

18. Cash is debited; Accounts Receivable is credited. (p. 272)

19. When a page is filled and totals are carried forward to a new page and always at the end of each month. (p. 273)

20. When a page is filled and totals are carried forward to a new page and always at the end of each month. (p. 273)

How often have you heard people complain about the rising costs of products? The tendency for prices to increase over time is referred to as inflation. Increasing prices reduce what an individual or company can purchase with the same amount of money.

INSTRUCTIONS:

The following table represents the prices for selected consumer goods in 1980. Copy the table and add a column for the current year and a column for the percent of change. Use the newspaper and identify current prices for the products listed. Determine the percentage change in the price of each item. If an item decreased in price, can you explain the reason for the decrease?

COMPARISON OF PRICES FOR SELECTED CONSUMER ITEMS 1980 AND 19--

Item	1980 Price
19-inch color television	$439.00
Cassette tape.	6.95
Milk (gallon)	1.99
Ground beef (pound)	1.69
Eggs, medium (dozen).	.69
Raisin bran	1.39
Film, 12 exposures	1.13
Theater ticket.	3.50
Motor oil (quart)	.84
Refrigerator (19.1 cu. ft.)	679.00

Surveys of business managers show that communication skills are one of the most desired traits in new employees. The APPLIED COMMUNICATIONS ACTIVITY provides an opportunity for students to practice their communication and language arts skills on topics that directly relate to accounting.

This APPLIED COMMUNICATIONS ACTIVITY requires students to research current prices of selected consumer items, calculate the percentage increase or decrease in price, and give reasons for the changes. Some items will show a price decrease which should challenge students to arrive at increased consumer demand, increased productivity, cheaper raw materials, global trade factors, and so on, to determine why the price has decreased.

DRILLS FOR UNDERSTANDING

EPT(c,d)

DRILL 12-D1 Analyzing transactions into debit and credit parts

TUTORIAL

INSTRUCTIONS:

Prepare T accounts for each of the following transactions. Use the T accounts to analyze each transaction. A 5% sales tax has been added to each sale. The first transaction is given as an example.

1. Recorded cash and credit card sales, $1,500.00, plus sales tax, $75.00; total, $1,575.00.

2. Sold merchandise on account to Steven Kramer, $300.00, plus sales tax, $15.00; total, $315.00.

3. Sold merchandise on account to Mark Fields, $360.00, plus sales tax, $18.00; total, $378.00.

4. Received cash on account from Jackson White, $157.50.

5. Received cash on account from Gloria Burton, $68.25.

6. Recorded cash and credit card sales, $1,750.00, plus sales tax, $87.50; total, $1,837.50.

The solution to Drill 12-D1 is needed to complete Drill 12-D3.

Cash	
1,575.00	

Sales	
	1,500.00

Sales Tax Payable	
	75.00

DRILL 12-D2 Analyzing sales transactions

MATHEMATICS

INSTRUCTIONS:

1. Prepare a T account for each of the following accounts: Cash, Accounts Receivable, Sales, and Sales Tax Payable.

2. Using the T accounts, analyze the following transactions. Add a 6% sales tax to each sale. Write the transaction number in parentheses to the left of each amount. The first transaction is given as an example.

CASES FOR CRITICAL THINKING

Case 1 Space and time can be saved by using an expanded journal for recording sales and purchases on account transactions. The journal in Chapter 5 does not provide special columns for recording sales and purchases on account. They would therefore have to be recorded in General Debit and General Credit columns. All journal entries to Sales, Purchases, Accounts Receivable, and Accounts Payable could be summarized in the special amount columns of an expanded journal.

Case 2 Credit card systems encourage people with good credit ratings to obtain and use credit cards. Most people with good credit ratings now have one or more credit cards. Business, therefore, could increase rather than decrease. The credit card fee charged by the bank should not be a major concern. The fee is minimal in comparison to a number of overdue accounts that may never be collected. When a credit card is used, the bank issuing the credit card assumes the responsibility for collecting amounts due from card holders. Accepting credit cards allows the business to record credit card sales as regular cash sales. An alternative to Miss Pryor's recommendations might be to continue to sell on account to selected regular customers with good payment records. Credit cards could then be used by other customers.

Students' solutions will vary depending on current price levels of the merchandise.

CHECK FIGURES

See Teacher's Edition of Working Papers for complete solutions to drills and problems.

Drill 12-D1 Cash is debited in 4 transactions; Sales is credited in 4 transactions; Accounts Receivable is debited in 2 and credited in 2 transactions.

Drill 12-D2 Cash is debited in Trans. (1), (4), (5), (6); Sales and Sales Tax Payable are credited in Trans. (1), (2), (3), (6); Accounts Receivable is debited in Trans. (2), (3) and credited (4), (5).

1. Recorded cash and credit card sales, $2,700.00.
2. Sold merchandise on account to Melissa Bedo, $180.00.
3. Sold merchandise on account to Kim Lea, $170.00.
4. Received cash on account from Maria Jones, $148.40.
5. Received cash on account from Jack Mumford, $79.50.
6. Recorded cash and credit card sales, $2,375.00.

Cash		
(1)	2,862.00	

Accounts Receivable		

Sales		
	(1)	2,700.00

Sales Tax Payable		
	(1)	162.00

DRILL 12-D3 Analyzing journal entries

The solution to Drill 12-D1 is needed to complete Drill 12-D3.

INSTRUCTIONS:

A form for analyzing journal entries is given in the working papers that accompany this textbook. Based on the answers in Drill 12-D1, write the amounts in the amount columns to be used to journalize each transaction. Transaction 1 is given as an example in the working papers.

APPLICATION PROBLEM   EPT(c,d,e)

PROBLEM 12-1 Journalizing sales and cash receipts

Mark Butler and Betty Rivers, partners, own a tennis equipment and clothing store.

INSTRUCTIONS:

1. Journalize the following transactions completed during September of the current year. Use page 16 of a journal similar to the one described in this chapter. A 4% sales tax has been added to each sale. Source documents are abbreviated as follows: receipt, R; sales invoice, S; cash register tape, T.

Sept. 1. Sold merchandise on account to Valerie Seeley, $50.00, plus sales tax, $2.00; total, $52.00. S66.

2. Sold merchandise on account to Jill Folker, $125.00, plus sales tax, $5.00; total, $130.00. S67.

4. Sold merchandise on account to Jerome Hodges, $85.00, plus sales tax, $3.40; total, $88.40. S68.

5. Received cash on account from Rita Picken, $140.40, covering S62. R93.

5. Recorded cash and credit card sales, $2,360.00, plus sales tax, $94.40; total, $2,454.40. T5.

7. Received cash on account from Karla Doyle, $182.00, covering S63. R94.

9. Sold merchandise on account to Anthony Zolte, $115.00, plus sales tax, $4.60; total, $119.60. S69.

12. Recorded cash and credit card sales, $2,890.00, plus sales tax, $115.60; total, $3,005.60. T12.

12. Received cash on account from Jonathan Ames, $50.40, covering S64. R95.

14. Received cash on account from Robert Hall, $67.60, covering S65. R96.

15. Sold merchandise on account to Beth Klein, $115.00, plus sales tax, $4.60; total, $119.60. S70.

Sept. 17. Received cash on account from Valerie Seeley, $52.00, covering S66. R97.

    19. Recorded cash and credit card sales, $2,810.00, plus sales tax, $112.40; total, $2,922.40. T19.

    25. Received cash on account from Jill Folker, $130.00, covering S67. R98.

    26. Sold merchandise on account to Jill Folker, $75.00, plus sales tax, $3.00; total, $78.00. S71.

    26. Recorded cash and credit card sales, $2,650.00, plus sales tax, $106.00; total, $2,756.00. T26.

    28. Received cash on account from Jerome Hodges, $88.40, covering S68. R99.

    29. Sold merchandise on account to Karla Doyle, $95.00, plus sales tax, $3.80; total, $98.80. S72.

    30. Recorded cash and credit card sales, $1,540.00, plus sales tax, $61.60; total, $1,601.60. T30.

2. Total the journal. Prove the equality of debits and credits.

3. Rule the journal.

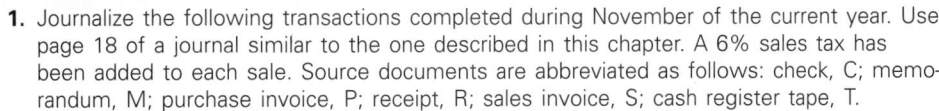

ENRICHMENT PROBLEMS   **EPT(c,d,e)**

CHECK FIGURES *(cont'd)*

Mastery Problem 12-M Journal totals page 18—4,556.00; 510.00; 1,577.28; 2,771.90; 12,448.00; 746.88; 2,793.00; 3,260.00; 3,641.00; 14,389.50; 7,220.00. Journal totals page 19— 4,942.00; 510.00; 1,969.48; 4,549.60; 16,138.00; 968.28; 2,793.00; 4,500.00; 4,881.00; 19,686.40; 7,606.00

MASTERY PROBLEM 12-M   Journalizing transactions

Kevin Sykes and David Webb, partners, own a bicycle and motorcycle store.

INSTRUCTIONS:

1. Journalize the following transactions completed during November of the current year. Use page 18 of a journal similar to the one described in this chapter. A 6% sales tax has been added to each sale. Source documents are abbreviated as follows: check, C; memorandum, M; purchase invoice, P; receipt, R; sales invoice, S; cash register tape, T.

Nov. 2. Paid cash for rent, $1,250.00. C244.

    2. Kevin Sykes, partner, withdrew cash for personal use, $600.00. C245.

    2. David Webb, partner, withdrew cash for personal use, $600.00. C246.

    3. Paid cash for electric bill, $130.00. C247.

    3. Purchased merchandise on account from Vista Cycle Co., $2,275.00. P58.

    4. Paid cash on account to Daley Motorcycles, $1,360.00, covering P56. C248.

    5. Sold merchandise on account to Loree Adams, $1,130.00, plus sales tax, $67.80; total, $1,197.80. S61.

    5. Paid cash for office supplies, $62.00. C249.

    6. Purchased merchandise for cash, $165.00. C250.

    7. Recorded cash and credit card sales, $5,850.00, plus sales tax, $351.00; total, $6,201.00. T7.

    9. Sold merchandise on account to Victor Droste, $358.00, plus sales tax, $21.48; total, $379.48. S62.

    9. Received cash on account from Wayne Ivory, $1,775.50, covering S57. R112.

    11. Bought office supplies on account from Walden Supply, $68.00. M43.

    12. Purchased merchandise for cash, $180.00. C251.

    12. Received cash on account from Robert Melvin, $996.40, covering S58. R113.

    13. Paid cash on account to Action Cycles, $1,365.00, covering P57. C252.

    14. David Webb, partner, withdrew merchandise for personal use, $385.00. M44.

Nov. 14. Recorded cash and credit card sales, $2,680.00, plus sales tax, $160.80; total, $2,840.80. T14.

16. Kevin Sykes, partner, withdrew cash for personal use, $600.00. C253.

16. David Webb, partner, withdrew cash for personal use, $600.00. C254.

17. Purchased merchandise on account from United Bicycle Co., $825.00. P59.

18. Purchased merchandise for cash, $196.00. C255.

18. Bought store supplies on account from Baker Supply, $92.00. M45.

19. Paid cash on account to Walden Supply, $68.00, covering M43. C256.

21. Recorded cash and credit card sales, $2,430.00, plus sales tax, $145.80; total, $2,575.80. T21.

23. Discovered that a payment of cash for advertising in October was journalized and posted in error as a debit to Miscellaneous Expense instead of Advertising Expense, $125.00. M46.

23. Paid cash for office supplies, $44.00. C257.

2. Prepare page 18 of the journal for forwarding. Total the amount columns. Prove the equality of debits and credits, and record the totals to be carried forward on line 32.

3. Record the totals brought forward on line 1 of page 19 of the journal. Prove the equality of debits and credits again.

4. Journalize the following transactions on page 19 of the journal.

Nov. 23. Received cash on account from Esther Lorand, $630.70, covering S59. R114.

24. Sold merchandise on account to Celia Sotelo, $325.00, plus sales tax, $19.50; total, $344.50. S63.

27. Purchased merchandise on account from Cycle World, $1,240.00. P60.

27. Paid cash for advertising, $85.00. C258.

28. Recorded cash and credit card sales, $2,680.00, plus sales tax, $160.80; total, $2,840.80. T28.

28. Received cash on account from Leonard Kane, $1,147.00, covering S60. R115.

30. Sold merchandise on account to Jonathan Hunt, $45.00, plus sales tax, $2.70; total, $47.70. S64.

30. Paid cash to replenish the petty cash fund, $301.00: office supplies, $62.00; store supplies, $71.00; advertising, $88.00; miscellaneous, $80.00. C259.

30. Recorded cash and credit card sales, $640.00, plus sales tax, $38.40; total, $678.40. T30.

5. Total page 19 of the journal. Prove the equality of debits and credits.

6. Prove cash. The November 1 cash account balance in the general ledger was $9,431.00. On November 30 the balance on the next unused check stub was $21,511.40.

7. Rule page 19 of the journal.

CHALLENGE PROBLEM 12-C Journalizing transactions

The columns of a journal may be arranged in different ways. For example, the journal used in this chapter is referred to as an expanded journal. All of the amount columns are to the right of the Account Title column. However, another arrangement is to have the amount columns divided by the Account Title column. Some of the amount columns are to the left and some are to the right of the Account Title column.

INSTRUCTIONS:

1. Use a journal with the columns arranged as follows.

Cash		Date	Account Title	Doc. No.	Post Ref.	General		Accts. Rec.		Sales Cr.	Sales Tax Pay. Cr.	Accts. Payable		Purchases Dr.
Dr.	Cr.					Dr.	Cr.	Dr.	Cr.			Dr.	Cr.	

2. Use the transactions and instructions for Mastery Problem 12-M. Complete all of the instructions using the journal above.

Chapter 13 describes the step-by-step process of posting from the multi-column journal to the general ledger and the accounts payable and accounts receivable subsidiary ledgers. Students review posting concepts presented in Chapter 6, including posting both individual items and column totals. The nature of controlling accounts in a general ledger that control accounts in a subsidiary ledger is explored. Posting to the accounts payable and receivable subsidiary ledgers is presented using the same steps for posting to a general ledger. Account numbers are used for customer and vendor accounts in the accounts

GUIDE TO ACHIEVING LEARNING OBJECTIVES

	TEACH	APPLY		EXTEND/ENRICH					
Enabling Performance Tasks	Lesson Plans	Drills for Understanding	Application Problems	Mastery Problems	Challenge Problems	Cases for Critical Thinking	Recycling Problems	Reinforcement Activity	
a. Define accounting terms related to posting to ledgers.	13-1, 13-3								
b. Identify accounting concepts related to posting to ledgers.	13-1, 13-2, 13-3					Cases 1, 2			
c. Post to a general ledger from a journal.	13-1	13D-2	13-1	13-M	13-C		13-R	2A	
d. Open accounts in ledgers.	13-1, 13-2		13-1				13-R		
e. Post to subsidiary ledgers from a journal.	13-2	13-D2	13-1	13-M	13-C		13-R	2A	
f. Prepare subsidiary schedules.	13-3		13-1	13-M	13-C		13-R	2A	

ENRICHMENT

SPECIAL FEATURES	TECHNOLOGY CONNECTION
Multicultural Awareness, page 286	*Automated Accounting 6.0* Problems 13-C
Personal Visions in Business, page 287	Integrating Automated Accounting Topic 4 Optional Problem DB-4A
	Electronic Study Guide

receivable and payable ledgers because automated accounting software references these accounts by account number and because it permits using account numbers for posting references the same way posting references are used in posting to the general ledger.

Challenge Problem 13-C includes both journalizing and posting for additional reinforcement. The solution to Drill 13-D1 is needed to complete Drill 13-D2.

	INFORMAL ASSESSMENT		FORMAL ASSESSMENT				
	Study Guide	Audit Your Understanding	Chapter MicroExam	Chapter Problem Test	Unit Problem Test	Unit Objective Test	Portfolio
	Unit A	✓	✓			✓	
	Unit B, C	✓	✓			✓	
				✓	✓		✓
				✓			
				✓	✓		✓
				✓	✓		✓

NEW, REVIEW, AND EXTENSION

ACTIVITIES/CONCEPTS/TRANSACTIONS	NEW	REVIEW/ EXTENSION
Ledgers and controlling accounts	✓	
Posting		✓
Posting from an 11-column multi-column journal		✓
Posting separate amounts individually		✓
Posting totals of special amount columns		✓
Opening a new page for a general ledger account		✓
File maintenance		✓
Assigning account numbers		✓
Assigning account numbers to subsidiary ledger accounts		✓
Posting to subsidiary ledgers	✓	
Proving cash		✓
Proving subsidiary ledgers	✓	

TEACHING MATERIALS

Teacher's Wraparound Edition of Text

Teacher's Resource Guide

Teacher's Edition of Working Papers

Teacher's Edition of Demonstration/Recycling Problems

Teaching Transparencies

MicroExam

13

Posting to General and Subsidiary Ledgers

ENABLING PERFORMANCE TASKS

After studying Chapter 13, you will be able to:

a Define accounting terms related to posting to ledgers.

b Identify accounting practices related to posting to ledgers.

c Post to a general ledger from a journal.

d Open accounts in ledgers.

e Post to subsidiary ledgers from a journal.

f Prepare subsidiary schedules.

TERMS PREVIEW

subsidiary ledger • accounts payable ledger • accounts receivable ledger • controlling account • schedule of accounts payable • schedule of accounts receivable

A journal provides a permanent record of transactions listed in chronological order. Journal entries are sorted and summarized by transferring information to ledger accounts. Transferring information from journal entries to ledger accounts is known as posting. Posting information from a journal to ledger accounts summarizes in one place transactions affecting each account.

LEDGERS AND CONTROLLING ACCOUNTS

A business' size, number of transactions, and type of transactions determine the number of ledgers used in an accounting system.

General Ledger

A ledger that contains all accounts needed to prepare financial statements is known as a general ledger. A general ledger sorts and summarizes all information affecting income statement and balance sheet accounts. A business with transactions involving mostly the receipt and payment of cash may use only a general ledger. Rugcare, described in Part 2, uses only a general ledger. CarLand also uses a general ledger. CarLand's general ledger chart of accounts is on page 244. However, because of the business' size and the number and type of transactions, CarLand also uses additional ledgers in its accounting system.

Subsidiary Ledgers

A business needs to know the amount owed each vendor as well as the amount to be collected from each charge customer. Therefore, a separate account is needed for each vendor and each customer. A general ledger could contain an account for each vendor and for each customer. However, a business with many vendors and customers would have a bulky general ledger and a long trial balance. CarLand eliminates these problems by keeping a separate ledger for vendors and a separate ledger for customers. Each separate ledger is summarized in a single general ledger account. A ledger that is summarized in a single general ledger account is called a **subsidiary ledger**. A subsidiary ledger containing only accounts for vendors from whom items are purchased or bought on account is called an **accounts payable ledger**. A subsidiary ledger containing only accounts for charge customers is called an **accounts receivable ledger**.

Controlling Accounts

The total amount owed to all vendors is summarized in a single general ledger account, Accounts Payable. The total amount to be collected from all charge customers is summarized in a single general ledger account, Accounts Receivable.

An account in a general ledger that summarizes all accounts in a subsidiary ledger is called a **controlling account**. The balance of a controlling account equals the total of all account balances in its related subsidiary ledger. Thus, the balance of the controlling account, Accounts Payable, equals the total of all vendor account balances in the accounts payable subsidiary ledger. The balance of the controlling account, Accounts Receivable, equals the total of all charge customer account balances in the accounts receivable subsidiary ledger.

POSTING TO A GENERAL LEDGER

Daily general ledger account balances are usually not necessary. Balances of general ledger accounts are needed only when financial statements are prepared. Posting from a journal to a general ledger can be done periodically throughout a month. The number of transactions determines how often to post to a general ledger. A business with many transactions would normally post more often than a business with few transactions. Posting often helps keep the work load evenly distributed throughout a month. However, posting must always be done at the end of a month. CarLand uses the same 4-column general ledger account form and posting procedures as described for Rugcare in Chapter 6.

Posting a Journal's General Amount Columns

Amounts recorded in a journal's general amount columns are amounts for which no special amount columns are provided. Therefore, separate amounts in a journal's General Debit and General Credit columns *ARE* posted individually to the accounts written in the journal's Account Title column. The posting of the General Debit entry on line 6 of CarLand's journal is shown in Illustration 13-1.

ILLUSTRATION 13-1   Posting from a journal's General Debit column

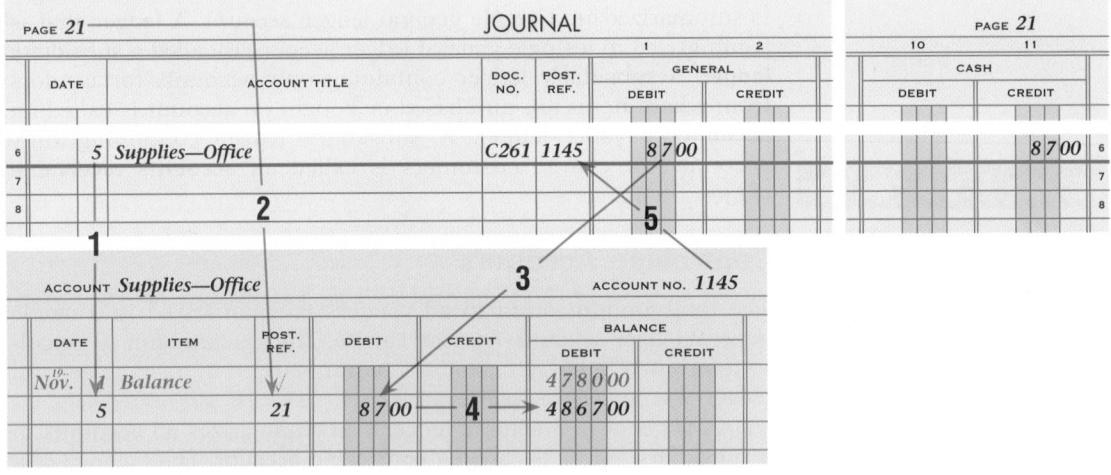

Five steps are followed to post the debit entry to the general ledger.

1 Write the date, *5*, in the Date column of the account.

2 Write the journal page number, *21*, in the Post. Ref. column of the account.

3 Write the debit amount, *$87.00*, in the account's Debit amount column.

4 Add the amount in the Debit amount column to the previous balance in the Balance Debit column ($4,780.00 + $87.00 = $4,867.00). Write the new account balance, *$4,867.00*, in the Balance Debit column.

5 Write the general ledger account number, *1145*, in the Post. Ref. column of the journal.

Posting a Journal's Special Amount Columns

CarLand's journal has nine special amount columns. Separate amounts written in these special amount columns *ARE NOT* posted individually to the general ledger. Separate amounts in a special

---

■ **Jan Robbins** ■

NAS, INC.

Jan Robbins owns NAS, Inc., a systems engineering company that specializes in government contracting. NAS, Inc. employs approximately 200 workers. Robbins is of Cherokee Indian heritage and wondered when she started her business whether she would encounter any discrimination. She was surprised to find that there was discrimination, not because she is a Native American, but because she is a woman. The industry she had entered, systems engineering for government contracts, was dominated by males who considered it to be an industry just for men. However, Robbins has worked hard and succeeded. She also finds that attitudes toward women in business are changing so that women starting out today should not face as much discrimination as she did.

Robbins worked as a sales representative for an adver-

tising agency before starting NAS, Inc. She also did some copywriting for an advertising agency. When she started her business, she started small because she had only a small amount of savings to invest. She began by being willing to work on even the smallest government contracts, usually as a subcontractor to the contractor who had won the contract.

Robbins attributes her ability to set up her business to the year of accounting she studied in high school. She says that it helped her set up her expenses and to understand the language that businesses use every day. Robbins strongly believes in the value of business courses for success and especially favors courses in accounting and banking as preparation for entrepreneurship.

Asked about her basic philosophy of business, Robbins replied, "No one plans to fail, they just fail to plan. A day doesn't pass that I don't think of that statement."

Personal Visions in Business

---

amount column all affect the same general ledger account. Therefore, only the totals of special amount columns *ARE* posted to the general ledger. Each special amount column total is posted to the general ledger account listed in the column heading. Posting of the Cash Credit amount column total is shown in Illustration 13-2.

ILLUSTRATION 13-2   Posting the Cash Credit column total

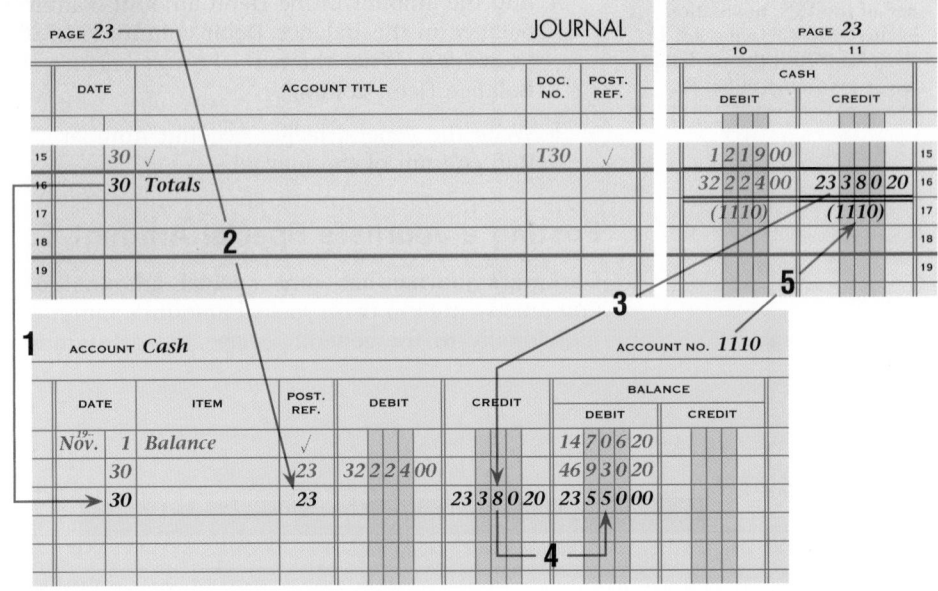

Five steps are followed to post the Cash Credit column total.

1 Write the date, *30*, in the Date column of the account.

2 Write the journal page number, *23*, in the Post. Ref. column of the account.

3 Write the Cash Credit column total, *$23,380.20*, in the account's Credit amount column.

4 Subtract the amount in the Credit amount column from the previous balance in the Balance Debit column ($46,930.20 − $23,380.20 = $23,550.00). Write the new account balance, *$23,550.00*, in the Balance Debit column.

5 Return to the journal and write the general ledger account number, *1110*, in parentheses below the Cash Credit column total.

Rules for Posting a Journal's Column Totals

Rules for posting a journal's column totals are shown in Illustration 13-3.

288   PART 3   Accounting for a Merchandising Business Organized as a Partnership

ILLUSTRATION 13-3   Rules for posting a journal's column totals

General amount column totals ARE NOT posted

Special amount column totals ARE posted

A check mark is placed in parentheses below the General Debit and General Credit column totals to indicate that the two amount column totals *ARE NOT* posted. The general ledger account number of the account listed in the column heading is written in parentheses below the special amount column totals to show that the totals *ARE* posted.

OPENING A NEW PAGE FOR AN ACCOUNT IN A GENERAL LEDGER

The number of entries that may be recorded on each general ledger account form depends on the number of lines provided. When all lines have been used, a new page is prepared. The account title, account number, and account balance are recorded on the new page.

On November 1 CarLand prepared a new page for Cash in the general ledger because the existing page was full. On that day, the account balance was $14,706.20. The new page for Cash in the general ledger is shown in Illustration 13-4.

ILLUSTRATION 13-4   Opening a new page for an account in a general ledger

Assess student understanding by checking solutions to Independent Practice activities.

Reteach

- Use Transparency 6-1 from Chapter 6 to review the five steps in posting. Posting from a 5-column journal is covered in Chapter 6. An expanded journal is used in this chapter. However, posting procedures do not change, and this should serve as review and reinforcement of posting to a general ledger. The only difference in Transparency 6-1 is that 4-digit account numbers are used and an expanded journal is used in this chapter.

- Use Transparency 6-2 to review posting the Cash Credit column total. The procedures for posting do not change. The only difference in this transparency is that 4-digit account numbers are used and an expanded journal is used in this chapter.

Extend

Assign students to read the MULTICULTURAL AWARENESS feature on page 286. Discuss with them how an understanding and appreciation of history and other cultures contributes to understanding civilization today.

Enrich

Ask students to write a brief report on CarLand's chart of accounts. Students should state the advantages of 4 digit account numbers over Rugcare's 3 digit account numbers. Students should also give examples of circumstances in which CarLand might go to 200s within a division (after 190 or when a new sub division is needed, such as 1100 for current assets and 1200 for plant assets).

CLOSURE

- Use Audit Your Understanding questions.

- Review the procedure for posting from a journal to a general ledger.

- Review the procedure for opening a new page for a general ledger account.

TEACHING STRATEGIES: TEACHING TIP

Review with students the process for opening a new page for a general ledger account. Then explain to students that a new page for a vendor or customer is opened in the same manner as a new page for a general ledger account.

Audit Your Understanding

1. What is a controlling account?
2. What is the relationship between a controlling account and a subsidiary ledger?
3. What are the four amount columns of the general ledger account form?
4. What accounts does an accounts payable ledger contain?
5. What accounts does an accounts receivable ledger contain?

FYI

Account numbers are assigned by 10s. A new account is assigned the unused middle number which places it in the correct alphabetic order.

The account title and account number are written on the heading at the top of the new page. The date, *19--, Nov. 1*, is recorded in the Date column. The word *Balance* is written in the Item column. A check mark is placed in the Post. Ref. column to show that the entry has been carried forward from a previous page rather than posted from a journal. The account balance, *$14,706.20*, is written in the Balance Debit column.

ASSIGNING ACCOUNT NUMBERS TO SUBSIDIARY LEDGER ACCOUNTS

CarLand assigns a vendor number to each account in the accounts payable ledger. A customer number is also assigned to each account in the accounts receivable ledger. A three-digit number is used. The first digit identifies the division in which the controlling account appears in the general ledger. The second two digits show each account's location within a subsidiary ledger. Accounts are assigned by 10s beginning with the second digit. Accounts in the subsidiary ledgers can be located by either number or name.

The vendor number for Antelo Supply is 210. The first digit, *2*, shows that the controlling account is a liability, Accounts Payable. The second and third digits, *10*, show the vendor number assigned to Antelo Supply.

The customer number for Ashley Delivery is 110. The first digit, *1*, shows that the controlling account is an asset, Accounts Receivable. The second and third digits, *10*, show the customer number assigned to Ashley Delivery.

The procedure for adding new accounts to subsidiary ledgers is the same as described for Rugcare's general ledger in Chapter 6. Accounts are arranged in alphabetic order within the subsidiary ledgers. New accounts are assigned the unused middle number. If the proper alphabetic order places a new account as the last account, the next number in the sequence of 10s is assigned. CarLand's chart of accounts for the subsidiary ledgers is on page 244.

POSTING TO AN ACCOUNTS PAYABLE LEDGER

When the balance of a vendor account in an accounts payable ledger is changed, the balance of the controlling account, Accounts Payable, is also changed. The total of all vendor account balances in the accounts payable ledger equals the balance of the controlling account, Accounts Payable. The relationship between the accounts payable ledger and the general ledger controlling account, Accounts Payable, is shown in Illustration 13-5.

TEACHING STRATEGIES: TEACHING TIP

Put vendor number 210 and customer number 110 on the board and explain the numbering system.

ILLUSTRATION 13-5 Relationship of accounts payable ledger and general ledger controlling account

Accounts Payable Ledger Form

CarLand uses the 3-column accounts payable subsidiary account form shown in Illustration 13-6.

ILLUSTRATION 13-6 Three-column account form used in an accounts payable ledger

VENDOR *Veloz Automotive*					VENDOR NO. *260*
DATE	ITEM	POST. REF.	DEBIT	CREDIT	CREDIT BALANCE

Information to be recorded in the accounts payable ledger is essentially the same as that recorded in the 4-column general ledger account. The information includes the date, posting reference, debit or credit amount, and new account balance. Accounts payable are liabilities, and liabilities have normal credit balances. Therefore, the Debit Balance column is usually not needed for the accounts payable ledger accounts. The accounts payable account form is the same as the general ledger account form except that there is no Debit Balance column.

Accounts in CarLand's accounts payable ledger are arranged in alphabetic order and kept in a loose-leaf binder. Periodically, accounts for new vendors are added and accounts no longer used are removed from the accounts payable ledger. If the number of accounts becomes large enough to make a loose-leaf binder inappropriate, ledger pages may be kept in a file cabinet.

CHAPTER 13   Posting to General and Subsidiary Ledgers   **291**

Cover student pages 290–300 "Assigning Account Numbers to Subsidiary Ledger Accounts," "Posting to an Accounts Payable Ledger," and "Posting to an Accounts Receivable Ledger." Put vendor number 210 and customer number 110 on the board and explain the numbering system. Refer students to the chart of accounts. Ask students to add Hall's Supplies to the Accounts Receivable ledger and Volmer and Company to the Accounts Payable ledger. Have students identify the similarities and differences in a 4-column general ledger account form and a 3-column accounts payable subsidiary ledger account form. Have students identify the similarities and differences in an accounts payable account form and an accounts receivable account form.

As the lesson progresses emphasize that (1) vendor accounts are opened by writing the vendor name and number, (2) accounts in the accounts payable ledger have a credit balance, (3) a new page for a vendor account is opened in the same manner as a new page for a general ledger account, (4) customer accounts are opened by writing the customer name and number, (5) accounts in the accounts receivable ledger have a debit balance, and (6) a new page for a customer account is opened in the same manner as a new page for a general ledger account.

Opening Vendor Accounts

Each new account is opened by writing the vendor name and vendor number on the heading of the ledger account. The account opened for Veloz Automotive is shown in Illustration 13-6.

The vendor name is obtained from the first purchase invoice received. The vendor number is assigned using the three-digit numbering system described on page 290. The correct alphabetic order for Veloz Automotive places the account as the sixth account in the accounts payable subsidiary ledger. Vendor number 260 is assigned to Veloz Automotive.

Some businesses record both the vendor name and vendor address on the ledger form. However, the address information is usually kept in a separate name and address file. This practice eliminates having to record the vendor address on the ledger form each time a new ledger page is opened or the address changes.

Posting from a Journal to an Accounts Payable Ledger

Each entry in the Accounts Payable columns of a journal affects the vendor named in the Account Title column. CarLand posts each amount in these two columns often. Posting often keeps each vendor account balance up to date. Totals of Accounts Payable special amount columns are posted to the general ledger at the end of each month.

Posting a Credit to an Accounts Payable Ledger. Posting a credit for a purchase on account from the journal to the accounts payable ledger is shown in Illustration 13-7.

ILLUSTRATION 13-7   Posting a credit to an accounts payable ledger

Five steps are followed to post the entry on line 2 of the journal to the accounts payable ledger.

1 Write the date, *19--, Nov. 2*, in the Date column of the account.

2 Write the journal page number, *21*, in the Post. Ref. column of the account.

3 Write the credit amount, *$1,754.00*, in the Credit amount column of the account for Veloz Automotive.

4 Add the amount in the Credit amount column to the previous balance in the Credit Balance column. (Veloz Automotive has no previous balance; therefore, $0 + $1,754.00 = $1,754.00.) Write the new account balance, *$1,754.00*, in the Credit Balance column.

5 Write the vendor number, *260*, in the Post. Ref. column of the journal. The vendor number shows that the posting for this entry is complete.

The controlling account in the general ledger, Accounts Payable, is also increased by this entry. At the end of the month, the journal's Accounts Payable Credit column total is posted to the controlling account, Accounts Payable.

Posting a Debit to an Accounts Payable Ledger. The same steps are followed to post a debit to a vendor account as are used to post a credit. However, the debit amount is entered in the Debit amount column of the vendor account. The debit amount is subtracted from the previous credit balance. Posting a cash payment on account from the journal to the accounts payable ledger is shown in Illustration 13-8.

The controlling account in the general ledger, Accounts Payable, is decreased by this entry. At the end of the month, the journal's

APPLY

- Use Transparency 13-1 to show the relationship of the accounts payable subsidiary accounts to the controlling account.

- Use Transparency 13-2 to demonstrate posting both a debit entry and a credit entry in an expanded journal to an accounts payable ledger. The steps in posting do not change.

- Use Transparency 13-3 to show the relationship of the accounts receivable subsidiary accounts to the controlling account.

- Use Transparency 13-4 to demonstrate posting both a debit entry and a credit entry from an expanded journal to an accounts receivable ledger.

Guided Practice

Guide students through Drill 13-D2, Instruction 2. Direct students to complete the form provided in the working papers. For each transaction, ask students which amounts are posted individually to the general, accounts receivable, or accounts payable ledger, and which amounts are not posted individually to any ledger. All students should agree with the posting analysis of each amount before proceeding to the next amount.

Independent Practice

Assign Questions 14–19 and Problem 13-1, Instructions 2, 3, 4(b) and (c), and 5.

ILLUSTRATION 13-8   Posting a debit to an accounts payable ledger

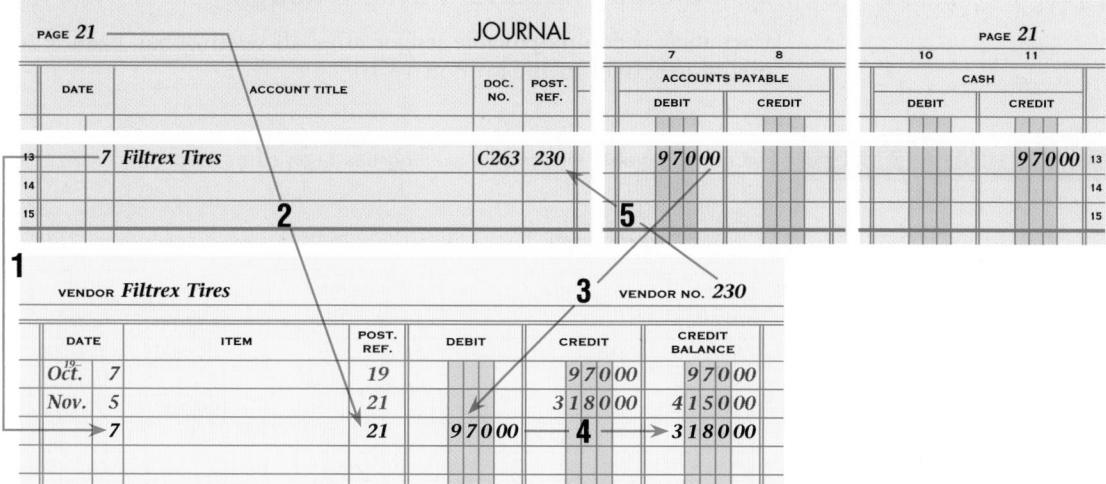

TEACHING STRATEGIES: TEACHING TIP

Emphasize to your students that accounts in the accounts payable ledger have a credit balance. To calculate a new balance after an amount has been posted to an account, add a credit entry to the previous balance and record the new balance in the balance column. Or subtract a debit entry from the previous balance and record the new balance in the balance column.

ASSESS

Assess student understanding by checking solutions to Independent Practice activities.

Reteach

Use Demonstration Problems 13A and 13B. These problems can be demonstrated on the overhead with the students completing the problems at their desks.

Extend

Assign Cases for Critical Thinking 1 and 2.

Enrich

Assign the PERSONAL VISIONS IN BUSINESS feature on page 287.

Accounts Payable Debit column total is posted to the controlling account, Accounts Payable.

Opening a New Page for a Vendor in an Accounts Payable Ledger

The number of entries that may be recorded on each account form depends on the number of lines provided. When all lines have been used, a new page is prepared. The vendor name, vendor number, and account balance are recorded on the new page.

On November 1 CarLand prepared a new page for Nilon Motor Parts in the accounts payable ledger because the existing page was full. On that day, the account balance was $4,840.00. The new page for Nilon Motor Parts in the accounts payable ledger is shown in Illustration 13-9.

FYI

When an account that is no longer used is removed from the accounts receivable ledger, that customer number is available for assignment to a new customer.

ILLUSTRATION 13-9

Opening a new page for a vendor in the accounts payable ledger

VENDOR Nilon Motor Parts						VENDOR NO. 240
DATE	ITEM	POST. REF.	DEBIT	CREDIT	CREDIT BALANCE
Nov. 19-- 1	Balance	✓			4 8 4 0 00

The vendor name and vendor number are written at the top of the account page. The date, *19--, Nov. 1,* is recorded in the Date column. The word *Balance* is written in the Item column. A check mark is placed in the Post. Ref. column to show that the amount has been carried forward from a previous page rather than posted from a journal. The account balance, *$4,840.00,* is written in the Credit Balance column.

Completed Accounts Payable Ledger

CarLand's accounts payable ledger after all posting has been completed is shown in Illustration 13-10.

ILLUSTRATION 13-10

Accounts payable ledger after posting has been completed

VENDOR Antelo Supply						VENDOR NO. 210
DATE	ITEM	POST. REF.	DEBIT	CREDIT	CREDIT BALANCE
Oct. 19-- 12		19		4 3 0 00	4 3 0 00
Nov. 6		21		1 6 0 00	5 9 0 00
12		21	4 3 0 00		1 6 0 00
23		22		5 9 0 00	7 5 0 00

TEACHING STRATEGIES: DIFFERENT LEARNING STYLES

Visual Learner. When learning how to post, the visual learner would prefer to see how the posting process works. To encourage visual learners, therefore, the instructor could use a transparency to assist in the lecture. The transparency could be (1) a blank transparency that the instructor completes or (2) a prepared transparency that uses arrows to trace the steps involved in posting.

CLOSURE

- Use Audit Your Understanding questions.
- Review the procedures for opening vendor and customer accounts.
- Review the procedures for posting to subsidiary ledgers.

VENDOR *Bell Office Products*   VENDOR NO. *220*

DATE		ITEM	POST. REF.	DEBIT	CREDIT	CREDIT BALANCE
Oct.	23		20		6 2 0 00	6 2 0 00
Nov.	23		22	6 2 0 00		
	24		22		8 3 0 00	8 3 0 00

VENDOR *Filtrex Tires*   VENDOR NO. *230*

DATE		ITEM	POST. REF.	DEBIT	CREDIT	CREDIT BALANCE
Oct.	7		19		9 7 0 00	9 7 0 00
Nov.	5		21		3 1 8 0 00	4 1 5 0 00
	7		21	9 7 0 00		3 1 8 0 00

VENDOR *Nilon Motor Parts*   VENDOR NO. *240*

DATE		ITEM	POST. REF.	DEBIT	CREDIT	CREDIT BALANCE
Nov.	1	Balance	✓			4 8 4 0 00
	4		21		3 4 5 6 00	8 2 9 6 00
	20		22	4 8 4 0 00		3 4 5 6 00

VENDOR *Q-Ban Distributors*   VENDOR NO. *250*

DATE		ITEM	POST. REF.	DEBIT	CREDIT	CREDIT BALANCE
Nov.	1	Balance	✓			3 9 6 0 00
	6		21	3 9 6 0 00		
	13		21		3 1 4 0 00	3 1 4 0 00
	20		22		2 7 6 0 00	5 9 0 0 00

VENDOR *Veloz Automotive*   VENDOR NO. *260*

DATE		ITEM	POST. REF.	DEBIT	CREDIT	CREDIT BALANCE
Nov.	2		21		1 7 5 4 00	1 7 5 4 00

TEACHING STRATEGIES: TEACHING TIP

Review with students the three guides to posting from journals.

a. Separate items in a General Debit or General Credit column are always posted individually to general ledger accounts.

b. Separate items in a special amount column are always posted individually if a subsidiary ledger is maintained for the account listed in the heading of the special amount column.

c. Totals of special amount columns are always posted if the heading of the amount column is the same as an account in the general ledger.

You should emphasize that posting separate items to subsidiary ledgers is done periodically during the month and is usually completed prior to the time that totals are posted at the end of a month.

FYI

An error in posting may cause a business to overpay or underpay its vendors.

POSTING TO AN ACCOUNTS RECEIVABLE LEDGER

When the balance of a customer account in an accounts receivable ledger is changed, the balance of the controlling account, Accounts Receivable, is also changed. The total of all customer account balances in the accounts receivable ledger equals the balance of the controlling account, Accounts Receivable. The relationship between the accounts receivable ledger and the general ledger controlling account, Accounts Receivable, is shown in Illustration 13-11.

ILLUSTRATION 13-11 Relationship of accounts receivable ledger and general ledger controlling account

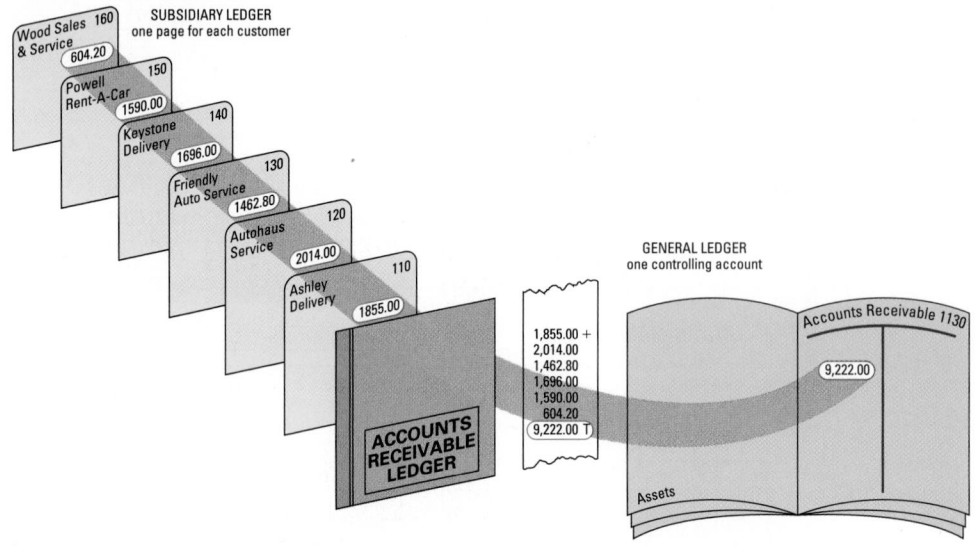

Accounts Receivable Ledger Form

CarLand uses the 3-column accounts receivable subsidiary account form shown in Illustration 13-12.

ILLUSTRATION 13-12 Three-column account form used in an accounts receivable ledger

CUSTOMER *Friendly Auto Service*					CUSTOMER NO. *130*
DATE	ITEM	POST. REF.	DEBIT	CREDIT	DEBIT BALANCE

The accounts receivable account form is similar to the one used for the accounts payable ledger. Accounts receivable are assets, and assets have normal debit balances. Therefore, the form used in the accounts receivable ledger has a Debit Balance column instead of a Credit Balance column.

Accounts in CarLand's accounts receivable ledger are arranged in alphabetic order and kept in a loose-leaf binder. Periodically,

TEACHING STRATEGIES: DIFFERENT LEARNING ABILITIES

Limited English Proficiency (LEP) Students. Recruit business persons willing to act as mentors for LEP students. These mentors should be invited to speak to the class and periodically meet with LEP students to assist with assignments. The instructor should be actively involved in any meetings with LEP students to show support for both the mentor and the students.

accounts for new customers are added and accounts no longer used are removed from the accounts receivable ledger. The customer number 130 had been assigned to a former customer. That account, however, had been removed from the ledger. Therefore, customer number 130 is available for assignment to Friendly Auto Service.

Some businesses record both the customer name and customer address on the ledger form. However, the address information is usually kept in a separate name and address file. This practice eliminates having to record the customer address on the ledger form each time a new ledger page is opened or the address changes.

Opening Customer Accounts

Procedures for opening customer accounts are similar to those used for opening vendor accounts. The customer name is obtained from the first sales invoice prepared for a customer. The customer number is assigned using the three-digit numbering system described on page 290. The customer name and customer number are written on the heading of the ledger account. The account opened for Friendly Auto Service is shown in Illustration 13-12.

Posting from a Journal to an Accounts Receivable Ledger

Each entry in the Accounts Receivable columns of a journal affects the customer named in the Account Title column. Each amount listed in these two columns is posted to a customer account in the accounts receivable ledger often. Posting often keeps each customer account balance up to date. Totals of Accounts Receivable special amount columns are posted to the general ledger at the end of each month.

Posting a Debit to an Accounts Receivable Ledger. Posting a debit for a sale on account from the journal to the accounts receivable ledger is shown in Illustration 13-13.

Five steps are followed to post the entry on line 4 of the journal to the accounts receivable ledger.

1 Write the date, *3,* in the Date column of the account.

2 Write the journal page number, *21,* in the Post. Ref. column of the account.

3 Write the debit amount, *$720.80,* in the Debit amount column of the account for Friendly Auto Service.

4 Add the amount in the Debit amount column to the previous balance in the Debit Balance column ($265.00 + $720.80 = $985.80). Write the new account balance, *$985.80,* in the Debit Balance column.

5 Write the customer number, *130,* in the Post. Ref. column of the journal. The customer number shows that the posting for this entry is completed.

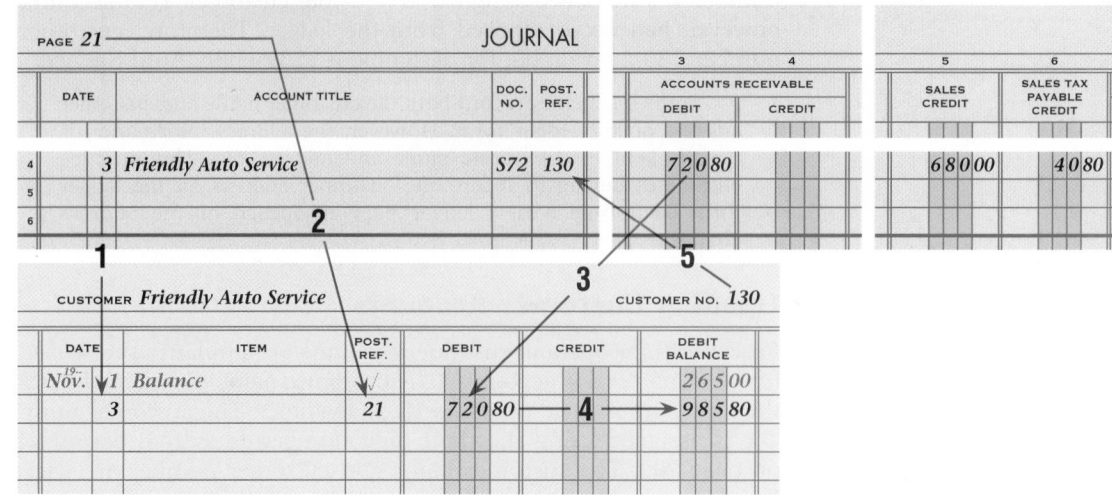

ILLUSTRATION 13-13 Posting a debit to an accounts receivable ledger

The controlling account in the general ledger, Accounts Receivable, is also increased by this entry. At the end of the month, the journal's Accounts Receivable Debit column total is posted to the controlling account, Accounts Receivable.

Posting a Credit to an Accounts Receivable Ledger. The same steps are followed to post a credit to a customer account as are used to post a debit. However, the credit amount is written in the Credit amount column of the customer account. The credit amount is subtracted from the previous debit balance. Posting a cash receipt on account from the journal to the accounts receivable ledger is shown in Illustration 13-14.

The controlling account in the general ledger, Accounts Receivable, is decreased by this entry. However, the amount is not posted individually to the accounts receivable account. At the end of the month, the amount, *$318.00*, is posted as part of the special amount column total to Accounts Receivable.

Opening a New Page for a Customer in an Accounts Receivable Ledger

Procedures for opening a new page in an accounts receivable ledger are similar to those for an accounts payable ledger. The customer name and customer number are written at the top of the new account page. The date is recorded in the Date column. The word *Balance* is written in the Item column. A check mark is placed in the Post. Ref. column to show that the amount has been carried forward from a previous page rather than posted from a journal. The account balance is recorded in the Debit Balance column.

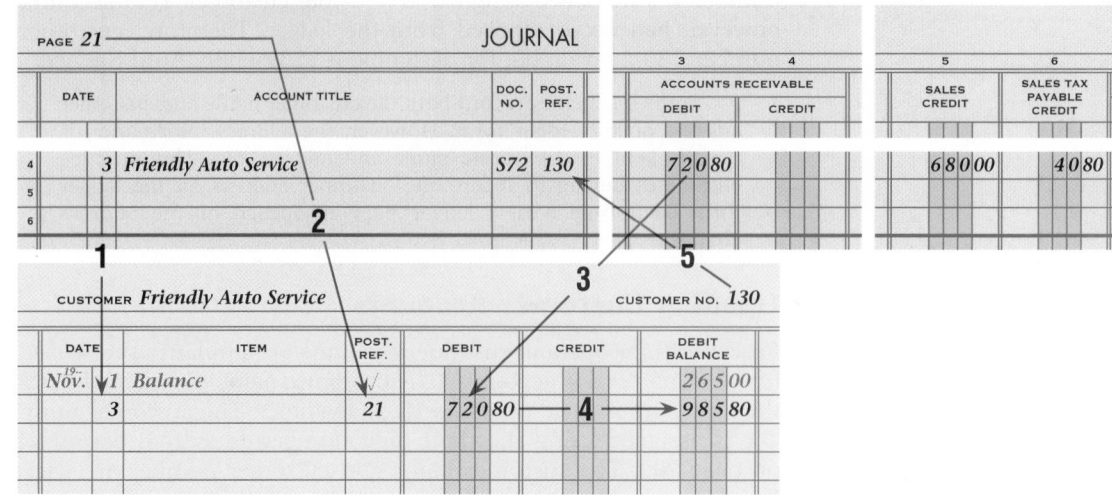

Audit Your Understanding

1. What is the title of the balance amount column of the accounts payable ledger form? Why?
2. How is a new vendor account opened?
3. List the five steps for posting to the accounts payable ledger.
4. What is the title of the balance amount column of the accounts receivable ledger form? Why?

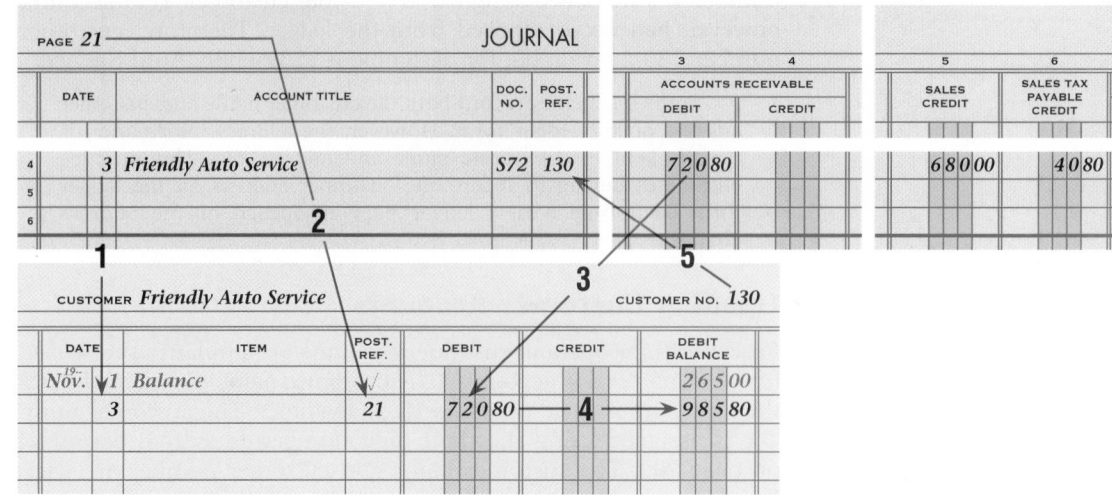

AUDIT YOUR UNDERSTANDING

1. Credit Balance. Because accounts payable are liabilities and liabilities have normal credit balances.
2. By writing the vendor name and vendor number on the heading of the ledger account.
3. (1) Write the date in the Date column of the account. (2) Write the journal page number in the Post. Ref. column of the account. (3) Write the amount in the appropriate amount column of the account. (4) Calculate the new account balance. Write the new account balance in the Credit Balance column. (5) Write the vendor number in the Post. Ref. column of the journal. The vendor number shows that the posting for this entry is completed.
4. Debit Balance. Because accounts receivable are assets and assets have normal debit balances.

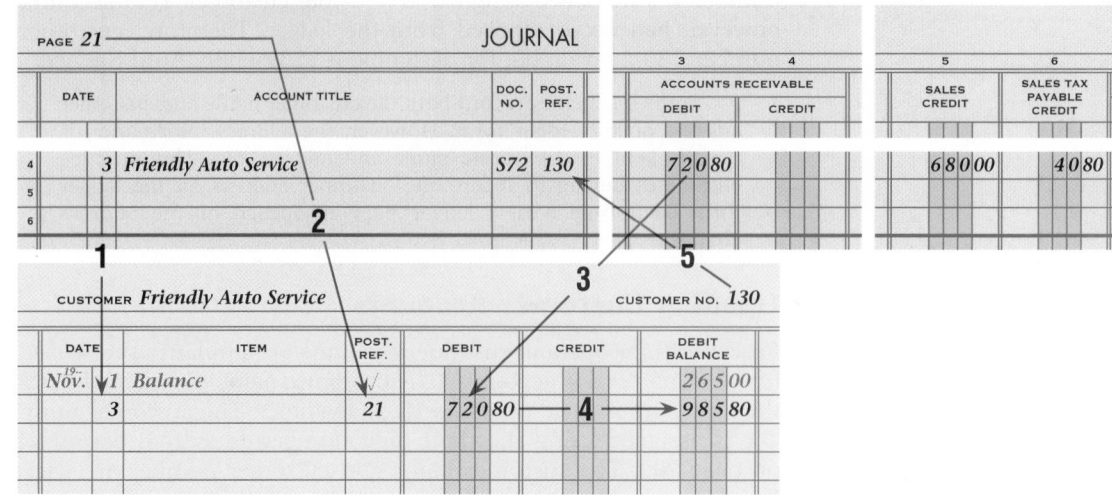

ILLUSTRATION 13-14   Posting a credit to an accounts receivable ledger

Completed Accounts Receivable Ledger

CarLand's accounts receivable ledger after all posting has been completed is shown in Illustration 13-15.

ILLUSTRATION 13-15   Accounts receivable ledger after posting has been completed

CUSTOMER **Ashley Delivery**   CUSTOMER NO. *110*

DATE		ITEM	POST. REF.	DEBIT	CREDIT	DEBIT BALANCE
Nov.	1	Balance	✓			2 4 9 1 00
	9		21	4 7 7 00		2 9 6 8 00
	16		22	1 3 7 8 00		4 3 4 6 00
	17		22		2 4 9 1 00	1 8 5 5 00

CUSTOMER **Autohaus Service**   CUSTOMER NO. *120*

DATE		ITEM	POST. REF.	DEBIT	CREDIT	DEBIT BALANCE
Nov.	1	Balance	✓			1 8 0 2 00
	6		21		1 8 0 2 00	——
	18		22	2 0 1 4 00		2 0 1 4 00

CHAPTER 13   Posting to General and Subsidiary Ledgers   **299**

TEACHING STRATEGIES: DIFFERENT LEARNING ABILITIES

At-Risk Students. Utilize the lesson plans provided in the teacher's edition to divide each chapter into smaller parts to create short units that provide frequent opportunities for assessment and goal attainment.

APPLIED SKILLS: LANGUAGE ARTS

Paraphrasing, writing complete sentences, and identifying prepositions. For additional practice in language arts skills, direct students to answer the Accounting Terms and Questions for Individual Study at the end of the chapter. Students should write the answers in their own words and in complete sentences. To further practice language arts skills, ask students to underline all prepositions in their answers.

CUSTOMER *Friendly Auto Service*   CUSTOMER NO. *130*

DATE		ITEM	POST. REF.	DEBIT	CREDIT	DEBIT BALANCE
Nov.	1	Balance	✓			265 00
	3		21	720 80		985 80
	24		22	742 00		1727 80
	25		22		265 00	1462 80

CUSTOMER *Keystone Delivery*   CUSTOMER NO. *140*

DATE		ITEM	POST. REF.	DEBIT	CREDIT	DEBIT BALANCE
Oct.	10		19	954 00		954 00
Nov.	10		21		954 00	—
	24		22	318 00		318 00
	29		22	1378 00		1696 00

CUSTOMER *Powell Rent-A-Car*   CUSTOMER NO. *150*

DATE		ITEM	POST. REF.	DEBIT	CREDIT	DEBIT BALANCE
Oct.	14		19	318 00		318 00
Nov.	5		21	1590 00		1908 00
	14		21		318 00	1590 00

CUSTOMER *Wood Sales & Service*   CUSTOMER NO. *160*

DATE		ITEM	POST. REF.	DEBIT	CREDIT	DEBIT BALANCE
Nov.	1	Balance	✓			2120 00
	11		21	604 20		2724 20
	13		21		901 00	1823 20
	20		22		1219 00	604 20

PROVING THE ACCURACY OF POSTING

A single error in posting to a ledger account may cause the trial balance to be out of balance. An error in posting may cause the cash account balance to disagree with the actual cash on hand. An error in posting may also cause the income to be understated or overstated on an income statement. An error in posting may also cause a business to overpay or underpay its vendors. Posting must be accurate to assure correct account balances. Therefore, to prove

---

LESSON PLAN 13-3

Materials

- Student pages 300–303
- Transparencies: 13-5, Chapter Summary
- Software: *Automated Accounting 6.0* or higher; Accounting Textbook Template first-year course; Electronic Study Guide
- Demonstration Problem: 13C, Preparing Subsidiary Schedules
- Assess: Problem Test Chapter 13, MicroExam Chapter 13, Objective Test 3, Unit Problem Test 3

Objectives (Enabling Performance Tasks)

a. Define accounting terms related to posting to ledgers.

b. Identify accounting practices related to posting to ledgers.

f. Prepare subsidiary schedules.

TEACHING STRATEGIES: TEACHING TIP

Emphasize to your students that three things must be done to prove posting.

1. Cash is proved.
2. Subsidiary schedules are prepared to prove that the total of the balances in the subsidiary ledgers equals the balance of the controlling account in the general ledger.
3. A trial balance is prepared to prove that debits equal credits in the general ledger.

the accuracy of posting, three things are done. (1) Cash is proved. (2) Subsidiary schedules are prepared to prove that the total of the balances in the subsidiary ledgers equals the balance of the controlling account in the general ledger. (3) A trial balance is prepared to prove that debits equal credits in the general ledger.

Preparation of a trial balance is described in Chapter 16.

Proving Cash

The method used to prove cash is described in Chapter 12. The cash proof total is compared with the balance on the next unused check stub in the checkbook.

Proving the Subsidiary Ledgers

A controlling account balance in a general ledger must equal the sum of all account balances in a subsidiary ledger. CarLand proves the accounts payable and accounts receivable subsidiary ledgers at the end of each month.

Proving Accounts Payable. A listing of vendor accounts, account balances, and total amount due all vendors is called a **schedule of accounts payable.** A schedule of accounts payable is prepared after all entries in a journal are posted. CarLand's schedule of accounts payable, prepared on November 30, is shown in Illustration 13-16.

ILLUSTRATION 13-16

Schedule of accounts payable

CarLand	
Schedule of Accounts Payable	
November 30, 19--	
Antelo Supply	750 00
Bell Office Products	830 00
Filtrex Tires	3180 00
Nilon Motor Parts	3456 00
Q-Ban Distributors	5900 00
Veloz Automotive	1754 00
Total Accounts Payable	15870 00

The balance of Accounts Payable in the general ledger is $15,870.00. The total of the schedule of accounts payable is $15,870.00. Because the two amounts are the same, the accounts payable ledger is proved.

Proving Accounts Receivable. A listing of customer accounts, account balances, and total amount due from all customers is called a **schedule of accounts receivable.** A schedule of accounts receivable is prepared after all entries in a journal are posted. CarLand's sched-

---

FYI

To prove the accuracy of posting: 1) cash is proved, 2) subsidiary schedules are prepared, and 3) a trial balance is prepared.

FOCUS

- Posting from a journal to the general and subsidiary ledgers was presented earlier in this chapter. In this lesson, we will prove the accuracy of the posting.

- Introduce new vocabulary: schedule of accounts payable, schedule of accounts receivable.

TEACH

Cover student pages 300–303 "Proving the Accuracy of Posting." During this lesson emphasize that three things must be done to prove posting. (1) Cash is proved. (2) Subsidiary schedules are prepared to prove that the total of the balances in the subsidiary ledgers equals the balance of the controlling account in the general ledger. (3) A trial balance is prepared to prove that debits equal credits in the general ledger.

TEACHING STRATEGIES: DIFFERENT LEARNING ABILITIES

Specific Learning Disability (SLD) Students. When asking questions during class, ask SLD students questions that they can likely answer successfully. Save more difficult or unstructured questions for better students.

APPLY

- Review the procedures for proving cash described in Chapter 12.

- Place on a chalkboard or overhead projector a trial balance that contains a number of accounts with vendors. Alongside this trial balance make a list of all vendor names and account balances. Total the list of vendor account balances. Then erase the vendor names from the trial balance and write the words "Accounts Payable" on one line in the trial balance. Record the total of the list of vendor account balances. Point out that the accounts payable account is a summary of all accounts with vendors and that a balance sheet can be kept within reasonable size when a controlling account takes the place of dozens, or possibly hundreds, of vendor accounts. Use the same trial balance and steps described above but use customer accounts instead of vendor accounts. Prepare a schedule of accounts payable and a schedule of accounts receivable.

Guided Practice

Guide students through Recycling Problem 13-R. Students should have the forms from the working papers (or use blackline masters from the TRG) to complete as you guide them through the drills. For each transaction, ask students which accounts are affected, and how. Ask them what columns are affected, and how. All students should agree with the analysis before proceeding to the next transaction.

Independent Practice

Assign Terms 5–6, Question 20, Problem 13-1, Instructions 6–7, Study Guide 13, and Mastery Problem 13-M.

ILLUSTRATION 13-17   Schedule of accounts receivable

CarLand		
Schedule of Accounts Receivable		
November 30, 19--		
Ashley Delivery	1 8 5 5	00
Autohaus Service	2 0 1 4	00
Friendly Auto Service	1 4 6 2	80
Keystone Delivery	1 6 9 6	00
Powell Rent-A-Car	1 5 9 0	00
Wood Sales & Service	6 0 4	20
Total Accounts Receivable	9 2 2 2	00

The balance of Accounts Receivable in the general ledger is $9,222.00. The total of the schedule of accounts receivable is $9,222.00. Because the two amounts are the same, the accounts receivable ledger is proved.

A summary of the posting steps from Rugcare's journal is in Chapter 6. The steps described for Rugcare also apply to posting from an expanded journal. However, special amount columns and controlling accounts require an additional set of posting steps.

SUMMARY ILLUSTRATION 13-18

Summary of posting

Separate amounts in General columns *ARE* posted individually. Totals of General Debit and Credit columns *ARE NOT* posted.

POST. REF.	GENERAL DEBIT	GENERAL CREDIT	
1150	2 5 00		+ → Separate amounts *ARE* posted individually
6110	1 5 00		+
6140	5 5 00		+
✓			
	1 5 6 8 6 22	2 0 2 9 02	← Totals *ARE NOT* posted
	(✓)	(✓)	

TEACHING STRATEGIES: Applying Visuals

Direct the students to Summary Illustration 13-18 to review posting.

SUMMARY ILLUSTRATION 13-18 (continued)

Summary of posting

Totals of special amount columns *ARE* posted to the account named in the column heading. Separate amounts in special columns *ARE NOT* posted individually unless the columns affect a controlling account.

Separate amounts and total amounts are posted from special columns for controlling accounts. Separate amounts in the Accounts Receivable Debit and Credit columns *ARE* posted individually to customer accounts. As the last posting step, a customer number is written in the Post. Ref. column of the journal.

Totals of special columns *ARE* posted to the controlling accounts named in the column headings. The total of an Accounts Receivable Debit column is posted as a debit to **Accounts Receivable** in the general ledger. The total of an Accounts Receivable Credit column is posted as a credit to **Accounts Receivable** in the general ledger. As a last posting step, an account number is placed in parentheses under the total of a special amount column.

The same principles used for Accounts Receivable amount columns also apply to Accounts Payable amount columns in a journal.

APPLIED SKILLS: WORD PROCESSING

If you wish to integrate word processing into your accounting course, you may direct students to answer the end-of-chapter Accounting Terms, Questions for Individual Study, and Cases for Critical Thinking using their word processing software.

- Assess student understanding by checking solutions to Independent Practice activities.
- Review Summary Illustration 13-18, "Summary of Posting."

Reteach

Use Demonstration Problem 13C. This problem can be demonstrated on the overhead with the students completing the problem at their desks.

Extend

Assign Challenge Problem 13-C (the challenge is that students must calculate sales tax).

Enrich

- Use the *Automated Accounting 6.0* or higher software with Challenge Problem 13-C to apply the concept of journalizing, posting, and preparing subsidiary schedules.
- Assign Electronic Study Guide Chapter 13 to complete the study guide from the working papers at the computer.

CLOSURE

- Use Audit Your Understanding questions.
- Review Summary Illustration 13-8. Use Transparency 13-5, Chapter Summary.

ASSESS

- Administer Problem Test Chapter 13.
- Administer a MicroExam test for Chapter 13.
- Administer Objective Test 3.
- Administer Unit Problem Test 3.

ACCOUNTING TERMS

1. subsidiary ledger: A ledger that is summarized in a single general ledger account. (p. 285)

2. accounts payable ledger: A subsidiary ledger containing only accounts for vendors from whom items are purchased or bought on account. (p. 285)

3. accounts receivable ledger: A subsidiary ledger containing only accounts for charge customers. (p. 285)

4. controlling account: An account in a general ledger that summarizes all accounts in a subsidiary ledger. (p. 285)

5. schedule of accounts payable: A listing of vendor accounts, account balances, and total amount due all vendors. (p. 301)

6. schedule of accounts receivable: A listing of customer accounts, account balances, and total amount due from all customers. (p. 301)

QUESTIONS FOR INDIVIDUAL STUDY

1. By transferring information to ledger accounts. (p. 285)

2. A business' size, number of transactions, and type of transactions. (p. 285)

3. General ledger. (p. 285)

4. A business with transactions involving mostly the receipt and payment of cash. (p. 285)

5. A business needs to know the amount owed each vendor as well as the amount due from each customer. (p. 285)

6. A business with many vendors and customers would have a bulky general ledger and a long trial balance. (p. 285)

7. Accounts Payable. (p. 285)

8. Accounts Receivable. (p. 285)

9. Because daily account balances are usually not necessary for general ledger accounts. Balances of general ledger accounts are needed only when financial statements are prepared. (p. 286)

10. The number of transactions. (p. 286)

11. Because amounts recorded in a journal's general columns are amounts for which no special amount columns are provided. (p. 286)

12. Because separate amounts recorded in special amount columns all affect the same account. (pp. 287–288)

ACCOUNTING TERMS   EPT(a)

What is the meaning of each of the following?

1. **subsidiary ledger**
2. **accounts payable ledger**
3. **accounts receivable ledger**
4. **controlling account**
5. **schedule of accounts payable**
6. **schedule of accounts receivable**

QUESTIONS FOR INDIVIDUAL STUDY   EPT(b)

1. How is journal entry information sorted and summarized?

2. What determines the number of ledgers used in an accounting system?

3. What ledger contains all accounts needed to prepare an income statement and a balance sheet?

4. What type of business would generally use a single ledger?

5. Why would a business keep a separate account for each vendor and each customer?

6. Why would a business keep a separate ledger for vendors and a separate ledger for customers?

7. What is the title of the general ledger controlling account for vendors?

8. What is the title of the general ledger controlling account for customers?

9. Why is posting to a general ledger done only periodically throughout the month?

10. What determines the frequency of posting to a general ledger?

11. Why are amounts recorded in a journal's general amount columns posted individually?

12. Why are separate amounts in special amount columns not posted individually to the general ledger?

13. Why is a check mark placed in parentheses below the General Debit and General Credit column totals?

14. What does the first digit in a vendor or customer number identify?

15. Why does the 3-column account form used in an accounts payable ledger have a Credit Balance column?

16. Why is posting of separate amounts in the Accounts Payable columns done often?

17. How often are the totals of the Accounts Payable columns of a journal posted?

18. Why is a check mark entered in the Post. Ref. column when a new page is opened for a vendor?

19. Why does the 3-column account form used in an accounts receivable ledger have a Debit Balance column?

20. How are subsidiary ledgers proved at the end of a month?

CASES FOR CRITICAL THINKING   EPT(b)

CASE 1 Automart purchased merchandise on account six weeks ago for $400.00 from Belview Supply. A check for $400.00 was sent three weeks ago in payment of the account. Although no additional purchases have been made, Automart recently received a bill from Belview Supply that listed the balance due as $800.00. What probably caused this error? When would the error probably be discovered?

CASE 2 Leon Reyes observes his accountant at work and says, "You post each individual accounts receivable entry in the journal. Then you post the totals of the Accounts Receivable columns. You are posting these entries twice, which will make the records wrong." The accountant does not agree that the posting procedure is incorrect. Is Mr. Reyes or his accountant correct? Why?

DRILL 13-D1 Analyzing transactions of a merchandising business

INSTRUCTIONS:

Prepare T accounts for each of the following transactions. Use the T accounts to analyze each transaction. A 6% sales tax has been added to each sale. The first transaction is given as an example.

Accounts Receivable	
127.20	

Sales	
	120.00

Sales Tax Payable	
	7.20

1. Sold merchandise on account to Sarah Burke, $120.00, plus sales tax, $7.20; total, $127.20.
2. Paid cash on account to Casa Enterprises, $950.00.
3. Paid cash for rent, $1,250.00.
4. Discovered that a payment for advertising was journalized and posted in error as a debit to Miscellaneous Expense instead of Advertising Expense, $125.00.
5. Paid cash for office supplies, $80.00.
6. Recorded cash and credit card sales, $1,850.00, plus sales tax, $111.00; total, $1,961.00.
7. Joyce Berling, partner, withdrew merchandise for personal use, $90.00.
8. Purchased merchandise on account from Irvine Products, $1,640.00.
9. Received cash on account from Carl Downing, $227.90.
10. Purchased merchandise for cash, $130.00.
11. Michael Zolty, partner, withdrew cash for personal use, $700.00.
12. Bought store supplies on account from Carter Supply, $315.00.

The solution to Drill 13-D1 is needed to complete Drill 13-D2.

DRILL 13-D2 Analyzing, journalizing, and posting transactions of a merchandising business

The solution to Drill 13-D1 is needed to complete Drill 13-D2.

INSTRUCTIONS:

A form for analyzing transactions is provided in the working papers that accompany the textbook.

1. Based on the answers in Drill 13-D1, place a check mark in the amount columns to be used to journalize each transaction.

A form for analyzing posting is provided in the working papers that accompany this textbook.

2. Based on the answers to Instruction 1, place a check mark in the proper column to indicate whether the amount will or will not be posted individually to the ledgers.

APPLICATION PROBLEM   EPT(c,d,e,f)

PROBLEM 13-1 Opening accounts and posting to ledgers from a journal

The journal for Carpet Magic is given in the working papers accompanying this textbook.

INSTRUCTIONS:

1. Open new pages for the following accounts in the general ledger. Record the balances as of September 1 of the current year.

CHAPTER 13 Posting to General and Subsidiary Ledgers   **305**

---

13. To indicate that the two amount column totals are not posted. (p. 289)
14. The division in which the controlling account appears in the general ledger. (p. 290)
15. Because accounts payable are liabilities, and liabilities have normal credit balances. Therefore, the Debit Balance column is usually not needed for the accounts payable ledger accounts. (p. 291)
16. Posting often keeps each vendor account balance up to date. (p. 292)
17. At the end of the month. (p. 292)
18. The check mark shows that the amount has been carried forward from a previous page rather than posted from a journal. (p. 294)
19. Because accounts receivable are assets, and assets have normal debit balances. (p. 296)
20. A schedule is prepared to show that the sum of all account balances in a subsidiary ledger equals the controlling account balance in the general ledger. (p. 301)

CASES FOR CRITICAL THINKING

Case 1 Since the accounts payable increased $400.00 rather than decreased $400.00, Belview likely made an error in posting by debiting rather than crediting the account of Automart when the payment was made. The error will probably be discovered when (1) Automart inquires about the bill or (2) Belview prepares a trial balance and the schedule of accounts receivable does not agree with the controlling account.

Case 2 The accountant is correct. Only the totals of the Accounts Receivable columns are posted to the general ledger controlling account, Accounts Receivable. Separate amounts are posted to individual accounts in the accounts receivable subsidiary ledger. This procedure only serves as detail for the controlling account so that the company will know the amounts owed by each customer. Amounts from the subsidiary ledger are not entered in the trial balance.

CHECK FIGURES

See Teacher's Edition of Working Papers for complete solutions to drills and problems.

Drill 13-D1 Cash is credited in 5 transactions. Cash is debited in 2 transactions.

Drill 13-D2 There are 6 check marks in the General Debit column; there are 13 check marks in the not posted column.

Problem 13-1 Schedule of Accounts Payable 11,150; Schedule of Accounts Receivable 4,851

Account No.	Account Title	Account Balance
1110	Cash	$ 18,300.00
1130	Accounts Receivable...................	8,470.00
1150	Supplies—Office......................	3,680.00
1160	Supplies—Store......................	4,260.00
1170	Prepaid Insurance	1,560.00
2110	Accounts Payable	10,555.00
2120	Sales Tax Payable	1,235.00
3120	Diane Engler, Drawing	8,000.00
3140	Paul Sisco, Drawing	8,340.00
4110	Sales	172,420.00
5110	Purchases............................	96,500.00
6110	Advertising Expense	1,860.00
6140	Miscellaneous Expense	1,310.00
6160	Rent Expense.........................	8,000.00

2. Open new pages for the following vendor accounts in the accounts payable ledger. Record the balances as of September 1 of the current year.

Vendor No.	Vendor Name	Purchase Invoice No.	Account Balance
210	Crown Carpet Co................	52	$2,575.00
220	Marlow Industries...............	53	4,220.00
230	Superior Carpeting	—	—
240	V & P Carpet Co.	51	3,760.00

3. Open new pages for the following customer accounts in the accounts receivable ledger. Record the balances as of September 1 of the current year.

Customer No.	Customer Name	Sales Invoice No.	Account Balance
110	Cameo Shoe Store	44	$3,680.00
120	Paula Hughs	42	1,850.00
130	Elsa Leyba.....................	43	2,940.00
140	Scott Ward	—	—

4. Post the separate items recorded in the following columns of the journal. (a) General Debit and Credit. (b) Accounts Receivable Debit and Credit. (c) Accounts Payable Debit and Credit.

5. Post the totals of the special columns of the journal.

6. Prepare a schedule of accounts payable. Compare the total of the schedule with the balance of the controlling account, Accounts Payable, in the general ledger. If the totals are not the same, find and correct the errors.

7. Prepare a schedule of accounts receivable. Compare the total of the schedule with the balance of the controlling account, Accounts Receivable, in the general ledger. If the totals are not the same, find and correct the errors.

ENRICHMENT PROBLEMS

EPT(c,e,f)

MASTERY PROBLEM 13-M Posting to ledgers from a journal

The journal and ledgers for Anton Leather Goods are given in the working papers accompanying this textbook.

INSTRUCTIONS:

1. Post the separate items recorded in the following columns of the journal. (a) General Debit and Credit. (b) Accounts Receivable Debit and Credit. (c) Accounts Payable Debit and Credit.

2. Post the totals of the special columns of the journal.
3. Prepare a schedule of accounts payable and a schedule of accounts receivable. Prove the accuracy of the subsidiary ledgers by comparing the schedule totals with the balances of the controlling accounts in the general ledger. If the totals are not the same, find and correct the errors.

CHALLENGE PROBLEM 13-C   Journalizing and posting business transactions

The general, accounts payable, and accounts receivable ledgers for Par Golf Products are given in the working papers accompanying this textbook. Use the following account titles.

CHECK FIGURES (cont'd)

Challenge Problem 13-C   Journal totals: 4,308.50; 258.00; 2,591.70; 1,706.60; 21,965.00; 1,317.90; 7,075.00; 5,450.00; 5,354.00; 22,397.80; 11,029.50. Schedule of Accounts Payable 6,398.00; Schedule of Accounts Receivable 3,752.40

GENERAL LEDGER

Account No.	Account Title	Account No.	Account Title
1110	Cash	3140	Lawrence Phipps, Drawing
1130	Accounts Receivable	3150	Income Summary
1140	Merchandise Inventory	4110	Sales
1150	Supplies—Office	5110	Purchases
1160	Supplies—Store	6110	Advertising Expenses
2110	Accounts Payable	6140	Miscellaneous Expenses
2120	Sales Tax Payable	6160	Rent Expense
3120	Maria Adolpho, Drawing	6190	Utilities Expense

ACCOUNTS PAYABLE LEDGER		ACCOUNTS RECEIVABLE LEDGER	
Vendor No.	Vendor Name	Customer No.	Customer Name
210	Artex Golf Products	110	William Backus
220	Ecola Golf Equipment	120	Linda Boge
230	Garcia Supply	130	Jonathan Dunbar
240	Patton Golf Co.	140	James Patco
250	Valiant Golf Co.	150	Bertha Welsh

INSTRUCTIONS:

1. Journalize the following transactions completed during November of the current year. Use page 18 of a journal similar to the one described in this chapter. Add a 6% sales tax to all sales transactions. Source documents are abbreviated as follows: check, C; memorandum, M; purchase invoice, P; receipt, R; sales invoice, S; cash register tape, T.

Nov. 2. Wrote a check for rent, $950.00. C275.
     3. Received an invoice from Valiant Golf Co. for merchandise purchased on account, $1,625.00. P76.
     4. Paid for merchandise, $119.00. C276.
     5. A check was received in payment on account from Linda Boge, $678.40, covering S50. R45.
     7. Ecola Golf Equipment was paid on account, $1,965.00, covering P72. C277.
     7. Cash and credit card sales, $4,730.00. T7.
        Posting. Post the items that are to be posted individually.
     9. Maria Adolfo, partner, withdrew merchandise for personal use, $165.00. M35.
    11. Merchandise was sold on account to James Patco, $255.00. S54.
    12. Discovered that a transaction for store supplies bought for cash was journalized and posted in error as a debit to Advertising Expense instead of Supplies—Store, $93.00. M36.
    14. Store supplies were bought on account from Garcia Supply, $215.00. M37.
    14. Cash and credit card sales, $4,840.00. T14.
        Posting. Post the items that are to be posted individually.
    16. Cash was withdrawn by Maria Adolfo, partner, for personal use, $1,200.00. C278.

Nov. 16. Cash was withdrawn by Lawrence Phipps, partner, for personal use, $1,200.00. C279.

17. Wrote a check for electric bill, $183.50. C280.

20. Wrote a check to Valiant Golf Co. on account, $2,680.00, covering P73. C281.

21. Recorded cash and credit card sales, $4,480.00. T21.

Posting. Post the items that are to be posted individually.

23. Artex Golf Products was paid on account, $2,430.00, covering P74. C282.

24. Jonathan Dunbar bought merchandise on account, $1,095.00. S55.

26. Received payment on account from Bertha Welsh, $233.20, covering S51. R46.

26. Merchandise was purchased on account from Patton Golf Co., $1,285.00. P77.

27. A check was received in payment on account from William Backus, $795.00, covering S52. R47.

28. Received an invoice on account from Artex Golf Products for merchandise purchased on account, $2,325.00. P78.

28. Merchandise was sold on account to Bertha Welsh, $1,095.00. S56.

28. Recorded cash and credit card sales, $4,630.00. T28.

Posting. Post the items that are to be posted individually.

30. Replenish the petty cash fund, $302.00: office supplies, $48.00; store supplies, $62.00; advertising, $74.00; miscellaneous, $118.00. C283.

30. Recorded cash and credit card sales, $840.00. T30.

Posting. Post the items that are to be posted individually.

2. Total the journal. Prove the equality of debits and credits.
3. Prove cash. The balance on the next unused check stub is $28,218.30.
4. Rule the journal.
5. Post the totals of the special columns of the journal.
6. Prepare a schedule of accounts payable and a schedule of accounts receivable. Prove the accuracy of the subsidiary ledgers by comparing the schedule totals with the balances of the controlling accounts in the general ledger. If the totals are not the same, find and correct the errors.

Recording Transactions for a Partnership

CarLand, the merchandising business described in Part 3, uses a manual accounting system. CarLand's manual journalizing procedures for purchases, cash payments, sales, and cash receipts are described in Chapters 11 and 12. Manual posting procedures are described in Chapter 13. Integrating Automated Accounting Topic 4 describes procedures for using automated accounting software to journalize and post CarLand's transactions. The Automated Accounting Problem contains instructions for using automated accounting software to solve Challenge Problem 13-C, Chapter 13.

AUTOMATED ACCOUNTING PROCEDURES FOR CARLAND

A group of journal entries is a **batch**. CarLand uses five input forms to batch transaction data for automated accounting.

1. Purchases journal input form for purchases on account.
2. Cash payments journal input form for cash payments.
3. Sales journal input form for sales on account.
4. Cash receipts journal input form for cash receipts.
5. General journal input form for all other transactions.

TEACHING STRATEGIES:
ACCOUNTING PEDAGOGY

This textbook introduces the manual accounting concept of journalizing purchases, cash payments, sales, and cash receipts before using the computer to journalize and post. It is important that students master accounting theory before using the computer.

LESSON PLAN A4-1

Materials

- Student pages 309–317
- Transparency AA-2, Blank General Journal Input Form
- Transparency AA-3, Blank Purchases Journal Input Form
- Transparency AA-4, Blank Cash Payments Journal Input Form
- Input forms for Automating Challenge Problem 13-C are provided in the working papers that accompany this textbook. If additional input forms are needed, blackline masters are provided in the Accounting Ruling Masters section of the Teacher's Resource Guide.
- Complete solutions for automated problems are provided in the Teacher's Resource Guide.
- Software: *Automated Accounting 6.0* or higher; Accounting Textbook Template, first-year course

Objective

Record and process purchases, cash payments, and other transactions for a partnership using an automated accounting system.

FILE MAINTENANCE

CarLand's chart of accounts for the general and subsidiary ledgers is on page 244. CarLand uses the same procedures as described for Rugcare in Part 2 to maintain its general ledger chart of accounts. The subsidiary ledgers are also a part of the general ledger data base on the template disk. Procedures for adding or changing a subsidiary account are the same as for a general ledger account. (1) An input form is prepared. (2) The data base is retrieved. (3) Data from the input form are keyed. (4) A revised chart of accounts, vendor list, or customer list is displayed to verify the accuracy of the data keyed. (5) The revised chart of accounts or subsidiary ledger lists are stored as part of the general ledger data base on the template disk.

RECORDING PURCHASES

CarLand batches purchases on account transactions and records them on a purchases journal input form.

Purchase of Merchandise on Account

November 2, 19--. Purchased merchandise on account from Veloz Automotive, $1,754.00. Purchase Invoice No. 74.

The journal entry to record this transaction is on line 1 of the purchases journal input form shown in Illustration T4-1.

ILLUSTRATION T4-1 Purchases journal input form with transactions recorded

RUN DATE 11/30/-- (MM DD YY)

PURCHASES JOURNAL
Input Form

	DATE MM/DD	VENDOR NO.	INVOICE NO.	INVOICE AMOUNT	ACCOUNT NO.	DEBIT	CREDIT	
1	11 02	260	P74	1754 00	5110	1754 00		1
2	05	240	P75	3456 00	5110	3456 00		2
3	05	230	P76	3180 00	5110	3180 00		3
4	13	250	P77	3140 00	5110	3140 00		4
5	20	250	P78	2760 00	5110	2760 00		5
25								25

NOTE: A credit to Accounts Payable is made automatically by the software.

The run date, *11/30/--*, is written in the space provided at the top of the input form.

On line 1, the date of the transaction, *11/02*, is recorded in the Date column. The vendor number, *260*, is entered in the Vendor No. column. The source document number, *P74*, is written in the

Invoice No. column. The invoice amount, *$1,754.00*, is recorded in the Invoice Amount column. The general ledger account number for Purchases, *5110*, is entered in the Account No. column. The debit amount, *$1,754.00*, is written in the Debit column. The Credit column is left blank. The software automatically records the credit to Accounts Payable for a purchases on account transaction.

RECORDING CASH PAYMENTS

CarLand batches cash payments and records them on a cash payments journal input form. CarLand has two types of cash payments. (1) Direct payments. (2) Payments on account. A direct payment transaction does not affect Accounts Payable. Whereas, a payment on account transaction does affect Accounts Payable.

Purchase of Merchandise for Cash

A purchase of merchandise for cash transaction is a direct payment not affecting Accounts Payable.

> *November 2, 19--. Purchased merchandise for cash, $483.00. Check No. 259.*

The journal entry to record this transaction is on line 1 of the cash payments journal input form shown in Illustration T4-2.

ILLUSTRATION T4-2   Cash payments journal input form with transactions recorded

RUN DATE 11, 30, -- (MM DD YY)

CASH PAYMENTS JOURNAL
Input Form

	DATE MM/DD	VENDOR NO.	CHECK NO.	ACCOUNTS PAY. DEBIT	ACCOUNT NO.	DEBIT	CREDIT	
1	11 02		C259		5110	483 00		1
2	02		C260		6160	1500 00		2
3	05		C261		1145	87 00		3
4	06	250	C262	3960 00				4
5	07	230	C263	970 00				5
6	09		C264		6190	300 00		6
7	09		C265		6110	125 00		7
8	09		C266		1145	58 00		8
9					1150	65 00		9
10	/				6110	92 00		10
11	/				6140	86 00		11
12	10		C267		3140	1500 00		12
13	12	210	C268	430 00				13
14	15		C272		3120	1500 00		14
15	20	240	C273	4840 00				15
16	23	220	C274	620 00				16
25	/							25

NOTE: A credit to Cash is made automatically by the software.

The run date, *11/30/--*, is written in the space provided at the top of the form.

On line 1, the date of the transaction, *11/02*, is entered in the Date column. The Vendor No. column is left blank because a purchase of merchandise for cash transaction does not affect a vendor account. The source document number, *C259*, is recorded in the Check No. column. The Accounts Pay. Debit column is left blank. The general ledger account number for Purchases, *5110*, is written in the Account No. column. The amount, *$483.00*, is entered in the Debit column. The software automatically makes the credit to Cash, *$483.00*. Therefore, the Credit column is left blank.

Buying Supplies for Cash

A buying supplies for cash transaction is a direct payment not affecting accounts payable.

> November 5, 19--. Paid cash for office supplies, $87.00. Check No. 261.

The journal entry to record this transaction is on line 3 of Illustration T4-2. The entry is similar to other direct payment transactions.

Cash Payment on Account

A cash payment on account transaction affects both the controlling account Accounts Payable and a vendor account in an accounts payable subsidiary ledger.

> November 6, 19--. Paid cash on account to Q-Ban Distributors, $3,960.00. Check No. 262.

The journal entry to record this transaction is on line 4 of Illustration T4-2.

The date of the transaction, *06*, is written in the Date column. The vendor number, *250*, is entered in the Vendor No. column. The check number, *C262*, is written in the Check No. column. The amount, *$3,960.00*, is recorded in the Accounts Pay. Debit column. The Account No., Debit, and Credit columns are left blank.

Cash Payment of an Expense

A cash payment of an expense transaction is a direct cash payment not affecting Accounts Payable.

> November 9, 19--. Paid cash for advertising, $125.00. Check No. 265.

The journal entry to record this transaction is on line 7 of Illustration T4-2. This journal entry is similar to other direct payments.

Cash Payment to Replenish Petty Cash

A cash payment to replenish petty cash transaction is a direct payment not affecting Accounts Payable.

FYI

The run date is usually the date of the last transaction or the last day of a fiscal period.

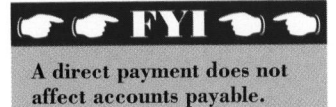

November 9, 19--. Paid cash to replenish the petty cash fund, $301.00: office supplies, $58.00; store supplies, $65.00; advertising, $92.00; miscellaneous, $86.00. Check No. 266.

The journal entry to record this transaction is on lines 8 through 11 of Illustration T4-2. This journal entry is similar to other direct payments.

A direct payment does not affect accounts payable.

RECORDING OTHER TRANSACTIONS

CarLand batches transactions that are not recorded on any of the other input forms and records them on a general journal input form.

Buying Supplies on Account

November 6, 19--. Bought store supplies on account from Antelo Supply, $160.00. Memorandum No. 43.

The run date, 11/30/--, is written in the space provided at the top of the form.

The journal entry to record this transaction is on lines 1 and 2 of the general journal input form shown in Illustration T4-3. Supplies—Store is debited and Accounts Payable is credited for $160.00.

ILLUSTRATION T4-3

General journal input form with transactions recorded

RUN DATE 11/30/-- MM DD YY

GENERAL JOURNAL Input Form

	DATE MM/DD	REFERENCE	ACCOUNT NO.	CUSTOMER/ VENDOR NO.	DEBIT	CREDIT	
1	11/06	M43	1150		160 00		1
2	/		2110	210		160 00	2
3	/12	M44	3140		200 00		3
4	/		5110			200 00	4
5	/13	M45	6110		120 00		5
6	/		6140			120 00	6
7	/20	M46	3120		250 00		7
8	/		5110			250 00	8
9	/23	M47	1150		590 00		9
10	/		2110	210		590 00	10
11	/24	M48	1145		830 00		11
12	/		2110	220		830 00	12
25	/						25

	DEBIT	CREDIT
PAGE TOTALS	2150 00	2150 00
FINAL TOTALS	2150 00	2150 00

Withdrawal of Merchandise by a Partner

November 12, 19--. Dario Mesa, partner, withdrew merchandise for personal use, $200.00. Memorandum No. 44.

INTEGRATING AUTOMATED ACCOUNTING—TOPIC 4   **313**

The journal entry to record this transaction is on lines 3 and 4 of the general journal input form shown in Illustration T4-3. Dario Mesa, Drawing is debited and Purchases is credited for $200.00.

Correcting Entry

November 13, 19--. Discovered that a payment of cash for advertising in October was journalized and posted in error as a debit to Miscellaneous Expense instead of Advertising Expense, $120.00. Memorandum No. 45.

The journal entry to record this transaction is on lines 5 and 6 of the general journal input form shown in Illustration T4-3. Advertising Expense is debited and Miscellaneous Expense is credited for $120.00.

PROCESSING PURCHASES, CASH PAYMENTS, AND OTHER TRANSACTIONS

The general ledger data base is retrieved from the template disk. To process purchases, the Journals menu is selected from the menu bar. The Purchases Journal command is chosen from the Journals menu to display the data entry window for keying transaction data.

After all transaction data have been keyed and posted, the Reports menu is selected from the menu bar. The Journals command is chosen to display the Report Selection window. The Purchases Journal report is selected from the Report Selection window. As CarLand wants to print all transactions from 11/01/-- to 11/30/--, the *Ok* button is pushed to display the purchases journal report. The displayed report is checked for accuracy by comparing the report with the purchases journal input form. The purchases journal report is printed, as shown in Illustration T4-4, and filed for future reference.

FYI

The petty cash account is only used when establishing petty cash.

ILLUSTRATION T4-4   Purchases journal report

```
                              CarLand
                         Purchases Journal
                            11/30/--
-----------------------------------------------------------------------
Date    Refer.   V/C Acct.  Title                      Debit     Credit
-----------------------------------------------------------------------
11/02   P74          5110   Purchases                 1754.00
11/02   P74      260 2110   AP/Veloz Automotive                  1754.00

11/05   P75          5110   Purchases                 3456.00
11/05   P75      240 2110   AP/Nilon Motor Parts                 3456.00

11/05   P76          5110   Purchases                 3180.00
11/05   P76      230 2110   AP/Filtrex Tires                     3180.00

11/13   P77          5110   Purchases                 3140.00
11/13   P77      250 2110   AP/Q-Ban Distributors                3140.00

11/20   P78          5110   Purchases                 2760.00
11/20   P78      250 2110   AP/Q-Ban Distributors                2760.00

                                                    ----------  ----------
                            Totals                   14290.00    14290.00
                                                    ==========  ==========
```

To process cash payments, the Journals menu is selected from the menu bar. The Cash Payments command is chosen from the Journals menu to display the data entry window for keying transaction data.

After all transactions have been keyed and posted, a cash payments journal report is displayed. The same steps are followed as for displaying the purchases journal report. However, Cash Payments Journal is selected from the Report Selection window. The displayed report is checked for accuracy by comparing the report with the cash payments journal input form. The cash payments report is printed, as shown in Illustration T4-5, and filed for future reference.

ILLUSTRATION T4-5	Cash payments journal report

```
                              CarLand
                       Cash Payments Journal
                            11/30/--
------------------------------------------------------------------------
Date   Refer.   V/C Acct.   Title                      Debit     Credit
------------------------------------------------------------------------
11/02  C259         5110    Purchases                 483.00
11/02  C259         1110    Cash                                 483.00

11/02  C260         6160    Rent Expense             1500.00
11/02  C260         1110    Cash                                1500.00

11/05  C261         1145    Supplies--Office           87.00
11/05  C261         1110    Cash                                  87.00

11/06  C262     250 2110    AP/Q-Ban Distributors    3960.00
11/06  C262         1110    Cash                                3960.00

11/07  C263     230 2110    AP/Filtrex Tires          970.00
11/07  C263         1110    Cash                                 970.00

11/09  C264         6190    Utilities Expense         300.00
11/09  C264         1110    Cash                                 300.00

11/09  C265         6110    Advertising Expense       125.00
11/09  C265         1110    Cash                                 125.00

11/09  C266         1145    Supplies--Office           58.00
11/09  C266         1150    Supplies--Store            65.00
11/09  C266         6110    Advertising Expense        92.00
11/09  C266         6140    Miscellaneous Expense      86.00
11/09  C266         1110    Cash                                 301.00

11/10  C267         3140    Dario Mesa, Drawing      1500.00
11/10  C267         1110    Cash                                1500.00

11/12  C268     210 2110    AP/Antelo Supply          430.00
11/12  C268         1110    Cash                                 430.00

11/15  C272         3120    Amy Kramer, Drawing      1500.00
11/15  C272         1110    Cash                                1500.00

11/20  C273     240 2110    AP/Nilon Motor Parts     4840.00
11/20  C273         1110    Cash                                4840.00

11/23  C274     220 2110    AP/Bell Office Products   620.00
11/23  C274         1110    Cash                                 620.00

                                                    ----------  ----------
                            Totals                  16616.00    16616.00
                                                    ==========  ==========
```

TEACHING STRATEGIES: USING VISUALS

Using Transparencies AA-2 Blank General Journal Input Form; AA-3 Blank Purchases Journal Input Form; AA-4 Blank Cash Payments Journal Input Form; AA-5 Blank Sales Journal Input Form; and AA-6 Blank Cash Receipts Journal Input Form will help students understand the journalizing process.

To process other transactions, the Journals menu is selected from the menu bar. The General Journal command is chosen from the Journals menu to display the data entry window for keying transactions.

After all transactions have been keyed and posted, a general journal report is displayed. The same steps are followed as for displaying the purchases journal report. However, General Journal is selected from the Report Selection window. The displayed general journal report is checked for accuracy by comparing the report totals, *$2,150.00*, with the totals on the general journal input form. Because the totals are the same, the general journal report is assumed to be correct. The general journal report is printed, as shown in Illustration T4-6, and filed for future reference.

SAFETY AND HEALTH

To prevent scratching the computer monitor, only use a soft cloth for cleaning the screen. A Safety and Health page is given in the Teacher's Resource Guide. This page may be duplicated and given to students.

ILLUSTRATION T4-6   General journal report

```
                              CarLand
                          General Journal
                            11/30/--
-----------------------------------------------------------------------
Date   Refer.    V/C Acct.  Title                     Debit     Credit
-----------------------------------------------------------------------
11/06  M43           1150   Supplies--Store           160.00
11/06  M43       210 2110   AP/Antelo Supply                    160.00

11/12  M44           3140   Dario Mesa, Drawing       200.00
11/12  M44           5110   Purchases                           200.00

11/13  M45           6110   Advertising Expense       120.00
11/13  M45           6140   Miscellaneous Expense               120.00

11/20  M46           3120   Amy Kramer, Drawing       250.00
11/20  M46           5110   Purchases                           250.00

11/23  M47           1150   Supplies--Store           590.00
11/23  M47       210 2110   AP/Antelo Supply                    590.00

11/24  M48           1145   Supplies--Office          830.00
11/24  M48       220 2110   AP/Bell Office Products             830.00

                                                    ----------  ----------
                            Totals                   2150.00    2150.00
                                                    ==========  ==========
```

PROVING THE ACCOUNTS PAYABLE SUBSIDIARY LEDGER

A general ledger controlling account balance must equal the sum of all account balances in a subsidiary ledger. CarLand proves the accounts payable subsidiary ledger at the end of each month.

To prove the accounts payable ledger, the Reports menu is selected from the menu bar. The Ledgers command is chosen to display the Report Selection window. General Ledger and Schedule of Accounts Payable are selected from the Report Selection window. As CarLand wants to print the transaction activity in only the general ledger controlling account, Accounts Payable, Account No. 2110 to 2110 is keyed as the account number range. After keying the account number range, the *Ok* button is pushed to display the general ledger account, Accounts Payable. The accounts payable account is printed as shown in Illustration T4-7. The schedule of accounts payable is then displayed. The total of the schedule of accounts payable is compared to the balance of the accounts payable account. As the two amounts are the same, *$15,870.00*, the accounts payable ledger is proved. The schedule of accounts payable is printed, as shown in Illustration T4-8, and filed for future reference.

ILLUSTRATION T4-7   Accounts payable account

```
                          CarLand
                       General Ledger
                         11/30/--
-------------------------------------------------------------------
Account          Journal  Date  Refer.    Debit     Credit    Balance
-------------------------------------------------------------------
2110-Accounts Payable
                 Bal. Fwd.                                   10820.00
                 Purchases 11/02 P74                1754.00  12574.00
                 Purchases 11/05 P75                3456.00  16030.00
                 Purchases 11/05 P76                3180.00  19210.00
                 Cash Pymt 11/06 C262    3960.00             15250.00
                 General   11/06 M43                 160.00  15410.00
                 Cash Pymt 11/07 C263     970.00             14440.00
                 Cash Pymt 11/12 C268     430.00             14010.00
                 Purchases 11/13 P77                3140.00  17150.00
                 Purchases 11/20 P78                2760.00  19910.00
                 Cash Pymt 11/20 C273    4840.00             15070.00
                 Cash Pymt 11/23 C274     620.00             14450.00
                 General   11/23 M47                 590.00  15040.00
                 General   11/24 M48                 830.00  15870.00
```

ILLUSTRATION T4-8   Schedule of accounts payable

```
                       CarLand
              Schedule of Accounts Payable
                        11/30/--
--------------------------------------------------------
Account
Number    Name                         Balance
--------------------------------------------------------
210       Antelo Supply                 750.00
220       Bell Office Products          830.00
230       Filtrex Tires                3180.00
240       Nilon Motor Parts            3456.00
250       Q-Ban Distributors           5900.00
260       Veloz Automotive             1754.00
                                      ----------
          Total                       15870.00
                                      ==========
```

LESSON PLAN A4-2

Materials

- Student pages 318–325
- Transparency AA-5, Blank Sales Journal Input Form
- Transparency AA-6, Blank Cash Receipts Journal Input Form
- Input forms for Automating Challenge Problem 13-C are provided in the working papers that accompany this textbook. If additional input forms are needed, blackline masters are provided in the Accounting Ruling Masters section of the Teacher's Resource Guide.
- Complete solutions for automated problems are provided in the Teacher's Resource Guide.
- Software: *Automated Accounting 6.0* or higher; Accounting Textbook Template, first-year course

Objective

Record and process sales and cash receipts transactions for a partnership using an automated accounting system.

RECORDING SALES ON ACCOUNT

CarLand batches sales on account transactions and records them on a sales journal input form.

November 3, 19--. Sold merchandise on account to Friendly Auto Service, $680.00, plus sales tax, $40.80; total, $720.80. Sales Invoice No. 72.

The journal entry to record this transaction is on lines 1 and 2 of the sales journal input form shown in Illustration T4-9.

ILLUSTRATION T4-9   Sales journal input form with transactions recorded

RUN DATE *11/30/--* (MM DD YY)

SALES JOURNAL Input Form

	DATE MM/DD	CUSTOMER NO.	INVOICE NO.	INVOICE AMOUNT	ACCOUNT NO.	DEBIT	CREDIT	
1	11 03	130	S72	720 80	4110		680 00	1
2	/				2140		40 80	2
3	05	150	S73	1590 00	4110		1500 00	3
4	/				2140		90 00	4
5	09	110	S74	477 00	4110		450 00	5
6	/				2140		27 00	6
7	11	160	S75	604 20	4110		570 00	7
8	/				2140		34 20	8
9	16	110	S76	1378 00	4110		1300 00	9
10	/				2140		78 00	10
11	18	120	S77	2014 00	4110		1900 00	11
12	/				2140		114 00	12
13	24	130	S78	742 00	4110		700 00	13
14	/				2140		42 00	14
15	24	140	S79	318 00	4110		300 00	15
16	/				2140		18 00	16
17	29	140	S80	1378 00	4110		1300 00	17
18	/				2140		78 00	18
25								25

NOTE: A debit to Accounts Receivable is made automatically by the software.

The run date, *11/30/--*, is written in the space provided at the top of the form.

On line 1, the date of the transaction, *11/03*, is entered in the Date column. The customer number, *130*, is recorded in the Customer No. column. The source document number, *S72*, is written in the Invoice No. column. The invoice amount, *$720.80*, is written in the Invoice Amount column. The general ledger account number for Sales, *4110*, is entered in the Account No. column. The Debit

318   INTEGRATING AUTOMATED ACCOUNTING—TOPIC 4

column is left blank. The software automatically makes the debit to the accounts receivable account. The sale on account amount, $680.00, is recorded in the Credit column.

On line 2 for a sales on account transaction, the Date, Customer No., and Invoice Amount columns are left blank. The general ledger account number for Sales Tax Payable, 2140, is written in the Account No. column. The sales tax amount, $40.80, is entered in the Credit column.

RECORDING CASH RECEIPTS

CarLand batches cash receipts and records them on a cash receipts journal input form. Two types of cash receipts are recorded. (1) Receipts on account. (2) Direct receipts. A receipt on account transaction affects Accounts Receivable. Whereas, a direct receipt transaction does not affect Accounts Receivable.

Cash Receipt on Account

November 6, 19--. Received cash on account from Autohaus Service, $1,802.00. Receipt No. 86.

The journal entry to record this transaction is on line 1 of the cash receipts journal input form shown in Illustration T4-10.

ILLUSTRATION T4-10 · Cash receipts journal input form with transactions recorded

	DATE MM/DD	CUSTOMER NO.	REFERENCE	ACCOUNTS REC. CREDIT	ACCOUNT NO.	DEBIT	CREDIT	
RUN DATE 11/30/-- MM DD YY			CASH RECEIPTS JOURNAL Input Form					
1	11/06	120	R86	1802 00				1
2	07		T7		4110		6450 00	2
3	/				2140		387 00	3
4	10	140	R87	954 00				4
5	13	160	R88	901 00				5
6	14	150	R89	318 00				6
7	14		T14		4110		5100 00	7
8	/				2140		306 00	8
9	17	110	R90	2491 00				9
10	20	160	R91	1219 00				10
11	21		T21		4110		5100 00	11
12	/				2140		306 00	12
13	25	130	R92	265 00				13
14	28		T28		4110		5100 00	14
15	/				2140		306 00	15
16	30		T30		4110		1150 00	16
17	/				2140		69 00	17
25	/							25

NOTE: A debit to Cash is made automatically by the software.

Cover student pages 318–325 "Recording Sales on Account," "Recording Cash
Receipts," "Processing Sales and Cash
Receipts," and "Proving the Accounts
Receivable Subsidiary Ledger." This lesson will show students step-by-step
how to record sales on account and
cash receipts. Students will also learn
to use the automated accounting software to prove the accounts receivable
subsidiary ledger. Explain the two types
of cash receipts. (1) Receipts on
account. (2) Direct receipts.

The run date, *11/30/--*, is written in the space provided at the top of the form.

On line 1, the date of the transaction, *11/06*, is entered in the Date column. The customer number, *120*, is recorded in the Customer No. column. The source document number, *R86*, is written in the Reference column. The amount of the cash receipt on account, *$1,802.00*, is entered in the Accounts Rec. Credit column. The software automatically makes the debit to *Cash*. Therefore, the Account No. and Debit columns are left blank.

Cash and Credit Card Sales

A cash or credit card sales transaction is a direct receipt not affecting Accounts Receivable.

> *November 7, 19--. Recorded cash and credit card sales, $6,450.00 plus sales tax, $387.00; total, $6,837.00. Cash Register Tape No. 7.*

The journal entry to record this transaction is on lines 2 and 3 of Illustration T4-10.

On line 2, the date of the transaction, *07*, is written in the Date column. The source document number, *T7*, is entered in the Reference column. The software automatically makes the debit to Cash. Therefore, the Debit column is left blank. The general ledger account number for Sales, *4110*, is recorded in the Account No. column. The amount of the sale, *$6,450.00*, is written in the Credit column.

On line 3, the general ledger account number for Sales Tax Payable, *2140*, is entered in the Account No. column. The sales tax payable amount, *$387.00*, is recorded in the Credit column.

PROCESSING SALES AND CASH RECEIPTS

To process sales on account, the Journals menu is selected from the menu bar. The Sales Journal command is chosen from the Journals menu to display the data entry window for keying transaction data.

After all sales on account transactions have been keyed and posted, the Reports menu is selected from the menu bar. The Journals command is chosen to display the Report Selection window. The Sales Journal report is selected from the Report Selection window. As CarLand wants to prints all transactions from 11/01/-- to 11/30/--, the *Ok* button is pushed to display the Sales Journal report. The displayed report is checked for accuracy by comparing the report with the sales journal input form. The sales journal report is printed, as shown in Illustration T4-11, and filed for future reference.

FYI

Display your work before printing to make sure the information is correct. This will save you time and paper.

```
                            CarLand
                         Sales Journal
                           11/30/--
-----------------------------------------------------------------------
Date   Refer.   V/C Acct.  Title                    Debit        Credit
-----------------------------------------------------------------------
11/03  S72      130 1130   AR/Friendly Auto Service  720.80
11/03  S72          4110   Sales                                  680.00
11/03  S72          2140   Sales Tax Payable                       40.80

11/05  S73      150 1130   AR/Powell Rent-A-Car     1590.00
11/05  S73          4110   Sales                                 1500.00
11/05  S73          2140   Sales Tax Payable                       90.00

11/09  S74      110 1130   AR/Ashley Delivery        477.00
11/09  S74          4110   Sales                                  450.00
11/09  S74          2140   Sales Tax Payable                       27.00

11/11  S75      160 1130   AR/Wood Sales & Service   604.20
11/11  S75          4110   Sales                                  570.00
11/11  S75          2140   Sales Tax Payable                       34.20

11/16  S76      110 1130   AR/Ashley Delivery       1378.00
11/16  S76          4110   Sales                                 1300.00
11/16  S76          2140   Sales Tax Payable                       78.00

11/18  S77      120 1130   AR/Autohaus Service      2014.00
11/18  S77          4110   Sales                                 1900.00
11/18  S77          2140   Sales Tax Payable                      114.00

11/24  S78      130 1130   AR/Friendly Auto Service  742.00
11/24  S78          4110   Sales                                  700.00
11/24  S78          2140   Sales Tax Payable                       42.00

11/24  S79      140 1130   AR/Keystone Delivery      318.00
11/24  S79          4110   Sales                                  300.00
11/24  S79          2140   Sales Tax Payable                       18.00

11/29  S80      140 1130   AR/Keystone Delivery     1378.00
11/29  S80          4110   Sales                                 1300.00
11/29  S80          2140   Sales Tax Payable                       78.00

                                                   ----------  ----------
                           Totals                    9222.00     9222.00
                                                   ==========  ==========
```

To process cash receipts, the Journals menu is selected from the menu bar. The Cash Receipts command is chosen from the Journals menu to display the data entry window for keying transaction data.

After all transactions have been keyed and posted, the Reports menu is selected from the menu bar. The Journals command is chosen to display the Report Selection window. The Cash Receipts Journal report is selected from the Report Selection window. As CarLand wants to print all transactions from 11/01/-- to 11/30/--, the *Ok* button is pushed to display the Cash Receipts report. The displayed report is checked for accuracy by comparing the report to the cash receipts journal input form. The cash receipts journal

Reteach

Give students a blank sales journal input form and a cash receipts journal input form. Read the transactions in the text and have students journalize each.

Enrich

Have the students discuss some of the ways computer technology has changed their everyday lives.

report is printed, as shown in Illustration T4-12, and is filed for future reference.

ILLUSTRATION T4-12   Cash receipts journal report

```
                              CarLand
                        Cash Receipts Journal
                             11/30/--
-----------------------------------------------------------------------
Date   Refer.    V/C Acct.  Title                      Debit      Credit
-----------------------------------------------------------------------
11/06  R86           1110   Cash                      1802.00
11/06  R86       120 1130   AR/Autohaus Service                  1802.00

11/07  T7            1110   Cash                      6837.00
11/07  T7            4110   Sales                                6450.00
11/07  T7            2140   Sales Tax Payable                     387.00

11/10  R87           1110   Cash                       954.00
11/10  R87       140 1130   AR/Keystone Delivery                  954.00

11/13  R88           1110   Cash                       901.00
11/13  R88       160 1130   AR/Wood Sales & Service               901.00

11/14  R89           1110   Cash                       318.00
11/14  R89       150 1130   AR/Powell Rent-A-Car                  318.00

11/14  T14           1110   Cash                      5406.00
11/14  T14           4110   Sales                                5100.00
11/14  T14           2140   Sales Tax Payable                     306.00

11/17  R90           1110   Cash                      2491.00
11/17  R90       110 1130   AR/Ashley Delivery                   2491.00

11/20  R91           1110   Cash                      1219.00
11/20  R91       160 1130   AR/Wood Sales & Service              1219.00

11/21  T21           1110   Cash                      5406.00
11/21  T21           4110   Sales                                5100.00
11/21  T21           2140   Sales Tax Payable                     306.00

11/25  R92           1110   Cash                       265.00
11/25  R92       130 1130   AR/Friendly Auto Service              265.00

11/28  T28           1110   Cash                      5406.00
11/28  T28           4110   Sales                                5100.00
11/28  T28           2140   Sales Tax Payable                     306.00

11/30  T30           1110   Cash                      1219.00
11/30  T30           4110   Sales                                1150.00
11/30  T30           2140   Sales Tax Payable            69.00

                                                    ---------- ----------
                            Totals                   32224.00   32224.00
                                                    ========== ==========
```

PROVING THE ACCOUNTS RECEIVABLE SUBSIDIARY LEDGER

CarLand proves the accounts receivable subsidiary ledger at the end of each month.

To prove the accounts receivable ledger, the Reports menu is selected from the menu bar. The Ledgers command is chosen to display the Report Selection window. General Ledger and Schedule of Accounts Receivable are selected from the Report Selection window. As CarLand wants to print the transaction activity only in the general ledger controlling account, Accounts Receivable, Account No. 1130 to 1130 is keyed as the account number range. After keying the account number range, the *Ok* button is pushed to display the general ledger account, Accounts Receivable. The accounts receivable account is printed as shown in Illustration T4-13. The schedule of accounts receivable is then displayed. The total of the schedule of accounts receivable is compared to the accounts receivable account balance. As the two amounts are the same, *$9,222.00*, the accounts receivable ledger is proved. The schedule of accounts receivable is printed, as shown in Illustration T4-14 on page 324, and is filed for future reference.

CLOSURE

Review the procedures for recording transactions on input forms and for using automated accounting software to process transactions.

ILLUSTRATION T4-13   Accounts receivable account

```
                              CarLand
                          General Ledger
                            11/30/--
---------------------------------------------------------------------
Account             Journal   Date   Refer.     Debit     Credit    Balance
---------------------------------------------------------------------
1130-Accounts Receivable
                    Bal. Fwd.                                       7950.00
                    Sales     11/03  S72       720.80               8670.80
                    Sales     11/05  S73      1590.00              10260.80
                    Cash Rcpt 11/06  R86                 1802.00    8458.80
                    Sales     11/09  S74       477.00               8935.80
                    Cash Rcpt 11/10  R87                  954.00    7981.80
                    Sales     11/11  S75       604.20               8586.00
                    Cash Rcpt 11/13  R88                  901.00    7685.00
                    Cash Rcpt 11/14  R89                  318.00    7367.00
                    Sales     11/16  S76      1378.00               8745.00
                    Cash Rcpt 11/17  R90                 2491.00    6254.00
                    Sales     11/18  S77      2014.00               8268.00
                    Cash Rcpt 11/20  R91                 1219.00    7049.00
                    Sales     11/24  S78       742.00               7791.00
                    Sales     11/24  S79       318.00               8109.00
                    Cash Rcpt 11/25  R92                  265.00    7844.00
                    Sales     11/29  S80      1378.00               9222.00
```

SOFTWARE FOCUS

The Automated Accounting Problem in this Integrating Automated Accounting topic uses Challenge Problem 13-C, Chapter 13, which students have already completed manually. Refer students back to this problem to complete the input forms. The problem instructions in *Automated Accounting 6.0* will lead students through automating the problem.

```
                    CarLand
          Schedule of Accounts Receivable
                   11/30/--
--------------------------------------------------
Account
Number    Name                           Balance
--------------------------------------------------
110       Ashley Delivery                1855.00
120       Autohaus Service               2014.00
130       Friendly Auto Service          1462.80
140       Keystone Delivery              1696.00
150       Powell Rent-A-Car              1590.00
160       Wood Sales & Service            604.20
                                       ----------
          Total                          9222.00
                                       ==========
```

AUTOMATED

OPTIONAL PROBLEM DB-4A

CarLand's general ledger data base is on the accounting textbook template. If you wish to process CarLand's purchases, cash payments, and other transactions using automated accounting software, load the *Automated Accounting 6.0* or higher software. Select Data Base 4A (DB-4A) from the template disk. Read the Problem Instructions screen. Use the completed purchases, cash payments, general journal input forms, Illustrations T4-1, T4-2, and T4-3, and follow the procedures described to process CarLand's purchases, cash payments, and other transactions.

AUTOMATED

OPTIONAL PROBLEM DB-4A

CarLand's general ledger data base is on the accounting textbook template. If you wish to process CarLand's sales and cash receipts transactions using automated accounting software, load the *Automated Accounting 6.0* or higher software. Continue using Data Base 4A (DB-4A) from the template disk. Use the completed sales and cash receipts journal input forms, Illustrations T4-9 and T4-10, and follow the procedures described to process CarLand's sales and cash receipts.

AUTOMATED ACCOUNTING PROBLEM

AUTOMATING CHALLENGE PROBLEM 13-C **Recording transactions for a partnership**

INSTRUCTIONS:

1. Journalize the transactions from Challenge Problem 13-C, Chapter 13 on the appropriate input forms. Use November 30 of the current year as the run date.
2. Load the *Automated Accounting 6.0* or higher software. Select data base F13-C (First-Year Course Problem 13-C) from the accounting textbook template. Read the Problem Instructions screen.
3. Select File from the menu bar and choose the Save As menu command. Key the path to the drive and directory that contains your data files. Save the data base with a file name of XXX13C (where XXX are your initials).
4. Key the data from the completed purchases journal input form.
5. Display/print the purchases journal report.
6. Key the data from the completed cash payments journal input form.
7. Display/print the cash payments journal report.
8. Key the data from the completed general journal input form.

9. Display/print the general journal report.
10. Display/print the accounts payable account.
11. Display/print the schedule of accounts payable.
12. Key the data from the completed sales journal input form.
13. Display/print the sales journal report.
14. Key the data from the cash receipts journal input form.
15. Display/print the cash receipts journal report.
16. Display/print the accounts receivable account.
17. Display/print the schedule of accounts receivable.

Chapter 14 is the first of two payroll chapters. The business in this accounting cycle is assumed to be large enough to include employees and, therefore, payroll procedures are introduced. This first chapter describes some basic payroll concepts, such as recording time worked using a time card and then calculating hours worked. The chapter narrative describes the basic kinds of payroll deductions withheld from an employee's wages and discusses an individual's withholding allowances and Form W-4. Procedures

GUIDE TO ACHIEVING LEARNING OBJECTIVES

Enabling Performance Tasks	TEACH	APPLY		EXTEND/ENRICH					
	Lesson Plans	Drills for Understanding	Application Problems	Mastery Problems	Challenge Problems	Cases for Critical Thinking	Recycling Problems	Reinforcement Activity	
a. Define accounting terms related to payroll records.	14-1, 14-2, 14-3, 14-4								
b. Identify accounting practices related to payroll records.	14-1, 14-2, 14-3, 14-4					Case 1			
c. Calculate employee earnings and deductions.	14-1, 14-2, 14-3	14-D1, 14-D2	14-1, 14-2 14-3	14-M	14-C		14-R		
d. Complete payroll records.	14-3, 14-4		14-1, 14-2 14-3	14-M	14-C		14-R		
e. Prepare payroll checks.	14-3		14-2	14-M		Case 2	14-R		

ENRICHMENT

SPECIAL FEATURES

Multicultural Awareness, page 332

Careers in Accounting, page 328

Applied Communications, page 346

Spreadsheet Options, page 333

TECHNOLOGY CONNECTION

Spreadsheet Template Problems 14-2, 14-3, 14-C

Electronic Study Guide

NEW, REVIEW, AND EXTENSION

ACTIVITIES/CONCEPTS/TRANSACTIONS	NEW	REVIEW/ EXTENSION
Calculating hours worked and total earnings from time cards	✓	
Calculating employee income tax	✓	
Calculating employee and employer social security tax	✓	
Preparing a payroll register	✓	
Writing payroll checks	✓	
Preparing employee earnings records	✓	
Processing a payroll using a pegboard	✓	

for using a payroll register to record an entire payroll and an earnings record to record an individual's payroll records are presented. Federal income tax withholding tables are illustrated and used to calculate the withholdings for each employee. Students who currently hold jobs will bring some of their own experiences in earning wages to the concepts in this chapter. Students who will be employed in the future will find personal relevance in this chapter.

	INFORMAL ASSESSMENT		FORMAL ASSESSMENT				
	Study Guide	Audit Your Understanding	Chapter MicroExam	Chapter Problem Test	Unit Problem Test	Unit Objective Test	Portfolio
	Unit B	✓	✓			✓	
	Units A, C	✓	✓			✓	
				✓	✓		
				✓	✓		
				✓			

TEACHING MATERIALS

Teacher's Wraparound Edition of the Text

Teacher's Resource Guide

Teacher's Edition of Working Papers

Teacher's Edition of the Demonstration/Recycling Problems

Teaching Transparencies

MicroExam

Applied Math Work Sheet

APPLIED MATHEMATICS

APPLIED MATH/ACCOUNTING SKILL	APPLICATION
Calculating hours worked	Prob. 14-1
Calculating employee total earnings	Drill 14-D1
Calculating FICA taxes	Drill 14-D2
Calculating deductions in a payroll register	Prob. 14-2
Calculating net pay in a payroll register	Prob. 14-2
Calculating accumulated earnings	Prob. 14-3

14

Preparing Payroll Records

ENABLING PERFORMANCE TASKS

After studying Chapter 14, you will be able to:

a Define accounting terms related to payroll records.

b Identify accounting practices related to payroll records.

c Calculate employee earnings and deductions.

d Complete payroll records.

e Prepare payroll checks.

TERMS PREVIEW

salary • pay period • payroll • total earnings • payroll taxes • withholding allowance • Medicare • FICA tax • federal unemployment tax • state unemployment tax • payroll register • tax base • net pay • automatic check deposit • employee earnings record • pegboard

326

CarLand employs several people to work in the business. These employees record the time they work for CarLand each day. Periodically CarLand pays its employees for the number of hours each employee has worked. The money paid for employee services is called a **salary**. The period covered by a salary payment is called a **pay period**. A business may decide to pay employee salaries every week, every two weeks, twice a month, or once a month. CarLand uses a semimonthly pay period. Employees are paid twice a month, on the 15th and last day of each month.

The total amount earned by all employees for a pay period is called a **payroll**. The payroll is reduced by state and federal taxes and other deductions, such as health insurance, to determine the amount paid to all employees. Special payroll records support the recording of payroll transactions in a journal. The business also uses these records to inform employees of their annual earnings and to prepare payroll reports for the government.

PAYROLL TIME CARDS

A payroll system must include an accurate record of the time each employee has worked. Several methods are used for keeping time records. One of the more frequently used methods is a time card. Time cards are used as the basic source of information to prepare a payroll.

Some time cards only require employees to record the total hours worked each day. Employees who record the total hours worked each day usually complete time cards by hand.

A business may use a time card that requires employees to record their arrival and departure times. CarLand uses a time clock to record the daily arrival and departure times of its employees. The time card for Patrick S. Turner for the pay period December 1–15 is shown in Illustration 14-1.

ILLUSTRATION 14-1

Payroll time card

CarLand

EMPLOYEE NO. ___4___
NAME __Patrick S. Turner__
PERIOD ENDING __December 15, 19--__

	MORNING		AFTERNOON		OVERTIME		HOURS	
	IN	OUT	IN	OUT	IN	OUT	REG	OT
1	758	12 02	12 59	5 06			8	
2	759	12 00	12 57	5 01			8	
3	755	12 01	12 56	5 02	7 01	9 33	8	2½
4	756	12 02					8	
14	754	12 04	12 59	5 01			8	
15	755	12 00	12 58	5 01	6 28	8 31	8	2

	HOURS	RATE	AMOUNT
REGULAR	88	8.00	704.00
OVERTIME	4½	12.00	54.00
TOTAL HOURS	92½	TOTAL EARNINGS	758.00

CAREERS IN ACCOUNTING

TIMEKEEPER

- *Reviews timecards*
- *Calculates total time worked by employees*
- *Calculates time worked and units produced by piecework employees*
- *Posts time worked to master records*

Compensation for employee services is known as wages. Wages are normally stated as hourly, weekly, or piecework. Employees who receive wages are usually paid for overtime.

Analyzing a Payroll Time Card

Mr. Turner's employee number is at the top of the card. Below the employee number are the employee name and the ending date of the pay period.

CarLand's time cards have three sections, Morning, Afternoon, and Overtime, with In and Out columns under each section. When Mr. Turner reported for work on December 1, he inserted the card in the time clock. The clock recorded his time of arrival, 7:58, on the first line of the time card. The other entries on this line indicate that he left for lunch at 12:02. He returned at 12:59 and left for the day at 5:06. On December 3 he worked overtime, starting at 7:01 and leaving at 9:33.

CarLand calculates overtime pay for each employee who works more than 8 hours in one day. No employee works more than 5 days in any one week.

Calculating Hours Worked

The first task in preparing a payroll is to calculate the number of hours worked by each employee. Four steps are followed to calculate employee hours worked.

1 Calculate the number of regular hours for each day and enter the amounts in the Hours Reg column.

> Mr. Turner works 8 hours during a normal day. The hours worked on December 3, the third line of the time card, are calculated using the arrival and departure times imprinted on the time card. Times are rounded to the nearest quarter hour to calculate the hours worked.

	Departure Time	−	Arrival Time	=	Hours Worked
Morning:					
Time card	12:01		7:55		
Nearest quarter hour	12:00	−	8:00	=	4:00
Afternoon:					
Time card	5:02		12:56		
Nearest quarter hour	5:00	−	1:00	=	4:00
Total regular hours worked on December 3					8:00

> The hours worked in the morning and afternoon are calculated separately. The morning departure time of 12:01 is rounded to the nearest quarter hour, 12:00. The rounded arrival time, 8:00, *subtracted* from the departure time, 12:00, *equals* the morning hours worked. Hours worked of 4:00 means that Mr. Turner worked 4 hours and no (00) minutes. The total regular hours worked, *8*, is recorded in the Hours Reg column on line 3 of the time card.

2 Calculate the number of overtime hours for each day and enter the amounts in the Hours OT column.

Overtime hours for December 3 are calculated using the same procedure as for regular hours.

	Departure Time	–	Arrival Time	=	Hours Worked
Time card	9:33		7:01		
Nearest quarter hour	9:30	–	7:00	=	2:30

The hours worked of 2:30 means that Mr. Turner worked 2 hours and 30 minutes (½ hour) of overtime. Therefore, 2½ is recorded in the Hours OT column.

3 Add the hours worked in the Hours Reg and OT columns. Enter the totals in the spaces provided at the bottom of the time card.

Mr. Turner worked 88 regular hours (8 hours × 11 days) and 4½ overtime hours during the semimonthly pay period. Therefore, *88* is recorded in the Regular Hours space at the bottom of the card and *4½* is recorded in the Overtime Hours space.

4 Add the Hours column to calculate the total hours. Enter the total in the Hours column at the bottom of the time card.

Mr. Turner worked 88 regular hours and 4½ overtime hours for a total of 92½ hours. Total hours, *92½*, are entered in the Total Hours space.

Calculating Employee Total Earnings

Once the total regular and overtime hours are determined, employee earnings can be calculated. The total pay due for a pay period before deductions is called **total earnings.** Total earnings are sometimes referred to as gross pay or gross earnings. Four steps are followed to calculate employee total earnings.

1 Enter the rate for regular time in the Rate column. Calculate the regular earnings by multiplying regular hours times the regular rate.

Mr. Turner's regular hourly rate, *$8.00*, is entered in the Regular Rate space. The regular earnings are calculated as shown below.

	Regular Hours	×	Regular Rate	=	Regular Earnings
	88	×	$8.00	=	$704.00

The amount of regular earnings, *$704.00*, is entered in the Regular Amount space.

APPLY

- Use Transparency 14-1 to describe Mr. Turner's time card shown in Illustration 14-1.

- Bring a time clock and time cards to class. During the days spent covering Chapter 14, have the students clock in when they arrive for class and clock out when they depart. Perhaps your school or a local business has a time clock that could be made available for classroom use.

Guided Practice

Guide students through Drill 14-D1. Students should have the forms from the working papers to complete as you guide them through the drill. For each employee ask the students to calculate the amount of regular, overtime, and total earnings. All students should agree with the calculations before proceeding to the next employee.

Independent Practice

Assign Terms 1–4, Questions 1–3, and Problem 14-1.

ASSESS

Assess student understanding by checking solutions to Independent Practice activities.

Reteach

- Use Demonstration Problem 14A. This problem can be demonstrated on the overhead with the students completing the problem at their desks.

- Duplicate and assign Math Work Sheet Chapter 14 Part A, Calculating Hours Worked and Part B, Calculating Employee Total Earnings from the Masters and Solutions to Enrichment/Application Activities Section in the Teacher's Resource Guide to provide additional practice on the mathematics of calculating hours worked and total earnings.

Extend

Assign Cases for Critical Thinking 1.

Enrich

Assign the APPLIED COMMUNICATIONS special feature on page 346.

APPLIED SKILLS: COMMUNICATIONS

Surveys of business managers show that communication skills are one of the most desired traits in new employees. The APPLIED COMMUNICATIONS activity provides an opportunity for students to practice their communication and language arts skills on topics that directly relate to accounting. This activity requires students to write a memo explaining a change in the way employees record their work time. The activity involves a badge reader, a computer device similar to credit card readers, increasingly used by large businesses to record work time.

- Use Audit Your Understanding questions.
- Review the procedures for calculating hours worked.
- Review the procedures for calculating employee total earnings.

2 Enter the rate for overtime in the Rate column.

Mr. Turner is paid 1½ times his regular rate for overtime work. The overtime rate for Mr. Turner is calculated as shown below.

Regular Rate	×	1½	=	Overtime Rate
$8.00	×	1½	=	$12.00

The overtime rate, *$12.00*, is entered in the Overtime Rate space.

3 Calculate the overtime earnings by multiplying overtime hours times the overtime rate.

The overtime earnings for Mr. Turner are calculated as shown below.

Overtime Hours	×	Overtime Rate	=	Overtime Earnings
4½	×	$12.00	=	$54.00

The amount of overtime earnings, $54.00, is entered in the Overtime Amount space.

4 Add the Amount column to calculate the total earnings.

The total earnings for Mr. Turner are calculated as shown below.

Regular Earnings	+	Overtime Earnings	=	Total Earnings
$704.00	+	$54.00	=	$758.00

The amount of total earnings, $758.00, is entered in the Total Earnings space.

CarLand owes Mr. Turner $758.00 for his work during the pay period ending December 15. However, taxes and other deductions must be subtracted from total earnings to determine the actual amount CarLand will pay Mr. Turner. Therefore, CarLand will not pay Mr. Turner the entire $758.00.

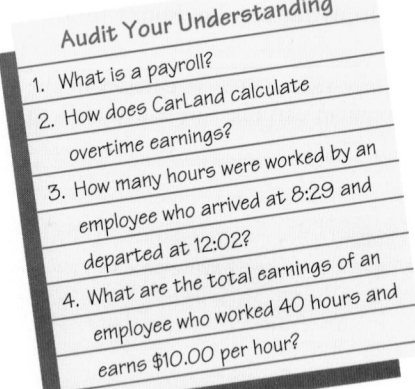

Audit Your Understanding

1. What is a payroll?
2. How does CarLand calculate overtime earnings?
3. How many hours were worked by an employee who arrived at 8:29 and departed at 12:02?
4. What are the total earnings of an employee who worked 40 hours and earns $10.00 per hour?

> **FYI**
>
> Total earnings are sometimes referred to as gross pay or gross earnings.

PAYROLL TAXES

Taxes based on the payroll of a business are called **payroll taxes.** A business is required by law to withhold certain payroll taxes from employee salaries. A business is also required to pay additional payroll taxes. All payroll taxes are based on employee total earnings. Therefore, accurate and detailed payroll records must be maintained. Errors in payroll records could cause incorrect payroll tax payments. Federal and state governments may charge a business a penalty for failure to pay correct payroll taxes when they are due.

Payroll taxes withheld represent a liability for the employer until payment is made. Federal payroll taxes may be paid to a Federal Reserve Bank. The taxes may also be paid to a bank authorized to receive such funds for the government. Local and state governments that assess payroll taxes also designate how, when, and where a business will pay the liability for employee taxes withheld.

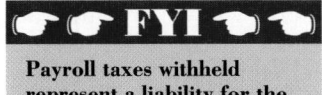

Payroll taxes withheld represent a liability for the employer until payment is made.

Employee Income Tax

A business must withhold federal income taxes from employee total earnings. Federal income taxes withheld must be forwarded periodically to the federal government. Federal income tax is withheld from employee earnings in all 50 states. Employers in many states also are required to withhold state, city, or county income taxes from employee earnings.

The information used to determine the amount of income tax withheld is identified on Form W-4, Employee's Withholding Allowance Certificate. The completed Form W-4 for Mr. Turner is shown in Illustration 14-2.

ILLUSTRATION 14-2   Form W-4, Employee's Withholding Allowance Certificate

Form **W-4** Department of the Treasury Internal Revenue Service	**Employee's Withholding Allowance Certificate** ▶ **For Privacy Act and Paperwork Reduction Act Notice, see reverse.**	OMB No. 1545-0010 **19 --**

1 Type or print your first name and middle initial   Last name   **2** Your social security number
Patrick S. Turner   450-70-6432

Home address (number and street or rural route)   **3** ☐ Single ☒ Married ☐ Married, but withhold at higher Single rate.
1625 Northland Drive   **Note:** *If married, but legally separated, or spouse is a nonresident alien, check the Single box.*

City or town, state, and ZIP code   **4** If your last name differs from that on your social security card,
Rockville, RI 02873   check here and call 1-800-772-1213 for more information . ▶ ☐

5 Total number of allowances you are claiming (from line G above or from the Worksheets on back if they apply)   **5** | 4

6 Additional amount, if any, you want deducted from each paycheck . . . .   **6** $ -0-

7 I claim exemption from withholding and I certify that I meet **ALL** of the following conditions for exemption:
● Last year I had a right to a refund of **ALL** Federal income tax withheld because I had **NO** tax liability; **AND**
● This year I expect a refund of **ALL** Federal income tax withheld because I expect to have **NO** tax liability; **AND**
● This year if my income exceeds $600 and includes nonwage income, another person cannot claim me as a dependent.
If you meet all of the above conditions, enter the year effective and "Exempt" here . . . ▶ **7** | 19

8 Are you a full-time student? (**Note:** *Full-time students are not automatically exempt.*) . . . . **8** ☒ Yes ☐ No

Under penalties of perjury, I certify that I am entitled to the number of withholding allowances claimed on this certificate or entitled to claim exempt status.

Employee's signature ▶ *Patrick S. Turner*   Date ▶ *June 27* , 19 --

9 Employer's name and address (Employer: Complete 9 and 11 only if sending to the IRS) | **10** Office code (optional) | **11** Employer identification number

---

TEACHING STRATEGIES: TEACHING TIP

Obtain the current year's Form W-4 and have students complete the form in class. Discuss the items which are available for employees to claim additional exemptions.

Cover student pages 330–334 "Payroll Taxes." Discuss state and local payroll taxes. Does your state have a tax? Does your local municipality have a tax? If so, what is the percentage? Emphasize that employees may claim allowances for themselves and for those people they legally support. Employees, if they like, may claim FEWER allowances which would result in more taxes being withheld each pay period. Explain that FICA taxes are also called Social Security taxes. Emphasize that employers pay federal and state unemployment tax so that if they lay off their employees, the employees may collect unemployment benefits while they are out of work.

APPLY

Using Illustration 14-2, Form W-4, Employee's Withholding Allowance Certificate, explain to students that this form is completed when someone begins employment and then is updated when their particular circumstances change.

Guided Practice

Guide students through completing a Form W-4 using fictitious information. Students should have a form to complete as you guide them through completing the Form W-4. W-4 forms can be obtained from your local post office, library, or perhaps the school office.

Independent Practice

● Assign Terms 5–10 and Questions 4–8.

● Assign students to complete a Form W-4 using their personal data.

Information from the completed Form W-4 is used when a business calculates the amount of federal income taxes to be withheld. Employers are required to have on file a current Form W-4 for all employees. The amount of income tax withheld is based on employee marital status and withholding allowances.

Marital Status. Employees identify on Form W-4 whether they are married or single. A married employee will have less income tax withheld than a single employee with the same total earnings.

Mr. Turner checked the married box for item 3 of the Form W-4 shown in Illustration 14-2.

Withholding Allowance. A deduction from total earnings for each person legally supported by a taxpayer is called a **withholding allowance.** The larger the number of the withholding allowances claimed, the smaller the income tax withheld from employee salaries.

Mr. Turner claimed four withholding allowances, one each for himself, his wife, and his two children. The number of withholding allowances was recorded in item 5 of the Form W-4.

Most employees are required to have federal income taxes withheld from their salaries. An exemption from withholding is available for certain low-income and part-time employees. The employee must meet the requirements listed in the instructions which accompany Form W-4. The requirements are very restrictive. Most students with part-time jobs who live with their parents do *not* qualify for the exemption. Students who earn over $500 in salary or any interest from a savings or checking account are not eligible to claim the exemption.

The federal government occasionally changes the way income taxes are withheld from employee total earnings. The Form W-4 shown in Illustration 14-2 was the form in use when the materials for this textbook were prepared. Employers must be aware of changes in tax laws and forms. If Form W-4 is changed, an employer must obtain a new W-4 from each employee.

Employee and Employer Social Security Tax

The federal social security law includes three programs.

1. Old-age, survivors, and disability insurance benefits for qualified employees and their spouses, widows or widowers, dependent children, and parents.
2. Payments to senior citizens for the cost of certain hospital and related services. The federal health insurance program for people who have reached retirement age is called **Medicare.**
3. Grants to states that provide benefits for persons temporarily unemployed and for certain relief and welfare purposes.

Each employee must have a social security number. Current law requires that most infants who are at least one year old by the

USING FUNCTIONS TO PREPARE A PAYROLL REGISTER

Many computations are required to prepare a payroll register. When computations require many values, formulas with individual cell references can become burdensome. For example, the formula to compute the total regular wages at G17 would be +G10+G11+G12+G13+G14+G15. A lengthy formula can sometimes by replaced with a function which is a short-cut formula. Functions make keying easier and more efficient.

A typical function begins with the @ sign, followed by the function name, and ending with cell references. The name of the function describes what calculation will be performed. The cell references identify the location of values to be used in the computation. The most common function, @SUM, computes the sum of the values in a range of cells. The function @SUM(G10..G15) would add the amounts in cells G10 through G15 to compute total regular wages.

In subsequent payroll periods, Ms. Bauch may have different earnings or change her number of withholding allowances. The electronic spreadsheet will use these new values to determine the correct income tax withholding from the data base. The electronic spreadsheet can perform this task instantly and accurately.

```
       A      B          C       D   E  F      G        H          I    J    K
1                                                                PAYROLL REGISTER
2     Semimonthly Period Ended:     December 15, 19--
3
4                                                 Earnings
5                                            ------------------------------       ---------
6                                No.                                              Federal
7     Empl.                      Mar. of                                          Income
8      No.   Employee's Name     St. All.   Regular  Overtime     Total            Tax
9            ------------------------------------------------------------------   ---------
10       2   Bauch, Mary R.       2   2     660.00                660.00          57.00
11       5   Clay, Richard P.     1   1      80.00                 80.00            .00
12       1   Javorski, Adam B.    2   2     384.00    18.00       402.00          17.00
13       6   Maggio, Brenda A.    1   1      40.00                 40.00            .00
14       4   Turner, Patrick S.   2   4     704.00    54.00       758.00          45.00
15       3   Wilkes, Samuel R.    1   1     616.00                616.00          73.00
16                                          ------------------------------       ---------
17                                        2,484.00    72.00     2,556.00         192.00
18                                        ==============================       =========
19
20
     G17    (,2) @SUM(G10..G15)
```

end of a tax year have a social security number. Therefore, most employees will have received their social security number as a child. Employees without social security numbers can apply for a number at the nearest Social Security office.

FICA Tax. A federal tax paid by employees and employers for old-age, survivors, disability, and hospitalization insurance is called **FICA tax.** FICA is the abbreviation for the Federal Insurance Contributions Act. FICA tax is based on the total earnings of the employees. Employers are required to withhold FICA tax from a specified amount of employee salary paid in a calendar year. In addition, employers must pay the same amount of FICA tax as withheld from employee salaries.

Federal Unemployment Tax. A federal tax used for state and federal administrative expenses of the unemployment program is

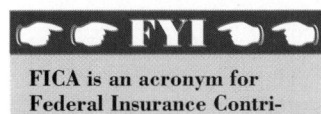

FYI

FICA is an acronym for Federal Insurance Contributions Act.

1. Marital status and withholding allowances.
2. Both the employer and employee.
3. Employer.
4. Employer.

called **federal unemployment tax.** This tax is paid entirely by employers.

State Unemployment Tax. A state tax used to pay benefits to unemployed workers is called **state unemployment tax.** This tax is usually paid by employers. The Social Security Act specifies certain standards for unemployment compensation laws. Therefore, a high degree of uniformity exists in state unemployment laws. However, details of state unemployment laws do differ. Because of these differences, employers must know the requirements of the states in which they operate.

Retention of Records. Employers are required to retain all payroll records showing payments and deductions. Some records must be retained longer than others. Records pertaining to social security tax payments and deductions must be retained for four years. The length of time state unemployment tax payment records must be retained varies from state to state.

Audit Your Understanding

1. Employee federal income tax withholdings are based on what two factors?
2. Does the employer or employee pay FICA tax?
3. Does the employer or employee pay federal unemployment tax?
4. Does the employer or employee pay state unemployment tax?

PAYROLL REGISTER

A business form used to record payroll information is called a **payroll register.** A payroll register summarizes the total earnings and payroll withholdings of all employees. CarLand's payroll register for the semimonthly period ended December 15 is shown in Illustration 14-3.

Regular, overtime, and total earnings are recorded in a payroll register from information on time cards. Amounts deducted for payroll taxes, health insurance, and charitable contributions are calculated and recorded in a payroll register. Also, the total amount

LESSON PLAN 14-3

Materials

- Student pages 334-341
- Transparency: 14-1, Payroll Time Card and Payroll Register
- Math Work Sheet Chapter 14: Part C: Calculating FICA Taxes; Part D: Calculating Deductions in a Payroll Register; Part E: Calculating Net Pay in a Payroll Register (TRG)
- Software: Spreadsheet Template
- Demonstration Problem: 14B, Preparing a Semimonthly Payroll

Objectives (Enabling Performance Tasks)

a. Define accounting terms related to payroll records.
b. Identify accounting practices related to payroll records.
c. Calculate employee earnings and deductions.
d. Complete payroll records.
e. Prepare payroll checks.

FOCUS

- Payroll taxes and calculating employee total earnings were presented earlier in this chapter. In this lesson, we will record employee earnings in a payroll register, calculate deductions, determine how much each employee will be paid, and prepare payroll checks.
- Introduce new vocabulary: payroll register, tax base, net pay, automatic check deposit.

ILLUSTRATION 14-3   Payroll register

SEMIMONTHLY PERIOD ENDED December 15, 19--   PAYROLL REGISTER   DATE OF PAYMENT December 15, 19--

					1	2	3	4	5	6	7		8	9	
	EMPL. NO.	EMPLOYEE'S NAME	MARITAL STATUS	NO. OF ALLOWANCES	EARNINGS			DEDUCTIONS					NET PAY	CHECK NO.	
					REGULAR	OVERTIME	TOTAL	FEDERAL INCOME TAX	FICA TAX	HEALTH INSURANCE	OTHER	TOTAL			
1	2	Bauch, Mary R.	M	2	660 00		660 00	57 00	52 80	38 00	B 5 00	152 80	507 20	419	1
2	5	Clay, Richard P.	S	1	80 00		80 00	00	6 40			6 40	73 60	420	2
3	1	Javorski, Adam B.	M	2	384 00	18 00	402 00	17 00	32 16	38 00		87 16	314 84	421	3
4	6	Maggio, Brenda A.	S	1	40 00		40 00	00	3 20			3 20	36 80	422	4
5	4	Turner, Patrick S.	M	4	704 00	54 00	758 00	45 00	60 64	50 00	B 1 0 00 UW 1 0 00	175 64	582 36	423	5
6	3	Wilkes, Samuel R.	S	1	616 00		616 00	73 00	49 28	32 00		154 28	461 72	424	6
7		Totals			2484 00	72 00	2556 00	192 00	204 48	158 00	B 1 5 00 UW 1 0 00	579 48	1976 52		7
8															8
9															9

TEACHING STRATEGIES: TEACHING TIP

Preparing a payroll register can be confusing. Use Transparency 14-1, Payroll Time Card and Payroll Register, to explain how to prove the register. The totals of columns 1 and 2 should equal the total of column 3. The totals of columns 4, 5, 6, and 7 should equal the total of column 8. The totals of columns 8 and 9 should equal the total of column 3.

to be paid to each employee and the check number of each payroll check are recorded in a payroll register.

The two partners of CarLand, Amy Kramer and Dario Mesa, are not listed on the payroll register. Owners of partnerships are not employees of the company. Cash payments to partners are recorded as withdrawals rather than as salaries.

Recording Earnings in a Payroll Register

The employee number, name, marital status, and withholding allowances are listed in a payroll register. Employee earnings for a pay period are written in the appropriate columns of a payroll register.

Recorded on line 5 of the payroll register are Mr. Turner's employee number, *4*, and name, *Turner, Patrick S.* Also recorded are Mr. Turner's marital status, *M* for married; the number of withholding allowances, *4*; regular earnings, *$704.00;* overtime earnings, *$54.00;* and total earnings, *$758.00.* This information is obtained from Mr. Turner's Form W-4 and time card.

Recording Deductions in a Payroll Register

The deductions section of a payroll register is used to record the payroll taxes and other deductions withheld from employee earnings. Also, some companies deduct amounts for retirement plans. These deductions will vary from one company to another depending on policies established between management and employees.

Five steps are followed to calculate and record deductions.

1 The Federal Income Tax column is used to record the amount of federal income tax withheld from employee earnings. This amount is determined from tables furnished by the federal government. Portions of the tables showing the tax to be withheld are shown in Illustration 14-4.

Mr. Turner's federal income tax on total earnings of $758.00 is found in the table for married persons. Since CarLand pays its payroll twice a month, the table for a semimonthly pay period is used. The proper wage bracket is from $740.00 to $760.00. The income tax to be withheld is the amount shown on this line under the column for four allowances, $45.00.

No federal income tax was withheld from the earnings of Richard Clay and Brenda Maggio. Although they are students who work part-time, they are not exempt from federal income tax withholding. They did not, however, have enough total earnings *in this pay period* to require any income tax to be withheld. Federal income tax withholding tables are also available for daily, weekly, biweekly, and monthly pay periods. The tables in Illustration 14-4 are those available when materials for this textbook were prepared.

2 The FICA Tax column is used to record the amount deducted for social security tax. FICA tax is calculated by multiplying

FYI

Businesses must withhold federal income tax from employee total earnings in all fifty states.

FYI

Businesses must withhold state and local income tax from employee total earnings in many states.

CHAPTER 14 Preparing Payroll Records

335

Use Transparency 14-1 to describe the entry in the payroll register for Mr. Turner. Trace each employee's federal income tax withholding amount back to the tax withholding tables shown in Illustration 14-4. Calculate the amount of FICA tax that should have been withheld for each employee and match it to the amount shown on the payroll register.

Guided Practice

Guide students through Drill 14-D2. Students should have the forms from the working papers to complete as you guide them through the drill. For each employee ask the students to determine the amount of federal income tax and FICA tax that must be withheld. All students should agree with the calculations before proceeding to the next employee.

Independent Practice

Assign Terms 11–14, Questions 9–16, and Problem 14-2.

ILLUSTRATION 14-4   Section of income tax withholding tables for semimonthly pay period

SEMIMONTHLY PAYROLL PERIOD — MARRIED PERSONS

And the wages are—		And the number of withholding allowances claimed is—										
At least	But less than	0	1	2	3	4	5	6	7	8	9	10
		The amount of income tax to be withheld shall be—										
$0	$130	1										
130	135	1										
135	140	2										
140	145	2										
145	150	3										
400	410	42	30	17	5							
410	420	43	31	19	7							
420	430	45	33	20	8							
430	440	46	34	22	10							
440	450	48	36	23	11							
450	460	49	37	25	13							
460	470	51	39	26	14	2						
470	480	52	40	28	16	3						
480	490	54	42	29	17	5						
490	500	55	43	31	19	6						
500	520	57	45	33	21	9						
520	540	60	48	36	24	12						
540	560	63	51	39	27	15	3					
560	580	66	54	42	30	18	6					
580	600	69	57	45	33	21	9					
600	620	72	60	48	36	24	12					
620	640	75	63	51	39	27	15	2				
640	660	78	66	54	42	30	18	5				
660	680	81	69	57	45	33	21	8				
680	700	84	72	60	48	36	24	11				
700	720	87	75	63	51	39	27	14	2			
720	740	90	78	66	54	42	30	17	5			
740	760	93	81	69	57	45	33	20	8			
760	780	96	84	72	60	48	36	23	11			
780	800	99	87	75	63	51	39	26	14	2		
800	820	102	90	78	66	54	42	29	17	5		
820	840	105	93	81	69	57	45	32	20	8		
840	860	108	96	84	72	60	48	35	23	11		
860	880	111	99	87	75	63	51	38	26	14	2	
880	900	114	102	90	78	66	54	41	29	17	5	
900	920	117	105	93	81	69	57	44	32	20	8	
920	940	120	108	96	84	72	60	47	35	23	11	
940	960	123	111	99	87	75	63	50	38	26	14	2
960	980	126	114	102	90	78	66	53	41	29	17	5
980	1,000	129	117	105	93	81	69	56	44	32	20	8
1,000	1,020	132	120	108	96	84	72	59	47	35	23	11
1,020	1,040	135	123	111	99	87	75	62	50	38	26	14
1,040	1,060	138	126	114	102	90	78	65	53	41	29	17
1,060	1,080	141	129	117	105	93	81	68	56	44	32	20
1,080	1,100	144	132	120	108	96	84	71	59	47	35	23
1,100	1,120	147	135	123	111	99	87	74	62	50	38	26
1,120	1,140	150	138	126	114	102	90	77	65	53	41	29
1,140	1,160	153	141	129	117	105	93	80	68	56	44	32
1,160	1,180	156	144	132	120	108	96	83	71	59	47	35
1,180	1,200	159	147	135	123	111	99	86	74	62	50	38
1,200	1,220	162	150	138	126	114	102	89	77	65	53	41
1,220	1,240	165	153	141	129	117	105	92	80	68	56	44
1,240	1,260	168	156	144	132	120	108	95	83	71	59	47
1,260	1,280	171	159	147	135	123	111	98	86	74	62	50
1,280	1,300	174	162	150	138	126	114	101	89	77	65	53
1,300	1,320	177	165	153	141	129	117	104	92	80	68	56
1,320	1,340	180	168	156	144	132	120	107	95	83	71	59
1,340	1,360	183	171	159	147	135	123	110	98	86	74	62
1,360	1,380	187	174	162	150	138	126	113	101	89	77	65
1,380	1,400	192	177	165	153	141	129	116	104	92	80	68

SEMIMONTHLY MARRIED PERSONS

---

total earnings by the tax rate. From time to time, Congress changes the tax rate used to calculate FICA taxes. A FICA tax rate of 8% is used to illustrate the FICA tax calculations in this textbook. The FICA tax for Mr. Turner is calculated as shown below.

	Total Earnings	×	FICA Tax Rate	=	FICA Tax Deduction
	$758.00	×	8%	=	$60.64

Congress has limited the amount of FICA tax that each individual must pay. The FICA tax is not calculated on total earnings over a specific maximum amount. The maximum amount of earnings on which a tax is calculated is called a **tax base**.

The FICA tax rate is a combination of two different tax rates: (1) a tax for old-age, survivors, and disability and (2) a

---

TEACHING STRATEGIES: APPLYING VISUALS

Reading tax tables is a difficult task. Direct students to look at the tax tables in the chapter. Spend time explaining how to read the tables.

ILLUSTRATION 14-4 Section of income tax withholding tables for semimonthly pay period

SEMIMONTHLY PAYROLL PERIOD — SINGLE PERSONS

And the wages are—		And the number of withholding allowances claimed is—										
At least	But less than	0	1	2	3	4	5	6	7	8	9	10
		The amount of income tax to be withheld shall be—										
$0	$45											
45	50	1										
50	55	1										
55	60	2										
60	65	3										
65	70	4										
70	75	4										
75	80	5										
80	85	6										
85	90	7										
380	390	51	39	27	15	2						
390	400	53	41	28	16	4						
400	410	54	42	30	18	5						
410	420	56	44	31	19	7						
420	430	57	45	33	21	8						
430	440	59	47	34	22	10						
440	450	60	48	36	24	11						
450	460	62	50	37	25	13	1					
460	470	63	51	39	27	14	2					
470	480	65	53	40	28	16	4					
480	490	66	54	42	30	17	5					
490	500	68	56	43	31	19	7					
500	520	70	58	46	33	21	9					
520	540	73	61	49	36	24	12					
540	560	76	64	52	39	27	15	3				
560	580	79	67	55	42	30	18	6				
580	600	82	70	58	45	33	21	9				
600	620	85	73	61	48	36	24	12				
620	640	88	76	64	51	39	27	15	3			
640	660	91	79	67	54	42	30	18	6			
660	680	94	82	70	57	45	33	21	9			
680	700	97	85	73	60	48	36	24	12			
700	720	100	88	76	63	51	39	27	15	2		
720	740	103	91	79	66	54	42	30	18	5		
740	760	106	94	82	69	57	45	33	21	8		
760	780	109	97	85	72	60	48	36	24	11		
780	800	112	100	88	75	63	51	39	27	14	2	
800	820	118	103	91	78	66	54	42	30	17	5	
820	840	123	106	94	81	69	57	45	33	20	8	
840	860	129	109	97	84	72	60	48	36	23	11	
860	880	135	112	100	87	75	63	51	39	26	14	2
880	900	140	118	103	90	78	66	54	42	29	17	5
900	920	146	123	106	93	81	69	57	45	32	20	8
920	940	151	129	109	96	84	72	60	48	35	23	11
940	960	157	134	112	99	87	75	63	51	38	26	14
960	980	163	140	117	102	90	78	66	54	41	29	17
980	1,000	168	146	123	105	93	81	69	57	44	32	20
1,000	1,020	174	151	128	108	96	84	72	60	47	35	23
1,020	1,040	179	157	134	111	99	87	75	63	50	38	26
1,040	1,060	185	162	140	117	102	90	78	66	53	41	29
1,060	1,080	191	168	145	122	105	93	81	69	56	44	32
1,080	1,100	196	174	151	128	108	96	84	72	59	47	35
1,100	1,120	202	179	156	134	111	99	87	75	62	50	38
1,120	1,140	207	185	162	139	116	102	90	78	65	53	41
1,140	1,160	213	190	168	145	122	105	93	81	68	56	44
1,160	1,180	219	196	173	150	128	108	96	84	71	59	47
1,180	1,200	224	202	179	156	133	111	99	87	74	62	50
1,200	1,220	230	207	184	162	139	116	102	90	77	65	53
1,220	1,240	235	213	190	167	144	122	105	93	80	68	56
1,240	1,260	241	218	196	173	150	127	108	96	83	71	59

SEMIMONTHLY SINGLE PERSONS

tax for Medicare. The two taxes also have different tax bases. The FICA tax rates and bases used in this text are shown below.

	Tax Rate	Tax Base
Old-age, survivors, and disability	6.5%	earnings up to $55,500
Medicare	1.5%	earnings up to $130,200
Total	8.0%	

Therefore, the effective FICA tax rate for earnings up to the tax base of $55,500 is 8.0% (6.5% + 1.5%). The additional FICA tax rate for earnings from $55,500 to $130,200 is 1.5%.

Before calculating Mr. Turner's FICA tax, his accumulated earnings are compared to the tax base. Between January 1 and December 1, Mr. Turner has earned $16,794.00. Since his earnings are less than either tax base, the total FICA tax of 8.0%

ASSESS

Assess student understanding by checking solutions to Independent Practice activities.

Reteach

- Use Demonstration Problem 14B. This problem can be done on the overhead with the students completing the problem at their desks.

- Duplicate and assign Math Work Sheet Chapter 14, Part C: Calculating FICA Taxes, Part D: Calculating Deductions in a Payroll Register, and Part E: Calculating Net Pay in a Payroll Register from the Masters and Solutions to Enrichment/Application Activities Section in the Teacher's Resource Guide to provide additional practice on the mathematics of calculating FICA taxes, deductions, and net pay in a payroll register.

Extend

- Assign Cases for Critical Thinking 2.

- Assign the Spreadsheet Template for Problem 14-2. Students may work at the computer at their own pace.

Enrich

- Assign students to read the MULTICULTURAL AWARENESS feature on page 332. Discuss with them how an understanding and appreciation of history and other cultures contributes to understanding civilization today.

CLOSURE

- Use Audit Your Understanding questions.

- Review the five steps used to calculate and record deductions.

- Review the procedures for completing a payroll register.

- Review the procedures for preparing payroll checks.

TEACHING STRATEGIES: DIFFERENT LEARNING ABILITIES

Visually-Impaired. Take time to orient visually impaired students with the classroom and their individual work stations. This will make them more comfortable and confident in their surroundings.

of earnings ($758.00 $\times$ 8% = $60.64) is recorded in the payroll register. If Mr. Turner had accumulated earnings over $55,500.00 but not yet $130,200.00, only the Medicare portion of FICA tax (1.5% of earnings) would be owed. If Mr. Turner had accumulated earnings over $130,200.00, no FICA tax would be owed and no amount would have been recorded in the payroll register.

Information from Form W-4 determines how much federal income tax is to be withheld.

3 The Health Insurance column is used to record health insurance premiums. Full-time employees of CarLand participate in a group health insurance plan to take advantage of lower group rates.

Mr. Turner's semimonthly health insurance premium is $50.00. Premiums are set by the insurance company and are usually based on the employee marital status and whether coverage is for an individual or a family. Some health insurance premiums may be based on the number of individuals covered.

4 The Other column is used to record voluntary deductions requested by an employee. Entries are identified by code letters. CarLand uses the letter *B* to identify amounts withheld for buying U.S. Savings Bonds. *UW* is used to identify amounts withheld for employee contributions to United Way.

Mr. Turner has authorized CarLand to withhold $10.00 each pay period to buy U.S. Savings Bonds for him. Mr. Turner has also authorized that $10.00 be withheld as a contribution to the United Way.

5 The Total column is used to record total deductions. All deductions on a line for each employee are added. The total deductions for Mr. Turner are calculated as shown below.

Federal Income Tax	+	FICA Tax	+	Health Insurance	+	Other	=	Total Deductions
$45.00	+	$60.64	+	$50.00	+	$20.00	=	$175.64

Calculating Net Pay in a Payroll Register

The total earnings paid to an employee after payroll taxes and other deductions is called **net pay.** Net pay is calculated by subtracting total deductions from total earnings. The Net Pay column is used to record the amount. The net pay for Mr. Turner is calculated as shown below.

Total Earnings	−	Total Deductions	=	Net Pay
$758.00	−	$175.64	=	$582.36

Completing a Payroll Register

After the net pay has been recorded for each employee, the word *Totals* is written in the Employee name column and each amount column is totaled. A separate total is shown for each different type of deduction in the Other column. Accuracy of these totals is verified by subtracting the Total Deductions column total from the Total Earnings column total as shown below.

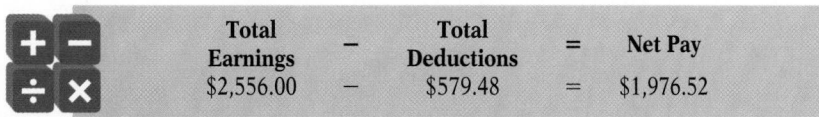

	Total Earnings	−	Total Deductions	=	Net Pay
	$2,556.00	−	$579.48	=	$1,976.52

The net pay calculated above, $1,976.52, is compared to the total of the Net Pay column. The payroll register is proved because these amounts are equal. After the payroll register is proved, a double rule is drawn below the totals, and the register is given to a partner of the company for approval.

Before checks are written for employee net pay, the payroll calculations are checked for accuracy. A partner approves the payroll after the accuracy is verified. After each check is written, the check number is recorded in the Ck. No. column.

PAYROLL CHECKS

CarLand pays its employees with checks written on a special payroll checking account. A check for the total net pay is written on CarLand's general checking account. The check is deposited in the payroll checking account. Illustration 14-5 shows the check written for the December 1-15 pay period. The check amount, $1,976.52, is the total of the Net Pay column of the payroll register in Illustration 14-3.

ILLUSTRATION 14-5 Check for total net pay

No. 287		
Date 12/15 19 -- $ 1,976.52		
To Payroll Account		
005972165		
For Payroll for December 1-15		

Bal. Bro't For'd	3,261	94
Amt. Deposited		
Total	3,261	94
Amt. This Check	1,976	52
Bal. Car'd For'd	1,285	42

GENERAL ACCOUNT   No. 287   57-63 / 115

CarLand   December 15, 19 --

Pay to the order of *Payroll Account 005972165* $ 1,976.52

One thousand nine hundred seventy-six and 52/100 Dollars

FOR CLASSROOM USE ONLY

FIRST SECURITY BANK OF ROCKVILLE

Dario Mesa

⑈011500638⑈ 0059721640

The information used to prepare payroll checks is taken from a payroll register. The payroll check for Mr. Turner is shown in Illustration 14-6. A special payroll check form is used that has a detachable stub for recording earnings and amounts deducted. Employees keep the stubs for a record of deductions and cash received.

ILLUSTRATION 14-6 Payroll check with detachable stub

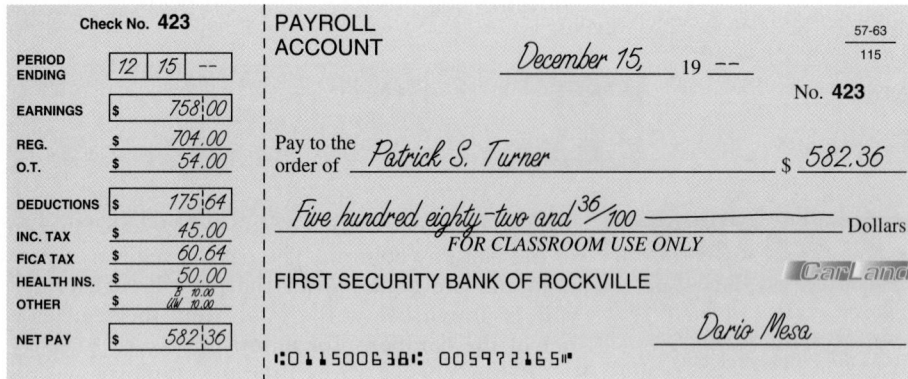

The two deductions for FICA tax would normally be shown separately on a payroll check stub. For simplicity, illustrations in this textbook will show the FICA tax as a single amount on payroll check stubs.

Payroll Bank Account

A separate checking account for payroll checks helps to protect and control payroll payments. The exact amount needed to pay the payroll is deposited in the special payroll account. If amounts on checks are altered or unauthorized payroll checks are prepared, the amount in the special payroll account would be insufficient to cover all the checks. Thus, the bank and CarLand would be alerted quickly to an unauthorized payroll check. Also, since payroll checks are drawn on the separate account, any balance in this account will correspond to the sum of outstanding payroll checks.

Automatic Check Deposit

Employees may authorize an employer to deposit payroll checks directly in their checking account at a specific bank. Depositing payroll checks directly to an employee's checking or savings account in a specific bank is called **automatic check deposit.** When automatic check deposit is used, the employer sends the check to the employee's bank for deposit.

Electronic Funds Transfer

A computerized cash payments system that uses electronic impulses to transfer funds is known as electronic funds transfer (EFT). Some businesses deposit employee net pay directly to each employee bank

Audit Your Understanding

1. What does the payroll register summarize?

2. How is federal income tax determined?

3. How is net pay calculated?

account through EFT. When EFT is used, the bank's computer deducts the amount of net pay from the business' bank account and adds the amount to each employee bank account. The payroll must still be calculated, but individual checks are not written and do not have to be distributed. Under this system, each employee receives a statement of earnings and deductions similar to the detachable stub on a payroll check.

EMPLOYEE EARNINGS RECORDS

A business form used to record details affecting payments made to an employee is called an **employee earnings record**. This information is recorded each pay period. The record includes earnings, deductions, net pay, and accumulated earnings for the calendar year. Employee earnings records enable the company to complete required tax forms at the end of the year.

Recording Information in an Employee Earnings Record

CarLand keeps all employee earnings records on cards. One card for each employee is used for each quarter in the calendar year. After a payroll register has been prepared, the payroll data for each employee are recorded on each employee earnings record. The December 15 payroll register data for Patrick S. Turner are recorded on his fourth quarter employee earnings record shown in Illustration 14-7, page 342.

Quarterly totals are used in the preparation of payroll reports required by the government. The accumulated earnings are also used to determine if the employee has earned more than the FICA tax base.

Analyzing an Employee Earnings Record

FYI

Accumulated earnings are also called year-to-date earnings.

Mr. Turner's employee number, name, social security number, and other payroll data are entered at the top of his fourth quarter employee earnings record.

Amount columns of an employee earnings record are the same as amount columns of a payroll register. Amounts opposite an employee name in a payroll register are recorded in the corresponding columns of the employee earnings record. The pay period ending December 15 is the fifth pay period in the fourth quarter. Therefore, Mr. Turner's earnings and deductions for that pay period are entered on line 5 of his employee earnings record.

The earnings record also has an Accumulated Earnings column. The first entry in this column is the accumulated earnings at the end of the previous quarter. Accumulated earnings of $13,918.00 were carried forward from the third quarter earnings record to the fourth quarter earnings record, as shown in Illustration 14-7.

ILLUSTRATION 14-7   Employee earnings record

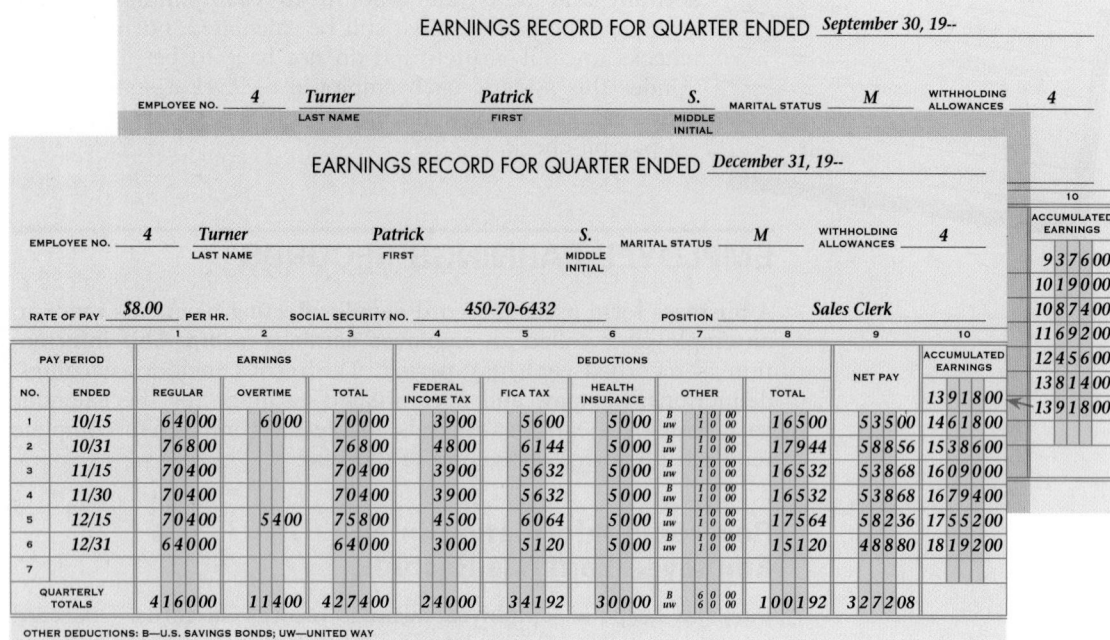

EARNINGS RECORD FOR QUARTER ENDED _September 30, 19--_

EARNINGS RECORD FOR QUARTER ENDED _December 31, 19--_

EMPLOYEE NO. 4 Turner (LAST NAME) Patrick (FIRST) S. (MIDDLE INITIAL) MARITAL STATUS M WITHHOLDING ALLOWANCES 4

RATE OF PAY $8.00 PER HR.   SOCIAL SECURITY NO. 450-70-6432   POSITION Sales Clerk

PAY PERIOD		EARNINGS			DEDUCTIONS					NET PAY	ACCUMULATED EARNINGS
NO.	ENDED	REGULAR (1)	OVERTIME (2)	TOTAL (3)	FEDERAL INCOME TAX (4)	FICA TAX (5)	HEALTH INSURANCE (6)	OTHER (7)	TOTAL (8)	(9)	(10)
1	10/15	640 00	60 00	700 00	39 00	56 00	50 00	B 10 00 / UW 10 00	165 00	535 00	14618 00
2	10/31	768 00		768 00	48 00	61 44	50 00	B 10 00 / UW 10 00	179 44	588 56	15386 00
3	11/15	704 00		704 00	39 00	56 32	50 00	B 10 00 / UW 10 00	165 32	538 68	16090 00
4	11/30	704 00		704 00	39 00	56 32	50 00	B 10 00 / UW 10 00	165 32	538 68	16794 00
5	12/15	704 00	54 00	758 00	45 00	60 64	50 00	B 10 00 / UW 10 00	175 64	582 36	17552 00
6	12/31	640 00		640 00	30 00	51 20	50 00	B 10 00 / UW 10 00	151 20	488 80	18192 00
7											
QUARTERLY TOTALS		4160 00	114 00	4274 00	240 00	341 92	300 00	B 60 00 / UW 60 00	1001 92	3272 08	

ACCUMULATED EARNINGS (10):
9376 00
10190 00
10874 00
11692 00
12456 00
13814 00
13918 00
13918 00

OTHER DEDUCTIONS: B—U.S. SAVINGS BONDS; UW—UNITED WAY

Total earnings for a pay period are added to the accumulated earnings in the previous line to calculate the new total accumulated earnings. Accumulated earnings are sometimes referred to as year-to-date earnings. Mr. Turner's accumulated earnings as of December 15 are calculated as shown below.

Accumulated Earnings as of December 1	+	Total Earnings for Pay Period Ended December 15	=	Accumulated Earnings as of December 15
$16,794.00	+	$758.00	=	$17,552.00

The Accumulated Earnings column shows the total earnings for Mr. Turner since the first of the year. The amounts in the Accumulated Earnings column supply an up-to-date reference for an employee's year-to-date earnings. When employee earnings reach the tax base, certain payroll taxes do not apply. For example, employers pay state and federal unemployment taxes only on a specified amount of each employee earnings. FICA taxes are also paid only on a specified amount of earnings.

Quarterly totals will be calculated on Mr. Turner's employee earnings record after the payroll for the pay period ended December 31 is recorded. The Quarterly Totals line provides space for the totals for the quarter. The accuracy of the quarterly totals is verified with the same steps used to verify payroll register totals. The Total Deductions column total is subtracted from the Total Earnings column total as shown below.

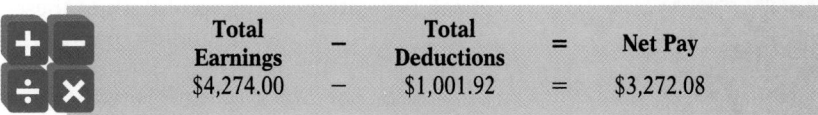

Total Earnings	−	Total Deductions	=	Net Pay
$4,274.00	−	$1,001.92	=	$3,272.08

The net pay calculated above, $3,272.08, is compared to the total of the Net Pay column. The earnings record is proved because these amounts are equal. These totals are needed to prepare required government reports.

PROCESSING A PAYROLL USING A PEGBOARD

A pegboard follows the write-it-once principle.

Preparing a payroll requires calculating, recording, and reporting payroll information. Each business selects a system for processing the payroll that results in adequate control for the least amount of cost.

A special device used to write the same information at one time on several forms is called a **pegboard**. One type of pegboard is shown in Illustration 14-8.

ILLUSTRATION 14-8   A pegboard

The name pegboard comes from the pegs along one side of the board. The forms used with this device have holes punched along one side. Each of the forms is placed on the pegs. Thus, the line

CHAPTER 14   Preparing Payroll Records   **343**

ASSESS

Assess student understanding by checking solutions to Independent Practice activities.

Reteach

- Duplicate and assign Math Work Sheet Chapter 14, Part F: Calculating Accumulated Earnings from the Masters and Solutions to Enrichment/Application Activities Section in the Teacher's Resource Guide to provide additional practice on the mathematics of calculating accumulated earnings on an employee earnings record.
- Assign Recycling Problem 14-R.

Extend

- Assign Challenge Problem 14-C (the challenge is that students must calculate a payroll using an alternate method of piecework).
- Assign the SPREADSHEET OPTIONS feature on page 333.

Enrich

- Assign the Spreadsheet Template for Problem 14-3. Students may work at the computer at their own pace.
- Assign the Spreadsheet Template for Challenge Problem 14-C. Students may work at the computer at their own pace.
- Assign Electronic Study Guide Chapter 14 to complete the study guide from the working papers at the computer.

CLOSURE

- Use Audit Your Understanding questions.
- Review Summary Illustration 14-9, "Summary of Preparing Payroll Records," and Transparency 14-3, Chapter Summary.

ASSESS

- Administer Problem Test Chapter 14.
- Administer a MicroExam test for Chapter 14.

Audit Your Understanding

1. Why do companies complete
employee earnings records?
2. What is the write-it-once principle?

on each form on which information is to be written is aligned one below the other.

When a payroll is recorded, a page of the payroll register is attached to the pegboard. Next, the employee earnings record is properly positioned on top of the payroll register page. Then the check is positioned on top of both of these sheets. As the check stub is written, the carbonless paper imprints the same information on the employee earnings record and the payroll register. The information is written only once. However, the information is recorded on three different records at the same time. Recording information on several forms with one writing is referred to as the write-it-once principle.

The pegboard has two major purposes. First, the pegboard provides a solid writing base for writing on the forms by hand. Second, information is recorded on several forms with one writing, thus saving time and reducing the chance of error.

SUMMARY ILLUSTRATION 14-9

Summary of preparing payroll records

1 A time card is used to record employee hours worked and to calculate regular, overtime, and total earnings. Payroll taxes are calculated using tax tables and information on the Form W-4. This information is recorded for each employee in a payroll register.

2 A check is written on a general checking account for the total of the Net Pay column on the payroll register. The check is deposited in a special payroll checking account.

3 Payroll checks are written on the special payroll checking account for the net pay of each employee.

4 Information from the payroll register is recorded on each employee earnings record.

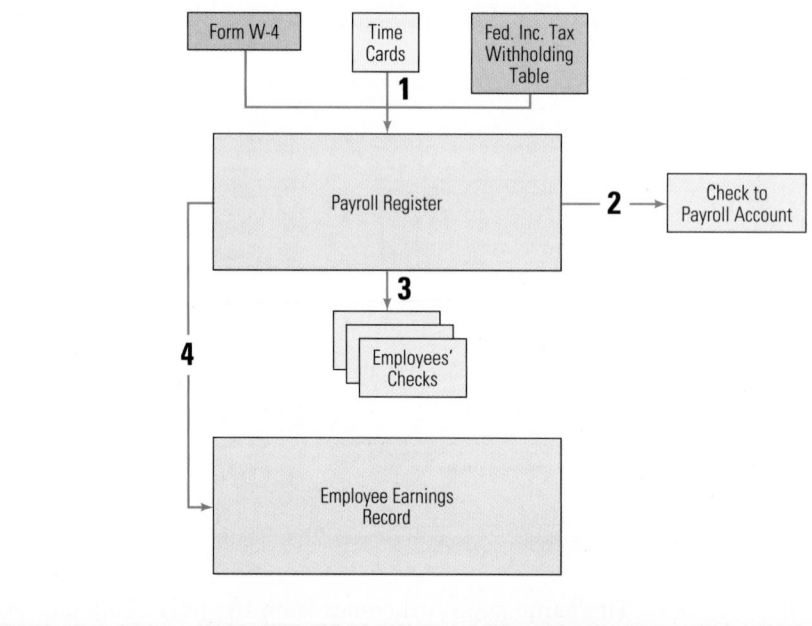

PART 3   Accounting for a Merchandising Business Organized as a Partnership

ACCOUNTING TERMS

What is the meaning of each of the following?

1. salary
2. pay period
3. payroll
4. total earnings
5. payroll taxes
6. withholding allowance
7. Medicare
8. FICA tax
9. federal unemployment tax
10. state unemployment tax
11. payroll register
12. tax base
13. net pay
14. automatic check deposit
15. employee earnings record
16. pegboard

QUESTIONS FOR INDIVIDUAL STUDY

1. How often may a business decide to pay its employees?
2. What information is presented at the top of a time card?
3. To calculate hours worked to the nearest quarter hour, how would an arrival time of 7:54 be rounded?
4. On what amount are employee payroll taxes based?
5. What factors determine the amount of federal income tax withheld from an employee?
6. How does the number of withholding allowances affect the amount of federal income tax withheld?
7. Who pays FICA tax?
8. How long must records pertaining to social security tax payments and deductions be retained?
9. What is the source of the earnings amounts reported in a payroll register?
10. Why are partners of a company not listed in the company's payroll register?
11. How is the amount of federal income tax withheld from employee salaries determined?
12. Under what circumstances can an employee who is not exempt from federal income tax withholding have no tax withheld on a payroll register?
13. What must an employer know to be able to calculate the amount of FICA tax to be withheld from the salary of an employee?
14. How is a payroll register proved?
15. What amount is deposited into a payroll checking account?
16. Where is the information obtained to prepare a payroll check?
17. What is the major purpose of the Accumulated Earnings column of an employee earnings record?
18. What are two major purposes for using a pegboard for processing a payroll?

CASES FOR CRITICAL THINKING

CASE 1 Kilton Hardware currently requires each employee to inform the accounting clerk of the total hours worked each day during the pay period. The total number of hours worked by all employees has been steadily increasing during the prior pay periods. The new store manager has suggested that a time clock be installed to record arrival and departure times. The accounting clerk believes the current system is satisfactory. Do you agree with the new manager or the accounting clerk? Explain your response.

CASE 2 A banker has recommended that Tillman Construction Company open a second checking account. The company would write payroll checks on the new checking account. The company's 50 employees are currently paid with checks written on its general checking account. Do you agree with the banker's recommendation? Explain the reason for your decision.

ACCOUNTING TERMS

1. **salary:** The money paid for employee services. (p. 327)
2. **pay period:** The period covered by a salary payment. (p. 327)
3. **payroll:** The total amount earned by all employees for a pay period. (p. 327)
4. **total earnings:** The total pay due for a pay period before deductions. (p. 329)
5. **payroll taxes:** Taxes based on the payroll of a business. (p. 330)
6. **withholding allowance:** A deduction from total earnings for each person legally supported by a taxpayer. (p. 332)
7. **Medicare:** The federal health insurance program for people who have reached retirement age. (p. 332)
8. **FICA tax:** A federal tax paid by employees and employers for old-age, survivors, disability, and hospitalization insurance. (p. 333)
9. **federal unemployment tax:** A federal tax used for state and federal administrative expenses of the unemployment program. (p. 334)
10. **state unemployment tax:** A state tax used to pay benefits to unemployed workers. (p. 334)
11. **payroll register:** A business form used to record payroll information. (p. 334)
12. **tax base:** The maximum amount of earnings on which a tax is calculated. (p. 336)
13. **net pay:** The total earnings paid to an employee after payroll taxes and other deductions. (p. 338)
14. **automatic check deposit:** Depositing payroll checks directly to an employee's checking or savings account in a specific bank. (p. 340)
15. **employee earnings record:** A business form used to record details affecting payments made to an employee. (p. 341)
16. **pegboard:** A special device used to write the same information at one time on several forms. (p. 343)

QUESTIONS FOR INDIVIDUAL STUDY

1. Every week, every two weeks, twice a month, or once a month. (p. 327)
2. The employee number, employee name, and the ending date of the pay period. (p. 328)
3. 8:00. (p. 328)
4. All payroll taxes are based on the total earnings of an employee. (p. 331)

5. The amount of total earnings, number of withholding allowances, and marital status. (p. 332)

6. The larger the number of withholding allowances claimed, the smaller the income tax withheld. (p. 332)

7. Both the employee and the employer pay an equal amount of FICA tax based on employee total earnings. (p. 333)

8. At least four years. (p. 334)

9. A time card. (p. 334)

10. Partners are not employees of the company. (p. 335)

11. The amount is determined from tables furnished by the federal government. (p. 335)

12. The employee could have small total earnings in a pay period for which the withholding amount is zero. (p. 335)

13. Employee total earnings for the pay period, accumulated earnings, the FICA tax rate, and the FICA tax base. (pp. 335–338)

14. The Total Deductions column is subtracted from the Total Earnings column. This amount should equal the total of the Net Pay column. (p. 339)

15. The total of the Net Pay column on the payroll register. (p. 339)

16. The payroll register. (p. 340)

17. To determine when an employee's earnings have reached the FICA tax base. (p. 341)

18. The pegboard (1) provides a solid writing base for writing on forms by hand and (2) records information on several forms with one writing. (p. 344)

CASES FOR CRITICAL THINKING

Case 1 The new manager. The time clock will force employees to record their arrival and departure times. The new system will prevent an employee from reporting hours worked when the employee was not working.

Case 2 Agree with the banker's recommendation. A separate payroll checking account offers a business several advantages. The business can more quickly detect any altered or unauthorized payroll checks. The balance in the account is equal to the amount of outstanding checks.

APPLIED COMMUNICATIONS

The employees of Ritter Company currently use time cards and a time clock to record their arrival and departure times. Management plans to replace the time clock with a device that reads a magnetic strip on the back of each employee's name badge. The name badge is scanned by the badge reader in the same manner that credit cards are scanned. Since the badge reader is connected to a computer, the information is recorded directly to a computer file. Thus, the new system will enable management to make daily analyses of employee hours and productivity. Management expects this information will allow its managers to make more timely decisions and increase profits.

INSTRUCTIONS:

Assume you are the payroll clerk for Ritter Company. Write a memo to the employees informing them of the new system. Because some employees may not be happy with this new system, be sure to include reasons why the policy is being implemented.

DRILLS FOR UNDERSTANDING   EPT(c)

DRILL 14-D1   Calculating employee total earnings

Information taken from employee time cards is given in the working papers accompanying this textbook.

INSTRUCTIONS:

For each employee, calculate the amount of regular, overtime, and total earnings. Overtime hours are paid at one and one-half times the regular rate.

DRILL 14-D2   Determining payroll taxes withholding

Information taken from a semimonthly payroll register is given in the working papers accompanying this textbook.

INSTRUCTIONS:

1. Determine the federal income tax that must be withheld for each of the eight employees. Use the tax withholding tables shown in Illustration 14-4.

2. Calculate the amount of FICA tax that must be withheld for each employee using an 8% tax rate. None of the eight employees has accumulated earnings greater than the tax base.

APPLICATION PROBLEMS   EPT(c,d,e)

PROBLEM 14-1   Completing payroll time cards

Employee time cards are given in the working papers accompanying this textbook.

INSTRUCTIONS:

1. Calculate the regular, overtime, and total hours worked by each employee. Any hours over the regular 8-hour day are considered overtime. Record the hours on the time cards.

2. Determine the regular, overtime, and total earnings for each employee. The overtime rate is 1½ times the regular rate. Complete the time cards.

APPLIED COMMUNICATIONS

Students' solutions will vary. The instructor should consider the following items when grading this activity: (1) writing style, and (2) mechanics (grammar, spelling, punctuation, sentence structure).

PROBLEM 14-2 Preparing a semimonthly payroll

The information for the semimonthly pay period April 1–15 of the current year is given in the working papers accompanying this textbook.

INSTRUCTIONS:

1. Prepare a payroll register. The date of payment is April 15. Use the federal income tax withholding tables in Illustration 14-4 to find the income tax withholding for each employee. Calculate FICA tax withholding using an 8% rate. None of the employee accumulated earnings has exceeded the FICA tax base.
2. Prepare a check for the total amount of the net pay. Make the check payable to Payroll Account, and sign your name as partner of City Hardware Company. The beginning check stub balance is $8,365.79.
3. Prepare payroll checks for Jill V. Gunter, Check No. 765, and Ronald E. Webb, Check No. 769. Sign your name as a partner of City Hardware Company. Record the two payroll check numbers in the payroll register.

PROBLEM 14-3 Preparing an employee earnings record

Derrick M. Hammond's earnings for the six semimonthly pay periods in April, May, and June of the current year are given in the working papers accompanying this textbook.

The following additional data about Derrick Hammond are needed to complete the employee earnings record.

1. Employee number: 32
2. Marital status: married
3. Withholding Allowances: 2
4. Rate of pay: regular, $14.00
5. Social security number: 218-78-2164
6. Position: service manager
7. Accumulated earnings for the first quarter: $7,928.00
8. Deductions from total earnings:
   a. Health insurance: $40.00 each semimonthly pay period
   b. U.S. Savings Bonds: $10.00 each semimonthly pay period
   c. Federal income tax: determined each pay period by using the withholding tables in Illustration 14-4
   d. FICA taxes: 8% of total earnings each pay period

INSTRUCTIONS:

1. Prepare an employee earnings record for Derrick Hammond for the second quarter of the year.
2. Verify the accuracy of the completed employee earnings record. The Quarter Total for Regular and Overtime Earnings should equal the Quarter Total for Net Pay plus Total Deductions. The Quarter Total for Total Earnings should equal the end-of-quarter Accumulated Earnings minus the beginning-of-quarter Accumulated Earnings.

ENRICHMENT PROBLEMS   EPT(c,d,e)

MASTERY PROBLEM 14-M Preparing a semimonthly payroll

The following information is for the semimonthly pay period May 15–31 of the current year.

CHECK FIGURES

See Teacher's Edition of Working Papers for complete solutions to drills and problems.

Drill 14-D1   Total earnings 249.00; 427.50; 195.00; 193.75; 391.00; 245.00

Drill 14-D2   Fed. inc. tax 87; 63; 82; 36; 79; 76; 79; 78; FICA tax 69.60; 62.40; 53.60; 60.80; 52.00; 56.80; 51.20; 71.20

Problem 14-1   Total earnings 722.40; 612.50; 542.85

Problem 14-2   Totals 7,733.40; 280.80; 8,014.20; 773.00; 641.13; 291.00; 60.00; 1,765.13; 6,249.07

Problem 14-3   Totals 6,888.00; 315.00; 7,203.00; 819.00; 576.24; 240.00; 60.00; 1,695.24; 5,507.76

Mastery Problem 14-M   Totals 5,543.00; 206.30; 5,749.30; 502.00; 459.95; 202.00; 55.00; 1,218.95; 4,530.35

| Employee | | Marital Status | No. of Allow-ances | Earnings | | Deductions | |
No.	Name			Regular	Overtime	Health Insurance	Savings Bonds
3	Abney, Patricia D.	M	2	$512.00	$12.80	$30.00	$10.00
6	Blanks, Wilma E.	S	1	576.00	21.60		
8	Fitts, Deborah S.	M	3	624.00	11.70	38.00	5.00
1	Greer, Daniel J.	M	2	399.00	34.20	30.00	5.00
5	Habig, Vincent W.	S	1	672.00			
9	Jones, Phyllis M.	M	2	608.00	79.80	30.00	10.00
10	Malloy, Timothy R.	S	2	544.00	10.20	30.00	10.00
2	Paxton, Alice Y.	M	4	496.00		44.00	
4	Tait, Michelle D.	S	1	640.00	36.00		
7	Walzak, Thomas T.	S	1	472.00			15.00

INSTRUCTIONS:

1. Prepare a payroll register. The date of payment is May 31. Use the income tax withholding tables in Illustration 14-4 to find the income tax withholding for each employee. Calculate FICA tax withholding using an 8% tax rate. None of the employee accumulated earnings has exceeded the FICA tax base.

2. Prepare a check for the total amount of the net pay. Make the check payable to Payroll Account, and sign your name as a partner of Mercer Company. The beginning check stub balance is $10,287.20.

3. Prepare payroll checks for Daniel Greer, Check No. 426, and Michelle Tait, Check No. 431. Sign your name as a partner of Mercer Company. Record the two payroll check numbers in the payroll register.

CHALLENGE PROBLEM 14-C Calculating piecework wages

SPREADSHEET

Production workers in factories are frequently paid on the basis of the number of units they produce. This payroll method is referred to as the piecework incentive wage plan. Most piecework incentive wage plans include a guaranteed hourly rate to employees regardless of the number of units they produce. This guaranteed hourly rate is referred to as the base rate.

Time and motion study engineers usually determine the standard time required for producing a single unit. Assume, for example, that time studies determine that one-third of an hour is the standard time required to produce a unit. Then the standard rate for an 8-hour day would be 24 units (8 hours divided by 1/3 hour = 24 units per day). If a worker's daily base pay is $66.00, the incentive rate per unit is $2.75 ($66.00 divided by 24 units = $2.75 per unit). Therefore, the worker who produces 24 or fewer units per day is paid the base pay, $66.00. However, each worker is paid an additional $2.75 for each unit over 24 produced each day.

Southern Woodworks Company has eight employees in production departments that are paid on a piecework incentive wage plan. The following standard and incentive wage rates are listed by department.

Department	Standard Production per Employee	Incentive Rate per Unit
Cutting	30 units per day	$2.30
Assembly	20 units per day	$4.10
Finishing	40 units per day	$1.80

Each employee worked eight hours a day during the semimonthly pay period, August 1–15. Payroll records for August 1–15 are summarized in the following table.

Employee		Marital Status	No. of Allow-ances	Guaranteed Daily Rate	Units Produced per Day									
No.	Name				Pay Period August 1–15									
					2	3	4	5	6	9	10	11	12	13
	Cutting Department													
C2	Simpson, Alan J.	S	1	$69.00	29	32	31	34	28	27	30	32	36	26
C4	Creek, Janice A.	M	1	$69.00	32	31	28	29	27	29	31	32	27	28
C8	Pate, Marie S.	M	2	$69.00	31	28	27	24	31	33	32	29	30	29
	Assembly Department													
A1	Meese, Frank K.	S	1	$82.00	20	21	19	19	18	18	19	21	20	21
A6	Harris, Kevin E.	M	3	$82.00	25	21	17	18	19	21	20	20	21	18
A7	Martin, Angela M.	S	1	$82.00	22	24	25	21	20	19	23	21	18	17
	Finishing Department													
F5	Quinn, Karen A.	M	2	$72.00	41	40	38	39	42	43	41	40	38	37
F3	Raines, Jon S.	M	2	$72.00	37	37	38	38	39	38	40	41	41	42

INSTRUCTIONS:

Prepare a payroll register. The earnings column headed *Incentive* is used instead of Overtime. The date of payment is August 16. Use the income tax withholding tables in Illustration 14-4. Calculate the employee FICA tax withholding using an 8% tax rate. None of the employees has health insurance or other deductions.

Chapter 15 presents payroll from the employer's point of view. Journal entries for recording the payment of salaries and the liabilities incurred by withholding tax and other deductions are described and illustrated. In addition, students see that employers must pay payroll taxes in addition to those withheld from employees' wages. The nature and calculation of the employer's FICA tax and federal and state unemployment taxes are presented along with the journal entries for recording these payroll tax expenses. Requirements for reporting and paying payroll tax liabilities are illustrated and described.

GUIDE TO ACHIEVING LEARNING OBJECTIVES

Enabling Performance Tasks	TEACH Lesson Plans	APPLY Drills for Understanding	APPLY Application Problems	EXTEND/ENRICH Mastery Problems	EXTEND/ENRICH Challenge Problems	EXTEND/ENRICH Cases for Critical Thinking	EXTEND/ENRICH Recycling Problems	EXTEND/ENRICH Reinforcement Activity	
a. Identify accounting concepts and practices related to payroll accounts, taxes, and reports.	15-1, 15-2, 15-3								
b. Analyze payroll transactions.	15-1, 15-2, 15-3	15-D1, 15-D2	15-1, 15-2, 15-4	15-M	15-C	Cases 1, 2	15-R	2A	
c. Journalize and post payroll transactions.	15-1, 15-2, 15-3		15-1, 15-2, 15-4	15-M	15-C		15-R	2A	
d. Prepare selected payroll tax reports.	15-3		15-3						

ENRICHMENT

SPECIAL FEATURES

Professional Business Ethics, page 358

Careers in Accounting, page 351

TECHNOLOGY CONNECTION

Automated Accounting 6.0 Problems 15-M, 15-C
Integrating Automated Accounting Topic 5 Optional Problem DB-5A

Accounting Tutorial Unit 4

Application Program Disk Problems 15-M, 15C

Spreadsheet Template Problem 15-2

Electronic Study Guide

NEW, REVIEW, AND EXTENSION

ACTIVITIES/CONCEPTS/TRANSACTIONS	NEW	REVIEW/ EXTENSION
Calculating employer payroll taxes		✓
Recording employer payroll taxes	✓	
Reporting withholding and payroll taxes	✓	
Paying withholding and payroll taxes	✓	

The general ledger accounts used in Problem 15-1 are needed to complete Problem 15-2. The use of the same ledger accounts for both problems combines the effects of the entries for both the taxes withheld from employees and those paid by the employer only.

	INFORMAL ASSESSMENT		FORMAL ASSESSMENT					
	Study Guide	Audit Your Understanding	Chapter MicroExam	Chapter Problem Test	Unit Problem Test	Unit Objective Test	Portfolio
Unit A		✓	✓			✓	
Unit B				✓	✓		✓
				✓	✓		✓
Unit C							

TEACHING MATERIALS

Teacher's Wraparound Edition of Text

Teacher's Resource Guide

Teacher's Edition of Working Papers

Teacher's Edition of the Demonstration/Recycling Problems

Teaching Transparencies

Accounting Tutorial Manual

MicroExam

Key for Stellar Attractions Pegboard Payroll Simulation

Applied Math Work Sheet

APPLIED MATHEMATICS

APPLIED MATH/ACCOUNTING SKILL	APPLICATION
Calculating unemployment taxes	Drill 15-D2
Calculating employer tax liabilities	Prob. 15-3

Payroll Accounting, Taxes, and Reports

ENABLING PERFORMANCE TASKS

After studying Chapter 15, you will be able to:

a Identify accounting concepts and practices related to payroll accounts, taxes, and reports.

b Analyze payroll transactions.

c Journalize and post payroll transactions.

d Prepare selected payroll tax reports.

Payroll information for each pay period is recorded in a payroll register. Each pay period the payroll information for each employee is also recorded on each employee earnings record. Separate payroll accounts for each employee are not kept in the general ledger. Instead, accounts are kept in the general ledger to summarize total earnings and deductions for all employees.

350

The payroll register and employee earnings records provide all the payroll information needed to prepare a payroll and payroll tax reports. Journal entries are made to record the payment of the payroll and the employer payroll taxes. In addition, various quarterly and annual payroll tax reports are required to report the payment of payroll taxes.

RECORDING A PAYROLL

The payroll register for CarLand's semimonthly pay period ended December 15 is shown in Illustration 15-1, on page 352.

Analyzing Payment of a Payroll

The column totals of a payroll register provide the debit and credit amounts needed to journalize a payroll. CarLand's December 15 payroll is summarized in the following T accounts.

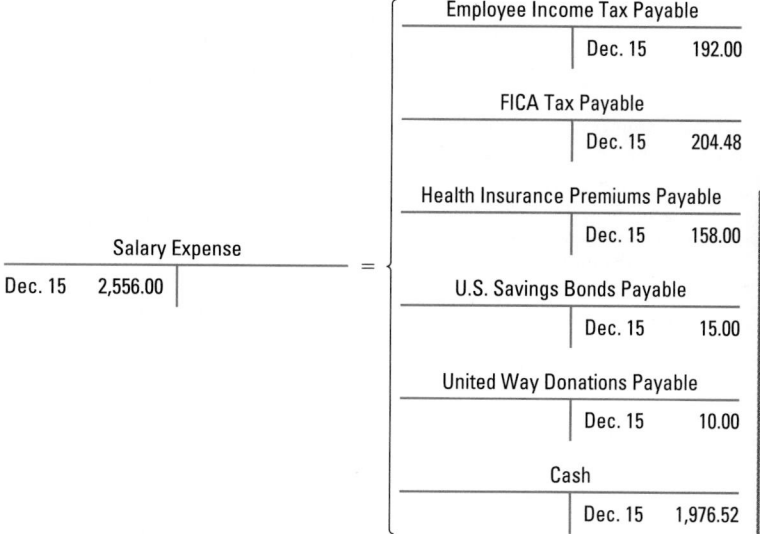

The Total Earnings column total, $2,556.00, is the salary expense for the period. Salary Expense is debited for this amount.

The Federal Income Tax column total, $192.00, is the amount withheld from employee salaries for federal income tax. The amount withheld is a liability of the business until the taxes are sent to the federal government. Employee Income Tax Payable is credited for $192.00 to record this liability.

The FICA Tax column total, $204.48, is the amount withheld from salaries of all employees for FICA tax. The amount withheld

---

CAREERS IN ACCOUNTING

PAYROLL CLERK

- *Compiles payroll data from time cards and personnel records*
- *Calculates wages and deductions*
- *Posts to payroll records*
- *Prepares and issues paychecks*
- *Prepares periodic reports of earnings, taxes, and deductions*
- *Records data concerning transfer of employees*

LESSON PLAN 15-1

Materials

- Student pages 351–354
- Transparency 15-1, Blank Expanded Journal (Partial)
- Software: Accounting Tutorial

Objectives (Enabling Performance Tasks)

a. Identify accounting concepts and practices related to payroll accounts, taxes, and reports.

b. Analyze payroll transactions.

c. Journalize and post payroll transactions.

CAREERS IN ACCOUNTING

The CAREERS IN ACCOUNTING feature box, PAYROLL CLERK, comes from the Dictionary of Occupational Titles (DOT). The entry number for this job title is D.O.T. 215.382-014. Bring this dictionary to class and explain its purpose and how to use it. The career feature is designed to expose students to the exploration of different careers in accounting. The feature gives a realistic description of actual job duties. This feature can be used to demonstrate that the skills learned in this course are relevant.

FOCUS

In Chapter 14, a payroll register was prepared. In this lesson, we will use information from the payroll register to record the payment of the payroll.

TEACH

Cover student pages 351–354 "Recording a Payroll." During this lesson, point out that the payroll register and employee earnings records provide all the payroll information needed to prepare a payroll and payroll tax reports. Emphasize that the total earnings column of the payroll register is the debit amount for Salary Expense. The net pay column is the credit amount for Cash. All other columns provide the credit parts of the entry. These credits become liabilities so add payable to the end of each column heading and you have your liability account. It is important during this lesson, which uses multiple-line journal entries, to reinforce that debits must always equal credits.

APPLY

Draw T accounts for the payroll transaction illustrated in the textbook. Use Transparency 15-1 to journalize this payroll entry. Or direct students to Illustration 15-2.

Guided Practice

Guide students through Drill 15-D1, Instructions 1 and 2a. Students should have the forms from the working papers to complete as you guide them through the drill. For each column, ask students which account is affected and how. All students should agree with the analysis before proceeding to the next column.

Independent Practice

Assign Questions 1–4 and Problem 15-1.

ILLUSTRATION 15-1 Payroll register

	EMPL. NO.	EMPLOYEE'S NAME	MARITAL STATUS	NO. OF ALLOWANCES	EARNINGS REGULAR	OVERTIME	TOTAL	DEDUCTIONS FEDERAL INCOME TAX	FICA TAX	HEALTH INSURANCE	OTHER		TOTAL	NET PAY	CHECK NO.	
1	2	Bauch, Mary R.	M	2	660 00		660 00	57 00	52 80	38 00	B	5 00	152 80	507 20	419	1
2	5	Clay, Richard P.	S	1	80 00		80 00	00	6 40				6 40	73 60	420	2
3	1	Javorski, Adam B.	M	2	384 00	18 00	402 00	17 00	32 16	38 00			87 16	314 84	421	3
4	6	Maggio, Brenda A.	S	1	40 00		40 00	00	3 20				3 20	36 80	422	4
5	4	Turner, Patrick S.	M	4	704 00	54 00	758 00	45 00	60 64	50 00	B / UW	10 00 / 10 00	175 64	582 36	423	5
6	3	Wilkes, Samuel R.	S	1	616 00		616 00	73 00	49 28	32 00			154 28	461 72	424	6
7		Totals			2484 00	72 00	2556 00	192 00	204 48	158 00	B / UW	15 00 / 10 00	579 48	1976 52		7

SEMIMONTHLY PERIOD ENDED *December 15, 19--*
PAYROLL REGISTER
DATE OF PAYMENT *December 15, 19--*

FYI

Other payroll deductions may include a deduction for savings bonds and United Way contributions.

is a liability of the business until the tax is paid to the government. FICA Tax Payable is credited for $204.48.

The Health Insurance column total, $158.00, is the amount withheld from salaries for health insurance premiums. The amount withheld is a liability of the business until the premiums are paid to the insurance company. Health Insurance Premiums Payable is credited for $158.00 to record this liability.

The Other column of the deductions section may contain more than one total. Two types of *Other* deductions are recorded in CarLand's payroll register. The $15.00 Other column total identified with the letter B is withheld to buy savings bonds for employees. The $10.00 total identified with the letters *UW* is withheld for employee United Way pledges. Until these amounts have been paid by the employer, they are liabilities of the business. U.S. Savings Bonds Payable is credited for $15.00. United Way Donations Payable is credited for $10.00.

The Net Pay column total, $1,976.52, is the net amount paid to employees. Cash is credited for $1,976.52. A check for the total net pay amount, $1,976.52, is written on CarLand's general checking account. This amount is deposited in a special payroll checking account used only for employee payroll checks. Individual payroll checks are then written on the special payroll checking account.

Journalizing Payment of a Payroll

December 15, 19--. Paid cash for semimonthly payroll, $1,976.52 (total payroll, $2,556.00, less deductions: employee income tax, $192.00; FICA tax, $204.48; health insurance premiums, $158.00; U.S. Savings Bonds, $15.00; United Way donations, $10.00). Check No. 287.

The journal entry to record payment of CarLand's December 15 payroll is shown in Illustration 15-2.

The date, *15*, is written in the Date column. The title of the account debited, *Salary Expense*, is recorded in the Account Title col-

---

APPLIED SKILLS: BUILDING STUDY SKILLS

Instruct students to prepare a Quick Reference Guide (QRG) for journalizing payroll.
1. Draw T accounts for Salary Expense, Employee Income Tax Payable, FICA Tax Payable, Health Insurance Premiums Payable, U.S. Savings Bonds Payable, and United Way Donations Payable.
2. Place a check mark on the debit side of Salary Expense and a check mark on the credit side of all payable accounts.

Students should use this QRG when analyzing transactions.

ILLUSTRATION 15-2   Journal entry to record a payroll

PAGE *24*				JOURNAL						
					1	2		10	11	
	DATE	ACCOUNT TITLE	DOC. NO.	POST. REF.	GENERAL			CASH		
					DEBIT	CREDIT		DEBIT	CREDIT	
21	15	Salary Expense	C287		2 5 5 6 00				1 9 7 6 52	21
22		Employee Income Tax Payable				1 9 2 00				22
23		FICA Tax Payable				2 0 4 48				23
24		Health Insurance Premiums Payable				1 5 8 00				24
25		U.S. Savings Bonds Payable				1 5 00				25
26		United Way Donations Payable				1 0 00				26

FYI

Total Earnings is the debit amount for Salary Expense. Net pay is the credit amount for cash.

umn. The check number, *C287,* is entered in the Doc. No. column. The amount debited to Salary Expense, *$2,556.00,* is written in the General Debit column. On the same line, the net amount paid to employees, *$1,976.52,* is written in the Cash Credit column. Five liability accounts are credited for the amounts deducted from employee salaries. The five account titles are written in the Account Title column. The five credit amounts are written in the General Credit column.

Posting the Journal Entry for Payment of a Payroll

Amounts recorded in the General columns of a journal are posted individually to general ledger accounts. After the December 15 payroll entry is posted, the liability and salary expense accounts appear as shown in Illustration 15-3.

ILLUSTRATION 15-3   General ledger accounts after journal entry for payment of a payroll is posted

ACCOUNT *Employee Income Tax Payable*   ACCOUNT NO. *2120*

DATE	ITEM	POST. REF.	DEBIT	CREDIT	BALANCE	
					DEBIT	CREDIT
15		24		1 9 2 00		1 9 2 00

ACCOUNT *FICA Tax Payable*   ACCOUNT NO. *2130*

DATE	ITEM	POST. REF.	DEBIT	CREDIT	BALANCE	
					DEBIT	CREDIT
15		24		2 0 4 48		2 0 4 48

CHAPTER 15   Payroll Accounting, Taxes, and Reports   **353**

TEACHING STRATEGIES: TEACHING TIP

Review the five steps of posting from the journal to the general ledger: date, posting reference from the journal, debit/credit amount, new account balance, posting reference from the ledger.

- Use Audit Your Understanding questions.

- Review the procedures for analyzing, recording, and posting the payment of a payroll.

ILLUSTRATION 15-3   General ledger accounts after journal entry for payment of a payroll is posted (concluded)

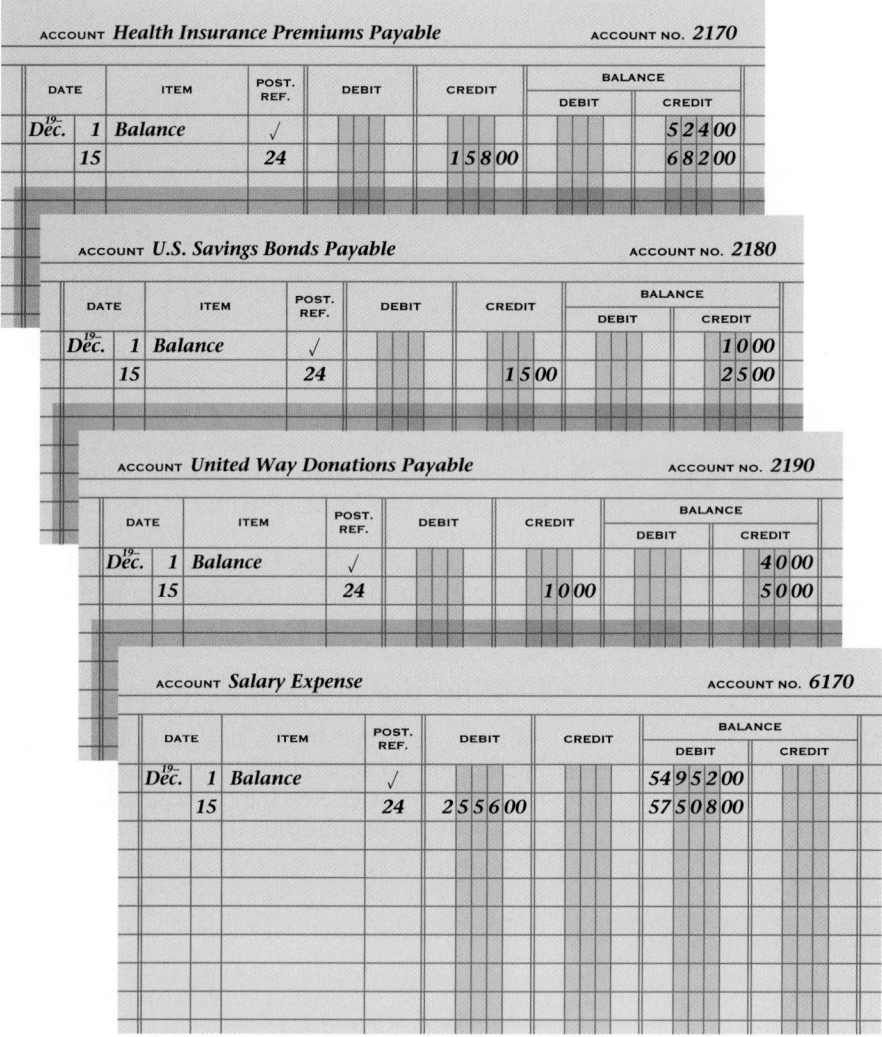

ACCOUNT Health Insurance Premiums Payable					ACCOUNT NO. 2170	
DATE	ITEM	POST. REF.	DEBIT	CREDIT	BALANCE DEBIT	BALANCE CREDIT
Dec. 1	Balance	√				52400
15		24		15800		68200

ACCOUNT U.S. Savings Bonds Payable					ACCOUNT NO. 2180	
DATE	ITEM	POST. REF.	DEBIT	CREDIT	BALANCE DEBIT	BALANCE CREDIT
Dec. 1	Balance	√				1000
15		24		1500		2500

ACCOUNT United Way Donations Payable					ACCOUNT NO. 2190	
DATE	ITEM	POST. REF.	DEBIT	CREDIT	BALANCE DEBIT	BALANCE CREDIT
Dec. 1	Balance	√				4000
15		24		1000		5000

ACCOUNT Salary Expense					ACCOUNT NO. 6170	
DATE	ITEM	POST. REF.	DEBIT	CREDIT	BALANCE DEBIT	BALANCE CREDIT
Dec. 1	Balance	√			549520 0	
15		24	255600		575080 0	

The credit to Cash, $1,976.52, is not posted separately to the cash account. The amount is included in the journal's Cash Credit column total that is posted at the end of the month.

RECORDING EMPLOYER PAYROLL TAXES

Employers must pay to the government the taxes withheld from employee earnings. CarLand has withheld federal income tax and FICA tax from employee salaries. The amounts withheld are liabil-

LESSON PLAN 15-2

Materials

- Student Pages 354–360

- Transparency: 15-1, Blank Expanded Journal (Partial)

- Math Work Sheet Chapter 15, Part A: Calculating Unemployment Taxes (TRG)

- 3-Step Checklist for Making Ethical Decisions (TRG)

- Software: Accounting Tutorial, Spreadsheet Template

Objectives (Enabling Performance Tasks)

a. Identify accounting concepts and practices related to payroll accounts, taxes, and reports.

b. Analyze payroll transactions.

c. Journalize and post payroll transactions.

ities to the business until they are actually paid to the government. In addition, employers must pay several of their own payroll taxes. Employer payroll taxes are business expenses.

Calculating Employer Payroll Taxes

Most employers must pay three separate payroll taxes. These taxes are (1) employer FICA tax, (2) federal unemployment tax, and (3) state unemployment tax. Employer payroll taxes expense is based on a percentage of employee earnings.

Employer FICA Tax. CarLand withheld $204.48 in FICA tax from employee wages for the pay period ended December 15. CarLand owes the same amount of FICA taxes as the amount withheld from employees. Therefore, CarLand's FICA tax for the pay period ended December 15 is also $204.48.

Congress sets the FICA tax rate for employees and employers. Periodically, Congress may change the tax rate and tax base. The FICA tax rate is a combination of two different tax rates: (1) a tax for old-age, survivors, and disability and (2) a tax for Medicare. The two taxes also have different tax bases. The FICA tax rates and bases used in this text are shown below.

	Tax Rate	Tax Base
Old-age, survivors, and disability	6.5%	earnings up to $55,500
Medicare	1.5%	earnings up to $130,200
Total	8.0%	

Therefore, the effective FICA tax rate for earnings up to the tax base of $55,500 is 8.0% (6.5% + 1.5%). The additional FICA tax rate for earnings from $55,500 to $130,200 is 1.5%.

The FICA tax is the only payroll tax paid by *both* the employees and the employer. Employees pay 8% of their total earnings up to a tax base of $55,500.00 and 1.5% of their total earnings up to $130,200.00 as a FICA tax. Employers also pay FICA tax on each employee's earnings using the same tax rates and tax bases.

Federal Unemployment Tax. Federal unemployment insurance laws require that employers pay taxes for unemployment compensation. These tax funds are used to pay workers benefits for limited periods of unemployment and to administer the unemployment compensation program. All of the federal unemployment tax is paid by the employer.

The federal unemployment tax for most businesses is 0.8% of total earnings of each employee up to a tax base of *$7,000.00* during a calendar year. The total earnings of CarLand's December 1-15 pay period subject to the federal unemployment tax is referred to

FYI

Employers must pay three taxes on employee earnings— FICA Tax, Federal Unemployment Tax, and State Unemployment Tax.

FOCUS

In Chapter 14, employer payroll taxes were introduced and the payroll register and employee earnings records were prepared. In this lesson, we will use information from these forms to calculate and record employer payroll taxes.

TEACH

Cover student pages 354–360 "Recording Employer Payroll Taxes." Emphasize that employers must pay three taxes on employee earnings—FICA Tax, Federal Unemployment Tax, and State Unemployment Tax. Explain that the FICA rate is 8% on the first $55,500 of earnings and 1.5% from $55,500 to $130,200 of earnings. Emphasize that even though FICA is a matching amount, when the rate is multiplied times total earnings, there can be several cents difference in amount paid by employees. To avoid rounding discrepancies, use the same amount employees pay.

Calculating federal unemployment tax is sometimes confusing for students. It is important to remember that the 0.8% federal unemployment tax is based on the first $7,000 made by each employee, not total earnings from the payroll register. Federal unemployment tax must be calculated after each employee earnings record has been examined. Once an employee earns $7,000, federal unemployment tax is not paid for that employee for the remainder of the year. Explain that in most states the state unemployment tax is 5.4% with a tax base of $7,000. These amounts will vary slightly from state to state.

Before journalizing the entry for employer payroll taxes, draw T accounts on the board and record the amount for each of the three taxes. The total of these three is the amount debited to Payroll Taxes Expense. Use Transparency 15-1 to journalize this payroll entry. Or direct students to Illustration 15-5.

Guided Practice

Guide students through Drill 15-D1, Instruction 2b. Students should have the forms from the working papers to complete as you guide them through the drill. For each column, ask students which account is affected and how. All students should agree with the analysis before proceeding to the next column.

Independent Practice

Assign Questions 5–9, Drill 15-D2, and Problem 15-2.

as unemployment taxable earnings. The amount of unemployment taxable earnings is calculated as shown in Illustration 15-4.

Accumulated earnings are calculated on each employee earnings record. Patrick S. Turner's accumulated earnings as of November 30, *$16,794.00*, are recorded in the first column. Total earnings for Mr. Turner for the December 15 pay period, *$758.00*, are recorded

ILLUSTRATION 15-4   Total earnings subject to federal unemployment tax

CarLand Taxable Earnings for December 15, 19-- Pay Period			
	Accumulated Earnings as of Nov. 30, 19--	**Total Earnings for Dec. 15, 19-- Pay Period**	**Unemployment Taxable Earnings**
Bauch, Mary R.	$14,520.00	$660.00	$ —
Clay, Richard P.	2,160.00	80.00	80.00
Javorski, Adam B.	5,792.50	402.00	402.00
Maggio, Brenda A.	1,680.00	40.00	40.00
Turner, Patrick S.	16,794.00	758.00	—
Wilkes, Samuel R.	4,976.50	616.00	616.00
			$1,138.00

in the second column. Since the accumulated earnings for Mr. Turner are greater than $7,000.00, none of his current earnings are subject to federal unemployment tax. Thus, the amount of unemployment taxable earnings recorded in the third column is zero, which is represented by a dash.

The accumulated earnings for Samuel R. Wilkes, $4,976.50, are less than $7,000.00. Therefore, his total earnings for the December 15 pay period are subject to federal unemployment tax. Total earnings for Mr. Wilkes for the December 15 pay period, *$616.00*, are recorded in the Unemployment Taxable Earnings column.

The total earnings for the pay period are entered in the Unemployment Taxable Earnings column for employees whose accumulated earnings are less than $7,000.00. The sum of the Unemployment Taxable Earnings Column, $1,138.00, is the amount used to calculate federal unemployment tax.

CarLand's federal unemployment tax is calculated as shown below.

◖◖ FYI ◗◗

Seniority is the amount of time an employee has been employed by a company.

	Unemployment Taxable Earnings	×	Federal Unemployment Tax Rate	=	Federal Unemployment Tax
	$1,138.00	×	0.8%	=	$9.10

APPLIED SKILLS: MATHEMATICS

Use the MATH WORK SHEETS in the Masters and Solutions to Enrichment/Application Activities Section of the Teacher's Resource Guide to integrate applied mathematics. In these work sheets, students will apply math concepts to calculate unemployment taxes and employer tax liabilities.

State Unemployment Tax. Most states require that employers pay unemployment tax of 5.4% on the first $7,000.00 earned by each employee. The unemployment taxable earnings used to calculate the federal unemployment tax are also used to calculate the state unemployment tax. The unemployment taxable earnings subject to the state unemployment tax are calculated in Illustration 15-4. Thus, the state employment tax to be paid by CarLand is calculated as shown below.

	Unemployment Taxable Earnings	×	State Unemployment Tax Rate	=	State Unemployment Tax
	$1,138.00	×	5.4%	=	$61.45

Journalizing Employer Payroll Taxes

Employer payroll taxes are paid to the government at a later date. However, the liability is incurred when salaries are paid. Therefore, the transaction to record employer payroll taxes expense is journalized on the same date the payroll is journalized. The salary expense and the employer payroll taxes expense are, therefore, both recorded in the same accounting period.

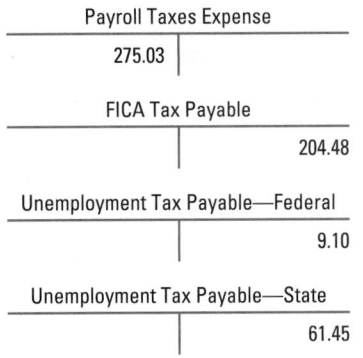

Payroll Taxes Expense
275.03

FICA Tax Payable
204.48

Unemployment Tax Payable—Federal
9.10

Unemployment Tax Payable—State
61.45

December 15, 19--. Recorded employer payroll taxes expense, $275.03, for the semimonthly pay period ended December 15. Taxes owed are: FICA tax, $204.48; federal unemployment tax, $9.10; state unemployment tax, $61.45. Memorandum No. 54.

Payroll Taxes Expense is debited for $275.03 to show the increase in the balance of this expense account. Three liability accounts are credited to show the increase in payroll tax liabilities. FICA Tax Payable is credited for $204.48. Unemployment Tax Payable—Federal is credited for $9.10. Unemployment Tax Payable—State is credited for $61.45.

CarLand's journal entry to record the employer payroll taxes expense is shown in Illustration 15-5.

ILLUSTRATION 15-5   Journal entry to record employer payroll taxes

					GENERAL		CASH		
	DATE	ACCOUNT TITLE	DOC. NO.	POST. REF.	DEBIT	CREDIT	DEBIT	CREDIT	
27	15	*Payroll Taxes Expense*	M54		275 03				27
28		*FICA Tax Payable*				204 48			28
29		*Unemployment Tax Payable—Federal*				9 10			29
30		*Unemployment Tax Payable—State*				61 45			30
31									31

PAGE 24   JOURNAL   PAGE 24

PROFESSIONAL BUSINESS ETHICS

Who Owns My Time?

Employers and their employees have a unique relationship. The employee agrees to provide the employer with a fair day's work. In return, the employer agrees to provide the employee with a fair day's wage and benefits.

As an accountant working for a public accounting firm, you spend a majority of your time working in your clients' offices. During your visits you have become aware of the following employment practices.

Situation 1. An office receptionist for Hammill Company is also assigned accounting tasks, such as checking the accuracy of purchase invoices and time cards. These tasks are not sufficient, however, to keep the recep-

The date, *15*, is written in the Date column. The title of the account debited, *Payroll Taxes Expense*, is written in the Account Title column. The memorandum number, *M54*, is entered in the Doc. No. column. The debit amount, *$275.03*, is entered in the General Debit column. The titles of the liability accounts are entered in the Account Title column. The amounts credited to the liability accounts are entered in the General Credit column.

Posting an Employer Payroll Taxes Entry

After the entry for the employer payroll taxes is posted, the accounts involved appear as shown in Illustration 15-6.

ILLUSTRATION 15-6 — General ledger accounts after journal entry for employer payroll taxes expense is posted

TEACHING STRATEGIES: TEACHING TIP

List on a chalkboard or overhead transparency all payroll related accounts. Have students analyze each account and answer the following questions. (a) Is the account an expense or a liability? (b) Is the account used for recording an employee tax, an employer tax, or both? (c) How is the payroll register used to determine the amount that goes into the account?

tionist busy. Thus, the receptionist frequently reads magazines and completes crossword puzzles to occupy the extra time.

Situation 2. Sandi's Hamburger Hut limits most of its employees to 32 hours per week. Only full-time employees who work 40 or more hours per week are eligible for the company's health insurance program.

Situation 3. Accountants of Adams and Associates, a CPA firm, receive a monthly salary. Although the accountants can work 60-70 hours per week during busy seasons, they do not receive overtime wages. Instead, they are able to take extra vacation after the busy season is over.

INSTRUCTIONS Use the three-step checklist to analyze whether the employment practices above demonstrate ethical behavior.

CLOSURE

- Use Audit Your Understanding questions.
- Review the procedures for calculating employer payroll taxes.
- Review the procedures for analyzing, recording, and posting the employer payroll taxes.

ILLUSTRATION 15-6	General ledger accounts after journal entry for employer payroll taxes expense is posted (concluded)

ACCOUNT **Unemployment Tax Payable—State**   ACCOUNT NO. **2160**

DATE		ITEM	POST. REF.	DEBIT	CREDIT	BALANCE	
						DEBIT	CREDIT
Dec.	1	Balance	✓				2 7 3 22
	15		24		6 1 45		3 3 4 67

ACCOUNT **Payroll Taxes Expense**   ACCOUNT NO. **6150**

DATE		ITEM	POST. REF.	DEBIT	CREDIT	BALANCE	
						DEBIT	CREDIT
Dec.	1	Balance	✓			6 7 3 8 96	
	15		24	2 7 5 03		7 0 1 3 99	

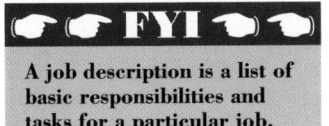

FYI

A job description is a list of basic responsibilities and tasks for a particular job.

The FICA Tax Payable account has two credits. The first credit, $204.48, is the FICA tax withheld from *employee* wages for the semi-monthly period ended December 15. This amount was posted from the journal entry that recorded payment of the payroll, Illustration 15-2. The second credit, $204.48, is the *employer* liability for FICA tax. This amount was posted from the journal entry that recorded the employer payroll taxes, Illustration 15-5.

Summary of Amounts Posted to the General Ledger

Both the employees and employer owe payroll taxes. Federal income tax and FICA tax are withheld from employee salaries. An equal amount of FICA tax is owed by the employer. The employer must also record federal and state unemployment taxes. The payroll taxes resulting from CarLand's December 1–15 pay period are summarized on page 360.

Audit Your Understanding

1. What account title is used to journalize the Total Earnings column of the payroll register?

2. What account title is used to journalize the Federal Income Tax column of the payroll register?

3. What account title is used to journalize the FICA Tax column of the payroll register?

	Employees	Employer
Federal Income Tax	$192.00	—
FICA Tax	204.48	$204.48
Federal Unemployment Tax	—	9.10
State Unemployment Tax	—	61.45
Total	$396.48	$275.03

Only the employer payroll taxes, $275.03, are recorded as payroll taxes expense in CarLand's general ledger accounts. The payroll taxes of both the employees and the employer create liabilities to the business which must be paid at times specified by the government.

REPORTING WITHHOLDING AND PAYROLL TAXES

Each employer is required by law to periodically report the payroll taxes withheld from employee salaries and the employer payroll taxes due the government. Some reports are submitted quarterly and others are submitted annually.

Employer Quarterly Federal Tax Return

Each employer must file a quarterly federal tax return showing the federal income tax and FICA taxes due the government. This information is submitted every three months on Form 941, Employer's Quarterly Federal Tax Return. Form 941 is filed before the last day of the month following the end of a calendar quarter. CarLand's Form 941 for the calendar quarter ended December 31 is shown in Illustration 15-7, page 361. The information needed to prepare Form 941 is obtained from employee earnings records.

Total earnings, *$15,192.85*, are recorded on line 2 of Form 941. This amount is the sum of the fourth quarter total earnings of all CarLand employees. The amount of total earnings, *$15,192.85*, is also recorded on the line to the left of line 6a and 7. The income tax withheld, *$1,168.00*, is recorded on line 3 of Form 941. The amount is the total of the fourth quarter federal income tax withheld from CarLand's employees.

The social security (FICA) taxes due are calculated as shown below.

FYI

Quarterly tax returns must be submitted every three months on Form 941.

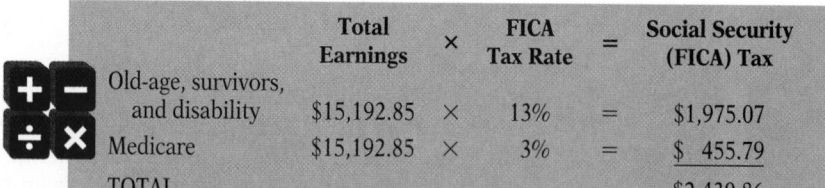

	Total Earnings	×	FICA Tax Rate	=	Social Security (FICA) Tax
Old-age, survivors, and disability	$15,192.85	×	13%	=	$1,975.07
Medicare	$15,192.85	×	3%	=	$ 455.79
TOTAL					$2,430.86

ILLUSTRATION 15-7   Form 941, Employer's Quarterly Federal Tax Return

Form **941** (Rev. January 19--)
Department of the Treasury
Internal Revenue Service

4141

Employer's Quarterly Federal Tax Return

▶ See Circular E for more information concerning employment tax returns.

Please type or print.

Your name, address, employer identification number, and calendar quarter of return. (If not correct, please change.) If address is different from prior return, check here ▶

Name (as distinguished from trade name): CarLand

Trade name, if any:

Address (number and street): 1374 Parklane

Date quarter ended: December 31, 19--

Employer identification number: 31-0429632

City, state, and ZIP code: Rockville, RI 02873 -4121

OMB No. 1545-0029
Expires 5-31-93

T
FF
FD
FP
I
T

If you do not have to file returns in the future, check here . . . ▶ ☐   Date final wages paid . . . ▶ _____

If you are a seasonal employer, see **Seasonal employers** on page 2 and check here . ▶ ☐

1	Number of employees (except household) employed in the pay period that includes March 12th ▶	1	6
2	Total wages and tips subject to withholding, plus other compensation . . . . ▶	2	$15,192 85
3	Total income tax withheld from wages, tips, pensions, annuities, sick pay, gambling, etc. ▶	3	1,168 00
4	Adjustment of withheld income tax for preceding quarters of calendar year (see instructions) ▶	4	-0-
5	Adjusted total of income tax withheld (line 3 as adjusted by line 4—see instructions)	5	1,168 00

6a	Taxable social security wages (Complete line 7)	$ 15,192 85	× 13% (.13) =	6a	1,975 07
b	Taxable social security tips	$ -0-	× 13% (.13) =	b	-0-
7	Taxable Medicare wages and tips	$ 15,192 85	× 3% (.03) =	7	455 79

8	Total social security and Medicare taxes (add lines 6a, 6b, and 7)	8	2,430 86
9	Adjustment of social security and Medicare taxes (see instructions for required explanation) .	9	-0-
10	Adjusted total of social security and Medicare taxes (line 8 as adjusted by line 9—see instructions) ▶	10	2,430 86
11	Backup withholding (see instructions)	11	-0-
12	Adjustment of backup withholding tax for preceding quarters of calendar year	12	-0-
13	Adjusted total of backup withholding (line 11 as adjusted by line 12)	13	-0-
14	**Total taxes** (add lines 5, 10, and 13)	14	3,598 86
15	Advance earned income credit (EIC) payments made to employees, if any . . . . ▶	15	-0-
16	Net taxes (subtract line 15 from line 14). **This should equal line IV below** (plus line IV of Schedule A (Form 941) if you have treated backup withholding as a separate liability)	16	3,598 86
17	**Total deposits for quarter**, including overpayment applied from a prior quarter, from your records . ▶	17	3,598 86
18	**Balance due** (subtract line 17 from line 16). This should be less than $500. Pay to Internal Revenue Service . ▶	18	-0-
19	**Overpayment**, if line 17 is more than line 16, enter excess here ▶ $ _____ and check if to be: ☐ Applied to next return **OR** ☐ Refunded.		

Record of Federal Tax Liability (You must complete if line 16 is $500 or more and Schedule B is not attached.) See instructions before checking these boxes.
If you made deposits using the 95% rule, check here ▶ ☐   If you are a first time 3-banking-day depositer, check here . . . ▶ ☐

Show tax liability here, **not deposits**. The IRS gets deposit data from FTD coupons.

Date wages paid		First month of quarter		Second month of quarter		Third month of quarter
1st through 3rd	A		I		Q	
4th through 7th	B		J		R	
8th through 11th	C		K		S	
12th through 15th	D	602.60	L	572.65	T	600.96
16th through 19th	E		M		U	
20th through 22nd	F		N		V	
23rd through 25th	G	592.65	O	596.80	W	633.20
26th through the last	H		P		X	
Total liability for month	I	1,195.25	II	1,169.45	III	1,234.16
IV Total for quarter (add lines **I**, **II**, and **III**). **This should equal line 16 above** . . . . ▶						3,598.86

DO NOT Show Federal Tax Deposits Here

Sign Here

Under penalties of perjury, I declare that I have examined this return, including accompanying schedules and statements, and to the best of my knowledge and belief, it is true, correct, and complete.

Signature ▶ *Amy Kramer*   Print Your Name and Title ▶ *Partner*   Date ▶ 1/24/--

For Paperwork Reduction Act Notice, see page 2.   Cat. No. 17001Z

FOCUS

- Recording both the payroll taxes withheld from employee salaries and the employer payroll taxes was presented earlier in this chapter. In this lesson, we will look at some of the forms the employer is required to submit to report these taxes.

- Earlier in this chapter, when journal entries for withholding and payroll taxes were recorded, liabilities were created for each of the taxes. In this lesson, we will record the entries to pay these withholding and payroll tax liabilities.

TEACH

Cover student pages 360–368 "Reporting Withholding and Payroll Taxes" and "Paying Withholding and Payroll Taxes." Explain the steps for preparing Form 941. Students will complete this form in Problem 15-3. Bring in a sample and explain a W-2 statement. Involve students in a discussion on W-2 statements. Ask working students about statements they have received. Remind students that Social Security taxes withheld are also referred to as FICA taxes. Explain a W-3 statement and its purpose.

Emphasize that employee income taxes and FICA tax are paid in one payment. A deposit coupon, Form 8109, accompanies the payment. Emphasize that federal unemployment tax is usually paid at the end of each quarter. Form 8109 accompanies the payment.

Draw T accounts for each transaction as it is presented. Use Transparency 15-1 to journalize each transaction.

Guided Practice

Guide students through Problem 15-3. Students should have the forms from the working papers to complete as you guide them through the problem. For each line of the form ask for a volunteer to read the directions aloud for the class. For each line, ask the students what the entry should be and how they arrived at that answer. All students should agree with the entry before proceeding to the next line.

Independent Practice

Assign Questions 10–17, Problem 15-4, Mastery Problem 15-M, and Study Guide 15.

The 13% tax rate is the sum of the *employee* 6.5% FICA tax rate and the employer 6.5% FICA tax rate for old-age, survivors, and disability tax. The 3% tax rate is the sum of the *employee* 1.5% FICA tax rate and the *employer* 1.5% FICA tax rate for Medicare tax. The total FICA tax amount, $2,430.86, is recorded on line 8 of Form 941.

CarLand is required to pay the federal government the sum of the FICA tax and federal income tax withheld. The amount of the payment is calculated as shown below.

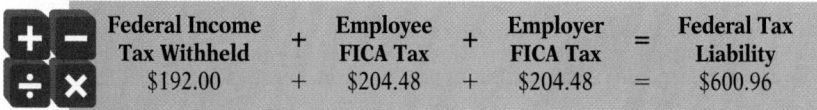

	Federal Income Tax Withheld	+	FICA Tax	=	Total Payment
	$1,168.00	+	$2,430.86	=	$3,598.86

Federal Income Tax withheld is copied from line 3 to line 5. FICA Tax is copied from line 8 to line 10. The total payment owed to the federal government, *$3,598.86*, is recorded on line 14 of Form 941.

The lower section of Form 941 lists the amounts and dates when payroll taxes were withheld from employees and are owed by the employer. For the pay period ended December 15, the amount of taxes owed is calculated as shown below.

	Federal Income Tax Withheld	+	Employee FICA Tax	+	Employer FICA Tax	=	Federal Tax Liability
	$192.00	+	$204.48	+	$204.48	=	$600.96

The federal tax liability for the December 15 pay period, *$600.96*, is recorded on line T of Form 941. The December 15 pay period ended in the third month of the quarter between the 12th and 15th of the month. The December 15 pay period is, therefore, recorded on line T.

Employer Annual Report to Employees of Taxes Withheld

Each employer who withholds income tax and FICA tax from employee earnings must furnish each employee with an annual report of these withholdings. The report shows total year's earnings and the amounts withheld for taxes for an employee. These amounts are obtained from the employee earnings records. The report is prepared on the Internal Revenue Service Form W-2, Wage and Tax Statement.

Employers are required to furnish Form W-2 to each employee by January 31 of the next year. If an employee ends employment before December 31, Form W-2 must be furnished within 30 days of the last date of employment.

☞☞ **FYI** ☞☞

Form W-2 shows the total year's earnings and the amounts withheld for taxes for each employee.

TEACHING STRATEGIES: DIFFERENT LEARNING ABILITIES

Visually-Impaired Students. Many visually impaired individuals are successful business professionals. It is important for visually impaired students to have confidence in their ability to participate fully within the business world. Require students to prepare an oral or written report which profiles a successful visually impaired business professional.

The Form W-2 prepared by CarLand for Patrick S. Turner is shown in Illustration 15-8.

ILLUSTRATION 15-8 Form W-2, Wage and Tax Statement

1 Control number	22222	For Official Use Only ▶ OMB No. 1545-0008		
2 Employer's name, address, and ZIP code		6 Statutory employee ☐ Deceased ☐ Pension plan ☐ Legal rep. ☐ 942 emp. ☐ Subtotal ☐ Deferred compensation ☐ Void ☐		
CarLand 1374 Parklane Rockville, RI 02873-4121		7 Allocated tips	8 Advance EIC payment	
		9 Federal income tax withheld 1,032.00	10 Wages, tips, other compensation 18,192.00	
3 Employer's identification number 31-0429632	4 Employer's state I.D. number	11 Social security tax withheld 1,182.48	12 Social security wages 18,192.00	
5 Employee's social security number 450-70-6432		13 Social security tips	14 Medicare wages and tips 18,192.00	
19a Employee's name (first, middle initial, last) Patrick S. Turner		15 Medicare tax withheld 272.88	16 Nonqualified plans	
1625 Northland Drive Rockville, RI 02873-5073		17 See Instrs. for Form W-2	18 Other	
19b Employee's address and ZIP code				
20	21	22 Dependent care benefits	23 Benefits included in Box 10	
24 State income tax	25 State wages, tips, etc.	26 Name of state	27 Local income tax	28 Local wages, tips, etc.	29 Name of locality

Copy A For Social Security Administration   Department of the Treasury—Internal Revenue Service

Form **W-2 Wage and Tax Statement 19--**

Four copies (A to D) of Form W-2 are prepared for each employee. Copies B and C are given to the employee. The employee attaches Copy B to a personal federal income tax return and keeps Copy C for a personal record. The employer sends Copy A to the Social Security Administration and keeps Copy D for the business' records.

Businesses in states with state income tax must prepare additional copies of Form W-2. The employee attaches the additional copy to the personal state income tax return.

Employer Annual Reporting of Payroll Taxes

Form W-3, Transmittal of Income and Tax Statements, is sent to the Social Security Administration by February 28 each year. Form W-3 reports the previous year's earnings and payroll taxes withheld for all employees. Attached to Form W-3 is Copy A of each employee Form W-2. A Form W-3 prepared by CarLand is shown in Illustration 15-9 on the next page.

Assess student understanding by checking solutions to Independent Practice activities.

Reteach

- Use Demonstration Problem 15A. This problem can be done on the overhead with the students completing the problem at their desks.

- Duplicate and assign Math Work Sheet Chapter 15, Part B: Calculating Employer Tax Liabilities from the Masters and Solutions to Enrichment/Application Activities Section in the Teacher's Resource Guide to provide additional practice on the mathematics of calculating employer tax liabilities.

- Assign Recycling Problem 15-R.

Extend

- Assign Challenge Problem 15-C (the challenge is that students must calculate liability amounts).

- Assign Reinforcement Activity 2, Part A.

Enrich

- Assign the Application Program Disk software to be used with Mastery Problem 15-M and Challenge Problem 15-C.

- Use Automated Accounting 6.0 or higher with Mastery Problem 15-M and Challenge Problem 15-C.

- Assign Electronic Study Guide Chapter 15.

- Assign the Stellar Attractions Pegboard Payroll Simulation.

- Use Audit Your Understanding questions.
- Review the steps for preparing Form 941.
- Review Summary Illustration 15-15, "Summary of Payroll Accounting, Taxes, and Reports." Use Transparency 15-2, Chapter Summary.

ILLUSTRATION 15-9   Form W-3, Transmittal of Income and Tax Statements

DO NOT STAPLE

1 Control number	33333	For Official Use Only ► OMB No. 1545-0008	

2 941/941E [X] Military 943 CT-1 942 Medicare govt. emp.	3 Employer's state I.D. number	5 Total number of statements

Kind of Payer ▶

4 | | 6

6 Establishment number	7 Allocated tips	8 Advance EIC payments

9 Federal income tax withheld 4,612.00	10 Wages, tips, and other compensation 60,153.00	11 Social security tax withheld 3,909.95
12 Social security wages 60,153.00	13 Social security tips	14 Medicare wages and tips 60,153.00
15 Medicare tax withheld 902.29	16 Nonqualified plans	17 Deferred compensation

18 Employer's identification number 31-0429632	19 Other EIN used this year
20 Employer's name CarLand	21 Dependent care benefits
1374 Parklane Rockville, RI 02873-4121	23 Adjusted total social security wages and tips 60,153.00
	24 Adjusted total Medicare wages and tips 60,153.00
	25 Income tax withheld by third-party payer

22 Employer's address and ZIP code (If available, place label over Boxes 18 and 20.)

Under penalties of perjury, I declare that I have examined this return and accompanying documents, and, to the best of my knowledge and belief, they are true, correct, and complete.

Signature ▶ *Amy Kramer*   Title ▶ *Partner*   Date ▶ *2/27/--*

Telephone number _(401) 555-9368_

Form **W-3 Transmittal of Income and Tax Statements 19--**   Department of the Treasury Internal Revenue Service

AUDIT YOUR UNDERSTANDING

1. Employers must pay 8% of each employee's total earnings up to the tax base.
2. Employers must pay 0.8% of total earnings of each employee up to a base of $7,000.00.

Audit Your Understanding

1. What is the FICA tax rate employers must pay on employees?

2. What is the federal unemployment tax rate employers must pay on employees?

At the end of a calendar year, employers must also report to the federal and state governments a summary of all earnings paid to employees during the twelve months.

Employers with more than 250 employees have different procedures for reporting withholding tax information. The information is sent to the Internal Revenue Service in computer files rather than the actual Forms W-2 and W-3.

PAYING WITHHOLDING AND PAYROLL TAXES

At least quarterly, employers must pay to the federal government the federal income taxes and FICA taxes withheld from employee salaries. The payment also includes the amount of employer FICA taxes.

TEACHING STRATEGIES: DIFFERENT LEARNING ABILITIES

Specific Learning Disability (SLD) Students.   Rotate instructional materials rather than trying to complete a single text. Supplemental instructional materials may include additional texts, business magazines, government publications, and so on.

Paying the Liability for Employee Income Tax and FICA Tax

Employee withheld income tax, employee FICA tax, and employer FICA tax are paid periodically in a combined payment. Tax payments are made to banks authorized by the Internal Revenue Service to accept these payments or to a Federal Reserve bank. The timing of these tax payments is based on the amount of taxes owed. A payment is accompanied by a Form 8109, Federal Tax Deposit Coupon, which shows the amount and purpose of the payment.

In December, CarLand withheld $402.00 from employee salaries for federal income taxes. The liability for FICA tax for December is $832.16. This amount includes both the employer share and the amounts withheld from employees. CarLand's federal tax payment is sent January 15 to an authorized bank with Form 8109 as shown in Illustration 15-10.

ILLUSTRATION 15-10 Form 8109, Federal Tax Deposit Coupon for withheld income tax and FICA taxes

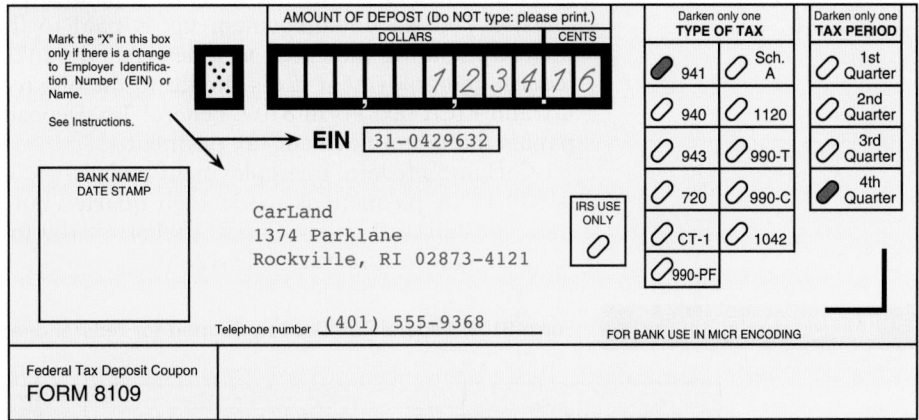

The type of tax, federal income and FICA taxes, is identified by marking the 941 circle. These taxes are reported to the government using Form 941. The calendar quarter is identified on the right side of the form.

Employee Income Tax Payable
402.00	

FICA Tax Payable
832.16	

Cash
	1,234.16

January 15, 19--. Paid cash for liability for employee income tax, $402.00, and for FICA tax, $832.16; total, $1,234.16. Check No. 305.

The balances of the liability accounts are reduced by this transaction. Therefore, Employee Income Tax Payable is debited for $402.00. FICA Tax Payable is debited for $832.16. The balance of the Cash account is decreased by a credit for the total payment, $1,234.16.

The journal entry to record payment of these liabilities is shown in Illustration 15-11 on the next page.

The date, *15,* is written in the Date column. The titles of the two accounts debited, *Employee Income Tax Payable* and *FICA Tax Payable,* are

TEACHING STRATEGIES: TEACHING TIP

It is important that transactions are always analyzed using T accounts. Students who establish the habit of analyzing transactions will have fewer problems understanding journalizing in future chapters. If working with the entire class, put the T accounts on the board and fill them in as students analyze a transaction. If working with an individual student, have that student put T accounts on a piece of paper. Avoid placing T accounts side by side on the board. Place T accounts one below another. With this stacked arrangement, students can more easily check the analysis to determine if debits equal credits for the transaction.

written in the Account Title column. The check number, *C305*, is entered in the Doc. No. column. The two debit amounts are entered in the General Debit column. The amount of the credit to Cash, *$1,234.16*, is recorded in the Cash Credit column.

ILLUSTRATION 15-11 Journal entry to record payment of liability for employee income tax and FICA tax

PAGE 27		JOURNAL							PAGE 27	
						1	2		10	11
DATE		ACCOUNT TITLE	DOC. NO.	POST. REF.	GENERAL				CASH	
					DEBIT	CREDIT			DEBIT	CREDIT
15		Employee Income Tax Payable	C305		4 0 2 00						25
		FICA Tax Payable			8 3 2 16					1 2 3 4 16	26
											27

Paying the Liability for Federal Unemployment Tax

Federal unemployment tax is usually paid after the end of each quarter. Federal unemployment tax is paid to the federal government by sending the check to a designated bank. The payment for federal unemployment tax is similar to the one required for income tax and FICA tax. Form 8109, Federal Tax Deposit Coupon, accompanies the unemployment tax payment.

CarLand's federal unemployment tax at the end of December 31 is $59.15. A payment is made each quarter but no report is due until the end of the year. CarLand's Form 8109 for the fourth quarter is shown in Illustration 15-12.

ILLUSTRATION 15-12 Form 8109, Federal Tax Deposit Coupon for federal unemployment tax

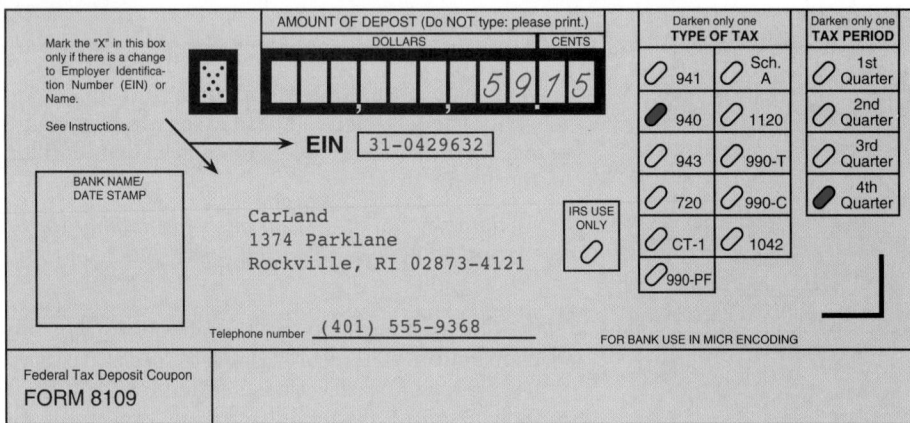

The type of tax, federal unemployment tax, is identified by marking the 940 circle since this tax is reported to the government using Form 940. The calendar quarter is identified on the right side of the form.

PART 3   Accounting for a Merchandising Business Organized as a Partnership

---

Unemployment Tax Payable—Federal

| 59.15 | |

Cash

| | 59.15 |

January 31, 19--. Paid cash for federal unemployment tax liability for quarter ended December 31, $59.15. Check No. 318.

The balance of the liability account is reduced by this transaction. Therefore, Unemployment Tax Payable—Federal is debited for $59.15. The balance of the asset account, Cash, is decreased by a credit for the payment, $59.15.

The journal entry to record payment of the liability for federal unemployment taxes is shown in Illustration 15-13.

The date, *31*, is written in the Date column. The title of the account debited, *Unemployment Tax Payable—Federal*, is written in the Account Title column. The check number, *C318*, is entered in the Doc. No. column. The check amount, *$59.15*, is entered in the General Debit and Cash Credit columns.

ILLUSTRATION 15-13

Journal entry to record payment of liability for federal unemployment tax

PAGE 28 — JOURNAL — PAGE 28

	DATE	ACCOUNT TITLE	DOC. NO.	POST. REF.	GENERAL DEBIT	GENERAL CREDIT	CASH DEBIT	CASH CREDIT	
27	31	Unemployment Tax Payable—Federal	C318		59 15			59 15	27
28									28

Paying the Liability for State Unemployment Tax

State requirements for reporting and paying state unemployment taxes vary. In general, employers are required to pay the state unemployment tax during the month following each calendar quarter.

Unemployment Tax Payable—State

| 399.26 | |

Cash

| | 399.26 |

January 31, 19--. Paid cash for state unemployment tax liability for quarter ended December 31, $399.26. Check No. 319.

The liability account is reduced by this transaction. Therefore, Unemployment Tax Payable—State is debited for $399.26. The balance of the asset account, Cash, is decreased by a credit, $399.26.

The journal entry to record payment of the liability for state unemployment tax is shown in Illustration 15-14.

ILLUSTRATION 15-14

Journal entry to record payment of liability for state unemployment tax

PAGE 28 — JOURNAL — PAGE 28

	DATE	ACCOUNT TITLE	DOC. NO.	POST. REF.	GENERAL DEBIT	GENERAL CREDIT	CASH DEBIT	CASH CREDIT	
28	31	Unemployment Tax Payable—State	C319		399 26			399 26	28

CHAPTER 15   Payroll Accounting, Taxes, and Reports   **367**

AUDIT YOUR UNDERSTANDING

1. Federal income tax and FICA taxes.
2. By January 31.
3. Federal income tax and FICA employee and employer taxes.

Audit Your Understanding

1. What taxes are included in the quarterly federal tax return filed by the employer?
2. When must employers furnish a W-2 statement to their employees?
3. What two taxes are paid to the government by the employer in one payment?

The date, *31*, is written in the Date column. The title of the account debited, *Unemployment Tax Payable—State*, is written in the Account Title column. The check number, *C319*, is entered in the Doc. No. column. The check amount, *$399.26*, is entered in the General Debit and Cash Credit columns.

The entries to journalize a payroll and payroll taxes are summarized in Illustration 15-15.

TEACHING STRATEGIES:
APPLYING VISUALS

Direct students to Summary Illustration 15-15 to review payroll journal entries.

SUMMARY ILLUSTRATION 15-15

Summary of payroll accounting, taxes, and reports

The payroll register provides the amounts required to journalize the payroll. Employer payroll taxes are calculated and recorded in the journal. Later, the employee and employer payroll taxes are paid to the federal and state governments.

ACCOUNT TITLE	GENERAL DEBIT (1)	GENERAL CREDIT (2)	CASH DEBIT (10)	CASH CREDIT (11)
Pay the Payroll:				
Salary Expense	X			X
Employee Income Tax Payable		X		
FICA Tax Payable		X		
Health Insurance Premiums Payable		X		
U.S. Savings Bonds Payable		X		
United Way Donations Payable		X		
Record Employer Payroll Taxes:				
Payroll Taxes Expense	X			
FICA Tax Payable		X		
Unemployment Tax Payable—Federal		X		
Unemployment Tax Payable—State		X		
Pay Employee and Employer Taxes:				
Employee Income Tax Payable	X			X
FICA Tax Payable	X			
Unemployment Tax Payable—Federal	X			X
Unemployment Tax Payable—State	X			X

Tax	Who Pays the Tax — Employee	Who Pays the Tax — Employer
Federal Income Tax	X	
FICA Tax	X	X
Federal Unemployment Tax		X
State Unemployment Tax		X

APPLIED SKILLS: WRITING ACROSS THE CURRICULUM

Writing paragraphs and short essays. The Cases for Critical Thinking are short, practical applications of the accounting principles developed in the chapter. Some cases are planned to present problems related to the chapter but not specifically discussed and answered in the chapter. These cases present an opportunity for critical thinking and decision making. These cases also require more than a short objective-type response. Therefore they provide ideal practice in writing paragraphs and short essays.

QUESTIONS FOR INDIVIDUAL STUDY

EPT(a)

1. Why does a business need to keep payroll information about individual employees?
2. What two business forms provide the payroll information needed about individual employees?
3. What accounts are affected, and how, by an entry to record a payroll?
4. Where is the amount obtained that is used to write a payroll check?
5. What are the three payroll taxes paid by most employers?
6. What is the only payroll tax paid by both the employee and the employer?
7. What amount is used to calculate federal unemployment tax?
8. When is the transaction to record employer payroll taxes expense journalized?
9. What accounts are affected, and how, by an entry to record employer payroll taxes?
10. Where is the information obtained that is needed to prepare a quarterly federal tax return, Form 941?
11. What amounts are used to calculate the tax liability for a pay period as reported on the quarterly federal tax return, Form 941?
12. What information is reported on a Form W-2, Wage and Tax Statement?
13. Who receives a completed Form W-2, Wage and Tax Statement?
14. What should an employee do with Copies B and C of Form W-2, Wage and Tax Statement, received from an employer?
15. What is the purpose of Form W-3, Transmittal of Income and Tax Statements?
16. What payroll taxes are deposited using Form 8109, Federal Tax Deposit Coupon?
17. What accounts are affected, and how, by an entry to record payment of an employer liability for federal unemployment tax?

CASES FOR CRITICAL THINKING

EPT(b)

CASE 1 The partners of Smith and Tyson have decided to hire a sales manager. They agree that the business can only afford to pay the manager a salary of $30,000.00. The accounting clerk informs the partners that hiring the manager will cost the business more than the $30,000.00 salary. Do you agree with the accounting clerk? Explain your response.

CASE 2 Miller Manufacturing had total salary expense for the month of November of $40,000.00. Sandra Peterson, accounting clerk, calculated the November employer FICA tax as $3,200.00 ($40,000.00 × 8%). Samuel Grissom, accountant, stated that the FICA taxes withheld from employee earnings were $2,850.00. What is the most likely reason for the difference between Ms. Peterson's and Mr. Grissom's calculations for FICA taxes? Explain.

DRILLS FOR UNDERSTANDING

EPT(b)

DRILL 15-D1 Analyzing payroll transactions

INSTRUCTIONS:

1. Prepare the following T accounts for four different businesses: Cash, Employee Income Tax Payable, FICA Tax Payable, Unemployment Tax Payable—Federal, Unemployment Tax Payable—State, Payroll Taxes Expense, and Salary Expense.

ACCOUNTING TERMS

No new terms are defined in Chapter 15.

QUESTIONS FOR INDIVIDUAL STUDY

1. To prepare a payroll and payroll tax reports. (p. 351)
2. The payroll register and employee earnings records. (p. 351)
3. Salary Expense is debited; Cash, Employee Income Tax Payable, FICA Tax Payable, Health Insurance Premiums Payable, U.S. Savings Bonds Payable, and United Way Donations Payable are credited. (pp. 351–352)
4. From the Net Pay column total of a payroll register. (p. 352)
5. Employer FICA tax, federal unemployment tax, and state unemployment tax. (p. 355)
6. FICA tax. (p. 355)
7. Unemployment taxable earnings. (pp. 355–356)
8. On the same date the payroll is journalized. (p. 357)
9. Payroll Taxes Expense is debited; FICA Tax Payable, Unemployment Tax Payable—Federal, and Unemployment Tax Payable—State are credited. (p. 357)
10. From employee earnings records. (p. 360)
11. Employee and employer FICA taxes, and employee federal income tax. (p. 362)
12. The total year's earnings and payroll taxes withheld for an employee. (p. 362)
13. Each employee receives a Form W-2. Copies are sent by the employee to state and federal governments. The employer sends a copy to the Social Security Administration. (p. 363)
14. Attach Copy B to a personal federal income tax return and keep Copy C for a personal record. (p. 363)
15. Form W-3 reports the earnings and taxes withheld for the previous year for all employees. (p. 363)
16. Federal income taxes, FICA taxes, and federal unemployment taxes. (pp. 365–366)
17. Unemployment Tax Payable—Federal is debited; Cash is credited. (p. 367)

CHECK FIGURES

See Teacher's Edition of Working Papers for complete solutions to drills and problems.

Drill 15-D1 For each business, dr. salary exp. for total earnings; dr. payroll taxes exp. for total of 3 employer taxes; cr. each tax; cr. cash.

Case 1 An employer must pay the employee salary and the employer payroll taxes. The employer must pay a FICA tax of 8% on the entire $30,000, federal unemployment tax of 0.8% on the first $7,000, and state unemployment tax of 5.4% on the first $7,000.00. The total cost of the sales manager is, therefore, $32,834.00 as follows: $30,000 × 8% = $2,400 FICA; $7,000 × 0.8% = $56 Federal Unemployment; $7,000 × 5.4% = $378 State Unemployment. $2,834 Total Taxes + $30,000 Salary = $32,834 Total Cost.

Case 2 FICA tax is figured as a percentage of an employee salary. However, the taxes apply only to a base amount for each employee. The tax base for FICA tax (as used in this textbook) is $55,500.00. FICA taxes are paid on the first $55,500.00 earned by each employee in a calendar year. FICA taxes are not paid on earnings above $55,500.00. A review of the payroll register shows that some employees had exceeded the $55,500.00 tax base. Earnings subject to FICA taxes are $35,625.00, resulting in FICA taxes of $2,850.00 ($35,625.00 x 8%). Ms. Peterson had multiplied the FICA tax rate by total earnings even though the entire earnings are not subject to the FICA tax.

Business	Total Earnings	Federal Income Tax Withheld	Employee FICA Tax	Employer FICA Tax	Federal Unemployment Tax	State Unemployment Tax
A	$ 9,000.00	$1,350.00	$ 720.00	$ 720.00	$ 72.00	$486.00
B	4,200.00	590.00	336.00	336.00	33.60	226.80
C	12,600.00	2,016.00	1,008.00	1,008.00	100.80	680.40
D	7,800.00	1,140.00	624.00	624.00	62.40	421.20

2. Use T accounts to analyze the following payroll entries for each business. (a) Entry to record payment of a payroll. (b) Entry to record employer payroll taxes.

DRILL 15-D2 Calculating employer payroll taxes

Payroll information taken from a payroll register and employee earnings records is given in the working papers accompanying this textbook.

INSTRUCTIONS:

1. Calculate the amount of earnings subject to unemployment taxes. Unemployment taxes are owed on the first $7,000.00 of earnings for each employee.
2. Calculate the amount of employer payroll taxes owed for the May 1–15 pay period. Employer payroll tax rates are as follows: FICA, 8%; federal unemployment, 0.8%; state unemployment, 5.4%.

APPLICATION PROBLEMS   EPT(b,c,d)

PROBLEM 15-1 Journalizing and posting payment of semimonthly payrolls

Lambert's payroll register has the following totals for two semimonthly pay periods, August 1–15 and August 16–31 of the current year.

Period	Total Earnings	Deductions				Net Pay
		Federal Income Tax	FICA Tax	Other	Total	
Aug. 1–15..........	$3,670.00	$514.00	$293.60	B $90.00	$897.60	$2,772.40
Aug. 16–31..........	$3,180.00	$437.00	$254.40	B $75.00	$766.40	$2,413.60

Other Deductions: B—U.S. Savings Bonds

INSTRUCTIONS:

1. Journalize payment of the two payrolls on page 17 of a journal. The first payroll was paid by Check No. 756 on August 15 of the current year. The second payroll was paid by Check No. 768 on August 31 of the current year.
2. Post the items that are to be posted individually. The balances in the general ledger as of August 1 of the current year are recorded in the accounts.

The general ledger accounts used in Problem 15-1 are needed to complete Problem 15-2.

PROBLEM 15-2 Calculating, journalizing, and posting employer payroll taxes

The general ledger accounts used in Problem 15-1 are needed to complete Problem 15-2.

Lambert's semimonthly payroll register totals are shown in Problem 15-1. Employer payroll tax rates are as follows: FICA, 8%; federal unemployment, 0.8%; state unemployment, 5.4%. Unemployment taxes are owed on the first $7,000.00 of earnings for each employee.

Information about accumulated earnings and total earnings for the August 1–15 pay period is given in the working papers accompanying this textbook.

INSTRUCTIONS:

1. Calculate the amount of earnings subject to unemployment taxes for the August 1–15 pay period.
2. Calculate the employer payroll tax amounts for the August 1–15 pay period.
3. Journalize the employer payroll taxes on page 18 of a journal. Use the date of August 15 of the current year. The source document is Memorandum No. 75.
4. Post the items that are to be posted individually.
5. Total earnings for the August 16–31 pay period are given in the working papers. Calculate the employer payroll taxes for the August 16–31 pay period. Calculate August 15 accumulated earnings by adding total earnings for the August 1–15 pay period to the July 31 accumulated earnings.
6. Journalize the employer payroll taxes on page 18 of a journal. Use the date of August 31 of the current year. The source document is Memorandum No. 82.
7. Post the items that are to be posted individually.

PROBLEM 15-3 Reporting employer quarterly withholding and payroll taxes

The following payroll data is for Jenson Clothing Company for the second quarter of the current year.

Date Paid	Total Earnings	Federal Income Tax Withheld	Employee FICA Tax Withheld
April 15	$2,825.00	$416.00	$226.00
April 30	2,987.00	438.00	238.96
May 15	3,142.00	468.00	251.36
May 31	2,936.00	428.00	234.88
June 15	3,212.00	489.00	256.96
June 30	2,849.00	422.00	227.92

Additional Data

1. Company address: 669 Eagle Street, Warrenville, IL 62325-4600
2. Employer identification number: 60-8909267
3. Number of employees: 5
4. Federal tax payments have been made on May 15, June 15, and July 15.

INSTRUCTIONS:

Prepare a Form 941, Employer's Quarterly Federal Tax Return, for Jenson Clothing Company. The return is for the second quarter of the current year. Use the date July 21. Sign your name as a partner of the company.

PROBLEM 15-4 Calculating and journalizing withholding and payroll taxes

The following payroll data is for Hawbecker Company for the first quarter of the current year.

Period	Total Earnings	Federal Income Tax Withheld
March	$12,537.00	$2,138.00
First Quarter	37,293.00	—

In addition, total earnings are subject to 8% employee and 8% employer FICA tax. The federal unemployment tax rate is 0.8% and the state unemployment tax rate is 5.4% of total earnings. No total earnings have exceeded the tax base for calculating unemployment taxes.

INSTRUCTIONS:

1. Calculate the appropriate liability amount of FICA tax for March. Journalize the payment of the federal income tax and FICA tax liabilities on page 7 of a journal. The taxes were paid by Check No. 785 on April 3 of the current year.

2. Calculate the appropriate federal unemployment tax liability for the first quarter. Journalize payment of this liability in the journal. The tax was paid by Check No. 802 on April 30 of the current year.

3. Calculate the appropriate state unemployment tax liability for the first quarter. Journalize payment of this liability in the journal. The tax was paid by Check No. 803 on April 30 of the current year.

ENRICHMENT PROBLEMS   EPT(b,c)

MASTERY PROBLEM 15-M   Journalizing and posting payroll transactions

AUTOMATED

APPLICATION

Star Equipment completed payroll transactions during the period April 1 to May 15 of the current year. Payroll tax rates are as follows: FICA, 8%; federal unemployment, 0.8%; state unemployment, 5.4%. The company buys savings bonds for employees as accumulated withholdings reach the necessary amount to purchase a bond. No total earnings have exceeded the tax base for calculating unemployment taxes.

The balances in the general ledger as of April 1 of the current year are recorded in the working papers accompanying this textbook.

CHART OF ACCOUNTS

Account Number	Account Title	Account Number	Account Title
1110	Cash	2150	Unemployment Tax Pay.—Fed.
1130	Accounts Receivable	2160	Unemployment Tax Pay.—St.
1140	Merchandise Inventory	2180	U.S. Savings Bonds Pay.
2110	Accounts Payable	3150	Income Summary
2120	Employee Income Tax Pay.	6150	Payroll Taxes Expense
2130	FICA Tax Payable	6170	Salary Expense

INSTRUCTIONS:

1. Journalize the following transactions on page 14 of a journal. Source documents are abbreviated as follows: check, C, and memorandum, M.

Apr. 15. Paid cash for liability for employee income tax, $945.00, and for FICA tax, $984.99; total, $1,929.99. C356.

15. Paid cash for semimonthly payroll, $2,463.52 (total payroll, $3,256.00, less deductions: employee income tax, $482.00; FICA tax, $260.48; U.S. Savings Bonds, $50.00). C357.

15. Recorded employer payroll taxes expense. M25.

15. Paid cash for U.S. Savings Bonds for employees, $250.00. C358.

30. Paid cash for semimonthly payroll, $2,527.36, (total payroll, $3,358.00, less deductions: employee income tax, $512.00; FICA tax, $268.64; U.S. Savings Bonds, $50.00). C376.

30. Recorded employer payroll taxes expense. M29.

30. Paid cash for federal unemployment tax liability for quarter ended March 31, $147.75. C377.

30. Paid cash for state unemployment tax liability for quarter ended March 31, $997.30. C378.

Posting. Post the items that are to be posted individually.

May 15. Paid cash for liability for employee income tax, $994.00, and for FICA tax, $1,058.24; total, $2,052.24. C405.

15. Paid cash for semimonthly payroll, $2,373.40 (total payroll, $3,145.00, less deductions: employee income tax, $470.00; FICA tax, $251.60; U.S. Savings Bonds, $50.00). C406.

372   PART 3   Accounting for a Merchandising Business Organized as a Partnership

SIMULATION

To give students an opportunity to apply payroll accounting concepts from the second accounting cycle, assign students Stellar Attractions Pegboard Payroll Simulation to demonstrate their understanding of payroll procedures.

May 15. Recorded employer payroll taxes expense. M36.

     Posting. Post the items that are to be posted individually.

2. Prove and rule the journal.

CHALLENGE PROBLEM 15-C Journalizing and posting payroll transactions

Danner Hardware completed payroll transactions during the period January 1 to April 30 of the current year. Payroll tax rates are as follows: FICA, 8%; federal unemployment, 0.8%; and state unemployment, 5.4%. The company buys savings bonds for employees as the accumulated withholdings reach the necessary amount to purchase a bond. No total earnings have exceeded the tax base for calculating unemployment taxes.

The balances in the general ledger as of January 1 of the current year are recorded in the working papers accompanying this textbook.

CHART OF ACCOUNTS

Account Number	Account Title	Account Number	Account Title
1110	Cash	2150	Unemployment Tax Pay.—Fed.
1130	Accounts Receivable	2160	Unemployment Tax Pay.—St.
1140	Merchandise Inventory	2180	U.S. Savings Bonds Pay.
2110	Accounts Payable	3150	Income Summary
2120	Employee Income Tax Pay.	6150	Payroll Taxes Expense
2130	FICA Tax Payable	6170	Salary Expense

INSTRUCTIONS:

1. Journalize the following transactions on page 1 of a journal. Source documents are abbreviated as follows: check, C, and memorandum, M.

Jan. 2. Wrote a check for 12 U.S. Savings Bonds at $25.00 each for employees. C143.
     15. Paid the December liability for employee income tax and for FICA tax. C152.
     31. Wrote a check for federal unemployment tax liability for quarter ended December 31. C158.
     31. Wrote a check for state unemployment tax liability for quarter ended December 31. C159.
     31. Paid January payroll, $6,283.04 (total payroll, $8,487.00, less deductions: employee income tax, $1,425.00; FICA tax, $678.96; U.S. Savings Bonds, $100.00). C164.
     31. Recorded employer payroll taxes expense. M95.
         Posting. Post the items that are to be posted individually.
Feb. 15. Wrote a check for January liability for employee income tax and for FICA tax. C170.
     28. Paid February payroll, $6,348.16 (total payroll, $8,598.00, less deductions: employee income tax, $1,462.00; FICA tax, $687.84; U.S. Savings Bonds, $100.00). C180.
     28. Recorded employer payroll taxes expense. M104.
         Posting. Post the items that are to be posted individually.
Mar. 15. Wrote a check for February liability for employee income tax and for FICA tax. C195.
     31. Paid March payroll, $6,660.76 (total payroll, $9,028.00, less deductions: employee income tax, $1,545.00; FICA tax, $722.24; U.S. Savings Bonds, $100.00). C206.
     31. Recorded employer payroll taxes expense. M113.
         Posting. Post the items that are to be posted individually.
Apr. 1. Paid cash for 12 U.S. Savings Bonds at $25.00 each for employees. C207.
     15. Wrote a check for March liability for employee income tax and for FICA tax. C218.
     30. Wrote a check for federal unemployment tax liability for quarter ended March 31. C224.
     30. Wrote a check for state unemployment tax liability for quarter ended March 31. C225.
         Posting. Post the items that are to be posted individually.

2. Prove and rule the journal.

Recording Payroll Transactions

CarLand's manual journalizing and posting procedures for payroll transactions are described in Chapter 15. Integrating Automated Accounting Topic 5 describes procedures for using automated accounting software to journalize and post CarLand's payroll transactions. The Automated Accounting Problems contain instructions for using automated accounting software to solve the April payroll transactions from Mastery Problem 15-M and Challenge Problem 15-C, Chapter 15.

SOFTWARE FOCUS

The Automated Accounting Problems in this Integrating Automated Accounting topic use Mastery Problem 15-M and Challenge Problem 15-C, Chapter 15, which students have already completed manually. Refer students back to these problems to complete the input forms. The problem instructions in *Automated Accounting 6.0* will lead students through automating these problems.

AUTOMATED PAYROLL ACCOUNTING PROCEDURES FOR CARLAND

CarLand uses two input forms to batch payroll transaction data for automated accounting.

1. Cash payments journal input form for all cash payments.
2. General journal input form for all other transactions.

Recording Payment of a Payroll

CarLand uses a cash payments journal input form to journalize payment of a payroll.

> *December 15, 19--. Paid cash for semimonthly payroll, $1,976.52 (total payroll, $2,556.00, less deductions: employee income tax, $192.00; FICA tax, $204.48; health insurance premiums, $158.00; U.S. Savings Bonds, $15.00; United Way donations, $10.00). Check No. 287.*

The journal entry to record this transaction is on lines 1 through 6 of the cash payments journal input form shown in Illustration T5-1.

Cash payments journal input form with payroll transactions recorded

RUN DATE *12,15,--*
MM DD YY

CASH PAYMENTS JOURNAL
Input Form

	DATE MM/DD	VENDOR NO.	CHECK NO.	ACCOUNTS PAY. DEBIT	ACCOUNT NO.	DEBIT	CREDIT	
1	12 15		C287		6170	2556 00		1
2	/				2120		192 00	2
3	/				2130		204 48	3
4	/				2170		158 00	4
5	/				2180		15 00	5
6	/				2190		10 00	6
25	/							25

NOTE: A credit to Cash is made automatically by the software.

The run date, *12/15/--*, is written in the space provided at the top of the form.

On line 1, the date of the transaction, *12/15*, is entered in the Date column. The source document number, *C287*, is recorded in the Check No. column. The general ledger account number for Salary Expense, *6170*, is written in the Account No. column. The debit amount, *$2,556.00*, is written in the Debit column.

On lines 2 through 6, the account numbers for the payroll liabilities are written in the Account No. column. The credit amounts

---

LESSON PLAN A5

Materials

- Student pages 375–380
- Transparency AA-2 Blank General Journal Input Form
- Transparency AA-4 Blank Cash Payments Input Form
- Input forms for Automating Problems 15-M and 15-C are provided in the working papers that accompany this textbook. If additional input forms are needed, blackline masters are provided in the Accounting Ruling Masters section of the Teacher's Resource Guide.
- Complete solutions for automated problems are provided in the Teacher's Resource Guide.
- Software: *Automated Accounting 6.0* or higher; Accounting Textbook Template, first-year course

Objective

Record payroll transactions using an automated accounting system.

OPTIONAL PROBLEM

The input forms illustrated in this topic can be keyed using *Automated Accounting 6.0*. Refer to the OPTIONAL PROBLEM at the end of the narrative for information about automating this topic.

TEACHING STRATEGIES: Using Visuals

Using Transparencies AA-2 Blank General Journal Input Form and AA-4 Blank Cash Payments Journal Input Form will help students understand the journalizing process.

TEACH

Cover student pages 375–380 "Automated Payroll Accounting Procedures for CarLand" and "Paying Withholding and Payroll Taxes." As the lesson progresses, review the definitions of pay period, payroll, payroll taxes, FICA taxes, federal unemployment tax, and state unemployment tax.

Use Transparency AA-4 to journalize each cash payment transaction and Transparency AA-2 to journalize the employer payroll taxes. It is important that students realize that the software automatically records the credit to Cash on a cash payments transaction.

Emphasize that payroll transactions are recorded along with other transactions throughout the fiscal period. Therefore, the dates selected in the Reports Selection window in the software would include the period desired for printing all transactions. For CarLand, the dates are 12/01/-- to 12/31/--.

are entered in the Credit column. The software automatically makes the credit to Cash, *$1,976.52*.

Recording Employer Payroll Taxes

CarLand journalizes employer payroll taxes on a general journal input form.

> *December 15, 19--. Recorded employer payroll taxes expense, $275.03, for the semimonthly pay period ended December 15. Taxes owed are: FICA tax, $204.48; federal unemployment tax, $9.10; state unemployment tax, $61.45. Memorandum No. 54.*

The journal entry to record this transaction is on lines 1 through 4 of the general journal input form shown in Illustration T5-2.

Each month's transactions begin on new input forms.

ILLUSTRATION T5-2

General journal input form with employer taxes recorded

RUN DATE 12,15,--		GENERAL JOURNAL			
MM DD YY		Input Form			

	DATE MM/DD	REFERENCE	ACCOUNT NO.	CUSTOMER/ VENDOR NO.	DEBIT	CREDIT	
1	12,15	M54	6150		275 03		1
2	/		2130			204 48	2
3	/		2150			9 10	3
4	/		2160			61 45	4
25	/						25
				PAGE TOTALS	275 03	275 03	
				FINAL TOTALS	275 03	275 03	

The run date, *12/15/--*, is written in the space provided at the top of the input form.

On line 1, the date of the transaction, *12/15*, is entered in the Date column. The source document number, *M54*, is recorded in the Reference column. The general ledger account number for Payroll Taxes Expense, *6150*, is written in the Account No. column. The debit amount, *$275.03*, is entered in the Debit column.

On lines 2 through 4, the account numbers for the payroll taxes are recorded in the Account No. column. The credit amounts are written in the Credit column.

After the employer payroll taxes transaction has been journalized, CarLand totals the Debit and Credit columns. The totals are recorded on the Page Totals and Final Totals lines provided at the bottom of the input form.

Processing a Payroll Payment and Employer Payroll Taxes

To process a cash payment, the Journals menu is selected from the menu bar. The Cash Payments Journal command is selected from

376

TEACHING STRATEGIES: DIFFERENT LEARNING ABILITIES

At-Risk Students. Teachers report that at-risk students are particularly successful when completing activities at the computer. Completing automated problems adds reality to the task at hand. Students can work at their own pace and experience immediate satisfaction. Encourage at-risk students to work at the computer as often as possible.

the Journals menu to display the data entry window for keying payroll data.

After the payroll payment has been keyed and posted, the Reports menu is selected from the menu bar. The Journals command is chosen to display the Report Selection window. The Cash Payments Journal is selected from the Report Selection window. As CarLand wants to print all transactions from 12/01/-- to 12/15/--, the *Ok* button is pushed to display the cash payments report. The report is checked for accuracy by comparing the report with the cash payments journal input form. The cash payments journal report is printed, as shown in Illustration T5-3, and filed for future reference.

APPLY

Guided Practice

Students should be at the computers. Guide students through booting the software and loading Optional Problem DB-5A from the template. Instruct students to journalize each transaction as you go step-by-step through the procedures.

Independent Practice

Assign Automating Problem 15-M. Explain that the May transactions for paying withholding and payroll taxes from Mastery Problem 15-M are not included with Automating Problem 15-M. The procedures for recording and processing these cash payments are the same as the cash payment procedures described for paying the payroll. If you would like to assign these transactions as an optional assignment, distribute input forms for students to journalize the transactions. Each month's transactions should begin on new input forms.

ILLUSTRATION T5-3   Cash payments journal report with a payroll payment recorded

```
                            CarLand
                    Cash Payments Journal
                          12/15/--
---------------------------------------------------------------------------
Date   Refer.   V/C Acct.  Title                    Debit       Credit
---------------------------------------------------------------------------
12/15  C287          6170  Salary Expense          2556.00
12/15  C287          2120  Employee Income Tax Pay.              192.00
12/15  C287          2130  FICA Tax Payable                      204.48
12/15  C287          2170  Health Ins. Premiums Pay.             158.00
12/15  C287          2180  U.S. Savings Bonds Pay.                15.00
12/15  C287          2190  United Way Donations Pay.              10.00
12/15  C287          1110  Cash                                 1976.52

                                             ----------  ----------
              Totals                           2556.00     2556.00
                                             ==========  ==========
```

To process general journal entries, the Journals menu is selected from the menu bar. The General Journal command is chosen from the Journals menu to display the data entry window for keying transaction data.

After all lines on the input form have been keyed and posted, the general journal report is displayed. The same steps are followed as for displaying the cash payments journal report. However, the General Journal is selected from the Report Selection window. The report is checked for accuracy by comparing the report totals, *$275.03*, with the totals on the general journal input form. Because the totals are the same, the general journal report is assumed to be correct. The general journal report is printed, as shown in Illustration T5-4, and is filed for future reference.

PAYING WITHHOLDING AND PAYROLL TAXES

CarLand journalizes the payment of withholding and payroll taxes on a cash payments journal input form.

Assess student understanding by checking solutions to Automating Problem
15-M.

Reteach

Give students blank cash payments and
general journal input forms. Read the
transactions in the text and have students journalize each.

Extend

Assign Automating Problem 15-C.
Explain that the February transactions
for paying withholding and payroll taxes
from Challenge Problem 15-C are not
included with Automating Problem 15-C.
The procedures for recording and processing these cash payments are the
same as the cash payment procedures
described for paying the payroll. If you
would like to assign these transactions
as an optional assignment, distribute
input forms for students to journalize
the transactions. Each month's transactions should begin on new input forms.

Enrich

Ask the students if their payroll check or
their parents' payroll check is generated
using an automated payroll system. Discuss some of the pros and cons of a
company's using an automated payroll
system.

ILLUSTRATION T5-4   General journal report with employer payroll taxes recorded

```
                              CarLand
                          General Journal
                             12/15/--
-----------------------------------------------------------------------
Date   Refer.   V/C Acct.   Title                      Debit    Credit
-----------------------------------------------------------------------
12/15  M54          6150    Payroll Taxes Expense      275.03
12/15  M54          2130    FICA Tax Payable                    204.48
12/15  M54          2150    Unemployment Tax Pay--Fed             9.10
12/15  M54          2160    Unemployment Tax Pay--St.            61.45

                                                     ---------- ----------
                            Totals                     275.03    275.03
                                                     ========== ==========
```

Recording Payment of Employee Income Tax and FICA Tax

January 15, 19--. Paid cash for liability for employee income tax, $402.00, and for FICA tax, $832.16; total, $1,234.16. Check No. 305.

The journal entry to record this transaction is on lines 1 and 2 of the cash payments journal input form shown in Illustration T5-5.

ILLUSTRATION T5-5   Cash payments journal input form with withholding and payroll taxes recorded

RUN DATE *01/31/--*   CASH PAYMENTS JOURNAL
MM DD YY   Input Form

	DATE MM/DD	VENDOR NO.	CHECK NO.	ACCOUNTS PAY. DEBIT	ACCOUNT NO.	DEBIT	CREDIT	
1	01 15		C305		2120	402 00		1
2	/				2130	832 16		2
3	31		C318		2150	59 15		3
4	31		C319		2160	399 26		4
25	/							25

NOTE: A credit to Cash is made automatically by the software.

![FYI]
For the purpose of this illustration, check numbers 306–317 have been omitted.

Paying the Liability for Federal Unemployment Tax

January 31, 19--. Paid cash for federal unemployment tax liability for quarter ended December 31, $59.15. Check No. 318.

The journal entry to record this transaction is on line 3 of Illustration T5-5.

TEACHING STRATEGIES: COOPERATIVE LEARNING

Using automated accounting software to complete accounting problems is an ideal cooperative learning
experience. Students working in groups can collaborate on completing input forms and keying data.

Paying the Liability for State Unemployment Tax

January 31, 19--. Paid cash for state unemployment tax liability for quarter ended December 31, $399.26. Check No. 319.

The journal entry to record this transaction is on line 4 of Illustration T5-5.

Processing the Payment of Withholding and Payroll Taxes

To process the cash payment for withholding and payroll taxes, the transaction data are keyed from the cash payments journal input form. After all lines have been keyed and posted, a cash payments report is displayed. The displayed cash payments report is checked for accuracy by comparing the report with the cash payments journal input form. After accuracy has been verified, the cash payments report is printed, as shown in Illustration T5-6, and is filed for future reference.

ILLUSTRATION T5-6

Cash payments journal report with withholding and payroll taxes recorded

```
                         CarLand
                    Cash Payments Journal
                        01/31/--
-----------------------------------------------------------------------
Date   Refer.  V/C Acct.  Title                    Debit      Credit
-----------------------------------------------------------------------
01/15  C305        2120   Employee Income Tax Pay.  402.00
01/15  C305        2130   FICA Tax Payable          832.16
01/15  C305        1110   Cash                                 1234.16

01/31  C318        2150   Unemployment Tax Pay--Fed  59.15
01/31  C318        1110   Cash                                   59.15

01/31  C319        2160   Unemployment Tax Pay--St. 399.26
01/31  C319        1110   Cash                                  399.26

                                                    ---------  ---------
                          Totals                    1692.57    1692.57
                                                    =========  =========
```

OPTIONAL PROBLEM DB-5A

CarLand's general ledger data base is on the accounting textbook template. If you wish to process CarLand's December payroll transactions using automated accounting software, load the *Automated Accounting 6.0* or higher software. Select Data Base 5A (DB-5A) from the template disk. Read the Problem Instructions screen. Using the completed cash payments and general journal input forms, Illustrations T5-1, T5-2, and T5-5, follow the procedures described to process CarLand's payroll transactions.

AUTOMATED

AUTOMATED ACCOUNTING PROBLEMS

AUTOMATING MASTERY PROBLEM 15-M Journalizing and posting payroll transactions

INSTRUCTIONS:

1. Journalize transactions for the month of April *only* from Mastery Problem 15-M, Chapter 15, on the appropriate input forms. Use April 30 of the current year as the run date.
2. Load the *Automated Accounting 6.0* or higher software. Select data base F15-M (First-Year Course Problem 15-M) from the accounting textbook template. Read the Problem Instructions screen.
3. Select File from the menu bar and choose the Save As menu command. Key the path to the drive and directory that contains your data files. Save the data base with a file name of XXX15M (where XXX are your initials).
4. Key the data from the completed cash payments journal input form.
5. Display/print the cash payments journal report.
6. Key the data from the completed general journal input form.
7. Display/print the general journal report.

AUTOMATED

AUTOMATING CHALLENGE PROBLEM 15-C Journalizing and posting payroll transactions

INSTRUCTIONS:

1. Journalize transactions for the month of January *only* from Challenge Problem 15-C, on the appropriate input forms. Use January 31 of the current year as the run date.
2. Load the *Automated Accounting 6.0* or higher software. Select data base F15-C from the accounting textbook template. Read the Problem Instructions screen.
3. Select File from the menu bar and choose the Save As menu command. Key the path to the drive and directory that contains your data files. Save the data base with a file name of XXX15C (where XXX are your initials).
4. Key the data from the completed cash payments journal input form.
5. Display/print the cash payments journal report.
6. Key the data from the completed general journal input form.
7. Display/print the general journal report.

An Accounting Cycle for a Partnership: Journalizing and Posting Transactions

AUTOMATED

Reinforcement Activity 2 reinforces learnings from Part 3, Chapters 11 through 18. Activities cover a complete accounting cycle for a merchandising business organized as a partnership. Reinforcement Activity 2 is a single problem divided into two parts. Part A includes learnings from Chapters 11 through 15. Part B includes learnings from Chapters 16 through 18.

The accounting work of a single merchandising business for the last month of a yearly fiscal period is used in this reinforcement activity. The records kept and reports prepared, however, illustrate the application of accounting concepts for all merchandising businesses.

TEACHING STRATEGIES:
REINFORCEMENT ACTIVITY

Reinforcement Activity 2 begins with Part A and continues with Part B after Chapter 18. Reinforcement Activity 2 presents the whole accounting cycle for a merchandising business organized as a partnership. You may prefer to have your students begin Part A at the end of Chapter 15 and continue with Part B later. Or you may reserve Part A to be completed with Part B after Chapter 18. Blackline masters for audit tests for Reinforcement Activity 2 are available in the Teacher's Resource Guide in three options: Part A only, Part B only, and Parts A and B combined. In addition, *Automated Accounting 6.0* or higher can be used to automate Reinforcement Activity 2.

CLEARVIEW OPTICAL

Tara Bruski and James Myler, partners, own and operate ClearView Optical, a merchandising business. The business sells a complete line of fashion, sun, and sport eyewear. ClearView is located in a downtown shopping area and is open for business Monday through Saturday. A monthly rent is paid for the building and fixtures. ClearView accepts credit cards from customers.

CHART OF ACCOUNTS

ClearView Optical uses the chart of accounts shown on the next page.

JOURNAL AND LEDGERS

The journal and ledgers used by ClearView Optical are listed in the following chart. Models of the journal and ledgers are shown in the textbook illustrations given in the chart.

Journal and Ledgers	Chapter	Illustration Number
Expanded journal	12	12-5
Accounts payable ledger	13	13-10
Accounts receivable ledger	13	13-15
General ledger	16	16-1

381

SOFTWARE FOCUS

Automated Accounting 6.0 can be used to complete Reinforcement Activity 2 using the computer.

CLEARVIEW OPTICAL
CHART OF ACCOUNTS

Balance Sheet Accounts

(1000) ASSETS
1110 Cash
1120 Petty Cash
1130 Accounts Receivable
1140 Merchandise Inventory
1145 Supplies—Office
1150 Supplies—Store
1160 Prepaid Insurance

(2000) LIABILITIES
2110 Accounts Payable
2120 Employee Income Tax Payable
2130 FICA Tax Payable
2140 Sales Tax Payable
2150 Unemployment Tax Payable—Federal
2160 Unemployment Tax Payable—State
2170 Health Insurance Premiums Payable
2180 U.S. Savings Bonds Payable
2190 United Way Donations Payable

(3000) OWNERS' EQUITY
3110 Tara Bruski, Capital
3120 Tara Bruski, Drawing
3130 James Myler, Capital
3140 James Myler, Drawing
3150 Income Summary

Income Statement Accounts

(4000) OPERATING REVENUE
4110 Sales

(5000) COST OF MERCHANDISE
5110 Purchases

(6000) OPERATING EXPENSES
6110 Advertising Expense
6120 Credit Card Fee Expense
6130 Insurance Expense
6140 Miscellaneous Expense
6150 Payroll Taxes Expense
6160 Rent Expense
6170 Salary Expense
6175 Supplies Expense—Office
6180 Supplies Expense—Store
6190 Utilities Expense

SUBSIDIARY LEDGERS

Accounts Receivable Ledger

110 Theresa Abbey
120 Nancy Bonner
130 Jonathan Doran
140 Irma Iznaga
150 Brian Patco
160 Norman Witte

Accounts Payable Ledger

210 A & B Optical Co.
220 Central Office Supply
230 Kosh Optical Lab
240 Optical Imports
250 Trend Optics Co.
260 Weaver Supply

TEACHING STRATEGIES:
ASSESSMENT BY PORTFOLIO

If you assign Reinforcement Activity 2, Part A and intend to use it as part of an assessment by portfolio evaluation, advise students that their work on this activity will be included in their portfolio.

RECORDING TRANSACTIONS

The December 1 account balances for the general and subsidiary ledgers are given in the working papers accompanying this textbook.

INSTRUCTIONS:

1. Journalize the following transactions on page 23 of a journal. A 6% sales tax has been added to each sale. Source documents are abbreviated as follows: check, C; memorandum, M; purchase invoice, P; receipt, R; sales invoice, S; cash register tape, T.

Dec. 1. Paid cash for rent, $1,000.00. C272.

1. Tara Bruski, partner, withdrew cash for personal use, $1,200.00. C273.

1. James Myler, partner, withdrew cash for personal use, $1,200.00. C274.

2. Paid cash for electric bill, $288.50. C275.

2. Received cash on account from Nancy Bonner, $344.50, covering S64. R82.

3. Paid cash for miscellaneous expense, $60.00. C276.

3. Paid cash on account to Trend Optics Co., $483.80, covering P73. C277.

4. Sold merchandise on account to Theresa Abbey, $375.00, plus sales tax, $22.50; total, $397.50. S67.

5. Recorded cash and credit card sales, $4,830.00, plus sales tax, $289.80; total, $5,119.80. T5.

    Posting. Post the items that are to be posted individually.

7. Sold merchandise on account to Jonathan Doran, $385.00, plus sales tax, $23.10; total, $408.10. S68.

7. Received cash on account from Norman Witte, $360.40, covering S65. R83.

8. Bought office supplies on account from Central Office Supply, $293.00. M43.

9. Purchased merchandise on account from Optical Imports, $1,125.00. P77.

9. Bought store supplies on account from Weaver Supply, $275.00. M44.

10. Tara Bruski, partner, withdrew merchandise for personal use, $250.00. M45.

10. Paid cash for office supplies, $145.00. C278.

10. Discovered that a payment of cash for advertising in November was journalized and posted in error as a debit to Miscellaneous Expense instead of Advertising Expense, $125.00. M46.

11. Paid cash on account to Kosh Optical Lab, $975.80, covering P74. C279.

11. Purchased merchandise on account from Trend Optics Co., $860.00. P78.

12. Paid cash for store supplies, $220.00. C280.

12. Recorded cash and credit card sales, $5,940.00, plus sales tax, $356.40; total, $6,296.40. T12.

    Posting. Post the items that are to be posted individually.

14. James Myler, partner, withdrew merchandise for personal use, $325.00. M47.

14. Purchased merchandise on account from Kosh Optical Lab, $2,730.00. P79.

14. Sold merchandise on account to Brian Patco, $140.00, plus sales tax, $8.40; total, $148.40. S69.

14. Paid cash for advertising, $345.00. C281.

15. Paid cash on account to A & B Optical Co., $1,060.40, covering P75. C282.

15. Received cash on account from Irma Iznaga, $683.70, covering S66. R84.

15. Sold merchandise on account to Nancy Bonner, $410.00, plus sales tax, $24.60; total, $434.60. S70.

    Posting. Post the items that are to be posted individually.

2. Prove and rule page 23 of the journal.

3. Carry the column totals forward to page 24 of the journal.

4. Journalize the following transactions on page 24 of the journal.

Dec. 15. Paid cash for semimonthly payroll, $1,751.80 (total payroll, $2,315.00, less deductions: employee income tax, $181.00; FICA tax, $185.20; health insurance, $142.00; U.S. Savings Bonds, $25.00; United Way donations, $30.00). C283.

Dec. 15. Recorded employer payroll taxes, $250.30, for the semimonthly pay period ended December 15. Taxes owed are: FICA tax, $185.20; federal unemployment tax, $8.40; and state unemployment tax, $56.70. M48.

19. Recorded cash and credit card sales, $5,760.00, plus sales tax, $345.60; total, $6,105.60. T19.

23. Paid cash on account to Optical Imports, $1,840.00, covering P76. C284.

26. Recorded cash and credit card sales, $5,820.00, plus sales tax, $349.20; total, $6,169.20. T26.

Posting. Post the items that are to be posted individually.

ClearView Optical's bank charges a fee for handling the collection of credit card sales deposited during the month. The credit card fee is deducted from ClearView Optical's bank account. The amount is then shown on the bank statement. The credit card fee is recorded in the journal as a reduction in cash.

Dec. 28. Recorded credit card fee expense, $285.20. M49. (Debit Credit Card Fee Expense; credit Cash.)

30. Purchased merchandise on account from A & B Optical Co., $1,620.00. P80.

31. Paid cash to replenish the petty cash fund, $304.00: office supplies, $62.00; store supplies, $59.00; advertising, $87.00; miscellaneous, $96.00. C285.

31. Paid cash for semimonthly payroll, $1,882.00 (total payroll, $2,460.00, less deductions: employee income tax, $184.20; FICA tax, $196.80; health insurance, $142.00; U.S. Savings Bonds, $25.00; United Way donations, $30.00). C286.

31. Recorded employer payroll taxes, $263.92, for the semimonthly pay period ended December 31. Taxes owed are: FICA tax, $196.80; federal unemployment tax, $8.66; and state unemployment tax, $58.46. M50.

31. Received bank statement showing December bank service charge, $4.50. M51.

31. Recorded cash and credit card sales, $3,240.00, plus sales tax, $194.40; total, $3,434.40. T31.

Posting. Post the items that are to be posted individually.

5. Total page 24 of the journal. Prove the equality of debits and credits.

6. Prove cash. The balance on the next unused check stub was $34,918.00.

7. Rule the journal.

8. Post the totals of the special columns of the journal.

9. Prepare a schedule of accounts payable and a schedule of accounts receivable. Prove the accuracy of the subsidiary ledgers by comparing the schedule totals with the balances of the controlling accounts in the general ledger. If the totals are not the same, find and correct the errors.

The ledgers used in Reinforcement Activity 2, Part A, are needed to complete Reinforcement Activity 2, Part B.

Stellar Attractions Pegboard Payroll System provides experience in preparing records using a pegboard and no-carbon-required forms. When data are entered on the statement of earnings and deductions stub on the check, the employee earnings record and the payroll register are simultaneously prepared. Posting is eliminated. The following activities are included in the accounting cycle for Stellar Attractions. This business simulation is available from the publisher.

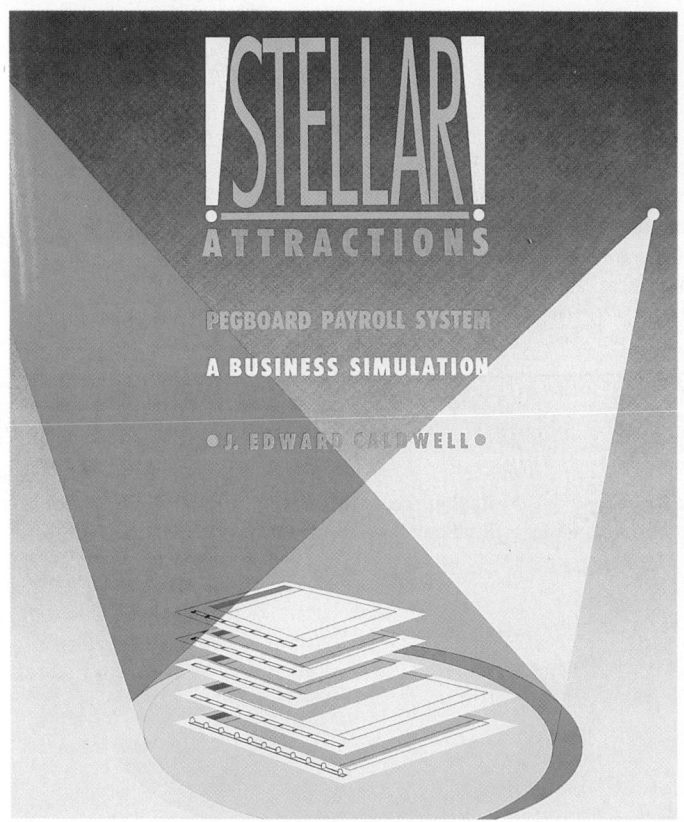

!STELLAR!
ATTRACTIONS

PEGBOARD PAYROLL SYSTEM

A BUSINESS SIMULATION

● J. EDWARD CALDWELL ●

Activities in Stellar Attractions:

1. Preparing necessary forms for new employees.

2. Completing time cards by entering summary data.

3. Assembling forms on a pegboard: checks with earnings and deductions stubs, employee earnings records, and payroll register. All records are completed with one writing.

4. Recording time card summary data on the statement of earnings and deductions stubs of checks on the pegboard.

5. Determining appropriate deductions using tax tables and figuring net pay.

6. Recording deductions and net pay on the statement of earnings and deductions stubs.

7. Totaling, proving, ruling, and filing the payroll register. Filing employee earnings records.

8. Separating, writing, and signing payroll checks.

9. Totaling and proving employee earnings records for the end of the quarter and year to date.

10. Preparing quarterly and annual reports.

Chapter 16 presents an 8-column work sheet for a merchandising business. This is the same work sheet covered in Chapter 8 in the first accounting cycle. However, this work sheet is expanded to cover the accounts and adjustments needed by a merchandising business. The adjustment for prepaid insurance and supplies are reviewed, and the supplies adjustment is expanded to include adjustments for two different kinds of supplies accounts. Then the merchandise inventory adjustment is presented. This new adjustment is shown to use exactly the same analysis process as the adjustments previously studied.

GUIDE TO ACHIEVING LEARNING OBJECTIVES

Enabling Performance Tasks	TEACH Lesson Plans	APPLY Drills for Understanding	APPLY Application Problems	EXTEND/ENRICH Mastery Problems	EXTEND/ENRICH Challenge Problems	EXTEND/ENRICH Cases for Critical Thinking	EXTEND/ENRICH Recycling Problems	EXTEND/ENRICH Reinforcement Activity	
a. Define accounting terms related to a work sheet for a merchandising business.	16-1								
b. Identify accounting concepts and practices related to a work sheet for a merchandising business.	16-1, 16-2, 16-3								
c. Plan adjustments on a work sheet for a merchandising business.	16-1, 16-3	16-D1	16-1, 16-2	16-M	16-C	Cases 1, 2	16-R	2B	
d. Complete a work sheet for a merchandising business.	16-2, 16-3	16-D2	16-1, 16-2	16-M	16-C		16-R	2B	

ENRICHMENT

SPECIAL FEATURES

Multicultural Awareness, page 393

Personal Visions in Business, page 403

TECHNOLOGY CONNECTION

Accounting Tutorial Unit 5

Application Program Disk Problem 16-M

Electronic Study Guide

NEW, REVIEW, AND EXTENSION

ACTIVITIES/CONCEPTS/TRANSACTIONS	NEW	REVIEW/ EXTENSION
Completing an 8-column work sheet for a merchandising business		✓
Merchandise inventory adjustment	✓	
Supplies adjustments		✓
Prepaid insurance adjustment		✓
Completing a 10-column work sheet	✓	

A 10-column work sheet is also illustrated as another type of work sheet that is used by some large merchandising businesses with many accounts to be adjusted and is used in the challenge problem. A 10-column work sheet may also be used for any problem in this chapter by duplicating the master form from the Teacher's Resource Guide.

	INFORMAL ASSESSMENT		FORMAL ASSESSMENT					
	Study Guide	Audit Your Understanding	Chapter MicroExam	Chapter Problem Test	Unit Problem Test	Unit Objective Test	Portfolio
		✓	✓			✓	
		✓	✓			✓	
Unit A				✓	✓		✓
Unit B				✓	✓		✓

TEACHING MATERIALS

Teacher's Wraparound Edition of the Text

Teacher's Resource Guide

Teacher's Edition of Working Papers

Teacher's Edition of Demonstration/Recycling Problems

Teaching Transparencies

Accounting Tutorial Manual

MicroExam

Applied Math Work Sheet

APPLIED MATHEMATICS

APPLIED MATH/ACCOUNTING SKILL	APPLICATION
Calculating net income	Drill 16-D2

Work Sheet for a Merchandising Business

ENABLING PERFORMANCE TASKS

After studying Chapter 16, you will be able to:

a Define accounting terms related to a work sheet for a merchandising business.

b Identify accounting concepts and practices related to a work sheet for a merchandising business.

c Plan adjustments on a work sheet for a merchandising business.

d Complete a work sheet for a merchandising business.

TERMS PREVIEW

inventory • merchandise inventory

386

Management decisions about future business operations are often based on financial information. Financial information shows whether a profit is being made or a loss is being incurred. Profit or loss information helps an owner or manager determine future changes. Financial information is also needed to prepare required tax reports. A business summarizes financial information at least once each fiscal period. CarLand uses a one-year fiscal period that begins on January 1 and ends on December 31. Therefore, CarLand summarizes its financial information on December 31 of each year.

GENERAL LEDGER WITH POSTING COMPLETED

CarLand's completed general ledger on December 31, after all transactions have been posted, is shown in Illustration 16-1, pages 388 through 393. No entries have been posted in the following accounts: Income Summary, Insurance Expense, Supplies Expense—Office, and Supplies Expense—Store. Transactions during the year did not affect these accounts.

AN 8-COLUMN WORK SHEET FOR A MERCHANDISING BUSINESS

A columnar accounting form on which the financial information needed to prepare financial statements is summarized is known as a work sheet. A work sheet is used to plan adjustments and sort financial statement information. A work sheet may be prepared whenever a business wishes to summarize and report financial information. A work sheet is always prepared at the end of each fiscal period because financial statements are prepared at the end of each fiscal period. (CONCEPT: Accounting Period Cycle) CarLand prepares a work sheet and financial statements annually.

Work sheets for service and merchandising businesses are similar. CarLand's work sheet is similar to the one used by Rugcare described in Chapter 8. CarLand's work sheet, however, also includes accounts for accounts receivable, merchandise inventory, accounts payable, sales tax, and purchases.

RECORDING A TRIAL BALANCE ON A WORK SHEET

To prove the equality of debits and credits in the general ledger, a trial balance is prepared. CarLand prepares a trial balance in the Trial Balance columns of a work sheet. CarLand's trial balance on December 31 is shown in Illustration 16-2, page 394.

CHAPTER 16   Work Sheet for a Merchandising Business   **387**

LESSON PLAN 16-1

Materials

- Student pages 387–399
- Transparency: C, Blank 8-Column Work Sheet
- Software: Accounting Tutorial, Unit 5
- Demonstration Problem: 16A, Analyzing Adjusting Entries

Objectives (Enabling Performance Tasks)

a. Define accounting terms related to a work sheet for a merchandising business.

b. Identify accounting concepts and practices related to a work sheet for a merchandising business.

c. Plan adjustments on a work sheet for a merchandising business.

FOCUS

- In the first cycle of the text, an 8-column work sheet was prepared for a service business organized as a proprietorship. The work sheet summarizes and reports financial information for the fiscal period. In this lesson, we will record a trial balance and plan adjustments on an 8-column work sheet for a merchandising business organized as a partnership.
- Introduce new vocabulary: inventory, merchandise inventory.

TEACHING STRATEGIES: TEACHING TIP

Review the definition of work sheet. A columnar accounting form used to summarize the general ledger information needed to prepare financial statements is called a work sheet.

Cover student pages 387–399 "General Ledger with Posting Completed," "An 8-Column Work Sheet for a Merchandising Business," "Recording a Trial Balance on a Work Sheet," and "Planning Adjustments on a Work Sheet." As the lesson progresses, review the definition and the purpose of a work sheet, adjustments, and adjusting entries. Establish the routine of asking the four questions to analyze adjustments. (1) What is the balance of the account being analyzed? (2) What should the balance be for this account? (3) What must be done to correct the account balance? (4) What adjustment is made?

Throughout the lesson emphasize: (1) that when the trial balance is recorded on a work sheet, all accounts must be listed whether they have a balance or not, (2) that the adjustment for supplies is the amount of supplies used, (3) that the balance in each account changes as a result of the adjustment—the new correct balance will be used for financial statements; (4) that the adjustment for prepaid insurance is the amount of insurance used or expired, and (5) Merchandise Inventory reflects the correct amount of ending inventory after the adjustment.

ILLUSTRATION 16-1   General ledger with posting completed

388   PART 3   Accounting for a Merchandising Business Organized as a Partnership

ILLUSTRATION 16-1

General ledger with posting completed (continued)

APPLY

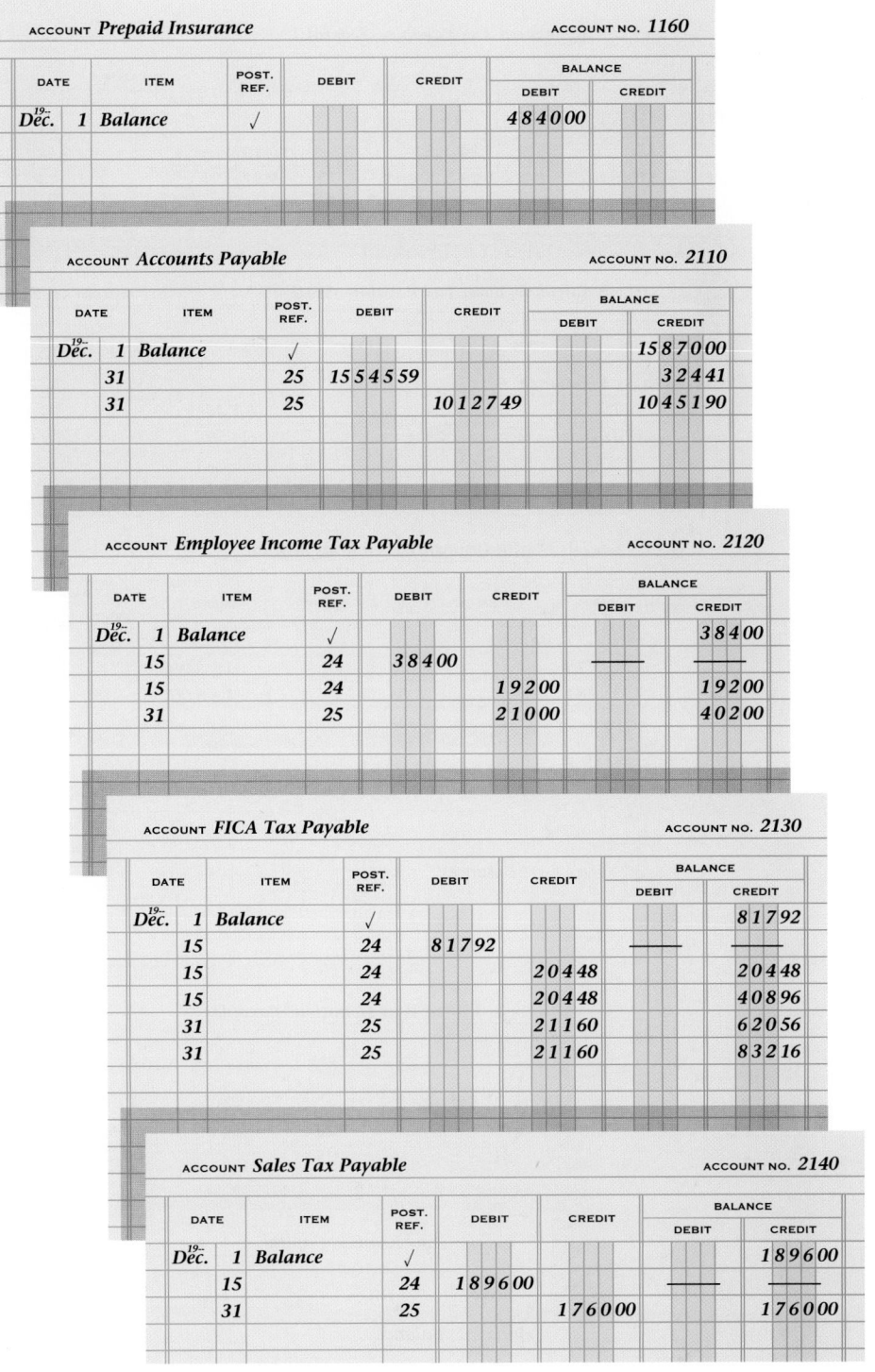

ACCOUNT *Prepaid Insurance*   ACCOUNT NO. *1160*

DATE	ITEM	POST. REF.	DEBIT	CREDIT	BALANCE DEBIT	BALANCE CREDIT
Dec. 1	Balance	✓			4 84 0 00	

ACCOUNT *Accounts Payable*   ACCOUNT NO. *2110*

DATE	ITEM	POST. REF.	DEBIT	CREDIT	BALANCE DEBIT	BALANCE CREDIT
Dec. 1	Balance	✓				15 8 7 0 00
31		25	15 5 4 5 59			3 24 41
31		25		10 1 27 49		10 4 51 90

ACCOUNT *Employee Income Tax Payable*   ACCOUNT NO. *2120*

DATE	ITEM	POST. REF.	DEBIT	CREDIT	BALANCE DEBIT	BALANCE CREDIT
Dec. 1	Balance	✓				3 84 00
15		24	3 84 00		—	—
15		24		1 92 00		1 92 00
31		25		2 10 00		4 02 00

ACCOUNT *FICA Tax Payable*   ACCOUNT NO. *2130*

DATE	ITEM	POST. REF.	DEBIT	CREDIT	BALANCE DEBIT	BALANCE CREDIT
Dec. 1	Balance	✓				8 17 92
15		24	8 17 92		—	—
15		24		2 04 48		2 04 48
15		24		2 04 48		4 08 96
31		25		2 11 60		6 20 56
31		25		2 11 60		8 32 16

ACCOUNT *Sales Tax Payable*   ACCOUNT NO. *2140*

DATE	ITEM	POST. REF.	DEBIT	CREDIT	BALANCE DEBIT	BALANCE CREDIT
Dec. 1	Balance	✓				1 89 6 00
15		24	1 89 6 00		—	—
31		25		1 76 0 00		1 76 0 00

Draw T accounts on the board for Merchandise Inventory, Income Summary, Supplies, Supplies Expense, Prepaid Insurance, and Insurance Expense. As the adjustments are presented, ask the four questions to analyze the adjustment. Record the adjustments in the T accounts. Use Transparency C to review the columns of the work sheet and to record the adjustments on the work sheet.

Guided Practice

Guide students through Drill 16-D1, Business A. Students should have the forms from the working papers to complete as you guide them through the drill. For each adjustment, ask the students the accounts affected and the amount of the adjustment. All students should agree with the analysis before proceeding to the next adjustment. Adjustments for Businesses B and C can be done as Independent Practice.

Independent Practice

Assign Terms 1–2, Questions 1–14, and Drill 16-D1, Businesses B and C.

CHAPTER 16   Work Sheet for a Merchandising Business   **389**

TEACHING STRATEGIES: WORK SHEET OVERLAY

Frequently refer to the work sheet overlay that appears in Chapter 8. This is an excellent step-by-step instructional method to review making adjustments and completing the work sheet.

ILLUSTRATION 16-1   General ledger with posting completed (continued)

Assess student understanding by checking solutions to Independent Practice activities.

Reteach

• Use Demonstration Problem 16A. This problem can be done on the overhead with the students completing the problem at their desks.

• Use Unit 5 of the Accounting Tutorial to reteach analyzing adjusting entries. Students may work at the computer at their own pace.

Extend

Assign Cases for Critical Thinking 1 and 2.

Enrich

Assign students to read the MULTICULTURAL AWARENESS feature on page 393. Discuss with them how an understanding and appreciation of history and other cultures contributes to understanding civilization today.

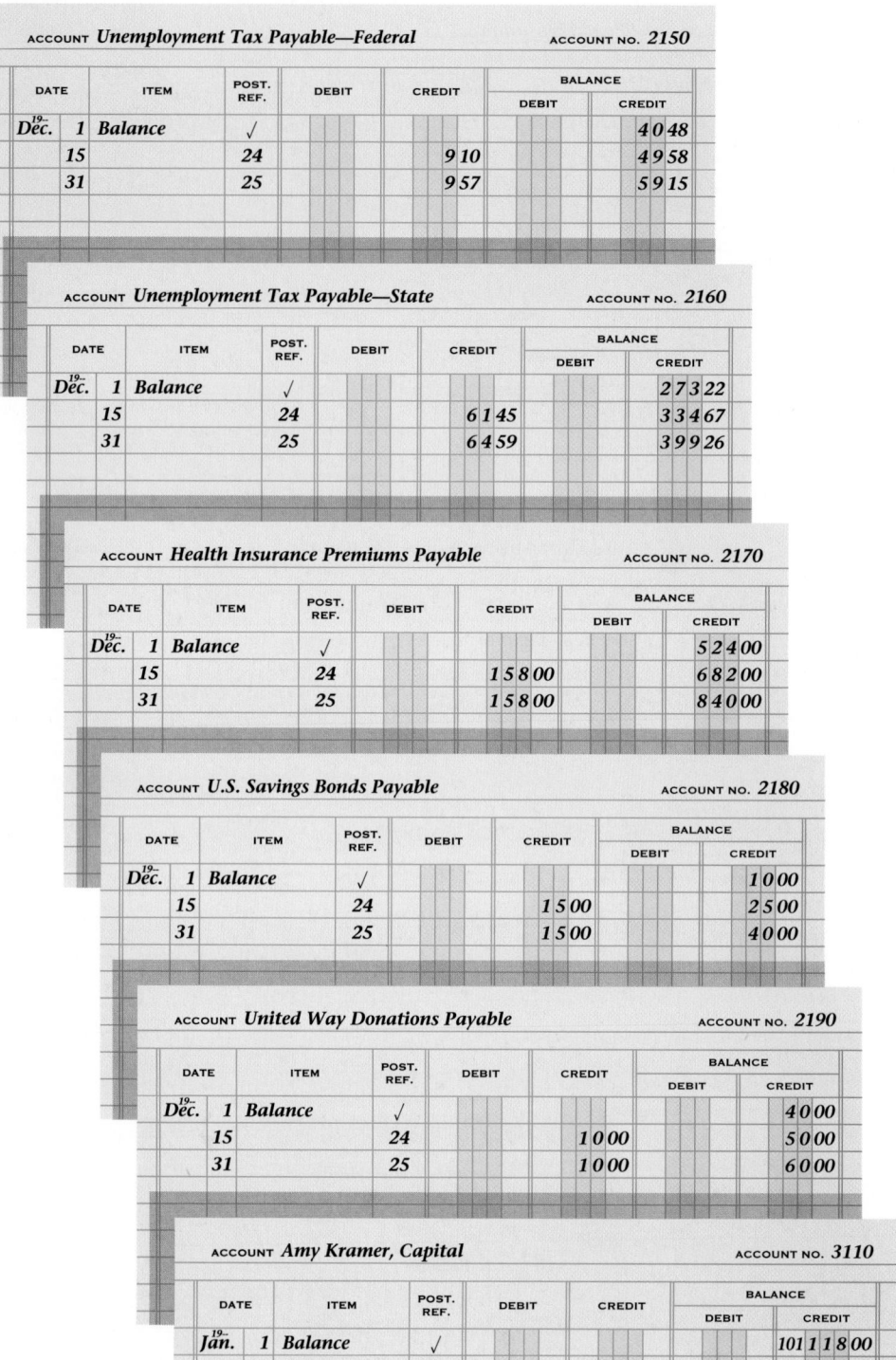

ACCOUNT *Unemployment Tax Payable—Federal* — **ACCOUNT NO.** *2150*

DATE		ITEM	POST. REF.	DEBIT	CREDIT	BALANCE DEBIT	BALANCE CREDIT
Dec. 19--	1	Balance	✓				40 48
	15		24		9 10		49 58
	31		25		9 57		59 15

ACCOUNT *Unemployment Tax Payable—State* — **ACCOUNT NO.** *2160*

DATE		ITEM	POST. REF.	DEBIT	CREDIT	BALANCE DEBIT	BALANCE CREDIT
Dec. 19--	1	Balance	✓				273 22
	15		24		61 45		334 67
	31		25		64 59		399 26

ACCOUNT *Health Insurance Premiums Payable* — **ACCOUNT NO.** *2170*

DATE		ITEM	POST. REF.	DEBIT	CREDIT	BALANCE DEBIT	BALANCE CREDIT
Dec. 19--	1	Balance	✓				524 00
	15		24		158 00		682 00
	31		25		158 00		840 00

ACCOUNT *U.S. Savings Bonds Payable* — **ACCOUNT NO.** *2180*

DATE		ITEM	POST. REF.	DEBIT	CREDIT	BALANCE DEBIT	BALANCE CREDIT
Dec. 19--	1	Balance	✓				10 00
	15		24		15 00		25 00
	31		25		15 00		40 00

ACCOUNT *United Way Donations Payable* — **ACCOUNT NO.** *2190*

DATE		ITEM	POST. REF.	DEBIT	CREDIT	BALANCE DEBIT	BALANCE CREDIT
Dec. 19--	1	Balance	✓				40 00
	15		24		10 00		50 00
	31		25		10 00		60 00

ACCOUNT *Amy Kramer, Capital* — **ACCOUNT NO.** *3110*

DATE		ITEM	POST. REF.	DEBIT	CREDIT	BALANCE DEBIT	BALANCE CREDIT
Jan. 19--	1	Balance	✓				101 118 00

PART 3   Accounting for a Merchandising Business Organized as a Partnership

TEACHING STRATEGIES: EXPANDING BEYOND THE CLASSROOM

Invite an auditor to talk about the importance of the accuracy of the data on the work sheet.

ILLUSTRATION 16-1   General ledger with posting completed (continued)

ACCOUNT *Amy Kramer, Drawing*   ACCOUNT NO. *3120*

DATE		ITEM	POST. REF.	DEBIT	CREDIT	BALANCE	
						DEBIT	CREDIT
Dec.¹⁹⁻	1	Balance	√			16 7 0 0 00	
	15		24	1 5 0 0 00		18 2 0 0 00	

ACCOUNT *Dario Mesa, Capital*   ACCOUNT NO. *3130*

DATE		ITEM	POST. REF.	DEBIT	CREDIT	BALANCE	
						DEBIT	CREDIT
Jan.¹⁹⁻	1	Balance	√				101 2 2 8 00

ACCOUNT *Dario Mesa, Drawing*   ACCOUNT NO. *3140*

DATE		ITEM	POST. REF.	DEBIT	CREDIT	BALANCE	
						DEBIT	CREDIT
Dec.¹⁹⁻	1	Balance	√			17 1 0 0 00	
	15		24	1 5 0 0 00		18 6 0 0 00	

ACCOUNT *Income Summary*   ACCOUNT NO. *3150*

DATE	ITEM	POST. REF.	DEBIT	CREDIT	BALANCE	
					DEBIT	CREDIT

ACCOUNT *Sales*   ACCOUNT NO. *4110*

DATE		ITEM	POST. REF.	DEBIT	CREDIT	BALANCE	
						DEBIT	CREDIT
Dec.¹⁹⁻	1	Balance	√				323 2 6 6 00
	31		25		29 3 3 4 00		352 6 0 0 00

ACCOUNT *Purchases*   ACCOUNT NO. *5110*

DATE		ITEM	POST. REF.	DEBIT	CREDIT	BALANCE	
						DEBIT	CREDIT
Dec.¹⁹⁻	1	Balance	√			148 1 7 2 51	
	31		25	10 1 2 7 49		158 3 0 0 00	

ACCOUNT *Advertising Expense*   ACCOUNT NO. *6110*

DATE		ITEM	POST. REF.	DEBIT	CREDIT	BALANCE	
						DEBIT	CREDIT
Dec.¹⁹⁻	1	Balance	√			4 8 6 0 00	
	4		24	1 6 5 00		5 0 2 5 00	
	16		25	8 3 00		5 1 0 8 00	
	22		25	3 9 2 00		5 5 0 0 00	

TEACHING STRATEGIES: COOPERATIVE LEARNING

Divide the class into groups of four or five students each. Using Cases for Critical Thinking, each group analyzes the cases and arrives at agreed-upon solutions. One member of each group is appointed the recorder and presents the group's analysis to the class. This cooperative learning activity should not take more than 20 to 25 minutes of class time.

ILLUSTRATION 16-1   General ledger with posting completed (continued)

ACCOUNT **Credit Card Fee Expense**   ACCOUNT NO. **6120**

DATE		ITEM	POST. REF.	DEBIT	CREDIT	BALANCE DEBIT	BALANCE CREDIT
Dec.¹⁹⁻	1	Balance	✓			2 1 7 5 00	
	28		25	7 1 5 00		2 8 9 0 00	

ACCOUNT **Insurance Expense**   ACCOUNT NO. **6130**

DATE	ITEM	POST. REF.	DEBIT	CREDIT	BALANCE DEBIT	BALANCE CREDIT

ACCOUNT **Miscellaneous Expense**   ACCOUNT NO. **6140**

DATE		ITEM	POST. REF.	DEBIT	CREDIT	BALANCE DEBIT	BALANCE CREDIT
Dec.¹⁹⁻	1	Balance	✓			1 7 3 2 15	
	9		24	3 9 00		1 7 7 1 15	
	17		25	1 6 3 00		1 9 3 4 15	
	22		25	1 0 6 00		2 0 4 0 15	
	31		25	1 4 2 00		2 1 8 2 15	

ACCOUNT **Payroll Taxes Expense**   ACCOUNT NO. **6150**

DATE		ITEM	POST. REF.	DEBIT	CREDIT	BALANCE DEBIT	BALANCE CREDIT
Dec.¹⁹⁻	1	Balance	✓			6 7 3 8 96	
	15		24	2 7 5 03		7 0 1 3 99	
	31		25	2 8 5 76		7 2 9 9 75	

ACCOUNT **Rent Expense**   ACCOUNT NO. **6160**

DATE		ITEM	POST. REF.	DEBIT	CREDIT	BALANCE DEBIT	BALANCE CREDIT
Dec.¹⁹⁻	1	Balance	✓			16 5 0 0 00	
	1		24	1 5 0 0 00		18 0 0 0 00	

ACCOUNT **Salary Expense**   ACCOUNT NO. **6170**

DATE		ITEM	POST. REF.	DEBIT	CREDIT	BALANCE DEBIT	BALANCE CREDIT
Dec.¹⁹⁻	1	Balance	✓			54 9 5 2 00	
	15		24	2 5 5 6 00		57 5 0 8 00	
	31		25	2 6 4 5 00		60 1 5 3 00	

ILLUSTRATION 16-1   General ledger with posting completed (concluded)

General ledger accounts are listed in the work sheet's Account Title column in the same order in which they appear in the general ledger. All accounts are listed regardless of whether there is a balance or not. Listing all accounts reduces the possibility of overlooking an account that needs to be brought up to date.

PLANNING ADJUSTMENTS ON A WORK SHEET

After posting is completed at the end of a fiscal period, some general ledger accounts, such as the two supplies accounts and the prepaid insurance account, are not up to date. Adjustments for supplies and prepaid insurance are described in Chapter 8. In addition to supplies and prepaid insurance, CarLand needs to adjust the merchandise inventory account. Changes recorded on a work sheet to update general ledger accounts at the end of a fiscal period are known as adjustments.

Adjustments are planned in the Adjustments columns of a work sheet. Adjustments recorded on a work sheet are for planning purposes only. The general ledger account balances are not changed until entries are journalized and posted. Journal entries made to bring general ledger accounts up to date are known as adjusting entries.

Merchandise Inventory Adjustment

The amount of goods on hand is called an **inventory**. The amount of goods on hand for sale to customers is called **merchandise inventory**. The general ledger account in which merchandise inventory is

ILLUSTRATION 16-2 Trial balance on a work sheet

CarLand
Work Sheet
For Year Ended December 31, 19--

	ACCOUNT TITLE	TRIAL BALANCE DEBIT	TRIAL BALANCE CREDIT
1	Cash	24 2 3 3 57	
2	Petty Cash	5 0 0 00	
3	Accounts Receivable	9 3 3 2 00	
4	Merchandise Inventory	225 4 0 0 00	
5	Supplies—Office	5 4 0 0 00	
6	Supplies—Store	5 7 8 0 00	
7	Prepaid Insurance	4 8 4 0 00	
8	Accounts Payable		10 4 5 1 90
9	Employee Income Tax Payable		4 0 2 00
10	FICA Tax Payable		8 3 2 16
11	Sales Tax Payable		1 7 6 0 00
12	Unemploy. Tax Payable—Federal		5 9 15
13	Unemploy. Tax Payable—State		3 9 9 26
14	Health Insurance Premiums Payable		8 4 0 00
15	U.S. Savings Bonds Payable		4 0 00
16	United Way Donations Payable		6 0 00
17	Amy Kramer, Capital		101 1 1 8 00
18	Amy Kramer, Drawing	18 2 0 0 00	
19	Dario Mesa, Capital		101 2 2 8 00
20	Dario Mesa, Drawing	18 6 0 0 00	
21	Income Summary		
22	Sales		352 6 0 0 00
23	Purchases	158 3 0 0 00	
24	Advertising Expense	5 5 0 0 00	
25	Credit Card Fee Expense	2 8 9 0 00	
26	Insurance Expense		
27	Miscellaneous Expense	2 1 8 2 15	
28	Payroll Taxes Expense	7 2 9 9 75	
29	Rent Expense	18 0 0 0 00	
30	Salary Expense	60 1 5 3 00	
31	Supplies Expense—Office		
32	Supplies Expense—Store		
33	Utilities Expense	3 1 8 0 00	
34		569 7 9 0 47	569 7 9 0 47
35			

recorded is titled *Merchandise Inventory*. Merchandise Inventory is an asset account with a normal debit balance, as shown in the T account.

Analyzing a Merchandise Inventory Adjustment. CarLand's merchandise inventory account on January 1, the beginning of the fiscal year, has a debit balance of $225,400.00, as shown in the T account.

Merchandise Inventory

Debit side Normal balance Increase	Credit side Decrease

Merchandise Inventory	
Jan. 1 Bal.	225,400.00

The balance of the merchandise inventory account on December 31, the end of the fiscal year, is the same amount, $225,400.00. The January 1 and December 31 balances are the same because no entries have been made in the account during the fiscal year. The changes in inventory resulting from purchases and sales transactions have not been recorded in the merchandise inventory account.

During a fiscal period, the amount of merchandise on hand increases each time merchandise is purchased. However, all purchases are recorded in the purchases account. The amount of merchandise on hand decreases each time merchandise is sold. However, all sales are recorded in the sales account. This procedure makes it easier to quickly determine the total purchases and sales during a fiscal period. The merchandise inventory account balance, therefore, must be adjusted to reflect the changes resulting from purchases and sales during a fiscal period.

FYI

When preparing a trial balance, all accounts must be listed whether they have a balance or not.

The two accounts used to adjust the merchandise inventory are Merchandise Inventory and Income Summary. The T accounts show the merchandise inventory and income summary accounts before the merchandise inventory adjustment is made.

Before the adjustment, the merchandise inventory account has a January 1 debit balance of $225,400.00. The merchandise inventory account balance, however, is not up to date. The actual count of merchandise on December 31 shows that the inventory is valued at $212,200.00. Therefore, the merchandise inventory account balance must be adjusted to show the current value of merchandise on hand.

Most accounts needing adjustment at the end of a fiscal period have a related temporary account. For example, when the account Supplies is adjusted, Supplies Expense is the related expense account, a temporary account. Merchandise Inventory, however, does not have a related expense account. Therefore, Income Summary, a temporary account, is used to adjust the merchandise inventory account at the end of a fiscal period.

Four questions are asked in analyzing the adjustment for merchandise inventory.

BEFORE ADJUSTMENT

Income Summary	

Merchandise Inventory	
Jan. 1 Bal.	225,400.00

FYI

When an account that requires adjusting does not have a related expense account, the temporary account Income Summary is used.

1. What is the balance of Merchandise Inventory?... $225,400.00
2. What should the balance be for this account? .. $212,200.00
3. What must be done to correct the account
   balance? Decrease .... $ 13,200.00
4. What adjustment is made?
   Debit Income Summary .... $ 13,200.00
   Credit Merchandise Inventory................ $ 13,200.00

AFTER ADJUSTMENT

Income Summary	
Adj. (a)	13,200.00

Merchandise Inventory			
Jan. 1 Bal.	225,400.00	Adj. (a)	13,200.00
(New Bal.	212,200.00)		

The merchandise inventory adjustment is shown in the T accounts.

Income Summary is debited and Merchandise Inventory is credited for $13,200.00. The beginning debit balance of Merchandise Inventory, $225,400.00, *minus* the adjustment credit amount, $13,200.00, *equals* the ending debit balance of Merchandise Inventory, $212,200.00.

Recording a Merchandise Inventory Adjustment on a Work Sheet.
The merchandise inventory adjustment is shown on lines 4 and 21 in the work sheet's Adjustments columns in Illustration 16-3.

ILLUSTRATION 16-3 Merchandise inventory adjustment on a work sheet

		1	2	3	4
	ACCOUNT TITLE	TRIAL BALANCE		ADJUSTMENTS	
		DEBIT	CREDIT	DEBIT	CREDIT
4	*Merchandise Inventory*	225 4 0 0 00		**3**	(a)13 2 0 0 00
21	*Income Summary*			(a)13 2 0 0 00	
22				**1**	**2**

Three steps are used to record CarLand's adjustment for merchandise inventory on a work sheet.

1 Write the debit amount, *$13,200.00,* in the Adjustments Debit column on the line with the account title Income Summary (line 21).

2 Write the credit amount, *$13,200.00,* in the Adjustments Credit column on the line with the account title Merchandise Inventory (line 4).

3 Label the two parts of this adjustment with the small letter a in parentheses, *(a).*

AFTER ADJUSTMENT

Merchandise Inventory

Jan. 1 Bal.	245,600.00	
Adj. (a)	5,200.00	
(New Bal.	250,800.00)	

Income Summary

		Adj. (a)	5,200.00

If the amount of merchandise inventory on hand is greater than the balance of Merchandise Inventory, opposite entries would be made—debit Merchandise Inventory and credit Income Summary. For example, Kobrin Company's merchandise inventory account on January 1 has a debit balance of $245,600.00. The count of merchandise on December 31 shows that the inventory is valued at $250,800.00. The merchandise on hand is $5,200.00 *greater* than the balance of Merchandise Inventory. This merchandise inventory adjustment is shown in the T accounts.

Merchandise Inventory is debited and Income Summary is credited for $5,200.00.

Supplies Adjustments

CarLand uses office and store supplies in the daily operation of the business. The amount of supplies *not used* during a fiscal period represents an asset. The amount of supplies used during a fiscal period represents an expense. Accurate financial reporting includes recording expenses in the fiscal period in which the expenses contribute to earning revenue. *(CONCEPT: Matching Expenses with Revenue)*

PART 3   Accounting for a Merchandising Business Organized as a Partnership

Supplies—Office

Dec. 31 Bal.	5,400.00

Analyzing an Office Supplies Inventory Adjustment. CarLand's office supplies account on December 31, the end of the fiscal period, has a debit balance of $5,400.00, as shown in the T account.

The account balance for Supplies—Office, $5,400.00, includes two items. (1) The account balance on January 1. (2) The cost of office supplies bought during the year. The account balance does not reflect the value of any office supplies *used* during the year (an expense). Therefore, the office supplies account balance must be adjusted to show the value of office supplies on hand on December 31. The amount of supplies on hand on December 31 is determined by counting the supplies on hand and calculating the value.

The two accounts used to adjust office supplies are Supplies—Office and Supplies Expense—Office. The T accounts show the two accounts before the adjustment is made.

Before the adjustment, the office supplies account has a December 31 debit balance of $5,400.00. However, office supplies have been used throughout the fiscal period. These changes in office supplies were not recorded in the office supplies account. Therefore, the office supplies account balance is not up to date. The actual count of office supplies on December 31 shows that the value of the office supplies inventory is $1,460.00. The office supplies account balance must be adjusted to show the current value of the office supplies inventory.

Four questions are asked in analyzing the adjustment for office supplies inventory.

FYI

The adjustment for supplies is the amount of supplies used.

TEACHING STRATEGIES:
DIFFERENT LEARNING ABILITIES

At-Risk Students. Together with the student, develop an individualized program that allows the student to attain both short-term and long-term goals. When identifying goals, consider the student's anticipated career goals.

BEFORE ADJUSTMENT
Supplies Expense—Office

Supplies—Office

Dec. 31 Bal.	5,400.00

1. What is the balance of Supplies—Office? $5,400.00
2. What should the balance be for this account? $1,460.00
3. What must be done to correct the account
   balance? Decrease $3,940.00
4. What adjustment is made?
   Debit Supplies Expense—Office. $3,940.00
   Credit Supplies—Office $3,940.00

AFTER ADJUSTMENT
Supplies Expense—Office

Adj. (b)	3,940.00

Supplies—Office

Dec. 31 Bal.	5,400.00	Adj. (b)	3,940.00
(New Bal.	*1,460.00)*		

The office supplies inventory adjustment is shown in the T accounts.

Supplies Expense—Office is debited and Supplies—Office is credited for $3,940.00. The beginning debit balance of Supplies—Office, $5,400.00, *minus* the adjustment credit amount, $3,940.00, *equals* the ending debit balance of Supplies—Office, $1,460.00.

Recording Supplies Inventory Adjustments on a Work Sheet. CarLand makes a similar adjustment for store supplies. The steps in recording the *two* supplies inventory adjustments are the same as those described for Rugcare in Chapter 8. The *two* supplies inventory adjustments are shown in the Adjustments columns of the work sheet in Illustration 16-4 on page 398. The adjustment for Supplies—Office is labeled *(b)* and is shown on lines 5 and 31. The adjustment for Supplies—Store is labeled *(c)* and is shown on lines 6 and 32.

CHAPTER 16   Work Sheet for a Merchandising Business   **397**

TEACHING STRATEGIES: WRITING ACROSS THE CURRICULUM

Writing paragraphs and short essays. The Cases for Critical Thinking are short, practical applications of the accounting principles developed in the chapter. Some cases are planned to present problems related to the chapter but not specifically discussed and answered in the chapter. These cases present an opportunity for critical thinking and decision making. These cases also require more than a short objective-type response. Therefore they provide ideal practice in writing paragraphs and short essays.

ILLUSTRATION 16-4   Supplies inventory adjustments on a work sheet

		1	2	3	4
	ACCOUNT TITLE	TRIAL BALANCE		ADJUSTMENTS	
		DEBIT	CREDIT	DEBIT	CREDIT
5	Supplies—Office	5 4 0 0 00			(b) 3 9 4 0 00
6	Supplies—Store	5 7 8 0 00			(c) 3 2 6 0 00
31	Supplies Expense—Office			(b) 3 9 4 0 00	
32	Supplies Expense—Store			(c) 3 2 6 0 00	
33					
34					

Prepaid Insurance Adjustment

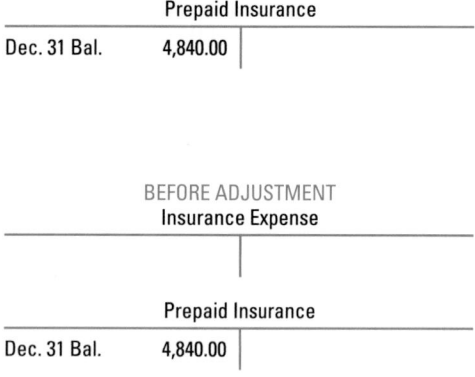

FYI

The adjustment for prepaid insurance is the amount of insurance used or expired.

Payment for insurance protection is paid in advance. The value of prepaid insurance *not expired* during a fiscal period is an asset. The value of prepaid insurance *expired* during a fiscal period is an expense.

Analyzing a Prepaid Insurance Adjustment. Car-Land's prepaid insurance account on December 31, the end of the fiscal period, has a debit balance of $4,840.00, as shown in the T account.

The account balance for Prepaid Insurance, $4,840.00, includes two items. (1) The account balance on January 1. (2) The cost of insurance premiums paid during the year. The account balance does not reflect the value of the insurance expired during the year (an expense). Therefore, the prepaid insurance account balance must be adjusted to bring the balance up to date. (CONCEPT: *Matching Expenses with Revenue*)

The two accounts used to adjust the prepaid insurance account are Prepaid Insurance and Insurance Expense. The T accounts show the two accounts before the adjustment is made.

Before the adjustment, the prepaid insurance account has a December 31 debit balance of $4,840.00. The account balance, however, is not up to date. The value of the prepaid insurance *not expired* is determined to be $2,200.00. The prepaid insurance account balance must be adjusted to show its current value.

Four questions are asked in analyzing the adjustment for prepaid insurance.

1. What is the balance of Prepaid Insurance?.............$4,840.00
2. What should the balance be for this account?.....$2,200.00
3. What must be done to correct the account
   balance? Decrease $2,640.00
4. What adjustment is made?
   Debit Insurance Expense.......................................$2,640.00
   Credit Prepaid Insurance.......................................$2,640.00

Prepaid Insurance

Dec. 31 Bal.   4,840.00

BEFORE ADJUSTMENT
Insurance Expense

Prepaid Insurance

Dec. 31 Bal.   4,840.00

Audit Your Understanding

1. What is a work sheet?
2. Why is a trial balance prepared?
3. What account must a merchandising business adjust that a service business does not?
4. What accounts are used for the adjustment for merchandise inventory?

AFTER ADJUSTMENT
Insurance Expense

Adj. (d)	2,640.00

Prepaid Insurance

Dec. 31 Bal.	4,840.00	Adj. (d)	2,640.00
(New Bal.	*2,200.00)*		

The prepaid insurance adjustment is shown in the T accounts.

Insurance Expense is debited and **Prepaid Insurance** is credited for $2,640.00. The beginning debit balance of Prepaid Insurance, $4,840.00, *minus* the adjustment credit amount, $2,640.00, *equals* the ending debit balance of Prepaid Insurance, $2,200.00.

Recording a Prepaid Insurance Adjustment on a Work Sheet. The steps in recording the prepaid insurance adjustment on a work sheet are the same as those followed by Rugcare in Chapter 8. The adjustment for Prepaid Insurance is labeled *(d)* and is shown in the Adjustments columns on lines 7 and 26 of the work sheet in Illustration 16-5.

ILLUSTRATION 16-5 Prepaid insurance adjustment on a work sheet

		1	2	3	4
	ACCOUNT TITLE	TRIAL BALANCE		ADJUSTMENTS	
		DEBIT	CREDIT	DEBIT	CREDIT
7	*Prepaid Insurance*	4 8 4 0 00			(d) 2 6 4 0 00
26	*Insurance Expense*			(d) 2 6 4 0 00	
27					
28					
29					

AUDIT YOUR UNDERSTANDING

1. Income Statement Debit or Credit column.
2. When the Income Statement Debit column total (costs and expenses) is larger than the Credit column total (revenue).
3. Balance Sheet Debit column.

COMPLETING A WORK SHEET

CarLand follows the same procedures for completing a work sheet as described for Rugcare in Chapter 8 with the exception of the income summary account. Rugcare sells a service, not merchandise. Therefore, Rugcare has no amount recorded in the income summary account, a related account used to adjust Merchandise Inventory. CarLand sells merchandise. Therefore, the income summary account is used as the related account to adjust Merchandise Inventory. The merchandise inventory adjustment reflects the increases and decreases in the amount of goods on hand resulting from sales and purchases. Therefore, the amount recorded in Income Summary is extended to the work sheet's Income Statement Debit or Credit column. An Income Summary debit amount is extended to the Income Statement Debit column. An Income Summary credit amount is extended to the Income Statement Credit column. CarLand's completed work sheet is shown in Illustration 16-6 on pages 400 and 401.

Illustration 16-7 on page 402 summarizes the steps followed in completing an 8-column work sheet for a merchandising business.

Audit Your Understanding

1. To what column is the Income Summary amount extended?
2. When does a net loss appear on a work sheet?
3. To which Balance Sheet column is a net loss amount extended?

LESSON PLAN 16-2

Materials

- Student pages 399–402
- Transparencies: C, Blank 8-Column Work Sheet; 16-1, Chapter Summary
- Software: Application Program Disk, Electronic Study Guide
- Demonstration Problem: 16B, Extending Balance Sheet and Income Statement Items

Objectives (Enabling Performance Tasks)

b. Identify accounting concepts and practices related to a work sheet for a merchandising business.

d. Complete a work sheet for a merchandising business.

TEACHING STRATEGIES: TEACHING TIP

As students work on end-of-chapter problems, have them analyze the adjustments in T accounts before recording the adjustments on the work sheet.

In Chapter 8, the procedures for completing a work sheet for a service business were presented. In this lesson, the same procedures will be used for a merchandising business with the exception of extending the merchandise inventory adjustment recorded in the income summary and merchandise inventory accounts.

Cover student pages 399–402 "Completing a Work Sheet." Review the procedures for completing a work sheet that were described in Chapter 8. Point out that the only exception is the use of the income summary account to adjust the related account Merchandise Inventory.

ILLUSTRATION 16-6 Completed work sheet for a merchandising business

CarLand
Work Sheet
For Year Ended December 31, 19--

	ACCOUNT TITLE	TRIAL BALANCE DEBIT	TRIAL BALANCE CREDIT	ADJUSTMENTS DEBIT	ADJUSTMENTS CREDIT	INCOME STATEMENT DEBIT	INCOME STATEMENT CREDIT	BALANCE SHEET DEBIT	BALANCE SHEET CREDIT	
1	Cash	2423357						2423357		1
2	Petty Cash	50000						50000		2
3	Accounts Receivable	933200						933200		3
4	Merchandise Inventory	22540000			(a)1320000			21220000		4
5	Supplies—Office	540000			(b)394000			146000		5
6	Supplies—Store	578000			(c)326000			252000		6
7	Prepaid Insurance	484000			(d)264000			220000		7
8	Accounts Payable		1045190						1045190	8
9	Employee Income Tax Payable		40200						40200	9
10	FICA Tax Payable		83216						83216	10
11	Sales Tax Payable		176000						176000	11
12	Unemployment Tax Payable—Federal		5915						5915	12
13	Unemployment Tax Payable—State		39926						39926	13
14	Health Insurance Premiums Payable		84000						84000	14
15	U.S. Savings Bonds Payable		4000						4000	15
16	United Way Donations Payable		6000						6000	16
17	Amy Kramer, Capital		10111800						10111800	17
18	Amy Kramer, Drawing	1820000						1820000		18
19	Dario Mesa, Capital		10122800							10122800	19
20	Dario Mesa, Drawing	1860000						1860000		20

SOFTWARE FOCUS

Software may be used for independent practice or enrichment/extension as the instructor deems appropriate. For this chapter, the following software may be used: Application Program Disk with Mastery Problem 16-M; Accounting Tutorial, Unit 5; Electronic Study Guide Chapter 16.

Work sheet (right portion — Adjustments, Income Statement, and Balance Sheet columns) for a merchandising business:

#	Account Title	Trial Balance Debit	Trial Balance Credit	Adjustments Debit	Adjustments Credit	Income Statement Debit	Income Statement Credit	Balance Sheet Debit	Balance Sheet Credit
21	Income Summary			(a) 1320000		1320000			
22	Sales		35260000				35260000		
23	Purchases	15830000				15830000			
24	Advertising Expense	550000				550000			
25	Credit Card Fee Expense	289000				289000			
26	Insurance Expense			(d) 264000		264000			
27	Miscellaneous Expense	218215				218215			
28	Payroll Taxes Expense	729975				729975			
29	Rent Expense	1800000				1800000			
30	Salary Expense	6015300				6015300			
31	Supplies Expense—Office			(b) 394000		394000			
32	Supplies Expense—Store			(c) 326000		326000			
33	Utilities Expense	318000				318000			
34		56979047	56979047	2304000	2304000	28054490	35260000	28924557	21719047
35	Net Income					7205510			7205510
36						35260000	35260000	28924557	28924557

APPLY

Use Transparency C to show how the amounts in Income Summary are extended to the work sheet's Income Statement columns.

Guided Practice

Guide students through Drill 16-D2. Students should have the forms from the working papers to complete as you guide them through the drill. For each account ask the students if it should be extended to the Income Statement columns or the Balance Sheet columns. All students should agree with the analysis before proceeding to the next account. Students should individually total the Income Statement and Balance Sheet columns. Calculate and record the net income as a group. Students should individually total and rule the Income Statement and Balance Sheet columns.

Independent Practice

Assign Problems 16-1, 16-2, Mastery Problem 16-M, and Study Guide 16.

ASSESS

Assess student understanding by checking solutions to Independent Practice activities.

Reteach

- Use Demonstration 16B. This problem can be demonstrated on the overhead with the students completing the problem at their desks.
- Assign Recycling Problem 16-R.

Extend

Assign the Application Program Disk software to be used with Problem 16-M.

Enrich

Assign Electronic Study Guide Chapter 16.

CLOSURE

- Use Audit Your Understanding questions.
- Review Summary Illustration 16-7, "Summary of an 8-Column Work Sheet for a Merchandising Business," and Transparency 16-1, Chapter Summary.

TEACHING STRATEGIES:
APPLYING VISUALS

Direct students to Summary Illustration 16-7 which reviews the steps followed in completing an 8-column work sheet for a merchandising business.

SUMMARY ILLUSTRATION 16-7

Summary of an 8-column work sheet for a merchandising business

1 Prepare a trial balance in the Trial Balance columns.

2 Analyze and record adjustments in the Adjustments columns.

3 Extend balance sheet items to the work sheet's Balance Sheet columns.

4 Extend income statement items, including Income Summary, to the work sheet's Income Statement columns.

5 Total the Income Statement and Balance Sheet columns.

6 Calculate the net income or net loss. If the Income Statement Credit column total (revenue) is larger than the Debit column total (costs and expenses), a net income has occurred. If the Income Statement Debit column total (costs and expenses) is larger than the Credit column total (revenue), a net loss has occurred. CarLand's net income is calculated as shown below.

Income Statement Credit Column Total	−	Income Statement Debit Column Total	=	Net Income
$352,600.00	−	$280,544.90	=	$72,055.10

7 Extend the amount of net income or net loss to the Balance Sheet Debit or Credit column. When a net income occurs, the net income amount is extended to the Balance Sheet Credit amount column, as shown on line 35. When a net loss occurs, the net loss amount is extended to the Balance Sheet Debit amount column.

8 Total the four Income Statement and Balance Sheet amount columns.

9 Check that the totals for each pair of columns are in balance. As shown on line 36, the totals for the Income Statement columns, $352,600.00, are the same. The totals for the Balance Sheet columns, $289,245.57, are also the same. CarLand's work sheet is in balance.

APPLIED SKILLS: LANGUAGE ARTS

Paraphrasing, writing complete sentences, and identifying direct objects. For additional practice in language arts skills, direct students to answer the Accounting Terms and Questions for Individual Study at the end of the chapter. Students should write the answers in their own words and in complete sentences. To further practice language arts skills, ask students to underline the direct objects in each sentence of their answers.

A 10-COLUMN WORK SHEET FOR A MERCHANDISING BUSINESS

Some large merchandising businesses *with many accounts to be adjusted* at the end of a fiscal period may use a 10-column work sheet. A 10-column work sheet includes an additional pair of amount columns titled *Adjusted Trial Balance*, as shown in the 10-column work sheet in Illustration 16-8, pages 404 and 405.

After adjustments have been recorded, the balance for each account listed in the Trial Balance columns is extended to the Adjusted Trial Balance columns. The Adjusted Trial Balance columns are then totaled to prove equality of debits and credits after adjustments. Following proof of debits and credits, amounts in the Adjusted Trial Balance columns are extended to the Balance Sheet and Income Statement columns. The Income Statement and Balance Sheet columns are totaled and ruled the same way as on an 8-column work sheet.

☞☞ FYI ☞☞

A 10-column work sheet is often used by large merchandising companies with many accounts to be adjusted.

■ Bryan Choi ■
ARCHITECTS ASSOCIATED, DAYTON OHIO

Bryan Choi has been an architect all of his professional life. Bryan Choi is also a planner; he sets goals and works toward them. Before he started his own architectural firm, he planned for fifteen years. He started working in a large company, then went to a medium-sized company, and then to a small company, to learn everything there was to know about going into business for yourself.

Choi also knew for a long time that he would eventually start his own business. Therefore he saved diligently for that day. Choi says, "I started small and took very few risks. That's why I succeeded where others had failed." Because he planned for so long, there were none of the surprises that first-time entrepreneurs often

encounter, such as underestimating the need for beginning capital.

Students who ask Choi what they need to do to succeed hear, "Learn to manage your time wisely. Set goals, establish good working habits, and continue to work at whatever it is you want to do until you master it."

Choi went to high school and also received his Bachelor's degree in his native Korea. He also earned a Master's degree in the United States, and was for a while an accounting major. He says that the hardest thing about American business that he had to learn was the culture, which was so different from Korea's. He says, "I learned early on to shut my mouth and open my ears. Listen and learn. In fact, that could be another rule for succeeding in business: Listen and learn."

Personal Visions in Business

LESSON PLAN 16-3

Materials

- Student pages 403–405
- Transparency: H, Blank 10-Column Work Sheet
- Math Work Sheet Chapter 16, Calculating Net Income (TRG)
- Assess: Problem Test Chapter 16, MicroExam Chapter 16

Objectives (Enabling Performance Tasks)

b. Identify accounting concepts and practices related to a work sheet for a merchandising business.

c. Plan adjustments on a work sheet for a merchandising business.

d. Complete a work sheet for a merchandising business.

FOCUS

Preparing an 8-column work sheet for a merchandising business was presented earlier in this chapter. In this lesson, a 10-column work sheet with Adjusted Trial Balance columns is introduced.

Personal Visions in Business

This special student feature introduces students to successful entrepreneurs or business professionals. Each profile gives a flavor of what the actual business world is like and some of the opportunities available to students who study accounting. These features can be used to motivate students to pursue professional business careers in a wide variety of fields. The subjects of these profiles have been carefully chosen to represent the full spectrum of diverse ethnic and racial backgrounds of professional business people. As an optional activity, students can be encouraged to seek out and interview successful business people in their own communities.

APPLIED SKILLS: MATHEMATICS

Use the MATH WORK SHEET in the Masters and Solutions to Enrichment/Application Section of the Teacher's Resource Guide to integrate applied mathematics. In this work sheet, students will apply math concepts to calculate net income/net loss.

APPLY

Direct students' attention to Illustration 16-8, 10-column work sheet. Explain that to complete a 10-column work sheet, the steps shown in Summary Illustration 16-7 for an 8-column work sheet should be followed. One additional step must be performed between steps 2 and 3.

Guided Practice

Guide the students through Problem 16-1 using a 10-column work sheet. (Problem 16-1 was previously completed using an 8-column work sheet. If students had particular difficulties with other problems you may want to substitute one of those problems for Problem 16-1.) Duplicate the 10-column work sheet blackline master from the Masters and Solutions to Enrichment/Application Activities Section in the Teacher's Resource Guide. Students should have the duplicated form from the TRG to complete as you guide them through the problem.

Independent Practice

Assign Questions 15–16 and Challenge Problem 16-C (the challenge is using a 10-column work sheet).

ILLUSTRATION 16-8   Ten-column work sheet (left page)

		TRIAL BALANCE		ADJUSTMENTS	
	ACCOUNT TITLE	1 DEBIT	2 CREDIT	3 DEBIT	4 CREDIT
1	Cash	24 23 3 57			
2	Petty Cash	5 0 0 00			
3	Accounts Receivable	9 33 2 00			
4	Merchandise Inventory	225 40 0 00			(a)13 2 0 0 00
5	Supplies—Office	5 40 0 00			(b) 3 9 4 0 00
6	Supplies—Store	5 78 0 00			(c) 3 2 6 0 00
7	Prepaid Insurance	4 84 0 00			(d) 2 6 4 0 00
8	Accounts Payable		10 45 1 90		
9	Employee Income Tax Payable		4 0 2 00		
10	FICA Tax Payable		8 3 2 16		
11	Sales Tax Payable		1 76 0 00		
29	Rent Expense	18 00 0 00			
30	Salary Expense	60 15 3 00			
31	Supplies Expense—Office			(b) 3 9 4 0 00	
32	Supplies Expense—Store			(c) 3 2 6 0 00	
33	Utilities Expense	3 18 0 00			
34		569 79 0 47	569 79 0 47	23 0 4 0 00	23 0 4 0 00
35	Net Income				
36					

CarLand
Work Sheet
For Year Ended December 31, 19--

Audit Your Understanding

1. List the column heads for a 10-column work sheet.

2. What extra step is required when a 10-column work sheet is prepared instead of an 8-column work sheet?

Any business with adjustments to make at the end of a fiscal period could use either an 8-column or a 10-column work sheet. However, completing two extra amount columns when most of the account balances *are not* adjusted requires extra time and work. Account balances not adjusted must be extended from the Trial Balance columns to the Adjusted Trial Balance columns. Whereas, with an 8-column work sheet, account balances *not* adjusted are extended directly to the Balance Sheet or Income Statement columns. CarLand prefers to use an 8-column work sheet because only four adjustments are needed at the end of each fiscal period.

AUDIT YOUR UNDERSTANDING

1. Trial Balance Debit and Credit columns; Adjustments Debit and Credit columns; Adjusted Trial Balance Debit and Credit columns; Income Statement Debit and Credit columns; and Balance Sheet Debit and Credit columns.
2. Trial balance amounts after adjustments are extended to the Adjusted Trial Balance columns and the Adjusted Trial Balance columns are proved before extending amounts to the Income Statement and Balance Sheet columns.

ILLUSTRATION 16-8   Ten-column work sheet (right page)

	5 ADJUSTED TRIAL BALANCE DEBIT	6 CREDIT	7 INCOME STATEMENT DEBIT	8 CREDIT	9 BALANCE SHEET DEBIT	10 CREDIT	
1	24 23 3 57				24 23 3 57		1
2	50 0 00				50 0 00		2
3	9 33 2 00				9 33 2 00		3
4	212 20 0 00				212 20 0 00		4
5	1 46 0 00				1 46 0 00		5
6	2 52 0 00				2 52 0 00		6
7	2 20 0 00				2 20 0 00		7
8		10 45 1 90				10 45 1 90	8
9		40 2 00				40 2 00	9
10		83 2 16				83 2 16	10
11		1 76 0 00				1 76 0 00	11
29	18 00 0 00		18 00 0 00				29
30	60 15 3 00		60 15 3 00				30
31	3 94 0 00		3 94 0 00				31
32	3 26 0 00		3 26 0 00				32
33	3 18 0 00		3 18 0 00				33
34	592 83 0 47	592 83 0 47	280 54 4 90	352 60 0 00	289 24 5 57	217 19 0 47	34
35			72 05 5 10			72 05 5 10	35
36			352 60 0 00	352 60 0 00	289 24 5 57	289 24 5 57	36

ACCOUNTING TERMS

1. **inventory:** The amount of goods on hand. (p. 393)
2. **merchandise inventory:** The amount of goods on hand for sale to customers. (p. 393)

QUESTIONS FOR INDIVIDUAL STUDY

1. Because transactions during the year did not affect these accounts. (p. 387)
2. To plan adjustments and sort information for financial statements. (p. 387)
3. Accounting Period Cycle. (p. 387)
4. To reduce the possibility of overlooking an account that needs to be brought up to date. (p. 393)
5. Merchandise Inventory, Supplies—Office, Supplies—Store, and Prepaid Insurance. (p. 393)
6. Merchandise Inventory is an asset account with a normal debit balance. (p. 394)
7. Because the changes in inventory resulting from purchases and sales transactions have not been recorded. (p. 395)
8. Income Summary is debited and Merchandise Inventory is credited for decreases in merchandise inventory. Merchandise Inventory is debited and Income Summary is credited for increases in merchandise inventory. (pp. 395–396)
9. An asset. (p. 396)
10. Matching Expenses with Revenue. (p. 396)
11. (1) The account balance on January 1. (2) The cost of office supplies bought during the year. (p. 397)
12. Supplies Expense—Office is debited; Supplies—Office is credited. (p. 397)
13. (1) The account balance on January 1. (2) The cost of insurance premiums paid during the year. (p. 398)
14. Insurance Expense is debited; Prepaid Insurance is credited. (p. 399s)
15. A large merchandising business with many accounts to be adjusted at the end of a fiscal period. (p. 403)
16. Adjusted Trial Balance Debit and Adjusted Trial Balance Credit. (p. 403)

ACCOUNTING TERMS   EPT(a)

What is the meaning of each of the following?

1. **inventory**
2. **merchandise inventory**

QUESTIONS FOR INDIVIDUAL STUDY   EPT(b)

1. Why do some general ledger accounts not have any entries posted and, therefore, zero balances at the end of a fiscal period?
2. Why is a work sheet used at the end of a fiscal period?
3. Which accounting concept is being applied when a work sheet is prepared at the end of each fiscal period?
4. Why are all general ledger accounts listed on the Trial Balance columns of a work sheet?
5. Which of CarLand's general ledger accounts need to be brought up to date at the end of a fiscal period?
6. What type of account is Merchandise Inventory, and what is its normal balance?
7. Why are the beginning and ending balances of the merchandise inventory account before adjustments the same?
8. What accounts are affected, and how, by the adjustment for merchandise inventory?
9. What does the amount of supplies not used during a fiscal period represent to a business?
10. Which accounting concept is being applied when expenses are recorded in the same accounting period in which the expenses contribute to earning revenue?
11. What two items are included in CarLand's office supplies account balance before adjustment?
12. What accounts are affected, and how, by the adjustment for office supplies inventory?
13. What two items are included in CarLand's prepaid insurance account balance before adjustment?
14. What accounts are affected, and how, by a prepaid insurance adjustment?
15. What type of merchandising business might use a 10-column work sheet?
16. What two additional amount columns are found on a 10-column work sheet?

CASES FOR CRITICAL THINKING   EPT(c)

CASE 1 After completing a work sheet, Kramer Merchandising Outlet finds that through an oversight, paper bags still in boxes were overlooked in calculating the supplies inventory. The value of the paper bags overlooked is $50.00. Joseph Kramer suggests that the accountant not worry about such a small amount because the oversight does not have any effect on balancing the Income Statement and Balance Sheet columns of the work sheet. Mr. Kramer further indicates that the oversight will be corrected anyway when the store supplies are counted at the end of the next fiscal period. The accountant recommends that the work sheet be redone to reflect the recalculated supplies inventory. Do you agree with Mr. Kramer or the accountant? Explain your answer.

CASE 2 Quality Shoes paid $1,440.00 for a one-year fire insurance policy. The company prepares an income statement and balance sheet every three months. However, the accountant prepares a prepaid insurance adjustment only at the end of the year. Rachel Delfield, one of the partners in the business, thinks the prepaid insurance should be adjusted every three months. Who is correct? Why?

DRILLS FOR UNDERSTANDING

DRILL 16-D1 Analyzing adjusting entries

The following chart contains adjustment information related to the preparation of work sheets for three businesses.

Business	Account Title and Balance		End-of-Fiscal-Period Information	
A	1. Merchandise Inventory	$148,000.00	Merchandise inventory	$134,000.00
	2. Supplies—Office	5,750.00	Office supplies inventory	4,200.00
	3. Supplies—Store	4,920.00	Store supplies inventory	3,840.00
	4. Prepaid Insurance	1,860.00	Value of prepaid insurance	1,240.00
B	1. Merchandise Inventory	$182,000.00	Merchandise inventory	$166,000.00
	2. Supplies—Office	4,680.00	Office supplies inventory	3,460.00
	3. Supplies—Store	5,930.00	Store supplies inventory	4,320.00
	4. Prepaid Insurance	2,520.00	Value of prepaid insurance	1,260.00
C	1. Merchandise Inventory	$166,500.00	Merchandise inventory	$178,000.00
	2. Supplies—Office	5,460.00	Office supplies inventory	4,520.00
	3. Supplies—Store	6,480.00	Store supplies inventory	4,960.00
	4. Prepaid Insurance	2,160.00	Value of prepaid insurance	1,080.00

A form for analyzing transactions is given in the working papers accompanying this textbook.

INSTRUCTIONS:

For each business, analyze the adjustments for merchandise inventory adjustment, office supplies inventory adjustment, store supplies inventory adjustment, and prepaid insurance adjustment. List the accounts affected and the amounts for each of the adjustments. List the account titles in Column 3 and the amounts in either Column 4 or 5. Adjustment 1 for Business A is given as an example in the working papers.

DRILL 16-D2 Extending balance sheet and income statement items

Madison Enterprise's partially completed work sheet is given in the working papers accompanying this textbook.

INSTRUCTIONS:

1. Extend the balance sheet items to the Balance Sheet columns of the work sheet.
2. Extend the income statement items to the Income Statement columns of the work sheet.
3. Complete the work sheet.
   a. Total the Income Statement and Balance Sheet columns.
   b. Calculate and record the net income or net loss.
   c. Total and rule the Income Statement and Balance Sheet columns.

APPLICATION PROBLEMS

PROBLEM 16-1 Completing a work sheet

Eastside Supply's trial balance as of December 31 of the current year is recorded on a work sheet in the working papers accompanying this textbook.

CHECK FIGURES *(cont'd)*

Problem 16-2 Adjustments:
(a) 3,000 (debit Inv.); (b) 3,940; (c) 3,870;
(d) 2,760. Net Loss: 3,770

Mastery Problem 16-M Adjustments: (a) 23,300 (debit Inv.); (b) 3,730;
(c) 3,380; (d) 2,700. Net Income: 96,560

Challenge Problem 16-C
Adjustments: (a) 10,500 (credit Inv.);
(b) 2,970; (c) 3,140; (d) 2,640. Net
Income: 53,660

INSTRUCTIONS:

1. Analyze the following adjustment information, and record the adjustments on the work sheet.

Adjustment Information, December 31

Merchandise inventory...............	$196,610.00
Office supplies inventory.............	1,410.00
Store supplies inventory..............	2,450.00
Value of prepaid insurance...........	1,935.00

2. Calculate and record the net income or net loss.

3. Complete the work sheet.

PROBLEM 16-2 Completing a work sheet

Jomar's trial balance as of December 31 of the current year is recorded on a work sheet in the working papers accompanying this textbook.

INSTRUCTIONS:

1. Analyze the following adjustment information, and record the adjustments on the work sheet.

Adjustment Information, December 31

Merchandise inventory...............	$246,600.00
Office supplies inventory.............	1,790.00
Store supplies inventory..............	1,510.00
Value of prepaid insurance...........	2,300.00

2. Calculate and record the net income or net loss.

3. Complete the work sheet.

ENRICHMENT PROBLEMS   EPT(c,d)

MASTERY PROBLEM 16-M Completing a work sheet

APPLICATION

Marine Supply's trial balance as of December 31 of the current year is recorded on a work sheet in the working papers accompanying this textbook.

INSTRUCTIONS:

Use the following adjustment information. Complete the work sheet.

Adjustment Information, December 31

Merchandise inventory...............	$208,600.00
Office supplies inventory.............	1,855.00
Store supplies inventory..............	2,355.00
Value of prepaid insurance...........	1,575.00

CHALLENGE PROBLEM 16-C Completing a 10-column work sheet

Ultimate Fashion's trial balance as of December 31 of the current year is recorded on a work sheet in the working papers accompanying this textbook.

INSTRUCTIONS:

Use the adjustment information given on the next page. Complete the 10-column work sheet.

Adjustment Information, December 31

Merchandise inventory.................	$205,370.00
Office supplies inventory..............	2,160.00
Store supplies inventory...............	2,195.00
Value of prepaid insurance............	1,320.00

Chapter 17 demonstrates the preparation of the financial statements typically prepared by a merchandising business organized as a partnership. The data in the Income Statement and Balance Sheet columns of the work sheet are used to prepare these statements. The income statement presented expands upon the income statement in Chapter 9 by including cost of merchandise sold and gross profit sections as would be expected for a merchandising business. Component percentage analysis is contin-

GUIDE TO ACHIEVING LEARNING OBJECTIVES

	TEACH	APPLY		EXTEND/ENRICH					
Enabling Performance Tasks	**Lesson Plans**	**Drills for Understanding**	**Application Problems**	**Mastery Problems**	**Challenge Problems**	**Cases for Critical Thinking**	**Recycling Problems**	**Reinforcement Activity**	
a. Define accounting terms related to financial statements.	17-1, 17-2								
b. Identify accounting concepts and practices related to financial statements.	17-1, 17-2					Case 2			
c. Prepare an income statement.	17-1	17-D1, 17-D2	17-1	17-M			17-R	2B	
d. Analyze an income statement using component percentages.	17-1	17-D3	17-1	17-M		Case 1	17-R	2B	
e. Prepare a distribution of net income statement.	17-1	17-D4	17-1, 17-2	17-M	17-C		17-R	2B	
f. Prepare an owners' equity statement.	17-2		17-1, 17-2, 17-3	17-M	17-C		17-R	2B	
g. Prepare a balance sheet.	17-2		17-1	17-M			17-R	2B	

ENRICHMENT

SPECIAL FEATURES

Global Perspective, page 415
Applied Communications, page 431

TECHNOLOGY CONNECTION

Spreadsheet Template Problem 17-M, 17-C
Electronic Study Guide

NEW, REVIEW, AND EXTENSION

ACTIVITIES/CONCEPTS/TRANSACTIONS	NEW	REVIEW/ EXTENSION
Preparing an income statement for a merchandising business		✓
Calculating component percentages		✓
Component percentage for cost of merchandise sold		✓
Component percentage for gross profit on sales		✓
Preparing a distribution of net income statement	✓	
Preparing an owners' equity statement	✓	
Preparing a balance sheet for a partnership		✓

ued for Chapter 8 and expanded to include more items. A distribution of net income statement for two partners is illustrated for both equal distribution and unequal distribution of partnership earnings. An owners' equity statement for two partners is illustrated for both net income and net loss situations. The balance sheet described and prepared in this chapter uses the report form of balance sheet to show alternatives to the account form of balance sheet shown in Chapter 9.

	INFORMAL ASSESSMENT		FORMAL ASSESSMENT				
	Study Guide	Audit Your Understanding	Chapter MicroExam	Chapter Problem Test	Unit Problem Test	Unit Objective Test	Portfolio
	Unit A		✓			✓	
	Units B, C	✓	✓			✓	
							✓
							✓
							✓
							✓
							✓

TEACHING MATERIALS

Teacher's Wraparound Edition of the Text

Teacher's Resource Guide

Teacher's Edition of Working Papers

Teacher's Edition of Demonstration/Recycling Problems

Teaching Transparencies

MicroExam

Applied Math Work Sheet

APPLIED MATHEMATICS

APPLIED MATH/ACCOUNTING SKILL	APPLICATION
Calculating cost of merchandise sold	Drill 17-D1
Calculating component percentages for an income statement	Drill 17-D3

17

Financial Statements for a Partnership

ENABLING PERFORMANCE TASKS

After studying Chapter 17, you will be able to:

a Define accounting terms related to financial statements for a merchandising business organized as a partnership.

b Identify accounting concepts and practices related to financial statements for a merchandising business organized as a partnership.

c Prepare an income statement for a merchandising business organized as a partnership.

d Analyze an income statement using component percentages for a merchandising business organized as a partnership.

e Prepare a distribution of net income statement for a merchandising business organized as a partnership.

f Prepare an owners' equity statement for a merchandising business organized as a partnership.

g Prepare a balance sheet for a merchandising business organized as a partnership.

TERMS PREVIEW

cost of merchandise sold • gross profit on sales • distribution of net income statement • owners' equity statement • supporting schedule

410

The financial activities of a business are recorded in journals and ledgers during a fiscal period. At the end of a fiscal period, a work sheet is prepared to organize and summarize this financial information. The completed work sheet is used to prepare financial statements. Financial statements provide the primary source of information needed by owners and managers to make decisions on the future activity of a business.

All financial information must be reported in order to make sound business decisions. The financial statements should provide information about a business' financial condition, changes in this financial condition, and the progress of operations. *(CONCEPT: Adequate Disclosure)*

Comparing financial condition and progress for more than one fiscal period also helps owners and managers make sound business decisions. Therefore, financial information must be reported the same way from one fiscal period to the next. *(CONCEPT: Consistent Reporting)*

FINANCIAL STATEMENTS FOR A PARTNERSHIP

A business organized as a partnership prepares four financial statements to report financial progress and condition. A partnership prepares an income statement and a balance sheet similar to those used by a proprietorship. A partnership also prepares two additional financial statements. One statement reports the distribution of net income or net loss for each partner. The other statement reports the changes in owners' equity for the fiscal period.

INCOME STATEMENT

FYI

An income statement is prepared using a completed work sheet.

An income statement is used to report a business' financial progress. Merchandising businesses report revenue, cost of merchandise sold, gross profit on sales, expenses, and net income or loss. Current and previous income statements can be compared to determine the reasons for increases or decreases in net income. This comparison is helpful in making management decisions about future operations.

Preparing an Income Statement

Information from a completed work sheet is used to prepare an income statement. CarLand's income statement information on a work sheet for the year ended December 31 is shown in Illustration 17-1 on page 412.

The income statement of a merchandising business has three main sections. (1) Revenue section. (2) Cost of merchandise sold section. (3) Expenses section. The total original price of all merchandise sold during a fiscal period is called the **cost of merchandise sold**. *(CONCEPT: Historical Cost)* Cost of merchandise sold is

LESSON PLAN 17-1

Materials

- Student pages 411–421

- Transparencies: D, Blank Income Statement; I, Blank One-Column Financial Form and Blank Three-Column Financial Form; 17-1, Income Statement; 17-2, Distribution of Income Statement and Owners' Equity Statement

- Math Work Sheet Chapter 17: Part A: Calculating Cost of Merchandise Sold (TRG); Part B: Calculating Component Percentages for an Income Statement (TRG)

- Demonstration Problems: 17A, Preparing an Income Statement; 17B, Preparing a Distribution of Net Income Statement

Objectives (Enabling Performance Tasks)

a. Define accounting terms related to financial statements for a merchandising business organized as a partnership.

b. Identify accounting concepts and practices related to financial statements for a merchandising business organized as a partnership.

c. Prepare an income statement for a merchandising business organized as a partnership.

d. Analyze an income statement using component percentages for a merchandising business organized as a partnership.

e. Prepare a distribution of net income statement for a merchandising business organized as a partnership.

- In the first cycle, the financial statements prepared by a service business organized as a proprietorship were presented. In this lesson, we will look at the first two financial statements prepared by a merchandising business organized as a partnership—an income statement and a distribution of net income statement.

- Introduce new vocabulary: cost of merchandise sold, gross profit on sales, distribution of net income statement.

ILLUSTRATION 17-1   Income statement information on a work sheet

	1	2	3	4	5	6	7	8	
ACCOUNT TITLE	TRIAL BALANCE		ADJUSTMENTS		INCOME STATEMENT		BALANCE SHEET		
	DEBIT	CREDIT	DEBIT	CREDIT	DEBIT	CREDIT	DEBIT	CREDIT	
4 Merchandise Inventory	225400 00			(a)13200 00			212200 00		4
22 Sales		352600 00				352600 00			22
23 Purchases	158300 00				158300 00				23
24 Advertising Expense	5500 00				5500 00				24
25 Credit Card Fee Expense	2890 00				2890 00				25
26 Insurance Expense			(d)2640 00		2640 00				26
27 Miscellaneous Expense	2182 15				2182 15				27
28 Payroll Taxes Expense	7299 75				7299 75				28
29 Rent Expense	18000 00				18000 00				29
30 Salary Expense	60153 00				60153 00				30
31 Supplies Expense—Office			(b)3940 00		3940 00				31
32 Supplies Expense—Store			(c)3260 00		3260 00				32
33 Utilities Expense	3180 00				3180 00				33
34	569790 47	569790 47	23040 00	23040 00	280544 90	352600 00	289245 57	217190 47	34
35 Net Income					72055 10			72055 10	35
36					352600 00	352600 00	289245 57	289245 57	36
37									37

sometimes known as cost of goods sold or cost of sales. CarLand's completed income statement is shown in Illustration 17-2.

CarLand uses seven steps in preparing an income statement.

1 Write the income statement heading on three lines.

2 Prepare the revenue section. Use the information from the Income Statement Credit column of the work sheet.

- Write the name of this section, *Revenue:*, at the extreme left of the wide column on the first line.
- Write the title of the revenue account, Sales, on the next line, indented about one centimeter.
- Write the balance of the sales account, *$352,600.00,* in the second amount column. For CarLand, this amount is also the total of the revenue section.

  For businesses with more than one source of revenue, each revenue account title is listed in the wide column. Each account balance is written in the first amount column. The words *Total Revenue* are written in the wide column on the next line below the last revenue account title. The total amount of revenue is written in the second amount column.

3 Prepare the cost of merchandise sold section.

- Write the name of this section, *Cost of Merchandise Sold:*, at the extreme left of the wide column.

FYI

Every financial form has a three-line heading.

ILLUSTRATION 17-2   Income statement for a merchandising business

CarLand				
Income Statement				
For Year Ended December 31, 19--				
				% OF SALES
Revenue:				
Sales			352 60 00 00	100.0
Cost of Merchandise Sold:				
Merchandise Inventory, January 1, 19--	225 40 00 00			
Purchases	158 30 00 00			
Total Cost of Mdse. Available for Sale	383 70 00 00			
Less Mdse. Inventory, December 31, 19--	212 20 00 00			
Cost of Merchandise Sold			171 50 00 00	48.6
Gross Profit on Sales			181 10 00 00	51.4
Expenses:				
Advertising Expense	5 50 00 00			
Credit Card Fee Expense	2 89 00 00			
Insurance Expense	2 64 00 00			
Miscellaneous Expense	2 18 2 15			
Payroll Taxes Expense	7 29 9 75			
Rent Expense	18 00 00 00			
Salary Expense	60 15 3 00			
Supplies Expense—Office	3 94 00 00			
Supplies Expense—Store	3 26 00 00			
Utilities Expense	3 18 00 00			
Total Expenses			109 04 4 90	30.9
Net Income			72 05 5 10	20.4

- Indent about one centimeter on the next line, and write the items needed to calculate cost of merchandise sold. Write the amount of each item in the first amount column.

Beginning merchandise inventory, January 1...... $ 225,400.00
(This amount is the debit balance of **Merchandise Inventory** in the Trial Balance Debit column of the work sheet.)

Plus purchases made during the fiscal period...... +158,300.00
(This amount is the debit balance of **Purchases** in the Income Statement Debit column of the work sheet.)

Equals total cost of merchandise available for sale during the fiscal period...................... $ 383,700.00

Less ending merchandise inventory, December 31.. −212,200.00
(This amount is the debit balance of **Merchandise Inventory** in the Balance Sheet Debit column of the work sheet.)

Equals cost of merchandise sold during the fiscal period................................... $ 171,500.00

TEACH

Cover student pages 411–421 "Financial Statements for a Partnership," "Income Statement," and "Distribution of Net Income Statement." This lesson reviews some important concepts regarding the preparation of an income statement, such as (1) account balances for the income statement are taken from the Income Statement columns of the work sheet; (2) all financial statements have a three-line heading; (3) account titles are indented; (4) the two columns on the income statement are not debit and credit columns; (5) account balances are listed in the first column, totals in the second column; and (6) it should always be verified that the amount of net income or net loss is the same as that on the work sheet.

This lesson introduces students to some important concepts regarding the preparation of an income statement for a merchandising business organized as a partnership, such as (1) preparing the cost of merchandise sold section of the income statement, (2) calculating gross profit on sales, and (3) calculating and analyzing component percentages for cost of merchandise sold and gross profit on sales. Emphasize that negative amounts are written within parentheses. Involve students in a discussion on how a business can increase revenue or decrease expenses.

During this lesson students should also be shown how to divide partnership net income or net loss and how to prepare a distribution of net income statement for a merchandising business organized as a partnership. Discuss why partners may divide net income or net loss in various ways.

APPLIED SKILLS: MATHEMATICS

Use the MATH WORK SHEET in the Masters and Solutions to Enrichment/Application Activities Section of the Teacher's Resource Guide to integrate applied mathematics. In this work sheet, students will apply math concepts to calculate cost of merchandise sold, and calculate component percentages for an income statement.

- Use Transparency D to demonstrate completing an income statement as the lesson progresses. Or use Transparency 17-1, which is a completed income statement, to explain how to prepare an income statement.

- Use Transparency I to demonstrate completing a distribution of net income statement. Or use Transparency 17-2, which is a completed statement, to explain how to prepare a distribution of net income statement.

Guided Practice

Guide students through Drills 17-D1; 17-D2; 17-D3; and 17-D4, Business A only. Businesses B and C can be assigned as Independent Practice. Students should have the forms from the working papers to complete as you guide them through the drills. For Drill 17-D1, ask the students how to calculate the cost of merchandise sold. For Drill 17-D2, ask the students how to calculate the net income or net loss. For Drill 17-D3, ask the students how to calculate the component percentages for cost of merchandise sold, gross profit on sales, total expenses, and net income. For Drill 17-D4, ask the students how to distribute the net income, and then the net loss. All students should agree with the calculations before proceeding to the next calculation.

Independent Practice

Assign Terms 1–3; Questions 1–16; Drills 17-D1, 17-D2, 17-D3, and 17-D4, Businesses B and C; Problem 17-1, Instructions 1–2; and Problem 17-2, Instruction 1.

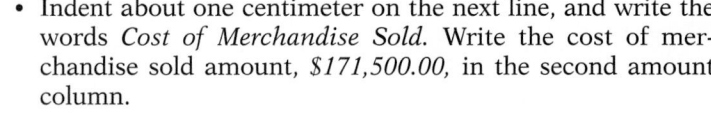

FYI

Amounts are listed in the first amount column of the financial statement and totaled in the second column. These are amount columns, not debit and credit columns.

- Indent about one centimeter on the next line, and write the words *Cost of Merchandise Sold*. Write the cost of merchandise sold amount, *$171,500.00*, in the second amount column.

4 Calculate the gross profit on sales. The revenue remaining after cost of merchandise sold has been deducted is called **gross profit on sales.**

- Write the words *Gross Profit on Sales* on the next line at the extreme left of the wide column.

- Write the gross profit on sales amount, *$181,100.00*, in the second amount column. (Total revenue, $352,600.00, *less* cost of merchandise sold, $171,500.00, *equals* gross profit on sales, $181,100.00.)

5 Prepare the expenses section. Use the information from the Income Statement Debit column of the work sheet.

- Write the name of this section, *Expenses:*, at the extreme left of the wide column.

- Indent about one centimeter on the next line, and list the expense account titles in the order in which they appear on the work sheet. Write the amount of each expense account balance in the first amount column.

- Indent about one centimeter, and write the words *Total Expenses* on the next line in the wide column below the last expense account title. Total the individual expense amounts and write the total, *$109,044.90*, in the second amount column on the total line.

6 Calculate the net income.

- Write the words *Net Income* on the next line at the extreme left of the wide column.

- Write the net income amount, *$72,055.10*, in the second amount column on the net income line. (Gross profit on sales, $181,100.00, *less* total expenses, $109,044.90, *equals* net income, $72,055.10.)

  Verify accuracy by comparing the amount of net income calculated on the income statement, $72,055.10, with the amount on the work sheet, $72,055.10. The two amounts must be the same.

7 Rule double lines across both amount columns to show that the income statement has been verified as correct.

Analyzing an Income Statement Showing a Net Income

For a merchandising business, every sales dollar reported on the income statement includes four components. (1) Cost of merchandise sold. (2) Gross profit on sales. (3) Total expenses. (4) Net income. To help make decisions about future operations, CarLand analyzes relationships between these four income statement com-

414

TEACHING STRATEGIES: TEACHING TIP

Emphasize to students that the net income or loss on the income statement must be the same as the net income or loss on the work sheet.

INTERNATIONAL TELEPHONE COMMUNICATION

When placing direct telephone or fax calls to the United States and Canada, a simple system is followed. Each telephone number is preceded by a "1," which allows direct dialing without the assistance of an operator. The number is then followed by a three-digit area code and a 7-digit telephone number as shown below:

```
  1      XXX     XXX-XXXX
Direct   Area    Telephone
 Dial    Code     Number
```

However, when calling other countries, the proce-dure is somewhat more involved. It is necessary to first dial the International Access Code, which is "011." This International Access Code allows you to dial a foreign country direct without the assistance of an operator.

The next set of digits that follows is the country code. Every country in the world has a country code. The country code can be one or more digits.

The country code is then followed by a city code. The city code can also be one or more digits. This is then followed by the telephone number of the receiving party as follows:

```
 011       XX      XX    XXX-XXXX
International
 Access  Country  City    Local
  Code    Code    Code   Number
```

Not all countries have direct dialing. So before making international phone calls, you should check with your local telephone company for information.

The chart below illustrates selected country codes and city codes.

CITY	COUNTRY CODE	CITY CODE
London, England (inner city)	44	71
Frankfurt, Germany	49	69
Keelung, Taiwan	886	32
Barcelona, Spain	34	3
Innsbruck, Austria	43	5222
Helsinki, Finland	358	0
Athens, Greece	30	1
Canberra, Australia	61	62
Cape Town, South Africa	27	21
Oslo, Norway	47	2

ponents and sales. The percentage relationship between one financial statement item and the total that includes that item is known as a component percentage. On an income statement, component percentages are calculated by dividing the amount of each component by the amount of sales. CarLand calculates a component percentage for cost of merchandise sold, gross profit on sales, total expenses, and net income. The relationship between each component and sales is shown in a separate column on the income statement.

Acceptable Component Percentages

Unacceptable component percentages serve as a warning that management action is necessary.

For a component percentage to be useful, a business must know acceptable percentages. This information is determined by making comparisons with prior fiscal periods as well as with industry standards that are published by industry organizations. Based on these sources, CarLand determines the acceptable component percentages shown in the following table.

TEACHING STRATEGIES: TEACHING TIP

Review the definition of component percentage. The percentage relationship between one financial statement item and the total that includes that item is called a component percentage. Give some everyday examples of component percentages (i.e., number of males/females in class, number of students wearing sweaters, number of students that participate in school-sponsored athletics, etc.).

ASSESS

- Assess student understanding by checking solutions to Independent Practice activities.

- Review the procedures for preparing the income statement. Use Transparency 17-1, the completed income statement.

- Review the procedures for preparing a distribution of net income statement. Use Transparency 17-2, the completed distribution of net income statement.

Reteach

- Use Demonstration Problems 17A and 17B. These problems can be completed on the overhead with the students completing the problems at their desks.

- Duplicate and assign Math Work Sheets Chapter 17 Parts A and B, Calculating Cost of Merchandise Sold, and Calculating Component Percentages for an Income Statement from the Masters and Solutions to Enrichment/Application Activities Section in the Teacher's Resource Guide to provide additional practice on the mathematics of calculating cost of merchandise sold and component percentages.

Extend

Assign Cases for Critical Thinking 1.

Enrich

Assign the APPLIED COMMUNICATIONS special feature on page 431.

Income Statement Items	Acceptable Component Percentages	Actual Component Percentages
Sales	100.0%	100.0%
Cost of merchandise sold	not more than 50.0%	48.6%
Gross profit on sales	not less than 50.0%	51.4%
Total expenses	not more than 32.0%	30.9%
Net income	not less than 18.0%	20.4%

Each percentage represents the amount of each sales dollar that is considered acceptable. For example, CarLand determines that no more than 50 cents, or 50.0%, of each sales dollar should be devoted to cost of merchandise sold.

Cost of Merchandise Sold Component Percentage. The cost of merchandise sold is a major cost. Therefore, this cost must be kept as low as possible. Analysis of CarLand's income statement, Illustration 17-2, shows that the cost of merchandise sold is 48.6% of sales. This component percentage is calculated as shown below.

Cost of Merchandise Sold	÷	Sales	=	Cost of Merchandise Sold Component Percentage
$171,500.00	÷	$352,600.00	=	48.6%

The component percentage for cost of merchandise sold, 48.6%, is *less than* the maximum acceptable percentage, 50.0%. Therefore, CarLand's component percentage for cost of merchandise sold is considered acceptable.

Gross Profit on Sales Component Percentage. Gross profit must be large enough to cover total expenses and the desired amount of net income. CarLand determines that at least 50 cents, or 50.0%, of each sales dollar should result in gross profit. Analysis of Car-Land's income statement shows that the component percentage for gross profit on sales is 51.4%. This component percentage is calculated as shown below.

Gross Profit on Sales	÷	Sales	=	Gross Profit on Sales Component Percentage
$181,100.00	÷	$352,600.00	=	51.4%

The component percentage for gross profit on sales, 51.4%, is *not less than* the minimum acceptable percentage, 50.0%. Therefore, CarLand's component percentage for gross profit on sales is considered acceptable.

FYI

Negative amounts are written in parentheses.

Total Expenses Component Percentage. Total expenses must be less than gross profit on sales to provide a desirable net income. CarLand determines that no more than 32 cents, or 32.0%, of each sales dollar should be devoted to total expenses. Analysis of Car-

---

TEACHING STRATEGIES: Cooperative Learning

Involve students in a discussion as to what component percentages mean and when they are acceptable or not acceptable. Make sure that students are aware that component percentages are useful only if the following are considered: (a) industry standards, (b) past performances of the company, (c) more than one fiscal period, and (d) company's goals and objectives.

Land's income statement shows that the component percentage for total expenses is 30.9%. This component percentage is calculated as shown below.

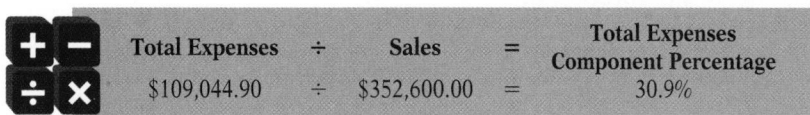

Total Expenses	÷	Sales	=	Total Expenses Component Percentage
$109,044.90	÷	$352,600.00	=	30.9%

The component percentage for total expenses, 30.9%, is *not more than* the maximum acceptable percentage, 32.0%. Therefore, CarLand's component percentage for total expenses is considered acceptable.

Net Income Component Percentage. The component percentage for net income shows the progress being made by a business. CarLand determines that at least 18 cents, or 18.0%, of each sales dollar should result in net income. Analysis of CarLand's income statement shows that the component percentage for net income is 20.4%. This component percentage is calculated as shown below.

Net Income	÷	Sales	=	Net Income Component Percentage
$72,055.10	÷	$352,600.00	=	20.4%

The component percentage for net income, 20.4%, is *not less than* the minimum acceptable percentage, 18.0%. Therefore, CarLand's component percentage for net income is considered acceptable.

Analyzing an Income Statement Showing a Net Loss

When a business' total expenses are greater than the gross profit on sales, the difference is known as a net loss. For example, the income statement shown in Illustration 17-3 on page 418 shows a net loss of $3,770.00 for the fiscal period.

Total expenses, $109,120.00, *less* gross profit on sales, $105,350.00, *equals* net loss, $3,770.00. The net loss amount, *$3,770.00*, is written in parentheses in the second amount column on the line with the words *Net Loss*. An amount written in parentheses on a financial statement indicates a negative amount.

Autoworks uses the same acceptable component percentages as CarLand. Analysis of the income statement, Illustration 17-3, indicates unacceptable component percentages. (1) The component percentage for cost of merchandise sold, 53.3%, is *more than* the maximum acceptable component percentage, 50.0%. (2) The component percentage for gross profit on sales, 46.7%, is *less than* the minimum acceptable component percentage, 50.0%. (3) The component percentage for total expenses, 48.4%, is *more than* the maximum acceptable component percentage, 32.0%. (4) Because a net loss occurred, the component percentage for net income, (1.67%), means that Autoworks lost 1.67 cents on each sales dollar. The net loss amount, $3,770.00, is considered unacceptable.

ILLUSTRATION 17-3 Income statement showing a net loss

Autoworks				
Income Statement				
For Year Ended December 31, 19--				
				% OF SALES
Revenue:				
Sales			225 40 0 00	100.0
Cost of Merchandise Sold:				
Merchandise Inventory, January 1, 19--	243 20 0 00			
Purchases	138 90 0 00			
Total Cost of Mdse. Available for Sale	382 10 0 00			
Less Mdse. Inventory, December 31, 19--	262 05 0 00			
Cost of Merchandise Sold			120 05 0 00	53.3
Gross Profit on Sales			105 35 0 00	46.7
Expenses:				
Advertising Expense		5 20 0 00		
Credit Card Fee Expense		3 12 0 00		
Insurance Expense		1 05 0 00		
Miscellaneous Expense		2 39 0 00		
Payroll Taxes Expense		8 34 0 00		
Rent Expense		14 40 0 00		
Salary Expense		62 31 0 00		
Supplies Expense—Office		4 62 0 00		
Supplies Expense—Store		4 28 0 00		
Utilities Expense		3 41 0 00		
Total Expenses			109 12 0 00	48.4
Net Loss			(3 77 0 00)	(1.67)

Actions to Correct Unacceptable Component Percentages

The goal of any business is to earn an acceptable net income. When component percentages are not acceptable, regardless of whether a net income or net loss occurred, management action is necessary.

Unacceptable Component Percentage for Gross Profit on Sales. The component percentage for gross profit on sales is directly related to sales revenue and cost of merchandise sold. An unacceptable component percentage for gross profit on sales requires one of three actions. (1) Increase sales revenue. (2) Decrease cost of merchandise sold. (3) Increase sales revenue and also decrease cost of merchandise sold.

Increasing sales revenue while keeping the cost of merchandise sold the same will increase gross profit on sales. To increase sales revenue, management may consider increasing the markup on merchandise purchased for sale. However, a business must be cautious on the amount of the markup increase. If the increase in markup is too large, a decrease in sales revenue could occur for two reasons. (1) The sales price is beyond what customers are willing to pay. (2) The sales price is higher than what competing businesses charge for the same merchandise.

Decreasing the cost of merchandise sold while keeping the sales revenue the same will also increase gross profit on sales. To decrease cost of merchandise sold, management should review purchasing practices. For example, would purchasing merchandise in larger quantities or from other vendors result in a lower cost?

Combining a small increase in sales revenue and a small decrease in the cost of merchandise sold may also result in an acceptable component percentage for gross profit on sales.

Unacceptable Component Percentage for Total Expenses. Each expense account balance must be reviewed to determine if major increases have occurred. This review should include comparisons with prior fiscal periods as well as with industry standards. Actions must then be taken to reduce any expenses for which major increases have occurred or that are beyond industry standards.

Unacceptable Component Percentage for Net Income. If the component percentages for cost of merchandise sold, gross profit on sales, and total expenses are brought within acceptable ranges, net income will also be acceptable.

DISTRIBUTION OF NET INCOME STATEMENT

A partnership's net income or net loss may be divided in any way agreed upon by the partners. Amy Kramer and Dario Mesa, partners in CarLand, agreed to share net income or net loss equally.

A partnership distribution of net income or net loss is usually shown on a separate financial statement. A partnership financial statement showing net income or loss distribution to partners is called a **distribution of net income statement**.

FYI

Partnerships must file tax returns with the IRS to report how income was divided among the partners.

Preparing a Distribution of Net Income Statement

The net income, $72,055.10, from the income statement shown in Illustration 17-2 is used to prepare the distribution of net income statement. CarLand's distribution of net income statement is shown in Illustration 17-4 on page 420.

CarLand uses seven steps in preparing a distribution of net income statement.

1 Write the heading of the distribution of net income statement on three lines.

ILLUSTRATION 17-4 Distribution of net income statement for a partnership

CarLand		
Distribution of Net Income Statement		
For Year Ended December 31, 19--		
Amy Kramer		
50.0% of Net Income		36 0 2 7 55
Dario Mesa		
50.0% of Net Income		36 0 2 7 55
Net Income		72 0 5 5 10

2 Write one partner's name, *Amy Kramer,* on the first line at the extreme left of the wide column.

3 Indent about one centimeter on the next line, and write Amy Kramer's share of net income as a percentage, *50.0% of Net Income.* Write Miss Kramer's share of net income, *$36,027.55* (50.0% × $72,055.10), in the amount column on the same line.

4 Write the other partner's name, *Dario Mesa,* on the next line at the extreme left of the wide column.

5 Indent about one centimeter on the next line, and write Dario Mesa's share of net income as a percentage, *50.0% of Net Income.* Write Mr. Mesa's share of net income, *$36,027.55* (50.0% × $72,055.10), in the amount column on the same line.

6 Write the words *Net Income* on the next line at the extreme left of the wide column. Add the distribution of net income for Amy Kramer, $36,027.55, and for Dario Mesa, $36,027.55. Write the total amount, *$72,055.10,* in the amount column. Verify accuracy by comparing the total amount, $72,055.10, with the net income reported on the income statement, $72,055.10. The two amounts must be the same.

7 Rule double lines across the amount column to show that the distribution of net income statement has been verified as correct.

Distribution of Net Income Statement with Unequal Distribution of Earnings

Regardless of how earnings are shared, the steps in preparing a distribution of net income statement are the same. The only difference is the description of how

Audit Your Understanding

1. What is the major difference between the income statement for a merchandising business and a service business?

2. How is the cost of merchandise sold calculated?

3. How can the amount of net income calculated on the income statement be verified?

4. What is the result if total expenses are greater than gross profit on sales?

the earnings are to be shared by the partners. A distribution of net income statement with unequal shares of earnings is shown in Illustration 17-5.

ILLUSTRATION 17-5

Distribution of net income statement with unequal distribution of earnings

Central Sporting Goods Distribution of Net Income Statement For Year Ended December 31, 19--	
Dolores Demski	
60.0% of Net Income	40 8 0 0 00
Linda Kemp	
40.0% of Net Income	27 2 0 0 00
Net Income	68 0 0 0 00

Dolores Demski and Linda Kemp are partners in a business. Because Mrs. Demski spends more time in the business than Ms. Kemp, the partners agree to share net income or loss unequally. Mrs. Demski gets 60.0% of net income or loss. Ms. Kemp gets 40.0% of net income or loss. With a net income of $68,000.00, Mrs. Demski receives 60.0%, or $40,800.00. Ms. Kemp receives 40.0%, or $27,200.00.

OWNERS' EQUITY STATEMENT

The amount of net income earned is important to business owners. Owners are also interested in changes that occur in owners' equity during a fiscal period. A financial statement that summarizes the changes in owners' equity during a fiscal period is called an **owners' equity statement.** Business owners can review an owners' equity statement to determine if owners' equity is increasing or decreasing and what is causing the change. Three factors can change owners' equity. (1) Additional investments. (2) Withdrawals. (3) Net income or net loss.

Preparing an Owners' Equity Statement

An owners' equity statement shows information about changes during a fiscal period in each partner's capital. Information needed to prepare an owners' equity statement is obtained from the distribution of net income statement and the general ledger capital and drawing accounts. The distribution of net income statement shows each partner's share of net income or net loss. Three kinds of information are obtained from each partner's capital and drawing account. (1) Beginning capital amount. (2) Any additional investments made during the fiscal period. (3) Each partner's withdrawal of assets during the fiscal period.

The general ledger capital and drawing accounts of Amy Kramer and Dario Mesa, partners, are shown in Illustration 17-6 on page 422.

Materials

- Student pages 421–429
- Transparencies: I, Blank One-Column Financial Form and Blank Three-Column Financial Form; J, Blank Two-Column Financial Form; 17-2, Distribution of Net Income Statement and Owners' Equity Statement; 17-3, Balance Sheet; 17-4, Chapter Summary
- Software: Spreadsheet Template, Electronic Study Guide
- Demonstration Problems: 17C, Preparing an Owners' Equity Statement; 17D, Preparing a Balance Sheet
- Global Perspective Activity Work Sheet (TRG)
- Assess: Problem Test Chapter 17; MicroExam Chapter 17

Objectives (Enabling Performance Tasks)

a. Define accounting terms related to financial statements for a merchandising business organized as a partnership.

b. Identify accounting concepts and practices related to financial statements for a merchandising business organized as a partnership.

f. Prepare an owners' equity statement for a merchandising business organized as a partnership.

g. Prepare a balance sheet for a merchandising business organized as a partnership.

- An income statement and a distribution of net income statement, the first two financial statements prepared by a merchandising business organized as a partnership, were discussed earlier in this chapter. In this lesson, we will look at the other two financial statements prepared by a merchandising business organized as a partnership—an owners' equity statement and a balance sheet. Supporting schedules for the balance sheet will also be introduced.

- Introduce new vocabulary: owners' equity statement, supporting schedule.

ILLUSTRATION 17-6   Partners' capital and drawing accounts

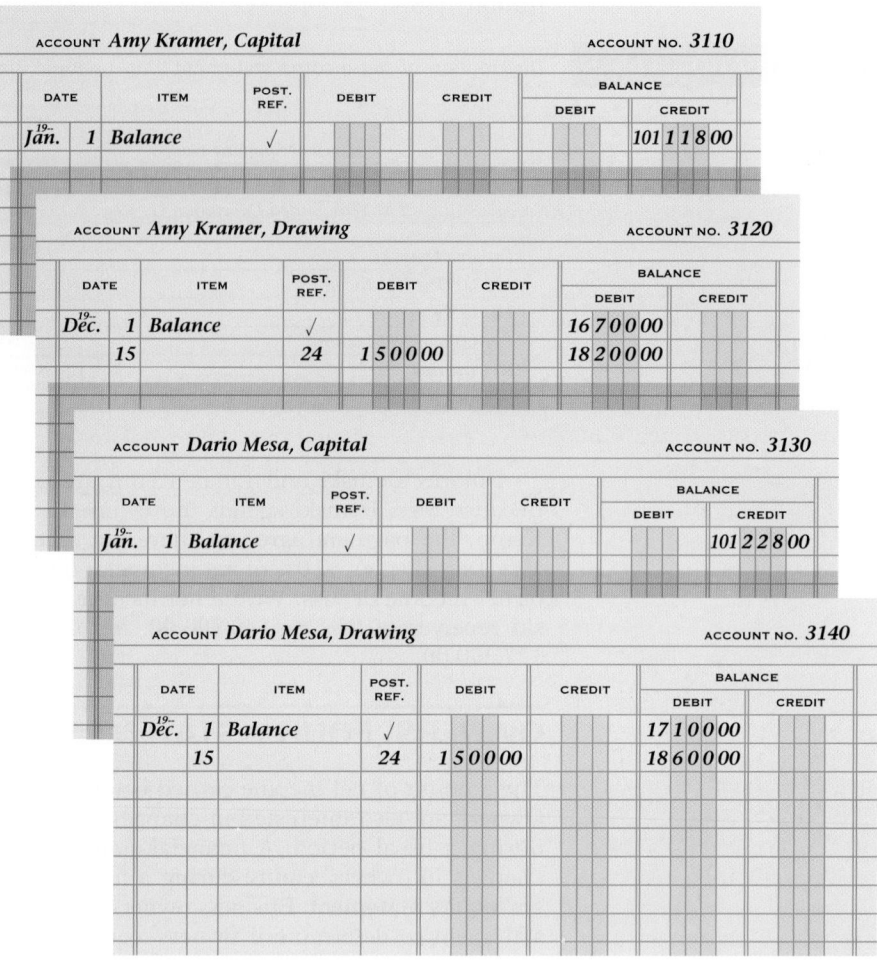

Neither Amy Kramer nor Dario Mesa invested any additional capital during the year ended December 31. The beginning and ending capital balances, therefore, are the same as recorded in the accounts on January 1. Both partners withdrew cash and merchandise during the year ended December 31.

CarLand's owners' equity statement, prepared for the year ended December 31, is shown in Illustration 17-7.

CarLand uses seven steps in preparing an owners' equity statement.

1 Write the heading of the owners' equity statement on three lines.

2 Write the name, *Amy Kramer*, on the first line at the extreme left of the wide column.

3 Calculate the net increase in capital for Amy Kramer.

ILLUSTRATION 17-7   Owners' equity statement

CarLand				
Owners' Equity Statement				
For Year Ended December 31, 19--				
Amy Kramer				
Capital, January 1, 19--			101 1 1 8 00	
Share of Net Income	36 0 2 7 55			
Less Withdrawals	18 2 0 0 00			
Net Increase in Capital			17 8 2 7 55	
Capital, December 31, 19--				118 9 4 5 55
Dario Mesa				
Capital, January 1, 19--			101 2 2 8 00	
Share of Net Income	36 0 2 7 55			
Less Withdrawals	18 6 0 0 00			
Net Increase in Capital			17 4 2 7 55	
Capital, December 31, 19--				118 6 5 5 55
Total Owners' Equity, December 31, 19--				237 6 0 1 10

TEACH

Cover student pages 421–429 "Owners' Equity Statement" and "Balance Sheet." When discussing the preparation of an owner's equity statement, emphasize that beginning capital is found in the capital account in the general ledger on January 1. Investments are any credit entries in the capital account. Point out that net income or loss is found on the distribution of net income statement. Emphasize that withdrawals are found in the drawing accounts in the general ledger.

When discussing the preparation of a balance sheet, explain that Chapter 9 used the account form of a balance sheet, which placed assets on the left side and liabilities and owners' equity on the right side. This chapter uses the report form in which all sections are listed on a 2-column financial form. Explain that each section title is centered. List amounts in the first column, totals in the second column. These are amount columns, not debit and credit columns. Emphasize that capital is found on the owners' equity statement.

- Indent about one centimeter on the next line, and write the words *Capital, January 1, 19--*. Write the beginning capital amount, *$101,118.00*, in the second amount column on the same line. (This amount is obtained from Miss Kramer's capital account in the general ledger.)

- Indent about one centimeter on the next line, and write the words *Share of Net Income*. On the same line, write Miss Kramer's share of net income amount, *$36,027.55*, in the first amount column. (This amount is obtained from the distribution of net income statement.)

- Indent about one centimeter on the next line, and write the words *Less Withdrawals*. On the same line, write the withdrawals amount, *$18,200.00*, in the first amount column. (This amount is obtained from Miss Kramer's drawing account in the general ledger.)

- Indent about one centimeter on the next line, and write the words *Net Increase in Capital*. Write the net increase in capital amount, *$17,827.55*, on the same line in the second amount column. (The share of net income, $36,027.55, *less* withdrawals, $18,200.00, *equals* the net increase in capital, $17,827.55.)

- Indent about one centimeter on the next line, and write the words *Capital, December 31, 19--*. Write the December 31 capital amount, *$118,945.55*, on the same line in the third amount column. (The January 1 capital, $101,118.00, *plus* the net increase in capital, $17,827.55, *equals* the December 31 capital, $118,945.55.)

TEACHING STRATEGIES: DIFFERENT LEARNING ABILITIES

Gifted Students. Students who are gifted often enjoy the challenge of getting to the heart of a problem. Assign Challenge Problem 17-C, which is preparing a distribution of net income and an owner's equity statement. Have the students complete the problem and then present it to the class, explaining the steps taken to prepare these financial statements.

4 Write the name, *Dario Mesa*, on the next line at the extreme left of the wide column.

5 Calculate the net increase in capital for Dario Mesa.

- Indent about one centimeter on the next line, and write the words *Capital, January 1, 19--*. On the same line, write the beginning capital amount, *$101,228.00*, in the second amount column.

- Indent about one centimeter on the next line, and write the words *Share of Net Income*. On the same line, write Mr. Dario's share of net income amount, *$36,027.55*, in the first amount column.

- Indent about one centimeter on the next line, and write the words *Less Withdrawals*. On the same line, write the withdrawals amount, *$18,600.00*, in the first amount column.

- Indent about one centimeter on the next line, and write the words *Net Increase in Capital*. On the same line, write the difference, *$17,427.55*, in the second amount column.

- Indent about one centimeter on the next line, and write the words *Capital, December 31, 19--*. On the same line, write the December 31 capital amount, *$118,655.55*, in the third amount column.

6 Write the words *Total Owners' Equity, December 31, 19--* on the next line at the extreme left of the wide column. On the same line, write the total amount, *$237,601.10*, in the third amount column.

7 Rule double lines across the three amount columns to show that the totals have been verified as correct.

Some businesses include the owners' equity statement information as part of the balance sheet. An example of this method of reporting changes in owner's equity is shown in Illustration 9-13, Chapter 9.

Owners' Equity Statement with an Additional Investment and a Net Loss

On December 31 the capital accounts of Kevin Blaine and David Lamont showed additional investments of $10,000.00 each. Also, the income statement, Illustration 17-3, showed a net loss of $3,770.00. The partners agreed to share net income or net loss equally. The owners' equity statement for Autoworks is shown in Illustration 17-8.

BALANCE SHEET

Some management decisions can best be made after owners have determined the amount of assets, liabilities, and owners' equity. Owners could obtain some of the information needed by inspect-

Autoworks			
Owners' Equity Statement			
For Year Ended December 31, 19--			
Kevin Blaine			
Capital, January 1, 19--	104 3 0 0 00		
Plus Additional Investment	10 0 0 0 00		
Total		114 3 0 0 00	
Share of Net Loss	1 8 8 5 00		
Plus Withdrawals	14 8 0 0 00		
Net Decrease in Capital		16 6 8 5 00	
Capital, December 31, 19--			97 6 1 5 00
David Lamont			
Capital, January 1, 19--	102 8 0 0 00		
Plus Additional Investment	10 0 0 0 00		
Total		112 8 0 0 00	
Share of Net Loss	1 8 8 5 00		
Plus Withdrawals	15 1 0 0 00		
Net Decrease in Capital		16 9 8 5 00	
Capital, December 31, 19--			95 8 1 5 00
Total Owners' Equity, December 31, 19--			193 4 3 0 00

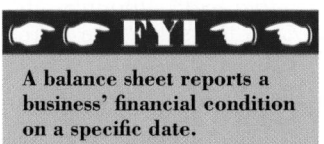

A balance sheet reports a business' financial condition on a specific date.

ing general ledger accounts. The information needed might also be found on a work sheet. However, the information is easier to use when organized and reported on a balance sheet. A balance sheet reports a business' financial condition on a specific date. A balance sheet may be prepared in account form or report form. Rugcare, described in Chapter 9, uses the account form. CarLand uses the report form.

Preparing a Balance Sheet

The information used to prepare a balance sheet is obtained from two sources. (1) The Balance Sheet columns of a work sheet, as shown in Illustration 17-9 on page 426. (2) The owners' equity statement, as shown in Illustration 17-7.

CarLand's completed balance sheet on December 31, the last day of the fiscal year, is shown in Illustration 17-10 on page 427.

CarLand uses six steps in preparing a balance sheet.

1 Write the balance sheet heading on three lines.

2 Prepare the assets section of the balance sheet. Use information from the work sheet given in Illustration 17-9.

- Write the section title, *Assets*, on the first line in the middle of the wide column.
- Beginning on the next line, at the extreme left of the wide column, write the asset account titles in the order in which

- Assess student understanding by checking solutions to Independent Practice activities.
- Review the procedures for preparing the owner's equity statement. Use Transparency 17-2, the completed owner's equity statement.
- Review the procedures for preparing a balance sheet. Use Transparency 17-3, the completed balance sheet.

Reteach

- Use Demonstration Problems 17-C and 17-D. These problems can be completed on the overhead with the students completing the problems at their desks.
- Assign Recycling Problem 17-R.

Extend

- Assign Cases for Critical Thinking 2.
- Assign Challenge Problem 17-C (the challenge is that the distribution of net income is uneven and an additional investment is included).

Enrich

- Assign the GLOBAL PERSPECTIVE ACTIVITY on page 415 to allow students to further explore this global topic. Use the GLOBAL PERSPECTIVE ACTIVITY work sheet in the Masters and Solutions to Enrichment/Application Activities Section in the Teacher's Resource Guide.
- Assign the Spreadsheet Template for Problems 17-M and 17-C.
- Assign Electronic Study Guide Chapter 17 to complete the study guide from the working papers at the computer.

APPLIED SKILLS: WORD PROCESSING

If you wish to integrate word processing in your accounting course, you may direct students to answer the end-of-chapter Accounting Terms, Questions for Individual Study, and Cases for Critical Thinking using their word processing software.

CLOSURE

- Use Audit Your Understanding questions.
- Review Summary Illustration 17-11, "Summary of Financial Statements for a Partnership," and Transparency 17-4, Chapter Summary.

ASSESS

- Administer Problem Test Chapter 17.
- Administer a MicroExam test for Chapter 17.

APPLIED SKILLS: LANGUAGE ARTS

Paraphrasing, writing complete sentences, and identifying objects of prepositional phrases. For additional practice in language arts skills, direct students to answer the Accounting Terms and Questions for Individual Study at the end of the chapter. Students should write the answers in their own words and in complete sentences. To further practice language arts skills, ask students to underline all the objects of prepositional phrases in their answers.

ILLUSTRATION 17-9   Balance sheet information on a work sheet

	ACCOUNT TITLE	TRIAL BALANCE DEBIT	TRIAL BALANCE CREDIT	ADJUSTMENTS DEBIT	ADJUSTMENTS CREDIT	INCOME STATEMENT DEBIT	INCOME STATEMENT CREDIT	BALANCE SHEET DEBIT	BALANCE SHEET CREDIT	
1	Cash	2423357						2423357		1
2	Petty Cash	50000						50000		2
3	Accounts Receivable	933200						933200		3
4	Merchandise Inventory	22540000			(a)1320000			21220000		4
5	Supplies—Office	540000			(b)394000			146000		5
6	Supplies—Store	578000			(c)326000			252000		6
7	Prepaid Insurance	484000			(d)264000			220000		7
8	Accounts Payable		1045190						1045190	8
9	Employee Income Tax Pay.		40200						40200	9
10	FICA Tax Payable		83216						83216	10
11	Sales Tax Payable		176000						176000	11
12	Unemploy. Tax Pay.—Fed.		5915						5915	12
13	Unemploy. Tax Pay.—State		39926						39926	13
14	Health Ins. Premiums Pay.		84000						84000	14
15	U.S. Savings Bonds Pay.		4000						4000	15
16	United Way Donations Pay.		6000						6000	16
17										17
18										18

they appear on the work sheet. Write the balance of each asset account in the first amount column.

- Write the words *Total Assets* on the next line below the last asset account title. Total the individual asset amounts, and write the total assets, *$252,445.57*, on the same line in the second amount column.

3 Prepare the liabilities section of the balance sheet. Use information from the work sheet given in Illustration 17-9.

- Write the section title, *Liabilities*, on the next line in the middle of the wide column.
- Beginning on the next line, at the extreme left of the wide column, write the liability account titles in the order in which they appear on the work sheet. Write the balance of each liability account in the first amount column.
- Write the words *Total Liabilities* on the next line below the last liability account title. Total the individual liability amounts, and write the total liabilities, *$14,844.47*, on the same line in the second amount column.

4 Prepare the owners' equity section of the balance sheet. Use information from the owners' equity statement given in Illustration 17-7.

- Write the section title, *Owners' Equity*, on the next line in the middle of the wide column.
- Write the account title, Amy Kramer, Capital, on the next line at the extreme left of the wide column. On the same line,

ILLUSTRATION 17-10 Balance sheet for a partnership

CarLand				
Balance Sheet				
December 31, 19--				
Assets				
Cash	24 2 3 3 57			
Petty Cash	5 0 0 00			
Accounts Receivable	9 3 3 2 00			
Merchandise Inventory	212 2 0 0 00			
Supplies—Office	1 4 6 0 00			
Supplies—Store	2 5 2 0 00			
Prepaid Insurance	2 2 0 0 00			
Total Assets			252 4 4 5 57	
Liabilities				
Accounts Payable	10 4 5 1 90			
Employee Income Tax Payable	4 0 2 00			
FICA Tax Payable	8 3 2 16			
Sales Tax Payable	1 7 6 0 00			
Unemployment Tax Payable—Federal	5 9 15			
Unemployment Tax Payable—State	3 9 9 26			
Health Insurance Premiums Payable	8 4 0 00			
U.S. Savings Bonds Payable	4 0 00			
United Way Donations Payable	6 0 00			
Total Liabilities			14 8 4 4 47	
Owners' Equity				
Amy Kramer, Capital	118 9 4 5 55			
Dario Mesa, Capital	118 6 5 5 55			
Total Owners' Equity			237 6 0 1 10	
Total Liabilities and Owners' Equity			252 4 4 5 57	

FYI

Verify accuracy of the balance sheet by comparing the total amount of assets and the total amount of liabilities and owner's equity. The two amounts must be the same.

write the amount of Amy Kramer's current capital, *$118,945.55,* in the first amount column.

- Write the account title, Dario Mesa, Capital, on the next line at the extreme left of the wide column. On the same line, write the amount of Dario Mesa's current capital, *$118,655.55,* in the first amount column.

- Write the words *Total Owners' Equity* on the next line at the extreme left of the wide column. Add the two capital amounts, and write the total, *$237,601.10,* on the same line in the second amount column.

5 Total the liabilities and owners' equity sections of the balance sheet.

- Write the words *Total Liabilities and Owners' Equity* on the next line at the extreme left of the wide column. Total the liabilities and owners' equity, and write the total, $252,445.57, on the same line in the second amount column.

Verify accuracy by comparing the total amount of assets and the total amount of liabilities and owners' equity. These two amounts must be the same. The two amounts, $252,445.57, are the same. The balance sheet is assumed to be correct.

6 Rule double lines across both amount columns below Total Assets and below Total Liabilities and Owners' Equity. These two sets of double lines show that the amounts have been verified as correct.

Supporting Schedules for a Balance Sheet

A report prepared to give details about an item on a principal financial statement is called a **supporting schedule**. A supporting schedule is sometimes referred to as a supplementary report or an exhibit.

CarLand prepares two supporting schedules to accompany the balance sheet. The supporting schedules are a schedule of accounts payable and a schedule of accounts receivable. A balance sheet shows only the accounts payable total amount. The account balance for each vendor is not shown. When detailed information is needed, a supporting schedule of accounts payable is prepared showing the balance for each vendor. A balance sheet also shows only the accounts receivable total amount. When information about the account balance for each customer is needed, a supporting schedule of accounts receivable is prepared. CarLand's supporting schedules on December 31 are similar to the supporting schedules for November 30 shown in Chapter 13.

The chart shown in Illustration 17-11 summarizes the financial statements for a partnership.

Audit Your Understanding

1. What information used to prepare an owners' equity statement is obtained from the distribution of net income statement?

2. What information used to prepare an owners' equity statement is obtained from the partners' capital and drawing accounts?

3. What are two supporting schedules that might accompany a balance sheet?

SUMMARY ILLUSTRATION 17-11

Summary of financial statements for a partnership

1 Information from the completed work sheet is used to prepare the income statement.

2 Information from the income statement is used to prepare the distribution of net income statement.

3 Information from the distribution of net income statement and the general ledger capital and drawing accounts is used to prepare the owners' equity statement.

4 Information from the completed work sheet and the owners' equity statement is used to prepare the balance sheet.

TEACHING STRATEGIES:
APPLYING VISUALS

Direct students to Summary Illustration 17-11 which reviews the financial statements for a partnership.

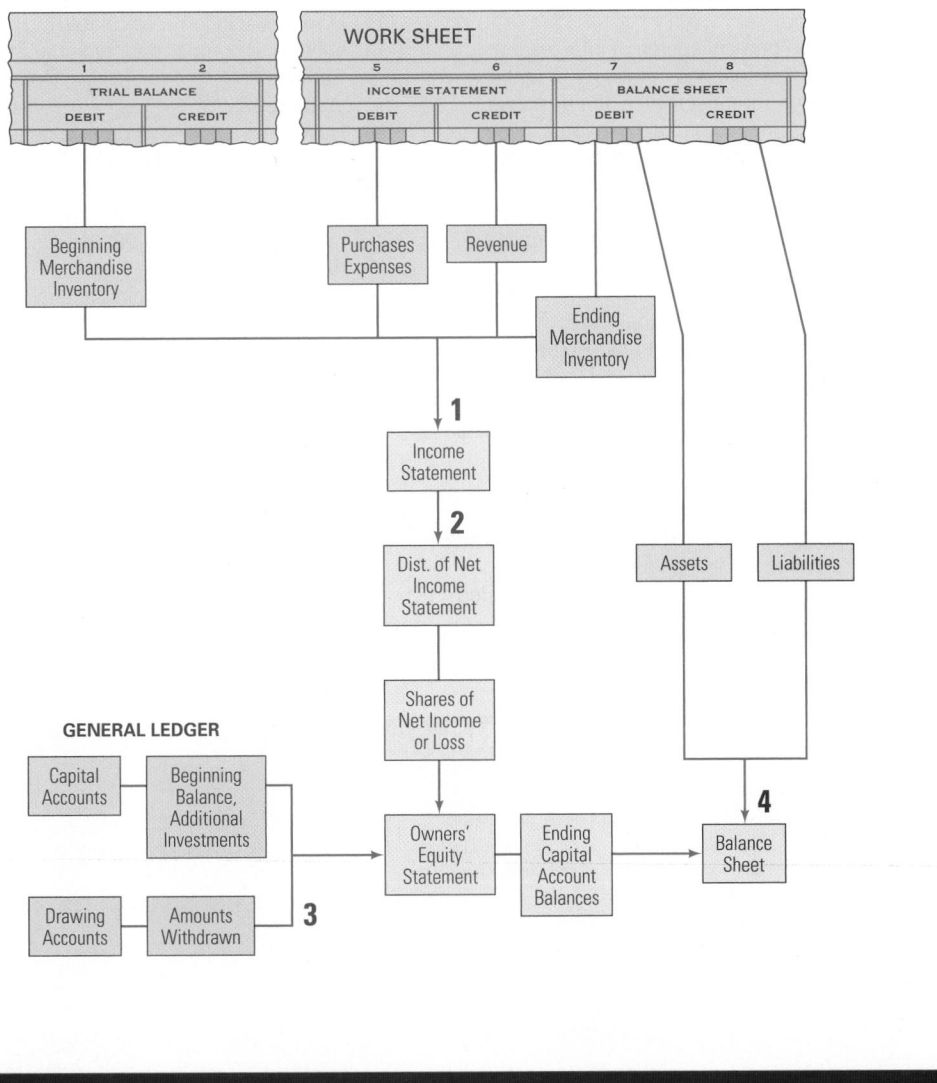

ACCOUNTING TERMS

1. cost of merchandise sold: The total original price of all merchandise sold during a fiscal period. (p. 411)

2. gross profit on sales: The revenue remaining after cost of merchandise sold has been deducted. (p. 414)

3. distribution of net income statement: A partnership financial statement showing net income or loss distribution to partners. (p. 419)

4. owners' equity statement: A financial statement that summarizes the changes in owners' equity during a fiscal period. (p. 421)

5. supporting schedule: A report prepared to give details about an item on a principal financial statement. (p. 428)

QUESTIONS FOR INDIVIDUAL STUDY

1. To organize and summarize financial information. (p. 411)

2. Financial statements. (p. 411)

3. Adequate Disclosure. (p. 411)

4. Consistent Reporting. (p. 411)

5. Income statement. (p. 411)

6. Current and previous income statements can be compared. (p. 411)

7. From a completed work sheet. (p. 411)

8. Revenue section, cost of merchandise sold section, and expenses section. (p. 411)

9. Purchases are added to beginning merchandise inventory to determine cost of merchandise available for sale. Ending merchandise inventory is then subtracted from cost of merchandise available for sale to determine cost of merchandise sold. (pp. 412–413)

10. Cost of merchandise sold is subtracted from total revenue. (p. 414)

11. Total expenses are subtracted from gross profit on sales. (p. 414)

12. Cost of merchandise sold, gross profit on sales, total expenses, and net income. (p. 414)

13. By making comparisons with prior fiscal periods as well as with industry standards. (p. 415)

14. Gross profit on sales is subtracted from total expenses. (p. 417)

15. (1) The sales price is beyond what customers are willing to pay. (2) The sales price is higher than what competing businesses charge for the same merchandise. (p. 419)

ACCOUNTING TERMS   EPT(a)

What is the meaning of each of the following?

1. **cost of merchandise sold**
2. **gross profit on sales**
3. **distribution of net income statement**
4. **owners' equity statement**
5. **supporting schedule**

QUESTIONS FOR INDIVIDUAL STUDY   EPT(b)

1. Why is a work sheet prepared at the end of a fiscal period?
2. What is the primary source of information needed by owners and managers to make decisions on future activities of a business?
3. Which accounting concept is being applied when financial statements contain all information necessary for a reader to understand a business' financial condition and progress?
4. Which accounting concept is being applied when accounting principles are applied the same way in preparing financial statements from one fiscal period to the next?
5. Which financial statement reports the financial progress of a business?
6. How may income statements be used to determine reasons for increases or decreases in net income?
7. Where does a business find the information needed to prepare an income statement?
8. What are the three main sections of an income statement for a merchandising business?
9. How is the cost of merchandise sold calculated?
10. How is the gross profit on sales calculated?
11. How is net income calculated?
12. What four component percentages does CarLand calculate to analyze its income statement?
13. How does a business determine acceptable component percentages?
14. How is net loss calculated?
15. What are two reasons why an increase in markup could result in a decrease in sales revenue?
16. Why does a partnership prepare a distribution of net income statement?
17. Why do businesses prepare an owners' equity statement?
18. What three factors can cause changes in owners' equity to occur?
19. Where does a business find the information needed to prepare an owners' equity statement?
20. Which financial statement reports the financial condition of a business?

CASES FOR CRITICAL THINKING   EPT(b,d)

CASE 1 Jun Mori and Victoria Leben, partners, compared their current income statement with their income statement of a year ago. They noted that sales were 15.0% higher than a year ago. They also noted that the total expenses were 20.0% higher than a year ago. What type of analysis should be done to determine whether the increase in expenses is justified?

CASE 2 Rhoda Chalupa and Jonathan Fulton are partners in a paint and decorating store. The store operates on a yearly fiscal period. At the end of each year, an accountant is hired to prepare financial statements. At the end of each month during the year, Mrs. Chalupa prepares a work sheet. The work sheet is prepared to determine if the business made or lost money that month. The accountant suggests that monthly financial statements also be prepared. Mrs. Chalupa believes, however, that the monthly work sheet is sufficient to determine how the business is doing. Do you agree with Mrs. Chalupa or the accountant? Why?

430   PART 3   Accounting for a Merchandising Business Organized as a Partnership

---

16. To report how the net income or net loss is distributed to the partners. (p. 419)

17. To show the changes in owners' equity during a fiscal period. (p. 421)

18. (1) Additional investments are made. (2) Cash, merchandise, or other assets are withdrawn. (3) Net income or net loss occurs from business operations. (p. 421)

19. From the distribution of net income statement and the general ledger capital and drawing accounts. (p. 421)

20. Balance sheet. (p. 425)

APPLIED COMMUNICATIONS

A long written report should contain numerous headings. A heading enables the reader to focus on the primary idea of the next section. An outline is a special document that lists only the headings of a report. By reviewing an outline before and after reading a report, the reader can gain a better understanding of the relationship among the topics being presented.

Each chapter of this textbook is similar to a long report. Headings are used to separate and emphasize major concepts.

INSTRUCTIONS:

Prepare an outline of this chapter.

DRILLS FOR UNDERSTANDING

EPT(c,d,e)

DRILL 17-D1   Calculating the cost of merchandise sold

Information from the work sheets of three businesses is given in the working papers accompanying this textbook.

INSTRUCTIONS:

Calculate the cost of merchandise sold for each business.

DRILL 17-D2   Calculating net income or loss

Information from the work sheets of three businesses is given in the working papers accompanying this textbook.

INSTRUCTIONS:

Calculate the net income or loss for each business.

DRILL 17-D3   Calculating component percentages

Information from the income statements of three businesses is given in the working papers accompanying this textbook.

INSTRUCTIONS:

Calculate component percentages for cost of merchandise sold, gross profit on sales, total expenses, and net income for each business. Round percentage calculations to the nearest 0.1%.

DRILL 17-D4   Calculating the distribution of net income or loss

Information concerning net income or loss distribution for three businesses is given in the working papers accompanying this textbook.

INSTRUCTIONS:

1. Assume that each business earned a net income of $64,000.00. What is the amount of income to be distributed to each partner in each business?
2. Assume that each business had a net loss of $8,000.00. What is the amount of loss to be distributed to each partner in each business?

APPLICATION PROBLEMS

EPT(c,d,e,f,g)

PROBLEM 17-1   Preparing financial statements

The work sheet for Midwest Supply for the year ended December 31 of the current year is provided in the working papers accompanying this textbook.

CHAPTER 17   Financial Statements for a Partnership   **431**

CASES FOR CRITICAL THINKING

Case 1   Compare the current net income with the net income for the previous year. If the current net income is also 15.0% higher than a year ago, the increase in total expenses may be justified. However, a more complete analysis may be made by calculating component percentages on the two income statements. Industry standards should be reviewed to determine acceptable component percentages. If the component percentages for cost of merchandise sold and gross profit on sales are both acceptable, total expenses and net income should then be analyzed. If the component percentages for total expenses and net income are both acceptable, the increase in total expenses may be justified. However, if either of these component percentages are unacceptable, individual expense accounts should be examined to determine which could be reduced without reducing sales. Also, even though the component percentage for net income may be acceptable, the percentage may have decreased due to the increase in total expenses. Therefore, individual expense accounts should regularly be reviewed for possible reductions.

Case 2   The monthly work sheet may not be sufficient. The work sheet does not separate and report information the same way financial statements do. For example, what items are contributing most to net income or net loss? This question can be best answered by comparing monthly income statements. What is happening to the business' financial condition? This question can be best answered by comparing monthly balance sheets. Even if the only comparison made is whether the business is making a net income or a net loss, owners may have difficulty determining specific, individual items that need attention from the work sheets alone. Therefore, the accountant's suggestion may be justified.

APPLIED COMMUNICATIONS

Students' solutions will vary slightly in format. The instructor should consider the following items when grading this activity: (1) completeness, and (2) mechanics (grammar, spelling, punctuation, sentence structure).

See Teacher's Edition of Working Papers for complete solutions to drills and problems.

Drill 17-D1 Cost of merchandise sold: (A) $17,800; (B) 20,200; (C) 37,400

Drill 17-D2 Net income/net loss: (A) 44,500; (B) (2,200); (C) 39,600

Drill 17-D3 (A) 100.0%; 48.9%; 51.1%; 22.0%; 29.0%; (B) 100.0%; 47.6%; 52.4%; 29.3%; 23.2%; (C) 100% 53.5%; 46.5%; 30.1%; 16.4%

Drill 17-D4 (A) 32,000; 4,000; 32,000; 4,000; (B) 25,600; 3,200; 38,400; 4,800; (C) 16,000; 2,000; 19,200; 2,400; 28,800; 3,600

Problem 17-1 49.2%; 50.8%; 17.8%; 33.0%. Capital Angulo 121,233.20; Capital Munoz 120,216.60. Total liab. and owner's eq. 251,125.

Problem 17-2 Capital Cova 166,180; Capital Landon 136,620

Problem 17-3 Capital Chapman 107,920; Capital Jaffa 99,060

Mastery Problem 17-M 55.9%; 44.1%; 16.4%; 27.7%. Capital Faust 159,657.50; Capital Mason 154,697.50. Total liab. and owner's eq. 324,557.

INSTRUCTIONS:

1. Prepare an income statement. Calculate and record the following component percentages: (a) cost of merchandise sold, (b) gross profit on sales, (c) total expenses, and (d) net income or loss. Round percentage calculations to the nearest 0.1%.
2. Prepare a distribution of net income statement. Net income or loss is to be shared equally.
3. Prepare an owners' equity statement. No additional investments were made.
4. Prepare a balance sheet in report form.

PROBLEM 17-2 **Preparing a distribution of net income statement and an owners' equity statement (net income)**

Louise Cova and Diane Landon are partners in a merchandising business. The following information was taken from the records on December 31 of the current year.

Partner	Balance of Capital Account January 1	Balance of Drawing Account	Distribution of Net Income
Cova	$138,000.00	$15,260.00	60.0%
Landon	$124,000.00	$16,340.00	40.0%

INSTRUCTIONS:

1. On December 31 the partnership had a net income of $72,400.00. Prepare a distribution of net income statement for the partnership of C.L. Sales.
2. Prepare an owners' equity statement. No additional investments were made.

PROBLEM 17-3 **Preparing an owners' equity statement (net loss)**

Paul Chapman and Lawrence Jaffa are partners in a merchandising business. The following information was taken from the records on December 31 of the current year.

Partner	Balance of Capital Account	Balance of Drawing Account	Distribution of Net Loss
Chapman	$113,000.00	$12,680.00	$3,400.00
Jaffa	$107,000.00	$13,540.00	$3,400.00

INSTRUCTIONS:

Prepare an owners' equity statement for Riverside Supply. Additional investments made during the year: Paul Chapman, $11,000.00; Lawrence Jaffa, $9,000.00.

ENRICHMENT PROBLEMS   EPT(c,d,e,f,g)

MASTERY PROBLEM 17-M **Preparing financial statements**

Gallery Furniture prepared the work sheet on the following page for the year ended December 31 of the current year.

INSTRUCTIONS:

1. Prepare an income statement. Calculate and record the following component percentages: (a) cost of merchandise sold, (b) gross profit on sales, (c) total expenses, and (d) net income or loss. Round percentage calculations to the nearest 0.1%.

Gallery Furniture

Work Sheet

For Year Ended December 31, 19--

	ACCOUNT TITLE	TRIAL BALANCE		ADJUSTMENTS		INCOME STATEMENT		BALANCE SHEET		
		DEBIT	CREDIT	DEBIT	CREDIT	DEBIT	CREDIT	DEBIT	CREDIT	
1	Cash	28792.00						28792.00		1
2	Petty Cash	500.00						500.00		2
3	Accounts Receivable	12835.00						12835.00		3
4	Merchandise Inventory	290600.00			(a)14510.00			276090.00		4
5	Supplies—Office	5375.00			(b)3360.00			2015.00		5
6	Supplies—Store	5840.00			(c)3720.00			2120.00		6
7	Prepaid Insurance	5145.00			(d)2940.00			2205.00		7
8	Accounts Payable		9130.00						9130.00	8
9	Sales Tax Payable		1072.00						1072.00	9
10	Jennifer Faust, Capital		142960.00						142960.00	10
11	Jennifer Faust, Drawing	18910.00						18910.00		11
12	David Mason, Capital		137450.00						137450.00	12
13	David Mason, Drawing	18360.00						18360.00		13
14	Income Summary			(a)14510.00		14510.00				14
15	Sales		257300.00				257300.00			15
16	Purchases	129280.00				129280.00				16
17	Advertising Expense	5585.00				5585.00				17
18	Credit Card Fee Expense	2360.00				2360.00				18
19	Insurance Expense			(d)2940.00		2940.00				19
20	Miscellaneous Expense	2640.00				2640.00				20
21	Rent Expense	19200.00				19200.00				21
22	Supplies Expense—Office			(b)3360.00		3360.00				22
23	Supplies Expense—Store			(c)3720.00		3720.00				23
24	Utilities Expense	2490.00				2490.00				24
25		547912.00	547912.00	24530.00	24530.00	186085.00	257300.00	361827.00	290612.00	25
26	Net Income					71215.00			71215.00	26
27						257300.00	257300.00	361827.00	361827.00	27
28										28

2. Prepare a distribution of net income statement. Net income or loss is to be shared equally.
3. Prepare an owners' equity statement. No additional investments were made.
4. Prepare a balance sheet in report form.

CHALLENGE PROBLEM 17-C Preparing financial statements (unequal distribution of net income; additional investment)

Gallery Furniture's work sheet is shown in Mastery Problem 17-M.

INSTRUCTIONS:

1. Prepare a distribution of net income statement. The net income is to be shared as follows: Jennifer Faust, 75.0%; David Mason, 25.0%.
2. Prepare an owners' equity statement. Mr. Mason made an additional investment of $15,000.00 during the year. He had a beginning capital of $122,450.00.

CHAPTER 18 OVERVIEW

Chapter 18 describes all aspects of recording the adjusting and closing entries for a merchandising business organized as a partnership. The procedures are identical to those studied in Chapter 10 for a service business organized as a proprietorship; only the account titles and number of accounts involved differ. Using the work sheet as the source of information for recording adjusting and closing entries helps

GUIDE TO ACHIEVING LEARNING OBJECTIVES

Enabling Performance Tasks	TEACH Lesson Plans	APPLY Drills for Understanding	APPLY Application Problems	EXTEND/ENRICH Mastery Problems	EXTEND/ENRICH Challenge Problems	EXTEND/ENRICH Cases for Critical Thinking	EXTEND/ENRICH Recycling Problems	EXTEND/ENRICH Reinforcement Activity
a. Identify accounting concepts and practices related to adjusting and closing entries for a merchandising business organized as a partnership.	18-1, 18-2							
b. Record adjusting entries for a merchandising business organized as a partnership.	18-1	18-D1	18-1	18-M	18-C	Case 1	18-R	2B
c. Record closing entries for a merchandising business organized as a partnership.	18-2	18-D2	18-1	18-M	18-C	Case 2	18-R	2B
d. Prepare a post-closing trial balance for a merchandising business organized as a partnership.	18-2		18-1	18-M	18-C			2B

ENRICHMENT

SPECIAL FEATURES	TECHNOLOGY CONNECTION
Multicultural Awareness, page 438	*Automated Accounting 6.0* Problems 18-1, 18-M, 18-C
Personal Visions in Business, page 443	Integrating Automated Accounting Topic 6 Optional Problem DB-6A
Careers in Accounting, page 460	Accounting Tutorial Units 5, 6
	Application Program Disk Problem 18-M
	Electronic Study Guide

demystify the process. This chapter reinforces the importance of adjusting and closing entries in the end-of-fiscal-period work for any accounting cycle.

Challenge Problem 18-C reinforces the completion of a 10-column work sheet introduced in Chapter 16.

	INFORMAL ASSESSMENT		FORMAL ASSESSMENT				
Study Guide	Audit Your Understanding	Chapter MicroExam	Chapter Problem Test	Unit Problem Test	Unit Objective Test	Portfolio
Unit B	✓	✓			✓	
Unit A			✓	✓		✓
Unit A			✓	✓		✓
			✓			✓

NEW, REVIEW, AND EXTENSION

ACTIVITIES/CONCEPTS/TRANSACTIONS	NEW	REVIEW/ EXTENSION
Recording adjusting entry for merchandise inventory	✓	
Recording adjusting entry for supplies inventories		✓
Recording adjusting entry for prepaid insurance		✓
Recording entry to close income statement accounts with credit balances		✓
Recording entry to close income statement accounts with debit balances		✓
Recording entry to record net income or loss and close income summary account		✓
Recording entry to close the partners' drawing accounts		✓
Preparing a post-closing trial balance		✓

TEACHING MATERIALS

Teacher's Wraparound Edition of the Text

Teacher's Resource Guide

Teacher's Edition of Working Papers

Teacher's Edition of the Demonstration/Recycling Problems

Teaching Transparencies

Accounting Tutorial Manual

MicroExam

Key for Viking Marine

18

Recording Adjusting and Closing Entries for a Partnership

ENABLING PERFORMANCE TASKS

After studying Chapter 18, you will be able to:

a Identify accounting concepts and practices related to adjusting and closing entries for a merchandising business organized as a partnership.

b Record adjusting entries for a merchandising business organized as a partnership.

c Record closing entries for a merchandising business organized as a partnership.

d Prepare a post-closing trial balance for a merchandising business organized as a partnership.

General ledger account balances are changed only by posting journal entries. Two types of journal entries change general ledger account balances at the end of a fiscal period. (1) Adjusting entries bring general ledger account balances up to date. (2) Closing entries prepare temporary accounts for the next fiscal period. *(CONCEPT: Matching Expenses with Revenue)* Information needed for journalizing adjusting entries is taken from the Adjustments columns of a work sheet. Information needed for journalizing closing entries is taken from the Income Statement and Balance Sheet columns of a work sheet and a distribution of net income statement.

RECORDING ADJUSTING ENTRIES

Four adjustments in the partial work sheet's Adjustments columns are shown in Illustration 18-1.

ILLUSTRATION 18-1   Partial work sheet showing adjustments

	1	2	3	4
	TRIAL BALANCE		ADJUSTMENTS	
ACCOUNT TITLE	DEBIT	CREDIT	DEBIT	CREDIT
4 Merchandise Inventory	225 4 0 0 00			(a)13 2 0 0 00
5 Supplies—Office	5 4 0 0 00			(b) 3 9 4 0 00
6 Supplies—Store	5 7 8 0 00			(c) 3 2 6 0 00
7 Prepaid Insurance	4 8 4 0 00			(d) 2 6 4 0 00
21 Income Summary			(a)13 2 0 0 00	
26 Insurance Expense			(d) 2 6 4 0 00	
31 Supplies Expense—Office			(b) 3 9 4 0 00	
32 Supplies Expense—Store			(c) 3 2 6 0 00	
33				

Remember to start a new page for adjusting entries.

Adjusting entries are recorded on the next journal page following the page on which the last daily transaction for the month is recorded. The adjusting entries are entered in the General Debit and Credit columns of a journal. CarLand's four adjusting entries are recorded in a journal as shown in Illustration 18-2 on page 436.

The heading, *Adjusting Entries,* is written in the middle of the journal's Account Title column. This heading explains all of the adjusting entries that follow. Therefore, indicating a source document is unnecessary. The first adjusting entry is recorded on the first two lines below the heading.

Adjusting Entry for Merchandise Inventory

The debit and credit parts of the merchandise inventory adjustment are identified on the work sheet by the letter (a), Illustration 18-1.

CHAPTER 18   Recording Adjusting and Closing Entries for a Partnership   **435**

LESSON PLAN 18-1

Materials

- Student pages 434–437
- Transparencies: F, Blank Journal; 18-1, Adjusting Entries
- Software: Accounting Tutorial
- Demonstration Problem: 18A, Journalizing and Posting Adjusting Entries

Objectives (Enabling Performance Tasks)

a. Identify accounting concepts and practices related to adjusting and closing entries for a merchandising business organized as a partnership.

b. Record adjusting entries for a merchandising business organized as a partnership.

FOCUS

In Chapter 16, the adjustments for a merchandising business organized as a partnership were analyzed and planned on a work sheet. In this lesson, we will journalize the adjusting entries.

TEACH

Cover student pages 434–437 "Recording Adjusting Entries." To begin this lesson, review the definition of adjustments and why they are necessary. Changes recorded on a work sheet to update general ledger accounts at the end of a fiscal period are called adjustments. Use Transparency 18-1 to describe journalizing adjusting entries. Explain that adjusting entries are recorded on a new journal page with the heading Adjusting Entries centered on the first line of the journal. Point out that no source document is necessary when journalizing adjusting entries. Explain that adjusting entries are journalized in pairs beginning with the letter (a). The debit is recorded first, and the credit second.

APPLY

Use Transparency F to journalize the entries as the lesson progresses. Draw T accounts to show the effect of posting each adjusting entry as it is presented.

Guided Practice

Guide students through Drill 18-D1. Students should have the form from the working papers to complete as you guide them through the drill. For each adjustment, ask the students the accounts affected and the amount of the adjustment. All students should agree with the analysis before entering the adjustment in the T accounts and proceeding to the next adjustment.

Independent Practice

Assign Questions 1–4 and Problem 18-1, Instructions 1–2.

ASSESS

Assess student understanding by checking solutions to Independent Practice activities.

Reteach

- Use Demonstration Problem 18A. This problem can be demonstrated on the overhead with the students completing the problem at their desks.
- Use Unit 5 of the Accounting Tutorial to reteach analyzing adjusting entries.

Extend

Assign Cases for Critical Thinking 1.

Enrich

- Assign the PERSONAL VISIONS IN BUSINESS feature on page 443.
- Assign students to read the MULTICULTURAL AWARENESS feature on page 438. Discuss with them how an understanding and appreciation of history and other cultures contributes to understanding civilization today.

ILLUSTRATION 18-2	Adjusting entries recorded in a journal

PAGE 26 — JOURNAL

	DATE		ACCOUNT TITLE	DOC. NO.	POST. REF.	GENERAL DEBIT	GENERAL CREDIT	ACCOUNTS RECEIVABLE DEBIT	ACCOUNTS RECEIVABLE CREDIT	
1			*Adjusting Entries*							1
2	Dec. 19—	31	Income Summary			13 2 0 0 00				2
3			Merchandise Inventory				13 2 0 0 00			3
4		31	Supplies Expense—Office			3 9 4 0 00				4
5			Supplies—Office				3 9 4 0 00			5
6		31	Supplies Expense—Store			3 2 6 0 00				6
7			Supplies—Store				3 2 6 0 00			7
8		31	Insurance Expense			2 6 4 0 00				8
9			Prepaid Insurance				2 6 4 0 00			9

Income Summary

Adj. (a)	13,200.00	

Merchandise Inventory

Bal.	225,400.00	Adj. (a)	13,200.00
(New Bal.	212,200.00)		

The merchandise inventory adjustment includes a debit to Income Summary and a credit to Merchandise Inventory of $13,200.00.

CarLand's adjusting entry for merchandise inventory is shown on lines 2 and 3 of the journal, Illustration 18-2.

The effect of posting the adjusting entry for merchandise inventory is shown in the T accounts.

Adjusting Entry for Office Supplies Inventory

Supplies Expense—Office

Adj. (b)	3,940.00	

Supplies—Office

Bal.	5,400.00	Adj. (b)	3,940.00
(New Bal.	1,460.00)		

The debit and credit parts of the office supplies adjustment are identified on the work sheet by the letter (b), Illustration 18-1. The office supplies inventory adjustment includes a debit to Supplies Expense—Office and a credit to Supplies—Office of $3,940.00.

CarLand's adjusting entry for office supplies inventory is shown on lines 4 and 5 of the journal, Illustration 18-2.

The effect of posting the adjusting entry for office supplies inventory is shown in the T accounts.

Adjusting Entry for Store Supplies Inventory

Supplies Expense—Store

Adj. (c)	3,260.00	

Supplies—Store

Bal.	5,780.00	Adj. (c)	3,260.00
(New Bal.	2,520.00)		

The debit and credit parts of the store supplies adjustment are identified on the work sheet by the letter (c), Illustration 18-1. The store supplies inventory adjustment includes a debit to Supplies Expense—Store and a credit to Supplies—Store of $3,260.00.

CarLand's adjusting entry for store supplies inventory is shown on lines 6 and 7 of the journal, Illustration 18-2.

The effect of posting the adjusting entry for store supplies inventory is shown in the T accounts.

The debit and credit parts of the prepaid insurance adjustment are identified on the work sheet by the letter (d), Illustration 18-1. The prepaid insurance adjustment includes a debit to Insurance Expense and a credit to Prepaid Insurance of $2,640.00.

CarLand's adjusting entry for prepaid insurance is shown on lines 8 and 9 of the journal, Illustration 18-2.

The effect of posting the adjusting entry for prepaid insurance is shown in the T accounts.

The four adjusting entries for a merchandising business organized as a partnership are summarized in Illustration 18-3.

Insurance Expense		
Adj. (d) 2,640.00		

Prepaid Insurance		
Bal. 4,840.00	Adj. (d)	2,640.00
(New Bal. 2,200.00)		

SUMMARY ILLUSTRATION 18-3

Summary of adjusting entries for a merchandising business organized as a partnership

Adjusting Entry	JOURNAL		
	Account Title	General	
		Debit	Credit
1. Adjust merchandise inventory (increase in inventory)	Merchandise Inventory	X	
	Income Summary		X
(decrease in inventory)	Income Summary	X	
	Merchandise Inventory		X
2. Adjust office supplies inventory	Supplies Expense—Office	X	
	Supplies—Office		X
3. Adjust store supplies inventory	Supplies Expense—Store	X	
	Supplies—Store		X
4. Adjust prepaid insurance	Insurance Expense	X	
	Prepaid Insurance		X

MULTICULTURAL AWARENESS ACTIVITY

Challenge students to create a list of documents that exist about themselves. To begin the process, remind them that the trail of records on their lives begins with a birth certificate. Students may think of social security numbers, employment records, driver's license, credit card information, medical records such as immunizations, dental records such as X-rays, and school records. After each student has had a few minutes to work on a list, compile a list using input from the class. The point is to demonstrate that societies keep records about each individual.

LESSON PLAN 18-2

Materials

- Student pages 438–452
- Transparencies: 18-2, Closing Entries for Income Statement Accounts with Credit Balances and Debit Balances; 18-3, Closing Entries for Income Summary and Drawing Accounts; 18-4, Closing Entries Recorded in a Journal; 18-5, Chapter Summary
- Software: Accounting Tutorial; Application Program Disk; *Automated Accounting 6.0* or higher; Accounting Textbook Template, first-year Course; Electronic Study Guide
- Demonstration Problems: 18B, Journalizing and Posting Closing Entries; 18C, Preparing a Post-Closing Trial Balance
- Assess: Problem Test Chapter 18, MicroExam Chapter 18, Objective Test No. 5, Unit Problem Test No. 5

Asia Minor

Over 7,000 years ago, the Assyrian, Sumerian, and Babylonian civilizations produced some of the oldest known governments, written languages, and business records. These cultures, located geographically in what is referred to as Asia Minor today, established some of the first businesses, including service businesses and small industries. These societies had banks, a standard system of assigning numerical values to goods, and the practice of drafts to be drawn in one place and paid in another.

The Babylonians are credited with creating the first formal legal codes. The codes required that most business transactions be put in writing and signed by the parties involved. This practice is the first verified use of source documents as evidence of transactions. The oldest known Babylonian documents date from 3,000 B.C.—over 5,000 years ago.

	Sales		
Closing	352,600.00	Bal.	352,600.00
		(New Bal. zero)	

	Income Summary		
Adj. (mdse. inv.)	13,200.00	Closing	
		(revenue)	352,600.00

RECORDING CLOSING ENTRIES

At the end of a fiscal period, the temporary accounts are closed to prepare the general ledger for the next fiscal period. *(CONCEPT: Matching Expenses with Revenue)* To close a temporary account, an amount equal to its balance is recorded on the side opposite the balance. CarLand records four kinds of closing entries.

1 An entry to close income statement accounts with credit balances.

2 An entry to close income statement accounts with debit balances.

3 An entry to record net income or loss and close the income summary account.

4 Entries to close the partners' drawing accounts.

The Income Summary Account

A temporary account is used to summarize the closing entries for revenue, cost, and expenses. The account is titled Income Summary because it is used to summarize information about net income. Income Summary is used only at the end of a fiscal period to help prepare other accounts for a new fiscal period. The income summary account is a unique account because it does not have a normal balance side.

Amounts needed for the closing entries are obtained from the Income Statement and Balance Sheet columns of the work sheet and from the distribution of net income statement.

Closing entries are recorded in the General Debit and Credit columns of a journal. The heading, *Closing Entries*, is written in the middle of the journal's Account Title column on the next line following the last adjusting entry. This heading explains all of the closing entries that follow. Therefore, indicating a source document is unnecessary. The first closing entry is recorded on the first two lines below the heading.

Closing Entry for an Income Statement Account with a Credit Balance

CarLand's work sheet has one income statement account with a credit balance, Sales, as shown in Illustration 18-4. This revenue account has a normal credit balance at the end of a fiscal period. This credit balance must be reduced to zero to prepare the account for the next fiscal period. *(CONCEPT: Matching Expenses with Revenue)* The closing entry for Sales is journalized as shown in Illustration 18-4.

To reduce the balance to zero, Sales is debited for the amount of the balance, $352,600.00. Income Summary is credited for $352,600.00 so that debits equal credits in this entry.

ILLUSTRATION 18-4

Closing entry for an income statement account with a credit balance

The effect of this closing entry on the general ledger accounts is shown in the T accounts.

The balance of Sales is now zero, and the account is ready for the next fiscal period.

Closing Entry for Income Statement Accounts with Debit Balances

CarLand's work sheet has eleven income statement accounts with debit balances, as shown in Illustration 18-5 on page 440. These eleven accounts are the cost account, Purchases, and the ten expense accounts. The cost and expense accounts have normal debit balances at the end of a fiscal period. These debit balances must be reduced to zero to prepare the accounts for the next fiscal period. (CONCEPT: *Matching Expenses with Revenue*) To reduce the balances to zero, the cost and expense accounts are credited for the amount of their balances. The account used for the debit of this closing entry is Income Summary. The closing entry for the cost and expense accounts is journalized as shown in Illustration 18-5.

The income summary amount shown on the work sheet, $13,200.00, is the amount of the adjustment for merchandise inventory. Income Summary is used to summarize the amounts that contribute to net income. The adjustment for merchandise inventory contributes to net income. However, Income Summary is not closed as part of this closing entry. Instead, the account is closed with the third closing entry when net income is recorded.

The debit to Income Summary is not entered in the amount column until all cost and expense balances have been journalized and the total amount calculated. The account title and balance of each cost and expense account is written in the Account Title and General Credit columns. After all cost and expense accounts and their

Cover student pages 438–452 "Record-ing Closing Entries" and "Checking a General Ledger's Accuracy after Posting Adjusting and Closing Entries." Review the purpose of the Income Summary account and discuss the four closing entries that CarLand makes. Emphasize that amounts for closing entries are taken from the Income Statement and Balance Sheet columns of the work sheet. Point out that the heading Clos-ing Entries is centered and no source document is necessary when journaliz-ing closing entries.

Students should understand that after posting closing entries, balance sheet accounts (permanent accounts) remain open but income statement accounts (temporary accounts) have zero balances. Emphasize that the post-clos-ing trial balance is prepared to prove equality of debits and credits in the gen-eral ledger. Only accounts with balances are listed.

ILLUSTRATION 18-5   Closing entry for income statement accounts with debit balances

		ACCOUNT TITLE	INCOME STATEMENT	
			DEBIT	CREDIT
21		Income Summary	1 3 2 0 0 00	
22		Sales		3 5 2 6 0 0 00
23		Purchases	1 5 8 3 0 0 00	
24		Advertising Expense	5 5 0 0 00	
25		Credit Card Fee Expense	2 8 9 0 00	
26		Insurance Expense	2 6 4 0 00	
27		Miscellaneous Expense	2 1 8 2 15	
28		Payroll Taxes Expense	7 2 9 9 75	
29		Rent Expense	1 8 0 0 0 00	
30		Salary Expense	6 0 1 5 3 00	
31		Supplies Expense—Office	3 9 4 0 00	
32		Supplies Expense—Store	3 2 6 0 00	
33		Utilities Expense	3 1 8 0 00	

(Credit to close)

PAGE 26 — JOURNAL

	DATE	ACCOUNT TITLE	DOC. NO.	POST. REF.	GENERAL DEBIT	GENERAL CREDIT
13	31	Income Summary			2 6 7 3 4 4 90	
14		Purchases				1 5 8 3 0 0 00
15		Advertising Expense				5 5 0 0 00
16		Credit Card Fee Expense				2 8 9 0 00
17		Insurance Expense				2 6 4 0 00
18		Miscellaneous Expense				2 1 8 2 15
19		Payroll Taxes Expense				7 2 9 9 75
20		Rent Expense				1 8 0 0 0 00
21		Salary Expense				6 0 1 5 3 00
22		Supplies Expense—Office				3 9 4 0 00
23		Supplies Expense—Store				3 2 6 0 00
24		Utilities Expense				3 1 8 0 00

balances have been written in the journal, add the credit amounts for this entry. Write the total of the cost and expense accounts, *$267,344.90,* in the General Debit column on the same line as the account title Income Summary.

The effect of this closing entry on the general ledger accounts is shown in the T accounts on the following page.

The cost account, Purchases, and the expense accounts are now closed and have zero balances. Income Summary has three amounts. (1) A debit of $13,200.00, the amount of the merchandise inventory adjust-ment. (2) A credit of $352,600.00, the amount of the entry to close the revenue account. (3) A debit of $267,344.90, the total amount of the entry to close the cost and expense accounts. The balance of Income Summary is the net income for the fiscal period, $72,055.10.

Income Summary

Adj. (mdse. inv.)	13,200.00	Closing	
Closing (cost and		(revenue)	352,600.00
expenses)	267,344.90	*(New Bal.*	*72,055.10)*

Purchases					**Rent Expense**			
Bal.	158,300.00	Closing	158,300.00		Bal.	18,000.00	Closing	18,000.00
(New Bal. zero)					*(New Bal. zero)*			

Advertising Expense					**Salary Expense**			
Bal.	5,500.00	Closing	5,500.00		Bal.	60,153.00	Closing	60,153.00
(New Bal. zero)					*(New Bal. zero)*			

Credit Card Fee Expense					**Supplies Expense—Office**			
Bal.	2,890.00	Closing	2,890.00		Bal.	3,940.00	Closing	3,940.00
(New Bal. zero)					*(New Bal. zero)*			

Insurance Expense					**Supplies Expense—Store**			
Bal.	2,640.00	Closing	2,640.00		Bal.	3,260.00	Closing	3,260.00
(New Bal. zero)					*(New Bal. zero)*			

Miscellaneous Expense					**Utilities Expense**			
Bal.	2,182.15	Closing	2,182.15		Bal.	3,180.00	Closing	3,180.00
(New Bal. zero)					*(New Bal. zero)*			

Payroll Taxes Expense			
Bal.	7,299.75	Closing	7,299.75
(New Bal. zero)			

Closing Entry to Record Net Income or Loss and Close the Income Summary Account

Net income increases the partners' equity and, therefore, must be credited to the partners' capital accounts. The share of the net income to be recorded for each partner is shown on the distribution of net income statement. The balance of the temporary account Income Summary must be reduced to zero to prepare the account for the next fiscal period. The distribution of net income statement and the closing entry to record net income and close Income Summary are shown in Illustration 18-6 on page 442.

The effect of this closing entry on the general ledger accounts is shown in the T accounts.

The credits to the two partners' capital accounts, $36,027.55, record the partners' share of the net income. The debit to the income summary account, $72,055.10, reduces the account balance to zero and prepares the account for the next fiscal period.

If the business has a net loss, the partners' capital accounts are debited for their share of the net loss. Income Summary is credited for the total net loss.

Income Summary

Adj. (mdse. inv.)	13,200.00	Closing	
Closing (cost and		(revenue)	352,600.00
expenses)	267,344.90		
Closing			
(net income)	72,055.10	*(New Bal. zero)*	

Amy Kramer, Capital

		Bal.	101,118.00
		Closing	
		(net income)	36,027.55

Dario Mesa, Capital

		Bal.	101,228.00
		Closing	
		(net income)	36,027.55

Reteach

- Use Demonstration Problems 18B and 18C. These problems can be demonstrated on the overhead with the students completing the problems at their desks.
- Assign Recycling Problem 18-R.
- Use Unit 6 of the Accounting Tutorial to reteach analyzing closing entries.

Extend

- Assign Cases for Critical Thinking 2.
- Assign the Application Program Disk to be used with Mastery Problem 18-M.
- Assign Challenge Problem 18-C (the challenge is that all end-of-fiscal-period work is completed).
- Assign Reinforcement Activity 2, Part B.

Enrich

- Use Automated Accounting 6.0 or higher with Problem 18-1, Mastery Problem 18-M, Challenge Problem 18-C, and Reinforcement Activity 2.
- Assign Electronic Study Guide Chapter 18.
- Assign VIKING MARINE: A Business Simulation.

ILLUSTRATION 18-6   Closing entry to record net income and close the income summary account

Closing Entries for the Partners' Drawing Accounts

The partners' drawing accounts are temporary accounts and must begin each fiscal period with zero balances. Because withdrawals are neither a revenue, cost, nor expense, the drawing accounts are not closed through Income Summary. The drawing account balances are closed directly to the partners' capital accounts.

A partial work sheet and the closing entries for the partners' drawing accounts are shown in Illustration 18-7. The closing entry is on lines 28-31 of the journal.

The credits to Amy Kramer, Drawing and Dario Mesa, Drawing reduce the account balances to zero. The accounts are prepared for the next fiscal period. The debits to Amy Kramer, Capital and Dario Mesa, Capital reduce the balances of these accounts by the amount of the partners' withdrawals during the fiscal period.

The effect of these closing entries on the general ledger accounts is shown in the T accounts.

After the closing entry for the partners' drawing accounts, the balances of the partners' capital accounts are the same as reported in the owners' equity section of the balance sheet, Illustration 18-8 on page 444.

ILLUSTRATION 18-7   Closing entries for the partners' drawing accounts

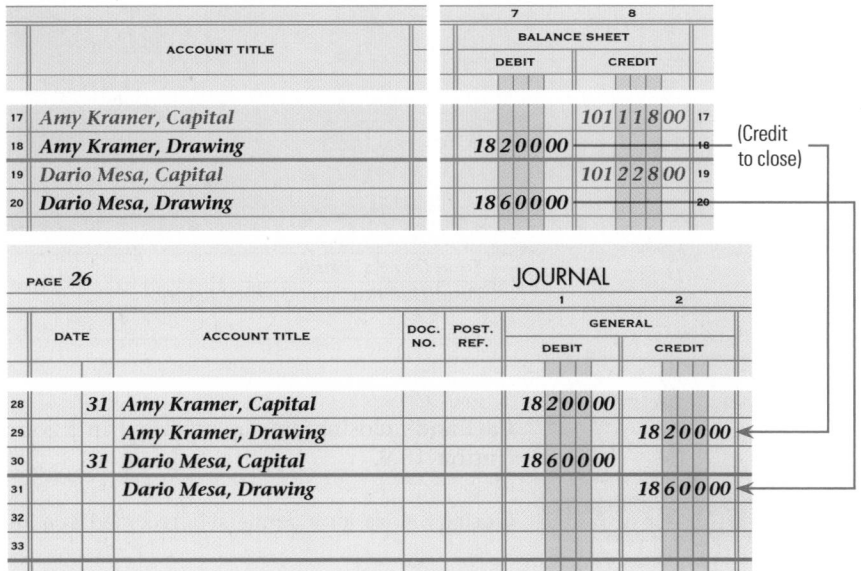

ACCOUNT TITLE	BALANCE SHEET	
	7 DEBIT	8 CREDIT
17 Amy Kramer, Capital		101 11 8 00
18 Amy Kramer, Drawing	18 20 0 00	
19 Dario Mesa, Capital		101 22 8 00
20 Dario Mesa, Drawing	18 60 0 00	

(Credit to close)

PAGE 26   JOURNAL

	DATE	ACCOUNT TITLE	DOC. NO.	POST. REF.	GENERAL 1 DEBIT	GENERAL 2 CREDIT
28	31	Amy Kramer, Capital			18 20 0 00	
29		Amy Kramer, Drawing				18 20 0 00
30	31	Dario Mesa, Capital			18 60 0 00	
31		Dario Mesa, Drawing				18 60 0 00
32						
33						

■ **Judy Sims** ■

SOFTWARE SPECTRUM, GARLAND, TEXAS

Judy Sims chairs the Board of Directors and is Chief Executive Officer of Software Spectrum Inc., a company she co-founded in 1983. Software Spectrum is a leading national reseller of microcomputer software and a provider of technical services to large corporations.

Sims majored in accounting at Texas Tech University and worked as a C.P.A. for eleven years for national accounting firms. She advanced to the position of Audit Partner, and provided small and larger corporations with audit services. In 1983, she and two partners pooled $40,000 of personal funds and started Software Spectrum.

"The biggest lesson we learned early was to listen to the customer and quickly make changes in response to their needs," says Sims. "We started as a retail store selling education and entertainment software. But in the first six weeks, the cash register hardly ever rang. We then decided to focus on selling business software to corporations. These corporate customers wanted their software delivered and they wanted to buy it on account. So we changed our policies immediately."

Sims's advice to students is to set goals. She says that you should not just think about goals but actually write them down on paper and review them frequently. "The great thing about our country," says Sims, "is that there are only self-imposed limitations. Don't limit yourself— set high goals."

Sims reports that when the company's focus changed from retail to corporate software sales, they gave up their retail location in a shopping center. That store is now occupied by a business named "Positively Magic." Sims says that that is appropriate because "that initial location was positively magic for us—it was the launching pad for what has grown into a $219 million company."

Personal Visions in Business

ILLUSTRATION 18-8   Owner's equity section of a balance sheet

CarLand		
Balance Sheet		
December 31, 19--		
Owners' Equity		
Amy Kramer, Capital	118 9 4 5 55	
Dario Mesa, Capital	118 6 5 5 55	
Total Owners' Equity		237 6 0 1 10
Total Liabilities and Owners' Equity		252 4 4 5 57

CarLand's closing entries recorded in a journal are shown in Illustration 18-9.

ILLUSTRATION 18-9   Closing entries for a partnership recorded in a journal

PAGE 26 — JOURNAL

	DATE	ACCOUNT TITLE	DOC. NO.	POST. REF.	GENERAL DEBIT	GENERAL CREDIT	ACCOUNTS RECEIVABLE DEBIT	ACCOUNTS RECEIVABLE CREDIT	
10		*Closing Entries*							10
11	31	Sales			352 6 0 0 00				11
12		Income Summary				352 6 0 0 00			12
13	31	Income Summary			267 3 4 4 90				13
14		Purchases				158 3 0 0 00			14
15		Advertising Expense				5 5 0 0 00			15
16		Credit Card Fee Expense				2 8 9 0 00			16
17		Insurance Expense				2 6 4 0 00			17
18		Miscellaneous Expense				2 1 8 2 15			18
19		Payroll Taxes Expense				7 2 9 9 75			19
20		Rent Expense				18 0 0 0 00			20
21		Salary Expense				60 1 5 3 00			21
22		Supplies Expense—Office				3 9 4 0 00			22
23		Supplies Expense—Store				3 2 6 0 00			23
24		Utilities Expense				3 1 8 0 00			24
25	31	Income Summary			72 0 5 5 10				25
26		Amy Kramer, Capital				36 0 2 7 55			26
27		Dario Mesa, Capital				36 0 2 7 55			27
28	31	Amy Kramer, Capital			18 2 0 0 00				28
29		Amy Kramer, Drawing				18 2 0 0 00			29
30	31	Dario Mesa, Capital			18 6 0 0 00				30
31		Dario Mesa, Drawing				18 6 0 0 00			31

The closing entries for a merchandising business organized as a partnership are summarized in Illustration 18-10.

Closing Entry	JOURNAL		
	Account Title	General	
		Debit	Credit
1. Transfers income statement accounts with credit balances to Income Summary	Revenue account Income Summary	X	X
2. Transfers income statement accounts with debit balances to Income Summary	Income Summary Cost and expense accounts	X	X
3. Transfers net income or loss to partners' capital accounts and closes Income Summary	Income Summary Partners' capital accounts (net income)	X	X
	Partners' capital accounts Income Summary (net loss)	X	X
4. Transfers partners' drawing account balances to partners' capital accounts	Partners' capital accounts Partners' drawing accounts	X	X

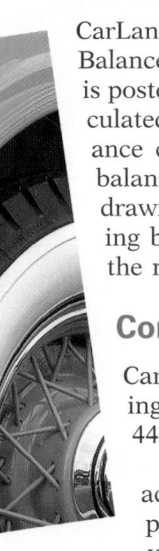

CHECKING A GENERAL LEDGER'S ACCURACY AFTER POSTING ADJUSTING AND CLOSING ENTRIES

CarLand's 4-column general ledger account form has separate Balance Debit and Balance Credit columns. Each time an entry is posted to a general ledger account, the account balance is calculated. The balance is then recorded in the appropriate balance column. Each general ledger account shows its current balance at all times. When an account is closed, a short line is drawn in both the Balance Debit and Credit columns. The ending balance for one fiscal period is the beginning balance for the next fiscal period.

Completed General Ledger

CarLand's completed general ledger after adjusting and closing entries are posted is shown in Illustration 18-11 on pages 446 through 451.

Balance sheet accounts (asset, liability, and capital accounts) have up-to-date balances to begin the new fiscal period. Balances in the balance sheet accounts agree with the amounts on the balance sheet, Illustration 17-10, Chapter 17. General ledger account balances on

December 31 of one year are the beginning balances for January 1 of the next year.

Income statement accounts (revenue, cost, and expense accounts) have zero balances to begin the new fiscal period. *(CONCEPT: Matching Expenses with Revenue)*

ILLUSTRATION 18-11 General ledger after adjusting and closing entries are posted

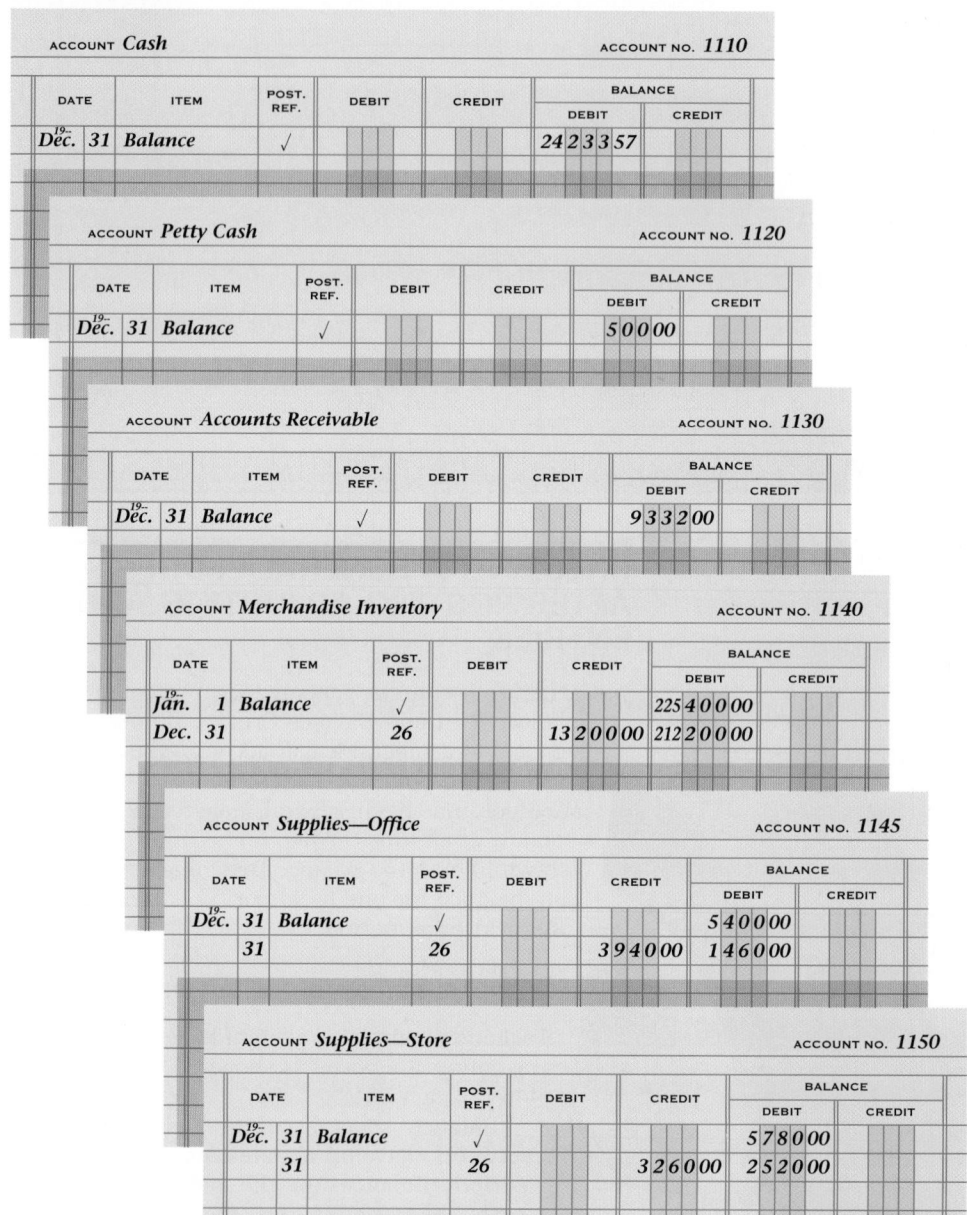

ACCOUNT *Cash* ACCOUNT NO. *1110*

DATE	ITEM	POST. REF.	DEBIT	CREDIT	BALANCE DEBIT	BALANCE CREDIT
Dec. 31	Balance	✓			24 23 3 57	

ACCOUNT *Petty Cash* ACCOUNT NO. *1120*

DATE	ITEM	POST. REF.	DEBIT	CREDIT	BALANCE DEBIT	BALANCE CREDIT
Dec. 31	Balance	✓			5 0 0 00	

ACCOUNT *Accounts Receivable* ACCOUNT NO. *1130*

DATE	ITEM	POST. REF.	DEBIT	CREDIT	BALANCE DEBIT	BALANCE CREDIT
Dec. 31	Balance	✓			9 33 2 00	

ACCOUNT *Merchandise Inventory* ACCOUNT NO. *1140*

DATE	ITEM	POST. REF.	DEBIT	CREDIT	BALANCE DEBIT	BALANCE CREDIT
Jan. 1	Balance	✓			225 40 0 00	
Dec. 31		26		13 20 0 00	212 20 0 00	

ACCOUNT *Supplies—Office* ACCOUNT NO. *1145*

DATE	ITEM	POST. REF.	DEBIT	CREDIT	BALANCE DEBIT	BALANCE CREDIT
Dec. 31	Balance	✓			5 40 0 00	
31		26		3 94 0 00	1 46 0 00	

ACCOUNT *Supplies—Store* ACCOUNT NO. *1150*

DATE	ITEM	POST. REF.	DEBIT	CREDIT	BALANCE DEBIT	BALANCE CREDIT
Dec. 31	Balance	✓			5 78 0 00	
31		26		3 26 0 00	2 52 0 00	

ACCOUNT *Prepaid Insurance*   ACCOUNT NO. *1160*

DATE		ITEM	POST. REF.	DEBIT	CREDIT	BALANCE	
						DEBIT	CREDIT
Dec.	31	Balance	✓			4 8 4 0 00	
	31		26		2 6 4 0 00	2 2 0 0 00	

ACCOUNT *Accounts Payable*   ACCOUNT NO. *2110*

DATE		ITEM	POST. REF.	DEBIT	CREDIT	BALANCE	
						DEBIT	CREDIT
Dec.	31	Balance	✓				10 4 5 1 90

ACCOUNT *Employee Income Tax Payable*   ACCOUNT NO. *2120*

DATE		ITEM	POST. REF.	DEBIT	CREDIT	BALANCE	
						DEBIT	CREDIT
Dec.	31	Balance	✓				4 0 2 00

ACCOUNT *FICA Tax Payable*   ACCOUNT NO. *2130*

DATE		ITEM	POST. REF.	DEBIT	CREDIT	BALANCE	
						DEBIT	CREDIT
Dec.	31	Balance	✓				8 3 2 16

ACCOUNT *Sales Tax Payable*   ACCOUNT NO. *2140*

DATE		ITEM	POST. REF.	DEBIT	CREDIT	BALANCE	
						DEBIT	CREDIT
Dec.	31	Balance	✓				1 7 6 0 00

ACCOUNT *Unemployment Tax Payable—Federal*   ACCOUNT NO. *2150*

DATE		ITEM	POST. REF.	DEBIT	CREDIT	BALANCE	
						DEBIT	CREDIT
Dec.	31	Balance	✓				5 9 15

ACCOUNT *Unemployment Tax Payable—State*   ACCOUNT NO. *2160*

DATE		ITEM	POST. REF.	DEBIT	CREDIT	BALANCE	
						DEBIT	CREDIT
Dec.	31	Balance	✓				3 9 9 26

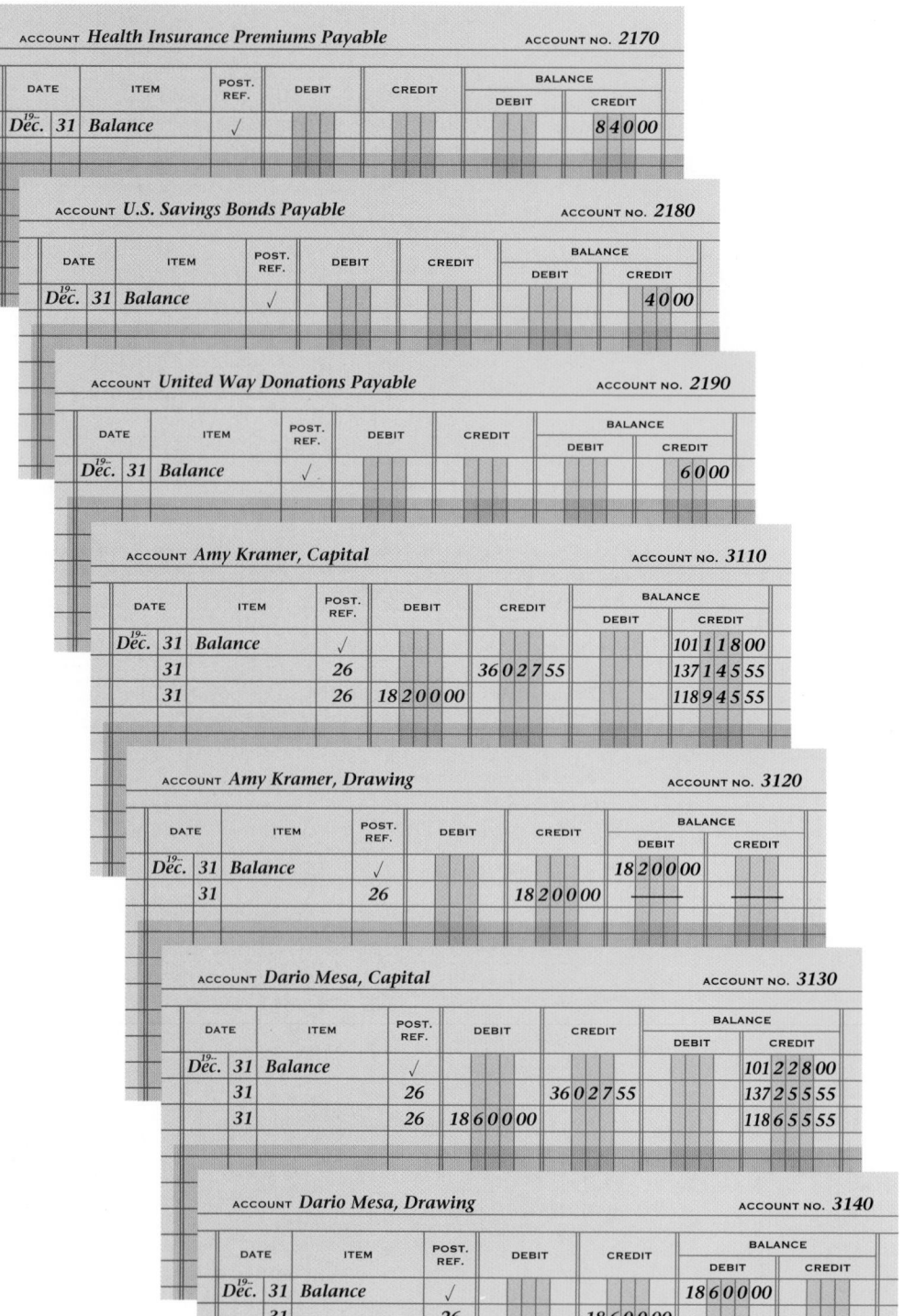

ACCOUNT *Health Insurance Premiums Payable*   **ACCOUNT NO.** *2170*

DATE	ITEM	POST. REF.	DEBIT	CREDIT	BALANCE DEBIT	BALANCE CREDIT
Dec. 31	Balance	✓				840 00

ACCOUNT *U.S. Savings Bonds Payable*   **ACCOUNT NO.** *2180*

DATE	ITEM	POST. REF.	DEBIT	CREDIT	BALANCE DEBIT	BALANCE CREDIT
Dec. 31	Balance	✓				40 00

ACCOUNT *United Way Donations Payable*   **ACCOUNT NO.** *2190*

DATE	ITEM	POST. REF.	DEBIT	CREDIT	BALANCE DEBIT	BALANCE CREDIT
Dec. 31	Balance	✓				60 00

ACCOUNT *Amy Kramer, Capital*   **ACCOUNT NO.** *3110*

DATE	ITEM	POST. REF.	DEBIT	CREDIT	BALANCE DEBIT	BALANCE CREDIT
Dec. 31	Balance	✓				101 118 00
31		26		36 027 55		137 145 55
31		26	18 200 00			118 945 55

ACCOUNT *Amy Kramer, Drawing*   **ACCOUNT NO.** *3120*

DATE	ITEM	POST. REF.	DEBIT	CREDIT	BALANCE DEBIT	BALANCE CREDIT
Dec. 31	Balance	✓			18 200 00	
31		26		18 200 00		

ACCOUNT *Dario Mesa, Capital*   **ACCOUNT NO.** *3130*

DATE	ITEM	POST. REF.	DEBIT	CREDIT	BALANCE DEBIT	BALANCE CREDIT
Dec. 31	Balance	✓				101 228 00
31		26		36 027 55		137 255 55
31		26	18 600 00			118 655 55

ACCOUNT *Dario Mesa, Drawing*   **ACCOUNT NO.** *3140*

DATE	ITEM	POST. REF.	DEBIT	CREDIT	BALANCE DEBIT	BALANCE CREDIT
Dec. 31	Balance	✓			18 600 00	
31		26		18 600 00		

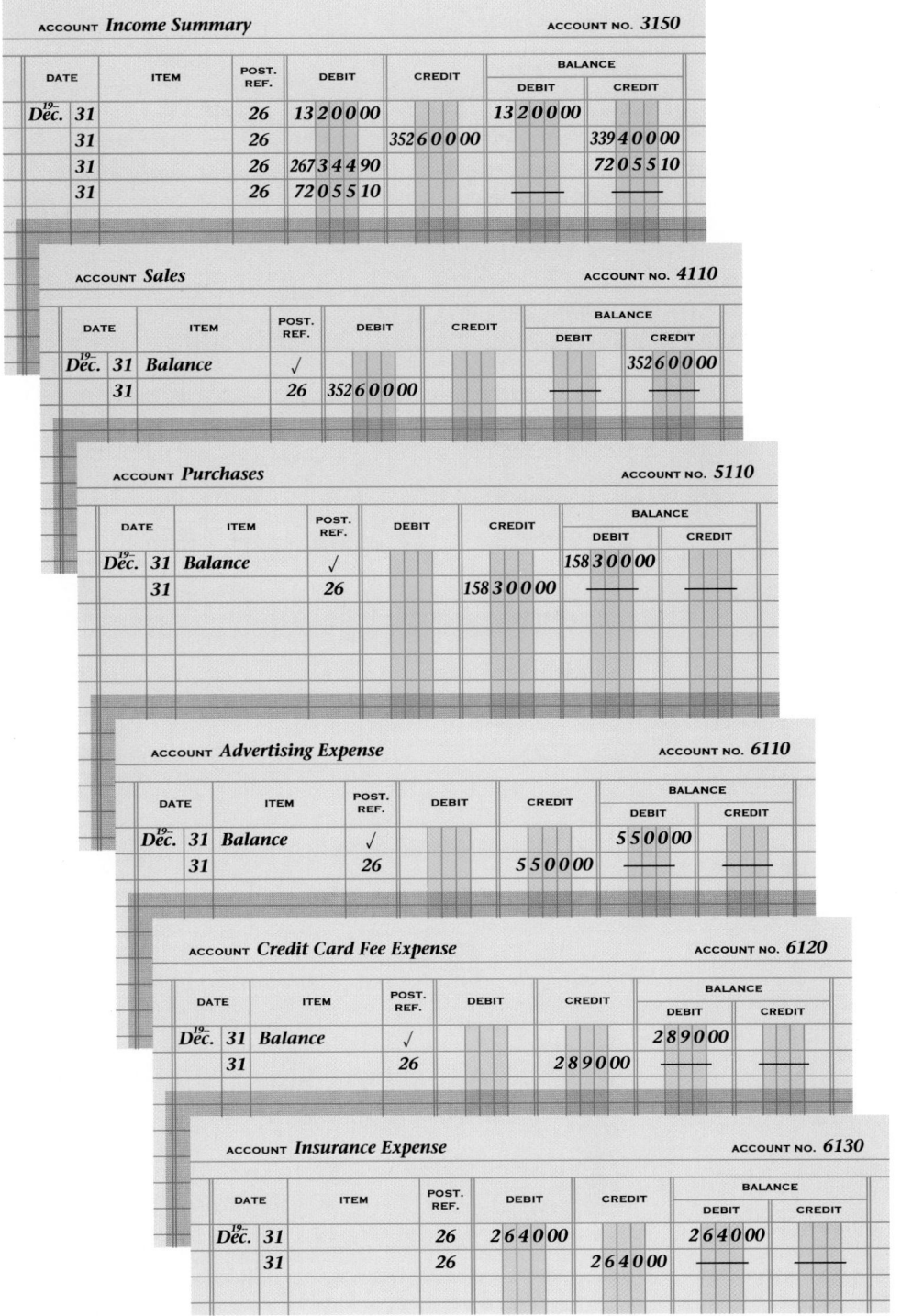

ACCOUNT **Income Summary**   ACCOUNT NO. *3150*

DATE		ITEM	POST. REF.	DEBIT	CREDIT	BALANCE DEBIT	BALANCE CREDIT
Dec.	31		26	13 2 0 0 00		13 2 0 0 00	
	31		26		352 6 0 0 00		339 4 0 0 00
	31		26	267 3 4 4 90			72 0 5 5 10
	31		26	72 0 5 5 10		———	

ACCOUNT **Sales**   ACCOUNT NO. *4110*

DATE		ITEM	POST. REF.	DEBIT	CREDIT	BALANCE DEBIT	BALANCE CREDIT
Dec.	31	Balance	✓				352 6 0 0 00
	31		26	352 6 0 0 00		———	

ACCOUNT **Purchases**   ACCOUNT NO. *5110*

DATE		ITEM	POST. REF.	DEBIT	CREDIT	BALANCE DEBIT	BALANCE CREDIT
Dec.	31	Balance	✓			158 3 0 0 00	
	31		26		158 3 0 0 00	———	

ACCOUNT **Advertising Expense**   ACCOUNT NO. *6110*

DATE		ITEM	POST. REF.	DEBIT	CREDIT	BALANCE DEBIT	BALANCE CREDIT
Dec.	31	Balance	✓			5 5 0 0 00	
	31		26		5 5 0 0 00	———	

ACCOUNT **Credit Card Fee Expense**   ACCOUNT NO. *6120*

DATE		ITEM	POST. REF.	DEBIT	CREDIT	BALANCE DEBIT	BALANCE CREDIT
Dec.	31	Balance	✓			2 8 9 0 00	
	31		26		2 8 9 0 00	———	———

ACCOUNT **Insurance Expense**   ACCOUNT NO. *6130*

DATE		ITEM	POST. REF.	DEBIT	CREDIT	BALANCE DEBIT	BALANCE CREDIT
Dec.	31		26	2 6 4 0 00		2 6 4 0 00	
	31		26		2 6 4 0 00	———	———

TEACHING STRATEGIES:
REINFORCEMENT ACTIVITY

Reinforcement Activity 2, Part B continues Reinforcement Activity 2 beginning with completing a trial balance on a work sheet through adjusting entries, financial statements, closing entries, and a post-closing trial balance. Reinforcement Activity 2, Part A was presented after Chapter 15 and included journalizing and posting daily transactions. Blackline masters for audit tests for Reinforcement Activity 2 are available in the Teacher's Resource Guide in three options: Part A only, Part B only, and Parts A and B combined. In addition, *Automated Accounting 6.0* or higher can be used to automate Reinforcement Activity 2.

ILLUSTRATION 18-11 General ledger after adjusting and closing entries are posted (continued)

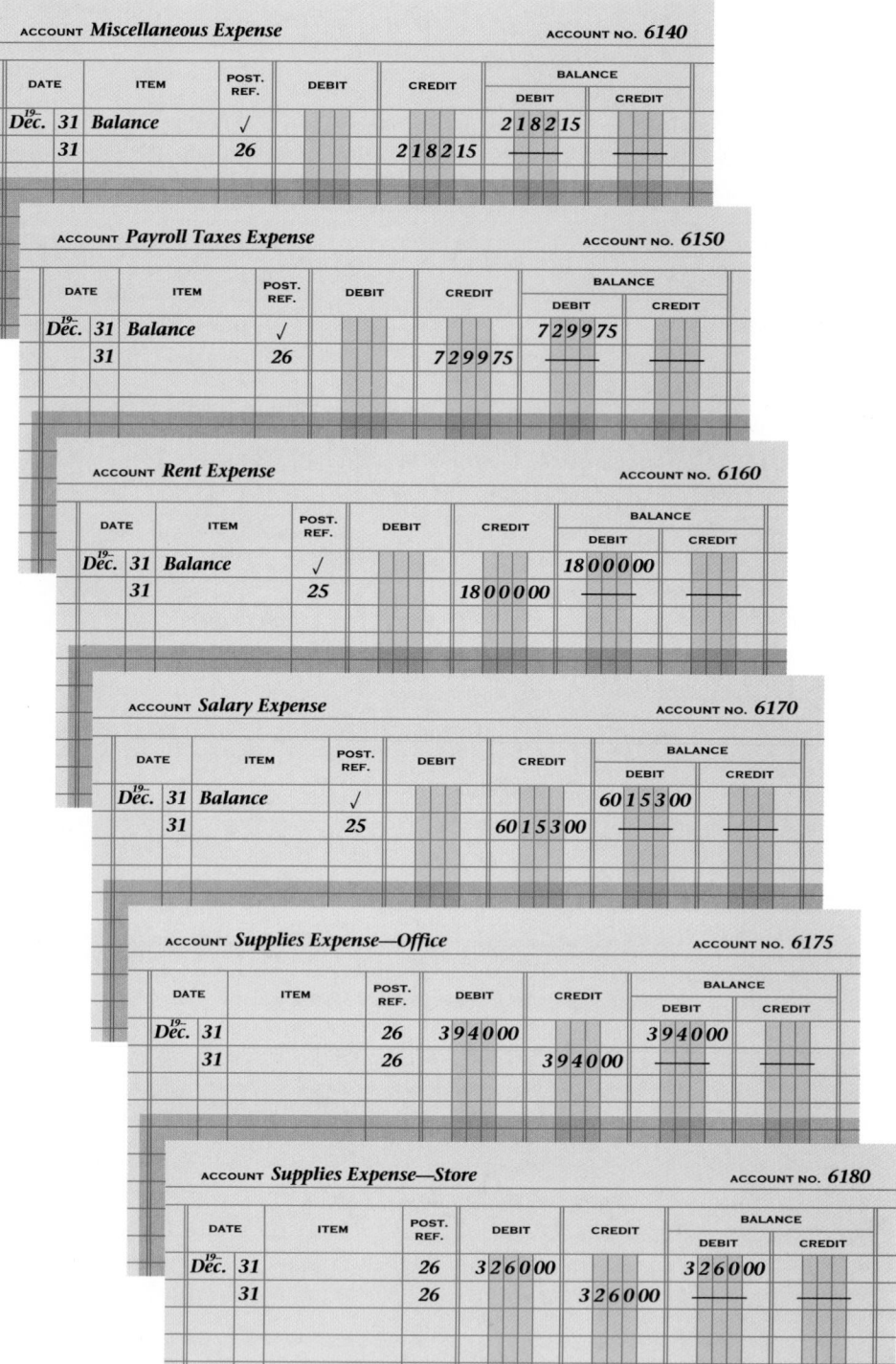

ACCOUNT Miscellaneous Expense   **ACCOUNT NO.** 6140

DATE		ITEM	POST. REF.	DEBIT	CREDIT	BALANCE DEBIT	BALANCE CREDIT
Dec.¹⁹⁻	31	Balance	✓			2 1 8 2 15	
	31		26		2 1 8 2 15	———	———

ACCOUNT Payroll Taxes Expense   **ACCOUNT NO.** 6150

DATE		ITEM	POST. REF.	DEBIT	CREDIT	BALANCE DEBIT	BALANCE CREDIT
Dec.¹⁹⁻	31	Balance	✓			7 2 9 9 75	
	31		26		7 2 9 9 75	———	———

ACCOUNT Rent Expense   **ACCOUNT NO.** 6160

DATE		ITEM	POST. REF.	DEBIT	CREDIT	BALANCE DEBIT	BALANCE CREDIT
Dec.¹⁹⁻	31	Balance	✓			18 0 0 0 00	
	31		25		18 0 0 0 00	———	———

ACCOUNT Salary Expense   **ACCOUNT NO.** 6170

DATE		ITEM	POST. REF.	DEBIT	CREDIT	BALANCE DEBIT	BALANCE CREDIT
Dec.¹⁹⁻	31	Balance	✓			60 1 5 3 00	
	31		25		60 1 5 3 00	———	———

ACCOUNT Supplies Expense—Office   **ACCOUNT NO.** 6175

DATE		ITEM	POST. REF.	DEBIT	CREDIT	BALANCE DEBIT	BALANCE CREDIT
Dec.¹⁹⁻	31		26	3 9 4 0 00		3 9 4 0 00	
	31		26		3 9 4 0 00	———	———

ACCOUNT Supplies Expense—Store   **ACCOUNT NO.** 6180

DATE		ITEM	POST. REF.	DEBIT	CREDIT	BALANCE DEBIT	BALANCE CREDIT
Dec.¹⁹⁻	31		26	3 2 6 0 00		3 2 6 0 00	
	31		26		3 2 6 0 00	———	———

SIMULATION

To give students an opportunity to apply accounting concepts from the second accounting cycle, assign students Reinforcement Activity 2, Part B and/or VIKING MARINE: A Business Simulation to demonstrate their understanding of the complete accounting cycle.

ILLUSTRATION 18-11

General ledger after adjusting and closing entries are posted (concluded)

ACCOUNT Utilities Expense							ACCOUNT NO. 6190

DATE	ITEM	POST. REF.	DEBIT	CREDIT	BALANCE DEBIT	BALANCE CREDIT
Dec. 31	Balance	✓			3 1 8 0 00	
31		26		3 1 8 0 00	— — —	

SOFTWARE FOCUS

Reinforcement Activity 2 and/or VIKING MARINE: A Business Simulation may be automated using *Automated Accounting 6.0* or higher.

Post-Closing Trial Balance

FYI

The post-closing trial balance is prepared to prove the equality of debits and credits in the general ledger. Only accounts with balances are listed.

After adjusting and closing entries have been posted, a post-closing trial balance is prepared. The post-closing trial balance is prepared to prove the equality of debits and credits in the general ledger. CarLand's post-closing trial balance prepared on December 31 is shown in Illustration 18-12.

All general ledger accounts that have balances are listed on a post-closing trial balance. Accounts are listed in the same order as they appear in the general ledger. Accounts with zero balances are not listed on a post-closing trial balance.

ILLUSTRATION 18-12

Post-closing trial balance

CarLand
Post-Closing Trial Balance
December 31, 19--

ACCOUNT TITLE	DEBIT	CREDIT
Cash	24 2 3 3 57	
Petty Cash	5 0 0 00	
Accounts Receivable	9 3 3 2 00	
Merchandise Inventory	212 2 0 0 00	
Supplies—Office	1 4 6 0 00	
Supplies—Store	2 5 2 0 00	
Prepaid Insurance	2 2 0 0 00	
Accounts Payable		10 4 5 1 90
Employee Income Tax Payable		4 0 2 00
FICA Tax Payable		8 3 2 16
Sales Tax Payable		1 7 6 0 00
Unemployment Tax Payable—Federal		5 9 15
Unemployment Tax Payable—State		3 9 9 26
Health Insurance Premiums Payable		8 4 0 00
U.S. Savings Bonds Payable		4 0 00
United Way Donations Payable		6 0 00
Amy Kramer, Capital		118 9 4 5 55
Dario Mesa, Capital		118 6 5 5 55
Totals	252 4 4 5 57	252 4 4 5 57

MILESTONE

The second accounting cycle has now been covered in its entirety. This is the second opportunity for students to experience the application of theory and practice for a complete accounting cycle. Chapters 11 through 18 of the textbook are the foundation for subsequent learning. It is assumed that these chapters have been mastered as the chapters to follow will expand upon this foundation with concepts of increasing complexity.

Audit Your Understanding

1. Where is the information obtained for journalizing closing entries?
2. What is the name of the temporary account that is used to summarize the closing entries for revenue, cost, and expenses?
3. How is a temporary account closed?
4. Which accounts are listed on a post-closing trial balance?

Account balances on the post-closing trial balance, Illustration 18-12, agree with the balances on the balance sheet, Illustration 17-10, Chapter 17. Also, because the post-closing trial balance debit and credit balance totals are the same, $252,445.57, the equality of debits and credits in the general ledger is proved. The general ledger is ready for the next fiscal period. *(CONCEPT: Accounting Period Cycle)*

SUMMARY OF AN ACCOUNTING CYCLE FOR A MERCHANDISING BUSINESS

Service and merchandising businesses use a similar accounting cycle. The accounting cycles are also similar for a proprietorship and a partnership. Variations occur when subsidiary ledgers are used. Variations also occur in preparing financial statements. Car-Land's accounting cycle for a merchandising business is summarized in Illustration 18-13.

QUESTIONS FOR INDIVIDUAL STUDY   EPT(a)

1. What two types of journal entries change general ledger account balances at the end of a fiscal period?

2. Where is the information obtained for journalizing adjusting entries?

3. Where is the information obtained for journalizing closing entries?

4. Where is the explanation for adjusting entries written in a journal?

5. Which accounting concept is being applied when temporary accounts are closed at the end of a fiscal period?

6. What four kinds of closing entries are recorded at the end of a fiscal period?

7. What is the title of the temporary account used to summarize information about net income at the end of a fiscal period?

8. Why is the income summary account considered a unique account?

9. Where is the explanation for closing entries written in a journal?

10. What are the three amounts recorded in the income summary account after closing the revenue, cost, and expense accounts?

11. Why are partners' withdrawals not closed to the income summary account?

12. What is recorded in the Balance Debit and Credit columns of a general ledger account when an account is closed?

13. Which accounting concept is being applied when revenue, cost, and expense accounts begin a new fiscal period with zero balances?

14. What accounts are listed on a post-closing trial balance?

Summary of an accounting cycle for a merchandising business

1 Source documents are checked for accuracy and transactions are analyzed into debit and credit parts.

2 Transactions, from information on source documents, are recorded in a journal.

3 Journal entries are posted to the accounts receivable ledger, the accounts payable ledger, and the general ledger.

4 Schedules of accounts receivable and accounts payable are prepared from the subsidiary ledgers.

5 Work sheet, including a trial balance, is prepared from the general ledger.

6 Financial statements are prepared from the work sheet.

7 Adjusting and closing entries are journalized from the work sheet.

8 Adjusting and closing entries are posted to the general ledger.

9 Post-closing trial balance of the general ledger is prepared.

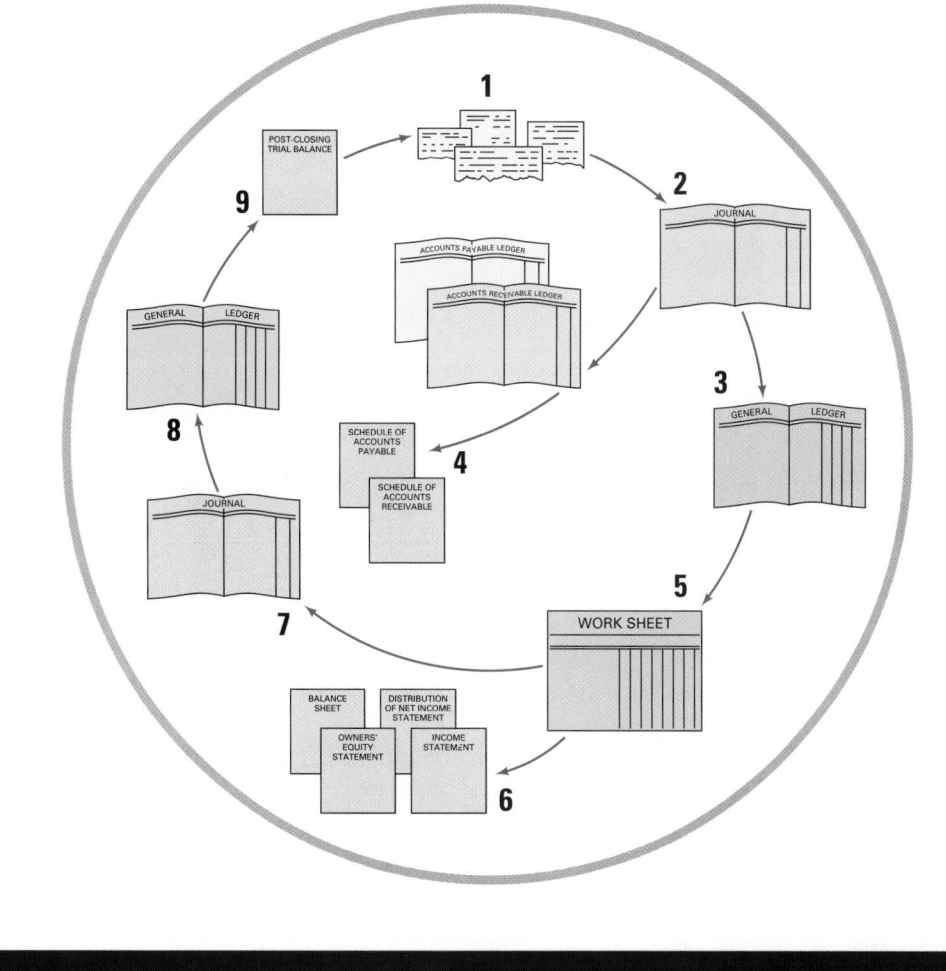

TEACHING STRATEGIES:
APPLYING VISUALS

Direct students to Summary Illustration 18-13 which reviews the accounting cycle for a merchandising business.

QUESTIONS *(cont'd)*

7. Income Summary. (p. 438)

8. Because the account does not have a normal balance side. (p. 438)

9. In the middle of the journal's Account Title column on the next line following the last adjusting entry. (p. 438)

10. (a) The amount of the merchandise inventory adjustment. (b) The amount of revenue. (c) The total amount of cost and expenses. (p. 440)

11. Because partners' withdrawals are neither a revenue, cost, nor expense. (p. 442)

12. A short line is drawn in both the Balance Debit and Credit columns. (p. 445)

13. Matching Expenses with Revenue. (p. 446)

14. All general ledger accounts that have balances. (p. 451)

CASES FOR CRITICAL THINKING
EPT(b,c)

Case 1 Agree with Miss Gray. The adjusting entry should be $600.00 and not the ending balance of the office supplies account. Recording an adjustment of $1,800.00 instead of $600.00 will mean that the assets (Supplies—Office) will be understated on the balance sheet. Also, the expenses (Supplies Expense—Office) will be overstated on the income statement. The amount of net income on the income statement will be understated. In summary, the accounting records for this fiscal period are incorrect.

Case 2 Either practice will give the correct results. Both the income summary and drawing accounts are closed to the capital accounts. Which accounts are closed first has no effect on the balances in the capital accounts. However, the income summary account is traditionally closed first.

CASE 1 Household Furniture's Trial Balance Debit column of the work sheet shows a debit balance of $2,400.00 for the office supplies account. The ending office supplies inventory is determined to be $1,800.00. The accounting clerk journalized the following adjusting entry: debit Supplies Expense—Office, $1,800.00; credit Supplies—Office, $1,800.00. Susan Gray, partner, discussed the entry with the accounting clerk and suggested that the adjusting entry should have been for $600.00 instead of $1,800.00. The clerk indicated that there is no problem because the amounts will be adjusted again at the end of the next fiscal period. Do you agree with Miss Gray or the accounting clerk? Explain your answer.

CASE 2 Two businesses have been using different accounting practices. One business first closes the income summary account to record the net income in the capital accounts and then closes the drawing accounts. The other business first closes the drawing accounts and then closes the income summary account to record the net income in the capital accounts. Which practice is correct? Explain.

CHECK FIGURES

See Teacher's Edition of Working Papers for complete solutions to drills and problems.

Drill 18-D1 Business 1 Income Summary Debit 23,000; Business 2 Income Summary Credit 12,000; Business 3 Income Summary Debit 14,000

Drill 18-D2 Income Summary Debits 12,000 and 124,180; Credit 236,000

Problem 18-1 Post-closing trial balance totals 318,450.

DRILLS FOR UNDERSTANDING

EPT(b,c)

DRILL 18-D1 Analyzing adjusting entries

The following information is related to adjustments needed at the end of a fiscal period for three businesses.

Business	Account Title	Account Balance in General Ledger	Adjustment Information	
			Ending Inventories	Ending Value
1	Merchandise Inventory	$388,000.00	$365,000.00	
	Supplies—Office	4,730.00	2,910.00	
	Supplies—Store	5,230.00	3,470.00	
	Prepaid Insurance	3,360.00		$840.00
2	Merchandise Inventory	$274,000.00	$286,000.00	
	Supplies—Office	3,620.00	1,840.00	
	Supplies—Store	3,950.00	2,110.00	
	Prepaid Insurance	2,850.00		$570.00
3	Merchandise Inventory	$292,000.00	$278,000.00	
	Supplies—Office	4,480.00	2,250.00	
	Supplies—Store	4,130.00	2,320.00	
	Prepaid Insurance	3,200.00		$800.00

INSTRUCTIONS:

1. Prepare eight T accounts for each of the three businesses. (1) Merchandise Inventory. (2) Supplies—Office. (3) Supplies—Store. (4) Prepaid Insurance. (5) Income Summary. (6) Insurance Expense. (7) Supplies Expense—Office. (8) Supplies Expense—Store. For those accounts that have a balance, enter the balance on the proper side of the T account.
2. Enter the adjusting entries in the appropriate T accounts for each business.

DRILL 18-D2 Analyzing closing entries

The following information is from the work sheet of Novak's Sport Center.

	ACCOUNT TITLE	5 INCOME STATEMENT DEBIT	6 CREDIT
21	Income Summary	12 00 0 00	
22	Sales		236 00 0 00
23	Purchases	94 40 0 00	
24	Advertising Expense	3 25 0 00	
25	Credit Card Fee Expense	2 13 0 00	
26	Insurance Expense	2 52 0 00	
27	Miscellaneous Expense	1 38 0 00	
28	Rent Expense	14 40 0 00	
29	Supplies Expense—Office	2 98 0 00	
30	Supplies Expense—Store	3 12 0 00	

INSTRUCTIONS:

1. Prepare a T account for each account. In each T account, enter the amount that is shown in the Income Statement columns.
2. Enter the debit and credit amounts to close the income statement credit balance account. Enter the debit and credit amounts to close the income statement debit balance accounts.

APPLICATION PROBLEM

PROBLEM 18-1 **Journalizing and posting adjusting and closing entries; preparing a post-closing trial balance**

AUTOMATED

Use the following partial work sheet of Jewel Box Company for the year ended December 31 of the current year. The general ledger accounts and their balances are in the working papers accompanying this textbook.

	ACCOUNT TITLE	3 ADJUSTMENTS DEBIT	4 CREDIT	5 INCOME STATEMENT DEBIT	6 CREDIT
4	Merchandise Inventory		(a)13 00 0 00		
5	Supplies—Office		(b) 2 14 0 00		
6	Supplies—Store		(c) 2 45 0 00		
7	Prepaid Insurance		(d) 2 64 0 00		
21	Income Summary	(a)13 00 0 00		13 00 0 00	
22	Sales				316 00 0 00
23	Purchases			126 45 0 00	
24	Advertising Expense			4 72 0 00	
25	Credit Card Fee Expense			3 26 0 00	
26	Insurance Expense	(d) 2 64 0 00		2 64 0 00	
27	Miscellaneous Expense			1 93 0 00	
28	Payroll Taxes Expense			6 77 3 00	
29	Rent Expense			15 60 0 00	
30	Salary Expense			56 78 7 00	
31	Supplies Expense—Office	(b) 2 14 0 00		2 14 0 00	
32	Supplies Expense—Store	(c) 2 45 0 00		2 45 0 00	
33	Utilities Expense			2 94 0 00	
34		20 23 0 00	20 23 0 00	238 69 0 00	316 00 0 00
35	Net Income			77 31 0 00	
36				316 00 0 00	316 00 0 00

INSTRUCTIONS:

1. Use page 25 of a journal. Journalize the adjusting entries using information from the partial work sheet.
2. Post the adjusting entries.
3. Continue using page 25 of the journal. Journalize the closing entries using information from the work sheet. The distribution of net income statement shows equal distribution of earnings. The partners' drawing accounts show the following debit balances in the work sheet's Balance Sheet Debit column: Paula Chaney, Drawing, $14,580.00; Scott Chaney, Drawing, $14,720.00.
4. Post the closing entries.
5. Prepare a post-closing trial balance.

ENRICHMENT PROBLEMS   EPT(b,c,d)

MASTERY PROBLEM 18-M Journalizing and posting adjusting and closing entries; preparing a post-closing trial balance

AUTOMATED

APPLICATION

Use the following partial work sheet of Robco Toys for the year ended December 31 of the current year. The general ledger accounts and their balances are in the working papers accompanying this textbook.

	ACCOUNT TITLE	3 ADJUSTMENTS DEBIT	4 ADJUSTMENTS CREDIT	5 INCOME STATEMENT DEBIT	6 INCOME STATEMENT CREDIT
4	Merchandise Inventory		(a)12 500 00		
5	Supplies—Office		(b) 2 430 00		
6	Supplies—Store		(c) 2 270 00		
7	Prepaid Insurance		(d) 2 280 00		
21	Income Summary	(a)12 500 00		12 500 00	
22	Sales				325 630 00
23	Purchases			130 450 00	
24	Advertising Expense			5 180 00	
25	Credit Card Fee Expense			3 420 00	
26	Insurance Expense	(d) 2 280 00		2 280 00	
27	Miscellaneous Expense			2 060 00	
28	Payroll Taxes Expense			7 124 00	
29	Rent Expense			15 600 00	
30	Salary Expense			59 360 00	
31	Supplies Expense—Office	(b) 2 430 00		2 430 00	
32	Supplies Expense—Store	(c) 2 270 00		2 270 00	
33	Utilities Expense			2 880 00	
34		19 480 00	19 480 00	245 554 00	325 630 00
35	Net Income			80 076 00	
36				325 630 00	325 630 00
37					

INSTRUCTIONS:

1. Use page 25 of a journal. Journalize the adjusting entries using information from the partial work sheet.
2. Post the adjusting entries.

3. Continue using page 25 of the journal. Journalize the closing entries using information from the work sheet. The distribution of net income statement shows equal distribution of earnings. The partners' drawing accounts show the following debit balances in the work sheet's Balance Sheet Debit column: Marcus Florie, Drawing, $18,230.00; Karen Rader, Drawing, $18,710.00.

4. Post the closing entries.

5. Prepare a post-closing trial balance.

CHALLENGE PROBLEM 18-C Completing end-of-fiscal-period work

Plaza Book Center's trial balance is recorded on a 10-column work sheet in the working papers accompanying this textbook. The general ledger accounts and their balances are also given.

AUTOMATED

INSTRUCTIONS:

1. Use the following adjustment information. Complete the 10-column work sheet.

Adjustment Information, December 31

Merchandise inventory	$204,680.00
Office supplies inventory	2,635.00
Store supplies inventory	2,310.00
Value of prepaid insurance	2,200.00

2. Prepare an income statement from the information on the work sheet. Calculate and record the following component percentages: (a) cost of merchandise sold, (b) gross profit on sales, (c) total expenses, and (d) net income or loss. Round percentage calculations to the nearest 0.1%.

3. Prepare a distribution of net income statement. Net income or loss is to be shared equally.

4. Prepare an owners' equity statement. No additional investments were made.

5. Prepare a balance sheet in report form.

6. Use page 25 of a journal. Journalize the adjusting entries.

7. Post the adjusting entries.

8. Continue using page 25 of the journal. Journalize the closing entries.

9. Post the closing entries.

10. Prepare a post-closing trial balance.

End-of-Fiscal-Period Work for a Partnership

Chapters 16 through 18 describe CarLand's manual accounting procedures for completing end-of-fiscal-period work. Integrating Automated Accounting Topic 6 describes procedures for using automated accounting software to complete CarLand's end-of-fiscal-period work. The Automated Accounting Problems contain instructions for using automated accounting software to solve Application Problem 18-1, Mastery Problem 18-M, and Challenge Problem 18-C, Chapter 18.

COMPLETING END-OF-FISCAL-PERIOD WORK

In automated accounting, end-of-fiscal-period reports are prepared by a computer based on instructions in the computer software. The run date used for all end-of-fiscal-period reports is the ending date of the accounting period. Before printing financial statements, the software is directed to prepare a trial balance. The trial balance is prepared to prove equality of general ledger debits and credits and to plan adjustments to general ledger accounts.

FYI

A trial balance proves the equality of the debits and credits in the general ledger. A trial balance taken after closing entries are performed is a post-closing trial balance. The Trial Balance command must be chosen to display a post-closing trial balance.

Preparing a Trial Balance

To prepare a trial balance the general ledger data base is retrieved. The Reports menu is selected from the menu bar. The Ledgers command is chosen from the Reports window. Trial Balance is selected from the Report Selection window to display the trial balance. The trial balance is printed as shown in Illustration T6-1.

ILLUSTRATION T6-1   Trial balance

```
                        CarLand
                      Trial Balance
                        12/31/--
--------------------------------------------------------------
Acct.   Account
Number  Title                          Debit          Credit
--------------------------------------------------------------
1110    Cash                         24233.57
1120    Petty Cash                     500.00
1130    Accounts Receivable           9332.00
1140    Merchandise Inventory       225400.00
1145    Supplies--Office               5400.00
1150    Supplies--Store                5780.00
1160    Prepaid Insurance              4840.00
2110    Accounts Payable                             10451.90
2120    Employee Income Tax Pay.                       402.00
2130    FICA Tax Payable                               832.16
2140    Sales Tax Payable                             1760.00
2150    Unemployment Tax Pay--Fed                       59.15
2160    Unemployment Tax Pay--St.                      399.26
2170    Health Ins. Premiums Pay.                      840.00
2180    U.S. Savings Bonds Pay.                         40.00
2190    United Way Donations Pay.                       60.00
3110    Amy Kramer, Capital                         101118.00
3120    Amy Kramer, Drawing          18200.00
3130    Dario Mesa, Capital                         101228.00
3140    Dario Mesa, Drawing          18600.00
4110    Sales                                       352600.00
5110    Purchases                   158300.00
6110    Advertising Expense           5500.00
6120    Credit Card Fee Expense       2890.00
6140    Miscellaneous Expense         2182.15
6150    Payroll Taxes Expense         7299.75
6160    Rent Expense                 18000.00
6170    Salary Expense               60153.00
6190    Utilities Expense             3180.00
                                   ----------      ----------
        Totals                     569790.47       569790.47
                                   ==========      ==========
```

LESSON PLAN A6

Materials

- Student pages 459–465
- Transparency AA-2 Blank General Journal Input Form
- Input forms for Automating Problems 18-M and 18-C are provided in the working papers that accompany this textbook. If additional input forms are needed, blackline masters are provided in the Accounting Ruling Masters section of the Teacher's Resource Guide.
- Complete solutions for automated problems are provided in the Teacher's Resource Guide.
- *Viking Marine An Automated Business Simulation*
- Software: *Automated Accounting 6.0* or higher; Accounting Textbook Template, first-year course

Objective

Complete end-of-fiscal period work for a partnership using an automated accounting system.

FOCUS

In Chapters 16 through 18, manual end-of-fiscal-period procedures for a partnership were described. Emphasize that using an automated accounting system speeds the processing of end-of-fiscal-period work by (1) eliminating the need to prepare a work sheet; (2) having all financial reports prepared by a computer; and (3) having the software generate closing entries. The end-of-fiscal-period procedures for Integrating Automated Accounting Topic 6 are very similar to procedures described in Integrating Automated Accounting Topic 3: End-of-Fiscal-Period Work for a Proprietorship.

Cover student pages 459–465 "Completing End-of-Fiscal-Period Work" and "Processing Financial Statements." This lesson introduces students to end-of-fiscal-period procedures for a partnership using automated accounting software. As the lesson progresses, review the definitions of inventory, merchandise inventory, cost of merchandise sold, gross profit on sales, distribution of net income statement, owners' equity statement, and supporting schedule.

End-of-fiscal-period work is completed using the same basic procedures for both manual and automated methods. However, the component percentages are automatically produced by the software. Analyzing acceptable component percentages is an important student critical thinking skill. Because using an automated accounting system speeds the processing of end-of-fiscal-period work, students can spend more time analyzing component percentages.

Remind students that a post-closing trial balance is a trial balance prepared after closing entries have been posted.

Reinforce to students that no additional input of data is necessary to record closing entries. The software contains instructions for closing temporary accounts.

CAREERS IN ACCOUNTING

The CAREERS IN ACCOUNTING feature box, COMPUTER PROGRAMMER, comes from the Dictionary of Occupational Titles (DOT). The entry number for this job title is D.O.T. 030.162-010. The career feature is designed to expose students to the exploration of different careers in accounting. The feature gives a realistic description of actual job duties. This feature can be used to demonstrate that the skills learned in this course are relevant.

CAREERS IN ACCOUNTING

COMPUTER PROGRAMMER

- *Writes, updates, and maintains computer programs*
- *Enters program codes into computer system and inputs test data into computer*
- *Interprets program operating codes while observing computer monitor screen*
- *Analyzes, reviews, and rewrites programs to increase operating efficiency*
- *Compiles and writes documentation of program development and subsequent revisions*

Recording Adjusting Entries

Adjusting entries are batched and recorded on a general journal input form. CarLand's completed general journal input form for the adjusting entries is shown in Illustration T6-2.

ILLUSTRATION T6-2

General journal input form with adjustments recorded

RUN DATE *12,31,--*
MM DD YY

GENERAL JOURNAL
Input Form

	DATE MM/DD	REFERENCE	ACCOUNT NO.	CUSTOMER/ VENDOR NO.	DEBIT	CREDIT	
1	12,31	Adj.Ent.	3150		13200 00		1
2	/		1140			13200 00	2
3	,31	Adj.Ent.	6175		3940 00		3
4	/		1145			3940 00	4
5	,31	Adj.Ent.	6180		3260 00		5
6	/		1150			3260 00	6
7	,31	Adj.Ent.	6130		2640 00		7
8	/		1160			2640 00	8
25	/						25
			PAGE TOTALS		23040 00	23040 00	
			FINAL TOTALS		23040 00	23040 00	

CarLand has the following adjustment data on December 31.

Adjustment Information, December 31

Merchandise inventory	$212,200.00
Office supplies inventory	1,460.00
Store supplies inventory	2,520.00
Value of prepaid insurance	2,200.00

The information needed to journalize the adjusting entries is obtained from the trial balance. Income Summary is debited and Merchandise Inventory is credited for $13,200.00, the decrease in merchandise inventory. The journal entry to record this adjustment is on lines 1 and 2 of the general journal input form shown in Illustration T6-2. The abbreviation for adjusting entries, *Adj.Ent.*, is written in the Reference column for each entry.

Supplies Expense—Office is debited and Supplies—Office is credited for $3,940.00, the value of office supplies used. The journal entry to record this adjustment is on lines 3 and 4 of Illustration T6-2.

Supplies Expense—Store is debited and Supplies—Store is credited for $3,260.00, the value of store supplies used. The journal entry to record this adjustment is on lines 5 and 6 of Illustration T6-2.

Insurance Expense is debited and Prepaid Insurance is credited for $2,640.00, the value of insurance used. The journal entry to record this adjustment is on lines 7 and 8 of Illustration T6-2.

After all adjusting entries have been recorded, the Debit and Credit columns are totaled. The totals are entered on the Page Totals and Final Totals lines provided at the bottom of the input

TEACHING STRATEGIES: USING VISUALS

Using Transparency AA-2, Blank General Journal Input Form, will help students understand the journalizing process.

form. The totals are compared to assure that debits equal credits. As the totals are the same, $23,040.00, the adjusting entries on the general journal input form are assumed to be correct.

Processing Adjusting Entries

The Journals menu is selected from the menu bar. The General Journal command is chosen from the Journals menu to display the data entry window for keying data.

After all lines on the input form have been keyed and posted, the Reports menu is selected from the menu bar. The Journals command is selected to display the Report Selection window. General Journal is selected from the Report Selection window. As CarLand wants to print only the adjusting entries, the abbreviation *Adj.Ent.* is keyed as a Reference restriction. The *Ok* button is pushed to display the general journal report. The report is checked for accuracy by comparing the report totals, $23,040.00, with the totals on the general journal input form. Because the totals are the same, the general journal report is assumed to be correct. The general journal report is printed, as shown in Illustration T6-3, and filed for future reference.

ILLUSTRATION T6-3   General journal report for adjusting entries

```
                              CarLand
                          General Journal
                             12/31/--
----------------------------------------------------------------------
Date   Refer.    V/C Acct.  Title                       Debit     Credit
----------------------------------------------------------------------
12/31  Adj.Ent.      3150   Income Summary            13200.00
12/31  Adj.Ent.      1140   Merchandise Inventory                13200.00

12/31  Adj.Ent.      6175   Supplies Expense--Office   3940.00
12/31  Adj.Ent.      1145   Supplies--Office                      3940.00

12/31  Adj.Ent.      6180   Supplies Expense--Store    3260.00
12/31  Adj.Ent.      1150   Supplies--Store                       3260.00

12/31  Adj.Ent.      6130   Insurance Expense          2640.00
12/31  Adj.Ent.      1160   Prepaid Insurance                     2640.00

                                                     ---------- ----------
                            Totals                    23040.00   23040.00
                                                     ========== ==========
```

PROCESSING FINANCIAL STATEMENTS

To prepare the income statement, the Reports menu is selected from the menu bar. The Financial Statements command is chosen to display the Report Selection window. Income Statement is selected from the Report Selection window. The income statement is printed, as shown in Illustration T6-4 on page 462, and filed for future reference.

To prepare the balance sheet, the same steps are followed as to prepare an income statement. However, Balance Sheet is selected

APPLY

Guided Practice

Students should be at the computers. Guide students through booting the software and loading Optional Problem DB-6A from the template. Instruct students to complete the end-of-fiscal-period work as you go step by step through the procedures.

Independent Practice

- Assign Automating Problem 18-1.
- Assign Automating Mastery Problem 18-M.

ASSESS

- Assess student understanding by checking solutions to Automating Problems 18-1 and 18-M.
- Have students list the steps for completing end-of-fiscal-period work.

Reteach

Use Transparency AA-2 to journalize CarLand's adjusting entries. For additional reteaching use Transparency AA-2 to journalize the adjusting entries from Automating Problems 18-1 and 18-M.

Extend

- Assign Automating Challenge Problem 18-C.
- Assign the students to complete Reinforcement Activity 2 using the automated accounting software.

Enrich

Have the students clip and bring to class newspaper want-ads that describe available accounting positions that require computer skills and knowledge. Have the students discuss the importance of having computer skills in today's job market.

Review the procedures for processing end-of-fiscal-period work using manual procedures and using automated accounting software.

Have the students complete *Viking Marine An Automated Business Simulation.*

ILLUSTRATION·T6-4   Income statement

```
                               CarLand
                          Income Statement
                      For Period Ended 12/31/--
-------------------------------------------------------------------------
                                *****Monthly*****    *****Yearly******
                                Amount    Percent    Amount    Percent
-------------------------------------------------------------------------
O p e r a t i n g   R e v e n u e
-------------------------------------------------------------------------
Sales                          352600.00   100.00  352600.00   100.00
                               ----------  ------  ----------  ------
Total Operating Revenue        352600.00   100.00  352600.00   100.00
C o s t   o f   M e r c h a n d i s e   S o l d
-------------------------------------------------------------------------
Beginning Inventory            225400.00    63.93  225400.00    63.93
Purchases                      158300.00    44.90  158300.00    44.90
                               ----------  ------  ----------  ------
Merchandise Available for Sale 383700.00   108.82  383700.00   108.82
Less Ending Inventory         -212200.00   -60.18 -212200.00   -60.18
                               ----------  ------  ----------  ------
Cost of Merchandise Sold       171500.00    48.64  171500.00    48.64
                               ----------  ------  ----------  ------
Gross Profit                   181100.00    51.36  181100.00    51.36
O p e r a t i n g   E x p e n s e s
-------------------------------------------------------------------------
Advertising Expense              5500.00     1.56    5500.00     1.56
Credit Card Fee Expense          2890.00      .82    2890.00      .82
Insurance Expense                2640.00      .75    2640.00      .75
Miscellaneous Expense            2182.15      .62    2182.15      .62
Payroll Taxes Expense            7299.75     2.07    7299.75     2.07
Rent Expense                    18000.00     5.10   18000.00     5.10
Salary Expense                  60153.00    17.06   60153.00    17.06
Supplies Expense--Office         3940.00     1.12    3940.00     1.12
Supplies Expense--Store          3260.00      .92    3260.00      .92
Utilities Expense                3180.00      .90    3180.00      .90
                               ----------  ------  ----------  ------
Total Operating Expenses       109044.90    30.93  109044.90    30.93
                               ----------  ------  ----------  ------
Net Income                      72055.10    20.44   72055.10    20.44
                               ==========  ======  ==========  ======
```

from the Report Selection window. The balance sheet is printed, as shown in Illustration T6-5, and filed for future reference.

CLOSING TEMPORARY ACCOUNTS

In automated accounting the software contains instructions for closing temporary accounts. After the balance sheet has been prepared, The Options menu is selected from the menu bar. The Period-End Closing command is chosen from the Options menu to close all temporary accounts.

PROCESSING A POST-CLOSING TRIAL BALANCE

After the financial statements have been prepared and period-end closing has been performed, a post-closing trial balance is

OPTIONAL PROBLEM

The input forms illustrated in this topic can be keyed using *Automated Accounting 6.0.* Refer to OPTIONAL PROBLEM DB-6A for information about automating this topic.

```
                          CarLand
                       Balance Sheet
                         12/31/--

A s s e t s
-----------
Cash                                24233.57
Petty Cash                            500.00
Accounts Receivable                  9332.00
Merchandise Inventory              212200.00
Supplies--Office                     1460.00
Supplies--Store                      2520.00
Prepaid Insurance                    2200.00
                                   ----------
Total Assets                                      252445.57
                                                  ==========
L i a b i l i t i e s
---------------------
Accounts Payable                    10451.90
Employee Income Tax Pay.              402.00
FICA Tax Payable                      832.16
Sales Tax Payable                    1760.00
Unemployment Tax Pay--Fed              59.15
Unemployment Tax Pay--St.             399.26
Health Ins. Premiums Pay.             840.00
U.S. Savings Bonds Pay.                40.00
United Way Donations Pay.              60.00
                                   ----------
Total Liabilities                                  14844.47

O w n e r ' s   E q u i t y
---------------------------
Amy Kramer, Capital                101118.00
Amy Kramer, Drawing                -18200.00
Dario Mesa, Capital                101228.00
Dario Mesa, Drawing                -18600.00
Net Income                          72055.10
                                   ----------
Total Owner's Equity                              237601.10
                                                  ----------
Total Liabilities & Equity                        252445.57
                                                  ==========
```

processed. The Reports menu is selected from the menu bar. The Ledgers command is chosen to display the Reports Selection window. Trial Balance is selected from the Report Selection window. The trial balance is printed, as shown in Illustration T6-6 on page 464, and filed for future reference.

OPTIONAL PROBLEM DB-6A

CarLand's general ledger data base is on the accounting textbook template. If you wish to complete Rugcare's end-of-fiscal-period work using automated accounting software, load the *Automated Accounting 6.0* or higher software. Select Data Base 6A (DB-6A) from the template disk. Read the Problem Instructions screen. Follow the procedures described to process CarLand's end-of-fiscal-period work.

```
                              CarLand
                            Trial Balance
                             12/31/--
---------------------------------------------------------------
Acct.   Account
Number  Title                           Debit         Credit
---------------------------------------------------------------
1110    Cash                          24233.57
1120    Petty Cash                      500.00
1130    Accounts Receivable            9332.00
1140    Merchandise Inventory        212200.00
1145    Supplies--Office               1460.00
1150    Supplies--Store                2520.00
1160    Prepaid Insurance              2200.00
2110    Accounts Payable                            10451.90
2120    Employee Income Tax Pay.                      402.00
2130    FICA Tax Payable                             832.16
2140    Sales Tax Payable                           1760.00
2150    Unemployment Tax Pay--Fed                      59.15
2160    Unemployment Tax Pay--St.                     399.26
2170    Health Ins. Premiums Pay.                     840.00
2180    U.S. Savings Bonds Pay.                        40.00
2190    United Way Donations Pay.                      60.00
3110    Amy Kramer, Capital                        118945.55
3130    Dario Mesa, Capital                        118655.55
                                      ----------    ----------
        Totals                       252445.57     252445.57
                                      ==========    ==========
```

AUTOMATED

AUTOMATED ACCOUNTING PROBLEMS

AUTOMATING APPLICATION PROBLEM 18-1 Journalizing and posting adjusting and closing entries; preparing a post-closing trial balance.

INSTRUCTIONS:

1. Use the end-of-fiscal-period work for Problem 18-1, Chapter 18. Use December 31 of the current year as the run date.
2. Load the *Automated Accounting 6.0* or higher software. Select data base F18-1 (First-Year Course Problem 18-1) from the accounting textbook template. Read the Problem Instructions Screen.
3. Select File from the menu bar and choose the Save As menu command. Key the path to the drive and directory that contains your data files. Save the data base with a file name of XXX181 (where XXX are your initials).
4. Display/print a trial balance.
5. Record the adjusting entries on a general ledger input form using the following information. Use the account numbers from the trial balance prepared in Instruction 4.

Adjustment Information, December 31

Merchandise inventory	$283,830.00
Office supplies inventory.	2,570.00
Store supplies inventory	2,130.00
Value of prepaid insurance	1,100.00

6. Key the adjusting entries from the general journal input form.
7. Display/print the general journal report.
8. Display/print the income statement and balance sheet.
9. Perform period-end closing.
10. Display/print the post-closing trial balance.

TEACHING STRATEGIES: TEACHING TIP

It is important for students to save a template file under another name before they begin work. This will keep the template file intact for future use.

AUTOMATED

AUTOMATING MASTERY PROBLEM 18-M Journalizing and posting adjusting and closing entries; preparing a post-closing trial balance

INSTRUCTIONS:

1. Use the end-of-fiscal-period work for Mastery Problem 18-M, Chapter 18. Use December 31 of the current year as the run date.
2. Load the *Automated Accounting 6.0* or higher software. Select data base F18-M (First-Year Course Mastery Problem 18-M) from the accounting textbook template. Read the Problem Instructions screen.
3. Select File from the menu bar and choose the Save As menu command. Key the path to the drive and directory that contains your data files. Save the data base with a file name of XXX18M (where XXX are your initials).
4. Display/print a trial balance.
5. Record the adjusting entries on a general journal input form using the following information. Use the account numbers from the trial balance prepared in Instruction 4.

Adjustment Information, December 31

Merchandise inventory	$276,140.00
Office supplies inventory.	2,400.00
Store supplies inventory	2,010.00
Value of prepaid insurance	750.00

6. Key the adjusting entries from the general journal input form.
7. Display/print the general journal report.
8. Display/print the income statement.
9. Display/print the balance sheet.
10. Perform period-end closing.
11. Display/print the post-closing trial balance.

AUTOMATED

AUTOMATING CHALLENGE PROBLEM 18-C Completing end-of-fiscal-period work

INSTRUCTIONS:

1. Use the end-of-fiscal-period work for Challenge Problem 18-C, Chapter 18. Use December 31 of the current year as the run date.
2. Load the *Automated Accounting 6.0* or higher software. Select data base F18-C from the accounting textbook template. Read the Problem Instructions screen.
3. Select File from the menu bar and choose the Save As menu command. Key the path to the drive and directory that contains your data files. Save the data base with a file name of XXX18C (where XXX are your initials).
4. Display/print a trial balance.
5. Record the adjusting entries on a general journal input form using the following information. Use the account numbers from the trial balance prepared in Instruction 4.

Adjustment Information, December 31

Merchandise inventory	$204,680.00
Office supplies inventory.	2,635.00
Store supplies inventory	2,310.00
Value of prepaid insurance	2,200.00

6. Key the adjusting entries from the general journal input form.
7. Display/print the general journal report.
8. Display/print the income statement and balance sheet.
9. Perform period-end closing.
10. Display/print the post-closing trial balance.

An Accounting Cycle for a Partnership: End-of-Fiscal-Period Work

The ledgers used in Reinforcement Activity 2, Part A, are needed to complete Reinforcement Activity 2, Part B.

Reinforcement Activity 2, Part B, includes those accounting activities needed to complete the accounting cycle of ClearView Optical.

END-OF-FISCAL-PERIOD WORK

INSTRUCTIONS:

10. Prepare a trial balance on a work sheet. Use December 31 of the current year as the date.

11. Complete the work sheet using the following adjustment information.

Adjustment Information, December 31

Merchandise inventory	$203,200.00
Office supplies inventory	2,370.00
Store supplies inventory	3,240.00
Value of prepaid insurance	260.00

12. Prepare an income statement. Figure and record the following component percentages: (a) cost of merchandise sold, (b) gross profit on sales, (c) total expenses, and (d) net income or loss. Round percentage calculations to the nearest 0.1%.

13. Prepare a distribution of net income statement. Net income or loss is to be shared equally.

14. Prepare an owners' equity statement. No additional investments were made.

15. Prepare a balance sheet in report form.

16. Use page 25 of a journal. Journalize and post the adjusting entries.

17. Continue using page 25 of the journal. Journalize and post the closing entries.

18. Prepare a post-closing trial balance.

466

Viking Marine is a merchandising business organized as a partnership. This business simulation covers the realistic transactions completed by Viking Marine, which sells personal watercraft and water sports items. Transactions are recorded in a journal similar to the one used by CarLand in Part 3. The following activities are included in the accounting cycle for Viking Marine. This business simulation is available from the publisher in either manual or automated versions.

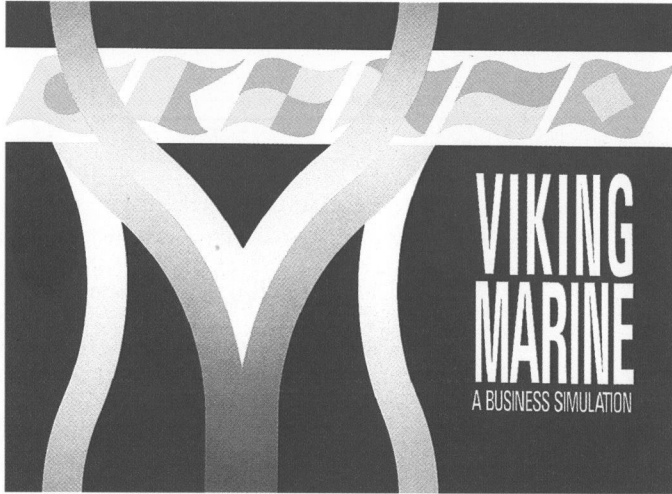

Activities in Viking Marine:

1. Recording transactions in a journal from source documents.

2. Posting items to be posted individually to a general ledger and subsidiary ledger.

3. Recording a payroll in a payroll register. Updating the employee earnings record. Recording payroll journal entries.

4. Posting column totals to a general ledger.

5. Preparing schedules of accounts receivable and accounts payable from subsidiary ledgers.

6. Preparing a trial balance on a work sheet.

7. Planning adjustments and completing a work sheet.

8. Preparing financial statements.

9. Journalizing and posting adjusting entries.

10. Journalizing and posting closing entries.

11. Preparing a post-closing trial balance.

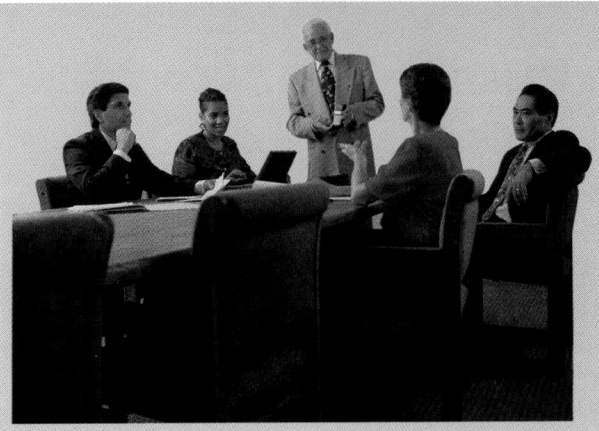

STUDENT EDITION

STUDENT FEATURES

Multicultural Awareness

Early Egypt, page 526
Ancient China, page 626
Historical Records, page 665

Professional Business Ethics

What Does The Policy Manual Say? page 594
Should Tax Fraud Be Reported? page 724

Global Perspective

International Weights and Measures, page 572
International Travel, page 687

Careers In Accounting

Letter-of-Credit Document Examiner, page 540
Credit Reporting Clerk, page 593
Tax Accountant, page 692

Personal Visions In Business

Philip Showalter, D.D.S., page 480
Bert N. Mitchell, page 632
Jean Myong VanHorn, page 670

Spreadsheet Options

Graphics Enhance Financial Statement Analysis, page 715

Audit Your Understanding

This student activity can be found on pages 476, 489, 496, 523,
531, 536, 542, 573, 579, 592, 598, 606, 609, 628, 635, 646, 651,
655, 671, 677, 688, 695, 716, 725

APPLIED SKILLS

Applied Communications

Pages 500, 613, 658

Applied Math

Pages 479, 481, 500, 527, 545, 551, 571, 574, 575, 582, 590,
591, 593, 596, 597, 600, 602, 604, 605, 606, 607, 608, 609, 613,
614, 616, 629, 630, 631, 633, 638, 639, 645, 646, 649, 650, 659,
662, 665, 668, 669, 672, 674, 676, 681, 682, 694, 700, 708, 711,
715, 716, 729

SOFTWARE APPLICATIONS

Automated Accounting 6.0 Problems 19-3, 19-M, (Optional
Problem DB-7A); 20-M, 20-C, (Optional Problem DB-8A); 22-6,
22-M, 22-C, (Optional Problem DB-9A); 27-C, (Optional Problem
DB-10A); Reinforcement Activity 3
Spreadsheet Template, Problems 22-M, 22-6, 23-1, 23-2, 24D-1,
24-D3, 27-M
Accounting Tutorial, Units 7–10
Application Program Disk, Problems 19-M, 20-M, 21-M, 22-5,
22-7, 24-M, 26-M
Study Guide Software for each chapter

APPLIED SKILLS

Communications, pages 500, 613, 614, 658

Language Arts, pages 489, 532, 574, 611, 629, 654, 669, 688, 710

Writing Across the Curriculum, pages 486, 538, 580, 600, 634, 650, 678, 695, 726

Building Study Skills, pages 482, 569, 588, 647, 666, 686

Mathematics, pages 479, 527, 571, 597, 636, 645, 665, 694, 708

Word Processing, pages 474, 539, 572, 604, 635, 656, 676, 696, 723

TEACHING STRATEGIES

Accounting Pedagogy, pages 470, 471, 507, 518, 554, 568, 586, 619, 624, 642, 664, 684, 702, 737

Assessment by Portfolio, pages 543, 564, 746

Different Learning Abilities, pages 477, 484, 488, 492, 495, 514, 529, 557, 576, 594, 599, 603, 621, 628, 651, 677, 697, 722, 740

Different Learning Styles, pages 473, 475, 483, 485, 487, 520, 521, 524, 528, 533, 535, 536, 537, 540, 541, 591, 593, 596, 602, 605, 707, 709, 711, 714, 715

Cooperative Learning, pages 472, 478, 515, 530, 534, 558, 566, 604, 620, 636, 672, 709, 711, 713, 741, 746

Expanding Beyond the Classroom, pages 579, 587, 630, 649

Applying Visuals, pages 498, 509, 543, 555, 580, 610, 636, 656, 678, 696, 717, 739

Teaching Tip, pages 470, 471, 473, 480, 481, 483, 490, 491, 493, 494, 516, 525, 560, 575, 577, 578, 589, 590, 595, 622, 623, 627, 631, 632, 643, 667, 668, 674, 689, 690, 692, 712, 718, 743

Software Focus, pages 471, 507, 518, 554, 565, 568, 586, 619, 633, 642, 664, 684, 702, 737, 745

Safety and Health, pages 515, 561, 623, 742

Simulation, page 735

Milestone, page 736

Optional Problem, pages 513, 556, 738

Reinforcement Activity, pages 563, 734, 745

ASSESSMENT

Assessment by Portfolio
MicroExam software for each chapter
Problem Test for each chapter
Unit Problem Test No. 6 (19–20)
Unit Problem Test No. 7 (21–23)
Unit Problem Test No. 8 (24–27)
Unit Objective Test No. 6 (19–20)
Unit Objective Test No. 7 (21–23)
Unit Objective Test No. 8 (24–27)

SOFTWARE

Automated Accounting 6.0
Accounting Tutorial
Electronic Auditor
Application Program Disk
Study Guide Software

MicroExam
Lotus (spreadsheet)
Ventura Publisher
  (desktop publishing software)
WordPerfect (word processing)

BIBLIOGRAPHY

Miller, Sidney R., and Patrick J. Schloss. *Career-Vocational Education for Handicapped Youth,* Aspen Systems Corporation, 1982.

Nattive, A. "Cooperative Learning: An Overview." *Journal of Humanistic Education.* 1988.

Parker, Jeanette Plauché. *Instructional Strategies for Teaching the Gifted.* Allyn and Bacon, 1989.

Periodicals

Accounting News, Warren, Gorham & Lamont, New York, NY.
Multinational Business, Economist Newspaper, New York, NY.
  (Global business)
Native Peoples, Phoenix, AZ. (Multicultural awareness)

Technology

AICPA. *The Bottom Line: Inside Accounting Today,* 1987. (Video)
Dun & Bradstreet Information Services. *Dun's Direct Access*
  (On-line database of U.S. companies)

PART 4 OPENER

PART 4

Accounting for a Merchandising Business Organized as a Corporation

GENERAL GOALS

1. Know accounting terminology related to an accounting system for a merchandising business organized as a corporation.

2. Understand accounting concepts and practices related to an accounting system for a merchandising business organized as a corporation.

3. Demonstrate accounting procedures used in an accounting system for a merchandising business organized as a corporation.

Part 4 presents the complete accounting cycle one more time, this time for a merchandising business organized as a corporation.

Chapters 19 and 20 describe how the basic kinds of daily transactions for purchases, sales, cash payments, and cash receipts are recorded in special journals. In addition, Chapter 20 features a new section on the procedures for arranging and accounting for international sales. After Chapter 19, Integrating Automated Accounting Topic 7 automates recording purchases and cash payments. After Chapter 20, Integrating Automated Accounting Topic 8 automates recording sales and cash receipts.

Chapter 21 covers the procedures for estimating uncollectible accounts expense at the end of a fiscal period.

Chapter 22 describes a full range of concepts and procedures related to accounting for and reporting plant assets. Straight-line depreciation is emphasized, but declining-balance and MACRS methods are also described. Disposal of plant assets is discussed, including the calculation and reporting of gains and losses on disposal. Property taxes are also covered. After Chapter 22, Integrating Automated Accounting Topic 9 automates accounting for plant assets.

Chapter 23 focuses on merchandise inventory. Inventory is costed using the fifo, lifo, and weighted average methods. The gross profit method of estimating an inventory is also presented.

Chapter 24 presents a range of topics related to notes payable and notes receivable.

Chapter 25 continues the discussion of notes payable and receivable, focusing on end-of-fiscal-period adjusting, closing, and reversing entries for accrued revenue and expenses.

Chapter 26 begins the end-of-fiscal-period work. Journal entries for distributing corporate earnings in the form of dividends are also illustrated.

Chapter 27 concludes the presentation of end-of-fiscal-period work for a corporation with the preparation of a financial statement followed by adjusting, closing, and reversing entries. After Chapter 27, Integrating Automated Accounting Topic 10 is presented to automate end-of-fiscal-period work for a corporation.

Chapters 19–27 present the entire accounting cycle for a corporation. Students may apply these concepts by completing a simulation, Western Rider, Inc., and/or the reinforcement activity. Reinforcement Activity 3 is divided into Parts A and B which may be completed separately or together after Chapter 27.

Chapter 19 describes and illustrates the use of two special journals—a purchases journal and a cash payments journal—and a two-column general journal. Cash and on account purchases of merchandise, previously studied in the second accounting cycle for a merchandising business, are reviewed. Cash payments on account with purchases discounts extend learning about cash payments. Purchases returns

GUIDE TO ACHIEVING LEARNING OBJECTIVES

Enabling Performance Tasks	TEACH Lesson Plans	APPLY Drills for Understanding	APPLY Application Problems	EXTEND/ENRICH Mastery Problems	EXTEND/ENRICH Challenge Problems	EXTEND/ENRICH Cases for Critical Thinking	EXTEND/ENRICH Recycling Problems	EXTEND/ENRICH Reinforcement Activity	
a. Define accounting terms related to purchases and cash payments.	19-1, 19-2, 19-3								
b. Identify accounting concepts and practices related to purchases and cash payments.	19-1, 19-2, 19-3					Cases 1, 2			
c. Analyze transactions affecting purchases and cash payments.	19-1, 19-2, 19-3	19-D1, 19-D2, 19-D3, 19-D4	19-1, 19-2, 19-3	19-M	19-C		19-R	RA3A	
d. Journalize and post transactions related to purchases and cash payments.	19-1, 19-2, 19-3	19-D5	19-1, 19-2, 19-3	19-M	19-C		19-R	RA3A	

ENRICHMENT

SPECIAL FEATURES

Personal Visions in Business, page 480

Applied Communications, page 500

TECHNOLOGY CONNECTION

Automated Accounting 6.0 Problems 19-3, 19-M

Integrating Automated Accounting Topic 7 Optional Problem DB-7A

Accounting Tutorial Unit 7

Application Program Disk Problem 19-M

Electronic Study Guide

NEW, REVIEW, AND EXTENSION

ACTIVITIES/CONCEPTS/TRANSACTIONS	NEW	REVIEW/ EXTENSION
Corporation accounting	✓	
Journalizing and posting using a purchases journal	✓	
Recording purchases of merchandise on account		✓
Journalizing and posting using a cash payments journal	✓	
Recording cash payments for expenses		✓
Recording purchase of merchandise for cash		✓
Recording cash payments for purchases on account		✓
Purchases discounts	✓	
Recording replenishing a petty cash fund		✓
Cash short and over	✓	
Journalizing and posting using a general journal	✓	
Recording purchases returns and allowances	✓	
Recording buying supplies on account		✓
Preparing a schedule of accounts payable		✓

and allowances and their affect on vendor accounts are discussed and illustrated. Replenishment of petty cash, which has been studied and applied since the first accounting cycle, is extended with coverage of cash short and over.

The solution to Drill 19-D4 is needed to complete Drill 19-D5.

	INFORMAL ASSESSMENT		FORMAL ASSESSMENT				
	Study Guide	Audit Your Understanding	Chapter MicroExam	Chapter Problem Test	Unit Problem Test	Unit Objective Test	Portfolio
Unit A		✓	✓			✓	
Unit C		✓	✓			✓	
Unit B				✓	✓		✓
				✓	✓		✓

TEACHING MATERIALS

Teacher's Wraparound Edition of the Text

Teacher's Resource Guide

Teacher's Edition of Working Papers

Teacher's Edition of Demonstration/Recycling Problems

Teaching Transparencies

Accounting Tutorial Manual

MicroExam

Applied Math Work Sheet

APPLIED MATHEMATICS

APPLIED MATH/ACCOUNTING SKILL	APPLICATION
Calculating Purchases Discounts	Drill 19-D1
Calculating Petty Cash Short and Over	Drill 19-D2

CHART OF ACCOUNTS

This third chart of accounts is for a merchandising business organized as a corporation. This chart of accounts is the most complicated form of business illustrated in this text.

In the Balance Sheet Accounts, the assets are divided into current and plant assets. The Stockholders' Equity section is similar to the owners' equity section of a proprietorship or partnership, but the accounts are named differently.

The Income Statement accounts section shows additional divisions for Other Revenue, Other Expenses, and Income Tax Expense. The Operating Revenue and Cost of Merchandise sections show the contra accounts for Sales and Purchases, the discount and returns and allowances accounts.

Balance Sheet Accounts

(1000) ASSETS

1100	Current Assets
1105	Cash
1110	Petty Cash
1115	Notes Receivable
1120	Interest Receivable
1125	Accounts Receivable
1130	Allowance for Uncollectible Accounts
1135	Merchandise Inventory
1140	Supplies
1145	Prepaid Insurance
1200	Plant Assets
1205	Office Equipment
1210	Accumulated Depreciation— Office Equipment
1215	Store Equipment
1220	Accumulated Depreciation— Store Equipment

(2000) LIABILITIES

2100	Current Liabilities
2105	Notes Payable
2110	Interest Payable
2115	Accounts Payable
2120	Employee Income Tax Payable
2125	Federal Income Tax Payable
2130	FICA Tax Payable
2135	Sales Tax Payable
2140	Unemployment Tax Payable—Federal
2145	Unemployment Tax Payable—State
2150	Health Insurance Premiums Payable
2155	Dividends Payable

(3000) STOCKHOLDERS' EQUITY

3105	Capital Stock
3110	Retained Earnings
3115	Dividends
3120	Income Summary

Income Statement Accounts

(4000) OPERATING REVENUE

4105	Sales
4110	Sales Discount
4115	Sales Returns and Allowances

(5000) COST OF MERCHANDISE

5105	Purchases
5110	Purchases Discount
5115	Purchases Returns and Allowances

(6000) OPERATING EXPENSES

6105	Advertising Expense
6110	Credit Card Fee Expense
6115	Depreciation Expense— Office Equipment
6120	Depreciation Expense— Store Equipment
6125	Insurance Expense
6130	Miscellaneous Expense
6135	Payroll Taxes Expense
6140	Rent Expense
6145	Salary Expense
6150	Supplies Expense
6155	Uncollectible Accounts Expense
6160	Utilities Expense

(7000) OTHER REVENUE

7105	Gain on Plant Assets
7110	Interest Income

(8000) OTHER EXPENSES

8105	Cash Short and Over
8110	Interest Expense
8115	Loss on Plant Assets

(9000) INCOME TAX EXPENSE

9105	Federal Income Tax Expense

The chart of accounts for Celluphone, Inc. is illustrated above for ready reference as you study Part 4 of this textbook.

19

Recording Purchases and Cash Payments Using Special Journals

ENABLING PERFORMANCE TASKS

After studying Chapter 19, you will be able to:

a Define accounting terms related to purchases and cash payments.

b Identify accounting concepts and practices related to purchases and cash payments.

c Analyze transactions affecting purchases and cash payments.

d Journalize and post transactions related to purchases and cash payments.

TERMS PREVIEW

corporation • share of stock • capital stock • special journal • purchases journal • cash payments journal • list price • trade discount • cash discount • purchases discount • cash short • cash over • general journal • purchases return • purchases allowance • debit memorandum

Reliable financial information is important for the successful operation of a business. However, the amount of information a business needs and can afford varies with the business' size and complexity. Several types of accounting systems may be used to record, summarize, and report a business' financial information. An accounting system may vary from a small manual system operated by one accounting clerk to a large computerized system that requires hundreds of accountants and clerks. A business should use an accounting system that provides the desired financial information with the least amount of effort and cost. Regardless of the accounting system used, financial information is reported for a specified period of time. (*CONCEPT: Accounting Period Cycle*)

CORPORATIONS

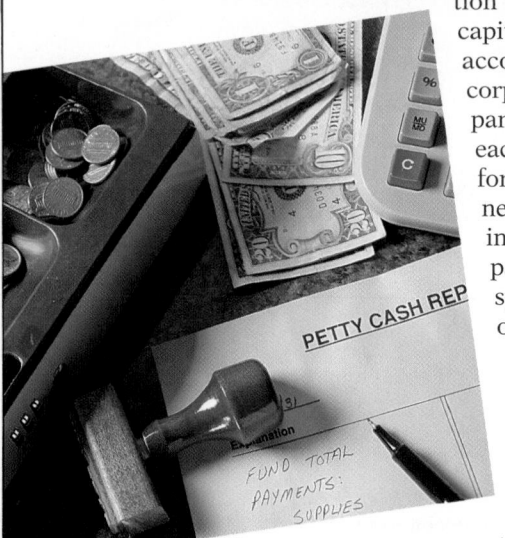

FYI

The term corporate culture describes the values, attitudes, and standards of a corporation.

Many businesses need amounts of capital that cannot be easily provided by a proprietorship or a partnership. An organization with the legal rights of a person and which may be owned by many persons is called a **corporation**. Many businesses are organized as corporations. A corporation is formed by receiving approval from a state or federal agency. A corporation can own property, incur liabilities, and enter into contracts in its own name. A corporation may also sell ownership in itself. Each unit of ownership in a corporation is called a **share of stock**. Total shares of ownership in a corporation are called **capital stock**.

Celluphone, Inc. is organized as a corporation. Celluphone, Inc. sells cellular phones to corporate customers for use in their company cars and trucks. Celluphone was formed as a corporation because several owners can provide larger amounts of capital than one owner. The principal difference among the accounting records of proprietorships, partnerships, and corporations is in the capital accounts. Proprietorships and partnerships have a single capital and drawing account for each owner. A corporation has separate capital accounts for the stock issued and for the earnings kept in the business. The use of the different capital accounts is explained in more detail in Chapter 26. As in proprietorships and partnerships, information in a corporation's accounting system is kept separate from the personal records of the owners. (*CONCEPT: Business Entity*)

SPECIAL JOURNALS

A business with few transactions may need only one bookkeeper or accounting clerk to record transactions. When one person records transactions, a business may record all entries in one journal. In Part 2, Rugcare used a 5-column journal to record all transactions. In Part 3, CarLand used an 11-column expanded journal to record all transactions. However, a

PART 4   Accounting for a Merchandising Business Organized as a Corporation

business with many daily transactions may use several different journals. A journal used to record only one kind of transaction is called a **special journal**. Using special journals allows the work of journalizing to be divided among several accounting clerks. The accounting clerks then specialize in the kind of transactions recorded. This specialization helps improve the efficiency of recording transactions.

Whether a single journal or several special journals are used, all business transactions are recorded in a common unit of measurement—the dollar. Recording all transactions in dollar values permits more meaningful comparisons with previous accounting periods and with other businesses. (CONCEPT: *Unit of Measurement*)

Celluphone uses four special journals along with a general journal to record its transactions.

1. Purchases journal—for all purchases on account
2. Cash payments journal—for all cash payments
3. Sales journal—for all sales on account
4. Cash receipts journal—for all cash receipts

A general journal is used for all other transactions.

FYI

When several journals are used, an abbreviation is used to show the journal from which the posting is made.

RECORDING PURCHASES ON ACCOUNT USING A PURCHASES JOURNAL

A special journal used to record *only* purchase on account transactions is called a **purchases journal**. The relationship between Celluphone's purchases journal and the expanded journal described in Chapter 11 is shown in Illustration 19-1.

ILLUSTRATION 19-1   Purchases journal

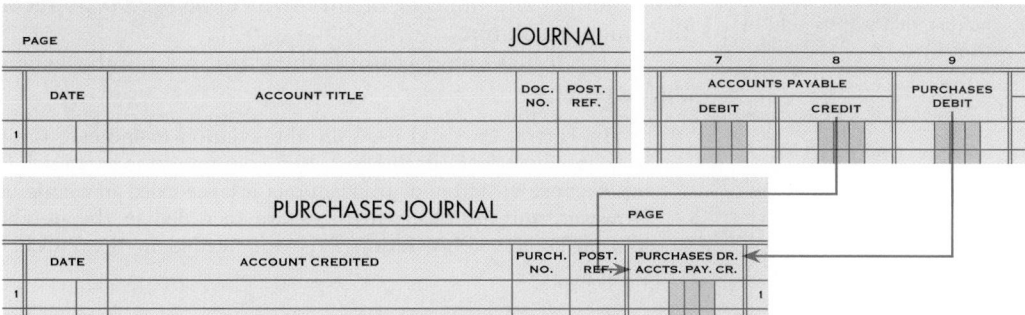

A purchase on account transaction can be recorded on one line of Celluphone's purchases journal. Each entry in the single amount column is both a debit to Purchases and a credit to Accounts Payable. The titles of both general ledger accounts are listed in the single amount column heading. Since the debit and credit entries always affect the same two accounts, recording time is reduced by using only one amount column.

CHAPTER 19   Recording Purchases and Cash Payments Using Special Journals   **473**

FOCUS

- In Part 2, the complete accounting cycle was presented for a service business organized as a proprietorship. In Part 3, the complete accounting cycle was presented for a merchandising business organized as a partnership. Explain that now we are going to work through the complete accounting cycle for a merchandising business organized as a corporation. In Parts 2 and 3, the businesses recorded all of their transactions in a single journal. Explain that the business in this part will use several different journals. In this lesson, we will record purchases on account in a special purchases journal.

- Introduce new vocabulary: corporation, share of stock, capital stock, special journal, purchases journal.

TEACHING STRATEGIES: TEACHING TIP

Review the difference between purchasing merchandise and buying supplies.

TEACHING STRATEGIES: DIFFERENT LEARNING STYLES

Auditory Learner. To reinforce the learning of journal entries, the auditory learner should verbally repeat the analysis of the transaction. The student should also verbally list the steps involved in making the entry.

Cover student pages 472–476 "Corporations," "Special Journals," and "Recording Purchases on Account Using a Purchases Journal." Involve students in a discussion of how a corporation differs from other types of ownership. Point out that a business will choose to use a single journal or special journal accounting system based on the volume and types of transactions that typically occur in the business. As the transaction volume and variety increases, the likelihood of a business using special journals increases. As the lesson progresses, draw T accounts on the board for the purchase on account transaction described in the textbook and demonstrate how to journalize the transaction. When discussing posting procedures explain that to abbreviate a journal in the Post. Ref. column of a ledger account, use a capital letter but no period after the abbreviation.

APPLY

- Use Transparency K to introduce the purchases journal or direct students to Illustration 19-1.
- Use Transparency 19-1 to explain the posting procedure from a purchases journal to an accounts payable ledger or direct students to Illustrations 19-3 and 19-4.

Guided Practice

Write several purchases on account transaction statements on the board. Guide students through analyzing and recording the transactions using a purchases journal. Have students draw T accounts at their desks. Give them blank journals and instruct them to journalize as you use Transparency K to journalize each transaction.

Independent Practice

Assign Terms 1–5, Questions 1–10, and Problem 19-1.

Journalizing Purchases on Account

The source document for recording a purchase on account is a purchase invoice received from a vendor. *(CONCEPT: Objective Evidence)* Celluphone dates, numbers, and verifies each purchase invoice.

March 1, 19--. Purchased merchandise on account from Cell Systems, $6,672.00. Purchase Invoice No. 39.

The balance of the purchases account is increased by this transaction. Thus, Purchases is debited for $6,672.00. The amount owed to a vendor is increased by this transaction. Therefore, Accounts Payable is credited for $6,672.00. The same amount is also credited to the account of Cell Systems in the accounts payable ledger.

Purchases are recorded at their cost. *(CONCEPT: Historical Cost)* The purchases journal entry to record this purchase on account transaction is shown in Illustration 19-2.

GENERAL LEDGER
Purchases

| 6,672.00 | |

Accounts Payable

| | 6,672.00 |

ACCOUNTS PAYABLE LEDGER
Cell Systems

| | 6,672.00 |

ILLUSTRATION 19-2

Purchases journal entry to record a purchase on account

			PURCHASES JOURNAL			PAGE 3	
	DATE		ACCOUNT CREDITED	PURCH. NO.	POST. REF.	PURCHASES DR. ACCTS. PAY. CR.	
1	Mar. 19--	1	Cell Systems	39		6 6 7 2 00	1
2							2
3							3
4							4

👀 FYI 👀

The purchases account is used to record only merchandise that will be sold to customers.

The date, *19--, Mar. 1,* is written in the Date column. The vendor name, *Cell Systems,* is written in the Account Credited column. The number stamped on the invoice, *39,* is entered in the Purch. No. column. The amount of the invoice, *$6,672.00,* is recorded in the amount column.

Each purchase on account is recorded in a purchases journal in the same way.

In Part 3, CarLand used an abbreviation to indicate the type of source document in the Post. Ref. column of the expanded journal because all kinds of transactions are recorded in one journal. However, only purchase invoices are recorded in the purchases journal so the abbreviation *P* is not needed in the Purch. No. column.

Posting from a Purchases Journal to an Accounts Payable Ledger

The amount on each line of a purchases journal is posted as a credit to the named vendor account in the accounts payable ledger.

Celluphone posts frequently to the accounts payable ledger. By posting frequently, each vendor account always shows an up-to-date balance. Posting from line 1 of a purchases journal to a vendor

APPLIED SKILLS: WORD PROCESSING

If you wish to integrate word processing into your accounting course, you may direct students to answer the end of chapter Accounting Terms, Questions for Individual Study, and Cases for Critical Thinking using their word processing software.

account in the accounts payable ledger is shown in Illustration 19-3.

- Assess student understanding by checking solutions to Independent Practice activities.

- Ask students to briefly summarize the procedure for journalizing and posting purchases on account using a purchases journal.

ILLUSTRATION 19-3

Posting from a purchases journal to an accounts payable ledger

The date, *1*, is recorded in the Date column of the vendor account. The abbreviation for the purchases journal and the page number of the journal, *P3*, is written in the Post. Ref. column of the account. The amount, *$6,672.00*, is entered in the Credit column of the vendor account. The amount in the Credit column is added to the previous balance in the Credit Balance column ($2,079.00 + $6,672.00 = $8,751.00). The new balance, *$8,751.00*, is recorded in the Credit Balance column. The vendor number for Cell Systems, *220*, is written in the Post. Ref. column of the purchases journal to show that posting has been completed for this line.

(a)(a)(a) FYI (a)(a)

To abbreviate a journal, use a capital letter but no period after the abbreviation.

When several journals are used, an abbreviation is used to show the journal from which the posting is made. The abbreviation *P* is used for the purchases journal. The abbreviation *P3* means page 3 of the purchases journal.

Posting from a purchases journal to an accounts payable ledger is the same as posting from an expanded journal's Accounts Payable Credit column, as described in Chapter 13.

Posting from a Purchases Journal to a General Ledger

At the end of each month, a purchases journal is totaled and ruled, as shown in Illustration 19-4 on page 476.

A single line is ruled across the amount column of the purchases journal under the last amount recorded. The date of the last day of the month, *31*, is entered in the Date column. The word *Total* is written in the Account Credited column. The amount column is added, and the total is written directly below the single line. Double lines are ruled across the amount column under the total amount.

Reteach

Use Demonstration Problem 19A. This problem can be demonstrated on the overhead with students completing the problem at their desks.

Extend

Have the students go to the library to find out the breakdown of businesses in the U.S. organized as proprietorships, partnerships, and corporations. The students should also determine the typical size, annual sales, and annual net income of the three types of business organizations. Have the students write a short report about their findings.

Enrich

Assign the PERSONAL VISIONS IN BUSINESS feature on page 480.

CHAPTER 19   Recording Purchases and Cash Payments Using Special Journals   **475**

TEACHING STRATEGIES: DIFFERENT LEARNING STYLES

Kinesthetic Learner. When covering journal entries with a kinesthetic learner, the instructor should give the student journal paper and have the student complete the entries as the instructor demonstrates on a transparency or chalkboard.

- Use Audit Your Understanding questions.
- Review Summary Illustration 19-5, Summary of Journalizing and Posting Using a Purchases Journal.

ILLUSTRATION 19-4   Posting from a purchases journal to a general ledger

AUDIT YOUR UNDERSTANDING

The AUDIT YOUR UNDERSTANDING feature appears at the end of each section of the chapter. Explain to your students that the word *audit* means to check or verify. AUDIT YOUR UNDERSTANDING may be used to check student comprehension of the section just studied. The answers are provided in Appendix D in the back of the textbook.

1. An organization with the legal rights of a person and which may be owned by many persons.
2. To allow accounting clerks to specialize in recording one kind of transaction to improve efficiency.
3. The purchase invoice received from a vendor.

Audit Your Understanding

1. What is a corporation?
2. Why are special journals used?
3. What is the source document for recording a purchase on account?

Illustration 19-4 also shows the posting of a purchases journal to a general ledger. The total amount of the purchases journal is posted to two general ledger accounts. The total amount, $108,046.00, is posted to Purchases as a debit and to Accounts Payable as a credit. This maintains the equality of debits and credits in the general ledger.

After the total is posted to Purchases, the account number, *5105*, is written under the total in the purchases journal. After this total is posted to Accounts Payable, the account number, *2115*, is written under the purchases journal total. Both account numbers are written in parentheses. This procedure is the same as posting totals of special amount columns in any journal.

Illustration 19-5 shows a summary of the procedure for journalizing and posting using a purchases journal.

RECORDING CASH PAYMENTS USING A CASH PAYMENTS JOURNAL

Celluphone uses another special journal for recording *only* cash payments. A special journal used to record only cash payment transactions is called a **cash payments journal**. The relationship

Materials

- Student pages 476–490
- Transparencies: L, Blank Cash Payments Journal (5-Column); 19-2, Posting from a Cash Payments Journal; 19-3, Posting Totals from a Cash Payments Journal
- Math Work Sheet Chapter 19: Part A: Calculating Purchases Discounts (TRG); Part B: Calculating Petty Cash Short and Over (TRG)
- Software: Accounting Tutorial
- Demonstration Problem: 19B, Journalizing and Posting Cash Payments Transactions

476

Objectives (Enabling Performance Tasks)

a. Define accounting terms related to purchases and cash payments.

b. Identify accounting concepts and practices related to purchases and cash payments.

c. Analyze transactions affecting purchases and cash payments.

d. Journalize and post transactions related to purchases and cash payments.

SUMMARY ILLUSTRATION 19-5

Summary of journalizing and posting using a purchases journal.

1 Celluphone records a purchase on account transaction on a single line of a one-column purchases journal.

2 Items in the purchases journal's amount column are posted separately to vendor accounts in the accounts payable ledger.

3 At the end of the month, the purchases journal amount column total is posted to two general ledger accounts. **Purchases** is debited; **Accounts Payable** is credited.

FOCUS

- Recording purchases transactions in a special purchases journal was presented earlier in this chapter. In this lesson, we will record cash payments transactions in a special cash payments journal.

- Introduce new vocabulary: cash payments journal, list price, trade discount, cash discount, purchases discount, cash short, cash over.

between Celluphone's cash payments journal and the expanded journal described in Chapter 11 is shown in Illustration 19-6.

ILLUSTRATION 19-6   Cash payments journal

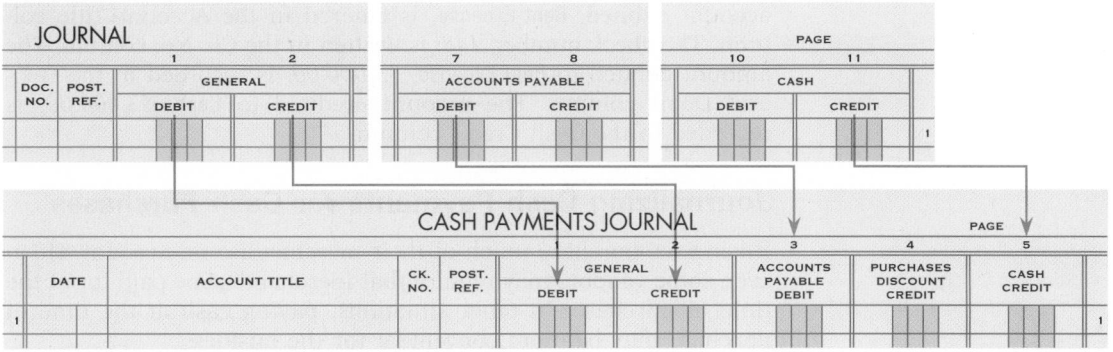

TEACHING STRATEGIES: DIFFERENT LEARNING ABILITIES

Visually-Impaired Students. The additional time required for visually impaired students to complete the previous cycles will minimize the time available to complete this cycle. The instructor should consider skipping Chapters 19 and 20 in favor of beginning chapters that present the new topics of uncollectible accounts receivable, plant assets, and inventory.

Cover student pages 476–490 "Record-ing Cash Payments Using a Cash Pay-ments Journal." Draw T accounts on the board or overhead for each transaction as it is presented in this lesson. Point out that most of Celluphone's cash pay-ments are for 1) expenses, 2) cash pur-chases, and 3) payments to vendors. The cash payments journal that is presented in this lesson is designed to effectively handle these types of payments.

During the lesson, emphasize that trade discounts are given for purchasing in quantity. Trade discounts are not jour-nalized. They are deducted from the invoice amount and that amount is recorded. Cash discounts are given for early payment of an invoice. Discuss the various terms of payment that may be offered. Distinguish the difference between cash and trade discounts. Emphasize that purchases discounts are recorded in a general ledger account, while trade discounts are not.

Review the four steps for replenish-ing the petty cash fund that were pre-sented in Chapter 7. Explain the use of the cash short and over account and why cash short and cash over may occur.

Those columns of an expanded journal needed to record only cash payments are included in Celluphone's cash payments journal. In addition, Celluphone has many cash payment transactions that include a discount on the purchases. Therefore, a special amount column is provided in the cash payments journal to record this dis-count. Transactions that do not occur often, such as monthly rent, are recorded in the General columns.

Journalizing Cash Payments for Expenses

All of Celluphone's cash payments are recorded in a cash payments journal. A few payments, such as bank service charges, are made as direct withdrawals from the company's bank account. For these payments not using a check, the source document is a memoran-dum. Most cash payments are for (1) expenses, (2) cash purchases, and (3) payments to vendors.

March 1, 19--. Paid cash for rent, $3,000.00. Check No. 148.

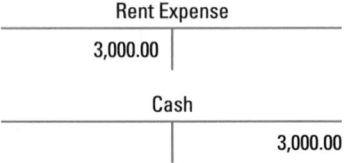

The amount of rent expense is increased by this transaction. Therefore, Rent Expense is debited for $3,000.00. The amount of cash is decreased by this transaction. Therefore, Cash is credited for $3,000.00.

The cash payments journal entry to record this cash payment for an expense is shown on line 1, Illustration 19-7.

ILLUSTRATION 19-7   Cash payments recorded in a cash payments journal

	DATE	ACCOUNT TITLE	CK. NO.	POST. REF.	GENERAL DEBIT	GENERAL CREDIT	ACCOUNTS PAYABLE DEBIT	PURCHASES DISCOUNT CREDIT	CASH CREDIT	
					1	2	3	4	5	
1	Mar. 1	Rent Expense	148		3 0 0 0 00				3 0 0 0 00	1
2	1	Purchases	149		4 8 0 00				4 8 0 00	2

CASH PAYMENTS JOURNAL   PAGE 6

The date, *19--, Mar. 1*, is written in the Date column. The account debited, Rent Expense, is entered in the Account Title col-umn. The check number, *148*, is written in the Ck. No. column. The amount debited to Rent Expense, *$3,000.00*, is recorded in the Gen-eral Debit column. The amount credited to Cash, *$3,000.00*, is recorded in the Cash Credit column.

Journalizing Cash Payments for Cash Purchases

Businesses purchase much of their merchandise on account. How-ever, some vendors may require that merchandise be paid for at the time of purchase. In other situations, paying cash at the time of purchase may be more convenient for the business.

Divide the class into auditing groups made up of three or four students per group. Each group serves as auditors for one of the chapters in Part 4. Each auditing group is responsible for assisting other class mem-bers as well as correcting homework assignments. A lead auditor is appointed by the group and is respon-sible for turning in completed homework assignments to the teacher.

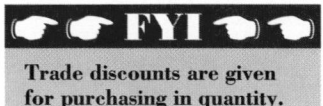

FYI

Trade discounts are given for purchasing in quantity.

Trade Discount. Many manufacturers and wholesalers print price lists and catalogs to describe their products. Generally, prices listed in catalogs are the manufacturers' suggested retail prices. A business' printed or catalog price is called a **list price.** When a merchandising business purchases a ,number of products from a manufacturer, the price frequently is quoted as "list price less trade discount." A reduction in the list price granted to customers is called a **trade discount.** Trade discounts are used to quote different prices for different quantities purchased without changing catalog or list prices.

When a trade discount is granted, the seller's invoice shows the actual amount charged. This amount after the trade discount has been deducted from the list price is referred to as the invoice amount. Only the invoice amount is used in a journal entry. *(CONCEPT: Historical Cost)* The invoice is recorded by both the seller and buyer at the same amount. No journal entry is made to show the amount of a trade discount.

Cash Purchases. Celluphone wishes to buy 80 cellular phone carrying cases for cash. The price quoted to Celluphone was $10.00 list price per case less 40% trade discount. The total invoice amount is calculated in three steps.

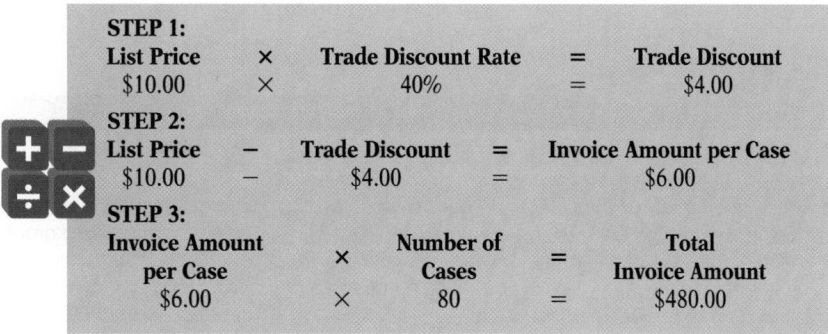

STEP 1:					
List Price	×	Trade Discount Rate	=	Trade Discount	
$10.00	×	40%	=	$4.00	
STEP 2:					
List Price	−	Trade Discount	=	Invoice Amount per Case	
$10.00	−	$4.00	=	$6.00	
STEP 3:					
Invoice Amount per Case	×	Number of Cases	=	Total Invoice Amount	
$6.00	×	80	=	$480.00	

Celluphone's purchase price for the 80 carrying cases will be $480.00, the list price less the trade discount.

March 1, 19--. Purchased merchandise for cash, $480.00. Check No. 149.

The amount of purchases is increased by this transaction. Thus, Purchases is debited for $480.00. The amount of cash is decreased by this transaction. Therefore, Cash is credited for $480.00.

The entry to record this cash purchase of merchandise is shown on line 2 of the cash payments journal, Illustration 19-7.

The date, *1,* is written in the Date column. The account debited, Purchases, is entered in the Account Title column. The check number, *149,* is written in the Ck. No. column. The amount debited to

Purchases	
480.00	

Cash	
	480.00

APPLIED SKILLS: MATHEMATICS

Use the MATH WORK SHEETS in the Masters and Solutions to Enrichment/Application Activities Section of the Teacher's Resource Guide to integrate applied mathematics. In this work sheet, students will apply math concepts to calculate purchases discounts and petty cash short and over.

Purchases, *$480.00*, is recorded in the General Debit column. The amount credited to Cash, $480.00, is recorded in the Cash Credit column.

Journalizing Cash Payments for Purchases on Account

Normally, the total amount shown on a purchase invoice is the amount that a customer is expected to pay by an agreed due date. However, some vendors offer their customers an incentive to pay before the due date.

A cash discount is given for early payment of an invoice.

Cash Discount. To encourage early payment, a vendor may allow a deduction from the invoice amount. A deduction that a vendor allows on the invoice amount to encourage prompt payment is called a **cash discount.** A cash discount is usually stated as a percentage that can be deducted from the invoice amount.

The terms of sale on an invoice may be written as *2/10, n/30.* These terms are commonly read *two ten, net thirty. Two ten* means 2% of the invoice amount may be deducted if the invoice is paid within 10 days of the invoice date. *Net thirty* means that the total invoice amount must be paid within 30 days. A business may also indicate the date for full payment of an invoice as *EOM.* Payment specified as *EOM* means that full payment is expected not later than the end of the month.

■ Philip Showalter ■
PHILIP SHOWALTER, D.D.S., GERMANTOWN, OHIO

Most people don't think of their dentist as a businessperson in the community. They don't stop to think that a dentist has to pay for office space, buy office and dental equipment, hire employees, and pay taxes just like any other businessperson.

Philip Showalter does know what kind of businessperson a dentist needs to be. Showalter is a dentist with his own practice. He says that people would be surprised—as he was—at the amount of time a dentist has to spend on the business side of the practice.

Showalter took a year of college accounting, figuring it would be useful no matter what business he went into.

When he started his own dental practice, he found that the accounting background helped him analyze the business side of the practice. Knowing the language of accounting along with having to analyze financial information helped him understand what his accountant was telling him and helped him make sound financial decisions.

Showalter was a dentist in the military and also worked as a dentist in the public health area. He saved just enough money to start his own practice. He says, however, "I had to work long, hard hours to make ends meet in the beginning, but eventually my persistence paid off and I was able to succeed."

When asked for advice to students, Showalter is very direct. He believes that students should stay in school and take their schoolwork seriously, just as they would a job. Persistence and determination are also key components of success.

Personal Visions in Business

TEACHING STRATEGIES: TEACHING TIP

Clarify the difference between a trade discount and a cash discount. A trade discount is deducted from the catalog price to calculate the invoice price. A cash discount is deducted from the invoice price as an incentive to pay the invoice before the due date. Trade discounts are not recorded in the journal.

FYI

An account that offsets a related account is a contra account. The normal balance of a contra account is the opposite of its related account.

Purchases	
Debit side	Credit side
Normal balance	
Increase	Decrease

Purchases Discount	
Debit side	Credit side
	Normal balance
Decrease	Increase

Purchases Discount. A cash discount on purchases taken by a customer is called a **purchases discount.** When a purchases discount is taken, the customer pays less cash than the invoice amount previously recorded in the purchases account. Therefore, purchases discounts are deducted from purchases. Purchases discounts are recorded in a general ledger account titled Purchases Discount.

In Celluphone's general ledger, the account Purchases Discount is numbered 5110. The purchases discount account is in the cost of merchandise division of Celluphone's general ledger. An account that offsets a related account is known as a contra account. Thus, on an income statement, the contra account, Purchases Discount, is deducted from the balance of its related account, Purchases.

Since contra accounts are deductions from their related accounts, contra account normal balances are opposite the normal balances of their related accounts. The normal balance for a purchases account is a debit. Therefore, the normal balance for Purchases Discount, a contra account to Purchases, is a credit.

Cash Payments on Account with Purchases Discounts. Celluphone's policy is to pay all vendors on or before the date for taking the purchases discount. This policy reduces the cost of merchandise purchased by Celluphone.

> *March 8, 19--. Paid cash on account to Cell Systems, $6,538.56, covering Purchase Invoice No. 39 for $6,672.00, less 2% discount, $133.44. Check No. 168.*

The cash amount paid after the purchases discount is calculated in two steps.

STEP 1:					
Purchase Invoice Amount (P39)	×	Purchases Discount Rate	=	Purchases Discount	
$6,672.00	×	2%	=	$133.44	
STEP 2:					
Purchase Invoice Amount (P39)	−	Purchases Discount	=	Cash Amount After Discount	
$6,672.00	−	$133.44	=	$6,538.56	

Accounts Payable is debited for the amount of the purchase invoice, $6,672.00. This debit decreases the amount owed to vendors. This same amount, $6,672.00, is also debited to the account of Cell Systems in the accounts payable ledger.

Cash is credited for the amount of the check, $6,538.56. Purchases Discount is credited for the amount of the purchases discount, $133.44.

CLOSURE

- Use Audit Your Understanding questions.

- Review Summary Illustration 19-17, Summary of Journalizing and Posting Using a Cash Payments Journal.

GENERAL LEDGER
Accounts Payable

| 6,672.00 | |

Cash

| | 6,538.56 |

Purchases Discount

| | 133.44 |

ACCOUNTS PAYABLE LEDGER
Cell Systems

| 6,672.00 | Bal. | 6,672.00 |

The cash payments journal entry to record this payment on account with a purchases discount is shown in Illustration 19-8.

The date, *8,* is written in the Date column. The vendor name, *Cell Systems,* is recorded in the Account Title column. The check number, *168,* is written in the Ck. No. column. The purchase invoice amount, *$6,672.00,* is entered in the Accounts Payable Debit column. The purchases discount amount, *$133.44,* is recorded in the Purchases Discount Credit column. The invoice amount less the purchases discount, *$6,538.56,* is entered in the Cash Credit column. The total of the two credits ($133.44 + $6,538.56) is $6,672.00, which is equal to the one debit of $6,672.00.

Purchases discounts are recorded frequently by Celluphone. Therefore, a special amount column, Purchases Discount Credit, is provided in the cash payments journal.

ILLUSTRATION 19-8 Cash payments journal entry to record a cash payment on account with a purchases discount

CASH PAYMENTS JOURNAL   PAGE 6

	DATE	ACCOUNT TITLE	CK. NO.	POST. REF.	GENERAL DEBIT	GENERAL CREDIT	ACCOUNTS PAYABLE DEBIT	PURCHASES DISCOUNT CREDIT	CASH CREDIT	
21	8	Cell Systems	168				6 672 00	1 33 44	6 538 56	21
22										22
23										23

Cash Payments on Account without Purchases Discounts. Some vendors do not provide purchases discounts. In this case the full invoice amount is paid. Celluphone purchased merchandise on account from Electro Sound on February 2. Electro Sound's credit terms are n/30. Therefore, Celluphone will pay the full amount of the purchase invoice, $1,740.00, within 30 days of the invoice date, February 2.

March 2, 19--. Paid cash on account to Electro Sound, $1,740.00, covering Purchase Invoice No. 21. Check No. 150.

GENERAL LEDGER
Accounts Payable

| 1,740.00 | |

Cash

| | 1,740.00 |

ACCOUNTS PAYABLE LEDGER
Electro Sound

| 1,740.00 | Bal. | 1,740.00 |

Accounts Payable is debited for the amount of the purchase invoice, $1,740.00. This debit decreases the amount owed to vendors. This same amount, $1,740.00, is also debited to the account of Electro Sound in the accounts payable ledger. Cash is decreased by this transaction. Therefore, Cash is credited for the amount of the check, $1,740.00, which is also the full amount of the purchase invoice.

The cash payments journal entry to record this payment on account without a purchases discount is shown in Illustration 19-9.

482

ILLUSTRATION 19-9   Cash payments journal entry to record a cash payment on account without a purchases discount

CASH PAYMENTS JOURNAL   PAGE 6

	DATE	ACCOUNT TITLE	CK. NO.	POST. REF.	GENERAL DEBIT	GENERAL CREDIT	ACCOUNTS PAYABLE DEBIT	PURCHASES DISCOUNT CREDIT	CASH CREDIT	
3	2	Electro Sound	150				1 7 4 0 00		1 7 4 0 00	3
4										4

The date, *2*, is written in the Date column. The vendor name, *Electro Sound*, is recorded in the Account Title column. The check number, *150*, is written in the Ck. No. column. The purchase invoice amount, *$1,740.00*, is entered in the Accounts Payable Debit column. The same amount, *$1,740.00*, is entered in the Cash Credit column.

Journalizing Cash Payments to Replenish a Petty Cash Fund

Establishing and replenishing a petty cash fund is described for Rugcare in Chapter 7. Celluphone follows procedures similar to those used by Rugcare to account for and safeguard its petty cash fund.

Regardless of how careful a petty cash custodian may be, errors may be made when making payments from a petty cash fund. These errors cause a difference between actual cash on hand and the custodian's record of the amount of cash that should be on hand. The amount of petty cash that should be on hand is the established amount of the petty cash fund less the amount of petty cash payments for the period. To keep the petty cash fund at a constant amount, differences are recorded at the end of a fiscal period as well as at other times when the petty cash fund is replenished. Differences are determined by comparing the amount that should be on hand with the amount of cash in the petty cash box.

Cash Short and Over Account.   Cash in the petty cash box may be less than what the cash balance should be according to the custodian's records. A petty cash on hand amount that is less than a recorded amount is called **cash short**. Cash in the petty cash box may also be more than the cash balance should be according to the custodian's records. A petty cash on hand amount that is more than a recorded amount is called **cash over**. Amounts of petty cash short and petty cash over are recorded in an account titled Cash Short and Over.

A cash short and over account is a temporary account. The account is used to record shortages and overages, if any, each time the petty cash fund is replenished throughout the year. At the end of the fiscal year, the cash short and over account is closed to Income

Summary. The cash short and over account is unique because it may have the characteristics of an expense account or the characteristics of a revenue account. If the balance of the account is a debit, similar to expense accounts, the account balance is an expense. If the balance of the account is a credit, similar to revenue accounts, the account balance is revenue. Therefore, the balance side of a cash short and over account determines whether it is an expense or revenue.

Cash Short and Over	
Debit side Increase cash short	Credit side Increase cash over

Cash short is an expense and, therefore, is debited to the account Cash Short and Over. Cash over is revenue and, therefore, is credited to Cash Short and Over.

Petty Cash Short. A petty cash on hand amount that is less than a recorded amount is known as cash short. Celluphone has an established petty cash fund of $300.00. Prior to replenishment of the petty cash fund on March 31, the custodian had receipts for the following total payments: supplies, $87.80; advertising, $43.75; and miscellaneous, $97.90. A cash count shows $66.55 in the petty cash box. A comparison is made between the cash that should be on hand and the amount actually on hand in the petty cash box. From the information above, Celluphone's petty cash custodian prepares a petty cash report, as shown in Illustration 19-10.

ILLUSTRATION 19-10

Petty cash report for replenishment of a petty cash fund with cash short

PETTY CASH REPORT Date: March 31, 19--

Explanation	Amounts	
Fund total		300 00
Payments:		
Supplies	87 80	
Advertising	43 75	
Miscellaneous	97 90	
Less total payments		229 45
Equals recorded amount on hand		70 55
Less actual amount on hand		66 55
Equals cash short		4 00
Total payments		229 45
Plus cash short		4 00
Equals amount to replenish		233 45

The petty cash report in Illustration 19-10 shows that the actual cash on hand ($66.55) is $4.00 less than the amount the records show should be on hand ($70.55). Therefore, the petty cash fund is short.

The petty cash fund is replenished for the amount paid out, $229.45, plus cash short, $4.00. This total amount, $233.45, restores the fund's cash balance to its original amount, $300.00 ($229.45 + $4.00 + $66.55 cash on hand).

FYI

Petty cash overages and shortages are recorded in the Cash Short and Over account.

Supplies
87.80	

Advertising Expense
43.75	

Miscellaneous Expense
97.90	

Cash Short and Over
4.00	

Cash
	233.45

March 31, 19--. Paid cash to replenish the petty cash fund, $233.45: supplies, $87.80; advertising, $43.75; miscellaneous, $97.90; cash short, $4.00. Check No. 209.

Debit entries include the accounts for which cash payments have been made plus Cash Short and Over. Cash is decreased by this transaction. Therefore, Cash is credited for the amount of the check to replenish the petty cash fund, $233.45, which is also the sum of the debit entries.

The cash payments journal entry to record this replenishment of the petty cash fund with cash short is shown in Illustration 19-11.

Petty Cash Over. A petty cash on hand amount that is more than a recorded amount is known as cash over.

ILLUSTRATION 19-11

Cash payments journal entry to record replenishment of a petty cash fund with cash short

CASH PAYMENTS JOURNAL

PAGE 8

	DATE	ACCOUNT TITLE	CK. NO.	POST. REF.	GENERAL DEBIT	GENERAL CREDIT	ACCOUNTS PAYABLE DEBIT	PURCHASES DISCOUNT CREDIT	CASH CREDIT	
19	31	Supplies	209		87 80				233 45	19
20		Advertising Expense			43 75					20
21		Miscellaneous Expense			97 90					21
22		Cash Short and Over			4 00					22
23										23

FYI

Most small corporations are privately owned and do not sell stock to outsiders.

Prior to Celluphone's replenishment of the petty cash fund on April 30, the custodian had receipts for the following total payments: supplies, $107.45; advertising, $57.00; and miscellaneous, $121.90. A cash count shows $16.20 in the petty cash box. A comparison is made between the cash that should be on hand and the amount actually on hand in the petty cash box. From the information above, Celluphone's petty cash custodian prepares a petty cash report, as shown in Illustration 19-12 on page 486.

The petty cash report in Illustration 19-12 shows that cash on hand ($16.20) is $2.55 more than what the records show should be on hand ($13.65). Therefore, the petty cash fund is over.

The petty cash fund will be replenished for the amount paid out, $286.35, less cash over, $2.55. This net amount, $283.80, will restore the fund's cash balance to its original amount, $300.00 ($286.35 − $2.55 + $16.20 cash on hand).

April 30, 19--. Paid cash to replenish the petty cash fund, $283.80: supplies, $107.45; advertising, $57.00; miscellaneous, $121.90; cash over, $2.55. Check No. 267.

TEACHING STRATEGIES: DIFFERENT LEARNING STYLES

Tactile Learner. Tactile learners may benefit from using the computer to key journal entries and then print reports. A ruler can be positioned on the input forms as a guide when keying the entries. The student should also be encouraged to place a finger on each account title in the journal entries report and trace it over to the amount in the amount column of the report to check it for accuracy. Tactile learners should also be given the opportunity to journalize transactions from at least one simulation that contains source documents which must be handled to analyze, journalize, and file.

ILLUSTRATION 19-12

Petty cash report for replenishment of a petty cash fund with cash over

PETTY CASH REPORT		Date: April 30, 19--	
Explanation		Amounts	
Fund total		300	00
Payments:			
Supplies	107 45		
Advertising	57 00		
Miscellaneous	121 90		
Less total payments		286	35
Equals recorded amount on hand		13	65
Less actual amount on hand		16	20
Equals cash over		2	55
Total payments		286	35
Less cash over		2	55
Equals amount to replenish		283	80

Writing paragraphs and short essays. The Cases for Critical Thinking are short, practical applications of the accounting principles developed in the chapter. Some cases are planned to present problems related to the chapter but not specifically discussed and answered in the chapter. These cases present an opportunity for critical thinking and decision making. These cases also require more than a short objective-type response. Therefore, they provide ideal practice in writing paragraphs and short essays.

Supplies

107.45	

Advertising Expense

57.00	

Miscellaneous Expense

121.90	

Cash Short and Over

	2.55

Cash

	283.80

Debit entries include the accounts for which cash payments have been made. Credit entries are Cash, $283.80, and Cash Short and Over, $2.55, since cash on hand was over this period. The sum of the debit entries equals the sum of the credit entries to Cash and Cash Short and Over.

The cash payments journal entry to record this replenishment of the petty cash fund with cash over is shown in Illustration 19-13.

Cash short is not an operating expense, nor is cash over operating revenue. Therefore, Cash Short and Over is not listed under operating expenses or operating revenue in a chart of accounts. Cash Short and Over is listed in the other expense division in a chart of accounts if the balance is a debit. If the account balance is a credit, the balance is listed in the other revenue division.

In Celluphone's general ledger, the account Cash Short and Over is numbered 8105. The cash short and over account may be an expense or a revenue, depending on whether it has a debit or credit

ILLUSTRATION 19-13

Cash payments journal entry to record replenishment of a petty cash fund with cash over

					GENERAL		ACCOUNTS PAYABLE DEBIT	PURCHASES DISCOUNT CREDIT	CASH CREDIT	
	DATE	ACCOUNT TITLE	CK. NO.	POST. REF.	DEBIT	CREDIT				
					1	2	3	4	5	
18	30	Supplies	267		107 45				283 80	18
19		Advertising Expense			57 00					19
20		Miscellaneous Expense			121 90					20
21		Cash Short and Over				2 55				21
22										22

CASH PAYMENTS JOURNAL   PAGE 11

486

balance. Celluphone lists the account in the other expense division of its general ledger, however, because the balance at year end normally is a debit, making the balance of the account an expense.

Posting from a Cash Payments Journal to an Accounts Payable Ledger

Illustration 19-14 shows the posting of a cash payments journal entry to a vendor account. Each entry in the Accounts Payable Debit column of a cash payments journal affects the vendor named in the Account Title column. Each amount listed in this column is posted separately to the proper vendor account in the accounts payable ledger. In this way, each vendor account shows an up-to-date balance.

ILLUSTRATION 19-14	Posting from a cash payments journal to an accounts payable ledger

CASH PAYMENTS JOURNAL — PAGE 6

	DATE	ACCOUNT TITLE	CK. NO.	POST. REF.	GENERAL DEBIT	GENERAL CREDIT	ACCOUNTS PAYABLE DEBIT	PURCHASES DISCOUNT CREDIT	CASH CREDIT	
3	2	Electro Sound	150	240			1 7 4 0 00		1 7 4 0 00	3
4										4

VENDOR **Electro Sound** — VENDOR NO. **240**

DATE	ITEM	POST. REF.	DEBIT	CREDIT	CREDIT BALANCE
Mar. 1	Balance	√			2 4 6 0 00
2		CP6	1 7 4 0 00		7 2 0 00

The date, *2*, is written in the Date column of the vendor account. *CP6* is entered in the Post. Ref. column. The abbreviation *CP6* means page 6 of the cash payments journal. The amount in the Accounts Payable Debit column, *$1,740.00*, is posted to the Debit column of the vendor account. The amount in the Debit column of the vendor account is subtracted from the previous balance in the Credit Balance column ($2,460.00 $ms $1,740.00 = $720.00). The new balance, *$720.00*, is recorded in the Credit Balance column. The vendor number for Electro Sound, *240*, is written in the Post. Ref. column of the cash payments journal. This last step shows completion of posting of this line.

Posting from a Cash Payments Journal to a General Ledger

Each amount in the General columns of a cash payments journal is posted separately to a general ledger account. Therefore, the totals of the general amount columns are not posted. However, the

CHAPTER 19   Recording Purchases and Cash Payments Using Special Journals   **487** monthly total of each special amount column is posted to a general ledger account.

Posting from the General Columns of a Cash Payments Journal. Separate amounts in the General columns are posted individually to the general ledger account named in the Account Title column. Illustration 19-15 shows the posting from a General column of a cash payments journal to a general ledger account.

ILLUSTRATION 19-15 — Posting from the general columns of a cash payments journal to a general ledger

TEACHING STRATEGIES: DIFFERENT LEARNING ABILITIES

Gifted Students. This cycle presents a variety of accounting concepts, such as accounts receivable, plant assets, and inventory. Using gifted students as tutors for other students can be an effective way of teaching the topics students find most difficult. Allow the gifted student to complete one of these chapters while the class completes the first two chapters of the cycle. The gifted students can then assist you in presenting the concepts and procedures on their chapter to the class. Encourage the students to use visual aids and develop methods to assess student learning.

The date, *Mar. 1*, is written in the Date column of the account Rent Expense. *CP6* is recorded in the Post. Ref. column to show that the amount is from page 6 of the cash payments journal. The amount in the General Debit column, *$3,000.00*, is posted to the Debit column of the general ledger account Rent Expense. The existing amount in the Balance Debit column, *$6,000.00*, is added to the March 1 debit entry, *$3,000.00*. The new balance, *$9,000.00*, is written in the Balance Debit column. The number of the rent expense account, *6140*, is entered in the Post. Ref. column of the cash payments journal. This account number shows that posting of the general amount on this line in the journal is complete.

Posting Totals from the Special Columns of a Cash Payments Journal. At the end of each month, equality of debits and credits is proved for a cash payments journal. The cash payments journal is ruled as shown in Illustration 19-16. The total of each special column is then posted to the account named in the journal's column headings. The date and CP8 are recorded in the Date and Post. Ref. columns of the account. The total is entered in the appropriate amount column, and the new account balance is recorded. As a last step, the account number is written in parentheses below the journal column total. This procedure is followed until all special amount column totals are posted.

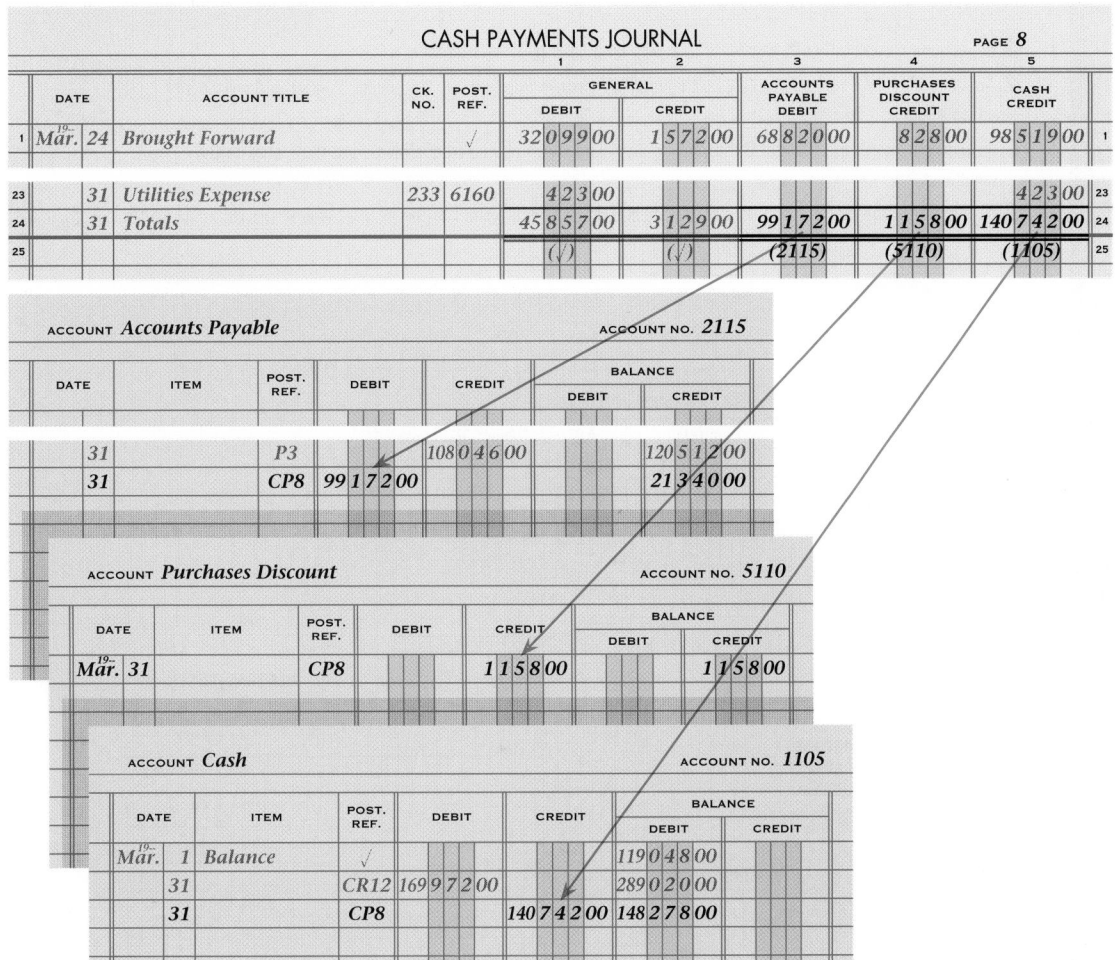

CASH PAYMENTS JOURNAL   PAGE 8

	DATE	ACCOUNT TITLE	CK. NO.	POST. REF.	GENERAL DEBIT	GENERAL CREDIT	ACCOUNTS PAYABLE DEBIT	PURCHASES DISCOUNT CREDIT	CASH CREDIT	
1	Mar. 24	Brought Forward		✓	32 099 00	1 572 00	68 820 00	828 00	98 519 00	1
23	31	Utilities Expense	233	6160	4 23 00				4 23 00	23
24	31	Totals			45 857 00	3 129 00	99 172 00	1 158 00	140 742 00	24
25					(✓)	(✓)	(2115)	(5110)	(1105)	25

ACCOUNT **Accounts Payable**   ACCOUNT NO. **2115**

DATE	ITEM	POST. REF.	DEBIT	CREDIT	BALANCE DEBIT	BALANCE CREDIT
31		P3		108 046 00		120 512 00
31		CP8	99 172 00			21 340 00

ACCOUNT **Purchases Discount**   ACCOUNT NO. **5110**

DATE	ITEM	POST. REF.	DEBIT	CREDIT	BALANCE DEBIT	BALANCE CREDIT
Mar. 31		CP8		1 158 00		1 158 00

ACCOUNT **Cash**   ACCOUNT NO. **1105**

DATE	ITEM	POST. REF.	DEBIT	CREDIT	BALANCE DEBIT	BALANCE CREDIT
Mar. 1	Balance	✓			119 048 00	
31		CR12	169 972 00		289 020 00	
31		CP8		140 742 00	148 278 00	

Audit Your Understanding

1. Why are trade discounts used?
2. Why are cash discounts used?
3. What accounts are credited when petty cash is replenished and petty cash is over?
4. What is the last step in posting special amount columns?

Posting from a cash receipts journal to the cash account, shown on line 2 of the cash account, Illustration 19-16, is described in Chapter 20.

The totals of the General columns are not posted. Each amount in these columns was posted separately to a general ledger account. To indicate that these totals are not to be posted, a check mark is placed in parentheses below each column total.

Illustration 19-17 on page 490 shows a summary of the procedure for journalizing and posting cash payments using a cash payments journal.

RECORDING TRANSACTIONS USING A GENERAL JOURNAL

Not all transactions are recorded in Celluphone's special journals. For example, when Celluphone buys supplies on account, the transaction is not recorded in any of the special journals. The transaction is not a cash payment transaction, so it is not recorded in the

FYI

General journals are used to record transactions that cannot be recorded in a special journal.

cash payments journal. The transaction is not a purchase of merchandise on account, so it is not recorded in the purchases journal.

A journal with two amount columns in which all kinds of entries can be recorded is called a **general journal**. A general journal has only two amount columns: a Debit amount column and a Credit amount column. Any journal entry can be recorded in a general journal by writing the account title and amount for each account affected. Celluphone uses a general journal for recording journal entries that cannot be recorded in any of the special journals. Celluphone records transactions for purchases returns and allowances and for buying supplies on account in its general journal. The relationship between Celluphone's general journal and the expanded journal described in Chapter 11 is shown in Illustration 19-18.

Objectives (Enabling Performance Tasks)

a. Define accounting terms related to purchases and cash payments.

b. Identify accounting concepts and practices related to purchases and cash payments.

c. Analyze transactions affecting purchases and cash payments.

d. Journalize and post transactions related to purchases and cash payments.

ILLUSTRATION 19-18   General journal

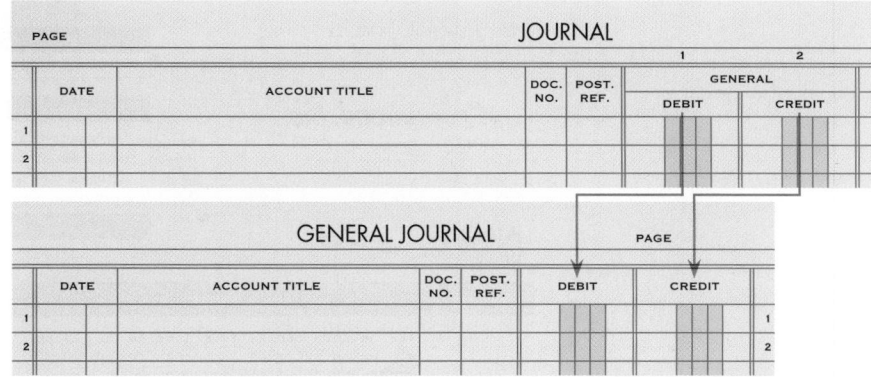

Purchases Returns and Allowances

> **FYI**
>
> A purchases return is made when a customer returns part or all of the merchandise purchased.

A customer may not want to keep merchandise that is inferior in quality or is damaged when received. A customer may be allowed to return part or all of the merchandise purchased. Credit allowed for the purchase price of returned merchandise, resulting in a decrease in the customer's accounts payable, is called a **purchases return**. When merchandise is damaged but still usable or is of a different quality than that ordered, the vendor may let the customer keep the merchandise at a reduced price. Credit allowed for part of the purchase price of merchandise that is not returned, resulting in a decrease in the customer's accounts payable, is called a **purchases allowance**.

A purchases return or allowance should be confirmed in writing. The details may be stated in a letter or on a form. A form prepared by the customer showing the price deduction taken by the customer for returns and allowances is called a **debit memorandum**. The form is called a debit memorandum because the customer records the amount as a debit (deduction) to the vendor account to show the decrease in the amount owed.

FOCUS

- Journalizing purchases and cash payments transactions in a purchases journal and a cash payments journal was presented earlier in this chapter. In this lesson, we will look at other transactions related to purchases that cannot be recorded in these special journals. These transactions will be recorded in a general journal.

- Introduce new vocabulary: general journal, purchases return, purchases allowance, debit memorandum.

TEACHING STRATEGIES: TEACHING TIP

Purchases Returns and Allowances is a new account introduced in this chapter. Draw a T account for Purchases and one for Purchases Returns and Allowances. Explain that Purchases Returns and Allowances is a contra account to Purchases and therefore has the opposite normal balance. Label the increase, decrease, and normal balance sides of both accounts.

During this lesson, give special emphasis to the difference between a return and an allowance and the difference between purchasing merchandise and buying supplies. Emphasize that both the controlling account and the subsidiary account are written on one line in the general journal. A slash divides the two accounts in the Account Title column and in the Post. Ref. column.

The customer may use a copy of the debit memorandum as the source document for journalizing purchases returns and allowances. However, the customer may wait for written confirmation from the vendor and use that confirmation as the source document. Celluphone issues a debit memorandum for each purchases return or allowance. This debit memorandum is used as the source document for purchases returns and allowances transactions. *(CONCEPT: Objective Evidence)* The transaction can be recorded immediately without waiting for written confirmation from the vendor. The original of the debit memorandum is sent to the vendor. The carbon copy is kept by Celluphone. The debit memorandum form used by Celluphone is shown in Illustration 19-19.

ILLUSTRATION 19-19

Debit memorandum for purchases returns and allowances

The FYI box:

> **A purchases allowance is made when a customer keeps the merchandise at a reduced price due to inferior quality or slight damage.**

Purchases	
Debit side	Credit side
Normal balance	
Increase	Decrease

Purchases Returns and Allowances	
Debit side	Credit side
	Normal balance
Decrease	Increase

Some businesses credit the purchases account for the amount of the purchases return or allowance. However, better information is provided if these amounts are credited to a separate account titled *Purchases Returns and Allowances*. A business can see how large its purchases returns and allowances are. Also, a business can see if purchases returns and allowances are increasing or decreasing from year to year. If the amounts are large, one account may be kept for purchases returns and another account for purchases allowances. Usually a single purchases returns and allowances account is satisfactory.

Purchases returns and allowances decrease the amount of purchases. Therefore, the account Purchases Returns and Allowances is a contra account to Purchases. Thus, the normal account balance of Purchases Returns and Allowances is a credit, the opposite of the normal account balance of Purchases, a debit.

TEACHING STRATEGIES: DIFFERENT LEARNING ABILITIES

Limited English Proficiency (LEP) Students.   At early levels, LEP students have limited comprehension of English and can respond with one or two word answers. Assess understanding by having students match, choose, move, draw, or point. Students at this level can respond to directions that require them to name, list, categorize, label, or reply with one or two words.

Journalizing Purchases Returns and Allowances

Celluphone uses a single account, Purchases Returns and Allowances. The account is in the cost of merchandise division of Celluphone's chart of accounts.

GENERAL LEDGER
Accounts Payable

375.00	

Purchases Returns and Allowances

	375.00

ACCOUNTS PAYABLE LEDGER
Interstate Com

375.00	Bal.	740.00
	(New Bal.	365.00)

March 8, 19--. Returned merchandise to Interstate Com, $375.00, covering Purchase Invoice No. 30. Debit Memorandum No. 18.

The amount owed to a vendor is decreased by this transaction. Therefore, Accounts Payable is debited for the amount of the return, $375.00. The same amount is also debited to the account of Interstate Com in the accounts payable ledger. This transaction increases the contra account, Purchases Returns and Allowances with a $375.00 credit.

The general journal entry to record this purchases returns and allowances transaction is shown in Illustration 19-20.

ILLUSTRATION 19-20

General journal entry to record purchases returns and allowances

The date, *19--, Mar. 8,* is written in the Date column. The single debit amount is posted both to the general ledger account and the accounts payable ledger account. Therefore, the accounts to be debited, *Accounts Payable/Interstate Com,* are entered in the Account Title column. A diagonal line is placed between the two account titles to separate them clearly. A diagonal line is also placed in the Post. Ref. column to show that the debit amount is to be posted to two accounts. The source document for the entry, *DM18,* is entered in the Doc. No. column. The amount of the debit, *$375.00,* is recorded in the Debit column. The account to be credited, *Purchases Returns and Allowances,* is written on the next line in the Account Title column. This account title is indented about one centimeter. The amount of the credit, *$375.00,* is recorded in the Credit column.

Journalizing Buying Supplies on Account

Celluphone generally buys supplies on account. Supplies are not merchandise. Only merchandise purchased on account is recorded in the purchases journal. Therefore, when any item that is not merchandise is bought on account, the transaction is recorded in the general journal.

FYI

The supplies account is used to record items that are bought for company use and are not to be sold to customers.

APPLY

- Draw T accounts for each transaction as it is presented in this lesson. Demonstrate how to journalize each transaction using Transparency M or direct students to Illustrations 19-20 and 19-21.

- Use Transparency 19-4 to explain the procedure for posting from a general journal or direct students to Illustration 19-22.

Guided Practice

- Guide students through 19-D4 and 19-D5. Students should have the forms from the working papers to complete as you guide them through the drills.

- Write several purchases returns and allowances and buying supplies on account transactions on the board. Guide students through analyzing and recording the transactions in a general journal. Have students draw T accounts at their desks. Give them blank journals and instruct them to journalize as you use Transparency M to journalize the transactions.

Independent Practice

Assign Terms 13–16, Questions 19–20, Problem 19-3, Mastery Problem 19-M, and Study Guide 19.

TEACHING STRATEGIES: TEACHING TIP

Explain that a slash dividing two account titles on the same line in a general journal means that the amount on that line is posted to both accounts. A diagonal line or slash is also placed in the Post. Ref. column to show that two different account numbers will be recorded as posting references.

Reteach

- Use Demonstration Problem 19C. This problem can be demonstrated on the overhead with the students completing the problem at their desks.

- Use the Application Program Disk software with Problem 19-M to reteach journalizing and posting purchases and cash payments transactions.

- Assign Recycling Problem 19-R.

Extend

- Assign Challenge Problem 19-C (the challenge is that the purchases and cash payments journals are combined into one journal).

Enrich

- Use *Automated Accounting 6.0* or higher with Problem 19-3 and Mastery Problem 19-M.

- Assign the Electronic Study Guide Chapter 19 to complete the study guide from the working papers at the computer.

March 9, 19--. Bought supplies on account from Kryger Supplies, $228.00. Memorandum No. 38.

GENERAL LEDGER
Supplies

| 228.00 | |

Accounts Payable

| | 228.00 |

ACCOUNTS PAYABLE LEDGER
Kryger Supplies

| | 228.00 |

A memorandum is used as the source document so that the supplies will not be recorded unintentionally as merchandise. The invoice received from Kryger Supplies is attached to the memorandum to confirm the price paid.

This transaction increases the balance of the supplies account. Therefore, Supplies is debited for $228.00. The amount owed to a vendor is also increased by this transaction. Therefore, Accounts Payable is credited for $228.00. The same amount is also credited to the account of Kryger Supplies in the accounts payable ledger.

The general journal entry to record this buying supplies on account transaction is shown in Illustration 19-21.

ILLUSTRATION 19-21   General journal entry to record buying supplies on account

		DATE	ACCOUNT TITLE	DOC. NO.	POST. REF.	DEBIT	CREDIT	
3		9	**Supplies**	M38		228 00		3
4			**Accounts Payable/Kryger Supplies**		/		228 00	4
5								5

GENERAL JOURNAL   PAGE 3

The date, 9, is written in the Date column. The account to be debited, Supplies, is recorded in the Account Title column. The source document, M38, is entered in the Doc. No. column. The amount of the debit, $228.00, is entered in the Debit column. The accounts to be credited, *Accounts Payable/Kryger Supplies,* are written on the next line in the Account Title column. These accounts are indented about one centimeter. A diagonal line is placed between the two account titles. A diagonal line is also placed in the Post. Ref. column to show that the credit is to be posted to two accounts. The amount of the credit, *$228.00,* is entered in the Credit column.

Posting from a General Journal

Each amount in the general journal Debit and Credit columns is posted separately to a general ledger account. The posting of an entry for supplies bought on account from a general journal is shown in Illustration 19-22.

The debit amount is posted first. The date, 9, is written in the Date column of the general ledger account Supplies. The abbreviation for the general journal, G3, is entered in the Post. Ref. column of the supplies account. The amount from the general journal Debit column, $228.00, is recorded in the Debit column of the supplies account. The amount in the Debit column is added to the previous balance in the Balance Debit column ($870.00 + $228.00 = $1,098.00). The new balance, *$1,098.00,* is recorded in the Balance

TEACHING STRATEGIES: TEACHING TIP

Explain that some accounting systems use a general journal that does not have a Doc. No. column for recording source documents. In such a system, a bookkeeper frequently writes a sentence describing each transaction as part of the journal entry. Demonstrate how this would be done and explain how much time is saved by simply writing a document number as the audit trail for a transaction.

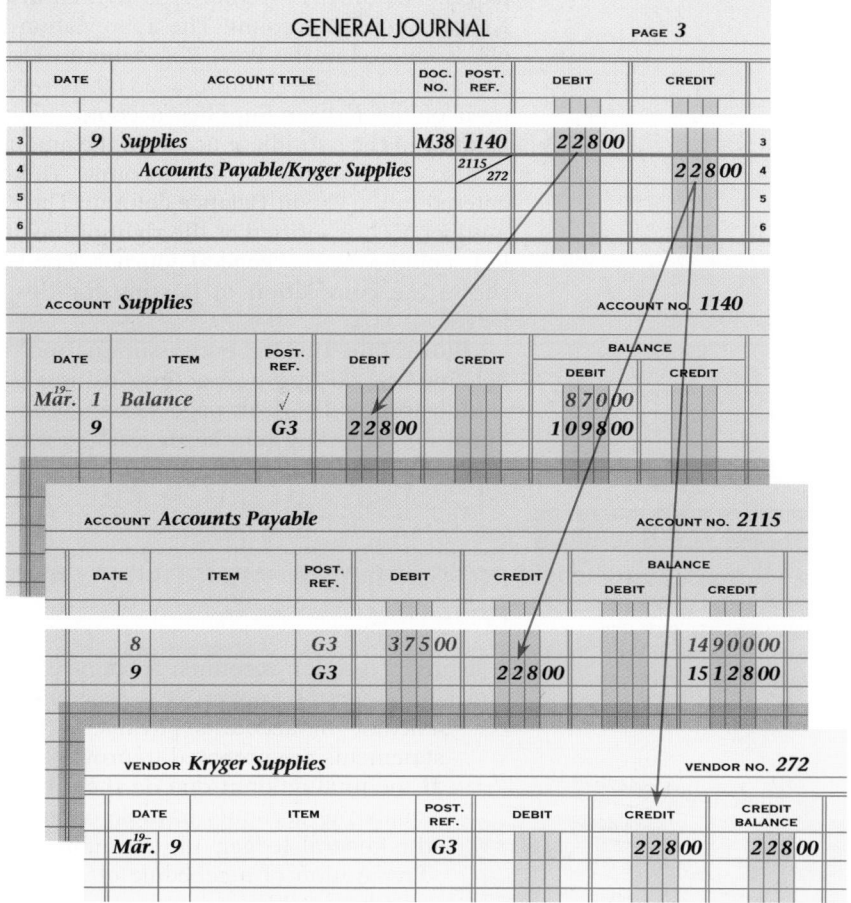

ILLUSTRATION 19-22   Posting a buying supplies on account entry from a general journal

Debit column. The supplies account number, *1140,* is written in the Post. Ref. column of the general journal to show the completion of posting for this line.

Next the credit amount is posted. The date, *9,* is written in the Date column of the general ledger account **Accounts Payable**. The abbreviation for the general journal, *G3,* is entered in the Post. Ref. column of the accounts payable account. The amount from the general journal Credit column, *$228.00,* is recorded in the Credit column of the accounts payable account. The amount in the Credit column is added to the previous balance in the Balance Credit column ($14,900.00 + $228.00 = $15,128.00). The new balance, *$15,128.00,* is recorded in the Balance Credit column. The accounts payable account number, *2115,* is written at the left of the diagonal line in the Post. Ref. column of the general journal. The account number shows the completion of posting for this line to the general ledger.

CHAPTER 19   Recording Purchases and Cash Payments Using Special Journals   **495**

After posting to the general ledger accounts is complete, the credit amount is also posted to the accounts payable subsidiary ledger. The date, *19--, Mar. 9*, is written in the Date column of the Kryger Supplies account. The abbreviation for the general journal, *G3*, is entered in the Post. Ref. column. The amount from the general journal Credit column, *$228.00*, is recorded in the Credit column of the Kryger Supplies account. Since there is no previous balance in the subsidiary account, the amount in the Credit column is also the balance of the account. Therefore, *$228.00*, is also entered in the Credit Balance column. The Kryger Supplies account number, *272*, is written at the right of the diagonal line in the Post. Ref. column of the general journal. The vendor account number shows the completion of posting for this line to the subsidiary ledger.

Illustration 19-23 shows a summary of the procedure for journalizing and posting transactions using a general journal.

Illustration 19-24 on page 498 shows a summary of the procedures for recording purchases, cash payments, and other transactions in special journals and a general journal.

PREPARING A SCHEDULE OF ACCOUNTS PAYABLE

A listing of vendor accounts, account balances, and total amount due all vendors is known as a schedule of accounts payable. A schedule of accounts payable is prepared before financial statements are prepared to prove the accounts payable ledger. If the total amount due on the schedule of accounts payable equals the accounts payable controlling account balance in the general ledger, the accounts payable ledger is proved. Preparation of a schedule of accounts payable is described in Chapter 13.

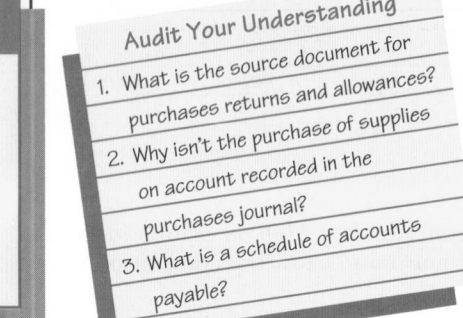

Audit Your Understanding

1. What is the source document for purchases returns and allowances?
2. Why isn't the purchase of supplies on account recorded in the purchases journal?
3. What is a schedule of accounts payable?

ACCOUNTING TERMS

1. **corporation:** An organization with the legal rights of a person and which may be owned by many persons. (p. 472)

2. **share of stock:** Each unit of ownership in a corporation. (p. 472)

3. **capital stock:** Total shares of ownership in a corporation. (p. 472)

4. **special journal:** A journal used to record only one kind of transaction. (p. 473)

5. **purchases journal:** A special journal used to record only purchase on account transactions. (p. 473)

6. **cash payments journal:** A special journal used to record only cash payment transactions. (p. 476)

7. **list price:** A business' printed or catalog price. (p. 479)

8. **trade discount:** A reduction in the list price granted to customers. (p. 479)

ACCOUNTING TERMS   EPT(a)

What is the meaning of each of the following?

1. corporation
2. share of stock
3. capital stock
4. special journal
5. purchases journal
6. cash payments journal
7. list price
8. trade discount
9. cash discount
10. purchases discount
11. cash short
12. cash over
13. general journal
14. purchases return
15. purchases allowance
16. debit memorandum

Summary of journalizing and posting using a general journal

1 Celluphone records in a general journal all transactions that cannot be recorded in any of the special journals.

2 Amounts in the Debit column are posted to the general ledger.

3 Amounts in the Credit column are posted to the genera ledger.

4 Amounts debited or credited to **Accounts Payable** are posted to the named vendor account in the accounts payable subsidiary ledger.

ACCOUNTING TERMS (cont'd)

9. cash discount: A deduction that a vendor allows on the invoice amount to encourage prompt payment. (p. 480)

10. purchases discount: A cash discount on purchases taken by a customer. (p. 481)

11. cash short: A petty cash on hand amount that is less than a recorded amount. (p. 483)

12. cash over: A petty cash on hand amount that is more than a recorded amount. (p. 483)

13. general journal: A journal with two amount columns in which all kinds of entries can be recorded. (p. 491)

14. purchases return: Credit allowed for the purchase price of returned merchandise, resulting in a decrease in the customer's accounts payable. (p. 491)

15. purchases allowance: Credit allowed for part of the purchase price of merchandise that is not returned, resulting in a decrease in the customer's accounts payable. (p. 491)

16. debit memorandum: A form prepared by the customer showing the price deduction taken by the customer for returns and allowances. (p. 491)

SUMMARY ILLUSTRATION 19-24

Summary of recording purchases and cash payments using special journals

Transaction	PURCHASES JOURNAL
	Purchases Debit Accts. Pay. Cr.
Purchases on account	X

Transactions	CASH PAYMENTS JOURNAL				
	1 General Debit	2 General Credit	3 Accounts Payable Debit	4 Purchases Discount Credit	5 Cash Credit
Cash payment for expenses	X				X
Cash purchases	X				X
Cash payment for purchases on account with purchases discount			X	X	X
Cash payment for purchases on account without purchases discount			X		X
Cash payment to replenish petty cash with cash short	X				X
Cash payment to replenish petty cash with cash over	X	X			X

Transactions	GENERAL JOURNAL	
	Debit	Credit
Purchases returns and allowances	X	X
Buying supplies on account	X	X

1. What kind of accounting system should a business use?

2. Which accounting concept is being applied when a business reports financial information for a specified period of time?

3. What are some business transactions a corporation can conduct in its own name?

4. What is the principal difference between the accounting records of a corporation and those of a proprietorship or partnership?

5. Which accounting concept is being applied when a corporation keeps only information in its accounting system that relates to the corporation?

6. What is the major purpose for applying the Unit of Measurement concept by recording all business transactions in a common unit of measurement—the dollar?

7. What is the source document for recording a purchase on account?

8. Which accounting concept is being applied when a business records purchases at cost?

9. What accounts are affected, and how, when the total amount of the purchases journal is posted?

10. What is the last step in posting a purchases journal to a general ledger to show that posting is complete?

11. Why would a vendor grant a cash discount to a customer?

12. What is meant by terms of sale 2/10, n/30?

13. What kind of account offsets a related account?

14. What accounts are affected, and how, when a check is issued as payment on account for a purchase with a purchases discount?

15. How is a balance in the cash short and over account treated at the end of a fiscal period?

16. If cash is short when a petty cash fund is replenished, what entry is made to Cash Short and Over to record the shortage?

17. If cash is over when a petty cash fund is replenished, what entry is made to Cash Short and Over to record the overage?

18. Why are the totals for the General Debit and Credit columns of a cash payments journal not posted?

19. If purchases returns and allowances are a decrease in purchases, why are returns and allowances credited to a separate account?

20. When supplies are bought on account, why is the entry made in a general journal instead of a purchases journal?

CASES FOR CRITICAL THINKING EPT(b)

CASE 1 McLain Florists, Inc. has employed an accounting firm to install a new accounting system using special journals. You and two other accountants are designing the special journals. Alisa Matthews, one of the accountants, recommends a cash payments journal with one special column—Cash Credit. Jose Ramundo, the other accountant, recommends a cash payments journal with three special columns—Accounts Payable Debit, Purchases Discount Credit, and Cash Credit. You have been asked to decide which cash payments journal should be used. Give your decision and the reason for that decision.

CASE 2 Gemini Company has established a $300.00 petty cash fund. During a routine review of the petty cash records, you discover that small shortages totaling $20.00 have occurred over the past four months. The fund custodian, Elaine Hilton, has not listed cash short or over on any of the reports prepared for replenishment. When asked about this practice, Miss Hilton said that she always waits until the amount of the shortage is significant—approximately $50.00. Then she requests replenishment for the amount of the shortage. What is your opinion of this practice? What action do you recommend?

19. Better information is provided if these amounts are credited to a separate account. A business can see how large its purchases returns and allowances are. Also, the business can see if purchases returns and allowances are increasing or decreasing from year to year. (p. 492)

20. Supplies are not merchandise. Only purchases of merchandise on account are recorded in a purchases journal. (p. 493)

1. One that provides the desired financial information with the least amount of effort and cost. (p. 472)

2. Accounting Period Cycle. (p. 472)

3. It can own property, incur liabilities, and enter into contracts. (p. 472)

4. The principal difference is in the capital accounts. A corporation has separate capital accounts for the stock issued and for the earnings kept in the business. Proprietorships and partnerships have a single capital and drawing account for each owner. (p. 472)

5. Business Entity. (p. 472)

6. Recording all transactions in dollar values permits more meaningful comparisons with previous accounting periods and with other businesses. (p. 473)

7. Purchase invoice. (p. 474)

8. Historical Cost. (p. 474)

9. Purchases is debited; Accounts Payable is credited. (p. 476)

10. Writing the account numbers for Purchases and Accounts Payable in parentheses under the total in the purchases journal. (p. 476)

11. To encourage early payment. (p. 480)

12. Two percent of the invoice amount may be deducted if the invoice is paid within 10 days of the invoice date. The total invoice amount must be paid within 30 days. (p. 480)

13. A contra account. (p. 481)

14. Accounts Payable is debited; Cash and Purchases Discount are credited. The account of the vendor in the accounts payable ledger is also debited. (p. 481)

15. Any balance in a cash short and over account is closed to Income Summary. (pp. 483–484)

16. Cash Short and Over is debited. (p. 485)

17. Cash Short and Over is credited. (p. 486)

18. Because each amount in the General Debit and General Credit columns is posted individually to a general ledger account. (p. 487)

500

Surveys of business managers show that communication skills are one of the most desired traits in new employees. The student activity APPLIED COMMUNICATIONS provides an opportunity for students to practice their communication and language arts skills on topics that directly relate to accounting. This Applied Communications activity gives students some background information on corporate annual reports and requires students to send a letter requesting an annual report from a public corporation. Several sources may be used to obtain an address: (1) investment reports in a library, (2) managers of local plants or businesses owned by the company, and (3) personal financial planners in your community. Most corporations will send the annual report within two or three weeks. When these reports are received, you may wish to use them when discussing financial reporting and analysis in Chapter 27.

CASES FOR CRITICAL THINKING

Case 1 Use the cash payments journal recommended by Mr. Ramundo. Special columns should be provided for entries that will occur frequently. Since the company is a merchandising company, probably many cash payments on account with purchases discounts will be made each month. Therefore, the special columns for Accounts Payable Debit and Purchases Discount Credit are justified.

Case 2 Miss Hilton's treatment of cash shortages is not recommended. An important control feature is to establish a fund at a fixed amount. When this control feature is followed, the accuracy of the amount in the petty cash fund can be verified at any time. The amount of cash on hand plus the total of petty cash slips should always equal the original amount of the fund. When Miss Hilton fails to replenish the fund for a shortage, the total amount in the fund will not equal the original fund amount. Whenever a shortage occurs that is not replenished, the fund balance will change. With a changing balance, it will be difficult to verify the correct amount of the fund because there is no control amount for purposes of comparison.

Miss Hilton should be instructed to include shortages or overages on the report each time the fund is replenished. In this way the fund balance should always have $300.00, the original amount. If the balance differs, you will know that the difference occurred since the fund was last replenished.

APPLIED COMMUNICATIONS

The common stock of many corporations is traded on national stock exchanges. These corporations are required by the government to publish their financial statements in an annual report. The annual report also includes management's analysis of the year's operations and its projection of future financial activity. Annual reports are used by bankers, stockholders, and investment advisers for making business decisions.

INSTRUCTIONS:

Write a letter to a corporation requesting a copy of its annual report. Your letter should include your return address, inside address, and request for the report.

DRILLS FOR UNDERSTANDING   EPT(c,d)

DRILL 19-D1 Calculating trade and purchases discounts

The list price, trade discount rate, and purchases discount rate for four different purchases are given below.

Purchase Invoice No.	List Price	Trade Discount Rate	Purchases Discount Rate
1	$1,000.00	40%	2%
2	400.00	30%	3%
3	600.00	25%	1%
4	250.00	50%	2%

INSTRUCTIONS:

For each purchase, calculate the (a) trade discount, (b) invoice amount, (c) purchases discount, and (d) cash amount after discounts.

DRILL 19-D2 Calculating petty cash short and petty cash over

Four different companies have the following information related to petty cash transactions.

Company	Petty Cash Record				Amount of Cash in Cash Box
	Beginning Balance	Distribution of Payments			
		Supplies	Advertising Expense	Miscellaneous Expense	
A	$300.00	$46.25	$76.32	$91.87	$ 85.56
B	250.00	24.76	82.35	18.21	120.68
C	150.00	12.43	51.45	14.15	78.97
D	200.00	53.98	25.34	34.25	84.43

INSTRUCTIONS:

For each company, determine the amount, if any, of petty cash short or petty cash over.

DRILL 19-D3 Analyzing replenishing a petty cash fund

Petty cash is replenished for the amounts and on the dates shown in the following table.

| Date on Which Replenished | Monthly Totals of Petty Cash Payment Records | | | | |
	Supplies	Advertising Expense	Miscellaneous Expense	Cash Short	Cash Over
May 31	$54.50	$15.30	$31.30	$4.01	
June 30	25.60	45.90	16.70	2.54	
July 31	14.20	64.00	42.20		$6.39
August 31	66.00	45.50	22.30	1.51	

INSTRUCTIONS:

For each date, prepare T accounts for the accounts affected by the cash payments journal entry to replenish petty cash. Record the amounts on the debit or credit side of each T account to show how the accounts are affected.

DRILL 19-D4 Analyzing the journalizing of purchases and cash payments transactions

A form for analyzing the journalizing of purchases and cash payments transactions is given in the working papers that accompany this textbook.

INSTRUCTIONS:

Complete the form for each of the following transactions. In Column A, write the title of the account(s) debited. In Column B, write the title of the account(s) credited. In Column C, write the name of the journal in which the transaction is recorded. In Columns D and E, write the names of the journal amount column(s) in which debit and credit amounts are recorded. Transaction 1 is given as an example in the working papers.

1. Paid cash on account to Hubburd Co.; no discount.
2. Purchased merchandise on account from Westward Company.
3. Bought supplies for cash.
4. Paid cash for rent.
5. Paid cash on account to Westward Company; no discount.
6. Purchased merchandise on account from Sadler, Inc.
7. Paid cash for advertising.
8. Returned merchandise to Westward Company.
9. Purchased merchandise for cash.
10. Returned merchandise to Sadler, Inc.
11. Paid cash on account to Olympus Gauge Company for a purchase invoice less discount.

The solution to Drill 19-D4 is needed to complete Drill 19-D5.

DRILL 19-D5 Analyzing the posting of purchases and cash payments transactions

The solution to Drill 19-D4 is needed to complete Drill 19-D5.

A form for analyzing the posting of purchases and cash payments is given in the working papers that accompany this textbook.

INSTRUCTIONS:

1. In Column A, write the titles of the accounts affected by each transaction in Drill 19-D4. These account titles are taken from Columns A and B of completed Drill 19-D4.
2. Place a check mark in Column B if the amount is posted individually to the general ledger. Place a check mark in Column C if the amount is posted individually to the accounts payable ledger. Place a check mark in Column D if the amount is not posted individually to any ledger. Transaction 1 is given as an example in the working papers.

Students' solutions will vary. The letter will have very little content and, therefore, should be graded primarily on mechanics (grammar, spelling, punctuation, and sentence structure).

See Teacher's Edition of Working Papers for complete solutions.

Drill 19-D1 (1) 400.00; 600.00; 12.00; 588.00. (2) 120.00; 280.00; 8.40; 271.60. (3) 150.00; 450.00; 4.50; 445.50. (4) 125.00; 125.00; 2.50; 122.50.

Drill 19-D2 (A) zero; (B) −$4.00; (C) +$7.00; (D) −$2.00

Drill 19-D3 Dr. each exp. acct. and cr. Cash for total on May 31, June 30, and Aug. 31. Dr. each exp. acct. and cr. Cash Short and Over and Cash for July 31.

Drill 19-D4 Cash is credited 7 times.

Drill 19-D5 8 check marks in col. (B); 7 check marks in col. (C); 15 check marks in col. (D).

CHECK FIGURES *(cont'd)*

Problem 19-1 Purch. Journal total 10,466.00.

Problem 19-2 Cash Pay. Journal totals 1,453.00; 5,573.00; 62.08; 6,963.92.

Problem 19-3 Purchases Journal total 22,454.00. Cash Pay. Journal totals 2,658.60; 3.40; 19,801.00; 228.19; 22,228.01. Sched. A/P total 10,193.00.

APPLICATION PROBLEMS
EPT(c,d)

PROBLEM 19-1 Journalizing and posting purchase on account transactions

The general ledger and accounts payable ledger accounts for Wholesale Office Supply Company are given in the working papers accompanying this textbook. The balances are recorded as of May 1 of the current year.

INSTRUCTIONS:

1. Journalize the following purchases on account completed during May of the current year. Use page 5 of a purchases journal. The abbreviation for purchase invoice is P.

May 2. Purchased merchandise on account from PXR, Inc., $1,500.00. P25.
    5. Purchased merchandise on account from Preston Office Supply, $154.00. P26.
    8. Purchased merchandise on account from Reznik Paper Company, $642.00. P27.
  11. Purchased merchandise on account from PXR, Inc., $414.00. P28.
  14. Purchased merchandise on account from Bird Enterprises, $2,268.00. P29.
  18. Purchased merchandise on account from Johnston Company, $1,849.00. P30.
  20. Purchased merchandise on account from PXR, Inc., $602.00. P31.
  24. Purchased merchandise on account from Preston Office Supply, $314.00. P32.
  26. Purchased merchandise on account from Reznik Paper Company, $1,988.00. P33.
  29. Purchased merchandise on account from Bird Enterprises, $735.00. P34.

2. Post each amount in the purchases journal to the accounts payable ledger.
3. Total and rule the purchases journal. Post the total.

PROBLEM 19-2 Journalizing and posting cash payment transactions

The general ledger and accounts payable ledger accounts for Jenson Company are given in the working papers that accompany this textbook. The balances are recorded as of July 1 of the current year.

INSTRUCTIONS:

1. Journalize the following cash payments completed during July of the current year. Use page 7 of a cash payments journal. The abbreviation for check is C.

July 1. Paid cash for rent, $600.00. C216.
    5. Paid cash on account to Gray's Decorum, $1,203.84, covering P127 for $1,216.00, less 1% discount, $12.16. C217.
    7. Paid cash for supplies, $128.00. C218.
    8. Paid cash on account to Lipson Company, $2,092.86, covering P128 for $2,114.00, less 1% discount, $21.14. C219.
    9. Paid cash for miscellaneous expense, $140.00. C220.
  12. Purchased merchandise for cash, $263.00. C221.
  14. Paid cash on account to Varsity Co., $1,410.22, covering P124 for $1,439.00, less 2% discount, $28.78. C222.
  19. Paid cash for supplies, $93.00. C223.
  23. Paid cash on account to Briggs Steel Company, $804.00, covering P126; no discount. C224.
  28. Paid cash for miscellaneous expense, $124.00. C225.
  30. Paid cash to replenish the petty cash fund, $105.00: advertising, $61.50; miscellaneous, $38.45; cash short, $5.05. C226.

2. Post accounts payable amounts to the appropriate accounts in the accounts payable ledger.
3. Post the amounts in the general columns to the appropriate general ledger accounts.
4. Prove and rule the cash payments journal. Post the totals of the special columns to the appropriate general ledger accounts.

PROBLEM 19-3 Journalizing and posting purchases and cash payment transactions

AUTOMATED

The general ledger and accounts payable ledger accounts for Sandy's Sewing Company are given in the working papers accompanying this textbook. The balances are recorded as of April 1 of the current year. Use the following account titles.

PARTIAL GENERAL LEDGER		ACCOUNTS PAYABLE LEDGER	
Account Number	**Account Title**	**Vendor Number**	**Vendor Name**
1105	Cash	210	Kelmans Supply
1110	Petty Cash	220	Office Emporium
1140	Supplies	230	Potters Equipment
2115	Accounts Payable	240	Threads, Inc.
5105	Purchases	250	York Company
5110	Purchases Discount		
5115	Purchases Returns and Allowances		
6105	Advertising Expense		
6130	Miscellaneous Expense		
6140	Rent Expense		
8105	Cash Short and Over		

INSTRUCTIONS:

1. Journalize the following transactions affecting purchases and cash payments completed during April of the current year. Use page 4 of a purchases journal, a general journal, and a cash payments journal. Source documents are abbreviated as follows: check, C; debit memorandum, DM; memorandum, M; purchase invoice, P.

April 1. Paid cash for rent, $1,450.00. C57.

2. Purchased merchandise on account from Threads, Inc., $2,565.00. P65.

2. Bought supplies on account from Office Emporium, $536.00. M15.

Posting. Post the items that are to be posted individually. Post from the journals in this order: purchases journal, general journal, and cash payments journal.

5. Purchased merchandise on account from York Company, $2,995.00. P66.

7. Paid cash on account to Potters Equipment, $5,197.50, covering P64 for $5,250.00, less 1% discount, $52.50. C58.

8. Returned merchandise to York Company, $188.00, from P66. DM7.

10. Paid cash on account to Kelmans Supply, $1,644.44 covering P63 for $1,678.00, less 2% discount, $33.56. C59.

Posting. Post the items that are to be posted individually.

12. Purchased merchandise on account from Kelmans Supply, $4,683.00. P67.

12. Paid cash on account to Threads, Inc., $597.96, covering P62 for $604.00, less 1% discount, $6.04. C60.

15. Paid cash to replenish the petty cash fund, $96.20: supplies, $21.40; advertising, $43.20; miscellaneous, $35.00; cash over, $3.40. C61.

16. Purchased merchandise for cash, $706.00. C62.

16. Purchased merchandise on account from Threads, Inc., $4,243.00. P68.

Posting. Post the items that are to be posted individually.

19. Paid cash for miscellaneous expense, $114.00. C63.

22. Paid cash on account to Kelmans Supply, $4,589.34, covering P67 for $4,683.00, less 2% discount, $93.66. C64.

22. Purchased merchandise on account from Kelmans Supply, $1,976.00. P69.

23. Purchased merchandise on account from Potters Equipment, $3,204.00. P70.

23. Purchased merchandise on account from Threads, Inc., $1,020.00. P71.

Posting. Post the items that are to be posted individually.

26. Returned merchandise to Threads, Inc., $340.00, from P71. DM8.

26. Paid cash on account to Office Emporium, $536.00, covering M15; no discount. C65.

April 28. Paid cash for miscellaneous expense, $214.00. C66.
   28. Purchased merchandise on account from York Company, $1,768.00. P72.
   30. Paid cash on account to York Company, $2,807.00, covering P66 for $2,995.00, less DM7, $188.00; no discount. C67.
   30. Paid cash on account to Threads, Inc., $4,200.57, covering P68 for $4,243.00, less 1% discount, $42.43. C68.
   30. Paid cash to replenish the petty cash fund, $75.00: supplies, $32.50; advertising, $16.40; miscellaneous, $23.25; cash short, $2.85. C69.
       Posting. Post the items that are to be posted individually.
2. Total and rule the purchases journal. Post the total.
3. Prove and rule the cash payments journal. Post the totals of the special columns.
4. Prepare a schedule of accounts payable similar to the one described in Chapter 13. Compare the schedule total with the balance of the accounts payable account in the general ledger. The total and balance should be the same.

ENRICHMENT PROBLEMS   EPT(b,c,d)

MASTERY PROBLEM 19-M Journalizing and posting purchases and cash payment transactions

AUTOMATED

APPLICATION

The general ledger and accounts payable ledger accounts of City Plumbing Supply Company are given in the working papers that accompany this textbook. The balances are recorded as of August 1 of the current year. Use the following account titles.

PARTIAL GENERAL LEDGER		ACCOUNTS PAYABLE LEDGER	
Account Number	**Account Title**	**Vendor Number**	**Vendor Name**
1105	Cash	210	Barker Pipe Co.
1110	Petty Cash	220	Edson Tools, Inc.
1140	Supplies	230	Fullers Tape Company
2115	Accounts Payable	240	Renson Supplies
5105	Purchases	250	TenCorp Tubing
5110	Purchases Discount		
5115	Purchases Returns and Allowances		
6105	Advertising Expense		
6130	Miscellaneous Expense		
6140	Rent Expense		
8105	Cash Short and Over		

INSTRUCTIONS:

1. Journalize the following transactions affecting purchases and cash payments completed during August of the current year. Use page 8 of a purchases journal, a cash payments journal, and a general journal.

Aug. 2. Returned merchandise to Fullers Tape Company, $152.00, from P72. DM17.
   2. Paid cash for rent, $690.00. C504.
   4. Paid cash on account to Barker Pipe Co., $361.35, covering P74 for $365.00, less 1% discount, $3.65. C505.
   6. Purchased merchandise on account from TenCorp Tubing, $602.00. P75.
   6. Paid cash on account to Renson Supplies, $942.00, covering M14; no discount. C506.
       Posting. Post the items that are to be posted individually. Post from the journals in this order: purchases journal, general journal, and cash payments journal.

Aug. 9. Purchased merchandise on account from Edson Tools, Inc., $446.00. P76.
10. Paid cash on account to Fullers Tape Company, $556.00, covering P72 for $708.00, less DM17, $152.00; no discount. C507.
13. Paid cash for miscellaneous expense, $147.00. C508.
13. Bought supplies on account from Renson Supplies, $206.00. M15.
16. Paid cash to replenish the petty cash fund, $165.35: supplies, $22.50; advertising, $34.00; miscellaneous, $114.00; cash over, $5.15. C509.
16. Purchased merchandise on account from Fullers Tape Company, $687.00. P77.
16. Paid cash on account to TenCorp Tubing, $589.96, covering P75 for $602.00, less 2% discount, $12.04. C510.
18. Paid cash on account to Edson Tools, Inc., $441.54, covering P76 for $446.00, less 1% discount, $4.46. C511.
    Posting. Post the items that are to be posted individually.
19. Returned merchandise to Fullers Tape Company, $88.00, from P77. DM18.
20. Purchased merchandise on account from TenCorp Tubing, $315.00. P78.
23. Purchased merchandise on account from Barker Pipe Co., $1,463.00. P79.
25. Paid cash on account to Renson Supplies, $206.00, covering M15; no discount. C512.
26. Bought supplies on account from Renson Supplies, $341.00. M16.
27. Paid cash for miscellaneous expense, $76.00. C513.
30. Purchased merchandise on account from Edson Tools, Inc., $1,161.00. P80.
30. Paid cash on account to TenCorp Tubing, $308.70, covering P78 for $315.00, less 2% discount, $6.30. C514.
31. Paid cash on account to Barker Pipe Co., $1,448.37, covering P79 for $1,463.00, less 1% discount, $14.63. C515.
31. Paid cash to replenish the petty cash fund, $201.75: supplies, $45.45; advertising, $80.40; miscellaneous, $72.40; cash short, $3.50. C516.
    Posting. Post the items that are to be posted individually.

2. Total and rule the purchases journal. Post the total.

3. Prove and rule the cash payments journal. Post the totals of the special columns.

4. Prepare a schedule of accounts payable. Compare the schedule total with the balance of the accounts payable account in the general ledger. The total and balance should be the same.

CHALLENGE PROBLEM 19-C Journalizing transactions in a combined purchases-cash payments journal

The accountant for City Plumbing Supply Company has suggested that time could be saved if the purchases journal and the cash payments journal were combined into one journal. The accountant suggests using a journal such as the following.

Purchases—Cash Payments Journal

				1	2	3	4	5	6	7
				General		Purchases Debit	Accounts Payable		Purchases Discount Credit	Cash Credit
Date	Account Title	Doc. No.	Post. Ref.	Debit	Credit		Debit	Credit		

Christopher Howard, manager, has asked the accountant to show him how the journal would appear after transactions have been recorded.

INSTRUCTIONS:

1. Use page 8 of a purchases-cash payments journal and a general journal. Journalize the transactions given in Mastery Problem 20-M.
2. Prove and rule the combined purchases-cash payments journal.
3. Do you agree with the accountant that the combined purchases-cash payments journal used in this problem saves time in journalizing and posting? Why?

Recording Purchases and Cash Payments for a Corporation

Celluphone, the merchandising business described in Part 4, uses a manual accounting system. Celluphone's manual journalizing and posting procedures for purchases and cash payments are described in Chapter 19. Integrating Automated Accounting Topic 7 describes procedures for using automated accounting software to journalize and post Celluphone's purchases and cash payments transactions. The Automated Accounting Problems contain instructions for using automated accounting software to solve Application Problem 19-3 and Mastery Problem 19-M, Chapter 19.

507

- Student pages 508–517
- Transparency AA-2, Blank General Journal Input Form
- Transparency AA-3, Blank Purchases Journal Input Form
- Transparency AA-4, Blank Cash Payments Journal Input Form
- Input forms for Automating Problems 19-3 and 19-M are provided in the working papers that accompany this textbook. If additional input forms are needed, blackline masters are provided in the Accounting Ruling Masters Section of the Teacher's Resource Guide.
- Complete solutions for automated problems are provided in the Teacher's Resource Guide.
- Software: *Automated Accounting 6.0* or higher; Accounting Textbook Template, first-year course

Objective

Record and process purchases, cash payments, and other transactions for a corporation using an automated accounting system.

FYI

File maintenance includes deleting accounts no longer needed and adding new accounts.

AUTOMATED ACCOUNTING PROCEDURES FOR CELLUPHONE

Celluphone uses three input forms to arrange purchases, cash payments, and other transaction data for automated accounting.

1. Purchases journal input form for purchases on account.
2. Cash payments journal input form for all cash payments.
3. General journal input form for all other transactions.

FILE MAINTENANCE

Celluphone's general ledger chart of accounts is on page 470. Celluphone uses the same procedures as described for Rugcare in Part 2 and Celluphone in Part 3 to maintain its general ledger chart of accounts. The subsidiary ledgers are also a part of the general ledger data base stored on the template disk. Procedures for adding or changing a subsidiary account are the same as for a general ledger account. (1) An input form is prepared. (2) The data base is retrieved. (3) Data from the input form are keyed. (4) A revised chart of accounts, vendor list, or customer list is prepared to verify the accuracy of the data keyed. (5) The revised chart of accounts or subsidiary ledger lists are stored as part of the general ledger data base on the template disk.

RECORDING PURCHASES ON ACCOUNT

Celluphone batches purchases on account transactions and records them on a purchases journal input form.

> *March 1, 19--. Purchased merchandise on account from Cell Systems, $6,672.00. Purchase Invoice No. 39.*

The journal entry to record this transaction is on line 1 of the purchases journal input form shown in Illustration T7-1.

The run date, *03/31/--*, is written in the space provided at the top of the input form.

On line 1, the date of the transaction, *03/01*, is recorded in the Date column. The vendor number, *220*, is entered in the Vendor No. column. The source document number, *P39*, is written in the Invoice No. column. The invoice amount, *$6,672.00*, is recorded in the Invoice Amount column. The general ledger account number for Purchases, *5105*, is entered in the Account No. column. The debit amount, *$6,672.00*, is written in the Debit column. The Credit column is left blank. The software automatically records the credit to Accounts Payable on a purchases on account transaction.

RECORDING CASH PAYMENTS

Celluphone batches cash payments and records them on a cash payments journal input form. Celluphone has two types of cash payments. (1) Direct payments. (2) Payments on account. A direct

Purchases journal input form with a purchase on account transaction recorded

RUN DATE 03/31/-- MM DD YY			PURCHASES JOURNAL Input Form				
	DATE MM/DD	VENDOR NO.	INVOICE NO.	INVOICE AMOUNT	ACCOUNT NO.	DEBIT	CREDIT
1	03/01	220	P39	6672 00	5105	6672 00		1
2	05	210	P40	2000 00	5105	2000 00		2
3	10	250	P41	39456 00	5105	39456 00		3
4	16	240	P42	1864 00	5105	1864 00		4
5	18	230	P50	17584 00	5105	17584 00		5
6	21	210	P51	16930 00	5105	16930 00		6
7	23	260	P59	21430 00	5105	21430 00		7
8	31	250	P61	2110 00	5105	2110 00		8
25								25

NOTE: A credit to Accounts Payable is made automatically by the software.

FOCUS

- Students completed manual journalizing and posting procedures for purchases and cash payments using special journals in Chapter 19. Emphasize that automated accounting software may be used to speed the journalizing and posting procedures. Explain that using automated accounting software, however, does not change accounting concepts. Only the methods change.

- Like CarLand in Integrating Automated Accounting Topic 4, Celluphone and the other businesses presented in this lesson batch account transaction data on input forms for processing.

payment transaction does not affect accounts payable, whereas a payment on account transaction does affect accounts payable.

Cash Payment of an Expense

A cash payment of an expense transaction is a direct cash payment not affecting accounts payable.

March 1, 19--. Paid cash for rent, $3,000.00. Check No. 148.

The journal entry to record this transaction is on line 1 of Illustration T7-2 on page 510.

The run date, *03/31/--*, is written in the space provided at the top of the form.

On line 1, the date of the transaction, *03/01*, is entered in the Date column. The Vendor No. column is left blank because a cash payment of an expense transaction does not involve a vendor. The source document number, *C148*, is recorded in the Check No. column. The Accounts Pay. Debit column is left blank. The general ledger account number for Rent Expense, *6140*, is written in the Account No. column. The amount of the expense, *$3,000.00*, is entered in the Debit column. The software automatically makes the credit to Cash, *$3,000.00*. Therefore, the Credit column is left blank.

Purchase of Merchandise for Cash

A purchase of merchandise for cash transaction is a direct payment not affecting accounts payable.

March 1, 19--. Purchased merchandise for cash, $480.00. Check No. 149.

FYI

For illustration purposes, some source document numbers have been omitted from input forms.

INTEGRATING AUTOMATED ACCOUNTING—TOPIC 7   **509**

TEACHING STRATEGIES: USING VISUALS

Using Transparencies AA-2, Blank General Journal Input Form; AA-3, Blank Purchases Journal Input Form; and AA-4, Blank Cash Payments Journal Input Form will help students understand the journalizing process.

Cover student pages 508–517 "Automated Accounting Procedures for Celluphone," "File Maintenance," "Recording Purchases on Account," "Recording Cash Payments," "Recording Other Transactions," and "Processing Purchases, Cash Payments, and Other Transactions." Review file maintenance procedures as described for Rugcare in Part 2 and CarLand in Part 3. Celluphone uses the same procedures.

As the lesson progresses, review the definitions of petty cash, cash discount, purchases discount, cash short, cash over, purchases return, purchases allowance, and debit memorandum.

The journal entry to record this transaction is on line 2 of the cash payments journal input form shown in Illustration T7-2. The entry is similar to other direct payment transactions.

ILLUSTRATION T7-2   Cash payments journal input form with transactions recorded

RUN DATE 03,31,-- MM DD YY

CASH PAYMENTS JOURNAL
Input Form

	DATE MM/DD	VENDOR NO.	CHECK NO.	ACCOUNTS PAY. DEBIT	ACCOUNT NO.	DEBIT	CREDIT	
1	03,01		C148		6140	3000,00		1
2	,01		C149		5105	480,00		2
3	,02	240	C150	1740,00				3
4	,05	220	C151	2437,00	5110		48,74	4
5	,07	210	C152	5921,00	5110		123,82	5
6	,08	220	C168	6672,00	5110		133,44	6
7	,08	260	C169	42600,00	5110		852,00	7
8	,12	272	C170	346,00				8
9	,16		C171		5105	200,00		9
10	,20	250	C172	39456,00				10
11	,28	230	C173	17584,00				11
12	,29	210	C208	16930,00				12
13	,31		C209		1140	87,80		13
14	/				6105	43,75		14
15	/				6130	97,90		15
16	/				8105	4,00		16
17	,31		C233		6160	423,00		17
25	/							25

NOTE: A credit to Cash is made automatically by the software.

Cash Payment on Account Without Purchases Discounts

A cash payment on account transaction affects both the controlling account Accounts Payable and a vendor account in an accounts payable subsidiary ledger.

March 2, 19--. Paid cash on account to Electro Sound, $1,740.00, covering Purchase Invoice No. 21. Check No. 150.

The journal entry to record this transaction is on line 3 of Illustration T7-2.

The date of the transaction, *02*, is written in the Date column. The vendor number, *240*, is entered in the Vendor No. column. The amount, *$1,740.00*, is recorded in the Accounts Pay. Debit column. The Account No., Debit, and Credit columns are left blank.

Cash Payment on Account with a Purchases Discount

Celluphone's policy is to pay all vendors on or before the date for taking the purchases discount. This procedure reduces the cost of merchandise purchased by Celluphone.

> *March 8, 19--. Paid cash on account to Cell Systems, $6,538.56, covering Purchase Invoice No. 39 for $6,672.00, less 2% discount, $133.44. Check No. 168.*

The journal entry to record this transaction is on line 6 of Illustration T7-2.

The date of the transaction, *08*, is written in the Date column. The vendor number, *220*, is entered in the Vendor No. column. The amount of the debit to Accounts Payable, *$6,672.00*, is recorded in the Accounts Pay. Debit column. The general ledger account number for *Purchases Discount, 5110*, is written in the Account No. column. The Debit column is left blank. The purchases discount amount, *$133.44*, is entered in the Credit column.

Cash Payment to Replenish Petty Cash

A cash payment to replenish petty cash transaction is a direct payment not affecting accounts payable. Establishing and replenishing a petty cash fund is described for Rugcare in Chapter 7. Celluphone follows procedures similar to those used by Rugcare.

Cash in the petty cash box may be less than what the petty cash balance should be. A petty cash on hand amount that is less than a recorded amount is cash short.

> *March 31, 19--. Paid cash to replenish the petty cash fund, $233.45: supplies, $87.80; advertising, $43.75; miscellaneous, $97.90; cash short, $4.00. Check No. 209.*

The journal entry to record this transaction is on lines 13 through 16 of Illustration T7-2. This journal entry is similar to other direct payments.

A petty cash on hand amount that is more than a recorded amount is cash over. Amounts of petty cash short and petty cash over are recorded in an account titled *Cash Short and Over*. An amount of petty cash short is debited and an amount of petty cash over is credited to *Cash Short and Over*.

RECORDING OTHER TRANSACTIONS

Celluphone uses a general journal input form to journalize transactions other than purchases on account and cash payments.

Purchases Returns and Allowances

> *March 8, 19--. Returned merchandise to Interstate Com, $375.00, covering Purchase Invoice No. 30. Debit Memorandum No. 18.*

FYI

The account title Petty Cash is only used when establishing the petty cash fund.

Use Transparency AA-3 to journalize each purchases transaction; Transparency AA-4 to journalize each cash payments transaction; and Transparency AA-2 to journalize each general journal entry. It is important that students realize that the *Automated Accounting 6.0* software automatically records the credit to Accounts Payable for a purchases on account transaction and the credit to Cash for a cash payments transaction. Emphasize that transactions not recorded on any of the other input forms are recorded on a general journal input form.

Guided Practice

Students should be at the computers. Guide students through booting the software and loading Optional Problem DB-7A from the template. Use the completed purchases, cash payments, and general journal input forms, Illustrations T7-1, T7-2, and T7-3, and follow the procedures described to process Celluphone's purchases, cash payments, and other transactions. Instruct students to journalize each transaction as you go step-by-step through the procedures.

Independent Practice

Assign Automating Problem 19-3.

ASSESS

Assess student understanding by checking solutions to Automating Problem 19-3.

Reteach

Give students a blank purchases journal input form, cash payments journal input form, and general journal input form. Read the transactions in the text and have students journalize each.

Extend

Assign Automating Mastery Problem 19-M.

Enrich

Assign students to write a paragraph or two about why businesses are willing to offer cash discounts to their customers.

The journal entry to record this transaction is on lines 1 and 2 of the general journal input form shown in Illustration T7-3.

The run date, *03/31/--*, is written in the space provided at the top of the form.

On line 1, the date of the transaction, *03/08*, is entered in the Date column. The source document number, *DM18*, is recorded in the Reference column. The general ledger account number for Accounts Payable, *2115*, is recorded in the Account No. column. The vendor number, *260*, is written in the Customer/Vendor No. column. The amount of the debit to the accounts payable subsidiary account, *$375.00*, is written in the Debit column.

ILLUSTRATION T7-3   General journal input form with transactions recorded

RUN DATE *03/31/--* MM DD YY

GENERAL JOURNAL
Input Form

	DATE MM/DD	REFERENCE	ACCOUNT NO.	CUSTOMER/ VENDOR NO.	DEBIT	CREDIT	
1	03 08	DM18	2115	260	375 00		1
2	/		5115			375 00	2
3	09	M38	1140		228 00		3
4	/		2115	272		228 00	4
5	22	DM19	2115	240	580 00		5
6	/		5115			580 00	6
7	24	M39	1140		375 00		7
8	/		2115	272		375 00	8
9	27	DM20	2115	260	6552 00		9
10	/		5115			6552 00	10
11	29	M40	1140		120 00		11
12	/		2115	272		120 00	12
25	/						25
				PAGE TOTALS	8230 00	8230 00	
				FINAL TOTALS	8230 00	8230 00	

On line 2, the general ledger account number for Purchases Returns and Allowances, *5115*, is entered in the Account No. column. The amount of the credit to the general ledger account, *$375.00*, is recorded in the Credit column.

Buying Supplies on Account

March 9, 19--. Bought supplies on account from Kryger Supplies, $228.00. Memorandum No. 38.

The journal entry to record this transaction is on lines 3 and 4 of Illustration T7-3.

On line 3, the date of the transaction, *09*, is written in the Date column. The source document number, *M38*, is recorded in the Reference column. The account number for Supplies, *1140*, is entered in the Account No. column. The amount, *$228.00*, is written in the Debit column.

On line 4, the account number for Accounts Payable, *2115*, is recorded in the Account No. column. The account number for Kryger Supplies, *272*, is entered in the Customer/Vendor No. column. The amount, *$228.00*, is written in the Credit column.

PROCESSING PURCHASES, CASH PAYMENTS, AND OTHER TRANSACTIONS

After all data from the input forms have been keyed and posted, three reports are displayed and printed. (1) A purchases journal report as shown in Illustration T7-4. (2) A cash payments journal report as shown in Illustration T7-5 on page 514. (3) A general journal report as shown in Illustration T7-6 on page 515. Each journal report is checked for accuracy by comparing the report with the appropriate journal input form.

After all journal reports have been verified and printed, the accounts payable account from the general ledger and the schedule of accounts payable are then printed as shown in Illustration T7-7

ILLUSTRATION T7-4   Purchases journal report

```
                            Celluphone, Inc.
                            Purchases Journal
                               03/31/--
-----------------------------------------------------------------------
Date    Refer.    V/C  Acct.   Title                  Debit      Credit
-----------------------------------------------------------------------
03/01   P39             5105   Purchases             6672.00
03/01   P39       220   2115   AP/Cell Systems                   6672.00

03/05   P40             5105   Purchases             2000.00
03/05   P40       210   2115   AP/Action Phone Co.               2000.00

03/10   P41             5105   Purchases            39456.00
03/10   P41       250   2115   AP/Hopkins Company               39456.00

03/16   P42             5105   Purchases             1864.00
03/16   P42       240   2115   AP/Electro Sound                  1864.00

03/18   P50             5105   Purchases            17584.00
03/18   P50       230   2115   AP/Dafoe Communications          17584.00

03/21   P51             5105   Purchases            16930.00
03/21   P51       210   2115   AP/Action Phone Co.              16930.00

03/23   P59             5105   Purchases            21430.00
03/23   P59       260   2115   AP/Interstate Com                21430.00

03/31   P61             5105   Purchases             2110.00
03/31   P61       250   2115   AP/Hopkins Company                2110.00
                                                    ----------  ----------
                Totals                              108046.00   108046.00
                                                    ==========  ==========
```

on page 515 and Illustration T7-8 on page 516. The accounts payable balance in the general ledger is compared to the total of the schedule of accounts payable. These two amounts must be the same. The schedule and all journal reports are filed for future reference.

on page 515 and Illustration T7-8 on page 516.

| ILLUSTRATION T7-5 | Cash payments journal report |

```
                          Celluphone, Inc.
                        Cash Payments Journal
                             03/31/--
-----------------------------------------------------------------------
Date    Refer.   V/C  Acct.  Title                      Debit     Credit
-----------------------------------------------------------------------
03/01   C148          6140   Rent Expense             3000.00
03/01   C148          1105   Cash                                3000.00

03/01   C149          5105   Purchases                 480.00
03/01   C149          1105   Cash                                 480.00

03/02   C150     240  2115   AP/Electro Sound         1740.00
03/02   C150          1105   Cash                                1740.00

03/05   C151     220  2115   AP/Cell Systems          2437.00
03/05   C151          5110   Purchases Discount                    48.74
03/05   C151          1105   Cash                                2388.26

03/07   C152     210  2115   AP/Action Phone Co.      5921.00
03/07   C152          5110   Purchases Discount                   123.82
03/07   C152          1105   Cash                                5797.18

03/08   C168     220  2115   AP/Cell Systems          6672.00
03/08   C168          5110   Purchases Discount                   133.44
03/08   C168          1105   Cash                                6538.56

03/08   C169     260  2115   AP/Interstate Com       42600.00
03/08   C169          5110   Purchases Discount                   852.00
03/08   C169          1105   Cash                               41748.00

03/12   C170     272  2115   AP/Kryger Supplies        346.00
03/12   C170          1105   Cash                                 346.00

03/16   C171          5105   Purchases                 200.00
03/16   C171          1105   Cash                                 200.00

03/20   C172     250  2115   AP/Hopkins Company      39456.00
03/20   C172          1105   Cash                               39456.00

03/28   C173     230  2115   AP/Dafoe Communications 17584.00
03/28   C173          1105   Cash                               17584.00

03/29   C208     210  2115   AP/Action Phone Co.     16930.00
03/29   C208          1105   Cash                               16930.00

03/31   C209          1140   Supplies                   87.80
03/31   C209          6105   Advertising Expense        43.75
03/31   C209          6130   Miscellaneous Expense      97.90
03/31   C209          8105   Cash Short and Over         4.00
03/31   C209          1105   Cash                                 233.45

03/31   C233          6160   Utilities Expense         423.00
03/31   C233          1105   Cash                                 423.00
                                                     ----------  ----------
                             Totals                 138022.45   138022.45
                                                     ==========  ==========
```

INTEGRATING AUTOMATED ACCOUNTING—TOPIC 7

TEACHING STRATEGIES:
DIFFERENT LEARNING ABILITIES

Physically-Challenged. You should set the work station up in a manner so that the physically challenged will not have to travel far to complete the automated problems. Encourage students to go to the computer with all input forms, template, and any other supplies that are needed. This will decrease the need to make many trips from the desk to the work station.

```
                        Celluphone, Inc.
                         General Journal
                            03/31/--
-------------------------------------------------------------------------
Date   Refer.   V/C  Acct.  Title                       Debit      Credit
-------------------------------------------------------------------------
03/03  DM18     260  2115   AP/Interstate Com           375.00
03/03  DM18          5115   Purchases Ret. and Allow.               375.00

03/09  M38           1140   Supplies                    228.00
03/09  M38      272  2115   AP/Kryger Supplies                      228.00

03/22  DM19     240  2115   AP/Electro Sound            580.00
03/22  DM19          5115   Purchases Ret. and Allow.               580.00

03/24  M39           1140   Supplies                    375.00
03/24  M39      272  2115   AP/Kryger Supplies                      375.00

03/27  DM20     260  2115   AP/Interstate Com          6552.00
03/27  DM20          5115   Purchases Ret. and Allow.              6552.00

03/29  M40           1140   Supplies                    120.00
03/29  M40      272  2115   AP/Kryger Supplies                      120.00

                                                       ----------  ----------
                            Totals                      8230.00     8230.00
                                                       ==========  ==========
```

ILLUSTRATION T7-7   General ledger report

```
                        Celluphone, Inc.
                         General Ledger
                            03/31/--
-------------------------------------------------------------------------
Account          Journal   Date    Refer.     Debit     Credit    Balance
-------------------------------------------------------------------------
2115-Accounts Payable
                 Op. Bal.  03/01  Balances              5921.00    5921.00
                 Op. Bal.  03/01  Balances              2437.00    8358.00
                 Op. Bal.  03/01  Balances              2460.00   10818.00
                 Op. Bal.  03/01  Balances             42600.00   53418.00
                 Op. Bal.  03/01  Balances               346.00   53764.00
                 Purchases 03/01  P39                   6672.00   60436.00
                 Cash Pymt 03/02  C150      1740.00                58696.00
                 General   03/03  DM18       375.00                58321.00
                 Purchases 03/05  P40                   2000.00    60321.00
                 Cash Pymt 03/05  C151      2437.00                57884.00
                 Cash Pymt 03/07  C152      5921.00                51963.00
                 Cash Pymt 03/08  C168      6672.00                45291.00
                 Cash Pymt 03/08  C169     42600.00                 2691.00
                 General   03/09  M38                    228.00     2919.00
                 Purchases 03/10  P41                  39456.00    42375.00
                 Cash Pymt 03/12  C170       346.00                42029.00
                 Purchases 03/16  P42                   1864.00    43893.00
                 Purchases 03/18  P50                  17584.00    61477.00
                 Cash Pymt 03/20  C172     39456.00                22021.00
                 Purchases 03/21  P51                  16930.00    38951.00
                 General   03/22  DM19       580.00                38371.00
                 Purchases 03/23  P59                  21430.00    59801.00
                 General   03/24  M39                    375.00    60176.00
                 General   03/27  DM20      6552.00                53624.00
                 Cash Pymt 03/28  C173     17584.00                36040.00
                 General   03/29  M40                    120.00    36160.00
                 Cash Pymt 03/29  C208     16930.00                19230.00
                 Purchases 03/31  P61                   2110.00    21340.00
```

INTEGRATING AUTOMATED ACCOUNTING—TOPIC 7   **515**

```
                Celluphone, Inc.
             Schedule of Accounts Payable
                    03/31/--
------------------------------------------------------
Account
Number      Name                          Balance
------------------------------------------------------
210         Action Phone Co.              2000.00
240         Electro Sound                 2004.00
250         Hopkins Company               2110.00
260         Interstate Com               14503.00
272         Kryger Supplies                723.00
                                        ----------
            Total                        21340.00
                                        ==========
```

OPTIONAL PROBLEM DB-7A

Celluphone's general ledger data base is on the accounting textbook template. If you wish to process Celluphone's purchases, cash payments, and other transactions using automated accounting software, load the *Automated Accounting 6.0* or higher software. Select Data Base 7A (DB-7A) from the template disk. Read the Problem Instructions screen. Use the completed purchases, cash payments, and general journal input forms, Illustrations T7-1, T7-2, and T7-3, and follow the procedures described to process Celluphone's purchases, cash payments, and other transactions.

AUTOMATED ACCOUNTING PROBLEMS

AUTOMATING APPLICATION PROBLEM 19-3 Recording purchases and cash payment transactions

INSTRUCTIONS:

1. Journalize transactions from Problem 19-3, Chapter 19, on the appropriate forms. Use April 30 of the current year as the run date.

2. Load the *Automated Accounting 6.0* or higher software. Select data base F19-3 (First-Year Course Problem 19-3) from the accounting textbook template. Read the Problem Instructions screen.

3. Select File from the menu bar and choose the Save As menu command. Key the path to the drive and directory that contains your data files. Save the data base with a file name of XXX193 (where XXX are your initials).

4. Key the data from each of the completed input forms.

5. Display/print the general journal report, purchases journal report, and the cash payments journal report.

6. Display/print the accounts payable account from the general ledger.

7. Display/print the schedule of accounts payable.

AUTOMATING MASTERY PROBLEM 19-M Recording purchases and cash payment transactions

INSTRUCTIONS:

1. Journalize transactions from Mastery Problem 19-M, Chapter 19, on the appropriate input forms. Use August 31 of the current year as the run date.

TEACHING STRATEGIES: TEACHING TIP

It is important for students to save a template file under another name before they begin work. This will keep the template file intact for future use.

2. Load the *Automated Accounting 6.0* or higher software. Select data base F19-M (First-Year Course Mastery Problem 19-M) from the accounting textbook template. Read the Problem Instructions screen.

3. Select File from the menu bar and choose the Save As menu command. Key the path to the drive and directory that contains your data files. Save the data base with a file name of XXX19M (where XXX are your initials).

4. Key the data from the completed input forms.

5. Display/print the general journal report, purchases journal report, and the cash payments journal report.

6. Display/print the accounts payable account from the general ledger.

7. Display/print the schedule of accounts payable.

CHAPTER 20 OVERVIEW

Chapter 20 describes and illustrates the use of two special journals—a sales journal and a cash receipts journal—and a two-column general journal. Cash, credit card, and on account sales of merchandise, previously studied in the second accounting cycle for a merchandising business, are reviewed. Cash receipts on account with sales discounts extend learning about cash receipts. Sales returns and allowances and their effect on customer accounts are discussed and illustrated. A new section on international sales describes the flow of paperwork, including letters of credit, that are involved in international sales, as well as the journal entries that are made at each stage of the process.

The solution to Drill 20-D1 is needed to complete Drill 20-D2. Challenge Problem 20-C includes transactions from Chapters 19 and 20 for additional reinforcement and realism.

GUIDE TO ACHIEVING LEARNING OBJECTIVES

Enabling Performance Tasks	TEACH — Lesson Plans	APPLY — Drills for Understanding	APPLY — Application Problems	EXTEND/ENRICH — Mastery Problems	EXTEND/ENRICH — Challenge Problems	EXTEND/ENRICH — Cases for Critical Thinking	EXTEND/ENRICH — Recycling Problems	EXTEND/ENRICH — Reinforcement Activity	
a. Define accounting terms related to sales and cash receipts.	20-1, 20-2, 20-3, 20-4								
b. Identify accounting concepts and practices related to sales and cash receipts.	20-1, 20-2, 20-3, 20-4	20-D3				Cases 1, 2			
c. Analyze transactions affecting sales and cash receipts.	20-1, 20-2, 20-3, 20-4	20-D1, 20-D2	20-1, 20-2, 20-3, 20-4	20-M	20-C		20-R	3A	
d. Journalize and post transactions related to sales and cash receipts.	20-1, 20-2, 20-3, 20-4		20-1, 20-2, 20-3, 20-4	20-M	20-C		20-R	3A	

ENRICHMENT

SPECIAL FEATURES

Multicultural Awareness, page 526

Careers in Accounting, page 540

TECHNOLOGY CONNECTION

Automated Accounting 6.0 Problems 20-M, 20-C

Integrating Automated Accounting Topic 8 Optional Problem DB-8A

Accounting Tutorial Unit 7

Application Program Disk Problem 20-M

Electronic Study Guide

NEW, REVIEW, AND EXTENSION

ACTIVITIES/CONCEPTS/TRANSACTIONS	NEW	REVIEW/ EXTENSION
Journalizing and posting using a sales journal	✓	
Recording sales of merchandise on account		✓
Journalizing and posting using a cash receipts journal	✓	
Recording cash and credit card sales		✓
Recording cash receipts for sales on account		✓
Sales discounts	✓	
Recording international sales	✓	
Journalizing and posting using a general journal		✓
Recording sales returns and allowances	✓	
Preparing a schedule of accounts receivable		✓

	INFORMAL ASSESSMENT		FORMAL ASSESSMENT				
	Study Guide	Audit Your Understanding	Chapter MicroExam	Chapter Problem Test	Unit Problem Test	Unit Objective Test	Portfolio
Unit A		✓	✓			✓	
Unit C		✓	✓			✓	
Unit B				✓	✓		✓
				✓	✓		✓

TEACHING MATERIALS

Teacher's Wraparound Edition of the Text

Teacher's Resource Guide

Teacher's Edition of Working Papers

Teacher's Edition of Demonstration/Recycling Problems

Teaching Transparencies

Accounting Tutorial Manual

MicroExam

Applied Math Work Sheet

APPLIED MATHEMATICS

APPLIED MATH/ACCOUNTING SKILL	APPLICATION
Calculating Sales Discounts	Drill 20-D3
Calculating Sales Tax Reductions for Sales Discounts	Drill 20-D3
Calculating Sales Tax on Sales Returns and Allowances	Drill 20-D3

20

Recording Sales and Cash Receipts Using Special Journals

ENABLING PERFORMANCE TASKS

After studying Chapter 20, you will be able to:

a Define accounting terms related to sales and cash receipts.

b Identify accounting concepts and practices related to sales and cash receipts.

c Analyze transactions affecting sales and cash receipts.

d Journalize and post transactions related to sales and cash receipts.

TERMS PREVIEW

sales journal • cash receipts journal • sales discount • sales return • sales allowance • credit memorandum • exports • imports • contract of sale • letter of credit • bill of lading • commercial invoice • draft • sight draft • time draft • trade acceptance

As the volume of business and the number of transactions increase for a business, efficiency of operation becomes more important in completing work accurately and on time. Celluphone has sales of about $2,000,000.00 annually and has numerous transactions to record each day. Because of the size and the numerous transactions of the business, Celluphone uses a system of special journals. Using special journals improves the efficiency of recording transactions and permits more than one accounting clerk to record transactions at the same time. Celluphone uses four special journals and a general journal. A sales journal, a cash receipts journal, and selected uses of a general journal are described in this chapter. A purchases journal, a cash payments journal, and selected uses of a general journal are described in Chapter 19.

RECORDING SALES ON ACCOUNT USING A SALES JOURNAL

FYI

The sales account is used only to record sales of merchandise. Occasionally a business may sell some other asset that is no longer needed, such as office equipment. The sales account is not used for this kind of transaction.

Celluphone sells much of its merchandise for cash. However, to encourage additional sales, Celluphone sells on account to customers with approved credit. Regardless of when cash is received, revenue should be recorded when merchandise is sold. *(CONCEPT: Realization of Revenue)* Since many sales are made on account, Celluphone uses a special journal to record *only* sales on account transactions. A special journal used to record only sales on account transactions is called a **sales journal**. The relationship between Celluphone's sales journal and the expanded journal described in Chapter 11 is shown in Illustration 20-1.

Those columns used in an expanded journal and needed to record *only* sales on account are included in Celluphone's sales journal. These amount columns are Accounts Receivable Debit, Sales Credit, and Sales Tax Payable Credit. With these special amount columns, each sale on account transaction can be recorded on one line in Celluphone's sales journal.

ILLUSTRATION 20-1   Sales journal

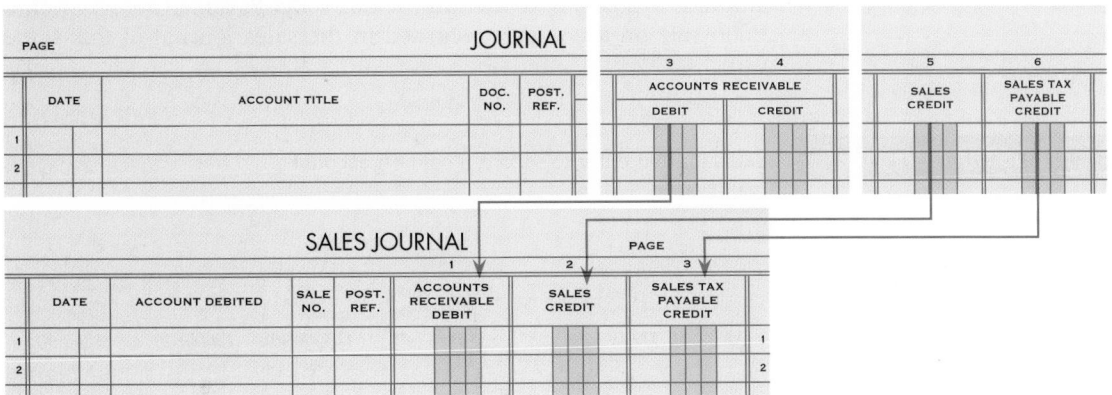

LESSON PLAN 20-1

Materials

- Student pages 519–523
- Transparencies: N, Blank Sales Journal; 20-1, Posting from a Sales Journal to a General Ledger
- Demonstration Problem: 20A, Journalizing and Posting Sales on Account Transactions

Objectives (Enabling Performance Tasks)

a. Define accounting terms related to sales and cash receipts.

b. Identify accounting concepts and practices related to sales and cash receipts.

c. Analyze transactions affecting sales and cash receipts.

d. Journalize and post transactions related to sales and cash receipts.

- In Chapter 19, special journals were introduced. In this lesson, we will record sales transactions in a special sales journal.

- Introduce new vocabulary: sales journal.

Cover student pages 519–523 "Recording Sales on Account Using a Sales Journal." Use Transparency N to introduce the sales journal or direct students to Illustration 20-1. Point out that the three columns used in the multi-column journal in Chapter 12 are used in the sales journal to record a sale on account. Remind students that the rules for posting from special amount columns also apply to the sales journal. Describe proving and ruling the sales journal and posting to the general and subsidiary ledgers.

Sales tax rates vary from state to state and may even vary within a state. An 8% sales tax is collected on items sold at retail in the city in which Celluphone is located. A retail business must collect the sales tax from customers and periodically send the sales tax collected to the state. Therefore, Celluphone uses a sales journal with a Sales Tax Payable Credit column to keep a separate record of sales tax.

Journalizing Sales on Account

Celluphone prepares a sales invoice in duplicate for each sale on account. The original copy is given to the customer. The carbon copy of the sales invoice is the source document for journalizing a sales on account transaction. *(CONCEPT: Objective Evidence)* Celluphone's sales invoice is similar to the one described in Chapter 12.

March 1, 19--. Sold merchandise on account to DTex Imports, $1,600.00, plus sales tax, $128.00; total, $1,728.00. Sales Invoice No. 148.

GENERAL LEDGER
Accounts Receivable

| 1,728.00 | |

Sales

| | 1,600.00 |

Sales Tax Payable

| | 128.00 |

ACCOUNTS RECEIVABLE LEDGER
DTex Imports

| 1,728.00 | |

Accounts Receivable is debited for $1,728.00, the amount of the sale plus the sales tax. Sales is credited for $1,600.00, the amount of the sale. Sales Tax Payable is credited for $128.00, the amount of sales tax on this sale. Celluphone owes the tax to the state government. Therefore, the amount of sales tax charged each customer is a liability. DTex Imports' account in the accounts receivable ledger is also debited for $1,728.00.

The sales journal entry to record this sales on account transaction is shown in Illustration 20-2.

The date, *19--, Mar. 1*, is written in the Date column. The customer name, *DTex Imports*, is recorded in the Account Debited column. The sales invoice number, *148*, is entered in the Sale No. column. The sale amount plus the sales tax, *$1,728.00*, is written in the Accounts Receivable Debit column. The sale amount, *$1,600.00*, is entered in the Sales Credit column. The sales tax amount, *$128.00*, is written in the Sales Tax Payable Credit column. Each sale on account is recorded in the sales journal in this same way.

ILLUSTRATION 20-2

Sales journal entry to record a sale on account

SALES JOURNAL   PAGE 8

	DATE		ACCOUNT DEBITED	SALE NO.	POST. REF.	ACCOUNTS RECEIVABLE DEBIT	SALES CREDIT	SALES TAX PAYABLE CREDIT	
1	Mar. 19--	1	DTex Imports	148		1 7 2 8 00	1 6 0 0 00	1 2 8 00	1
2									2

TEACHING STRATEGIES: DIFFERENT LEARNING STYLES

Auditory Learner. To reinforce the learning of journal entries, the auditory learner should verbally repeat the analysis of the transaction. The student should also verbally list the steps involved in making the entry.

Since the source document for all entries in the sales journal is a sales invoice, it is not necessary to use an *S* with the document number.

Posting from a Sales Journal to an Accounts Receivable Ledger

Each amount in a sales journal's Accounts Receivable Debit column is posted individually to the customer account in the accounts receivable ledger. Each amount is posted as a debit to the customer account listed in the Account Debited column. Celluphone posts frequently to the accounts receivable ledger so that each customer account will show an up-to-date balance. Illustration 20-3 shows the posting of this entry on line 1 of the sales journal.

ILLUSTRATION 20-3

Posting from a sales journal to an accounts receivable ledger

SALES JOURNAL   PAGE **8**

	DATE	ACCOUNT DEBITED	SALE NO.	POST. REF.	ACCOUNTS RECEIVABLE DEBIT (1)	SALES CREDIT (2)	SALES TAX PAYABLE CREDIT (3)	
1	Mar. 1	DTex Imports	148	120	1 7 2 8 00	1 6 0 0 00	1 2 8 00	1
2								2

CUSTOMER **DTex Imports**   CUSTOMER NO. **120**

DATE	ITEM	POST. REF.	DEBIT	CREDIT	DEBIT BALANCE
Mar. 1	Balance	✓			4 8 6 00
1		S8	1 7 2 8 00		2 2 1 4 00

The date, *1,* is written in the Date column of the account. The abbreviation for the sales journal and the page number, *S8,* are recorded in the Post. Ref. column. The amount, *$1,728.00,* is entered in the Debit column of the customer account. The amount in the Debit column is added to the previous balance in the Debit Balance column ($486.00 + $1,728.00 = $2,214.00). The new balance, *$2,214.00,* is written in the Debit Balance column. The customer number for DTex Imports, *120,* is recorded in the Post. Ref. column of the sales journal to show that posting has been completed for this line.

Posting from a Sales Journal to a General Ledger

Equality of debits and credits is proved for a sales journal at the end of each month. The sales journal is then ruled, and the totals of special columns are posted, as shown in Illustration 20-4 on page 522.

TEACHING STRATEGIES: DIFFERENT LEARNING STYLES

Auditory Learner. When learning how to post, the auditory learner would prefer to hear the steps involved in posting. This can be done via a live lecture or a taped tutorial. To reinforce learning, the student could recite the posting steps to another student or group of students.

ASSESS

Assess student understanding by checking solutions to Independent Practice activities.

Reteach

Use Demonstration Problem 20A. This problem can be done on the overhead with students completing the problem at their desks.

Extend

Assign Cases for Critical Thinking 1.

Enrich

Assign students to read the MULTICULTURAL AWARENESS feature on page 526.

CLOSURE

- Use Audit Your Understanding questions.
- Review Summary Illustration 20-5, Summary of Journalizing and Posting Using a Sales Journal.

ILLUSTRATION 20-4   Posting from a sales journal to a general ledger

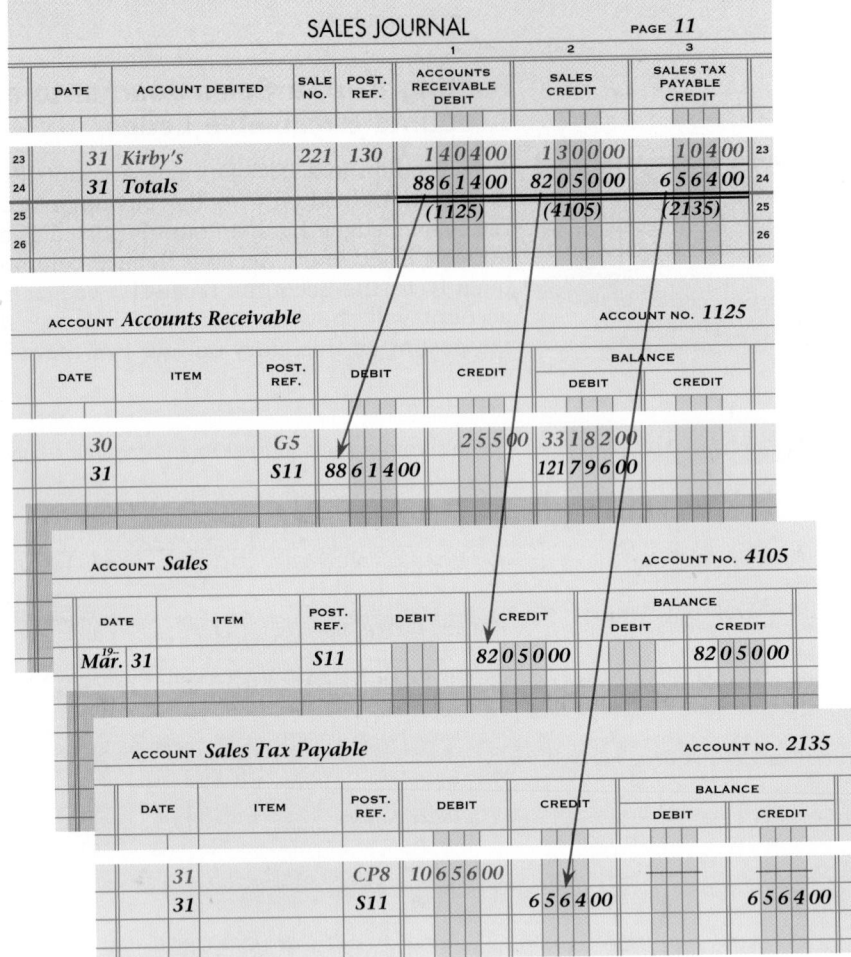

FYI

Account numbers in parentheses under the totals of special amount columns in a journal show the general ledger accounts to which the totals have been posted. This cross-reference provides an audit trail.

A single line is ruled across the amount columns of the sales journal under the last amounts recorded. The date of the last day of the month, *31*, is written in the Date column. The word *Totals* is written in the Account Debited column. The column totals are written below the single line. Double lines are ruled across the amount columns under the totals. Next, each amount column total is posted to the general ledger account named in the sales journal column headings.

When each sales journal amount column total is posted, *S11* is written in the Post. Ref. column of the account. The account number is written in parentheses under the amount column total in the sales journal. The accounts receivable account number, *1125*, is written under the Accounts Receivable Debit column total in the sales journal. The sales account number, *4105*, is written under the Sales Credit column total. The sales tax payable account number,

2135, is written under the Sales Tax Payable Credit column total.

A summary of the procedure for journalizing and posting using a sales journal is shown in Illustration 20-5.

RECORDING CASH RECEIPTS USING A CASH RECEIPTS JOURNAL

Celluphone has many transactions involving the receipt of cash. Because of the numerous transactions involving sizable amounts of cash, Celluphone has two objectives. (1) To avoid the loss of any cash. (2) To efficiently account for the cash. To help meet these objectives, Celluphone uses a special journal to record *only* cash receipt transactions. A special journal used to record only cash receipt transactions is called a **cash receipts journal.**

SUMMARY ILLUSTRATION 20-5

Summary of journalizing and posting using a sales journal

1 All sales on account are recorded in a 3-column sales journal.

2 Individual items in the sales journal are posted frequently to the customer accounts in the accounts receivable ledger.

3 At the end of each month, each amount column total is posted. The Accounts Receivable Debit column total is posted to **Accounts Receivable** as a debit. The Sales Credit column total is posted to **Sales** as a credit. The Sales Tax Payable Credit column total is posted to **Sales Tax Payable** as a credit.

- Journalizing sales on account transactions in a special sales journal
was presented earlier in this chapter. In this lesson, we will record
cash receipts transactions in a special cash receipts journal.

- Introduce new vocabulary: cash
receipts journal, sales discount.

Using a cash receipts journal permits Celluphone to record all cash receipts in one location—the cash receipts journal. Thus the amount of cash received can be determined much more quickly and easily.

The relationship between Celluphone's cash receipts journal and the expanded journal described in Chapter 11 is shown in Illustration 20-6.

ILLUSTRATION 20-6   Cash receipts journal

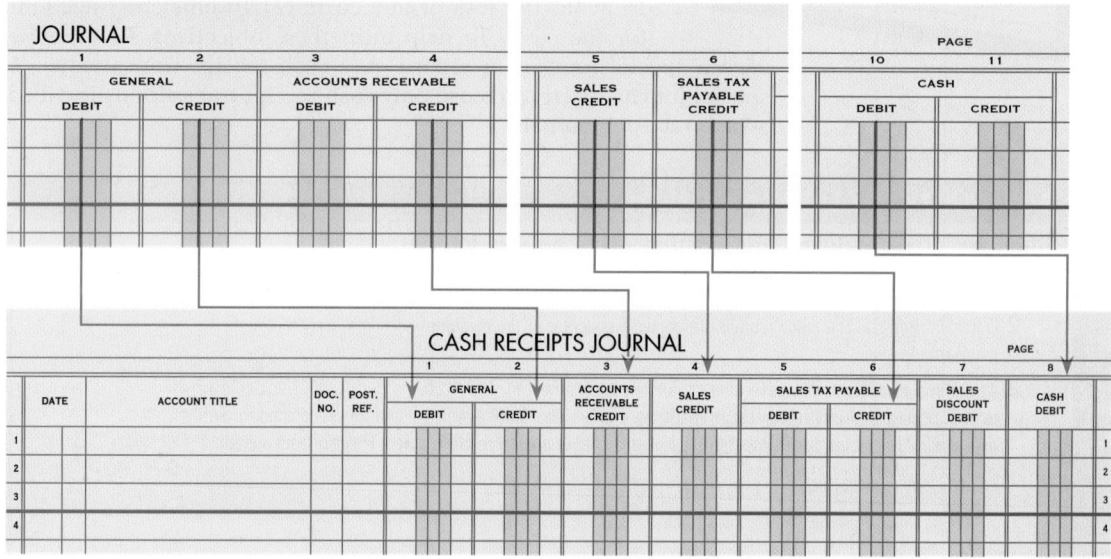

Those columns used in an expanded journal and needed to record *only* cash receipts are included in Celluphone's cash receipts journal. In addition, Celluphone has many transactions with cash discounts. Two additional special amount columns are provided in the cash receipts journal for recording cash received on account with a cash discount. These special amount columns are Sales Tax Payable Debit and Sales Discount Debit. With these additional special amount columns, each cash receipt transaction can be recorded on one line in Celluphone's cash receipts journal.

All cash receipts are recorded in a cash receipts journal. Most cash receipts are for (1) cash and credit card sales and (2) cash received from customers on account.

Journalizing Cash and Credit Card Sales

March 1, 19--. Recorded cash and credit card sales, $2,870.00, plus sales tax, $229.60; total, $3,099.60. Cash Register Tape No. 1.

524   PART 4   Accounting for a Merchandising Business Organized as a Corporation

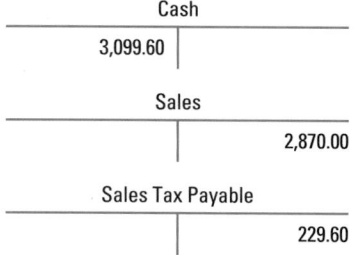

Cash | 3,099.60

Sales | 2,870.00

Sales Tax Payable | 229.60

Cash is debited for $3,099.60. Sales is credited for $2,870.00, and Sales Tax Payable is credited for $229.60.

The cash receipts journal entry to record this cash receipt transaction is shown in Illustration 20-7.

The date, *19--, Mar. 1*, is written in the Date column. A check mark is recorded in the Account Title column to show that no account title needs to be written. The cash register tape number, *T1*, is entered in the Doc. No. column. A check mark is also recorded in the Post. Ref. column to show that separate amounts on this line are not posted individually. The amount credited to Sales, *$2,870.00*, is written in the Sales Credit column. The amount credited to Sales Tax Payable, *$229.60*, is recorded in the Sales Tax Payable Credit column. The amount of cash received, *$3,099.60*, is written in the Cash Debit column.

ILLUSTRATION 20-7   Cash receipts journal entry to record cash and credit card sales

CASH RECEIPTS JOURNAL   PAGE 9

	DATE	ACCOUNT TITLE	DOC. NO.	POST. REF.	GENERAL DEBIT	GENERAL CREDIT	ACCOUNTS RECEIVABLE CREDIT	SALES CREDIT	SALES TAX PAYABLE DEBIT	SALES TAX PAYABLE CREDIT	SALES DISCOUNT DEBIT	CASH DEBIT	
1	Mar. 1	√	T1	√				2 8 7 0 00		2 2 9 60		3 0 9 9 60	1
2													2

Sales Discounts

Selling merchandise on account usually helps a business increase the volume of its sales by providing more convenience to the customer. The sales transaction can be made by telephone or mail. The merchandise can be shipped to a customer when a sales agreement is reached. A customer can then pay for the merchandise after it is received. Because of this convenience, many sales are made on account. A customer is expected to pay the amount due within the credit period agreed upon.

To encourage early payment for a sale on account, a deduction on the invoice amount may be allowed. A deduction on the invoice amount to encourage prompt payment is known as a cash discount. A cash discount on sales is called a **sales discount**. When a sales discount is taken, a customer pays less cash than the invoice amount previously recorded in the sales account. Therefore, the amount of a sales discount is deducted from sales. Sales discounts are recorded in a general ledger account titled *Sales Discount*. The contra account Sales Discount follows the account to which it is related, Sales, in Celluphone's general ledger operating revenue division. The account is numbered 4110. Since sales discounts decrease sales, the account Sales Dis-

Sales	
Debit side	Credit side
	Normal balance
Decrease	Increase

Sales Discount	
Debit side	Credit side
Normal balance	
Increase	Decrease

CHAPTER 20   Recording Sales and Cash Receipts Using Special Journals   **525**

MULTICULTURAL AWARENESS

The MULTICULTURAL AWARENESS feature is intended to expose students to the concept that our society is composed of people from many different cultural backgrounds. These features show both past contributions of many cultures and benefits of a culturally diverse society. (1) Read the feature. (2) Discuss the specific information in the feature. (3) Clarify any terms or questions. (4) Do the Multicultural Awareness Activity.

MULTICULTURAL AWARENESS ACTIVITY

The invention of paper advanced the possibility of keeping records as well as the artistic and cultural aspects of civilization. If a paper factory is located in your community, a field trip would be worthwhile. Your community may also have artists who make their own paper who would be willing to speak to your class and give a demonstration. Students could also research the history of paper through various civilizations. Students could also prepare a presentation on what is meant by a "paperless office" in today's work world and how close we are to achieving a paperless office. The results of this research should reemphasize the importance of the invention of paper to commerce.

MULTICULTURAL AWARENESS

Early Egypt

The Egyptian invention of **papyrus**, *a form of paper, facilitated the development of accounting in early Egypt. The Egyptians were able to keep more extensive and detailed records than the Babylonians because papyrus was easier to handle than clay tablets.*

Egypt had an elaborate tax system in which taxes were paid in commodities such as wheat and sent to local district storehouses. Less perishable items were transferred to a central treasury. All of these transfers were meticulously recorded by the scribes. There was an auditing system in which the records of each scribe were compared and had to match. Scribes were very careful to be accurate because irregularities could be punished by mutilation or death. Financial communities around the world today depend on the accuracy of accounting records that have been verified by auditors.

FYI

Most states have sales taxes. Many states also permit local governments, such as cities and counties, to levy additional percentages or fractions of a percent to the state rate.

count is a contra account to Sales. Therefore, the normal account balance of Sales Discount is a debit, the opposite of the normal account balance of Sales, a credit.

Some businesses debit the sales account for the amount of the sales discount. However, better information is provided if these amounts are debited to a separate account, Sales Discount. A separate account shows the amount being given as a sales discount. The amount of sales, sales discounts, and time of collections can be analyzed to determine whether sales discounts are effective and worth the cost.

Calculating and Journalizing Cash Receipts on Account with Sales Discounts

To encourage prompt payment, Celluphone gives credit terms of 1/10, n/30. When a customer pays the amount owed within 10 days, the sales invoice amount is reduced 1%.

On March 1, as shown in Illustration 20-2, Celluphone sold merchandise on account to DTex Imports for $1,600.00 plus 8% sales tax, $128.00, for a total invoice amount of $1,728.00. On March 11 Celluphone received payment for this sale on account within the discount period.

In the state where Celluphone is located, state regulations require that sales taxes be paid only on actual sales realized. When Celluphone prepares an invoice for a sale on account, the company does not know whether the customer will pay within the sales discount period. Therefore, the customer is invoiced for the full sales amount plus sales tax on that amount. Thus, on March 1, DTex Imports was invoiced for the full amount of the sale, $1,600.00, plus sales tax on that amount, $128.00, for a total invoice amount of $1,728.00. If payment for a sale on account is received within the discount period, the sales amount is reduced by the amount of the sales discount. The amount of sales tax is also reduced because the amount of the sale is reduced.

> In some states sales taxes must be paid on the original invoice amount of sale. In these states a sales discount would not result in a reduction in the sales tax liability.

Three amounts must be calculated to prepare the journal entry and verify that the customer paid the correct amount. (1) The amount of the sales discount, which is a percentage of the amount originally credited to Sales. (2) The amount the sales tax liability is reduced, which is the amount of sales tax on the sales discount. (3) The amount of cash received, which is the original total invoice amount (the Accounts Receivable Debit amount at the time of the sale) less the sales discount and the reduction in sales tax liability. These three amounts are calculated as shown on page 527 for cash received on account within the discount period for Sales Invoice No. 148 to DTex Imports.

(1) *Sales Discount:*

Sales Invoice Amount	×	Sales Discount Rate	=	Sales Discount
$1,600.00	×	1%	=	$16.00

(2) *Sales Tax Liability Reduction:*

Sales Discount	×	Sales Tax Rate	=	Reduction in Sales Tax Payable
$16.00	×	8%	=	$1.28

(3) *Cash Received:*

Total Invoiced Amount	–	Sales Discount	–	Sales Tax Reduction	=	Cash Received
$1,728.00	–	$16.00	–	$1.28	=	$1,710.72

GENERAL LEDGER
Cash

Mar. 11	1,710.72	

Sales Discount

Mar. 11	16.00	

Sales Tax Payable

Mar. 11	1.28	Mar. 1	128.00

Accounts Receivable

Mar. 1	1,728.00	Mar. 11	1,728.00

ACCOUNTS RECEIVABLE LEDGER
DTex Imports

Mar. 1	1,728.00	Mar. 11	1,728.00

March 11, 19--. Received cash on account from DTex Imports, $1,710.72, covering Sales Invoice No. 148 for $1,728.00 ($1,600.00 plus sales tax, $128.00), less 1% discount, $16.00, and less sales tax, $1.28. Receipt No. 232.

Cash is debited for the total amount received, $1,710.72. Sales Discount is debited for the sales discount amount, $16.00. Sales Tax Payable is debited for $1.28, the amount of the reduction in sales tax liability. The sales tax payable on this discounted sale is now $126.72 ($128.00 less $1.28). Accounts Receivable is credited for $1,728.00, the amount debited to Accounts Receivable at the time of the sale on account. DTex Imports' account is also credited for the same amount as Accounts Receivable, $1,728.00.

The amounts for this transaction can be proved by making the calculations shown below.

Sales invoice amount............................	$1,600.00
Less sales discount..............................	– 16.00
($1,600.00 × 1%)	
Equals reduced invoice amount	$1,584.00
Plus sales tax on reduced invoice amount	+ 126.72
($1,584.00 × 8%)	
Equals cash received	$1,710.72

The cash receipts journal entry to record this cash receipt on account with a sales discount is shown in Illustration 20-8 on page 528.

The date, *11,* is written in the Date column. The customer name, *DTex Imports,* is entered in the Account Title column. The receipt number, *R232,* is written in the Doc. No. column. The amount credited to Accounts Receivable, *$1,728.00,* is recorded in the Accounts Receivable Credit column. The reduction in Sales Tax Payable, *$1.28,* is written in the Sales Tax Payable Debit column. The debit to Sales Discount, *$16.00,* is entered in the Sales Discount Debit column. The debit to Cash, *$1,710.72,* is written in the Cash Debit column. The

ASSESS

Assess student understanding by checking solutions to Independent Practice activities.

Reteach

- Use Demonstration Problem 20B. This problem can be done on the overhead with the students completing the problem at their desks.

- Duplicate and assign Math Work Sheet Chapter 20 Part A, Calculating Sales Discounts, and Part B, Calculating Sales Tax Reductions for Sales Discounts, from the Masters and Solutions to Enrichment/Application Activities Section in the Teacher's Resource Guide to provide additional practice on the mathematics of calculating sales discounts and sales tax on sales discounts.

Extend

Use the Accounting Tutorial, Unit 7, to teach analyzing sales and cash receipts transactions.

Enrich

Ask students to research and report on various characteristics of sales taxes in your state and local community. Students should research the rate, local options for rates, goods that are taxable, exempt organizations, and so on. In some states, the use tax may replace the sales tax.

| ILLUSTRATION 20-8 | Cash receipts journal entry to record a cash receipt on account with sales discount |

CASH RECEIPTS JOURNAL   PAGE 9

	DATE	ACCOUNT TITLE	DOC. NO.	POST. REF.	GENERAL DEBIT	GENERAL CREDIT	ACCOUNTS RECEIVABLE CREDIT	SALES CREDIT	SALES TAX PAYABLE DEBIT	SALES TAX PAYABLE CREDIT	SALES DISCOUNT DEBIT	CASH DEBIT	
20	11	DTex Imports	R232				1 728 00		1 28		16 00	1 710 72	20
21													21

total of the three debits ($1.28 + $16.00 + $1,710.72) is $1,728.00 and is equal to the one credit of $1,728.00.

    If a customer does not pay the amount owed within the sales discount period, the full invoice amount is due. If DTex Imports had not taken the sales discount, the journal entry would be a debit to Cash, $1,728.00, and a credit to Accounts Receivable, $1,728.00. The same amount, $1,728.00, would also be credited to the account of DTex Imports in the accounts receivable ledger.

Posting from a Cash Receipts Journal to an Accounts Receivable Ledger

Each entry in the Accounts Receivable Credit column affects the account of the customer named in the Account Title column. Each amount listed in the Accounts Receivable Credit column is posted individually to the proper customer account in the accounts receivable ledger. Illustration 20-9 shows the posting of a cash receipts journal entry to a customer account.

| ILLUSTRATION 20-9 | Posting from a cash receipts journal to an accounts receivable ledger |

CASH RECEIPTS JOURNAL   PAGE 9

	DATE	ACCOUNT TITLE	DOC. NO.	POST. REF.	GENERAL DEBIT	GENERAL CREDIT	ACCOUNTS RECEIVABLE CREDIT	SALES CREDIT	SALES TAX PAYABLE DEBIT	SALES TAX PAYABLE CREDIT	SALES DISCOUNT DEBIT	CASH DEBIT	
20	11	DTex Imports	R232	120			1 728 00		1 28		16 00	1 710 72	20
21													21

CUSTOMER **DTex Imports**   CUSTOMER NO. **120**

DATE	ITEM	POST. REF.	DEBIT	CREDIT	DEBIT BALANCE
1		S8	1 728 00		2 214 00
4		CR9		486 00	1 728 00
11		CR9		1 728 00	——

TEACHING STRATEGIES: DIFFERENT LEARNING STYLES

Kinesthetic Learner. When learning how to post, the kinesthetic learner would prefer to participate in the posting process. This can be done by using a transparency of the ledger account and having each student complete one or more steps of the posting process at the overhead projector. Other students can be completing the posting process individually on printed ledger accounts.

The date, *11*, is written in the Date column of the customer account. The abbreviation and page number of the cash receipts journal, *CR9*, is recorded in the Post. Ref. column. The amount in the Accounts Receivable Credit column, *$1,728.00*, is written in the Credit column of the customer account. The amount in the Credit column of the customer account is subtracted from the previous balance in the Debit Balance column ($1,728.00 − $1,728.00 = 0). A horizontal line is drawn in the Debit Balance column to indicate a new balance of zero. The customer number for DTex Imports, *120*, is recorded in the Post. Ref. column of the cash receipts journal to show that posting has been completed for this line.

Posting from a Cash Receipts Journal to a General Ledger

Each amount in the General amount columns of a cash receipts journal is posted individually to a general ledger account named in the Account Title column. However, only the total of each special amount column is posted to the general ledger account given in the column heading. Posting the special amount column totals of Celluphone's cash receipts journal is shown in Illustration 20-10 on page 530.

Posting from the General Columns of a Cash Receipts Journal. Each amount in the General columns is posted individually to the general ledger account named in the Account Title column. Entries that are recorded in the General columns are described in Chapter 24.

Posting Totals from the Special Columns of a Cash Receipts Journal. At the end of each month, equality of debits and credits is proved for a cash receipts journal. Cash is then proved as shown below.

Cash on hand at the beginning of the month . . . . (March 1, 19--, balance of cash account in general ledger)	$119,048.00
Plus total cash received during the month . . . . (Cash Debit column total, cash receipts journal, Illustration 20-10)	+169,972.00
Total	$289,020.00
Less total cash paid during the month . . . . (Cash Credit column total, cash payments journal, Illustration 19-16, Chapter 19)	−140,742.00
Equals cash on hand at the end of the month	$148,278.00
Checkbook balance on the next unused check stub. . .	$148,278.00

After cash is proved, the cash receipts journal is ruled as shown in Illustration 20-10 on page 530. Each special amount column total is posted to the account named in the cash receipts journal column heading.

Posting from a cash payments journal to the cash account is described in Chapter 19.

CLOSURE

- Use Audit Your Understanding questions.

- Review Summary Illustration 20-11, Summary of Journalizing and Posting Using a Cash Receipts Journal.

☞☞ FYI ☜☜

The abbreviation *CR* is used when posting from the cash receipts journal. The abbreviation provides a reference back to the cash receipts journal in case the original entry needs to be examined.

TEACHING STRATEGIES: DIFFERENT LEARNING ABILITIES

Gifted Students. This cycle presents a variety of accounting concepts, such as accounts receivable, plant assets, and inventory. Using gifted students as tutors for other students can be an effective way of teaching the topics students find most difficult. Allow the gifted student to complete one of these chapters while the class completes the first two chapters of the cycle. The gifted students can then assist you in presenting the concepts and procedures on their chapter to the class. Encourage the students to use visual aids and develop methods to assess student learning.

ILLUSTRATION 20-10 Posting totals of the special amount columns in a cash receipts journal to a general ledger

530   PART 4   Accounting for a Merchandising Business Organized as a Corporation

530

Audit Your Understanding

1. Why are cash and credit card sales recorded in a cash receipts journal instead of a sales journal?

2. How is a sales discount calculated?

3. How is the cash receipt amount for a sale on account with sales tax and sales discount calculated?

4. Why does the cash receipts journal have both Debit and Credit columns for Sales Tax Payable?

When each special amount column total is posted, *CR12* is written in the Post. Ref. column of the account. The general ledger account number is written below the related cash receipts journal column total. The account number, written in parentheses, shows that posting of a column total is complete.

The totals of the General amount columns are not posted. Each amount in these columns was posted individually to a general ledger account. To indicate that these totals are not posted, a check mark is placed in parentheses below each column total.

A summary of the procedure for journalizing and posting using a cash receipts journal is shown in Illustration 20-11 on page 532.

AUDIT YOUR UNDERSTANDING

1. Because the sales journal is used only for sales on account and because they are receipts of cash.

2. Sales invoice amount times sales discount rate.

3. Total invoiced amount, less sales discount, less sales tax reduction equals cash received.

4. The Debit column is used for cash receipts on account with sales discounts and the Credit column is used for cash and credit card sales.

RECORDING TRANSACTIONS USING A GENERAL JOURNAL

Purchases related transactions recorded in a general journal are described in Chapter 19. Celluphone also records two sales related transactions in a general journal. These two transactions are not sales on account or cash receipts. Thus, they are not appropriate for either the sales journal or the cash receipts journal. These two transactions are (1) sales returns and allowances and (2) correcting entries that affect customer accounts but not the controlling account.

Sales Returns and Allowances

> **FYI**
>
> A credit memorandum is prepared by the vendor and sent to the customer. In the vendor's records, the credit memorandum authorizes a credit to the customer's account in the accounts receivable ledger.

Most merchandising businesses expect to have some merchandise returned because a customer decides not to keep the merchandise. A customer may have received the wrong style, the wrong size, or damaged goods. A customer may return merchandise and ask for a credit on account or a cash refund. Credit allowed a customer for the sales price of returned merchandise, resulting in a decrease in the vendor's accounts receivable, is called a **sales return.**

Credit may be granted to a customer without asking for the return of damaged or imperfect merchandise. Credit also may be given because of a shortage in a shipment. Credit allowed a customer for part of the sales price of merchandise that is not returned, resulting in a decrease in the vendor's accounts receivable, is called a **sales allowance.**

A vendor usually informs a customer in writing when a sales return or a sales allowance is granted. A form prepared by the vendor showing the amount deducted for returns and allowances is called a **credit memorandum.** The form is called a credit memorandum because the vendor records the amount as a credit to the customer account to show the decrease in Accounts Receivable.

LESSON PLAN 20-3

Materials

- Student pages 531–537

- Transparencies: M, Blank General Journal

- Math Work Sheet Chapter 20: C: Calculating Sales Tax on Sales Returns and Allowances (TRG)

- Software: *Automated Accounting 6.0* or higher; Accounting Textbook Template, first-year course; Accounting Tutorial; Application Program Disk; Electronic Study Guide

- Demonstration Problem: 20C Recording Transactions Using a General Journal

Objectives (Enabling Performance Tasks)

a. Define accounting terms related to sales and cash receipts.

b. Identify accounting concepts and practices related to sales and cash receipts.

c. Analyze transactions affecting sales and cash receipts.

d. Journalize and post transactions related to sales and cash receipts.

CHAPTER 20   Recording Sales and Cash Receipts Using Special Journals   **531**

- Recording sales and cash receipts transactions in special sales and cash receipts journals was presented earlier in this chapter. In this lesson, we will look at other transactions related to sales and cash receipts that are recorded in a general journal.

- Introduce new vocabulary: sales return, sales allowance, credit memorandum.

APPLIED SKILLS:
LANGUAGE ARTS

Practicing punctuation skills.
Special handouts for practicing punctuation skills can be created easily using word processing software. Key in some text, either something that you have written yourself or that has appeared in a newspaper or magazine. After checking to be sure you have keyed it correctly, use the change feature of the word processor to change all punctuation to an underline. This will create an answer space for students to supply the correct punctuation. Student solutions can then be compared with the original copy for correctness. For additional challenge, the answer blanks can be omitted.

SUMMARY ILLUSTRATION 20-11

Summary of journalizing and posting using a cash receipts journal

1 All cash receipts are recorded in an 8-column cash receipts journal.

2 Amounts in the Accounts Receivable Credit column are posted frequently to the customer accounts in the accounts receivable ledger.

3 At the end of the month, the totals of the special columns are posted to the general ledger.

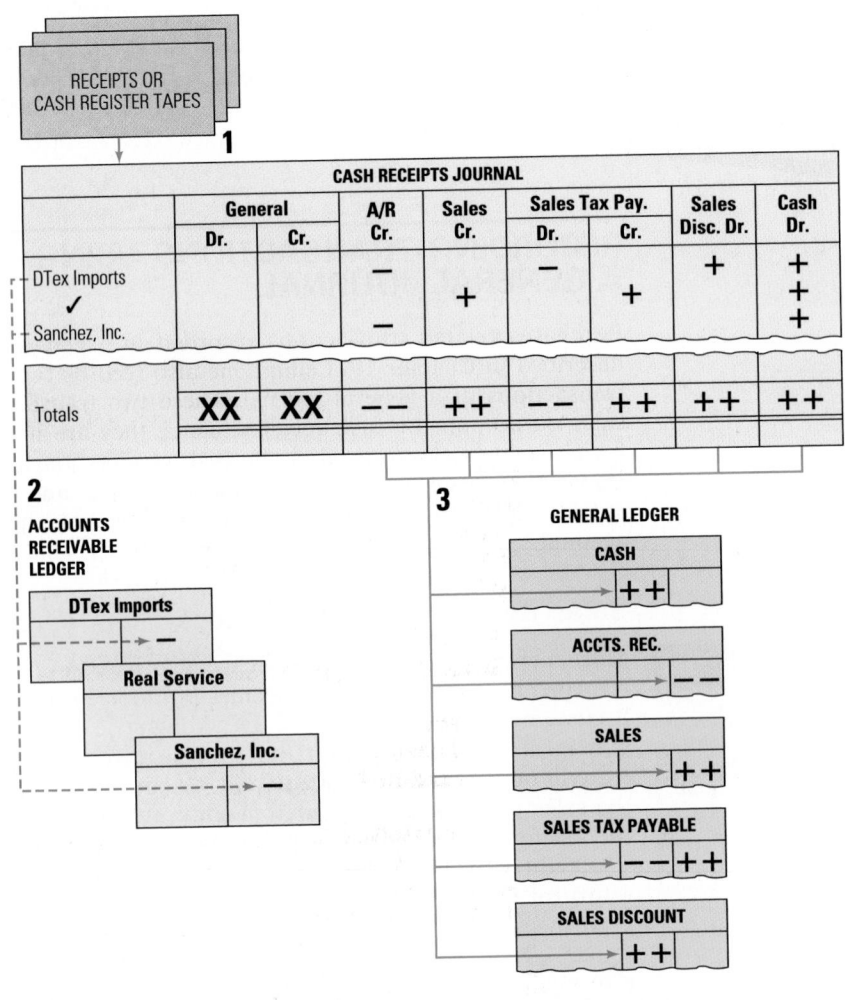

Celluphone issues a credit memorandum in duplicate for each sales return or sales allowance. The original copy is given to the customer. The second copy is used as the source document for sales returns and allowances. *(CONCEPT: Objective Evidence)* The credit memorandum form used by Celluphone is shown in Illustration 20-12.

ILLUSTRATION 20-12

Credit memorandum

CREDIT MEMORANDUM NO. 41

	DATE
	March 11, 19--

Celluphone, Inc.
12610 Hillcrest Road
Dallas, TX 75230-8623

TO
ALAMO COMPANY
2101 WEST APOLLO ROAD
GARLAND TX 74631-0879

We have this day credited your account as follows:

ACCOUNT NO.
110

Quantity	Description	Price	Total
1	Battery pack, Invoice No. 160	180.00	
	Sales tax	14.40	194.40

If the above is incorrect, please return stating difference.

Sales returns and sales allowances decrease the amount of sales. Therefore, the account Sales Returns and Allowances is a contra account to the revenue account Sales. Thus, the normal account balance of Sales Returns and Allowances is a debit, the opposite of the normal balance of Sales, a credit.

Some businesses debit the sales account for the amount of a return or allowance. However, better information is provided if these amounts are debited to a separate account, Sales Returns and Allowances. A separate account shows how large the sales returns and allowances are. Also, a business can see if returns and allowances are increasing or decreasing from year to year. If the amounts are large, separate accounts may be kept for sales returns and for sales allowances. Usually a single, combined account is sufficient.

Celluphone uses a single contra revenue account, Sales Returns and Allowances. The account is in the general ledger's operating revenue division.

Sales	
Debit side	Credit side
	Normal balance
Decrease	Increase

Sales Returns and Allowances	
Debit side	Credit side
Normal balance	
Increase	Decrease

Journalizing Sales Returns and Allowances

On March 8 Celluphone sold merchandise on account to Alamo Company for $360.00. Alamo's account was debited for $388.80 ($360.00 sales and $28.80 sales tax). Later, Alamo returned part of

- Draw T accounts on the board for each transaction as it is presented in the lesson.

- Use Transparency M to journalize transactions in the general journal. Or direct students to Illustrations 20-13 and 20-14.

Guided Practice

Guide students through Drills 20-D1 and 20-D2. Students should have the forms from the working papers to complete as you guide them through each transaction. All students should agree with the analysis of each transaction before proceeding to the next transaction.

Independent Practice

Assign Terms 4–6, Questions 11–12, Drill 20-D3, Problem 20-3, Mastery Problem 20-M, and Study Guide 20.

the merchandise. A customer is entitled to credit for the amount of a sales return or allowance. The credit must include the sales tax on the return or allowance.

March 11, 19--. Granted credit to Alamo Company for merchandise returned, $180.00, plus sales tax, $14.40, from S160; total, $194.40. Credit Memorandum No. 41.

Because Sales has a normal credit balance, the contra revenue account, Sales Returns and Allowances, has a normal debit balance. Therefore, the sales returns and allowances account is increased by a debit. This transaction increases the balance of the account. Therefore, Sales Returns and Allowances is debited for $180.00, the amount of the sale that was returned.

The sales tax payable account, a liability account, has a normal credit balance. Therefore, the sales tax payable account is increased by a credit. However, this transaction decreases the balance of this account. Therefore, Sales Tax Payable is debited for $14.40, the amount of tax on the returned merchandise.

The amount to be collected from the customer is decreased. Alamo is entitled to a $180.00 credit for the merchandise returned and a $14.40 credit for sales tax. Therefore, Accounts Receivable is credited for the total amount of the return, $194.40. The same amount is also credited to Alamo's account in the accounts receivable ledger.

The general journal entry to record this sales returns and allowances transaction is shown in Illustration 20-13.

GENERAL LEDGER
Sales Returns and Allowances

Mar. 11	180.00	

Sales Tax Payable

Mar. 11	14.40	Mar. 8	28.80

Accounts Receivable

Mar. 8	388.80	Mar. 11	194.40

ACCOUNTS RECEIVABLE LEDGER
Alamo Company

Mar. 8	388.80	Mar. 11	194.40

ILLUSTRATION 20-13   General journal entry to record sales returns and allowances

	DATE	ACCOUNT TITLE	DOC. NO.	POST. REF.	DEBIT	CREDIT	
12	11	*Sales Returns and Allowances*	CM41		1 8 0 00		12
13		*Sales Tax Payable*			1 4 40		13
14		*Accounts Receivable/Alamo Co.*				1 9 4 40	14
15							15
16							16
17							17

The date, *11*, is written in the Date column. *Sales Returns and Allowances* is recorded in the Account Title column. The source document, *CM41*, is entered in the Doc. No. column. The amount of the debit, *$180.00*, is entered in the Debit column. *Sales Tax Payable* is written on the next line in the Account Title column. The amount of the debit, *$14.40*, is recorded in the Debit column. The accounts credited, *Accounts Receivable/Alamo Company*, are written on the next line in the Account Title column. These account titles are indented about one centimeter. A diagonal line is placed between the two

TEACHING STRATEGIES: COOPERATIVE LEARNING

Divide the class into groups of two students each. Using Drill 20-D1, have students orally analyze transactions 1 through 8 to each other, alternating transactions. This cooperative learning activity should not take more than 10 to 15 minutes of class time.

account titles. A diagonal line also is placed in the Post. Ref. column to show that the credit is posted to two accounts. The amount of the credit, $194.40, is entered in the Credit column.

Journalizing Correcting Entries Affecting Customer Accounts

Errors may be made in recording amounts in subsidiary ledgers that do not affect the general ledger controlling account. For example, a sale on account may be recorded to the wrong customer in the sales journal. The column total posted from the sales journal to the general ledger is correct. The accounts receivable account shows the correct balance. However, two of the customer accounts in the accounts receivable ledger show incorrect balances. To correct this error, only the subsidiary ledger accounts need to be corrected.

March 12, 19--. Discovered that a sale on account to Ridgecrest Co. on February 26, S133, was incorrectly charged to the account of Ridgepoint Co., $297.00. Memorandum No. 40.

On February 28 the total of the Accounts Receivable Debit column in the sales journal was posted correctly. Accounts Receivable was debited for the amount of the column total which included the $297.00 involved in this transaction. No correction is needed for this amount.

The account of Ridgepoint Co. was debited for $297.00 when the account of Ridgecrest Co. should have been debited. The correcting entry involves only subsidiary ledger accounts. Ridgecrest Co.'s account is debited for $297.00 to record the charge sale in the correct account. Ridgepoint Co.'s account is credited for $297.00 to cancel the incorrect entry. The general journal entry to record this correcting entry is shown in Illustration 20-14.

ACCOUNTS RECEIVABLE LEDGER
Ridgecrest Co.

Mar. 12	297.00	

Ridgepoint Co.

Feb. 26	297.00	Mar. 12	297.00

FYI

Errors in the accounts receivable ledger are usually discovered when customer statements are prepared or after a customer examines the statement and reports an error.

ILLUSTRATION 20-14

General journal entry to record a correcting entry affecting customer accounts

	DATE	ACCOUNT TITLE	DOC. NO.	POST. REF.	DEBIT	CREDIT	
15	12	Ridgecrest Co.	M40		297 00		15
16		Ridgepoint Co.				297 00	16
17							17
18							18

GENERAL JOURNAL   PAGE 3

The date, *12*, is written in the Date column. The name of the correct customer, *Ridgecrest Co.,* is entered in the Account Title column. The source document, *M40,* is entered in the Doc. No. column. The debit amount, *$297.00,* is recorded in the Debit column.

CLOSURE

1. Use Audit Your Understanding questions.
2. Review Summary Illustration 20-15, Summary of Journalizing and Posting Using a General Journal.

On the next line, the name of the incorrectly charged customer, *Ridgepoint Co.*, is entered in the Account Title column. This account name is indented about one centimeter. The credit amount, *$297.00*, is recorded in the Credit column.

Posting from a General Journal

Each amount in the Debit and Credit columns of a general journal is posted to the account or accounts named in the Account Title column. The two general journal entries discussed in this chapter are posted in the same way as described in Chapter 19.

A summary of the procedure for journalizing and posting transactions using a general journal is shown in Summary Illustration 20-15.

PREPARING A SCHEDULE OF ACCOUNTS RECEIVABLE

FYI

A schedule of accounts receivable is prepared before financial statements are prepared to prove the accounts receivable ledger.

A listing of customer accounts, account balances, and total amount due from all customers is known as a schedule of accounts receivable. A schedule of accounts receivable is prepared before financial statements are prepared to prove the accounts receivable ledger. If the total amount shown on a schedule of accounts receivable equals the accounts receivable controlling account balance in the general ledger, the accounts receivable ledger is proved. Preparation of a schedule of accounts receivable is described in Chapter 13.

ORDER OF POSTING FROM SPECIAL JOURNALS

AUDIT YOUR UNDERSTANDING

1. Contra revenue account in the operating revenue division.
2. Sales Tax Payable is debited (decreased).
3. Accounts receivable ledger.

Audit Your Understanding

1. What kind of account is Sales Returns and Allowances and what is its chart of accounts division?
2. What is the effect on Sales Tax Payable when a sales return is recorded?
3. What ledger needs to be corrected if a sale on account has been journalized and posted to the wrong customer?

Items affecting customer or vendor accounts are posted often during the month. Some businesses post daily so that the balances of the subsidiary ledger accounts will be up to date. Since general ledger account balances are needed only when financial statements are prepared, the general ledger accounts may be posted less often during the month. All items, including the totals of special columns, must be posted before a trial balance is prepared.

The best order in which to post the journals is listed below.

1. Sales journal.
2. Purchases journal.
3. General journal.
4. Cash receipts journal.
5. Cash payments journal.

This order of posting usually puts the debits and credits in the accounts in the order the transactions occurred.

TEACHING STRATEGIES: DIFFERENT LEARNING STYLES

Tactile Learner. The tactile learner can use a group of index cards to represent the general ledger. Each card should represent an account and should have 3 vertical lines to distinguish between the debit and credit columns and balance columns. Have the tactile learner post each example of a journal entry to the appropriate cards (accounts).

Summary of journalizing and posting using a general journal

1 All transactions that cannot be recorded in any of the special journals are recorded in the general journal.

2 Amounts in the Debit column are posted frequently to the general ledger.

3 Amounts in the Credit column are posted frequently to the general ledger.

4 Amounts debited or credited to **Accounts Receivable** are posted to the named customer account in the accounts receivable ledger.

5 Correcting entries involving only subsidiary ledger accounts are posted only to the appropriate subsidiary ledger.

INTERNATIONAL SALES

With the improvement in communications and transportation, international trade has increased. Businesses throughout the world are finding it necessary to buy and sell products and services to and from businesses in foreign countries.

CHAPTER 20   Recording Sales and Cash Receipts Using Special Journals   **537**

TEACHING STRATEGIES: DIFFERENT LEARNING STYLES

Visual Learner. When learning how to post, the visual learner would prefer to see how the posting process works. To encourage visual learners, therefore, the instructor could use a transparency to assist in the lecture. The transparency could be (1) a blank transparency that the instructor completes or (2) a prepared transparency that uses arrows to trace the steps involved in posting.

LESSON PLAN 20-4

Materials

- Student pages 537–543
- Transparencies: M, Blank General Journal; O, Blank Cash Receipts Journal; 20-2, Chapter Summary
- Assess: Problem Test Chapter 20, MicroExam Chapter 20, Unit Problem Test 6, Objective Test 6

Objectives (Enabling Performance Tasks)

a. Define accounting terms related to sales and cash receipts.

b. Identify accounting concepts and practices related to sales and cash receipts.

c. Analyze transactions affecting sales and cash receipts.

d. Journalize and post transactions related to sales and cash receipts.

- Recording sales and cash receipts transactions in special sales and cash receipts journals was presented earlier in this chapter. In this lesson, we will look at how international sales transactions are arranged between countries.

- Introduce new vocabulary: exports, imports, contract of sale, letter of credit, bill of lading, commercial invoice, draft, sight draft, time draft, trade acceptance.

FYI

As the business environment becomes more international, college accounting programs are adding international courses to the curriculum. These courses will enable accountants to appreciate and adapt to different cultures.

FYI

The International Chamber of Commerce publishes *Incoterms* to attempt to coordinate international sales. This set of international rules interprets common sales terms used in foreign trade which are adopted by most international trade associations.

Goods or services shipped out of a seller's home country to a foreign country are called **exports**. Businesses may increase their volume of sales by expanding into the export markets.

Goods or services bought from a foreign country and brought into a buyer's home country are called **imports**. Businesses may be able to import materials or services that are not available or are less expensive than within their own country. Thus, many companies have entered into the export and import markets to maintain their competitiveness and provide the products and services to meet customer demand.

International Sales

Selling merchandise to individuals or other businesses within one's own country, generally referred to as domestic sales, is much simpler than international sales.

Most domestic sales are sold for cash or on account after reviewing and approving a customer's credit. Because all transactions in the U. S. are covered by the same universal commercial law code and the same accounting standards, many transactions are based on trust. A customer with approved credit orders merchandise. The merchandise is shipped and an invoice is sent by the vendor. After receiving the merchandise and invoice, the customer pays the vendor.

However, because of the increased complexities of international sales, several issues must be considered. The lack of a uniform commercial law code among countries makes settlement of disputes more difficult. Greater distances and sometimes more complex transportation methods increase the time to complete the transaction. The reduced ability to determine a customer's financial condition and ability to take legal action if a customer does not pay increases the risk of uncollected amounts. Unstable political conditions in some countries may affect the ability to receive payments from those countries. Therefore, most businesses dealing in exports and/or imports follow a general process in international trade that insures the vendor receives payment for merchandise sold and the customer receives the merchandise ordered.

Processing and Accounting for International Sales

World Wide, Inc., located in Minneapolis, Minnesota, contracts to sell $20,000.00 of merchandise to Gonzalez Compañía in Mexico City, D. F., Mexico. World Wide and Gonzalez follow a procedure for their transaction that is used frequently for international sales. The summary of general procedures for international sales is shown in Illustration 20-16.

A document that details all the terms agreed to by seller and buyer for a sales transaction is called a **contract of sale**. World Wide and Gonzalez agreed to the terms of a contract of sale. The contract includes a description and quantity of merchandise, price, point of delivery, packing and marking instructions, shipping information, insurance provisions, and method of payment. The contract

538

PART 4   Accounting for a Merchandising Business Organized as a Corporation

---

APPLIED SKILLS: WRITING ACROSS THE CURRICULUM

Writing paragraphs and short essays. The Cases for Critical Thinking are short, practical applications of the accounting principles developed in the chapter. Some cases are planned to present problems related to the chapter but not specifically discussed and answered in the chapter. These cases present an opportunity for critical thinking and decision making. These cases also require more than a short objective-type response. Therefore, they provide ideal practice in writing paragraphs and short essays.

SUMMARY ILLUSTRATION 20-16

General procedures for international sales

1 Seller and buyer prepare a contract of sale.

2 Buyer applies for letter of credit to buyer's bank. Buyer's bank approves application and sends letter of credit to seller's bank. Seller's bank delivers letter of credit to seller.

3 Seller verifies letter of credit and ships merchandise.

4 Seller submits documents to seller's bank including (a) bill of lading, (b) commercial invoice, and (c) draft. Seller's bank forwards documents to buyer's bank.

5 Buyer's bank deducts amount of draft from buyer's account and sends amount to seller's bank.

6 Buyer's bank forwards documents to buyer. Buyer presents bill of lading and approved letter of credit to transportation company and receives merchandise.

7 Seller's bank receives payment from buyer's bank and deposits receipts in seller's account.

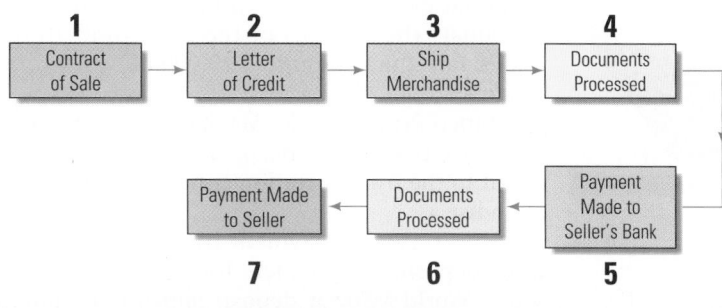

Cover student pages 537–543 "International Sales." Explain the definitions of exports and imports and the complex issues related to international sales. Explain the definitions of letter of credit and contract of sale. Explain the definitions of bill of lading, commercial invoice, draft, and sight draft. Explain why letters of credit are frequently used for international sales transactions.

price is $20,000.00 in U.S. dollars, and merchandise is to be delivered to Mexico City, D. F. The Gonzalez Compañía is to pay transportation charges. A letter issued by a bank guaranteeing that a named individual or business will be paid a specified amount provided stated conditions are met is called a **letter of credit**. The contract of sale specified a letter of credit as the method of payment.

Gonzalez prepared an application with its bank, Banco Nacional de Mexico, to issue a letter of credit. Banco Nacional de Mexico approved Gonzalez's application and issued the letter of credit. Banco Nacional de Mexico forwarded the letter of credit to a bank in the vicinity of the seller, First Bank in Minneapolis, Minnesota.

First Bank delivered the letter of credit to World Wide. World Wide reviewed the letter of credit to insure that the provisions in the letter agreed with the contract of sale. World Wide then shipped the merchandise.

In order for World Wide to collect payment, three documents specified in the letter of credit must be submitted to First Bank: (1) bill of lading, (2) commercial invoice, and (3) draft. A receipt signed by the authorized agent of a transportation company for merchandise received that also serves as a contract for the delivery of the merchandise is called a **bill of lading**. The transportation company

The United States federal government does not collect a sales tax. However, many countries of the world do collect what is referred to as a "value added tax" or VAT. A value added tax is basically a national sales tax.

CHAPTER 20   Recording Sales and Cash Receipts Using Special Journals   **539**

APPLIED SKILLS: WORD PROCESSING

If you wish to integrate word processing into your accounting course, you may direct students to answer the end-of-chapter Accounting Terms, Questions for Individual Study, and Cases for Critical Thinking using their word processing software.

CAREERS IN ACCOUNTING

LETTER-OF-CREDIT DOCUMENT EXAMINER

- *Examines letters of credit for accuracy and completeness*
- *Verifies document calculations*
- *Instructs workers in preparing amendments to letters of credit*
- *Contacts foreign banks to obtain required documents*
- *Authorizes method of payment against letter of credit*

GENERAL LEDGER

Cash

| Apr. 1 | 20,000.00 | |

Sales

| | Apr. 1 | 20,000.00 |

ILLUSTRATION 20-17

sends the bill of lading to World Wide when the merchandise is shipped. World Wide then prepares the other two documents. A statement prepared by the seller of merchandise addressed to the buyer showing a detailed listing and description of merchandise sold, including prices and terms, is called a **commercial invoice**. A written, signed, and dated order from one party ordering another party, usually a bank, to pay money to a third party is called a **draft**. A draft is sometimes referred to as a bill of exchange. A draft payable on sight, when the holder presents it for payment is called a **sight draft**.

First Bank examines the documents submitted by World Wide to insure that all terms of sale are in compliance with the letter of credit. First Bank then forwards the documents to Gonzalez Compañía's bank, Banco Nacional de Mexico. Banco Nacional de Mexico examines the documents to insure they are in compliance with the terms and conditions of the letter of credit. When Banco Nacional de Mexico determines all documents are in compliance, it deducts the amount of the sight draft from Gonzalez's account and sends that amount, $20,000.00, to World Wide's bank, First Bank.

Banco Nacional de Mexico then forwards the documents to Gonzalez Compañía. By presenting the bill of lading and letter of credit to the transportation company, Gonzalez can receive the merchandise.

After receiving payment from Banco Nacional de Mexico, First Bank deposits the payment for the sale in World Wide's account and sends World Wide a deposit slip for the amount deposited. After receiving the deposit slip from First Bank, World Wide prepares a memorandum as a source document for the cash received. The sale is then recorded as a cash sale.

April 1, 19--. Recorded international cash sale, $20,000.00. Memorandum 482.

Cash is debited to show the increase in the balance of this asset account. Sales is credited to show the increase in this revenue account.

The cash receipts journal entry to journalize this sales transaction is shown in Illustration 20-17.

Journalizing a cash sales transaction is described in more detail in Chapter 12.

Cash receipts journal entry to record a sight draft for an international sales transaction

						GENERAL		ACCOUNTS RECEIVABLE CREDIT	SALES CREDIT	SALES TAX PAYABLE		SALES DISCOUNT DEBIT	CASH DEBIT	
						1	2	3	4	5	6	7	8	
	DATE	ACCOUNT TITLE	DOC. NO.	POST. REF.		DEBIT	CREDIT			DEBIT	CREDIT			
1	Apr. 1	√	M482	√					20 000 00				20 000 00	1
2														2

CASH RECEIPTS JOURNAL — PAGE *48*

Sales taxes are normally paid only on sales to a consumer. World Wide's sale is to Gonzalez Compañía, another business. Therefore, sales tax is not collected.

The sales and collection process World Wide followed assured World Wide of receiving payment for its sale and Gonzalez Compañía of receiving the merchandise it ordered.

Time Drafts

World Wide, Inc. sold $10,000.00 of merchandise to Alvarez Hermanos, located in Merida, Yucatan, Mexico. The contract of sale with Alvarez was similar to the contract with Gonzalez Compañía, with one exception. World Wide agreed to delay receipt of payment 60 days. A draft that is payable at a fixed or determinable future time after it is accepted is called a **time draft**.

> A time draft is similar to a promissory note. Promissory notes are described in Chapter 24.

The sales process with Alvarez is the same as with Gonzalez except World Wide submits with the documentation a time draft due 60 days from the date the draft is accepted. On April 10, all documentation for the Alvarez sale is verified to be correct by the seller's and buyer's banks, and World Wide's time draft is accepted.

After verifying the documentation, Alvarez's bank, Banco Nacional de Mexico, returns the accepted time draft to World Wide and forwards the other documents to Alvarez Hermanos. Alvarez can receive the merchandise by presenting the bill of lading and letter of credit to the transportation company.

April 10, 19--. Received a 60-day, time draft from Alvarez Hermanos for international sale of merchandise, $10,000.00. Time Draft No. 8.

Time Drafts Receivable is debited for $10,000.00 to show the increase in this asset account. Sales is credited to show the increase in this revenue account.

The general journal entry to record this transaction is shown in Illustration 20-18.

When Alvarez Hermanos' time draft is due and presented to Alvarez's bank, Banco Nacional de Mexico, the bank pays the draft. The payment process is the same as the payment of Gonzalez Compañía's sight draft.

At least 83 countries in the world have a value added tax (VAT), including 21 of the 24 major industrial powers. The European Community adopted VAT in 1967 and Canada and Japan also have VATs.

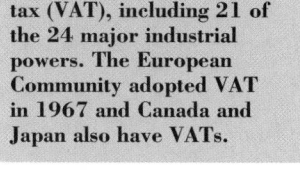

GENERAL LEDGER
Time Drafts Receivable

| Apr. 10 | 10,000.00 | |

Sales

| | Apr. 10 | 10,000.00 |

ILLUSTRATION 20-18

General journal entry to record a time draft receivable for a sale of merchandise

			GENERAL JOURNAL				PAGE 3	
	DATE		ACCOUNT TITLE	DOC. NO.	POST. REF.	DEBIT	CREDIT	
6	*Apr.*	*10*	*Time Draft Receivable*	TD8		10000 00		6
7			*Sales*				10000 00	7

ASSESS

- Administer Problem Test Chapter 20.
- Administer a MicroExam for Chapter 20.
- Administer Objective Test 6.
- Administer Unit Problem Test 6.

GENERAL LEDGER
Cash

| June 9 | 10,000.00 | |

Time Drafts Receivable

| | June 9 | 10,000.00 |

June 9, 19--. Received cash for the value of Time Draft No. 8, $10,000.00. Receipt No. 962.

Cash is debited for $10,000.00 to show the increase in the balance of this asset account. Time Drafts Receivable is credited for $10,000.00 to show the decrease in the balance of this asset account.

The cash receipts journal entry to record this transaction is shown in Illustration 20-19.

ILLUSTRATION 20-19   Cash receipts journal entry to record receipt of cash for a time draft receivable

CASH RECEIPTS JOURNAL   PAGE 61

					1	2	3	4	5	6	7	8
	DATE	ACCOUNT TITLE	DOC. NO.	POST. REF.	GENERAL DEBIT	GENERAL CREDIT	ACCOUNTS RECEIVABLE CREDIT	SALES CREDIT	SALES TAX PAYABLE DEBIT	SALES TAX PAYABLE CREDIT	SALES DISCOUNT DEBIT	CASH DEBIT
9	June 9 19--	Time Draft Receivable	R962			10000 00						10000 00	9
10													10
11													11

FYI

The minimum value added tax (VAT) in the European Community is 15%; however, there is usually no additional local sales tax.

AUDIT YOUR UNDERSTANDING

1. Bill of lading.
2. Receiving payment for the sale.
3. Receiving the merchandise.

Audit Your Understanding

1. What kind of receipt can also serve as a contract for the delivery of merchandise?

2. In international sales, what is the main concern of the business that is selling merchandise?

3. In international sales, what is the main concern of the business that is purchasing merchandise?

The process used by World Wide, Inc. for international sales relies upon letters of credit from banks to assure receipt of payment for those sales. Occasionally, World Wide grants an extension of time for payment to long-time international customers by submitting a time draft.

Trade Acceptances

A form signed by a buyer at the time of a sale of merchandise in which the buyer promises to pay the seller a specified sum of money usually at a stated time in the future is called a **trade acceptance**. A trade acceptance is similar to a draft except a draft is generally paid by a bank and a trade acceptance by the buyer. A seller generally has much more assurance of receiving payment from a bank than from a buyer. Because of the many complexities, few businesses use trade acceptances in international sales. Some businesses, however, use trade acceptances for domestic sales to very reliable customers.

SUMMARY OF RECORDING SALES AND CASH RECEIPTS USING SPECIAL JOURNALS

The charts shown in Summary Illustration 20-20 on page 543 summarize the entries for sales, cash receipts, and other transactions in special journals and a general journal.

SUMMARY ILLUSTRATION 20-20

Summary of recording sales and cash receipts using special journals

Transaction	SALES JOURNAL		
	1	2	3
	Accounts Receivable Debit	Sales Credit	Sales Tax Payable Credit
Sales on account	X	X	X

Transactions	CASH RECEIPTS JOURNAL							
	1	2	3	4	5	6	7	8
	General		Accounts Receivable Credit	Sales Credit	Sales Tax Payable		Sales Discount Debit	Cash Debit
	Debit	Credit			Debit	Credit		
Cash receipts from sales				X		X		X
Cash receipts on account with sales discount			X		X		X	X
Cash receipts from sight drafts for international sales				X				X
Cash receipts from time draft receivables		X						X

Transactions	GENERAL JOURNAL	
	Debit	Credit
Sales returns and allowances	X	X
Correcting entry	X	X
International sale with a time draft receivable	X	X

1. **sales journal:** A special journal used to record only sales on account transactions. (p. 519)

2. **cash receipts journal:** A special journal used to record only cash receipt transactions. (p. 523)

3. **sales discount:** A cash discount on sales. (p. 525)

4. **sales return:** Credit allowed a customer for the sales price of returned merchandise, resulting in a decrease in the vendor's accounts receivable. (p. 531)

5. **sales allowance:** Credit allowed a customer for part of the sales price of merchandise that is not returned, resulting in a decrease in the vendor's accounts receivable. (p. 531)

6. **credit memorandum:** A form prepared by the vendor showing the amount deducted for returns and allowances. (p. 531)

7. **exports:** Goods or services shipped out of a seller's home country to a foreign country. (p. 538)

8. **imports:** Goods or services bought from a foreign country and brought into a buyer's home country. (p. 538)

9. **contract of sale:** A document that details all the terms agreed to by seller and buyer for a sales transaction. (p. 538)

10. **letter of credit:** A letter issued by a bank guaranteeing that a named individual or business will be paid a specified amount provided stated conditions are met. (p. 539)

11. **bill of lading:** A receipt signed by the authorized agent of a transportation company for merchandise received that also serves as a contract for the delivery of the merchandise. (p. 539)

12. **commercial invoice:** A statement prepared by the seller of merchandise addressed to the buyer showing a detailed listing and description of merchandise sold, including prices and terms. (p. 540)

13. **draft:** A written, signed, and dated order from one party ordering another party, usually a bank, to pay money to a third party. (p. 540)

14. **sight draft:** A draft payable on sight, when the holder presents it for payment. (p. 540)

15. **time draft:** A draft that is payable at a fixed or determinable future time after it is accepted. (p. 541)

16. **trade acceptance:** A form signed by a buyer at the time of a sale of merchandise in which the buyer promises to pay the seller a specified sum of money, usually at a stated time in the future. (p. 542)

ACCOUNTING TERMS   EPT(a)

What is the meaning of each of the following?

1. sales journal	7. exports	13. draft
2. cash receipts journal	8. imports	14. sight draft
3. sales discount	9. contract of sale	15. time draft
4. sales return	10. letter of credit	16. trade acceptance
5. sales allowance	11. bill of lading	
6. credit memorandum	12. commercial invoice	

QUESTIONS FOR INDIVIDUAL STUDY   EPT(b)

1. Why do some companies sell merchandise on account?
2. Which accounting concept is being applied when revenue is recorded as merchandise is sold regardless of when cash is received?
3. Why does Celluphone post frequently to customer accounts?
4. What objectives do companies with numerous transactions involving sizable amounts of cash frequently have?
5. Why do companies offer sales discounts?
6. What is the normal account balance of the sales discount account?
7. Are businesses that offer sales discounts required to use a sales discount account?
8. When cash is received on account within the discount period and sales tax is charged on the amount less the discount, what amounts must be calculated to prepare the journal entry for receipt of cash?
9. What general ledger accounts are affected, and how, by a cash receipt from a customer on account when there is a sales discount and sales tax?
10. Which amounts in a cash receipts journal are posted separately to general ledger accounts?
11. What general ledger accounts are affected, and how, by a sales returns and allowances transaction?
12. How can an error involving posting a debit amount to the wrong customer account be corrected?
13. Why have many businesses entered into the export and import business?
14. What are some of the issues that must be considered before making international sales?
15. What two purposes does a bill of lading serve?
16. How does a sight draft differ from a time draft?
17. Why do many companies dealing in international sales rely upon letters of credit from banks?
18. How does a trade acceptance differ from a draft?

CASES FOR CRITICAL THINKING   EPT(b)

CASE 1 Latson Company uses a 3-column sales journal with special amount columns similar to the one in this chapter. The company records sales tax payable at the time a sale on account is made. Christopher Chenault, the office manager, questions this practice. He suggests that sales tax payable not be recorded until cash is actually collected for a sale. Which procedure is preferable? Why?

CASE 2 Regents Office Supply sells office supplies to many local firms. Most of the store's sales are made on account. In order to encourage prompt payment, Regents offers a sales discount for those who pay within the discount period. Regents is considering changing its payroll policy for sales personnel from a salary plan to a commission-on-sales plan in order to encourage sales personnel to increase their sales efforts. Commissions would be 5% of sales. Various sales personnel have asked you, the manager, whether commissions would be based on gross sales or on sales after sales discounts and returns and allowances. What should your response be? Explain.

DRILL 20-D1   Analyzing the journalizing of sales and cash receipts transactions

A form for analyzing transactions is given in the working papers that accompany this textbook.

INSTRUCTIONS:

Complete the form for each of the following transactions. In Column A, write the title of the account(s) debited. In Column B, write the title of the account(s) credited. In Column C, write the name of the journal in which the transaction is recorded. In Columns D and E, write the names of the journal amount column(s) in which debit and credit amounts are recorded. Transaction 1 is given as an example.

1. Sold merchandise on account to James Harding plus sales tax.
2. Recorded cash and credit card sales plus sales tax.
3. Received cash on account from Accent Company; no sales discount.
4. Granted credit to Richco for merchandise returned plus sales tax.
5. Sold merchandise on account to Kennel Co. plus sales tax.
6. Granted credit to Silver Star for damaged merchandise plus sales tax.
7. Discovered that a sale on account to Rebecca Hind was incorrectly charged to Rebecca Hindle.
8. Received cash on account from Forms Co. less sales discount and sales tax.

The solution to Drill 20-D1 is needed to complete Drill 20-D2.

DRILL 20-D2   Analyzing the posting of sales and cash receipts transactions

The solution to Drill 20-D1 is needed to complete Drill 20-D2.

A form for analyzing transactions is given in the working papers that accompany this textbook.

INSTRUCTIONS:

1. In Column A, write the titles of the accounts affected by each transaction in Drill 20-D1.

2. Place a check mark in Column B if the amount is posted individually to the general ledger. Place a check mark in Column C if the amount is posted individually to the accounts receivable ledger. Place a check mark in Column D if the amount is not posted individually to any ledger. Transaction 1 is given as an example.

DRILL 20-D3   Calculating sales discounts and cash receipts

A form for recording the answers to this drill is given in the working papers that accompany this textbook.

INSTRUCTIONS:

1. Information about six sales invoices is given at the top of the next page. Use a sales tax rate of 6% and a cash discount rate of 2%. For Sales No. S1, S2, S3, and S4, calculate the sales discount amount, sales tax reduction, and amount of the cash receipt after the discount is taken.

2. For Sales No. S5 and S6, calculate the sales tax on the credit memorandum amount. Also calculate the sales discount amount, sales tax reduction, and amount of the cash receipt for the invoices less the credit memorandums.

CHAPTER 20   Recording Sales and Cash Receipts Using Special Journals   **545**

1. To encourage additional sales. (p. 519)
2. Realization of Revenue. (p. 519)
3. So that each customer account will show an up-to-date balance. (p. 521)
4. (a) To avoid the loss of any cash. (b) To efficiently account for the cash. (p. 523)
5. To encourage prompt payment of sales on account. (p. 525)
6. A debit. (pp. 525–526)
7. No. The sales account could be debited for the amount of the discount. However, better information is provided if these amounts are debited to a separate account, Sales Discount. (p. 526)
8. (1) Sales discount. (2) Sales tax liability reduction. (3) Cash received. (p. 526)
9. Cash, Sales Discount, and Sales Tax Payable are debited; Accounts Receivable is credited. (p. 527)
10. The amounts entered in the General amount columns of the cash receipts journal. (p. 529)
11. Sales Returns and Allowances and Sales Tax Payable are debited; Accounts Receivable is credited. (p. 534)
12. By recording a correcting entry in the general journal. Debit the customer account that should have been debited; credit the customer account that was incorrectly debited. (pp. 535–536)
13. To maintain their competitiveness and provide the products and services to meet customer demand. (p. 538)
14. The lack of a uniform commercial law code among countries makes settlement of disputes more difficult. Greater distances and sometimes more complex transportation methods increase the time to complete the transaction. The reduced ability to determine a customer's financial condition and ability to take legal action if a customer does not pay increases the risk of uncollected amounts. Unstable political conditions in some countries may affect the ability to receive payments from those countries. (p. 538)
15. (1) As a receipt signed by an authorized agent of a transportation company for merchandise received. (2) As a contract for the delivery of the merchandise. (p. 539)
16. A sight draft is payable on sight when the holder presents it for payment. A time draft is payable at a fixed or determinable future time after it is accepted. (pp. 540–541)
17. To assure receipt of payment for those sales. (p. 542)
18. A draft is generally paid by a bank and a trade acceptance is generally paid by the buyer. (p. 542)

Drill 20-D1   Journal recorded for Trans. 1, Sales; 2, Cash Receipts; 3, Cash Receipts; 4, General; 5, Sales; 6, General; 7, General; 8, Cash Receipts

Drill 20-D2   Accts. posted to General Ledger: Trans. 4, Sales R & A, Sales Tax Pay., Accts. Rec.; Trans. 6, Sales R and A, Sales Tax Pay., Accts. Rec.; Accts. posted to Accts. Rec. Ledger: James Harding, Accent Co., Richco, Kennel Co., Silver Star, Rebecca Hind, Rebecca Hindle, Forms Co.

Drill 20-D3   Cash receipt amount column: $1,817.90; $992.05; $2,665.77; $3,761.49; $1,532.23; $2,770.48

Case 1 The company is currently using the preferred procedure. The sales tax is based on a percentage of sales. The Realization of Revenue concept emphasizes that revenue (sales) is recorded when merchandise is sold. Therefore, sales tax is owed when the sale is made. Sales tax payable should be recorded at the same time the sale is recorded. Since the tax is owed, liabilities will be understated if Sales Tax Payable is not credited.

Case 2 The company needs to decide what amount the commissions will be based on. Then everyone concerned should be provided with that information. Actual revenue realized by the company is sales less sales discounts and sales returns and allowances. Therefore, if commissions are based on the company's realized sales, commissions will be based on sales less discounts and returns and allowances. However, this may result in loss of employee goodwill. Also, the additional administrative efforts required to relate all discounts and returns and allowances to the salesperson who sold the merchandise in order to determine that salesperson's net sales may not be worth the extra effort.

If the company decides to pay commissions on gross sales, management should be alert for excessive returns and allowances. A salesperson, in an effort to increase commissions, could persuade customer friends to order excessive amounts of merchandise and then return them. If sales commissions are paid only on net sales (gross sales less discounts, returns, and allowances), this type of collusion between a salesperson and customers would not be possible.

Sale No.	Sale Amount	Sales Tax Amount	Invoice Amount	Credit Memo. Amount
S1	1,750.00	105.00	1,855.00	—
S2	955.00	57.30	1,012.30	—
S3	2,566.20	153.97	2,720.17	—
S4	3,621.00	217.26	3,838.26	—
S5	1,625.00	97.50	1,722.50	150.00
S6	2,892.00	173.52	3,065.52	225.00

APPLICATION PROBLEMS   EPT(c,d)

PROBLEM 20-1   Journalizing and posting sales on account transactions

The general ledger and accounts receivable ledger accounts for Capitol Sales Company are given in the working papers accompanying this textbook. The balances are recorded as of March 1 of the current year.

INSTRUCTIONS:

1. Journalize the following sales on account transactions completed during March of the current year. Use page 3 of a sales journal. The sales tax rate is 8%. The abbreviation for sales invoice is S.

Mar. 1. Sold merchandise on account to Daniel Noble, $204.00, plus sales tax, $16.32; total, $220.32. S58.

  3. Sold merchandise on account to Austin Equipment Co., $330.65, plus sales tax, $26.45; total, $357.10. S59.

  5. Sold merchandise on account to Crawford Company, $145.25, plus sales tax, $11.62; total, $156.87. S60.

  8. Sold merchandise on account to Theresa Briggs, $215.90, plus sales tax, $17.27; total, $233.17. S61.

  10. Sold merchandise on account to Tensil Company, $154.00, plus sales tax, $12.32; total, $166.32. S62.

  12. Sold merchandise on account to Crawford Company, $198.55, plus sales tax, $15.88; total, $214.43. S63.

  15. Sold merchandise on account to Midori Saga, $114.00, plus sales tax, $9.12; total, $123.12. S64.

  20. Sold merchandise on account to Austin Equipment Co., $234.90, plus sales tax, $18.79; total, $253.69. S65.

  26. Sold merchandise on account to Midori Saga, $233.00, plus sales tax, $18.64; total, $251.64. S66.

  31. Sold merchandise on account to Daniel Noble, $164.25, plus sales tax, $13.14; total, $177.39. S67.

2. Post each amount in the Accounts Receivable Debit column of the sales journal to the accounts receivable ledger.

3. Prove and rule the sales journal. Post the totals of the special columns.

PROBLEM 20-2 Journalizing and posting cash receipts transactions

The general ledger and accounts receivable ledger accounts for The General Store are given in the working papers accompanying this textbook. The balances are recorded as of May 1 of the current year.

INSTRUCTIONS:

1. Journalize the following cash receipts transactions completed during May of the current year. Use page 5 of a cash receipts journal. The General Store offers terms of 1/10, n/30. The sales tax rate is 8%. Source documents are abbreviated as follows: receipt, R; sales invoice, S; cash register tape, T.

May 2. Received cash on account from Brandon Company, $641.52, covering S219 for $648.00 ($600.00 plus sales tax, $48.00), less discount, $6.00, and less sales tax, $0.48. R65.

5. Received cash on account from Kitchen Kettle, $157.00, covering S223; no discount. R66.

7. Received cash on account from Jason Denison, $213.84, covering S218 for $216.00 ($200.00 plus sales tax, $16.00), less discount, $2.00, and less sales tax, $0.16. R67.

8. Received cash on account from Cynthia Anson, $320.76, covering S217 for $324.00 ($300.00 plus sales tax, $24.00), less discount, $3.00, and less sales tax, $0.24. R68.

14. Recorded cash and credit card sales, $7,177.00, plus sales tax, $574.16; total, $7,751.16. T14.

21. Received cash on account from Stan's Eatery, $463.00, covering S220; no discount. R69.

31. Recorded cash and credit card sales, $6,947.00, plus sales tax, $555.76; total, $7,502.76. T31.

2. Post each amount in the Accounts Receivable Credit column of the cash receipts journal to the accounts receivable ledger.

3. Prove the equality of debits and credits for the cash receipts journal.

4. Prove cash. The cash balance on hand on May 1 was $10,233.00. The total of the Cash Credit column of the cash payments journal for The General Store is $14,003.83. The balance on the next unused check stub on May 31 is $13,279.21.

5. Rule the cash receipts journal. Post the totals of the special columns.

PROBLEM 20-3 Journalizing and posting sales and cash receipts transactions

The general ledger and accounts receivable ledger accounts for Pierce Imports are given in the working papers accompanying this textbook. The balances are recorded as of June 1 of the current year.

INSTRUCTIONS:

1. Journalize the following transactions affecting sales and cash receipts completed during June of the current year. Use page 6 of a sales journal, a general journal, and a cash receipts journal. Pierce Imports offers terms of 1/10, n/30. The sales tax rate is 8%. Source documents are abbreviated as follows: credit memorandum, CM; memorandum, M; receipt, R; sales invoice, S; cash register tape, T.

June 3. Received cash on account from Beverly's Gift Shop, $300.22, covering S136 for $303.25 ($280.79 plus sales tax, $22.46), less discount, $2.81, and less sales tax, $0.22. R83.

4. Sold merchandise on account to Geno's, $416.25, plus sales tax, $33.30; total, $449.55. S152.

June 4. Recorded cash and credit card sales, $3,556.00, plus sales tax, $284.48; total, $3,840.48. T4.

7. Received cash on account from Geno's, $342.54, covering S147 for $346.00 ($320.37 plus sales tax, $25.63), less discount, $3.20, and less sales tax, $0.26. R84.

9. Received cash on account from Hana Victor, $614.79, covering S149 for $621.00 ($575.00 plus sales tax, $46.00), less discount, $5.75, and less sales tax, $0.46. R85.

9. Discovered that a sale on account to Nan and Jenkins Decorators on May 26, S145, was incorrectly charged to the account of Frank Finnely, $415.00 ($384.26 plus sales tax, $30.74). M27.

10. Received cash on account from Frank Finnely, $273.72, covering S150 for $276.48 ($256.00 plus sales tax, $20.48), less discount, $2.56, and less sales tax, $0.20. R86.

11. Sold merchandise on account to Hana Victor, $604.15, plus sales tax, $48.33; total, $652.48. S153.

11. Recorded cash and credit card sales, $4,122.00, plus sales tax, $329.76; total, $4,451.76. T11.

   Posting. Post the items that are to be posted individually. Post from the journals in this order: sales journal, general journal, and cash receipts journal.

14. Granted credit to The Import Shop for merchandise returned, $67.00, plus sales tax, $5.36, from S151; total, $72.36. CM31.

15. Sold merchandise on account to Beverly's Gift Shop, $414.00, plus sales tax, $33.12; total, $447.12. S154.

15. Sold merchandise on account to Susan Malta, $305.80, plus sales tax, $24.46; total, $330.26. S155.

17. Received cash on account from Nan and Jenkins Decorators, $415.00, covering M27; no discount. R87.

18. Recorded cash and credit card sales, $2,997.00, plus sales tax, $239.76; total, $3,236.76. T18.

   Posting. Post the items that are to be posted individually.

21. Sold merchandise on account to Frank Finnely, $348.00, plus sales tax, $27.84; total, $375.84. S156.

21. Received cash on account from The Import Shop, $851.64 (covering S151 less CM31), no discount. R88.

21. Received cash on account from Hana Victor, $645.96, covering S153 for $652.48 ($604.15 plus sales tax, $48.33), less discount, $6.04, and less sales tax, $0.48. R89.

22. Received cash on account from Geno's, $449.55, covering S152; no discount. R90.

24. Sold merchandise on account to Frank Finnely, $149.80, plus sales tax, $11.98; total, $161.78. S157.

25. Sold merchandise on account to The Import Shop, $415.50, plus sales tax, $33.24; total, $448.74. S158.

27. Sold merchandise on account to Nan and Jenkins Decorators, $637.00, plus sales tax, $50.96; total, $687.96. S159.

30. Received cash on account from Susan Malta, $475.75, covering S146; no discount. R91.

30. Recorded cash and credit card sales, $1,582.00, plus sales tax, $126.56; total, $1,708.56. T30.

   Posting. Post the items that are to be posted individually.

2. Prove and rule the sales journal. Post the totals of the special columns.
3. Prove the equality of debits and credits for the cash receipts journal.
4. Prove cash. The cash balance on hand on June 1 was $9,211.00. The total of the Cash Credit column of the cash payments journal for Pierce Imports is $15,672.58. The balance on the next unused check stub on June 30 is $11,145.15.
5. Rule the cash receipts journal. Post the totals of the special columns.
6. Prepare a schedule of accounts receivable similar to the one described in Chapter 13. Compare the schedule total with the balance of the accounts receivable account in the general ledger. The total and balance should be the same.

PROBLEM 20-4 Journalizing international sales transactions

INSTRUCTIONS:

1. Journalize the following international sales completed by Exports, Ltd. during April of the current year. Use page 8 of a cash receipts journal and a general journal. Sales tax is not charged on these sales. Source documents are abbreviated as follows: memorandum, M; time draft, TD, and receipt, R.

April 1. Recorded international cash sale, $25,000.00. M123.
    5. Received a 30-day time draft from Lih Fen Hwang for international sale of merchandise, $18,000.00. TD12.
    9. Received cash for the value of Time Draft No. 10, $23,000.00. R421.
   12. Recorded domestic cash sale, $17,500.00. M124.
   13. Received cash for the value of Time Draft No. 11, $15,000.00. R422.
   16. Recorded international cash sale, $32,800.00. M125.
   19. Received a 60-day time draft from Kittika Kamarsu for international sale of merchandise, $10,000.00. TD13.
   27. Recorded international cash sale, $41,200.00. M126.

2. Prove and rule the cash receipts journal.

ENRICHMENT PROBLEMS   EPT(c,d)

MASTERY PROBLEM 20-M Journalizing and posting sales and cash receipts transactions

The general ledger and accounts receivable accounts for Founders Corporation are given in the working papers accompanying this textbook. The balances are recorded as of February 1 of the current year. Use the following account titles.

PARTIAL GENERAL LEDGER		ACCOUNTS RECEIVABLE LEDGER	
Account No.	Account Title	Customer No.	Customer Name
1105	Cash	110	Andrew Anderson
1125	Accounts Receivable	120	Brady and Co.
2135	Sales Tax Payable	130	Jessica Howe
4105	Sales	140	Kindercraft
4110	Sales Discount	150	Alford Lein
4115	Sales Returns and Allowances	160	Mandon, Inc.
		170	Platter Company
		180	Glenda Stevens

INSTRUCTIONS:

1. Journalize the following transactions affecting sales and cash receipts completed during February of the current year. Use page 2 of a sales journal, a general journal, and a cash

receipts journal. Founders Corporation offers terms of 2/10, n/30. The sales tax rate is 8%. Source documents are abbreviated as follows: credit memorandum, CM; memorandum, M; receipt, R; sales invoice, S; cash register tape, T.

Feb. 1. Sold merchandise on account to Jessica Howe, $330.00, plus sales tax, $26.40; total, $356.40. S96.

1. Granted credit to Mandon, Inc., for merchandise returned, $48.00, plus sales tax, $3.84, from S90; total, $51.84. CM27.

5. Received cash on account from Platter Company, $423.36, covering S92 for $432.00 ($400.00 plus sales tax, $32.00), less discount, $8.00, and less sales tax, $0.64. R42.

8. Received cash on account from Glenda Stevens, $383.67, covering S95 for $391.50 ($362.50 plus sales tax, $29.00), less discount, $7.25, and less sales tax, $0.58. R43.

8. Recorded cash and credit card sales, $1,420.00, plus sales tax, $113.60; total, $1,533.60. T8.

Posting. Post the items that are to be posted individually. Post from the journals in this order: sales journal, general journal, and cash receipts journal.

9. Sold merchandise on account to Mandon, Inc., $214.00, plus sales tax, $17.12; total, $231.12. S97.

11. Received cash on account from Jessica Howe, $367.20, covering S88; no discount. R44.

11. Granted credit to Andrew Anderson for merchandise returned, $112.50, plus sales tax, $9.00, from S91; total $121.50. CM28.

12. Received cash on account from Kindercraft, $150.00, covering S87; no discount. R45.

12. Received cash on account from Mandon, Inc., $326.16 (covering S90 less CM27), no discount. R46.

12. Recorded cash and credit card sales, $2,215.00, plus sales tax, $177.20; total, $2,392.20. T12.

Posting. Post the items that are to be posted individually.

15. Received cash on account from Brady and Co., $404.56, covering S94; no discount. R47.

18. Sold merchandise on account to Platter Company, $205.00, plus sales tax, $16.40; total, $221.40. S98.

18. Received cash on account from Mandon, Inc., $226.50, covering S97 for $231.12 ($214.00 plus sales tax, $17.12), less discount, $4.28, and less sales tax, $0.34. R48.

19. Sold merchandise on account to Brady and Co., $420.00, plus sales tax, $33.60; total, $453.60. S99.

19. Recorded cash and credit card sales, $1,897.00, plus sales tax, $151.76; total, $2,048.76. T19.

Posting. Post the items that are to be posted individually.

22. Received cash on account from Jessica Howe, $356.40, covering S96; no discount. R49.

22. Discovered that a sale on account to Platter Company on January 15, S93, was incorrectly charged to the account of Alford Lein, $216.00 ($200.00 plus sales tax, $16.00). M52.

23. Sold merchandise on account to Kindercraft, $296.00, plus sales tax, $23.68; total, $319.68. S100.

23. Received cash on account from Andrew Anderson, $108.00 (covering S91 less CM28), no discount. R50.

Feb. 23. Received cash on account from Brady and Co., $444.53, covering S99 for $453.60 ($420.00 plus sales tax, $33.60), less discount, $8.40, and less sales tax, $0.67. R51.

25. Sold merchandise on account to Andrew Anderson, $356.00, plus sales tax, $28.48; total, $384.48. S101.

28. Received cash on account from Kindercraft, $313.29, covering S100 for $319.68 ($296.00 plus sales tax, $23.68), less discount, $5.92, and less sales tax, $0.47. R52.

28. Recorded cash and credit card sales, $2,197.00, plus sales tax, $175.76; total, $2,372.76. T28.

   Posting. Post the items that are to be posted individually.

2. Prove and rule the sales journal. Post the totals of the special columns.

3. Prove the equality of debits and credits for the cash receipts journal.

4. Prove cash. The cash balance on hand on February 1 was $6,354.00. The total of the Cash Credit column of the cash payments journal for Founders Corporation is $11,234.00. The balance on the next unused check stub on February 28 is $6,970.99.

5. Rule the cash receipts journal. Post the totals of the special columns.

6. Prepare a schedule of accounts receivable similar to the one described in Chapter 13. Compare the schedule total with the balance of the accounts receivable account in the general ledger. The total and balance should be the same.

CHALLENGE PROBLEM 20-C Journalizing and posting sales, purchases, cash receipts, and cash payments transactions

The general ledger, accounts receivable ledger, and accounts payable ledger accounts for Princess Company are given in the working papers accompanying this textbook. The balances are recorded as of April 1 of the current year.

AUTOMATED

MATHEMATICS

PARTIAL GENERAL LEDGER

Account No.	Account Title
1105	Cash
1110	Petty Cash
1125	Accounts Receivable
1140	Supplies
2115	Accounts Payable
2135	Sales Tax Payable
4105	Sales
4110	Sales Discount
4115	Sales Returns and Allowances
5105	Purchases
5110	Purchases Discount
5115	Purchases Returns and Allowances
6105	Advertising Expense
6130	Miscellaneous Expense
6140	Rent Expense
8105	Cash Short and Over

ACCOUNTS RECEIVABLE LEDGER

Customer No.	Customer Name
110	Barbra Almon
120	Bland Company
130	James Hart
140	Jefferson Co.
150	Linda Ponder

ACCOUNTS PAYABLE LEDGER

Vendor No.	Vendor Name
210	Dunn Supplies
220	Gibson Electric Co.
230	Roland and Barnes
240	Webb Co.

INSTRUCTIONS:

1. Journalize the following transactions affecting sales, purchases, cash receipts, and cash payments completed during April of the current year. Calculate and record sales tax on all sales and sales returns and allowances as described in this chapter. Use page 4 of a sales journal, a purchases journal, a general journal, a cash receipts journal, and a cash

CHECK FIGURES *(cont'd)*

Challenge Problem 20-C Sales journal totals: $3,534.84, $3,273.00, $261.84; Purchases journal total: $4,851.00; Cash receipts journal totals: $2,415.96, $9,991.00, $2.83, $799.28, $35.52, $13,167.89; Cash payments journal totals: $1,635.25, $6,481.68, $56.65, $8,060.28.

payments journal. Princess Company offers its customers terms of 2/10, n/30. The sales tax rate is 8%. Source documents are abbreviated as follows: check, C; credit memorandum, CM; debit memorandum, DM; memorandum, M; purchase invoice, P; receipt, R; sales invoice, S; cash register tape, T.

Apr. 1. Wrote a check for April rent, $850.00. C84.
1. Wrote a check to pay on account to Roland and Barnes, covering P74 for $366.00, less 1% discount. C85.
2. Cash was received on account from Jefferson Co., $545.08, covering S53 for $556.20 ($515.00 plus sales tax, $41.20), less discount and less sales tax on discount. R26.
2. Cash and credit card sales, $1,926.00, plus sales tax. T2.
  Posting. Post the items that are to be posted individually. Post the journals in this order: sales journal, purchases journal, general journal, cash receipts journal, and cash payments journal.
5. Merchandise was returned to Webb Co., $468.32, from P75. DM9.
6. Bland Company bought merchandise on account, $247.00, plus sales tax. S55.
6. Wrote a check for money owed to Gibson Electric Co., $1,945.00, covering P64; no discount. C86.
6. Received payment on account from Linda Ponder, $417.01, covering S54 for $425.52 ($394.00 plus sales tax, $31.52), less discount and less sales tax on discount. R27.
7. Bought supplies on credit from Dunn Supplies, $537.00. M15.
9. Cash was received on account from Barbra Almon, $330.48, covering S51; no discount. R28.
9. Recorded cash and credit card sales, $1,820.00, plus sales tax. T9.
  Posting. Post the items that are to be posted individually.
12. Merchandise was purchased on account from Gibson Electric Co., $1,675.00. P77.
13. Wrote a check for money owed to Webb Co., covering P75 for $3,010.00, less DM9, $468.32, and less 2% discount. C87.
14. Jefferson Co. bought merchandise on credit, $746.00, plus sales tax. S56.
14. Paid for advertising, $450.00. C88.
14. Issued a check on account to Dunn Supplies, $1,413.00, covering M14; no discount. C89.
15. Bland Company returned merchandise for credit, $126.00, plus sales tax, from S55. CM18.
16. Sold merchandise on account to Barbra Almon, $742.00, plus sales tax. S57.
16. Received a check on account from Bland Company, $128.07, covering S55 for $266.76 ($247.00 plus sales tax, $19.76), less CM18 ($126.00 plus sales tax), less discount and less sales tax on discount. R29.
16. Recorded cash and credit card sales, $2,246.00, plus sales tax. T16.
  Posting. Post the items that are to be posted individually.
19. Cash was received on account from James Hart, $167.40, covering S50; no discount. R30.
20. Merchandise was purchased on account from Roland and Barnes, $216.00. P78.
21. Sold merchandise on credit to Linda Ponder, $623.00, plus sales tax. S58.
23. Wrote a check for miscellaneous expense, $205.00. C90.
23. Received on account from Jefferson Co., $789.57, covering S56 for $805.68 ($746.00 plus sales tax, $59.68), less discount and less sales tax on discount. R31.
23. Cash and credit card sales, $2,152.00, plus sales tax. T23.
  Posting. Post the items that are to be posted individually.
26. Sold merchandise on account to Bland Company, $915.00, plus sales tax. S59.
26. Merchandise was purchased on account from Gibson Electric Co., $1,975.00. P79.
29. Paid cash on account to Roland and Barnes, covering P78 for $216.00, less 1% discount. C91.
29. Purchased merchandise on account from Webb Co., $985.00. P80.
30. Recorded cash and credit card sales, $1,847.00, plus sales tax. T30.

Apr. 30. Issued a check to replenish the petty cash fund, $130.25: supplies, $45.15; advertising, $60.00; miscellaneous, $22.50; cash short, $2.60. C92.

Posting. Post the items that are to be posted individually.

2. Prove and rule the sales journal. Post the totals of the special columns.
3. Total and rule the purchases journal. Post the total.
4. Prove the equality of debits and credits for the cash receipts and cash payments journals.
5. Prove cash. The cash balance on hand on April 1 was $7,690.00. The balance on the next unused check stub on April 30 is $12,797.61.
6. Rule the cash receipts journal. Post the totals of the special columns.
7. Rule the cash payments journal. Post the totals of the special columns.
8. Prepare a schedule of accounts receivable and a schedule of accounts payable similar to the ones described in Chapter 13. Compare each schedule total with the balance of the controlling account in the general ledger. The total and balance should be the same.

Recording Sales and Cash Receipts for a Corporation

Celluphone's manual journalizing and posting procedures for sales and cash receipts are described in Chapter 20. Integrating Automated Accounting Topic 8 describes procedures for using automated accounting software to journalize and post Celluphone's transactions. The Automated Accounting Problems contain instructions for using automated accounting software to solve Mastery Problem 20-M and Challenge Problem 20-C, Chapter 20.

AUTOMATED ACCOUNTING PROCEDURES FOR CELLUPHONE

Celluphone uses three input forms to batch sales and cash receipts transaction data for automated accounting.
1. Sales journal input form for sales on account.
2. Cash receipts journal input form for all cash receipts.
3. General journal input form for all other transactions.

554

RECORDING SALES ON ACCOUNT

Celluphone batches sales on account transactions and records them on a sales journal input form.

> *March 1, 19--. Sold merchandise on account to DTex Imports, $1,600.00, plus sales tax, $128.00; total, $1,728.00. Sales Invoice No. 148.*

The journal entry to record this transaction is on lines 1 and 2 of the sales journal input form shown in Illustration T8-1.

The run date, *03/31/--*, is written in the space provided at the top of the form.

On line 1, the date of the transaction, *03/01*, is entered in the Date column. The customer number, *120*, is recorded in the Customer No. column. The source document number, *S148*, is written in the Invoice No. column. The general ledger account number for Sales, *4105*, is entered in the Account No. column. The Debit column is left blank. The automated accounting software automatically makes the debit to Accounts Receivable. The sale on account amount, *$1,600.00*, is recorded in the Credit column.

On line 2 for a sales on account transaction, the Date, Customer No., and Invoice Amount columns are left blank. The general ledger account number for Sales Tax Payable, *2135*, is written in the Account No. column. The sales tax amount, *$128.80*, is entered in the Credit column.

ILLUSTRATION T8-1

Sales journal input form with a sale on account transaction entered

RUN DATE __03/31/--__
MM DD YY

SALES JOURNAL
Input Form

	DATE MM/DD	CUSTOMER NO.	INVOICE NO.	INVOICE AMOUNT	ACCOUNT NO.	DEBIT	CREDIT	
1	03 01	120	S148	1728 00	4105		1600 00	1
2	/				2135		128 00	2
3	02	150	S149	11546 80	4105		10691 48	3
4	/				2135		855 32	4
5	03	140	S150	39463 20	4105		36540 00	5
6					2135		2923 20	6
7	05	110	S160	10368 00	4105		9600 00	7
8	/				2135		768 00	8
9	22	140	S161	18360 00	4105		17000 00	9
10					2135		1360 00	10
11	25	150	S162	4453 50	4105		4123 61	11
12	/				2135		329 89	12
13	27	120	S163	1484 90	4105		1374 91	13
14	/				2135		109 99	14
15	31	130	S221	1404 00	4105		1300 00	15
16	/				2135		104 00	16
25	/							25

NOTE: A debit to Accounts Receivable is made automatically by the software.

TEACHING STRATEGIES: USING VISUALS

Using Transparencies AA-2 Blank General Journal Input Form, AA-5 Blank Sales Journal Input Form, and AA-6 Blank Cash Receipts Journal Input Form will help students understand the journalizing process.

Cover student pages 554–562 "Automated Accounting Procedures for Celluphone," "Recording Sales on Account," "Recording Cash Receipts," "Recording Other Transactions," and "Processing Sales, Cash Receipts, and Other Transactions." This lesson focuses on recording and processing sales on account, cash receipts, and sales returns and allowances transactions.

As the lesson progresses, review the definitions of sales discount, sales return, sales allowance, and credit memorandum. The two types of cash receipts should also be reviewed during this lesson.

RECORDING CASH RECEIPTS

Celluphone batches cash receipts and records them on a cash receipts journal input form. Two types of cash receipts are recorded. (1) Direct receipts. (2) Receipts on account. A direct receipt transaction does not affect Accounts Receivable, whereas a receipt on account transaction does affect Accounts Receivable.

Cash and Credit Card Sales

A cash or credit card sales transaction is a direct receipt not affecting Accounts Receivable.

March 1, 19--. Recorded cash and credit card sales, $2,870.00, plus sales tax, $229.60; total, $3,099.60. Cash Register Tape No. 1.

The journal entry to record this transaction is on lines 1 and 2 of Illustration T8-2.

The run date, *03/31/--*, is written in the space provided at the top of the form.

On line 1, the date of the transaction, *03/01*, is written in the Date column. The source document number, *T1*, is entered in the

Each month's transactions begin on new input forms.

ILLUSTRATION T8-2

Cash receipts journal input form with transactions entered

RUN DATE **03,31,--**
MM DD YY

CASH RECEIPTS JOURNAL
Input Form

	DATE MM/DD	CUSTOMER NO.	REFERENCE	ACCOUNTS REC. CREDIT	ACCOUNT NO.	DEBIT	CREDIT	
1	03,01		T1		4105		2870 00	1
2	/				2135		229 60	2
3	,02	150	R227	297 00				3
4	,03	130	R228	14525 35	4110	134 49		4
5	/				2135	10 76		5
6	,04	120	R229	486 00				6
7	,05	150	R230	7462 45				7
8	,06	110	R231	10411 20	4110	104 11		8
9	/				2135	8 33		9
10	,11	120	R232	1728 00	4110	16 00		10
11	/				2135	1 28		11
12	,12	150	R233	11546 80				12
13	,13	140	R234	39463 20	4110	365 40		13
14	/				2135	29 23		14
15	,15		T15		4105		63540 00	15
16	/				2135		5083 20	16
17	,31		T31		4105		2840 00	17
18	/				2135		227 20	18
25	/							25

NOTE: A debit to Cash is made automatically by the software.

OPTIONAL PROBLEM

The input forms illustrated in this topic can be keyed using *Automated Accounting 6.0.* Refer to OPTIONAL PROBLEM DB-8A at the end of the narrative for information about automating this topic.

Reference column. The general ledger account number for Sales, *4105*, is recorded in the Account No. column. The automated accounting software automatically makes the debit to Cash. Therefore, the Debit column is left blank. The amount of the sale, *$2,870.00*, is written in the Credit column.

On line 2, the general ledger account number for Sales Tax Payable, *2135*, is entered in the Account No. column. The sales tax payable amount, *$229.60*, is recorded in the Credit column.

Cash Receipt on Account

> *March 11, 19--. Received cash on account from DTex Imports, $1,710.72, covering Sales Invoice No. 148 for $1,728.00 ($1,600.00 plus sales tax, $128.00), less 1% discount, $16.00, and less sales tax, $1.28. Receipt No. 232.*

The journal entry to record this transaction is on lines 10 and 11 of the cash receipts journal input form shown in Illustration T8-2.

On line 10, the date of the transaction, *11*, is entered in the Date column. The customer number, *120*, is recorded in the Customer No. column. The source document number, *R232*, is written in the Reference column. The amount of the cash receipt on account, *$1,728.00*, is entered in the Accounts Rec. Credit column. The account number for Sales Discount, *4110*, is recorded in the Account No. column. The sales discount amount, *$16.00*, is written in the Debit column. The software automatically makes the debit to *Cash*.

On line 11, the account number for Sales Tax Payable, *2135*, is entered in the Account No. column. The sales tax payable amount, *$1.28*, is recorded in the Debit column.

RECORDING OTHER TRANSACTIONS

Celluphone uses a general journal input form to journalize transactions other than sales and cash receipts.

Sales Returns and Allowances

> *March 11, 19--. Granted credit to Alamo Company for merchandise returned, $180.00, plus sales tax, $14.40 from S160; total, $194.40. Credit Memorandum No. 41.*

The run date, *03/31/--*, is written in the space provided at the top of the form.

The journal entry to record this transaction is on lines 1 through 3 of the general journal input form shown in Illustration T8-3.

Correcting Entries Affecting Customer Accounts

> *March 12, 19--. Discovered that a sale on account to Ridgecrest Co. on February 26 was incorrectly charged to the account of Ridgepoint Co., $297.00. Memorandum No. 40.*

FYI

The run date is usually the date of the last transaction or the last day of a fiscal period.

Use Transparency AA-5 Blank Sales Journal Input Form to journalize each sales transaction; Transparency AA-6 Blank Cash Receipts Journal Input Form to journalize each cash receipts transaction; and Transparency AA-2 Blank General Journal Input Form to journalize each general journal entry. It is important that students realize that the *Automated Accounting 6.0* software automatically records the debit to Accounts Receivable for a sale on account transaction and the debit to Cash for a cash receipts transaction. Emphasize that transactions not recorded on any of the other input forms are recorded on a general journal input form.

Guided Practice

Students should be at the computers. Guide students through booting the software and loading Optional Problem DB-8A from the template. Use the completed sales, cash receipts, general journal input forms, Illustrations T8-1, T8-2, and T8-3; and follow the procedures described to process Celluphone's sales, cash receipts, and other transactions. Instruct students to journalize each transaction as you go step by step through the procedures.

Independent Practice

Assign Automating Mastery Problem 20-M.

TEACHING STRATEGIES: DIFFERENT LEARNING ABILITIES

Limited English Proficiency (LEP) Students. Teachers report that LEP students are particularly successful using software to complete accounting problems. LEP students are independent, work at their own pace, and do not feel the need to compete with other students in the classroom. LEP students can successfully complete automated problems because the problems do not require strong verbal skills.

Reteach

Give students a blank sales, cash receipts, and general journal input form. Read the transactions in the text and have students journalize each.

Extend

Assign Automating Challenge Problem 20-C. This problem also includes purchases and cash payments transactions. To complete this problem successfully students will need a blank sales, cash receipts, purchases, cash payments, and general journal input form.

Enrich

Assign students to write a paragraph or two about the difference between sales returns and sales allowances and why businesses are willing to grant sales allowances.

CLOSURE

Review the procedures for recording sales, purchases, cash receipts, cash payments, and other transactions on input forms and for using *Automated Accounting 6.0* software to process the transactions.

ILLUSTRATION T8-3 General journal input form with transactions entered

	DATE MM/DD	REFERENCE	ACCOUNT NO.	CUSTOMER/ VENDOR NO.	DEBIT	CREDIT	
RUN DATE 03/31/-- MM DD YY				GENERAL JOURNAL Input Form			
1	03/11	CM41	4115		180 00		1
2	/		2135		14 40		2
3	/		1125	110		194 40	3
4	/12	M40	1125	140	297 00		4
5	/		1125	150		297 00	5
6	/						6
25	/						25
				PAGE TOTALS	491 40	491 40	
				FINAL TOTALS	491 40	491 40	

The journal entry to record this transaction is on lines 4 and 5 of Illustration T8-3.

PROCESSING SALES, CASH RECEIPTS, AND OTHER TRANSACTIONS

After all data from the input forms have been keyed and posted, three reports are displayed and printed. (1) A sales journal report as shown in Illustration T8-4. (2) A cash receipts journal report as shown in Illustration T8-5. (3) A general journal report as shown in Illustration T8-6. Each report is checked for accuracy by comparing the report with the appropriate journal input form.

After all journal reports have been verified and printed, the accounts receivable account from the general ledger and the schedule of accounts receivable is displayed and printed as shown in Illustrations T8-7 and T8-8. The accounts receivable balance in the general ledger is compared to the total of the schedule of accounts receivable. These two amounts must be the same. The schedule and all journal reports are filed for future reference.

FYI

When the cents are zero (.00), key only the dollar amount. For example, if the amount is 15.00, key 15. The software automatically assigns the .00.

OPTIONAL PROBLEM DB-8A

AUTOMATED

Celluphone's general ledger data base is on the accounting textbook template. If you wish to process Celluphone's sales, cash receipts, and other transactions using automated accounting software, load the *Automated Accounting 6.0* or higher software. Select Data Base 8A (DB-8A) from the template disk. Read the Problem Instructions Screen. Use the completed sales, cash receipts, and general journal input forms, Illustrations T8-1, T8-2, and T8-3, and follow the procedures described to process Celluphone's sales, cash receipts, and other transactions.

TEACHING STRATEGIES: Cooperative Learning

Using automated accounting software to complete accounting problems is an ideal cooperative learning experience. Students working in groups can collaborate on completing input forms and keying data.

```
                          Celluphone, Inc.
                           Sales Journal
                             03/31/--
-----------------------------------------------------------------------
Date   Refer.  V/C  Acct.  Title                    Debit        Credit
-----------------------------------------------------------------------
03/01  S148    120  1125   AR/DTex Imports         1728.00
03/01  S148         4105   Sales                                1600.00
03/01  S148         2135   Sales Tax Payable                     128.00

03/02  S149    150  1125   AR/Ridgepoint Co.      11546.80
03/02  S149         4105   Sales                               10691.48
03/02  S149         2135   Sales Tax Payable                     855.32

03/03  S150    140  1125   AR/Ridgecrest Co.      39463.20
03/03  S150         4105   Sales                               36540.00
03/03  S150         2135   Sales Tax Payable                    2923.20

03/05  S160    110  1125   AR/Alamo Company       10368.00
03/05  S160         4105   Sales                                9600.00
03/05  S160         2135   Sales Tax Payable                     768.00

03/22  S161    140  1125   AR/Ridgecrest Co.      18360.00
03/22  S161         4105   Sales                               17000.00
03/22  S161         2135   Sales Tax Payable                    1360.00

03/25  S162    150  1125   AR/Ridgepoint Co.       4453.50
03/25  S162         4105   Sales                                4123.61
03/25  S162         2135   Sales Tax Payable                     329.89

03/27  S163    120  1125   AR/DTex Imports         1484.90
03/27  S163         4105   Sales                                1374.91
03/27  S163         2135   Sales Tax Payable                     109.99

03/31  S221    130  1125   AR/Kirby's              1404.00
03/31  S221         4105   Sales                                1300.00
03/31  S221         2135   Sales Tax Payable                     104.00


                           Totals               88808.40      88808.40
                                               ==========    ==========
```

AUTOMATED ACCOUNTING PROBLEMS

AUTOMATED

AUTOMATING MASTERY PROBLEM 20-M Recording sales and cash receipts transactions

INSTRUCTIONS:

1. Journalize transactions from Mastery Problem 20-M, Chapter 20 on the appropriate input forms. Use February 28 of the current year as the run date.
2. Load the *Automated Accounting 6.0* or higher software. Select data base F20-M (First-Year Course Mastery Problem 20-M) from the accounting textbook template. Read the Problem Instructions screen.
3. Select File from the menu bar and choose the Save As menu command. Key the path to the drive and directory that contains your data files. Save the data base with a file name of XXX20M (where XXX are your initials).
4. Key the data from each of the completed input forms.
5. Display/print the general journal report, sales journal report, and the cash receipts journal report.

```
                              Celluphone, Inc.
                            Cash Receipts Journal
                                  03/31/--
------------------------------------------------------------------------
Date    Refer.   V/C Acct.  Title                      Debit      Credit
------------------------------------------------------------------------
03/01 T1            1105   Cash                       3099.60
03/01 T1            4105   Sales                                 2870.00
03/01 T1            2135   Sales Tax Payable                      229.60

03/02 R227          1105   Cash                        297.00
03/02 R227      150 1125   AR/Ridgepoint Co.                      297.00

03/03 R228          1105   Cash                      14380.10
03/03 R228          4110   Sales Discount              134.49
03/03 R228          2135   Sales Tax Payable            10.76
03/03 R228      130 1125   AR/Kirby's                           14525.35

03/04 R229          1105   Cash                        486.00
03/04 R229      120 1125   AR/DTex Imports                        486.00

03/05 R230          1105   Cash                       7462.45
03/05 R230      150 1125   AR/Ridgepoint Co.                     7462.45

03/06 R231          1105   Cash                      10298.76
03/06 R231          4110   Sales Discount              104.11
03/06 R231          2135   Sales Tax Payable             8.33
03/06 R231      110 1125   AR/Alamo Company                     10411.20

03/11 R232          1105   Cash                       1710.72
03/11 R232          4110   Sales Discount               16.00
03/11 R232          2135   Sales Tax Payable             1.28
03/11 R232      120 1125   AR/DTex Imports                       1728.00

03/12 R233          1105   Cash                      11546.80
03/12 R233      150 1125   AR/Ridgepoint Co.                    11546.80

03/13 R234          1105   Cash                      39068.57
03/13 R234          4110   Sales Discount              365.40
03/13 R234          2135   Sales Tax Payable            29.23
03/13 R234      140 1125   AR/Ridgecrest Co.                    39463.20

03/15 T15           1105   Cash                      68623.20
03/15 T15           4105   Sales                                63540.00
03/15 T15           2135   Sales Tax Payable                     5083.20

03/31 T31           1105   Cash                       3067.20
03/31 T31           4105   Sales                                 2840.00
03/31 T31           2135   Sales Tax Payable                      227.20

                           Totals                    160710.00  160710.00
```

6. Display/print the accounts receivable account from the general ledger.
7. Display/print the schedule of accounts receivable.

AUTOMATING CHALLENGE PROBLEM 20-C Recording sales, purchases, cash receipts, and cash payment transactions

INSTRUCTIONS:

1. Journalize transactions from Challenge Problem 20-C, Chapter 20 on the appropriate forms. Use April 30 of the current year as the run date.

AUTOMATED

```
                      Celluphone, Inc.
                      General Journal
                         03/31/--
----------------------------------------------------------------
Date    Refer.   V/C Acct.  Title                 Debit    Credit
----------------------------------------------------------------
03/11   CM41         4115   Sales Returns and Allow.  180.00
03/11   CM41         2135   Sales Tax Payable          14.40
03/11   CM41     110 1125   AR/Alamo Company                    194.40

03/12   M40      140 1125   AR/Ridgecrest Co.         297.00
03/12   M40      150 1125   AR/Ridgepoint Co.                   297.00

                                                   ---------- ----------
                            Totals                     491.40     491.40
                                                   ========== ==========
```

2. Load the *Automated Accounting 6.0* or higher software. Select data base F20-C (First-Year Course Challenge Problem 20-C) from the accounting textbook template. Read the Problem Instructions screen.
3. Select File from the menu bar and choose the Save As menu command. Key the path to the drive and directory that contains your data files. Save the data base with a file name of XXX20C (where XXX are your initials).
4. Key the data from each of the completed input forms.

SAFETY AND HEALTH

Always store diskettes in the storage envelope to prevent dust from collecting on the surface. A Safety and Health page is given in the Teacher's Resource Guide. This page may be duplicated and given to students.

ILLUSTRATION T8-7   General ledger report

```
                         Celluphone, Inc.
                         General Ledger
                            03/31/--
----------------------------------------------------------------
Account          Journal  Date  Refer.   Debit    Credit   Balance
----------------------------------------------------------------
1125-Accounts Receivable
                 Op. Bal. 03/01 Balances 10411.20          10411.20
                 Op. Bal. 03/01 Balances   486.00          10897.20
                 Op. Bal. 03/01 Balances 14525.35          25422.55
                 Op. Bal. 03/01 Balances  7759.45          33182.00
                 Sales    03/01 S148      1728.00          34910.00
                 Sales    03/02 S149     11546.80          46456.80
                 Cash Rcpt 03/02 R227               297.00 46159.80
                 Sales    03/03 S150     39463.20          85623.00
                 Cash Rcpt 03/03 R228            14525.35  71097.65
                 Cash Rcpt 03/04 R229              486.00  70611.65
                 Sales    03/05 S160     10368.00          80979.65
                 Cash Rcpt 03/05 R230             7462.45  73517.20
                 Cash Rcpt 03/06 R231            10411.20  63106.00
                 Cash Rcpt 03/11 R232             1728.00  61378.00
                 General  03/11 CM41               194.40  61183.60
                 Cash Rcpt 03/12 R233            11546.80  49636.80
                 General  03/12 M40        297.00          49933.80
                 General  03/12 M40                297.00  49636.80
                 Cash Rcpt 03/13 R234            39463.20  10173.60
                 Sales    03/22 S161     18360.00          28533.60
                 Sales    03/25 S162      4453.50          32987.10
                 Sales    03/27 S163      1484.90          34472.00
                 Sales    03/31 S221      1404.00          35876.00
```

   Schedule of accounts receivable report

```
                         Celluphone, Inc.
                    Schedule of Accounts Receivable
                             03/31/--
-----------------------------------------------------------
Account
Number      Name                              Balance
-----------------------------------------------------------
110         Alamo Company                    10173.60
120         DTex Imports                      1484.90
130         Kirby's                           1404.00
140         Ridgecrest Co.                   18657.00
150         Ridgepoint Co.                    4156.50
                                            ----------
            Total                            35876.00
                                            ==========
```

5. Display/print the general journal report, cash payments journal report, sales journal report, and the cash receipts journal report.
6. Display/print the accounts payable account from the general ledger.
7. Display/print the schedule of accounts payable.
8. Display/print the accounts receivable account from the general ledger.
9. Display print the schedule of accounts receivable.

An Accounting Cycle for a Corporation: Journalizing and Posting Transactions

AUTOMATED

Reinforcement Activity 3 reinforces learnings from Part 4, Chapters 19 through 27, and covers a complete accounting cycle for a merchandising business organized as a corporation. Part A reinforces learnings from Chapters 19 and 20. Part B reinforces learnings from Chapters 21 through 27.

The general ledger account balances summarize transactions for the first eleven months of a fiscal year. The transactions given for December of the current year are for the last month of the fiscal year.

HARDWARE MART

Reinforcement Activity 3 includes accounting records for Hardware Mart. Hardware Mart sells home repair materials, electrical supplies, and small hand and power tools. The business, which is located in a shopping center, is open Monday through Saturday. Space for the business is rented. However, the corporation owns the office and store equipment.

CHART OF ACCOUNTS

Hardware Mart uses the chart of accounts shown on the next page.

JOURNALS AND LEDGERS

Hardware Mart uses the following journals and ledgers. Models of journals and ledgers are shown in the textbook illustrations given in the following chart.

Journals and Ledgers	Chapter	Illustration Number
Sales journal	20	20-4
Purchases journal	19	19-4
General journal	19	19-22
Cash receipts journal	20	20-10
Cash payments journal	19	19-16
Accounts receivable ledger	20	20-9
Accounts payable ledger	19	19-14
General ledger	19	19-4

RECORDING TRANSACTIONS

The account balances for the general and subsidiary ledgers are given in the working papers accompanying this textbook.

563

HARDWARE MART
CHART OF ACCOUNTS

Balance Sheet Accounts

(1000) ASSETS

1100 Current Assets

1105 Cash
1110 Petty Cash
1115 Notes Receivable
1120 Interest Receivable
1125 Accounts Receivable
1130 Allowance for Uncollectible Accounts
1135 Merchandise Inventory
1140 Supplies
1145 Prepaid Insurance

1200 Plant Assets

1205 Office Equipment
1210 Accumulated Depreciation—Office Equipment
1215 Store Equipment
1220 Accumulated Depreciation—Store Equipment

(2000) LIABILITIES

2100 Current Liabilities

2105 Notes Payable
2110 Interest Payable
2115 Accounts Payable
2120 Employee Income Tax Payable
2125 Federal Income Tax Payable
2130 FICA Tax Payable
2135 Sales Tax Payable
2140 Unemployment Tax Payable—Federal
2145 Unemployment Tax Payable—State
2150 Health Insurance Premiums Payable
2155 Dividends Payable

(3000) STOCKHOLDERS' EQUITY

3105 Capital Stock
3110 Retained Earnings
3115 Dividends
3120 Income Summary

Income Statement Accounts

(4000) OPERATING REVENUE

4105 Sales
4110 Sales Discount
4115 Sales Returns and Allowances

(5000) COST OF MERCHANDISE

5105 Purchases
5110 Purchases Discount
5115 Purchases Returns and Allowances

(6000) OPERATING EXPENSES

6105 Advertising Expense
6110 Credit Card Fee Expense
6115 Depreciation Expense—Office Equipment
6120 Depreciation Expense—Store Equipment
6125 Insurance Expense
6130 Miscellaneous Expense
6135 Payroll Taxes Expense
6140 Rent Expense
6145 Salary Expense
6150 Supplies Expense
6155 Uncollectible Accounts Expense
6160 Utilities Expense

(7000) OTHER REVENUE

7105 Gain on Plant Assets
7110 Interest Income

(8000) OTHER EXPENSES

8105 Cash Short and Over
8110 Interest Expense
8115 Loss on Plant Assets

(9000) INCOME TAX EXPENSE

9105 Federal Income Tax Expense

INSTRUCTIONS:

1. Journalize the following transactions completed during December of the current year. Use page 12 of a sales journal, a purchases journal, a general journal, and a cash receipts journal. Use pages 23 and 24 of a cash payments journal. Hardware Mart offers its customers terms of 1/10, n/30. The sales tax rate is 8%. Source documents are abbreviated as follows: check, C; credit memorandum, CM; debit memorandum, DM; memorandum, M; purchase invoice, P; receipt, R; sales invoice, S; cash register tape, T.

Dec. 1. Paid cash for rent, $1,750.00. C310.
    1. Received cash on account from Gerald Bell, $3,143.45, covering S180 for $3,175.20 ($2,940.00 plus sales tax, $235.20), less 1% discount, $29.40, and less sales tax, $2.35. R169.
    1. Purchased merchandise on account from Granger Company, $11,728.00. P95.
    2. Granted credit to Linda Franz for merchandise returned, $555.00, plus sales tax, $44.40, from S170; total, $599.40. CM23.
    2. Received cash on account from Linda Franz, $2,975.40 (covering S170 less CM23), no discount. R170.
    3. Sold merchandise on account to Paul Rodriguez, $2,130.00, plus sales tax, $170.40; total, $2,300.40. S188.
    3. Paid cash on account to Beta Hardware Supplies, $4,176.37, covering P92 for $4,261.60, less 2% discount, $85.23. C311.
    3. Recorded cash and credit card sales, $7,755.80, plus sales tax, $620.46; total, $8,376.26. T3.

    > **Posting.** Post the items that are to be posted individually. Post the journals in this order: sales journal, purchases journal, general journal, cash receipts journal, and cash payments journal.

    5. Returned merchandise to Granger Company, $1,620.00, from P90. DM25.
    6. Paid cash on account to Sunbelt Corp., $3,132.86, covering P93 for $3,196.80, less 2% discount, $63.94. C312.
    7. Received cash on account from Paul Rodriguez, $5,116.12, covering S185 for $5,167.80 ($4,785.00 plus sales tax, $382.80), less 1% discount, $47.85, and less sales tax, $3.83. R171.
    7. Purchased merchandise on account from Western Tools, $5,730.00. P96.
    8. Sold merchandise on account to Roy Heflin, $2,481.00, plus sales tax, $198.48; total, $2,679.48. S189.
    8. Paid cash on account to Western Tools, $2,637.76, covering P94 for $2,664.40, less 1% discount, $26.64. C313.
    9. Received cash on account from Roy Heflin, $4,374.00, covering S183; no discount. R172.
    10. Paid cash for liability for November health insurance premiums, $625.00. C314.
    10. Recorded cash and credit card sales, $14,542.20, plus sales tax, $1,163.38; total, $15,705.58. T10.

    > **Posting.** Post the items that are to be posted individually.

    12. Purchased merchandise on account from Sunbelt Corp., $11,652.00. P97.
    13. Paid cash for miscellaneous expense, $227.50. C315.
    13. Paid cash for supplies, $176.10. C316.
    13. Received cash on account from Paul Rodriguez, $2,277.40, covering S188 for $2,300.40 ($2,130.00 plus sales tax, $170.40), less 1% discount, $21.30, and less sales tax, $1.70. R173.
    14. Sold merchandise on account to Patricia Nielsen, $750.00, plus sales tax, $60.00; total, $810.00. S190.
    14. Paid cash for advertising, $579.50. C317.
    15. Paid cash for semimonthly payroll, $3,247.50 (total payroll, $4,450.00, less deductions: employee income tax, $534.00; FICA tax, $356.00; health insurance premiums, $312.50). C318.
    15. Recorded employer payroll taxes expense, $405.60 (FICA tax, $356.00; federal unemployment tax, $6.40; state unemployment tax, $43.20). M31.

SOFTWARE FOCUS

Automated Accounting 6.0 can be used to complete Reinforcement Activity 3 using the computer.

Dec. 15. Paid cash for liability for employee income tax, $1,075.00, and for FICA tax, $1,360.00; total, $2,435.00. C319.

15. Paid cash for quarterly estimated federal income tax, $3,500.00. C320. (Debit **Federal Income Tax Expense**; credit **Cash.**)

15. Paid cash to replenish the petty cash fund, $178.50: supplies, $26.75; advertising, $44.00; miscellaneous, $109.75; cash over, $2.00. C321.

16. Paid cash on account to Western Tools, $5,672.70, covering P96 for $5,730.00, less 1% discount, $57.30. C322.

16. Received cash on account from Patricia Nielsen, $2,381.40, covering S186; no discount. R174.

17. Received cash on account from Roy Heflin, $2,652.69, covering S189 for $2,679.48 ($2,481.00 plus sales tax, $198.48), less 1% discount, $24.81, and less sales tax, $1.98. R175.

17. Purchased merchandise for cash, $470.00. C323.

17. Recorded cash and credit card sales, $18,096.00, plus sales tax, $1,447.68; total, $19,543.68. T17.

    Posting. Post the items that are to be posted individually.

19. Paid cash for miscellaneous expense, $124.60. C324.

19. Sold merchandise on account to Linda Franz, $2,675.00, plus sales tax, $214.00; total, $2,889.00. S191.

20. Paid cash on account to Granger Company, $2,464.70, covering P90 for $4,084.70, less DM25, $1,620.00; no discount. C325.

21. Paid cash on account to Decorator Systems, $3,552.50, covering P91; no discount. C326.

2. Prove and rule page 23 of the cash payments journal.

3. Forward the totals from page 23 to page 24 of the cash payments journal.

4. Continue recording the following transactions.

Dec. 21. Paid cash for miscellaneous expense, $288.00. C327.

22. Purchased merchandise on account from Beta Hardware Supplies, $7,165.00. P98.

22. Paid cash on account to Sunbelt Corp., $11,418.96, covering P97 for $11,652.00, less 2% discount, $233.04. C328.

23. Purchased merchandise for cash, $617.50. C329.

24. Sold merchandise on account to Roy Heflin, $650.00, plus sales tax, $52.00; total, $702.00. S192.

24. Recorded cash and credit card sales, $14,003.60, plus sales tax, $1,120.29; total, $15,123.89. T24.

    Posting. Post the items that are to be posted individually.

26. Bought supplies on account from HiValue Electrical Co., $339.00. M32.

27. Sold merchandise on account to Gerald Bell, $1,854.00, plus sales tax, $148.32; total, $2,002.32. S193.

27. Paid cash for advertising, $441.30. C330.

28. Purchased merchandise on account from Western Tools, $11,474.00. P99.

29. Received cash on account from Linda Franz, $2,860.11, covering S191 for $2,889.00 ($2,675.00 plus sales tax, $214.00), less 1% discount, $26.75, and less sales tax, $2.14. R176.

29. Paid cash on account to Granger Company, $11,728.00, covering P95; no discount. C331.

30. Sold merchandise on account to Paul Rodriguez, $875.00, plus sales tax, $70.00; total, $945.00. S194.

30. Paid cash for liability for sales tax, $4,932.60. C332. (Debit **Sales Tax Payable**; credit **Cash.**)

31. Paid cash for semimonthly payroll, $3,170.50 (total payroll, $4,300.00, less deductions: employee income tax, $473.00; FICA tax, $344.00; health insurance premiums, $312.50). C333.

31. Recorded employer payroll taxes expense, $368.80 (FICA tax, $344.00; federal unemployment tax, $3.20; state unemployment tax, $21.60). M33.

Dec. 31. Recorded credit card fee expense for December, $776.60. M34. (Debit **Credit Card Fee Expense**; credit **Cash**.)

31. Paid cash to replenish the petty cash fund, $171.20: supplies, $21.80; advertising, $52.00; miscellaneous, $96.40; cash short, $1.00. C334.

31. Recorded cash and credit card sales, $4,524.00, plus sales tax, $361.92; total, $4,885.92. T31.

Posting. Post the items that are to be posted individually.

5. Prove and rule the sales journal. Post the totals of the special columns.
6. Total and rule the purchases journal. Post the total.
7. Prove the equality of debits and credits for the cash receipts and cash payments journals.
8. Prove cash. The balance on the next unused check stub on December 31 is $54,777.45.
9. Rule the cash receipts journal. Post the totals of the special columns.
10. Rule the cash payments journal. Post the totals of the special columns.
11. Prepare a schedule of accounts receivable and a schedule of accounts payable. Compare each schedule total with the balance of the controlling account in the general ledger. The total and balance should be the same.

The general ledger used in Reinforcement Activity 3, Part A, is needed to complete Reinforcement Activity 3, Part B.

An allowance method of recording uncollectible accounts expense, based on a percentage of total sales on account, is presented in this chapter. The allowance method affects both the method of writing off accounts and reinstating them and also the adjustment for uncollectible accounts expense.

GUIDE TO ACHIEVING LEARNING OBJECTIVES

Enabling Performance Tasks	TEACH Lesson Plans	APPLY Drills for Understanding	APPLY Application Problems	Mastery Problems	Challenge Problems	Cases for Critical Thinking	Recycling Problems	Reinforcement Activity
a. Define accounting terms related to uncollectible accounts.	21-1, 21-2							
b. Identify accounting concepts and practices related to uncollectible accounts.	21-1, 21-2					Cases 1, 2		
c. Calculate estimated uncollectible accounts expense.	21-1	21-D1	21-1	21-M	21-C		21-R	3B
d. Journalize and post entries related to uncollectible accounts.	21-1, 21-2	21-D2	21-1, 21-2, 21-3	21-M	21-C		21-R	3B

ENRICHMENT

SPECIAL FEATURES

Global Perspective, page 572

TECHNOLOGY CONNECTION

Accounting Tutorial Unit 8

Application Program Disk Problem 21-M

Electronic Study Guide

NEW, REVIEW, AND EXTENSION

ACTIVITIES/CONCEPTS/TRANSACTIONS	NEW	REVIEW/ EXTENSION
Calculating estimated uncollectible accounts expense	✓	
Adjustment for uncollectible accounts expense	✓	
Writing off an uncollectible account	✓	
Calculating book value of accounts receivable	✓	
Reopening a customer account	✓	
Collecting a written-off account receivable	✓	

INFORMAL ASSESSMENT		FORMAL ASSESSMENT					
Study Guide	Audit Your Understanding	Chapter MicroExam	Chapter Problem Test	Unit Problem Test	Unit Objective Test	Portfolio	
Units A, B	✓	✓			✓		
Units A, B	✓	✓			✓		
			✓	✓		✓	
			✓	✓		✓	

TEACHING MATERIALS

Teacher's Wraparound Edition of the Text

Teacher's Resource Guide

Teacher's Edition of Working Papers

Teacher's Edition of Demonstration/Recycling Problems

Teaching Transparencies

Accounting Tutorial Manual

MicroExam

Applied Math Work Sheet

APPLIED MATHEMATICS

APPLIED MATH/ACCOUNTING SKILL	APPLICATION
Calculating Estimated Uncollectible Accounts Expense	Drill 21-D1
Calculating Book Value of Accounts Receivable	Prob. 21-1

21

Accounting for Uncollectible Accounts Receivable

ENABLING PERFORMANCE TASKS

After studying Chapter 21, you will be able to:

a Define accounting terms related to uncollectible accounts.

b Identify accounting concepts and practices related to uncollectible accounts.

c Calculate estimated uncollectible accounts expense.

d Journalize and post entries related to uncollectible accounts.

TERMS PREVIEW

uncollectible accounts • allowance method of recording losses from uncollectible accounts • book value of accounts receivable • writing off an account

568

A business generally sells on account to encourage sales. If sales on account are offered, customers may buy merchandise today even though they will not have the cash needed until later. Also, when sales on account are offered, sales can be made over the telephone or by mail more easily without requiring immediate cash payment.

Although many businesses sell on account, they do expect full payment within the terms of sale. Most businesses thoroughly investigate customers before selling to them on credit. Even with a thorough credit investigation, however, some accounts receivable will be uncollectible. Accounts receivable that cannot be collected are called **uncollectible accounts**. Uncollectible accounts are also referred to as bad debts.

If a business fails to collect from a customer, the business loses part of the asset *Accounts Receivable*. The amount of the accounts receivable not collected is recorded as an expense. Celluphone records the expense caused by uncollectible accounts in an account titled *Uncollectible Accounts Expense*. Uncollectible Accounts Expense is also referred to as bad debts expense. An uncollectible amount does not decrease revenue. Instead, the loss is considered a regular expense of doing business. Revenue was earned when the sale was made. *(CONCEPT: Realization of Revenue)* Failing to collect an account does not cancel the sale. Therefore the loss is treated as an expense.

FYI

Note that the word "uncollectible" is spelled "-ible."

ESTIMATING AND RECORDING UNCOLLECTIBLE ACCOUNTS EXPENSE

Risk of loss occurs when a business sells on account. This potential loss is present even though several months may pass before the actual loss becomes known. Accurate financial reporting requires that expenses be recorded in the fiscal period in which the expenses contribute to earning revenue. *(CONCEPT: Matching Expenses with Revenue)* The balance of Accounts Receivable, a controlling account, must equal the sum of the customer accounts in the subsidiary ledger. A business does not know at the time sales are made which customer accounts will become uncollectible. If a business knew exactly which accounts would become uncollectible in the future, it could credit Accounts Receivable and each customer account for the uncollectible amounts. Uncollectible Accounts Expense could then be debited for the same amount. However, businesses do not know which customers will not pay their accounts in the future. Therefore, specific customer accounts cannot be credited for uncollectible amounts. The accounts receivable general ledger account also cannot be credited for these amounts. However, at the end of each fiscal period, a business can calculate and record an *estimated* amount of uncollectible accounts expense.

Estimating and recording uncollectible accounts expense at the end of a fiscal period accomplishes two objectives. (1) An up-to-date value of uncollectible accounts prevents an overstatement of the

LESSON PLAN 21-1

Materials

- Student Pages 569–574
- Transparencies: C, Blank 8-column Work Sheet; M, Blank General Journal
- Software: Accounting Tutorial
- Math Work Sheets for Chapter 21: A: Calculating Estimated Uncollectible Accounts Expense (TRG); B: Calculating Book Value of Accounts Receivable (TRG)
- Global Perspective Activity Work Sheet (TRG)
- Demonstration Problem: 21A, Estimating and Journalizing Entries for Uncollectible Accounts Expense

Objectives (Enabling Performance Tasks)

After studying Chapter 21, students will be able to:

a. Define accounting terms related to uncollectible accounts.

b. Identify accounting concepts and practices related to uncollectible accounts.

c. Calculate estimated uncollectible accounts expense.

d. Journalize and post entries related to uncollectible accounts.

- Sales on account and cash receipts for these sales were recorded in Chapter 20. Explain that not all customers pay within the terms of sale. If a business cannot collect from customers, that amount becomes an expense to the business. In this lesson, we will look at how a business calculates and records the estimated amount for this expense.

- Introduce new vocabulary: uncollectible accounts, allowance method of recording losses from uncollectible accounts, book value of accounts receivable.

Cover student pages 569–574 "Estimating and Recording Uncollectible Accounts Expense." Explain that uncollectible accounts are the same as bad debts. Review the definition of contra account. Emphasize that uncollectible accounts expense is an estimated amount. Explain that the adjusting entry affects an expense account, Uncollectible Accounts Expense, and a contra asset, Allowance for Uncollectible Accounts. Explain book value. Review percentages used in calculating uncollectible accounts expense; remind students that multiplying by 1% is the same as multiplying by the decimal equivalent .01; 0.1% (one-tenth of a percent) is the same as the decimal equivalent .001. Emphasize that the adjusting entry is a debit to the expense account, Uncoll. Accts. Exp., and a credit to the contra asset account, Allow. for Uncoll. Accts. Explain that the adjusting entry is journalized as are other adjusting entries.

Uncollectible Accounts Expense	
Debit side Normal balance Increase	Credit side Decrease

Accounts Receivable	
Debit side Normal balance Increase	Credit side Decrease

Allowance for Uncollectible Accounts	
Debit side Decrease	Credit side Normal balance Increase

FYI

Some companies use a predetermined number of past-due days to determine when an account is uncollectible. For example, all accounts more than 90 days overdue may be considered uncollectible.

FYI

Corporations that have important operations in more than one country are known as multinational corporations. Sometimes they are referred to simply as multinationals.

value of accounts receivable on the balance sheet. (2) Recording the estimated uncollectible accounts expense prevents an understatement of expenses on the income statement.

To record estimated uncollectible accounts, an adjusting entry is made affecting two accounts: Uncollectible Accounts Expense and Allowance for Uncollectible Accounts. The estimated value of uncollectible accounts is debited to Uncollectible Accounts Expense. An expense account has a normal debit balance. Therefore, the uncollectible accounts expense account is increased by a debit and decreased by a credit.

The estimated value of uncollectible accounts is also credited to an account titled Allowance for Uncollectible Accounts. An account that reduces a related account is known as a contra account. Allowance for Uncollectible Accounts is a contra account to its related asset account, Accounts Receivable. A contra asset account has a normal credit balance because it reduces the balance of an asset account. Therefore, Allowance for Uncollectible Accounts is increased by a credit and decreased by a debit.

Allowance for Bad Debts and Allowance for Doubtful Accounts are account titles sometimes used instead of Allowance for Uncollectible Accounts.

Crediting the estimated value of uncollectible accounts to a contra account is called the **allowance method of recording losses from uncollectible accounts.** The difference between the balance of Accounts Receivable and its contra account, Allowance for Uncollectible Accounts, is called the **book value of accounts receivable.** The book value of accounts receivable is reported on a balance sheet as shown in Chapter 27.

A contra account is usually assigned the next number of the account number sequence after its related account in the chart of accounts. Celluphone numbers its accounts in sequences of five. Celluphone's accounts receivable account is numbered 1125. Therefore Allowance for Uncollectible Accounts is numbered 1130.

Estimating Uncollectible Accounts Expense

Many businesses use a percentage of total sales on account to estimate uncollectible accounts expense. Each sale on account represents a risk of loss from an uncollectible account. Therefore, if the estimated percentage of loss is accurate, the amount of uncollectible accounts expense will be accurate regardless of when the actual losses occur. Since a sale on account creates a risk of loss, estimating the percentage of uncollectible accounts expense for the same period matches sales revenue with the related uncollectible accounts expense. (CONCEPT: Matching Expenses with Revenue)

Celluphone estimates uncollectible accounts expense by calculating a percentage of total sales on account. A review of Celluphone's previous experience in collecting sales on account shows that actual uncollectible accounts expense has been about 1% of total sales on account. The company's total sales on account for the year is $922,700.00. Thus, Celluphone's uncollectible accounts expense is calculated as shown on the next page.

	Total Sales on Account	×	Percentage	=	Estimated Uncollectible Accounts Expense
	$922,700.00	×	1%	=	$9,227.00

APPLY

- Draw a T account for Allowance for Uncollectible Accounts and label the normal balance side.

- Draw a T account for Uncollectible Accounts Expense and label the normal balance side.

- Use Transparency C to demonstrate entering the adjustment for uncollectible accounts expense on the work sheet or direct students to Illustration 21-1.

- Use Transparency M to journalize the adjusting entry or direct students to Illustration 21-2.

Guided Practice

Guide students through Drill 21-D1. Students should have the forms from the working papers to complete as you guide them through the calculations for each of the six stores. All students should agree with the answers for each store before proceeding to the next step.

Independent Practice

Assign Terms 1–3, Questions 1–12, and Problem 21-1.

Celluphone estimates that of the $922,700.00 sales on account during the year, $9,227.00 will eventually be uncollectible.

Analyzing an Adjustment for Uncollectible Accounts Expense

An adjustment is made to record estimated uncollectible accounts expense for a fiscal year. The effect of Celluphone's uncollectible accounts expense adjustment is shown in the T accounts.

Uncollectible Accounts Expense is debited for $9,227.00 to show the increase in the balance of this expense account. The balance of this account, $9,227.00, is the uncollectible accounts expense for the fiscal period.

Allowance for Uncollectible Accounts is credited for $9,227.00 to show the increase in the balance of this contra asset account. The previous balance, $265.00, plus the fiscal year increase, $9,227.00, equals the December 31 balance, $9,492.00. After the adjustment, Celluphone estimates that $9,492.00 of accounts receivable will be uncollectible.

> **FYI**
>
> When the allowance method is used, the amount recorded as an expense for a year is an estimated amount.

Uncollectible Accounts Expense

Dec. 31 Adj.	9,227.00	

Allowance for Uncollectible Accounts

	Bal.	265.00
	Dec. 31 Adj.	9,227.00
	(New Bal.	*9,492.00)*

Entering an Adjustment for Uncollectible Accounts Expense on a Work Sheet

At the end of a fiscal period, an adjustment for uncollectible accounts expense is planned on a work sheet. Celluphone's adjustment for uncollectible accounts expense is shown in the Adjustments columns of the partial work sheet in Illustration 21-1.

> **ILLUSTRATION 21-1**   Uncollectible accounts expense adjustment on a work sheet

		1	2	3	4
	ACCOUNT TITLE	TRIAL BALANCE		ADJUSTMENTS	
		DEBIT	CREDIT	DEBIT	CREDIT
6	*Allowance for Uncollectible Accounts*		265 00		(b) 9 2 2 7 00
45	*Uncollectible Accounts Expense*			(b) 9 2 2 7 00	

On line 45 of the work sheet, Uncollectible Accounts Expense is debited for $9,227.00 in the Adjustments Debit column. On line 6 Allowance for Uncollectible Accounts is credited for $9,227.00 in the Adjustments Credit column.

APPLIED SKILLS: MATHEMATICS

Use the MATH WORK SHEETS in the Masters and Solutions to Enrichment/Application section of the Teacher's Resource Guide to integrate applied mathematics. In these work sheets, students will apply math concepts to calculate estimated uncollectible accounts expense and book value of accounts receivable.

Global Perspective

The GLOBAL PERSPECTIVE feature is intended to expose students to some of the ways in which accounting and business in general differ in other countries. Use the GLOBAL PERSPECTIVE ACTIVITY in the Masters and Solutions to Enrichment/Application Activities Section in the Teacher's Resource Guide to allow students to apply the concept of converting to and from metric measurements.

Global Perspective

INTERNATIONAL WEIGHTS AND MEASURES

The United States is one of the few major industrial countries that does not use the metric system exclusively. In order to conduct international business, it is sometimes necessary to convert to the metric system. Some American

TO CHANGE	TO	MULTIPLY BY
meter	inches	39.37
decimeter	inches	3.94
centimeter	inches	0.39
millimeter	inches	0.04
liter	quart (dry)	.908
liter	quart (liquid)	1.057

To convert, simply take the original weight or measure and multiply by the conversion factor. For example, 10 centimeters × 0.39 = 3.90 inches.

industries have already converted or specify measurements in both the U.S.

equivalent and metric measures. For example, beverages are routinely packaged

in liter containers. Automobile mechanics frequently need two sets of socket wrenches—one in the U.S. system and an additional metric set. Most industries that do any international business have had to adapt to the metric system of measures.

The metric system is based on a decimal system like our currency.

Above is a partial metric conversion chart.

☞☞ FYI ☞☞

Uncollectible accounts are also known as "bad debts" or "doubtful accounts."

The percentage of total sales on account method of estimating uncollectible accounts expense assumes that a portion of every sale on account dollar will become uncollectible. An Allowance for Uncollectible Accounts balance in the Trial Balance Credit column means that previous fiscal period estimates have not yet been identified as uncollectible. When the allowance account has a previous credit balance, the amount of the adjustment is added to the previous balance. The new balance is then extended to the Balance Sheet Credit column. This new balance of the allowance account is the estimated amount of accounts receivable that will eventually become uncollectible.

Journalizing an Adjusting Entry for Uncollectible Accounts Expense

Information used to journalize an uncollectible accounts expense adjusting entry is obtained from a work sheet's Adjustments columns. The adjusting entry for uncollectible accounts expense is shown in the general journal in Illustration 21-2.

ILLUSTRATION 21-2

Adjusting entry for uncollectible accounts expense

GENERAL JOURNAL   PAGE 15

	DATE	ACCOUNT TITLE	DOC. NO.	POST. REF.	DEBIT	CREDIT	
1		*Adjusting Entries*					1
4	31	*Uncollectible Accounts Expense*			9 2 2 7 00		4
5		*Allow. for Uncollectible Accts.*				9 2 2 7 00	5

Posting an Adjusting Entry for Uncollectible Accounts Expense

After the adjusting entry is posted, Accounts Receivable, Allowance for Uncollectible Accounts, and Uncollectible Accounts Expense appear as shown in Illustration 21-3.

ILLUSTRATION 21-3

General ledger accounts after adjusting entry for uncollectible accounts expense is posted

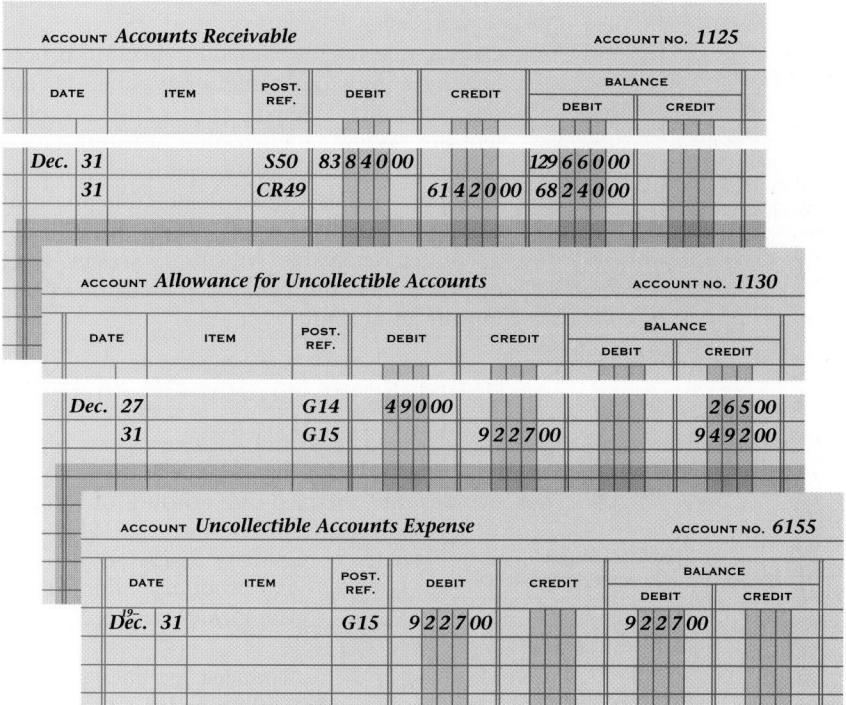

ACCOUNT *Accounts Receivable*   **ACCOUNT NO.** *1125*

DATE	ITEM	POST. REF.	DEBIT	CREDIT	BALANCE DEBIT	BALANCE CREDIT
Dec. 31		S50	83 8 4 0 00		129 6 6 0 00	
31		CR49		61 4 2 0 00	68 2 4 0 00	

ACCOUNT *Allowance for Uncollectible Accounts*   **ACCOUNT NO.** *1130*

DATE	ITEM	POST. REF.	DEBIT	CREDIT	BALANCE DEBIT	BALANCE CREDIT
Dec. 27		G14	4 9 0 00			2 6 5 00
31		G15		9 2 2 7 00		9 4 9 2 00

ACCOUNT *Uncollectible Accounts Expense*   **ACCOUNT NO.** *6155*

DATE	ITEM	POST. REF.	DEBIT	CREDIT	BALANCE DEBIT	BALANCE CREDIT
Dec. 31		G15	9 2 2 7 00		9 2 2 7 00	

Audit Your Understanding

1. Why does a business estimate uncollectible accounts expense?

2. Why is an estimated amount used for uncollectible accounts expense instead of the actual amount?

3. What is the normal balance side of Allowance for Uncollectible Accounts?

4. What is the normal balance side of Uncollectible Accounts Expense?

Accounts Receivable has a debit balance of $68,240.00, the total amount due from customers on December 31. Allowance for Uncollectible Accounts has a credit balance of $9,492.00 on December 31. The balance of this contra account is to be subtracted from the balance of its related account, Accounts Receivable, on the balance sheet. The debit balance of Uncollectible Accounts Expense is $9,227.00. This amount is the estimated uncollectible accounts expense for the current fiscal year ended December 31.

The December 27 Allowance for Uncollectible Accounts entry, $490.00, is the amount of an account that was determined to be uncollectible. Canceling uncollectible accounts is described in the next section of this chapter.

The book value of accounts receivable on December 31 is calculated as shown on the next page.

CLOSURE

- Use Audit Your Understanding questions.
- Review the procedures for calculating uncollectible accounts expense.
- Review the procedures for analyzing and recording the adjusting entry for uncollectible accounts expense.

AUDIT YOUR UNDERSTANDING

The AUDIT YOUR UNDERSTANDING feature appears at the end of each section of the chapter. Explain to your students that the word *audit* means to check or verify. AUDIT YOUR UNDERSTANDING may be used to check student comprehension of the section just studied. The answers are provided in Appendix D in the back of the textbook.

1. To record the expense in the same fiscal period in which the sales were made. This is an application of the Matching Expenses with Revenue accounting concept.
2. At the time the expense is recorded, the actual amount is not known because the accounts have not yet become uncollectible. Therefore, an estimate is needed.
3. Credit.
4. Debit.

	Accounts Receivable	–	Balance of Allowance for Uncollectible Accounts	=	Book Value of Accounts Receivable
	$68,240.00	–	$9,492.00	=	$58,748.00

CANCELING UNCOLLECTIBLE ACCOUNTS RECEIVABLE

👉👉 FYI 👈👈

The journals and ledgers of a business are known as the company's "books"; therefore, the book value is the value as it is recorded in the "books."

Celluphone uses a planned collection procedure to collect customer accounts. Most customers pay when accounts are due. However, a few accounts, regardless of collection efforts, prove to be uncollectible. When a customer account is determined to be uncollectible, a journal entry is made to cancel the uncollectible account. This entry cancels the uncollectible amount from the general ledger account Accounts Receivable as well as the customer account in the accounts receivable subsidiary ledger. Canceling the balance of a customer account because the customer does not pay is called **writing off an account.**

Journalizing Writing Off an Uncollectible Account Receivable

After several months of unsuccessful collection efforts, Celluphone decides that the past-due account of North Star Co. is uncollectible.

GENERAL LEDGER
Allowance for Uncollectible Accounts

Jan. 3	556.00	Bal.	9,492.00
		(New Bal.	*8,936.00)*

Accounts Receivable

Bal.	68,240.00	Jan. 3	556.00
(New Bal.	*67,684.00)*		

ACCOUNTS RECEIVABLE LEDGER
North Star Co.

Bal.	556.00	Jan. 3	556.00

January 3, 19--. Wrote off North Star Co.'s past-due account as uncollectible, $556.00. Memorandum No. 2.

Allowance for Uncollectible Accounts is debited for $556.00 to reduce the balance of this contra asset account. This specific amount, $556.00, is no longer an estimate because the account of North Star Co. has been determined to be uncollectible. Therefore, the amount of the uncollectible account is deducted from the allowance account. The new balance of the allowance account is $8,936.00 ($9,492.00 less $556.00).

Accounts Receivable is credited for $556.00 to reduce the balance due from customers. The new balance of the accounts receivable account is $67,684.00 ($68,240.00 less $556.00).

North Star's account in the accounts receivable ledger is also credited for $556.00. This entry cancels the debit balance of the account. North Star's account is written off.

The book value of accounts receivable is the same both before and after writing off an uncollectible account. The book value of accounts receivable before writing off North Star's account is calculated as shown on the next page.

👉👉 FYI 👈👈

Some businesses use the direct write-off method for uncollectible accounts without using an allowance account. An account is then written off by debiting Uncollectible Accounts Expense.

LESSON PLAN 21-2

Materials

- Student pages 574–580
- Transparencies: M, Blank General Journal; O, Blank Cash Receipts Journal; 21-1, Chapter Summary
- Software: Application Program Disk, Electronic Study Guide
- Demonstration Problems: 21B, Recording Entries to Write Off Uncollectible Accounts Receivable; 21C, Recording Collection of Written-Off Accounts Receivable
- Tests: Problem Test Chapter 21, MicroExam Chapter 21

Objectives (Enabling Performance Tasks)

After studying Chapter 21, students will be able to:

a. Define accounting terms related to uncollectible accounts.

b. Identify accounting concepts and practices related to uncollectible accounts.

d. Journalize and post entries related to uncollectible accounts.

APPLIED SKILLS: LANGUAGE ARTS

Paraphrasing, writing complete sentences, and identifying subjects. For additional practice in language arts skills, direct students to answer the Questions for Individual Study at the end of the chapter. Students should write the answers in their own words and in complete sentences. To further practice language arts skills, ask students to underline the subject(s) in each sentence of their answers.

Accounts Receivable	−	Balance of Allowance for Uncollectible Accounts	=	Book Value of Accounts Receivable
$68,240.00	−	$9,492.00	=	$58,748.00

The book value of accounts receivable after writing off North Star's account is calculated as shown below.

Accounts Receivable	−	Balance of Allowance for Uncollectible Accounts	=	Book Value of Accounts Receivable
$67,684.00	−	$8,936.00	=	$58,748.00

Segregation of duties for internal control means that no one person or department should perform all phases of a transaction.

The book value remains the same because the same amount is deducted from both the accounts receivable account and the allowance account.

The general journal entry to write off North Star's account is shown in Illustration 21-4.

ILLUSTRATION 21-4

General journal entry to write off an uncollectible account

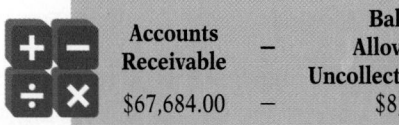

GENERAL JOURNAL PAGE *18*

	DATE	ACCOUNT TITLE	DOC. NO.	POST. REF.	DEBIT	CREDIT	
8	3	Allow. for Uncollectible Accts.	M2		5 5 6 00		8
9		Accts. Rec./North Star Co.				5 5 6 00	9
10							10
11							11
12							12
13							13
14							14

Allowance for Uncollectible Accounts is debited for $556.00. Accounts Receivable and North Star's account are both credited for $556.00.

Posting an Entry to Write Off an Uncollectible Account Receivable

After the journal entry to write off an uncollectible account is posted, the two general ledger accounts, Accounts Receivable and Allowance for Uncollectible Accounts, and the customer account appear as shown in Illustration 21-5 on page 576. The words *Written off* are written in the Item column of the customer account to show the full credit history for the customer.

CHAPTER 21 Accounting for Uncollectible Accounts Receivable **575**

- Draw T accounts on the board for the entry to write off an uncollectible account receivable. Use Transparency M to demonstrate how to journalize the transaction. Or direct students to Illustration 21-4.

- Demonstrate by drawing T accounts that when a customer pays an account that has been written off, the account is reopened by doing the opposite of the entry to write off.

- Use Transparency M to journalize the entry to reopen the customer account or direct the students to Illustration 21-6.

- Use Transparency O to journalize the receipt of cash on account entry or direct students to Illustration 21-7.

Guided Practice

- Guide students through Drill 21-D2. Students should have the forms from the working papers to complete as you guide them through the drills. All students should agree with the analysis of how each account is affected by each transaction before proceeding to the next transaction.

Independent Practice

Assign Term 4, Questions 13–18, Problems 21-2 and 21-3, Study Guide 21, and Mastery Problem 21-M.

ILLUSTRATION 21-5   General ledger and customer accounts after entry for writing off an uncollectible account is posted

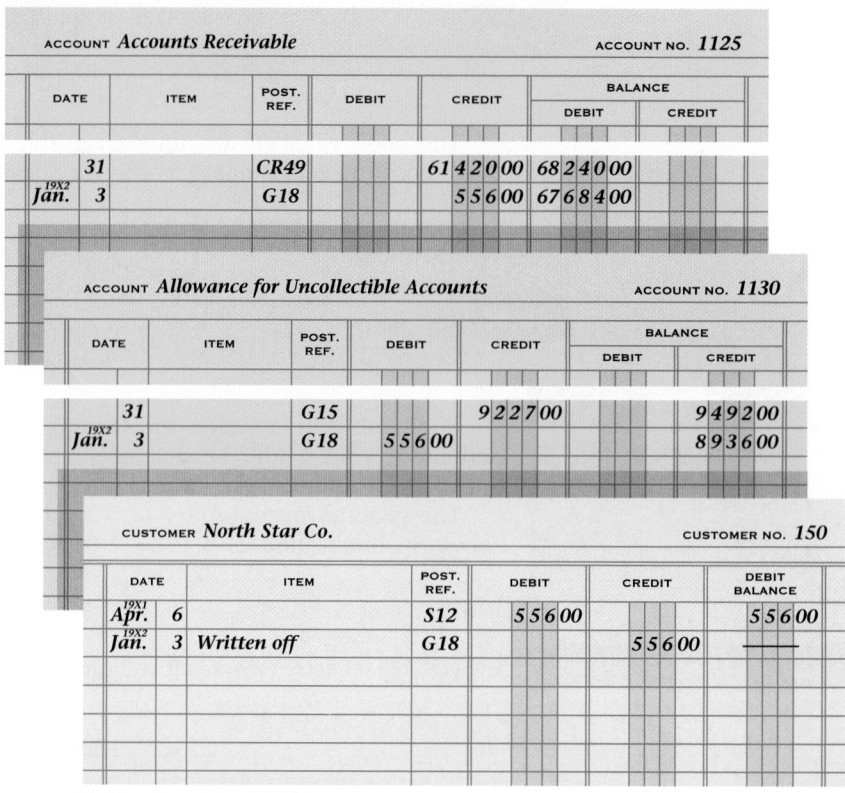

COLLECTING WRITTEN-OFF ACCOUNTS RECEIVABLE

A business writes off a specific account receivable after determining that the account probably will not be collected. Occasionally, after an account has been written off, the customer pays the delinquent account. Several accounts must be changed to recognize payment of a written-off account receivable.

Journalizing Collecting a Written-Off Account Receivable

> January 7, 19--. Received cash in full payment of North Star Co.'s account, previously written off as uncollectible, $556.00. Memorandum No. 3 and Receipt No. 4.

The accounts must be changed to show that North Star did pay its account. The accounts also should be changed to show a complete credit history of North Star's dealings with Celluphone. Two journal entries are recorded for the collection of a written-off account

---

TEACHING STRATEGIES: DIFFERENT LEARNING ABILITIES

Limited English Proficiency (LEP) Students. LEP students, like visual learners, require a variety of visual clues to support the lesson and help them understand abstract ideas. Use transparencies, textbook illustrations, and software demonstrations to provide these clues.

GENERAL LEDGER
Accounts Receivable

| Bal. | 68,240.00 | Jan. 3 | 556.00 |
| Jan. 7 | 556.00 | | |

Allowance for Uncollectible Accounts

| Jan. 3 | 556.00 | Bal. | 9,492.00 |
| | | Jan. 7 | 556.00 |

ACCOUNTS RECEIVABLE LEDGER
North Star Co.

Bal.	556.00	Jan. 3	556.00
Jan. 7	556.00		
(New Bal.	556.00)		

receivable. (1) A general journal entry to reopen the customer account. (2) A cash receipts journal entry to record the cash received on account.

General Journal Entry to Reopen the Customer Account. To show an accurate credit history, North Star's account is reopened.

Accounts Receivable is debited for $556.00. This debit entry replaces the amount previously written off in the general ledger account Accounts Receivable. Allowance for Uncollectible Accounts is credited for $556.00. This credit entry replaces the amount in the allowance account that was removed when North Star's account was previously written off. Also, North Star's account in the accounts receivable ledger is debited for $556.00. This entry to reopen the account is the exact reverse of the entry to write off North Star's account.

The general journal entry to reopen North Star's account in the accounts receivable ledger is shown in Illustration 21-6.

ILLUSTRATION 21-6   General journal entry to reopen customer account previously written off

		GENERAL JOURNAL				PAGE 18	
	DATE	ACCOUNT TITLE	DOC. NO.	POST. REF.	DEBIT	CREDIT	
16	7	Accts. Receivable/North Star Co.	M3	/	556 00		16
17		Allow. for Uncollectible Accts.				556 00	17
18							18
19							19
20							20
21							21
22							22

GENERAL LEDGER
Cash

| Jan. 7 | 556.00 | | |

Accounts Receivable

| Bal. | 68,240.00 | Jan. 3 | 556.00 |
| Jan. 7 | 556.00 | Jan. 7 | 556.00 |

ACCOUNTS RECEIVABLE LEDGER
North Star Co.

Bal.	556.00	Jan. 3	556.00
Jan. 7	556.00	Jan. 7	556.00
		(New Bal.	zero)

Cash Receipts Journal Entry to Record Cash Received for an Account Previously Written Off. After the entry to reopen North Star's account is recorded, an entry is made to record the cash received on North Star's account.

Cash is debited for $556.00. Accounts Receivable is credited for $556.00. North Star's account in the accounts receivable ledger is also credited for $556.00.

The cash receipts journal entry to record the receipt of cash on account from North Star Co. is shown in Illustration 21-7.

TEACHING STRATEGIES: TEACHING TIP

Annual reports from a number of companies may be collected. Students can review the income statements, balance sheets, and footnote explanations to the financial statements. Students should be directed to observe how these companies report uncollectible accounts expense and to note the significance of the amount of the expense.

CLOSURE

- Use Audit Your Understanding questions.
- Cover "Summary of Accounting for Uncollectible Accounts Receivable." Use Transparency 21-1, Chapter Summary.

ASSESS

- Administer Problem Test Chapter 21.
- Administer a MicroExam test for Chapter 21.

ILLUSTRATION 21-7

Cash receipts journal entry to record cash received for an account previously written off

CASH RECEIPTS JOURNAL

PAGE 51

	DATE	ACCOUNT TITLE	DOC. NO.	POST. REF.	GENERAL DEBIT	GENERAL CREDIT	ACCOUNTS RECEIVABLE CREDIT	SALES CREDIT	SALES TAX PAYABLE DEBIT	SALES TAX PAYABLE CREDIT	SALES DISCOUNT DEBIT	CASH DEBIT	
1	Jan. 7 (19X2)	North Star Co.	R4				5 5 6 00					5 5 6 00	1
2													2

Posting an Entry for Collecting a Written-Off Account Receivable

After posting the two entries to reopen North Star's account and to record collection of the account, the accounts affected appear as shown in Illustration 21-8.

ILLUSTRATION 21-8

General ledger and customer accounts after collection of a previously written-off account

ACCOUNT **Accounts Receivable**   ACCOUNT NO. 1125

DATE	ITEM	POST. REF.	DEBIT	CREDIT	BALANCE DEBIT	BALANCE CREDIT
31		CR49		61 4 2 0 00	68 2 4 0 00	
Jan. 3 (19X2)		G18		5 5 6 00	67 6 8 4 00	
7		G18	5 5 6 00		68 2 4 0 00	

ACCOUNT **Allowance for Uncollectible Accounts**   ACCOUNT NO. 1130

DATE	ITEM	POST. REF.	DEBIT	CREDIT	BALANCE DEBIT	BALANCE CREDIT
31		G15		9 2 2 7 00		9 4 9 2 00
Jan. 3 (19X2)		G18	5 5 6 00			8 9 3 6 00
7		G18		5 5 6 00		9 4 9 2 00

CUSTOMER **North Star Co.**   CUSTOMER NO. 150

DATE	ITEM	POST. REF.	DEBIT	CREDIT	DEBIT BALANCE
Apr. 6 (19X1)		S12	5 5 6 00		5 5 6 00
Jan. 3 (19X2)	Written off	G18		5 5 6 00	—
7	Reopen account	G18	5 5 6 00		5 5 6 00
7		CR51		5 5 6 00	—

TEACHING STRATEGIES: TEACHING TIP

In this chapter, students are instructed to make entries in the Item column of the customer ledger accounts. Remind students that this is a special procedure used to provide a historical record of customer payment history in the event a customer seeks additional credit in the future. "Written off" is recorded when an account is written off. "Reopen account" is recorded when the account is later reopened to record subsequent payment by the customer.

North Star's account balance is zero. The entries in North Star's account show a complete history of North Star's credit dealings with Celluphone. The account shows the April 6 balance, $556.00, and the balance written off on January 3. On January 7 the account is debited for the same amount, $556.00, to reopen North Star's account. The words *Reopen account* are written in the Item column to describe this entry. Also, on January 7 the account is credited for $556.00 to record payment of the account.

Entries resulting from cash received for a previously written-off account are recorded in a cash receipts journal's special amount columns. These amounts are posted to the general ledger accounts at the end of the month as part of the column totals.

SUMMARY OF ACCOUNTING FOR UNCOLLECTIBLE ACCOUNTS RECEIVABLE

Summary Illustration 21-9 on page 580 shows four entries that affect Accounts Receivable and its related expense and contra accounts when there are uncollectible accounts.

1. *Adjusting entry for uncollectible accounts expense.* The expense account, Uncollectible Accounts Expense, is debited for the amount of estimated uncollectible accounts expense for the fiscal period. The contra asset account, Allowance for Uncollectible Accounts, is credited for the estimated amount of uncollectible accounts expense.

2. *Writing off an uncollectible account receivable.* When a specific account is determined to be uncollectible, the balance of the account must be removed. The specific account in the accounts receivable ledger has a debit balance; therefore, it is credited for the uncollectible amount. In the general ledger, the controlling account, Accounts Receivable, is also credited. The contra asset account, Allowance for Uncollectible Accounts, is debited.

3. *Collecting a previously written off account receivable (first entry).* When a previously written off account is collected, it is first reinstated. Accounts Receivable is debited to restore the amount, and the customer's account in the accounts receivable ledger is also debited. The contra asset account, Allowance for Uncollectible Accounts, is credited for the same amount. This amount was debited to the account when the customer's account was written off.

4. *Collecting a previously written off account receivable (second entry).* Once the customer's account is reinstated, the cash receipt on account is recorded using the usual procedures. Cash is debited for the amount of the cash receipt and Accounts Receivable and the customer's account in the accounts receivable ledger are credited.

TEACHING STRATEGIES:
APPLYING VISUALS

Direct students to Summary Illustration 21-9 and review the effects on the accounts of entries for uncollectible accounts receivable.

By using two entries to record collection of a previously written off account, the accounts receivable ledger shows a complete history of the customer's account.

SUMMARY ILLUSTRATION 21-9

Summary of entries for uncollectible accounts receivable

Transactions		GENERAL LEDGER								Accts. Rec. Subsidiary Ledger	
		Cash		Accts. Rec.		Allow. for Uncoll. Accts.		Uncoll. Accts. Expense		Customer Account	
		Debit	Credit	Debit	Credit	Debit	Credit	Debit	Credit	Debit	Credit
Adjusting entry for uncollectible accounts expense							X	X			
Write off uncollectible account receivable					X	X					X
Collect previously written off account receivable	Entry 1			X			X			X	
	2	X			X						X

PART 4   Accounting for a Merchandising Business Organized as a Corporation

APPLIED SKILLS: WRITING ACROSS THE CURRICULUM

Writing paragraphs and short essays.   The Cases for Critical Thinking are short, practical applications of the accounting principles developed in the chapter. Some cases are planned to present problems related to the chapter but not specifically discussed and answered in the chapter. These cases present an opportunity for critical thinking and decision making. These cases also require more than a short objective-type response. Therefore, they provide ideal practice in writing paragraphs and short essays.

What is the meaning of each of the following?

1. **uncollectible accounts**
2. **allowance method of recording losses from uncollectible accounts**
3. **book value of accounts receivable**
4. **writing off an account**

QUESTIONS FOR INDIVIDUAL STUDY   EPT(b)

1. Why might a business sell merchandise on account?
2. Why is an uncollectible account recorded as an expense rather than a reduction in revenue?
3. When does the risk of loss from a sale on account occur?
4. Which accounting concept is being applied when uncollectible accounts expense is recorded in the same fiscal period in which the expense contributes to earning revenue?
5. When do businesses normally estimate the amount of their uncollectible accounts expense?
6. What two objectives will be accomplished by recording an estimated amount of uncollectible accounts expense?
7. Why is Allowance for Uncollectible Accounts called a contra account?
8. Why would a business use a percentage of total sales on account to estimate uncollectible accounts expense?
9. What is the procedure for estimating uncollectible accounts expense based on total sales on account?
10. What accounts are affected, and how, when an adjusting entry is made to record uncollectible accounts expense?
11. What kind of situation would cause Allowance for Uncollectible Accounts to have a balance in the work sheet's Trial Balance Credit column?
12. How is the book value of accounts receivable calculated?
13. What accounts are affected, and how, when an uncollectible account is written off?
14. Why is Allowance for Uncollectible Accounts debited when a customer account is written off?
15. Does the book value of accounts receivable differ before and after writing off an account? Explain.
16. Why is a customer account reopened when the account is paid after being previously written off?
17. What accounts are affected, and how, when a written-off account receivable is collected?
18. How does the journal entry for reopening an account previously written off differ from an entry for writing off an account?

CASES FOR CRITICAL THINKING   EPT(b)

CASE 1 CompuCraft Corporation has always assumed that an account receivable is good until the account is proven to be uncollectible. When an account proves to be uncollectible, the credit manager notifies the accounting clerk to write off the account. The accounting clerk then debits Uncollectible Accounts Expense and credits Accounts Receivable. Recently the company's new accountant, Diane Wilson, suggested that the method be changed for recording uncollectible accounts expense. Mrs. Wilson recommended that the company estimate uncollectible accounts expense based on a percentage of total sales on account. Mrs. Wilson stated that the change would provide more accurate information on the income statement and balance sheet. Do you agree with Mrs. Wilson that her recommended method would provide more accurate information? Explain.

CASE 2 Ulrick Corporation credits Accounts Receivable for the amount of estimated uncollectible accounts expense at the end of each fiscal period. Lindsey Company credits Allowance for Uncollectible Accounts for the amount of estimated uncollectible accounts expense at the end of each fiscal period. Which company is using the better method? Why?

1. **uncollectible accounts:** Accounts receivable that cannot be collected. (p. 569)
2. **allowance method of recording losses:** Crediting the estimated value of uncollectible accounts to a contra account. (p. 570)
3. **book value of accounts receivable:** The difference between the balance of Accounts Receivable and its contra account, Allowance for Uncollectible Accounts. (p. 570)
4. **writing off an account:** Canceling the balance of a customer account because the customer does not pay. (p. 574)

QUESTIONS FOR INDIVIDUAL STUDY

1. To encourage sales. (p. 569)
2. An uncollectible amount does not decrease revenue. Instead, the loss is considered a regular expense of doing business. Revenue was earned when the sale was made. Failing to collect an account does not cancel the sale. Therefore, the loss is treated as an expense. (p. 569)
3. When a business sells on account. (p. 569)
4. Matching Expenses with Revenue. (p. 569)
5. At the end of each fiscal period. (p. 569)
6. (a) An up-to-date value of uncollectible accounts expense prevents an overstatement of the value of accounts receivable on the balance sheet. (b) Recording the estimated uncollectible accounts expense prevents an understatement of expenses on the income statement. (p. 569–570)
7. Because it reduces the balance of its related account, Accounts Receivable. (p. 570)
8. Each sale on account represents a risk of loss from an uncollectible account. Therefore, if the estimated percentage of loss is accurate, the amount of uncollectible accounts expense will be accurate regardless of when the actual losses occur. Since a sale on account creates a risk of loss, estimating the percentage of uncollectible accounts expense for the same period matches sales revenue with related uncollectible accounts expense. (p. 570)
9. Multiply the total sales on account for a fiscal period by an estimated percentage of uncollectible accounts expense. (p. 570)
10. Uncollectible Accounts Expense is debited; Allowance for Uncollectible Accounts is credited. (p. 571)

11. Previous fiscal period estimates have not yet been identified as uncollectible. (p. 572)

12. The balance of Accounts Receivable minus the balance of Allowance for Uncollectible Accounts. (p. 574)

13. Allowance for Uncollectible Accounts is debited; Accounts Receivable and the customer account are credited. (p. 574)

14. The specific amount written off is no longer an estimate. Therefore, the amount of the uncollectible account is deducted from the allowance account. (p. 574)

15. No, the book value does not differ. The book value of accounts receivable is the same because the same amount is deducted from both the accounts receivable account and the allowance account. (pp. 574–575)

16. To show that the customer did pay the account and to show a complete credit history. (pp. 576–577)

17. Two entries are made. (a) To reopen the customer account, Accounts Receivable and the customer account are debited; Allowance for Uncollectible Accounts is credited. (b) To record the cash received on account, Cash is debited; Accounts Receivable and the customer account are credited. (p. 577)

18. The journal entry to reopen an account is the exact reverse of the entry to write off an account. (p. 577)

CASES FOR CRITICAL THINKING

Case 1 The percentage of total sales on account method recommended by Mrs. Wilson should provide more accurate financial statements. Risk of loss occurs when a business makes a sale on account. This potential loss is present even though several months may pass before the actual uncollectible account is determined. Recording uncollectible accounts expense in the same fiscal period the revenue is earned is an application of the Matching Expenses with Revenue concept. Accurate financial reporting requires that expenses be included in the accounting period in which the expenses contribute to earning revenue.

DRILLS FOR UNDERSTANDING

EPT(c,d)

DRILL 21-D1 Calculating estimated uncollectible accounts expense

TUTORIAL

MATHEMATICS

The accounting records of six stores show the following summary information for the fiscal period ended December 31 of the current year.

Store	Total Sales on Account	Estimated Uncollectible Accounts as Percentage of Sales on Account	Balance of Allowance for Uncollectible Accounts Before Adjustment
1	$48,700.00	0.6%	$32.00 Credit
2	73,900.00	0.5%	63.00 Credit
3	95,200.00	1.0%	24.00 Debit
4	61,400.00	0.7%	79.00 Credit
5	54,800.00	0.4%	Zero
6	89,600.00	0.8%	57.00 Debit

INSTRUCTIONS:

For each of the six stores, calculate the following:

a. Uncollectible accounts expense.

b. Balance of Allowance for Uncollectible Accounts after adjustment.

c. Book value of accounts receivable after adjustment. Use a balance of $25,000.00 for accounts receivable for each store.

DRILL 21-D2 Analyzing entries for uncollectible accounts

INSTRUCTIONS:

Use a form similar to the following. Analyze each entry. For each entry, indicate how each account is affected by writing one of the following: *DR* if debited, *CR* if credited, or *NE* if no entry is made.

Transaction	General Ledger				Accounts Receivable Ledger Customer Account
	Cash	Accounts Receivable	Allowance for Uncollectible Accounts	Uncollectible Accounts Expense	
A. Adjusting entry for uncollectible accounts expense at end of fiscal period					
B. Wrote off an uncollectible account					
C. Collected account previously written off 1) Entry 1:					
2) Entry 2:					

APPLICATION PROBLEMS

EPT(c,d)

PROBLEM 21-1 Estimating and journalizing entries for uncollectible accounts expense

Use the following information from the records of Caraway Company for three successive years.

Year	Total Sales on Account	Balance of Allowance for Uncollectible Accounts Before Adjustment
19X1	$473,221.00	$171.00 Credit
19X2	495,074.00	279.00 Credit
19X3	516,978.00	392.80 Credit

Caraway Company estimates uncollectible accounts expense as 1.0% of its total sales on account.

INSTRUCTIONS:

1. For each year record the uncollectible accounts expense adjustment on a work sheet.
2. For each year journalize the adjusting entry on page 13 of a general journal.

PROBLEM 21-2 Recording entries to write off uncollectible accounts receivable

During June of the current year, Alphacom Corporation determined that three accounts were uncollectible.

INSTRUCTIONS:

1. Journalize the entries to write off the following accounts. Use page 6 of a general journal.

June 4. Wrote off Davidson Corporation's past-due account as uncollectible, $347.00. M13.
     15. Wrote off Jordan Equipment Co.'s past-due account as uncollectible, $521.00. M20.
     30. Wrote off Porter, Inc.'s past-due account as uncollectible, $179.00, M27.

2. Post each entry to the customer accounts in the accounts receivable ledger.

PROBLEM 21-3 Recording transactions for collection of written-off accounts receivable

Abbott Electronics received payment for accounts that had previously been written off.

INSTRUCTIONS:

1. Journalize the following transactions completed during August of the current year. Use page 8 of a general journal and page 15 of a cash receipts journal.

Aug. 6. Received cash in full payment of Hargrove Inc.'s account, previously written off as uncollectible, $715.00. M4 and R34.
     20. Received cash in full payment of Andrews Corp.'s account, previously written off as uncollectible, $384.00. M27 and R92.
     27. Received cash in full payment of Tyler Co.'s account, previously written off as uncollectible, $443.00. M38 and R121.

2. Post each entry to the customer accounts in the accounts receivable ledger.

ENRICHMENT PROBLEMS

EPT(c,d)

MASTERY PROBLEM 21-M Recording entries for uncollectible accounts

APPLICATION

The accounts receivable ledger accounts for Travis Industries are given in the working papers accompanying this textbook.

INSTRUCTIONS:

1. Journalize the transactions on page 584 completed during October, November, and December of the current year. Use pages 10, 11, and 12 of a general journal and pages 11 and 12 of a cash receipts journal.

CHAPTER 21 Accounting for Uncollectible Accounts Receivable **583**

CASES FOR CRITICAL THINKING (cont'd)

Case 2 Lindsey Company is using the better method. As long as the amount being recorded is only an estimate, it should not be charged to the accounts receivable account. Only when it is known for sure that a customer cannot or will not pay the amount owed should the amount be credited to Accounts Receivable. Also, the total of Ulrick Corporation's accounts receivable ledger will not balance with the controlling account.

CHECK FIGURES

See Teacher's Edition of Working Papers for solutions.

Drill 21-D1 (1) 292.20, 324.20; (2) 369.50, 432.50; (3) 952, 928; (4) 429.80, 508.80; (5) 219.20, 219.20; (6) 716.80, 659.80.

Drill 21-D2 (A) NE, NE, CR, DR, NE; (B) NE, CR, DR, NE, CR; (C-1) NE, DR, CR, NE, DR; (C-2) DR, CR, NE, NE, CR.

Problem 21-1 Adjustments 4,732.21; 4,950.74; 5,169.78.

Problem 21-2 For each entry, dr. Allow. for Uncoll. Accts., cr. Accts. Rec.

Problem 21-3 For each entry, dr. Accts. Rec., cr. Allow. for Uncoll. Accts. Then record cash received.

Mastery Problem 21-M Adjusting entry 10,510.80.

Oct. 7. Wrote off Kingston Corporation's past-due account as uncollectible, $247.60. M202.
18. Wrote off Gentry Corporation's past-due account as uncollectible, $482.50. M206.
   Posting. Post each entry to the customer accounts in the accounts receivable ledger.
Nov. 8. Wrote off Burrell Company's past-due account as uncollectible, $714.15. M219.
17. Received cash in full payment of Kingston Corporation's account, previously written off as uncollectible, $247.60. M223 and R461.
   Posting. Post each entry to the customer accounts in the accounts receivable ledger.
Dec. 3. Wrote off Fiber-Tech's past-due account as uncollectible, $829.35. M226.
9. Received cash in full payment of Burrell Company's account, previously written off as uncollectible, $714.15. M229 and R514.
28. Received cash in full payment of Gentry Corporation's account, previously written off as uncollectible, $482.50. M235 and R547.
   Posting. Post each entry to the customer accounts in the accounts receivable ledger.

2. Journalize the December 31 adjusting entry for estimated uncollectible accounts expense for the year. Use page 13 of the general journal. Uncollectible accounts expense is estimated as 1.0% of total sales on account. Total sales on account for the year were $1,051,080.00.

CHALLENGE PROBLEM 21-C Recording entries for uncollectible accounts

Sunrise Nursery has general ledger accounts for account number 1130, Allowance for Uncollectible Accounts, and account number 6165, Uncollectible Accounts Expense. At the beginning of the current year, the credit balance of Allowance for Uncollectible Accounts was $1,573.25. Uncollectible accounts expense is estimated as 0.75% of the total sales on account each quarter.

INSTRUCTIONS:

1. Journalize entries for the following transactions and adjusting entries completed during the current year. Use page 1 of a general journal and a cash receipts journal. (Usually a new journal page is started each month and adjusting entries are also recorded on a new journal page. To conserve space in the working papers, record all of the year's entries on the same page of the appropriate journal.)

Jan. 11. Received a check in full payment of Taylor Corporation's account, previously written off as uncollectible, $317.40. M2 and R4.
Mar. 3. Gibson Company's past-due account was written off as uncollectible, $629.80. M7.
31. Record the adjusting entry for estimated uncollectible accounts expense for the end of the first quarterly fiscal period. Total sales on account for the first quarterly fiscal period were $174,920.00.
   Posting. Post entries to Allowance for Uncollectible Accounts and Uncollectible Accounts Expense.
May 5. Bowman, Inc.'s account, previously written off as uncollectible, was paid in full, $62.15. M13 and R39.
18. Wrote off Kirkwood Corporation's past-due account as uncollectible, $281.75. M16.
June 14. Liberty Landscapes' past-due account was written off as uncollectible, $753.40. M19.
30. End of second quarterly fiscal period. Record the adjusting entry for estimated uncollectible accounts expense. Sales on account for the second quarterly fiscal period totaled $195,800.00.
   Posting. Post entries to Allowance for Uncollectible Accounts and Uncollectible Accounts Expense.
July 6. Wrote off Plant Dimension Co.'s past-due account as uncollectible, $594.30. M20.
28. The past-due account of Parker Fertilizer Company was written off as uncollectible, $256.10. M24.

Sept. 28. Jacobsen Corporation's past-due account was written off as uncollectible, $74.80. M37.

30. Record the adjusting entry for estimated uncollectible accounts expense for the end of the third quarterly fiscal period. Total sales on account for the third quarterly fiscal period were $201,760.00.

Posting. Post entries to Allowance for Uncollectible Accounts and Uncollectible Accounts Expense.

Nov. 1. The past-due account of Superior Design was written off as uncollectible, $789.20. M38.

23. Cash was received in full payment of Parker Fertilizer Company's account, previously written off as uncollectible, $256.10. M41 and R114.

Dec. 31. End of fourth quarterly fiscal period. Record the adjusting entry for estimated uncollectible accounts expense. Total sales on account for the fourth quarterly fiscal period were $219,860.00.

Posting. Post entries to Allowance for Uncollectible Accounts and Uncollectible Accounts Expense.

2. Assume that you are the accountant for Sunrise Nursery. You have determined that all possible procedures are now being used to reduce uncollectible accounts. Examine the year's activity in the account Allowance for Uncollectible Accounts. Are the accounting procedures for uncollectible accounts adequate and accurate? Should any changes in procedure be recommended? If so, what? Explain the reason for your response.

A depreciation method used for the preparation of financial statements should be selected that most nearly allocates the cost of a plant asset over its useful life and in proportion to its decrease in value. Several depreciation methods comply with generally accepted accounting practices. Two of those accepted methods, straight-line depreciation and declining-balance depreciation, are presented in this text. This chapter is also expanded to include disposal of plant assets with both gains and losses.

GUIDE TO ACHIEVING LEARNING OBJECTIVES

Enabling Performance Tasks	TEACH Lesson Plans	APPLY Drills for Understanding	Application Problems	EXTEND/ENRICH Mastery Problems	Challenge Problems	Cases for Critical Thinking	Recycling Problems	Reinforcement Activity
a. Define accounting terms related to plant assets, depreciation, and property tax expense.	22-1, 22-2, 22-3, 22-4							
b. Identify accounting concepts and practices related to accounting for plant assets, depreciation, and property tax expense.	22-1, 22-2, 22-3, 22-4					Cases 1, 2		
c. Calculate depreciation expense and book value of a plant asset.	22-1, 22-2, 22-3, 22-4	22-D1, 22-D2	22-2, 22-6	22-M	22-C		22-R	
d. Record plant asset information in a plant asset record.	22-1, 22-2, 22-3		22-3					
e. Record entries related to accounting for plant assets, depreciation, and property tax expense.	22-1, 22-2, 22-3, 22-4		22-1, 22-4, 22-5, 22-7	22-M	22-C		22-R	3B

ENRICHMENT

SPECIAL FEATURES

Professional Business Ethics, page 594

Careers in Accounting, page 593

Applied Communications, page 613

TECHNOLOGY CONNECTION

Automated Accounting 6.0 Problems 22-6, 22-M, 22-C

Integrating Automated Accounting Topic 9 Optional Problem DB-9A

Accounting Tutorial Unit 8

Application Program Disk Problems 22-5, 22-7

Spreadsheet Template Problems 22-6, 22-M

Electronic Study Guide

NEW, REVIEW, AND EXTENSION

ACTIVITIES/CONCEPTS/TRANSACTIONS	NEW	REVIEW/ EXTENSION
Plant assets and depreciation	✓	
Recording buying plant assets	✓	
Calculating depreciation	✓	
Straight-line method of depreciation	✓	
Preparing plant asset records	✓	
Calculating book value of a plant asset	✓	
Adjustment for depreciation	✓	
Disposing of a plant asset	✓	
Gain and loss on plant assets	✓	
Declining-balance method of depreciation	✓	
Calculating and recording property tax	✓	

The Internal Revenue Service requires that for most plant assets placed in service after 1986, the IRS' Modified Accelerated Cost Recovery System (MACRS) depreciation method be used for income tax computation purposes. A brief discussion of this method is included in this chapter. However, the MACRS method is generally used only for the preparation of federal income tax returns.

	INFORMAL ASSESSMENT		FORMAL ASSESSMENT				
Study Guide	Audit Your Understanding	Chapter MicroExam	Chapter Problem Test	Unit Problem Test	Unit Objective Test	Portfolio
Unit A		✓			✓	
Unit C	✓	✓			✓	
	✓		✓	✓		
			✓			
Unit B			✓	✓		✓

TEACHING MATERIALS

Teacher's Wraparound Edition of the Text

Teacher's Resource Guide

Teacher's Edition of Working Papers

Teacher's Edition of Demonstration/Recycling Problems

Teaching Transparencies

Accounting Tutorial Manual

MicroExam

Applied Math Work Sheet

APPLIED MATHEMATICS

APPLIED MATH/ACCOUNTING SKILL	APPLICATION
Calculating Depreciation Expense for a Year (Straight-Line Method)	Drill 22-D1
Calculating Depreciation Expense for a Partial Year (Straight-Line Method)	Drill 22-D2
Calculating Book Value of Plant Assets	Drill 22-D2
Calculating Gain or Loss on a Plant Asset	Prob. 22-5
Calculating Depreciation Expense (Declining-Balance Method)	Prob. 22-6
Calculating Property Tax	Prob. 22-7

22

Accounting for Plant Assets and Depreciation

ENABLING PERFORMANCE TASKS

After studying Chapter 22, you will be able to:

a Define accounting terms related to plant assets, depreciation, and property tax expense.

b Identify accounting concepts and practices related to accounting for plant assets, depreciation, and property tax expense.

c Calculate depreciation expense and book value of a plant asset.

d Record plant asset information in a plant asset record.

e Record entries related to accounting for plant assets, depreciation, and property tax expense.

TERMS PREVIEW

current assets • plant assets • depreciation expense • estimated salvage value • straight-line method of depreciation • plant asset record • accumulated depreciation • book value of a plant asset • gain on plant assets • loss on plant assets • declining-balance method of depreciation • real property • personal property • assessed value

586

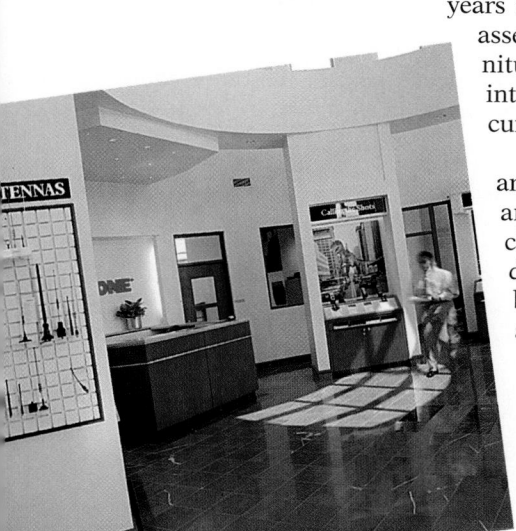

Most businesses use two broad categories of assets in the operations of their businesses. Cash and other assets expected to be exchanged for cash or consumed within a year are called **current assets.** Assets which will be used for a number of years in the operation of a business are called **plant assets.** Some of the more significant current assets used by Celluphone are cash, accounts receivable, merchandise inventory, supplies, and prepaid insurance. Celluphone also has plant assets that will be used for a number of years in the operation of its business. Some of Celluphone's plant assets are computers, cash registers, sales display cases, and furniture. These assets are used in the business and are not intended for sale to its customers. Celluphone's complete list of current and plant assets is in the chart of accounts, page 470.

The telephones Celluphone uses in operating the business are classified as plant assets. The telephones Celluphone buys and resells to its customers are merchandise inventory and classified as current assets. The difference in classification is determined by the way the asset is used. Assets purchased to be resold are merchandise inventory and classified as current assets. Assets bought to be used in operating the business are classified as plant assets.

Businesses may have three major types of plant assets—equipment, buildings, and land. Celluphone owns equipment, such as computers, cash registers, and sales display cases, that it uses to operate the business. However, the company rents the building and the land where the business is located. Therefore, Celluphone has accounts for equipment, which is the only type of plant asset it owns.

To provide more detailed financial information, Celluphone records its equipment in two different equipment accounts—Office Equipment and Store Equipment. *(CONCEPT: Adequate Disclosure)*

BUYING AND RECORDING PLANT ASSETS

Office Equipment	
Debit Side Normal Balance Increase	Credit Side Decrease

Procedures for recording the buying of a plant asset are similar to procedures for recording the buying of current assets such as supplies. The amount paid for a plant asset is debited to a plant asset account with a title such as Office Equipment. *(CONCEPT: Historical Cost)* A plant asset account has a normal debit balance. Therefore, a plant asset account such as Office Equipment is increased by a debit and decreased by a credit.

January 2, 19X1. Paid cash for a new printer, $820.00. Check No. 4.

Office Equipment	
820.00	

Cash	
	820.00

Celluphone has a separate plant asset account for office equipment. Therefore, Office Equipment is increased by an $820.00 debit. Cash is decreased by an $820.00 credit.

The cash payments journal entry to record this transaction is shown in Illustration 22-1 on page 588.

TEACHING STRATEGIES: EXPANDING BEYOND THE CLASSROOM

The instructor could invite a car dealer or bank loan officer to discuss the financing options available when a car is being purchased. This would be of personal interest to several students. The speaker should also address how businesses would finance such a purchase.

- The term asset was defined in Chapter 2. As each new business was studied, new asset accounts were included in the chart of accounts. In this lesson, the two basic categories of assets used by most businesses will be introduced: current assets and plant assets. Buying a plant asset is presented in this lesson. A plant asset is used for a number of years in the operation of a business. However, a plant asset decreases in value because of use and the passage of time. Therefore, a portion of the cost of a plant asset should be allocated to an expense each year that the plant asset is used to earn revenue. In this lesson, we will look at how to calculate this expense.

- Introduce new vocabulary: current assets, plant assets, depreciation expense, estimated salvage value, straight-line method of depreciation.

TEACH

Cover student pages 587–592 "Buying and Recording Plant Assets," "Effects of Depreciation on Plant Assets," and "Calculating Depreciation Expense." Emphasize the difference between current and plant assets. Ask students to give examples of current and plant assets. Discuss depreciation of an asset students can relate to such as a car. Emphasize that depreciation is an estimate. Also emphasize that depreciation does not necessarily represent the actual decline in the value of an asset; instead it is a method of allocating the cost of the asset over the years it will be used to generate revenue. Thus, expenses are matched with revenue.

ILLUSTRATION 22-1   Cash payments journal entry to record the buying of a plant asset

						1	2	3	4	5
						GENERAL		ACCOUNTS PAYABLE DEBIT	PURCHASES DISCOUNT CREDIT	CASH CREDIT
	DATE	ACCOUNT TITLE	CK. NO.	POST. REF.		DEBIT	CREDIT			
4	2	Office Equipment	4			82000				82000	4
5											5

After the entry for buying a printer is posted, the office equipment account in the general ledger appears as shown in Illustration 22-2.

ILLUSTRATION 22-2   A plant asset account in the general ledger

ACCOUNT Office Equipment						ACCOUNT NO. 1205			
DATE		ITEM	POST. REF.	DEBIT	CREDIT	BALANCE			
						DEBIT		CREDIT	
Jan. 19X1	1	Balance	✓			1283000			
	2		CP1	82000		1365000			

The $12,830.00 balance of Office Equipment is the original cost of office equipment owned on January 1. The $13,650.00 balance of Office Equipment is the original cost of office equipment owned on January 2. The debit balance of Office Equipment always shows the original cost of all office equipment owned. *(CONCEPT: Historical Cost)*

EFFECTS OF DEPRECIATION ON PLANT ASSETS

A business buys plant assets to use in earning revenue. Celluphone bought a new printer to use for preparing invoices and other correspondence for the business. Celluphone plans to use the printer for its entire useful life. However, plant assets such as Celluphone's printer decrease in value because of use. Plant assets also decrease in value with the passage of time as they become older and newer models become available. All plant assets, with the exception of land, have a limited useful life. However, plant assets generally have a useful life of several years.

In order to match revenue with the expenses used to earn the revenue, the cost of a plant asset should be allocated to an expense over the plant asset's useful life. Therefore, a portion of a plant asset's cost is transferred to an expense account in each fiscal period that a plant asset is used to earn revenue. *(CONCEPT: Matching Expenses with Revenue)* The portion of a plant asset's cost that is

APPLIED SKILLS: BUILDING STUDY SKILLS

Three new accounts, Office Equipment, Accumulated Depreciation, and Depreciation Expense are introduced in this chapter. Direct students to create a Quick Reference Guide (QRG) on a small card or sheet of paper to use as an aid in analyzing transactions. T accounts should be used to show normal balance sides. Students might also wish to write out the formulas for calculating depreciation expense and book value on the QRG.

transferred to an expense account in each fiscal period during a plant asset's useful life is called **depreciation expense.**

Depreciation expense differs from many other business expenses in one significant way. For many business expenses, cash is paid out in the same fiscal period in which the expense is recorded. For example, cash is generally paid for salaries during the same fiscal period in which salary expense is recorded for those salaries. However, cash is generally paid out when a plant asset is bought, but depreciation expense is recorded over several years. Celluphone paid $820.00 for a new printer in 19X1, but a portion of the new printer's cost will be recorded as depreciation expense each year during the estimated useful life of the printer.

Two factors affect the useful life of a plant asset: (1) physical depreciation and (2) functional depreciation. Physical depreciation is caused by wear from use and deterioration from aging and weathering. Functional depreciation occurs when a plant asset becomes inadequate or obsolete. An asset is inadequate when it can no longer satisfactorily perform needed service. An asset is obsolete when a newer machine can operate more efficiently or produce better service.

Land, because of its permanent nature, generally is not subject to depreciation. Buildings, after years of use, eventually become unusable to a business. However, the building may be torn down and a new building constructed on the same land. Since land can be used indefinitely, it is considered permanent and is not depreciated.

> **☞☞ FYI ☞☞**
> Deterioration causes physical depreciation. Obsolescence causes functional depreciation.

CALCULATING DEPRECIATION EXPENSE

Depreciation expense is recorded for each fiscal period a plant asset is used. *(CONCEPT: Accounting Period Cycle)* Several factors are considered in calculating depreciation expense.

Factors Affecting Depreciation Expense

Three factors affect the amount of depreciation expense for a plant asset.

1. The original cost of a plant asset.
2. The estimated salvage value of a plant asset.
3. The estimated useful life of a plant asset.

Original Cost. The original cost of a plant asset includes all costs paid to make the asset usable to a business. These costs include the price of the asset, delivery costs, and any necessary installation costs. The original cost of the new printer bought by Celluphone is $820.00.

Estimated Salvage Value. Generally, a business removes a plant asset from use and disposes of it when the asset is no longer usable. The amount that will be received for an asset at the time of its

> **☞☞ FYI ☞☞**
> Depreciation does not represent the actual decline in value of an asset. Instead, it is an allocation of the asset's cost over several fiscal periods.

APPLY

- Draw T accounts on the board for the buying of a plant asset transaction. Use Transparency L to demonstrate how to journalize the transaction or direct students to Illustration 22-1.

- Place the two formulas for calculating total depreciation expense and annual depreciation expense on the board and explain.

- Demonstrate calculating straight-line depreciation using the two formulas on the board. Use the problem: Cost $450, salvage $50, life 4 years (total depreciation is $400 and annual depreciation is $100). Use additional problem data as needed. When finished, do not erase.

- Use the problems on the board to extend the calculations to calculating depreciation for part of a year if each asset was bought June 1; August 1; December 1.

Guided Practice

Guide students through Drill 22-D1. Students should have the forms from the working papers to complete as you guide them through the calculations for each plant asset. All students should agree with the calculation for each plant asset before proceeding to the next plant asset.

Independent Practice

Assign Terms 1–5, Questions 1–10, Problems 22-1 and 22-2.

TEACHING STRATEGIES: TEACHING TIP

Point out that 19-- is used through most of the textbook to indicate the year a transaction occurs. The hyphens are used instead of actual years to avoid dating the textbook. In this chapter, 19X1 and 19X2 are used to designate the first year a transaction occurs (19X1) and the second year in which another transaction occurs (19X2). This method of indicating the years is used when it is important to show the time relationship between one transaction and another.

Reteach

Duplicate and assign Math Work Sheet Chapter 22 Parts A and B, Calculating Depreciation Expense for a Year (Straight-Line Method) and Calculating Depreciation Expense for a Partial Year (Straight-Line Method) from the Masters and Solutions to Enrichment/Application Activities section in the Teacher's Resource Guide to provide additional practice on the mathematics of calculating depreciation expense.

Extend

Use Demonstration Problem 22A, Instructions 1 and 2.

Enrich

Discuss the PROFESSIONAL BUSINESS ETHICS feature on page 594. You may wish to distribute copies of the 3-step Checklist for Making Ethical Decisions. A blackline master is furnished in the Masters and Solutions to Enrichment/Application Activities Section in the Teacher's Resource Guide.

FYI

Salvage value is also called residual value or scrap value.

disposal is not known when the asset is bought. Thus, the amount that may be received at disposal must be estimated. The amount an owner expects to receive when a plant asset is removed from use is called **estimated salvage value**. Estimated salvage value may also be referred to as residual value or scrap value.

Celluphone estimates a salvage value of $100.00 for the new printer at the end of its useful life.

Estimated Useful Life. The total amount of depreciation expense is distributed over the estimated useful life of a plant asset. When a plant asset is bought, the exact length of useful life is impossible to predict. Therefore, the number of years of useful life must be estimated.

Celluphone estimates that the useful life of a printer is five years. An estimate of useful life should be based on prior experience with similar assets and on available guidelines. Trade associations frequently publish guidelines for specialized plant assets. For tax purposes the Internal Revenue Service also publishes depreciation guidelines for plant assets.

Calculating Depreciation Expense for a Fiscal Year

The total cost of a plant asset that should be allocated to an expense over the asset's useful life is the amount paid for the asset (original cost) less the estimated salvage value. This difference, original cost less estimated salvage value, is the estimated total depreciation expense for the asset's entire useful life.

The total amount of estimated depreciation expense for the printer bought on January 2 is calculated as shown below.

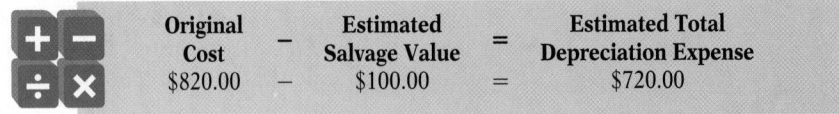

	Original Cost	−	Estimated Salvage Value	=	Estimated Total Depreciation Expense
	$820.00	−	$100.00	=	$720.00

Charging an equal amount of depreciation expense for a plant asset in each year of useful life is called the **straight-line method of depreciation**. Celluphone uses the straight-line method to calculate depreciation.

Depreciation expense for a fiscal year is calculated by dividing a plant asset's estimated total depreciation expense by the estimated useful life in years.

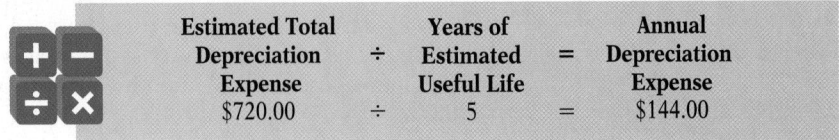

	Estimated Total Depreciation Expense	÷	Years of Estimated Useful Life	=	Annual Depreciation Expense
	$720.00	÷	5	=	$144.00

The depreciation expense for Celluphone's printer is $144.00 each year of use. Since Celluphone used the printer for all of the

TEACHING STRATEGIES: TEACHING TIP

Teach the arithmetic of depreciation. Additional exercises similar to Drill 22-D1 may be used for chalkboard drills. Place three headings on the chalkboard: (a) Original Cost, (b) Estimated Salvage Value, and (c) Estimated Useful Life. Place amounts under columns for a plant asset. Instruct students to calculate annual depreciation expense (or a specific portion of a year's depreciation). Have students raise their hands when they have calculated the answer. Call on various students to verify the correct answer. Repeat until all students can calculate depreciation expense.

year it was bought, January 2 to December 31, one year's depreciation expense, $144.00, is charged as an expense for the year.

There are other methods of calculating depreciation expense. However, the straight-line method is widely used because it allocates a plant asset's original cost equally to each accounting period and is simple to calculate.

Calculating Depreciation Expense for Part of a Fiscal Year

Depreciation expense is calculated for a fiscal year for those plant assets used throughout the entire fiscal year. However, if a plant asset is bought during the year, the asset will be used only part of that fiscal year. Thus, depreciation expense should be calculated for only the part of the year the asset is used. To calculate depreciation expense for part of a year, the annual depreciation expense is divided by 12 to determine the depreciation expense for a month. The monthly depreciation expense is then multiplied by the number of months the plant asset is used that year.

Celluphone bought a new computer on July 1, 19X1. The original cost is $4,600.00, the estimated salvage value is $1,000.00, and the estimated useful life is four years. Celluphone calculated the computer depreciation expense for 19X1 by following four steps. The first two steps are similar to those illustrated previously for Celluphone's printer. The third and fourth steps are used to calculate depreciation expense for part of a year.

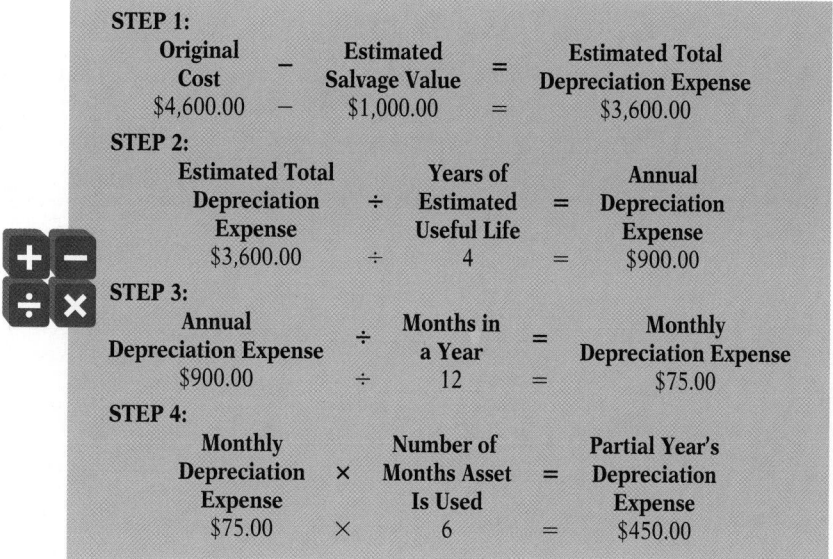

STEP 1:

Original Cost	−	Estimated Salvage Value	=	Estimated Total Depreciation Expense
$4,600.00	−	$1,000.00	=	$3,600.00

STEP 2:

Estimated Total Depreciation Expense	÷	Years of Estimated Useful Life	=	Annual Depreciation Expense
$3,600.00	÷	4	=	$900.00

STEP 3:

Annual Depreciation Expense	÷	Months in a Year	=	Monthly Depreciation Expense
$900.00	÷	12	=	$75.00

STEP 4:

Monthly Depreciation Expense	×	Number of Months Asset Is Used	=	Partial Year's Depreciation Expense
$75.00	×	6	=	$450.00

The depreciation expense for the part of the year Celluphone used the new computer is $450.00.

CHAPTER 22 Accounting for Plant Assets and Depreciation **591**

LESSON PLAN 22-2

Materials

- Student pages 592–598
- Transparencies: 22-1, Blank Plant Asset Record; C, Blank 8-column Work Sheet; M, Blank General Journal
- Math Work Sheet Chapter 22: Part C: Calculating Book Value of Plant Assets (TRG)
- Demonstration Problems: 22A Calculating Depreciation Expense and Preparing a Plant Asset Record, 22B Recording Work Sheet Adjustments and Journal Entries for Depreciation Expense
- Software: Accounting Tutorial

Objectives (Enabling Performance Tasks)

a. Define accounting terms related to plant assets, depreciation, and property tax expense.

b. Identify accounting concepts and practices related to accounting for plant assets, depreciation, and property tax expense.

c. Calculate depreciation expense and book value of a plant asset.

d. Record plant asset information in a plant asset record.

e. Record entries related to accounting for plant assets, depreciation, and property tax expense.

Audit Your Understanding

1. What are three major types of plant assets?
2. What is the normal balance of a plant asset account?
3. What two factors affect the useful life of a plant asset?
4. What three factors affect the amount of depreciation expense?
5. How is the estimated total depreciation expense for a plant asset's entire useful life calculated?

FYI

Always record the original cost of the asset in the plant asset account when new equipment is bought.

When determining the number of months to use in calculating depreciation for part of a year, most businesses round to the nearest whole month. For example, if an asset is bought on July 7, the asset is used for more than half the month. Thus, depreciation expense would be calculated for all of July. If an asset is bought on July 19, the asset is used for less than half the month. Thus, depreciation expense is not calculated for any of July.

PREPARING PLANT ASSET RECORDS

A separate record is kept for each plant asset. An accounting form on which a business records information about each plant asset is called a **plant asset record.**

Plant asset records may vary in arrangement for different businesses, but most records contain similar information. Celluphone's plant asset record, shown in Illustration 22-3, has three sections. Section 1 is prepared when a plant asset is bought. Information in this section shows the description, general ledger account title and number, date bought, serial number, and information needed to calculate annual depreciation expense for the plant asset. Section 2 provides space for recording disposition of the plant asset. This information will be filled in when the asset is disposed of. Section 3 provides space for recording annual depreciation expense and the changing book value of the asset each year it is used.

ILLUSTRATION 22-3   Plant asset record

PLANT ASSET RECORD

General Ledger Account No.		1205
Description	Computer	General Ledger Account	Office Equipment
Date Bought	July 1, 19X1	Serial Number	19X5-24867	Original Cost	$4,600.00
Estimated Useful Life	4 years	Estimated Salvage Value	$1,000.00	Annual Depreciation	$900.00

Disposed of: _____ Discarded _____ Sold _____ Traded _____
Date _____ Disposal Amount _____

YEAR	ANNUAL DEPRECIATION EXPENSE	ACCUMULATED DEPRECIATION	ENDING BOOK VALUE
19X1	450.00	450.00	4,150.00
19X2	900.00	1,350.00	3,250.00
19X3	900.00	2,250.00	2,350.00
19X4	900.00	3,150.00	1,450.00
19X5	450.00	3,600.00	1,000.00

Continue record on back of card

At the end of each fiscal period, Celluphone brings each plant asset record up to date by calculating and recording three amounts:

592

592

(1) annual depreciation expense, (2) accumulated depreciation, and (3) ending book value.

The amount recorded in the Annual Depreciation Expense column is always the amount recorded for the fiscal year. The annual depreciation expense for the computer bought July 1, 19X1, is $900.00. However, the amount recorded for the year 19X1 in the Annual Depreciation Expense column is $450.00, the amount of depreciation expense for the part of the year Celluphone actually used the computer.

Depreciation is the portion of a plant asset's cost that is transferred to an expense account at the end of each fiscal period during the plant asset's useful life. Therefore, as the amount of depreciation expense increases, the remaining value of the plant asset decreases. However, important information would be lost if the plant asset account is reduced each time depreciation expense is recorded. Thus, information about the original cost of a plant asset and the total amount of depreciation expense recorded over the life of a plant asset should be retained. Therefore, the cumulative total of depreciation expense is recorded. The total amount of depreciation expense that has been recorded since the purchase of a plant asset is called **accumulated depreciation.**

At the end of the fiscal year 19X1, Celluphone has used its computer six months, or half a year. Since the computer had no previous depreciation expense in 19X1, the accumulated depreciation for 19X1 is the same amount as the depreciation expense, $450.00, as shown in Illustration 22-3.

A plant asset's accumulated depreciation each fiscal period is calculated as shown below for the first two years of life for Celluphone's computer.

Year	Previous Year's Balance of Accumulated Depreciation	+	Current Year's Depreciation Expense	=	Current Year's Balance of Accumulated Depreciation
19X1	0	+	$450.00	=	$ 450.00
19X2	$450.00	+	$900.00	=	$1,350.00

For 19X1, $450.00 is recorded and for 19X2, $1,350.00 is recorded in the plant asset record's Accumulated Depreciation column.

The original cost of a plant asset minus accumulated depreciation is called the **book value of a plant asset.** To complete the end-of-fiscal-period updating of a plant asset record, the ending book value is calculated. The ending book value for Celluphone's computer is calculated as shown below.

Year	Original Cost	–	Accumulated Depreciation	=	Ending Book Value
19X1	$4,600.00	–	$ 450.00	=	$4,150.00
19X2	$4,600.00	–	$1,350.00	=	$3,250.00

CHAPTER 22   Accounting for Plant Assets and Depreciation   **593**

CAREERS IN ACCOUNTING

The CAREERS IN ACCOUNTING feature box, CREDIT REPORTING CLERK, comes from the Dictionary of Occupational Titles (DOT). The entry number for this job title is D.O.T. 203.362-014. The career feature is designed to expose students to the exploration of different careers in accounting. The feature gives a realistic description of actual job duties. This feature can be used to demonstrate that the skills learned in this course are relevant.

FOCUS

- Buying a plant asset and calculating depreciation expense for a plant asset were presented earlier in this chapter. In this lesson, we will record information about a plant asset in a special accounting form called a plant asset record. Explain that the annual depreciation expense is recorded on this form. Book value of accounts receivable was presented in Chapter 21; in this lesson, book value of a plant asset is described.

- Introduce new vocabulary: plant asset record; accumulated depreciation; book value of a plant asset.

TEACHING STRATEGIES: DIFFERENT LEARNING STYLES

Kinesthetic Learner. The kinesthetic learner should have the opportunity to perform the calculations to solve the formula. One way to accomplish this is to develop a work sheet with several depreciable assets listed. The student should calculate the amount of annual depreciation for each asset.

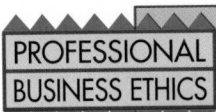

PROFESSIONAL BUSINESS ETHICS

What Does the Policy Manual Say?

Pathanos Technologies sells and services business communication equipment. The company purchases plant assets to make its employees more productive and earn more income for its stockholders. A statement from the company policies and procedures manual reads: "Company-owned assets shall not be used by employees or their dependents for any purpose other than for the economic benefit of the company. Exceptions to this policy must be approved by written permission of the board of directors."

Like most companies, Pathanos Technologies has an informal communication system often referred to as a grapevine. While eating lunch in the company's cafeteria, you learn of the following situations through the grapevine.

Situation 1. Ella Huckaby, the accounts payable clerk, uses the company's WATTS line to call relatives and friends. The cost of calls made on a WATTS line is considerably less than the cost of calls made on her personal phone. The company is billed for each minute the WATTS line is used.

Situation 2. Janice Iverson, an administrative assistant, uses a company computer to key university students' term papers for which she receives

---

FYI

Book value is what the asset is worth in the "books" of the business. It is the difference between original cost (an actual amount) and accumulated depreciation (an estimated amount).

The book value is recorded each year in the plant asset record's Ending Book Value column, as shown in Illustration 22-3.

A plant asset is never depreciated below its estimated salvage value. Therefore, when a plant asset's book value equals its estimated salvage value, no further depreciation expense is recorded. The book value of Celluphone's computer at the end of 19X4, as shown in Illustration 22-3, is $1,450.00. Only $450.00 depreciation expense is needed to reduce the book value to the estimated salvage value, $1,000.00. Therefore, on December 31, 19X5, only $450.00 depreciation expense is recorded for Celluphone's computer. Thus, at the end of 19X5, and thereafter, the book value for the computer will remain at $1,000.00.

ACCOUNTS AFFECTING THE VALUATION OF PLANT ASSETS

Three general ledger accounts are used to record information about each kind of plant asset. (1) An asset account is used to record the original cost of the asset. (2) An expense account is used to record the amount of depreciation expense. (3) A contra asset account is used to record the accumulated depreciation.

Plant Asset Accounts

Celluphone uses two plant asset accounts: Office Equipment and Store Equipment. The appropriate plant asset account is debited for the

---

TEACHING STRATEGIES: DIFFERENT LEARNING ABILITIES

Limited English Proficiency (LEP) Students. Allow for longer pauses when you ask questions. Non-native speakers need more time to formulate their answers.

APPLY

- Use Transparency 22-1 to describe a plant asset record or direct students to Illustration 22-3.
- Place the formula on the board for calculating book value.
- Draw T accounts for Accumulated Depreciation and Depreciation Expense and label the normal balance sides.
- Use Transparency C to demonstrate recording adjustments for depreciation on a work sheet or direct students to Illustration 22-4.
- Use Transparency M to demonstrate journalizing the adjusting entries or direct students to Illustration 22-5.

Guided Practice

Guide students through Drill 22-D2. Students should have the forms from the working papers to complete as you guide them through the calculations for each plant asset. All students should agree with the calculation for each plant asset before proceeding to the next plant asset.

Independent Practice

Assign Terms 6–8, Questions 11–14, Problems 22-3 and 22-4.

original cost when equipment is bought. The account is credited for the original cost when equipment is disposed of. Therefore, the balance of a plant asset account always shows the original cost of all equipment in current use.

Depreciation Expense Accounts

Depreciation is an expense to a business. To record depreciation expense for a fiscal period, an adjusting entry is made to two accounts. The amount of depreciation for a fiscal period is debited to an expense account titled Depreciation Expense.

Celluphone uses two depreciation expense accounts: Depreciation Expense—Office Equipment and Depreciation Expense—Store Equipment. The location of these expense accounts is shown in Celluphone's chart of accounts.

Accumulated Depreciation Accounts

Accumulated Depreciation	
Debit side	Credit side
	Normal balance
Decrease	Increase

The adjusting entry for the amount of depreciation for a fiscal period also has a credit to a contra asset account titled Accumulated Depreciation. A contra asset account has a normal credit balance. Therefore, the accumulated depreciation account is increased by a credit and decreased by a debit.

The account title Allowance for Depreciation is sometimes used instead of Accumulated Depreciation.

Celluphone uses two accumulated depreciation accounts: Accumulated Depreciation—Office Equipment and Accumulated Depreciation —

CHAPTER 22   Accounting for Plant Assets and Depreciation   **595**

TEACHING STRATEGIES: TEACHING TIP

Link new learning with previous learnings. Explain how the contra asset account, Accumulated Depreciation, is similar to the contra asset account, Allowance for Uncollectible Accounts, described in Chapter 21. Describe how plant assets accounts have a book value just as accounts receivable have a book value. Describe the calculation of book value as asset account minus contra account equals book value to draw the parallel between book value of accounts receivable and plant assets.

Assess student understanding by checking solutions to Independent Practice activities.

Reteach

- Use Demonstration Problem 22A, Instructions 3 and 4. This problem can be done on the overhead with the students completing the problem at their desks.

- Use Demonstration Problem 22B. This problem can be done on the overhead with the students completing the problem at their desks.

- Duplicate and assign Math Work Sheet Chapter 22, Part C, Calculating Book Value of Plant Assets from the Masters and Solutions to Enrichment/Application Activities section in the Teacher's Resource Guide to provide additional practice on the mathematics of calculating book value of plant assets.

Extend

- Assign Cases for Critical Thinking 1.
- Assign the Accounting Tutorial, Unit 8.

Enrich

Assign the Applied Communications special feature on page 613.

Store Equipment. The location of these contra asset accounts is shown in Celluphone's chart of accounts.

RECORDING DEPRECIATION EXPENSE

At the end of the fiscal year, Celluphone calculates the depreciation expense for each plant asset. Next, the total depreciation expense is calculated for all plant assets of the same kind. For example, in 19X1 the depreciation expense for the new printer is $144.00. The depreciation expense for other office equipment is $1,606.00. Thus, the total office equipment depreciation expense for the year is $1,750.00. Celluphone's accumulated depreciation for each kind of plant asset on December 31, 19X1, is calculated as shown below.

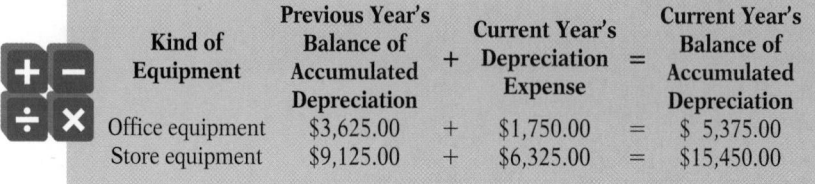

Kind of Equipment	Previous Year's Balance of Accumulated Depreciation	+	Current Year's Depreciation Expense	=	Current Year's Balance of Accumulated Depreciation
Office equipment	$3,625.00	+	$1,750.00	=	$ 5,375.00
Store equipment	$9,125.00	+	$6,325.00	=	$15,450.00

Analyzing an Adjustment for Depreciation Expense

An adjusting entry is made to record depreciation expense for a fiscal period. The T accounts show the office equipment account, depreciation expense account, and accumulated depreciation account before and after the adjustment for depreciation expense is made.

Depreciation Expense—Office Equipment is debited for $1,750.00 to show the increase in the balance of this expense account. The balance of this account, $1,750.00, is the estimated depreciation expense for the accounting period.

Accumulated Depreciation—Office Equipment is credited for $1,750.00 to show the increase in the balance of this contra asset account. The January 1 balance, $3,625.00, plus the annual increase, $1,750.00, equals the December 31 balance, $5,375.00. The office equipment account balance, $18,250.00, *minus* the accumulated depreciation account balance, $5,375.00, *equals* the office equipment book value, $12,875.00.

A similar adjusting entry is made to record depreciation expense for store equipment. The book value of each kind of plant asset after the adjustments on December 31, 19X1, is calculated as shown on the next page.

BEFORE ADJUSTMENT
Office Equipment

Jan. 1 Bal.	12,830.00	
Jan. 2	820.00	
July 1	4,600.00	
Dec. 31 Bal.	*18,250.00*	

Depreciation Expense—Office Equipment

Accumulated Depreciation—Office Equipment

	Jan. 1 Bal.	3,625.00

AFTER ADJUSTMENT
Office Equipment

Jan. 1 Bal.	12,830.00	
Jan. 2	820.00	
July 1	4,600.00	
Dec. 31 Bal.	*18,250.00*	

Depreciation Expense—Office Equipment

Dec. 31 Adj.	1,750.00	

Accumulated Depreciation—Office Equipment

	Jan. 1 Bal.	3,625.00
	Dec. 31 Adj.	1,750.00
	Dec. 31 Bal.	*5,375.00*

TEACHING STRATEGIES: DIFFERENT LEARNING STYLES

Print Learner. When learning formulas, the print learner would prefer to be able to study the formula as given in the textbook or as printed on a separate handout. The print material should show the formula as well as an example of performing the calculations.

	Kind of Equipment	Balance of Asset Account	−	Total Accumulated Depreciation	=	Ending Book Value 12/31/X1
	Office equipment	$18,250.00	−	$ 5,375.00	=	$12,875.00
	Store equipment	$77,190.00	−	$15,450.00	=	$61,740.00

CLOSURE

- Use Audit Your Understanding questions.

- Review the formula for calculating accumulated depreciation: Previous Year's Balance of Accumulated Depreciation + Current Year's Depreciation Expense = Current Year's Balance of Accumulated Depreciation.

- Review the formula for calculating book value: Original Cost − Accumulated Depreciation = Ending Book Value.

Planning Depreciation Expense Adjustments on a Work Sheet

Celluphone plans the adjustments for depreciation expense in the Adjustments columns of a work sheet. The adjustments for depreciation expense are on the partial work sheet shown in Illustration 22-4.

ILLUSTRATION 22-4   Adjustments for depreciation expense on a work sheet

Celluphone, Inc.
Work Sheet
For Year Ended December 31, 19X1

	ACCOUNT TITLE	TRIAL BALANCE DEBIT	TRIAL BALANCE CREDIT	ADJUSTMENTS DEBIT	ADJUSTMENTS CREDIT
10	Office Equipment	18 2 5 0 00			
11	Accum. Depr.—Office Equipment		3 6 2 5 00		(f) 1 7 5 0 00
12	Store Equipment	77 1 9 0 00			
13	Accum. Depr.—Store Equipment		9 1 2 5 00		(g) 6 3 2 5 00
37	Depr. Exp.—Office Equipment			(f) 1 7 5 0 00	
38	Depr. Exp.—Store Equipment			(g) 6 3 2 5 00	
39					

APPLIED SKILLS:
MATHEMATICS

Use the MATH WORK SHEETS in the Masters and Solutions to Enrichment/Application Activities Section of the Teacher's Resource Guide to integrate applied mathematics. In these work sheets, students will apply math concepts to calculate depreciation expense for a year using the straight-line method, depreciation expense for a partial year using the straight-line method, book value of plant assets, gain or loss on disposal of a plant asset, declining-balance depreciation expense, and property tax.

Adjustment for Depreciation of Office Equipment. On line 37 the increase in Depreciation Expense—Office Equipment, *$1,750.00*, is entered in the Adjustments Debit column. On line 11 the increase in Accumulated Depreciation—Office Equipment, *$1,750.00*, is entered in the Adjustments Credit column.

Adjustment for Depreciation of Store Equipment. On line 38 the increase in Depreciation Expense—Store Equipment, *$6,325.00*, is entered in the Adjustments Debit column. On line 13 the increase in Accumulated Depreciation—Store Equipment, *$6,325.00*, is entered in the Adjustments Credit column.

Journalizing Adjusting Entries for Depreciation Expense

Information needed to journalize adjustments for depreciation expense is obtained from the work sheet's Adjustments columns.

CHAPTER 22   Accounting for Plant Assets and Depreciation   **597**

Celluphone's two adjusting entries to record depreciation expense are shown in Illustration 22-5.

ILLUSTRATION 22-5   Adjusting entries to journalize depreciation expense

	DATE	ACCOUNT TITLE	DOC. NO.	POST. REF.	DEBIT	CREDIT	
	GENERAL JOURNAL					PAGE 15	
12	31	Depr. Exp.—Office Equipment			1 7 5 0 00		12
13		Accum. Depr.—Office Equipment				1 7 5 0 00	13
14	31	Depr. Exp.—Store Equipment			6 3 2 5 00		14
15		Accum. Depr.—Store Equipment				6 3 2 5 00	15
16							16
17							17

Posting Adjusting Entries for Depreciation Expense

After adjusting entries for depreciation expense are posted, the accounts appear as shown in Illustration 22-6.

Office Equipment and Store Equipment have debit balances showing the original cost of equipment. The two contra accounts for the equipment accounts have credit balances showing the accumulated depreciation recorded to date. The two depreciation expense accounts have debit balances showing depreciation expense for the current fiscal period.

DISPOSING OF A PLANT ASSET

A business uses a plant asset for its useful life. A plant asset may no longer be useful to a business for a number of reasons. The asset may not be needed. The asset may be worn out or more productive new assets may be available. Whatever the reason, when a plant asset is no longer useful to a business, the asset may be disposed of. The old plant asset may be sold, traded for a new asset, or discarded.

When a plant asset is disposed of, a journal entry is recorded that achieves the following three effects in the accounts.

1. Removes the original cost of the plant asset and its related accumulated depreciation.
2. Recognizes any cash or other asset received for the old plant asset.
3. Recognizes the gain or loss on the disposal, if any.

Sidebar content:

AUDIT YOUR UNDERSTANDING

1. (1) Annual depreciation expense, (2) accumulated depreciation, and (3) ending book value.
2. None.
3. Credit.
4. No effect on the plant asset account; the amount is recorded in the accumulated depreciation account.
5. Debit Depreciation Expense, credit Accumulated Depreciation.

LESSON PLAN 22-3

Materials

- Student pages 598–606
- Transparencies: M, Blank General Journal; O, Blank Cash Receipts Journal
- Software: Application Program Disk
- Math Work Sheet Chapter 22: Part D: Calculating Gain or Loss on a Plant Asset (TRG)
- Demonstration Problem: 22C Calculating Depreciation Expense and Book Value of Plant Assets; Journalizing Depreciation Expense and Disposing of a Plant Asset

Objectives (Enabling Performance Tasks)

a. Define accounting terms related to plant assets, depreciation, and property tax expense.
b. Identify accounting concepts and practices related to accounting for plant assets, depreciation, and property tax expense.
c. Calculate depreciation expense and book value of a plant asset.
d. Record plant asset information in a plant asset record.
e. Record entries related to accounting for plant assets, depreciation, and property tax expense.

598

Audit Your Understanding

1. What three amounts are calculated at the end of each fiscal period to bring each plant asset record up to date?
2. How much depreciation expense is recorded after a plant asset's book value equals its estimated salvage value?
3. What is the normal balance of an accumulated depreciation account?
4. How is a plant asset account affected by the adjustment for depreciation expense?
5. What is the adjusting entry to record depreciation expense for the period?

ILLUSTRATION 22-6

General ledger accounts after posting adjusting entries for depreciation expense

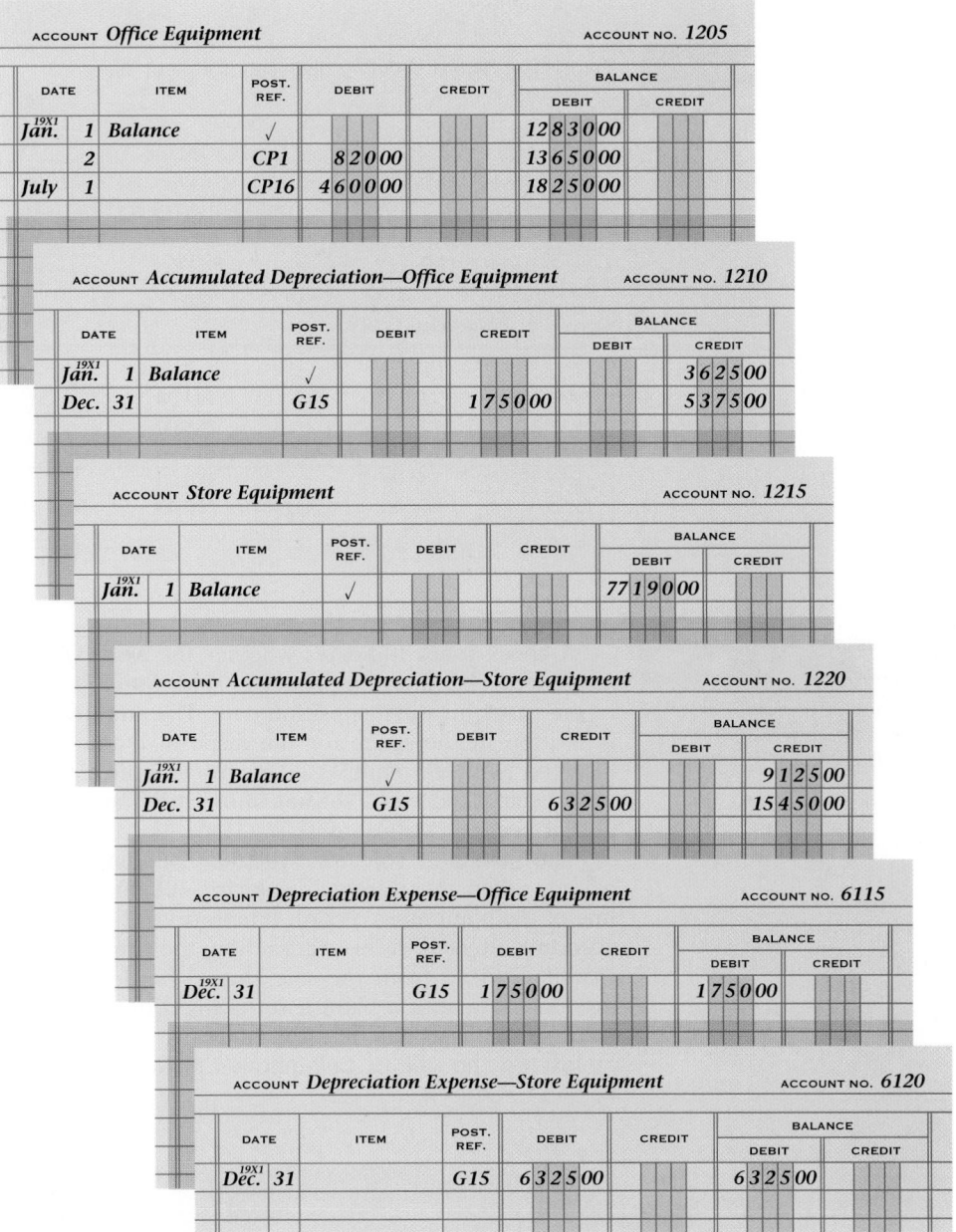

Sale of a Plant Asset for Book Value

After five years of use, Celluphone sold a printer.

> *January 3, 19X6. Received cash from sale of the printer bought on January 2, 19X1, $100.00: original cost, $820.00; total accumulated depreciation through December 31, 19X5, $720.00. Receipt No. 4.*

CHAPTER 22   Accounting for Plant Assets and Depreciation   **599**

Cover student pages 598–606 "Disposing of a Plant Asset." Explain that plant assets can be discarded, sold, or traded. When an asset is discarded, any remaining book value is a loss to the company. When an asset is sold, the difference between the asset received, usually cash, and the book value of the asset sold is the gain or loss on the disposal of the asset. Emphasize that the plant asset's accumulated depreciation and depreciation expense accounts must be up to date before the disposal can be recorded; therefore, an adjusting entry may be necessary if the disposal occurs at some time other than the end of the fiscal period. Emphasize the three effects in accounts achieved by the journal entries to dispose of a plant asset.

A notation is made in the second section of the plant asset record for this printer, as shown in Illustration 22-7.

ILLUSTRATION 22-7   Plant asset record showing disposal of a plant asset

PLANT ASSET RECORD		General Ledger Account No.	1205
Description	Printer	General Ledger Account	Office Equipment

Date Bought	January 2, 19X1	Serial Number	48C79623	Original Cost	$820.00
Estimated Useful Life	5 years	Estimated Salvage Value	$100.00	Annual Depreciation	$144.00

Disposed of:	Discarded		Sold ✓	Traded	
Date	January 3, 19X6		Disposal Amount	$100.00	

YEAR	ANNUAL DEPRECIATION EXPENSE	ACCUMULATED DEPRECIATION	ENDING BOOK VALUE
19X1	144.00	144.00	676.00
19X2	144.00	288.00	532.00
19X3	144.00	432.00	388.00
19X4	144.00	576.00	244.00
19X5	144.00	720.00	100.00

When an asset is sold for book value, no gain or loss results.

A check mark indicates whether the asset was discarded, sold, or traded. The date the printer is sold, *January 3, 19X6*, is written in the space for the disposition date. The amount received, *$100.00*, is written in the space for the disposal amount. Celluphone then files the printer's plant asset record in a file for plant assets that have been disposed of so that information about the asset is available if needed.

The printer is sold for $100.00. The ending book value of the printer when the printer is sold is $100.00, as shown on the last line of the plant asset record, Illustration 22-7. Before analyzing the accounts affected in this transaction, the amount of any gain or loss that is realized from the sale should be determined. The gain or loss on the sale of a plant asset is the difference between the book value of the asset sold and the value of the asset received. The gain or loss on the sale of Celluphone's printer is calculated as shown below.

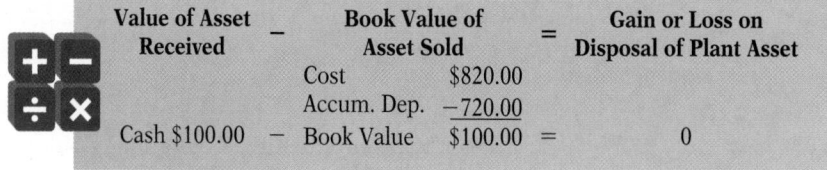

Value of Asset Received	−	Book Value of Asset Sold	=	Gain or Loss on Disposal of Plant Asset
		Cost $820.00		
		Accum. Dep. −720.00		
Cash $100.00	−	Book Value $100.00	=	0

Celluphone sold its printer for the printer's book value. Therefore, no gain or loss exists. The journal entry for the sale of a plant

600   PART 4   Accounting for a Merchandising Business Organized as a Corporation

APPLIED SKILLS: WRITING ACROSS THE CURRICULUM

Writing paragraphs and short essays. The Cases for Critical Thinking are short, practical applications of the accounting principles developed in the chapter. Some cases are planned to present problems related to the chapter but not specifically discussed and answered in the chapter. These cases present an opportunity for critical thinking and decision making. These cases also require more than a short objective-type response. Therefore, they provide ideal practice in writing paragraphs and short essays.

asset for book value must achieve the following two effects in the accounts.

1. Remove the original cost of the plant asset and its related accumulated depreciation.
2. Recognize the cash received.

Cash

100.00	

Accumulated Depreciation—Office Equipment

720.00	Bal.	720.00

Office Equipment

Bal.	820.00		820.00

Cash is debited for $100.00 to show the increase in the balance of this asset account.

The accumulated depreciation account should show only the depreciation for plant assets still in use. Therefore, Accumulated Depreciation—Office Equipment is debited for $720.00 to show the decrease in this contra asset account's balance. The amount, $720.00, is the total depreciation recorded during the printer's entire life.

Office Equipment is credited for $820.00 to show the decrease in the balance of this plant asset account. This entry cancels the original cost, $820.00, that was debited to the office equipment account when the printer was bought.

The cash receipts journal entry to record the sale of the printer is shown in Illustration 22-8.

ILLUSTRATION 22-8   Cash receipts journal entry to record the sale of a plant asset for book value

CASH RECEIPTS JOURNAL   PAGE *1*

						GENERAL		ACCOUNTS RECEIVABLE CREDIT	SALES CREDIT	SALES TAX PAYABLE		SALES DISCOUNT DEBIT	CASH DEBIT	
	DATE	ACCOUNT TITLE	DOC. NO.	POST. REF.		DEBIT	CREDIT			DEBIT	CREDIT			
8	3	Accum. Depr.—Office Equipment	R4			720 00							100 00	8
9		Office Equipment					820 00							9
10														10

Sale of a Plant Asset for More than Book Value

Revenue that results when a plant asset is sold for more than book value is called **gain on plant assets**. After five years of use, Cellu-phone sold a cash register for $150.00.

> *April 1, 19X7. Received cash from sale of the cash register bought on April 1, 19X2, $150.00: original cost, $470.00; total accumulated depreciation through December 31, 19X6, $399.00; additional depreciation to be recorded through April 1, 19X7, $21.00. Memorandum No. 14 and Receipt No. 38.*

The source documents for this transaction are a memorandum, detailing the need for an additional three months' depreciation, and a receipt. *(CONCEPT: Objective Evidence)*

Journalizing Depreciation for Part of a Year.   A plant asset may be disposed of at any time during the asset's useful life. When a plant

Assess student understanding by checking solutions to Independent Practice
activities.

Reteach

- Duplicate and assign Math Work
  Sheet Chapter 22 Part D, Calculating
  Gain or Loss on a Plant Asset from
  the Masters and Solutions to Enrich-
  ment/Application Activities section
  in the Teacher's Resource Guide to
  provide additional practice on the
  mathematics of calculating gain or
  loss on disposal of plant assets.

- Use Demonstration Problem 22C.
  This problem can be done on the
  overhead with the students completing the problem at their desks.

Extend

Assign Cases for Critical Thinking 2.

Enrich

Assign the Application Program Disk
software with Problem 22-5.

asset is disposed of, its depreciation from the beginning of the current fiscal year to the date of disposal is recorded. For example,
Celluphone last recorded adjusting entries for depreciation expense
on December 31, 19X6. The cash register is sold on April 1, 19X7.
Before entries are made for the sale of the cash register, three
months' depreciation must be recorded for the period January 1
through April 1. The additional depreciation for the cash register is
calculated as shown below.

Annual Depreciation Expense	÷	Months in a Year	=	Monthly Depreciation Expense
$84.00	÷	12	=	$7.00

Monthly Depreciation Expense	×	Number of Months Asset Is Used	=	Partial Year's Depreciation Expense
$7.00	×	3	=	$21.00

Depreciation Expense—Store Equipment

Add. Depr.	21.00	

Accumulated Depreciation— Store Equipment

	Bal.	399.00
	Add. Depr.	21.00
	(New Bal.	*420.00)*

Depreciation Expense—Store Equipment is debited for $21.00 to
show the increase in the balance of this expense account. Accumulated Depreciation—Store Equipment is credited for $21.00 to show
the increase in this contra asset account.

The general journal entry to record the three months' depreciation is shown in Illustration 22-9.

ILLUSTRATION 22-9   General journal entry to record depreciation for part of a year

	DATE		ACCOUNT TITLE	DOC. NO.	POST. REF.	DEBIT	CREDIT	
1	*19X7 Apr.*	*1*	*Depr. Exp.—Store Equipment*	M14		2 1 00		1
2			*Accum. Depr.—Store Equipment*				2 1 00	2
3								3

GENERAL JOURNAL   PAGE 4

Journalizing the Sale of a Plant Asset. After the partial year's
depreciation is recorded, a journal entry is made to record the sale
of the cash register. The cash register is sold for $150.00. The end-
ing book value when the cash register is sold is $50.00. The gain
on the sale of Celluphone's cash register is calculated as shown
below.

Value of Asset Received	−	Book Value of Asset Sold		=	Gain on Disposal
		Cost	$470.00		
		Accum. Dep.	−420.00		
Cash $150.00	−	Book Value	$ 50.00	=	$100.00 Gain

TEACHING STRATEGIES: DIFFERENT LEARNING STYLES

Tactile Learner. Suggest using a calculator with a printed tape to perform mathematical calculations.
Better calculators also print the operational signs of calculations (+, −, etc.) for students to trace the
steps in a calculation.

Celluphone sold its cash register for $100.00 more than its book value. Since the asset received has greater value than the book value of the plant asset disposed of, the difference is recognized as a gain on plant assets. The gain is calculated as $150.00 cash received, *less* $50.00 book value of plant asset, *equals* $100.00 gain on plant asset.

The amount of gain realized on the disposal of a plant asset is credited to a revenue account titled *Gain on Plant Assets*. A revenue account has a normal credit balance. Therefore, the gain on plant assets account is increased by a credit and decreased by a debit.

Gain on Plant Assets	
Debit side	Credit side
	Normal balance
Decrease	Increase

A gain from the sale of plant assets is not an operating revenue. Therefore, Gain on Plant Assets is not listed under Operating Revenue in a chart of accounts. Gain on Plant Assets is listed in a classification titled *Other Revenue* in a chart of accounts.

The journal entry for the sale of a plant asset for more than book value must achieve the following three effects in the accounts.

1. Remove the original cost of the plant asset and its related accumulated depreciation.
2. Recognize the cash received.
3. Recognize the gain on disposal of the asset.

Cash	
150.00	

Accumulated Depreciation— Store Equipment	
420.00	Bal. 420.00

Store Equipment	
Bal. 470.00	470.00

Gain on Plant Assets	
	100.00

Cash is debited for $150.00 to show the increase in the balance of this asset account. Accumulated Depreciation—Store Equipment is debited for $420.00 to show the decrease in this contra asset account. This amount, $420.00, is the sum of all depreciation expense recorded during the entire time Celluphone has used this cash register. Store Equipment is credited for $470.00 to show the decrease in the balance of this plant asset account. This entry removes the original cost, $470.00, that was debited to the store equipment account when the cash register was bought. Gain on Plant Assets is credited for $100.00 to show the increase in this other revenue account.

The cash receipts journal entry to record the sale of the cash register is shown in Illustration 22-10.

Notations are made on the plant asset record to record the partial year's depreciation and disposal information.

ILLUSTRATION 22-10 — Cash receipts journal entry to record the sale of a plant asset for more than book value

CASH RECEIPTS JOURNAL — PAGE 10

	DATE	ACCOUNT TITLE	DOC. NO.	POST. REF.	GENERAL DEBIT	GENERAL CREDIT	ACCOUNTS RECEIVABLE CREDIT	SALES CREDIT	SALES TAX PAYABLE DEBIT	SALES TAX PAYABLE CREDIT	SALES DISCOUNT DEBIT	CASH DEBIT	
1	19X7 Apr. 1	Accum. Depr.—Store Equipment	R38		420 00							150 00	1
2		Store Equipment				470 00							2
3		Gain on Plant Assets				100 00							3

Sale of a Plant Asset for Less than Book Value

Loss that results when a plant asset is sold for less than book value is called **loss on plant assets.** Celluphone sold a computer for $800.00 after four years of use.

September 1, 19X5. Received cash from sale of the computer bought on September 1, 19X1, $800.00: original cost, $4,000.00; total accumulated depreciation through December 31, 19X4, $2,000.00; additional depreciation to be recorded through September 1, 19X5, $400.00. Memorandum No. 82 and Receipt No. 281.

Journalizing Depreciation for Part of a Year. Celluphone last recorded adjusting entries for depreciation expense on December 31, 19X4. Celluphone sold its computer on September 1, 19X5. Before entries are made for the sale of the computer, eight months' depreciation must be recorded. The eight months' depreciation is for the period January 1 through September 1. The additional depreciation for the computer is calculated as shown below.

Annual Depreciation Expense	÷	Months in a Year	=	Monthly Depreciation Expense
$600.00	÷	12	=	$50.00

Monthly Depreciation Expense	×	Number of Months Asset Is Used	=	Partial Year's Depreciation Expense
$50.00	×	8	=	$400.00

Depreciation Expense—Office Equipment

Add. Depr.	400.00	

Accumulated Depreciation— Office Equipment

	Bal.	2,000.00
	Add. Depr.	400.00
	(New Bal.	2,400.00)

Depreciation Expense—Office Equipment is debited for $400.00 to show the increase in the balance of this expense account. Accumulated Depreciation—Office Equipment is credited for $400.00 to show the increase in this contra asset account.

The general journal entry to record the eight months' depreciation is shown in Illustration 22-11.

Journalizing the Sale of a Plant Asset. After the partial year's depreciation is recorded, a journal entry is made to record the

ILLUSTRATION 22-11

General journal entry to record depreciation for part of a year

	DATE		ACCOUNT TITLE	DOC. NO.	POST. REF.	DEBIT	CREDIT	
1	*Sept.*	*1*	*Depr. Exp.—Office Equipment*	M82		400 00		1
2			*Accum. Depr.—Office Equip.*				400 00	2
3								3

GENERAL JOURNAL   PAGE 9

sale of the computer. The computer is sold for $800.00. The ending book value when the computer is sold is $1,600.00. The loss on the sale of Celluphone's computer is calculated as shown below.

	Book Value of Asset Sold	−	Value of Asset Received	=	Loss on Disposal
Cost	$4,000.00				
Accum. Dep.	−2,400.00				
Book Value	$1,600.00	−	Cash $800.00	=	$800.00 Loss

Celluphone sold its computer for $800.00 less than its book value. Since the asset received has less value than the book value of the plant asset disposed of, the difference is recognized as a loss on plant assets. The loss is calculated as $1,600.00 book value of plant asset, *less* $800.00 cash received, *equals* $800.00 loss on plant asset.

The amount of loss realized on the disposal of a plant asset is debited to an expense account titled *Loss on Plant Assets*. An expense account has a normal debit balance. Therefore, Loss on Plant Assets is increased by a debit and decreased by a credit, as shown in the T account.

A loss from the sale of plant assets is not an operating expense. Therefore, Loss on Plant Assets is listed in a classification titled *Other Expenses* in a chart of accounts.

The journal entry for the sale of a plant asset for less than book value must achieve the following three effects in the accounts.

1. Remove the original cost of the plant asset and its related accumulated depreciation.
2. Recognize the cash received.
3. Recognize the loss on disposal of the asset.

Cash

800.00	

Accumulated Depreciation— Office Equipment

2,400.00	Bal. 2,400.00

Loss on Plant Assets

800.00	

Office Equipment

Bal. 4,000.00	4,000.00

Cash is debited for $800.00 to show the increase in the balance of this asset account. Accumulated Depreciation—Office Equipment is debited for $2,400.00 to show the decrease in this contra asset account. This amount, $2,400.00, is the sum of all depreciation expense recorded during the entire period Celluphone has used this computer. Loss on Plant Assets is debited for $800.00 to show the increase in this expense account. Office Equipment is credited for $4,000.00 to show the decrease in the balance of this plant asset account. This entry removes the original cost, $4,000.00, which was debited to the office equipment account when the computer was bought.

The cash receipts journal entry to record the sale of Celluphone's computer is shown in Illustration 22-12.

Notations are made on the plant asset record to record the partial year's depreciation and disposal information.

TEACHING STRATEGIES:
DIFFERENT LEARNING STYLES

Visual Learner. Formulas, such as those used to calculate depreciation expense, should be illustrated on the chalkboard to assist visual learners. The instructor should also complete the calculations for a few depreciable assets to show the process to visual learners.

AUDIT YOUR UNDERSTANDING

1. (1) Original cost and accumulated depreciation are removed from the accounts. (2) Cash or other asset received is recognized. (3) Gain or loss on the disposal is recognized.
2. By calculating the difference between the book value of the asset disposed of and the value of the asset received.
3. When additional depreciation expense should be recorded for the time from the last adjustment for depreciation expense and the date of disposal.
4. Annual depreciation expense divided by 12 equals monthly depreciation expense. Monthly depreciation expense is multiplied by the number of months in the partial year.

LESSON PLAN 22-4

Materials

- Student pages 606–611
- Transparencies: L, Blank Cash Payments Journal; 22-2, Chapter Summary
- Software: *Automated Accounting 6.0* or higher; Accounting Textbook Template, first-year course; Spreadsheet Template; Electronic Study Guide
- Demonstration Problems: 22D, Calculating Depreciation Expense and Book Value Using the Declining-Balance Method of Depreciation; 22E, Calculating and Journalizing Property Tax
- Math Work Sheet Chapter 22: Part E: Calculating Depreciation Expense (Declining-Balance Method) (TRG); Part F: Calculating Property Tax (TRG)
- Assess: Problem Test Chapter 22, MicroExam Chapter 22

Objectives (Enabling Performance Tasks)

a. Define accounting terms related to plant assets, depreciation, and property tax expense.

b. Identify accounting concepts and practices related to accounting for plant assets, depreciation, and property tax expense.

c. Calculate depreciation expense and book value of a plant asset.

e. Record entries related to accounting for plant assets, depreciation, and property tax expense.

ILLUSTRATION 22-12

Cash receipts journal entry to record the sale of a plant asset for less than book value

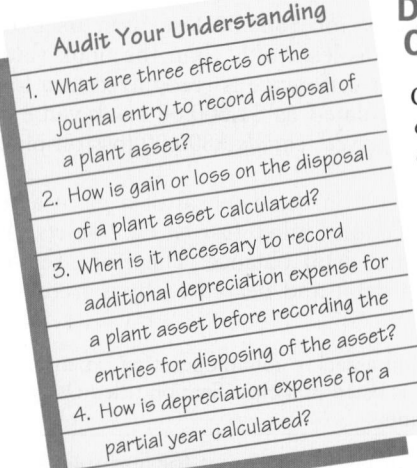

					1	2	3	4	5	6	7	8	
	DATE	ACCOUNT TITLE	DOC. NO.	POST. REF.	GENERAL DEBIT	GENERAL CREDIT	ACCOUNTS RECEIVABLE CREDIT	SALES CREDIT	SALES TAX PAYABLE DEBIT	SALES TAX PAYABLE CREDIT	SALES DISCOUNT DEBIT	CASH DEBIT	
1	*Sept.* 1	*Accum. Depr.—Office Equipment*	R281		2 4 0 0 00							8 0 0 00	1
2		*Loss on Plant Assets*			8 0 0 00								2
3		*Office Equipment*				4 0 0 0 00							3

CASH RECEIPTS JOURNAL   PAGE 19

Audit Your Understanding

1. What are three effects of the journal entry to record disposal of a plant asset?
2. How is gain or loss on the disposal of a plant asset calculated?
3. When is it necessary to record additional depreciation expense for a plant asset before recording the entries for disposing of the asset?
4. How is depreciation expense for a partial year calculated?

FYI

Under the declining-balance method of depreciation, more depreciation is recorded in the earlier years of the asset's life.

DECLINING-BALANCE METHOD OF CALCULATING DEPRECIATION

Celluphone uses the straight-line method of depreciation. An equal amount of depreciation expense is recorded each year during the useful life of a plant asset. However, not all assets depreciate the same amount each year. Many plant assets depreciate more in the early years of useful life than in later years. For example, a truck's value will decrease more the first year of service than in later years. Therefore, charging more depreciation expense in the early years of a plant asset may be more accurate than charging the same amount each year. *(CONCEPT: Matching Expenses with Revenue)*

Multiplying the book value at the end of each fiscal period by a constant depreciation rate is called the **declining-balance method of depreciation**. Although the rate is the same each year, the book value declines from one year to the next because of the increasing accumulated depreciation. The greatest book value exists during the first year. Therefore, the greatest depreciation expense is recorded in the first year. Because the smallest book value exists during the last year, the least depreciation expense is recorded in the last year.

The declining-balance depreciation rate, or percentage, is a multiple of the straight-line rate. Because of the ease in calculating, many businesses use a declining-balance rate that is two times the straight-line rate. For example, if a plant asset has an estimated useful life of five years, then the declining-balance rate is calculated as shown below.

Estimated Total Depreciation Expense	÷	Years of Estimated Useful Life	=	Straight-Line Rate
100%	÷	5	=	20%

Straight-Line Rate	×	2	=	Declining-Balance Rate
20%	×	2	=	40%

The straight-line rate is generally stated when identifying the declining-balance method rate. Thus, if the rate is to be twice the straight-line rate, the rate would be stated as *double declining-balance*. Depreciation expense calculated using both the straight-line and the declining-balance methods is shown in Illustration 22-13.

ILLUSTRATION 22-13 Comparison of the straight-line and declining-balance methods of calculating annual depreciation expense for the same plant asset

	Plant asset: Truck Original cost: $20,000.00 Estimated salvage value: $2,000.00 Estimated useful life: 5 years					
Year	Straight-Line Method			Declining-Balance Method		
	Beg. Book Value	Annual Depr.	End. Book Value	Beg. Book Value	Annual Depr.	End. Book Value
1	$20,000.00	$3,600.00	$16,400.00	$20,000.00	$8,000.00	$12,000.00
2	16,400.00	3,600.00	12,800.00	12,000.00	4,800.00	7,200.00
3	12,800.00	3,600.00	9,200.00	7,200.00	2,880.00	4,320.00
4	9,200.00	3,600.00	5,600.00	4,320.00	1,728.00	2,592.00
5	5,600.00	3,600.00	2,000.00	2,592.00	592.00	2,000.00
Total Depr.	—	$18,000.00	—	—	$18,000.00	—

FYI

Over 75% of all businesses use the straight-line method of depreciation.

When using the declining-balance method, the annual depreciation expense is calculated using the beginning book value for each year. The beginning book value is the same as the ending book value from the previous year. More depreciation expense is recorded in the earlier years of a plant asset. The annual depreciation expense and ending book value for the first year using the declining-balance method are calculated as shown below.

Year 1 Beginning Book Value	×	Rate	=	Year 1 Depreciation Expense
$20,000.00	×	40%	=	$8,000.00

Year 1 Beginning Book Value	−	Year 1 Depreciation Expense	=	Year 1 Ending Book Value
$20,000.00	−	$8,000.00	=	$12,000.00

The annual depreciation expense and ending book value for the second year using the declining-balance method are calculated as shown on the next page.

CHAPTER 22 Accounting for Plant Assets and Depreciation **607**

FOCUS

- The straight-line method of calculating depreciation was presented earlier in this chapter. This method records an equal amount of depreciation each year. Explain that not all assets depreciate the same amount each year. Therefore, some businesses use a method that charges more depreciation in the early years of a plant asset's life. In this lesson, a method of calculating depreciation that charges more depreciation in the early years will be introduced. Also, calculating and paying property taxes on plant assets will be presented.

- Introduce new vocabulary: declining-balance method of depreciation; real property; personal property; assessed value.

TEACH

Cover student pages 606–611 "Declining-Balance Method of Calculating Depreciation" and "Calculating and Paying Property Tax." Emphasize that the declining-balance depreciation rate is a multiple of the straight-line rate, generally double. Explain that to calculate depreciation expense using the declining-balance method, multiply the depreciation rate times the plant asset's book value at the beginning of the year. Emphasize that salvage value is not a factor in calculating annual depreciation using the declining-balance method. Salvage value is used only to determine the minimum book value to which the plant asset should be reduced. Explain that property tax on plant assets is calculated by multiplying the tax rate times assessed valuation of the property, not market value.

APPLY

- Demonstrate the calculation of declining-balance depreciation on the board. First show how to calculate the rate to be used. Then calculate the first year's depreciation using that rate. Then show how the book value that results is the amount used to calculate the next year's depreciation.

- Direct students to Illustration 22-13 for a comparison of straight-line and declining-balance methods.

- Use Transparency L to journalize the entry to pay property tax. Or direct students to Illustration 22-14.

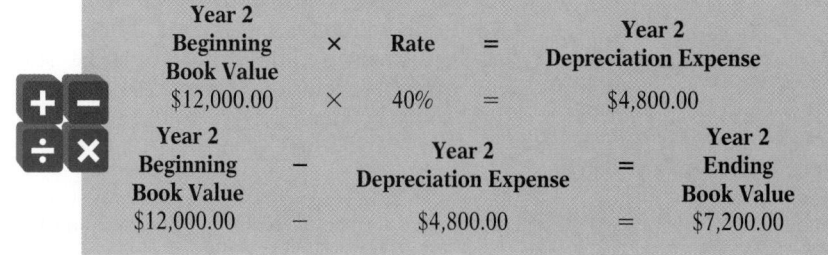

	Year 2 Beginning Book Value	×	Rate	=	Year 2 Depreciation Expense
	$12,000.00	×	40%	=	$4,800.00

Year 2 Beginning Book Value	−	Year 2 Depreciation Expense	=	Year 2 Ending Book Value
$12,000.00	−	$4,800.00	=	$7,200.00

608

Guided Practice

Guide students through calculating depreciation expense using the declining-balance method. Use the following problem: Cost $675, salvage $75, life 5 years. Have students calculate the declining-balance rate as twice the straight-line rate. On the board or overhead, prepare a depreciation table similar to Illustration 22-13 while students are doing the same activity at their desks. Show beginning book value, annual depreciation expense, and ending book value. Be sure all students agree on each part of the calculation before proceeding to the next part.

Independent Practice

Assign Terms 11–14, Questions 17–20, Problems 22-6 and 22-7, Mastery Problem 22-M, and Study Guide 22.

ASSESS

Assess student understanding by checking solutions to Independent Practice activities.

Reteach

- Duplicate and assign Math Work Sheet Chapter 22 Parts E and F, Calculating Depreciation Expense (Declining-Balance Method) and Calculating Property Tax from the Masters and Solutions to Enrichment/Application Activities Section in the Teacher's Resource Guide to provide additional practice on the mathematics of calculating declining-balance depreciation and property taxes.

- Use Demonstration Problems 22D and 22E. These problems can be demonstrated on the overhead with the students completing the problems at their desks.

- Assign Recycling Problem 22-R.

- Assign the Electronic Study Guide Chapter 22 to complete the study guide from the working papers at the computer.

Extend

Assign Challenge Problem 22-C. (The challenge is that students must calculate accumulated depreciation and recognize that the assets disposed of on Mar. 15 and Aug. 1 should not be depreciated below their salvage values.)

When using the declining-balance method, a different amount of depreciation expense is recorded each year. Special care must be taken in calculating depreciation expense for the last year of useful life. A plant asset is never depreciated below its estimated salvage value. Therefore, in the last year, only enough depreciation expense is recorded to reduce the book value of the plant asset to its salvage value. For example, in Illustration 22-13, depreciation expense in the fifth year is only $592.00, the amount that will reduce the ending book value to $2,000.00, the estimated salvage value of the plant asset.

Regardless of the method used to calculate the amount of depreciation expense, the general ledger accounts affected are the same. The appropriate depreciation expense account is debited and the related accumulated depreciation account is credited for the amount of depreciation for the period.

CALCULATING AND PAYING PROPERTY TAX

Property taxes are a major source of funds for education in many states.

For tax purposes, state and federal governments define two kinds of property—real and personal. Land and anything attached to the land is called **real property.** Real property is sometimes referred to as real estate. All property not classified as real property is called **personal property.** For tax purposes, these definitions apply whether the property is owned by a business or an individual.

Assessed Value of Property

The value of an asset determined by tax authorities for the purpose of calculating taxes is called the **assessed value.** Assessed value is usually based on the judgment of persons referred to as assessors. Assessors are elected by citizens or are specially trained employees of a governmental unit.

The assessed value of an asset may not be the same as the book value on the business' or individual's records. The assessed value is assigned to an asset for tax purposes only. Often the assessed value is only a part of the true value of the asset.

Calculating Property Tax on Plant Assets

Most governmental units with taxing power have a tax based on the value of real property. The real property tax is used on buildings and land. Some governmental units also tax personal property such as cars, boats, trailers, and airplanes.

A governmental taxing unit determines a tax rate to use in calculating taxes. The tax rate is multiplied by an asset's *assessed value*, not the book value recorded on a business' records.

PhoneLand's buildings and land have been assessed for a total of $250,000.00. The city tax rate is 1.5%. PhoneLand's annual property tax is calculated as shown below.

	Assessed Value	×	Tax Rate	=	Annual Property Tax
	$250,000.00	×	1.5%	=	$3,750.00

PhoneLand is required to pay current year property taxes not later than December 31.

Paying Property Tax on Plant Assets

On December 30, PhoneLand paid its property tax.

Property Tax Expense	
3,750.00	

Cash	
	3,750.00

December 30, 19--. Paid cash for property tax, $3,750.00. Check No. 487.

Property Tax Expense is increased by a $3,750.00 debit. Cash is decreased by a $3,750.00 credit.

The journal entry to record payment of property tax is shown in Illustration 22-14 on page 610.

Payment of all assessed taxes is necessary if a firm is to continue in business. Therefore, PhoneLand classifies property tax as an operating expense.

The first chart in Summary Illustration 22-15 on pages 610 and 611 analyzes the entries for transactions related to plant assets, depreciation, and property taxes. The second chart summarizes the calculations for amounts related to depreciation and sale of plant assets.

Audit Your Understanding

1. When is the most depreciation expense recorded when the declining-balance method is used?

2. When the declining-balance method of depreciation is used, how much depreciation is recorded in the last year of the plant asset's useful life?

3. Who usually determines the assessed value of property for tax purposes?

ASSESS (cont'd)

Enrich

- Use the Application Program Disk software with Problem 22-7.
- Use *Automated Accounting 6.0* and Accounting Textbook Template, first-year course with Problem 22-6, Mastery Problem 22-M, and Challenge Problem 22-C.
- Use the Spreadsheet Template with Problem 22-6 and Mastery Problem 22-M.

CLOSURE

- Use Audit Your Understanding questions.
- Review calculating depreciation expense using the declining-balance method.
- Review Summary Illustration 22-15, "Summary of Entries and Calculations Related to Plant Assets, Depreciation, and Property Taxes." Use Transparency 22-2, Chapter Summary.

ASSESS

- Administer Problem Test Chapter 22
- Administer a MicroExam for Chapter 22

AUDIT YOUR UNDERSTANDING

1. In the earlier years of the plant asset's life.
2. Only enough depreciation expense to reduce the book value to the salvage value.
3. Assessors who are elected by citizens or trained by the government.

ILLUSTRATION 22-14   Journal entry to record payment of property tax

CASH PAYMENTS JOURNAL

PAGE 24

	DATE	ACCOUNT TITLE	CK. NO.	POST. REF.	GENERAL DEBIT	GENERAL CREDIT	ACCOUNTS PAYABLE DEBIT	PURCHASES DISCOUNT CREDIT	CASH CREDIT	
1	Dec. 30	Property Tax Expense	487		3 7 5 0 00				3 7 5 0 00	1
2										2

SUMMARY ILLUSTRATION 22-15

Summary of entries and calculations related to plant assets, depreciation, and property taxes

Transactions	GENERAL LEDGER														
	Cash		Equipment		Accumulated Depreciation		Depreciation Expense		Property Tax Expense		Gain on Plant Assets		Loss on Plant Assets	
	Debit	Credit	Debit	Credit	Debit	Credit	Debit	Credit	Debit	Credit	Debit	Credit	Debit	Credit
Buying a plant asset		X	X											
Recording depreciation expense for a fiscal period							X							
Sale of plant asset for book value	X				X	X								
Sale of plant asset for more than book value	X				X	X						X		
Sale of plant asset for less than book value	X				X	X								X
Paying property tax on plant assets		X							X					

Summary of entries and calculations related to plant assets, depreciation, and property taxes

AMOUNTS	CALCULATIONS				
Annual Depreciation Expense	Original Cost	− Estimated Salvage Value	= Estimated Total Depreciation Expense	÷ Years of Estimated Useful Life	= Annual Depreciation Expense
Partial Year's Depreciation Expense	Annual Depreciation Expense	÷ Months in a Year	= Monthly Depreciation Expense	× Number of Months Asset Is Used	= Partial Year's Depreciation Expense
Current Year's Balance of Accumulated Depreciation	Previous Year's Balance of Accumulated Depreciation	+ Current Year's Depreciation Expense	= Current Year's Balance of Accumulated Depreciation		
Book Value of a Plant Asset	Original Cost	− Accumulated Depreciation	= Ending Book Value		
Gain on Sale of a Plant Asset	Value of Asset Received	− Book Value of Asset Sold	= Gain on Disposal		
Loss on Sale of a Plant Asset	Book Value of Asset Sold	− Value of Asset Received	= Loss on Disposal		

**APPLIED SKILLS:
LANGUAGE ARTS**

Paraphrasing, writing complete sentences, and identifying direct objects. For additional practice in language arts skills, direct students to answer the Accounting Terms and Questions For Individual Study at the end of the chapter. Students should write the answers in their own words and in complete sentences. To further practice language arts skills, ask students to underline the direct object(s) in each sentence of their answers.

1. **current assets:** Cash and other assets expected to be exchanged for cash or consumed within a year. (p. 587)

2. **plant assets:** Assets which will be used for a number of years in the operation of a business. (p. 587)

3. **depreciation expense:** The portion of a plant asset's cost that is transferred to an expense account in each fiscal period during a plant asset's useful life. (p. 589)

4. **estimated salvage value:** The amount an owner expects to receive when a plant asset is removed from use. (p. 590)

5. **straight-line method of depreciation:** Charging an equal amount of depreciation expense for a plant asset in each year of useful life. (p. 590)

6. **plant asset record:** An accounting form on which a business records information about each plant asset. (p. 592)

7. **accumulated depreciation:** The total amount of depreciation expense that has been recorded since the purchase of a plant asset. (p. 593)

8. **book value of a plant asset:** The original cost of a plant asset minus accumulated depreciation. (p. 593)

9. **gain on plant assets:** Revenue that results when a plant asset is sold for more than book value. (p. 601)

10. **loss on plant assets:** Loss that results when a plant asset is sold for less than book value. (p. 604)

11. **declining-balance method of depreciation:** Multiplying the book value at the end of each fiscal period by a constant depreciation rate. (p. 606)

12. **real property:** Land and anything attached to the land. (p. 608)

13. **personal property:** All property not classified as real property. (p. 608)

14. **assessed value:** The value of an asset determined by tax authorities for the purpose of calculating taxes. (p. 608)

QUESTIONS FOR INDIVIDUAL STUDY

1. Current assets and plant assets. (p. 587)

2. To transfer a portion of a plant asset's cost to an expense account in each fiscal period that a plant asset is used to earn revenue. (p. 588)

3. Matching Expenses with Revenue. (p. 588)

ACCOUNTING TERMS EPT(a)

What is the meaning of each of the following?

1. **current assets**
2. **plant assets**
3. **depreciation expense**
4. **estimated salvage value**
5. **straight-line method of depreciation**
6. **plant asset record**
7. **accumulated depreciation**
8. **book value of a plant asset**
9. **gain on plant assets**
10. **loss on plant assets**
11. **declining-balance method of depreciation**
12. **real property**
13. **personal property**
14. **assessed value**

QUESTIONS FOR INDIVIDUAL STUDY EPT(b)

1. What are the two broad categories of assets used by most businesses in the operations of their businesses?

2. What is the reason for recording depreciation expense?

3. Which accounting concept is being applied when depreciation is recorded?

4. In what significant way does depreciation expense differ from many other business expenses?

5. Why is land generally not subject to depreciation?

6. What three factors affect the amount of depreciation expense for a plant asset?

7. What is included in the original cost of a plant asset?

8. Why is the estimated salvage value used in determining depreciation expense rather than the actual salvage value?

9. If, when purchased, the useful life of an asset cannot be reasonably estimated from past experience, where might this information be obtained?

10. How is the annual depreciation expense calculated for a plant asset using the straight-line method of depreciation?

11. When a plant asset record is brought up to date, what three amounts are generally recorded on the record?

12. How is the book value of a plant asset calculated?

13. When a plant asset's book value equals its estimated salvage value, how is the depreciation expense for the succeeding periods recorded?

14. On a work sheet, what accounts are affected, and how, in planning adjustments for depreciation of a plant asset?

15. What accounts are affected, and how, when a plant asset is sold for more than book value?

16. What accounts are affected, and how, when a plant asset is sold for less than book value?

17. What method of depreciation would be more accurate, straight-line or declining-balance, if a plant asset's value decreases more in the first year of service than in later years?

18. How does real property differ from personal property?

19. Who determines the assessed value of property?

20. What accounts are affected, and how, by an entry to pay property tax?

---

4. For many business expenses, cash is paid out in the same fiscal period in which the expense is recorded. Cash is generally paid out when a plant asset is bought, but depreciation expense is recorded over several years. (p. 589)

5. Because of land's permanent nature. Land can be used indefinitely. (p. 589)

6. (a) Original cost. (b) Estimated salvage value. (c) Estimated useful life. (p. 589)

7. All costs paid to make the asset usable to a business. These costs include the price of the asset, delivery costs, and any necessary installation costs. (p. 589)

8. The amount that will be received for an asset at the time of its disposal is not known when the asset is bought. Thus, the amount that may be received at disposal must be estimated. (pp. 589–590)

CASE 1 Carol Ebener, owner of a small business, does not record depreciation expense for the business' plant assets. Ms. Ebener says that she does not make actual cash payments for depreciation. Therefore, she records an expense for the use of plant assets only when cash is paid for a plant asset. Do you agree with Ms. Ebener's method? Explain.

CASE 2 TriState Company sold a printer for $100.00 after using it for five years. TriState paid $800.00 for the printer and at that time estimated the useful life to be five years with an estimated salvage value of $50.00. When the printer was sold, a total of $750.00 accumulated depreciation had been recorded in its plant asset record. Jonathan Yancey, a new accounting clerk, recorded the sale as a $100.00 debit to **Cash** and a $100.00 credit to **Gain on Plant Assets.** When asked why he made that entry, Mr. Yancey said that since the printer had been used for its full estimated useful life, he thought any amount realized from its sale should be recorded as a gain. Is Mr. Yancey correct? Explain.

APPLIED COMMUNICATIONS

Financing expensive plant assets can be a complicated process for both individuals and businesses. Buying a car, for example, requires the buyer to evaluate numerous combinations of rebates, loan interest rates, and loan payment terms. Car dealers often offer the buyer either a cash rebate or a low interest loan.

INSTRUCTIONS:

1. For the car of your choice, identify two available financing options. Obtain financing information from a local bank or a car dealer. Using their estimated monthly payment, calculate the total money paid using each alternative.

2. Prepare a table summarizing your analysis. The table should include: purchase price, cash rebate, amount to be financed, financing terms (interest rate and payment term), estimated monthly payment, and total payments. Write a paragraph describing which alternative you would select, and support your answer.

DRILLS FOR UNDERSTANDING

EPT(c)

DRILL 22-D1 Calculating depreciation expense

INSTRUCTIONS:

Use the straight-line method of calculating depreciation described in this chapter. Calculate the amount of annual depreciation expense for each of the following plant assets.

Plant Asset	Original Cost	Estimated Salvage Value	Estimated Useful Life
1	$ 730.00	$ 50.00	4 years
2	5,200.00	1,400.00	5 years
3	2,170.00	250.00	3 years
4	1,610.00	170.00	6 years
5	8,950.00	2,350.00	8 years
6	17,480.00	950.00	10 years
7	12,600.00	3,150.00	9 years
8	57,200.00	5,500.00	25 years
9	9,220.00	480.00	4 years
10	26,500.00	5,950.00	15 years

CHAPTER 22 Accounting for Plant Assets and Depreciation **613**

QUESTIONS *(cont'd)*

13. When a plant asset's book value equals its estimated salvage value, no further depreciation expense is recorded. (p. 594)

14. The depreciation expense account for the plant asset being adjusted is debited; the accumulated depreciation account for the plant asset being adjusted is credited. (p. 597)

15. Cash is debited. The accumulated depreciation account for the plant asset being sold is debited; the plant asset account for the plant asset being sold is credited. Gain on Plant Assets is credited. (p. 603)

16. Cash is debited. The accumulated depreciation account for the plant asset being sold is debited. Loss on Plant Assets is debited. The plant asset account for the plant asset being sold is credited. (p. 605)

17. Declining-balance method of depreciation. (p. 606)

18. Real property, sometimes referred to as real estate, includes land and anything attached to the land while personal property is all property not classified as real property. (p. 608)

19. Assessed value is usually based on the judgment of persons referred to as assessors. Assessors are elected by citizens or are specially trained employees of a governmental unit. (p. 608)

20. Property Tax Expense is debited; Cash is credited. (p. 609)

QUESTIONS *(cont'd)*

9. Trade associations frequently publish guidelines for specialized plant assets. For tax purposes the Internal Revenue Service also publishes depreciation guidelines for plant assets. (p. 590)

10. Original cost minus estimated salvage value equals estimated total depreciation expense. Estimated total depreciation expense divided by years of estimated useful life equals annual depreciation expense. (p. 590)

11. (a) Annual depreciation expense. (b) Accumulated depreciation. (c) Ending book value. (pp. 592–593)

12. Original cost of a plant asset minus accumulated depreciation. (p. 593)

CASES FOR CRITICAL THINKING

Case 1   No. A portion of a plant asset's cost should be transferred to an expense account in each fiscal period that a plant asset is used to earn revenue. In this way expenses are recorded in the same fiscal period the related revenue is earned. If Ms. Ebener records an expense only when cash is paid for an asset, the total cost will be expensed in a single fiscal period. This procedure violates the Matching Expenses with Revenue concept. A portion of the total depreciation expense should be charged to each fiscal period if a reasonably accurate net income is to be reported on the income statement.

Case 2   No, Mr. Yancey is not correct. At the time of sale, the printer has a recorded book value of $50.00 (original cost, $800.00, less accumulated depreciation, $750.00). Therefore, the gain that should be recorded would be the amount the cash received exceeds the book value of the asset sold ($100.00 cash received less $50.00 book value of asset sold). Also, when the printer is disposed of, all amounts related to that asset should be closed (equipment account and accumulated depreciation). Therefore, to close those amounts, recognize the cash received, and recognize the correct amount of gain, the correct entry would be as follows: Debit: Cash, $100.00; Accumulated Depreciation, $750.00. Credit: Office Equipment, $800.00; Gain on Plant Assets, $50.00.

APPLIED COMMUNICATIONS

Students' solutions will vary. The table should include: purchase price, cash rebate, amount to be financed, financing terms (interest rate and payment term), estimated monthly payment, total payments. The instructor should consider the following items when grading this activity: (1) accuracy of the calculations; (2) appropriateness of the decision; and (3) mechanics (grammar, spelling, punctuation, and sentence structure).

DRILL 22-D2   Calculating book value of plant assets

MATHEMATICS

INSTRUCTIONS:

Calculate two amounts for each of the following plant assets.

a. Using the straight-line method of depreciation, calculate the amount of total accumulated depreciation that should be recorded through December 31, 19X6. Calculate the time of depreciation to the nearest number of months. Round amounts to the nearest cent.

b. Calculate the ending book value as of December 31, 19X6.

Plant Asset	Date Bought	Original Cost	Estimated Salvage Value	Estimated Useful Life
1	Jan. 1, 19X1	$ 1,050.00	$ 150.00	6 years
2	July 1, 19X1	4,700.00	400.00	10 years
3	Apr. 1, 19X2	25,500.00	1,500.00	15 years
4	Sept. 1, 19X2	12,800.00	1,250.00	7 years
5	Mar. 1, 19X3	10,700.00	1,100.00	8 years
6	Aug. 1, 19X4	6,200.00	500.00	5 years
7	Dec. 31, 19X4	930.00	110.00	4 years
8	Oct. 1, 19X5	2,700.00	300.00	3 years
9	May 1, 19X6	15,600.00	3,600.00	8 years
10	Nov. 1, 19X6	7,800.00	240.00	9 years

APPLICATION PROBLEMS   EPT(c,d,e)

PROBLEM 22-1   Journalizing the buying of plant assets

Holloway Company records plant assets in two accounts: **Office Equipment** and **Store Equipment**.

INSTRUCTIONS:

Journalize the following transactions completed during the current year. Use page 12 of a cash payments journal. (Usually a new journal page is started each month. However, to conserve space in the working papers, record all of the year's entries on the same page of the cash payments journal.) The abbreviation for check is C.

Jan. 1. Paid cash for office equipment, $9,270.00. C127.

Feb. 1. Paid cash for store equipment, $12,850.00. C159.

May 1. Paid cash for office equipment, $313.00. C228.

June 1. Paid cash for office equipment, $1,740.00. C263.

Nov. 1. Paid cash for store equipment, $3,684.00. C401.

Dec. 1. Paid cash for office equipment, $920.00. C442.

PROBLEM 22-2   Calculating depreciation expense

Creative Concepts, Inc. owns the following plant assets.

Plant Asset	Date Bought	Original Cost	Estimated Salvage Value	Estimated Useful Life
1	July 1, 19X1	$ 5,600.00	$ 800.00	12 years
2	Nov. 1, 19X1	5,000.00	380.00	7 years

CHECK FIGURES

See the Teacher's Edition of Working Papers for solutions.

Drill 22-D1   170, 760, 640, 240, 825, 1,653, 1,050, 2,068, 2,185, 1,370.

Drill 22-D2   900/150; 2,365/2,335; 7,599.97/17,900.03; 7,150/5,650; 4,600/6,100; 2,755/3,445; 410/520; 1,000.01/1,699.99; 1,000/14,600; 140/7,660.

Problem 22-1   General Debit amounts: 9,270, 12,850, 313, 1,740, 3,684, 920.

Problem 22-2   400, 660, 1,290, 916.63, 450, 258.35.

Plant Asset	Date Bought	Original Cost	Estimated Salvage Value	Estimated Useful Life
3	May 1, 19X2	21,600.00	2,250.00	15 years
4	Feb. 1, 19X3	10,750.00	1,750.00	9 years
5	Apr. 1, 19X3	3,820.00	220.00	6 years
6	Aug. 1, 19X3	1,440.00	200.00	2 years

INSTRUCTIONS:

For each plant asset, calculate the depreciation expense to be recorded for the year ended December 31, 19X3. Use the straight-line method of calculating depreciation.

PROBLEM 22-3 Preparing a plant asset record

PhotoCraft bought a new high-speed photocopying machine on July 1 of the current year. Use the following additional information pertaining to the copier.

> Account number: 1225
>
> General ledger account: Store Equipment
>
> Serial number of copier: KP3044987
>
> Cost: $12,500.00
>
> Estimated useful life: 7 years
>
> Estimated salvage value: $2,000.00

INSTRUCTIONS:

Prepare a plant asset record. For each year of the plant asset's life, record year-end date, annual depreciation expense, accumulated depreciation, and ending book value. Use the straight-line method of calculating depreciation.

PROBLEM 22-4 Recording work sheet adjustments and journal entries for depreciation expense

Landmark Contractors' general ledger has the following accounts and balances on December 31 of the current year.

PARTIAL GENERAL LEDGER

Account Title	Balance Debit	Credit
Office Equipment	$ 8,740.00	—
Accumulated Depreciation—Office Equipment	—	$2,130.00
Store Equipment.	37,820.00	—
Accumulated Depreciation—Store Equipment	—	7,564.00
Depreciation Expense—Office Equipment	—	—
Depreciation Expense—Store Equipment.	—	—

INSTRUCTIONS:

1. Record the account titles and balances in a work sheet's Account Title and Trial Balance columns for the current year ended December 31.

2. Record on the work sheet the adjustments for estimated depreciation for the year. Annual depreciation expenses are office equipment, $1,150.00, and store equipment, $1,890.00.

3. Journalize the adjusting entries on page 13 of a general journal.

CHAPTER 22 Accounting for Plant Assets and Depreciation **615**

PROBLEM 22-5 Journalizing the disposing of plant assets

APPLICATION

MATHEMATICS

Horizon Company records plant assets in two accounts: **Office Equipment** and **Store Equipment**.

INSTRUCTIONS:

Journalize the following transactions completed during 19X2. Use page 12 of a general journal and a cash receipts journal. Source documents are abbreviated as follows: memorandum, M; receipt, R.

Feb. 1. Received cash from sale of office equipment, $1,400.00: original cost, $10,700.00; total accumulated depreciation through December 31, 19X1, $9,000.00; additional depreciation to be recorded through February 1, 19X2, $300.00. M25 and R43.

Apr. 1. Received cash from sale of store equipment, $500.00: original cost, $5,200.00; total accumulated depreciation through December 31, 19X1, $4,500.00; additional depreciation to be recorded through April 1, 19X2, $200.00. M52 and R74.

June 1. Received cash from sale of office equipment, $200.00: original cost, $3,800.00; total accumulated depreciation through December 31, 19X1, $3,500.00; additional depreciation to be recorded through June 1, 19X2, $100.00. M97 and R133.

Aug. 1. Received cash from sale of office equipment, $1,200.00: original cost, $8,100.00; total accumulated depreciation through December 31, 19X1, $6,120.00; additional depreciation to be recorded through August 1, 19X2, $400.00. M132 and R206.

Oct. 1. Received cash from sale of store equipment, $600.00: original cost, $1,450.00; total accumulated depreciation through December 31, 19X1, $1,050.00; additional depreciation to be recorded through October 1, 19X2, $50.00. M197 and R289.

PROBLEM 22-6 Calculating depreciation expense using the straight-line and declining-balance methods

AUTOMATED

SPREADSHEET

MATHEMATICS

The following data, relating to a drill press, are obtained from the accounting records of Machine Works, Inc.

Original cost	$4,000.00
Estimated salvage value	300.00
Estimated useful life	4 years

INSTRUCTIONS:

Prepare a depreciation table similar to Illustration 22-13 showing annual depreciation expense, beginning book value, and ending book value. Calculate these amounts using the straight-line and the declining-balance methods. Use twice the straight-line rate for the declining-balance method.

PROBLEM 22-7 Calculating and journalizing property tax

MATHEMATICS

Excel Graphics has real property with an assessed value of $450,000. The tax rate in the city where the property is located is 2.5% of assessed value.

INSTRUCTIONS:

1. Calculate Excel Graphics' total annual property tax for the current year.
2. Journalize the payment of the property tax on March 1. Use page 4 of a cash payments journal. Check No. 187.

ENRICHMENT PROBLEMS

EPT(c,e)

MASTERY PROBLEM 22-M Calculating depreciation expense and book value of plant assets; journalizing entries affecting plant assets

AUTOMATED

SPREADSHEET

Taylor Lumber records plant assets in two accounts: Office Equipment and Store Equipment. Taylor Lumber owns the following plant assets.

Plant Asset	Asset Account	Date Bought	Original Cost	Estimated Salvage Value	Estimated Useful Life
1	Office Equipment	Apr. 1, 19X1	$ 7,300.00	$ 700.00	6 years
2	Store Equipment	July 1, 19X1	6,900.00	600.00	9 years
3	Store Equipment	Oct. 1, 19X1	5,700.00	840.00	3 years
4	Store Equipment	Aug. 1, 19X2	2,600.00	500.00	5 years
5	Store Equipment	Sept. 1, 19X2	3,100.00	700.00	4 years
6	Office Equipment	Nov. 1, 19X3	10,800.00	1,800.00	10 years
7	Office Equipment	May 1, 19X4	1,400.00	200.00	4 years
8	Office Equipment	July 1, 19X4	22,500.00	1,500.00	14 years

INSTRUCTIONS:

1. Calculate each plant asset's depreciation expense for the year ended December 31, 19X4. Use the straight-line method of calculating depreciation. Round amounts to the nearest cent.
2. Calculate each plant asset's ending book value as of December 31, 19X4.
3. Journalize the two adjusting entries for depreciation expense for the year ended December 31, 19X4. Use page 13 of a general journal.
4. Journalize the following transaction. Use page 4 of a cash receipts journal. Source documents are abbreviated as follows: memorandum, M; receipt, R.

19X5
Apr. 2. Received cash from sale of plant asset number 2, $4,200.00: original cost, $6,900.00; total accumulated depreciation through December 31, 19X4, $2,450.00; additional depreciation to be recorded through April 2, 19X5, $175.00. M125 and R193.

CHALLENGE PROBLEM 22-C Calculating depreciation expense and book value of plant assets; journalizing entries affecting plant assets

AUTOMATED

Candlewick Company records plant assets in two accounts: Office Equipment and Store Equipment. Candlewick Company owns the following plant assets.

Plant Asset	Asset Account	Date Bought	Original Cost	Estimated Salvage Value	Estimated Useful Life
1	Office Equipment	Jan. 1, 19X1	$ 1,750.00	$ 250.00	5 years
2	Store Equipment	Jan. 1, 19X2	7,250.00	1,000.00	5 years
3	Store Equipment	Apr. 1, 19X2	12,500.00	1,500.00	10 years
4	Office Equipment	July 1, 19X2	3,500.00	300.00	4 years
5	Office Equipment	Apr. 1, 19X3	4,400.00	500.00	6 years
6	Store Equipment	July 1, 19X3	1,400.00	200.00	3 years
7	Store Equipment	July 1, 19X5	6,050.00	800.00	7 years
8	Office Equipment	Oct. 1, 19X5	3,000.00	600.00	8 years

INSTRUCTIONS:

1. Calculate each plant asset's depreciation expense for the year ended December 31, 19X5. Use the straight-line method of calculating depreciation. Round amounts to the nearest cent.
2. Calculate each plant asset's total accumulated depreciation as of December 31, 19X5.
3. Calculate each plant asset's ending book value as of December 31, 19X5.
4. Journalize the two adjusting entries for depreciation expense for the year ended December 31, 19X5. Use page 13 of a general journal.
5. Journalize the following transactions completed during 19X6. Use page 25 of a cash receipts journal. Continue using page 13 of the general journal. Source documents are abbreviated as follows: memorandum, M; receipt, R.

19X6
Mar. 15. Sold plant asset number 1, $250.00. R72.
Apr. 30. Received cash from sale of plant asset number 2, $2,000.00. M97 and R115.
Aug. 1. Sold plant asset number 4, $850.00. M173 and R209.

Automated Accounting
for Depreciation

TEACHING STRATEGIES:
ACCOUNTING PEDAGOGY

This textbook introduces manual methods for calculating depreciation before using automated accounting to journalize and post the entries. It is important that students master accounting theory before relying on the computer to perform the repetitive functions.

Celluphone's manual methods for calculating depreciation and preparing depreciation schedules are described in Chapter 22. Integrating Automated Accounting Topic 9 describes procedures for using automated accounting software to calculate depreciation and prepare depreciation schedules for the straight-line and double declining-balance methods. The Automated Accounting Problems contain instructions for using automated accounting software to solve Application Problem 22-6, Mastery Problem 22-M, and Challenge Problem 22-C, Chapter 22.

PREPARING DEPRECIATION SCHEDULES

A separate record is kept for each plant asset when using either a manual or an automated accounting system. The arrangement of a plant asset record may vary for different businesses. Celluphone bought two plant assets during the current year.

Plant Asset	Description	Date Bought	Original Cost	Estimated Salvage Value	Estimated Useful Life
1	Printer	01/02/X1	$ 820.00	$ 100.00	5 Years
2	Computer	07/01/X1	4,600.00	1,000.00	4 Years

619

LESSON PLAN A9

Materials

- Student pages 619–623
- If input forms are needed to customize this lesson, blackline masters are provided in the Accounting Ruling Masters section of the Teacher's Resource Guide.
- Complete solutions for automated problems are provided in the Teacher's Resource Guide.
- Software: *Automated Accounting 6.0* or higher; Accounting Textbook Template, first-year course

Objective

Calculate depreciation and prepare depreciation schedules using an automated accounting system.

SOFTWARE FOCUS

The Automated Accounting Problems in this Integrating Automated Accounting Topic use Problem 22-6, Mastery Problem 22-M, and Challenge Problem 22-C, Chapter 22, which students have already completed manually. Refer students back to these problems to complete the problems. The problem instructions in *Automated Accounting 6.0* will lead students through automating the problems.

FYI

When the cents are zero (.00), key only the dollar amount. For example, if the amount is 15.00, key 15. The software automatically assigns the .00.

Straight-Line Depreciation Method

To prepare a plant asset record for each of Celluphone's plant assets using automated accounting software, the second module, Payroll/Assets/Bank Rec., must be loaded. The Payroll/Assets/Bank Rec. command is selected from the File menu. File is again selected from the menu bar. The Open Data File command is then chosen to retrieve the plant assets data base from the template disk.

The Assets menu command is selected from the menu bar. The Maintain Assets command is then chosen to display the data entry window for keying plant asset data. The information is keyed and the straight-line method is selected. Illustration T9-1 shows a completed data entry window for Celluphone's printer. The second plant asset information is entered in the same way.

ILLUSTRATION T9-1 A completed data entry for a plant asset

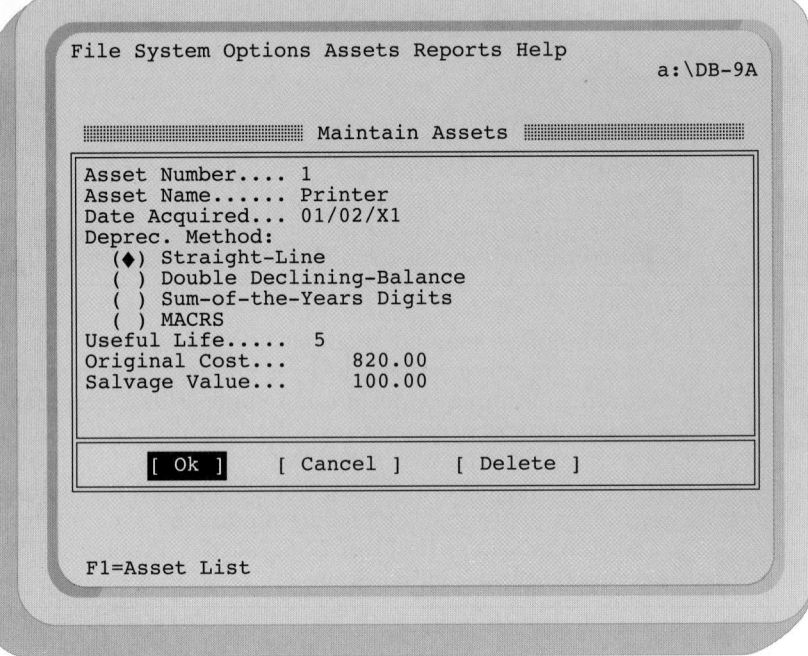

After all plant asset data have been keyed, the Reports menu is selected from the menu bar. The Plant Assets Report command is then chosen and printed, as shown in Illustration T9-2, and filed for future reference.

To prepare the straight-line depreciation schedule, the Reports menu is selected from the menu bar. The Depreciation Schedule is chosen from the Reports menu. As Celluphone wants depreciation schedules prepared for both plant assets, the *OK* check box is

PART 4   Accounting for a Merchandising Business Organized as a Corporation

ILLUSTRATION T9-2   Plant Asset Report for straight-line depreciation method

```
                        Celluphone, Inc.
                       Plant Assets Report
                          12/31/X1
-----------------------------------------------------------------------
Asset        Asset            Date    Depr. Useful   Original    Salvage
Number       Name             Acquired Meth. Life    Cost        Value
-----------------------------------------------------------------------
  1          Printer          01/02/X1  SL    5        820.00     100.00
  2          Computer         07/01/X1  SL    4       4600.00    1000.00
                                                      ----------
             Total                                    5420.00
                                                      ==========
```

selected from the Reports Selection Options menu to display the depreciation schedules. The schedules are printed and filed for future reference. The schedules for both plant assets are shown in Illustration T9-3.

ILLUSTRATION T9-3   Depreciation Schedules for straight-line depreciation method

```
                        Celluphone, Inc.
                      Depreciation Schedule
                          12/31/X1

Asset Number..........1
Asset Name...........Printer
Date Acquired........01/02/X1
Depreciation Method...Straight-Line
Useful Life..........5
Original Cost........   820.00
Salvage Value........   100.00

-----------------------------------------------------
            Annual        Accumulated       Book
Year        Depreciation  Depreciation      Value
-----------------------------------------------------
19X1          144.00        144.00         676.00
19X2          144.00        288.00         532.00
19X3          144.00        432.00         388.00
19X4          144.00        576.00         244.00
19X5          144.00        720.00         100.00


Asset Number..........2
Asset Name...........Computer
Date Acquired........07/01/X1
Depreciation Method...Straight-Line
Useful Life..........4
Original Cost........  4600.00
Salvage Value........  1000.00

-----------------------------------------------------
            Annual        Accumulated       Book
Year        Depreciation  Depreciation      Value
-----------------------------------------------------
19X1          450.00        450.00        4150.00
19X2          900.00       1350.00        3250.00
19X3          900.00       2250.00        2350.00
19X4          900.00       3150.00        1450.00
19X5          450.00       3600.00        1000.00
```

CHAPTER 22   Accounting for Plant Assets and Depreciation   **621**

CLOSURE

Review the procedures for recording depreciation using automated accounting software. Discuss the effect of using the straight-line or declining-balance methods of depreciation.

Other Depreciation Methods

To prepare Celluphone's plant asset records using other depreciation methods, follow the same steps as those for straight-line depreciation. However, push the appropriate depreciation button in the data entry window for keying plant asset data.

OPTIONAL PROBLEM DB-9A

Celluphone's plant asset data base is on the accounting textbook template. If you wish to prepare Celluphone's depreciation schedules using automated accounting software, load the *Automated Accounting 6.0* or higher software and select the second module, Payroll/Assets/Bank Rec. Select Data Base 9A (DB-9A) from the template disk. Read the Problem Instructions screen. Follow the procedures described to prepare Celluphone's depreciation schedules.

AUTOMATED ACCOUNTING PROBLEMS

AUTOMATING APPLICATION PROBLEM 22-6 Preparing depreciation schedules

The following data, relating to a drill press bought on January 3 of the current year, are obtained from the accounting records of Machine Works, Inc. (This information is found in Application Problem 22-6, Chapter 22.)

Plant Asset	Description	Date Bought	Original Cost	Estimated Salvage Value	Estimated Useful Life
1	Drill Press	01/03/–	$4,000.00	$300.00	4 Years

INSTRUCTIONS:

1. Load the *Automated Accounting 6.0* or higher software. Bring up the Payroll/Assets/Bank Rec. module.
2. Select data base F22-6 (First-Year Course Application Problem 22-6) from the accounting textbook template. Read the Problem Instructions screen.
3. Pull down the File menu and choose the Save As menu command. Key the path to the drive and directory that contains your data files. Save the data base with a file name of XXX226 (where XXX are your initials).
4. Key the data for the plant asset for the straight-line depreciation method.
5. Display/Print a plant asset report for the straight-line depreciation method.
6. Display/Print a depreciation schedule.

AUTOMATING MASTERY PROBLEM 22-M Preparing depreciation schedules

INSTRUCTIONS:

1. Load the *Automated Accounting 6.0* or higher software. Bring up the Payroll/Assets/Bank Rec. module.
2. Select data base F22-M from the accounting textbook template. Read the Problem Instructions screen.
3. Pull down the File menu and choose the Save As menu command. Key the path to the drive and directory that contains your data files. Save the data base with a file name of XXX22M (where XXX are your initials).
4. Use the plant asset data given in Mastery Problem 22-M, Chapter 22. Key the data for the plant assets for the straight-line depreciation method.
5. Display/Print a plant asset report for the straight-line depreciation method.
6. Display/Print a depreciation schedule.

AUTOMATED

AUTOMATING CHALLENGE PROBLEM 22-C Preparing depreciation schedules

INSTRUCTIONS:

1. Load the *Automated Accounting 6.0* or higher software. Bring up the Payroll/Assets/Bank Rec. module.

2. Select data base F22-C from the accounting textbook template. Read the Problem Instructions screen.

3. Pull down the File menu and choose the Save As menu command. Key the path to the drive and directory that contains your data files. Save the data base with a file name of XXX22C (where XXX are your initials).

4. Use the plant asset data given in Challenge Problem 22-C, Chapter 22. Key the data for the plant assets for the straight-line depreciation method.

5. Display/Print a plant asset report for the straight-line depreciation method.

6. Display/Print a depreciation schedule.

CHAPTER 23 OVERVIEW

This chapter focuses on merchandise inventory, often the largest dollar-value asset for a merchandising company, and brings the discussion within the accounting cycle. Inventory is costed using the fifo, lifo, and weighted-average methods. For interim reporting, the gross profit method of estimating an inventory is also presented.

GUIDE TO ACHIEVING LEARNING OBJECTIVES

Enabling Performance Tasks	TEACH Lesson Plans	APPLY Drills for Understanding	Application Problems	Mastery Problems	Challenge Problems	EXTEND/ENRICH Cases for Critical Thinking	Recycling Problems	Reinforcement Activity
a. Define accounting terms related to inventory.	23-1, 23-2							
b. Identify accounting concepts and practices related to inventory.	23-1, 23-2	23-D1				Cases 1, 2		
c. Determine the cost of merchandise inventory using the fifo, lifo, and weighted-average inventory costing methods.	23-2	23-D2	23-1	23-M			23-R	
d. Estimate the cost of merchandise inventory using the gross profit method of estimating inventory.	23-2		23-2		23-C			

ENRICHMENT

SPECIAL FEATURES

Multicultural Awareness, page 626

Personal Visions in Business, page 632

TECHNOLOGY CONNECTION

Spreadsheet Template Problems 23-1, 23-2

Electronic Study Guide

NEW, REVIEW, AND EXTENSION

ACTIVITIES/CONCEPTS/TRANSACTIONS	NEW	REVIEW/ EXTENSION
Determining the quantity of merchandise inventory	✓	
Completing an inventory record	✓	
Completing a stock record	✓	
Calculating cost of merchandise sold	✓	
First-in, first-out inventory costing method	✓	
Last-in, first-out inventory costing method	✓	
Weighted-average inventory costing method	✓	
Gross profit method of estimating merchandise inventory	✓	

	INFORMAL ASSESSMENT		FORMAL ASSESSMENT					
	Study Guide	Audit Your Understanding	Chapter MicroExam	Chapter Problem Test	Unit Problem Test	Unit Objective Test	Portfolio
Unit A	✓	✓				✓	
Units B, C	✓	✓				✓	
Unit C				✓	✓		
				✓			

TEACHING MATERIALS

- Teacher's Wraparound Edition of the Text
- Teacher's Resource Guide
- Teacher's Edition of Working Papers
- Teacher's Edition of Demonstration/Recycling Problems
- Teaching Transparencies
- MicroExam
- Applied Math Work Sheet

APPLIED MATHEMATICS

APPLIED MATH/ACCOUNTING SKILL	APPLICATION
Calculating Inventory Using the First-in, First-Out Inventory Costing Method	Drill 23-D2
Calculating Inventory Using the Last-in, First-Out Inventory Costing Method	Drill 23-D2
Calculating Inventory Using the Weighted-Average Inventory Costing Method	Drill 23-D2
Estimating Inventory Using the Gross Profit Method	Prob. 23-2

23

Accounting for Inventory

ENABLING PERFORMANCE TASKS

After studying Chapter 23, you will be able to:

a Define accounting terms related to inventory.

b Identify accounting concepts and practices related to inventory.

c Determine the cost of merchandise inventory using the fifo, lifo, and weighted-average inventory costing methods.

d Estimate the cost of merchandise inventory using the gross profit method of estimating inventory.

TERMS PREVIEW

periodic inventory • perpetual inventory • inventory record • stock record • stock ledger • first-in, first-out inventory costing method • last-in, first-out inventory costing method • weighted-average inventory costing method • gross profit method of estimating inventory

624

Merchandise inventory on hand is typically the largest asset of a merchandising business. Successful businesses must have merchandise available for sale that customers want. A business, therefore, needs controls that assist managers in maintaining a merchandise inventory of sufficient quantity, variety, and price.

The cost of merchandise inventory is reported on both the balance sheet and the income statement. An accurate cost of merchandise inventory is required to correctly report current assets and retained earnings on the balance sheet. The accuracy of the inventory cost will also assure that gross profit and net income are reported correctly on the income statement. *(CONCEPT: Adequate Disclosure)*

CONTROLLING THE QUANTITY OF MERCHANDISE INVENTORY

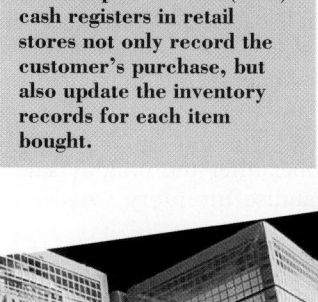

Modern point-of-sale (POS) cash registers in retail stores not only record the customer's purchase, but also update the inventory records for each item bought.

To determine the most efficient size of inventory, a business makes frequent analysis of purchases, sales, and inventory records. Many businesses fail because too much or too little merchandise inventory is kept on hand. A business that stocks merchandise that does not satisfy the demand of its customers is also likely to fail.

A merchandise inventory that is larger than needed may decrease the net income of a business for several reasons.

1. Excess inventory requires that a business spend money for expensive store and warehouse space.
2. Excess inventory uses capital that could be invested in other assets to earn a profit for the business.
3. Excess inventory requires that a business spend money for expenses, such as taxes and insurance premiums, that increase with the cost of the merchandise inventory.
4. Excess inventory may become obsolete and unsaleable.

Merchandise inventory that is smaller than needed may also decrease the net income of a business for several reasons.

1. Sales may be lost to competitors if items wanted by customers are not on hand.
2. Sales may be lost to competitors if there is an insufficient variety of merchandise to satisfy customers.
3. When a business frequently orders small quantities of an item, the price paid is often more per unit than when merchandise is ordered in large quantities.

DETERMINING THE QUANTITY OF MERCHANDISE INVENTORY

The quantity of items in inventory at the end of a fiscal period must be determined in order to calculate the cost of merchandise sold.

CHAPTER 23   Accounting for Inventory **625**

LESSON PLAN 23-1

Materials
- Student pages 625–628
- Transparencies: 23-1, Inventory Record and Stock Record

Objectives (Enabling Performance Tasks)
a. Define accounting terms related to inventory.
b. Identify accounting concepts and practices related to inventory.

FOCUS

- Merchandise inventory on hand is typically the largest asset of a merchandising business. Students should be familiar with the term "inventory" because they have seen advertisements for after-inventory and pre-inventory sales by local stores. In this lesson, we will learn how merchandising businesses keep records about their inventory.
- Introduce new vocabulary: periodic inventory, perpetual inventory, inventory record, stock record, stock ledger.

TEACH

Cover student pages 625–628 "Controlling the Quantity of Merchandise Inventory" and "Determining the Quantity of Merchandise Inventory." Explain the two principal methods to determine merchandise inventory, periodic and perpetual inventory. Describe an inventory record. An inventory record is used for periodic inventory. Describe a stock record. A stock record is used for perpetual inventory.

Two principal methods are used to determine the quantity of each item of merchandise on hand.

1. A merchandise inventory determined by counting, weighing, or measuring items of merchandise on hand is called a **periodic inventory.** A periodic inventory is also referred to as a physical inventory.
2. A merchandise inventory determined by keeping a continuous record of increases, decreases, and balance on hand is called a **perpetual inventory.** A perpetual inventory is also referred to as a book inventory.

Periodic Inventory

Counting, weighing, or measuring merchandise on hand for a periodic inventory is commonly referred to as "taking an inventory." Employees count each item of inventory and record the quantities on special forms. To assure an accurate and complete count, a business will typically be closed during the periodic inventory. Taking an inventory is often a large and expensive task. Therefore, a periodic inventory usually is taken only at the end of a fiscal period.

Businesses frequently establish their fiscal period to end when inventory is at a minimum because it takes less time to count a smaller inventory. For example, a department store may take an inventory at the end of December. The amount of merchandise on hand is smaller because of holiday sales. Few purchases of additional merchandise are made in December after the holiday sales. All of these activities make the merchandise inventory smaller at the end of December.

Celluphone has found from past experience that relatively few sales are made after the holiday season. Thus, the quantity of merchandise on hand is relatively small at the end of December. Therefore, Celluphone ends its annual fiscal period on December 31. Celluphone takes its periodic inventory during the last week of December.

A form used during a periodic inventory to record information about each item of merchandise on hand is called an **inventory record.** The inventory record has space to record the stock number, unit description, number of units on hand, unit price, and total cost of each item. The inventory record used by Celluphone is shown in Illustration 23-1 on page 627.

Information is typed in the Stock Number column and Description column before the periodic inventory begins. Employees taking the inventory write the actual count in the No. of Units on Hand column. Inventory records are then sent to the accounting department where the Unit Price and Total Cost columns are completed.

Perpetual Inventory

Some businesses keep inventory records that show continuously the quantity on hand for each kind of merchandise. A form used to show the kind of merchandise, quantity received, quantity sold, and

ILLUSTRATION 23-1

Inventory record

INVENTORY RECORD

DATE	December 31, 19--		ITEM	Antennas	
1	2		3	4	5
STOCK NUMBER	DESCRIPTION		NO. OF UNITS ON HAND	UNIT PRICE	TOTAL COST
3410	Standard		32	9.80	313.60
3420	Deluxe		28	10@12.20 }	
				18@12.50 }	347.00
3600	Retractable		13	21.40	278.20
	Total				938.80

balance on hand is called a **stock record**. A separate stock record is prepared for each kind of merchandise on hand. A file of stock records for all merchandise on hand is called a **stock ledger**. A stock record for Celluphone is shown in Illustration 23-2.

ILLUSTRATION 23-2

Stock record

STOCK RECORD

Description	Hand Sets			Stock No.	4516B	
Reorder	40		Minimum	10	Location	Aisle F
1	2	3	4	5	6	7
	INCREASES			DECREASES		BALANCE
DATE	PURCHASE INVOICE NO.	QUANTITY	DATE	SALES INVOICE NO.	QUANTITY	QUANTITY
Jan. 1 (19--)						23
			Jan. 12 (19--)	3269	15	8
Feb. 1	9281	40				48
			Feb. 4	3461	5	43
			Feb. 12	3489	10	33
			Feb. 20	3511	8	25

A perpetual inventory system provides day-to-day information about the quantity of merchandise on hand. The minimum balance allowed before a reorder must be placed is also shown on each stock record. The minimum balance is the quantity of merchandise that will typically last until the ordered merchandise can be received from the vendors. When the quantity falls below the minimum, additional merchandise is ordered in the quantity shown on the reorder line of the stock record. A stock record shows the quantity but usually not the cost of the merchandise.

When a perpetual inventory of merchandise is kept, entries are made on the stock records to show the following information.

CHAPTER 23   Accounting for Inventory   **627**

1. Increases in the quantity on hand when additional merchandise is received.
2. Decreases in the quantity on hand when merchandise is sold.
3. The balance on hand after each increase or decrease is recorded. The quantity of merchandise on hand is the last amount in the Balance column of a stock record.

When a perpetual inventory is kept, errors may be made in recording or calculating amounts. Also, some stock records may be incorrect because merchandise is taken from stock and not recorded on stock records. A customary practice is to take a periodic inventory at least once a fiscal period. The periodic inventory is then compared with the perpetual inventory records. The perpetual records are corrected to reflect the actual quantity on hand as determined by the periodic inventory.

Perpetual Inventory Using a Computer

Many merchandising businesses use a computer to keep perpetual inventory records. Special cash registers and checkout counters are used. The checkout counters have devices to read the Universal Product Codes (UPC codes) marked on products. An example of a UPC code is shown in Illustration 23-3.

ILLUSTRATION 23-3

Universal Product Code (UPC code)

A stock ledger for all merchandise on hand is stored in the computer. Each time a UPC code is read at the checkout counter, the computer checks the stock ledger to obtain the product description and the sales price. The product description and price are then displayed on the cash register. At the same time, the computer reduces the units on hand to reflect the item sold. In complex inventory systems the computer is programmed to periodically check the quantities in the stock ledger and print a list of the items that need to be reordered.

DETERMINING THE COST OF MERCHANDISE INVENTORY

Costs are not recorded on inventory records at the time a periodic inventory is taken. After the quantities of merchandise on hand are counted, purchase invoices are used to find merchandise unit

Audit Your Understanding

1. What are the two principal methods used to determine the quantity of each item of merchandise on hand?
2. When are periodic inventories usually taken?
3. What does UPC represent?

AUDIT YOUR UNDERSTANDING

The AUDIT YOUR UNDERSTANDING feature appears at the end of each section of the chapter. Explain to your students that the word *audit* means to check or verify. AUDIT YOUR UNDERSTANDING may be used to check student comprehension of the section just studied. The answers are provided in Appendix D in the back of the textbook.

1. Periodic inventory, perpetual inventory.
2. At the end of a fiscal period.
3. Universal Product Code.

LESSON PLAN 23-2

Materials

- Student pages 628–636
- Transparency: 23-2, Chapter Summary
- Software: Spreadsheet Template, Electronic Study Guide

PART 4   Accounting for a Merchandising Business Organized as a Corporation

TEACHING STRATEGIES: DIFFERENT LEARNING ABILITIES

Limited English Proficiency (LEP) Students. Stress accounting terms so that LEP students learn the language of accounting.

prices. The total costs are then calculated using the quantities and unit prices recorded on the inventory records. Most businesses use one of three inventory costing methods to calculate the cost of merchandise inventory: (1) first-in, first-out, (2) last-in, first-out, or (3) weighted-average.

First-In, First-Out Inventory Costing Method

The account Merchandise Inventory is shown on both the balance sheet and the income statement. Therefore, an accurate value is important to financial reporting.

The term fifo is an acronym. An acronym is a word formed by using the first letter or letters of a longer group of words.

Celluphone takes a periodic inventory at the end of each fiscal period. The quantity of each item on hand is recorded on an inventory record. The inventory records are sent to the accounting department to determine the unit price and total cost of each item on hand. Celluphone uses the most recent invoices for purchases to determine the unit price of an item. The earliest invoices for purchases, therefore, are used to determine the cost of merchandise sold.

Using the price of merchandise purchased first to calculate the cost of merchandise sold first is called the **first-in, first-out inventory costing method**. The cost of the ending inventory, therefore, consists of the most recent cost of merchandise purchased. The first-in, first-out method is frequently abbreviated as *fifo* (the first letter of each of the four words). On December 31 a periodic inventory of Model 88 cellular phone batteries, Stock No. MS130, showed 16 batteries on hand. Purchase information for this item during the fiscal period is shown below.

Purchase Dates	Units	Unit Price	Total Cost
January 1, beginning inventory..........	4	$40.00	$ 160.00
April 14, purchases....................	10	42.00	420.00
June 22, purchases....................	8	44.00	352.00
September 6, purchases................	16	45.00	720.00
November 28, purchases	12	48.00	576.00
Totals...........................	50		$2,228.00

During the fiscal period, 34 batteries were sold. Using the fifo method, the cost of the 16 inventory units on hand on December 31 is determined using the most recent unit prices. The most recent unit prices are $48.00 and $45.00. The inventory cost using the fifo method is calculated as shown below.

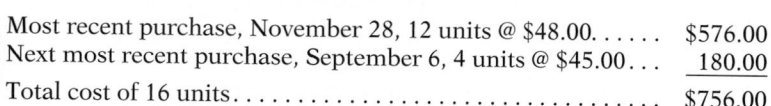

Most recent purchase, November 28, 12 units @ $48.00......	$576.00
Next most recent purchase, September 6, 4 units @ $45.00...	180.00
Total cost of 16 units................................	$756.00

The most recent purchase, November 28, is used to cost 12 of the 16 units in ending inventory. The remaining 4 units in ending inventory are costed using the next most recent purchase, September 6.

On the inventory record, the 16 batteries are shown as having a total cost of $756.00. The cost of the 34 batteries sold is calculated as shown on the following page.

LESSON PLAN 23-2 *(cont'd)*

- Math Work Sheet Chapter 23: Part A: Calculating Inventory and Cost of Merchandise Sold Using the First-in, First-out Inventory Costing Method; Part B: Calculating Inventory and Cost of Merchandise Sold Using the Last-in, First-out Inventory Costing Method; Part C: Calculating Inventory and Cost of Merchandise Sold Using the Weighted-Average Inventory Costing Method; Part D: Estimating Inventory Using the Gross Profit Method (TRG)

- Demonstration Problems: 23A, Determining Cost of Ending Inventory Using the Fifo, Lifo, and Weighted-Average Methods; 23B, Estimating Inventory using the Gross Profit Method of Estimating Inventory

- Assess: Problem Test Chapter 23, MicroExam Chapter 23, Objective Test No. 7, Unit Problem Test No. 7

Objectives (Enabling Performance Tasks)

a. Define accounting terms related to inventory.

b. Identify accounting concepts and practices related to inventory.

c. Determine the cost of merchandise inventory using the fifo, lifo, and weighted-average inventory costing methods.

d. Estimate the cost of merchandise inventory using the gross profit method of estimating inventory.

APPLIED SKILLS: LANGUAGE ARTS

Exploring spelling checker software. Students may wish to rely too heavily on the spelling checker feature of their word processing software. A word may be spelled correctly, but it may not be the word that should be used. Spend some time giving examples of incorrect words that the spelling checker cannot identify as misspelled. ("if" instead of "is"; "its" instead of "it's"; "the" instead of "them"; etc.) Ask students to supply other pairs of words.

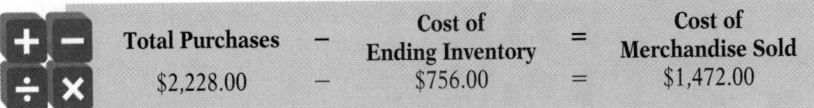

	Total Purchases	−	Cost of Ending Inventory	=	Cost of Merchandise Sold
	$2,228.00	−	$756.00	=	$1,472.00

Last-In, First-Out Inventory Costing Method

Using the price of merchandise purchased last to calculate the cost of merchandise sold first is called the **last-in, first-out inventory costing method.** The last-in, first-out method is frequently abbreviated as *lifo*. This method is based on the idea that the most recent costs of merchandise should be charged against current revenue. *(CONCEPT: Matching Expenses with Revenue)*

Using the lifo method, each item on the inventory records is recorded at the earliest prices paid for the merchandise. The lifo inventory cost for the 16 batteries previously described is calculated as shown below.

Beginning inventory, January 1, 4 units @ $40.00	$160.00
Next earliest purchase, April 14, 10 units @ $42.00	420.00
Next earliest purchase, June 22, 2 units @ $44.00	88.00
Total cost of 16 units.................................	$668.00

The earliest prices consist of the 4 units in the January 1 beginning inventory. The next earliest purchase, April 14, of 10 units is then used to cost 10 units in ending inventory. The remaining 2 units in ending inventory are costed using the next earliest purchase, June 22.

On the inventory record, the 16 batteries would show a total cost of $668.00. The cost of merchandise sold for the 34 batteries sold would be recorded as $1,560.00, the difference between total purchases, $2,228.00, and the cost of ending inventory, $668.00.

Weighted-Average Inventory Costing Method

Using the average cost of beginning inventory plus merchandise purchased during a fiscal period to calculate the cost of merchandise sold is called the **weighted-average inventory costing method.** The average unit price of the total inventory available is calculated. This average unit price is used to calculate both ending inventory and cost of merchandise sold. The average cost of merchandise is then charged against current revenue. *(CONCEPT: Matching Expenses with Revenue)*

Using the weighted-average method, the inventory is costed at the average price per unit of the beginning inventory plus the cost of all purchases during the fiscal year. The weighted-average inventory cost for the 16 batteries previously described is calculated as shown on the following page.

TEACHING STRATEGIES: EXPANDING BEYOND THE CLASSROOM

Invite two or three local business people to class for a panel discussion on the advantages and disadvantages of various inventory costing methods. The persons selected should represent businesses that use different inventory costing methods.

- In the first part of this chapter, students learned the importance of keeping inventory records. In the second accounting cycle, students also learned to record an adjusting entry for merchandise inventory based on the ending inventory amount. In this lesson, we will explore the different methods of determining what value to use for the ending merchandise inventory.

- Introduce new vocabulary: first-in, first-out inventory costing method; last-in, first-out inventory costing method; weighted-average inventory costing method; gross profit method of estimating inventory.

Weighted-Average Inventory Costing Method
Quantity on Hand, 16 Units

Date	Purchase Units	Unit Price	Total Cost
January 1, beginning inventory.......	4	$40.00	$160.00
April 14, purchases.................	10	42.00	420.00
June 22, purchases	8	44.00	352.00
September 6, purchases	16	45.00	720.00
November 28, purchases.............	12	48.00	576.00
Totals................................	50		$2,228.00

Total of Beginning Inventory and Purchases	÷	Total Units	=	Weighted-Average Price per Unit
$2,228.00	÷	50	=	$44.56

Units in Ending Inventory	×	Weighted-Average Price per Unit	=	Cost of Ending Inventory
16	×	$44.56	=	$712.96

On the inventory record, the 16 batteries would show a total cost of $712.96. The cost of merchandise sold for the 34 units sold would be recorded as $1,515.04, the difference between total purchases, $2,228.00, and the cost of ending inventory, $712.96. Since the weighted-average method uses an average unit price, the same unit price may be used to calculate the cost of both ending inventory and cost of merchandise sold. Thus, the cost of merchandise sold could also be calculated as shown below.

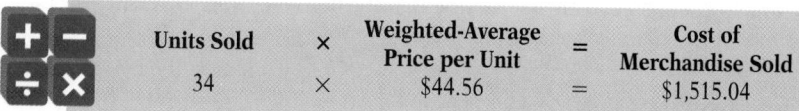

	Units Sold	×	Weighted-Average Price per Unit	=	Cost of Merchandise Sold
	34	×	$44.56	=	$1,515.04

A business usually determines the order in which products are sold based on the type of inventory. A grocery store, for example, must sell its earliest purchases first. A hardware store, however, could sell its most recent purchases first. The inventory costing method used to calculate the cost of merchandise sold should not, however, be determined by the order in which items are sold. A business should choose the inventory costing method that provides its managers with the best accounting information.

A comparison of the three inventory methods used in determining the cost of merchandise sold is shown in Illustration 23-4 on page 632.

The fifo method gives the highest possible ending inventory cost and the lowest cost of merchandise sold. The lifo method gives the lowest possible ending inventory cost and the highest cost of merchandise sold. The weighted-average method gives ending inventory cost and cost of merchandise sold between fifo and lifo. As the cost of merchandise sold increases, gross profit and net income decrease.

TEACH

Cover student pages 628–635 "Determining the Cost of Merchandise Inventory" and "Estimating the Cost of Merchandise Inventory." First describe the fifo and lifo methods of costing inventory because they are both based on assumptions about the order in which merchandise is sold, either the first-in or the last-in. Emphasize that businesses do not necessarily decide which method to use based on how their inventory actually is sold but instead usually decide on the basis of the best effect on the financial statements.

Remind students that businesses often need financial statements more often than once a year and that the cost of taking a physical inventory often would be too expensive. Therefore, the gross profit method provides an inexpensive alternative to taking periodic inventory or maintaining a perpetual inventory.

TEACHING STRATEGIES:
TEACHING TIP

Place quantity and cost information on a chalkboard for one or two inventory items similar to the information provided with Problem 23-1. Ask students to calculate at their desks the value of inventory from the information on the chalkboard. First calculate using fifo, then lifo, and weighted-average. After students have calculated a value using the fifo method, ask two or three students to give their answers. Write the answers on the chalkboard. If there are questions, work the solution on the chalkboard. Repeat the process for each method. After inventory values have been calculated using each method, discuss the reasons why the amounts are different.

ILLUSTRATION 23-4   Comparison of inventory costing methods

	Fifo	Lifo	Weighted Average
Cost of Merchandise Sold:			
Merchandise Inventory, Jan. 1	$ 160.00	$ 160.00	$ 160.00
Net Purchases	2,068.00	2,068.00	2,068.00
Merchandise Available for Sale	$2,228.00	$2,228.00	$2,228.00
Less Ending Inventory, Dec. 31	756.00	668.00	712.96
Cost of Merchandise Sold	$1,472.00	$1,560.00	$1,515.04
Relative Cost of Ending Inventory	highest	lowest	intermediate
Relative Cost of Merchandise Sold	lowest	highest	intermediate

Thus, net income is highest under the fifo method, lowest under the lifo method, and intermediate under the weighted-average method.

All three inventory costing methods are acceptable accounting practices. However, a business should select one method and use

Personal Visions in Business

This special student feature introduces students to successful entrepreneurs or business professionals. Each profile gives a flavor of what the actual business world is like and some of the opportunities available to students who study accounting. These features can be used to motivate students to pursue professional business careers in a wide variety of fields. The subjects of these profiles have been carefully chosen to represent the full spectrum of diverse ethnic and racial backgrounds of professional business people. As an optional activity, students can be encouraged to seek out and interview successful business people in their own communities.

■ Bert N. Mitchell ■
MITCHELL, TITUS & CO.

Bert N. Mitchell is the co-founder and CEO of Mitchell, Titus & Co., the nation's largest minority-controlled CPA firm. Mitchell and his partner, Robert P. Titus, founded the firm in 1974 and built it to become a national leader among domestic CPA firms. Not only is it the largest minority-controlled CPA firm, but it also ranks among the top 40 out of 50,000 CPA firms in the U.S. The firm has more than 200 employees in offices in New York, Washington, D.C., and Philadelphia.

Mitchell is a native of Jamaica who came to America in 1958. While working full-time as a clerk, he went to school at the Bernard M. Baruch School of Business of the City University of New York. Although he originally wanted to become an engineer, he did so well in business courses that he turned to accounting instead.

Mitchell worked as a bookkeeper for a union and later as an accountant at Lucas, Tucker & Co., the oldest black accounting firm in the nation. Eventually he and Robert Titus joined to form their own firm.

In the firm's first years, Mitchell found that he could not always convince the people he wanted to come work for him. In fact, he sometimes found it difficult to attract good people to the firm. He was also surprised that some clients would not pay on time. He said, "I always paid my bills on time and I expected my customers to do the same. I was surprised to find that that's not always the case."

Mitchell and Titus still manage the firm, but they recruit young talent to be sure the firm will grow and prosper. With its excellent record of growth and position in the industry, the firm now attracts top candidates from top colleges and universities. All the professional staff have bachelor degrees; many are CPAs and hold advanced degrees. Mitchell, Titus & Co. has provided a fast track to executive-level opportunities that were traditionally closed to minority professionals, as evidenced by the fact that many of the firm's partners are in their 30s. The firm realizes that one of its most important assets is its people, so training and personal development are important to the firm.

The firm has a very international feel. About 30% of the partnership's employees are not native-born Americans.

Mitchell advises young people to set high standards for themselves and then live up to those standards. He said, "Some people will tell you that you won't or can't make it. But you have to put your faith in yourself and your abilities."

Personal Visions in Business

TEACHING STRATEGIES: TEACHING TIP

Discuss the circumstances under which it might be advantageous for a business to change from one inventory costing method to another. Emphasize that a change cannot be made without permission from the Internal Revenue Service.

that same method continuously for each fiscal period. Using the same inventory costing method for all fiscal periods provides financial statements that can be compared with other fiscal period statements. If a business changes inventory costing methods, part of the difference in gross profit and net income may be caused by the change in methods. Therefore, to provide financial statements that can be analyzed and compared with statements of other fiscal periods, the same inventory costing method should be used each fiscal period. *(CONCEPT: Consistent Reporting)*

ESTIMATING THE COST OF MERCHANDISE INVENTORY

Estimating inventory by using the previous years' percentage of gross profit on operations is called the **gross profit method of estimating inventory**. The gross profit method of estimating inventory is often used to estimate the cost of the monthly ending inventory. The ending inventory cost is used to prepare monthly financial statements. The gross profit method of estimating inventory provides a business with a method of calculating inventory costs that is less expensive than taking a periodic inventory or maintaining a perpetual inventory system.

Celluphone prepares an income statement at the end of each month. *(CONCEPT: Accounting Period Cycle)* To estimate the ending merchandise inventory on January 31, the following information is obtained.

Beginning inventory, January 1	$205,160.00
Net purchases for the period, January 1 to 31 . .	119,900.00
Net sales for the period, January 1 to 31	168,400.00
Gross profit on operations (percentage based on records of previous year's operations)	30.0%

Celluphone's fiscal year ends on December 31. A periodic inventory was taken on December 31 to provide an accurate cost of ending inventory for annual financial statements. The ending inventory on December 31 of the prior fiscal period, $205,160.00, is also the beginning inventory on January 1 for the next fiscal period. Therefore, the January 1 inventory cost, which has been verified by taking a periodic inventory, is used as the basis for estimating monthly ending inventory.

In the prior fiscal period, Celluphone's gross profit was 30.0% of its net sales. Celluphone can use this percentage in the current fiscal period to estimate the cost of merchandise sold and gross profit.

Four steps are followed to estimate the ending merchandise inventory for Celluphone on January 31.

1 Determine the cost of merchandise available for sale.

Beginning inventory, January 1	$205,160.00
Plus net purchases, January 1 to 31	+119,900.00
Equals cost of merchandise available for sale . . .	$325,060.00

ASSESS

Assess student understanding by checking solutions to Independent Practice activities.

Reteach

- From the Masters and Solutions to Enrichment/Application Activities Section in the Teacher's Resource Guide, duplicate and assign Math Work Sheet Chapter 23 Part A: Calculating Inventory and Cost of Merchandise Sold Using the First-in, First-out Inventory Costing Method; Part B: Calculating Inventory and Cost of Merchandise Sold Using the Last-in First-out Inventory Costing Method; Part C: Calculating Inventory and Cost of Merchandise Sold Using the Weighted-Average Inventory Costing Method; Part D: Estimating Inventory Using the Gross Profit Method.

- Use Demonstration Problems 23A and 23B. These problems can be demonstrated on the overhead with the students completing the problem at their desks.

- Assign Recycling Problem 23-R.

Extend

- Assign Cases for Critical Thinking 1 and 2.

- Assign Challenge Problem 23-C. (The challenge is calculating the value of merchandise destroyed in a fire using techniques from the gross profit method of estimating inventory.)

Enrich

- Assign the PERSONAL VISIONS IN BUSINESS feature on page 632.

- Assign the Spreadsheet Template for Problems 23-1 and 23-2.

- Assign the Electronic Study Guide Chapter 23.

CLOSURE

- Use Audit Your Understanding questions.

- Review Summary Illustration 23-6, "Summary of Fifo, Lifo, and Weighted-Average Inventory Costing Methods" or use Transparency 23-2, Chapter Summary.

2 Estimate the gross profit on operations.

Net sales for January 1 to 31	$168,400.00
Times previous year's gross profit percentage. . . .	× 30.0%
Equals estimated gross profit on operations	$ 50,520.00

3 Estimate the cost of merchandise sold.

Net sales for January 1 to 31	$168,400.00
Less estimated gross profit on operations (from Step 2)	−50,520.00
Equals estimated cost of merchandise sold	$117,880.00

4 Estimate the cost of ending merchandise inventory.

Cost of merchandise available for sale (from Step 1)	$325,060.00
Less estimated cost of merchandise sold (from Step 3)	−117,880.00
Equals estimated ending merchandise inventory	$207,180.00

The estimated ending merchandise inventory for Celluphone on January 31, $207,180.00, is used to prepare the January income statement. Celluphone's income statement prepared on January 31 is shown in Illustration 23-5.

ILLUSTRATION 23-5   Income statement with estimated inventory

Celluphone, Inc. Income Statement For Month Ended January 31, 19--			
			% of Net Sales
Operating Revenue:			
Net Sales		$168,400.00	100.0
Cost of Merchandise Sold:			
Beginning Inventory, January 1.	$205,160.00		
Net Purchases.	119,900.00		
Merchandise Available for Sale	$325,060.00		
Less Est. Ending Inv., January 31 . . .	207,180.00		
Cost of Merchandise Sold.		117,880.00	70.0
Gross Profit on Operations		$ 50,520.00	30.0
Operating Expenses.		37,385.00	22.2
Net Income		$ 13,135.00	7.8

APPLIED SKILLS: WRITING ACROSS THE CURRICULUM

Writing paragraphs and short essays.   The Cases for Critical Thinking are short, practical applications of the accounting principles developed in the chapter. Some cases are planned to present problems related to the chapter but not specifically discussed and answered in the chapter. These cases present an opportunity for critical thinking and decision making. These cases also require more than a short objective-type response. Therefore, they provide ideal practice in writing paragraphs and short essays.

The beginning inventory on January 1, $205,160.00, is the ending inventory from the income statement on December 31 of the prior year. The amount of merchandise inventory purchased in January, $119,900.00, is obtained from the general ledger. By using the $207,180.00 estimate of ending merchandise inventory, Celluphone calculated its estimated cost of merchandise sold to be $117,880.00.

An estimated inventory is not completely accurate. The actual rate of gross profit on operations may not be exactly the percentage used in the estimate. Also, some merchandise may have been stolen or damaged. However, an estimated ending inventory is accurate enough for management to prepare a monthly income statement without taking the time to count the inventory. Businesses using a monthly estimate of the merchandise inventory usually take an annual periodic inventory. This is necessary in order to have accurate information for the end-of-year financial statements and tax reports.

Audit Your Understanding

1. Which inventory costing method uses the price of merchandise purchased first to calculate cost of merchandise sold?

2. Which inventory costing method uses the cost of merchandise purchased last to calculate cost of merchandise sold?

3. Which inventory costing method uses the average cost of beginning inventory plus merchandise purchased to calculate cost of merchandise sold?

4. How can a cost be assigned to merchandise inventory when it is too expensive to take a periodic inventory?

SUMMARY OF AN INVENTORY SYSTEM

At the end of the fiscal year, a merchandising business will usually determine the actual quantity of each item by taking a periodic inventory. The cost of merchandise inventory can be calculated using the fifo, lifo, or weighted-average inventory costing method, as shown in Illustration 23-6 on page 636.

A merchandising business can control its merchandise inventory by maintaining a continuous record of item quantities known as a perpetual inventory. At any time a business can determine the quantity of any inventory item on hand by examining the stock record in the stock ledger.

A merchandising business can also estimate monthly ending merchandise inventory costs by using the gross profit method of estimating inventory. The previous years' percentage of gross profit on operations is used to estimate the cost of merchandise inventory sold during the period. This estimate is subtracted from the merchandise available for sale to calculate the estimated ending merchandise inventory.

AUDIT YOUR UNDERSTANDING

1. Fifo.
2. Lifo.
3. Weighted-average.
4. By estimating inventory using the gross profit method of estimating inventory.

SUMMARY ILLUSTRATION 23-6

Summary of fifo, lifo, and weighted-average inventory costing methods

INVENTORY COSTS FOR DECEMBER 31
ENDING INVENTORY OF 16 UNITS

	Units	Unit Price	Total Cost
January 1, beginning inventory	4	$16.00	$ 64.00
March 3, purchases	10	18.00	180.00
April 15, purchases	10	20.00	200.00
June 17, purchases	12	22.00	264.00
November 29, purchases	12	24.00	288.00
Totals	48		$996.00

Lifo Inventory
4 units @ $16.00 = $ 64.00
10 units @ $18.00 = 180.00
2 units @ $20.00 = 40.00
Total $284.00

Fifo Inventory
12 units @ $24.00 = $288.00
4 units @ $22.00 = 88.00
Total $376.00

Weighted-Average Inventory
Weighted-average price per unit:
$996.00 ÷ 48 = $20.75

Cost of ending inventory:
16 units × $20.75 = $332.00

Use the MATH WORK SHEETS in the Masters and Solutions to Enrichment/Application Activities Section of the Teacher's Resource Guide to integrate applied mathematics. In these work sheets, students will apply math concepts to calculate inventory and cost of merchandise sold using the First-in, First-out, Last-in, First-out, and weighted-average inventory costing methods, and estimated inventory using the gross profit method.

PART 4 Accounting for a Merchandising Business Organized as a Corporation

TEACHING STRATEGIES: COOPERATIVE LEARNING

Divide the class into two groups. Each group stands and faces each other. Teacher chooses selected Accounting Terms from Chapters 19 through 23. Teacher gives the term. The first student who raises his/her hand has the opportunity to give the correct definition. The group with the most correctly defined terms is declared the winner. This cooperative learning activity should not take more than 20 to 25 minutes of class time.

ACCOUNTING TERMS

What is the meaning of each of the following?

1. periodic inventory
2. perpetual inventory
3. inventory record
4. stock record
5. stock ledger
6. first-in, first-out inventory costing method
7. last-in, first-out inventory costing method
8. weighted-average inventory costing method
9. gross profit method of estimating inventory

QUESTIONS FOR INDIVIDUAL STUDY

1. What item is typically the largest asset of a merchandising business?
2. Why do successful businesses need an effective inventory system?
3. Identify four reasons why a merchandise inventory that is larger than needed may decrease the net income of a business.
4. What two methods can be used to determine the quantity of each item of merchandise on hand?
5. When are periodic inventories normally taken?
6. How do inventory levels affect the period a business selects for its fiscal year? Why?
7. What action should a business take when the minimum balance is reached on a stock record?
8. When a perpetual inventory of merchandise is kept, entries are made on a stock record to show what information?
9. How is the accuracy of a perpetual inventory checked?
10. When the fifo method is used, how is the price of each kind of merchandise determined?
11. On what idea is the lifo method based?
12. When the weighted-average method is used, how is the cost of each kind of merchandise determined?
13. Which inventory costing method gives the highest cost of merchandise sold?
14. Why should a business select one inventory costing method and use that same method continuously for each fiscal period?
15. When neither a perpetual system is maintained nor a periodic inventory is taken, how can an ending merchandise inventory be determined that is accurate enough for a monthly income statement?

CASES FOR CRITICAL THINKING

CASE 1   Marshall Company uses the fifo method of costing its merchandise inventory. The manager is considering a change to the lifo method. Costs have increased steadily over the past three years. What effect will the change have on the following items? (1) The amount of net income on the income statement. (2) The amount of income taxes to be paid. (3) The quantity of each item of merchandise that must be kept in stock. Why?

CASE 2   The Craft Shop stocks many kinds of merchandise. The store has always taken a periodic inventory at the end of a fiscal year. The store has not kept a perpetual inventory because of the cost. However, the manager wants a reasonably accurate cost of merchandise inventory at the end of each month. The manager needs the amount to prepare monthly income statements and to help in making decisions about the business. What would you recommend?

DRILLS FOR UNDERSTANDING

DRILL 23-D1   Determining quantities of merchandise on hand using a perpetual inventory

Accounting records at Blette Company show the following inventory increases and decreases for one item of merchandise. Beginning inventory on July 1 was 68 units.

CHAPTER 23   Accounting for Inventory   **637**

ACCOUNTING TERMS

1. **periodic inventory:** A merchandise inventory determined by counting, weighing, or measuring items of merchandise on hand. (p. 626)
2. **perpetual inventory:** A merchandise inventory determined by keeping a continuous record of increases, decreases, and balance on hand. (p. 626)
3. **inventory record:** A form used during a periodic inventory to record information about each item of merchandise on hand. (p. 626)
4. **stock record:** A form used to show the kind of merchandise, quantity received, quantity sold, and balance on hand. (p. 627)
5. **stock ledger:** A file of stock records for all merchandise on hand. (p. 627)
6. **first-in, first-out inventory costing method:** Using the price of merchandise purchased first to calculate the cost of merchandise sold first. (p. 629)
7. **last-in, first-out inventory costing method:** Using the price of merchandise purchased last to calculate the cost of merchandise sold first. (p. 630)
8. **weighted-average inventory costing method:** Using the average cost of beginning inventory plus merchandise purchased during a fiscal period to calculate the cost of merchandise sold. (p. 630)
9. **gross profit method of estimating inventory:** Estimating inventory by using the previous years' percentage of gross profit on operations. (p. 633)

QUESTIONS FOR INDIVIDUAL STUDY

1. Merchandise inventory. (p. 625)
2. Successful businesses must have merchandise available for sale that customers want. A business needs controls that assist managers in maintaining a merchandise inventory of sufficient quantity, variety, and price. (p. 625)
3. (a) Excess inventory requires that a business spend money for expensive store and warehouse space.
   (b) Excess inventory uses capital that could be invested in other assets to earn a profit for the business.
   (c) Excess inventory requires that a business spend money for expenses, such as taxes and insurance premiums, that increase with the cost of the merchandise inventory.
   (d) Excess inventory may become obsolete and unsaleable. (p. 625)

---

4. Periodic inventory and perpetual inventory. (p. 626)

5. At the end of a fiscal period. (p. 626)

6. A business frequently establishes its fiscal period to end when inventory normally is at a minimum because it takes less time to count a smaller inventory. (p. 626)

7. Additional merchandise should be ordered to bring the balance up to the maximum. (p. 627)

8. (a) Increases in the quantity on hand when additional merchandise is received. (b) Decreases in the quantity on hand when merchandise is sold. (c) The balance on hand after each increase or decrease is recorded. (pp. 627–628)

9. A customary practice is to take a periodic inventory at least once a fiscal period. The periodic inventory is then compared with the perpetual inventory records. (p. 628)

10. The most recent invoices for purchases are used in recording prices for each item on the inventory record. (p. 629)

11. The most recent costs of merchandise should be charged against current revenue. (p. 630)

12. An inventory is recorded using the average cost of the beginning inventory plus all purchases during the fiscal period. (p. 630)

13. Lifo. (p. 631)

14. Using the same inventory costing method for all fiscal periods provides financial statements that can be compared with other fiscal period statements. If a business changes inventory costing methods, part of the difference in gross profit and net income may be caused by the change in methods. (pp. 632–633)

15. By using the gross profit method of estimating inventory. (p. 633)

Increases		Decreases	
Date	Quantity	Date	Quantity
		July 5	34
		July 7	25
July 8	50		
		July 12	15
July 15	125		
		July 16	108
		July 23	52
July 28	100		

INSTRUCTIONS:

1. Use a stock record similar to the one in the chapter. Record the increases and decreases.
2. Calculate and record the balance of units on hand for each date a transaction occurred.

DRILL 23-D2 Calculating cost of ending inventory using fifo, lifo, and weighted-average methods

Accounting records at Zapata Company show the following beginning inventory and purchases for Inventory Item No. 87.

Purchase Dates	Units	Unit Price	Total Cost
January 1, beginning inventory	5	$20.00	$100.00
March 20, purchases	7	22.00	154.00
May 12, purchases	8	24.00	192.00
September 24, purchases	12	25.00	300.00
November 16, purchases	8	27.00	216.00
Total available	40		$962.00
Units sold	26		
Units in inventory, December 31	14		

INSTRUCTIONS:

Calculate the total cost of ending inventory on December 31 using the fifo, lifo, and weighted-average methods.

APPLICATION PROBLEMS   EPT(c,d)

PROBLEM 23-1 Determining cost of ending inventory using the fifo, lifo, and weighted-average methods

Accounting records at Wimberly Company show the following purchases and periodic inventory counts.

Model No.	Beginning Inventory January 1	First Purchase	Second Purchase	Third Purchase	Periodic Inventory Count December 31
A48	15 @ $12.00	24 @ $14.00	20 @ $15.00	16 @ $18.00	29
G56	6 @ $40.00	8 @ $42.00	4 @ $44.00	9 @ $45.00	12
Q392	24 @ $ 7.00	18 @ $ 6.00	30 @ $ 6.00	26 @ $ 5.00	42
S49	6 @ $40.00	8 @ $45.00	10 @ $45.00	5 @ $48.00	16
P32	14 @ $12.00	12 @ $10.00	22 @ $ 9.00	10 @ $ 8.00	30
K235	4 @ $30.00	16 @ $35.00	8 @ $35.00	10 @ $38.00	19

INSTRUCTIONS:

1. Calculate the total cost of ending inventory on December 31 using the fifo method. The inventory cost for Model No. A48 is given as an example in the working papers that accompany this textbook. Use the following procedure to complete the form.
   a. Record the model number and number of units of each model on hand on December 31.
   b. Record the unit price of each model. When more than one unit price is used, list the units and unit prices on separate lines as shown in the example.
   c. Calculate the cost of ending inventory of each model, and write the amount in the Cost of Ending Inventory column.
   d. Add the amounts in the Cost of Ending Inventory column to calculate the total cost of ending inventory.
2. On another form in the working papers, calculate the total cost of ending inventory using the lifo method. Follow the steps given in Instruction 1.
3. On another form in the working papers, calculate the total cost of ending inventory using the weighted-average method. Use the following procedure.
   a. Record the model number and number of units of each model on hand on December 31.
   b. Calculate the weighted-average price per unit for each model. Round the amount per unit to the nearest cent. Write the amount in the Unit Price column.
   c. Calculate the cost of ending inventory of each model, and write the amount in the Cost of Ending Inventory column.
   d. Add the amounts in the Cost of Ending Inventory column to calculate the total cost of ending inventory.
4. Compare the total cost of ending inventory obtained in Instructions 1, 2, and 3. Which method, fifo, lifo, or weighted-average, resulted in the lowest cost of ending inventory?

PROBLEM 23-2 Estimating ending inventory using the gross profit method of estimating inventory

The following information is from the accounting records of two different companies for July of the current year.

	Companies	
	Daniel	**Pearson**
Beginning inventory, July 1	$12,900.00	$32,900.00
Net purchases for July	32,300.00	63,200.00
Net sales for July	76,500.00	98,500.00
Gross profit on operations as a percent of sales . . .	60.0%	45.0%
Operating expenses for July	25,400.00	37,600.00

INSTRUCTIONS:

1. For each company, estimate the ending inventory for July of the current year using the gross profit method of estimating inventory.
2. For each company, prepare an income statement for the month ended July 31 of the current year similar to the one shown in Illustration 23-5.

ENRICHMENT PROBLEMS
EPT(c,d)

MASTERY PROBLEM 23-M Determining cost of ending inventory using the fifo, lifo, and weighted-average methods

Accounting records at SummerSport Company show the following purchases and periodic inventory counts.

Model No.	Beginning Inventory January 1	First Purchase	Second Purchase	Third Purchase	Periodic Inventory Count December 31
23B2	4 @ $4.50	12 @ $4.75	8 @ $4.90	15 @ $5.20	22
13M2	3 @ $3.50	6 @ $3.30	2 @ $3.20	5 @ $3.10	8
45V23	23 @ $1.20	45 @ $1.25	35 @ $1.30	40 @ $1.40	35
90F2	12 @ $7.40	15 @ $7.50	16 @ $7.80	20 @ $7.90	30
10K3	32 @ $5.40	38 @ $5.10	19 @ $4.90	26 @ $4.80	40
34P2	2 @ $2.50	5 @ $2.70	4 @ $2.80	3 @ $3.00	4

INSTRUCTIONS:

1. Calculate the total cost of ending inventory on December 31 using the fifo method. The inventory cost for Model No. 23B2 is given as an example in the working papers that accompany this textbook. Use the following procedure to complete the form.

   a. Record the model number and number of units of each model on hand on December 31.

   b. Record the unit price of each model. When more than one unit price is used, list the units and unit prices on separate lines as shown in the example.

   c. Calculate the cost of ending inventory of each model, and write the amount in the Cost of Ending Inventory column.

   d. Add the amounts in the Cost of Ending Inventory column to calculate the total cost of ending inventory.

2. On another form in the working papers, calculate the total cost of ending inventory using the lifo method. Follow the steps given in Instruction 1.

3. On another form in the working papers, calculate the total cost of ending inventory using the weighted-average method. Use the following procedure.

   a. Record the model number and number of units of each model on hand on December 31.

   b. Calculate the weighted-average price per unit for each model. Round the amount per unit to the nearest cent. Write the amount in the Unit Price column.

   c. Calculate the cost of ending inventory of each model, and write the amount in the Cost of Ending Inventory column.

   d. Add the amounts in the Cost of Ending Inventory column to calculate the total cost of ending inventory.

4. Compare the total cost of ending inventory obtained in Instructions 1, 2, and 3. Which method, fifo, lifo, or weighted-average, resulted in the lowest cost of ending inventory?

CHALLENGE PROBLEM 23-C Determining the cost of merchandise inventory destroyed in a fire

A fire completely destroyed the warehouse of Fleming Lighting Company on the night of October 12. The accounting records of the company and $6,500 of merchandise inventory remained safe in the company's showroom. The company does not maintain a perpetual inventory system. The insurance company, therefore, has requested an estimate of the merchandise inventory destroyed in the fire.

The following income statement is for the previous fiscal year.

Fleming Lighting Company
Income Statement
For Year Ended July 31, 19--

Operating Revenue:		
Net Sales		$746,900.00
Cost of Merchandise Sold:		
Beginning Merchandise Inventory, Aug. 1	$ 72,430.00	
Net Purchases	291,300.00	
Merchandise Available for Sale	$363,730.00	
Less Ending Inventory, July 31	79,610.00	
Cost of Merchandise Sold		284,120.00
Gross Profit on Operations		$462,780.00
Operating Expenses		416,900.00
Net Income		$ 45,880.00

The following additional financial information is obtained from the current year's accounting records.

Net purchases, August 1 to October 12	$ 70,190.00
Net sales, August 1 to October 12	162,790.00
Operating expenses, August 1 to October 12	87,280.00

INSTRUCTIONS:

1. Calculate the prior year's gross profit on operations as a percentage of net sales. Round the percentage calculation to the nearest whole percent.

2. Use the percentage calculated in Instruction 1 and the current year's financial information to calculate an estimate of the total merchandise inventory as of October 12.

3. To calculate the cost of the inventory destroyed in the fire, subtract the cost of the merchandise inventory from the estimate of the total merchandise inventory as of October 12.

4. Prepare an income statement for the period August 1 to October 12.

Procedures for accounting for notes payable and notes receivable are presented in this chapter. Detailed procedures for calculating maturity dates and interest on notes are illustrated. Banks and some businesses have computer services available to calculate interest and maturity dates. However, numerous businesses continue to calculate interest and maturity dates manually. Regardless of how the calculations are performed, journal entries are required to recognize these other revenues and expenses in the books of the business.

GUIDE TO ACHIEVING LEARNING OBJECTIVES

Enabling Performance Tasks	TEACH	APPLY		EXTEND/ENRICH					
	Lesson Plans	Drills for Understanding	Application Problems	Mastery Problems	Challenge Problems	Cases for Critical Thinking	Recycling Problems	Reinforcement Activity	
a. Define accounting terms related to notes and interest.	24-1, 24-2, 24-3								
b. Identify accounting concepts and practices related to notes and interest.	24-1, 24-2, 24-3					Cases 1, 2			
c. Calculate interest and maturity dates for notes.	24-1, 24-2, 24-3	24-D1, 24-D2, 24-D3			24-C	Cases 1, 2			
d. Analyze and record transactions for notes payable and notes receivable.	24-2, 24-3	24-D4, 24-D5	24-1, 24-2, 24-3	24-M	24-C		24-R	3B	

ENRICHMENT

SPECIAL FEATURES

Applied Communications, page 658

TECHNOLOGY CONNECTION

Accounting Tutorial Unit 7

Application Program Disk Problem 24-M

Spreadsheet Template Drills 24-D1, 24-D3

Electronic Study Guide

NEW, REVIEW, AND EXTENSION

ACTIVITIES/CONCEPTS/TRANSACTIONS	NEW	REVIEW/ EXTENSION
Promissory notes	✓	
Calculating maturity date on promissory notes	✓	
Calculating interest on promissory notes	✓	
Issuing a note payable to borrow money from a bank	✓	
Paying principal and interest on a note payable at maturity	✓	
Issuing a note payable for an extension of time on account	✓	
Issuing a discounted note payable for cash	✓	
Paying a discounted note payable	✓	
Accepting a note receivable from a customer	✓	
Collecting principal and interest on a note receivable at maturity	✓	
Receiving a dishonored note receivable	✓	

	INFORMAL ASSESSMENT		FORMAL ASSESSMENT				
	Study Guide	Audit Your Understanding	Chapter MicroExam	Chapter Problem Test	Unit Problem Test	Unit Objective Test	Portfolio
Unit A	✓	✓				✓	
Unit C	✓	✓				✓	
Unit C	✓			✓			
Unit B				✓	✓		✓

TEACHING MATERIALS

Teacher's Wraparound Edition of the Text
Teacher's Resource Guide
Teacher's Edition of Working Papers
Teacher's Edition of Demonstration/Recycling Problems
Teaching Transparencies
Accounting Tutorial Manual
MicroExam
Applied Math Work Sheet

APPLIED MATHEMATICS

APPLIED MATH/ACCOUNTING SKILL	APPLICATION
Calculating Interest for a Year	Drill 24-D1
Calculating Interest for a Fraction of a Year	Drill 24-D1
Calculating Maturity Date	Drill 24-D2
Calculating Maturity Value of a Note	Prob. 24-C
Calculating Bank Discount and Proceeds for a Discounted Note	Prob. 24-C

24

Accounting for Notes and Interest

ENABLING PERFORMANCE TASKS

After studying Chapter 24, you will be able to:

a Define accounting terms related to notes and interest.

b Identify accounting concepts and practices related to notes and interest.

c Calculate interest and maturity dates for notes.

d Analyze and record transactions for notes payable and notes receivable.

TERMS PREVIEW

promissory note • date of a note • time of a note • payee of a note • principal of a note • interest rate of a note • maturity date of a note • maker of a note • number of a note • interest • interest-bearing note • non-interest-bearing note • maturity value • creditor • notes payable • current liabilities • interest expense • bank discount • discounted note • proceeds • notes receivable • interest income • dishonored note

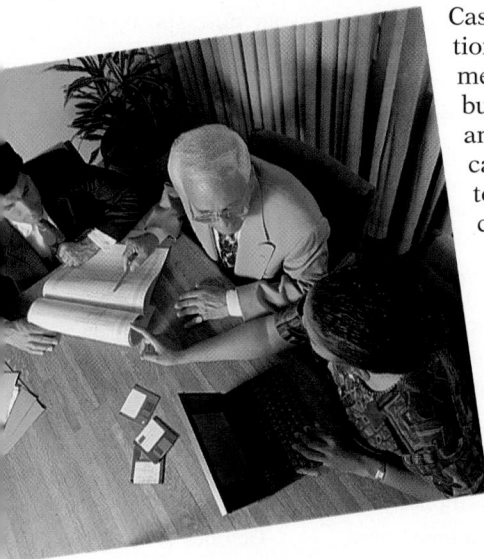

Cash is the primary medium of exchange for business transactions. *(CONCEPT: Unit of Measurement)* Cash is used to purchase merchandise and to pay salaries and other expenses. In turn, businesses receive cash when they sell their products or services and collect payment. The cash received for products or services can be used to purchase more merchandise and continue to pay salaries and other expenses. Thus, the business cycle continues.

Sometimes a business receives more cash from sales than is needed to pay for purchases and expenses. When this occurs, a business may deposit the extra cash in a bank or other financial in stitution for a short period. At other times, the receipt of cash from sales does not occur at the same time and in sufficient amounts to pay for needed purchases and expenses. When this occurs, a business needs to borrow additional cash or make arrangements with its vendors to delay payment for a period of time. Generally, when a bank or other business lends money to another business, the loan agreement is made in writing.

PROMISSORY NOTES

A written and signed promise to pay a sum of money at a specified time is called a **promissory note**. A promissory note frequently is referred to as a note.

Promissory notes are used when money is borrowed for a period of time from a bank or other lending agency. Sometimes a business requests a note from a customer who wants credit beyond the usual time given for sales on account. Notes have an advantage over oral promises and accounts receivable or payable. A note, like a check, can be endorsed and transferred to a bank in return for cash. Thus, the business can get its money before the note is due. Notes can also be useful in a court of law as written evidence of a debt. One form of a promissory note is shown in Illustration 24-1.

ILLUSTRATION 24-1   A promissory note

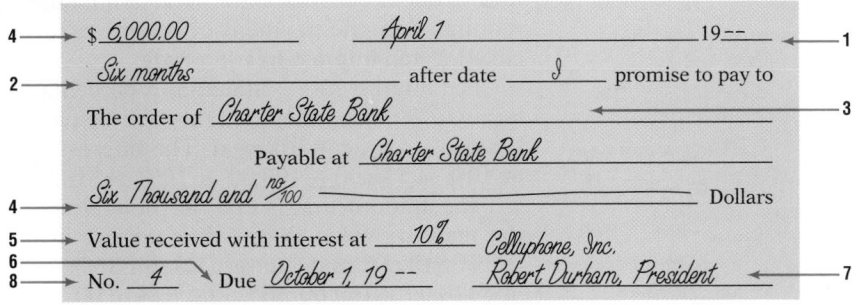

TEACHING STRATEGIES: TEACHING TIP

Copies of notes may be secured from local banks. Using the note forms, a bulletin board can be prepared highlighting the parts of a note and/or illustrating the completion of a note.

LESSON PLAN 24-1

Materials

- Student pages 643–646
- Transparency: 24-1, Promissory Note
- Software: Spreadsheet Template
- Math Work Sheet Chapter 24: Part A: Calculating Interest for a Year; Part B: Calculating Interest for a Fraction of a Year; Part C: Calculating Maturity Date (TRG)
- Demonstration Problem: 24A, Calculating Interest and Maturity Dates on Notes

Objectives (Enabling Performance Tasks)

a. Define accounting terms related to notes and interest.

b. Identify accounting concepts and practices related to notes and interest.

c. Calculate interest and maturity dates for notes.

FOCUS

- In earlier chapters, cash has been presented as the primary medium of exchange for business transactions. Cash was used to pay vendors for merchandise and to pay expenses. A business received cash from customers as payment for services and merchandise. Explain that when cash is not available to make these payments, the business or the customers may borrow the money they need. In this lesson, we will look at the written agreement to repay the borrowed money and the procedures for calculating the amount paid for using the borrowed money.

- Introduce new vocabulary: promissory note, date of a note, time of a note, payee of a note, principal of a note, interest rate of a note, maturity date of a note, maker of a note, number of a note, interest, interest-bearing note, non-interest-bearing note, maturity value.

Cover student pages 643–646 "Promissory Notes" and "Interest on Promissory Notes." Explain that interest is usually charged whenever money is loaned or credit is extended. Interest is a fee for the use of the money. Ask students for examples of interest charges they know about, e.g., car loans, mortgages, department store credit cards. Explain that a note is the source document for a loan and proves the transaction occurred. Review the use of percentages in calculations: depending on the equipment being used and the numbers involved, some students may prefer to use percentages, such as 10%, some decimals, such as 0.10, and some may prefer fractions, such as 1/10. Explain the basic formula for interest—principal times rate times time—that will be used for all interest calculations. Describe the different ways of expressing the time in the interest formula, e.g., in years (1, 2, or more years), a fraction of a year in even months (1/12, 2/12, 3/12, etc.), or a fraction of a year in days (65/360, 90/360, etc.) Explain that 360 days is used for calculations in this text, although many agencies use 365 days. (Using 360 days makes some calculations simpler if calculators are not available.) Explain how the maturity date is calculated: (1) if expressed in days, the actual days are counted; (2) if expressed in months, the note is due on the same day in some subsequent month.

APPLY

- Use Transparency 24-1 to identify and describe each part of the promissory note or direct students to Illustration 24-1.

- Write the formulas for interest calculations on the board. Work through the examples.

- Work through the examples for calculating the maturity date of notes.

Guided Practice

Guide students through Drills 24-D1, 24-D2, and 24-D3. Students should have the forms from the working papers to complete as you guide them through the drills. Complete each calculation aloud in class. Have volunteers share their answers with the class. All students should agree with the calculations for each item before proceeding to the next one.

Independent Practice

Assign Terms 1–13 and Questions 1–6.

The terms defined below apply to the promissory note shown in Illustration 24-1.

Term	Definition	Illustration
1 **Date of a note**	The day a note is issued.	April 1, 19--
2 **Time of a note**	The days, months, or years from the date of issue until a note is to be paid.	Six months
3 **Payee of a note**	The person or business to whom the amount of a note is payable.	Charter State Bank
4 **Principal of a note**	The original amount of a note. Sometimes referred to as face amount of a note.	$6,000.00
5 **Interest rate of a note**	The percentage of the principal that is paid for use of the money.	10%
6 **Maturity date of a note**	The date a note is due.	October 1, 19--
7 **Maker of a note**	The person or business who signs a note and thus promises to make payment.	Celluphone, Inc. Robert Durham, President
8 **Number of a note**	The number assigned by the maker to identify a specific note.	4

INTEREST ON PROMISSORY NOTES

An amount paid for the use of money for a period of time is called **interest**. Banks and other lending institutions generally charge interest on money loaned to their customers.

When businesses borrow money from banks, other lending institutions, or other businesses, promissory notes generally are prepared to provide written evidence of the transaction. Most promissory notes require the payment of interest. A promissory note that requires the payment of principal plus interest when the note is due is called an **interest-bearing note**. A promissory note that requires only the payment of the principal when the note is due is called a **non-interest-bearing note**.

The interest rate is stated as a percentage of the principal. *Interest at 10%* means that 10 cents will be paid for the use of each dollar borrowed for a full year. The interest on $100.00 for a full year at 10% is $10.00 ($100.00 × 10% = $10.00).

The amount that is due on the maturity date of a note is called the **maturity value**. A one-year interest-bearing note with a principal of $100.00 and interest rate of 10% will have a maturity value of $110.00 ($100.00 principal + $10.00 interest).

Sometimes partial payments on a note are made each month. This arrangement is particularly true when an individual buys a car and signs a note for the amount owed. The monthly payment includes part of the principal and part of the interest to be paid.

When multiplying by 12%, convert the percentage to the decimal .12.

Calculating Interest

To calculate interest for one year, the principal is multiplied by the interest rate. The interest on a $1,000.00, 12% interest-bearing note for one year is calculated as shown below.

	Principal	×	Interest Rate	×	Time in Years	=	Interest for One Year
	$1,000.00	×	12%	×	1	=	$120.00

When the time of a note is expressed in months, the time used in calculating interest is stated as a fraction of 12 months. The interest on a $1,000.00, 12% interest-bearing note for three months (3/12 of a year) is calculated as shown below.

	Principal	×	Interest Rate	×	Time as Fraction of Year	=	Interest for Fraction of Year
	$1,000.00	×	12%	×	$\frac{3}{12}$	=	$\frac{\$360.00}{12} = \$30.00$

The time of a note is often stated as a number of days, such as 30 days, 60 days, or 90 days. When the time of a note is stated in days, the time used in calculating interest is stated as a fraction of 360 days. The interest on a $1,000.00, 12% interest-bearing note for 60 days (60/360 of a year) is calculated as shown below.

	Principal	×	Interest Rate	×	Time as Fraction of Year	=	Interest for Fraction of Year
	$1,000.00	×	12%	×	$\frac{60}{360}$	=	$\frac{\$7,200.00}{360} = \$20.00$

A 360-day year is used for all interest calculations in this text.

Agencies of the federal government generally use a 365-day year when calculating interest. Consumer interest is also generally calculated on a 365-day year. However, many banks use a 360-day year when calculating interest. Therefore, the interest calculations in this textbook use a 360-day year.

CHAPTER 24   Accounting for Notes and Interest   **645**

Audit Your Understanding

1. What is the difference between the maturity value of an interest-bearing note and a non-interest-bearing note?
2. What is the interest on $500 at 10% for a full year?
3. What is the maturity value of a $400 6-month note at 8%?
4. What is the maturity date of a 3-month note dated November 22?
5. What is the maturity date of a 60-day note dated March 23?

Calculating Maturity Date

The time between the date a note is issued and the date a note is due may be expressed in either years, months, or days. When the time of a note is stated in months, the maturity date is calculated by counting the number of months from the date of issuance. For example, a six-month note dated April 11 would be due on October 11.

When the time of a note is expressed in days, the maturity date is calculated by counting the exact number of days. The date the note is written is not counted, but the maturity date is counted. To calculate this maturity date, find the number of days remaining in the month the note was written. Then add the days in the following months until the total equals the required number of days. For example, a 60-day note dated March 3 is due on May 2. The maturity date is calculated as shown below.

March 3 through 31	28 days (31 − 3 = 28)
April 1 through 30	30 days
May 1 through 2	2 days (Maturity date: May 2)
	60 days

NOTES PAYABLE

A person or organization to whom a liability is owed is called a **creditor.** Promissory notes that a business issues to creditors are called **notes payable.** Liabilities due within a short time, usually within a year, are called **current liabilities.** Since notes payable generally are paid within one year, they are classified as current liabilities.

Issuing a Note Payable to Borrow Money from a Bank

When a business issues a note payable, the principal or face amount of the note is credited to a liability account titled *Notes Payable.* A liability account has a normal credit balance. Therefore, the notes payable account is increased by a credit and decreased by a debit, as shown in the T account.

On April 1 Celluphone arranges to borrow money from its bank. A note payable is issued to the bank as evidence of the debt. The bank deposits the principal amount of the note in Celluphone's checking account.

April 1, 19--. Issued a 6-month, 10% note, $6,000.00. Note Payable No. 4.

FYI

To calculate a maturity date, remember that April, June, September, and November have 30 days; all other months, except February, have 31 days.

Notes Payable	
Debit side	Credit side
	Normal balance
Decrease	Increase

646

```
                Cash
Apr. 1    6,000.00  |

            Notes Payable
                   |  Apr. 1    6,000.00
```

The bank retains the original of the note until Celluphone pays the maturity value. A copy of the note payable is the source document used by Celluphone to record this transaction. *(CONCEPT: Objective Evidence)*

Cash is debited for $6,000.00 to show the increase in the balance of this asset account. Notes Payable is credited for $6,000.00 to show the increase in the balance of this liability account. No entry is made for interest until a later date when the interest is paid.

The cash receipts journal entry to record this transaction is shown in Illustration 24-2.

ILLUSTRATION 24-2 Cash receipts journal entry to record cash received for the issuance of a note payable

CASH RECEIPTS JOURNAL

					GENERAL		ACCOUNTS RECEIVABLE CREDIT	SALES CREDIT	SALES TAX PAYABLE		SALES DISCOUNT DEBIT	CASH DEBIT	
	DATE	ACCOUNT TITLE	DOC. NO.	POST. REF.	DEBIT	CREDIT			DEBIT	CREDIT			
					1	2	3	4	5	6	7	8	
6	1	Notes Payable	NP4			6 000 00						6 000 00	6
7													7
8													8
9													9

PAGE 13

```
            Interest Expense
   Debit side        |  Credit side
   Normal balance    |
   Increase          |  Decrease
```

Paying Principal and Interest on a Note Payable at Maturity

When a note payable reaches its maturity date, the maker of the note pays the maturity value to the payee. The maturity value of a note is the principal (original amount borrowed) plus the interest that has accrued during the time of the note. The interest accrued on money borrowed is called **interest expense.**

The interest accrued on a note payable is debited to an expense account titled *Interest Expense.* An expense account has a normal debit balance. Therefore, the interest expense account is increased by a debit and decreased by a credit, as shown in the T account.

Interest expense is a financial expense rather than an expense of the business' normal operations. Therefore, Interest Expense is listed in a classification titled *Other Expenses* in a chart of accounts.

Celluphone paid the six-month note payable it had issued on April 1.

October 1, 19--. Paid cash for the maturity value of Note Payable No. 4: principal, $6,000.00, plus interest, $300.00; total, $6,300.00. Check No. 573.

APPLIED SKILLS: BUILDING STUDY SKILLS

Four new accounts, Notes Payable, Interest Expense, Notes Receivable, and Interest Income are introduced in this chapter. Direct students to create a Quick Reference Guide (QRG) on a small card or sheet of paper to use as an aid in analyzing transactions. T accounts should be used to show normal balance sides. Students may also wish to record the formula for calculating interest.

- Draw a T account for Notes Payable and label the normal balance side.
- Draw T accounts for each transaction as it is presented in this lesson.
- Use Transparency O to journalize issuing a note to borrow money. Or direct students to Illustration 24-2.
- Use Transparency L to journalize paying a note to borrow money. Or direct students to Illustration 24-3.
- Use Transparency M to journalize issuing a note for an extension of time. Or direct students to Illustration 24-4.
- Use Transparency L to journalize paying a note for an extension of time. Or direct students to Illustration 24-5.
- Use Transparency O to journalize issuing a discounted note payable. Or direct students to Illustration 24-6.
- Use Transparency L to journalize paying a discounted note payable. Or direct students to Illustration 24-7.

Guided Practice

Guide students through Drill 24-D4. Students should have the forms from the working papers to complete as you guide them through each transaction. All students should agree with the analysis of each transaction before proceeding to the next transaction.

Independent Practice

Assign Terms 14–20, Questions 7–15, and Problems 24-1 and 24-2.

Notes Payable

Oct. 1	6,000.00	Apr. 1 6,000.00

Interest Expense

Oct. 1	300.00

Cash

	Oct. 1 6,300.00

Notes Payable is debited for $6,000.00 to show the decrease in the balance of this liability account. Interest Expense is debited for $300.00 to show the increase in the balance of this other expense account. Cash is paid for the maturity value of the note. Thus, Cash is credited for $6,300.00 ($6,000.00 principal + $300.00 interest) to show the decrease in the balance of this asset account.

The cash payments journal entry to record this transaction is shown in Illustration 24-3.

ILLUSTRATION 24-3   Cash payments journal entry to record payment of maturity value of a note payable

CASH PAYMENTS JOURNAL   PAGE 28

	DATE		ACCOUNT TITLE	CK. NO.	POST. REF.	GENERAL DEBIT	GENERAL CREDIT	ACCOUNTS PAYABLE DEBIT	PURCHASES DISCOUNT CREDIT	CASH CREDIT	
1	Oct.	1	Notes Payable	573		6 0 0 0 00				6 3 0 0 00	1
2			Interest Expense			3 0 0 00					2
3											3
4											4
5											5
6											6
7											7

Issuing and Paying a Note Payable for an Extension of Time

FYI

A promissory note given to a vendor changes an account payable to a note payable.

GENERAL LEDGER
Accounts Payable

2,000.00	

Notes Payable

	2,000.00

ACCOUNTS PAYABLE LEDGER
Action Phone Company

2,000.00	Bal.	2,000.00

A business may ask for an extension of time if it is unable to pay an account when due. When a request for more time is made, sometimes the business is asked to issue a note payable. The note payable does not pay the amount owed to the vendor. However, the form of the liability is changed from an account payable to a note payable.

April 5, 19--. Issued a 60-day, 12% note to Action Phone Company for an extension of time on this account payable, $2,000.00. Note Payable No. 5.

Accounts Payable is debited for $2,000.00 to show the decrease in the balance of this liability account. Notes Payable is credited for $2,000.00 to show the increase in the balance of this liability account. The vendor account, Action Phone Company, is debited for $2,000.00 to show the decrease in the balance of this accounts payable ledger account. Whenever Accounts Payable is decreased, the vendor account in the accounts payable ledger is also decreased by the same amount. No entry is made for interest expense until a later date when interest is paid.

The general journal entry to record this transaction is shown in Illustration 24-4.

ILLUSTRATION 24-4

General journal entry to record issuing a note payable for an extension of time on an account payable

	DATE	ACCOUNT TITLE	DOC. NO.	POST. REF.	DEBIT	CREDIT	
		GENERAL JOURNAL				PAGE 5	
17	5	Accounts Payable/Action Phone Co.	NP5	╱	2 0 0 0 00		17
18		Notes Payable				2 0 0 0 00	18

When this entry is posted, the balance of the accounts payable account for Action Phone Company will be zero. One liability, Accounts Payable, is replaced by another liability, Notes Payable.

Note Payable No. 5 is due on June 4. The maturity date for Note Payable No. 5 is calculated as shown below.

April 5 through 30	25 days (30 − 5 = 25)
May 1 through 31	31 days
June 1 through 4	4 days (Maturity date: June 4)
	60 days

June 4, 19--. Paid cash for the maturity value of Note Payable No. 5: principal, $2,000.00, plus interest, $40.00; total, $2,040.00. Check No. 328.

The interest expense is calculated as shown below.

	Principal	×	Interest Rate	×	Time as Fraction of Year	=	Interest for Fraction of Year
	$2,000.00	×	12%	×	$\frac{60}{360}$	=	$\frac{\$14,400.00}{360} = \$40.00$

Notes Payable

June 4	2,000.00	Apr. 5	2,000.00

Interest Expense

June 4	40.00	

Cash

	June 4	2,040.00

Notes Payable is debited for $2,000.00 to show the decrease in the balance of this liability account. Interest Expense is debited for $40.00 to show the increase in the balance of this other expense account. Cash is credited for the principal of the note plus the interest, $2,040.00, to show the decrease in the balance of this asset account.

The cash payments journal entry to record this transaction is shown in Illustration 24-5.

CHAPTER 24 Accounting for Notes and Interest **649**

CLOSURE

- Use Audit Your Understanding questions.
- Review calculating interest and maturity dates of notes payable.
- Review calculating bank discount and proceeds for discounted notes payable.
- Review the entries to issue and pay notes payable.

ILLUSTRATION 24-5	Cash payments journal entry to record payment of maturity value of a note payable issued for an extension of time

CASH PAYMENTS JOURNAL — PAGE 15

	DATE	ACCOUNT TITLE	CK. NO.	POST. REF.	GENERAL DEBIT	GENERAL CREDIT	ACCOUNTS PAYABLE DEBIT	PURCHASES DISCOUNT CREDIT	CASH CREDIT	
1	19-- June 4	Notes Payable	328		2 0 0 0 00				2 0 4 0 00	1
2		Interest Expense			4 0 00					2
3										3
4										4
5										5
6										6

Issuing and Paying a Discounted Note Payable

FYI

A discounted note is a non-interest-bearing note because the interest is paid in advance.

Some banks require that the interest be paid at the time a note is issued. Interest collected in advance on a note is called **bank discount**. A note on which interest is paid in advance is called a **discounted note**. The amount received for a note after the bank discount has been deducted is called **proceeds**.

May 3, 19--. Discounted at 10% a 3-month non-interest-bearing note, $3,000.00; proceeds, $2,925.00, interest, $75.00. Note Payable No. 6.

The bank deposited the proceeds, $2,925.00, in Celluphone's checking account. The amount of the discount and the proceeds are calculated as shown below.

Maturity Value	×	Discount Rate	×	Time as Fraction of Year	=	Bank Discount
$3,000.00	×	10%	×	$\frac{3}{12}$	=	$\frac{\$900.00}{12} = \$75.00$

Maturity Value	−	Bank Discount	=	Proceeds
$3,000.00	−	$75.00	=	$2,925.00

Cash

May 3	2,925.00	

Interest Expense

May 3	75.00	

Notes Payable

	May 3	3,000.00

Cash is debited for $2,925.00 ($3,000.00 − $75.00 interest expense) to show the increase in the balance of this asset account. Interest Expense is debited for the discount, $75.00, to show the increase in the balance of this other expense account. Notes Payable is credited for $3,000.00 to show the increase in the balance of this liability account.

The cash receipts journal entry to record this transaction is shown in Illustration 24-6.

APPLIED SKILLS: WRITING ACROSS THE CURRICULUM

Writing paragraphs and short essays. The Cases for Critical Thinking are short, practical applications of the accounting principles developed in the chapter. Some cases are planned to present problems related to the chapter but not specifically discussed and answered in the chapter. These cases present an opportunity for critical thinking and decision making. These cases also require more than a short objective-type response. Therefore, they provide ideal practice in writing paragraphs and short essays.

ILLUSTRATION 24-6

Cash receipts journal entry to record cash received for a discounted note payable

CASH RECEIPTS JOURNAL

PAGE *17*

	DATE	ACCOUNT TITLE	DOC. NO.	POST. REF.	GENERAL DEBIT	GENERAL CREDIT	ACCOUNTS RECEIVABLE CREDIT	SALES CREDIT	SALES TAX PAYABLE DEBIT	SALES TAX PAYABLE CREDIT	SALES DISCOUNT DEBIT	CASH DEBIT	
6	3	Interest Expense	NP6		75 00							2925 00	6
7		Notes Payable				3000 00							7
8													8
9													9
10													10

Audit Your Understanding

1. What is the normal balance side of Notes Payable?
2. Why is Interest Expense classified as an "Other Expense" in a chart of accounts?
3. Under what circumstances can a borrower receive less cash than the principal of a note?

When Note Payable No. 6 is paid on August 3, Check No. 450 is issued to the bank. This check is in payment of the principal. No payment of interest expense is necessary at this time because the bank collected the interest in advance when the note was discounted. Therefore, the maturity value of a discounted note is the principal of the note. Because no interest is paid on the maturity date, a discounted note is considered a non-interest-bearing note.

August 3, 19--. Paid cash for the maturity value of non-interest-bearing Note Payable No. 6, $3,000.00. Check No. 450.

Notes Payable is debited for $3,000.00 to show the decrease in the balance of this liability account. Cash is credited for the amount paid, $3,000.00, to show the decrease in the balance of this asset account.

The cash payments journal entry to record this transaction is shown in Illustration 24-7.

Notes Payable			
Aug. 3	3,000.00	May 3	3,000.00

Cash			
		Aug. 3	3,000.00

ILLUSTRATION 24-7

Cash payments journal entry to record payment of a discounted note payable

CASH PAYMENTS JOURNAL

PAGE *20*

	DATE	ACCOUNT TITLE	CK. NO.	POST. REF.	GENERAL DEBIT	GENERAL CREDIT	ACCOUNTS PAYABLE DEBIT	PURCHASES DISCOUNT CREDIT	CASH CREDIT	
3	3	Notes Payable	450		3000 00				3000 00	3
4										4
5										5
6										6
7										7

TEACHING STRATEGIES: DIFFERENT LEARNING ABILITIES

Limited English Proficiency (LEP) Students. Speak directly. Avoid sentences with negative constructions, such as "Don't forget that Cash is not debited in this transaction." Instead, say "Remember that Cash is credited in this transaction." Use active verbs in your sentences rather than passive verbs.

Materials

- Student pages 652–657

- Transparencies: M, Blank General Journal; O, Blank Cash Receipts Journal; 24-2, Chapter Summary

- Software: Accounting Tutorial, Unit 7; Application Program Disk; Electronic Study Guide

- Demonstration Problem: 24C, Journalizing Notes Receivable Transactions

- Assess: Problem Test Chapter 24, MicroExam Chapter 24

Objectives (Enabling Performance Tasks)

a. Define accounting terms related to notes and interest.

b. Identify accounting concepts and practices related to notes and interest.

c. Calculate interest and maturity dates for notes.

d. Analyze and record transactions for notes payable and notes receivable.

FOCUS

- Promissory notes, calculating interest on notes, and calculating the maturity date of notes were presented earlier in this chapter. Explain that a customer who is unable to pay an account when it is due may ask the business for additional time. The business may agree to accept a promissory note from the customer. In this lesson, we will analyze and journalize the transactions for a business that accepts a note from a customer to extend a payment period.

- Introduce new vocabulary: notes receivable, interest income, dishonored note.

NOTES RECEIVABLE

Promissory notes that a business accepts from customers are called **notes receivable.** Notes receivable generally are paid within one year. Therefore, they are classified as current assets.

Accepting a Note Receivable from a Customer

A customer who is unable to pay an account on the due date may request additional time. When a request for more time is made, a business may agree to accept a note receivable. A note receivable does not pay the amount the customer owes. However, the form of the asset is changed from an account receivable to a note receivable.

If a customer needs extra time to pay, most businesses prefer a note receivable over an account receivable for several reasons. A note receivable usually earns interest whereas an account receivable does not. By signing the promissory note, the customer provides a written confirmation of the amount owed, which provides evidence of the debt in case legal action is required to collect.

When a business accepts a note receivable, the principal or face amount of the note is debited to an asset account titled *Notes Receivable*. An asset account has a normal debit balance. Therefore, the notes receivable account is increased by a debit and decreased by a credit, as shown in the T account.

Celluphone agrees to accept a promissory note from Ann Nance. Celluphone accepts the note because Ms. Nance is unable to pay the account receivable when due. The note Ms. Nance issues, which will be payable to Celluphone, is an interest-bearing note. Although Celluphone has not yet collected the cash Ms. Nance owes, the promissory note does provide a written promise to pay the amount owed plus interest.

As defined earlier, a promissory note is a written and signed promise to pay a sum of money at a specified time. A note is recorded as a note receivable by the person or business to whom the amount of the note is payable. A note is recorded as a note payable by the maker of the note, the person or business who signs the note and thus promises to make payment. Therefore, the note issued by Ms. Nance to Celluphone is recorded by Celluphone as a note receivable. This same note is recorded by Ms. Nance as a note payable.

April 22, 19--. Received a 2-month, 12% note from Ann Nance for an extension of time on her account, $800.00. Note Receivable No. 10.

Notes Receivable is debited for $800.00 to show the increase in the balance of this asset account. Accounts Receivable is credited for $800.00 to show the decrease in the balance of this asset account. The customer account, Ann Nance, is also credited for $800.00 to

FYI

A promissory note signed by a customer changes an account receivable to a note receivable.

Notes Receivable	
Debit side	Credit side
Normal balance	
Increase	Decrease

GENERAL LEDGER
Notes Receivable

Apr. 22	800.00	

Accounts Receivable

		Apr. 22	800.00

ACCOUNTS RECEIVABLE LEDGER
Ann Nance

Bal.	800.00	Apr. 22	800.00

show the decrease in the balance of this accounts receivable ledger account. Whenever Accounts Receivable is decreased, the customer account in the accounts receivable ledger is also decreased by the same amount.

The general journal entry to record this transaction is shown in Illustration 24-8.

ILLUSTRATION 24-8

General journal entry to record a note receivable for an extension of time on an account

	DATE	ACCOUNT TITLE	DOC. NO.	POST. REF.	DEBIT	CREDIT	
6	22	Notes Receivable	NR10		800 00		6
7		Accounts Receivable/Ann Nance				800 00	7
8							8
9							9
10							10
11							11

GENERAL JOURNAL — PAGE 6

FYI

For a non-interest-bearing note, the interest is paid when the note is issued; therefore, the maturity value equals the principal.

When this entry is posted, the balance of the accounts receivable account for Ms. Nance will be zero. One asset, Accounts Receivable, is replaced by another asset, Notes Receivable.

Collecting Principal and Interest on a Note Receivable at Maturity

When a note receivable reaches its maturity date, the payee of the note receives the maturity value from the maker of the note. The maturity value of a note is the principal (original amount of the note) plus the interest earned during the time of the note. The interest earned on money loaned is called **interest income.**

The interest earned on a note receivable is credited to a revenue account titled *Interest Income.* A revenue account has a normal credit balance. Therefore, the interest income account is increased by a credit and decreased by a debit, as shown in the T account.

Interest income is investment revenue rather than revenue from the business' normal operations. Therefore, Interest Income is listed in a classification titled *Other Revenue* in a chart of accounts.

Celluphone received cash from Ann Nance for the principal and interest of the note accepted from Ms. Nance on April 22.

June 22, 19--. Received cash for the maturity value of Note Receivable No. 10: principal, $800.00, plus interest, $16.00; total, $816.00. Receipt No. 497.

Interest Income	
Debit side	Credit side
	Normal balance
Decrease	Increase

TEACH

Cover student pages 652–657 "Notes Receivable." Emphasize that notes receivable are issued when a customer needs additional time to pay an account receivable. Emphasize that when a note is issued, only the original amount is recorded; the interest is not recorded at this time because it is not yet due. When a note is dishonored, the amount is removed from notes receivable and returned to accounts receivable because the amount is still owed. The customer owes principal plus interest. That total is recorded in the account receivable.

APPLY

- Draw a T account for Notes Receivable and label the normal balance side.

- Draw T accounts on the board for each transaction as it is presented in this lesson.

- Use Transparency M to journalize the receipt of a note from a customer or direct students to Illustration 24-8.

- Draw a T account for Interest Income and label the normal balance side.

- Use Transparency O to journalize collecting a note receivable or direct students to Illustration 24-9.

- Use Transparency M to record a dishonored note receivable or direct students to Illustration 24-10.

Guided Practice

Guide students through Drill 24-D5. Students should have the forms from the working papers to complete as you guide them through each transaction. All students should agree with the analysis of each transaction before proceeding to the next transaction.

Independent Practice

Assign Terms 21–23, Questions 16–19, Problem 24-3, Mastery Problem 24-M, and Study Guide 24.

Reteach

- Use Demonstration Problem 24C. This problem can be done on the overhead with the students completing the problem at their desks.

- Assign Recycling Problem 24-R.

Extend

- Assign the Application Program Disk software with Problem 24-M.

- Assign the Electronic Study Guide Chapter 24 to complete the study guide from the working papers at the computer.

- Assign the Accounting Tutorial Unit 7.

Enrich

Assign Challenge Problem 24-C. (The challenge is that students calculate the interest and journalize complex transactions.)

```
                Cash
June 22    816.00  |

            Notes Receivable
Apr. 22   800.00  |  June 22    800.00

            Interest Income
                  |  June 22     16.00
```

Cash is debited for $816.00 ($800.00 principal + $16.00 interest income) to show the increase in the balance of this asset account. Notes Receivable is credited for $800.00 to show the decrease in the balance of this asset account. Interest Income is credited for $16.00 ($800.00 × 12% × 2/12 = $16.00) to show the increase in the balance of this other revenue account.

The cash receipts journal entry to record this transaction is shown in Illustration 24-9.

After the entry is recorded, the original copy of Note Receivable No. 10 is marked *Paid* and returned to Ann Nance, the maker.

ILLUSTRATION 24-9 Cash receipts journal entry to record receipt of maturity value of a note receivable

	DATE	ACCOUNT TITLE	DOC. NO.	POST. REF.	GENERAL DEBIT	GENERAL CREDIT	ACCOUNTS RECEIVABLE CREDIT	SALES CREDIT	SALES TAX PAYABLE DEBIT	SALES TAX PAYABLE CREDIT	SALES DISCOUNT DEBIT	CASH DEBIT	
18	22	Notes Receivable	R497			800 00						816 00	18
19		Interest Income				16 00							19
20													20
21													21
22													22
23													23

CASH RECEIPTS JOURNAL — PAGE 22

Recording a Dishonored Note Receivable

A note that is not paid when due is called a **dishonored note**. The balance of the notes receivable account should show only the total amount of notes that probably will be collected. The amount of a dishonored note receivable should therefore be removed from the notes receivable account. The amount of the note plus interest income earned on the note is still owed by the customer. Therefore, the total amount owed should be debited to the accounts receivable account in the general ledger. The amount owed should also be debited to the customer account in the accounts receivable ledger. The customer account will then show the total amount owed by the customer, including the amount of the dishonored note and interest earned. This information may be important if the customer requests credit in the future or if collection is achieved later.

> **FYI**
>
> Interest income is recorded even for a dishonored note because the interest has been earned even if it will not be collected.

May 12, 19--. Keith Leising dishonored Note Receivable No. 9, a 1-month, 12% note, maturity value due today: principal, $200.00; interest, $2.00; total, $202.00. Memorandum No. 65.

Accounts Receivable is debited for $202.00 ($200.00 principal + $2.00 interest income) to show the increase in the balance of this

---

APPLIED SKILLS: LANGUAGE ARTS

Paraphrasing, writing complete sentences, and identifying active and passive verbs. For additional practice in language arts skills, direct students to answer the Accounting Terms and Questions for Individual Study at the end of the chapter. Students should write the answers in their own words and in complete sentences. To further practice language arts skills, ask students to underline all active verbs and circle all passive verbs in their answers.

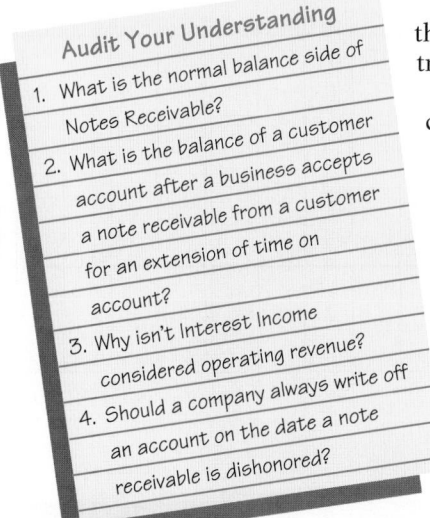

GENERAL LEDGER
Accounts Receivable

May 12	202.00	

Notes Receivable

Apr. 12	200.00	May 12	200.00

Interest Income

		May 12	2.00

ACCOUNTS RECEIVABLE LEDGER
Keith Leising

May 12	202.00	

asset account. Notes Receivable is credited for $200.00 to show the decrease in the balance of this asset account. Interest Income is credited for $2.00 ($200.00 × 12% × 1/12 = $2.00) to show the increase in the balance of this other revenue account. The customer account, Keith Leising, is also debited for $202.00 ($200.00 principal + $2.00 interest) to show the increase in the balance of this accounts receivable ledger account.

The interest income has been earned even though it has not been paid. Keith Leising owes the principal amount of the note plus the interest earned. Therefore, the total of principal plus interest ($200.00 + $2.00 = $202.00) is debited to Accounts Receivable and to the customer account.

The general journal entry to record this transaction is shown in Illustration 24-10.

CLOSURE

- Use Audit Your Understanding questions.
- Review Summary Illustration 24-11, "Summary of Accounting for Notes and Interest." Use Transparency 24-2, Chapter Summary.

ASSESS

- Administer Problem Test Chapter 24
- Administer a MicroExam for Chapter 24

ILLUSTRATION 24-10   General journal entry to record a dishonored note receivable

GENERAL JOURNAL   PAGE 8

	DATE	ACCOUNT TITLE	DOC. NO.	POST. REF.	DEBIT	CREDIT	
9	12	Accounts Receivable/Keith Leising	M65		202 00		9
10		Notes Receivable				200 00	10
11		Interest Income				2 00	11
12							12
13							13
14							14

Audit Your Understanding

1. What is the normal balance side of Notes Receivable?

2. What is the balance of a customer account after a business accepts a note receivable from a customer for an extension of time on account?

3. Why isn't Interest Income considered operating revenue?

4. Should a company always write off an account on the date a note receivable is dishonored?

Celluphone does not write off Mr. Leising's account when the note is dishonored. Instead, the company continues to try to collect the account.

Later Celluphone may decide that the account cannot be collected from Mr. Leising. At that time the balance of the account will be written off as an uncollectible account. Allowance for Uncollectible Accounts will be debited, and Accounts Receivable and Keith Leising's account will be credited.

The chart shown in Illustration 24-11 on pages 656 and 657 summarizes the journal entries for recording notes payable and notes receivable transactions and the calculations for interest and discounted notes.

AUDIT YOUR UNDERSTANDING

1. Debit.
2. Zero.
3. Because it is revenue from investment rather than normal operations.
4. Not necessarily; they may continue to try to collect the account before writing it off.

SUMMARY ILLUSTRATION 24-11

Summary of accounting for notes and interest

Transactions	Cash Dr.	Cash Cr.	Notes Rec. Dr.	Notes Rec. Cr.	Accts. Rec. Dr.	Accts. Rec. Cr.	Notes Pay. Dr.	Notes Pay. Cr.	Accts. Pay. Dr.	Accts. Pay. Cr.	Interest Income Dr.	Interest Income Cr.	Interest Expense Dr.	Interest Expense Cr.	Accts. Rec. Dr.	Accts. Rec. Cr.	Accts. Pay. Dr.	Accts. Pay. Cr.
Issuing a note payable to borrow money from a bank	X							X										
Paying principal and interest on a note payable at maturity		X					X						X					
Issuing a note payable for an extension of time							X	X										X
Paying principal and interest on a note for an extension of time		X					X						X					
Issuing a discounted note payable for cash	X							X					X					
Paying a discounted note payable		X					X											
Accepting a note receivable from a customer			X			X										X		
Collecting principal and interest on a note receivable at maturity	X			X								X						
Recording a dishonored note receivable				X	X							X			X			

The header spans: **GENERAL LEDGER** covers Cash, Notes Rec., Accts. Rec., Notes Pay., Accts. Pay., Interest Income, Interest Expense. **SUBSIDIARY LEDGERS** covers the final Accts. Rec. and Accts. Pay.

Summary of accounting for notes and interest

AMOUNTS	CALCULATIONS				
Interest for Years	Principal	× Interest Rate	× Time in Years	=	Interest for Years
Interest for Fraction of Year	Principal	× Interest Rate	× Time as Fraction of Year	=	Interest for Fraction of Year
Bank Discount	Maturity Value	× Discount Rate	× Time as Fraction of Year	=	Bank Discount
Proceeds	Maturity Value	− Bank Discount		=	Proceeds

# ACCOUNTING TERMS
EPT(a)

What is the meaning of each of the following?

1. promissory note
2. date of a note
3. time of a note
4. payee of a note
5. principal of a note
6. interest rate of a note
7. maturity date of a note
8. maker of a note

9. number of a note
10. interest
11. interest-bearing note
12. non-interest-bearing note
13. maturity value
14. creditor
15. notes payable
16. current liabilities

17. interest expense
18. bank discount
19. discounted note
20. proceeds
21. notes receivable
22. interest income
23. dishonored note

# QUESTIONS FOR INDIVIDUAL STUDY
EPT(b)

1. What conditions would cause a business to have extra cash to deposit in a bank, yet at another time of year, need to borrow extra cash from a bank?
2. Why does a business sometimes request a promissory note from a credit customer?
3. What is the advantage of a promissory note over an account receivable?
4. What is the difference between the payee and the maker of a note?
5. What does interest at 10% mean?
6. How is interest calculated for a fraction of a year?
7. Why are notes payable generally classified as current liabilities?

8. Which accounting concept is being applied when a copy of a note payable is used as the source document for recording the issuance of a note payable?
9. What accounts are affected, and how, when a business issues a note payable to borrow money from a bank?
10. When an interest-bearing note is paid, why is the credit to **Cash** greater than the debit to **Notes Payable**?
11. What accounts are affected, and how, when a business issues an interest-bearing note payable for an extension of time on its account payable?

1. **promissory note:** A written and signed promise to pay a sum of money at a specified time. (p. 643)
2. **date of a note:** The day a note is issued. (p. 644)
3. **time of a note:** The days, months, or years from the date of issue until a note is to be paid. (p. 644)
4. **payee of a note:** The person or business to whom the amount of a note is payable. (p. 644)
5. **principal of a note:** The original amount of a note. (p. 644)
6. **interest rate of a note:** The percentage of the principal that is paid for use of the money. (p. 644)
7. **maturity date of a note:** The date a note is due. (p. 644)
8. **maker of a note:** The person or business who signs a note and thus promises to make payment. (p. 644)
9. **number of a note:** The number assigned by the maker to identify a specific note. (p. 644)
10. **interest:** An amount paid for the use of money for a period of time. (p. 644)
11. **interest-bearing note:** A promissory note that requires the payment of principal plus interest when the note is due. (p. 644)
12. **non-interest-bearing note:** A promissory note that requires only the payment of the principal when the note is due. (p. 644)
13. **maturity value:** The amount that is due on the maturity date of a note. (p. 644)
14. **creditor:** A person or organization to whom a liability is owed. (p. 646)
15. **notes payable:** Promissory notes that a business issues to creditors. (p. 646)
16. **current liabilities:** Liabilities due within a short time, usually within a year. (p. 646)
17. **interest expense:** The interest accrued on money borrowed. (p. 647)
18. **bank discount:** Interest collected in advance on a note. (p. 650)
19. **discounted note:** A note on which interest is paid in advance. (p. 650)
20. **proceeds:** The amount received for a note after the bank discount has been deducted. (p. 650)
21. **notes receivable:** Promissory notes that a business accepts from customers. (p. 652)
22. **interest income:** The interest earned on money loaned. (p. 653)
23. **dishonored note:** A note that is not paid when due. (p. 654)

1. Sometimes a business receives more cash from sales than is needed to pay for purchases and expenses. When this occurs, a business may deposit the extra cash in a bank or other financial institution for a short period. At other times, the receipt of cash from sales does not occur at the same time and in sufficient amounts to pay for needed purchases and expenses. When this occurs, a business needs to borrow additional cash or make arrangements with its vendors to delay payment for a period of time. (p. 643)

2. Generally because the customer wants credit beyond the usual time given for sales on account. (p. 643)

3. A note, like a check, can be endorsed and transferred to a bank in return for cash. Notes can also be useful in a court of law as written evidence of a debt. (p. 643)

4. The payee is the person or business to whom a note is payable. The maker is the person or business who signs a note and promises to make payment. (p. 644)

5. Ten cents will be paid for the use of each dollar borrowed for a full year. (p. 644)

6. Multiply the principal times the interest rate times the time stated as a fraction of a year. (p. 645)

7. Notes payable are generally paid within one year. (p. 646)

8. Objective Evidence. (p. 647)

9. Cash is debited; Notes Payable is credited. (p. 647)

10. Cash is paid for the principal of the note plus the interest. Thus, Cash is credited for the sum of the amounts debited to Notes Payable and Interest Expense. (p. 648)

11. Accounts Payable and the vendor account in the accounts payable ledger are debited for the principal of the note payable. Notes Payable is credited for the same amount. (p. 648)

12. Notes Payable is debited for the principal of the note payable. Interest Expense is debited for the interest. Cash is credited for the principal plus interest. (p. 649)

12. What accounts are affected, and how, when a business pays an interest-bearing note payable that had been issued for an extension of time on its account payable?

13. How much will the maker receive from a one-year non-interest-bearing note with a face value of $1,000.00, discounted at 10%?

14. What accounts are affected, and how, when a non-interest-bearing note payable is discounted at a bank?

15. What accounts are affected, and how, when a discounted note payable is paid at maturity?

16. When a business accepts a note receivable from a credit customer for an extension of time on the customer's account receivable, how does the amount and form of the business asset change?

17. What accounts are affected, and how, when a business receives the principal and interest on a note receivable at maturity?

18. What accounts are affected, and how, when a customer dishonors an interest-bearing note receivable?

19. Why is interest income recorded at the time a note is dishonored even though cash has not been received?

CASES FOR CRITICAL THINKING   EPT(b,c)

CASE 1 Because of a temporary cash shortage, Jupiter Company requested an extension of time on its purchases on account. Jupiter's regular vendor, Custom Suppliers, requires that a 12% interest-bearing note be issued to them for any extension of time over one month. Jupiter usually needs 3 months from time of purchase to time of payment. Because of the extra costs for interest expense, Jupiter has been exploring other vendor options. Another vendor, Page Supplies, has been located that will sell merchandise on account with credit terms of net due in 3 months. For the same quantity and brand of merchandise, Custom Suppliers' cost is $10,000.00; for Page Supplies, $10,250.00. Since Page Supplies offers 3 months credit terms without any interest charges and the merchandise is only 2.5% higher than that from Custom Suppliers, Jupiter's purchasing manager, Robert Jimerson, has decided to buy the merchandise from Page. When asked why he is buying from the company with costs 2.5% higher, he said, "A 2.5% higher price is better than the 12% interest we would have to pay Custom Suppliers." Do you agree with Mr. Jimerson? Explain.

CASE 2 Alexandra Davis requested a $1,000.00 bank loan for one year. The loan officer agreed to the loan and offered Miss Davis her choice of a 10% interest-bearing note or a note discounted at 10%. Which choice should Miss Davis accept?

APPLIED COMMUNICATIONS

As a bookkeeper for a corporation, you have been asked to assist the president in making a presentation to the board of directors. The president wants to report the 4-year growth in sales of four major products. The following table presents product sales (in thousands of dollars) from 19X1 to 19X4.

	19X1	19X2	19X3	19X4
Stereo Receivers	$235	$312	$322	$284
Speakers	197	211	187	205
CD-Players	62	156	199	276
Telephones	155	143	135	132

INSTRUCTIONS:
Prepare a graph depicting the data presented in the table.

APPLIED SKILLS: COMMUNICATIONS

Surveys of business managers show that communication skills are one of the most desired traits in new employees. The student activity APPLIED COMMUNICATIONS provides an opportunity for students to practice their communication and language arts skills on topics that directly relate to accounting. This activity requires students to prepare a graph of accounting information. Students should be encouraged to use computer software, such as an electronic spreadsheet, to prepare the graph. Either a comparative bar or line graph is an effective graph style to illustrate product sales information.

DRILL 24-D1 Calculating interest on notes

INSTRUCTIONS:

Calculate the interest for each of the following notes.

No. of Note	Principal of Note	Interest Rate	Time of Note
1	$ 700.00	8%	1 year
2	1,200.00	12%	6 months
3	500.00	15%	30 days
4	800.00	9%	4 months
5	600.00	10%	60 days

DRILL 24-D2 Calculating maturity dates of notes

INSTRUCTIONS:

Calculate the maturity date for each of the following notes.

No. of Note	Date of Note	Time of Note
1	Jan. 11	90 days
2	Feb. 5	1 year
3	May 17	30 days
4	July 1	3 months
5	Oct. 20	6 months

DRILL 24-D3 Calculating maturity dates and interest on notes

INSTRUCTIONS:

For each of the following notes, calculate (1) the maturity date and (2) the interest.

No. of Note	Date of Note	Principal of Note	Interest Rate	Time of Note
1	Jan. 4	$ 400	9%	30 days
2	Mar. 21	800	11%	1 year
3	May 8	1,200	13%	60 days
4	July 15	1,700	12%	6 months
5	Sept. 1	2,000	10%	90 days

DRILL 24-D4 Analyzing recording notes payable transactions

INSTRUCTIONS:

A form for analyzing recording notes payable transactions is given in the working papers that accompany this text. For each transaction, write the title of the accounts affected in the Account Title column. For each account title, place a check mark in the Debit or Credit column to show whether the account is debited or credited. The abbreviation for note payable is NP. Transaction 1 is given as an example in the working papers.

1. Discounted at 14% a 60-day non-interest-bearing note. NP135.
2. Issued a 1-year, 12% note. NP136.
3. Issued a 6-month, 10% note. NP137.
4. Discounted at 11% a 90-day non-interest-bearing note. NP138.
5. Discounted at 13% a 2-month non-interest-bearing note. NP139.
6. Issued a 30-day, 15% note for an extension of time on an account payable. NP140.
7. Paid cash for the maturity value of non-interest-bearing NP135.
8. Paid cash for the maturity value of NP136.

13. $900.00. Maturity value, $1,000.00, less bank discount, $100.00, equals proceeds, $900.00. Bank discount is calculated as follows: maturity value, $1,000.00, times discount rate, 10%, times time, 1 year, equals bank discount, $100.00. (p. 650)

14. Cash is debited for the proceeds. Interest Expense is debited for the interest. Notes Payable is credited for the principal of the note payable. (p. 650)

15. Notes Payable is debited for the principal of the note. Cash is credited for the same amount. No payment of interest expense is necessary because the bank collected the interest in advance. (p. 651)

16. A note receivable does not pay the amount the customer owes. Therefore, the amount of the asset does not change at the time the note is accepted. The form of the asset does change from an account receivable to a note receivable. However, the asset will remain classified as a current asset. (p. 652)

17. Cash is debited for the principal of the note receivable and the interest. Notes Receivable is credited for the principal. Interest Income is credited for the interest. (p. 654)

18. Accounts Receivable and the customer account are each debited for the principal of the note and the interest. Notes Receivable is credited for the principal of the note. Interest Income is credited for the interest. (pp. 654–655)

19. Because the interest has been earned. (p. 655)

CASES FOR CRITICAL THINKING

Case 1 No. Mr. Jimerson's reasoning is incorrect. To make a fair comparison, the total cost of merchandise from both suppliers must be compared for the same items and same payment requirements. The cost comparisons are as follows (with payment 3 months after purchase as Jupiter requires):

1. Page Supplies, payable in 3 months with no interest	$10,250.00
2. Custom Suppliers	$10,000.00
*Interest: $10,000.00 × 12% × 2/12 =	+ 200.00
Total cost	$10,200.00

*Since Custom Suppliers provides credit terms of one month for sales on account, the note payable will be issued at the end of one month so that the time of the note needs to be for 2 months only.

The total cost to buy the merchandise from Page Supplies will be $50.00 more than from Custom Suppliers. Mr. Jimerson drew an incorrect conclusion when he compared only the two percentages—2.5% and 12%. The 2.5% higher cost is a percentage of the total merchandise cost—$10,000.00. The 12% interest is a percentage of the $10,000.00 but for only 2/12 of a year, resulting in a smaller amount.

Case 2 Accept the 10% interest-bearing note. The interest will be $100.00 for either choice. However, the interest-bearing note will provide the use of $1,000.00. The discounted note will provide the use of only $900.00 (principal, $1,000.00, less discount, $100.00, equals proceeds, $900.00). The actual interest rate paid on cash available for use is calculated as follows:

1. Interest-bearing:

Interest	−	Amount Available for Use	=	Comparable Interest Rate
$100.00	−	$1,000.00	=	.10 (10%)

2. Discounted:

$100.00	−	$ 900.00	=	.111 (11.1%)

The actual interest rate for money available for use for the discounted note is 11.1%. For the interest-bearing note the rate is 10%.

APPLIED COMMUNICATIONS

Students' solutions will vary slightly depending on the method of graph preparation. The graph should be graded on neatness and accuracy.

CHECK FIGURES *(cont'd)*

Drill 24-D5 Notes Receivable is credited in Trans. 6, 7, and 8; debited in the rest; Interest Income is credited in Trans. 6, 7, and 8.

Problem 24-1 Cash Receipts Journal totals, 11,500, 11,500. Cash Payments Journal totals, 37,803.33, 37,803.33.

Problem 24-2 Cash Receipts Journal totals, 219.17, 20,500, 20,280.83; Cash Payments Journal totals, 30,864.16, 30,864.16.

DRILL 24-D5   Analyzing recording notes receivable transactions

INSTRUCTIONS:

A form for analyzing notes receivable transactions is given in the working papers that accompany the text. For each transaction, write the title of the accounts affected in the Account Title column. For each account title, place a check mark in the Debit or Credit column to show whether the account is debited or credited. The abbreviation for note receivable is NR. Transaction 1 is given as an example.

1. Received a 60-day, 14% note for an extension of time on an account. NR26.
2. Received a 1-year, 10% note for an extension of time on an account. NR27.
3. Received a 3-month, 12% note for an extension of time on an account. NR28.
4. Received a 90-day, 11% note for an extension of time on an account. NR29.
5. Received a 6-month, 13% note for an extension of time on an account. NR30.
6. Received cash for the maturity value of NR26.
7. Received cash for the maturity value of NR27.
8. Maker dishonored NR28, a 3-month, 12% note, maturity value due today.

APPLICATION PROBLEMS   EPT(d)

PROBLEM 24-1   Journalizing notes payable transactions

The following transactions were completed by Coastal Construction during the current year.

INSTRUCTIONS:

1. Journalize the following transactions. Use page 10 of a general journal, page 20 of a cash receipts journal, and page 18 of a cash payments journal. (Usually a new journal page is started each month. However, to conserve space in the working papers, record all of the year's entries on the same page of each journal.) Source documents are abbreviated as follows: check, C; note payable, NP.

Mar.   3. Issued a 90-day, 13% note, $6,000.00. NP179.
        12. Paid cash for the maturity value of NP169: principal, $3,500.00, plus interest, $35.00; total, $3,535.00. C2117.
        31. Issued a 30-day, 12% note to Santa Fe Company for an extension of time on this account payable, $1,500.00. NP180.
Apr.   8. Paid cash for the maturity value of NP158: principal, $12,500.00, plus interest, $375.00; total, $12,875.00. C2189.
        30. Paid cash for the maturity value of NP180: principal, $1,500.00, plus interest, $15.00; total, $1,515.00. C2234.
May 13. Issued a 60-day, 12% note, $5,500.00. NP181.
June 1. Paid cash for the maturity value of NP179: principal, $6,000.00, plus interest, $195.00; total, $6,195.00. C2415.
        17. Issued a 30-day, 11% note to Universal Lumber for an extension of time on this account payable, $8,000.00. NP182.
July 12. Paid cash for the maturity value of NP181: principal, $5,500.00, plus interest, $110.00; total, $5,610.00. C2543.
        17. Paid cash for the maturity value of NP182: principal, $8,000.00, plus interest, $73.33; total, $8,073.33. C2561.

2. Prove the cash receipts and cash payments journals.

PROBLEM 24-2   Journalizing notes payable transactions

The following transactions were completed by Manhattan Concepts, Inc., during the current year.

INSTRUCTIONS:

1. Journalize the following transactions. Use page 16 of a general journal, page 23 of a cash receipts journal, and page 20 of a cash payments journal.

Jan. 17. Issued a 90-day, 12% note, $9,000.00. NP134.
    29. Paid cash for the maturity value of NP112: principal, $2,000.00, plus interest, $18.33; total, $2,018.33. C1073.
Feb. 2. Discounted at 13% a 60-day non-interest-bearing note, $7,000.00; proceeds, $6,848.33, interest, $151.67. NP135.
    9. Paid cash for the maturity value of NP120: principal, $3,000.00, plus interest, $30.00; total, $3,030.00. C1103.
    21. Issued a 30-day, 11% note to Newport Company for an extension of time on this account payable, $5,000.00. NP136.
Mar. 8. Discounted at 12% a 45-day non-interest-bearing note, $4,500.00; proceeds, $4,432.50, interest, $67.50. NP137.
    23. Paid cash for the maturity value of NP136: principal, $5,000.00, plus interest, $45.83; total, $5,045.83. C1234.
Apr. 3. Paid cash for the maturity value of non-interest-bearing NP135, $7,000.00. C1279.
    17. Paid cash for the maturity value of NP134: principal, $9,000.00, plus interest, $270.00; total, $9,270.00. C1312.
    22. Paid cash for the maturity value of non-interest-bearing NP137, $4,500.00. C1335.

2. Prove the cash receipts and cash payments journals.

PROBLEM 24-3 Journalizing notes receivable transactions

The following transactions were completed by Westport Company during the current year.

INSTRUCTIONS:

1. Journalize the following transactions. Use page 19 of a general journal and page 22 of a cash receipts journal.

Jan. 10. Received a 90-day, 11% note from Gary Shelton for an extension of time on his account, $1,500.00. NR67.
    18. Received cash for the maturity value of NR49: principal, $500.00, plus interest, $25.00; total, $525.00. R37.
Feb. 3. Received a 30-day, 10% note from Joanne Davis for an extension of time on her account, $800.00. NR68.
    12. Received cash for the maturity value of NR53: principal, $4,000.00, plus interest, $80.00; total, $4,080.00. R83.
    27. Received a 60-day, 12% note from Andrew McCormick for an extension of time on his account, $2,400.00. NR69.
Mar. 5. Received cash for the maturity value of NR68: principal, $800.00, plus interest, $6.67; total, $806.67. R99.
Apr. 10. Gary Shelton dishonored NR67, a 90-day, 11% note, maturity value due today: principal, $1,500.00; interest, $41.25; total, $1,541.25. M251.
    28. Received cash for the maturity value of NR69: principal, $2,400.00, plus interest, $48.00; total, $2,448.00. R154.

2. Prove the cash receipts journal.

CHECK FIGURES (cont'd)

Problem 24-3   Cash Receipts Journal totals, 7,859.67, 7,859.67.

Mastery Problem 24-M   Cash Receipts Journal totals, 330, 20,887.79, 20,557.79; Cash Payments Journal totals, 32,250, 32,250.

ENRICHMENT PROBLEMS   EPT(c,d)

MASTERY PROBLEM 24-M   Journalizing notes payable and notes receivable transactions

APPLICATION

The following transactions were completed by Peterson Sporting Goods during the current year.

INSTRUCTIONS:

1. Journalize the following transactions. Use page 14 of a general journal, page 20 of a cash receipts journal, and page 16 of a cash payments journal.

Apr. 2. Issued a 30-day, 12% note to Devco Supply Company for an extension of time on this account payable, $6,500.00. NP120.

7. Received a 90-day, 13% note from Jill Bankston for an extension of time on her account, $700.00. NR154.

14. Discounted at 11% a 90-day non-interest-bearing note, $12,000.00; proceeds, $11,670.00, interest, $330.00. NP121.

26. Issued a 30-day, 13% note to Dayton Corporation for an extension of time on this account payable, $4,000.00. NP122.

30. Received a 60-day, 12% note from Jeremy Hicks for an extension of time on his account, $300.00. NR155.

May 2. Paid cash for the maturity value of NP120: principal, $6,500.00, plus interest, $65.00; total, $6,565.00. C175.

5. Received a 30-day, 11% note from Suzanne Johnson for an extension of time on her account, $550.00. NR156.

11. Issued a 60-day, 10% note, $7,000.00. NP123.

26. Paid cash for the maturity value of NP122: principal, $4,000.00, plus interest, $43.33; total, $4,043.33. C189.

June 4. Received cash for the maturity value of NR156: principal, $550.00, plus interest, $5.04; total, $555.04. R225.

8. Issued a 30-day, 12% note to Winston Company for an extension of time on this account payable, $2,500.00. NP124.

17. Received a 60-day, 10% note from Melissa Albertson for an extension of time on her account, $600.00. NR157.

29. Jeremy Hicks dishonored NR155, a 60-day, 12% note, maturity value due today: principal, $300.00; interest, $6.00; total $306.00. M310.

July 6. Received cash for the maturity value of NR154: principal, $700.00, plus interest, $22.75; total, $722.75. R253.

8. Paid cash for the maturity value of NP124: principal, $2,500.00, plus interest, $25.00; total, $2,525.00. C251.

10. Paid cash for the maturity value of NP123: principal, $7,000.00, plus interest, $116.67; total, $7,116.67. C262.

13. Paid cash for the maturity value of non-interest-bearing NP121, $12,000.00. C274.

Aug. 16. Received cash for the maturity value of NR157: principal, $600.00, plus interest, $10.00; total, $610.00. R278.

2. Prove the cash receipts and cash payments journals.

CHALLENGE PROBLEM 24-C   Journalizing notes payable and notes receivable transactions

The following transactions were completed by Briarcraft Apparel Company during the current year.

INSTRUCTIONS:

1. Journalize the following transactions. Use page 20 of a general journal, page 27 of a cash receipts journal, and page 31 of a cash payments journal.

Feb. 3. A 90-day, 13% note was issued to Rainbow Manufacturing. This is for an extension of time on this account payable, $7,550.00. NP158.

7. We discounted a 10%, 6-month non-interest-bearing note, $15,000.00. NP159.

9. We received a note dated February 6 from William Andrews. This note is a 30-day, 12% note for an extension of time on his account, $985.00. NR84.

24. A note dated February 23 was received from Elizabeth Townsend. This is a 2-month, 13% note for an extension of time on her account, $1,275.00. NR85.

Mar. 1. A 3-month, 12% note was issued to Livingston Company for an extension of time on this account payable, $6,995.00. NP160.

Mar. 8. A check was received for the maturity value of NR84. R273.

15. Store equipment was bought from Warner Company, $2,875.00. Paid cash, $1,200.00, and issued a 4-month, 11% note for the balance, $1,675.00. C124 and NP161. Journalize the transaction in the cash payments journal in one combined entry. Record the check number in the Ck. No. column. Write *NP161* in parentheses after the account title for notes payable to complete the audit trail.

Apr. 24. Elizabeth Townsend dishonored NR85, maturity value due today. M64.

May 4. Issued a check for the maturity value of NP158. C172.

June 1. Paid cash for the maturity value of NP160. C183.

July 15. The maturity value of NP161 is due today. Issued a check. C197.

21. Elizabeth Townsend sent a check for $600.00 for part of the balance charged to her account on April 24. R325. Wrote off the remainder of this account receivable as uncollectible. M99. Journalize the check in the cash receipts journal. Journalize the write-off of the customer account in the general journal.

Aug. 7. Wrote a check for the maturity value of non-interest-bearing NP159. C215.

2. Prove the cash receipts and cash payments journals.

Chapter 25 illustrates the procedures for adjusting, closing, and reversing entries for accrued revenues and expenses related to notes payable and notes receivable. Reversing entries have the following benefits: (a) improved efficiency because reversing entries are prepared as a part of end-of-period activities and (b) improved accuracy because entries for notes receivable and notes payable are recorded the same way regardless of whether or not part of the interest was recorded at the end of the previous year.

GUIDE TO ACHIEVING LEARNING OBJECTIVES

	TEACH	APPLY		EXTEND/ENRICH					
Enabling Performance Tasks	Lesson Plans	Drills for Understanding	Application Problems	Mastery Problems	Challenge Problems	Cases for Critical Thinking	Recycling Problems	Reinforcement Activity	
a. Define accounting terms related to accrued revenue and accrued expenses.	25-1, 25-2								
b. Identify accounting concepts and practices related to accrued revenue and accrued expenses.	25-1, 25-2					Cases 1, 2			
c. Record adjusting, closing, and reversing entries for accrued revenue.	25-1	25-D1	25-1	25-M	25-C		25-R	3B	
d. Record adjusting, closing, and reversing entries for accrued expenses.	25-2	25-D2	25-2	25-M	25-C		25-R	3B	

ENRICHMENT

SPECIAL FEATURES

Multicultural Awareness, page 665

Personal Visions in Business, page 670

TECHNOLOGY CONNECTION

Accounting Tutorial Units 8, 9, 10

Electronic Study Guide

NEW, REVIEW, AND EXTENSION

ACTIVITIES/CONCEPTS/TRANSACTIONS	NEW	REVIEW/ EXTENSION
Adjustment for accrued interest income	✓	
Closing entry for interest income	✓	
Reversing entry for accrued interest income	✓	
Recording collection of a note receivable issued in a previous fiscal period	✓	
Adjustment for accrued interest expense	✓	
Closing entry for interest expense	✓	
Reversing entry for accrued interest expense	✓	
Recording payment of a note payable issued in a previous fiscal period	✓	

INFORMAL ASSESSMENT		FORMAL ASSESSMENT				
Study Guide	Audit Your Understanding	Chapter MicroExam	Chapter Problem Test	Unit Problem Test	Unit Objective Test	Portfolio
Unit A	✓	✓			✓	
Units B, D	✓	✓			✓	
Unit C			✓	✓		✓
Unit C			✓	✓		✓

TEACHING MATERIALS

Teacher's Wraparound Edition of the Text

Teacher's Resource Guide

Teacher's Edition of Working Papers

Teacher's Edition of Demonstration/Recycling Problems

Teaching Transparencies

Accounting Tutorial Manual

MicroExam

Applied Math Work Sheet

APPLIED MATHEMATICS

APPLIED MATH/ACCOUNTING SKILL	APPLICATION
Calculating Accrued Interest Income	Prob. 25-1
Calculating Maturity Value of a Note	Prob. 25-C
Calculating Accrued Interest Expense	Prob. 25-2

Accounting for Accrued Revenue and Expenses

ENABLING PERFORMANCE TASKS

After studying Chapter 25, you will be able to:

a Define accounting terms related to accrued revenue and accrued expenses.

b Identify accounting concepts and practices related to accrued revenue and accrued expenses.

c Record adjusting, closing, and reversing entries for accrued revenue.

d Record adjusting, closing, and reversing entries for accrued expenses.

TERMS PREVIEW

accrued revenue • accrued interest income • reversing entry • accrued expenses • accrued interest expense

Generally accepted accounting procedures require that revenue and expenses be recorded in the accounting period in which revenue is earned and expenses are incurred. *(CONCEPT: Matching Expenses with Revenue)* Some revenues, however, are earned each day but are usually recorded only when cash is actually received. For example, interest is earned for each day an interest-bearing note receivable is held. However, the interest may not be received until the maturity date of the note. Likewise, some expenses may be incurred before they are actually paid. An interest-bearing note payable incurs interest expense each day the note is outstanding. Yet, the interest generally is not paid until the note's maturity date. At the end of the fiscal period, adjusting entries are recorded for these revenues and expenses.

ACCRUED REVENUE

Revenue earned in one fiscal period but not received until a later fiscal period is called **accrued revenue.** At the end of a fiscal period, accrued revenue is recorded by an adjusting entry. *(CONCEPT: Realization of Revenue)* The adjusting entry for accrued revenue increases the accrued revenue account, an other revenue account. The adjusting entry also increases the accrued revenue receivable account, an asset account. The income statement will then report all revenue earned for the period even though some of the revenue has not yet been received. The balance sheet will report all the assets, including the accrued revenue receivable. *(CONCEPT: Adequate Disclosure)*

Adjusting Entry for Accrued Interest Income

At the end of each fiscal period, Celluphone examines the notes receivable on hand. The amount of interest income earned but not yet collected is calculated. Interest earned but not yet received is called **accrued interest income.** On December 31 Celluphone has one note receivable on hand, Note Receivable No. 15. Note Receivable No. 15 is a 3-month, $550.00, 12% note from J. T. Monroe, dated October 31. The accounting records should show all the interest income for the fiscal period. *(CONCEPT: Adequate Disclosure)* Therefore, an adjusting entry must be made to record the amount of interest earned to date on this note.

The time period from October 31 to December 31 is two months. Therefore, the time stated as a fraction of a year is $^2/_{12}$. Accrued interest on this note to the end of the fiscal year is calculated as shown below.

	Principal	×	Interest Rate	×	Time as Fraction of Year	=	Accrued Interest Income
	$550.00	×	12%	×	$\frac{2}{12}$	=	$11.00

CHAPTER 25   Accounting for Accrued Revenue and Expenses   **665**

Objectives (Enabling Performance Tasks)

a. Define accounting terms related to accrued revenue and accrued expenses.

b. Identify accounting concepts and practices related to accrued revenue and accrued expenses.

c. Record adjusting, closing, and reversing entries for accrued revenue.

FOCUS

- In Chapter 24, accounting for notes and interest was presented. Interest is earned for each day an interest-bearing note receivable is held. However, the interest may not be received until the maturity date of the note. Accepted accounting procedures require that revenue and expenses be recorded in the accounting period in which revenue is earned and expenses are incurred. In this lesson, we will look at the entries made to record revenue that has been earned but not yet received.

- Introduce new vocabulary: accrued revenue, accrued interest income, reversing entry.

Interest Receivable	
Dec. 31 Adj. 11.00	

Interest Income	
	Dec. 31 Bal. 203.00
	Dec. 31 Adj. 11.00
	(New Bal. 214.00)

Interest Receivable is debited for $11.00 to show the increase in the balance of this asset account. The interest receivable account balance is the amount of interest income that has accrued at the end of the fiscal period. However, this revenue will not be collected until the next fiscal period.

Interest Income is credited for $11.00 to show the increase in the balance of this other revenue account. The new interest income account balance, $214.00, is the total amount of interest income earned during the fiscal period.

The adjustment for accrued interest income is planned on a work sheet. Celluphone's accrued interest income adjustment for the year ended December 31 is shown in Illustration 25-1.

ILLUSTRATION 25-1   Accrued interest income adjustment on a work sheet

Celluphone, Inc.
Work Sheet
For Year Ended December 31, --

		1	2	3	4	5	6	7	8	
	ACCOUNT TITLE	TRIAL BALANCE		ADJUSTMENTS		INCOME STATEMENT		BALANCE SHEET		
		DEBIT	CREDIT	DEBIT	CREDIT	DEBIT	CREDIT	DEBIT	CREDIT	
4	*Interest Receivable*			(a) 11 00				11 00		4
48	*Interest Income*		203 00		(a) 11 00		214 00			48

FYI

The interest receivable balance will appear on the balance sheet as an asset.

On line 4 of the work sheet, Interest Receivable is debited for $11.00 in the Adjustments Debit column. This amount, $11.00, is extended to the Balance Sheet Debit column. On line 48 Interest Income is credited for $11.00 in the Adjustments Credit column. The interest income adjustment, $11.00, is added to the previous balance in the Trial Balance Credit column, $203.00. The new balance, $214.00 ($11.00 + $203.00), is extended to the Income Statement Credit column.

Information used to journalize an adjustment for accrued interest income is obtained from the Adjustments columns of a work sheet. The adjusting entry is shown in Illustration 25-2.

After the adjusting entry is posted, the interest receivable and interest income accounts appear as shown in Illustration 25-3.

The interest receivable account has a debit balance of $11.00 and will appear on the balance sheet as a current asset. This debit balance is the accrued interest income earned but not yet collected at the end of the year. The interest income account has a credit balance of $214.00 and will appear on the income statement as other revenue. This amount is the total interest income for the year.

FYI

The interest income balance will appear on the income statement as other revenue.

APPLIED SKILLS: BUILDING STUDY SKILLS

Two new accounts, Interest Receivable and Interest Payable, are introduced in this chapter. Direct students to create a Quick Reference Guide (QRG) on a small card or sheet of paper to use as an aid in analyzing transactions. T accounts should be used to show normal balance sides.

ILLUSTRATION 25-2

Adjusting entry for accrued interest income

Cover student pages 665–671 "Accrued Revenue." Explain that the adjusting entry for accrued interest income is debit Interest Receivable, credit Interest Income. Reinforce that the adjustment is planned on the work sheet in the usual manner. Review closing entries for accounts with credit balances; information for closing entries is always taken from the work sheet. Explain that Interest Income is closed to Income Summary (debit Interest Income, credit Income Summary). Reversing entries are a new concept in this chapter. Explain that reversing entries are only needed if an adjusting entry creates a balance in an asset or liability account. Then the reversing entry is the opposite of the adjusting entry that created the balance.

		GENERAL JOURNAL				PAGE 15
DATE		ACCOUNT TITLE	DOC. NO.	POST. REF.	DEBIT	CREDIT
1		*Adjusting Entries*					1
2	*Dec.* ¹⁹⁻ 31	*Interest Receivable*			1 1 00		2
3		*Interest Income*				1 1 00	3
4							4
5							5

Interest Income

Dec. 31 Closing	214.00	Dec. 31 Bal.	203.00
		Dec. 31 Adj.	11.00
		(New Bal. zero)	

Income Summary

	Dec. 31 Closing	214.00

Closing Entry for Interest Income

Information needed to record closing entries is obtained from the Income Statement columns of a work sheet. Interest Income is closed to the income summary account.

Interest Income is closed as part of the regular closing entry for income statement accounts with credit balances. Interest Income is debited for $214.00 to reduce the account balance to zero. The $214.00 is also credited to Income Summary as part of the entry to close all income statement accounts with credit balances. After the closing entry is posted, the interest income account is closed. Closing entries for all revenue and expense accounts are described in Chapter 27.

ILLUSTRATION 25-3

General ledger accounts after adjusting entry for accrued interest income is posted

CHAPTER 25   Accounting for Accrued Revenue and Expenses   **667**

- Write the formula on the board for calculating accrued interest income.

- Draw a T account on the board for the new account, Interest Receivable. Label the normal balance side.

- Draw T accounts on the board for each transaction as it is presented in this lesson.

- Use Transparency C to record the adjustment on the work sheet or direct students to Illustration 25-1.

- Use Tranasparency M to journalize the adjusting entry or direct students to Illustration 25-2.

- Use Transparency M to journalize the reversing entry for accrued interest income or direct students to Illustration 25-4.

- Write the formula on the board for calculating maturity value.

- Use Transparency O to journalize the receipt of cash for a note receivable when reversing entries are used or direct students to Illustration 25-5.

Guided Practice

Guide students through Drill 25-D1. Students should have the forms from the working papers to complete as you guide them through each entry. All students should agree with the analysis of each entry before proceeding to the next entry.

Independent Practice

Assign Terms 1–3, Questions 1–9, and Problem 25-1.

Reversing Entry for Accrued Interest Income

Adjusting entries for accrued revenues have an effect on transactions to be recorded in the following fiscal period. For example, on the maturity date of Note Receivable No. 15, January 31, Celluphone will receive cash for the note's principal and interest. Total interest earned for the 3-month note is $16.50, calculated as shown below.

	Principal	×	Interest Rate	×	Time as Fraction of Year	=	Interest
	$550.00	×	12%	×	$\frac{3}{12}$	=	$16.50

However, an adjusting entry was made to record the amount of interest earned last year, $11.00, by debiting Interest Receivable and crediting Interest Income. Thus, $11.00 of the $16.50 total interest income has already been recorded as revenue. The remaining $5.50 of the $16.50 total interest was earned during the current year. Determining how much of the cash received is for interest income earned and accrued during the previous year and how much is earned during the current year is inconvenient. To avoid this inconvenience, a reversing entry is made at the beginning of the new fiscal period. An entry made at the beginning of one fiscal period to reverse an adjusting entry made in the previous fiscal period is called a **reversing entry**.

The reversing entry results in a debit balance of $11.00 in Interest Income. A debit balance is the opposite of the normal balance of the interest income account. When the full amount of interest is received, $16.50, this amount will be credited to Interest Income. The account will then have a credit balance of $5.50 ($16.50 credit − $11.00 debit), the amount earned in the new year.

The reversing entry to Interest Receivable reduces that account to a zero balance. Thus, when the interest is received, no credit entry will be required to recognize collection of the balance of Interest Receivable. The total amount of interest received will be credited to Interest Income. Celluphone's reversing entry for accrued interest income is shown in Illustration 25-4.

The reversing entry is the opposite of the adjusting entry shown in Illustration 25-2.

Celluphone uses the following rule of thumb to determine whether or not reversing entries are made. If an adjusting entry creates a balance in an asset or liability account that initially had a zero balance, the adjusting entry is reversed. The adjusting entry for accrued interest income creates a balance in the asset account, Interest Receivable. Therefore, Celluphone uses reversing entries for all accrued interest income adjusting entries.

FYI

A reversing entry is the opposite of an adjusting entry.

Interest Income

Dec. 31 Closing	214.00	Dec. 31 Bal.	203.00
Jan. 1. Rev.	11.00	Dec. 31 Adj.	11.00
(New Bal.	*11.00)*	*(New Bal. zero)*	

Interest Receivable

Dec. 31 Adj.	11.00	Jan. 1 Rev.	11.00
(New Bal. zero)			

FYI

A reversing entry is made if an adjusting entry creates a balance in an asset or liability account.

TEACHING STRATEGIES: TEACHING TIP

Reversing entries do not need to be difficult. Teach students two rules for reversing entries: (1) Reversing entries are recorded when an adjusting entry creates a balance in an asset or liability account. (2) The reversing entry is exactly the opposite of the adjusting entry it reverses.

A balance is "created" in an account when the account balance is changed from a zero balance to an amount.

ILLUSTRATION 25-4   Reversing entry for accrued interest income

	DATE		ACCOUNT TITLE	DOC. NO.	POST. REF.	DEBIT	CREDIT	
1			Reversing Entries					1
2	Jan. 19--	1	Interest Income			11 00		2
3			Interest Receivable				11 00	3
4								4

GENERAL JOURNAL   PAGE 17

Collecting a Note Receivable Issued in a Previous Fiscal Period

On January 31 Celluphone received the maturity value (principal plus interest) of the only note receivable on hand December 31, the end of the previous fiscal year. The maturity value for Note Receivable No. 15 is calculated as shown below.

Principal	×	Interest Rate	×	Time as Fraction of Year	=	Interest
$550.00	×	12%	×	$\frac{3}{12}$	=	$16.50

Principal	+	Interest	=	Maturity Value
$550.00	+	$16.50	=	$566.50

January 31, 19--. Received cash for the maturity value of Note Receivable No. 15: principal, $550.00, plus interest, $16.50; total, $566.50. Receipt No. 38.

Cash			
Jan. 31 Rec'd	566.50		

Notes Receivable			
Oct. 31 NR15	550.00	Jan. 3 Rec'd	550.00

Interest Income			
Dec. 31 Closing	214.00	Dec. 31 Bal.	203.00
Jan. 1 Rev.	11.00	Dec. 31 Adj.	11.00
		(New Bal. zero)	
		Jan. 31 Rec'd	16.50
		(New Bal.	5.50)

The total interest, $16.50, was earned during two fiscal periods, $11.00 during the previous fiscal period and $5.50 during the current fiscal period. Since Celluphone uses reversing entries, the entry to record the collection of this note receivable and interest is the same as the entry to record a note accepted and collected in a single fiscal year.

When Note Receivable No. 15 is collected on January 31, Cash is debited for the total amount received, $566.50, to record the increase in this asset account. Notes Receivable is credited for the principal of the note, $550.00, to record the decrease in the balance of this asset account. Interest Income is credited

CHAPTER 25 Accounting for Accrued Revenue and Expenses   **669**

CLOSURE

- Use Audit Your Understanding questions.
- Review the adjusting, closing, and reversing entries for accrued interest income.

FYI

Many CPA firms end their fiscal years on August 31 because most of the year's tax and fiscal year work for clients has been completed.

for the total amount of interest, $16.50, to record the increase in this other revenue account. The interest income account now has a credit balance of $5.50 ($16.50 credit − $11.00 debit), the amount of interest earned during the current fiscal period.

The cash receipts journal entry to record this receipt of cash for a note receivable when reversing entries are used is shown in Illustration 25-5.

ILLUSTRATION 25-5 Cash receipts journal entry to record note receivable accepted in previous fiscal period when reversing entries are used

	DATE	ACCOUNT TITLE	DOC. NO.	POST. REF.	GENERAL		ACCOUNTS RECEIVABLE CREDIT	SALES CREDIT	SALES TAX PAYABLE		SALES DISCOUNT DEBIT	CASH DEBIT	
					DEBIT	CREDIT			DEBIT	CREDIT			
12	31	Notes Receivable	R38			5 5 0 00						5 6 6 50	12
13		Interest Income				1 6 50							13
14													14

CASH RECEIPTS JOURNAL — PAGE 53

■ Jean Myong VanHorn ■
AMKOR CLEANERS

Jean Myong VanHorn was a sales representative for the import/export business in Korea. She also has a degree in animal husbandry from a university in Korea and worked in that area for a while. When she came to America she worked many jobs and saved her money in order to start her own business.

VanHorn started a business called AMKOR Cleaners. In addition to providing laundry and drycleaning services, AMKOR also specializes in customer alterations. VanHorn's business also has a contract with a large local department store to furnish their custom alterations. VanHorn continues to work hard. She says she still works for other companies in addition to running her own business. "It is as if I have two full-time careers," VanHorn says.

VanHorn got some understanding of American business procedures from an accounting course she took at the University of Cincinnati. However, other factors helped contribute to her success. In addition to her hard work, VanHorn says of her experiences: "I was surprised at how American people, especially my competitors, helped me. I spoke very little English and so many people came to my aid to help me learn the language. Everyone wanted me to succeed. I was also surprised at how my competitors were willing to trade their expertise for my expertise. It was as if we all wanted to see one another succeed."

VanHorn advises students, "Be logical; choose a career because it interests you, not just because it pays well. Personal satisfaction and knowing that you are in a career that you enjoy will bring you greater rewards than money can bring." She also strongly emphasizes the value of an education.

Personal Visions in Business

Personal Visions in Business

This special student feature introduces students to successful entrepreneurs or business professionals. Each profile gives a flavor of what the actual business world is like and some of the opportunities available to students who study accounting. These features can be used to motivate students to pursue professional business careers in a wide variety of fields. The subjects of these profiles have been carefully chosen to represent the full spectrum of diverse ethnic and racial backgrounds of professional business people. As an optional activity, students can be encouraged to seek out and interview successful business people in their own communities.

After the cash receipts journal entry is posted, the notes receivable, interest receivable, and interest income accounts appear as shown in Illustration 25-6.

Notes Receivable has a zero balance. This account will be used again when additional notes receivable are accepted. After the reversing entry is recorded, Interest Receivable has a zero balance. Interest Receivable will not be used again until it is needed for an adjusting entry at the end of the current fiscal year. Interest Income has a credit balance of $5.50, the amount of interest earned on Note Receivable No. 15 in the current year.

ACCRUED EXPENSES

Expenses incurred in one fiscal period but not paid until a later fiscal period are called **accrued expenses.** At the end of a fiscal period, accrued expense is recorded by an adjusting entry. *(CONCEPT: Matching Expenses with*

ILLUSTRATION 25-6 General ledger accounts after posting cash receipt for note receivable accepted in previous fiscal period when reversing entries are used

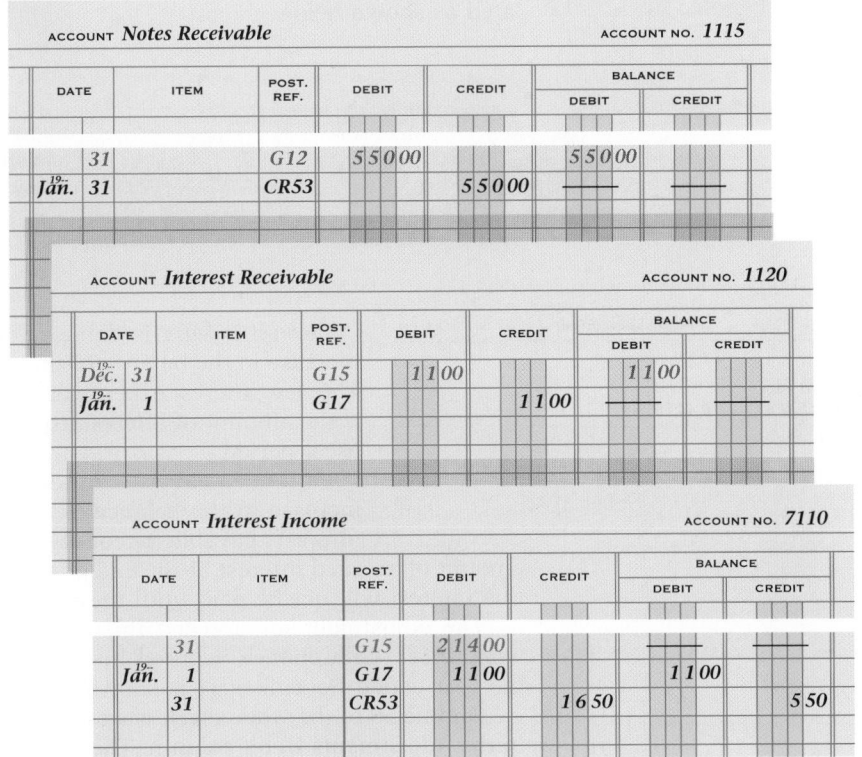

- An interest-bearing note payable incurs interest expense each day the note is outstanding. However, the interest generally is not paid until the maturity date of the note. Accepted accounting procedures require that revenue and expenses be recorded in the accounting period in which revenue is earned and expenses are incurred. In this lesson, we will look at the entries made to record expenses that have been incurred but not yet paid.

- Introduce new vocabulary: accrued expenses, accrued interest expense.

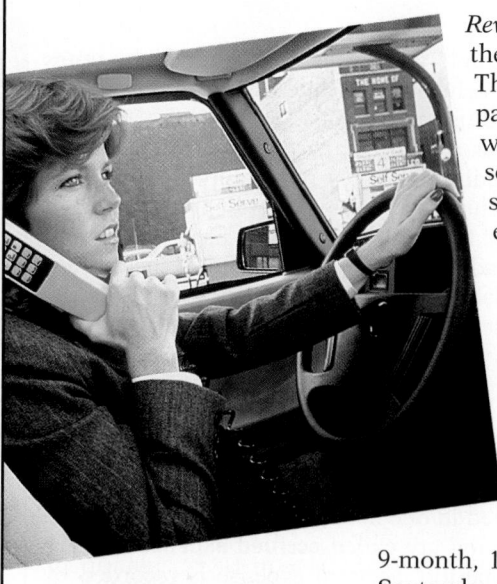

FYI

Many colleges end their fiscal years on June 30 because the school year is over for most students.

Revenue) The adjusting entry for accrued expense increases the accrued expense account, an other expense account. The adjusting entry also increases the accrued expense payable account, a liability account. The income statement will then report all expenses for the period even though some of the expenses have not yet been paid. The balance sheet will report all liabilities, including the accrued expenses payable. *(CONCEPT: Adequate Disclosure)*

Adjusting Entry for Accrued Interest Expense

Interest incurred but not yet paid is called **accrued interest expense.** At the end of each fiscal period, Celluphone examines the notes payable outstanding and calculates the accrued interest expense. On December 31, Celluphone has one note payable outstanding, Note Payable No. 10. Note Payable No. 10 is a 9-month, 10% note for $2,800.00 issued to First National Bank on September 30. The accounting records should show all the interest expense for the fiscal period. *(CONCEPT: Adequate Disclosure)* Therefore, an adjusting entry is made to record the amount of accrued interest expense to date on this note.

The time period from September 30 to December 31 is three months. Therefore, the time stated as a fraction of a year is $3/12$. Accrued interest on this note at the end of the fiscal year is calculated as shown below.

Principal	×	Interest Rate	×	Time as Fraction of Year	=	Accrued Interest Expense
$2,800.00	×	10%	×	$\frac{3}{12}$	=	$70.00

Interest Expense

Dec. 31 Bal.	1,375.00	
Dec. 31 Adj.	70.00	
(New Bal.	*1,445.00)*	

Interest Payable

| | | Dec. 31 Adj. | 70.00 |

Interest Expense is debited for $70.00 to show the increase in the balance of this other expense account. The new interest expense account balance, $1,445.00, is the amount of interest expense incurred during the fiscal period.

Interest Payable is credited for $70.00 to show the increase in the balance of this liability account. The interest payable account balance, $70.00, is the amount of accrued interest at the end of the fiscal period. However, this interest will not be paid until the next fiscal period.

The adjustment for accrued interest expense is planned on a work sheet. Celluphone's accrued interest expense adjustment for the year ended December 31 is shown in Illustration 25-7.

On line 50 of the work sheet, Interest Expense is debited for $70.00 in the Adjustments Debit column. The interest expense adjustment,

ILLUSTRATION 25-7 Accrued interest expense adjustment on a work sheet

Celluphone, Inc.
Work Sheet
For Year Ended December 31, 19--

	ACCOUNT TITLE	TRIAL BALANCE		ADJUSTMENTS		INCOME STATEMENT		BALANCE SHEET		
		DEBIT	CREDIT	DEBIT	CREDIT	DEBIT	CREDIT	DEBIT	CREDIT	
15	Interest Payable				(h) 70 00				70 00	15
50	Interest Expense	1 3 7 5 00		(h) 70 00		1 4 4 5 00				50

TEACH

Cover student pages 671–678 "Accrued Expenses." The adjusting entry for accrued interest expense is debit Interest Expense, credit Interest Payable. The adjustment for accrued interest expense is planned on the work sheet in the usual manner. Review closing entries for accounts with debit balances; information for closing entries is always taken from the work sheet. Explain that Interest Expense is closed to Income Summary (debit Income Summary, credit Interest Expense). Reversing entries are the opposite of adjusting entries and are needed whenever an adjusting entry creates a balance in an asset or liability account.

$70.00, is added to the previous balance in the Trial Balance Debit column, $1,375.00. The new balance, $1,445.00 ($70.00 + $1,375.00), is extended to the Income Statement Debit column. On line 15 Interest Payable is credited for $70.00 in the Adjustments Credit column. This amount, $70.00, is extended to the Balance Sheet Credit column.

Information used to journalize an adjustment for accrued interest expense is obtained from the Adjustments columns of a work sheet. The adjusting entry is shown in Illustration 25-8.

ILLUSTRATION 25-8 Adjusting entry for accrued interest expense

GENERAL JOURNAL   PAGE 15

	DATE	ACCOUNT TITLE	DOC. NO.	POST. REF.	DEBIT	CREDIT	
1		*Adjusting Entries*					1
16	31	Interest Expense			70 00		16
17		Interest Payable				70 00	17
18							18
19							19
20							20

After the adjusting entry is posted, the interest payable and interest expense accounts appear as shown in Illustration 25-9.

The interest payable account has a credit balance of $70.00 and will appear on the December 31 balance sheet as a current liability. This credit balance is the accrued interest expense incurred but not yet paid at the end of the year. The interest expense account has a debit balance of $1,445.00 and will appear on the income statement for the year ended December 31 as an other expense. This amount is the total interest expense for the year.

FYI

The interest payable balance will appear on the balance sheet as a liability.

- Write the formula on the board for calculating accrued interest expense.

- Draw a T account on the board for the new account, Interest Payable. Label the normal balance side.

- Draw T accounts on the board for each transaction as it is presented in this lesson.

- Use Transparency C to record the adjustment on the work sheet or direct students to Illustration 25-7.

- Use Transparency M to journalize the adjusting entry or direct students to Illustration 25-8.

- Write the formula on the board for calculating interest.

- Use Transparency M to journalize the reversing entry for accrued interest expense or direct students to Illustration 25-10.

- Write the formula on the board for calculating maturity value.

- Use Transparency L to journalize the cash payment of a note payable when reversing entries are used or direct students to Illustration 25-11.

Guided Practice

Guide students through Drill 25-D2. Students should have the forms from the working papers to complete as you guide them through each entry. All students should agree with the analysis of each entry before proceeding to the next entry.

Independent Practice

Assign Terms 4–5, Questions 10–13, Problem 25-2, Mastery Problem 25-M, and Study Guide 25.

| **ILLUSTRATION 25-9** | General ledger accounts after adjusting entry for accrued interest expense is posted |

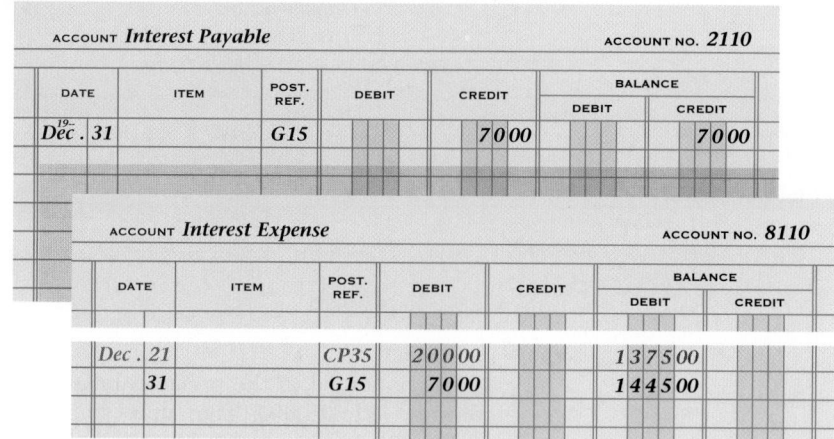

Closing Entry for Interest Expense

Income Summary	
Dec. 31 Closing 1,445.00	

Interest Expense	
Dec. 31 Bal. 1,375.00	Dec. 31 Closing 1,445.00
Dec. 31 Adj. 70.00	
(New Bal. zero)	

FYI

The interest expense account will appear on the income statement as an other expense.

Information needed to record closing entries is obtained from the Income Statement columns of a work sheet. Interest Expense is closed to the income summary account.

Interest Expense is closed as part of the regular closing entries. The $1,445.00 will also be a part of the debit entry to Income Summary to close all income statement accounts with debit balances. Interest Expense is credited for $1,445.00 to reduce the account balance to zero. After the closing entry is posted, the interest expense account is closed.

Reversing Entry for Accrued Interest Expense

On the maturity date of Note Payable No. 10, June 30, Celluphone will pay the note's maturity value (principal and interest). Total interest incurred for the 9-month note is $210.00, calculated as shown below.

Principal	×	Interest Rate	×	Time as Fraction of Year	=	Interest
$2,800.00	×	10%	×	$\frac{9}{12}$	=	$210.00

However, an adjusting entry was made to record the amount of accrued interest expense last year, $70.00, by debiting Interest Expense and crediting Interest Payable. Thus, $70.00 of the $210.00 total inter-

TEACHING STRATEGIES: TEACHING TIP

Reversing entries are recorded to facilitate recording subsequent entries. Students may not realize from the text examples that include only a few accrued revenue or expense items how useful a reversing entry can be. Emphasize that a large company may have hundreds or more notes payable and receivable maturing every day after the accrued revenue and expenses have been recorded.

est expense was incurred and recorded in the previous year. The remaining $140.00 of the $210.00 total interest expense was incurred during the current year. Determining how much of the cash paid is for accrued interest expense and how much applies to the current year is an inconvenience. To avoid this inconvenience, a reversing entry is made at the beginning of the new fiscal period.

The adjusting entry for accrued interest expense creates a balance in the liability account Interest Payable. Therefore, Celluphone uses reversing entries for all accrued interest expense adjusting entries.

The reversing entry results in a credit balance of $70.00 in Interest Expense. A credit balance is the opposite of the normal balance of the interest expense account. When the full amount of interest is paid, $210.00, this amount will be debited to Interest Expense. The account will then have a debit balance of $140.00 ($210.00 debit − $70.00 credit), the amount of interest expense incurred in the new year.

The reversing entry to Interest Payable reduces that account to a zero balance. Thus, when the interest is received, no debit entry will be required to recognize payment of the balance of Interest Payable. The total amount of interest paid will be debited to Interest Expense. Celluphone's reversing entry for accrued interest expense is shown in Illustration 25-10.

The reversing entry is the opposite of the adjusting entry shown in Illustration 25-8.

Interest Payable

Jan. 1 Rev.	70.00	Dec. 31 Adj.	70.00
		(New Bal. zero)	

Interest Expense

Dec. 31 Bal.	1,375.00	Dec. 31 Closing	1,445.00
Dec. 31 Adj.	70.00	Jan. 1 Rev.	70.00
(New Bal.	*70.00)*		

ASSESS

Assess student understanding by checking solutions to Independent Practice activities.

Reteach

• Use Demonstration Problem 25B. This problem can be done on the overhead with the students completing the problem at their desks.

• Assign Recycling Problem 25-R.

Extend

• Assign the Accounting Tutorial Units 8, 9, and 10.

• Assign the Electronic Study Guide, Chapter 25.

• Assign Challenge Problem 25-C. (The challenge is calculating a partial month's interest expense and calculating and recording a dishonored note receivable and the maturity value of a note payable.)

Enrich

• Assign students to read the MULTICULTURAL AWARENESS feature on page 665.

• Assign Cases for Critical Thinking 2.

ILLUSTRATION 25-10

Reversing entry for accrued interest expense

	DATE		ACCOUNT TITLE	DOC. NO.	POST. REF.	DEBIT	CREDIT	
1			*Reversing Entries*					1
4		1	*Interest Payable*			70 00		4
5			*Interest Expense*				70 00	5
6								6
7								7
8								8
9								9
10								10

GENERAL JOURNAL   PAGE *17*

Paying a Note Payable Issued in a Previous Fiscal Period

On June 30 Celluphone paid the maturity value (principal plus interest) of the only note payable on hand December 31, the end of

CLOSURE

- Use Audit Your Understanding questions.
- Review Summary Illustration 25-13, "Summary of Journal Entries for Recording Accrued Revenue and Expenses." Use Transparency 25-1, Chapter Summary.

ASSESS

- Administer Problem Test Chapter 25.
- Administer a MicroExam test for Chapter 25.

the previous fiscal year. The maturity value for Note Payable No. 10 is calculated as shown below.

Principal	$\times$	Interest Rate	$\times$	Time as Fraction of Year	$=$	Interest
$2,800.00	$\times$	10%	$\times$	$\frac{9}{12}$	$=$	$210.00

Principal	$+$	Interest	$=$	Maturity Value
$2,800.00	$+$	$210.00	$=$	$3,010.00

Notes Payable

June 30 Paid	2,800.00	Sept. 30 NP10	2,800.00

Interest Expense

Dec. 31 Bal.	1,375.00	Dec. 31 Closing	1,445.00
Dec. 31 Adj.	70.00	Jan. 1 Rev.	70.00
(New Bal. zero)			
June 30 Paid	210.00		
(New Bal.	*140.00)*		

Cash

		June 30 Paid	3,010.00

June 30, 19--. Paid cash for the maturity value of Note Payable No. 10: principal, $2,800.00, plus interest, $210.00; total, $3,010.00. Check No. 982.

The total interest, $210.00, was incurred during two fiscal periods, $70.00 during the previous fiscal period and $140.00 during the current fiscal period. Since Celluphone uses reversing entries, the entry to record the payment of this note payable and interest is the same as the entry to record a note issued and paid in a single fiscal year.

Notes Payable is debited for the principal of the note, $2,800.00, to record the decrease in the balance of this current liability account. Interest Expense is debited for the total amount of interest, $210.00, to record the increase in this other expense account. The interest expense account now has a debit balance of $140.00, the amount of interest expense incurred during the current fiscal period. Cash is credited for the total amount paid, $3,010.00, to record the decrease in this asset account.

The cash payments journal entry to record this payment of a note payable when reversing entries are used is shown in Illustration 25-11.

ILLUSTRATION 25-11

Cash payments journal entry to record note payable issued in previous fiscal period when reversing entries are used

CASH PAYMENTS JOURNAL PAGE 55

	DATE	ACCOUNT TITLE	CK. NO.	POST. REF.	GENERAL DEBIT	GENERAL CREDIT	ACCOUNTS PAYABLE DEBIT	PURCHASES DISCOUNT CREDIT	CASH CREDIT	
21	30	*Notes Payable*	982		2800 00				3010 00	21
22		*Interest Expense*			210 00					22
23										23
24										24
25										25

APPLIED SKILLS: WORD PROCESSING

If you wish to integrate word processing into your accounting course, you may direct students to answer the end-of-chapter Accounting Terms, Questions for Individual Study, and Cases for Critical Thinking using their word processing software.

Audit Your Understanding

1. What is the adjusting entry for accrued interest expense?

2. What is the closing entry for interest expense?

3. What type of entry is the opposite of an adjusting entry?

After the cash payments journal entry is posted, the notes payable, interest payable, and interest expense accounts appear as shown in Illustration 25-12.

Notes Payable has a zero balance. This account will be used again when additional notes payable are issued. After the reversing entry is recorded, Interest Payable has a zero balance. Interest Payable will not be used again until it is needed for an adjusting entry at the end of the current fiscal year. Interest Expense has a debit balance of $140.00, the amount of interest incurred on Note Payable No. 10 in the current year.

The chart shown in Summary Illustration 25-13 on the next page summarizes the journal entries for recording accrued revenue and expenses.

AUDIT YOUR UNDERSTANDING

1. Debit Interest Expense, credit Interest Payable.
2. Debit Income Summary, credit Interest Expense.
3. A reversing entry.

ILLUSTRATION 25-12   General ledger accounts after posting cash payment for note payable issued in previous fiscal period when reversing entries are used

ACCOUNT **Notes Payable**   ACCOUNT NO. **2105**

DATE	ITEM	POST. REF.	DEBIT	CREDIT	BALANCE DEBIT	BALANCE CREDIT
30		CR26		2 80 0 00		2 80 0 00
June 30		CP55	2 80 0 00		—	—

ACCOUNT **Interest Payable**   ACCOUNT NO. **2110**

DATE	ITEM	POST. REF.	DEBIT	CREDIT	BALANCE DEBIT	BALANCE CREDIT
Dec. 31		G15		70 00		70 00
Jan. 1		G17	70 00		—	—

ACCOUNT **Interest Expense**   ACCOUNT NO. **8110**

DATE	ITEM	POST. REF.	DEBIT	CREDIT	BALANCE DEBIT	BALANCE CREDIT
31		G16		1 44 5 00		
Jan. 1		G17		70 00		70 00
June 30		CP55	2 10 00		1 40 00	

CHAPTER 25   Accounting for Accrued Revenue and Expenses   **677**

TEACHING STRATEGIES: DIFFERENT LEARNING ABILITIES

Limited English Proficiency (LEP) Students.   Rather than asking students whether they understand what you have said, ask them to restate what you have said in their own words.

TEACHING STRATEGIES:
APPLYING VISUALS

Direct students to Summary Illustration 25-13 and review the journal entries for recording accrued revenue and expenses.

SUMMARY ILLUSTRATION 25-13

Summary of journal entries for recording accrued revenue and expenses

Journal Entries	GENERAL LEDGER															
	Cash		Notes Receivable		Interest Receivable		Notes Payable		Interest Payable		Income Summary		Interest Income		Interest Expense	
	DR	CR	DR	CR	DR	CR	DR	CR	DR	CR	DR	CR	DR	CR	DR	CR
Adjusting entry for accrued interest income on note receivable					X									X		
Entry to close interest income account												X	X			
Reversing entry for accrued interest income						X							X			
Received cash for note receivable accepted in previous fiscal period when reversing entries are used	X			X										X		
Adjusting entry for accrued interest expense on note payable										X					X	
Entry to close interest expense account											X					X
Reversing entry for accrued interest expense									X							X
Paid cash for note payable issued in previous fiscal period when reversing entries are used		X					X								X	

APPLIED SKILLS: WRITING ACROSS THE CURRICULUM

Writing paragraphs and short essays. The Cases for Critical Thinking are short, practical applications of the accounting principles developed in the chapter. Some cases are planned to present problems related to the chapter but not specifically discussed and answered in the chapter. These cases present an opportunity for critical thinking and decision making. These cases also require more than a short objective-type response. Therefore, they provide ideal practice in writing paragraphs and short essays.

What is the meaning of each of the following?

1. **accrued revenue**
2. **accrued interest income**
3. **reversing entry**
4. **accrued expenses**
5. **accrued interest expense**

QUESTIONS FOR INDIVIDUAL STUDY

1. When do generally accepted accounting procedures require that revenue and expenses be recorded?
2. Which accounting concept is being applied when an adjusting entry is made at the end of the fiscal period to record accrued revenue?
3. Why should accrued revenue be recorded by an adjusting entry before financial statements are prepared at the end of a fiscal period?
4. What accounts are affected, and how, by the adjusting entry for accrued interest income?
5. Where is the information obtained that is needed to journalize an adjustment for accrued interest income?
6. After closing entries are posted, what is the balance of the interest income account?
7. Why does a business use reversing entries as part of its procedures for accounting for accrued interest income?
8. What accounts are affected, and how, by the reversing entry for accrued interest income?

9. Interest of $15.00 on a note receivable is earned and accrued on December 31 and an additional $25.00 interest is earned by the note's maturity date. What entry will be made to Interest Income when the maturity value of the note is received? (The business uses reversing entries for all accrual adjusting entries.)
10. Why should accrued expenses be recorded by an adjusting entry before financial statements are prepared at the end of a fiscal period?
11. What accounts are affected, and how, by the adjusting entry for accrued interest expense?
12. What accounts are affected, and how, by the reversing entry for accrued interest expense?
13. Immediately after a reversing entry for accrued interest expense is recorded, what is the balance of the interest payable account?

CASES FOR CRITICAL THINKING

CASE 1 As a new accounting clerk at The Print Shop, you discover that $80.00 accrued interest income on notes receivable was not recorded at the end of the current fiscal period. When you consult with the manager, the manager says, "Don't worry about recording the interest income. It will be recorded when we collect the note and interest." Is the manager's approach acceptable? Explain your answer. What effect will the omission of accrued interest income have on the current fiscal year's (a) income statement and (b) balance sheet?

CASE 2 At the end of each fiscal period, Jet-Air prepares adjusting entries to record accrued interest expense. However, the company does not record reversing entries for the accrued interest expense. At the end of the current fiscal year, Jet-Air had Note Payable No. 12 outstanding, a $3,000.00, 3-month, 10% note issued October 31. Jet-Air made the following journal entries related to Note Payable No. 12.

ACCOUNTING TERMS

1. **accrued revenue:** Revenue earned in one fiscal period but not received until a later fiscal period. (p. 665)
2. **accrued interest income:** Interest earned but not yet received. (p. 665)
3. **reversing entry:** An entry made at the beginning of one fiscal period to reverse an adjusting entry made in the previous fiscal period. (p. 668)
4. **accrued expenses:** Expenses incurred in one fiscal period but not paid until a later fiscal period. (p. 671)
5. **accrued interest expense:** Interest incurred but not yet paid. (p. 672)

QUESTIONS FOR INDIVIDUAL STUDY

1. In the accounting period in which revenue is earned and expenses are incurred. (p. 665)
2. Realization of Revenue. (p. 665)
3. So that the income statement will report all revenue earned for the period even though some of the revenue has not yet been received. Also, so that the balance sheet will report all assets, including the accrued revenue receivable. (p. 665)
4. Interest Receivable is debited; Interest Income is credited. (p. 666)
5. From the Adjustments columns of a work sheet. (p. 666)
6. Zero. (p. 667)
7. To avoid the inconvenience of determining how much of the cash received is for interest income earned and accrued during the previous year and how much is earned during the current year. (p. 668)
8. Interest Income is debited; Interest Receivable is credited. (p. 668)
9. Interest Income is credited for $40.00, the total amount of interest earned. (p. 669–670)
10. So that the income statement will report all expenses for the period even though some of the expenses have not yet been paid. Also, so that the balance sheet will report all liabilities, including the accrued expenses payable. (p. 672)
11. Interest Expense is debited; Interest Payable is credited. (p. 672)
12. Interest Payable is debited; Interest Expense is credited. (p. 675)
13. Zero. (p. 675)

Case 1 The manager's approach is not acceptable. Good accounting practice requires that a business record revenue in the fiscal period in which it is earned. *(CONCEPT: Realization of Revenue)* The $80.00 interest amount was earned in the current year. Thus, it should be recorded as revenue in the current year or the financial statements will not be accurate for the current fiscal period. By omitting the accrued interest income, The Print Shop's current year's income statement will understate its revenue; thus net income will be understated. When accrued interest revenue is recorded, Interest Receivable, an asset account, is debited and Interest Income, a revenue account, is credited. Since $80.00 was not recorded in these accounts, the balance sheet will understate assets and capital. Since net income was understated, the amount of net income closed to the capital accounts will be understated.

Case 2 Ms. Harwick is not correct in stating that generally accepted accounting principles require that reversing entries be used for all accrued expenses. The procedure now used by Jet-Air does provide correct information on the financial statements. Therefore, a business has the option of using or not using reversing entries in conjunction with accrued expenses. If correct procedures are followed, results will be the same for either option. However, if reversing entries are used, the accounting clerk will avoid the inconvenience of determining how much of the cash paid is for expenses incurred and accrued during the previous year and how much is incurred during the current year.

(Continued on p. 681)

Issued Oct. 31		
Cash	$3,000.00	
Notes Payable		$3,000.00
Adj. Entry Dec. 31		
Interest Expense	50.00	
Interest Payable		50.00
Clos. Entry Dec. 31		
Income Summary	50.00	
Interest Expense		50.00
Paid Note Jan. 31		
Notes Payable	3,000.00	
Interest Payable	50.00	
Interest Expense	25.00	
Cash		3,075.00

Winifred Harwick, a newly employed accounting supervisor, says that generally accepted accounting principles require that reversing entries be used in conjunction with adjusting entries for accrued expenses. Thus, Ms. Harwick says Jet-Air must begin using reversing entries for all accrued expenses. Is Ms. Harwick correct? Do the procedures Jet-Air has been using result in incorrect financial statements? Explain your answer.

DRILLS FOR UNDERSTANDING   EPT(c,d)

DRILL 25-D1 **Analyzing entries for notes receivable and accrued revenue**

A form for analyzing transactions is given in the working papers that accompany this textbook.

INSTRUCTIONS:

For each of the following entries, indicate by a check mark which account(s) should be debited and which account(s) should be credited.

1. Received a note receivable from a customer for an extension of time on account.
2. Recorded an adjusting entry at the end of the fiscal period for interest earned but not yet received.
3. Closed interest income account.
4. Recorded reversing entry for accrued interest income.
5. Received cash for maturity value of a note receivable accepted in previous fiscal period for a business that uses reversing entries.

DRILL 25-D2 **Analyzing entries for notes payable and accrued expenses**

A form for analyzing transactions is given in the working papers that accompany this textbook.

INSTRUCTIONS:

For each of the following entries, indicate by a check mark which account(s) should be debited and which account(s) should be credited.

1. Issued a note payable to a vendor for an extension of time on an account payable.
2. Recorded an adjusting entry at the end of the fiscal period for interest incurred but not yet paid.
3. Closed interest expense account.
4. Recorded reversing entry for accrued interest expense.
5. Paid cash for maturity value of a note payable issued in previous fiscal period for a business that uses reversing entries.

APPLICATION PROBLEMS
EPT(c,d)

PROBLEM 25-1 Journalizing and posting entries for accrued revenue

The general ledger accounts for Citation Corporation are given in the working papers accompanying this textbook. The balances are recorded as of December 31 of the current year before adjusting entries.

Citation Corporation completed the following transactions related to notes receivable during the current year and the following year. The first transaction has already been journalized and posted. Note Receivable No. 11 is the only note receivable on hand at the end of the fiscal period. Source documents are abbreviated as follows: note receivable, NR; receipt, R.

19X1
Nov. 1. Received a 3-month, 12% note from Peter Mendoza for an extension of time on his account, $800.00. NR11.

19X2
Feb. 1. Received cash for the maturity value of NR11: principal, $800.00, plus interest, $24.00; total, $824.00. R110.

INSTRUCTIONS:

1. Use page 14 of a general journal. Journalize the adjusting entry for accrued interest income on December 31. Post this entry.
2. Continue to use page 14 of a general journal. Journalize the closing entry for interest income. Post this entry.
3. Use page 15 of a general journal. Journalize the reversing entry for accrued interest income. Post this entry.
4. Use page 18 of a cash receipts journal. Journalize the receipt of cash for the maturity value of NR11. Post this entry.

PROBLEM 25-2 Journalizing and posting entries for accrued expenses

The general ledger accounts for Charter Corporation are given in the working papers accompanying this textbook. The balances are recorded as of December 31 of the current year before adjusting entries.

Charter Corporation completed the following transactions related to notes payable during the current year and the following year. The first transaction has already been journalized and posted. Note Payable No. 5 is the only note payable on hand at the end of the fiscal period. Source documents are abbreviated as follows: check, C; note payable, NP.

19X1
Sept. 1. Issued a 6-month, 12% note, $4,000.00. NP5.

19X2
Mar. 1. Paid cash for the maturity value of NP5: principal, $4,000.00, plus interest, $240.00; total, $4,240.00. C189.

INSTRUCTIONS:

1. Use page 15 of a general journal. Journalize the adjusting entry for accrued interest expense on December 31. Post this entry.
2. Continue to use page 15 of a general journal. Journalize the closing entry for interest expense. Post this entry.
3. Use page 16 of a general journal. Journalize the reversing entry for accrued interest expense. Post this entry.
4. Use page 20 of a cash payments journal. Journalize the cash payment for the maturity value of NP5. Post this entry.

Following is a comparison of Jet-Air's entries for Note Payable No. 12 without and with reversing entries.

Without Reversing Entries

Issued Oct. 31:		
Cash	$3,000.00	
Notes Payable		$3,000.00
Adj. Entry Dec. 31:		
Interest Expense	$50.00	
Interest Payable		$50.00
Clos. Entry Dec. 31:		
Income Summary	$50.00	
Interest Expense		$50.00
Rev. Entry Jan. 1:	None	
Paid Note Jan. 31:		
Notes Payable	$3,000.00	
Interest Payable	50.00	
Interest Expense	25.00	
Cash		$3,075.00

With Reversing Entries

Issued Oct. 31:		
Same entry as above		
Adj. Entry Dec. 31:		
Same entry as above		
Clos. Entry Dec. 31:		
Same entry as above		
Rev. Entry Jan. 1:		
Interest Payable	$50.00	
Interest Expense		$50.00
Paid Note Jan. 31:		
Notes Payable	$3,000.00	
Interest Expense	75.00	
Cash		$3,075.00

Both methods result in recording $50.00 interest expense in the first year and $25.00 in the second year. However, when reversing entries are used, the accounting clerk does not need to search the accounts when the note is paid to determine how much was accrued last period so that the interest payable account can be credited for that amount. The reversing entry has already reduced Interest Payable. So the entire amount of interest paid is debited to Interest Expense. Consequently, using reversing entries usually reduces the number of errors in recording payment of accrued expenses.

Problem 25-1 Int. Rec. 800 × 12% × 2/12 = 16; End. Bal. of Interest Income, $8.00; Cash receipts journal Cash Debit column, 824.

Problem 25-2 Int. Pay. 4,000 × 12% × 4/12 = 160; End. Bal. of Interest Expense, $80.00; Cash payments journal Cash Credit column, 4,240.

MASTERY PROBLEM 25-M Journalizing and posting entries for accrued revenue and expenses

The general ledger accounts for Hahn Company are given in the working papers accompanying this textbook. The balances are recorded as of December 31 of the current year before adjusting entries.

Hahn Company completed the following transactions related to notes receivable and notes payable during the current year and the following year. The first two transactions have already been journalized and posted. Note Receivable No. 8 and Note Payable No. 4 are the only notes on hand at the end of the fiscal period.

19X1
Oct. 31. Received a 3-month, 12% note from Donald Ritter for an extension of time on his account, $600.00. NR8.
  31. Issued a 4-month, 14% note, $2,400.00. NP4.

19X2
Jan. 31. Received cash for the maturity value of NR8: principal, $600.00, plus interest, $18.00; total, $618.00. R207.
Feb. 28. Paid cash for the maturity value of NP4: principal, $2,400.00, plus interest, $112.00; total, $2,512.00. C423.

INSTRUCTIONS:

1. Use page 15 of a general journal. Journalize the adjusting entries for accrued interest income and accrued interest expense on December 31. Post these entries.
2. Continue to use page 15 of a general journal. Journalize the closing entries for interest income and interest expense. Post these entries.
3. Use page 16 of a general journal. Journalize the reversing entries for accrued interest income and accrued interest expense. Post these entries.
4. Use page 19 of a cash receipts journal. Journalize the receipt of cash for the maturity value of NR8. Post this entry.
5. Use page 25 of a cash payments journal. Journalize the cash payment for the maturity value of NP4. Post this entry.

CHALLENGE PROBLEM 25-C Journalizing and posting entries for accrued revenue and expenses

The general ledger accounts for Castoldo Corporation are given in the working papers accompanying this textbook. The balances are recorded as of December 31 of the current year before adjusting entries.

Castoldo Corporation completed the following transactions related to notes receivable and notes payable during the current year and the following year. The first two transactions have already been journalized and posted. Note Receivable No. 6 and Note Payable No. 11 are the only notes on hand at the end of the fiscal period.

19X1
Nov. 30. We received a note from Margaret Snider. This note is a 4-month, 12% note for an extension of time on her account, $400.00. NR6.
Dec. 15. A 5-month, 12% note was issued, $2,500.00. NP11.

19X2
Mar. 31. Margaret Snider dishonored NR6, maturity value due today. M83.
May 15. Paid cash for the maturity value of NP11. C465.

INSTRUCTIONS:

1. Use page 13 of a general journal. Journalize the adjusting entries for accrued interest income and accrued interest expense on December 31. Post these entries.

2. Continue to use page 13 of a general journal. Journalize the closing entries for interest income and interest expense. Post these entries.

3. Use page 14 of a general journal. Journalize the reversing entries for accrued interest income and accrued interest expense. Post these entries.

4. Use page 16 of a general journal. Journalize the dishonored note, NR6. Post this entry to the general ledger accounts.

5. Use page 33 of a cash payments journal. Journalize the cash payment for the maturity value of NP11. Post this entry.

End-of-fiscal-period work for a corporation is divided into two chapters. Chapter 26 includes distributing dividends and preparing a work sheet. Journal entries for the declaration and the payment of dividends to distribute a corporation's earnings to stockholders are illustrated. Adjustments presented in individual chapters earlier in this cycle are tied together on one work sheet in this chapter, including adjustments for uncollectible accounts, depreciation on plant assets, merchandise inventory, and accrued interest

GUIDE TO ACHIEVING LEARNING OBJECTIVES

	TEACH	APPLY		EXTEND/ENRICH					
Enabling Performance Tasks	Lesson Plans	Drills for Understanding	Application Problems	Mastery Problems	Challenge Problems	Cases for Critical Thinking	Recycling Problems	Reinforcement Activity	
a. Define accounting terms related to distributing dividends and preparing a work sheet.	26-1								
b. Identify accounting concepts and practices related to distributing dividends and preparing a work sheet.	26-1, 26-2					Cases 1, 2			
c. Journalize the declaration and payment of a dividend.	26-1		26-1	26-M			26-R		
d. Plan end-of-fiscal-period adjustments.	26-2	26-D1	26-2	26-M	26-C		26-R	3B	
e. Complete a work sheet.	26-2	26-D2	26-2	26-M	26-C		26-R	3B	

ENRICHMENT

SPECIAL FEATURES

Global Perspective, page 687

Careers in Accounting, page 692

TECHNOLOGY CONNECTION

Accounting Tutorial Unit 8

Application Program Disk Problem 26-M

Electronic Study Guide

NEW, REVIEW, AND EXTENSION

ACTIVITIES/CONCEPTS/TRANSACTIONS	NEW	REVIEW/ EXTENSION
Stockholders' equity accounts used by a corporation	✓	
Declaring a corporate dividend to stockholders	✓	
Paying a corporate dividend to stockholders	✓	
Completing a work sheet		✓
Adjustment for accrued interest income		✓
Adjustment for uncollectible accounts expense		✓
Adjustment for merchandise inventory		✓
Adjustment for supplies		✓
Adjustment for prepaid insurance		✓
Adjustment for depreciation expense		✓
Adjustment for accrued interest expense		✓
Adjustment for federal income tax expense	✓	

income and expense. The adjustment for a corporation's federal income tax is presented as a new adjustment.

Challenge Problem 26-C uses a 10-column work sheet to provide practice with an alternative work sheet format. However, a 10-column work sheet may be used for any of the problems in this chapter. A master ruling of a 10-column work sheet is available in the Teacher's Resource Guide for this purpose.

	INFORMAL ASSESSMENT		FORMAL ASSESSMENT				
	Study Guide	Audit Your Understanding	Chapter MicroExam	Chapter Problem Test	Unit Problem Test	Unit Objective Test	Portfolio
Unit B		✓	✓			✓	
Unit C		✓	✓			✓	
Unit A				✓	✓		
Unit A				✓	✓		✓
				✓			✓

TEACHING MATERIALS

Teacher's Wraparound Edition of the Text

Teacher's Resource Guide

Teacher's Edition of Working Papers

Teacher's Edition of Demonstration/Recycling Problems

Teaching Transparencies

Accounting Tutorial Manual

MicroExam

Applied Math Work Sheet

APPLIED MATHEMATICS

APPLIED MATH/ACCOUNTING SKILL	APPLICATION
Calculating Net Income Before Federal Income Tax Expense	Prob. 26-C
Calculating the Adjustment for Federal Income Tax Expense	Prob. 26-2

26

Distributing Dividends and Preparing a Work Sheet for a Corporation

ENABLING PERFORMANCE TASKS

After studying Chapter 26, you will be able to:

a Define accounting terms related to distributing dividends and preparing a work sheet for a merchandising business organized as a corporation.

b Identify accounting concepts and practices related to distributing dividends and preparing a work sheet for a merchandising business organized as a corporation.

c Journalize the declaration and payment of a dividend for a merchandising business organized as a corporation.

d Plan end-of-fiscal-period adjustments for a merchandising business organized as a corporation.

e Complete a work sheet for a merchandising business organized as a corporation.

TERMS PREVIEW

stockholder • retained earnings • dividends • board of directors • declaring a dividend

Many accounting procedures used for a corporation are similar to the procedures used for a proprietorship or a partnership. Consequently, preparing a work sheet for a corporation is similar to preparing a work sheet for a proprietorship or a partnership.

There are, however, three principal differences between accounting for a proprietorship or partnership and accounting for a corporation. (1) Different accounts are used to record owners' equity. (2) Different procedures are used to distribute income to owners. (3) Corporations calculate and pay federal income tax. Corporations must pay income tax on their net income. Proprietorship and partnership net income is treated as part of each owner's personal income for income tax purposes. Thus, income tax is not calculated for a proprietorship or partnership business.

STOCKHOLDERS' EQUITY ACCOUNTS USED BY A CORPORATION

A corporation's ownership is divided into units. Each unit of ownership in a corporation is known as a share of stock. An owner of one or more shares of a corporation is called a **stockholder.** Each stockholder is an owner of a corporation.

Separate general ledger owners' equity accounts are maintained for each owner of a proprietorship or a partnership. However, a corporation may have many stockholders. Therefore, a separate owners' equity account is not maintained for each owner of a corporation. Instead, a single owners' equity account, titled Capital Stock, is used for the investment of all owners.

Owners' equity accounts for a corporation normally are listed under a major chart of accounts division titled *Stockholders' Equity.* The stockholders' equity section of Celluphone's chart of accounts is shown in Illustration 26-1.

ILLUSTRATION 26-1

Stockholders' equity section of a corporation chart of accounts

(3000) STOCKHOLDERS' EQUITY
3105 Capital Stock
3110 Retained Earnings
3115 Dividends
3120 Income Summary

A second stockholders' equity account is used to record a corporation's earnings. An amount earned by a corporation and not yet distributed to stockholders is called **retained earnings.** Retained Earnings is the title of the account used to record a corporation's earnings.

A third stockholders' equity account is used to record the distribution of a corporation's earnings to stockholders. Earnings distributed to stockholders are called **dividends.** A corporation's

FYI

At the end of each fiscal period, the balance in the dividends account is closed to Retained Earnings.

dividend account is a temporary account similar to a proprietorship's or partnership's drawing account. Each time a dividend is declared, an account titled Dividends is debited. At the end of each fiscal period, the balance in the dividends account is closed to Retained Earnings. Dividends could be recorded as debits to a corporation's retained earnings account. However, many corporations record dividends in a separate account so that the total amounts are easily determined for each fiscal period.

DISTRIBUTING CORPORATE DIVIDENDS TO STOCKHOLDERS

Net income increases a corporation's total stockholders' equity. Some income may be retained by a corporation for business expansion. Also, some income may be given to stockholders as a return on their investments. Dividends can be distributed to stockholders ONLY by formal action of a corporation's board of directors. (CONCEPT: Business Entity) A group of persons elected by the stockholders to manage a corporation is called a **board of directors.**

Declaring a Dividend

FYI

Dividends are declared on one date and paid on another date.

Action by a board of directors to distribute corporate earnings to stockholders is called **declaring a dividend.** Dividends normally are declared on one date and paid on a later date. A corporation's board of directors is not required to declare a dividend. In fact, dividends cannot be declared that would exceed the balance of the retained earnings account. However, when a board of directors does declare a dividend, the corporation is then obligated to pay the dividend. The dividend is a liability that must be recorded in the corporation's accounts.

Celluphone's board of directors declares a dividend every three months so that stockholders can share the corporation's earnings throughout the year. Celluphone declares dividends each March 15, June 15, September 15, and December 15. The dividends are then paid on the 15th of the month following the declaration.

> December 15, 19--. Celluphone's board of directors declared a quarterly dividend of $2.00 per share; capital stock issued is 10,000 shares; total dividend, $20,000.00. Date of payment is January 15, 19--. Memorandum No. 195.

A dividend declaration increases the balance of the dividends account. The stockholders' equity account, Dividends, has a normal debit balance and is increased by a debit. Dividends, therefore, is debited for $20,000.00 (10,000 shares × $2.00 per share). Dividends Payable is credited for $20,000.00 to show the increase in this liability account.

Dividends	
3/15 Decl.	20,000.00
6/15 Decl.	20,000.00
9/15 Decl.	20,000.00
12/15 Decl.	**20,000.00**

Dividends Payable			
4/15 Paid	20,000.00	3/15 Decl.	20,000.00
7/15 Paid	20,000.00	6/15 Decl.	20,000.00
10/15 Paid	20,000.00	9/15 Decl.	20,000.00
		12/15 Decl.	20,000.00

INTERNATIONAL TRAVEL

When traveling internationally, a passport is usually required. A passport is a formal document that allows exit from and reentry into the country. It proves citizenship and provides identity for the traveler.

For the first-time passport applicant to receive a passport, a passport application must be completed. The application may be obtained from the United States Postal Service office and submitted with the following.

1. Proof of U.S. citizenship. Proof of U.S. citizenship is usually a certified birth certificate.
2. Proof of identity. Proof of identity is a document such as a driver's license.
3. Two photographs. Two photographs must be submitted that are identical and $2'' \times 2''$ in size. These photos cannot be snapshots as they must meet certain criteria. There are many local photo studios that advertise passport photos service.
4. Fee. The applicable fee when this textbook was written was $65. The passport is valid for ten years.

This information must be sent to a designated postal service employee at a selected post office; a clerk of a Federal or State court of record or a judge or clerk of a probate court who accepts applications; a U.S. consular official; or an agent at a Passport Agency in Boston, Chicago, Honolulu, Houston, Los Angeles, Miami, New Orleans, New York, Philadelphia, San Francisco, Seattle, Stamford, or Washington D.C.

Some countries require an additional endorsement or stamp by foreign country officials to be placed on the U.S. passport that allows entrance into that country. This stamp is known as a visa. Visas may be obtained from the appropriate embassy of the country being visited.

Immunizations are sometimes required by countries under the International Health Regulations adopted by the World Health Organization. Be sure to check with the Center for Disease Control to see if vaccinations such as those to prevent yellow fever or cholera are necessary before entering a particular country.

FYI

The general journal is used to record declaration of a dividend.

A transaction for a declaration of a dividend is not appropriately journalized in any of the special journals. Therefore, the entry is journalized in a general journal. The general journal entry to record Celluphone's quarterly declaration of a dividend is shown in Illustration 26-2.

ILLUSTRATION 26-2

General journal entry to record the declaration of a dividend by a corporation

	DATE		ACCOUNT TITLE	DOC. NO.	POST. REF.	DEBIT	CREDIT	
1	Dec. 19–	15	Dividends	M195		20 00 00 00		1
2			Dividends Payable				20 00 00 00	2
3								3
4								4
5								5
6								6

GENERAL JOURNAL PAGE 14

Dividends is debited for the dividend declared, $20,000.00. Dividends Payable is credited for the liability incurred by the dividend declaration, $20,000.00.

CHAPTER 26   Distributing Dividends and Preparing a Work Sheet   **687**

CLOSURE

- Use Audit Your Understanding questions.
- Review the three stockholders' equity accounts used by a corporation: (a) Capital Stock, (b) Retained Earnings, (c) Dividends.
- Review the procedures for journalizing dividends.

A corporation may declare a cash dividend even when there is not enough net income, as long as there is enough cash to make the payment.

Paying a Dividend

Celluphone issues one check for the amount of the total dividend to be paid. This check is deposited in a special dividend checking account. A separate check for each stockholder is drawn on this special account. The special account avoids a large number of cash payments journal entries and also reserves cash specifically for paying dividends.

A check is often made payable to an agent, such as a bank. The agent then handles the details of sending dividend checks to individual stockholders.

Dividends Payable

4/15 Paid	20,000.00	3/15 Decl.	20,000.00
7/15 Paid	20,000.00	6/15 Decl.	20,000.00
10/15 Paid	20,000.00	9/15 Decl.	20,000.00
1/15 Paid	**20,000.00**	12/15 Decl.	20,000.00

Cash

1/15 Paid	20,000.00

January 15, 19--. Paid cash for quarterly dividend declared December 15, 19--, $20,000.00. Check No. 794.

In this transaction the balance of the liability account, Dividends Payable, is decreased. The balance of the asset account, Cash, is also decreased. Therefore, Dividends Payable is debited for $20,000.00 and Cash is credited for $20,000.00.

The cash payments journal entry to record Celluphone's quarterly dividend payment of $20,000.00 is shown in Illustration 26-3.

Dividends Payable is debited for the amount of dividends paid, $20,000.00. Cash is credited for the total amount of cash paid, $20,000.00. When this entry is posted, the dividends payable account has a zero balance.

AUDIT YOUR UNDERSTANDING

The AUDIT YOUR UNDERSTANDING feature appears at the end of each section of the chapter. Explain to your students that the word *audit* means to check or verify. AUDIT YOUR UNDERSTANDING may be used to check student comprehension of the section just studied. The answers are provided in Appendix D in the back of the textbook.

1. The board of directors.
2. Debit Dividends, credit Dividends Payable.
3. Debit Dividends Payable, credit Cash.

Audit Your Understanding

1. Who is responsible for declaring dividends?
2. What is the entry to record declaration of a dividend?
3. What is the entry to record payment of a dividend?

ILLUSTRATION 26-3   Cash payments journal entry to record the payment of a dividend

CASH PAYMENTS JOURNAL   PAGE 37

	DATE		ACCOUNT TITLE	CK. NO.	POST. REF.	GENERAL DEBIT	GENERAL CREDIT	ACCOUNTS PAYABLE DEBIT	PURCHASES DISCOUNT CREDIT	CASH CREDIT	
1	Jan.	15	Dividends Payable	794		20000 00				20000 00	1
2											2
3											3
4											4
5											5
6											6
7											7
8											8

PREPARING A WORK SHEET FOR A CORPORATION

Work sheets for proprietorships, partnerships, and corporations are similar. Businesses use work sheets to plan adjustments and provide information needed to prepare financial statements. Celluphone may prepare a work sheet at any time financial statements are needed. However, Celluphone always prepares a work sheet and financial statements at the end of a fiscal year. *(CONCEPT: Accounting Period Cycle)*

Entering a Trial Balance on a Work Sheet

To prepare a work sheet, a trial balance is first entered in the Trial Balance columns. All general ledger accounts are listed in the same order as they appear in the general ledger. Trial Balance columns are totaled to prove equality of debits and credits.

Celluphone's trial balance on December 31 is shown on the work sheet, Illustration 26-4 on pages 690 and 691. A corporation's accounts are similar to those of a proprietorship or partnership except for the capital stock, retained earnings, dividends, and federal income tax accounts.

Planning Adjustments on a Work Sheet

Some general ledger accounts need to be brought up to date before financial statements are prepared. Accounts are brought up to date by planning and entering adjustments on a work sheet. Most adjustments on a corporation's work sheet are similar to those for proprietorships and partnerships.

The adjustments for merchandise inventory, supplies, and prepaid insurance are described in earlier chapters. Celluphone also makes six other adjustments. (1) Interest Income. (2) Uncollectible Accounts Expense. (3) Depreciation Expense—Office Equipment. (4) Depreciation Expense—Store Equipment. (5) Interest Expense. (6) Federal Income Tax Expense.

Adjustments for depreciation expense, uncollectible accounts expense, interest income, and interest expense could also be made by proprietorships and partnerships. However, the adjustment for federal income tax is unique to corporations. This adjustment is not made for proprietorships and partnerships because taxes are paid by the owners, not the business. Adjustments generally are made in the order that accounts are listed on a work sheet.

Interest Income Adjustment. Interest income earned during the current fiscal period but not yet received needs to be recorded. Two accounts are used for the adjustment for accrued interest income: Interest Receivable and Interest Income. An analysis of Celluphone's adjustment for accrued interest income is described in Chapter 25. Celluphone's accrued interest income adjustment is labeled *(a)* on

LESSON PLAN 26-2

Materials

- Student pages 689–697
- Transparencies: 26-1, Chapter Summary
- Software: Accounting Tutorial, Application Program Disk, Electronic Study Guide
- Math Work Sheet Chapter 25: Part A: Calculating Net Income Before Federal Income Tax Expense; Part B: Calculating the Adjustment for Federal Income Tax Expense
- Demonstration Problem: 26B, Preparing a Work Sheet for a Corporation
- Assess: Problem Test Chapter 26, MicroExam Chapter 26

Objectives (Enabling Performance Tasks)

b. Identify accounting concepts and practices related to distributing dividends and preparing a work sheet for a merchandising business organized as a corporation.

d. Plan end-of-fiscal-period adjustments for a merchandising business organized as a corporation.

e. Complete a work sheet for a merchandising business organized as a corporation.

TEACHING STRATEGIES: TEACHING TIP

Adjusting entries often prove difficult for students. For additional practice in analyzing adjusting entries, the teacher and students together should analyze in T accounts all the adjustments on the work sheet in Illustration 26-4.

In Part 2, a work sheet was prepared for a service business organized as a proprietorship. In Part 3, a work sheet was prepared for a merchandising business organized as a partnership. Preparing a work sheet for a corporation is similar to preparing a work sheet for a proprietorship or a partnership. In this lesson, we will prepare a work sheet for a merchandising business organized as a corporation. Also, we will look at how corporations calculate and pay federal income tax—the third principal difference between accounting for a proprietorship or partnership and a corporation. The first two differences were presented earlier in this chapter.

ILLUSTRATION 26-4 Completed work sheet for a corporation

Celluphone, Inc.
Work Sheet
For Year Ended December 31, 19--

#	ACCOUNT TITLE	TRIAL BALANCE Debit	TRIAL BALANCE Credit	ADJUSTMENTS Debit	ADJUSTMENTS Credit	INCOME STATEMENT Debit	INCOME STATEMENT Credit	BALANCE SHEET Debit	BALANCE SHEET Credit
1	Cash	4096800						4096800	
2	Petty Cash	30000						30000	
3	Notes Receivable	55000						55000	
4	Interest Receivable			(a) 1100				1100	
5	Accounts Receivable	6824000						6824000	
6	Allowance for Uncollectible Accounts		26500		(b) 922700				949200
7	Merchandise Inventory	20516000		(c) 701800				21217800	
8	Supplies	1545500			(d) 1169000			376500	
9	Prepaid Insurance	1355000			(e) 859800			495200	
10	Office Equipment	1825000						1825000	
11	Accumulated Depreciation—Office Equip.		362500		(f) 175000				537500
12	Store Equipment	7719000						7719000	
13	Accumulated Depreciation—Store Equip.		912500		(g) 632500				1545000
14	Notes Payable		280000						280000
15	Interest Payable				(h) 7000				7000
16	Accounts Payable		8396575						8396575
17	Employee Income Tax Payable		234000						234000
18	Federal Income Tax Payable				(i) 221923				221923
19	FICA Tax Payable		269500						269500
20	Sales Tax Payable		1098200						1098200
21	Unemployment Tax Payable—Federal		4700						4700
22	Unemployment Tax Payable—State		31725						31725
23	Health Insurance Premiums Payable		99500						99500
24	Dividends	2000000						2000000	
25	Capital Stock		100000000						100000000

TEACHING STRATEGIES: TEACHING TIP

Have students inspect the corporation's work sheet trial balance shown in Illustration 26-4. Determine which of the accounts might be the same regardless of the form of business organization and which accounts will be found only on the trial balance of a corporation.

#	Account Title	Trial Balance Debit	Trial Balance Credit	Adjustments Debit	Adjustments Credit	Income Statement Debit	Income Statement Credit	Balance Sheet Debit	Balance Sheet Credit
26	Retained Earnings		14911800						14911800
27	Dividends	8000000						8000000	
28	Income Summary				(e) 701800		701800		
29	Sales		205044000				205044000		
30	Sales Discount	564200				564200			
31	Sales Returns and Allowances	2431800				2431800			
32	Purchases	145479800				145479800			
33	Purchases Discount		1076600				1076600		
34	Purchases Returns and Allowances		531000				531000		
35	Advertising Expense	3260000				3260000			
36	Credit Card Fee Expense	2046800				2046800			
37	Depr. Expense—Office Equipment			(f) 175000		175000			
38	Depr. Expense—Store Equipment			(g) 632500		632500			
39	Insurance Expense			(c) 859800		859800			
40	Miscellaneous Expense	2235000				2235000			
41	Payroll Taxes Expense	2372000				2372000			
42	Rent Expense	5640000				5640000			
43	Salary Expense	25193200				25193200			
44	Supplies Expense			(d) 1169000		1169000			
45	Uncollectible Accounts Expense			(b) 922700		922700			
46	Utilities Expense	4890000				4890000			
47	Gain on Plant Assets		22500				22500		
48	Interest Income		20300		(a) 1100		21400		
49	Cash Short and Over	300				300			
50	Interest Expense	1437500		(h) 7000		1444500			
51	Loss on Plant Assets	46000				46000			
52	Federal Income Tax Expense	3460000		(i) 221923		3681923			
53		245321900	245321900	4690823	4690823	197343523	207397300	506404400	496350623
54	Net Income after Federal Income Tax					10053777			10053777
55						207397300	207397300	506404400	506404400

TEACH

Cover student pages 689–697 "Preparing a Work Sheet for a Corporation." A trial balance is prepared on the work sheet in the usual manner, as are adjustments. Emphasize that the adjustment for federal income tax is for corporations only. Review adjustments presented in earlier chapters. The adjustment for interest income is debit Interest Receivable, credit Interest Income. The adjustment for uncollectible accounts expense is debit Uncollectible Accounts Expense, credit Allowance for Uncollectible Accounts. Merchandise Inventory, Supplies, and Prepaid Insurance are adjusted in the usual manner. The adjustment for depreciation is debit depreciation expense account, credit accumulated depreciation account. The adjustment for interest expense is debit Interest Expense, credit Interest Payable. Explain quarterly installments used for paying estimated income tax. At the end of the fiscal year, when net income is known, federal income tax for the year can be calculated. The amount of federal income tax in the Trial Balance column is the amount of tax that was paid in quarterly installments. The adjustment is how much additional tax must be paid. Ask the questions: What is the balance of Federal Income Tax Expense? What should the balance be? The amount extended to the Income Statement column is the total amount of tax for the period.

The CAREERS feature box, ACCOUN-TANT, TAX, comes from the Diction-ary of Occupational Titles (DOT). The entry number for this job title is D.O.T. 160.162-010. Bring this dictionary to class and explain its purpose and how to use it. The career feature is designed to expose students to the exploration of different careers in accounting. The feature gives a real-istic description of actual job duties. This feature can be used to demon-strate that the skills learned in this course are relevant.

APPLY

- Draw T accounts for Federal Income Tax Payable and Federal Income Tax Expense. Label the normal balance sides.

- Demonstrate on the board how to calculate the amount of federal income tax expense adjustment when the total amount of tax is known.

- Direct students to Illustration 26-4 as you discuss the adjustments pre-sented in this lesson.

Guided Practice

Guide students through Drills 26-D1 and 26-D2. Students should have the forms from the working papers to complete as you guide them through each adjust-ment and account balance extension. All students should agree with the analysis of each adjustment and each account balance extension before proceeding to the next item.

Independent Practice

Assign Questions 11–16, Problem 26-2, Mastery Problem 26-M, and Study Guide 26.

CAREERS IN ACCOUNTING

ACCOUNTANT, TAX

- *Uses accounting records to calculate taxes*
- *Ensures that business complies with periodic tax payment, reporting, and other requirements*
- *Advises management regarding tax effect of business activities*
- *Develops strategies for minimizing tax liability*

👉👉 FYI 👉👉

Corporate dividends may also be paid in additional capital stock, known as a "stock dividend." Dividends Payable is debited for the value of the stock and Capital Stock is credited.

lines 4 and 48 in the work sheet Adjustments columns, Illustration 26-4, pages 690 and 691.

Interest Receivable is debited for the amount of accrued interest income, $11.00. Interest Income is credited for the same amount.

Uncollectible Accounts Expense Adjustment. The estimated amount of uncollectible accounts expense for a fiscal period needs to be brought up to date. Two accounts are used for the adjustment for uncollectible accounts expense: Uncollectible Accounts Expense and Allowance for Uncollectible Accounts. An analysis of Celluphone's uncol-lectible accounts expense adjustment is described in Chapter 21. The uncollectible accounts expense adjustment is labeled *(b)* on lines 6 and 45 in the work sheet Adjustments columns, Illustration 26-4. Uncollectible Accounts Expense is debited for the amount of esti-mated uncollectible accounts expense, $9,227.00. Allowance for Uncol-lectible Accounts is credited for the same amount.

Merchandise Inventory Adjustment. The merchandise inventory account balance in a trial balance is the beginning inventory for a fiscal period. The amount of the ending inventory is determined by counting the merchandise on hand at the end of the fiscal period. An adjusting entry is made to bring merchandise inventory up to date so that the end-of-fiscal-period balance will be shown in the merchandise inventory account. The merchandise inventory adjust-ment is labeled *(c)* on lines 7 and 28 in the work sheet Adjustments columns, Illustration 26-4.

The process used to adjust Celluphone's merchandise inventory account is the same as that described for a partnership business in Chapter 16.

Celluphone's beginning merchandise inventory, $205,160.00, is shown on line 7 in the Trial Balance Debit column on the work sheet. Celluphone's ending merchandise inventory on December 31 is counted and determined to be $212,178.00. To bring Celluphone's merchandise inventory account up to date, the balance of Merchan-dise Inventory needs to be increased by $7,018.00 ($212,178.00 end-ing inventory less $205,160.00 beginning inventory). Merchandise Inventory is debited for the amount of the increase, $7,018.00. Income Summary is credited for the same amount.

If the ending merchandise inventory is less than the beginning merchandise inventory, the difference (decrease) is debited to Income Summary and credited to Merchandise Inventory.

Supplies Adjustment. Two accounts are used for the adjustment for supplies: Supplies and Supplies Expense. The supplies adjustment is labeled *(d)* on lines 8 and 44 in the work sheet Adjustments columns, Illustration 26-4. Supplies Expense is debited for the value of supplies used, $11,690.00. Supplies is credited for the same amount.

Prepaid Insurance Adjustment. Insurance premiums are debited to a prepaid insurance account when paid. Insurance expense, how-

692

ever, must be recorded for the fiscal period in which the insurance is used. *(CONCEPT: Matching Expenses with Revenue)* Therefore, Prepaid Insurance and Insurance Expense are adjusted at the end of the fiscal period. The prepaid insurance adjustment is labeled *(e)* on lines 9 and 39 in the work sheet Adjustments columns, Illustration 26-4. Insurance Expense is debited for the value of insurance used, $8,598.00. Prepaid Insurance is credited for the same amount.

Depreciation Expense Adjustments. An analysis of Celluphone's depreciation expense adjustments is described in Chapter 22. The depreciation expense adjustments are labeled *(f)* and *(g)* on lines 11, 13, 37, and 38 in the work sheet Adjustments columns, Illustration 26-4.

Depreciation Expense—Office Equipment is debited for the amount of office equipment depreciation expense, $1,750.00. Accumulated Depreciation—Office Equipment is credited for the same amount. Depreciation Expense—Store Equipment is debited for the amount of store equipment depreciation expense, $6,325.00. Accumulated Depreciation—Store Equipment is credited for the same amount.

Interest Expense Adjustment. Interest expense incurred during the current fiscal period but not yet paid needs to be recorded. Two accounts are used for the adjustment for accrued interest expense: Interest Payable and Interest Expense. An analysis of Celluphone's adjustment for accrued interest expense is described in Chapter 25. The interest expense adjustment is labeled *(h)* on lines 15 and 50 in the work sheet Adjustments columns, Illustration 26-4.

Interest Expense is debited for the amount of accrued interest expense, $70.00. Interest Payable is credited for the same amount.

Federal Income Tax Expense Adjustment

Corporations anticipating annual federal income taxes of $500.00 or more are required to pay their estimated taxes each quarter. Estimated income tax is paid in quarterly installments in April, June, September, and December. However, the actual income tax owed is calculated at the end of a fiscal year. Based on the actual tax owed for a year, a corporation must file an annual return. Any additional tax owed that was not paid in quarterly installments must be paid when the final return is sent.

Early in the current year, Celluphone estimated $34,600.00 federal income tax for the year. Celluphone paid $8,650.00 in each quarterly installment for a total of $34,600.00. Each tax payment is recorded as a debit to Federal Income Tax Expense and a credit to Cash.

Federal income tax is an expense of a corporation. However, the amount of tax depends on net income before the tax is recorded. Five steps are used to calculate the total amount of federal income tax expense and the amount of the adjustment needed on a work sheet.

1 Complete all adjustments on a work sheet except the federal income tax expense adjustment.

FYI

After paying quarterly taxes, a corporation must still file an annual tax return and send any additional tax owed with the return.

Assess student understanding by checking solutions to Independent Practice activities.

Reteach

- Duplicate and assign Math Work Sheets Chapter 26 Parts A and B, Calculating Net Income Before Federal Income Tax Expense and Calculating the Adjustment for Federal Income Tax Expense from the Masters and Solutions to Enrichment/Application Activities Section in the Teacher's Resource Guide. These will provide additional practice on the mathematics of calculating federal income tax.

- Use Demonstration Problem 26B. This problem can be demonstrated on the overhead with the students completing the problem at their desks.

- Assign Recycling Problem 26-R.

Extend

- Assign Accounting Tutorial Unit 8.
- Assign the Application Program Disk software with Problem 26-M.
- Assign the Electronic Study Guide Chapter 26.
- Assign Cases for Critical Thinking 2.
- Assign Challenge Problem 26-C. (The challenge is calculating federal income tax using a tax rate table and completing a 10-column work sheet.)

Enrich

Assign students to read the CAREERS IN ACCOUNTING feature on page 692.

CLOSURE

• Use Audit Your Understanding questions.

• Review Summary Illustration 26-5, "Summary of Preparing a Work Sheet for a Corporation." Use Transparency 26-1, Chapter Summary.

ASSESS

• Administer Problem Test Chapter 26.

• Administer a MicroExam test for Chapter 26.

2 Extend all amounts except the federal income tax expense account balance to the appropriate Income Statement or Balance Sheet columns.

3 On a separate sheet of paper, total the work sheet's Income Statement columns. Calculate the difference between the two totals. This difference is the net income before federal income tax expense. Celluphone's net income before federal income tax is calculated from the Income Statement columns of the work sheet, Illustration 26-4.

Total of Income Statement Credit column $2,073,973.00
Less total of Income Statement Debit column
    before federal income tax . . . . −1,936,616.00
Equals net income before federal income tax . . . . . . $ 137,357.00

4 Calculate the amount of federal income tax expense using a tax rate table furnished by the Internal Revenue Service. Celluphone's federal income tax for the current year is $36,819.23.

Tax rate tables showing income tax rates for corporations are distributed by the Internal Revenue Service. Each corporation should check a current table to find the applicable rates. Corporation tax rates in effect when this text was written were used to calculate Celluphone's federal income tax expense.

5 Calculate the amount of the federal income tax expense adjustment.

The difference between the total federal income tax expense and the estimated tax already paid is the amount of the adjustment, $2,219.23 ($36,819.23 − $34,600.00 = $2,219.23).

Celluphone's federal income tax expense adjustment is shown in the T accounts. Celluphone paid quarterly federal income tax installments of $8,650.00 each. Federal Income Tax Expense has a debit balance of $34,600.00 at the end of the fiscal period before the adjustment is made.

To enter the adjustment for income tax expense, Celluphone debits Federal Income Tax Expense for $2,219.23 to show the increase in the balance of this expense account. The new balance of this account, $36,819.23, is the total federal income tax expense for the fiscal period. Federal Income Tax Payable is credited for $2,219.23 to show the increase in this liability account. Celluphone's federal income tax payable account balance, $2,219.23, is the amount of income tax expense still unpaid at year end. Celluphone's federal income tax expense adjustment is labeled *(i)* on lines 18 and 52 in the work sheet Adjustments columns, Illustration 26-4.

Federal Income Tax Expense is debited for the amount of the increase, $2,219.23. Federal Income Tax Payable is credited for the same amount.

FYI

The adjustment for federal income tax is the difference between the tax owed on the actual net income before federal income tax and the estimated amounts paid for the year.

Federal Income Tax Expense

4/15	8,650.00	
6/15	8,650.00	
9/15	8,650.00	
12/15	8,650.00	
(12/15 Bal.	*34,600.00*	
12/31 Adj. (i)	2,219.23	
(New Bal.	*36,819.23)*	

Federal Income Tax Payable

| | 12/31 Adj. (i) | 2,219.23 |

APPLIED SKILLS: MATHEMATICS

Use the MATH WORK SHEETS in the Masters and Solutions to Enrichment/Application Activities Section of the Teacher's Resource Guide to integrate applied mathematics. In these work sheets, students will apply math concepts to calculate net income before federal income tax and the adjustment for federal income tax expense.

Federal Income Tax Expense is an expense account. The account appears under a major division titled *Income Tax Expense* as the last item in Celluphone's chart of accounts. **Federal Income Tax Payable**, a liability account, appears under the heading *Current Liabilities*.

After the federal income tax expense adjustment is recorded, the Adjustments columns are totaled and ruled. Next, the balances of the income tax accounts are extended to the appropriate work sheet columns. The federal income tax expense account balance is extended to the Income Statement Debit column. The federal income tax payable account balance is extended to the Balance Sheet Credit column.

Completing a Work Sheet

The Income Statement and Balance Sheet columns are totaled. Totals are written as shown on line 53 of Celluphone's work sheet, Illustration 26-4. The Income Statement Credit column total for Celluphone is $2,073,973.00, which is more than the Income Statement Debit column total of $1,973,435.23. (The Credit column total, $2,073,973.00, *less* the Debit column total, $1,973,435.23, *equals* the difference, $100,537.77.) This amount, *$100,537.77*, is written in the Income Statement Debit column on line 54 of the work sheet. *Net Income after Federal Income Tax* is written in the Account Title column on the same line. Income Statement columns are then totaled as shown on line 55 of the work sheet.

The net income after federal income tax amount, $100,537.77, is written in the Balance Sheet Credit column, line 54. Balance Sheet columns are totaled as shown on line 55. The totals of both the Balance Sheet Debit and Balance Sheet Credit columns are the same and assumed to be correct. Double lines are ruled across the Income Statement and Balance Sheet columns on line 55 to show that the totals have been verified as correct.

The chart shown in Summary Illustration 26-5 on pages 696 and 697 summarizes the steps followed in preparing an 8-column work sheet for a corporation.

Audit Your Understanding

1. What type of adjusting entry is unique to corporations?

2. If a physical inventory shows that ending inventory is greater than beginning inventory, what is the entry to record the adjustment?

3. How is the amount of the federal income tax expense adjustment calculated?

AUDIT YOUR UNDERSTANDING

1. The adjustment for federal income tax expense.
2. Debit Merchandise Inventory, credit Income Summary.
3. Total federal income tax expense minus estimated taxes already paid in quarterly installments.

APPLIED SKILLS: WRITING ACROSS THE CURRICULUM

Writing paragraphs and short essays. The Cases for Critical Thinking are short, practical applications of the accounting principles developed in the chapter. Some cases are planned to present problems related to the chapter but not specifically discussed and answered in the chapter. These cases present an opportunity for critical thinking and decision making. These cases also require more than a short objective-type response. Therefore, they provide ideal practice in writing paragraphs and short essays.

SUMMARY ILLUSTRATION 26-5

Summary of preparing a work sheet for a corporation

1 Prepare a trial balance in the Trial Balance columns.

2 Analyze and record all adjustments except the federal income tax expense adjustment in the Adjustments columns.

3 Extend all amounts except the federal income tax expense account balance to the appropriate Income Statement or Balance Sheet columns.

4 On a separate sheet of paper, total the work sheet's Income Statement columns. Calculate the difference between the two totals. This difference is the net income before federal income tax.

Income Statement Credit column	$2,073,973.00
Less total of Income Statement Debit column	−1,936,616.00
Equals net income before federal income tax	$ 137,357.00

5 Calculate the amount of federal income tax expense.

6 Calculate and enter the federal income tax expense adjustment in the Adjustments columns.

Total federal income tax expense	$36,819.23
Less balance of Federal Income Tax Expense	−34,600.00
Equals federal income tax expense adjustment	$ 2,219.23

7 Total and rule the Adjustments columns.

8 Extend the federal income tax expense account balance to the Income Statement Debit column. Extend the federal income tax payable account balance to the Balance Sheet Credit column.

9 Total the Income Statement and Balance Sheet columns.

10 Calculate the net income or net loss.

11 Enter the amount of net income in the Income Statement Debit column and in the Balance Sheet Credit column. If there is a net loss, enter the amount of net loss in the Income Statement Credit column and in the Balance Sheet Debit column.

12 Total the four Income Statement and Balance Sheet amount columns.

13 Check that both totals of the Income Statement columns are the same and that both totals of the Balance Sheet columns are the same.

14 Rule double lines across the Income Statement and Balance Sheet column totals to show that the totals have been verified as correct.

PART 4   Accounting for a Merchandising Business Organized as a Corporation

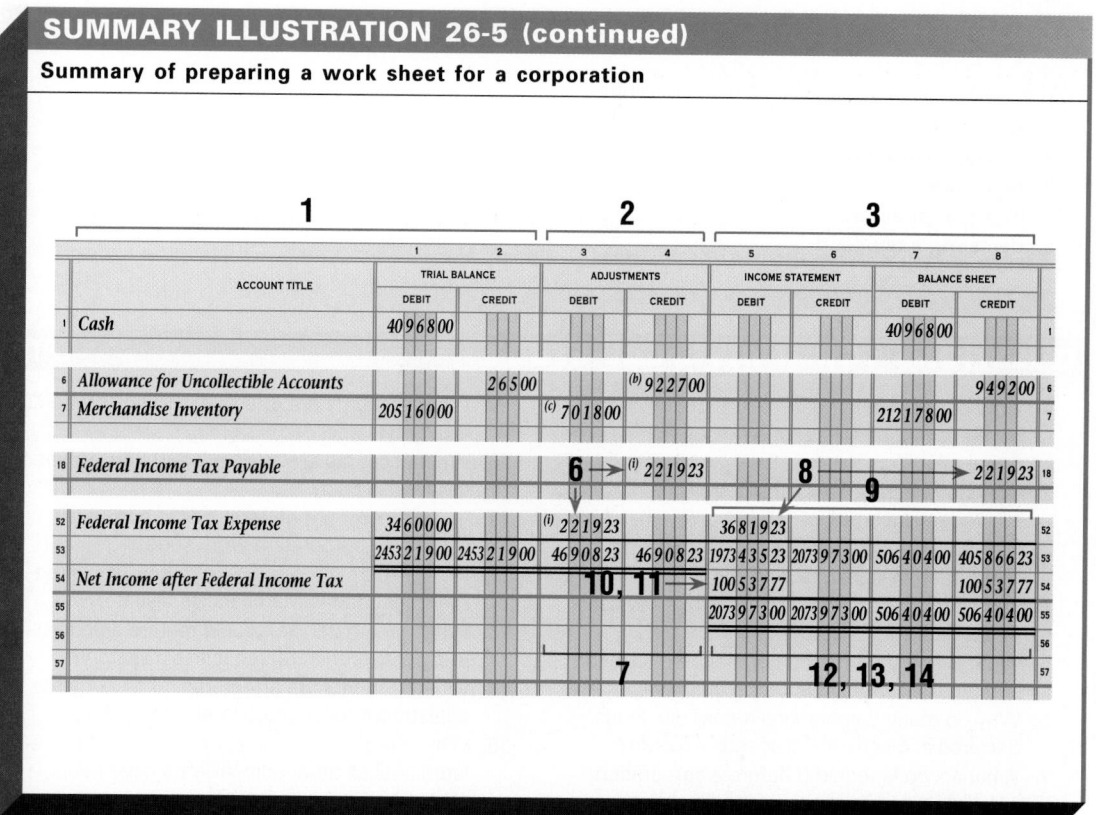

	1		2		3			
	TRIAL BALANCE		ADJUSTMENTS		INCOME STATEMENT		BALANCE SHEET	
ACCOUNT TITLE	DEBIT	CREDIT	DEBIT	CREDIT	DEBIT	CREDIT	DEBIT	CREDIT
1 Cash	40 96 8 00						40 96 8 00	
6 Allowance for Uncollectible Accounts		2 6 5 00		(b) 9 2 2 7 00				9 4 9 2 00
7 Merchandise Inventory	205 16 0 00		(c) 7 0 1 8 00				212 17 8 00	
18 Federal Income Tax Payable			**6** →	(i) 2 2 1 9 23		**8**	**9** →	2 2 1 9 23
52 Federal Income Tax Expense	34 6 0 0 00		(i) 2 2 1 9 23		36 8 1 9 23			
53	2453 2 1 9 00	2453 2 1 9 00	46 9 0 8 23	46 9 0 8 23	1973 4 3 5 23	2073 9 7 3 00	506 4 0 4 00	405 8 6 6 23
54 Net Income after Federal Income Tax			**10, 11** →		100 5 3 7 77			100 5 3 7 77
55					2073 9 7 3 00	2073 9 7 3 00	506 4 0 4 00	506 4 0 4 00
56								
57			**7**		**12, 13, 14**			

TEACHING STRATEGIES:
DIFFERENT LEARNING ABILITIES

Limited English Proficiency (LEP) Students. Adjust the length of time allotted to complete assignments and tests. Remember that the primary objective is to assess knowledge of accounting rather than the ability to translate and comprehend the question or problem.

ACCOUNTING TERMS

1. stockholder: An owner of one or more shares of a corporation. (p. 685)

2. retained earnings: An amount earned by a corporation and not yet distributed to stockholders. (p. 685)

3. dividends: Earnings distributed to stockholders. (p. 685)

4. board of directors: A group of persons elected by the stockholders to manage a corporation. (p. 686)

5. declaring a dividend: Action by a board of directors to distribute corporate earnings to stockholders. (p. 686)

QUESTIONS FOR INDIVIDUAL STUDY

1. (a) Different accounts are used to record owners' equity. (b) Different procedures are used to distribute income to owners. (c) Corporations calculate and pay federal income tax. (p. 685)

2. Proprietorship and partnership net income is treated as part of each owner's personal income for income tax purposes. Thus, federal income tax is not calculated for a proprietorship or partnership business. (p. 685)

3. One capital stock account. (p. 685)

4. In the stockholders' equity section. (p. 685)

5. Retained Earnings. (p. 685)

6. So that the total amounts of dividends are easily determined for each fiscal period. (p. 686)

7. Formal action, called declaring a dividend, by a corporation's board of directors. (p. 686)

8. When a corporation's board of directors declares a dividend, the liability for the dividend must be recorded in the accounts. (p. 686)

9. Dividends is debited; Dividends Payable is credited. (p. 686)

10. Dividends Payable is debited; Cash is credited. (p. 688)

11. All general ledger accounts are listed in the same order as they appear in the general ledger. (p. 689)

12. An ending merchandise inventory that is larger than the beginning merchandise inventory. (p. 692)

13. An ending merchandise inventory that is less than the beginning merchandise inventory. (p. 692)

14. Interest Expense is debited; Interest Payable is credited. (p. 693)

ACCOUNTING TERMS $\qquad$ EPT(a)

What is the meaning of each of the following?

1. **stockholder**
2. **retained earnings**
3. **dividends**
4. **board of directors**
5. **declaring a dividend**

QUESTIONS FOR INDIVIDUAL STUDY $\qquad$ EPT(b)

1. How does accounting for a corporation differ from accounting for a proprietorship or partnership?
2. Why don't partnerships and proprietorships pay federal income tax?
3. How many accounts are kept for the investment of all owners of a corporation?
4. In which chart of accounts division is the capital stock account listed?
5. What account does a corporation use to record earnings not yet distributed to stockholders?
6. Why do many corporations record dividends declared in a separate dividends account?
7. What action is required before a corporation can distribute income to its stockholders?
8. When is a dividend recorded as a liability in a corporation's general ledger accounts?
9. What accounts are affected, and how, when a dividend is declared?
10. What accounts are affected, and how, when a dividend is paid?
11. In what order are general ledger accounts listed on a corporation work sheet?
12. What circumstances would require an adjustment that debits **Merchandise Inventory**?
13. What circumstances would require an adjustment that credits **Merchandise Inventory**?
14. What accounts are affected, and how, by the adjustment for accrued interest expense?
15. Why is federal income tax expense not calculated until all other adjustments have been planned on a work sheet?
16. What accounts are affected, and how, by the adjustment for federal income tax expense?

CASES FOR CRITICAL THINKING $\qquad$ EPT(b)

CASE 1 Fahle Company's net income has been fluctuating between a small net income and a small net loss during the first four years of the corporation's existence. The company is hoping to earn $12.00 per share during its fifth year. Janet Riley, newly appointed president of Fahle Company, believes the corporation needs to take some positive action to regain the confidence of the stockholders. She suggests the corporation declare a $10.00 per share dividend December 15 to be paid February 1. By February 1 financial statements for Fahle's fifth year ending December 31 will be completed so the net income earned for the year will be known. Mrs. Riley also suggests that if the net income is not as high as expected, the board of directors can cancel the declared dividend before it is paid. Do you agree with Mrs. Riley's proposal? Explain.

CASE 2 At the beginning of the current year, Bower Company changed its organization from a partnership to a corporation. The president suggested that since the same six individuals owned the corporation as had owned the partnership, the same procedures should be used for paying income tax on the earnings of the business. The net income of the corporation would be treated as part of each corporation owner's personal income for income tax purposes. "If this procedure is followed," said the president, "the corporation will not need to pay any income tax." Do you agree with the president's suggestion? Explain.

DRILLS FOR UNDERSTANDING

EPT(d,e)

DRILL 26-D1 Analyzing adjustments on a work sheet

TUTORIAL

A form for analyzing adjustments is given in the working papers that accompany this textbook.

INSTRUCTIONS:

For each of the following adjustments, write the title of the account debited and the title of the account credited.

1. Supplies
2. Accrued interest income
3. Merchandise inventory (increased)
4. Merchandise inventory (decreased)
5. Uncollectible accounts expense
6. Prepaid insurance
7. Depreciation expense—store equipment
8. Accrued interest expense
9. Additional federal income tax owed

DRILL 26-D2 Extending account balances on a work sheet

A form for analyzing extending account balances on a work sheet is given in the working papers that accompany this textbook.

INSTRUCTIONS:

For each of the following accounts, place a check mark in the work sheet column to which the account balance should be extended.

1. Allowance for Uncollectible Accounts
2. Sales Returns and Allowances
3. Notes Payable
4. Retained Earnings
5. Accounts Receivable
6. Purchases Discount
7. Merchandise Inventory
8. Dividends
9. Federal Income Tax Expense
10. Accumulated Depreciation—Store Equipment

APPLICATION PROBLEMS

EPT(c,d,e)

PROBLEM 26-1 Journalizing dividends

Century Center Corporation completed the following transactions during December of the current year and January of the next year.

Dec. 15. The board of directors declared a dividend of $10.00 per share; capital stock issued is 1,500 shares; total dividend, $15,000.00. Date of payment is January 15. M126.

Jan. 15. Paid cash for dividend declared December 15, $15,000.00. C432.

INSTRUCTIONS:

1. Use page 12 of a general journal. Journalize the dividend declared on December 15.
2. Use page 15 of a cash payments journal. Journalize payment of the dividend.

15. The amount of tax is based on the amount of net income before the tax is recorded. Therefore, all other adjustments must be planned and net income before federal income tax must be calculated before federal income tax expense can be determined. (p. 693)

16. Federal Income Tax Expense is debited; Federal Income Tax Payable is credited. (p. 694)

CASES FOR CRITICAL THINKING

Case 1   Mrs. Riley's proposal is not acceptable for two major reasons. (1) A corporation cannot declare dividends that exceed the retained earnings account balance. The retained earnings account balance represents the corporation's earnings that have been retained in the corporation. Dividends are a distribution of a corporation's earnings to its stockholders. If there are no earnings available, dividends cannot be declared. Since Fahle Company apparently has earned little net income in its first four years, the current year's earnings would need to be sufficient to cover any dividends declared. Since the current year's earnings are not yet known on December 15, there probably is an insufficient balance in the retained earnings account to cover the dividends declared. (2) When dividends are declared, the corporation is obligated to pay the dividend and a liability is recorded in the accounts. The board of directors is not required to declare a dividend. However, after a dividend is declared and the liability created, the liability must be paid. Therefore, Mrs. Riley's proposal to cancel the dividend if net income is not adequate cannot be done. The corporation has a legal obligation to pay this liability just as it is obligated to pay other liabilities.

Case 2   The president's suggestion is not acceptable. Partnership income is correctly treated as part of the owners' personal income for income tax purposes. However, corporations are required to calculate and pay income tax on their net income.

PROBLEM 26-2 Preparing a work sheet for a corporation

Eagle System Corporation's general ledger accounts and balances are recorded on a work sheet in the working papers.

INSTRUCTIONS:

Complete the work sheet for the current year ended December 31. Record the adjustments on the work sheet using the following information.

Adjustment Information, December 31

Accrued interest income	$ 277.20
Uncollectible accounts expense estimated as 1.5% of sales on account. Sales on account for year, $499,000.00.	
Merchandise inventory	90,066.26
Supplies inventory	327.88
Value of prepaid insurance	3,023.60
Annual depreciation expense—office equipment	2,690.00
Annual depreciation expense—store equipment	1,607.60
Accrued interest expense	545.16
Federal income tax expense for the year	21,446.41

ENRICHMENT PROBLEMS   EPT(c,d,e)

MASTERY PROBLEM 26-M Journalizing dividends and preparing a work sheet for a corporation

Universal Corporation's general ledger accounts and balances are recorded on a work sheet in the working papers.

INSTRUCTIONS:

1. Complete the work sheet for the current year ended December 31. Record the adjustments on the work sheet using the following information.

Adjustment Information, December 31

Accrued interest income	$ 118.00
Uncollectible accounts expense estimated as 1.0% of sales on account. Sales on account for year, $407,800.00.	
Merchandise inventory	123,952.00
Supplies inventory	1,592.10
Value of prepaid insurance	5,906.00
Annual depreciation expense—office equipment	1,386.00
Annual depreciation expense—store equipment	9,800.00
Accrued interest expense	94.00
Federal income tax expense for the year	12,950.28

2. Use page 36 of a cash payments journal. Journalize the following transaction completed during the next year. The abbreviation for check is C.

Jan. 15. Paid cash for quarterly dividend declared December 15, $10,500.00. C604.

CHALLENGE PROBLEM 26-C Preparing a 10-column work sheet for a corporation

Austin Sports Center's general ledger accounts and balances are recorded on a 10-column work sheet in the working papers.

INSTRUCTIONS:

Complete the 10-column work sheet for the current year ended December 31. Record the adjustments on the work sheet using the following information.

Adjustment Information, December 31

Accrued interest income....................................... $ 119.25
Uncollectible accounts expense estimated as 1.5% of sales on account.
   Sales on account for year, $306,933.33.
Merchandise inventory 81,356.00
Supplies inventory 1,872.00
Value of prepaid insurance 4,440.00
Annual depreciation expense—office equipment 1,360.00
Annual depreciation expense—store equipment................... 15,304.00
Accrued interest expense...................................... 57.00
Federal income tax for the year is calculated at the following rates:
   15% of net income before taxes, zero to $50,000.00.
   Plus 25% of net income before taxes, $50,000.00 to $75,000.00.
   Plus 34% of net income before taxes, $75,000.00 to $100,000.00.
   Plus 39% of net income before taxes, $100,000.00 to $335,000.00.
   Plus 34% of net income before taxes over $335,000.00.

Chapter 27 includes the preparation of financial statements and journalizing adjusting, closing and re-versing entries. Reversing entries for accrued interest income and accrued interest expense are first de-scribed in Chapter 25 and reinforced in this chapter. The end-of-fiscal-period activities in the problems in this chapter include these reversing entries. Financial statement analysis is expanded in this chapter from the presentation in the first two accounting cycles. Income statement component percentages are

GUIDE TO ACHIEVING LEARNING OBJECTIVES

Enabling Performance Tasks	TEACH Lesson Plans	APPLY Drills for Understanding	Application Problems	Mastery Problems	Challenge Problems	Cases for Critical Thinking	Recycling Problems	Reinforcement Activity
a. Define accounting terms related to financial statements.	27-1							
b. Identify accounting concepts and practices related to financial statements and end-of-fiscal-period entries.	27-1, 27-2	27-D1, 27-D2				Cases 1, 2		
c. Prepare and analyze an income statement.	27-1		27-1	27-M	27-C		27-R	3B
d. Prepare a statement of stockholders' equity.	27-1		27-1	27-M	27-C		27-R	3B
e. Prepare and analyze a balance sheet.	27-1		27-1	27-M	27-C		27-R	3B
f. Record adjusting and closing entries.	27-2		27-2	27-M	27-C		27-R	3B
g. Record reversing entries.	27-2		27-2	27-M	27-C		27-R	3B

ENRICHMENT

SPECIAL FEATURES
Professional Business Ethics, page 724

Spreadsheet Options, page 715

TECHNOLOGY CONNECTION
Automated Accounting 6.0 Problem 27-C
Integrating Automated Accounting Topic 10 Optional Problem DB-10A

Accounting Tutorial Units 8, 9, 10

Spreadsheet Template Problem 27-M

Electronic Study Guide

NEW, REVIEW, AND EXTENSION

ACTIVITIES/CONCEPTS/TRANSACTIONS	NEW	REVIEW/EXTENSION
Preparing an income statement for a corporation		✓
Preparing a statement of stockholders' equity	✓	
Preparing a balance sheet for a corporation		✓
Calculating component percentages		✓
Calculating financial strength: Working capital Current ratio	✓ ✓	
Recording adjusting entries for a corporation		✓
Recording closing entries for a corporation		✓
Recording reversing entries for a corporation		✓

calculated for six items: (a) cost of merchandise sold; (b) gross profit on operations; (c) total operating expenses; (d) income from operations; (e) net addition or deduction from other revenue and expenses; and (f) net income before federal income tax. In addition, financial strength is analyzed from the balance sheet by calculating (a) working capital and (b) current ratio.

	INFORMAL ASSESSMENT		FORMAL ASSESSMENT				
	Study Guide	Audit Your Understanding	Chapter MicroExam	Chapter Problem Test	Unit Problem Test	Unit Objective Test	Portfolio
Unit A		✓	✓			✓	
Unit B		✓	✓			✓	
				✓			✓
							✓
				✓			✓
Unit C				✓	✓		✓
Unit C				✓	✓		✓

TEACHING MATERIALS

Teacher's Wraparound Edition of the Text

Teacher's Resource Guide

Teacher's Edition of Working Papers

Teacher's Edition of Demonstration/Recycling Problems

Teaching Transparencies

Accounting Tutorial Manual

MicroExam

Key for Western Rider, Inc.

Applied Math Work Sheet

APPLIED MATHEMATICS

APPLIED MATH/ACCOUNTING SKILL	APPLICATION
Calculating Component Percentages	Prob. 27-1
Calculating Retained Earnings	Prob. 27-1
Calculating Working Capital and the Current Ratio	Prob. 27-1

Financial Statements and End-of-Fiscal-Period Entries for a Corporation

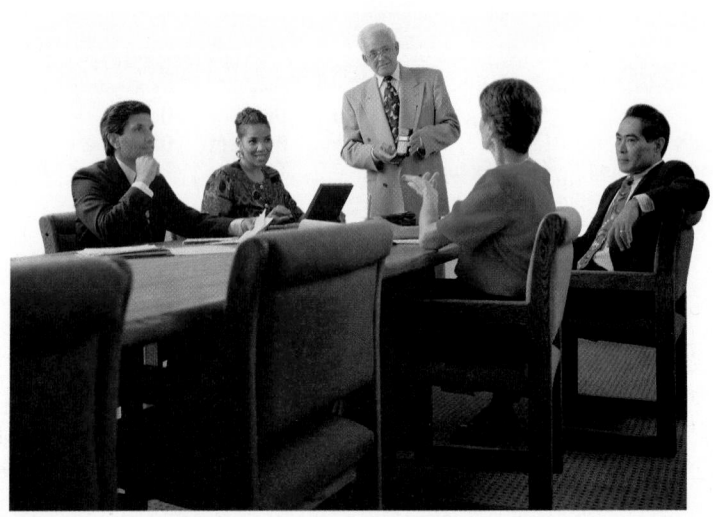

ENABLING PERFORMANCE TASKS

After studying Chapter 27, you will be able to:

a Define accounting terms related to financial statements for a merchandising business organized as a corporation.

b Identify accounting concepts and practices related to financial statements and end-of-fiscal-period entries for a merchandising business organized as a corporation.

c Prepare and analyze an income statement for a merchandising business organized as a corporation.

d Prepare a statement of stockholders' equity for a merchandising business organized as a corporation.

e Prepare and analyze a balance sheet for a merchandising business organized as a corporation.

f Record adjusting and closing entries for a merchandising business organized as a corporation.

g Record reversing entries for a merchandising business organized as a corporation.

702

net sales • net purchases • statement of stockholders' equity • book value • long-term liabilities • working capital • ratio • current ratio

Corporations prepare financial statements that report financial information similar to the information reported by proprietorships and partnerships. To provide the corporation's managers and stockholders with information on how well the corporation is progressing, financial statements are prepared annually and sometimes monthly or quarterly. *(CONCEPT: Accounting Period Cycle)*

FINANCIAL STATEMENTS FOR A CORPORATION

Financial statements are used to report a business' financial progress and condition as well as changes in the owners' equity. To report this information, Celluphone prepares three financial statements. (1) Income statement. (2) Statement of stockholders' equity. (3) Balance sheet.

A corporation prepares an income statement and a balance sheet similar to those used by proprietorships and partnerships. However, a corporation reports changes in owners' equity differently. First, owners' equity for all owners is reported as a single amount rather than for each owner. Second, owners' equity is reported in two categories. (1) Capital contributed by the owners. (2) Capital earned by the corporation.

Income Statement

An income statement reports financial progress of a business during a fiscal period. *(CONCEPT: Accounting Period Cycle)* Revenue, cost of merchandise sold, gross profit on operations, operating expenses, and net income or net loss are reported on an income statement. *(CONCEPT: Adequate Disclosure)* To help make decisions about current and future operations, Celluphone also analyzes relationships between revenue and expense items. Based on this analysis, Celluphone reports component percentages for all major income statement items.

Component percentages help analyze the relationships between revenue and expense items.

Preparing an Income Statement. Celluphone's income statement is prepared from information found in the Trial Balance, Income Statement, and Balance Sheet columns of the work sheet, Illustration 27-1, shown on pages 704–705.

Procedures for preparing Celluphone's income statement are similar to those used by any merchandising business. Celluphone's income statement for the current year ended December 31 is shown in Illustration 27-2 on page 706.

LESSON PLAN 27-1

Materials

- Student pages 703–716
- Transparency: 27-1, Chapter Summary
- Software: Spreadsheet Template
- Math Work Sheet Chapter 27: Part A: Calculating Component Percentages; Part B: Calculating Retained Earnings; Part C: Calculating Working Capital and the Current Ratio (TRG)
- Demonstration Problems: 27A, Preparing an Income Statement for a Corporation; 27B, Preparing a Statement of Stockholders' Equity; 27C, Preparing a Balance Sheet for a Corporation

Objectives (Enabling Performance Tasks)

a. Define accounting terms related to financial statements for a merchandising business organized as a corporation.

b. Identify accounting concepts and practices related to financial statements and end-of-fiscal-period entries for a merchandising business organized as a corporation.

c. Prepare and analyze an income statement for a merchandising business organized as a corporation.

d. Prepare a statement of stockholders' equity for a merchandising business organized as a corporation.

e. Prepare and analyze a balance sheet for a merchandising business organized as a corporation.

- In Parts 2 and 3, financial statements used by proprietorships and partnerships were presented. Explain that a corporation prepares an income statement and a balance sheet similar to those used by proprietorships and partnerships. However, a corporation reports changes in owners' equity differently. In this lesson, we will prepare the three financial statements used by a corporation.

- Introduce new vocabulary: net sales, net purchases, statement of stockholders' equity, book value, long-term liabilities, working capital, ratio, current ratio.

ILLUSTRATION 27-1   Work sheet for a corporation

Celluphone, Inc.
Work Sheet
For Year Ended December 31, 19--

ACCOUNT TITLE	TRIAL BALANCE DEBIT	TRIAL BALANCE CREDIT	ADJUSTMENTS DEBIT	ADJUSTMENTS CREDIT	INCOME STATEMENT DEBIT	INCOME STATEMENT CREDIT	BALANCE SHEET DEBIT	BALANCE SHEET CREDIT
1 Cash	4096800						4096800	
2 Petty Cash	30000						30000	
3 Notes Receivable	55000						55000	
4 Interest Receivable			(a) 1100				1100	
5 Accounts Receivable	6824000						6824000	
6 Allowance for Uncollectible Accounts		26500		(b) 922700				949200
7 Merchandise Inventory	20516000		(c) 701800				21217800	
8 Supplies	1545500			(d) 1169000			376500	
9 Prepaid Insurance	1355000			(e) 859800			495200	
10 Office Equipment	1825000						1825000	
11 Accumulated Depreciation—Office Equip.		362500		(f) 175000				537500
12 Store Equipment	7719000						7719000	
13 Accumulated Depreciation—Store Equip.		912500		(g) 632500				1545000
14 Notes Payable		2800000						2800000
15 Interest Payable				(h) 7000				7000
16 Accounts Payable		8396575						8396575
17 Employee Income Tax Payable		234000						234000
18 Federal Income Tax Payable				(i) 221923				221923
19 FICA Tax Payable		269500						269500
20 Sales Tax Payable		1098200						1098200
21 Unemployment Tax Payable—Federal		4700						4700
22 Unemployment Tax Payable—State		31725						31725
23 Health Insurance Premiums Payable		99500						99500
24 Dividends Payable		2000000						2000000
25 Capital Stock		10000000						10000000

#	Account Title	Trial Balance Dr	Trial Balance Cr	Adjustments Dr	Adjustments Cr	Income Statement Dr	Income Statement Cr	Balance Sheet Dr	Balance Sheet Cr
26	Retained Earnings		149 11800						149 11800
27	Dividends	8000000						8000000	
28	Income Summary				(c) 701800		701800		
29	Sales		2050 44000				2050 44000		
30	Sales Discount	564200				564200			
31	Sales Returns and Allowances	2431800				2431800			
32	Purchases	1454 79800				1454 79800			
33	Purchases Discount		1076600				1076600		
34	Purchases Returns and Allowances		531000				531000		
35	Advertising Expense	3260000				3260000			
36	Credit Card Fee Expense	2046800				2046800			
37	Depr. Expense—Office Equipment			(f) 175000		175000			
38	Depr. Expense—Store Equipment			(g) 632500		632500			
39	Insurance Expense			(e) 859800		859800			
40	Miscellaneous Expense	2235000				2235000			
41	Payroll Taxes Expense	2372000				2372000			
42	Rent Expense	5640000				5640000			
43	Salary Expense	251 93200				251 93200			
44	Supplies Expense			(d) 1169000		1169000			
45	Uncollectible Accounts Expense			(b) 922700		922700			
46	Utilities Expense	489000				489000			
47	Gain on Plant Assets		22500				22500		
48	Interest Income		20300		(a) 1100		21400		
49	Cash Short and Over	300				300			
50	Interest Expense	137500		(h) 7000		144500			
51	Loss on Plant Assets	46000				46000			
52	Federal Income Tax Expense	3460000		(i) 221923		3681923			
53		2453 21900	2453 21900	4690823	4690823	1973 43523	2073 97300	5064 0400	4058 6623
54	Net Income after Federal Income Tax					100 53777			100 53777
55						2073 97300	2073 97300	5064 0400	5064 0400
56									

- List the three financial statements on the board.
- Present the income statement. Direct students to Illustrations 27-3 and 27-4. (1) Explain how to calculate net sales. (2) Explain how to calculate net purchases.
- Present the statement of stockholders' equity. Direct students to Illustration 27-7. Place the formula on the board for determining capital stock: Beginning Balance of Capital Stock + Shares Issued during Year = Ending Balance of Capital Stock. Place the formula on the board for determining retained earnings: Beginning Balance of Retained Earnings + Net Income after Tax − Dividends Declared = Ending Balance of Retained Earnings.
- List the formula for working capital on the board: Total Current Assets − Total Current Liabilities = Working Capital.
- List the formula for the current ratio on the board: Total Current Assets ÷ Total Current Liabilities = Current Ratio.

Guided Practice

Guide students through Drills 27-D1 and 27-D2. Students should have the forms from the working papers to complete as you guide them through classifying each account. All students should agree with the classification for each account before proceeding to the next account.

Independent Practice

Assign Terms 1–8, Questions 1–17, and Problem 27-1.

ILLUSTRATION 27-2   Income statement for a corporation

Celluphone, Inc.
Income Statement
For Year Ended December 31, 19--

				% of Net Sales
Operating Revenue:				
Sales.............................			$2,050,440.00	
Less: Sales Discount	$ 5,642.00			
Sales Ret. and Allow.	24,318.00		29,960.00	
Net Sales........................			$2,020,480.00	100.0
Cost of Merchandise Sold:				
Merchandise Inv., Jan. 1, 19--........			$ 205,160.00	
Purchases........................		$1,454,798.00		
Less: Purchases Discount	$10,766.00			
Purch. Ret. and Allow.	5,310.00	16,076.00		
Net Purchases....................			1,438,722.00	
Total Cost of Mdse. Avail. for Sale			$1,643,882.00	
Less Mdse. Inventory, Dec. 31, 19--...			212,178.00	
Cost of Merchandise Sold..........			1,431,704.00	70.9
Gross Profit on Operations...........			$ 588,776.00	29.1
Operating Expenses:				
Advertising Expense..............		$ 32,600.00		
Credit Card Fee Expense		20,468.00		
Depreciation Exp.—Office Equip......		1,750.00		
Depreciation Exp.—Store Equip.......		6,325.00		
Insurance Expense		8,598.00		
Miscellaneous Expense		22,350.00		
Payroll Taxes Expense		23,720.00		
Rent Expense....................		56,400.00		
Salary Expense...................		251,932.00		
Supplies Expense		11,690.00		
Uncollectible Accounts Expense......		9,227.00		
Utilities Expense.................		4,890.00		
Total Operating Expenses..........			449,950.00	22.3
Income from Operations			$ 138,826.00	6.9
Other Revenue:				
Gain on Plant Assets..............	$ 225.00			
Interest Income..................	214.00			
Total Other Revenue..............		$ 439.00		
Other Expenses:				
Cash Short and Over..............	$ 3.00			
Interest Expense.................	1,445.00			
Loss on Plant Assets	460.00			
Total Other Expenses.............		1,908.00		
Net Deduction....................			1,469.00	0.1
Net Income before Fed. Inc. Tax			$ 137,357.00	6.8
Less Federal Income Tax Exp.			36,819.23	1.8
Net Income after Fed. Inc. Tax			$ 100,537.77	5.0

Celluphone's income statement differs in four ways from Car-Land's income statement shown in Part 3.

1. Net sales is listed in the Operating Revenue section. Total sales less sales discount and sales returns and allowances is called **net sales**. Net sales is reported in the Operating Revenue section of Celluphone's income statement, as shown in Illustration 27-3.

ILLUSTRATION 27-3   Net sales reported on an income statement

			% of Net Sales
Operating Revenue:			
Sales.............................		$2,050,440.00	
Less: Sales Discount	$ 5,642.00		
Sales Ret. and Allow.	24,318.00	29,960.00	
Net Sales........................		$2,020,480.00	100.0

2. Net purchases is reported in the Cost of Merchandise Sold section. Total purchases less purchases discount and purchases returns and allowances is called **net purchases**. Net purchases is reported in the Cost of Merchandise Sold section of Celluphone's income statement, as shown in Illustration 27-4.

ILLUSTRATION 27-4   Net purchases reported on an income statement

Cost of Merchandise Sold:			
Merchandise Inv., Jan. 1, 19--.........		$ 205,160.00	
Purchases........................	$1,454,798.00		
Less: Purchases Discount	$10,766.00		
Purch. Ret. and Allow.	5,310.00	16,076.00	
Net Purchases....................		1,438,722.00	

3. Income from operations is reported separately from net income. Income from operations is the income earned only from normal business activities. Celluphone's normal business activities are selling cellular phones to corporate customers. Other revenue and expenses, such as interest income, interest expense, and gains or losses on plant assets, are not normal business activities. Other revenue and expenses are not included in calculating income from operations.

4. Net income before and net income after federal income tax are reported separately. Reporting net income before and after federal income tax is unique to corporation income statements. Corporations pay federal income tax on their net income. However, federal income taxes are not paid by proprietorships and

☞☞ FYI ☞☞

Corporations report net income before and after federal income taxes.

TEACHING STRATEGIES: DIFFERENT LEARNING STYLES

Auditory Learner. The auditory learner can reinforce the learning of formulas by verbally explaining the formula and/or calculations to other students in a small group. In a group of three, for example, each student should get the opportunity to "teach" the formula to the other two students. Through this process, each student in the group will "teach" the formula once and "learn" the formula two times.

CLOSURE

- Use Audit Your Understanding questions.

- Review Summary Illustration 27-11, "Summary of Financial Statements for a Corporation" or use Transparency 27-1 Chapter Summary.

partnerships because they are paid by the owners. Thus, proprietorships and partnerships do not report federal income tax on their income statements. Net income is reported in the Net Income section of Celluphone's income statement as shown in Illustration 27-5.

ILLUSTRATION 27-5   Federal income tax reported on an income statement

Net Income before Fed. Inc. Tax	$ 137,357.00	6.8
Less Federal Income Tax Exp.	36,819.23	1.8
Net Income after Fed. Inc. Tax	$ 100,537.77	5.0

Analyzing an Income Statement. For a business to determine whether it is progressing satisfactorily, results of operations are compared with industry standards and/or previous fiscal periods. To provide meaningful comparisons, the same accounting concepts must be followed for preparing the income statements for each fiscal period. *(CONCEPT: Consistent Reporting)*

To help management improve future fiscal periods, items contributing to net income should be analyzed. By analyzing items of revenue, cost, and expense, items that should be improved can be identified.

The percentage relationship between one financial statement item and the total that includes that item is known as a component percentage. Celluphone prepares component percentages for six major items on its income statement. Celluphone uses net sales as the base for calculating component percentages. The amount of each item on the income statement is divided by the amount of net sales. Thus, each component percentage shows the percentage that item is of net sales. For example, Celluphone's cost of merchandise sold component percentage is calculated as shown below.

	Cost of Merchandise Sold	÷	Net Sales	=	Cost of Merchandise Sold Component Percentage
	$1,431,704.00	÷	$2,020,480.00	=	70.9%

FYI

A limited liability company (LLC) provides the limited protection of a corporation.

This component percentage indicates that during the current fiscal year, Celluphone spent 70.9 cents out of each $1.00 of sales for the merchandise sold. Component percentages for each major item on Celluphone's income statement are listed in a separate column in Illustration 27-2.

When analyzing an income statement, Celluphone first reviews the component percentages for the six major items. (1) Cost of merchandise sold. (2) Gross profit on operations. (3) Total operating expenses. (4) Income from operations. (5) Net addition or deduction from other revenue and expenses. (6) Net income before federal income tax. The last two items on the income statement, federal income tax expense and net income after federal income tax, are important. Celluphone does not have much control over these two items because the tax rate, set by the Internal Revenue Service, determines these amounts. However, the company is interested in what portion of each sales dollar is paid to the federal government for income taxes. Therefore, the component percentage for federal income tax is calculated. Celluphone also calculates the component percentage for net income after federal income tax.

Acceptable Component Percentages. Based on comparisons with industry standards as well as previous accounting periods, Celluphone has determined acceptable component percentages for each major item of cost and expense on its income statement. For comparative purposes, Celluphone's acceptable and actual component percentages are shown in Illustration 27-6.

ILLUSTRATION 27-6   Income statement acceptable component percentages

Income Statement Items	Acceptable Component Percentages	Actual Component Percentages
Net sales	100.0%	100.0%
Cost of merchandise sold	not more than 71.0%	70.9%
Gross profit on operations	not less than 29.0%	29.1%
Total operating expenses	not more than 22.4%	22.3%
Income from operations	not less than 6.6%	6.9%
Net deduction	not more than 0.1%	0.1%
Net income before federal income tax	not less than 6.5%	6.8%

If the component percentage of any cost or expense item for a fiscal period exceeds the acceptable percentage, that cost or expense is reviewed further to determine the reason. After determining the reason why a cost or expense exceeded the acceptable percentage, ways are sought to bring the expense within acceptable limits.

Achieving acceptable component percentages for the six major income statement items indicates that the business is keeping costs and expenses at an acceptable level compared with revenue. For the current year ended December 31, Celluphone has achieved acceptable percentages for all six major items. Component percentages for cost of merchandise sold, 70.9%, total operating expenses, 22.3%, and deductions for other revenue and expenses, 0.1%, are all equal to or less than the maximum acceptable level for each item, a positive result. The component percentages for gross profit on operations, 29.1%, income from operations, 6.9%, and net income before federal income tax, 6.8%, are all more than the minimum acceptable percentage for each item, a positive result.

However, if a major item shows a negative result, further analysis should be made of each item to determine and correct any negative results of individual income statement items. For example, in the previous fiscal period, the component percentage for Celluphone's total operating expenses was more than the acceptable level, a negative result. A further review of each expense item showed that component percentages for salary expense and payroll taxes expense were higher than the acceptable percentages, a negative result. Further investigation revealed that Celluphone had employed additional temporary employees during the company's busy season. However, during the year, Celluphone retained these temporary employees two months longer than needed because of a lack of coordination between managers. Since the cause of the excessive salary expense was identified, Celluphone took action to more carefully control these expenses in the future.

Statement of Stockholders' Equity

A financial statement that shows changes in a corporation's ownership for a fiscal period is called a **statement of stockholders' equity.** A statement of stockholders' equity is similar to the owners' equity statement for a partnership.

A statement of stockholders' equity contains two major sections. (1) Capital stock. (2) Retained earnings. Celluphone's statement of stockholders' equity for the current year ended December 31 is shown in Illustration 27-7.

👈👈 **FYI** 👉👉

A statement of stockholder's equity is similar to the owner's equity statement for a partnership.

ILLUSTRATION 27-7   Statement of stockholders' equity for a corporation

Celluphone, Inc.
Statement of Stockholders' Equity
For Year Ended December 31, 19--

Capital Stock:			
$100.00 Per Share			
January 1, 19--, 1,000 Shares Issued		$100,000.00	
Issued during Current Year, None.		0	
Balance, December 31, 19--, 1,000 Shares Issued			$100,000.00
Retained Earnings:			
Balance, January 1, 19--		$149,118.00	
Net Income after Federal Income Tax for 19--	$100,537.77		
Less Dividends Declared during 19--.	80,000.00		
Net Increase during 19--		20,537.77	
Balance, December 31, 19--			169,655.77
Total Stockholders' Equity, December 31, 19--.			$269,655.77

The first section of Celluphone's statement of stockholders' equity shows that the corporation started the current fiscal year on January 1 with $100,000.00 in capital stock. This capital stock consisted of 1,000 shares of stock issued in previous years at $100.00 per share. During the current fiscal year, no additional capital stock was issued. Thus, at the end of the current fiscal year, Celluphone still has $100,000.00 capital stock issued. This information is obtained from the previous year's statement and the capital stock account.

The second section of Celluphone's statement of stockholders' equity shows that Celluphone started the current fiscal year on January 1 with $149,118.00 retained earnings. This amount represents previous years' earnings that have been kept in the business and not distributed to stockholders. For the current fiscal year ended December 31, Celluphone earned net income after federal income tax of $100,537.77. This amount is obtained from line 54 of the work sheet, Illustration 27-1.

Net income increases a corporation's total capital. Some income may be retained by a corporation for business expansion. Some income may be distributed to stockholders as a return on their investments.

During the year, Celluphone's board of directors declared $80,000.00 in dividends. The amount of dividends declared is obtained from line 27 of the work sheet's Balance Sheet Debit column. Changes in Celluphone's retained earnings during the current fiscal year are calculated as shown below.

Retained earnings balance, January 1, 19--		$149,118.00
Net income after federal income tax for 19--	$100,537.77	
Less dividends declared during 19--	− 80,000.00	
Net increase during 19--		+ 20,537.77
Retained earnings balance, December 31, 19--		$169,655.77

Celluphone's capital stock, $100,000.00, plus retained earnings, $169,655.77, equals total stockholders' equity on December 31, $269,655.77.

Balance Sheet

A corporation balance sheet reports assets, liabilities, and stockholders' equity on a specific date. *(CONCEPT: Accounting Period Cycle)*

Celluphone's balance sheet, shown in Illustration 27-8 on page 712, is prepared from information found in the Balance Sheet columns of the work sheet, Illustration 27-1, and the statement of stockholders' equity, Illustration 27-7.

Classifying Assets. Celluphone classifies its assets into two categories. (1) Current assets. (2) Plant assets. These categories are based on the length of time the assets will be in use. A business owning both current assets and plant assets usually lists them under separate headings on a balance sheet.

Cash and other assets expected to be exchanged for cash or consumed within a year are known as current assets. Current assets

---

FYI

Many business people refer to watching the "bottom line." The bottom line usually refers to the net income amount on the income statement, the last or "bottom" line of the statement.

FYI

The balance sheet can be used to determine the financial strength of a business.

TEACHING STRATEGIES: DIFFERENT LEARNING STYLES

Print Learner. When learning formulas, the print learner would prefer to be able to study the formula as given in the textbook or as printed on a separate handout. The print material should show the formula as well as an example of performing the calculations.

TEACHING STRATEGIES: COOPERATIVE LEARNING

Develop a better way to classify assets: Assign students to groups of three. Give students a deck of cards with one asset listed on each card. Ask each group to physically group these asset cards to develop a better system of classifying assets. Each group should explain their system to one other group. Time frame: 30 minutes.

ILLUSTRATION 27-8   Balance sheet for a corporation

Celluphone, Inc.
Balance Sheet
December 31, 19--

ASSETS

Current Assets:			
Cash		$ 40,968.00	
Petty Cash		300.00	
Notes Receivable		550.00	
Interest Receivable		11.00	
Accounts Receivable	$68,240.00		
Less Allowance for Uncollectible Accounts	9,492.00	58,748.00	
Merchandise Inventory		212,178.00	
Supplies		3,765.00	
Prepaid Insurance		4,952.00	
Total Current Assets			$321,472.00
Plant Assets:			
Office Equipment	$18,250.00		
Less Accumulated Depreciation—Office Equipment	5,375.00	$ 12,875.00	
Store Equipment	$77,190.00		
Less Accumulated Depreciation—Store Equipment	15,450.00	61,740.00	
Total Plant Assets			74,615.00
Total Assets			$396,087.00

LIABILITIES

Current Liabilities:		
Notes Payable	$ 2,800.00	
Interest Payable	70.00	
Accounts Payable	83,965.75	
Employee Income Tax Payable	2,340.00	
Federal Income Tax Payable	2,219.23	
FICA Tax Payable	2,695.00	
Sales Tax Payable	10,982.00	
Unemployment Tax Payable—Federal	47.00	
Unemployment Tax Payable—State	317.25	
Health Insurance Premiums Payable	995.00	
Dividends Payable	20,000.00	
Total Liabilities		$126,431.23

STOCKHOLDERS' EQUITY

Capital Stock	$100,000.00	
Retained Earnings	169,655.77	
Total Stockholders' Equity		269,655.77
Total Liabilities and Stockholders' Equity		$396,087.00

include such items as cash, accounts receivable, merchandise inventory, supplies, and prepaid insurance. Assets that will be used for a number of years in the operation of a business are known as plant assets. Plant assets include such items as cash registers, computers, and display cases.

Reporting Book Value of Assets. An account that reduces a related account on financial statements is known as a contra account. Celluphone reports three contra accounts on its balance sheet. (1) Allowance for Uncollectible Accounts. (2) Accumulated Depreciation—Office Equipment. (3) Accumulated Depreciation—Store Equipment. The difference between an asset's account balance and its related contra account balance is called **book value.** Celluphone reports the book value for Accounts Receivable and the two equipment accounts on its balance sheet. An asset's book value is reported on a balance sheet by listing three amounts. (1) The balance of the asset account. (2) The balance of the asset's contra account. (3) Book value. Book value of Celluphone's accounts receivable and plant asset accounts is reported as shown on the partial balance sheet, Illustration 27-9.

ILLUSTRATION 27-9   Book value of asset accounts reported on a balance sheet

Celluphone, Inc. Balance Sheet December 31, 19--			
ASSETS			
Current Assets:			
Accounts Receivable.	$68,240.00		
Less Allowance for Uncollectible Accounts.	9,492.00	58,748.00	
Plant Assets:			
Office Equipment	$18,250.00		
Less Accumulated Depreciation—Office Equipment	5,375.00	$ 12,875.00	
Store Equipment	$77,190.00		
Less Accumulated Depreciation—Store Equipment	15,450.00	61,740.00	
Total Plant Assets			74,615.00

Celluphone uses the following procedure to report the book value of accounts receivable on the balance sheet. The total amount of accounts receivable, *$68,240.00,* is written in the first amount column of the balance sheet. *Less Allowance for Uncollectible Accounts* is written on the next line, indented about one centimeter. The amount, *$9,492.00,* is written below the $68,240.00. The difference between the two amounts, *$58,748.00,* is written in the second amount column on the same line. The amount of the difference, $58,748.00, is the book value of accounts receivable on December 31. Similar procedures are followed to report book values of the plant asset accounts. The total of the two individual book values, *$74,615.00,* is written in the third amount column of the balance sheet.

Classifying Liabilities.   Liabilities are classified according to the length of time until they are due. Liabilities due within a short time, usually within a year, are known as current liabilities. All of Celluphone's liabilities are listed on the balance sheet in Illustration 27-8 as current liabilities because they come due within a year.

Liabilities owed for more than a year are called **long-term liabilities.** An example of a long-term liability is Mortgage Payable. On

December 31 of the current year, Celluphone does not have any long-term liabilities.

Electro Company has both current liabilities and long-term liabilities. A portion of Electro's balance sheet is shown in Illustration 27-10.

ILLUSTRATION 27-10

Liabilities section of a balance sheet showing current and long-term liabilities

LIABILITIES		
Current Liabilities:		
Notes Payable	$ 12,560.00	
Dividends Payable	25,000.00	
Total Current Liabilities		$ 48,369.00
Long-term Liabilities:		
Mortgage Payable		86,000.00
Total Liabilities.		$134,369.00

FYI

The forerunner of today's annual report was first published in 1902. Today, annual reports contain much more information than that first report.

Reporting a Corporation's Stockholders' Equity. A major difference between corporation balance sheets and proprietorship or partnership balance sheets is the owners' equity section. The owners' equity section of Celluphone's balance sheet, Illustration 27-8, is labeled *Stockholders' Equity.* Some corporations use the same label, Owners' Equity, as proprietorships and partnerships. Either label is acceptable.

The Stockholders' Equity section contains accounts related to capital stock and earnings kept in the business. For Celluphone, these accounts are Capital Stock and Retained Earnings. Total stockholders' equity on Celluphone's balance sheet, Illustration 27-8, is $269,655.77, the same as on Celluphone's statement of stockholders' equity, Illustration 27-7.

Analyzing a Balance Sheet. To continue operating successfully, a business must have adequate financial resources. A business must be able to buy additional merchandise, pay employee salaries, and pay for other operating expenses. Financial strength analysis measures the ability of a business to pay its debts. The balance sheet is the primary source of data to determine the financial strength of a business.

Celluphone analyzes its financial strength to assist the company in planning for future periods and to insure that adequate resources are available to operate the business. Creditors and investors also use financial strength analysis to determine if the company is a good credit and investment risk. Before a creditor sells merchandise to a company on account, the creditor must believe that the company will later pay for the merchandise. A company that is considered to be a poor credit risk is usually a bad investment for an investor.

Celluphone uses two analyses to evaluate financial strength. (1) Working capital. (2) Current ratio.

SPREADSHEET OPTIONS

GRAPHICS ENHANCE FINANCIAL STATEMENT ANALYSIS

The electronic spreadsheet is an effective tool for preparing financial statements. The income statement of Celluphone, Inc. in Illustration 27-2 is keyed on a spreadsheet. The printed spreadsheet would closely resemble the income statement in Illustration 27-2. In future fiscal periods, Celluphone's accountants can quickly prepare income statements by inputting new values. Formulas use these values to calculate other income statement values, such as net sales and cost of merchandise sold, and all the component percentages.

The electronic spreadsheet provides management with an additional valuable feature—the ability to view financial information in graphic form. **Graphs** are an effective way to communicate summary information such as component percentages.

A variety of graph styles is available to display different types of financial information. A **pie graph** is an appropriate graph style to illustrate how several values together comprise another value. In this graph, the total pie represents the net sales component percentage. Each slice represents the component percentage for an income statement item. The component percentages together equal the net sales component percentage.

Celluphone, Inc.
Income Statement Component Percentages

Net Deductions (0.1%)
Operating Exp. (22.3%)
Net Income (5.0%)
Income Taxes (1.8%)
Cost of Mdse. Sold (70.9%)

The software automatically determines the size of each slice using the component percentages. To emphasize the net income component percentage, the accountant preparing this graph instructed the software to "explode" the net income value. The graph can be displayed on the computer monitor or printed. The graph can also be inserted into reports created using other software such as a word processor.

FYI

Current financial reporting requirements include a statement of cash flows. A similar statement, no longer required, is the statement of changes in financial position.

Current assets less current liabilities is the amount of financial resources a company has available to conduct its daily operations. Current assets include cash, notes receivable, interest receivable, accounts receivable, merchandise inventory, supplies, and prepaid insurance. Current liabilities include notes payable, interest payable, accounts payable, taxes payable, health insurance premiums payable, and dividends payable. For a company to operate efficiently, an adequate supply of resources must be available after current liabilities are paid.

The amount of total current assets less total current liabilities is called **working capital**. Working capital is the amount of current assets available for use in the business after current liabilities are paid. The amount is stated in dollars. Celluphone's working capital for December 31 of the current year is calculated as shown below.

	Total Current Assets	−	Total Current Liabilities	=	Working Capital
	$321,472.00	−	$126,431.23	=	$195,040.77

TEACHING STRATEGIES: DIFFERENT LEARNING STYLES

Visual Learner. Formulas, such as those used to calculate component percentages, should be illustrated on the chalkboard to assist visual learners. The instructor should also complete the calculations for a few financial statement items to show the process to visual learners.

716

Working capital should not be confused with cash. Celluphone does not have $195,040.77 of excess cash. However, Celluphone does have $195,040.77 of assets that will be converted to cash and will be available for use in daily operations during the next fiscal year.

Working capital is a measure of the amount of financial resources available for the daily operations of the business. Although working capital is a useful measure, working capital does not permit a business to compare itself to its industry or to provide a convenient relative measurement from year to year.

A more useful measure results from comparing the amount of total current assets to total current liabilities. A comparison between two numbers showing how many times one number exceeds the other is called a **ratio**. A ratio that shows the numeric relationship of current assets to current liabilities is called the **current ratio**. The current ratio is a measure of a company's ability to pay its current liabilities. Creditors use the ratio to determine if merchandise should be sold to a company on account.

Based on the balance sheet information, Celluphone's current ratio is calculated as shown below.

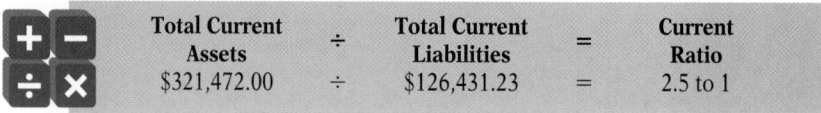

	Total Current Assets	÷	Total Current Liabilities	=	Current Ratio
	$321,472.00	÷	$126,431.23	=	2.5 to 1

Celluphone's current ratio is stated as 2.5 to 1, which means that total current assets are 2.5 times total current liabilities.

Based on previous experience and industry guidelines, Celluphone has established a minimum acceptable current ratio of 2.0 to 1. On December 31 of the current year, Celluphone's current ratio, 2.5 to 1, exceeds the minimum acceptable ratio. This year's current ratio indicates a favorable condition of financial strength.

The chart shown in Summary Illustration 27-11 summarizes the financial statements for a corporation.

Audit Your Understanding

1. What is the percentage relationship called between one financial statement item and the total that includes that item?

2. What is a financial statement called that shows changes in a corporation's ownership for a fiscal period?

3. What items are included as current assets?

4. What are two analyses used to evaluate financial strength?

ADJUSTING, CLOSING, AND REVERSING ENTRIES FOR A CORPORATION

The end-of-fiscal-period work of corporations is similar to the work of proprietorships and partnerships except for differences in the equity accounts. After corporate financial statements are prepared,

Summary of financial statements for a corporation

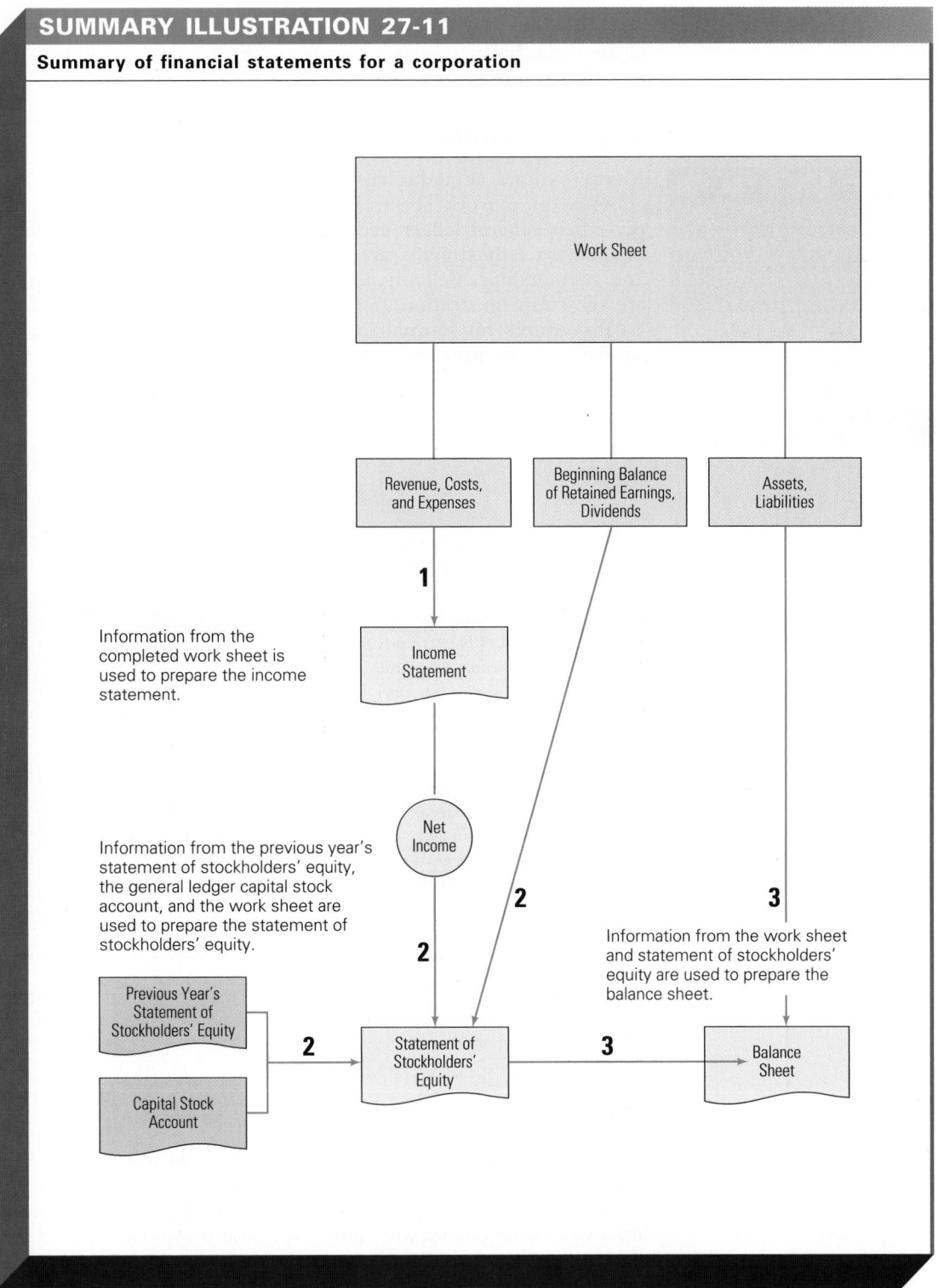

Information from the completed work sheet is used to prepare the income statement.

Information from the previous year's statement of stockholders' equity, the general ledger capital stock account, and the work sheet are used to prepare the statement of stockholders' equity.

Information from the work sheet and statement of stockholders' equity are used to prepare the balance sheet.

TEACHING STRATEGIES:
APPLYING VISUALS

Direct students to Summary Illustration 27-11 and review financial statements for a corporation; use Summary Illustration 27-19 to review the end-of-fiscal-period entries for a corporation.

FOCUS

In Parts 2 and 3, the end-of-fiscal-period work of proprietorships and partnerships was presented. Explain that the end-of-fiscal-period work for corporations is similar to that of proprietorships and partnerships. In this lesson, we will journalize adjusting, closing, and reversing entries for a corporation.

CHAPTER 27   Financial Statements and End-of-Fiscal-Period Entries   **717**

Cover student pages 716–726 "Adjusting, Closing, and Reversing Entries for a Corporation." Review the definition of adjusting entries and how they are journalized. The adjusting entry for federal income tax is journalized in the same manner as other adjusting entries. Review steps in journalizing closing entries. The first two closing entries follow the same procedure as those for proprietorships and partnerships. The third closing entry for a corporation records net income or net loss in the retained earnings account and closes the income summary account. The last closing entry closes the dividends account into retained earnings. Review journalizing reversing entries for accrued interest income and accrued interest expense.

adjusting and closing entries are journalized and posted. A post-closing trial balance is then prepared. Finally, reversing entries are journalized and posted.

Adjusting Entries

American corporations donated 5.9 billion dollars to charitable organizations in 1990.

A corporation's adjusting entries are made from the Adjustments columns of a work sheet. Each adjustment is journalized and posted to general ledger accounts. With the exception of federal income tax, adjustments are similar to those for proprietorships and partnerships. Celluphone's adjusting entries for December 31 are shown in Illustration 27-12.

Procedures for journalizing Celluphone's adjusting entries are similar to those previously described for other businesses.

ILLUSTRATION 27-12

Adjusting entries for a corporation

GENERAL JOURNAL — PAGE 15

	DATE		ACCOUNT TITLE	DOC. NO.	POST. REF.	DEBIT	CREDIT	
1			*Adjusting Entries*					1
2	Dec. 19--	31	Interest Receivable			1 1 00		2
3			Interest Income				1 1 00	3
4		31	Uncollectible Accounts Expense			9 2 2 7 00		4
5			Allowance for Uncoll. Accts.				9 2 2 7 00	5
6		31	Merchandise Inventory			7 0 1 8 00		6
7			Income Summary				7 0 1 8 00	7
8		31	Supplies Expense			11 6 9 0 00		8
9			Supplies				11 6 9 0 00	9
10		31	Insurance Expense			8 5 9 8 00		10
11			Prepaid Insurance				8 5 9 8 00	11
12		31	Depreciation Exp.—Office Equip.			1 7 5 0 00		12
13			Accum. Depr.—Office Equip.				1 7 5 0 00	13
14		31	Depreciation Exp.—Store Equip.			6 3 2 5 00		14
15			Accum. Depr.—Store Equip.				6 3 2 5 00	15
16		31	Interest Expense			7 0 00		16
17			Interest Payable				7 0 00	17
18		31	Federal Income Tax Expense			2 2 1 9 23		18
19			Federal Income Tax Payable				2 2 1 9 23	19
20								20

Closing Entries

Closing entries for a corporation are made from information in a work sheet. Closing entries for revenue and expense accounts are similar to those for proprietorships or partnerships. A corporation's last two closing entries are similar to those previously studied but affect different accounts. A corporation records the following four closing entries.

718   PART 4 Accounting for a Merchandising Business Organized as a Corporation

TEACHING STRATEGIES: TEACHING TIP

Review closing entries by comparing them to the closing entries for the merchandising business in the second accounting cycle. The first two entries are the same: Credit the income statement accounts with credit balances and debit the income statement accounts with debit balances. The third entry is similar to closing income summary to the partners' capital accounts, except Retained Earnings is used instead. The fourth entry is similar to closing the partners' drawing accounts, except Dividends is closed instead.

1. Closing entry for income statement accounts with credit balances (revenue and contra cost accounts).
2. Closing entry for income statement accounts with debit balances (cost, contra revenue, and expense accounts).
3. Closing entry to record net income or net loss in the retained earnings account and close the income summary account.
4. Closing entry for the dividends account.

Closing Entry for Income Statement Accounts with Credit Balances.   The closing entry for Celluphone's income statement credit balance accounts on December 31 is shown in Illustration 27-13, page 720. Income statement credit balance accounts are revenue (Sales, Gain on Plant Assets, and Interest Income) and the contra cost accounts (Purchases Discount and Purchases Returns and Allowances). Information needed for closing income statement credit balance accounts is obtained from the work sheet's Income Statement Credit column as shown in Illustration 27-13.

Celluphone begins its closing entries on a new page of the general journal. Thus, all the closing entries are together on one page.

Closing Entry for Income Statement Accounts with Debit Balances.   The closing entry for Celluphone's income statement debit balance accounts on December 31 is shown in Illustration 27-14 on page 721. Income statement debit balance accounts are the contra revenue accounts (Sales Discount and Sales Returns and Allowances) and the cost (Purchases) and expense accounts. Information needed for closing income statement debit balance accounts is obtained from the work sheet's Income Statement Debit column, as shown in Illustration 27-14, page 721.

If Cash Short and Over has a credit balance, the account balance amount is closed to Income Summary with the credit balance accounts.

After closing entries for the income statement debit balance accounts are posted, Income Summary has a credit balance of $100,537.77. This credit balance is the amount of net income. This amount is the same as on line 54 of Celluphone's work sheet.

Closing Entry to Record Net Income or Net Loss in the Retained Earnings Account and Close the Income Summary Account.   A corporation's net income is recorded in the retained earnings account. The closing entry to record Celluphone's net income and close Income Summary is shown in Illustration 27-15. Information needed for this entry is obtained from line 54 of Celluphone's work sheet, as shown in Illustration 27-15 on page 722.

After the entry to record net income is posted, Income Summary has a zero balance. The net income, $100,537.77, has been recorded as a credit to Retained Earnings.

- Direct students to Illustration 27-12 to review journalizing adjusting entries.
- Direct students to Illustrations 27-13, 27-14, 27-15, and 27-16 to review journalizing closing entries.
- Direct students to Illustration 27-17 to review preparing a post-closing trial balance.
- Direct students to Illustration 27-18 to review journalizing reversing entries.

Guided Practice

Assign Problem 27-2 and guide students through it in class. Students should have the forms from the working papers to complete as you guide them through each adjusting, closing, and reversing entry. Ask students to volunteer which entry should be done next and what the entry is. Discuss each entry before recording it. All students should agree with the analysis of each entry before proceeding to the next entry.

Independent Practice

Assign Questions 18–19, Mastery Problem 27-M, and Study Guide 27.

Reteach

- Use Demonstration Problem 27D. This problem can be demonstrated on the overhead with the students completing the problem at their desks.

- Assign the Accounting Tutorial, Units 8, 9, and 10.

- Assign Recycling Problem 27-R.

Extend

- Assign *Automated Accounting 6.0* or higher with Problem 27-C.

- Assign the Electronic Study Guide Chapter 27.

- Assign Problem 27-C. (The challenge is completing a 10-column work sheet and calculating federal income tax using a tax table.)

Enrich

- Discuss the PROFESSIONAL BUSINESS ETHICS feature on page 724. You may wish to distribute copies of the 3-step Checklist for Making Ethical Decisions. A blackline master is furnished in the Masters and Solutions to Enrichment/Application Activities Section in the Teacher's Resource Guide.

ILLUSTRATION 27-13   Closing entry for a corporation's income statement accounts with credit balances

Celluphone, Inc.
Work Sheet
For Year Ended December 31, 19--

	ACCOUNT TITLE	INCOME STATEMENT DEBIT	INCOME STATEMENT CREDIT
28	Income Summary		7 01 8 00
29	Sales		2050 4 4 0 00
30	Sales Discount	5 6 4 2 00	
31	Sales Returns and Allowances	24 3 1 8 00	
32	Purchases	1454 7 9 8 00	
33	Purchases Discount		10 7 6 6 00
34	Purchases Returns and Allowances		5 3 1 0 00
35	Advertising Expense	32 6 0 0 00	
36	Credit Card Fee Expense	20 4 6 8 00	
37	Depr. Expense—Office Equipment	1 7 5 0 00	
38	Depr. Expense—Store Equipment	6 3 2 5 00	
39	Insurance Expense	8 5 9 8 00	
40	Miscellaneous Expense	22 3 5 0 00	
41	Payroll Taxes Expense	23 7 2 0 00	
42	Rent Expense	56 4 0 0 00	
43	Salary Expense	251 9 3 2 00	
44	Supplies Expense	11 6 9 0 00	
45	Uncollectible Accounts Expense	9 2 2 7 00	
46	Utilities Expense	4 8 9 0 00	
47	Gain on Plant Assets		2 2 5 00
48	Interest Income		2 1 4 00
49	Cash Short and Over	3 00	
50	Interest Expense	1 4 4 5 00	
51	Loss on Plant Assets	4 6 0 00	
52	Federal Income Tax Expense	36 8 1 9 23	
53		1973 4 3 5 23	2073 9 7 3 00
54	Net Income after Fed. Inc. Tax	100 5 3 7 77	
55		2073 9 7 3 00	2073 9 7 3 00
56			
57			

GENERAL JOURNAL   PAGE 16

	DATE	ACCOUNT TITLE	DOC. NO.	POST. REF.	DEBIT	CREDIT	
1		Closing Entries					1
2	Dec. 31	Sales			2050 4 4 0 00		2
3		Purchases Discount			10 7 6 6 00		3
4		Purchases Returns and Allowances			5 3 1 0 00		4
5		Gain on Plant Assets			2 2 5 00		5
6		Interest Income			2 1 4 00		6
7		Income Summary				2066 9 5 5 00	7
8							8
9							9

ILLUSTRATION 27-14

Closing entry for a corporation's income statement accounts with debit balances

CLOSURE

- Use Audit Your Understanding questions.
- Review Summary Illustration 27-19 "Summary of End-of-Fiscal-Period Entries for a Corporation."

ASSESS

- Administer Problem Test Chapter 27.
- Administer a MicroExam test for Chapter 27.
- Administer Objective Test No. 8.
- Administer Unit Problem Test No. 8.

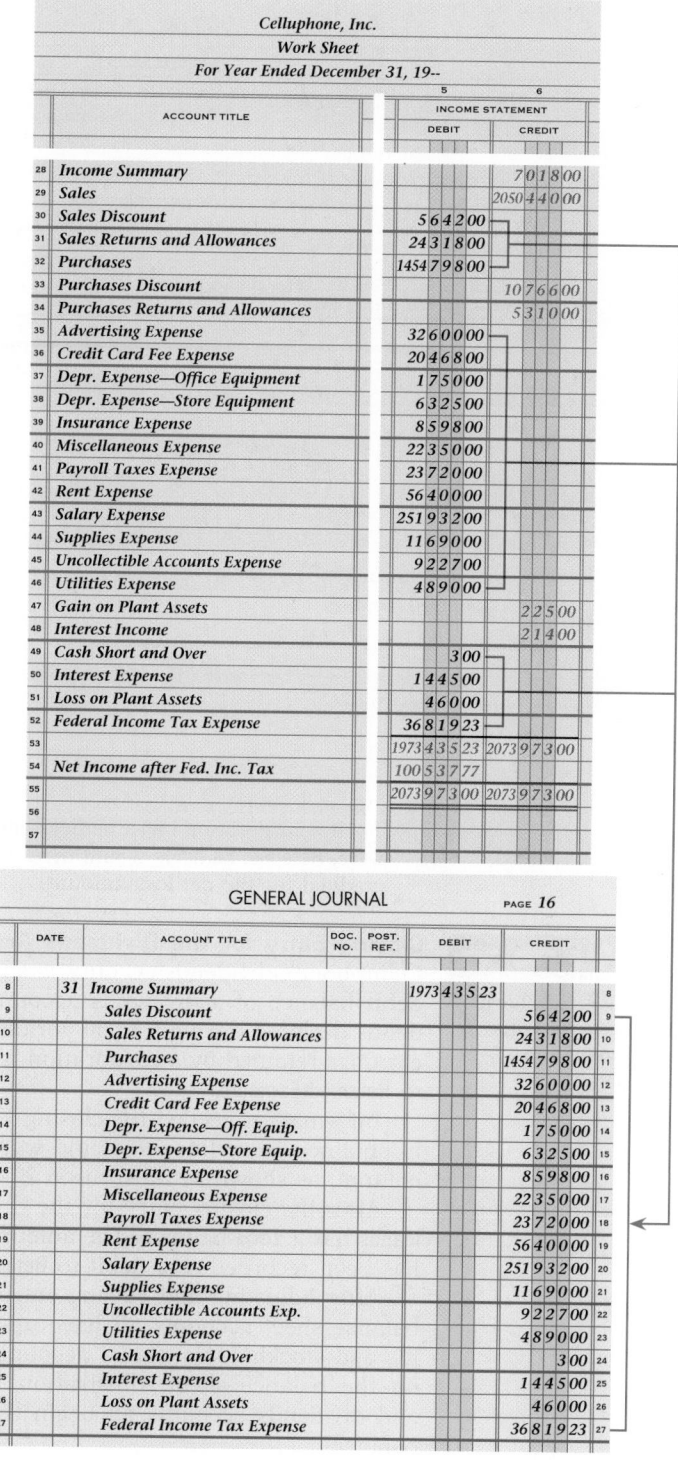

Celluphone, Inc.
Work Sheet
For Year Ended December 31, 19--

	ACCOUNT TITLE	5 INCOME STATEMENT DEBIT	6 CREDIT
28	Income Summary		7 0 1 8 00
29	Sales		2050 4 4 0 00
30	Sales Discount	5 6 4 2 00	
31	Sales Returns and Allowances	24 3 1 8 00	
32	Purchases	1454 7 9 8 00	
33	Purchases Discount		10 7 6 6 00
34	Purchases Returns and Allowances		5 3 1 0 00
35	Advertising Expense	32 6 0 0 00	
36	Credit Card Fee Expense	20 4 6 8 00	
37	Depr. Expense—Office Equipment	1 7 5 0 00	
38	Depr. Expense—Store Equipment	6 3 2 5 00	
39	Insurance Expense	8 5 9 8 00	
40	Miscellaneous Expense	22 3 5 0 00	
41	Payroll Taxes Expense	23 7 2 0 00	
42	Rent Expense	56 4 0 0 00	
43	Salary Expense	251 9 3 2 00	
44	Supplies Expense	11 6 9 0 00	
45	Uncollectible Accounts Expense	9 2 2 7 00	
46	Utilities Expense	4 8 9 0 00	
47	Gain on Plant Assets		2 2 5 00
48	Interest Income		2 1 4 00
49	Cash Short and Over	3 00	
50	Interest Expense	1 4 4 5 00	
51	Loss on Plant Assets	4 6 0 00	
52	Federal Income Tax Expense	36 8 1 9 23	
53		1973 4 3 5 23	2073 9 7 3 00
54	Net Income after Fed. Inc. Tax	100 5 3 7 77	
55		2073 9 7 3 00	2073 9 7 3 00
56			
57			

GENERAL JOURNAL   PAGE 16

	DATE	ACCOUNT TITLE	DOC. NO.	POST. REF.	DEBIT	CREDIT	
8	31	Income Summary			1973 4 3 5 23		8
9		Sales Discount				5 6 4 2 00	9
10		Sales Returns and Allowances				24 3 1 8 00	10
11		Purchases				1454 7 9 8 00	11
12		Advertising Expense				32 6 0 0 00	12
13		Credit Card Fee Expense				20 4 6 8 00	13
14		Depr. Expense—Off. Equip.				1 7 5 0 00	14
15		Depr. Expense—Store Equip.				6 3 2 5 00	15
16		Insurance Expense				8 5 9 8 00	16
17		Miscellaneous Expense				22 3 5 0 00	17
18		Payroll Taxes Expense				23 7 2 0 00	18
19		Rent Expense				56 4 0 0 00	19
20		Salary Expense				251 9 3 2 00	20
21		Supplies Expense				11 6 9 0 00	21
22		Uncollectible Accounts Exp.				9 2 2 7 00	22
23		Utilities Expense				4 8 9 0 00	23
24		Cash Short and Over				3 00	24
25		Interest Expense				1 4 4 5 00	25
26		Loss on Plant Assets				4 6 0 00	26
27		Federal Income Tax Expense				36 8 1 9 23	27

ILLUSTRATION 27-15

Closing entry to record a corporation's net income in the retained earnings account and close the income summary account

Celluphone, Inc.

Work Sheet

For Year Ended December 31, 19--

	ACCOUNT TITLE	INCOME STATEMENT		BALANCE SHEET		
		5 DEBIT	6 CREDIT	7 DEBIT	8 CREDIT	
51	Loss on Plant Assets	4 6 0 00				51
52	Federal Income Tax Expense	36 8 1 9 23				52
53		1973 4 3 5 23	2073 9 7 3 00	506 4 0 4 00	405 8 6 6 23	53
54	Net Income after Fed. Inc. Tax	100 5 3 7 77			100 5 3 7 77	54
55		2073 9 7 3 00	2073 9 7 3 00	506 4 0 4 00	506 4 0 4 00	55
56						56
57						57

GENERAL JOURNAL   PAGE 16

	DATE	ACCOUNT TITLE	DOC. NO.	POST. REF.	DEBIT	CREDIT	
28	31	Income Summary			100 5 3 7 77		28
29		Retained Earnings				100 5 3 7 77	29
30							30
31							31
32							32

If a corporation has a net loss, Income Summary has a debit balance. Retained Earnings would then be debited and Income Summary credited for the net loss amount.

Closing Entry for the Dividends Account. The closing entry for Celluphone's dividends account is shown in Illustration 27-16. The debit balance of a dividends account is the total amount of dividends declared during a fiscal period. Since dividends decrease the earnings retained by a corporation, the dividends account is closed to Retained Earnings.

Information needed for closing Celluphone's dividends account is obtained from line 27 of the work sheet's Balance Sheet Debit column, as shown in Illustration 27-16.

After the closing entry for the dividends account is posted, Dividends has a zero balance. The amount of the dividends, $80,000.00, has been recorded as a debit to Retained Earnings.

After adjusting and closing entries are journalized and posted, balance sheet accounts all have up-to-date balances. Asset, liability, and stockholders' equity account balances agree with amounts on the balance sheet, Illustration 27-8. Revenue, cost, expense, and dividends accounts all begin the new fiscal period with zero balances.

FYI

The last closing entry for a corporation is to close the dividends account into retained earnings.

ILLUSTRATION 27-16   Closing entry for a corporation's dividends account

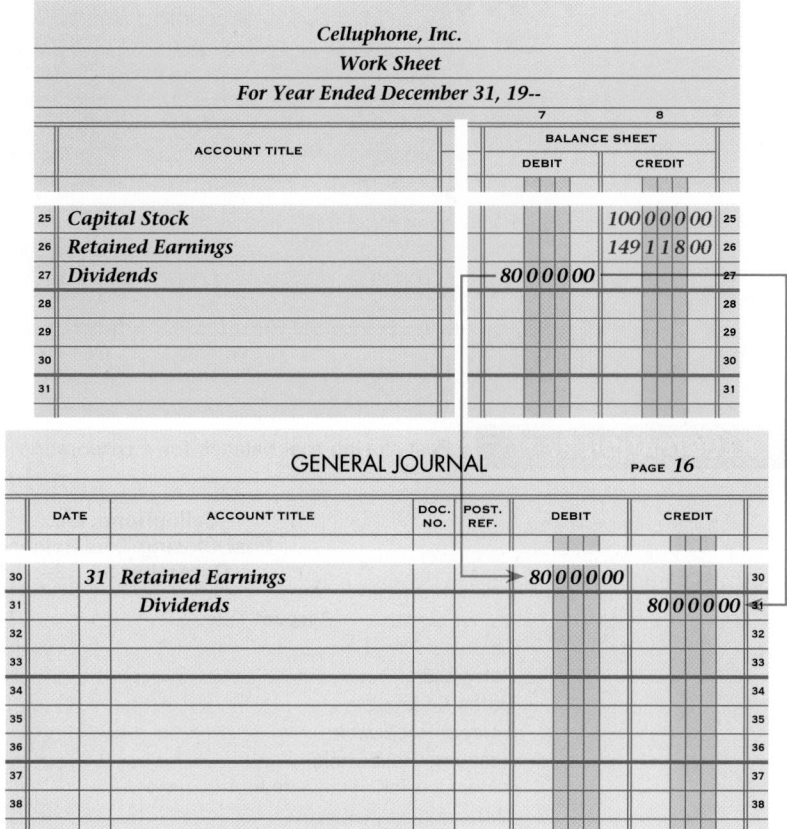

Post-Closing Trial Balance

A post-closing trial balance is prepared to prove the equality of debits and credits in the general ledger after adjusting and closing entries have been posted. Celluphone's December 31 post-closing trial balance is shown in Illustration 27-17 on page 724. Celluphone's general ledger is ready for the next fiscal period. *(CONCEPT: Accounting Period Cycle)*

Reversing Entries

If an adjusting entry creates a balance in an asset or liability account, Celluphone reverses the adjusting entry. A review of Celluphone's adjusting entries shows that the adjusting entry for accrued interest income created a balance in the interest receivable account. The adjusting entry for accrued interest expense created a balance in the interest payable account. Therefore, reversing entries are recorded for these two adjusting entries, as shown in Illustration 27-18 on page 725.

APPLIED SKILLS:
WORD PROCESSING

If you wish to integrate word processing into your accounting course, you may direct students to answer the end-of-chapter Accounting Terms, Questions for Individual Study, and Cases for Critical Thinking using their word processing software.

PROFESSIONAL BUSINESS ETHICS

Should Tax Fraud Be Reported?

Rhonda Bender, CPA, is an accountant for Sutton and Associates, a public accounting firm. While reviewing the quarterly financial statements of Walker Company, she discovers that the company's prior year tax return was prepared incorrectly. The accounting records show that sales were $946,000. However, the tax return shows sales of only $746,000. When Ms. Bender asked the chief financial officer about the discrepancy, he sternly replied "Your firm doesn't do our tax return, so it's none of your business!"

Ms. Bender knows that accountants are not required to notify the government if they become aware of fraudulent tax returns. In addition, professional accounting standards require accountants to keep client

ILLUSTRATION 27-17	Post-closing trial balance for a corporation

Celluphone, Inc.
Post-Closing Trial Balance
December 31, 19--

Account Title	Debit	Credit
Cash	$ 40,968.00	
Petty Cash	300.00	
Notes Receivable	550.00	
Interest Receivable	11.00	
Accounts Receivable	68,240.00	
Allowance for Uncollectible Accounts		$ 9,492.00
Merchandise Inventory	212,178.00	
Supplies	3,765.00	
Prepaid Insurance	4,952.00	
Office Equipment	18,250.00	
Accumulated Depreciation—Office Equipment		5,375.00
Store Equipment	77,190.00	
Accumulated Depreciation—Store Equipment		15,450.00
Notes Payable		2,800.00
Interest Payable		70.00
Accounts Payable		83,965.75
Employee Income Tax Payable		2,340.00
Federal Income Tax Payable		2,219.23
FICA Tax Payable		2,695.00
Sales Tax Payable		10,982.00
Unemployment Tax Payable—Federal		47.00
Unemployment Tax Payable—State		317.25
Health Insurance Premiums Payable		995.00
Dividends Payable		20,000.00
Capital Stock		100,000.00
Retained Earnings		169,655.77
Totals	$426,404.00	$426,404.00

information confidential. Therefore, Ms. Bender decides to write a letter to Walker's board of directors reporting the error and relaying the chief financial officer's response to her inquiry. The letter states that Sutton and Associates will be forced to resign unless the company reports and corrects the tax return.

Upon learning that the board of directors has decided not to correct the tax return, Ms. Bender informs the company that Sutton and Associates has resigned as its accountants.

INSTRUCTIONS Use the three-step checklist to determine whether Sutton and Associates' resignation as Walker Company's accountants demonstrates ethical behavior.

ILLUSTRATION 27-18   Reversing entries

	DATE		ACCOUNT TITLE	DOC. NO.	POST. REF.	DEBIT	CREDIT	
1			*Reversing Entries*					1
2	Jan. 19--	1	*Interest Income*			1 1 00		2
3			*Interest Receivable*				1 1 00	3
4		1	*Interest Payable*			7 0 00		4
5			*Interest Expense*				7 0 00	5
6								6
7								7
8								8
9								9
10								10
11								11

GENERAL JOURNAL   PAGE *17*

Audit Your Understanding

1. Where is information needed for closing income statement credit balance accounts obtained from?

2. In what account is a corporation's net income recorded?

3. Why is a post-closing trial balance prepared after adjusting and closing entries have been posted?

Celluphone's adjusting entry for federal income tax expense does create a balance in the federal income tax payable account. During the new year, cash will be paid for accrued income tax expense for the previous year plus periodic payments for the current year's income tax expense. To avoid confusing the amount of income tax expense recorded for each of these years and to provide year-to-date income tax expense information for each year, Celluphone does not reverse this adjusting entry. For similar reasons many corporations do not reverse accrued income tax adjusting entries.

The chart shown in Summary Illustration 27-19, page 726, summarizes the end-of-fiscal-period entries for a corporation.

AUDIT YOUR UNDERSTANDING

1. The work sheet's Income Statement Credit column.
2. Retained Earnings.
3. To prove the equality of debits and credits in the general ledger.

SUMMARY ILLUSTRATION 27-19

Summary of end-of-fiscal-period entries for a corporation

Work Sheet

1
Record adjusting entries from information in the Adjustments columns of the work sheet.

1
GENERAL JOURNAL
Adjusting Entries

2
GENERAL JOURNAL
Closing Entries

1. Closing entry for income statement accounts with credit balances (revenue and contra cost accounts).

2. Closing entry for income statement accounts with debit balances (cost, contra revenue, and expense accounts).

3. Closing entry to record net income or net loss in the retained earnings account and close the income summary account.

4. Closing entry for the dividends account.

2
Record the closing entries from information on the work sheet.

GENERAL LEDGER

4
At the beginning of the next fiscal year, record the reversing entries.

4
GENERAL JOURNAL
Reversing Entries

3
After all adjusting and closing entries are journalized and posted, prepare a post-closing trial balance to prove the equality of debits and credits.

POST-CLOSING TRIAL BALANCE

# ACCOUNTING TERMS
EPT(a)

What is the meaning of each of the following?

1. **net sales**

2. **net purchases**

3. **statement of stockholders' equity**

4. **book value**

5. **long-term liabilities**

6. **working capital**

7. **ratio**

8. **current ratio**

# QUESTIONS FOR INDIVIDUAL STUDY
EPT(b)

1. Which accounting concept is being applied when a corporation prepares financial statements annually and sometimes monthly or quarterly?

2. In what two ways does a corporation report changes in owners' equity differently from a proprietorship or partnership?

3. What financial information does an income statement report?

4. Where is the information found to prepare a corporation income statement?

5. What is the difference between sales and net sales reported on an income statement?

6. Why are other revenue and other expenses reported separately on the income statement from sales, cost of merchandise sold, and operating expenses?

7. How may the information on an income statement be used to determine whether the business is progressing satisfactorily?

8. Which accounting concept is being applied when the same accounting concepts are used for preparing income statements for each fiscal period?

9. What information is shown by component percentages on an income statement?

10. What financial information does a statement of stockholders' equity report?

11. Where is the information found to prepare a statement of stockholders' equity?

12. What financial information does a corporation balance sheet report?

13. Where is the information found to prepare a balance sheet?

14. What three amounts are reported on a balance sheet to show book value of a plant asset?

15. What determines whether a liability on a balance sheet is classified as current or long term?

16. For what purposes is the financial strength of a business analyzed?

17. What is working capital?

18. What kind of balances do income statement accounts have immediately after adjusting and closing entries are journalized and posted?

19. Why is a post-closing trial balance prepared?

ACCOUNTING TERMS

1. **net sales:** Total sales less sales discount and sales returns and allowances. (p. 707)

2. **net purchases:** Total purchases less purchases discount and purchases returns and allowances. (p. 707)

3. **statement of stockholders' equity:** A financial statement that shows changes in a corporation's ownership for a fiscal period. (p. 710)

4. **book value:** The difference between an asset's account balance and its related contra account balance. (p. 713)

5. **long-term liabilities:** Liabilities owed for more than a year. (p. 713)

6. **working capital:** The amount of total current assets less total current liabilities. (p. 715)

7. **ratio:** A comparison between two numbers showing how many times one number exceeds the other. (p. 716)

8. **current ratio:** A ratio that shows the numeric relationship of current assets to current liabilities. (p. 716)

QUESTIONS FOR INDIVIDUAL STUDY

1. Accounting Period Cycle. (p. 703)

2. (a) Owners' equity for all owners is reported as a single amount rather than for each owner. (b) Owners' equity is reported in two categories: (1) capital contributed by the owners and (2) capital earned by the corporation. (p. 703)

3. Information showing the financial progress of a business during a fiscal period: revenue, cost of merchandise sold, gross profit on operations, operating expenses, and net income or net loss. (p. 703)

4. In the Trial Balance, Income Statement, and Balance Sheet columns of a work sheet. (p. 703)

5. Net sales is total sales less sales discount and sales returns and allowances. (p. 707)

6. Sales, cost of merchandise sold, and operating expenses are part of the items used to determine income from operations. Other revenue and other expenses, such as interest income, interest expense, and gains or losses on plant assets, are not normal business activities. Therefore, they are not included in calculating income from operations and are reported separately. (p. 707)

QUESTIONS (cont'd)

7. The results reported on the income statement may be compared with industry standards and/or previous fiscal periods. (p. 708)

8. Consistent Reporting. (p. 708)

9. Each component percentage shows the percentage that each item is of net sales. (p. 708)

10. The changes in a corporation's ownership for a fiscal period. (p. 710)

11. On the previous year's statement, in the capital stock account, and on the work sheet. (p. 710–711)

12. The assets, liabilities, and stockholders' equity on a specific date. (p. 711)

13. In the Balance Sheet columns of a work sheet and the statement of stockholders' equity. (p. 711)

14. (a) The balance of the asset account. (b) The balance of the asset's contra account. (c) Book value (asset's account balance less contra account balance). (p. 713)

15. The length of time until they are due. Liabilities due within a short time, usually within a year, are classified as current. Liabilities owed for more than a year are classified as long term. (p. 713)

16. To assist the company in planning for future periods and to insure that adequate resources are available to operate the business. Creditors and investors also use financial strength analysis to determine if the company is a good credit and investment risk. (p. 714)

17. The amount of current assets available for use in the business after current liabilities are paid. (p. 715)

18. Revenue, cost, and expense accounts all have zero balances to begin the new fiscal period. (p. 722)

19. To prove the equality of debits and credits in the general ledger after adjusting and closing entries have been posted. (p. 723)

CASES FOR CRITICAL THINKING

Case 1 Do not agree with the accountant. The income statement does report each of the revenue and expense amounts and net income for the current accounting period. However, if component percentages are added for each amount, better relative comparisons can

CASES FOR CRITICAL THINKING   EPT(b)

CASE 1 The president of Kalikow Company asked the accounting department to provide as much information as possible to help management improve the company's net income. Paul Jayroe, a senior accountant, suggests that an income statement showing all the revenue and expense amounts should provide all the information management needs to analyze the company's results of operations. Do you agree with the accountant's suggestion? If not, what additional information do you recommend? Explain your answer.

CASE 2 Riverside Company recently organized as a corporation with five stockholders. Tamara Connell, the bookkeeper, is developing the accounting system. She suggested that although there are five stockholders, only one equity account be used. The account would be titled **Corporation Capital**. The president of Riverside questions the bookkeeper's recommendation. Is the bookkeeper's recommendation acceptable? If not, how should capital be recorded and reported? Explain your answer.

DRILLS FOR UNDERSTANDING   EPT(b)

DRILL 27-D1 **Classifying a corporation's revenue, cost, and expense accounts**

A form for classifying a corporation's revenue, cost, and expense accounts is given in the working papers that accompany this textbook.

INSTRUCTIONS:

For each of the following accounts, place a check mark in the column that correctly classifies the account.

1. Advertising Expense
2. Sales
3. Interest Income
4. Salary Expense
5. Sales Returns and Allowances
6. Purchases
7. Depreciation Expense
8. Purchases Discount
9. Interest Expense
10. Sales Discount
11. Uncollectible Accounts Expense
12. Purchases Returns and Allowances
13. Gain on Plant Assets
14. Utilities Expense
15. Cash Short and Over (cash short)

DRILL 27-D2 **Classifying a corporation's assets, liabilities, and stockholders' equity accounts**

A form for classifying a corporation's assets, liabilities, and stockholders' equity accounts is given in the working papers that accompany this textbook.

INSTRUCTIONS:

For each of the following accounts, place a check mark in the column that correctly classifies the account.

1. Cash
2. Accumulated Depreciation—Office Equipment
3. Federal Income Tax Payable
4. Prepaid Insurance

5. Notes Payable
   6. Interest Receivable
   7. Accounts Payable
   8. Notes Receivable
   9. Office Equipment
  10. Interest Payable
  11. Capital Stock
  12. Mortgage Payable
  13. Employee Income Tax Payable
  14. Dividends Payable
  15. Retained Earnings
  16. Petty Cash
  17. Accumulated Depreciation—Store Equipment
  18. FICA Tax Payable
  19. Merchandise Inventory
  20. Allowance for Uncollectible Accounts

APPLICATION PROBLEMS   EPT(c,d,e,f,g)

PROBLEM 27-1   Preparing financial statements for a corporation

AmTech Company completed the work sheet shown on pages 730–731 for the current year ended December 31.

INSTRUCTIONS:

1. Prepare an income statement. Calculate and record the following component percentages. (a) Cost of merchandise sold. (b) Gross profit on operations. (c) Total operating expenses. (d) Income from operations. (e) Net addition or deduction resulting from other revenue and expenses. (f) Net income before federal income tax. Round percentage calculations to the nearest 0.1%.

2. Analyze AmTech's income statement by determining if component percentages are within acceptable levels. If any component percentage is not within an acceptable level, suggest steps that the company should take. AmTech considers the following component percentages acceptable.

Cost of merchandise sold	Not more than 73.0%
Gross profit on operations	Not less than 27.0%
Total operating expenses	Not more than 24.9%
Income from operations	Not less than 2.1%
Net deduction from other revenue and expenses	Not more than 0.1%
Net income before federal income tax	Not less than 2.0%

3. Prepare a statement of stockholders' equity. Use the following additional information.

January 1 balance of capital stock account	$100,000.00
(1,000 shares issued for $100.00 per share)	
January 1 balance of retained earnings account	68,085.20

4. Prepare a balance sheet.

5. Calculate AmTech's (a) working capital and (b) current ratio. Determine if these items are within acceptable levels. AmTech considers the following levels acceptable.

Working capital	Not less than $100,000.00
Current ratio	Between 2.2 to 1 and 2.8 to 1

---

be made of each expense as a percentage of net sales. These percentages can be compared with the company's previous accounting periods as well as industry standard percentages. This additional information will help management identify expense items that are higher than they should be compared with industry standards. This information will also help identify undesirable trends earlier by comparing component percentages for each expense item with percentages for previous periods.

Case 2   The bookkeeper is correct. Since a corporation has the legal rights of one individual, separate capital accounts are not kept for each owner (stockholder). However, corporations normally are required to keep separate accounts for stock issued (capital contributed by the stockholders) and for earnings kept in the business. This permits any interested person reading the balance sheet to determine how much equity was contributed by the stockholders and how much was earned. Riverside Company should have at least two equity accounts: Capital Stock and Retained Earnings.

CHECK FIGURES

Drill 27-D1   Operating Rev.: Sales; Contra Operating Rev.: Sales R&A, Sales Disc.; Cost of Mdse.: Purchases; Contra Cost of Mdse.: Purch. R&A, Purch. Disc.; Operating Exp.: Adv. Exp., Salary Exp., Depr. Exp., Uncoll. Accts. Exp.; Other Rev.: Interest Inc.; Gain on Plant Assets; Other Exp.: Interest Exp., Cash Short and Over (Short).

Drill 27-D2   Curr. Assets: Cash, Prepaid Ins., Interest Rec., Notes Rec., Petty Cash, Mdse. Inventory; Contra Curr. Asset: Allow. for Uncoll. Accts. Plant Asset: Office Equip.; Contra Plant Asset: Accum. Deprec.—Office Equip., Accum. Deprec.—Store Equip.; Curr. Liabilities: Fed. Inc. Tax Pay., Notes Pay., Accounts Pay., Interest Pay., Empl. Inc. Tax Pay., Dividends Pay., and FICA Tax Pay.; Long-term Liability: Mortgage Pay.; SE: Capital Stock, Retained Earnings.

Problem 27-1   Component Percentages: 73.3%, 26.7%, 24.6%, 2.1%, 0.0%, 2.2%; Net Inc. after Fed. Inc. Tax, 26,154.59; Total SE, 170,239.79; Total Assets, 244,739; Working Cap., 115,391.59; Current Ratio, 2.6 to 1.

AmTech Company
Work Sheet
For Year Ended December 31, 19--

	Account Title	Trial Balance Debit	Trial Balance Credit	Adjustments Debit	Adjustments Credit	Income Statement Debit	Income Statement Credit	Balance Sheet Debit	Balance Sheet Credit
1	Cash	8539900						8539900	
2	Petty Cash	25000						25000	
3	Notes Receivable	350000						350000	
4	Interest Receivable			(a) 13100				13100	
5	Accounts Receivable	5561800						5561800	
6	Allowance for Uncollectible Accounts		37800		(b) 506400				544200
7	Merchandise Inventory	4053700		(c) 295460				4349160	
8	Supplies	772640			(d) 566720			205920	
9	Prepaid Insurance	1465200			(e) 976800			488400	
10	Office Equipment	1282160						1282160	
11	Accumulated Depr.—Office Equipment		257400		(f) 149600				407000
12	Store Equipment	7788000						7788000	
13	Accumulated Depr.—Store Equipment		1494900		(g)1683440				3178340
14	Notes Payable		165000						165000
15	Interest Payable				(h) 6270				6270
16	Accounts Payable		5695350						5695350
17	Employee Income Tax Payable		153500						153500
18	Federal Income Tax Payable				(i) 41551				41551
19	FICA Tax Payable		80600						80600
20	Sales Tax Payable		625600						625600
21	Unemployment Tax Payable—Federal		3800						3800
22	Unemployment Tax Payable—State		25650						25650
23	Health Insurance Premiums Payable		52600						52600
24	Dividends Payable		600000						600000
25	Capital Stock		100000000						100000000

#	Account Title	Trial Balance Debit	Trial Balance Credit	Adjustments Debit	Adjustments Credit	Income Statement Debit	Income Statement Credit	Balance Sheet Debit	Balance Sheet Credit
26	*Retained Earnings*								6808520
27	*Dividends*	2400000						2400000	
28	*Income Summary*			(c) 295460		295460			
29	*Sales*		14439 6120				14439 6120		
30	*Sales Discount*	443190				443190			
31	*Sales Returns and Allowances*	1751700				1751700			
32	*Purchases*	105629000				105629000			
33	*Purchases Discount*		782430				782430		
34	*Purchases Returns and Allowances*		385000				385000		
35	*Advertising Expense*	2335520				2335520			
36	*Credit Card Fee Expense*	1303500				1303500			
37	*Depr. Expense—Office Equipment*			(f) 149600		149600			
38	*Depr. Expense—Store Equipment*			(g) 1683440		1683440			
39	*Insurance Expense*			(e) 976800		976800			
40	*Miscellaneous Expense*	2773540				2773540			
41	*Payroll Taxes Expense*	1629210				1629210			
42	*Rent Expense*	4620000				4620000			
43	*Salary Expense*	18103100				18103100			
44	*Supplies Expense*			(d) 566720		566720			
45	*Uncollectible Accounts Expense*			(b) 506400		506400			
46	*Utilities Expense*	346500				346500			
47	*Gain on Plant Assets*		26400				26400		
48	*Interest Income*		39400		(a) 13100		52500		
49	*Cash Short and Over*	880				880			
50	*Interest Expense*	18480		(h) 6270		24750			
51	*Loss on Plant Assets*	17050				17050			
52	*Federal Income Tax Expense*	4200000		(i) 41551		4615 51			
53		171630 0070	171630 0070	4239341	4239341	1433224 51	14593 7910	310034 40	28387981
54	*Net Income after Federal Income Tax*					2615459			2615459
55						14593 7910	14593 7910	310034 40	310034 40
56									
57									

PROBLEM 27-2 Journalizing adjusting, closing, and reversing entries for a corporation

Use the completed work sheet shown in Problem 27-1 to complete Problem 27-2.

INSTRUCTIONS:

1. Use page 18 of a general journal. Journalize the adjusting entries.

2. Use page 19 of a general journal. Journalize the closing entries.

3. Use page 20 of a general journal. Journalize the reversing entries for the accrued interest income and accrued interest expense.

ENRICHMENT PROBLEMS   EPT(c,d,e,f,g)

MASTERY PROBLEM 27-M Preparing financial statements and end-of-fiscal-period entries for a corporation

Accent, Inc., completed the work sheet shown on pages 734–735 for the current year ended December 31.

INSTRUCTIONS:

1. Prepare an income statement. Calculate and record the following component percentages. (a) Cost of merchandise sold. (b) Gross profit on operations. (c) Total operating expenses. (d) Income from operations. (e) Net addition or deduction resulting from other revenue and expenses. (f) Net income before federal income tax. Round percentage calculations to the nearest 0.1%.

2. Analyze Accent's income statement by determining if component percentages are within acceptable levels. If any component percentage is not within an acceptable level, suggest steps that the company should take. Accent considers the following component percentages acceptable.

Cost of merchandise sold	Not more than 72.0%
Gross profit on operations	Not less than 28.0%
Total operating expenses	Not more than 22.0%
Income from operations	Not less than 6.0%
Net deduction from other revenue and expenses	Not more than 0.1%
Net income before federal income tax	Not less than 5.9%

3. Prepare a statement of stockholders' equity. Use the following additional information.

January 1 balance of capital stock account	$150,000.00
(15,000 shares issued for $10.00 per share)	
January 1 balance of retained earnings account	42,387.20

4. Prepare a balance sheet.

5. Calculate Accent's (a) working capital and (b) current ratio. Determine if these items are within acceptable levels. Accent considers the following levels acceptable.

Working capital	Not less than $125,000.00
Current ratio	Between 2.0 to 1 and 2.6 to 1

6. Use page 20 of a general journal. Journalize the adjusting entries.

7. Use page 21 of a general journal. Journalize the closing entries.

8. Use page 22 of a general journal. Journalize the reversing entries for the accrued interest income and accrued interest expense.

CHALLENGE PROBLEM 27-C Preparing financial statements and end-of-fiscal-period entries for a corporation

AUTOMATED

Glass Design Corporation's general ledger accounts and balances are recorded on a 10-column work sheet in the working papers.

INSTRUCTIONS:

1. Complete a 10-column work sheet for the current year ended December 31. Record the adjustments on the work sheet using the following information.

CHECK FIGURES *(cont'd)*

Challenge Problem 27-C Component Percentages: 65.8%, 34.2%, 25.0%, 9.2%, 0.2%, 9.0%; Total SE, 164,219.05; Total assets, 269,276.64; Working Capital, 136,543.39; Current Ratio, 2.3 to 1.

Adjustment Information, December 31

Accrued interest income..	$ 250.00
Uncollectible accounts expense estimated as 1.2% of sales on account. Sales on account for year, $561,375.00.	
Merchandise inventory	85,059.56
Supplies inventory	295.12
Value of prepaid insurance	2,720.80
Annual depreciation expense—office equipment	2,421.00
Annual depreciation expense—store equipment....................	1,446.84
Accrued interest expense...	490.64

Federal income tax for the year is calculated at the following rates:
15% of net income before taxes, zero to $50,000.00.
Plus 25% of net income before taxes, $50,000.00 to $75,000.00.
Plus 34% of net income before taxes, $75,000.00 to $100,000.00.
Plus 39% of net income before taxes, $100,000.00 to $335,000.00.
Plus 34% of net income before taxes over $335,000.00.

2. Prepare an income statement. Calculate and record the following component percentages. (a) Cost of merchandise sold. (b) Gross profit on operations. (c) Total operating expenses. (d) Income from operations. (e) Net addition or deduction resulting from other revenue and expenses. (f) Net income before federal income tax. Round percentage calculations to the nearest 0.1%.

3. Analyze Glass Design's income statement by determining if component percentages are within acceptable levels. If any component percentage is not within an acceptable level, suggest steps that the company should take. Glass Design considers the following component percentages acceptable.

Cost of merchandise sold	Not more than 70.0%
Gross profit on operations.....................	Not less than 30.0%
Total operating expenses	Not more than 24.0%
Income from operations......................	Not less than 6.0%
Net deduction from other revenue and expenses.....................	Not more than 0.1%
Net income before federal income tax...............................	Not less than 5.9%

4. Prepare a statement of stockholders' equity. Use the following additional information.

January 1 balance of capital stock account......	$100,000.00
(10,000 shares issued for $10.00 per share)	
January 1 balance of retained earnings account. .	33,028.87

CHAPTER 27 Financial Statements and End-of-Fiscal-Period Entries **733**

TEACHING STRATEGIES: REINFORCEMENT ACTIVITY

Reinforcement Activity 3, Part B continues Reinforcement Activity 3 beginning with completing a trial balance on a work sheet through adjusting entries, financial statements, closing entries, a post-closing trial balance, and reversing entries. Reinforcement Activity 3, Part A was presented after Chapter 20 and included journalizing and posting daily transactions. Blackline masters for audit tests for Reinforcement Activity 3 are available in the Teacher's Resource Guide in three options: Part A only, Part B only, and Parts A and B combined. In addition, *Automated Accounting 6.0* or higher can be used to automate Reinforcement Activity 3.

Accent, Inc.
Work Sheet
For Year Ended December 31, 19--

	ACCOUNT TITLE	TRIAL BALANCE DEBIT	TRIAL BALANCE CREDIT	ADJUSTMENTS DEBIT	ADJUSTMENTS CREDIT	INCOME STATEMENT DEBIT	INCOME STATEMENT CREDIT	BALANCE SHEET DEBIT	BALANCE SHEET CREDIT
1	Cash	5228300						5228300	
2	Petty Cash	30000						30000	
3	Notes Receivable	440000						440000	
4	Interest Receivable			(a) 12980				12980	
5	Accounts Receivable	5909640						5909640	
6	Allowance for Uncollectible Accounts		38610		(b) 448580				487190
7	Merchandise Inventory	10556410		(c) 1278310				11834720	
8	Supplies	823240			(d) 648109			175131	
9	Prepaid Insurance	1559250			(e) 909590			649660	
10	Office Equipment	1362130						1362130	
11	Accumulated Depr.—Office Equipment		273460		(f) 152460				425920
12	Store Equipment	8274640						8274640	
13	Accumulated Depr.—Store Equipment		1588290		(g) 1078000				2666290
14	Notes Payable		274340						274340
15	Interest Payable				(h) 10340				10340
16	Accounts Payable		6826500						6826500
17	Employee Income Tax Payable		162910						162910
18	Federal Income Tax Payable				(i) 150560				150560
19	FICA Tax Payable		197780						197780
20	Sales Tax Payable		664730						664730
21	Unemployment Tax Payable—Federal		3400						3400
22	Unemployment Tax Payable—State		22950						22950
23	Health Insurance Premiums Payable		55660						55660
24	Dividends Payable		1200000						1200000
25	Capital Stock		15000000						15000000

Work Sheet (partial — rows 26–57)

#	Account	Trial Balance Debit	Trial Balance Credit	Adjustments Debit	Adjustments Credit	Income Statement Debit	Income Statement Credit	Balance Sheet Debit	Balance Sheet Credit
26	Retained Earnings		4238720						4238720
27	Dividends	4800000						4800000	
28	Income Summary				(c)1278310		1278310		
29	Sales		150698570				150698570		
30	Sales Discount	759330				759330			
31	Sales Returns and Allowances	1786730				1786730			
32	Purchases	107741480				107741480			
33	Purchases Discount		589050				589050		
34	Purchases Returns and Allowances		392700				392700		
35	Advertising Expense	2074270				2074270			
36	Credit Card Fee Expense	1355530				1355530			
37	Depr. Expense—Office Equipment			(f) 152460		152460			
38	Depr. Expense—Store Equipment			(g)1078000		1078000			
39	Insurance Expense			(e) 909590		909590			
40	Miscellaneous Expense	2828980				2828980			
41	Payroll Taxes Expense	1735580				1735580			
42	Rent Expense	4800000				4800000			
43	Salary Expense	18465040				18465040			
44	Supplies Expense			(d) 648109		648109			
45	Uncollectible Accounts Expense			(b) 448580		448580			
46	Utilities Expense	361900				361900			
47	Gain on Plant Assets		22500				22500		
48	Interest Income		39050		(a) 12980		52030		
49	Cash Short and Over	1210				1210			
50	Interest Expense	30910		(h) 10340		41250			
51	Loss on Plant Assets	34650				34650			
52	Federal Income Tax Expense	1330000		(i) 150560		1480560			
53		182289220	182289220	4688929	4688929	146703249	153033160	38717201	32387290
54	Net Income after Federal Income Tax					6329911			6329911
55						153033160	153033160	38717201	38717201
56									
57									

SIMULATION

To give students an opportunity to apply accounting concepts from the third accounting cycle, assign students to complete *Western Rider, Inc.: A Business Simulation*. *Western Rider, Inc.* may also be automated using *Automated Accounting 6.0* or higher.

TEACHING STRATEGIES: ASSESSMENT BY PORTFOLIO

If you assign Reinforcement Activity 3, Parts A and B, or *Western Rider, Inc.: A Business Simulation* and intend to use it as part of an assessment by portfolio evaluation, advise students that their work on this activity will be included in their portfolio.

5. Prepare a balance sheet.

6. Calculate Glass Design's (a) working capital and (b) current ratio. Determine if these items are within acceptable levels. Glass Design considers the following levels acceptable.

   Working capital . . . .   Not less than $125,000.00
   Current ratio . . . .   Between 2.0 to 1 and 2.5 to 1

7. Use page 13 of a general journal. Journalize the adjusting entries.
8. Use page 14 of a general journal. Journalize the closing entries.
9. Use page 15 of a general journal. Journalize the reversing entries for the accrued interest income and accrued interest expense.

End-of-Fiscal-Period Work for a Corporation

Celluphone's manual accounting procedures for completing a corporation's end-of-fiscal-period work are described in Chapter 27. Integrating Automated Accounting Topic 10 describes procedures for using automated accounting software to complete Celluphone's end-of-fiscal-period work. The Automated Accounting Problem contains instructions for using automated accounting software to solve Challenge Problem 27-C, Chapter 27.

PLANNING ADJUSTMENTS

A trial balance is prepared by the software to check the equality of debits and credits in the general ledger. Celluphone's trial balance is shown in Illustration T10-1 on page 738.

The trial balance also serves as the basis for planning adjusting entries. Adjusting entries are batched and recorded on a general journal input form. Celluphone's December 31 adjustment data is shown at the bottom of the next page.

SOFTWARE FOCUS

The Automated Accounting Problem in this Integrating Automated Accounting Topic uses Challenge Problem 27-C, Chapter 27, which students have already completed manually. Refer students back to this problem to complete the input forms. The problem instructions in *Automated Accounting 6.0* will lead students through automating the problem.

In Chapter 27, manual end-of-fiscal-period procedures for a corporation were described. Emphasize that using an automated accounting system speeds the processing of end-of-fiscal-period work by (1) eliminating the need to prepare a work sheet, (2) having all financial reports prepared by a computer, and (3) having the software generate closing entries. The end-of-fiscal-period procedures for Integrating Automated Accounting Topic 10 are very similar to procedures described in Integrating Automated Accounting Topic 6: End-of-Fiscal-Period Work for a Partnership.

ILLUSTRATION T10-1   Trial balance prepared by automated accounting software

```
                        Celluphone, Inc.
                         Trial Balance
                           12/31/--
---------------------------------------------------------------
Acct.   Account
Number  Title                             Debit         Credit
---------------------------------------------------------------
1105    Cash                            40968.00
1110    Petty Cash                        300.00
1115    Notes Receivable                  550.00
1125    Accounts Receivable             68240.00
1130    Allow. for Uncoll. Accts.                        265.00
1135    Merchandise Inventory          205160.00
1140    Supplies                        15455.00
1145    Prepaid Insurance               13550.00
1205    Office Equipment                18250.00
1210    Acc. Depr.--Office Equip.                       3625.00
1215    Store Equipment                 77190.00
1220    Acc. Depr.--Store Equip.                        9125.00
2105    Notes Payable                                   2800.00
2115    Accounts Payable                               83965.75
2120    Employee Income Tax Pay.                        2340.00
2130    FICA Tax Payable                                2695.00
2135    Sales Tax Payable                              10982.00
2140    Unemployment Tax Pay--Fed                         47.00
2145    Unemployment Tax Pay--St.                        317.25
2150    Health Ins. Premiums Pay.                        995.00
2155    Dividends Payable                              20000.00
3105    Capital Stock                                 100000.00
3110    Retained Earnings                             149118.00
3115    Dividends                       80000.00
4105    Sales                                        2050440.00
4110    Sales Discount                   5642.00
4115    Sales Ret. and Allowances       24318.00
5105    Purchases                     1454798.00
5110    Purchases Discount                             10766.00
5115    Purchases Ret. and Allow.                       5310.00
6105    Advertising Expense             32600.00
6110    Credit Card Fee Expense         20468.00
6130    Miscellaneous Expense           22350.00
6135    Payroll Taxes Expense           23720.00
6140    Rent Expense                    56400.00
6145    Salary Expense                 251932.00
6160    Utilities Expense                4890.00
7105    Gain on Plant Assets                             225.00
7110    Interest Income                                  203.00
8105    Cash Short and Over                 3.00
8110    Interest Expense                 1375.00
8115    Loss on Plant Assets              460.00
9105    Federal Income Tax Exp.         34600.00
                                      ----------      ----------
        Totals                       2453219.00      2453219.00
                                      ==========      ==========
```

Adjustment Information, December 31

Accrued interest income...............................	$ 11.00
Uncollectible accounts expense.......................	9,227.00
Merchandise inventory...............................	212,178.00
Supplies inventory...................................	3,765.00
Value of prepaid insurance	4,952.00
Annual depreciation expense—office equipment	1,750.00
Annual depreciation expense—store equipment........	6,325.00
Accrued interest expense	70.00
Federal income tax expense for the year	36,819.23

OPTIONAL PROBLEM

The input forms illustrated in this topic can be keyed using *Automated Accounting 6.0*. Refer to OPTIONAL PROBLEM DB-10A at the end of the narrative for information about automating this topic.

After all adjusting entries have been recorded on the general journal input form, the Debit and Credit columns are totaled. The totals are entered on the Page Totals and Final Totals lines provided at the bottom of the input form. The totals are compared to assure that debits and credits are equal. As the totals are the same, $46,908.23, the adjusting entries on the general journal input form are assumed to be correct. Celluphone's completed general journal input form for the adjusting entries is shown in Illustration T10-2.

ILLUSTRATION T10-2

General journal input form with adjusting entries recorded

RUN DATE 12,31,--
MM DD YY

GENERAL JOURNAL
Input Form

	DATE MM/DD	REFERENCE	ACCOUNT NO.	CUSTOMER/ VENDOR NO.	DEBIT	CREDIT	
1	12,31	Adj.Ent.	1120		11 00		1
2	/		7110			11 00	2
3	31	Adj.Ent.	6155		9227 00		3
4	/		1130			9227 00	4
5	31	Adj.Ent.	1135		7018 00		5
6	/		3120			7018 00	6
7	31	Adj.Ent.	6150		11690 00		7
8	/		1140			11690 00	8
9	31	Adj.Ent.	6125		8598 00		9
10	/		1145			8598 00	10
11	31	Adj.Ent.	6115		1750 00		11
12	/		1210			1750 00	12
13	31	Adj.Ent.	6120		6325 00		13
14	/		1220			6325 00	14
15	31	Adj.Ent.	8110		70 00		15
16	/		2110			70 00	16
17	31	Adj.Ent.	9105		2219 23		17
18	/		2125			2219 23	18
19	/						19
25	/						25
				PAGE TOTALS	46908 23	46908 23	
				FINAL TOTALS	46908 23	46908 23	

After all lines on the input form have been keyed and posted, a general journal report is prepared. Celluphone's general journal report is shown in Illustration T10-3 on page 740.

PREPARING END-OF-FISCAL-PERIOD REPORTS

After the general journal report for adjusting entries has been prepared, an income statement is displayed and printed. Celluphone's income statement is shown in Illustration T10-4 on page 741.

In Celluphone's manual accounting system, a statement of stockholders' equity is prepared to show changes in stockholders'

TEACH

Cover student pages 737–744, "Planning Adjustments," "Preparing End-of-Fiscal-Period Reports," and "Recording Reversing Entries." This lesson introduces students to end-of-fiscal-period procedures for a corporation using automated accounting software. As the lesson progresses, review the definitions of merchandise inventory, cost of merchandise sold, gross profit on sales, and statement of stockholders' equity.

End-of-fiscal-period work is completed using the same basic procedures for both manual and automated methods. However, the component percentages are automatically produced by the software. Analyzing acceptable component percentages is an important student critical thinking skill. Because using an automated accounting system speeds the processing of end-of-fiscal-period work, students can spend more time analyzing component percentages.

Remind students that a post-closing trial balance is a trial balance prepared after closing entries have been posted.

Reinforce to students that no additional input of data is necessary to record closing entries. The software contains instructions for closing temporary accounts.

Emphasize that if an adjusting entry creates a balance in an asset or liability account, a reversing entry is completed.

TEACHING STRATEGIES: USING VISUALS

Using Transparency AA-2 Blank General Journal Input Form will help students understand the journalizing process for adjusting and reversing entries.

Guided Practice

Students should be at the computers. Guide students through booting the software and loading Optional Problem DB-10A from the template. Instruct students to complete the end-of-fiscal-period work as you go step-by-step through the procedures.

Independent Practice

Assign Automating Challenge Problem 27-C.

ILLUSTRATION T10-3   General journal report for adjusting entries

```
                          Celluphone, Inc.
                           General Journal
                             12/31/--
------------------------------------------------------------------------
Date   Refer.   V/C  Acct.  Title                      Debit       Credit
------------------------------------------------------------------------
12/31  Adj.Ent.      1120   Interest Receivable        11.00
12/31  Adj.Ent.      7110   Interest Income                         11.00

12/31  Adj.Ent.      6155   Uncoll. Accounts Expense  9227.00
12/31  Adj.Ent.      1130   Allow. for Uncoll. Accts.              9227.00

12/31  Adj.Ent.      1135   Merchandise Inventory     7018.00
12/31  Adj.Ent.      3120   Income Summary                         7018.00

12/31  Adj.Ent.      6150   Supplies Expense         11690.00
12/31  Adj.Ent.      1140   Supplies                              11690.00

12/31  Adj.Ent.      6125   Insurance Expense         8598.00
12/31  Adj.Ent.      1145   Prepaid Insurance                      8598.00

12/31  Adj.Ent.      6115   Depr. Exp.--Office Equip. 1750.00
12/31  Adj.Ent.      1210   Acc. Depr.--Office Equip.              1750.00

12/31  Adj.Ent.      6120   Depr. Exp.--Store Equip.  6325.00
12/31  Adj.Ent.      1220   Acc. Depr.--Store Equip.               6325.00

12/31  Adj.Ent.      8110   Interest Expense            70.00
12/31  Adj.Ent.      2110   Interest Payable                         70.00

12/31  Adj.Ent.      9105   Federal Income Tax Exp.   2219.23
12/31  Adj.Ent.      2125   Federal Income Tax Pay.                2219.23

                            Totals                   46908.23    46908.23
                                                    ==========  ==========
```

equity during the fiscal period. In Celluphone's automated accounting system, changes in stockholders' equity are shown on the balance sheet. Celluphone's balance sheet is shown in Illustration T10-5 on page 742.

After the balance sheet has been prepared, the software is directed to perform period-end closing.

After the financial statements have been prepared and period-end closing has been performed, a post-closing trial balance is prepared. Celluphone's post-closing trial balance is shown in Illustration T10-6 on page 743.

RECORDING REVERSING ENTRIES

FYI

Reversing entries are completed at the beginning of the next fiscal period.

Celluphone records two reversing entries after the post-closing trial balance is prepared. (1) An entry to reverse the adjusting entry for accrued interest income. (2) An entry to reverse the adjusting entry for accrued interest expense. The reversing entries are batched and recorded on a general journal input form. Celluphone's reversing entries are on the general journal input form shown in Illustration T10-7 on page 743.

TEACHING STRATEGIES: DIFFERENT LEARNING ABILITIES

Physically-Challenged.   You should set the work station up in a manner that the physically challenged will not have to travel far to complete the automated problems. Encourage students to go to the computer with all input forms, template, and any other supplies that are needed. This will decrease the need to make many trips from the desk to the work station.

```
                          Celluphone, Inc.
                          Income Statement
                      For Period Ended 12/31/--
-----------------------------------------------------------------------
                          *****Monthly*****   *****Yearly******
                          Amount    Percent    Amount    Percent
-----------------------------------------------------------------------
O p e r a t i n g    R e v e n u e
--------------------------------------------
Sales                     2050440.00  101.48 2050440.00   101.48
Sales Discount              -5642.00    -.28   -5642.00     -.28
Sales Ret. and Allowances -24318.00   -1.20  -24318.00    -1.20
                          ----------  ------ ----------   ------
Total Operating Revenue   2020480.00  100.00 2020480.00   100.00

C o s t   o f   M e r c h a n d i s e   S o l d
-------------------------------------------------
Beginning Inventory        205160.00   10.15  205160.00    10.15
Purchases                 1454798.00   72.00 1454798.00    72.00
Purchases Discount         -10766.00    -.53  -10766.00     -.53
Purchases Ret. and Allow.   -5310.00    -.26   -5310.00     -.26
                          ----------  ------ ----------   ------
Merchandise Available for Sale 1643882.00 81.36 1643882.00  81.36
Less Ending Inventory     -212178.00  -10.50 -212178.00   -10.50
                          ----------  ------ ----------   ------
Cost of Merchandise Sold  1431704.00   70.86 1431704.00    70.86
                          ----------  ------ ----------   ------
Gross Profit               588776.00   29.14  588776.00    29.14

O p e r a t i n g    E x p e n s e s
--------------------------------------------
Advertising Expense         32600.00    1.61   32600.00     1.61
Credit Card Fee Expense     20468.00    1.01   20468.00     1.01
Depr. Exp.--Office Equip.    1750.00     .09    1750.00      .09
Depr. Exp.--Store Equip.     6325.00     .31    6325.00      .31
Insurance Expense            8598.00     .43    8598.00      .43
Miscellaneous Expense       22350.00    1.11   22350.00     1.11
Payroll Taxes Expense       23720.00    1.17   23720.00     1.17
Rent Expense                56400.00    2.79   56400.00     2.79
Salary Expense             251932.00   12.47  251932.00    12.47
Supplies Expense            11690.00     .58   11690.00      .58
Uncoll. Accounts Expense     9227.00     .46    9227.00      .46
Utilities Expense            4890.00     .24    4890.00      .24
                          ----------  ------ ----------   ------
Total Operating Expenses   449950.00   22.27  449950.00    22.27
                          ----------  ------ ----------   ------
Net Income from Operations 138826.00    6.87  138826.00     6.87

O t h e r    R e v e n u e
----------------------------
Gain on Plant Assets          225.00     .01     225.00      .01
Interest Income               214.00     .01     214.00      .01

O t h e r    E x p e n s e
----------------------------
Cash Short and Over             3.00               3.00
Interest Expense             1445.00     .07    1445.00      .07
Loss on Plant Assets          460.00     .02     460.00      .02
                          ----------  ------ ----------   ------
Net Income before Income Tax 137357.00  6.80  137357.00     6.80

I n c o m e    T a x
----------------------
Federal Income Tax Exp.     36819.23    1.82   36819.23     1.82
                          ----------  ------ ----------   ------
Net Income after Income Tax 100537.77   4.98  100537.77     4.98
                          ==========  ====== ==========   ======
```

Assess student understanding by checking solutions to Automating Problem 27-C. Have students list the steps for completing end-of-fiscal-period work.

Reteach

Use Transparency AA-2 to journalize Celluphone's adjusting and reversing entries from Automating Problem 27-C. Give each student two general journal input forms and have them complete the input forms while you complete the forms using the overhead.

Extend

Create a template file using the information provided in Problem 27-1, Chapter 27. Have the students complete the end-of-fiscal-period work following the procedures discussed in this lesson.

Enrich

Invite an accounting professional from the local area to come to class and discuss the procedures they use to perform end-of-fiscal-period work.

TEACHING STRATEGIES: COOPERATIVE LEARNING

Using automated accounting software to complete accounting problems is an ideal cooperative learning experience. Students working in groups can collaborate on completing input forms and keying data.

CLOSURE

Review the procedures for processing end-of-fiscal-period work using manual procedures and using automated accounting software.

ILLUSTRATION T10-5   Balance sheet prepared by automated accounting software

```
                     Celluphone, Inc.
                     Balance Sheet
                        12/31/--

A s s e t s
-----------
Cash                               40968.00
Petty Cash                           300.00
Notes Receivable                     550.00
Interest Receivable                   11.00
Accounts Receivable                68240.00
Allow. for Uncoll. Accts.          -9492.00
Merchandise Inventory             212178.00
Supplies                            3765.00
Prepaid Insurance                   4952.00
                                  ----------
Total Current Assets              321472.00

Office Equipment                   18250.00
Acc. Depr.--Office Equip.          -5375.00
Store Equipment                    77190.00
Acc. Depr.--Store Equip.          -15450.00
                                  ----------
Total Plant Assets                 74615.00
                                  ----------
Total Assets                                    396087.00
                                                ==========
L i a b i l i t i e s
---------------------
Notes Payable                       2800.00
Interest Payable                      70.00
Accounts Payable                   83965.75
Employee Income Tax Pay.            2340.00
Federal Income Tax Pay.             2219.23
FICA Tax Payable                    2695.00
Sales Tax Payable                  10982.00
Unemployment Tax Pay--Fed             47.00
Unemployment Tax Pay--St.            317.25
Health Ins. Premiums Pay.            995.00
Dividends Payable                  20000.00
                                  ----------
Total Liabilities                               126431.23

S t o c k h o l d e r s '   E q u i t y
---------------------------------------
Capital Stock                     100000.00
Retained Earnings                 149118.00
Dividends                         -80000.00
Net Income                        100537.77
                                  ----------
Total Stockholders' Equity                      269655.77
                                                ----------
Total Liabilities & Equity                      396087.00
                                                ==========
```

After all lines on the input form have been keyed and posted, a general journal report is prepared. Celluphone's general journal report for reversing entries is shown in Illustration T10-8 on page 744.

OPTIONAL PROBLEM DB-10A

Celluphone's general ledger data base is on the accounting textbook template. If you wish to process Celluphone's end-of-fiscal-period work using automated accounting software, load the

Post-closing trial balance prepared by automated accounting software

```
                    Celluphone, Inc.
                      Trial Balance
                        12/31/--
-----------------------------------------------------------
Acct.   Account
Number  Title                          Debit          Credit
-----------------------------------------------------------
1105    Cash                         40968.00
1110    Petty Cash                     300.00
1115    Notes Receivable               550.00
1120    Interest Receivable             11.00
1125    Accounts Receivable          68240.00
1130    Allow. for Uncoll. Accts.                     9492.00
1135    Merchandise Inventory       212178.00
1140    Supplies                      3765.00
1145    Prepaid Insurance             4952.00
1205    Office Equipment             18250.00
1210    Acc. Depr.--Office Equip.                     5375.00
1215    Store Equipment              77190.00
1220    Acc. Depr.--Store Equip.                     15450.00
2105    Notes Payable                                 2800.00
2110    Interest Payable                                70.00
2115    Accounts Payable                             83965.75
2120    Employee Income Tax Pay.                      2340.00
2125    Federal Income Tax Pay.                       2219.23
2130    FICA Tax Payable                              2695.00
2135    Sales Tax Payable                            10982.00
2140    Unemployment Tax Pay--Fed                       47.00
2145    Unemployment Tax Pay--St.                      317.25
2150    Health Ins. Premiums Pay.                      995.00
2155    Dividends Payable                            20000.00
3105    Capital Stock                               100000.00
3110    Retained Earnings                           169655.77
                                     ----------     ----------
        Totals                       426404.00      426404.00
                                     ==========     ==========
```

TEACHING STRATEGIES:
TEACHING TIP

It is important for students to save a template file under another name before they begin work. This will keep the template file intact for future use.

Automated Accounting 6.0 or higher software. Select Data Base 10A (DB-10A) from the template disk. Read the Problem Instructions screen. Using the completed general journal input forms, Illustrations T10-2 and T10-7, follow the procedures described to process Celluphone's end-of-fiscal-period work.

General journal input form with reversing entries recorded

RUN DATE 01 01 --
MM DD YY

GENERAL JOURNAL
Input Form

	DATE MM/DD	REFERENCE	ACCOUNT NO.	CUSTOMER/ VENDOR NO.	DEBIT	CREDIT	
1	01 01	Rev.Ent.	7110		11 00		1
2	/		1120			11 00	2
3	01	Rev.Ent.	2110		70 00		3
4	/		8110			70 00	4
5	/						5
25	/						25
				PAGE TOTALS	81 00	81 00	
				FINAL TOTALS	81 00	81 00	

```
                              Celluphone, Inc.
                              General Journal
                                 01/01/--
-------------------------------------------------------------------------
Date   Refer.    V/C Acct.  Title                          Debit     Credit
-------------------------------------------------------------------------
01/01  Rev.Ent.      7110   Interest Income                11.00
01/01  Rev.Ent.      1120   Interest Receivable                       11.00

01/01  Rev.Ent.      2110   Interest Payable               70.00
01/01  Rev.Ent.      8110   Interest Expense                          70.00

                                                        ----------  ----------
                            Totals                          81.00      81.00
                                                        ==========  ==========
```

AUTOMATED ACCOUNTING PROBLEM

AUTOMATED

AUTOMATING CHALLENGE PROBLEM 27-C   Preparing financial statements and end-of-fiscal-period entries for a corporation

INSTRUCTIONS:

1. Load the *Automated Accounting 6.0* or higher software. Select data base F27-C (First-Year Course Challenge Problem 27-C) from the accounting textbook template. Read the Problem Instructions screen.
2. Select File from the menu bar and choose the Save As menu command. Key the path to the drive and directory that contains your data files. Save the data base with a file name of XXX27C (where XXX are your initials).
3. Display/print a trial balance.
4. Display/print the chart of accounts.
5. Record the adjusting entries on a general journal input form using the information given below. Net income before federal income tax for the year is $87,030.57. Use December 31 of the current year as the run date.

Adjustment Information, December 31

Accrued interest income	$ 250.00
Uncollectible accounts expense estimated at 1.2% of sales on account.	
Sales on account for the year, $561,375.00.	
Merchandise inventory	85,059.56
Supplies inventory	295.12
Value of prepaid insurance	2,720.80
Annual depreciation expense—office equipment	2,421.00
Annual depreciation expense—store equipment.	1,446.84
Accrued interest expense	490.64
Federal income tax expense for the year.	17,840.39

6. Key the adjusting entries from the completed general journal input form.
7. Display/print the general journal report.
8. Display/print the income statement and balance sheet.
9. Perform period-end closing.
10. Display/print the post-closing trial balance.
11. Record the reversing entries on a general journal input form. Use January 1 of the following year as the run date.
12. Key the reversing entries from the completed general journal input form.
13. Display/print the general journal report.

An Accounting Cycle for a Corporation: End-of-Fiscal-Period Work

AUTOMATED

The general ledger used in Reinforcement Activity 3, Part A, is needed to complete Reinforcement Activity 3, Part B.

Reinforcement Activity 3, Part B, includes those accounting activities needed to complete an accounting cycle for a corporation. In Part A Hardware Mart's transactions were recorded for the last month of a fiscal year. In Part B end-of-fiscal-period work is completed.

END-OF-FISCAL-PERIOD WORK

INSTRUCTIONS:

12. Prepare a work sheet for the fiscal year ended December 31 of the current year. Use the following adjustment information.

Adjustment Information, December 31

Accrued interest income	$ 84.00
Uncollectible accounts expense is estimated as 1.5% of sales on account.	
Sales on account for the year, $120,800.00.	
Merchandise inventory	65,661.20
Supplies inventory	242.50
Value of prepaid insurance	2,160.00
Annual depreciation expense—office equipment	2,130.00
Annual depreciation expense—store equipment.	3,410.00
Accrued interest expense	500.00
Federal income tax for the year.	14,579.41

13. Prepare an income statement. Calculate and record the following component percentages as a percent of net sales: (a) cost of merchandise sold; (b) gross profit on operations; (c) total operating expenses; (d) income from operations; (e) net additions/deductions from other revenue and expenses; and (f) net income before federal income tax. Round percentage calculations to the nearest 0.1%.

14. Analyze Hardware Mart's income statement by determining if component percentages are within acceptable levels. If any component percentage is not within an acceptable level, suggest steps that the company should take. Hardware Mart considers the following percentages acceptable.

Cost of merchandise sold	Not more than 66.0%
Gross profit on operations	Not less than 34.0%
Total operating expenses	Not more than 25.0%
Income from operations	Not less than 9.0%
Net deductions from other revenue and expenses	Not more than 0.5%
Net income before federal income tax	Not less than 8.5%

15. Prepare a statement of stockholders' equity. Use the following additional information.

January 1 balance of capital stock account $40,000.00
    (4,000 shares issued for $10.00 per share)
January 1 balance of retained earnings account 34,894.40

16. Prepare a balance sheet.

17. Calculate Hardware Mart's (a) working capital and (b) current ratio. Determine if these items are within acceptable levels. Hardware Mart considers the following amounts acceptable.

Working capital	Not less than $50,000.00
Current ratio	Between 2.0 to 1 and 2.5 to 1

18. Journalize the adjusting entries on page 13 of a general journal. Post the adjusting entries.

19. Journalize the closing entries on page 14 of a general journal. Post the closing entries.

20. Prepare a post-closing trial balance.

21. Journalize the reversing entries on page 15 of a general journal for the accrued interest income and accrued interest expense adjusting entries. Post the reversing entries.

Western Rider, Inc. is a merchandising business organized as a corporation. This business simulation covers the realistic transactions completed by Western Rider, Inc., which sells clothing, tack, and other items to those who own and show horses or who simply ride horses for pleasure. Transactions are recorded in special journals and a general journal similar to the ones used by Celluphone, Inc. in Part 4. The following activities are included in the accounting cycle for Western Rider, Inc. This business simulation is available from the publisher in either manual or automated versions.

Activities in Western Rider, Inc.:

1. Recording transactions in special journals from source documents.

2. Posting items to be posted individually to a general ledger and subsidiary ledger

3. Posting column totals to a general ledger.

4. Preparing schedules of accounts receivable and accounts payable from subsidiary ledgers.

5. Preparing a trial balance on a work sheet.

6. Planning adjustments and completing a work sheet.

7. Preparing financial statements.

8. Journalizing and posting adjusting entries.

9. Journalizing and posting closing entries.

10. Preparing a post-closing trial balance.

11. Journalizing and posting reversing entries.

PART 5 OVERVIEW

STUDENT EDITION

STUDENT FEATURES

Multicultural Awareness

Ancient Accounting, page 751

Professional Business Ethics

Can You Make Too Much Money? page 754

Audit Your Understanding

This student activity can be found on pages 755, 760, 763

APPLIED SKILLS

Applied Communications

Page 765

Applied Math

Pages 753, 758, 766

SOFTWARE APPLICATIONS

Study Guide Software

TEACHER'S EDITION

APPLIED SKILLS

Applied Communications, page 765

Language Arts, page 756

Writing Across the Curriculum, page 762

Building Study Skills, page 763

Mathematics, page 753

Word Processing, page 759

TEACHING STRATEGIES

Accounting Pedagogy, page 750

Different Learning Abilities, page 760

Expanding Beyond the Classroom, page 758

Applying Visuals, page 764

Teaching Tip, pages 751, 757, 761

Software Focus, page 750

ASSESSMENT

MicroExam software

SOFTWARE

Study Guide Software
MicroExam
WordPerfect (word processing)
Windows (operating system)

BIBLIOGRAPHY

Gelinas, Ulric J., Jr., Allan E. Oram, and William P. Wiggins. *Accounting Information Systems.* Second Edition. Cincinnati: South-Western Publishing Co., 1993.

Hamilton, D. *Cooperative Learning in the Classroom.* Bloomington, IN: Phi Delta Kappa Educational Foundation, 1990.

Johnson, D., and R. Johnson. *Social Skills for Successful Group Work.* Educational Leadership, 1990.

Sarkees, Michelle Donnelly, and John L. Scott. *Vocation Special Needs,* Second Edition. American Technical Publishers, 1986.

Skousen, K. Fred, Harold Q. Langenderfer, and W. Steve Albrecht. *Accounting Principles and Applications.* Cincinnati: South-Western Publishing Co., 1993.

Wallace, Wanda A. *Financial Accounting.* Second Edition. Cincinnati: South-Western Publishing Co., 1993.

Periodicals

Accounting Horizons, American Accounting Association, Sarasota, FL.

CPA Journal, New York State Society of CPAs, New York, NY.

Journal of Business Ethics, Kluwer Academic Publishers, Norwell, CA.

Management Accounting, National Association of Accountants, 10 Paragon Drive, Montvale, NJ.

Multicultural Review, Greenwood Press Inc., Westport, CT. (Multicultural awareness)

Technology

AICPA. *Serving America: A Tradition of Excellence,* 1986. (Video)

Mead Data Central, Inc. *LEXIS/NEXIS* (On-line database)

747B

The Legal Environment of Business

Part 5 explores events that do not occur as regular parts of the accounting cycle. The formation and dissolution of a business are singular events in the life of a business and, therefore, may not be experienced by many accounting workers. However, an understanding of how businesses are formed and how they are dissolved at the end of their lives is important to understanding the nature of business ownership.

In the one chapter in this part, the formation and liquidation of a proprietorship, a partnership, and a corporation are discussed and illustrated. The formation of a proprietorship is essentially a review of the transactions presented at the start of the first accounting cycle in Chapter 2. The formation of a partnership closely parallels the formation of a proprietorship, except that there are capital accounts for each of the partners. The formation of a corporation is also similar, except that different kinds of account titles are used for the capital accounts of the stockholders who own the corporation.

Dissolving a business is a new concept presented in this part. Again there are parallels between the dissolving of a proprietorship and a partnership and the primary difference is in the distribution of the proceeds to the owners. The procedures illustrated also allow for both a gain and a loss on dissolution, just as there are gains and losses on disposal of plant assets previously covered in Chapter 22.

It is rare that corporations are truly liquidated. Instead, the ownership is transferred by selling shares of stock. In the rare instance that a corporation is liquidated, the accounting for the liquidation is complex. Any gains/losses on the sale of noncash assets are subject to taxation.

In addition, the advantages and disadvantages of each kind of business organization are discussed in this part.

GENERAL GOALS

1. Know terminology related to forming and dissolving business organizations.

2. Understand the legal requirements for forming and dissolving business organizations.

3. Demonstrate accounting procedures for forming and liquidating various forms of business organizations.

Chapter 28 looks only at how proprietorships, partnerships, and corporations are formed and dissolved. The transactions are covered in their simplest form. The advantages and disadvantages of each type of business organization are presented to enhance understanding of why business owners choose one form of organization over another.

Part 5 is a one-chapter part. Therefore, there is no unit objective test or unit problem test.

GUIDE TO ACHIEVING LEARNING OBJECTIVES

Enabling Performance Tasks	TEACH Lesson Plans	APPLY Drills for Understanding	APPLY Application Problems	EXTEND/ENRICH Mastery Problems	EXTEND/ENRICH Challenge Problems	EXTEND/ENRICH Cases for Critical Thinking	EXTEND/ENRICH Recycling Problems	EXTEND/ENRICH Reinforcement Activity	
a. Define accounting terms related to forming and liquidating business organizations.	28-1, 28-2, 28-3								
b. Identify the legal requirements for forming and dissolving various foms of business organizations.	28-1, 28-2, 28-3					Case 1			
c. Journalize entries for initial investment for a proprietorship, partnership, and corporation.	28-1, 28-2, 28-3		28-1, 28-2, 28-3	28-M			28-R		
d. Journalize entries for liquidation of a proprietorship and a partnership.	28-1, 28-2	28-D1, 28-D2	28-1, 28-2, 28-3	28-M	28-C		28-R		

ENRICHMENT

SPECIAL FEATURES

Professional Business Ethics, page 754

Multicultural Awareness, page 751

Applied Communications, page 765

TECHNOLOGY CONNECTION

Electronic Study Guide

NEW, REVIEW, AND EXTENSION

ACTIVITIES/CONCEPTS/TRANSACTIONS	NEW	REVIEW/ EXTENSION
Legal requirements for forming a proprietorship	✓	
Accounting transactions for forming a proprietorship		✓
Legal requirements for dissolving a proprietorship	✓	
Liquidation of a proprietorship	✓	
Legal requirements for forming a partnership	✓	
Accounting transactions for forming a partnership		✓
Legal requirements for dissolving a partnership		✓
Liquidation of a partnership		✓
Legal requirements for forming a corporation	✓	
Accounting transactions for forming a corporation		✓
Legal requirements for dissolving a corporation	✓	
Liquidation of a corporation	✓	

	INFORMAL ASSESSMENT		FORMAL ASSESSMENT				
Study Guide	Audit Your Understanding	Chapter MicroExam	Chapter Problem Test	Unit Problem Test	Unit Objective Test	Portfolio
Unit A	✓	✓				
Unit C	✓	✓				
Unit B			✓			
Unit B			✓			

TEACHING MATERIALS

Teacher's Wraparound Edition of the Text

Teacher's Resource Guide

Teacher's Edition of Working Papers

Teacher's Edition of Demonstration/Recycling Problems

Teaching Transparencies

MicroExam

Applied Math Work Sheet

APPLIED MATHEMATICS

APPLIED MATH/ACCOUNTING SKILL	APPLICATION
Calculating the Loss on Sale of Assets	Drill 28-D1
Calculating the Gain on Sale of Assets	Drill 28-D2

28
Forming and Dissolving Business Organizations

ENABLING PERFORMANCE TASKS

After studying Chapter 28, you will be able to:

a Define accounting terms related to forming and liquidating business organizations.

b Identify the legal requirements for forming and dissolving various forms of business organizations.

c Journalize entries for initial investment for a proprietorship, partnership, and corporation.

d Journalize entries for liquidation of a proprietorship and a partnership.

TERMS PREVIEW

dissolution • liquidation • partnership agreement • articles of incorporation • par value • par-value stock

750

One of the disadvantages of a proprietorship is unlimited liability.

When starting a business, one of three basic forms of ownership can be chosen. A business can be organized as a proprietorship, partnership, or corporation. Each form of business ownership has legal and accounting implications that the owners must consider when making a choice.

A business organization may stop operations at any time for a variety of reasons. The process of stopping the operation of a business is called **dissolution.** The process of paying all liabilities of a business and distributing remaining cash to the owner(s) is called **liquidation.**

FORMING A PROPRIETORSHIP

A business owned by one person is known as a proprietorship. Roger Moher is starting a sporting goods business called SportsLure. Because Mr. Moher is the only owner, SportsLure is a proprietorship. Mr. Moher will have total control over the business and will be able to make all decisions for SportsLure. The advantages of a proprietorship include:

1. Ease of formation. A proprietorship is relatively easy to form.
2. Total control. Mr. Moher has total control of the proprietorship.
3. Unshared profits. Mr. Moher gets all profits made by SportsLure.

Mr. Moher has also considered the disadvantages of a proprietorship. The disadvantages include:

1. Limited resources. Since Mr. Moher is the only owner, he is the only person who can invest cash and other assets in the business.
2. Unlimited liability. Mr. Moher is totally responsible for the liabilities of SportsLure. Mr. Moher's personal assets, such as his house and car, can be claimed by creditors to pay SportsLure's liabilities.
3. Limited time, energy, and experience. The amount of time, energy, and experience that Mr. Moher will be able to put into the business is limited.
4. Limited life. A proprietorship must be dissolved when the owner dies or decides to stop doing business.

When Mr. Moher started SportsLure, he was required to follow the laws of the federal government as well as the laws of the state and city in which the business was formed.

Legal Requirements for Forming a Proprietorship

A proprietorship is the simplest form of business to organize. The legal requirements for organizing a proprietorship vary from state to state. However, most cities and states have few, if any, legal procedures to follow. In some states, if the name of the business is different from the name of the owner, the name of the business must be registered with the Secretary of State. In addition, some cities

Some cities require a proprietorship to obtain an operating license before beginning operations.

- In Part 2, the accounting cycle for a service business organized as a proprietorship was presented. In this lesson, we will look at the legal requirements and journal entries for forming and liquidating a proprietorship. Remind students that they learned how to record the initial investment of an owner in a proprietorship in the first accounting cycle.

- Introduce new vocabulary: dissolution, liquidation.

TEACH

Cover student pages 751–755 "Forming a Proprietorship" and "Dissolving a Proprietorship." Explain the advantages and disadvantages of a proprietorship. The transaction to pay creditors for amounts owed is the same as paying on account when the business is not being liquidated. The entry to distribute remaining cash to the owner is not the same as an owner's withdrawal—when the owner withdraws cash, the drawing account is debited; when the business is liquidated, the owner's capital account is debited.

require a proprietorship to obtain an operating license to run a business in that locality. Once these legal requirements have been met, the proprietorship can officially begin business. To begin operation of SportsLure, the owner, Mr. Moher, filed the name of the business with the state and obtained the required city operating license.

Accounting Transaction for Forming a Proprietorship

Once SportsLure was legally established, Mr. Moher invested $10,000.00 of his own money in the business.

Cash

10,000.00	

Roger Moher, Capital

	10,000.00

April 1, 19--. Received cash from owner as an investment, $10,000.00. Receipt No. 1.

Cash is debited for $10,000.00. Roger Moher, Capital is credited for $10,000.00.

The journal entry to record this transaction is shown in Illustration 28-1.

ILLUSTRATION 28-1   Journal entry to record receiving cash from owner as an investment

CASH RECEIPTS JOURNAL

PAGE 1

	DATE	ACCOUNT TITLE	DOC. NO.	POST. REF.	GENERAL DEBIT	GENERAL CREDIT	ACCOUNTS RECEIVABLE CREDIT	SALES CREDIT	SALES TAX PAYABLE DEBIT	SALES TAX PAYABLE CREDIT	SALES DISCOUNT DEBIT	CASH DEBIT	
1	Apr. 1	Roger Moher, Capital	R1			10000.00						10000.00	1
2													2
3													3

DISSOLVING A PROPRIETORSHIP

A proprietor may choose to dissolve the proprietorship at any time. Legal requirements must be completed and correct accounting procedures must be followed when a proprietorship is dissolved.

Legal Requirements for Dissolving a Proprietorship

To dissolve a business, the proprietor merely stops doing business and settles all the affairs of the business. If the business has employees, the owner must notify the appropriate federal and state tax authorities that the business has terminated operations.

Liquidation of a Proprietorship

Once a proprietorship is legally dissolved, the liquidation process can begin. When a proprietorship is liquidated, noncash assets are

FYI

Bankruptcy is a legal procedure in which a company that cannot meet its financial obligations is relieved of its debts. The assets are distributed to the creditors.

usually sold and the cash is used to pay creditors. Any remaining cash is distributed to the owner.

After many years of business, Mr. Moher decided to terminate SportsLure. Necessary legal documents were filed, and on June 30 financial statements were prepared and adjusting and closing entries were journalized and posted. After the end-of-fiscal-period work was completed, the business had account balances as shown in the T accounts.

Cash			Accounts Payable	
21,000.00				9,000.00

Supplies			Roger Moher, Capital	
5,000.00				17,000.00

Selling Noncash Assets for Less than Book Value. Noncash assets are sometimes sold for less than the recorded book value.

July 1, 19--. Received cash from sale of supplies, $3,500.00; book value of supplies, $5,000.00. Receipt No. 744.

Cash			Supplies	
Bal. 21,000.00			Bal. 5,000.00	5,000.00
3,500.00			(New Bal. zero)	
(New Bal. 24,500.00)				

Roger Moher, Capital	
1,500.00	Bal. 17,000.00
	(New Bal. 15,500.00)

The loss on the sale of the supplies is calculated as shown below.

	Book Value of Asset Sold	−	Value of Asset Received	=	Loss on Sale
	Supplies $5,000.00	−	Cash $3,500.00	=	$1,500.00

Because the business is in the process of liquidation, the loss on sale is recorded directly in the owner's capital account.

Cash is debited for the amount received, $3,500.00. Roger Moher, Capital is debited for $1,500.00, the loss on the sale of the supplies. Supplies is credited for the recorded book value of the supplies sold, $5,000.00.

The journal entry to record this transaction is shown in Illustration 28-2 on page 754.

The loss on sale could be recorded in an expense account. Recording the loss in an expense account would provide management with better information regarding the effect of the transaction on owner's equity. However, when a business is being liquidated, this additional information is unnecessary. Therefore, the loss on sale is recorded directly in the owner's capital account.

APPLIED SKILLS: MATHEMATICS

Use the MATH WORK SHEET in the Masters and Solutions to Enrichment/Application Activities Section of the Teacher's Resource Guide to integrate applied mathematics. In this work sheet, students will apply math concepts to calculate gain or loss on the sale of assets.

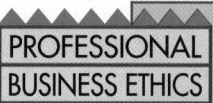

PROFESSIONAL BUSINESS ETHICS

Can You Make Too Much Money?

A majority of the chief executive officers of the nation's largest corporations earn more than $1 million dollars annually. Whereas worker pay increased 53% during the 1980s, chief executive officer pay increased by 212%. As a result, the average chief executive officer earns 85 times the pay of a typical American worker. In contrast, the chief executive officer of a Japanese company receives only 17 times the pay of a worker.

Assume you have recently purchased stock in a company that has experienced substantial growth during the past five years. You expect the company to continue this growth trend, thus increasing the value of your stock. Upon receiving the company's annual financial report, you discover that the chief executive officer earned $3 million dollars last year.

INSTRUCTIONS Use the three-step checklist to determine whether the amount paid to the chief executive officer demonstrates ethical behavior by the company. What action, if any, would you consider taking as a new stockholder?

ILLUSTRATION 28-2   Journal entry to record loss on liquidation of noncash assets

CASH RECEIPTS JOURNAL

PAGE 13

	DATE	ACCOUNT TITLE	DOC. NO.	POST. REF.	GENERAL DEBIT	GENERAL CREDIT	ACCOUNTS RECEIVABLE CREDIT	SALES CREDIT	SALES TAX PAYABLE DEBIT	SALES TAX PAYABLE CREDIT	SALES DISCOUNT DEBIT	CASH DEBIT	
1	19-- July 1	Roger Moher, Capital	R744		1 50 0 00							3 50 0 00	1
2		Supplies				5 00 0 00							2
3													3

GENERAL LEDGER
Accounts Payable

9,000.00	Bal. 9,000.00
	(New Bal. zero)

Cash

Bal. 24,500.00	9,000.00
(New Bal. 15,500.00)	

ACCOUNTS PAYABLE LEDGER
Sampe Sports

5,000.00	Bal. 5,000.00
	(New Bal. zero)

Sports Supply Co.

4,000.00	Bal. 4,000.00
	(New Bal. zero)

Distributing Cash to Creditors. Once all noncash assets have been sold, cash is used to pay all creditors.

> July 2, 19--. Paid cash to all creditors: Sampe Sports, $5,000.00; Sports Supply Co., $4,000.00. Check Numbers 711-712.

Accounts Payable is debited for $9,000.00. Each subsidiary ledger account is debited for the account balance. Cash is credited for $9,000.00.

The journal entry to record this transaction is shown on lines 1 and 2 of Illustration 28-3.

CASH PAYMENTS JOURNAL

PAGE 13

	DATE	ACCOUNT TITLE	CK. NO.	POST. REF.	GENERAL DEBIT	GENERAL CREDIT	ACCOUNTS PAYABLE DEBIT	PURCHASES DISCOUNT CREDIT	CASH CREDIT	
1	July 2	Sampe Sports	711				5 0 0 0 0		5 0 0 0 0	1
2		Sports Supply Co.	712				4 0 0 0 0		4 0 0 0 0	2
3	3	Roger Moher, Capital	713		15 5 0 0 00				15 5 0 0 00	3

When a proprietorship is liquidated, all creditors must be satisfied before the owner can take the remaining cash.

Distributing Remaining Cash to Owner. The last step in the liquidation of a proprietorship is to distribute the remaining cash to the owner.

> *July 3, 19--. Recorded final distribution of remaining cash to Roger Moher, $15,500.00. Check No. 713.*

Roger Moher, Capital is debited for $15,500.00. Cash is credited for $15,500.00.

Roger Moher, Capital	
15,500.00	Bal. 15,500.00
	(New Bal. zero)

Cash	
Bal. 15,500.00	15,500.00
(New Bal. zero)	

The journal entry to record this transaction is shown on line 3 of Illustration 28-3.

After this journal entry is posted, all general ledger accounts will have zero balances. The proprietorship is now liquidated.

Audit Your Understanding

1. Which form of business is the simplest to organize?
2. What is the entry to record investing money to start a proprietorship?
3. What is the last step in liquidating a proprietorship?
4. When a proprietorship is being liquidated, and an asset is sold for less than book value, what is the effect on the proprietor's capital account?

FORMING A PARTNERSHIP

A business in which two or more persons combine their assets and skills is known as a partnership. Michelle Marier and Ron Morgan started a partnership called Rosebud Nursery. The partners chose to form the business as a partnership because of the advantages a partnership has as compared to a proprietorship. The advantages include:

One of the advantages of a partnership is that more resources are available to the business.

1. More resources. Both Ms. Marier and Mr. Morgan will be investing cash and other assets in the business.
2. More time, energy, and experience. Rosebud Nursery will benefit by having two owners who can invest time and energy in the business. Also, both partners will bring experience and skill to the new partnership.

CHAPTER 28 Forming and Dissolving Business Organizations **755**

CLOSURE

- Use Audit Your Understanding questions.
- Review the advantages and disadvantages of a proprietorship.
- Review the entries for initial investment and liquidation of a proprietorship.

AUDIT YOUR UNDERSTANDING

The AUDIT YOUR UNDERSTANDING feature appears at the end of each section of the chapter. Explain to your students that the word *audit* means to check or verify. AUDIT YOUR UNDERSTANDING may be used to check student comprehension of the section just studied. The answers are provided in Appendix D in the back of the textbook.

1. A proprietorship.
2. Debit Cash, credit Capital.
3. Distributing remaining cash to the owner.
4. Capital is decreased with a debit for the amount of loss.

LESSON PLAN 28-2

Materials

- Student pages 755–760
- Transparencies: L, Blank cash payments journal; O, Blank cash receipts journal
- Math Work Sheet Chapter 28: Part B: Calculating Gain on Sale of Assets
- Demonstration Problem: 28B, Journalizing Entries to Form and Liquidate a Partnership

Objectives (Enabling Performance Tasks)

a. Define accounting terms related to forming and liquidating business organizations.
b. Identify the legal requirements for forming and dissolving various forms of business organizations.
c. Journalize entries for initial investment for a proprietorship, partnership, and corporation.
d. Journalize entries for liquidation of a proprietorship and a partnership.

FOCUS

- In Part 3, the accounting cycle of a merchandising business organized as a partnership was presented. In this lesson, we will look at the legal requirements and journal entries for forming and liquidating a partnership.

- Introduce new vocabulary: partnership agreement.

3. Transfer of ownership. If a partnership wants to admit a new partner or if a partner dies or a partner wants to leave the business, the partnership must be dissolved and a new partnership formed. However, the assets of the partnership can be transferred to the new partnership. The assets do not have to be liquidated.

Michelle Marier and Ron Morgan also considered the disadvantages of a partnership. The disadvantages include:

1. Shared decision making. Business decisions must be discussed and agreement reached by both partners.
2. Unlimited liability. *Each* partner is totally responsible for the liabilities of Rosebud Nursery, even those liabilities incurred by the other partner. Therefore, either partner's personal assets may be claimed by creditors to pay all of the partnership's liabilities.
3. Shared profits. Any profits earned by Rosebud Nursery must be divided between the partners based on the agreement between the partners. Losses must also be shared.

When Ms. Marier and Mr. Morgan started Rosebud Nursery, they were required to follow the laws of the state in which the business was formed.

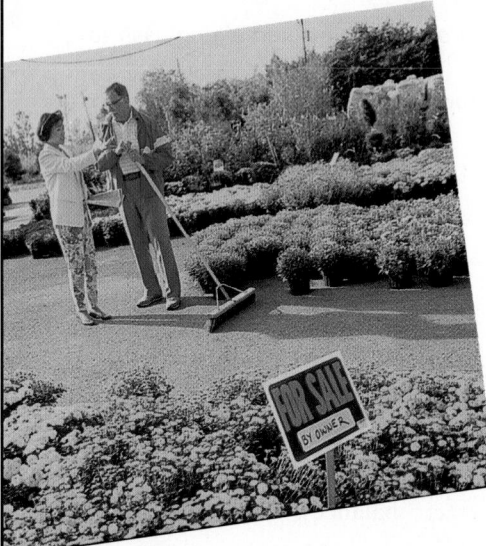

Legal Requirements for Forming a Partnership

In most states, the minimum legal requirement to form a partnership is to file a document to register the name of the partnership with the state in which it is located. An additional document should be created by the partners. A written agreement setting forth the conditions under which a partnership is to operate is called a **partnership agreement.** Although not required by law, it is in the best interest of the partners to sign a partnership agreement. The partnership agreement includes the name and description of the business, capital investments of each partner, distribution of profits and losses, duties and responsibilities of each partner, and provisions for dissolving the partnership. If a partnership agreement is not signed, the laws of the state will determine the conditions under which the partnership is to operate.

Accounting Transactions for Forming a Partnership

☞ ☞ FYI ☞ ☞

Partnership agreements are not required by law but are in the best interests of both partners.

Michelle Marier and Ron Morgan completed the legal requirements to form a partnership named Rosebud Nursery. The partnership agreement called for each partner to invest $5,000.00 in the business.

Cash	
10,000.00	

Michelle Marier, Capital	
	5,000.00

Ron Morgan, Capital	
	5,000.00

May 2, 19--. Received cash from partners as initial investment: from Michelle Marier, $5,000.00; from Ron Morgan, $5,000.00. Receipt Nos. 1 and 2.

In a partnership, a capital account is established for each partner. Cash is debited for the total investment, $10,000.00. Michelle Marier, Capital is credited for $5,000.00. Ron Morgan, Capital is credited for $5,000.00.

The journal entry to record this transaction is shown in Illustration 28-4.

ILLUSTRATION 28-4	Journal entry to record partners' initial investment

CASH RECEIPTS JOURNAL   PAGE 1

					GENERAL		ACCOUNTS RECEIVABLE CREDIT	SALES CREDIT	SALES TAX PAYABLE		SALES DISCOUNT DEBIT	CASH DEBIT	
	DATE	ACCOUNT TITLE	DOC. NO.	POST. REF.	DEBIT	CREDIT			DEBIT	CREDIT			
1	May 19 2	Michelle Marier, Capital	R1			5 00 0 00						5 00 0 00	1
2	2	Ron Morgan, Capital	R2			5 00 0 00						5 00 0 00	2
3													3
4													4
5													5

DISSOLVING A PARTNERSHIP

FYI

In some bankruptcies, a company may continue to exist, satisfying its creditors by a plan for paying part of the debts and writing off the rest.

A partnership may be dissolved for any of several reasons. One or more of the partners may want to discontinue doing business. The partners may need more capital and agree to admit an additional partner. The partners may disagree on how to operate the business. The partnership agreement may call for the partnership to be dissolved on a specific date. When a partnership is dissolved, legal requirements must be met and correct accounting procedures must be followed.

Legal Requirements for Dissolving a Partnership

The terms of the dissolution may be set forth in the partnership agreement if one was created when the partnership was formed. Any terms of dissolution set forth in the partnership agreement must be followed when the partnership is dissolved. If no partnership agreement was created for the business, the laws of the state will govern the dissolution of the partnership.

Whenever a partnership has a change in partners—bringing in additional partners or current partners leaving—the partnership must be legally dissolved and a new partnership established. However, a change in partners does not require the partnership to be liquidated.

Two basic legal actions are usually taken to dissolve a partnership. First, if the name of the partnership was registered with the state when formed, a document should be filed notifying the state

CHAPTER 28   Forming and Dissolving Business Organizations   **757**

- Before actually discussing the advantages/disadvantages of a partnership, have students suggest what could be the advantages/disadvantages of a partnership.

- Draw T accounts on the board for each transaction as it is presented in this lesson.

- Use Transparency O to journalize the partners' initial investments or direct students to Illustration 28-4.

- Write the formula for calculating gain on sale on the chalkboard or overhead.

- Use Transparency O to journalize the sale of noncash assets for more than book value or direct students to Illustration 28-5.

- Use Transparency L to journalize the liquidation of liabilities and distribution of remaining cash to partners or direct students to Illustration 28-6.

Guided Practice

Guide students through Drill 28-D2. Students should have the forms from the working papers to complete as you guide them through calculating the gain on each sale of noncash assets. All students should agree with the calculation for each sale before proceeding to the next item.

Independent Practice

Assign Term 3, Questions 10–15, and Problem 28-2.

that the partnership is being dissolved. If the business has employees, the partners must notify the appropriate federal and state tax authorities that the business has terminated operations.

Liquidation of a Partnership

> **FYI**
>
> Most distributions to partners are made according to the partnership agreement. However, in the final step of liquidation, each partner receives the balance of that partner's capital account.

Once a partnership is dissolved, the liquidation process can begin. When a partnership is liquidated, noncash assets are usually sold and the available cash is used to pay creditors. Any remaining cash is distributed to the partners.

After many years of business, Ms. Marier and Mr. Morgan agreed to dissolve and liquidate Rosebud Nursery. Necessary legal documents were filed, and on August 31 financial statements were prepared and adjusting and closing entries were journalized and posted. After the end-of-fiscal-period work was completed, the partnership had account balances as shown in the T accounts.

Cash		Accounts Payable	
17,000.00			4,000.00

Equipment		Michelle Marier, Capital	
10,000.00			9,000.00

Accumulated Depreciation—Equipment		Ron Morgan, Capital	
	7,000.00		7,000.00

Selling Noncash Assets for More than Book Value. Noncash assets are sometimes sold for more than the recorded book value. When this occurs, the amount received in excess of the book value is added to the partners' capital accounts.

> *September 1, 19--. Received cash from sale of equipment, $5,000.00; original cost, $10,000.00; total accumulated depreciation recorded to date, $7,000.00. Receipt No. 512.*

The gain on the sale of the equipment is calculated as shown below.

Value of Asset Received	−	Book Value of Asset Sold		=	Gain on Sale
		Cost	$10,000.00		
		Accum. Depr.	−7,000.00		
Cash $5,000.00	−	Book Value	$ 3,000.00	=	$2,000.00

Because the partnership is in the process of liquidation, the gain on sale is recorded directly in the partners' capital accounts. The partnership agreement for Rosebud Nursery calls for the partners to share equally in any liquidation gains or losses. Therefore, the $2,000.00 gain is divided equally between the two partners.

TEACHING STRATEGIES: EXPANDING BEYOND THE CLASSROOM

Ask a local small business owner/partner to share with the class the process the owner/partner followed when determining the kind of business to organize.

Cash is debited for the amount received, $5,000.00. Accumulated Depreciation—Equipment is debited for the total depreciation recorded to date, $7,000.00. Equipment is credited for the cost of the equipment, $10,000.00. Michelle Marier, Capital is credited for $1,000.00, her share of the gain. Ron Morgan, Capital is credited for $1,000.00, his share of the gain.

ASSESS

Assess student understanding by checking solutions to Independent Practice activities.

Cash	
Bal. 17,000.00	
5,000.00	
(New Bal. 22,000.00)	

Equipment	
Bal. 10,000.00	10,000.00
(New Bal. zero)	

Accumulated Depreciation—Equipment	
7,000.00	Bal. 7,000.00
	(New Bal. zero)

Michelle Marier, Capital	
	Bal. 9,000.00
	1,000.00
	(New Bal. 10,000.00)

Ron Morgan, Capital	
	Bal. 7,000.00
	1,000.00
	(New Bal. 8,000.00)

Reteach

- Duplicate and assign Math Work Sheet Chapter 28 Part B, Calculating Gain on Sale of Assets from the Masters and Solutions to Enrichment/Application Activities Section in the Teacher's Resource Guide to provide additional practice on the mathematics of calculating gain on sale of assets during liquidation of a business.

- Use Demonstration Problem 28B. This problem can be demonstrated on the overhead with the students completing the problem at their desks.

Extend

Have students name local businesses that they think are partnerships. Ask why they think the businesses are partnerships.

Enrich

- Ask students if they know of any partnerships that have been dissolved. Discuss possible reasons for the dissolution.

- Discuss the PROFESSIONAL BUSINESS ETHICS feature on page 754. You may wish to distribute copies of the 3-Step Checklist for Making Ethical Decisions. A blackline master is furnished in the Masters and Solutions to Enrichment/Application Activities Section in the Teacher's Resource Guide.

The journal entry to record this transaction is shown in Illustration 28-5.

ILLUSTRATION 28-5   Journal entry to record gain on liquidation of noncash assets

CASH RECEIPTS JOURNAL   PAGE 17

	DATE	ACCOUNT TITLE	DOC. NO.	POST. REF.	GENERAL DEBIT	GENERAL CREDIT	ACCOUNTS RECEIVABLE CREDIT	SALES CREDIT	SALES TAX PAYABLE DEBIT	SALES TAX PAYABLE CREDIT	SALES DISCOUNT DEBIT	CASH DEBIT	
1	Sept. 1	Accum. Depr.—Equipment	R512		7 0 0 0 00							5 0 0 0 00	1
2		Equipment				10 0 0 0 00							2
3		Michelle Marier, Capital				1 0 0 0 00							3
4		Ron Morgan, Capital				1 0 0 0 00							4
5													5

The gain on sale could be recorded in an other revenue account. Recording the gain in an other revenue account would provide management with better information regarding the effect of the transaction on partners' equity. However, when a business is being liquidated, this additional information is unnecessary. Therefore, the gain on sale is recorded in the partners' capital accounts.

Distributing Cash to Creditors.   Once all noncash assets have been sold, cash is used to pay all creditors.

CHAPTER 28   Forming and Dissolving Business Organizations   **759**

APPLIED SKILLS: WORD PROCESSING

If you wish to integrate word processing into your accounting course, you may direct students to answer the end-of-chapter Accounting Terms, Questions for Individual Study, and Cases for Critical Thinking using their word processing software.

CLOSURE

- Use Audit Your Understanding questions.
- Review the advantages and disadvantages of a partnership.
- Review the entries for initial investment and liquidation of a partnership.

GENERAL LEDGER
Accounts Payable

4,000.00		Bal.	4,000.00
		(New Bal. zero)	

Cash

Bal.	22,000.00		4,000.00
(New Bal.	18,000.00)		

ACCOUNTS PAYABLE LEDGER
American Tree Company

2,300.00		Bal.	2,300.00
		(New Bal. zero)	

Waltham Sod Farm

1,700.00		Bal.	1,700.00
		(New Bal. zero)	

September 3, 19--. Paid cash to all creditors: American Tree Company, $2,300.00; Waltham Sod Farm, $1,700.00. Check Numbers 589-590.

Accounts Payable is debited for $4,000.00. Each subsidiary ledger account is debited for the account balance. Cash is credited for $4,000.00.

The journal entry to record this transaction is shown on lines 1 and 2 of Illustration 28-6.

Distributing Remaining Cash to Partners. The last step in the liquidation of a partnership is to distribute the remaining cash to the partners. The balance in each partner's capital account is distributed to each partner.

ILLUSTRATION 28-6   Journal entries to record liquidation of liabilities and distribution of remaining cash to partners

CASH PAYMENTS JOURNAL — PAGE 17

	DATE		ACCOUNT TITLE	CK. NO.	POST. REF.	GENERAL DEBIT	GENERAL CREDIT	ACCOUNTS PAYABLE DEBIT	PURCHASES DISCOUNT CREDIT	CASH CREDIT	
1	Sept.	3	American Tree Company	589				2 3 0 0 00		2 3 0 0 00	1
2			Waltham Sod Farm	590				1 7 0 0 00		1 7 0 0 00	2
3		4	Michelle Marier, Capital	591		10 0 0 0 00				10 0 0 0 00	3
4			Ron Morgan, Capital	592		8 0 0 0 00				8 0 0 0 00	4

AUDIT YOUR UNDERSTANDING

1. A partnership agreement.
2. The partnership must be legally dissolved and a new partnership established.
3. The balance of the cash account which includes cash received from buyers of the noncash assets.
4. The partnership's creditors are paid first and any remaining cash is distributed to the partners.

Audit Your Understanding

1. What is a written agreement called that sets forth the conditions under which a partnership is to operate?
2. What is required if a partnership has a change in partners?
3. When a partnership is liquidated, what are the most common sources of cash?
4. During the process of liquidating a partnership, who usually receives cash?

September 4, 19--. Recorded final distribution of remaining cash to partners: to Michelle Marier, $10,000.00; to Ron Morgan, $8,000.00. Check Numbers 591 and 592.

Michelle Marier, Capital

10,000.00		Bal. 10,000.00	
		(New Bal. zero)	

Cash

Bal. 18,000.00		18,000.00
(New Bal. zero)		

Ron Morgan, Capital

8,000.00		Bal. 8,000.00	
		(New Bal. zero)	

Michelle Marier, Capital is debited for $10,000.00. Ron Morgan, Capital is debited for $8,000.00. Cash is credited for $18,000.00.

The journal entry to record this transaction is shown on lines 3 and 4 of Illustration 28-6.

After this journal entry is posted, all general ledger accounts will have zero balances. The partnership is now liquidated.

TEACHING STRATEGIES: DIFFERENT LEARNING ABILITIES

Specific Learning Disability (SLD) Students. Incorporate current literature (magazines and newspapers) to identify current topics of interest to students.

FORMING A CORPORATION

An organization with the legal rights of a person and which may be owned by many persons is known as a corporation. Each unit of ownership in a corporation is known as a share of stock. An owner of one or more shares of a corporation is known as a stockholder.

A group of owners is starting a corporation called LakeShore, Inc. The owners considered the advantages and disadvantages of a corporate form of business.

The advantages of a corporation include:

One advantage of a corporation is limited liability.

1. Expanded resources. Corporations such as LakeShore, Inc. raise funds by selling stock. The sale of stock means that LakeShore, Inc. may be able to acquire more capital than would be possible as a proprietorship or partnership.
2. Limited liability. Stockholders of LakeShore, Inc. are not usually personally responsible for the liabilities of the corporation.
3. Ease of transfer of ownership. Ownership is transferred when a share of stock is sold. The process of selling stock does not affect the continuation of the corporation.
4. Legal rights. Since a corporation has the legal rights of a person, the corporation may buy, own, and sell property in its corporate name.

The disadvantages of a corporation include:

1. High organization cost. A corporation is the most complex and expensive form of business to establish.
2. Extensive government regulation. Corporations must comply with numerous government regulations, which often require the completion of extensive reports.
3. Double taxation. As a separate legal entity, corporations are subject to taxation. In addition, the profits distributed to a stockholder are subject to taxation as personal income for the stockholder.

When LakeShore, Inc. was formed, the owners were required to follow the laws of the state in which the business was formed and the states in which it intended to operate.

Legal Requirements for Forming a Corporation

A merger occurs when two or more companies combine to form one new company.

A corporation is the most complex kind of business to form. Many laws must be followed to legally form a corporation. Several legal documents must be created and filed. A written application requesting permission to form a corporation is called the **articles of incorporation.** The articles of incorporation are filed with the Secretary of State where the corporation is formed. The articles of incorporation contain the name and nature of the business, the number of shares of stock authorized, the names of incorporators and officers, and other conditions about the new corporation. The articles of incorporation is just one of many legal documents necessary for incorporating a business. Failure to comply with these laws can

Materials

- Student pages 761–764
- Transparencies: O, Blank cash receipts journal; 28-1, Chapter Summary
- Software: Electronic Study Guide
- Demonstration Problem: 28C, Journalizing Entries to Form a Corporation
- Assess: Problem Test Chapter 28, MicroExam Chapter 28

Objectives (Enabling Performance Tasks)

a. Define accounting terms related to forming and liquidating business organizations.

b. Identify the legal requirements for forming and dissolving various forms of business organizations.

c. Journalize entries for initial investment for a proprietorship, partnership, and corporation.

FOCUS

- In Part 4, the accounting cycle of a merchandising business organized as a corporation was presented. In this lesson we will look at the legal requirements and journal entries for forming a corporation.
- Introduce new vocabulary: articles of incorporation, par value, par-value stock.

TEACH

Cover student pages 761– 764 "Forming a Corporation" and "Dissolving a Corporation." Review the definition of share of stock and stockholder. Discuss the advantages and disadvantages of a corporation. Proprietorships and partnerships are not taxed as legal entities; the owners of a proprietorship or a partnership pay taxes on the profits of the businesses through their individual tax return, while a corporation pays taxes on its earnings. The transaction to form a corporation is similar to those for forming a proprietorship or partnership. A corporation is rarely dissolved; the corporate form of ownership is based on the idea of a perpetual life. The accounting aspects of liquidating a corporation are extremely complex and should be handled by a professional accounting service.

TEACHING STRATEGIES: Teaching Tip

Emphasize the similarities in the entries for forming a proprietorship, a partnership, and a corporation. In each transaction, the business is receiving cash and records an increase in equity account(s).

APPLY

- Draw T accounts on the board for the sale of stock transaction.

- Use Transparency O to journalize the entry to record sale of stock at par value or direct students to Illustration 28-7.

Guided Practice

Guide students through a comparison of the advantages and disadvantages of the three forms of business organization. Assign students to each type of organization to record the items the rest of the class will name. Have the students write "Proprietorships," "Partnerships," and "Corporations" as headings across the top of the board. Ask students to list the advantages of each form of business organization under the appropriate heading. Then, ask them to list the disadvantages.

Independent Practice

Assign Terms 4–6, Questions 16–20, Problem 28-3, Mastery Problem 28-M, and Study Guide 28.

ASSESS

Assess student understanding by checking solutions to Independent Practice activities.

Reteach

- Use Demonstration Problem 28C. This problem can be demonstrated on the overhead with the students completing the problem at their desks.

- Assign Recycling Problem 28-R.

Extend

- Have students name local businesses that they think are corporations.

- Assign the Electronic Study Guide Chapter 28.

Enrich

- Assign Case for Critical Thinking 1.

- Assign Challenge Problem 28-C. (The challenge is that gain on sale of equipment is divided unequally between the partners.)

- Assign students to read the MULTI-CULTURAL AWARENESS feature on page 751.

result in loss of corporate status for the business. Since the forming of a corporation is complex, the incorporators should seek legal advice.

Accounting Transactions for Forming a Corporation

Once a corporation is legally established, the corporation may begin selling shares of stock. Shares of stock are frequently assigned a value as part of the articles of incorporation. A value assigned to a share of stock and printed on the stock certificate is called **par value.** A share of stock that has an authorized value printed on the stock certificate is called **par-value stock.**

The incorporators of Lakeshore, Inc. completed the legal requirements for a corporation. The corporation received $100,000.00 in cash for which 100,000 shares of common stock are to be issued.

March 1, 19--. Received cash for 100,000 shares of $1.00 par-value common stock, $100,000.00. Receipt Nos. 1–7.

In a corporation, a capital account is *not* established for each owner. Instead, one summary general ledger capital account titled Capital Stock is used for all stock issued. Cash is debited for $100,000.00. Capital Stock is credited for $100,000.00.

The journal entry to record this transaction is shown in Illustration 28-7.

```
            Cash
    100,000.00  |
    _____|_____

         Capital Stock
                |
                |  100,000.00
```

| ILLUSTRATION 28-7 | Journal entry to record sale of stock at par value |

CASH RECEIPTS JOURNAL PAGE 1

					GENERAL		ACCOUNTS RECEIVABLE CREDIT	SALES CREDIT	SALES TAX PAYABLE		SALES DISCOUNT DEBIT	CASH DEBIT	
	DATE	ACCOUNT TITLE	DOC. NO.	POST. REF.	DEBIT	CREDIT			DEBIT	CREDIT			
					1	2	3	4	5	6	7	8	
1	Mar. 1	Capital Stock	R1–7			100 000 00						100 000 00	1
2													2
3													3

DISSOLVING A CORPORATION

👉👉 **FYI** 👈👈

In an acquisition, a company or group buys another company; the identity of the acquired company may be absorbed into the existing one.

When a corporation is dissolved, legal requirements must be met and correct accounting procedures must be followed. Legal and accounting procedures have been established for the dissolution of a corporation. However, it is rare that a corporation is dissolved. The proprietorship and partnership forms of business are both tied very closely to the owner(s). When the owner(s) die or decide to stop doing business, the business is legally dissolved. A corporate form of ownership, however, is based on the idea of a perpetual life *(CONCEPT: Going Concern)*. When an owner (stockholder) decides not to participate in the corporation, the stockholder merely sells all shares of stock owned. The corporation is not dissolved.

762   PART 4   Accounting for a Merchandising Business Organized as a Corporation

APPLIED SKILLS: WRITING ACROSS THE CURRICULUM

Writing paragraphs and short essays. The Cases for Critical Thinking are short, practical applications of the accounting principles developed in the chapter. Some cases are planned to present problems related to the chapter but not specifically discussed and answered in the chapter. These cases present an opportunity for critical thinking and decision making. These cases also require more than a short objective-type response. Therefore, they provide ideal practice in writing paragraphs and short essays.

Legal Requirements for Dissolving a Corporation

The corporation is also the most complex form of business to dissolve. The dissolution of a corporation involves many legal procedures and documents. Documents that must be filed include a notice to the state in which the business was incorporated and a notice to all creditors of the corporation. Since the dissolution of a corporation is complex, the board of directors should seek legal advice.

Liquidation of a Corporation

Once a corporation is dissolved, the liquidation process can begin. When a corporation is liquidated, noncash assets are usually sold and the available cash is used to pay creditors. The procedure for selling noncash assets is similar to that for proprietorships and partnerships. However, since a corporation is a taxable entity, the gains and losses on the sale of noncash assets are subject to taxation. Therefore, additional tax reports for the corporation must be filed.

The accounting aspects of actually liquidating a corporation are extremely complex. Therefore, obtaining professional accounting services to assist in the liquidation of a corporation is recommended.

The chart shown in Summary Illustration 28-8 on page 764 summarizes the processes of forming and liquidating business organizations.

Audit Your Understanding

1. What is each unit of ownership in a corporation called?
2. What is a written application requesting permission to form a corporation called?
3. What is meant by "double taxation" for corporations?
4. What is the entry to record the issuance of stock for a corporation?
5. Why are corporations rarely dissolved?

- Use Audit Your Understanding questions.
- Review the advantages and disadvantages of a corporation.
- Review Summary Illustration 28-8, "Summary of Forming and Liquidating Business Organizations." Use Transparency 28-1, Chapter Summary.

ASSESS

- Administer Problem Test Chapter 28.
- Administer a MicroExam test for Chapter 28.

AUDIT YOUR UNDERSTANDING

1. A share of stock.
2. The articles of incorporation.
3. Corporations pay federal income tax on their net income and stockholders pay an additional personal income tax on profits distributed to them as dividends.
4. Debit Cash, credit Capital Stock.
5. Because they are based on the idea of perpetual life.

APPLIED SKILLS: BUILDING STUDY SKILLS

Chapter summary illustrations describe the important points within a chapter. The summary illustration in this chapter describes the entries necessary to form and liquidate different kinds of business organizations. Students should develop the habit of studying the summary illustrations and making certain that they understand the points that are summarized.

SUMMARY ILLUSTRATION 28-8

Summary of forming and liquidating business organizations

	Proprietorship	Partnership	Corporation
Ownership	1 person	2 or more partners	All stockholders
Legal Requirements to Establish	Simple	Moderate	Complex
Investment Account	1 capital account	1 capital account for each partner	1 capital stock account
Entry for Cash Investment	Debit: Cash Credit: Owner's Capital Account	Debit: Cash Credit: Each Partner's Capital Account	Debit: Cash Credit: Capital Stock
Steps for Liquidation	1. Sell noncash assets 2. Pay creditors 3. Distribute remaining cash to owner	1. Sell noncash assets 2. Pay creditors 3. Distribute remaining cash to partners	Complex process requiring the help of legal and accounting professionals

ACCOUNTING TERMS   EPT(a)

What is the meaning of each of the following?

1. **dissolution**
2. **liquidation**
3. **partnership agreement**
4. **articles of incorporation**
5. **par value**
6. **par-value stock**

1. What are the advantages of the proprietorship form of business?

2. What are the disadvantages of the proprietorship form of business?

3. What is the simplest form of business to organize?

4. What accounts are affected, and how, when an owner invests in a proprietorship?

5. What is the formula for calculating a loss on sale?

6. In the liquidation of a proprietorship, what accounts are affected, and how, when supplies are sold for less than the recorded book value?

7. In a liquidation, what general ledger accounts are affected, and how, when cash is distributed to creditors?

8. What is the last step in the liquidation of a proprietorship?

9. In the liquidation of a proprietorship, what accounts are affected, and how, when the remaining cash is distributed to the owner?

10. What are the advantages of the partnership form of business as compared to a proprietorship?

11. What are the disadvantages of the partnership form of business as compared to a proprietorship?

12. What is the formula for calculating a gain on sale?

13. In the liquidation of a partnership, what accounts are affected, and how, when equipment is sold for more than the recorded book value?

14. How are liquidation gains or losses divided between partners?

15. In the liquidation of a partnership, what accounts are affected, and how, when the remaining cash is distributed to the partners?

16. What is the owner of one or more shares of a corporation called?

17. What are the advantages of the corporate form of business?

18. What are the disadvantages of the corporate form of business?

19. What accounts are affected, and how, when stock is sold?

20. Why is it recommended that professional accounting services be employed to assist in the liquidation of a corporation?

CASE FOR CRITICAL THINKING
EPT(b)

CASE 1 Barbara Sather wants to open a hair salon. She also knows several people who would like to go into the business with her. What should Ms. Sather consider when deciding the form of ownership that is most appropriate for her?

APPLIED COMMUNICATIONS

Public speakers are judged by the ability of their audience to remember important points of their presentation. Effective public speakers use a variety of techniques to encourage the audience to listen to their message.

INSTRUCTIONS:

Contact an instructor in your school or a local businessperson you have heard speak at school or community functions. Ask the person to describe the techniques used to help the audience listen and retain the message. Write a short report summarizing these techniques. Be prepared to present your report orally in class.

1. Ease of formation, total control, and unshared profits. (p. 751)

2. Limited resources; unlimited liability; limited time, energy, and experience; and limited life. (p. 751)

3. A proprietorship. (p. 751)

4. Cash is debited; Capital is credited. (p. 752)

5. Book value of asset sold − value of asset received = loss on sale. (p. 753)

6. Cash and Capital are debited; Supplies is credited. (p. 753)

7. Accounts Payable is debited; Cash is credited. (p. 754)

8. Distribute the remaining cash to the owner. (p. 755)

9. Capital is debited; Cash is credited. (p. 755)

10. More resources; more time, energy, and experience; transfer of ownership. (pp. 755–756)

11. Shared decision making, unlimited liability, and shared profits. (p. 756)

12. Value of asset received − book value of asset sold = gain on sale. (p. 758)

13. According to the partnership agreement. (p. 758)

14. Cash and Accumulated Depreciation—Equipment are debited; Equipment and each partner's capital account are credited. (p. 759)

15. Each partner's capital account is debited; Cash is credited. (p. 760)

16. Stockholder. (p. 761)

APPLIED SKILLS:
COMMUNICATIONS

Surveys of business managers show that communication skills are one of the most desired traits in new employees. The student activity APPLIED COMMUNICATIONS provides an opportunity for students to practice their communication and language arts skills on topics that directly relate to accounting. This activity requires students to prepare a short report summarizing the techniques effective public speakers use to help their audience remember the important points of their presentation.

QUESTIONS (cont'd)

17. Expanded resources, limited liability, ease of transfer of ownership, and legal rights. (p. 761)

18. High organization cost, extensive government regulation, and double taxation. (p. 761)

19. Cash is debited; Capital Stock is credited. (p. 762)

20. The accounting aspects of liquidating a corporation are extremely complex. (p. 763)

CASE FOR CRITICAL THINKING

Case 1 Barbara Sather should consider several items: (1) Does she want to give up total control of the hair salon? (2) Does she have enough capital to invest in the business without taking in any other partners? (3) Does she have enough time, energy, and experience to successfully operate the business by herself? (4) Is she willing to be personally responsible for the liabilities of the hair salon? (5) Will the anticipated profits from the hair salon be enough to support more than one owner? (6) Can she trust any of the potential partners to incur liabilities for the business? (7) Can she work closely with any of the potential co-owners? (8) Do the advantages of a corporation outweigh the double taxation? (9) Which form of ownership would be easiest to transfer if she chooses to get out of the business? (10) How much would it cost to form a partnership or corporation instead of starting a proprietorship? (11) Is she willing to conform to the government regulations for corporations?

APPLIED COMMUNICATIONS

Student solutions will vary. The instructor should consider the following items when grading this activity: (1) completeness, and (2) mechanics (grammar, spelling, punctuation, sentence structure).

DRILLS FOR UNDERSTANDING   EPT(d)

DRILL 28-D1 Calculating loss on sale

INSTRUCTIONS:

Calculate the amount of loss on sale for each transaction listed below.

Transaction 1. Received cash from sale of supplies, $1,000.00; book value of supplies, $1,600.00.

Transaction 2. Received cash from sale of equipment, $1,500.00; original cost, $4,000.00; total accumulated depreciation recorded to date, $2,200.00.

Transaction 3. Received cash from sale of truck, $5,000.00; original cost, $12,000.00; total accumulated depreciation recorded to date, $4,000.00.

DRILL 28-D2 Calculating gain on sale

INSTRUCTIONS:

Calculate the amount of gain on sale for each transaction listed below.

Transaction 1. Received cash from sale of supplies, $1,200.00; book value of supplies, $1,100.00.

Transaction 2. Received cash from sale of equipment, $2,100.00; original cost, $6,000.00; total accumulated depreciation recorded to date, $4,500.00.

Transaction 3. Received cash from sale of truck, $8,000.00; original cost, $15,000.00; total accumulated depreciation recorded to date, $9,000.00.

APPLICATION PROBLEMS   EPT(c,d)

PROBLEM 28-1 Journalizing entries to form and liquidate a proprietorship

INSTRUCTIONS:

Journalize the following transactions completed during the first and last years of operation. Use page 1 of a cash receipts journal for the first transaction. Use page 17 of a cash receipts journal and a cash payments journal for all remaining transactions.

Mar. 1, 19X1. Received cash from James McKimmy as an investment, $3,000.00. R1.

Sept. 1, 19X9. Received cash from sale of supplies, $1,250.00; book value of supplies, $1,400.00. R258.

Sept. 1, 19X9. Paid cash to all creditors: Cline Carpet, $1,250.00; Carpet Wholesalers, $2,450.00. C541-542.

Sept. 2, 19X9. Recorded final distribution of remaining cash to James McKimmy, $6,500.00. C543.

PROBLEM 28-2 Journalizing entries to form and liquidate a partnership

INSTRUCTIONS:

Journalize the following transactions completed during the first and last years of operation. Use page 1 of a cash receipts journal for the first transaction. Use page 5 of a cash receipts journal and a cash payments journal for all remaining transactions. The partnership agreement states that all losses or gains on sale are to be divided equally between the partners.

Nov. 1, 19X1. Received cash from partners as initial investment: from Laura Erickson, $4,000.00; from Kent Dodge, $6,000.00. R1-2.

Mar. 1, 19X8. Received cash from sale of equipment, $11,000.00; original cost, $20,000.00; total accumulated depreciation recorded to date, $12,000.00. R329.

CHECK FIGURES

See Teacher's Edition of Working Papers for solutions.

Drill 28-D1   600, 300, 3,000.

Drill 28-D2   100.00, 600, 2,000.

Problem 28-1   Loss on Sale: 150; Cash distributed to owner: 6,500.

Problem 28-2   Gain on Sale: 3,000; Cash distributed to partners: Erickson, 5,000; Dodge, 9,500.

Mar. 1, 19X8. Paid cash to all creditors: Precision Supplies, $4,100.00; Wacher Florist, $1,100.00. C492-493.

Mar. 2, 19X8. Recorded final distribution of remaining cash to partners: to Laura Erickson, $5,000.00; to Kent Dodge, $9,500.00. C494-495.

PROBLEM 28-3 Journalizing entries to form a corporation

INSTRUCTIONS:

Journalize the following transaction completed during the current year. Use page 1 of a cash receipts journal. Source documents are abbreviated as follows: receipt, R.

June 1. Received cash for 120,000 shares of $1.00 par-value common stock, $120,000.00. R1-6.

ENRICHMENT PROBLEMS   EPT(c,d)

MASTERY PROBLEM 28-M Journalizing entries to form and liquidate business organizations

INSTRUCTIONS:

1. Journalize the following transaction. Use page 1 of a cash receipts journal.

Jan. 1, 19X1. Received cash from Dennis Moen as an investment, $4,000.00. R1.

Dennis Moen has decided to liquidate his business and start a partnership with his sister.

2. Journalize the following transactions. Use page 7 of a cash receipts journal and a cash payments journal.

April 1, 19X3. Received cash from sale of supplies, $1,000.00; book value of supplies, $1,200.00. R175.

April 1, 19X3. Paid cash to all creditors: Industrial Cleaners, $550.00; Neiman Interiors, $650.00. C233-234.

April 2, 19X3. Recorded final distribution of remaining cash to Dennis Moen, $1,500.00. C235.

Dennis Moen and Dorothy Moen agree to form a partnership called Moen Music Company.

3. Journalize the following transaction. Use page 1 of a cash receipts journal.

April 15, 19X3. Received cash from partners as initial investment: from Dennis Moen, $1,500.00; from Dorothy Moen, $2,000.00. R1-2.

Dennis and Dorothy Moen have agreed to liquidate their business and form a corporation with other business associates.

4. Journalize the following transactions. Use page 9 of a cash receipts journal and a cash payments journal. The partnership agreement states that all losses or gains on sale are to be divided equally between the partners.

May 1, 19X7. Received cash from sale of equipment, $8,000.00; original cost, $22,000.00; total accumulated depreciation recorded to date, $15,000.00. R222.

May 1, 19X7. Paid cash to all creditors: Burke Piano Movers, $250.00; Thomas Musical Instruments, $2,950.00. C256-257.

May 2, 19X7. Recorded final distribution of remaining cash to partners: to Dennis Moen, $6,000.00; to Dorothy Moen, $8,000.00. C258-259.

Dennis Moen and four other business associates agree to form a corporation called Moen, Inc.

5. Journalize the following transaction. Use page 1 of a cash receipts journal.

June 1, 19X7. Received cash for 75,000 shares of $1.00 par-value common stock, $75,000.00. R1-6.

CHECK FIGURES (cont'd)

Challenge Problem 28-C Distribution of gain on sale of equipment: Stone, 600; Vance, 400.

CHALLENGE PROBLEM 28-C Journalizing entries to liquidate a partnership

INSTRUCTIONS:

1. Journalize the following transactions completed during June of the current year. Use page 11 of a cash receipts journal and a cash payments journal. The partnership agreement states that all losses or gains on sale are to be divided 60% to Vivian Stone and 40% to Carol Vance.

June 15. Received cash from sale of equipment, $2,000.00; original cost, $12,000.00; total accumulated depreciation recorded to date, $11,000.00. R321.

June 16. Paid cash to all creditors: Hunter Company, $1,320.00; Twain Inc., $3,880.00. C765-766.

June 16. Recorded final distribution of remaining cash to partners: to Vivian Stone, $2,000.00; to Carol Vance, $3,500.00. C767-768.

Accounting Concepts

The following accounting concepts and their definitions are provided in this appendix for ready reference.

ACCOUNTING CONCEPTS

Accounting personnel are guided in their work by generally accepted accounting concepts. Ten commonly accepted accounting concepts are described in this appendix. Each concept is fully explained in the text the first time an application of the concept is described. Throughout the textbook, each time a concept application occurs, a concept reference is given, such as *(CONCEPT: Business Entity)*.

1. ACCOUNTING PERIOD CYCLE. [Chapter 8]
   Changes in financial information are reported for a specific period of time in the form of financial statements.

2. ADEQUATE DISCLOSURE. [Chapter 9]
   Financial statements contain all information necessary to understand a business' financial condition.

3. BUSINESS ENTITY. [Chapter 2]
   Financial information is recorded and reported separately from the owner's personal financial information.

4. CONSISTENT REPORTING. [Chapter 8]
The same accounting procedures are followed in the same way in each accounting period.

5. GOING CONCERN. [Chapter 2]
Financial statements are prepared with the expectation that a business will remain in operation indefinitely.

6. HISTORICAL COST. [Chapter 11]
The actual amount paid for merchandise or other items bought is recorded.

7. MATCHING EXPENSES WITH REVENUE. [Chapter 8]
Revenue from business activities and expenses associated with earning that revenue are recorded in the same accounting period.

8. OBJECTIVE EVIDENCE. [Chapter 5]
A source document is prepared for each transaction.

9. REALIZATION OF REVENUE. [Chapter 12]
Revenue is recorded at the time goods or services are sold.

10. UNIT OF MEASUREMENT. [Chapter 2]
Business transactions are stated in numbers that have common values, that is, using a common unit of measurement.

Using a Calculator and Computer Keypad

KINDS OF CALCULATORS

Many different models of calculators, both desktop and hand held, are available. All calculators have their own features and particular placement of operating keys. Therefore, it is necessary to refer to the operator's manual for specific instructions and locations of the operating keys for the calculator being used. A typical keyboard of a desktop calculator is shown in Illustration B-1.

ILLUSTRATION B-1   Typical desktop calculator keyboard

DESKTOP CALCULATOR SETTINGS

Several operating switches on a desktop calculator must be engaged before the calculator will produce the desired results.

The *decimal selector* sets the appropriate decimal places necessary for the numbers that will be entered. For example, if the decimal selector is set at 2, both the numbers entered and the answer will have two decimal places. If the decimal selector is set at F, the calculator automatically sets the decimal places. The F setting allows the answer to be unrounded and carried out to the maximum number of decimal places possible.

The *decimal rounding selector* rounds the answers. The down arrow position will drop any digits beyond the last digit desired. The up arrow position will drop any digits beyond the last digit desired and round the last digit up. In the 5/4 position, the calculator rounds the last desired digit up only when the following digit is 5 or greater. If the following digit is less than 5, the last desired digit remains unchanged.

The *GT* or *grand total switch* in the on position accumulates totals.

KINDS OF COMPUTER KEYBOARDS

The computer has a keypad on the right side of the keyboard called the **numeric keypad.** Even though several styles of keyboards for the IBM® and compatible computers are found, there are two basic layouts for the numeric keypad. The standard layout and enhanced layout are shown in Illustration B-2 on page B-3. On the standard keyboard the directional arrow keys are found on the number keys. To use the numbers, press the key called **Num Lock.** (This key is found above the "7" key.) When the Num Lock is turned on, numbers are entered when the keys on the keypad are pressed. When the Num Lock is off, the arrow, Home, Page Up, Page Down, End, Insert, and Delete keys can be used.

The enhanced keyboards have the arrow keys and the other directional keys mentioned above to the left of the numeric keypad. When using the keypad on an enhanced keyboard, Num Lock can remain on.

The asterisk (*) performs a different function on the computer than the calculator. The asterisk on the calculator is used for the total while the computer uses it for multiplication.

Another difference is the division key. The computer key is the forward slash key (/). The calculator key uses the division key (÷).

TEN-KEY TOUCH SYSTEM

Striking the numbers 0 to 9 on a calculator or numeric keypad without looking at the keyboard is called the **touch system.** Using the touch system develops both speed and accuracy.

Standard
Keyboard Layout

Enhanced
Keyboard Layout

The 4, 5, and 6 keys are called the **home row.** If the right hand is used for the keyboard, the index finger is placed on the 4 key, the middle finger on the 5 key, and the ring finger on the 6 key. If the left hand is used, the ring finger is placed on the 4 key, the middle finger on the 5 key, and the index finger on the 6 key.

Place the fingers on the home row keys. Curve the fingers and keep the wrist straight. These keys may feel slightly concaved or the 5 key may have a raised dot. The differences in the home row allow the operator to recognize the home row by touch rather than by sight.

Maintain the position of the fingers on the home row. The finger used to strike the 4 key will also strike the 7 key and the 1 key. Stretch the finger up to reach the 7; then stretch the finger down to reach the 1 key. Visualize the position of these keys.

Again, place the fingers on the home row. Stretch the finger that strikes the 5 key up to reach the 8 key, then down to reach the 2 key. Likewise, stretch the finger that strikes the 6 key up to strike the 9 and down to strike the 3 key. This same finger will stretch down again to hit the decimal point.

If the right hand is used, the thumb will be used to strike the 0 and 00 keys and the little finger to strike the addition key. If the left hand is used, the little finger will be used to strike the 0 and 00 keys and the thumb to strike the addition key.

HAND-HELD CALCULATORS

Hand-held calculators are slightly different from desktop calculators, not only in their size and features but also in their operation. Refer to the operator's manual for specific instructions for the calculator being used.

On a hand-held calculator, the numeric keys are usually very close together. In addition, the keys do not respond to touch as easily as on a desktop calculator. Therefore, the touch system is usually not used on a hand-held calculator.

PERFORMING MATHEMATICAL OPERATIONS ON DESKTOP CALCULATORS

Mathematical operations can be performed on a calculator both quickly and efficiently. The basic operations of addition, subtraction, multiplication, and division are used frequently on a calculator.

Addition

Each number to be added is called an **addend**. The answer to an addition problem is called the **sum**.

Addition is performed by entering an addend and striking the addition key (+). All numbers are entered on a calculator in the exact order they are given. To enter the number 4,455.65, strike the 4, 4, 5, 5, decimal, 6, and 5 keys in that order, and then strike the addition key. Commas are not entered. Continue in this manner until all addends have been entered. To obtain the sum, strike the total key on the calculator.

Subtraction

The top number or first number of a subtraction problem is called the **minuend**. The number to be subtracted from the minuend is called the **subtrahend**. The answer to a subtraction problem is called the **difference**.

Subtraction is performed by first entering the minuend and striking the addition key (+). The subtrahend is then entered, followed by the minus key (−), followed by the total key.

Multiplication

The number to be multiplied is called the **multiplicand**. The number of times the multiplicand will be multiplied is called the **multiplier**. The answer to a multiplication problem is called the **product**.

Multiplication is performed by entering the multiplicand and striking the multiplication key (×). The multiplier is then entered, followed by the equals key (=). The calculator will automatically multiply and give the product.

Division

The number to be divided is called the **dividend**. The number the dividend will be divided by is called the **divisor**. The answer to a division problem is called the **quotient**.

Division is performed by entering the dividend and striking the division key (÷). The divisor is then entered, followed by the equals key (=). The calculator will automatically divide and give the quotient.

Correcting Errors

If an error is made while using a calculator, several methods of correction may be used. If an incorrect number has been entered and the addition key or equals key has not yet been struck, strike the clear entry (CE) key one time. This key will clear only the last number that was entered. However, if the clear entry key is depressed more than one time, the entire problem will be cleared on some calculators. If an incorrect number has been entered and the addition key has been struck, strike the minus key one time only. This will automatically subtract the last number added, thus removing it from the total.

PERFORMING MATHEMATICAL OPERATIONS ON COMPUTERS AND HAND-HELD CALCULATORS

On a computer keypad or a hand-held calculator, addition is performed in much the same way as on a desktop calculator. However, after the + key is depressed, the display usually shows the accumulated total. Therefore, the total key is not found. Some computer programs will not calculate the total until Enter is pressed.

Subtraction is performed differently on many computer keypads and hand-held calculators. The minuend is usually entered, followed by the minus (−) key. Then the subtrahend is entered. Pressing either the + key or the = key will display the difference. Some computer programs will not calculate the difference until Enter is pressed.

Multiplication and division are performed the same way on a computer keypad and hand-held calculator as on a desktop calculator. Keep in mind that computers use the * for multiplication and / for division.

SAFETY CONCERNS

Whenever electrical equipment such as a calculator or computer is being operated in a classroom or office, several safety rules apply. These rules protect the operator of the equipment, other persons in the environment, and the equipment itself.

1. Do not unplug equipment by pulling on the electrical cord. Instead, grasp the plug at the outlet and remove it.

2. Do not stretch electrical cords across an aisle where someone might trip over them.

3. Avoid food and beverages near the equipment where a spill might result in an electrical short.

4. Do not attempt to remove the cover of a calculator, computer, or keyboard for any reason while the power is turned on.

5. Do not attempt to repair equipment while it is plugged in.

6. Always turn the power off or unplug equipment when finished using it.

CALCULATION DRILLS

INSTRUCTIONS FOR DESKTOP CALCULATORS

Complete each drill using the touch method. Set the decimal selector at the setting indicated in each drill. Compare the answer on the calculator to the answer in the book. If the two are the same, progress to the next problem. It is not necessary to enter 00 in the cents column if the decimal selector is set at 0-F. However, digits other than zeros in the cents column must be entered preceded by a decimal point.

INSTRUCTIONS FOR COMPUTER KEYPADS

Complete each drill using the touch method. There is no decimal selector on computer keypads. Set the number of decimal places as directed in the instructions for the computer program. In spreadsheets, for example, use the formatting options to set the number of decimal places. When the drill indicates "F" for floating, leave the computer application in its default format. Compare the answer on the computer monitor to the answer in the book. If the two are the same, progress to the next problem. It is not necessary to enter 00 in the cents column. However, digits other than zeros in the cents column must be entered preceded by a decimal point.

DRILL D-1 **Performing addition using the home row keys**
Decimal Selector—2

4.00	44.00	444.00	4,444.00	44,444.00
5.00	55.00	555.00	5,555.00	55,555.00
6.00	66.00	666.00	6,666.00	66,666.00
5.00	45.00	455.00	4,455.00	44,556.00
4.00	46.00	466.00	4,466.00	44,565.00
5.00	54.00	544.00	5,544.00	55,446.00
6.00	56.00	566.00	5,566.00	55,664.00
5.00	65.00	655.00	6,655.00	66,554.00
4.00	64.00	644.00	6,644.00	66,555.00
5.00	66.00	654.00	6,545.00	65,465.00
49.00	561.00	5,649.00	56,540.00	565,470.00

DRILL D-2 Performing addition using the 0, 1, 4, and 7 keys
Decimal Selector—2

4.00	11.00	444.00	4,440.00	44,000.00
7.00	44.00	777.00	7,770.00	77,000.00
4.00	74.00	111.00	1,110.00	11,000.00
1.00	71.00	741.00	4,400.00	41,000.00
4.00	70.00	740.00	1,100.00	71,000.00
7.00	10.00	101.00	4,007.00	10,000.00
4.00	14.00	140.00	7,001.00	10,100.00
1.00	17.00	701.00	1,007.00	40,100.00
4.00	40.00	700.00	1,004.00	70,100.00
7.00	77.00	407.00	7,700.00	74,100.00
43.00	428.00	4,862.00	39,539.00	448,400.00

DRILL D-3 Performing addition using the 2, 5, and 8 keys
Decimal Selector—2

5.00	58.00	588.00	8,888.00	88,855.00
8.00	52.00	522.00	5,555.00	88,822.00
5.00	85.00	888.00	2,222.00	88,852.00
2.00	52.00	222.00	8,525.00	88,222.00
5.00	25.00	258.00	2,585.00	85,258.00
8.00	58.00	852.00	8,258.00	22,255.00
5.00	82.00	225.00	8,585.00	22,288.00
2.00	28.00	885.00	5,258.00	22,258.00
5.00	88.00	882.00	2,852.00	22,888.00
8.00	22.00	228.00	2,288.00	25,852.00
53.00	550.00	5,550.00	55,016.00	555,550.00

DRILL D-4 Performing addition using the 3, 6, 9, and decimal point keys
Decimal Selector—2

6.00	66.66	666.66	6,666.99	66,699.33
9.00	99.99	999.99	9,999.66	99,966.66
6.00	33.33	333.33	3,333.99	33,366.33
3.00	33.66	666.99	3,366.99	36,963.36
6.36	33.99	999.66	6,699.33	69,636.36
3.36	99.66	333.66	9,966.33	33,333.66
9.36	99.33	696.36	9,636.69	66,666.99
9.63	33.36	369.63	3,696.36	99,999.33
6.33	33.69	336.69	6,963.99	96,369.63
9.93	69.63	963.36	6,699.33	36,963.36
68.97	603.30	6,366.33	67,029.66	639,965.01

DRILL D-5 Performing subtraction using all number keys
Decimal Selector—F

456.73	789.01	741.00	852.55	987.98
−123.21	−456.00	−258.10	−369.88	−102.55
333.52	333.01	482.90	482.67	885.43

DRILL D-6 Performing multiplication using all number keys
Decimal Selector—F

654.05	975.01	487.10	123.56	803.75
× 12.66	× 27.19	× 30.21	× 50.09	× 1.45
8,280.273	26,510.5219	14,715.291	6,189.1204	1,165.4375

DRILL D-7 Performing division using all number keys
Decimal Selector—F

900.56	÷	450.28	=	2.
500.25	÷	100.05	=	5.
135.66	÷	6.65	=	20.4
269.155	÷	105.55	=	2.550023685*
985.66	÷	22.66	=	43.49779346*

Number of decimal places may vary due to machine capacity.

APPENDIX C

Recycling Problems

NOTE: No recycling problems are provided for Chapter 1.

RECYCLING PROBLEM 2-R Determining how transactions change an accounting equation and preparing a balance sheet

Kim Suomi is starting Suomi Service Center, a telephone-answering business. Suomi Service Center uses the accounts shown in the following accounting equation. Use a form similar to the following to complete this problem.

Trans. No.	Assets			=	Liabilities	+	Owner's Equity
	Cash +	Supplies +	Prepaid Insurance	=	Olson Office Supply	+	Kim Suomi, Capital
Beg. Bal.	0	0	0		0		0
1.	+700						+700 (investment)
New Bal.	700	0	0		0		700
2.							

Transactions
1. Received cash from owner as an investment, $700.00.
2. Bought supplies on account from Olson Office Supply, $100.00.
3. Paid cash for insurance, $150.00.
4. Paid cash for supplies, $50.00.
5. Paid cash on account to Olson Office Supply, $50.00.

1. For each transaction, complete the following. Transaction 1 is given as an example.
   a. Analyze the transaction to determine which accounts in the accounting equation are affected.
   b. Write the amount in the appropriate columns, using a plus (+) if the account increases or a minus (−) if the account decreases.
   c. For transactions that change owner's equity, write in parentheses a description of the transaction to the right of the amount.
   d. Calculate the new balance for each account in the accounting equation.
   e. Before going on to the next transaction, determine that the accounting equation is still in balance.

Check figures: Final New Bal.: 450; 150; 150; 50; 700

2. Using the final balances in the accounting equation, prepare a balance sheet. Use February 7 of the current year as the date of the balance sheet.

RECYCLING PROBLEM 3-R Determining how transactions change an accounting equation and preparing a balance sheet

Steve Bird operates a service business called Office Plants Company. Office Plants Company uses the accounts shown in the following accounting equation. Use a form similar to the following to complete the problem.

Trans. No.	Assets			=	Liabilities	+	Owner's Equity
	Cash +	Supplies +	Prepaid Insurance	=	Stanton Company	+	Steve Bird, Capital
Beg. Bal.	1,600	200	400		500		1,700
1.	−90						−90 (expense)
New Bal.	1,510	200	400		500		1,610
2.							

Transactions
1. Paid cash for telephone bill, $90.00.
2. Received cash from sales, $230.00.
3. Paid cash for equipment repair, $25.00.
4. Received cash from owner as an investment, $300.00.
5. Paid cash for rent, $400.00.
6. Received cash from sales, $250.00.
7. Paid cash for advertising, $100.00.
8. Paid cash on account to Stanton Company, $500.00.
9. Paid cash for water bill, $60.00.
10. Paid cash for miscellaneous expense, $10.00.
11. Bought supplies on account from Stanton Company, $300.00.
12. Paid cash for supplies, $200.00.
13. Received cash from sales, $270.00.
14. Paid cash to owner for personal use, $600.00.
15. Paid cash for insurance, $150.00.

INSTRUCTIONS:

1. For each transaction, complete the following. Transaction 1 is given as an example.
   a. Analyze the transaction to determine which accounts in the accounting equation are affected.
   b. Write the amount in the appropriate columns, using a plus (+) if the account increases or a minus (−) if the account decreases.

c. For transactions that change owner's equity, write in parentheses a description of the transaction to the right of the amount.

d. Calculate the new balance for each account in the accounting equation.

e. Before going on to the next transaction, determine that the accounting equation is still in balance.

Check figures: Final New Bal.: 515; 700; 550; 300; 1,465

2. Using the final balances in the accounting equation, prepare a balance sheet. Use the date November 15 of the current year.

RECYCLING PROBLEM 4-R Analyzing transactions into debit and credit parts

Alicia Valdez owns a business called QuickWash. QuickWash uses the following accounts.

Cash	Sales
Supplies	Advertising Expense
Prepaid Insurance	Miscellaneous Expense
Kishler Office Supplies	Rent Expense
Travis Office Supplies	Repair Expense
Alicia Valdez, Capital	Utilities Expense
Alicia Valdez, Drawing	

Transactions

Mar. 1. Received cash from owner as an investment, $3,000.00.
    2. Paid cash for supplies, $60.00.
    5. Paid cash for rent, $200.00.
    5. Received cash from sales, $350.00.
    6. Bought supplies on account from Travis Office Supplies, $500.00.
    9. Paid cash for repairs, $10.00.
   12. Received cash from sales, $200.00.
   13. Paid cash for insurance, $100.00.
   17. Bought supplies on account from Kishler Office Supplies, $50.00.
   19. Paid cash for miscellaneous expense, $5.00.
   19. Received cash from owner as an investment, $800.00.
   19. Received cash from sales, $300.00.
   20. Paid cash on account to Travis Office Supplies, $50.00.
   24. Paid cash for telephone bill (utilities expense), $25.00.
   25. Paid cash for advertising, $35.00.
   26. Received cash from sales, $320.00.
   30. Paid cash to owner for personal use, $500.00.
   31. Received cash from sales, $100.00.

INSTRUCTIONS:

1. Prepare a T account for each account.

Check figures: Cash account has 7 debits and 9 credits.

2. Analyze each transaction into its debit and credit parts. Write the debit and credit amounts in the proper T accounts to show how each transaction changes account balances. Write the date of the transaction in parentheses before each amount.

RECYCLING PROBLEM 5-R Journalizing transactions

Mary Ching owns a service business called Ching's Accounting. Ching's Accounting uses the following accounts.

Cash	Sales
Supplies	Advertising Expense
Prepaid Insurance	Miscellaneous Expense
West Supplies	Rent Expense
Wilson's Office Supplies	Repair Expense
Mary Ching, Capital	Utilities Expense
Mary Ching, Drawing	

INSTRUCTIONS:

1. Journalize the following transactions completed during October of the current year. Use page 1 of a journal similar to the one described in Chapter 5 for Rugcare. Source documents are abbreviated as follows: check, C; memorandum, M; receipt, R; calculator tape, T.

Oct. 1. Received cash from owner as an investment, $14,000.00. R1.
    2. Paid cash for rent, $700.00. C1.
    5. Paid cash for supplies, $500.00. C2.
    6. Paid cash for insurance, $1,500.00. C3.
    7. Bought supplies on account from West Supplies, $2,000.00. M1.
    9. Paid cash for miscellaneous expense, $5.00. C4.
  12. Paid cash on account to West Supplies, $1,000.00. C5.
  12. Received cash from sales, $450.00. T12.
  13. Received cash from sales, $400.00. T13.
  14. Paid cash for telephone bill, $60.00. C6.
  14. Received cash from sales, $480.00. T14.
  15. Paid cash for repairs, $80.00. C7.
  15. Paid cash to owner for personal use, $400.00. C8.
  15. Received cash from sales, $550.00. T15.
  16. Received cash from sales, $480.00. T16.
  19. Received cash from sales, $380.00. T19.
  20. Received cash from sales, $520.00. T20.
  21. Bought supplies on account from Wilson's Office Supplies, $600.00. M2.
  21. Received cash from sales, $400.00. T21.
  22. Paid cash for supplies, $1,200.00. C9.
  22. Received cash from sales, $550.00. T22.
  23. Received cash from sales, $450.00. T23.

2. Prove and rule page 1 of the journal. Carry the column totals forward to page 2 of the journal.

3. Use page 2 of the journal. Journalize the following transactions completed during October of the current year.

Oct. 26. Paid cash for advertising, $100.00. C10.
  26. Bought supplies on account from West Supplies, $60.00. M3.
  26. Received cash from sales, $460.00. T26.
  27. Received cash from sales, $370.00. T27.
  28. Paid cash for electric bill, $40.00. C11.
  28. Received cash from sales, $400.00. T28.
  29. Paid cash on account to West Supplies, $60.00. C12.
  29. Received cash from sales, $330.00. T29.
  30. Paid cash for supplies, $50.00. C13.
  30. Received cash from sales, $550.00. T30.
  31. Paid cash to owner for personal use, $400.00. C14.

4. Prove page 2 of the journal.

5. Prove cash. The beginning cash balance on October 1 is zero. The balance on the next unused check stub is $14,675.00.

6. Rule page 2 of the journal.

Check figures:
Page 1: 8,045;
16,600; 4,660;
18,660; 5,445

Page 2: 8,755;
16,660; 6,770;
20,770; 6,095

RECYCLING PROBLEM 6-R Journalizing and posting to a general ledger

Al Burns owns a service business called Burns Cleaning. Burns Cleaning uses the same journal used by Rugcare in Chapter 6.

INSTRUCTIONS:

1. Open a general ledger account for each of the following accounts.

	Assets			Revenue
110	Cash		410	Sales
120	Supplies			**Expenses**
130	Prepaid Insurance		510	Advertising Expense
	Liabilities		520	Miscellaneous Expense
210	Mitchell Office Supplies		530	Rent Expense
	Owner's Equity		540	Utilities Expense
310	Al Burns, Capital			
320	Al Burns, Drawing			

2. Journalize the following transactions completed during November of the current year. Use page 1 of a journal. Source documents are abbreviated as follows: check, C; memorandum, M; receipt, R; calculator tape, T.

Nov. 1. Received cash from owner as an investment, $7,000.00. R1.
3. Paid cash for insurance, $250.00. C1.
5. Paid cash for miscellaneous expense, $5.00. C2.
6. Received cash from sales, $410.00. T6.
9. Paid cash for rent, $400.00. C3.
11. Paid cash for supplies, $550.00. C4.
13. Bought supplies on account from Mitchell Office Supplies, $700.00. M1.
13. Received cash from sales, $380.00. T13.
16. Paid cash for electric bill, $50.00. C5.
18. Paid cash on account to Mitchell Office Supplies, $350.00. C6.
20. Paid cash for advertising, $35.00. C7.
20. Received cash from sales, $1,020.00. T20.
25. Paid cash for supplies, $100.00. C8.
27. Paid cash for supplies, $120.00. C9.
27. Received cash from sales, $1,660.00. T27.
30. Paid cash to owner for personal use, $500.00. C10.
30. Received cash from sales, $450.00. T30.

Check figures: 3,060; 7,700; 3,920; 10,920; 2,360

3. Prove the journal.
4. Prove cash. The beginning cash balance on November 1 is zero. The balance on the next unused check stub is $8,560.00.
5. Rule the journal.
6. Post from the journal to the general ledger.

RECYCLING PROBLEM 7-R Reconciling a bank statement; journalizing a bank service charge, a dishonored check, and petty cash transactions

Sarah Getz owns a business called Quick Service. Quick Service completed the following transactions during August of the current year.

INSTRUCTIONS:

1. Journalize the following transactions completed during August of the current year. Use page 8 of a journal. Source documents are abbreviated as follows: check, C; memorandum, M.

Aug. 24. Paid cash to establish a petty cash fund, $200.00. C81.
25. Received notice from the bank of a dishonored check, $50.00, plus $5.00 fee; total, $55.00. M28.
26. Paid cash for miscellaneous expense, $18.00. C82.
27. Paid cash for supplies, $60.00. C83.
28. Paid cash for repairs, $35.00. C84.
31. Paid cash to owner for personal use, $500.00. C85.
31. Paid cash to replenish the petty cash fund, $105.00: supplies, $65.00; miscellaneous expense, $40.00. C86.

2. On August 31 of the current year, Quick Service received a bank statement dated August 30. Prepare a bank statement reconciliation. Use August 31 of the current year as the

date. The following information is obtained from the August 30 bank statement and from the records of the business.

Bank statement balance	$1,970.00
Bank service charge.	6.00
Outstanding deposit, August 31.	520.00
Outstanding checks, Nos. 85 and 86	
Checkbook balance on Check Stub No. 87	1,891.00

Check figure: adjusted balance $1,885

3. Continue using the journal and journalize the following transaction.

Aug. 31. Received bank statement showing August bank service charge, $6.00. M29.

RECYCLING PROBLEM 8-R Completing a work sheet

On May 31 of the current year, ServiceAll has the following general ledger accounts and balances. The business uses a monthly fiscal period.

Account Title	Account Balances	
	Debit	**Credit**
Cash	$3,900.00	
Petty Cash	100.00	
Supplies	3,400.00	
Prepaid Insurance	850.00	
Gordon Supplies.		$ 170.00
Weil Company		90.00
James McCurdy, Capital.		6,000.00
James McCurdy, Drawing	340.00	
Income Summary	—	—
Sales		3,500.00
Advertising Expense	270.00	
Insurance Expense	—	
Miscellaneous Expense.	120.00	
Rent Expense.	400.00	
Supplies Expense	—	
Utilities Expense	380.00	

INSTRUCTIONS:

1. Prepare the heading and trial balance on a work sheet.
2. Analyze the following adjustment information into debit and credit parts. Record the adjustments on the work sheet.

Adjustment Information, May 31

Supplies on hand	$2,000.00
Value of prepaid insurance	350.00

Check figure: Net Income $430

3. Extend the up-to-date account balances to the Balance Sheet or Income Statement columns.
4. Complete the work sheet.

RECYCLING PROBLEM 9-R Preparing financial statements

See the following page for information obtained from the work sheet of Best Delivery Service for the month ended December 31 of the current year.

INSTRUCTIONS:

Check figure: Total Liab. and Owner's Eq. $14,675

1. Prepare an income statement for the month ended December 31 of the current year. Calculate and record the component percentages for total expenses and net income. Round percentage calculations to the nearest 0.1%.
2. Prepare a balance sheet for December 31 of the current year.

ACCOUNT TITLE		INCOME STATEMENT DEBIT	INCOME STATEMENT CREDIT	BALANCE SHEET DEBIT	BALANCE SHEET CREDIT	
		5	6	7	8	
1	Cash			6 07 5 00		1
2	Petty Cash			2 00 00		2
3	Supplies			6 30 0 00		3
4	Prepaid Insurance			2 10 0 00		4
5	Dale Supplies				3 80 0 00	5
6	Niles Office Supplies				9 70 00	6
7	Evert Pole, Capital				9 70 0 00	7
8	Evert Pole, Drawing			1 00 0 00		8
9	Income Summary					9
10	Sales		4 56 0 00			10
11	Advertising Expense	3 00 0 00				11
12	Insurance Expense	1 50 0 00				12
13	Miscellaneous Expense	1 20 0 00				13
14	Rent Expense	2 50 0 00				14
15	Supplies Expense	1 65 00				15
16	Utilities Expense	1 20 00				16
17		3 35 5 00	4 56 0 00	15 67 5 00	14 47 0 00	17
18	Net Income	1 20 5 00			1 20 5 00	18
19		4 56 0 00	4 56 0 00	15 67 5 00	15 67 5 00	19
20						20
21						21
22						22
23						23

RECYCLING PROBLEM 10-R Journalizing adjusting and closing entries

The following information is obtained from the partial work sheet of Lawn Services for the month ended September 30 of the current year.

ACCOUNT TITLE		ADJUSTMENTS DEBIT	ADJUSTMENTS CREDIT	INCOME STATEMENT DEBIT	INCOME STATEMENT CREDIT	BALANCE SHEET DEBIT	BALANCE SHEET CREDIT	
		3	4	5	6	7	8	
1	Cash					3 15 0 00		1
2	Supplies		(a) 1 75 00			6 75 00		2
3	Prepaid Insurance		(b) 2 30 00			2 50 00		3
4	Lodge Supplies						4 50 00	4
5	Verner Supplies						1 00 00	5
6	Norman Eli, Capital						3 13 0 00	6
7	Norman Eli, Drawing					3 15 00		7
8	Income Summary							8
9	Sales				1 61 5 00			9
10	Insurance Expense	(b) 2 30 00		2 30 00				10
11	Miscellaneous Expense			7 5 00				11
12	Rent Expense			4 25 00				12
13	Supplies Expense	(a) 1 75 00		1 75 00				13
14		4 05 00	4 05 00	9 05 00	1 61 5 00	4 39 0 00	3 68 0 00	14
15	Net Income			7 10 00			7 10 00	15
16				1 61 5 00	1 61 5 00	4 39 0 00	4 39 0 00	16
17								17
18								18

INSTRUCTIONS:

1. Use page 3 of a journal. Journalize the adjusting entries.

2. Continue to use page 3 of the journal. Journalize the closing entries.

RECYCLING PROBLEM 11-R Journalizing purchases, cash payments, and other transactions

Eva Akemi and Daniel Marino, partners, own a furniture store.

INSTRUCTIONS:

Journalize the following transactions completed during November of the current year. Use page 11 of a journal similar to the one described in Chapter 11. Source documents are abbreviated as follows: check, C; memorandum, M; purchase invoice, P.

Nov. 2. Paid cash for rent, $1,200.00. C251.
      2. Purchased merchandise on account from Baines Furniture Co., $2,335.00. P88.
      3. Paid cash for office supplies, $66.00. C252.
      5. Paid cash on account to Decor-Concepts, $985.00, covering P85. C253.
      7. Purchased merchandise for cash, $130.00. C254.
      9. Purchased merchandise on account from Metaline Co., $950.00. P89.
      9. Bought store supplies on account from Gateway Supply, $140.00. M40.
      10. Purchased merchandise for cash, $83.00. C255.
      12. Paid cash on account to Furniture Industries, $1,400.00, covering P86. C256.
      12. Bought office supplies on account from Scott Supply, $95.00. M41.
      14. Discovered that a transaction for store supplies bought in October was journalized and posted in error as a debit to Purchases instead of Supplies—Store, $74.00. M42.
      16. Eva Akemi, partner, withdrew cash for personal use, $1,000.00. C257.
      17. Daniel Marino, partner, withdrew cash for personal use, $1,000.00. C258.
      17. Paid cash for advertising, $75.00. C259.
      19. Paid cash on account to Classic Furniture, $1,345.00, covering P87. C260.
      19. Purchased merchandise on account from Metaline Co., $1,250.00. P90.
      20. Daniel Marino, partner, withdrew merchandise for personal use, $152.00. M43.
      22. Purchased merchandise for cash, $60.00. C261.
      24. Paid cash on account to Baines Furniture Co., $2,335.00, covering P88. C262.
      25. Eva Akemi, partner, withdrew merchandise for personal use, $225.00. M44.
      27. Paid cash for store supplies, $78.00. C263.
      30. Paid cash to replenish the petty cash fund, $301.00: office supplies, $78.00; store supplies, $52.00; advertising, $125.00; miscellaneous, $46.00. C264.
      30. Paid cash on account to Metaline Co., $950.00, covering P89. C265.

*Check figures:
There will be four
blank lines left on
the journal. Cash is
credited 15 times.*

RECYCLING PROBLEM 12-R Journalizing sales and cash receipts

Ana Lamas and Alex Keyser, partners, own an office supply store.

INSTRUCTIONS:

1. Journalize the following transactions completed during September of the current year. Use page 9 of a journal similar to the one described in Chapter 12. A 4% sales tax has been added to each sale. Source documents are abbreviated as follows: receipt, R; sales invoice, S; cash register tape, T.

Sept. 1. Sold merchandise on account to Samuel Quist, $75.00, plus sales tax, $3.00; total, $78.00. S53.
       1. Received cash on account from David Plouff, $85.28, covering S49. R85.
       2. Sold merchandise on account to Carmen Estevez, $125.00, plus sales tax, $5.00; total, $130.00. S54.

Sept. 5. Sold merchandise on account to Keith Aldrich, $265.00, plus sales tax, $10.60; total, $275.60. S55.

5. Recorded cash and credit card sales, $1,940.00, plus sales tax, $77.60; total, $2,017.60. T5.

7. Received cash on account from Edward Jarmen, $249.60, covering S50. R86.

9. Sold merchandise on account to Perez Accounting Co., $345.00, plus sales tax, $13.80; total, $358.80. S56.

10. Sold merchandise on account to Nancy Cain, $85.00, plus sales tax, $3.40; total, $88.40. S57.

11. Received cash on account from Bonner Secretarial Service, $249.60, covering S51. R87.

12. Recorded cash and credit card sales, $2,350.00, plus sales tax, $94.00; total, $2,444.00. T12.

14. Received cash on account from David Doran, $187.20, covering S52. R88.

15. Sold merchandise on account to Hazel Ervin, $65.00, plus sales tax, $2.60; total, $67.60. S58.

18. Received cash on account from Samuel Quist, $78.00, covering S53. R89.

19. Recorded cash and credit card sales, $2,450.00, plus sales tax, $98.00; total, $2,548.00. T19.

21. Received cash on account from Carmen Estevez, $130.00, covering S54. R90.

25. Received cash on account from Keith Aldrich, $275.60, covering S55. R91.

26. Recorded cash and credit card sales, $2,140.00, plus sales tax, $85.60; total, $2,225.60. T26.

29. Sold merchandise on account to Susan Gates, $145.00, plus sales tax, $5.80; total, $150.80. S59.

30. Recorded cash and credit card sales, $1,285.00, plus sales tax, $51.40; total, $1,336.40. T30.

Check figures:
1,149.20; 1,255.28;
11,270.00; 450.80;
11,826.88

2. Total the journal. Prove the equality of debits and credits.

3. Rule the journal.

RECYCLING PROBLEM 13-R Opening accounts and journalizing and posting business transactions

INSTRUCTIONS:

1. Open the following accounts in the general ledger of Catalina Shoes. Record the balances as of September 1 of the current year.

Account No.	Account Title	Account Balance
1110	Cash	$ 13,200.00
1130	Accounts Receivable	441.00
1140	Supplies—Office	1,830.00
1150	Supplies—Store	1,560.00
2110	Accounts Payable	3,820.00
2120	Sales Tax Payable	937.50
3120	Sophia Kizer, Drawing	9,820.00
3140	Brian Rankin, Drawing	9,600.00
4110	Sales	150,000.00
5110	Purchases	88,000.00
6110	Advertising Expense	2,310.00
6140	Miscellaneous Expense	1,260.00
6160	Rent Expense	7,600.00
6190	Utilities Expense	1,620.00

2. Open the following vendor accounts in the accounts payable ledger. Record the balances as of September 1 of the current year.

Vendor No.	Vendor Name	Purchase Invoice No.	Account Balance
210	A & J Shoes............................	P66	$1,480.00
220	Colormate Shoes......................	—	—
230	Sanz Supply..........................	—	—
240	Suave Shoe Co........................	P65	2,340.00

3. Open the following customer accounts in the accounts receivable ledger. Record the balances as of September 1 of the current year.

Customer No.	Customer Name	Sales Invoice No.	Account Balance
110	Joyce Abler..........................	S53	$178.50
120	Helen Gorthy.........................	—	—
130	Joshua Lentz.........................	—	—
140	Earl Ward............................	S52	262.50

4. Journalize the following transactions completed during September of the current year. Use page 9 of a journal similar to the one described in Chapter 13. A 5% sales tax has been added to each sale. Source documents are abbreviated as follows: check, C; memorandum, M; purchase invoice, P; receipt, R; sales invoice, S; cash register tape, T.

Sept. 1. Paid cash for rent, $950.00. C225.
2. Purchased merchandise on account from Colormate Shoes, $1,650.00. P67.
4. Received cash on account from Earl Ward, $262.50, covering S52. R33.
5. Recorded cash and credit card sales, $3,350.00, plus sales tax, $167.50; total, $3,517.50. T5.
   Posting. Post the items that are to be posted individually.
7. Paid cash for electric bill, $158.10. C226.
9. Bought office supplies on account from Sanz Supply, $135.00. M32.
10. Paid cash on account to Suave Shoe Co., $2,340.00, covering P65. C227.
12. Recorded cash and credit card sales, $4,140.00, plus sales tax, $207.00; total, $4,347.00. T12.
   Posting. Post the items that are to be posted individually.
14. Sold merchandise on account to Helen Gorthy, $260.00, plus sales tax, $13.00; total, $273.00. S54.
15. Sold merchandise on account to Joshua Lentz, $125.00, plus sales tax, $6.25; total, $131.25. S55.
15. Sophia Kizer, partner, withdrew cash for personal use, $1,200.00. C228.
15. Brian Rankin, partner, withdrew cash for personal use, $1,200.00. C229.
18. Purchased merchandise on account from A & J Shoes, $940.00. P68.
19. Recorded cash and credit card sales, $4,080.00, plus sales tax, $204.00; total, $4,284.00. T19.
   Posting. Post the items that are to be posted individually.
21. Discovered that a transaction for office supplies bought for cash was journalized and posted in error as a debit to Supplies—Store instead of Supplies—Office, $118.00. M33.
22. Sophia Kizer, partner, withdrew merchandise for personal use, $125.00. M34.
24. Sold merchandise on account to Earl Ward, $135.00, plus sales tax, $6.75; total, $141.75. S56.
25. Sold merchandise on account to Joyce Abler, $95.00, plus sales tax, $4.75; total, $99.75. S57.
26. Recorded cash and credit card sales, $4,530.00, plus sales tax, $226.50; total, $4,756.50. T26.
   Posting. Post the items that are to be posted individually.
28. Received cash on account from Joyce Abler, $178.50, covering S53. R34.
28. Paid cash on account to A & J Shoes, $1,480.00, covering P66. C230.
30. Paid cash to replenish the petty cash fund, $201.50: office supplies, $42.00; store supplies, $57.50; advertising, $64.00; miscellaneous, $38.00. C231.

Sept. 30. Purchased merchandise on account from Suave Shoe Co., $860.00. P69.

30. Recorded cash and credit card sales, $1,970.00, plus sales tax, $98.50; total, $2,068.50. T30.

Posting. Post the items that are to be posted individually.

Check figures:
Journal Totals
4,087.60; 243.00;
645.75; 441.00;
18,685.00; 934.25;
3,820.00; 3,585.00;
3,450.00;
19,414.50;
7,529.60. Total
Accounts Payable
$3,585.00. Total
Accounts
Receivable
$645.75.

5. Total the journal. Prove the equality of debits and credits.
6. Prove cash. The balance on the next unused check stub is $25,084.90.
7. Rule the journal.
8. Post the totals of the special columns of the journal.
9. Prepare a schedule of accounts payable and a schedule of accounts receivable. Prove the accuracy of the subsidiary ledgers by comparing the schedule totals with the balances of the controlling accounts in the general ledger. If the totals are not the same, find and correct the errors.

RECYCLING PROBLEM 14-R Preparing a semimonthly payroll

The following information is for the semimonthly pay period June 1–15 of the current year.

Employee		Marital Status	No. of Allow-ances	Earnings		Deductions
No.	Name			Regular	Overtime	Health Insurance
3	Cahill, Bryan M.	S	2	$598.40	$40.00	$25.00
4	Dykes, Eleanor S.	M	3	525.60		30.00
7	Holcomb, David K.	S	1	624.00		
1	Kirby, Sharon A.	S	1	552.00	9.30	
5	Mendez, Thomas T.	M	2	545.60		25.00
6	Salassi, Carol W.	M	3	576.00		30.00
8	Tsang, Elaine C.	M	2	651.20	44.40	25.00

INSTRUCTIONS:

1. Prepare a payroll register. The date of payment is June 16. Use the federal income tax withholding tables in Illustration 14-4 to find the income tax withholding for each employee. Calculate FICA tax withholding using an 8% tax rate. None of the employee accumulated earnings has exceeded the FICA tax base.

Check figures:
4,072.80; 93.70;
4,166.50; 360.00;
333.32; 135.00;
828.32; 3,338.18

2. Prepare a check for the total amount of the net pay. Make the check payable to Payroll Account, and sign your name as a partner of Riddley Company. The beginning check stub balance is $7,687.89.
3. Prepare payroll checks for David Holcomb, Check No. 332, and Carol Salassi, Check No. 335. Sign your name as a partner of Riddley Company. Record the two payroll check numbers in the payroll register.

RECYCLING PROBLEM 15-R Journalizing payroll taxes

Johnson Manufacturing completed payroll transactions during the period February 28 to April 30 of the current year. Payroll tax rates are as follows: FICA, 8%; federal unemployment, 0.8%; and state unemployment, 5.4%. No total earnings have exceeded the tax base for calculating unemployment taxes.

INSTRUCTIONS:

1. Journalize the following transactions on page 4 of a journal. Source documents are abbreviated as follows: check, C, and memorandum, M.

Feb. 28. Paid cash for monthly payroll, $3,312.16 (total payroll, $4,298.00, less deductions: employee income tax, $642.00; FICA tax, $343.84). C167.

28. Recorded employer payroll taxes expense. M34.

Mar. 15. Paid cash for liability for employee income tax, $642.00, and for FICA tax, $687.68; total, $1,329.68. C192.

15. 31. Paid cash for monthly payroll, $3,328.84 (total payroll, $4,327.00, less deductions: employee income tax, $652.00; FICA tax, $346.16). C235.

31. Recorded employer payroll taxes expense. M39.

Apr. 15. Paid cash for liability for employee income tax, $652.00, and for FICA tax, $692.32; total, $1,344.32. C251.

30. Paid cash for federal unemployment tax liability for quarter ended March 31, $103.62. C272.

30. Paid cash for state unemployment tax liability for quarter ended March 31, $699.41. C273.

Check figures:
13,326.78;
3,208.75; 10,118.03

2. Prove and rule the journal.

RECYCLING PROBLEM 16-R Completing a work sheet

On December 31 of the current year, Klimer has the following general ledger accounts and balances.

Account Title	Balance
Cash	$ 19,865.00
Petty Cash	500.00
Accounts Receivable	9,260.00
Merchandise Inventory	226,320.00
Supplies—Office	5,085.00
Supplies—Store	5,420.00
Prepaid Insurance	4,300.00
Accounts Payable	9,720.00
Sales Tax Payable	950.00
Dorothy Klimer, Capital	107,365.00
Dorothy Klimer, Drawing	15,880.00
Howard Klimer, Capital	106,190.00
Howard Klimer, Drawing	15,730.00
Income Summary	—
Sales	189,540.00
Purchases	85,250.00
Advertising Expense	4,735.00
Credit Card Fee Expense	1,930.00
Insurance Expense	—
Miscellaneous Expense	2,360.00
Rent Expense	14,400.00
Supplies Expense—Office	—
Supplies Expense—Store	—
Utilities Expense	2,730.00

Check figures:
Adjustments (a)
$7,550, (b) 2,890,
(c) 3,215, (d) 2,580;
Net Income
$61,900

INSTRUCTIONS:

Prepare Klimer's work sheet for the fiscal period ended December 31 of the current year.

Adjustment Information, December 31

Merchandise inventory	$218,770.00
Office supplies inventory	2,195.00
Store supplies inventory	2,205.00
Value of prepaid insurance	1,720.00

RECYCLING PROBLEM 17-R Preparing financial statements

Discount Footwear prepared the work sheet on page C-13 for the year ended December 31 of the current year.

Discount Footwear

Work Sheet

For Year Ended December 31, 19--

	ACCOUNT TITLE	TRIAL BALANCE DEBIT	TRIAL BALANCE CREDIT	ADJUSTMENTS DEBIT	ADJUSTMENTS CREDIT	INCOME STATEMENT DEBIT	INCOME STATEMENT CREDIT	BALANCE SHEET DEBIT	BALANCE SHEET CREDIT	
1	Cash	1939500						1939500		1
2	Petty Cash	30000						30000		2
3	Accounts Receivable	893000						893000		3
4	Merchandise Inventory	25720000			(a) 975000			24745000		4
5	Supplies—Office	512000			(b) 298000			214000		5
6	Supplies—Store	487500			(c) 314000			173500		6
7	Prepaid Insurance	483000			(d) 276000			207000		7
8	Accounts Payable		836000						836000	8
9	Sales Tax Payable		98000						98000	9
10	Joseph Kane, Capital		11164000						11164000	10
11	Joseph Kane, Drawing	1584000						1584000		11
12	Gail Miles, Capital		11036000						11036000	12
13	Gail Miles, Drawing	1593000						1593000		13
14	Income Summary			(a) 975000		975000				14
15	Sales		23545000				23545000			15
16	Purchases	10595000				10595000				16
17	Advertising Expense	496500				496500				17
18	Credit Card Fee Expense	213000				213000				18
19	Insurance Expense			(d) 276000		276000				19
20	Miscellaneous Expense	228500				228500				20
21	Rent Expense	1680000				1680000				21
22	Supplies Expense—Office			(b) 298000		298000				22
23	Supplies Expense—Store			(c) 314000		314000				23
24	Utilities Expense	224000				224000				24
25		46679000	46679000	1863000	1863000	15300000	23545000	31379000	23134000	25
26	Net Income					8245000			8245000	26
27						23545000	23545000	31379000	31379000	27
28										28

INSTRUCTIONS:

Check figures:
49.1%, 50.9%,
15.8%, 35.0%.
Joseph Kane,
Capital 137,025.00;
Gail Miles, Capital
135,655.00.

1. Prepare an income statement. Calculate and record the following component percentages: (a) cost of merchandise sold, (b) gross profit on sales, (c) total expenses, and (d) net income or loss. Round percentage calculations to the nearest 0.1%.
2. Prepare a distribution of net income statement. Net income or loss is to be shared equally.
3. Prepare an owners' equity statement. No additional investments were made.
4. Prepare a balance sheet in report form.

RECYCLING PROBLEM 18-R Journalizing adjusting and closing entries

Use the following partial work sheet of Cook & Latzco Paints for the year ended December 31 of the current year.

	ACCOUNT TITLE	ADJUSTMENTS		INCOME STATEMENT	
		3 DEBIT	**4** CREDIT	**5** DEBIT	**6** CREDIT
4	*Merchandise Inventory*		(a) 9 8 4 0 00		
5	*Supplies—Office*		(b) 2 5 1 0 00		
6	*Supplies—Store*		(c) 2 6 3 0 00		
7	*Prepaid Insurance*		(d) 2 5 8 0 00		
21	*Income Summary*	(a) 9 8 4 0 00		9 8 4 0 00	
22	*Sales*				310 9 2 0 00
23	*Purchases*			124 3 5 0 00	
24	*Advertising Expense*			4 7 8 0 00	
25	*Credit Card Fee Expense*			3 9 8 0 00	
26	*Insurance Expense*	(d) 2 5 8 0 00		2 5 8 0 00	
27	*Miscellaneous Expense*			2 1 4 0 00	
28	*Payroll Taxes Expense*			7 0 7 0 00	
29	*Rent Expense*			13 2 0 0 00	
30	*Salary Expense*			58 9 2 0 00	
31	*Supplies Expense—Office*	(b) 2 5 1 0 00		2 5 1 0 00	
32	*Supplies Expense—Store*	(c) 2 6 3 0 00		2 6 3 0 00	
33	*Utilities Expense*			2 7 6 0 00	
34		17 5 6 0 00	17 5 6 0 00	234 7 6 0 00	310 9 2 0 00
35	*Net Income*			76 1 6 0 00	
36				310 9 2 0 00	310 9 2 0 00
37					
38					
39					
40					
41					

Check figures: 4
adjusting entries; 5
closing entries

INSTRUCTIONS:

1. Use page 25 of a journal. Journalize the adjusting entries using information from the partial work sheet.
2. Continue using page 25 of the journal. Journalize the closing entries using information from the work sheet. The distribution of net income statement shows equal distribution of earnings. The partners' drawing accounts show the following debit balances in the work sheet's Balance Sheet Debit column: Angela Cook, Drawing, $14,780.00; Alan Latzco, Drawing, $15,120.00.

RECYCLING PROBLEM 19-R Journalizing and posting purchases and cash payment transactions

INSTRUCTIONS:

1. Open the following accounts in the general ledger of Dunhill Corporation. Record the balances as of October 1 of the current year.

PARTIAL GENERAL LEDGER

Account No.	Account Title	Account Balance
1105	Cash....................................	$23,410.00
1110	Petty Cash	250.00
1140	Supplies................................	957.00
2115	Accounts Payable.........................	1,382.00
5105	Purchases	—
5110	Purchases Discounts	—
5115	Purchases Returns and Allowances	—
6105	Advertising Expense	—
6130	Miscellaneous Expense.....................	—
6140	Rent Expense............................	—
8105	Cash Short and Over......................	—

2. Open the following vendor accounts in the accounts payable ledger. Record the balances as of October 1 of the current year.

ACCOUNTS PAYABLE LEDGER

Vendor No.	Vendor Name	Terms	Purchase Invoice Number	Account Balance
210	Adkin Supplies	n/15	—	—
220	Blair Company	n/30	—	—
230	Friedmans Company	n/30	P92	$625.00
240	Hargrove, Inc	1/10, n/30	P100	757.00
250	Stovall Company	2/10, n/30	—	—
260	Winston Company	1/10, n/30	—	—

3. Journalize the following transactions affecting purchases and cash payments completed during October of the current year. Use page 10 of a purchases journal, a general journal, and a cash payments journal. Source documents are abbreviated as follows: check, C; debit memorandum, DM; memorandum, M; purchase invoice, P.

Oct. 1. Paid cash for rent, $1,500.00. C163.
  1. Purchased merchandise on account from Blair Company, $1,482.00. P101.
  5. Purchased merchandise on account from Winston Company, $225.00. P102.
  5. Returned merchandise to Friedmans Company, $70.00, from P92. DM61.
   Posting. Post the items that are to be posted individually. Post from the journals in this order: purchases journal, general journal, and cash payments journal.
  8. Paid cash on account to Friedmans Company, $555.00, covering P92 for $625.00, less DM61, $70.00; no discount. C164.
  8. Paid cash on account to Hargrove, Inc., $749.43, covering P100 for $757.00, less 1% discount, $7.57. C165.
  12. Purchased merchandise for cash, $720.00. C166.
  14. Purchased merchandise on account from Winston Company, $1,296.00. P103.
  15. Paid cash on account to Winston Company, $222.75, covering P102 for $225.00, less 1% discount, $2.25. C167.
  15. Paid cash to replenish the petty cash fund, $158.80: supplies, $47.50; advertising, $53.60; miscellaneous, $61.75; cash over, $4.05. C168.
  15. Bought supplies on account from Adkin Supplies, $304.00. M17.
   Posting. Post the items that are to be posted individually.
  18. Paid cash for miscellaneous expense, $218.00. C169.

Oct. 20. Purchased merchandise on account from Friedmans Company, $350.00. P104.
  20. Returned merchandise to Blair Company, $177.00, from P101. DM62.
  21. Paid cash on account to Winston Company, $1,283.04, covering P103 for $1,296.00, less 1% discount, $12.96. C170.
  22. Paid cash for advertising, $345.00. C171.
  25. Purchased merchandise on account from Winston Company, $817.00. P105.
  27. Paid cash on account to Blair Company, $1,305.00, covering P101 for $1,482.00, less DM62, $177.00; no discount. C172.
  28. Returned merchandise to Winston Company, $34.00, from P105. DM63.
  29. Paid cash on account to Adkin Supplies, $304.00, covering M17; no discount. C173.
  29. Purchased merchandise on account from Stovall Company, $925.00. P106.
  29. Paid cash to replenish the petty cash fund, $187.80: supplies, $14.30; advertising, $78.60; miscellaneous, $90.00; cash short, $4.90. C174.
      Posting. Post the items that are to be posted individually.

Check figures: Purchases journal total $5,095.00. Cash payments journal totals 3,133.65; 4.05; 4,442.00; 22.78; 7,548.82. Schedule of accounts payable total $2,058.00.

4. Total and rule the purchases journal. Post the total.
5. Prove and rule the cash payments journal. Post the totals of the special columns.
6. Prepare a schedule of accounts payable. Compare the schedule total with the balance of the accounts payable account in the general ledger. The total and balance should be the same.

RECYCLING PROBLEM 20-R Journalizing and posting sales and cash receipts transactions

INSTRUCTIONS:

1. Open the following accounts in the general ledger of Thompson Company. Record the balances as of June 1 of the current year.

PARTIAL GENERAL LEDGER

Account No.	Account Title	Account Balance
1105	Cash	$9,216.00
1125	Accounts Receivable	3,024.01
2135	Sales Tax Payable	—
4105	Sales	—
4110	Sales Discount	—
4115	Sales Returns and Allowances	—

2. Open the following customer accounts in the accounts receivable ledger. Record the balances as of June 1 of the current year.

ACCOUNTS RECEIVABLE LEDGER

Customer No.	Customer Name	Sale No.	Account Balance
110	Bolero Company	S84	$616.45
120	Franklin, Inc.	S88	448.20
130	Mooney and Associates	S85	398.76
140	Powers Company	S89	702.00
150	David Reed	S90	858.60

3. Journalize the following transactions affecting sales and cash receipts completed during June of the current year. Use page 6 of a sales journal, a general journal, and a cash receipts journal. Thompson Company offers its customers terms of 2/10, n/30. The sales tax rate is 8%. Source documents are abbreviated as follows: credit memorandum, CM; receipt, R; sales invoice, S; cash register tape, T.

June 1. Received cash on account from Franklin, Inc., $439.24, covering S88 for $448.20 ($415.00 plus sales tax, $33.20), less discount, $8.30, and less sales tax, $0.66. R21.

June 4. Granted credit to David Reed for merchandise returned, $126.00, plus sales tax, $10.08, from S90; total, $136.08. CM8.

7. Received cash on account from Powers Company, $687.96, covering S89 for $702.00 ($650.00 plus sales tax, $52.00), less discount, $13.00, and less sales tax, $1.04. R22.

7. Recorded cash and credit card sales, $1,980.00, plus sales tax, $158.40; total, $2,138.40. T7.

Posting. Post the items that are to be posted individually. Post from the journals in this order: sales journal, general journal, and cash receipts journal.

9. Received cash on account from David Reed, $722.52 (covering S90 less CM8), no discount. R23.

9. Received cash on account from Mooney and Associates, $398.76, covering S85; no discount. R24.

11. Recorded cash and credit card sales, $2,358.00, plus sales tax, $188.64; total, $2,546.64. T11.

Posting. Post the items that are to be posted individually.

13. Sold merchandise on account to Franklin, Inc., $1,236.00, plus sales tax, $98.88; total, $1,334.88. S91.

15. Granted credit to Franklin, Inc., for merchandise returned, $36.40, plus sales tax, $2.91, from S91; total, $39.31. CM9.

15. Received cash on account from Bolero Company, $616.45, covering S84; no discount. R25.

18. Recorded cash and credit card sales, $2,678.00, plus sales tax, $214.24; total, $2,892.24. T18.

Posting. Post the items that are to be posted individually.

21. Sold merchandise on account to David Reed, $540.00, plus sales tax, $43.20; total, $583.20. S92.

22. Sold merchandise on account to Bolero Company, $415.00, plus sales tax, $33.20; total, $448.20. S93.

22. Sold merchandise on account to Powers Company, $643.00, plus sales tax, $51.44; total, $694.44. S94.

25. Recorded cash and credit card sales, $1,916.00, plus sales tax, $153.28; total, $2,069.28. T25.

Posting. Post the items that are to be posted individually.

28. Sold merchandise on account to Bolero Company, $756.00, plus sales tax, $60.48; total, $816.48. S95.

29. Received cash on account from Franklin, Inc., $1,295.57 (covering S91 less CM9), no discount. R26.

29. Received cash on account from David Reed, $571.54, covering S92 for $583.20 ($540.00 plus sales tax, $43.20), less discount, $10.80, and less sales tax, $0.86. R27.

30. Sold merchandise on account to Franklin, Inc., $772.50, plus sales tax, $61.80; total, $834.30. S96.

30. Recorded cash and credit card sales, $1,606.00, plus sales tax, $128.48; total, $1,734.48. T30.

Posting. Post the items that are to be posted individually.

4. Prove and rule the sales journal. Post the totals of the special columns.

5. Prove the equality of debits and credits for the cash receipts journal.

6. Prove cash. The cash balance on hand on June 1 was $9,216.00. The total of the Cash Credit column of the cash payments journal for Thompson Company is $14,753.00. The balance on the next unused check stub on June 30 is $10,576.08.

7. Rule the cash receipts journal. Post the totals of the special columns.

8. Prepare a schedule of accounts receivable similar to the one described in Chapter 13. Compare the schedule total with the balance of the accounts receivable account in the general ledger. The total and the balance should be the same.

RECYCLING PROBLEM 21-R Recording entries for uncollectible accounts

Colonial Plastics has the following accounts in its accounts receivable ledger.

PARTIAL ACCOUNTS RECEIVABLE LEDGER

Account No. and Title	Date	Post. Ref.	Debit	Debit Balance
125 Dixon Company	May 19	S5	$ 621.00	$ 621.00
135 Fire Star Co.	Mar. 25	S3	1,295.00	1,295.00
140 Haber Corporation	Jan. 26	S1	916.00	916.00
190 Tri-State Corporation	Feb. 1	S2	384.00	384.00

INSTRUCTIONS:

1. Journalize the following transactions completed during October, November, and December of the current year. Use pages 10, 11, and 12 of a general journal and pages 11 and 12 of a cash receipts journal. Source documents are abbreviated as follows: memorandum, M; receipt, R.

Oct. 2. Wrote off Tri-State Corporation's past-due account as uncollectible, $384.00. M332.
    14. Wrote off Haber Corporation's past-due account as uncollectible, $916.00. M336.
        Posting. Post each entry to the customer accounts in the accounts receivable ledger.
Nov. 17. Wrote off Dixon Company's past-due account as uncollectible, $621.00. M342.
    22. Received cash in full payment of Tri-State Corporation's account, previously written off as uncollectible, $384.00. M347 and R409.
        Posting. Post each entry to the customer accounts in the accounts receivable ledger.
Dec. 13. Wrote off Fire Star Co.'s past-due account as uncollectible, $1,295.00. M355.
    21. Received cash in full payment of Dixon Company's account, previously written off as uncollectible, $621.00. M362 and R476.
    26. Received cash in full payment of Haber Corporation's account, previously written off as uncollectible, $916.00. M368 and R482.
        Posting. Post each entry to the customer accounts in the accounts receivable ledger.

Check figures: Tri-State Corporation Nov. 22 balance, $0; Haber Corporation Dec. 26 balance, $0. Adjusting entry for Uncol. Accts. Exp. $12,064.70.

2. Journalize the December 31 adjusting entry for estimated uncollectible accounts expense for the year. Use page 13 of the general journal. Uncollectible accounts expense is estimated as 1.0% of total sales on account. Total sales on account for the year were $1,206,470.00.

RECYCLING PROBLEM 22-R Calculating depreciation expense and book value of plant assets; journalizing entries affecting plant assets

Magnolia Company records plant assets in two accounts: **Office Equipment** and **Store Equipment**. Magnolia Company owns the following plant assets.

Plant Asset	Asset Account	Date Bought	Original Cost	Estimated Salvage Value	Estimated Useful Life
1	Office Equipment	Apr. 1, 19X1	$ 7,500.00	$ 500.00	7 years
2	Store Equipment	Sept. 1, 19X1	18,900.00	2,400.00	10 years
3	Office Equipment	Oct. 1, 19X1	6,300.00	300.00	5 years
4	Store Equipment	Mar. 1, 19X2	5,200.00	1,240.00	6 years
5	Store Equipment	July 1, 19X2	13,700.00	1,100.00	12 years
6	Store Equipment	June 1, 19X3	9,600.00	2,040.00	9 years
7	Office Equipment	Nov. 1, 19X4	1,250.00	350.00	3 years
8	Office Equipment	July 1, 19X5	2,800.00	800.00	4 years

INSTRUCTIONS:

1. Calculate each plant asset's depreciation expense for the year ended December 31, 19X5. Use the straight-line method of calculating depreciation. Round amounts to the nearest cent.

2. Calculate each plant asset's ending book value as of December 31, 19X5.

3. Journalize the two adjusting entries for depreciation expense for the year ended December 31, 19X5. Use page 13 of a general journal.

4. Journalize the following transaction. Use page 4 of a cash receipts journal. Source documents are abbreviated as follows: memorandum, M; receipt, R.

19X6

Apr. 2. Received cash from sale of plant asset number 2, $12,200.00: original cost, $18,900.00; total accumulated depreciation through December 31, 19X5, $7,150.00; additional depreciation to be recorded through April 2, 19X6, $412.50. M125 and R193.

RECYCLING PROBLEM 23-R Determining cost of ending inventory using the fifo, lifo, and weighted-average methods

Accounting records at Northland Company show the following purchases and periodic inventory counts.

Model No.	Beginning Inventory January 1	First Purchase	Second Purchase	Third Purchase	Periodic Inventory Count December 31
C23	10 @ $15.00	8 @ $16.00	12 @ $18.00	16 @ $20.00	20
R79	15 @ $ 9.00	18 @ $10.00	20 @ $12.00	12 @ $14.00	25
C152	8 @ $ 6.25	12 @ $ 6.00	15 @ $ 5.90	10 @ $ 5.75	14
D34	42 @ $23.00	35 @ $22.00	40 @ $20.00	40 @ $18.00	67
R493	8 @ $ 5.20	9 @ $ 5.80	5 @ $ 6.30	7 @ $ 6.50	15
G549	20 @ $10.00	15 @ $11.00	15 @ $12.00	25 @ $12.00	35

INSTRUCTIONS:

1. Calculate the total cost of ending inventory on December 31 using the fifo method. Use a form similar to the following. The inventory cost for Model No. C23 is given as an example.

Model No.	No. of Units on Hand	Unit Price	Cost of Ending Inventory
C23	20	16 @ $20.00 ⎱ 4 @ 18.00 ⎰	$392.00

Use the following procedure to complete the form.

(a) Record the model number and number of units of each model on hand on December 31.

(b) Record the unit price of each model. When more than one unit price is used, list the units and unit prices on separate lines as shown in the example.

(c) Calculate the cost of ending inventory of each model, and write the amount in the Cost of Ending Inventory column.

(d) Add the amounts in the Cost of Ending Inventory column to calculate the total cost of ending inventory.

2. On another form, calculate the total cost of ending inventory using the lifo method. Follow the steps given in Instruction 1.

Check figure: total weighted-average cost $2,587.82

3. On another form, calculate the total cost of ending inventory using the weighted-average method. Use the following procedure.
   (a) Record the model number and number of units of each model on hand on December 31.
   (b) Calculate the weighted-average price per unit for each model. Round the amount per unit to the nearest cent. Write the amount in the Unit Price column.
   (c) Calculate the cost of ending inventory of each model, and write the amount in the Cost of Ending Inventory column.
   (d) Add the amounts in the Cost of Ending Inventory column to calculate the total cost of ending inventory.
4. Compare the total cost of ending inventory obtained in Instructions 1, 2, and 3. Which method, fifo, lifo, or weighted-average, resulted in the lowest cost of ending inventory?

RECYCLING PROBLEM 24-R Journalizing notes payable and notes receivable transactions

The following transactions were completed by Arrowhead Manufacturing during July of the current year.

INSTRUCTIONS:

1. Journalize the following transactions. Use page 7 of a general journal, page 14 of a cash receipts journal, and page 18 of a cash payments journal. Source documents are abbreviated as follows: check, C; memorandum, M; note payable, NP; note receivable, NR; receipt, R.

July 2. Received cash for the maturity value of NR95: principal, $1,100.00, plus interest, $11.00; total, $1,111.00. R132.
   5. Issued a 60-day, 10% note, $3,000.00. NP155.
   6. Paid cash for the maturity value of NP149: principal, $7,000.00, plus interest, $140.00; total, $7,140.00. C1043.
   8. Discounted at 11% a 30-day non-interest-bearing note, $2,500.00; proceeds, $2,477.08, interest, $22.92. NP156.
   11. Received cash for the maturity value of NR92: principal, $600.00, plus interest, $12.00; total, $612.00. R147.
   13. Received cash for the maturity value of NR94: principal, $575.00, plus interest, $5.75; total, $580.75. R152.
   17. Paid cash for the maturity value of NP151: principal, $4,500.00, plus interest, $90.00; total, $4,590.00. C1212.
   18. Issued a 3-month, 12% note to McKinney Company for an extension of time on this account payable, $1,700.00. NP157.
   21. Melinda Blair dishonored NR80, a 6-month, 12% note, maturity value due today: principal, $500.00; interest, $30.00; total, $530.00. M113.
   25. Discounted at 11% a 6-month non-interest-bearing note, $12,500.00; proceeds, $11,812.50, interest, $687.50. NP158.
   27. Received a 30-day, 13% note from Miles Browning for an extension of time on his account, $1,500.00. NR96.
   29. Paid cash for the maturity value of NP131: principal, $3,500.00, plus interest, $192.50; total, $3,692.50. C1235.

Check figures: Cash Receipts Journal totals, $710.42; $20,303.75; $19,593.33. Cash Payments Journal totals, $15,422.50; $15,422.50

2. Prove the cash receipts and cash payments journals.

RECYCLING PROBLEM 25-R Journalizing and posting entries for accrued revenue and expenses

The following accounts are from Willem Corporation's general ledger. The balances are recorded as of December 31 of the current year before adjusting entries.

PARTIAL GENERAL LEDGER

Account No.	Account Title	Account Balance
1115	Notes Receivable.....................................	$ 720.00
1120	Interest Receivable	—
2105	Notes Payable	4,000.00
2110	Interest Payable.....................................	—
3120	Income Summary.....................................	—
7110	Interest Income	132.00
8110	Interest Expense	575.00

Willem Corporation completed the following transactions related to notes receivable and notes payable during the current year and the following year. The first two transactions have already been journalized and posted. Note Receivable No. 7 and Note Payable No. 10 are the only notes on hand at the end of the fiscal period. Source documents are abbreviated as follows: check, C; note payable, NP; note receivable, NR; receipt, R.

19X1

Oct. 1. Received a 4-month, 15% note from Joseph Dowd for an extension of time on his account, $720.00. NR7.

Nov. 1. Issued a 6-month, 14% note, $4,000.00. NP10.

19X2

Feb. 1. Received cash for the maturity value of NR7: principal, $720.00, plus interest, $36.00; total, $756.00. R194.

May 1. Paid cash for the maturity value of NP10: principal, $4,000.00, plus interest, $280.00; total, $4,280.00. C426.

Check figures: Interest Income $720 × 15% × 3/12 = $27. Interest Expense $4,000 × 14% × 2/12 = $93.33. Closing entries: Dr. Int. Inc. 159.00, Cr. Inc. Sum. 159.00; Dr. Inc. Sum. 668.33, Cr. Int. Exp. 668.33. Cash receipts journal, Cash Debit col. 756.00. Cash payments journal, Cash Credit col. 4,280.00.

INSTRUCTIONS:

1. Open the seven general ledger accounts and record the balances.
2. Use page 14 of a general journal. Journalize the adjusting entries for accrued interest income and accrued interest expense on December 31. Post these entries.
3. Continue to use page 14 of a general journal. Journalize the closing entries for interest income and interest expense. Post these entries.
4. Use page 15 of a general journal. Journalize the reversing entries for accrued interest income and accrued interest expense. Post these entries.
5. Use page 21 of a cash receipts journal. Journalize the receipt of cash for the maturity value of NR7. Post this entry.
6. Use page 22 of a cash payments journal. Journalize the cash payment for the maturity value of NP10. Post this entry.

RECYCLING PROBLEM 26-R Journalizing dividends and preparing a work sheet for a corporation

On December 31 of the current year, Specialty Design Corporation has the following general ledger accounts and balances.

Account Title	Account Balance
Cash	$ 67,277.00
Petty Cash...	300.00
Notes Receivable	5,937.00
Interest Receivable....................................	—
Accounts Receivable	26,115.00
Allowance for Uncollectible Accounts	36.00
Merchandise Inventory.................................	142,806.00
Supplies	3,450.00
Prepaid Insurance	12,300.00
Office Equipment	8,787.50

Account Title	Account Balance
Accumulated Depreciation—Office Equipment	1,175.00
Store Equipment	27,125.00
Accumulated Depreciation—Store Equipment	6,251.00
Notes Payable	12,500.00
Interest Payable	—
Accounts Payable	38,945.00
Employee Income Tax Payable	1,732.00
Federal Income Tax Payable	—
FICA Tax Payable	2,000.00
Sales Tax Payable	4,980.00
Unemployment Tax Payable—Federal	35.00
Unemployment Tax Payable—State	236.25
Health Insurance Premiums Payable	1,487.00
Dividends Payable	7,000.00
Capital Stock	100,000.00
Retained Earnings	60,487.25
Dividends	28,000.00
Income Summary	—
Sales	1,340,500.00
Sales Discount	3,361.00
Sales Returns and Allowances	3,415.00
Purchases	982,935.00
Purchases Discount	4,807.00
Purchases Returns and Allowances	3,678.00
Advertising Expense	4,039.00
Credit Card Fee Expense	13,446.00
Depreciation Expense—Office Equipment	—
Depreciation Expense—Store Equipment	—
Insurance Expense	—
Miscellaneous Expense	2,225.00
Payroll Taxes Expense	16,910.00
Rent Expense	42,600.00
Salary Expense	179,890.00
Supplies Expense	—
Uncollectible Accounts Expense	—
Utilities Expense	3,227.00
Gain on Plant Assets	75.00
Interest Income	690.00
Cash Short and Over (cash short)	14.00
Interest Expense	1,460.00
Loss on Plant Assets	95.00
Federal Income Tax Expense	10,900.00

INSTRUCTIONS:

1. Complete a work sheet for the current year ended December 31. Record the adjustments on the work sheet using the following information.

Adjustment Information, December 31

Accrued interest income	$ 140.00
Uncollectible accounts expense estimated as 2.0% of sales on account. Sales on account for year, $453,800.00.	
Merchandise inventory	140,700.00
Supplies inventory	450.00
Value of prepaid insurance	4,100.00
Annual depreciation expense—office equipment	950.00

Adjustment Information, December 31

Annual depreciation expense—store equipment.	4,065.00
Accrued interest expense	290.00
Federal income tax for the year	12,146.50

2. Use page 1 of a cash payments journal. Journalize the following transaction completed during the next year. The abbreviation for check is C.

Jan. 20. Paid cash for quarterly dividend declared December 20, $7,000.00. C568.

RECYCLING PROBLEM 27-R Preparing financial statements and end-of-fiscal-period entries for a corporation

Just-In-Time Supplies completed the work sheet on pages C-24 and C-25 for the current year ended December 31.

INSTRUCTIONS:

1. Prepare an income statement. Calculate and record the following component percentages. (a) Cost of merchandise sold. (b) Gross profit on operations. (c) Total operating expenses. (d) Income from operations. (e) Net addition or deduction resulting from other revenue and expenses. (f) Net income before federal income tax. Round percentage calculations to the nearest 0.1%.

2. Analyze Just-In-Time's income statement by determining if component percentages are within acceptable levels. If any component percentage is not within an acceptable level, suggest steps that the company should take. Just-In-Time considers the following component percentages acceptable.

Cost of merchandise sold	Not more than 73.0%
Gross profit on operations	Not less than 27.0%
Total operating expenses	Not more than 20.0%
Income from operations	Not less than 7.0%
Net deduction from other revenue and expenses	Not more than 0.5%
Net income before federal income tax	Not less than 6.5%

3. Prepare a statement of stockholders' equity. Use the following additional information.

January 1 balance of capital stock account	$80,000.00
(16,000 shares issued for $5.00 per share)	
January 1 balance of retained earnings account	25,928.60

4. Prepare a balance sheet.

5. Calculate Just-In-Time's (a) working capital and (b) current ratio. Determine if these items are within acceptable levels. Just-In-Time considers the following levels acceptable.

Working capital	Not less than $90,000.00
Current ratio	Between 2.0 to 1 and 2.5 to 1

6. Use page 13 of a general journal. Journalize the adjusting entries.

7. Use page 14 of a general journal. Journalize the closing entries.

8. Use page 1 of a general journal. Journalize the reversing entries for the accrued interest income and accrued interest expense.

RECYCLING PROBLEM 28-R Journalizing entries to form and liquidate business organizations

INSTRUCTIONS:

1. Journalize the following transaction. Use page 1 of a cash receipts journal. Source documents are abbreviated as follows: receipt, R.

Feb. 1, 19x1. Received cash from Paul Edwall as an investment, $2,500.00. R1.

Paul Edwall has decided to terminate his business and start a partnership with a friend.

2. Journalize the following transactions. Use page 7 of a cash receipts journal and a cash payments journal. Source documents are abbreviated as follows: check, C; receipt, R. (*Continued on page C-26.*)

Just-In-Time Supplies
Work Sheet
For Year Ended December 31, 19--

	1 TRIAL BALANCE DEBIT	2 TRIAL BALANCE CREDIT	3 ADJUSTMENTS DEBIT	4 ADJUSTMENTS CREDIT	5 INCOME STATEMENT DEBIT	6 INCOME STATEMENT CREDIT	7 BALANCE SHEET DEBIT	8 BALANCE SHEET CREDIT
1 Cash	3081700						3081700	
2 Petty Cash	30000						30000	
3 Notes Receivable	540000						540000	
4 Interest Receivable			(a) 10800				10800	
5 Accounts Receivable	2350300						2350300	
6 Allowance for Uncollectible Accts.		3200		(b) 484056				487256
7 Merchandise Inventory	8852540		(c) 791400				9643940	
8 Supplies	310000			(d) 270000			40000	
9 Prepaid Insurance	1107000			(e) 738000			369000	
10 Office Equipment	791000						791000	
11 Accum. Depr.—Office Equipment		105700		(f) 855500				191200
12 Store Equipment	4441200						4441200	
13 Accum. Depr.—Store Equipment		562590		(g) 365850				928440
14 Notes Payable		1125000						1125000
15 Interest Payable				(h) 28125				28125
16 Accounts Payable		3444590						3444590
17 Employee Income Tax Payable		155800						155800
18 Federal Income Tax Payable				(i) 100710				100710
19 FICA Tax Payable		180000						180000
20 Sales Tax Payable		448200						448200
21 Unemployment Tax Payable—Federal		3200						3200
22 Unemployment Tax Payable—State		21600						21600
23 Health Insurance Premiums Payable		133830						133830
24 Dividends Payable		600000						600000
25 Capital Stock		8000000						8000000

#	Account	Trial Balance Debit	Trial Balance Credit	Adjustments Debit	Adjustments Credit	Income Statement Debit	Income Statement Credit	Balance Sheet Debit	Balance Sheet Credit
26	*Retained Earnings*								2592860
27	*Dividends*	2400000						2400000	
28	*Income Summary*				(c) 791400		791400		
29	*Sales*		119764000				119764000		
30	*Sales Discount*	302490				302490			
31	*Sales Returns and Allowances*	307350				307350			
32	*Purchases*	88464150				88464150			
33	*Purchases Discount*		432630				432630		
34	*Purchases Returns and Allowances*		331020				331020		
35	*Advertising Expense*	363500				363500			
36	*Credit Card Fee Expense*	1210140				1210140			
37	*Depr. Expense—Office Equipment*			(f) 85500		85500			
38	*Depr. Expense—Store Equipment*			(g) 365850		365850			
39	*Insurance Expense*			(e) 738000		738000			
40	*Miscellaneous Expense*	200250				200250			
41	*Payroll Taxes Expense*	1521900				1521900			
42	*Rent Expense*	3840000				3840000			
43	*Salary Expense*	16190100				16190100			
44	*Supplies Expense*			(d) 270000		270000			
45	*Uncollectible Accounts Expense*			(b) 484056		484056			
46	*Utilities Expense*	290400				290400			
47	*Gain on Plant Assets*		7000				7000		
48	*Interest Income*		60000		(a) 10800		70800		
49	*Cash Short and Over*		750				750		
50	*Interest Expense*	382950		(h) 28125		411075			
51	*Loss on Plant Assets*	8500				8500			
52	*Federal Income Tax Expense*	985000		(i) 100710		1085710			
53		1379771220	1379771220	2874441	2874441	116139721	121396850	23697940	18440811
54	*Net Income after Federal Inc. Tax*					5257129			5257129
55						121396850	121396850	23697940	23697940
56									
57									

April 1, 19x3. Received cash from sale of supplies, $1,500.00; book value of supplies, $1,850.00. R145.

April 1, 19x3. Paid cash to all creditors: Addams Supply, $900.00; Burnstein and Associates, $1,000.00. C322-323.

April 2, 19x3. Recorded final distribution of remaining cash to Paul Edwall, $3,500.00. C324.

Paul Edwall and Leonard Simm agree to form a partnership called OfficeMart.

3. Journalize the following transaction. Use page 1 of a cash receipts journal. Source documents are abbreviated as follows: receipt, R.

April 15, 19x3. Received cash from partners as initial investment: from Paul Edwall, $4,500.00; from Leonard Simm, $2,500.00. R1-2.

Mr. Edwall and Mr. Simm agreed to terminate their business and form a corporation with other business associates.

Check figures: Loss on sale of supplies, $350.00. Distribution of gain on sale of equipment: Edwall, $500.00; Simm, $500.00.

4. Journalize the following transactions. Use page 9 of a cash receipts journal and a cash payments journal. The partnership agreement states that all losses or gains on sale are to be divided equally between the partners. Source documents are abbreviated as follows: check, C; receipt, R.

May 1, 19x7. Received cash from sale of equipment, $4,000.00; original cost, $10,000.00; total accumulated depreciation recorded to date, $7,000.00. R122.

May 1, 19x7. Paid cash to all creditors: Douglas Distributors, $2,200.00; Irwin Supply Company, $500.00. C187-188.

May 2, 19x7. Recorded final distribution of remaining cash to partners: to Paul Edwall, $5,600.00; to Leonard Simm, $8,000.00. C189-190.

Paul Edwall and five associates agree to form a corporation, Office Supplies, Inc.

5. Journalize the following transaction. Use page 1 of a cash receipts journal. Source documents are abbreviated as follows: receipt, R.

June 1, 19x7. Received cash for 125,000 shares of $1.00 par-value common stock, $125,000.00. R1-6.

Answers to Audit Your Understanding

CHAPTER 1, PAGE 11

1. The language of business.
2. Accountants, bookkeepers, accounting clerks, and other general office workers.
3. The American Institute of Certified Public Accountants (AICPA).

CHAPTER 1, PAGE 13

1. Communication is the transfer of information between two or more individuals.
2. When an individual disregards his or her principles of right and wrong by choosing the wrong action.
3. **(1)** Is the action illegal? **(2)** Does the action violate company or professional standards? **(3)** Who is affected, and how, by the action?

CHAPTER 2, PAGE 21

1. A business owned by one person.
2. Assets = Liabilities + Owner's Equity.
3. Assets.
4. Liabilities and Owner's Equity.

CHAPTER 2, PAGE 26

1. The left side equals the right side.
2. The right side must be increased.
3. An account is increased by the same amount another account on the same side is decreased.

CHAPTER 2, PAGE 29

1. Assets, liabilities, and owner's equity.
2. Assets.
3. Liabilities and owner's equity.
4. Find the errors before completing any more work.

CHAPTER 3, PAGE 41

1. Increased.
2. Decreased.
3. Decreased.

CHAPTER 3, PAGE 43

1. Assets.
2. Liabilities and owner's equity.
3. Total assets.
4. Total liabilities and owner's equity.

CHAPTER 4, PAGE 55

1.   Assets = Liabilities + Owner's Equity

2. **(1)** Account balances increase on the normal balance side of an account. **(2)** Account balances decrease on the side opposite the normal balance side of an account.

CHAPTER 4, PAGE 64

1. **(1)** What accounts are affected? **(2)** How is each account classified? **(3)** How is each account balance changed? **(4)** How is each amount entered in the accounts?
2. Debit.
3. Credit.
4. Debit.
5. Credit.
6. Debit.

CHAPTER 5, PAGE 76

1. General Debit, General Credit, Sales Credit, Cash Debit, and Cash Credit.
2. By date.
3. Checks, calculator tapes, receipts, memorandums.
4. Source documents are one way to verify the accuracy of a specific journal entry.

CHAPTER 5, PAGE 83

1. Date, debit, credit, source document.

CHAPTER 5, PAGE 87

1. Cash on hand at the beginning of the month, plus total cash received, less total cash paid.

2. (1) Rule a single line across all amount columns directly below the last entry to indicate that the columns are to be added. **(2)** On the next line, write the date in the Date column. **(3)** Write the word, *Totals*, in the Account Title column. **(4)** Write each column total below the single line. **(5)** Rule double lines below the column totals across all amount columns. The double lines mean that the totals have been verified as correct.

CHAPTER 6, PAGE 103

1. The first digit indicates in which general ledger division the account is located. The second and third digits indicate the location of the account within that division.

2. (1) Write the account title in the heading. **(2)** Write the account number in the heading.

CHAPTER 6, PAGE 112

1. (1) Write the date in the Date column of the account. **(2)** Write the journal page number in the Post. Ref. column of the account. **(3)** Write the amount in the Debit or Credit column. **(4)** Calculate and write the new account balance in the Balance Debit or Balance Credit column. **(5)** Write the account number in the Post. Ref. column of the journal.

CHAPTER 7, PAGE 140

1. Blank endorsement, special endorsement, and restrictive endorsement.

2. (1) Write the amount of the check in the space after the dollar sign at the top of the stub. **(2)** Write the date of the check on the Date line at the top of the stub. **(3)** Write to whom the check is to be paid on the To line at the top of the stub. **(4)** Record the purpose of the check on the For line. **(5)** Write the amount of the check in the amount column at the bottom of the stub on the line with the words "Amt. this Check." **(6)** Calculate the new checking account balance and record the new balance in the amount column on the last line of the stub.

CHAPTER 7, PAGE 147

1. (1) Calculate the adjusted check stub balance. **(2)** Calculate the adjusted bank balance. **(3)** Compare adjusted balances.

2.

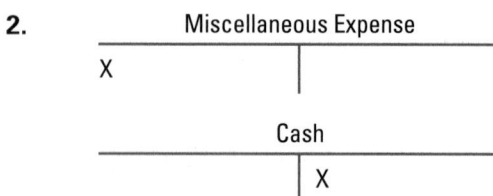

CHAPTER 7, PAGE 153

1.

2.

3.

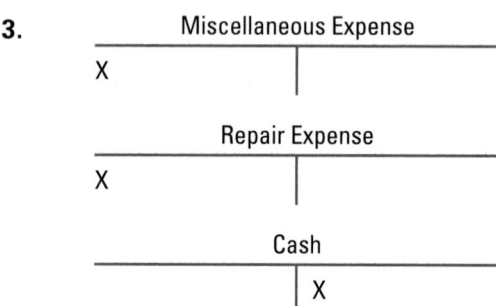

CHAPTER 8, PAGE 183

1. One year.
2. Name of business, name of report, and date of report.
3. (1) What is the balance of the account? **(2)** What should the balance be for this account? **(3)** What must be done to correct the account balance? **(4)** What adjustment is made?
4. Assets, liabilities, and owner's equity accounts.
5. Revenue and expense accounts.

CHAPTER 8, PAGE 187

1. Subtract the smaller total from the larger total to find the difference.
2. The difference between two column totals can be divided evenly by 9.
3. A slide.

CHAPTER 9, PAGE 199

1. Heading, revenue, expenses, and net income or net loss.
2. Total Expenses ÷ Total Sales = Total Expenses Component Percentage.
3. Net Income ÷ Total Sales = Net Income Component Percentage.

CHAPTER 9, PAGE 204

1. Heading, assets, liabilities, and owner's equity.
2. Capital Account Balance + Net Income − Drawing Account Balance = Current Capital.

CHAPTER 10, PAGE 213

1. To update general ledger accounts.
2. Adjustments column of the work sheet.
3. Insurance Expense and Supplies Expense.

CHAPTER 10, PAGE 223

1. Beginning balances.
2. Changes in the owner's capital account for a single fiscal period.
3. **(1)** An entry to close income statement accounts with credit balances. **(2)** An entry to close income statement accounts with debit balances. **(3)** An entry to record net income or net loss and close the income summary account. **(4)** An entry to close the drawing account.

CHAPTER 10, PAGE 227

1. To assure a reader that a balance has not been omitted.
2. Only those with balances (permanent accounts).
3. Because they are closed and have zero balances.

CHAPTER 11, PAGE 253

1. To save time and space in journalizing transactions.
2.

Purchases	
dr.	cr.
+	−

Accounts Payable	
dr.	cr.
−	+

3. To show that no account title needs to be written.
4. To show that amounts on that line are not to be posted individually.
5. A business purchases merchandise to sell but buys supplies for use in the business. Supplies are not intended for sale.

CHAPTER 11, PAGE 259

1. Cash is decreased by a credit.
2. Cash and merchandise.
3. A journal entry made to correct an error in the ledger.

CHAPTER 12, PAGE 273

1. Price of Goods × Sales Tax Rate = Sales Tax
2.

Sales Tax Payable	
dr.	cr.
−	+

Accounts Receivable	
dr.	cr.
+	−

3. Cash is increased; Accounts Receivable and the customer's account are decreased.

CHAPTER 12, PAGE 277

1. The columns are totaled and the equality of debits and credits is verified.
2. **(1)** Write the page number at the top of the journal. **(2)** Write the date in the Date column. **(3)** Write the words, Brought Forward, in the Account Title column. A check mark is also placed in the Post. Ref. column to show that nothing on this line needs to be posted. **(4)** Record the column totals brought forward from page 21 of the journal.
3. Cash on hand at the beginning of the month, *plus* total cash received during the month, *less* total cash paid during the month, *equals* cash balance on hand at end of the month. Cash is proved if the balance on the next unused check stub is the same as the cash proof.

CHAPTER 13, PAGE 290

1. An account in a general ledger that summarizes all accounts in a subsidiary ledger.
2. The balance of a controlling account equals the total of all account balances in its related subsidiary ledger.
3. Debit, Credit, Debit Balance, and Credit Balance.
4. Accounts for vendors from whom items are purchased or bought on account.
5. Accounts for charge customers.

CHAPTER 13, PAGE 298

1. Credit Balance. Because accounts payable are liabilities and liabilities have normal credit balances.
2. By writing the vendor name and vendor number on the heading of the ledger account.
3. **(1)** Write the date in the Date column of the account. **(2)** Write the journal page number in the Post. Ref. column of the account. **(3)** Write the credit amount in the Credit amount column of the account. **(4)** Add the amount in the Credit amount column to the previous balance in the Credit Balance column. Write the new account balance in the Credit Balance column. **(5)** Write the vendor number in the Post. Ref. column of the journal. The vendor number shows that the posting for this entry is completed.
4. Debit Balance. Because accounts receivable are assets and assets have normal debit balances.

CHAPTER 13, PAGE 302

1. By preparing a schedule of accounts receivable and schedule of accounts payable.
2. All vendor accounts that have balances.
3. When the total of the schedule of accounts receivable equals the balance of the accounts receivable general ledger account.

CHAPTER 14, PAGE 330

1. The total amount earned by all employees for a pay period.
2. Overtime hours X overtime rate (time and one half).
3. 3½.
4. $400.00.

CHAPTER 14, PAGE 334

1. Marital status and withholding allowance.
2. Both the employer and employee.
3. Employer.
4. Employer.

CHAPTER 14, PAGE 341

1. The total earnings and payroll withholdings of all employees.
2. By using tax tables provided by the federal government.
3. By subtracting total deductions from total earnings.

CHAPTER 14, PAGE 344

1. To enable the company to complete required tax forms at the end of the year.
2. Recording information on several forms with one writing.

CHAPTER 15, PAGE 359

1. Salary Expense.
2. Employee Income Tax Payable.
3. FICA Tax Payable.

CHAPTER 15, PAGE 363

1. Employers must pay 8% of each employee's total earnings up to the tax base.
2. Employers must pay 0.8% of total earnings of each employee up to a base of $7,000.00.

CHAPTER 15, PAGE 367

1. Federal income tax and FICA taxes.
2. By January 31.
3. Federal income tax and FICA employee and employer taxes.

CHAPTER 16, PAGE 398

1. A columnar form on which the financial information needed to prepare financial statements is summarized.
2. To prove the equality of debits and credits in the general ledger.
3. Merchandise Inventory.
4. Merchandise Inventory and Income Summary.

CHAPTER 16, PAGE 399

1. Income Statement Debit or Credit column.
2. When the Income Statement Debit column total (costs and expenses) is larger than the Credit column total (revenue).

3. Balance Sheet Debit.

CHAPTER 16, PAGE 404

1. Trial Balance Debit and Credit columns; Adjustments Debit and Credit columns; Adjusted Trial Balance Debit and Credit columns; Income Statement Debit and Credit columns; and Balance Sheet Debit and Credit columns.
2. Trial balance amounts after adjustments are extended to the Adjusted Trial Balance columns and the Adjusted Trial Balance columns are proved before extending amounts to the Income Statement and Balance Sheet columns.

CHAPTER 17, PAGE 420

1. The cost of merchandise sold section.
2. Beginning merchandise inventory, *plus* purchases, *equals* total cost of merchandise available for sale, *less* ending merchandise inventory, *equals* cost of merchandise sold.
3. By comparing it with the amount calculated on the work sheet.
4. Net loss.

CHAPTER 17, PAGE 428

1. Each partner's share of net income or net loss.
2. Beginning capital, additional investments, and withdrawal of assets.
3. Schedules of accounts receivable and schedule of accounts payable.

CHAPTER 18, PAGE 437

1. Insurance Expense and Income Summary.
2. Because the explanation "Adjusting Entries" is recorded in the Account Title column to explain all of the adjusting entries that follow.
3. Adjusting entry for merchandise inventory.

CHAPTER 18, PAGE 452

1. Income Statement and Balance Sheet columns of the work sheet and a distribution of net income statement.
2. Income Summary.
3. An amount equal to its balance is recorded on the side opposite the balance.
4. General ledger accounts with balances.

CHAPTER 19, PAGE 476

1. An organization with the legal rights of a person and which may be owned by many persons.
2. To allow accounting clerks to specialize in recording one kind of transaction to improve efficiency.
3. The purchase invoice received from a vendor.

CHAPTER 19, PAGE 489

1. To quote different prices for different quantities purchased without changing catalog or list prices.
2. To encourage prompt payment.

3. Cash, Cash Short and Over.
4. Writing the account number in parentheses below the journal column total.

CHAPTER 19, PAGE 496
1. A debit memorandum.
2. Only merchandise purchased on account is recorded in the purchases journal. Supplies are not merchandise.
3. A listing of vendor accounts, account balances, and total amount due all vendors.

CHAPTER 20, PAGE 523
1. Accounts Receivable is debited; Sales Tax Payable and Sales are credited.
2. Posted individually to the customer account in the accounts receivable ledger.
3. Individual items should be posted frequently to the customer accounts in the accounts receivable ledger. Column totals are posted to the general ledger at the end of each month.

CHAPTER 20, PAGE 531
1. Because the sales journal is used only for sales on account and because they are receipts of cash.
2. Sales invoice amount times sales discount rate.
3. Total invoiced amount, *less* sales discount, *less* sales tax reduction *equals* cash received.
4. The Debit column is used for cash receipts on account with sales discounts and the Credit column is used for cash and credit card sales.

CHAPTER 20, PAGE 536
1. Contra revenue account in the operating revenue division.
2. Sales Tax Payable is debited (decreased).
3. Accounts receivable ledger.

CHAPTER 20, PAGE 542
1. Bill of lading.
2. Receiving payment for the sale.
3. Receiving the merchandise.

CHAPTER 21, PAGE 573
1. To record the expense in the same fiscal period in which the sales were made. This is an application of the Matching Expenses with Revenue accounting concept.
2. At the time the expense is recorded, the actual amount is not known because the accounts have not yet become uncollectible. Therefore, an estimate is needed.
3. Credit.
4. Debit.

CHAPTER 21, PAGE 579
1. General ledger and accounts receivable ledger.

2. The words "Written off" are written in the Item column. To show the full credit history for the customer.
3. Record an entry for reopening the customer account. Record an entry for the cash receipt.

CHAPTER 22, PAGE 592
1. Equipment, buildings, and land.
2. Debit.
3. Physical depreciation and functional depreciation.
4. Original cost, estimated salvage value, and estimated useful life.
5. Original cost less estimated salvage value.

CHAPTER 22, PAGE 598
1. (1) Annual depreciation expense, (2) accumulated depreciation, and (3) ending book value.
2. None.
3. Credit.
4. No effect on the plant asset account; the amount is recorded in the accumulated depreciation account.
5. Debit Depreciation Expense, credit Accumulated Depreciation.

CHAPTER 22, PAGE 606
1. (1) Original cost and accumulated depreciation are removed from the accounts. (2) Cash or other asset received is recognized. (3) Gain or loss on the disposal is recognized.
2. By calculating the difference between the book value of the asset disposed of and the value of the asset received.
3. When additional depreciation expense should be recorded for the time from the last adjustment for depreciation expense and the date of disposal.
4. Annual depreciation expense divided by 12 equals monthly depreciation expense. Monthly depreciation expense is multiplied by the number of the months in the partial year.

CHAPTER 22, PAGE 609
1. In the earlier years of the plant asset's life.
2. Only enough depreciation expense to reduce the book value to the salvage value.
3. Assessors who are elected by citizens or trained by the government.

CHAPTER 23, PAGE 628
1. Periodic inventory, perpetual inventory.
2. At the end of a fiscal period.
3. Universal Product Code.

CHAPTER 23, PAGE 635
1. Fifo.
2. Lifo.
3. Weighted-average.

4. By estimating inventory using the gross profit method of estimating inventory.

CHAPTER 24, PAGE 646

1. The maturity value of an interest-bearing note is the principal plus the interest; the maturity value of a non-interest-bearing note is the principal only.

2. $50 ($500 × 10% × 1).

3. $416 ($400 × 8% × ⁹⁄₁₂).

4. February 22.

5. May 22 (March 23–31, 8 days; April 1–30, 30 days; May 1–22, 22 days).

CHAPTER 24, PAGE 651

1. Credit.

2. Because it is a financial expense rather than an expense of normal operations.

3. When the note is discounted; it is a non-interest-bearing note.

CHAPTER 24, PAGE 655

1. Debit.

2. Zero.

3. Because it is revenue from investment rather than normal operations.

4. Not necessarily; they may continue to try to collect the account before writing it off.

CHAPTER 25, PAGE 671

1. Debit Interest Receivable, credit Interest Income.

2. Debit Interest Income, credit Income Summary.

3. A reversing entry.

4. Principal + Interest = Maturity Value.

CHAPTER 25, PAGE 677

1. Debit Interest Expense, credit Interest Payable.

2. Debit Income Summary, credit Interest Expense.

3. A reversing entry.

CHAPTER 26, PAGE 688

1. The board of directors.

2. Debit Dividends, credit Dividends Payable.

3. Debit Dividends Payable, credit Cash.

CHAPTER 26, PAGE 695

1. The adjustment for federal income tax expense.

2. Debit Merchandise Inventory, credit Income Summary.

3. Total federal income tax expense minus estimated taxes already paid in quarterly installments.

CHAPTER 27, PAGE 716

1. A component percentage.

2. A statement of stockholders' equity.

3. Cash, accounts receivable, merchandise inventory, supplies, and prepaid insurance.

4. Working capital and current ratio.

CHAPTER 27, PAGE 725

1. The work sheet's Income Statement Credit column.

2. Retained Earnings.

3. To prove the equality of debits and credits in the general ledger.

CHAPTER 28, PAGE 755

1. A proprietorship.

2. Debit Cash, Credit Capital.

3. Distributing remaining cash to the owner.

4. Capital is decreased with a debit for the amount of loss.

CHAPTER 28, PAGE 760

1. A partnership agreement.

2. The partnership must be legally dissolved and a new partnership established.

3. The balance of the cash account which includes cash received from buyers of the noncash assets.

4. The partnership's creditors are paid first and any remaining cash is distributed to the partners.

CHAPTER 28, PAGE 763

1. A share of stock.

2. The articles of incorporation.

3. Corporations pay federal income tax on their net income and stockholders pay an additional personal income tax on profits distributed to them as dividends.

4. Debit Cash, credit Capital Stock.

5. Because they are based on the idea of perpetual life.

Glossary

Account: a record summarizing all the information pertaining to a single item in the accounting equation. (p. 22)

Accountant: a person who plans, summarizes, analyzes, and interprets accounting information. (p. 6)

Account balance: the amount in an account. (p. 22)

Accounting: planning, recording, analyzing, and interpreting financial information. (p. 5)

Accounting clerk: a person who records, sorts, and files accounting information. (p. 7)

Accounting cycle: the series of accounting activities included in recording financial information for a fiscal period. (p. 227)

Accounting equation: an equation showing the relationship among assets, liabilities, and owner's equity. (p. 21)

Accounting period: see *fiscal period*.

Accounting records: organized summaries of a business' financial activities. (p. 5)

Accounting system: a planned process for providing financial information that will be useful to management. (p. 5)

Account number: the number assigned to an account. (p. 100)

Accounts payable ledger: a subsidiary ledger containing only accounts for vendors from whom items are purchased or bought on account. (p. 285)

Accounts receivable ledger: a subsidiary ledger containing only accounts for charge customers. (p. 285)

Account title: the name given to an account. (p. 22)

Accrued expenses: expenses incurred in one fiscal period but not paid until a later fiscal period. (p. 671)

Accrued interest expense: interest incurred but not yet paid. (p. 672)

Accrued interest income: interest earned but not yet received. (p. 665)

Accrued revenue: revenue earned in one fiscal period but not received until a later fiscal period. (p. 665)

Accumulated depreciation: the total amount of depreciation expense that has been recorded since the purchase of a plant asset. (p. 593)

Addend: each number to be added. (p. B-4)

Adjusting entries: journal entries recorded to update general ledger accounts at the end of a fiscal period. (p. 211)

Adjustments: changes recorded on a work sheet to update general ledger accounts at the end of a fiscal period. (p. 175)

Allowance method of recording losses from uncollectible accounts: crediting the estimated value of uncollectible accounts to a contra account. (p. 570)

Articles of incorporation: a written application requesting permission to form a corporation. (p. 761)

Assessed value: the value of an asset determined by tax authorities for the purpose of calculating taxes. (p. 608)

Asset: anything of value that is owned. (p. 20)

Automated accounting: an accounting system in which data are recorded and reported mostly by using automated machines. (p. 123)

Automated accounting system: a collection of computer programs designed to computerize accounting procedures. (p. 124)

Automatic check deposit: depositing payroll checks directly to an employee's checking or savings account in a specific bank. (p. 340)

Bad debts: see *uncollectible accounts*.

Balance ruled account: see *account*.

Balance sheet: a financial statement that reports assets, liabilities, and owner's equity on a specific date. (p. 26)

Bank discount: interest collected in advance on a note. (p. 650)

Bank statement: a report of deposits, withdrawals, and bank balance sent to a depositor by a bank. (p. 140)

Batch: a group of journal entries. (p. 309)

Bill of exchange: see *draft.*

Bill of lading: a receipt signed by the authorized agent of a transportation company for merchandise received that also serves as a contract for the delivery of merchandise. (p. 593)

Blank endorsement: an endorsement consisting of only the endorser's signature. (p. 137)

Board of directors: a group of persons elected by the stockholders to manage a corporation. (p. 686)

Book inventory: see *perpetual inventory.*

Bookkeeper: a person who does general accounting work plus some summarizing and analyzing of accounting information. (p. 7)

Book value: the difference between an asset's account balance and its related contra account balance. (p. 713)

Book value of accounts receivable: the difference between the balance of Accounts Receivable and its contra account, Allowance for Uncollectible Accounts. (p. 574)

Book value of a plant asset: the original cost of a plant asset minus accumulated depreciation. (p. 593)

Business ethics: the use of personal ethics in making business decisions. (p. 12)

Capital: the account used to summarize the owner's equity in the business. (p. 202)

Capital stock: total shares of ownership in a corporation. (p. 472)

Cash discount: a deduction that a vendor allows on the invoice amount to encourage prompt payment. (p. 480)

Cash over: a petty cash on hand amount that is more than a recorded amount. (p. 485)

Cash payments journal: a special journal used to record only cash payment transactions. (p. 476)

Cash receipts journal: a special journal used to record only cash receipt transactions. (p. 523)

Cash sale: a sale in which cash is received for the total amount of the sale at the time of the transaction. (p. 268)

Cash short: a petty cash on hand amount that is less than a recorded amount. (p. 483)

Cell: the space on an electronic spreadsheet where a column intersects with a row. (p. 145)

Cell address: the column letter and row number of a cell. (p. 145)

Charge sale: see *sale on account.*

Chart of accounts: a list of accounts used by a business. (p. 55)

Check: a business form ordering a bank to pay cash from a bank account. (p. 74)

Checking account: a bank account from which payments can be ordered by a depositor. (p. 135)

Closing entries: journal entries used to prepare temporary accounts for a new fiscal period. (p. 215)

Commercial invoice: a statement prepared by the seller of merchandise addressed to the buyer showing a detailed listing and description of merchandise sold, including prices and terms. (p. 540)

Component percentage: the percentage relationship between one financial statement item and the total that includes that item. (p. 197)

Computer program: a set of instructions followed by a computer to process data. (p. 124)

Contra account: an account that reduces a related account on a financial statement. (p. 63)

Contract of sale: a document that details all the terms agreed to by seller and buyer for a sales transaction. (p. 538)

Controlling account: an account in a general ledger that summarizes all accounts in a subsidiary ledger. (p. 285)

Corporation: an organization with the legal rights of a person and which may be owned by many persons. (p. 472)

Correcting entry: a journal entry made to correct an error in the ledger. (p. 258)

Cost of goods sold: see *cost of merchandise sold.*

Cost of merchandise: the price a business pays for goods it purchases to sell. (p. 247)

Cost of merchandise sold: the total original price of all merchandise sold during a fiscal period. (pp. 411–412)

Credit: an amount recorded on the right side of a T account. (p. 54)

Credit card sale: a sale in which a credit card is used for the total amount of the sale at the time of the transaction. (p. 268)

Credit memorandum: a form prepared by the vendor showing the amount deducted for returns and allowances. (p. 531)

Creditor: a person or organization to whom a liability is owed. (p. 646)

Current assets: cash and other assets expected to be exchanged for cash or consumed within a year. (p. 587)

Current liabilities: liabilities due within a short time, usually within a year. (p. 646)

Current ratio: a ratio that shows the numeric relationship of current assets to current liabilities. (p. 716)

Customer: a person or business to whom merchandise or services are sold. (p. 267)

Data base: a prearranged file in which data can be entered and retrieved. (p. 124)

Date of a note: the day a note is issued. (p. 644)

Debit: an amount recorded on the left side of a T account. (p. 54)

Debit memorandum: a form prepared by the customer showing the price deduction taken by the customer for returns and allowances. (p. 491)

Declaring a dividend: action by a board of directors to distribute corporate earnings to stockholders. (p. 686)

Declining-balance method of depreciation: multiplying the book value at the end of each fiscal period by a constant depreciation rate. (p. 606)

Depreciation expense: the portion of a plant asset's cost that is transferred to an expense account in each fiscal period during a plant asset's useful life. (p. 589)

Difference: the answer to a subtraction problem. (p. B-4)

Discounted note: a note on which interest is paid in advance. (p. 650)

Dishonored check: a check that a bank refuses to pay. (p. 146)

Dishonored note: a note that is not paid when due. (p. 654)

Dissolution: the process of stopping the operation of a business. (p. 751)

Distribution of net income statement: a partnership financial statement showing distribution of net income or net loss to partners. (p. 419)

Dividend: the number to be divided. (p. B-5)

Dividends: earnings distributed to stockholders. (p. 685)

Divisor: the number the dividend will be divided by. (p. B-5)

Double-entry accounting: the recording of debit and credit parts of a transaction. (p. 74)

Draft: a written, signed, and dated order from one party ordering another party, usually a bank, to pay money to a third party. (p. 540)

Electronic funds transfer: a computerized cash payment system that uses electronic impulses to transfer funds. (p. 148)

Electronic spreadsheet: a group of rows and columns displayed on a computer monitor. (p. 145)

Employee earnings record: a business form used to record details affecting payments made to an employee. (p. 341)

Endorsement: a signature or stamp on the back of a check transferring ownership. (p. 137)

Endorsement in full: see *special endorsement*.

Entry: information for each transaction recorded in a journal. (p. 74)

Equities: financial rights to the assets of a business. (p. 21)

Estimated salvage value: the amount an owner expects to receive when a plant asset is removed from use. (p. 590)

Ethics: the principles of right and wrong that guide an individual in making decisions. (p. 12)

Exhibit: see *supporting schedule*.

Expense: a decrease in owner's equity resulting from the operation of a business. (p. 38)

Exports: goods or services shipped out of a seller's home country to a foreign country. (p. 538)

Face amount: see *principal of a note*.

Federal Insurance Contributions Act: see *FICA tax*.

Federal unemployment tax: a federal tax used for state and federal administrative expenses of the unemployment program. (pp. 333–334)

FICA tax: a federal tax paid by employees and employers for old-age, survivors, disability, and hospitalization insurance. (p. 333)

Fifo: see *first-in, first-out inventory costing method*.

File maintenance: the procedure for arranging accounts in a general ledger, assigning account numbers, and keeping records current. (pp. 101–104)

First-in, first-out inventory costing method: using the price of merchandise purchased first to calculate the cost of merchandise sold first. (p. 629)

Fiscal period: the length of time for which a business summarizes and reports financial information. (p. 171)

Gain on plant assets: revenue that results when a plant asset is sold for more than book value. (p. 601)

General amount column: a journal amount column that is not headed with an account title. (p. 73)

General journal: a journal with two amount columns in which all kinds of entries can be recorded. (p. 491)

General ledger: a ledger that contains all accounts needed to prepare financial statements. (p. 100)

General office clerk: a person who does general kinds of office tasks, including some accounting tasks. (p. 8)

Gross earnings: see *total earnings*.

Gross pay: see *total earnings*.

Gross profit method of estimating an inventory: estimating inventory by using the previous years' percentage of gross profit on operations. (p. 633)

Gross profit on sales: the revenue remaining after cost of merchandise sold has been deducted. (p. 414)

Imports: goods or services brought from a foreign country and brought into a buyer's home country. (p. 538)

Income statement: a financial statement showing the revenue and expenses for a fiscal period. (p. 178)

Interest: an amount paid for the use of money for a period of time. (p. 644)

Interest-bearing note: a promissory note that requires the payment of principal plus interest when the note is due. (p. 644)

Interest expense: the interest accrued on money borrowed. (p. 746)

Interest income: the interest earned on money loaned. (p. 653)

Interest rate of a note: the percentage of the principal that is paid for use of the money. (p. 644)

Internal Revenue Service (IRS): the branch of the U.S. Treasury Department concerned with enforcement and collection of income taxes. (pp. 171, 635, 694)

Inventory: the amount of goods on hand. (p. 393)

Inventory card: see *stock record*.

Inventory record: a form used during a periodic inventory to record information about each item of merchandise on hand. (p. 626)

Invoice: a form describing the goods sold, the quantity, and the price. (p. 249)

Journal: a form for recording transactions in chronological order. (p. 73)

Journal entry: see *entry*.

Journalizing: recording transactions in a journal. (p. 73)

Last-in, first-out inventory costing method: using the price of merchandise purchased last to calculate the cost of merchandise sold first. (p. 630)

Ledger: a group of accounts. (p. 100)

Letter of credit: a letter issued by a bank guaranteeing that a named individual or business will be paid a specified amount provided stated conditions are met. (p. 539)

Liability: an amount owed by a business. (p. 21)

Lifo: see *last-in, first-out inventory costing method*.

Liquidation: the process of paying all liabilities of a business and distributing remaining cash to the owner(s). (p. 751)

List price: a business' printed or catalog price. (p. 479)

Long-term liabilities: liabilities owed for more than a year. (p. 713)

Loss on plant assets: loss that results when a plant asset is sold for less than book value. (p. 604)

Maker of a note: the person or business who signs a note and thus promises to make payment. (p. 644)

Management accountant: see *private accountant*.

Manual accounting: an accounting system in which data are recorded and reported mostly by hand. (p. 123)

Markup: the amount added to the cost of merchandise to establish the selling price. (p. 247)

Maturity date of a note: the date a note is due. (p. 644)

Maturity value: the amount that is due on the maturity date of a note. (p. 644)

Medicare: the federal health insurance program for people who have reached retirement age. (p. 332)

Memorandum: a form on which a brief message is written describing a transaction. (p. 76)

Menu: a list of options from which an activity may be selected. (p. 126)

Merchandise: goods that a merchandising business purchases to sell. (p. 246)

Merchandise inventory: the amount of goods on hand for sale to customers. (p. 393)

Merchandising business: a business that purchases and sells goods. (p. 246)

Minuend: the top number or first number of a subtraction problem. (p. B-4)

Multiplicand: the number to be multiplied. (p. B-4)

Multiplier: the number of times the multiplicand will be multiplied. (p. B-4)

Net income: the difference between total revenue and total expenses when total revenue is greater. (p. 180)

Net loss: the difference between total revenue and total expenses when total expenses is greater. (p. 182)

Net pay: the total earnings paid to an employee after payroll taxes and other deductions. (p. 337)

Net purchases: total purchases less purchases discount and purchases returns and allowances. (p. 707)

Net sales: total sales less sales discount and sales returns and allowances. (p. 707)

Nominal account: see *temporary accounts.*

Non-interest-bearing note: a promissory note that requires only the payment of the principal when the note is due. (p. 644)

Note: see *promissory note.*

Notes payable: promissory notes that a business issues to creditors. (p. 646)

Notes receivable: promissory notes that a business accepts from customers. (p. 652)

Number of a note: the number assigned by the maker to identify a specific note. (p. 644)

Opening an account: Writing an account title and number on the heading of an account. (p. 102)

Owner's equity: the amount remaining after the value of all liabilities is subtracted from the value of all assets. (p. 21)

Owners' equity statement: a financial statement that summarizes the changes in owners' equity during a fiscal period. (p. 421)

Partner: each member of a partnership. (p. 246)

Partnership: a business in which two or more persons combine their assets and skills. (p. 246)

Partnership agreement: a written agreement setting forth the conditions under which a partnership is to operate. (p. 756)

Par value: a value assigned to a share of stock and printed on the stock certificate. (p. 762)

Par-value stock: a share of stock that has an authorized value printed on the stock certificate. (p. 762)

Payee of a note: the person or business to whom the amount of a note is payable. (p. 644)

Pay period: the period covered by a salary payment. (p. 327)

Payroll: the total amount earned by all employees for a pay period. (p. 327)

Payroll register: a business form used to record payroll information. (p. 334)

Payroll taxes: taxes based on the payroll of a business. (p. 330)

Pegboard: a special device used to write the same information at one time on several forms. (p. 343)

Periodic inventory: a merchandise inventory determined by counting, weighing, or measuring items of merchandise on hand. (p. 626)

Permanent accounts: accounts used to accumulate information from one fiscal period to the next. (p. 214)

Perpetual inventory: a merchandise inventory determined by keeping a continuous record of increases, decreases, and balance on hand. (p. 626)

Personal property: all property not classified as real property. (p. 608)

Petty cash: an amount of cash kept on hand and used for making small payments. (p. 149)

Petty cash slip: a form showing proof of a petty cash payment. (p. 151)

Physical inventory: see *periodic inventory.*

Plant asset record: an accounting form on which a business records information about each plant asset. (p. 592)

Plant assets: assets which will be used for a number of years in the operation of a business. (p. 587)

Post-closing trial balance: a trial balance prepared after the closing entries are posted. (pp. 226, 237)

Postdated check: a check with a future date on it. (p. 139)

Posting: transferring information from a journal entry to a ledger account. (p. 103)

Principal of a note: the original amount of a note. (p. 103)

Private accountant: an accountant who is employed by a single business. (p. 7)

Proceeds: the amount received for a note after the bank discount has been deducted. (p. 650)

Product: the answer to a multiplication problem. (p. B-4)

Profit: see *net income.*

Promissory note: a written and signed promise to pay a sum of money at a specified time. (p. 643)

Proprietorship: a business owned by one person. (p. 20)

Proving cash: determining that the amount of cash agrees with the accounting records. (p. 86)

Public accounting firm: a business selling accounting services to the general public. (p. 6)

Purchase invoice: an invoice used as a source document for recording a purchase on account transaction. (p. 249)

Purchase on account: a transaction in which the merchandise purchased is to be paid for later. (p. 249)

Purchases allowance: credit allowed for part of the purchase price of merchandise that is not returned, resulting in a decrease in the customer's accounts payable. (p. 491)

Purchases discount: a cash discount on purchases taken by a customer. (p. 481)

Purchases journal: a special journal used to record only purchase on account transactions. (p. 473)

Purchases return: credit allowed for the purchase price of returned merchandise, resulting in a decrease in the customer's accounts payable. (p. 491)

Quotient: the answer to a division problem. (p. B-5)

Ratio: a comparison between two numbers showing how many times one number exceeds the other. (p. 716)

Real accounts: see *permanent accounts.*

Real estate: see *real property.*

Real property: land and anything attached to the land. (p. 608)

Receipt: a business form giving written acknowledgement for cash received. (p. 75)

Residual value: see *estimated salvage value.*

Restrictive endorsement: an endorsement restricting further transfer of a check's ownership. (p. 138)

Retained earnings: an amount earned by a corporation and not yet distributed to stockholders. (p. 685)

Revenue: an increase in owner's equity resulting from the operation of a business. (p. 37)

Reversing entry: an entry made at the beginning of one fiscal period to reverse an adjusting entry made in the previous fiscal period. (p. 668)

Run date: the date to be printed on reports prepared by a computer. (p. 125)

Salary: the money paid for employee services. (p. 327)

Sale on account: a sale for which cash will be received at a later date. (p. 269)

Sales allowance: credit allowed a customer for part of the sales price of merchandise that is not returned, resulting in a decrease in the vendor's accounts receivable. (p. 531)

Sales discount: a cash discount on sales. (p. 525)

Sales invoice: an invoice used as a source document for recording a sale on account. (p. 269)

Sales journal: a special journal used to record only sales on account transactions. (p. 519)

Sales return: credit allowed a customer for the sales price of returned merchandise, resulting in a decrease in the vendor's accounts receivable. (p. 531)

Sales slip: see *sales invoice.*

Sales tax: a tax on a sale of merchandise or services. (p. 267)

Salvage value: see *estimated salvage value.*

Schedule of accounts payable: a listing of vendor accounts, account balances, and total amount due all vendors. (p. 301)

Schedule of accounts receivable: a listing of customer accounts, account balances, and total amount due from all customers. (p. 301)

Scrap value: see *estimated salvage value.*

Service business: a business that performs an activity for a fee. (p. 20)

Share of stock: each unit of ownership in a corporation. (p. 472)

Sight draft: a draft payable on sight when the holder presents it for payment. (p. 540)

Social security taxes: see *FICA tax.*

Software: programs used to direct the operations of a computer. (p. 124)

Sole proprietorship: see *proprietorship.*

Source document: a business paper from which information is obtained for a journal entry. (p. 74)

Special amount column: a journal amount column headed with an account title. (p. 73)

Special endorsement: an endorsement indicating a new owner of a check. (p. 137)

Special journal: a journal used to record only one kind of transaction. (p. 473)

State unemployment tax: a state tax used to pay benefits to unemployed workers. (p. 334)

Statement of stockholders' equity: a financial statement that shows changes in a corporation's ownership for a fiscal period. (p. 710)

Stockholder: an owner of one or more shares of a corporation. (p. 685)

Stock ledger: a file of stock records for all merchandise on hand. (p. 627)

Stock record: a form used to show the kind of merchandise, quantity received, quantity sold, and balance on hand. (p. 627)

Straight-line method of depreciation: charging an equal amount of depreciation expense for a plant asset in each year of useful life. (p. 590)

Subsidiary ledger: a ledger that is summarized in a single general ledger account. (p. 285)

Subtrahend: the number to be subtracted from the minuend. (p. B-4)

Sum: the answer to an addition problem. (p. B-4)

Supplementary report: see *supporting schedule.*

Supporting schedule: a report prepared to give details about an item on a principal financial statement. (p. 428)

T account: an accounting device used to analyze transactions. (p. 53)

Taking an inventory: see *periodic inventory.*

Tax base: the maximum amount of earnings on which a tax is calculated. (p. 336)

Template: a model of a computer application stored on a computer disk for repeated use. (p. 124)

Temporary accounts: accounts used to accumulate information until it is transferred to the owner's capital account. (p. 215)

Terms of sale: an agreement between a buyer and a seller about payment for merchandise. (p. 250)

Time draft: a draft that is payable at a fixed or determined future time after it is accepted. (p. 541)

Time of a note: the days, months, or years from the date of issue until a note is to be paid. (p. 644)

Total earnings: the total pay due for a pay period before deductions. (p. 329)

Trade acceptance: a form signed by a buyer at the time of a sale of merchandise in which the buyer promises to pay the seller a specified sum of money usually at a stated time in the future. (p. 542)

Trade discount: a reduction in the list price granted to customers. (p. 479)

Trade-in value: see *estimated salvage value.*

Transaction: a business activity that changes assets, liabilities, or owner's equity. (p. 21)

Trial balance: a proof of the equality of debits and credits in a general ledger. (p. 172)

Uncollectible accounts: accounts receivable that cannot be collected. (p. 569)

Vendor: a business from which merchandise is purchased or supplies or other assets are bought. (p. 248)

Vertical analysis: see *component percentage.*

Weighted-average inventory costing method: using the average cost of beginning inventory plus merchandise purchased during a fiscal period to calculate the cost of merchandise sold. (p. 630)

Withdrawal: asset taken out of a business for the owner's personal use. (p. 40)

Withholding allowance: a deduction from total earnings for each person legally supported by a taxpayer. (p. 332)

Working capital: the amount of total current assets less total current liabilities. (p. 715)

Work sheet: a columnar accounting form used to summarize the general ledger information needed to prepare financial statements. (p. 172)

Writing off an account: canceling the balance of a customer account because the customer does not pay. (p. 574)

Index

Bold page numbers indicate illustrations.